THE
ENCYCLOPEDIA
OF
MYTHS AND LEGENDS

Also by Stuart Gordon

Smile on the Void
Fire in the Abyss
Archon
The Hidden World
The Mask
Down the Drain
The Paranormal: An Illustrated Encyclopedia*

* Available from Headline

THE ENCYCLOPEDIA OF MYTHS AND LEGENDS

Stuart Gordon

HEADLINE

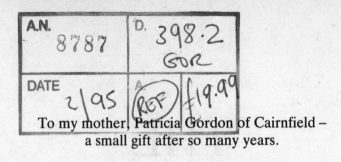
To my mother, Patricia Gordon of Cairnfield –
a small gift after so many years.

First published in 1993
by HEADLINE BOOK PUBLISHING PLC

10 9 8 7 6 5 4 3 2 1

British Library Cataloguing in Publication Data

Gordon, Stuart
 Encyclopedia of Myths and Legends
 I. Title
 398.2

 ISBN 0-7472-0623-6

Typeset by
Letterpart Limited, Reigate, Surrey

Printed and bound in Great Britain by
Mackays of Chatham PLC, Chatham, Kent

HEADLINE BOOK PUBLISHING PLC
Headline House
79 Great Titchfield Street
London W1P 7FN

Contents

Acknowledgements

Thanks are due to my brother and sister-in-law, David and Fiona Gordon, for the long-term loan of source material, also (once again) to Constance Marcham of the Findhorn Foundation Library; to Moray District Council's Department of Libraries for supplying texts I could not afford to buy, and to Bonnie McCalla for reminding me that the written word is only a shadow.

Introduction: Ancient or Modern?

Myths, as developed and transmitted orally or in writing by virtually every culture on earth, consist of legends, allegories, traditions and cycles of tales by which we human folk have long tried to explain to ourselves who we are, how the world and we were created, how we relate with nature and the elements, where we come from (as particular tribes or races), and what is the origin of our social institutions, laws, rites and codes of conduct.

Though most myths are obviously fabulous or metaphoric, in some cases (*see* **Flood Myth**) the similarity in accounts of a specific mythic event as given by societies wholly remote from one another may suggest an historical basis in some dimly remembered collective cataclysm. So too, myths of the overthrow of an older pantheon of deities by a new race of gods may be a metaphoric encoding of an historic event in which an indigenous race and its deities were destroyed and absorbed by invaders. Thus the Greek tale of how the sky-god **Zeus** married the goddess **Hera** (the 'Lady') suggests the conquest *c.*1300 BC by invading Achaean nomads of the older goddess-worshipping Cretan culture. Hera's continual rage at Zeus suggests the fury of a defeated culture. Likewise the Irish tale of how the Milesians overcame and drove underground the magical **Tuatha dé Danaan**, who became the **fairy** race, suggests an attempt by later Christian mythographers not only to explain how the Gaels came to possess Ireland, but to marry popular need to believe in the old pagan religion with the demands of Christianity.

Yet most myths are so inherently fantastic that now the word 'mythical' is applied to anything that is unbelievable. Tales of winged horses, heroes returning alive from the Land of the Dead, shape-shifting **witches**, tricksy fairies, evil **giants** and fabulous **dragons** or **unicorns**, as told from Britain to Greece, Egypt to China, New Zealand to Nova Scotia, are clearly the product of imagination. But to dismiss them as meaningless on this account is to miss the point. Many myths (as in the Indian *Puranas*) were created in the first place in an attempt to adapt esoteric, philosophic or religious teachings to popular needs by cloaking the teaching in fantastic romance, full of horror or humour, so engaging the imagination of those hearing the tale. In many cultures from generation to generation the **bards**, *rhapsodes*, and itinerant storytellers passed down such tales so as to edify by entertaining. Those later recording such tales in writing (so fixing them forever in one form) may often have missed the hidden, esoteric educational purpose originally intended, or may have distorted the original tale to serve present political need. The biblical myth of **Eden**, in which both **serpent** and **Eve** are demonised by patriarchal Judaic scribes, denies the Sumerian original, in which the Earth Mother is married to the Serpent (cosmic fertilising principle) and in which no jealous Jehovah or sense of **original sin** or **Fall** exists.

Many myths have gone through innumerable local cultural, political and social changes before reaching their present fixed form, in which they now appear as holy writ, having become the dogma of accepted religious beliefs. Others, especially those long denied by the Christian Church (at least in the West) have maintained an underground **pagan** life, and today live again.

Either way, many have survived to be enjoyed as well as analysed. They live because the process of edification via entertainment long predates the modern era of television. Mythic tales enduring today are those anciently found not only morally meaningful but entertaining. No storyteller ever held a fireside audience by preaching alone. It was always necessary (at least in cultures not ruled by fear) to cloak bald metaphysics in mystery and romance. Who would hear tales of how the world was created, how the gods warred, how humanity was born, how fire was stolen, how land was first tilled so that civilisation began, if such tales had no human interest?

In 3000 BC as now, people wanted to know how heroes slay dragons and how Beauty beats the Beast. They wanted to hear about bravery, about mercy in victory and courage in adversity: in other words, how to live life well.

As for the annual mystery of seasonal change and fertility, spring to summer to winter, life to death, it made no sense unless described in human terms. So, the world over is found the essential myth of the beautiful **corn-god** (**Adonis, Attis**) who, annually slain, goes to **hell** (winter), to be resurrected each spring by the efforts of his goddess-lover who descends to hell to resurrect or reincarnate him. The annual cycle is personified in myth and **Mystery**-rite, so those toiling on the soil and hearing the tale gained consolation and a sense of meaning. Their work was not for nothing.

So many myths are **archetypal**, welling spontaneously from common human experience of life since time immemorial. How to tell a child about birth, death and rebirth? How to explain the annual death of the sun in winter save by a cosmic **wolf** that chases then swallows it? How to talk of the phases of the **moon** save in human terms: youth, middle age and death?

Thus the personification of natural processes and cosmic cycles. Pagan gods and goddesses are a projection into nature of the human need to perceive the powers of this bewildering world in human terms, i.e., as friendly, hostile or merely remote. In pagan terms, every tree, stream or mountain is possessed by a particular spirit, to be invoked or placated, while the boundaries between different natural realms (shoreline or twilight, spring or winter) are as ambiguous as the boundary between life and death. Pagan deities and myth are amoral. *Pagans* (from *paganus*: Latin, 'countryman' or 'rustic') imposed no intellectual order on Nature, but took orders from their nature. In this, they were naively honest, not self-conscious.

The growth of self-conscious religion and philosophy from **Akhenaton** to **Pythagoras**, **Plato** to **Christ**, the **Cathars** to **Paracelsus**, and **Faust** to the modern era, is among the themes covered in this book.

It may not seem so at first glance, but myth, religion, philosophy and science are closely related. All try to understand or reconnect with the primal nature of things. Old myths may seem absurd to a modern audience, but that is because of their social context. The context dies, the tale remains. In every case, a myth is the manufactured attempt to understand a status quo, a rite by which folk try to understand themselves and their era – a rite all too often manufactured by the priests of that era to bend the common mind into a required way of thought, for local political purposes. Yet even modern priests ('spin-doctors') must work with popular myth.

In the modern West, the **Beatles** and **John F. Kennedy** are already as mythic as **Theseus** and **Perseus** were to the ancient Greeks. It matters not what they actually did; what matters is what we believe, i.e., what they represent in the common realm of modern myth. Few of us have proof that US astronauts did actually land on the **moon**, yet most of us accept that they did. Why? Because we saw it on TV? Why deride our ancestors for accepting that King **Arthur** and **Guinevere** were buried at **Glastonbury**, or that the founders of Rome (**Romulus** and Remus) were suckled by a she-wolf, or even that the **Hindu** god **Vishnu** sleeps on the back of a giant serpent, **Ananta-Shesha**, during the aeon-long cosmic night of **Brahma**? At heart we still live as much by myth as by 'common sense' or reason. Pragmatic knowledge as proved by sensory experience alone is all very well, but any culture that denies its deeper, darker, wider, higher dreams purely for the sake of a mess of pottage (material wealth) is already walking the mythic plank.

We are not just consumers, citizens, or serfs. Every one of us, no matter what our personal attainment or happiness, is a being thrown into a confusing world without obvious purpose or destination. We know not where we came from nor what happens when we die, and even during our living we are frequently in confusion. The purpose of religion, philosophy, science and myth is (ultimately) to try to win sense out of the conundrum, to steal some fire from heaven, to find some peace on earth. However sophisticated or safe we may feel today in our centrally heated homes, there is no way to avoid the ultimate mystery.

Who or what are we?
Where did we come from?
What are we here for?
Where are we going?
What must we do?

How to Use This Book

Within this book's A to Z format the themes considered include: (1) myths, legends and mythic beings; (2) the religions, cultures and traditions of their origin; (3) old texts recording (*Edda, Mabinogion, Mahabharata*) and mythical bards said to have originated (**Homer, Merlin, Taliesin**) myth and legend and modern authors adopting or adapting mythic themes (The **Brothers Grimm, James Joyce, Edgar Rice Burroughs**); (4) the myths and folklore attached to flora, fauna, minerals, etc.; (5) how cultures use myth, or are moved by it, or define themselves in terms of it (**Bonnie Prince Charlie, Hollywood, Nazi Myth, Wild West**); and (6) the psychology, symbolism and interpretation of myth (*see* **Campbell, Graves, Freud, Jung**).

Given the subject's complexity and the many individual entries and themes, the internal cross-referencing is organised on several levels, as follows: (1) Within each specific racial/regional mythology (**Greek, Norse, Oceanic**, etc.), individual entries (gods, heroes, local themes) all refer to a core-essay on the culture concerned (thus **Isis, Ra, Thoth** to **Egyptian Myth**; **Cuchulainn, Finn, Lug** to **Irish Myth**). A **Concordance** of related themes is included at the back to aid cross-referencing. (2) Related individual entries refer across race and region (thus **Noah** to **Manu** to **Gilgamesh**), and all these to **Flood Myth** or, again, **Indra** to **Zeus, Jupiter, Thor**, and these to **Hammer, Thunder, Oak**, etc.). (3) Other generally related themes are also cross-referenced. The entry on **Tricksters** refers to the **Yoruba** god Edshu, also to **Coyote, Raven** and the Islamic folk-hero **Nasruddin**; each of these entries in turn refers elsewhere. Thus **Coyote** to **Dog, Native American Myth, Wind**; **Raven** to **Divination, Eskimo Myth, Whale**; and **Nasruddin** to **Islam, Jalaluddin Rumi** and **Sufis**.

Thus any entry leads in many directions to create a multi-dimensional web, to be followed this way or that as required. The entry on the theme of the **Labyrinth** may be consulted if dizziness intervenes. References in the text which are not headlined are **highlighted** via terms set in bold face.

A

ABAKULU-BANTU (*See* **AFRICAN MYTH, REINCARNATION, ZULU**)

Buddhism is not alone in its concept of **bodhisattvas** ('enlightened ones'). The **theosophist** P.G. Bowen claimed to have learned from one of the Zulu Isanusi ('Wise Men') of an ancient pan-African brotherhood, the Bonabakulu abase-Khemu (Brotherhood of the Higher Ones of Egypt). Said to have been founded by a priest of **Isis** in the reign of Cheops (legendary builder of the Great **Pyramid**, *c*.2600 BC), this secret order has apparently survived, with at least one member in every tribe and nation of Africa. The highest of its seven grades comprise the Abakulu-bantu ('Perfect Men'). As with the bodhisattvas, they 'dwell on earth in physical form by their own will, and can retain or relinquish that form as they choose.'[1]

1. *'The Ancestral Wisdom in Africa'*, P.G. Bowen, from the *Theosophist*, Madras, August 1927.

ABAROS (*See* **PYTHAGORAS**)

Abaros (or Abaris) of the Hyperboreans, a race the ancient Greeks supposed to live in the far north, is said to have been the high priest of a 'winged temple' dedicated to **Apollo** the sun-god. He rode a golden arrow south to Greece to visit the philosopher Pythagoras (*c*.590–520 BC), who **initiated** him into the **Mysteries**. But into what did Abaros initiate Pythagoras?

Diodorus Siculus, quoting the historian Hecateus (6th century BC), mentions the visit, and connects Hyperborea with Britain, home of many of Europe's great **megalithic** henges. A survey of such sites by Prof. Alexander Thom has established the use in their construction of Pythagorean geometric principles, but over a millennium before Pythagoras lived.[1]

As to the identity of the 'winged temple', some say it was **Stonehenge**. Another candidate is Callanish on Lewis in the Outer Hebrides: a circle not only pre-dating Stonehenge, but contained within the 'wings' of an avenue and three subsidiary arms: i.e., within a **cross**.

1. *Megalithic Sites in Britain*, Alexander Thom, OUP, 1967.

ABDUCTIONS (*See* **FAIRIES, OTHERWORLD, SACRIFICE, UFOs, UNDERWORLD**)

In ancient myth the abduction of mortals or gods by **underworld** deities epitomises nature's annual death and rebirth. **Sumerian, Babylonian** and **Greek** lore tells of the abduction or forced descent of fertility-goddesses (**Inanna, Ishtar, Persephone**) to the underworld, whence each spring they are released to renew the world. The Greek account is that **Hades** stole Persephone, daughter of the **sky-god Zeus**, who made Hades return her to her distraught mother, the goddess **Demeter**, for half of each year.

The murdered **corn-gods** (**Adonis, Osiris, Tammuz**) likewise descend to the underworld, to be resurrected as spring's new growth. Egyptian **Set** murders Osiris, who becomes Lord of the Underworld. **Christ** crucified is dead three days (dark of the **moon**) before rising again: Jonah spends a similar period in the **whale**'s belly. The prophet **Enoch, Methuselah**'s father, was taken by God, aged 365 years.[1] Does this imply the year's death and rebirth? In **Norse myth** the **Fimbulwinter**, lasting three years, begins when the **wolf** Skoll swallows ('abducts') the **sun**. In **Welsh myth** Gwion Bach is eaten up by the hag **Cerridwen**, who nine months later bears him as **Taliesin**. The **Aztecs** appointed a youth king for a year, then tore out his heart. The old king (year) is sacrificed: the new king (year) is duly anointed (reborn).

This basic myth became part of folk belief. The **Pied Piper**, denied payment for ridding Hamelin of its rats, in revenge abducts the children, **Orpheus**-like charming them with his music into the sea to drown, or into a magic **mountain** from which one day (like **Arthur, Charlemagne** or Frederick **Barbarossa**) he and they may return.

Celtic folklore is likewise rich in tales of mortals charmed away by **fairies** into the **otherworld**, or of fairies stealing human babies, leaving wizened **changelings** instead. In 1692 the **Rev. Robert Kirk**, a Scot, was found dead on a fairy knowe. Folk said he was not dead, but seized by the fairies (*see* **Kirk**).[2] So, too, in a well-known ballad the thirteenth-century Scots poet and seer **True Thomas** (Thomas the Rhymer) one day meets 'the queen of fair Elfland'. Warned not to kiss her, he does. 'Now, ye maun go wi' me,' she says, 'And ye maun serve me seven years.'[3]

The 'seven-year' period is typical. The abductee's otherworld visit may seem to last but hours, yet on return he finds 'seven years', or 'a hundred years and a day' gone by. In the Irish voyage of **Bran MacFebal**, the mariners returning from the West (Land of the Dead) are warned not to set foot on land which, to them, they left only months earlier, for many years have passed. One homesick sailor wades ashore, and crumbles into dust. Similarly, **Oisin**, much like True Thomas abducted to **Tir nan Og** by Niav of the Golden Hair, returns to Ireland to find three centuries gone; he too crumbles into dust when his horse throws him on the shore.

The modern version of the myth involves the abduction of mortals by entities associated with **UFOs**. In some such reports, as in the case of Barney and Betty Hill, supposedly abducted while driving late at night through the New Hampshire mountains (USA, September 1961), the event is recalled only later under hypnosis, following time-loss and nervous crisis.

In *Communion* (1987) the American novelist Whitley Streiber tells how he was abducted by 'visitors' in upstate New York in December 1985. Under hypnosis he recalled being enticed from his house into a 'black iron cot'. Levitated into a little round room, he underwent medical and sexual examination by four types of entity: one robot-like; the second, short and stocky beings in blue coveralls (the 'good army'); the third, frail beings with vestigial mouth, nose and hypnotic black slanted eyes; the fourth, bald and small with black button-like eyes. His 'examination' was overseen by a third-category female with yellow-brown leathery skin. She seemed old, wise and insectile. Later he associated her big slanted eyes with images of the Babylonian goddess **Ishtar**. He implied that these entities are physically 'real' yet somehow rooted in the human unconscious. They can enter the mind, affect perception and draw the **soul** from the body. He felt they had occupied earth a long time and might be involved with human evolution. They said this world 'is a school', that they 'recycle souls'.

He asks if (1) they are a modern manifestation of the fairy race; (2) **spirits** of the dead; (3) creations of the human collective unconscious; (4) from other **dimensions**; (5) an archaic, group-minded, insectile species sharing the world with us; superior, yet afraid of human unpredictability.[4]

The sense of proximity to alien species, fearful yet glamorous, runs through all folklore. Certain beliefs typify every age. One is that the abductors seek sexual union with humanity, to create a superior hybrid, or to ensure racial survival. There are the tales of (typically) poets (True Thomas), magicians (**Merlin**), sacred kings (Arthur, Charlemagne) removed to an otherworldly realm whence they may return if required or released by correct ritual. Finally, the myths of fertility-gods/goddesses: their abduction epitomising Nature's annual seasonal death and rebirth.

1. Genesis v: 21.
2. *The Secret Commonwealth of Elves, Fauns and Fairies,* Robert Kirk, Observer Press, Stirling, 1933 (1691).
3. 'The Ballad of Thomas the Rhymer' (anon.), as in *The Edinburgh Book of Scottish Verse,* ed. W. MacNeile Dixon, Meiklejohn & Holden, London, 1910.
4. *Communion,* Whitley Streiber, Arrow Books, London, 1988, p.95.

ABOMINABLE SNOWMAN (*See* YETI)

ABORIGINES (*See* ARANDA, OCEANIC MYTHOLOGY, YURLUNGUR)

On arrival in Australia in 1788 the British found nomadic folk who, seemingly isolated on the continent over 30,000 years before, numbered some 300,000. Divided into over 400 tribes, these 'Aborigines' were hunters and fruit-gatherers. Lacking technology or agriculture, they had a complex mythology and ritual culture, believing in a distant **sky-god**, and in local animistic deities and culture-heroes. Via initiation rites and group ceremonies they sustained tribal life by continually reaffirming the mythic events of the alchera, or Dreamtime: a legendary era not so much in the past as in what **Jung** terms the collective unconscious. In it, the Wondjina (ancestral spirits) rose from sleep, walked and shaped the land, created all birds and beasts (Man included) and taught Man how to survive. Then they returned to sleep in the earth, or (say other traditions), married into humanity.

Figures (some over 10,000 years old) said to represent the Wondjina are found in the Australian outback, painted on open rock, faces and shoulders white, eyes and nose black, a red band invariably circling their heads like a halo or helmet. These haloes carry marks like writing, as also found in South American rock carvings. It is said the artists came from the sky and long ago returned to it, now to be seen as lights moving among the stars.

The Aborigines say that a tree (as with the Norse **Yggdrasil** or the **Christian cross**) joins earth to heaven, and that Man has two **souls**. The 'real' one is the eternal soul of the Dreamtime; the other appears 'in dreams, [and] may take up its abode within another person after its owner's death, or may lie in the bush and play tricks'.[1]

They say material goods harm their owners unless always in motion. So, such goods were once continually traded in a continent-wide game, the land itself the game-board, all its inhabitants players. The value of the goods exchanged lay in token of intent: to meet and trade again, to fix frontiers and share ideas, to mark and maintain psychic highways called 'Songlines'.[2]

These, formed during the legendary continent-wide journeys made by the Dreamtime **ancestors**, define not only the land's features but the relations between different tribes. Thus each tribe came to guard part of the common ancestral myth: members of other tribes walking the Songlines through alien territory had to learn (and sing) the local Song to pass safely, to trade, or to find a wife. So each tribe held part of the jigsaw of knowledge laid down in the Dreamtime: none could be despised or destroyed by another, or the knowledge they alone held would be lost.

Holding Dreamtime myth-events to be as 'real' as factual phenomena, the Aborigines maintained rites to reaffirm this primal knowledge in each new generation. Of rites paralleling Christian ceremony, one involved 'eating' the primal father, involving **cannibalism**, or at least drinking **blood** from older men by the initiates. They were intrigued by the Christian Communion, in which Christ's body and blood is (symbolically) eaten and drunk.

Creation accounts vary, but one says the **sun-goddess** Yhi, alerted by the whispering of Baiame, the Great Spirit, descended to earth, fertilising it wherever her heat touched. With the whole earth clad in flowers, trees and grass, she rested. Baiame was pleased. Then she went under the earth where dim forms stirred to life. Wings sprouting, the insects followed her to the outer world, to begin their work. Baiame sent her to the mountains, to melt the ice. From the flowing water emerged fish, snakes and reptiles; rivers rushed down to the plains, feeding plants, encouraging reptiles to leap on to the dry land. Next she entered mountain caves, to find the latent soul of birds and beasts. Her light awoke them, and down the mountain they flew and ran. Yhi told them what she had done, and who they were, and that Baiame would guard them. Soon she would send the seasons, but first she must leave them for the sky, where their spirits would join her when their bodies died. So she rose, a dwindling ball of light that fell in the west. The first night scared her creatures. After long hours, the birds welcomed her return in the east. After this, they knew she would leave at night but return at dawn. To encourage them, she sent the Morning Star to herald her daily return. But the star was lonely, so she created Bahloo, the moon, to sail the night, giving birth to the other stars, and making each night majestic.

Yet another task remained, for none of the creatures made by Baiame and Yhi were satisfied: the fishes wanted to walk, the animals wished to fly. For the last time Yhi descended to the earth to meet her creatures. All demanded new forms, which they thought would make them happy. Knowing she had failed, she went back to the sky, leaving the rest to Baiame, the Great Spirit who, bodiless, fashioned an animal in which his mind lived.

So Man was made, secretly, amid a great darkness, as **Flood** ravaged the land. The animals hid in the hills until the mists parted and the Flood fell. Yhi again shone; and the animals, leaving their cave, saw standing before them Baiame in the form of Man who has since ruled all creation, for he has Baiame's soul in a human body. Yet Man was lonely. He went for company to Kangaroo, Wombat, Snake and Lizard, but they had too little of Baiame in them. The beauty of trees, grasses and flowers did not satisfy his soul. One night he slept beneath a grass yacca tree, troubled by strange dreams. He awoke to find Yhi shining into the yacca tree. Even as he watched, the tree changed into a shape like yet unlike him. Shorter, rounder, smoother, softer: it was Woman! He came to her, and she stepped out of the tree to join him. Then the animals, who had gathered to watch, danced with delight to see the loneliness of Man ended.[3]

1. *The Secret Life of Humans*, Stan Gooch, Dent, London, 1981, p.29.
2. *The Songlines*, Bruce Chatwin, Picador, London, 1988, p.63.
3. Adapted from *Myths and Legends of Australia*, A.W. Reed, A.H. & A.W. Reed, Sydney, 1965, pp.15–25.

ACHILLES (*See* **ACHILLES HEEL, GREEK MYTH, HERO MYTH**)
In Greek myth the **Nereid** (sea-nymph) Thetis **shape-shifted** many times to
evade the amorous advances of the Thessalian hero Peleus: becoming a fish,
an animal, a wave and a flame (much as, in Welsh myth, young **Gwion Bach**
shifts shape in futile flight from **Cerridwen**). But Peleus, aided by the
centaur Chiron, seized and married her. In time she bore a son, Achilles,
who, being half-mortal, was doomed to die. Thetis dipped him in the River
Styx, rendering his entire body **invulnerable**, save for the heel by which she
held him. Aged nine, it was foretold of him by the seer Calchas that he would
conquer Troy. Fearing his death there, Thetis disguised him as a girl in the
palace of Lycomedes, king of Skyros. But the Greek champion **Odysseus**
entered the palace and sounded war-cries. Thinking they were being
attacked, Achilles seized his weapons and so betrayed himself. Taken to
Troy, he killed the Trojan hero **Hector** in single combat, before himself
being slain, shot through the heel by an arrow fired either by Apollo or by
Paris. Thus, an early statement of the theme known as the 'Achilles heel'.

ACHILLES HEEL (*See* **ACHILLES, BALDUR, CUCHULAINN,
SIEGFRIED**)
The theme of one flaw dooming an otherwise **invulnerable** hero says as much
about human imperfectability as the need to limit the power of individuals.
Thus the **Teutonic** hero **Siegfried** became invulnerable by washing in the
blood of the **dragon Fafnir**, except for a spot under his left shoulder where a
leaf stuck while he bathed. Unwittingly betrayed by Kriemhild, he is speared
through that spot and slain by Hagen (*see* *Nibelungenlied*). In **Norse myth**,
Baldur, most beautiful of the **Aesir**, is so well loved that all beasts, plants,
minerals, poisons and sicknesses on earth swear to the goddess **Frigga** not to
harm him. Only the **mistletoe**, growing not on earth but on the **oak** (between
earth and sky), made no promise, Frigga having forgotten to ask it. Learning
this, the jealous god **Loki**, hating Baldur, tricks Baldur's blind brother
Hodur into hurling the fatal **mistletoe** dart.

In **Irish myth**, kings and heroes are bound by contradictory *geasa* (the
plural form of *geis*), or magical prohibitions. To obey one *geis* means to
disobey another, leading to fated death. So **Cuchulainn** ('the Hound of
Chulainn') cannot refuse a feast yet must not eat **dog**, his totem animal.
Warned by **omens** (a cup brimming with blood, a ford where the *bean-nighe*
scrubs bloody clothes) that his **fate** is near, he meets three old crones who ask
him to join in eating a dog roasting over a spit. He must break one *geis* to obey
the other. As he eats, the strength goes out of him.

So too with mechanical or monstrous men. In Greek myth, Talos is the
giant guardian of Crete met by **Jason** and the Argonauts. Made of bronze,
created by **Daedalus**, his only weakness is that 'beneath the sinew of his
ankle was a blood-red vein; and this, with its issues of life and death, was
covered by a thin skin'.[1] Through this weak point Talos met his doom, just as
Frankenstein's monster is doomed by human emotions, or **Superman** by
kryptonite. Even modern **superheroes** must have their Achilles heel.

1. *Argonautica*, Apollonius of Rhodes (IV, 1638–48).

ACTAEON (*See* **ARTEMIS, GREEK MYTH, TRANSFORMATION**)
Pursuing a **stag** with his hounds, this Greek hunter came to the fountain of
Parthenius in the valley of Gargaphia. Here the goddess Artemis was bathing
naked as part of her *anados* (yearly reappearance), by which she renewed her
virginity. Smitten by her beauty, Actaeon peeped, but was seen. Enraged,

she changed him into a stag and set his own hounds on him.

This myth may refer to the fate of the 'stag king', 'horned god' or **Green Man**, alias **Cernunnos**. In the Welsh *Mabinogion*, Pwyll, Prince of Dyfed, hunts a stag which is his own soul. The doomed god Llew Llaw Gyffes (also Mabinogion), sees a stag being baited to death: it too is his soul. The tradition of a man wearing stag-skins being chased, killed and eaten (a punishment for trespass) survived into Roman times. **Graves** suggests that this ancient stag-cult (the hunter becoming the hunted) dates back to at least 20,000 BC, as indicated by paleolithic cave-paintings at Altamira in Spain and in the French Ariège.[1]

1. *The White Goddess*, Robert Graves, Faber & Faber, London, 1961, p.217.

ADAM (*See* CADUCEUS, CREATION MYTH, EDEN, EVE, SERPENT, YAHWEH)

'So God created man in his own image, in the image of God created he him; male and female created he them.'[1] It seems odd to many that in the Bible **creation** myth the first man, Adam, is said to have given birth to Woman! Yet the Jewish Midrash says this primal Adam was an androgyne, or **hermaphrodite**; both male and female, as is the Adam Kadmon of **Qabalah**. Likewise the word 'man' derives from the Sanskrit *manas*, 'mind', implying no original gender discrimination. So by this account the division of the sexes caused the **Fall** from unity into multiplicity, leading to knowledge of Good and Evil, and expulsion from **Eden** into the world of birth, death and sorrow.

Variants of the myth of the first man exist the world over. **Aborigines** tell how Baiame created the first Man, and how Woman came out of the yacca tree to join him. The Efik of Africa tell how the **sky-god** Abassi set the first man and woman on earth. Fearing they might excel him in wisdom, his wife Atai forbade them to procreate or work. But they ignored the gods by tilling the soil and mating, so Atai sent death, and made their children fight (*see* **Cain**). In **Slavonic myth** the evil spirit **Erlik** was sometimes seen as the first man, like Adam fallen from grace. Banished to the depths (expelled from Eden), he became Lord of the **underworld**. Yet to the Tartars he remained 'the father' of humankind. So too in **Vedic** belief **Yama**, the first man, was also the first man to die, and likewise became Lord of the Dead. In **Persian myth**, the father and mother of humanity, Mashye and Mashyane, denied the wise lord **Ahura Mazda** for the evil one, **Ahriman**.

The Biblical Adam is not original. He appears first as Adapa, son of the Sumerian god **Ea**, Lord of the **Apsu**, the fresh-water ocean on which the earth was thought to float. King of Eridu, Adapa invented speech (Adam names only the beasts and fowl) but was not **immortal**, declining the god **Anu**'s offer of the 'food of life' and the 'water of life', preferring human kingship, accepting humanity's fate to be disease and death (duality: expulsion from the Garden). Adam is a scribal creation from *c*.1000 BC or even later, from the time of the Jewish captivity in Babylon. Nor was he originally in Eden at all. Akkadian seals from long before Genesis was written portray the primal Garden of Immortality as inhabited by two female figures, **Demeter–Persephone**, the **mother-goddess**, accompanied by the **Serpent**, the cosmic spirit that fertilises Mother Earth.[2]

So Adam and Eve are fathered by the Serpent and mothered by the earth. The jealous god **Yahweh** is a late insertion. The patriarchal scribes of Genesis demonise both the Serpent and the Woman, presenting an interloper, Yahweh, as the true god, but failed to expel all the contradictions. So the Lord God, having told Adam and Eve that they will die if they eat of the Tree of the Knowledge of Good and Evil, is contradicted by the Serpent: 'Ye shall not surely die.' They eat, and do not die (save esoterically, in that by falling into duality they lose their primal androgynous spirit-life). There is also evidence throughout the text that Yahweh himself is but a (disguised) aspect of the Serpent power.[3]

1. Genesis i: 27.
2. *Occidental Mythology*, Joseph Campbell, Penguin, London, 1976, p.13.
3. *Ibid.*, pp.29–30.

ADAPA (*See* **ADAM, CREATION MYTH, SUMERIAN MYTH**)

ADDER (*See* **ASP, SERPENT, SNAKE**)
The only poisonous snake in the British Isles retains a reputation for sly cunning ('a snake in the grass'). **Druid** amulets called 'gloine nathair' appear to have been adder stones. A man of Lewis in the Outer Hebrides describes how, 'A number of serpents (adders) congregrating at certain times form themselves into a knot and move round and round on the stone until a hole is worn. They pass and re-pass each other through the stone, which by-and-by becomes hard. It is this slime which gives the stone the healing properties it is supposed to possess.'[1]
   The rarity of poisonous snakes in Britain, and their absence in Ireland (since **St Patrick** drove them out), does not explain the British tradition and horror of the **'loathly worm'**: another story.

1. *The Silver Bough*, F. Marian McNeill, MacLellan, Glasgow, 1977.

ADONIS (*See* **CORN-GODS, PHOENICIAN MYTH**)
Born of a **tree** into which his mother transformed herself, like the Norse **Baldur**, this vegetation-god (his name comes from the Canaanite *adon*, or 'lord') grew up a young man of great beauty. Identified in the Bible by Ezekiel as the Mesopotamian **corn-god Tammuz**, his myth was adopted by the Greeks. It is said that at his birth **Aphrodite** put him in a coffer which she gave to **Persephone**, goddess of the **underworld** – thus, that he was planted in the earth. Opening the coffer, transfixed by his beauty, Persephone would not give him up. **Zeus** settled the dispute by ordering him to spend half the year on earth and the other half (winter) in the underworld.
   His cult, widespread throughout Phoenicia, was special to the temple of **Astarte** at Byblos in Syria. Here were celebrated his annual death (after the harvest) and rebirth (when the red anemone bloomed).
   It was said his death occurred in a gorge near the source of the Nahr Ibrahim, called the River Adonis by the Greeks. Here every year he was gored by a wild boar (sacred to the Syrians), his mortal wound changing the waters to blood. This phenomenon is said to be due to the washing into the river of particles of red ochre (known as **'blood** of the earth') at times when the river runs high.

ADU OGYINAE (*See* **AFRICAN MYTH, ASHANTI, CREATION MYTH**)
This bold hero and leader of the first people, say the Ashanti of Ghana, brought the first people to earth through holes in the ground. On arriving above the ground they were terrified, but Adu Ogyinae laid his hands on them and they were calmed. Next day, as he and his company were building the first houses, he was killed by a falling tree.

This echoes the myth of **Christ**, crucified on the **cross** (a **tree**), or of **Odin**, self-impaled on the world-tree **Yggdrasil** by his own **spear**. It seems the creators of culture are invariably sacrificed by the culture they create. Not for the first or last time: 'Long live the King, the King must die.' Life is invariably **abducted** by death: mythic heroes are those who not only live well, but who bravely face the inevitability of death.

ADVERTISING AND PROPAGANDA (*See* ARTHURIAN MYTH)

Today public opinion and belief are manipulated on a vast scale by those named 'hidden persuaders' or 'people shapers' by the American author Vance Packard. Operating through the mass media, these technicians mould public perception of political parties and commercial products alike. Political moulding is called propaganda, the commercial variety, advertising. Either form plays on the collective human susceptibility to myth, ancient or modern. In the 1960 US Presidential election, **John F. Kennedy**'s campaign managers tried to persuade folk that the candidate was of mythic status: a glamorous war-hero, a new **King Arthur**. They succeeded so well that, when Kennedy came to power, his White House 'court' was soon called '**Camelot**', after the Arthurian court. Henry VII, first Tudor King of England (1485–1509), justified his seizure of the throne by claiming descent from King Arthur. Naming his first son Arthur, he damned his predecessor, Richard III, as a hunchbacked tyrant who had murdered the two young 'Princes in the Tower'. This worked so well that even today Richard's true nature remains in dispute. So too Kennedy's 1960 Republican opponent, Richard M. Nixon, was slighted as 'an hairy man' who had to shave twice a day. In 1968, Nixon got his revenge. In *The Selling of the President*, Joe McGinniss described how Nixon's election managers reinstated his mythic image.[1]

More dangerously, during the 1930s Hitler's **Nazi** Party stage-managed mass rallies that drowned the German mind in **Teutonic** myth. Searchlights spearing the night sky like temple pillars and bloody banners stimulated emotion so potent that few could resist. In *Mein Kampf*, Hitler wrote: 'one deals with the problem of influencing the human will . . . In the morning and during the day it seems that the power of the human will rebels with its strongest energy against any attempt to impose upon it the will or opinion of another. On the other hand, in the evening it easily succumbs to the domination of a stronger will . . . The mysterious artificial dimness of the Catholic churches also serves this purpose . . .'[2]

For the **Christian** Church has been in the business of mythic propaganda and advertising at least since the time of **St Paul**, at whose door may be laid the supernaturalisation of Christ; the creation of a divine image for a new **religion** which, to succeed, had to compete in a crowded marketplace with already popular died-and-reborn gods such as **Adonis, Mithras** or **Attis**. Following the institutionalisation of Christianity, abbeys and monasteries competed for the lucrative pilgrim trade by advertising their possession of relics (*see* **Shroud of Turin**). The healing powers, real or imagined, of old pagan **wells** were sanctified as Christian; the old gods and goddesses were converted into the saints of the Church; the myth of hellfire for the sinner was promoted; the promise of salvation was sold as pragmatically as today, when we are subjected to 30-second mythic tv dramas persuading us that if we buy this car or that perfume we become **Superman** or Superwoman. Such claims play on the same hopes and fears that led the medieval pilgrim to seek a cure by touching a holy relic; all are myths, in the negative sense of myth as a lie or false expression of life as it actually is. The point here is simply this: if collectively we were not affected by such false romances, nobody would try to foist them on us. As it is, advertising myths flourish today as never before. So who are we to despise the beliefs and superstitions of those who lived before us? There's *still* one born every minute.[3]

1. *The Selling of the President*, Joe McGinniss, Penguin, London, 1970.
2. *The Messianic Legacy*, Baigent Leigh & Lincoln, Corgi, London, 1987, p.196.
3. *The People Shapers*, Vance Packard, Macdonald, London, 1978.

AENEAS (*See* GREEK MYTH, HOMER, ROMAN MYTH, VIRGIL)

Son of Anchises and the goddess **Aphrodite**, this warrior led his followers from the fallen city of Troy in Asia Minor to the Tiber in Italy. Here he married Lavinia, daughter of the local king, Latinus. Founding a town, Lavinium, he succeeded Latinus but died in war after a short reign. Later revered as founder of the Roman race and state, in the first century BC the poet **Virgil** celebrated him as the **archetypal** Roman hero in *The Aeneid*.

Crucial to this epic poem (which celebrates the destiny of the Romans as **Fate**-appointed rulers of the ancient world) is Virgil's description of the hero's descent to the **underworld**. Armed by the **Sibyl** with the **Golden Bough** (which Virgil compares with the **mistletoe**), Aeneas accompanies her to 'the land of shades'. There (after passing through a vast, gloomy wood lit up only by the Golden Bough), he meets Queen Dido of Carthage and tries to speak to her, but she ignores him. He meets his father Anchises, who with the prophetic power of the dead tells him of the future unity of the Trojans and Latins, culminating in Rome's glory under Augustus.

Virgil wrote his epic during the reign of Augustus, the first emperor after Julius Caesar had ended the republic by assuming godhood. Augustus wrote from Spain in 26 BC, asking Virgil to send him an early draft of *The Aeneid*, which was a good **advertisement** for the new imperial authority.[1]

Around AD 1135 the English fabulist **Geoffrey of Monmouth** claimed, in *The History of the Kings of Britain*, that the Britons were descended from **Brutus**, the great-grandson of Aeneas.

1. *The Golden Bough*, Sir James Frazer, Macmillan, London, 1963, p.703.

AESCHYLUS (*See* GREEK MYTH (1))

AESIR (*See* CREATION MYTH, NORSE MYTH, RAGNORAK, VANIR)

In **Norse myth** two races of gods exist, each always quarrelling with the other, each in perpetual enmity with the Frost **Giants**, and both inevitably moving towards their final hour – **Ragnorak**, the 'Twilight of the Gods'.

These two races are the Aesir and the Vanir. The war with the giants seemingly began soon after the northern ice began to melt. From below this melting ice appeared a giant, **Ymir**. From his feet came the Frost Giants: from his left armpit, a living being, Búri, who had a son, Borr. His marriage to Ymir's daughter, Bestla, produced the first three Aesir – **Odin**, Vili and Vé. These three young gods slew Ymir, whose blood flooded the world. In the **Flood** all the Frost Giants died save Bergelmir, who escaped to father a new giant race, forever hostile to the Aesir.

From Ymir's corpse the Aesir formed Midgard (Middle Earth), the world of Man. This lies between **Muspelheim**, the southern (higher) fire-world, and **Nifleim**, the northern (underworld) realm of ice and darkness.

The seas and lakes of Midgard came from Ymir's blood, its earth from his flesh, mountains from his bones, rocks and pebbles from his teeth and jaws. From his eyebrows the Aesir made a wall to keep the Frost Giants out. From his skull they created the dome of the sky, supported at the four corners by four **dwarves**, and by the world-tree, the **ash Yggdrasil**, round the roots of which coils the **serpent** Nidhögg, and where the three **Norns** (the Norse **Fates**) sit spinning the destiny of men.

Setting the sea in a ring round Midgard, they made stars from sparks flying from Muspelheim. With gold from the realm of the fire-demon Surtur they formed the sun-chariot, before which sped the moon-chariot. Neither dared rest a moment, being pursued by the **wolf** Skoll which at Ragnorak will consume them both, darkening the world for three years before a rebirth.

By now new gods had joined the Aesir. Their origin is not explained, but in addition to the original three they included **Baldur**, Bregi, Hodur, **Heimdall**, Hermod, **Loki, Thor, Tyr** and Vali; also their wives – **Frigga**, Iduna, Nanna and Sif. They met daily under the shade of Yggdrasil to talk of all they were doing . . . but still the world was empty of life.

The Aesir now built themselves a home, Asgard, joined to Midgard by the **rainbow** bridge, Bifrost. Less imposing than the abode of the Greek gods at **Olympus**, it was still impressive. Here the gods ate, drank, made love and squabbled while, high above it on Lidskialf, or Heaven's Crag, Odin sat and surveyed the world, two tame **ravens**, Hugin and Munin, on his shoulder.

Each day they flew the world, returning every evening to report how the giants plotted revenge. So Odin had a wall built round Asgard, guarded by the silent god Heimdall, who would blow his great Gjallarhorn should the giants ever attack. Its blast could be heard through all the worlds.

Yet soon enough, with men toiling on the earth, the Aesir had to fight a war, not with the giants, but with a race of invaders. These were the Vanir, or fertility-gods. In time a truce was declared with the upstarts, and the two races of gods intermarried. The Vanir **Frey, Freya** and Njord settled at Asgard, carousing in Odin's great hall, Valhalla. Yet (many contradictions in the myth persist), still the Aesir squabbled. The tales of these squabbles, including how jealous Loki tricked Baldur to his death, are given elsewhere. And though the Aesir are gods, it is a main part of the myth that all will die at the dreadful day of **Ragnorak,** and that only after the sun has been swallowed for three years will a new world be born.

Snorri Sturluson (1179–1241), the Icelandic author of the *Prose Eddas* in which many traditions are drawn together, thought the word *aesir* derived from 'Asia'. As **Geoffrey of Monmouth** euhemerised the **Aeneas** myth to create a genealogy for the kings of Britain, so Snorri makes **Thor** the grandson of Priam of Troy, and Odin his twentieth-generation descendant. Also he claims that the Vanir originally came from the Don region of Russia.

Today this is thought unlikely. Yet it represents an early attempt to explain Norse myth in terms of distorted historical memory of the northern movement of hunter-warrior peoples after the last Ice Age. Also it may be that the Ragnorak myth expresses an **archetypal** fear of the ice returning.

AESOP (*See* GREEK MYTH)

After **Homer**, *Aesop's Fables* may be the world's longest-running bestseller. Yet Aesop himself is probably as fabulous as his fables, in which moral and ethical tales (like 'The Tortoise and the Hare') are based on the imagined activity of beasts, as in the twentieth-century *Just-So Stories* of **Kipling**.

It is likely that Aesop never existed, and that he is an invention, a convenient assumption, the fictitious author of tales gathered by many.

The myth of Aesop begins in the fifth century BC, when the Greek historian Herodotus claimed Aesop's fables were penned a century earlier by a slave of this name. Likewise, an Egyptian biography of the first century AD describes Aesop as a slave on the isle of Samos who, freed by his master, served King Lycurgus of Babylon as **riddle**-solver before returning to Greece to die at **Delphi**. Also in the first century AD, the Roman writer Plutarch identified Aesop as an adviser in the court of the Lydian king **Croesus** (sixth century BC).

The earliest known compendium of *Aesop's Fables* was collated in the fourth century BC by Demetrius Philareus. The last known copy of this version vanished shortly after AD 800. Surviving into modern times, the edition by Phaedrus, a first-century AD Roman author, influenced all later ones. The first version to treat the fables as consecutive literature, it certainly influenced the seventeenth-century French fabulist and poet, Jean de la Fontaine.

Yet 'The **Tortoise** and the **Hare**' survives, no matter who originated it.

AFRICAN MYTH (*see* CONCORDANCE)

How, briefly, can one encompass the breadth and depth of mythic belief in a vast continent with over a thousand different languages (excluding dialects), a huge diversity of local traditions, and many ethnic religions other than **Islam** and **Christianity**. The task is made even more difficult by the Western tendency to reject African religions as inherently primitive compared to the great world religions developed in the northern hemisphere. For centuries European colonisers, insisting that African **ancestor-worship** was idolatrous nonsense, not only despised African beliefs but effectively destroyed the social fabric of traditional morality based on them, causing much subsequent turbulence. Nor does the general lack of written tradition assist the recall of ancient myths orally transmitted. The sophisticated cultures flourishing a millennium ago in western Africa and at Great Zimbabwe left nothing in writing. For knowledge of their beliefs we rely on surviving artefacts and on notes by medieval Arab travellers. Likewise, much of what is known about many pre-colonial beliefs derives from the work of Western scholars.

But some generalisations can be made. The first is that – despite the huge diversity of separate ethnic groups, from the **Zulu**, Lovedu, **Bushmen** and **Hottentots** in the south to the Berbers on the Mediterranean shore; from the **Ashanti, Fon, Dogon** and **Yoruba** in the west to the Congo pygmies and the **Masai, Kikuyu** and Ethiopian Copts in the east – almost all African peoples believe in an omniscient, omnipresent supreme sky-god. The Kikuyu and Masai of Kenya call this god **Ngai**, 'the Apportioner'; the Zulu call him uKqili, 'the wise one'; the Ganda of Uganda insist that his 'great eye' never blinks and sees everything; in Nigeria the Yoruba agree that Olodumare the Creator sees 'both the inside and outside of man'. Yet this god is not a personal or loving god; he is remote and to be approached only through the mediation of special people, medicine men who communicate with him via dream, trance and **omen**. Among the Masai these hereditary initiates, corresponding to the Siberian **shaman**, are called *iloibonok*.

Many local gods and goddesses exist, especially in West Africa, where the pantheons of the Ashanti, Fon, Yoruba and many others are more complex than those found elsewhere. The Fon gods known as *vodu* seemingly provide one root of Haitian **voodoo** worship. **Trickster**-gods like Edshu among the Yoruba, **Anansi** (Mr **Spider**) in Sierra Leone, or **Tule**, the Sudanese spider-god, love to make folk quarrel, and remain popular in folklore.

In many regions the ancestors are worshipped. It is commonly believed that they survive death to linger near their graves, emanating beneficial influence so long as they are remembered and if animal sacrifices are made. So too, many Africans are **animists**, attributing distinct spirits to every object, be it animal, vegetable or mineral. Only living things have their own spirits: stones may be inhabited by spirits, while in some trees, like the Kenyan baobab, whole families of spirits are thought to live. Spirits also inhabit *asuman*, talismen of beads or horn: the Masai say the souls of the dead may **reincarnate** in certain **snakes**, which must not be killed.

Belief in evil spirits abounds, from the **ifrit** or *djinns* of Islamic cultures in the north to the *angatch* of Madagascar. The Hottentots of the southern deserts speak of odd man-eating monsters, the Aigamuxa, who with eyes on their instep have to get down on hands and knees and hold up one foot to see. Likewise belief in **magic** is widespread, though defined in negative terms, its methods non-physical, its results invisibly acquired. The Kalahari Bushmen say that magic is the art of manipulating the spirit-world, which can be seen only by **sorcerers**. In other ways their beliefs match those of the Australian **Aborigines**. 'You know,' a Bushman told Laurens van der Post, 'there is a dream dreaming us.'[1] Elsewhere, diviners called *nganga* prophesy or perceive distant events by tossing bones or their *hakata* sticks. These are sometimes incorrectly called witchdoctors.

Belief in magic, in **witches** and **witchdoctors**, was derided by European missionaries and doctors, who saw in it only deception and charlatanry. It was noted how individuals **cursed** to death would simply wait to die, which they duly did, but this was taken to be but auto-suggestion. The negative image of the witchdoctor became a stock European cliché in assessing the Africans as unsophisticated. In fact, though the term 'witchdoctor' is used to mean a healer using magic medicines or harming folk by sorcery, its only correct use is of one who exorcises witches by driving out evil **spirits**.

In Africa witches are always evil, though not necessarily female: their urge is to cause misfortune by **black magic**, or to 'eat' people by devouring their spiritual strength. Belief that witchcraft may run in the family is found from Zaïre to South Africa, where 'witch-smellers' seek out witches by smelling the aura of death and magic poison surrounding them.[2]

1. *Jung and the Story of our Time*, Laurens van der Post, Penguin, London, 1978.
2. *African Mythology*, Jan Knappert, Aquarian Press, Wellingborough, 1990.

AFTERLIFE (*See* OTHERWORLD, UNDERWORLD)

Throughout the world the individual **soul** is said to survive death, though in what state is unclear. This belief goes back a long time. Neanderthal burials from 80,000 BC imply preparation for the afterlife. The Phoenician myth of the murdered **Adonis** reborn in spring restates the idea. Egyptians saw the *ba* (soul) as a bird taking flight at physical death. Homeric Greeks saw the dead as shades condemned to endless misery in **Hades**. Africans thought the dead flutter as bats in jungle caves. **Christian** dogmas of heaven and hell use the concept to coerce morality. *The Tibetan Book of the Dead* advises the newly-dead how to avoid rebirth. The *Koran* states that those who doubt immortality are dead and do not know when they will be born again. Based perhaps on fear of death, the belief persists despite lack of proof.

AGAMEMNON (*See* HOMER, *ILIAD*, ORESTES)

AGHARTI (*See* ATLANTIS, CAVES, HOLLOW EARTH, LOST WORLDS, SHAMBHALA)

The notion of a lost subterranean world inhabited by superbeings possessed of potent secret science still exercises a powerful fascination. Perhaps it merely restates classical myths of the **underworld**, from **Tartarus** to **Hades**, or **Celtic** tales of the **fairy**-folk, or maybe it is no more than unrealised metaphor for our own unconscious underworld – but it persists.

The myth of Agharti – a subterranean kingdom linked to the four corners of the earth by a network of tunnels, and inhabited by a peace-loving folk who try to moderate the excesses of us aboveground dwellers – appears to be ancient. **Plato**, the mythologer of Atlantis, also speaks of 'tunnels both broad and narrow, in the interior of the earth', and of a great ruler, 'who sits in the centre, on the navel of the earth, and he is the interpreter of religion to all mankind'. The Roman writer Pliny, in his *Natural History*, likewise mentions folk who fled underground after Atlantis was destroyed.[1]

The twelfth-century Welsh historian Walter Map, in *De Nugis Curialium*, tells how a British king, Herla, was led by a handsome man to an underworld realm from which, after a stay of just three days, he returns to find two hundred years passed in the mortal world (*see* **Abductions**).

In short, Agharti is the Land of the Dead.

Yet the theme is powerful, and has persisted in numerous romances since the mid-nineteenth century. **Bulwer-Lytton**, Conan Doyle, **Jules Verne**, **Edgar Rice Burroughs** and many other fantasists have made free with it, while esoteric traditionalists continue to assert that Agharti is fact, not fiction. They claim that the Atlanteans migrated to Asia where they tunnelled under the Himalayas to create the mystical city of Agharti. There to this day dwell the mystical 'White Brotherhood' or 'White Lodge', awaiting the Last Days when they may emerge again to rule the world.[2]

1. *The Lost World of Agharti*, Alec Maclellan, Corgi, London, 1983.
2. *The Subterranean Kingdom*, Nigel Pennick, Turnstone Press, 1981.

AGNI (*See* FIRE, HESTIA, INDIAN MYTH, VESTA)

The **Vedic** god of **fire**: identified as **Indra**'s twin brother and as an **avatar** of **Brahma**; the fire-god and 'vital spark' of life, personifying solar fire, lightning, and the fire by which men burned down the forests of ancient India to clear ground. His altar is oriented to the rising sun. He is the Indian god of marriage: bride and groom walk seven times round the fire to sanctify their union. He is invoked by lovers as a source of virility. He knows what goes on in every house, because he is honoured in every house as the hearth fire. Some say that if he is present, the mother must be sick or have died. He is honest as fire is honest: he cleanses sin, so the **Hindus** burn their dead. He is the divine priest: Indra the divine warrior.

Lotus-born, he is depicted with two red faces (sun-fire, earth-fire). His seven arms reach the seven continents. His three legs represent the sacrificial, nuptial, and funeral fires of a person's life. His seven tongues of flame lick up the sacrificial butter. In the *Mahabharata* it is told how, exhausting himself by consuming too many offerings, he recovered by burning down the Khandava Forest, aided by **Krishna** and **Arjuna**, despite Indra's displeasure. In this guise, as destructive fire, he is identified with **Rudra**, the roaring god, an aspect of **Shiva**.

AGRIPPA, CORNELIUS (1486–1535) (*See* BLACK MAGIC, FAUST, PARACELSUS)

After his death and even during his life, this restless German Renaissance occultist became the very symbol of the myth of the black magician or evil magus. Yet the facts of his life suggest another interpretation.

Court secretary to the Holy Roman Emperor at the age of nineteen, he was sent as an imperial spy to France. Study of gematria and **Qabalah** brought him a Doctorship in Divinity. Yet his unorthodox views led to denunciation by the Franciscans. He had to move, and keep moving. His *De occulta philosophia* (*On Occult Philosophy*), a major survey of Renaissance magic, was written by 1510 but went unpublished until 1533. In it he divides the universe into three worlds: elemental, celestial and intellectual; each affected by that above it. Magicians may draw upper-world virtues down by manipulating the lower ones. The elemental world is revealed via medicine and natural philosophy, the celestial world via astrology and mathematics and the intellectual world by religious ceremony.[1] Though denying the evil uses of knowledge so gained, he advocated demonic magic to attract intellectual power. He said bodily health is subject to imaginative will, and that impure thought guarantees a corresponding bodily impurity: the practice of ceremonial religion leads to pure thought and firm spirit, without which disaster is inevitable.

Denouncing the ancient Magi as false compared with Catholic faith, he still said their teachings were valuable – to those able to sift truth from lies. No surprise that notoriety pursued him. The **Wandering Jew** was said to have visited him: another myth claims that a student, secretly using his book of spells, inadvertently summoned a **demon** and was strangled. Finding the corpse, Agrippa apparently ordered the demon to revive the student who, walking in the marketplace, collapsed dead of a heart-attack. Examination of the corpse indicated strangulation. Agrippa was again forced to flee.

Ruined by endless conflict with the Church, unable (like **Paracelsus**) to keep quiet, driven from every town he tried to settle in, his desire for peace proved elusive: unsurprising, given his rash claims that he contacted the dead and talked to demons. Yet he died not in jail or at the stake, but of bitterness and exhaustion, at Grenoble in 1535. In a late book, *De vanitate scientarium* (*On the Vanity of Sciences and Arts*) (1530) he claimed, Faust-like, that knowledge brings only disillusionment. He would have been even more upset to learn how, in nineteenth-century books of nursery rhymes (like Strüwwelpeter) he figured as the epitome of the black magician, and as one of the founder fathers of the modern myth of Faust.[1]

1. *Giordano Bruno and the Hermetic Tradition*, Frances A. Yates, Routledge & Kegan Paul, London, 1964.

AH PUCH (*See* MAYAN MYTH)

AHALYA (*See* INDIAN MYTH, INDRA)

The first woman ever created (by **Brahma**), she married the priest Gautama. The sky-god Indra fell in love with her, and persuaded the **moon** to take the form of a **cock** and crow while it was still night. Hearing it, Gautama rose to go to prayer. As soon as he left the room Indra took his shape, and seduced Ahalya who, suspecting his identity, begged protection against Gautama's wrath. But Gautama appeared and cursed Indra, so that the god's testicles fell off, and also cursed Ahalya (her name means 'Night') so that for 10,000 years she was invisible. At length, though, the hero **Rama** restored her to visibility and reconciled Gautama to her.

AHOEITU (*See* **CREATION MYTH, OCEANIC MYTH**)

The legendary king of Tonga (southwest of Samoa, west of Tahiti), descended from Kohai, the first man, who was the offspring of a **worm**, or grub. One day the **sky-god** Eitumatupua climbed down to earth on a great **tree** and married Ilaheva, one of the worm's descendants. He returned to the sky while Ilaheva bore their child, Ahoeitu, meaning 'Day Has Dawned'. Growing up, Ahoeitu climbed the tree to meet his father, who was glad to see him. They pressed noses. But Eitumatupua's other sons, sky-born, were so jealous that they ambushed, dismembered, cooked and ate Ahoeitu. Making them vomit up the pieces, Eitumatupua restored his earthly son to life with magic herbs, and sent him back down to earth as the Tongan king. His sky-born brothers begged forgiveness, and in time were allowed to descend the great tree. But Ahoeitu's descendants thereafter ruled as Tui Tonga, or kings.

AHRIMAN (*See* **AHURA MAZDA, DEVIL, DUALISM, PERSIAN MYTH, ZOROASTER**)

Also called Angra Mainya, 'the destructive spirit', or Druj, 'the lie', in **Persian–Zoroastrian** mythology of the **Zend-Avesta**, Ahriman was created by the 'Wise Lord', Ahura Mazda, as twin brother of Spenta Mainya, 'the living spirit'. But like **Satan** he turned against his maker. In his greed, wrath and envy he created **demons** (*devas*) to prosecute his war against the Wise Lord. Devoted to trickery and lies, they existed to thwart the good. He created the **dragon** Azhi Dahaka, and when Ahura Mazda made the stars, leapt like a **snake** into the sky to form the planets, whose evil influence then fell over the world. Bringing frost to winter and heat to summer, he also created insects and all other diseases and misfortunes that folk endure.

This myth, perhaps from the seventh century BC, led to a dualism so stern that the Persian Sassanians (AD 226–652) tried to alleviate it, explaining that Ahriman and Spenta Mainya were in fact the children of Zurvan Akarana, 'Infinite Time'. Zurvan had promised the firstborn kingship but, as Ahriman had 'ripped the womb open' to claim the title, his worldly reign would only last 9,000 years. Then Ahura Mazda would triumph and Ahriman perish.

This dualism deeply influenced the **Manichaean** heresy. Troubling the Church from the fourth century to the thirteenth, its final expression as Catharism was at last bloodily suppressed. Today the **Parsees**, inheriting Zoroastrian belief, explain Ahriman as an **allegory** of humanity's dark side. Yet it seems that Ahriman had once been an underworld god. Dedications to *Deo Arimanio* exist in **caves** used by devotees of **Mithra**: the **Aryan** Mitra who became Ahura Mazda.

AHURA MAZDA (*See* **AHRIMAN, FIRE-WORSHIP, MITHRA, ZOROASTER**)

This 'Wise Lord' of Zoroastrian belief, also called Ormuzd, reigned supreme in Persia after Zoroaster promoted monotheism (seventh century BC). Worshipped by Darius I (522–486 BC) and his successors, he may once have been connected with Mithra before his elevation as the sole symbol of moral purity. Seen as light and fire (as with the Indian **Agni** representing truth, also as the divine spark indwelling humanity), he was forever opposed to Ahriman's dark deceit. His son Atar (sky-fire) defeated the three-headed **dragon** Azhi Dahaka, burying him under the ocean. But the dragon was destined to escape, destroying a third of mankind before being slain (as in Revelation) at the end of time.

All the elements of the dualistic war between Ahura Mazda and Ahriman, light and dark, existed in the Indian mind. But where in **Indian myth** unity underlies the multiplicity of gods, those settling the Iranian plateau were inspired by Zoroaster to a monotheism admitting of no shades between light and dark. Once the magi, his priestly followers, realised that absolute righteousness cannot be attained on earth, they could personify good and evil only in increasingly opposed terms: thus Ahriman and Ahura Mazda. This dualism the **Christian** Church has never quite escaped: thus God and **Devil**.

AINU (*See* JAPANESE MYTH)

Maybe Caucasian in origin, renowned for their hairiness, the Ainu occupied Hokkaido, Sakhalin and the Kiril Isles long before the Japanese. **Animists** claiming descent from a **bear** or an **eagle**, today no more than 12,000 Ainu are still identified as such, none of pure blood.

Their legends say they were once cannibals, eating their own relations raw. But the divine Aioina ('teacher'), who created the first Ainu (meaning 'man'), again descended from heaven to warn them against **cannibalism** and to teach them how to catch and cook game. To do this he put on human clothes. When he returned to heaven still wearing them, the other gods were so disgusted by his human stench that he had to descend again and remove them before returning.

They also say they were made imperfect as Aioina, in a hurry to get back to heaven, told Otter to tell another god to come and finish the job, but Otter forgot, being too busy catching fish. So the work was unfinished.

Yet it is also said by the mountain Ainu that their creator was the God of the Mountains, meaning Bear, who took human form to console a childless woman whose husband had died. Her child became a great hunter, the father of many children. Other Ainu claimed that their progenitor was Eagle.[1]

1. *The Ainu and their Folk-Lore*, John Batchelor, Religious Tract Society, London, 1901.

AKHENATON (ruled *c*.1377–1358 BC) (*See* EGYPTIAN MYTH, FREUD, MOSES)

Succeeding his father Amenhotep III, this eighteenth Dynasty Egyptian pharaoh denied many old gods to worship one god, **Aton**, characterised as the **sun**. Rejecting the name Amenhotep IV and the Theban capital, he took the name Akhenaton (variant: Ikhnaton) and built a new capital at Tell al-Amarna, 'City of the Horizon'. His nature and purpose remain as enigmatic as his relationship (incestuous father?) to the boy-king Tutankhamun. The claim that he birthed **Judaic** monotheism remains controversial. Though historic, dispute over his mythic imprint persists. **Freud** argues that **Moses** was an Egyptian noble who served him and who, after Akhenaton's death and failure, led from Egypt a band of monotheistic Semites (Habiru: Hebrews). Argument persists not only as to the date of Exodus (traditionally *c*.1250 BC, under Rameses II), but also as to whether Akhenaton created the new monotheism or got it from the Habiru. Yet his reform precedes Exodus: oddly, the idea that he 'invented' monotheism still horrifies many. Some Egyptologists call him a 'heretic . . . possibly even insane' (Hoving); a 'transvestite' (Lefebvre); a 'religious fanatic' whose monotheism was historically immaterial (Hayes); his reforms being 'insane' and 'disastrous' (Aldred). **Velikovsky** throws the psychoanalytic book at him, calling him, 'autistic . . . narcissistic . . . a homosexual . . . with sadism suppressed and feminine traits . . . to the fore.'[1]

Yet Sir Alan Gardiner, calling him a 'genuine monotheist', refers to, 'the moral courage with which the reformer strove to sweep away the vast accumulation of mythological rubbish inherited from the past.' Sir Wallis Budge says that this 'individualist and idealist . . . attempted to establish a positive religion [and] would not tolerate the traditional forms in which [Egyptian] spiritual feelings were embodied.'[2]

Chaos followed his death. The old gods regrouped. The capital returned to Thebes. His name was deleted from the records. His tomb and remains are undiscovered. Yet it is odd how, 3,350 years later, this early heretic, this weak lantern-jawed transvestite, still upsets some modern scholars as much as he upset the old priests of ram-headed Amun (**Amon**).

1. _Oedipus and Akhenaton_, Immanuel Velikovsky, Abacus Books, London.
2. _The Search for the Gold of Tutankhamen_, Arnold C. Brackman, Hale, London, 1978.

ALADDIN (_See **ARABIAN NIGHTS**_, DJINNS)

ALBION (_See_ **BLAKE, GIANTS**)
An old name for Britain (Scotland in Gaelic is called Alba). William Blake (1757–1827) personified Albion as a giant symbolising British history and all Britons – past, present and future. Developing the image from the **Qabalistic Adam** Kadmon (Primordial Man), Blake identifies Albion as the Greek **Atlas**, one of the **Titans**. But in Blake's epic, 'Jerusalem: The Emanation of the Giant Albion', this old free spirit of Britain now lies buried in a landscape of 'dark satanic mills', asleep and dreaming, locked up in 'single vision and Newton's sleep', all primordial liberty lost.

ALCHERA (_See_ **ABORIGINES**)

ALDER (_See_ **BRAN**, _MABINOGION_, **TREE ALPHABET, TREES, WILLOW**)
Once feared from China to Western Europe for the bloody tint of its cut wood, the alder was thought to embody evil spirits, like the Erlkönig ('alder king', or '**elf king**') of German legend. In Celtic myth it is the tree of **Bran**; in the Beth-Luis-Nion **tree alphabet** it holds fourth place, representing the consonant F, for Fearn. Called 'the very battle-witch of all woods, tree that is hottest in the fight' in the Irish Ossianic _Song of the Forest Trees_, it was prized as yielding the best charcoal. In the Welsh _Romance of Branwen_, 'Gwern' (alder), the son of Bran's sister, is burned in a bonfire; in rural Ireland to burn a sacred alder was held to lead to the burning of one's house – which, typically, would once have been built by a lakeside on piles of alder, which resists water-rot.

The Celtic **riddle**: 'What can no house ever contain?' is answered: 'The pile on which it is built.' So it was said of Bran: 'No house could contain him.' His 'singing head' (kept seven years at Harlech) was the mummified, oracular head of a sacred king; also the 'head' of the alder tree.

The Rialto at Venice and several medieval cathedrals were founded on alder piles: jetties, bridges and causeways were built on alder.

In _The Odyssey_ the alder is one of the three trees of resurrection (with white poplar and cypress) forming the wood round the cave of Calypso, daughter of **Atlas**. In _The Aeneid_, Virgil converts the lamenting sisters of the slain solar hero **Phaethon** into an alder thicket on the banks of the Po.[1]

Yielding crimson dye from its bark, the alder offers a green dye from its leaves and brown from its twigs. The green is associated with fairies' clothes and with the 'Lincoln Green' of **Robin Hood** and other semi-mythic forest-dwelling outlaws.

1. *The White Goddess*, Robert Graves, Faber & Faber, London, 1961, pp.169–72.

ALEXANDER THE GREAT (356–323 BC)

Alexander's career was meteoric. In ten years he conquered territory from Macedonia to India. Called son of **Zeus** in his own time, even today he is recalled in legend from Iceland and Africa to China. Afghani hillsmen and Greek fishermen on stormy nights in the Aegean invoke his protection as an **ancestral** spirit. Founder of eighteen cities in three continents (naming one after his **horse** Bucephalos, another for his **dog**), when he died in Babylon at the age of thirty-two he ruled over two million square miles of land.

Son of Philip, king of Macedon, taught by Aristotle, when in 336 BC his father was murdered he liquidated potential rivals, he consolidated his power in Greece by sacking Thebes, then set out to win glory by conquering lands beyond the known world. Seeking to excel the mythic heroes **Achilles** and **Hercules**, he wore armour from the Homeric past. Conquering western Asia Minor and Persia by 333, in 332 he stormed Tyre. Seizing Egypt and founding the greatest of his many cities called Alexandria, a forty-day Saharan march led him to the **oracle** of the god Ammon (associated with the Egyptian **ram**-god **Amon**) at Siwah in Libya. Coins later showed him with ram's-horns: in the biblical Book of Daniel he appears as a ram-horned conqueror.

Islamic lore says he reached Ethiopia and the Jabali Lamma, or Gleaming Mountain (maybe Ruwenzori). More certain is that in 331 he crossed Mesopotamia and occupied Babylon. Overcoming Scythian resistance by 328, he marched north of the Hindu Kush. Turning southeast to invade India, he crossed the Indus in spring 329. His homesick Macedonians threatened mutiny, and control of this vast empire proved impossible. Reaching the Indian Ocean at modern Karachi, founding more cities, he turned west past Persepolis to Hamadan. Now outnumbered ten to one in the army by orientals, the Macedonians looked on askance at his ever more imperial rule. Reaching Babylon after one last march, further alienating his countrymen by promoting their marriages to the women of Babylon, on 10 June 323 BC he died ten days after falling ill at a banquet. That he was poisoned remains unproved. To the last, the man and his myth are impossible to separate. He was laid to rest in a golden coffin in Egyptian Alexandria, the greatest of the cities he had founded.[1]

1. *Alexander the Great*, Robin Lane-Fox, Allen Lane, London, 1973.

ALGONQUIN (*See* GLOOSCAP, HIAWATHA, KICI MANITOU)

ALICE IN WONDERLAND (*See* CARROLL, CAT)

ALLEGORIES

Originally the Roman deification of virtues such as equity, chastity, hope, courage and many others, the term in the singular (allegory) came to refer to the expression of truths about the human experience by means of symbolic or mythic narrative. Thus in *The Faerie Queene* (1589–96), the Anglo-Irish poet

Edmund Spenser developed his allegory of the Garden of Love by using mythic themes to interest those otherwise immune to such arcane concepts. So too in medieval **mystery** plays (*Everyman*), typically the characters personify moral conditions, virtues or vices such as Good Deeds, Gluttony, Avarice, Anger or Hypocrisy. The device is also traditionally used by authors who wish to make political points without getting their throats cut.

The fourteenth-century author of *Piers Plowman* used the fable of mice scared to bell the **cat** to condemn the failure of the House of Commons to control John of Gaunt. In *Animal Farm* (1945), **George Orwell** satirised Stalinist Bolshevism by telling how the revolution of the farm animals leads only to a new tyranny, the **pigs** succeeding the farmer as tyrant.

Many myths contain allegorical elements: the gods and goddesses being but depictions of human tendencies and natural events. Yet **Robert Graves** defined allegory as inferior to true myth, and distinct from it.[1]

1. *The Greek Myths*, Robert Graves, Penguin, London, 1960, vol.1, p.12.

ALTAR

The altar is the symbolic table in a temple upon which the priest, or intermediary between man and god, makes sacrifice, offering, prayer or thanksgiving to the invoked deity. A gate between the daily world and the surrounding yet invisible world of spirit, it is usually sited at the east end of the place of worship, facing the rising sun, thus symbolising daily rebirth. Table-shaped, it symbolises spiritual nutrition, the Communion cup and wafer (in **Christianity**) being dedicated upon it. Tomb-shaped, it symbolises passage from material life to eternity. If of stone, it implies divinity's endurance and indestructibility. If of wood, it signifies the **tree** or **cross**, implying not only (in a Christian church) the crucifixion of Spirit in Matter, but the continual annual rebirth of Nature.

The approach to the altar is as meaningful as the altar itself. Steps up to it symbolise stages of growth to spiritual realisation. Three steps symbolise the Trinity; seven, the gifts of the Holy Spirit. The high altar is the Hill of Calvary: redemption through self-sacrifice. The linen cloth on it is the shroud of Christ: the vault above it the heavens. It is the world-navel, **omphalos**, the four-sided building about it the world's four corners. Though now a device to focus the mind on spiritual matters, in origin, from Abraham to the **Aztecs**, it was literally a sacrificial table, on which human or animal victims were killed and offered up to the god.

AMANITA MUSCARIA (*See* DIONYSUS, HAOMA, SOMA)

Was '**Jesus Christ**' not a man but a hallucinogenic toadstool? This theory, advanced by the English scholar John M. Allegro, is one of the more astonishing claims made for *Amanita muscaria*. Portrayed by Tenniel in his drawings for **Carroll**'s *Alice in Wonderland* as seating a hookah-smoking caterpillar, the white-spotted red cap of this remarkable fungus is commonly found under birch or pine – and in it may lie the secret of the **Mysteries** of **Dionysus** and other ancient ecstatic **shamanic** cults from Siberia to Greece, Norway to Mexico. Also called 'Food of the Gods', the 'Hundred-Spotted Toad' or 'Fly Agaric' (from the belief that crumbled into water in a bowl it kills domestic flies), it is related to *Amanita virosa* (the Destroying Angel) and *Amanita phalloides* (the Death-Cap) – both of them deadly. Yet it differs from these in that, in a regulated dose, not death but hallucinatory vision results. So, for millennia, this fungus has been eaten to induce prophecy, religious vision, erotic potency or (by Norse **berserkers**), battle-rage.

Its danger was always known. Thus in every land its use was hedged in secrecy, ambiguity and **allegory**. Ambrosia, **haoma**, nectar, **soma** and other obscure mystical foods may refer to it, or to its combination in a brew with other similarly hallucinogenic plants or fungi.

In **Greek myth** it is said that at their autumn orgy, the 'Ambrosia', the **Maenads**, followers of **Dionysus**, raged through the woods, decapitating those they met. **Robert Graves** has suggested that in fact what was torn off (and eaten) was the head of the *Amanita*. Nobody seeking vision via this or other hallucinogenic mushrooms eats the stalk, or body. Graves also suggests that the lightning-engendered **Mexican** god **Tlaloc** was this same *Amanita*, and points out that Greek hero **Perseus** (a Dionysus worshipper) named the city of Mycenae for a toadstool he found on the site.[1]

All of which provides background for Allegro's contentious claim that primitive Christianity arose from an *Amanita* cult. This is widely thought absurd. Yet there is little doubt that consumption of *Amanita muscaria* and other such natural drugs was crucial in stimulating religious ecstasy, and not only in the ancient world. But experimentation is ill advised. Over-dosage of this toadstool can kill, slowly and horribly.

1. *The Greek Myths*, Robert Graves, Penguin, London, 1960, vol.1, p.10.

AMARANTH
An immortal flower symbolising the constancy of true love.

AMATERASU (*See* JAPANESE MYTH, SHINTO, SUN)
The myth of this Shinto goddess may reflect some ancient rivalry between a brother and his sister, a priestess-queen. Certainly it is unusual to find a female solar deity. The Japanese tale is that Amaterasu and her brother, the storm-god Susanowo, between them created three goddesses and five gods. The eight children were venerated as **ancestors**, the eight 'princes': the eldest male being the ancestor of the emperors. But Susanowo was so self-satisfied that he lost all control. Terrorising humanity by destroying rice-fields and forests, he drove Amaterasu to shut herself into a cave.

With the sun thus vanished, darkness and evil spirits ruled the world. The good gods decided she must return. Before her cave they made offerings – a **mirror**, a **sword**, a jewelled **tree**, crowing **cocks**. They lit bonfires and danced. In ecstasy the goddess Ama no Uzume stripped naked, at which the gods all laughed. Hearing this, Amaterasu opened the door to find out why they were laughing. 'Because,' cried Uzume, 'we have found a better goddess than you.' Thus tantalised, Amaterasu saw the mirror. Amazed at her own reflection she emerged further. The god of force grabbed her as another god drew the *shimenawa* (straw-rope) over the cave-door behind her.

Unable to go back, the sun reappeared. Order and peace returned. She was forbidden to vanish again. Susanowo was expelled from heaven for his crimes, to become a fertility-god associated with **serpent**-worship.

AMAZONS (*See* GREEK MYTH, THESEUS)
The name of this mythic race of female warriors is from the Greek *amazona*, 'woman without breast' (*mazos*). It is said they cut off the right breast the better to draw their bowstrings. Some Arab authors insist that they were born with one male and one female breast, or again that their one breast was more like a cow's udder, set amid the body.

In Greek myth, they were born of **Ares** by the Naiad Harmonia. Tanais, son of their queen Lysippe, offended **Aphrodite** by scorning marriage: in revenge Aphrodite made him fall in love with his mother, so that he killed himself. To escape his ghost Lysippe led the Amazons round the Black Sea to Phrygia. They formed a society in which men did domestic work; women fought and ruled. Founding Ephesus and Smyrna, briefly they took **Troy**.

Sent on his ninth labour to steal the golden girdle of Ares worn by the Amazonian queen Hippolyte, **Hercules** was accompanied by the **bull**-hero and later Athenian king **Theseus**. Hippolyte was slain and her girdle stolen by Hercules. The Amazons were slaughtered. As his prize Theseus got Antiope, ruler of one of the three Amazon cities on the river Thermodon. Her sister Oreithyia swore vengeance, allied with the Scythians, and led her Amazons over the Danube into Greece. Theseus won a four-month battle: the surviving Amazons settled in Scythia to the east. As for Antiope, when for political reasons Theseus married Phaedra of Crete, she burst armed into the wedding, jealously threatening to kill the guests. Theseus killed her, though she had borne him Hippolytus and had remained faithful to him alone.[1]

In Africa it is said the Amazons lived on one bank of a river in the western desert (in Senegal?), the men on the other. Only once a year could the men wade the diminished river to impregnate the women. It is also said the climate was so bad that only daughters survived, and that the women became pregnant by bathing in a holy pool. Islamic writers insist that the Amazons were faithful Muslim women who lacked sexual desire yet could give birth without ordinary masculine insemination, God's will being sufficient.[2]

The myth of the self-sufficient Amazonian woman persists in modern feminism and **science fiction** tales by authors like John Wyndham (*Consider Her Ways*), Joanna Russ (*The Female Man*) and Margaret Attwood (*The Handmaiden's Tale*). The theme seems **archetypal**, due to both innate male fear of the domineering female, and innate female desire for a world in which men do not always have the final bloody say.

1. *The Greek Myths*, Robert Graves, Penguin, London, 1960.
2. *African Mythology*, Jan Knappert, Aquarian Press, Wellingborough, 1990.

AMBROSIA (*See AMANITA*, **HAOMA, SOMA**)

AMBROSIUS AURELIANUS (*See* **ARTHUR**)

AMERINDIAN MYTH (*See* **CONCORDANCE, NATIVE AMERICAN MYTH**)

AMIDA (*See* **BUDDHISM, JAPANESE MYTH**)
In Japan this 'Buddha of Infinite Light' protects humanity, comforting all who call on him in terror or fear of death. His Western Paradise is open to all. He will not enter **Nirvana** until all humanity is saved. As such, he provides in the East the closest approximation to the Judaeo-Christian notion in the West of a personal saviour, a personal salvation. Shown with uncovered head and in Indian dress he is coloured red, legs crossed, rising behind the mountains or enthroned amid the Paradise of the Pure Land. Here amid jewelled, bell-hung trees perch marvellous spiritual birds, above them the **Buddha** and what in the West we call saints and **angels**.

This sect of the 'Pure Land' (Jodo) dates from the twelfth century, based on the teachings of Honen, who developed a pietistic doctrine teaching that those of pure heart and childlike simplicity will, in their last days, find peace by attainment to the merciful kindness of Amida's Western Paradise.

As in other **allegories** of the 'West' (Land of the Setting Sun), this mythology offers emotional peace to those heartstruck by fear of death. A degeneration of pure Buddhist philosophy, none the less it proved popular.

AMMA (*See* AFRICAN MYTH, DOGON)

AMON (*See* ALEXANDER, EGYPTIAN MYTH)

This Egyptian **ram**-headed **creator**-god (also Amun or later Ammon) gained his greatest popularity in the sixteenth century BC as 'King of the Gods'. The patron of Middle Kingdom pharaohs ruling at Thebes, he was identified with the older **sun**-god **Ra**, thus taking the title of Amon-Ra. During the fourteenth century BC, the revolutionary pharaoh Akhenaton tried to eclipse Amon-Ra by setting up instead the new sun-god **Aton**, progenitor of the Mosaic-Judaic **Jehovah** or Yahweh – the One God. Akhenaton's peculiar reign ended with his son Tutankhamun ('Living Image of Amon') who, prior to his early death, was encouraged to restore the old rule of Amon.

Yet **Isis** had already made this old god reveal his secret name. Nothing could be the same again . . . even if, a millennium later, the Macedonian Alexander re-established the degenerate Amon as the romantic new Ammon-**Zeus**.

AMULETS (*See* CHARMS, MAGIC, TALISMAN)

Worn the world over to protect against **witchcraft** or **sorcery**, or simply as good luck **charms**, amulets are objects in which inherent power to ward off evil is thought to reside. From the Greek *amylon*, 'food', the original amulet was a piece of food set out to feed and thus propitiate or befriend potentially harmful **spirits**. The Latin *amuletum* derives from *amolire*, 'to ward off, avoid, protect'. Thus a lucky rabbit's foot or a St Christopher medallion are amulets no less than those made by Hausa magicians from the skin of an electric eel, *munjiriyya*, found in Niger. It is said the owners of these cannot be caught by robbers, arrested by the police or harmed by any weapon.[1]

1. *African Mythology*, Jan Knappert, Aquarian Press, Wellingborough, 1990.

ANANSI (*See* AFRICAN MYTH, SPIDER, TRICKSTERS)

The exploits of Anansi (Mr Spider), West Africa's great trickster-god, are told in many stories. Anansi is rarely lost for an answer. One day, with fire raging through the savannah and all the animals in flight, he leapt from a branch into the ear of an **antelope**, and told her which way to run to escape the inferno. Thus both survived. Thanking her for her kindness, Anansi said they would meet again. She gave birth, but one day two hunters saw her. With her infant hiding in the shrubs, she fled. Returning later, she could not find her baby until Anansi led her to a thicket surrounded by the web he had woven to hide the baby antelope from the hunters.

ANANTA (*See* HINDU MYTH, SERPENT)

Meaning 'endless', 'infinity', in Hindu mythology Ananta is the epithet of Shesha, the world-serpent on the back of which the **sun**-god **Vishnu** sleeps during the Night of **Brahma**.

Ananta-Shesha's thousand heads (or, by another account, seven) protect the dreaming god (also known as Ananta-Shayana, 'Sleeping on Ananta'). At the end of this period Vishnu awakens into the activity of a new *kalpa*, or Day of Brahma.

As Balarama, **Krishna**'s half-brother, Ananta assumes human form, until a **serpent** crawls from his mouth and leaves him bodiless. Returned to the primal cosmic sea, Ananta spits out the cosmic fire that destroys creation at the end of each *kalpa*. He is also used by the gods as a rope to churn the ocean in their search for the **elixir** of **immortality**, amrita.

ANCESTOR-WORSHIP

Ancestor-worship persists as a natural response to the mystery of our fate after death, and to the sensation that the dead survive in ghostly form, requiring respectful propitiation if they are to help and not harm their living descendants. It also implies recognition that the purposeful life of humanity as a whole is not measured by the doings of the living alone: that our present successes are those of pygmies standing on the shoulders of past **giants**. We are individuals but also a collective organism in time as well as space. So when we invoke the example of past national heroes, from King **Arthur** to Winston Churchill in Britain, from Davy Crockett to **John F. Kennedy** in the USA, from Roland to De Gaulle in France, or **Siegfried** to Frederick the Great in Germany, in effect we call upon these figures as ancestors or epitomes of a particular national spirit. What is implied is not so much superstition as a reminder of how to live.

Thus Australian **Aborigines** tell how their ancestral spirits, Wondjina, arose from sleep to shape the land and teach man the arts of survival, then went away into the sky, now to be seen as lights moving amid the stars.

Again, the **fairy** faith of **Celtic** lands seems in the first place to represent ancestor-worship, the fey folk being firmly connected with green mounds or tumuli associated with neolithic burials. They are, in other words, the dead, with whom liberties cannot be taken. Even if not actually worshipped, they must be feared or respected. Those too familiar with them, like the Rev. **Robert Kirk**, vanish into fairy-land, either never to return to life or, like **Oisin**, to return only to find many centuries have passed.

So too in ancient Rome as in many parts of modern Africa and elsewhere the relationship seems basically commercial. If offerings are made to the ancestors, they provide a service to the living. It is a matter of trade or, at least, of buying power or good fortune. To ignore the ancestors is to risk ill-luck, just as it is to ignore one's **dreams**. In this sense the ancestors are the primordial forces of the collective unconscious, and in approaching them we approach our own hidden depths in which (as in the fairy world) time and the laws of the material world do not exist.

ANDERSEN, HANS CHRISTIAN (1805–75) (*See* FAIRY-TALES)

Tales like 'The Princess and the Pea' by this Danish master-fabulist remain among the most often translated in all literary history. Born in a slum in Odense, he entered the University of Copenhagen (1828), and in 1829 had his first success with a romance in the style of the German E.T.A. Hoffman.

For long known as a playwright and novelist, the first of his 'Tales told for Children' appeared in the 1830s. Though based on folk legends, the moral realism of stories like 'The Tinderbox' led to mounting acclaim, and to further collections in 1843, 1847 and 1852. Though some tales like 'The Snow Queen' express an optimistic belief in the triumph of beauty and good, others are deeply pessimistic. This in part seems due to his unhappy personal life (he never married, though often in love), but may also have arisen from his perception of the nature of the world. 1848 saw the 'Year of Revolutions' in Europe: Andersen did not indulge mere wish-fulfilment in his writings, but achieved his lasting success by innovation.

ANDROGYNE (*See* HERMAPHRODITES)

ANDROMEDA (*See* **PERSEUS**)

ANFORTAS (*See* **ARTHURIAN MYTH, FISHER KING, HOLY GRAIL**)

ANGELS (*See* **DEMONS, DEVIL, ST MICHAEL**)

Belief in angels (Greek: *angelos*, 'messenger'), supernal beings who mediate between God and man, is ancient. Where **demons** work to harm us, angels offer protection, guidance or spiritual insight. That they epitomise a linkage of higher and lower spheres of consciousness is seen in Jacob's **dream** of the ladder, on which angels both climb and descend. In wrestling with the angel, Jacob engaged in **shamanic** battle with his own inner self.

The names of the great archangels are known to Muslims as well as to **Christians**. The prophet **Mohammed** received the **Koran** from God via the archangel Gabriel, who also told Mary she would bear Christ. Mohammmed tells how Gabriel 'descended in his own form, of such beauty, of such sacred glory, of such majesty, that all my dwelling was illuminated.'

Vision of angels as shining winged human beings is found world-wide. The Peruvian Campu **shaman** sees the hawk-spirit Koakiti as a winged man; the Four Thunderbirds of the North American **Sioux** are seen as winged men. 'I looked up at the clouds,' said Sioux visionary Black Elk, 'and two men were coming there, headfirst like arrows slanting down; and as they came, they sang a sacred song and the thunder was like drumming.'[1]

Angels are often seen as **birds**. **Raven** the **trickster** both enlightens and confuses the Tlingit of North America. In ancient Egypt man's soul or higher self was seen as **hawk** or **eagle**. The Old Testament prophet Ezekiel describes certain angels as 'a wheel in the middle of a wheel', moving amid a firmament the colour of a 'terrible crystal'.[2] At Fatima, Portugal, in 1917, three shepherd children met a beautiful young woman who appeared amid blinding light and said she came from heaven. Subsequent visions led to a crowd of 70,000 witnessing the sun descend to earth. As at Knock in Ireland, Lourdes in France and (recently) Medugorje in the former Yugoslavia, mass healings followed this event, which was initiated by a childlike vision of an entity usually identified as the **Virgin Mary**. Close encounters with **UFOs** have led to similar phenomena. Whatever the culture and its background, the 'miracle' of transcendental visitation by winged messengers persists.

Angels belong to another order of being, but the boundary is vague. Those like **Lucifer**, refusing to bow to God's new creation, **Adam**, are cast down even as humans ascend, climbing Jacob's ladder (Tree of Life) up to angelic status. The prophet **Enoch**, charged by God to warn the Watchers who sinned by taking human wives, becomes the archangel Metatron. **Hermes Trismegistus** (Mercurius, the winged youth of alchemical transformation), inhabits the mythic terrain between angel and human. Angels represent idealised projections of positive human imagination, just as **demons** represent the negative pole.

Angelic functions were once organised in hierarchies reflecting human values. The **Neoplatonist**, Dionysus the Areopagite, writes in his *Celestial Hierarchies* that angels exist in nine orders: Seraphim, Kerubim, Wheels; Orders, Dominions and Powers; Principalities, Archangels and mere Angels.

Of these, the Seraphim represent divine love; the Kerubim, wisdom; the Wheels or Thrones bound this upper triad, corresponding symbolically to the supernal triad in the Qabalistic Tree of Life. These symbolise primordial psychic forces. The other six orders represent further stages connecting personal consciousness to the Absolute. Each sphere on the Tree has its resident 'angel', **Tarot** trump, vibratory colours and other correspondences with minerals, **totem** animals, and so on. By ritual the magician tries to tap into these pre-established images, which operate like a road-map. Thus the angel Uriel (earth and material matters) rules the North; Michael (fire and high places) the East; Gabriel (water and the subconscious) the South; and Raphael (air and spirit) the West.[2]

Lucifer represents the human ego, 'fallen' through intellectual pride, yet capable of being 'saved' (raised again). Likewise the Angel of Death (in **Jewish** myth standing between heaven and earth with a poison-dripping **sword**) is not evil *per se*, but an expression of universal law.

1. *Black Elk Speaks*, John G. Neihardt, Penguin, London.
2. *Angels*, Peter Lamborn Wilson, Thames & Hudson, London, 1980.

ANGLO-SAXON MYTH (*See* CONCORDANCE, TEUTONIC MYTH)

ANGUS MAC OG (*See* TUATHA DÉ DANAAN)

Son of the **Dagda** and the goddess Boann, this Irish god of youth and love was one of the **Tuatha dé Danaan** or **fairy** race, his home said to be the 6,000-year-old neolithic mound at New Grange in Meath, the Bruigh na Boinne. Otherwise named Aengus or Oengus, he was called Mac Og ('Young Son') after his magical begetting at break of day. The eighth-century text *Aislinge Oenguso* (*Dream of Angus*) tells how, visited in dream by Caer Ibormeith, a supernatural maiden, he so fell in love with her that he was ill until he found her at Loch Bel Dracon at the time of the feast called **Samhain**. In **swan**-form one year, she was human the next. When he met her she was with 149 other swan-maidens. He took similar shape: they circled the loch three times singing so wondrously that all who heard them fell asleep for three days and nights. Then he returned with her to Bruigh na Boinne.

Given power over time, he also owned a magic cloak of **invisibility**, and was foster-father to the **Fenian** hero Diarmuid.

ANIMALS (*See* CONCORDANCE)

In mythology animals may be **totemic** gods, **tricksters**, moral exemplars, **shape-shifting** wizards, the dead **reincarnated**, or **spirits** to be propitiated if hunted so that their ghosts do not haunt their killers. When men of the Bear clan in the Ottawa tribe killed a **bear**, they made him a feast of his own flesh and apologised to him, explaining their need to eat him. The Finns would tell a slain bear they had not killed him: his death was accidental. Madagascar whalers would apologise to the mother **whales** for killing their offspring. Ajumba hunters in West Africa, killing a **hippopotamus**, would bathe in its blood and excretions while praying to its soul to bear no grudge. Sables caught by Siberian hunters were not to be seen or spoken about, for fear that other sables would hear what had happened and avoid capture. The Dyaks of Borneo would kill a **crocodile** only if it had killed a man. Sumatrans did not hunt a tiger save in self-defence: if Europeans set traps, local folk would tell the **tigers** that the traps had been set without their consent.

No Masai of Kenya willingly killed a **snake**, believing that the souls of the dead **reincarnate** in snake-form. If the Seminole and Cherokee of North America had to kill a rattlesnake, they begged pardon of its ghost, or else the dead snake's kin would track down and kill the murderer. The myth of the cunning serpent is universal.

Likewise, the qualities ascribed to particular animals typically take on a mythic cast. **Dogs** guard the domestic door and so also the door to the underworld (*see* **Anubis, Cerberus**). The **lion** ('King of the Beasts') is tawny and native to hot lands: so becomes associated with the **sun**. The **spider**, like **Anansi**, may be a **trickster**-god, weaving subtle webs. On the turtle's broad back a world may rest. In India, the **elephant**-god Ganesh is the god of practical wisdom, remover of obstacles: the monkey-king **Hanuman** can not only fly but is a master doctor and poet.

Shape-shifting between human and animal form is common. The **cat** may be a **witch**: so too the lunar **hare**. In Shetland it was believed that some women were really **seals**, or selkies, who could be taken by men as wives if caught without their seal-skins. Some men at full moon turn into **were-wolves**; the undead may take the form of the bloodsucking **vampire** bat.

The mystery of our own humanity and its relationship with the animal kingdom stimulates persisting fascination with allegorical tales in which animals are granted human attributes and concerns. From *Aesop's Fables* to *The Wind in the Willows* and *Watership Down*, the fascination persists.

ANIMISM

This old belief holds (1) that all life arises from the action of soul ('anima') on matter; and (2) that spirit ('animus') indwells all supposedly inanimate objects and natural phenomena. Thus to the animist, wind, wave, storm, mountain and forest are alive with the particular spirit or spirits indwelling them. Personifications of such nature **spirits** include **sylphs** (air); undines (water); **gnomes** (earth) and **salamanders** (fire). All who embrace **pagan** beliefs or practise **shamanistic** tradition may be said to be animistic in outlook. That such belief may be held as arising out of the projection of unconscious content on to the environment does not invalidate it – in fact, the opposite, given increasing evidence as to the degree to which our perception of the world is organised by unconscious forces, and given the parallel evidence that our denial of such forces makes us sick. Animism at least demands that minimum respect for the natural world without which we are unlikely to survive as a species. Not so much a philosophy as an intuitive attitude, animistic belief is not reducible to logic.

ANNUNCIATION (*See* CHRISTIANITY, VIRGIN MARY, VIRGINITY)

ANNWN (*See MABINOGION*, PWYLL, UNDERWORLD, WELSH MYTH, WILD HUNT)

The **pagan** Welsh/British **underworld** ruled by Arawn, with whom **Pwyll** the king of Dyfed (*see* **Mabinogion**) exchanged places for a year in penance for baiting his hounds on a **stag** slain by Arawn's pack. Sometimes spelt Anwfn, in medieval Welsh poetry it is said to lie under the mortal world, and to be divided into several planes or kingdoms. The name may mean the 'Not-World'; it was also called Anghar ('Loveless Place'). Affwys ('Abyss') and Affan ('Invisible Land'). In the esoteric tradition it was regarded as the lowest sphere of existence; more popularly it came to be viewed as a world invisible, the **fairy**-realm, the supernatural realm from which the **Wild Hunt** rode out on stormy nights. 'The Spoiling of Annwn', a Welsh poem attributed to **Taliesin**, describes how **Arthur** and his comrades raid Annwn to seize the **cauldron** of inspiration and plenty; one of its treasures. This accentuates the fairy-land motif: one of the chief treasures of the Irish **Tuatha dé Danaan**, who became the fairies, was the cauldron of the Good God, the **Dagda**. Another gift that came to humanity out of Annwn was the **pig**, traditionally an **otherworld** beast.

ANTELOPE (*See* **AFRICAN MYTH, ANANSI, ANIMALS, DEER**)
Unsurprisingly, given the grace of this fleet-footed tropical deer, it has been associated with the divine from the Kalahari to India. In **Egyptian myth** the antelope, though sacrificed to **Set**, also represented **Osiris** and **Horus** as Set's opponents. In Asia Minor and Europe it was associated with worship of the Great Mother as a lunar symbol; specifically with **Astarte**, the Canaanite goddess. In India it was an emblem of the god **Shiva**: Pavana the god of winds rides an antelope. In Babylonia it was taken to be a form of the gods **Ea** and **Marduk**, Ea-Oannes being called 'the antelope of the subterranean ocean' or 'the antelope of creation'.

In heraldry the antelope is depicted with tusks on the head of a tiger, with the body of a stag and the tail of a **unicorn**.

ANTICHRIST (*See* **APOCALYPSE, DEVIL**)
Denying **dualism**, Christianity invokes duality. **Christ** as Saviour implies Antichrist, the Destroyer. Fair enough: destruction and creation belong to each other, as most traditions recognise. From Mexico (Ah Puch) to India (**Shiva**) the Destroyer is seen as necessary. But exoteric Christianity has never accepted this. Inheriting **Zoroastrian** ideas, it denies that God can be involved with evil – despite Old Testament evidence to the contrary.

Antichrist, like **Ahriman**, was invented as the image of the Evil One, seeking to destroy God's plan, as if that plan never included destruction.

The symbol of Antichrist seems to arise in the Old Testament **prophecy** of Daniel's **dream**, telling of a king 'who shall exalt himself, and magnify himself above every god'.[1] That this referred to the megalomaniac Antiochus Epiphanes was forgotten: the God-hating tyrant of the Last Days became part of Jewish-Christian myth, merging with the figure of **Satan**, the ten-horned **dragon**, 'that old **serpent**', to fascinate the Middle Ages as an image of demonic tyranny. Overbearing monarchs and popes were called Antichrist, as was Luther. Only with the dawn of the Age of Reason did this stock insult fall into disuse – for a time. For now the image is revived by Christian fundamentalists like Hal Lindsay and Jeanne Dixon in the USA.[2]

Insisting that Last Days are nigh and that **Armageddon** nears, Lindsay has reached a vast audience. The seeress Jeanne Dixon claims that Antichrist, born in the Middle East in 1962, will soon engulf the world in **apocalyptic** war. But in 1999 the image of the cross will be seen in the eastern skies, Antichrist and his legions will be destroyed at the Battle of Armageddon (Megiddo, near Haifa in Israel). Amid worldwide carnage Jesus will return, physically, to establish the millennium. Meanwhile the Righteous will have been saved from the carnage by the **Rapture**, literally rising 'in the middle of the air' to meet Jesus and go to heaven. Some fundamentalists say the Rapture occurs only after the final defeat of the Antichrist.

This is potent myth . . . for some.

1. *The Pursuit of the Millennium*, Norman Cohn, Paladin, London, 1970, p.33.
2. *The Late Great Planet Earth*, Hal Lindsay, Zondervan Books, Michigan, 1970.

ANU (*See* **BABYLONIAN MYTH, CREATION MYTH, GILGAMESH, SUMERIAN MYTH**)
As An, an early Sumerian personification of heaven, this shadowy deity was named Anu ('Sky') in the later Assyrio-Babylonian pantheon. To him as the supreme god came the other deities when they were in danger (as during the **Flood**) or if they had complaints to set before him. The stars of heaven,

created to destroy the wicked, were called the 'soldiers of Anu'.

Remaining remote, he never descended to earth. When forced to confront **Tiamat**, the female **dragon** of Chaos or 'Watery Wastes', he delegated the task to the solar god **Bel-Marduk**. Despite this personal avoidance of duty, he remained so venerated that the newer gods had to assume his name to gain respect among the seething, sceptical populations of a new Mesopotamia that dates from the nineteenth-century BC reign of Hammurabi. Anu was already ancient.

ANUBIS (*See* DOG, DOORS, EGYPTIAN MYTH, GUARDIANS)

Later identified with the Greek **Hermes**, from the earliest dynasties and prior to the rise of **Osiris** this jackal-headed Egyptian god was considered the guide or conductor of the souls of the newly-dead to the **otherworld**. In the pyramid texts he is the 'fourth son of **Ra**' the **sun**-god. It is said that he went with Osiris on the latter's conquest of the world, and later, when **Set** murdered Osiris, helped **Isis** and **Nepthys** (who perhaps bore him to Osiris) to bury him. It was then, binding up the corpse of Osiris as a mummy to prevent bodily corruption, that Anubis became known as 'Lord of the Mummy Wrappings'. In later Egyptian myth, Anubis takes the hand of the dead, leading them before the judges who weigh up their souls. In this role his image survived into Greek times: in *The Golden Ass* the Roman author **Apuleius** places Anubis in the forefront of the great procession honouring Isis. Yet it may be that in the first place the jackal Anubis was chosen as the 'Conductor of Souls' because of the capacity of this **animal** to smell life-giving water over vast stretches of otherwise deadly desert. To the Egyptian mind, such talent suggested a capacity to overwhelm death, thus to guide the thirsty souls of the dead to a new oasis in the afterlife.

ANUNNAKI (*See* INANNA, SUMERIAN MYTH)

When **Inanna**, the Sumerian Queen of Heaven and Earth, descended to the lower or **underworld**, she found herself surrounded by the Anunnaki, the Judges. They said:

> *No one ascends from the underworld unmarked.*
> *If Inanna wishes to return from the underworld,*
> *She must provide someone in her place.*[1]

From the third millennium BC, this text expresses the first surviving written version of the **archetypal** belief that (a) the newly-dead are judged by the acts of their life (feather in the scale, as in **Egypt**); (b) that they may return to life, so long as appropriate **sacrifice** is made.

Of the Anunnaki we learn nothing. They are forces beyond humanity: the lords of the **underworld**, as mysterious now as 4,000 years ago. All we know is that they make no easy bargain. Their kingdom is harsh.

1. *Inanna*, Diane Wolkstein and Samuel Noah Kramer, Rider, London, 1984, p.68.

APHRODITE (*See* GREEK MYTH, VENUS)

Castrating his father **Ouranos** at the wish of his mother **Gaia**, **Cronus** threw the severed phallus into the sea. From the white foam thus produced arose the Greek goddess of love, Aphrodite ('Foam-Born'). Carried by the West Wind, Zephyrus, she landed on Cyprus. Richly dressed and jewelled by the Horae ('Hours': fertility divinities), seductively lovely and sweet-natured, she brought amorous chaos to Olympus. All the gods wanted her. Marrying **Hephaestus**, the lame ugly smith-god, she had affairs with **Hermes** and the war god **Ares**, and got all the immortals (save **Artemis** and Hestia) so worked up that even **Zeus** began chasing mortal women. In revenge he made her fall for the mortal Anchises, by whom she bore **Aeneas**. For his *hubris* Anchises was blinded by bees. Meanwhile the jealousy of **Hera** (the haughty wife of Zeus) and **Athene** (warlike goddess of wisdom) was exploited by Eris ('Discord'). Excluded from the wedding of Thetis and Peleus, he threw into the hall a golden **apple** inscribed: 'For the fairest.' All three claimed it. Zeus made them submit to the mortal judgement of the shepherd **Paris**, son of King Priam of **Troy**. Hera promised Paris the lordship of Asia if he found her loveliest; Athene promised him victory in every battle. But Aphrodite unloosed her **girdle**, promising him possession of the most lovely of mortal women. So she got the apple: Paris got **Helen**, wife of Menelaus. So the vengeance of Hera and Athene led to the bitter Trojan war. Aphrodite tried to defend the fated city and her son Aeneas, yet was wounded. She fled to Olympus. Zeus told her to forget war and deal with love alone. For in this she was supreme. Even Hera, wishing to hold wayward Zeus, borrowed Aphrodite's girdle, which enslaved the affections of men and gods alike.

Falling in love with the beautiful Canaanite god **Adonis**, she disputed with **Persephone**, goddess of the **underworld**, to possess him. **Eros** was said to be her son; her retinue also included the three **Graces**, who delighted all men and aided her in her seductions.

A Greek metamorphosis of the Sumerian goddess **Inanna**, she originally came from the East, not the West, and by the Athenians was regarded as the senior of the **Fates**, or Moirai. Not only the goddess of sexual love, like her Roman counterpart Venus, Aphrodite also represented social affections.

APIS (*See* BULL, EGYPTIAN MYTH, GREEK MYTH, PTAH)

The **bull** Hapi ('Apis' is the Greek rendering) was sacred to the Egyptian **creator**-god **Ptah** (also associated by the Greeks with **Hephaestus**), whose cult centre was at Memphis. Believed to be Ptah's **reincarnation**, only one Apis bull lived at a time, being recognised by specific marks. Black and with double hairs on its tail, its forehead bore a white triangle, its back the figure of a vulture, its right flank a crescent **moon**, its tongue the image of a scarab. Released daily in its sacred enclosure to attract not only the devout but also Graeco-Roman tourists in Egypt, Apis usually died of old age, to be worshipped as **Osiris** Apis. This Greek Osarapis became confused with the foreign Serapis, an **underworld** god worshipped at Alexandria.

APOCALYPSE (*See* ANTICHRIST, NEW JERUSALEM)

Meaning revelation (Greek *apokalupsis*, 'to uncover'), this term is often associated with End Times via the last book of the New Testament: the Revelation of St John, written by a second-century Greek **Christian** mystic. His imagery – the Breaking of the Seals; War in Heaven; the Beast numbered 666; the Fall of **Babylon** and a **New Jerusalem** – has ever since fascinated and terrified folk, especially in connection with the myth of Antichrist.

Whenever doom is in the air; when war, plague, famine and strife rage out of hand, St John's imagery is eagerly applied by fundamentalists who insist that the End Times are at hand: that the Rider on the White **Horse** is due to descend from heaven to trample the nations, cast **Satan** into the abyss for a millennium and raise those who have not bowed to the Beast.

APOLLO (*See* DELPHI, GREEK MYTH, SUN-GODS)

Son of **Zeus** and the **Titaness** Leto, twin brother of **Artemis** the virgin huntress, also called Phoebus ('Shining'), this Greek god has affinities with other solar deities, from the Egyptian **Ra** to the Celtic **Lug**. Fed not on mother's milk but **nectar** and **ambrosia**, when he was only four days old at Pytho (Greek, 'to rot') he fought a female **dragon** which had molested his mother during her pregnancy. Slaying it, he renamed Pytho **Delphi** (from *Delphyne*, 'Womb-like'). The myth implies how male solar power overthrew the **oracle** here; the 'dragon' being a **pythoness** (priestess) who uttered **prophecies**. The name Delphi also implies how, in **dolphin**-form Apollo captured a Cretan ship, sending its sailors to Delphi to guard the temple he had seized.

Each winter Apollo went far north to **Hyperborea**; each spring returning to Delphi in a chariot drawn by white **swans** or **griffons**. Master of lyre and bow, in war his arrows slew both gods and mortals. When **Hercules** stole Delphi's sacred tripod, **Zeus** himself made Hercules restore it. Apollo twice enraged his father. Joining **Hera**'s plot against Zeus, he was exiled to Troy for a year. When Zeus murdered Apollo's son **Asclepius**, Apollo killed the **Cyclopes** who had made the murder weapon, a **thunderbolt**, and was sent to serve Admetus, mortal king of Pherae, but did so peacefully, playing the lyre (his invention) to his flocks so sweetly that even wild beasts joined the dance. As god of music he was usually accompanied by the nine **Muses**, deities of poetic inspiration – nymphs whose cult originated in Thrace. Of his many love-affairs, that with Koronis led to the birth of Asclepius, and in Lybia the lion-wrestling nymph Cyrene bore him Aristaeus. Yet to escape him the river-nymph Daphne called upon **Gaia**, who turned her into a laurel tree, while the mortal woman Castalia of Delphi drowned herself in the fountain that later took her name. A figure embracing many traditions, today Apollo seems most of all to represent the novel masculine logic and reason which so thoroughly remade the ancient world of the **Great Goddess**.

APPLE (*See* SILVER BOUGH, TREE ALPHABET)

Forbidden fruit of the **Fall** in **Eden**, cause of discord when thrown by Eris among the gods (*see* **Aphrodite**), fruit of **immortality** in the garden of the **Hesperides** and (Norse) **Freya**'s garden, the apple symbolises both life and death. Dying, **King Arthur** goes to **Avalon**, the Isle of Apples: ducking for apples at **Hallowe'en** symbolises the dying old year. Yet the death of the king implies rebirth: Arthur is not dead, only sleeping. Held by **Christ** or the **Virgin Mary** it symbolises salvation; the Celtic god **Bran** is called to the Land of Youth by a white-blossomed apple branch (*see* **Silver Bough**).

The etymology is uncertain, but the word is known from the Balkans to Ireland in a form similar to Apol: the apple is sacred to **Apollo**. In the Celtic Beth-Luis-Nion tree alphabet, the apple-tree is Q, for *Quert*: one of the 'seven noble trees'. The Celtic *nemeton*, 'sacred grove', is represented by an apple bough, as used in the rites of **Diana**, called Diana Nemetona in Gaul. In old Irish lore, death is the fate of those felling apple-trees or **hazel** (due to the value of their fruit and nuts?). Sacred to **Aphrodite** as a symbol of love and desire, in China it represented peace and concord.[1]

1. *The White Goddess*, Robert Graves, Faber & Faber, London, 1961, pp.253–61.

APSU (*See* ENKI, MARDUK, SUMERIAN MYTH, TIAMAT, WATER)

APULEIUS, LUCIUS (*c*.AD 130–*c*.180) (*See* **ISIS**)
Born in North Africa and later a rhetorician and priest of **Asclepius**, this widely travelled Roman author left one work still widely read today despite the efforts of the medieval Inquisition to destroy all copies: *The Golden Ass*, or *Transformations of Lucius*. This bawdy satire tells of a young man transformed into an ass to observe every kind of human folly before being restored to human form by the goddess **Isis**. The passage describing this final transformation offers perhaps the finest Classical description of the **mysteries** of Isis. The tale of **Cupid** (**Eros**) and Psyche forming the mid-part of this entertaining work demonstrates the author's comedic power.[1]

Also surviving is his *Apologia*, or *A Discourse on Magic*, written in self-defence when accused of using **witchcraft** to marry a young widow.

1. *The Golden Ass*, Apuleius (trans. R. Graves), Penguin, London, 1950.

ARABIAN NIGHTS (*See* **ISLAM**)
In 1704, the Frenchman Antoine Galland published his translation of the tales now known as the *Arabian Nights*. The best known ('Aladdin and his Magic Lamp'; 'Ali Baba and the Forty Thieves'; and 'The Voyages of Sinbad the Sailor') remain pantomime's staple fare. Probably first collected *c*.1450, they came from India, Persia, Egypt and Arabia. Their tales of **giants**, **djinns** and languishing princesses often revolve around the historical figure of the Caliph Haroun al Raschid who ruled in Baghdad in the late eighth century AD. Forming a vast mosaic with one tale budding out of another, Sir Richard Burton's nineteenth-century translation runs to ten dense volumes. Galland's own collection was as incomplete as most other editions: many of the stories being repetitious and of interest only to folklorists.

The tale of Scheherazade runs like **Ariadne**'s thread through the maze of the others. It tells how a Sassanian sultan (Persian dynasty: AD 226–652) had two sons, Schahriar and Schahzenan. When Schahriar became sultan at Baghdad, he gave Schahzenan the kingdom of Great Tartary. Invited to Baghdad years later, Schahzenan set out but, wishing to see his queen again, secretly returned to find her in bed with a slave. Enraged, he killed them both. Telling nobody, he came to Baghdad, keeping his grief to himself. When Schahriar went out hunting, Schahzenan saw his brother's wife meet another man in the palace gardens. Realising he was not the world's only cuckold, he felt better. Returning, Schahriar asked him why he seemed happier. Schahzenan admitted how he had killed his own wife. 'I would not have killed just one woman,' said Schahriar, 'but should have sacrificed a thousand to my resentment.' Then Schahzenan said what he had seen. In a fury, Schahriar slew his wife and her lover. From then on he married a new wife each night and each morning had her killed to avoid further infidelity. He had his grand vizier rake the city for new brides, all to die after one night of marriage. Panic spread. The caliph became hated. But the vizier had two daughters: Scheherazade and Dinarzade. One day Scheherazade told her father she would marry Schahriar, saying she knew how to end the terror.

On the fatal night Scheherazade asked the sultan if Dinarzade too could sleep in the bridal chamber, as one last favour. Overcome by her tears, Schahriar agreed. At dawn Dinarzade awoke the royal couple and asked her sister, 'to relate to me one of those delightful tales you know'. Schahriar agreed. Scheherazade began her first tale, which so delighted the sultan that he delayed her execution so that she might finish the tale the next night – then die. So for the next 1,000 nights Scheherazade told tales that never quite ended, so that every morning Schahriar spared her, until his admiration for her courage and ingenuity persuaded him he had judged women wrongly, and he revoked his vow. Thus, it is said, the tales that still delight millions were all told by a woman battling male prejudice.

ARACHNE (*See* **SPIDER, ZODIAC**)

ARANDA (*See* **ABORIGINES**)
This central Australian people speak of a primordial celestial being, 'him none made', existing before the alchera or 'Dreamtime'. This primal father is still ritually consumed in an act of communion whereby the initiation of youths into manhood involves drinking blood drawn from older men. Once this blood came from a man **sacrificially** killed, his flesh also being eaten. The rite also involved the **circumcision** of the initiates and, a year later, the subincision of the phallus, symbolically creating a vagina or womb-opening in the male organ, reminiscent of the centurion's spear-thrust into the body of the crucified **Christ**, even as the women wept (bled) below.

ARAWN (*See* **ANNWN**, *MABINOGION*, **UNDERWORLD**)

ARCHETYPES (*See* **COLLECTIVE UNCONSCIOUS, DREAMS, JUNG**)
Early in his career the Swiss psychologist C.G. **Jung** found potent primordial images manifesting in his patients' **dreams** and fantasies. These did not arise from personal experience, but seemingly from an ancient store of collective unconscious imagery. Freud considered them 'archaic residues': psychic equivalents of the appendix; Jung decided they were vital centres of psychic life arising from a primal pre-conscious level. As archetypes, as Jung named them, they exist in every cultural era. **Trickster**, **Earth Mother** and Wise Old Man: these archetypes inform the conscious individual mind. Mythic gods and devils intuitively represent archetypes; Greek myth offers perhaps the most detailed model. Jung thought the denial of archetypal values and messages were the source of that (peculiarly modern) sense of life as empty: a state which Africans call 'loss of soul' and which they consider the worst disaster that can befall a human being. Derangement and neurosis thus measure individual estrangement from the full unconscious self.[1]

1. *Man and his Symbols*, ed. C.G. Jung, Aldus Books, London, 1964, pp.67ff.

ARES (*See* **GREEK MYTH**)
Tempestuous and cruel, this Greek god of war was as hated by the Olympians as by men. Even his father **Zeus** found him odious. Clad in bronze armour and attended by his sons Phobos ('Fright') and Deimos ('Fear') he ranged battlefields in a swift chariot, killing with every blow of his spear. Yet this 'scourge of mortals' was rarely victorious. **Athene** continually got the better of him: even mortals such as **Hercules** on occasion bested him. Nor was he luckier in love. Fathering the **Amazons** on the Naiad Harmonia, his affair with **Aphrodite** was discovered by her husband **Hephaestus**, who netted and humiliated the sleeping pair. The Olympians were delighted.

He had a temple in Athens and was worshipped in Thrace, but was widely regarded as an unscrupulous and cowardly killer. His Roman equivalent, **Mars**, is an altogether more dignified deity. It may be that the name of Ares, like Mars, is derived from the Sanskrit root *mar*, giving rise to the Vedic **Maruts**, or storm-divinities.

ARGONAUTS (*See* GOLDEN FLEECE, JASON)

ARHAT (*See* ABAKULU-BANTU, BUDDHISM)
An Arhat (or Arahat) is a Buddhist ascetic who, having attained the highest
peak of self-control, is exempt from rebirth.

ARIADNE (*See* ARIANRHOD, LABYRINTH, MINOTAUR,
THESEUS)

ARIANRHOD (*See MABINOGION*)
Daughter of Don and sister of **Gwydion**, this Welsh goddess appears in the
Mabinogion in the tale of 'Math, Son of Mathonwy'. Applying for the post of
Math's footholder, she has to prove her virginity by stepping over his magic
wand. On so doing she gives birth to two infants, **Dylan** and **Llew**. Thus
publicly shamed, she lays a *geis* on Llew: that he shall have no name, no arms
and no human wife. Through Gwydion's magic these prohibitions are
overcome, though Llew is later slain by the treachery of **Blodeuwedd**.
  Arianrhod, 'Silver Wheel', was associated with the constellation Corona
Borealis ('Northern Crown'), in the starry regions of which she maintained
Caer Sidi, an **otherworld** castle of initiation where the dead went between
incarnations. In the Welsh *Hanes Taliesin* (*The Tale of Taliesin*), **Gwion-
Taliesin**, whose 'original country is in the summer stars', spends 'three
periods' in Arianrhod's 'prison' while awaiting resurrection.
  A similar connection of the Corona Borealis with **Ariadne** (daughter of
King **Minos** of Crete who aided **Theseus** in slaying the **Minotaur**) suggests
that she and Arianrhod were one and the same. It is said Theseus gave her
this crown in gratitude for her help, or that **Bacchus** gave it to her, and cast it
into the sky when she died.

ARISTOPHANES (*See* GREEK MYTH (1))

ARJUNA (*See BHAGAVAD GITA*, KRISHNA)
In the *Bhagavad Gita*, this Indian **Achilles**, son of the Pandavas, reluctant to
make war on his cousins the Kauravas, is persuaded to do so by the god
Krishna, his charioteer. 'Do your duty as a Kshatriya (warrior), and do not
fear to kill: I have already killed them,' Krishna consoles him.

ARK (*See* BOAT, FLOOD MYTH, GILGAMESH, NOAH)

ARK OF THE COVENANT (*See* BIBLE, HOLY GRAIL, JUDAISM)
Holding the two stone tablets on which the Ten Commandments were
inscribed, this acacia wood chest (measuring 45in × 27in × 18in) was
constructed *c*.1250 BC under Mount **Sinai** after the Israelite Exodus from
Egypt. Gold-lined inside and out, with two golden cherubim (angels) facing
each other on the 'mercy seat' atop it, it was kept in the 'Holy of Holies', the
innermost sanctuary of the Israelite god **Yahweh**. For the three centuries of
their wanderings in the wilderness, this sanctuary – the Tabernacle – was a
tent. So heavy that four men were needed to carry it, the Ark's sides had
rings through which were permanently set two gold-plated poles of acacia
wood, it being so dangerous that its handlers had to keep their distance.
When King David took the Ark to Jerusalem, it was put on a new cart, but
the oxen stumbled by 'the threshing-place of Nacon'. Uzzah, one of the
guides of the cart, reached out to steady it, but on touching it was struck dead
by Yahweh, 'because of his irreverence'.[1]

David, furious, was also afraid. Charged with divine energy, the Ark could level mountains, knock down the walls of cities and strike Israel's enemies with cancerous tumours and fiery bolts. Rather than carry it on, he left it for three months. On learning that its local guardians still lived (blessed by Yahweh), he dared take it on to Jerusalem where it was housed (955 BC) in the Temple of **Solomon** built by **Hiram Abiff**, the mythic founder of **Freemasonry**. Yet it had vanished sometime before Nebuchadnezzar sacked Jerusalem (587 BC). The Bible is mute about how, why or where it vanished. Jewish tradition says it is buried under the Dome of the Rock in Jerusalem where no excavation is allowed. Ethiopian lore claims it was removed by Menelik, son of Solomon and the **Queen of Sheba**. Author Graham Hancock claims it was taken away during the reign of the idolator Manasseh (687–642 BC), to be guarded in Egypt then in Ethiopia, first by Jewish then by Christian protectors. Today it is said to rest in the Church of St Mary of Zion at Axum in Ethiopia. Hancock also claims that the **Knights Templar** sought it, and that the stone tablets are the true **Holy Grail** (in *Parzival c.*1195–1216, Wolfram von Eschenbach refers to the Grail as a 'stone').[2]

One tradition suggests that the stone tablets were meteoric in origin, and that the Ark's gold casing shielded against radioactive corruption. Yet maybe its power was primarily symbolic, it being a relic in which lay the self-confidence of the Israelite spirit. No surprise, if so, that it vanished soon before the humiliation of the Babylonish captivity.

Fascination with the Ark persists, as in the 1982 **Hollywood** movie, *Raiders of the Lost Ark*, starring Harrison Ford.

1. *Good News Bible*, 2 Samuel vi:6.
2. *The Sign and the Seal*, Graham Hancock, Heinemann, London, 1992.

ARMAGEDDON (*See* ANTICHRIST, APOCALYPSE)
In Christian apocalyptic myth, it is said the final battle between Good and Evil will take place at Armageddon, as derived from the New Testament Book of Revelation (xvi:16). This 'place that in Hebrew is called Armageddon' is probably Megiddo, near Haifa in modern Israel, once a Canaanite fortress at which many biblical battles occurred. This history seems to have commended it to St John, author of Revelation, as a useful metaphor for the site of his final visionary battle. Yet centuries of fundamentalist interpretation have led to the perception (by some) of Armageddon as a location in literal space-time, rather than as visionary metaphor of internal or psychological conflict of a sort that perpetually reoccurs in every human heart.

ART AND MYTH
Art and myth go hand-in-hand. The first surviving visual arts (neolithic Lascaux cave-paintings, etc.) depict hunters as the animals they hunt, or as ancestral gods. The earliest surviving sculptures are of deep-breasted pot-bellied fertility-goddesses. The earliest literature, from Sumeria to Greece, describes relations between humankind and the gods. In the first place, 'art' depicts the human quest for self-knowledge (knowledge of the gods) and the attempt to portray or magically control the forces that rule life. The skill the Egyptians exercised in pyramids, painted mummies and in text (*The Book of the Dead*) speaks of their concern with the **afterlife**. Ancient **fetish** masks and recent Shona sculptures from Zimbabwe gain their primary 'artistic' power not from 'market economy' but from a concern with racial and personal identity. Bas-reliefs of the victories of **Assyrian** kings express an urgent desire to render their local glory immortal.

In Greece and Rome sculptors like Phidias moulded stone into god-shapes in which men saw themselves: later Byzantine mosaics show Justinian and Theodora equal to the conquering **Christ**. Should we in the West wonder now why **Islam** still resists the *human* portrayal of the deity?

For a millennium all art was controlled by the Church. Not until the Renaissance did Giotto, Masagna, **Dante**, Boccaccio and Ariosto again dare to express the old pagan themes. Botticelli, Leonardo, Michelangelo and others drew on Classical myth even as – protected by merchant princes in Germany and Flanders – Breughel and Vermeer began to celebrate everyday life and material wealth. Yet Classical myth remained potent. Caravaggio, Bernini and other baroque masters drew on it. Jacques-Louis David used classic Roman themes to epitomise the values of the French Revolution – but, a century later, inspiration from the Classical past was dead. Thus Gauguin went to Tahiti to discover a new painterly **Eden**. Picasso, Dali, Chagall and Magritte reinterpreted myths in modern terms; Warhol continued the process, portraying soup-cans or **Marilyn Monroe** as modern deities.

So too in writing and music. From Dante, Chaucer and **Shakespeare** to **Blake**, **Joyce** and **Yeats**; from medieval troubadours to Berlioz, **Wagner**, and Philip Glass in the USA today – all are one in that myth inspires them. Without myth no artist works. Yet frequently, and not just today, the prevailing myths are politically dangerous. They speak of a freedom which the worldly powers-that-be not only reject, but destroy, if given a chance.

The art of myth is owned by nobody, but is expressed by all with heart.

ARTEMIS (*See* ACTAEON, DIANA, GREEK MYTH, VIRGINITY)

Born on the isle of Delos to **Zeus** and Leto, twin sister of **Apollo**, this many-breasted Greek fertility- and **moon**-goddess was originally a Phrygian nature-goddess, her cult taken up by Greek settlers. She was worshipped in rural areas by *arktoi*, '**bear** virgins', who sometimes drew **blood** from the throat of a male victim in her honour. The myth of how the hunter **Actaeon** spied on her as she bathed naked, and was turned into a **stag** torn apart by his own hounds, amplifies her nature as a 'virgin' huntress. 'Virgin' here is *parthenos*, 'unmarried'. To sleeping Endymion she bore fifty daughters yet remained 'virgin'. Like **Athene**, she sometimes wore a **Gorgon**-mask: turning men to stone by her gaze alone. **Aphrodite**, carnal love, had no power over her, though in Asia Minor Aphrodite too was seen as an aspect of Artemis. **Hecate** and Selene were later identified with her, as was the great **Diana** of the Ephesians, against whom **St Paul** rails in his Epistles.

ARTHURIAN MYTH (*See* CONCORDANCE)

The commonly agreed tale of King Arthur is as follows: aided by the magic of the wizard **Merlin**, King **Uther Pendragon** assumed the appearance of King Gorlois of Cornwall in order to seduce Ygraine, the wife of Gorlois. From this union Arthur was born, earning the undying hatred of his step-sister, the enchantress **Morgan Le Fay**. Removed by Merlin into the keeping of Sir Hector of the Forest Sauvage, as a youth he became king by doing what no one else could do: pulling the sword **Excalibur** from the stone into which Uther had plunged it as he died. Gaining the allegiance of many unruly knights, Arthur established his court at Camelot. He married **Guinevere**, and set about stabilising the kingdom. As his fame grew, more knights joined him, including **Lancelot**, **Perceval**, **Galahad**, **Gawain** and **Bedivere**. These were the knights of the **Round Table**. For a time the land flourished. The **Holy Grail** appeared at Camelot, leading to a great **Quest** by all the knights for this elusive object. Meanwhile the appearance of Arthur's illegitimate and incestuous son, **Mordred** (his mother was **Morgause**, a sister of Morgan Le Fay, thus a half-sister of Arthur), the affair of Guinevere and Lancelot, and the petrification of Merlin in a crystal cave, all contributed to the decline in the fortunes of the land, a decline symbolised by Arthur's own loss of power even as the Grail-Quest led to the deaths of many knights.

Lancelot, Gawain, Perceval, Bors and Galahad came close to the Grail, but only Galahad (Lancelot's son) gained the true vision of it, thus passing away from this world. Summoning up all his strength as Mordred invaded, Arthur defeated his son's army at Camlan. He killed Mordred but himself was mortally wounded. Three mysterious queens came on a black barge and took him to Avalon to be healed.

It is said that one day he will return when the land needs him. So he is known as *Rex Quondam Rex Futurus* – 'The Once and Future King'.

How did this famous British legend take shape? In 1485, soon after the first publication of *Le Morte d'Arthur* by **Sir Thomas Malory**, in which the myth assumed its final form, the printer Caxton remarked: 'Divers men hold opinion that there was no such Arthur.'[1] For by then the tale was already old. In his *History of the Kings of Britain* (1135) **Geoffrey of Monmouth**, tracing British kingship back to Brutus the Trojan, drew for his main theme on the legend of one *Arth Vawr mab Uthr* (Welsh: 'The Terrible Great Bear'). Mistranslating *'mab Uthr'* as 'son of Uther', Geoffrey's romance of Arthur took Europe by storm. Lewis Spence believed 'Arth Vawr' to be the central figure of a British **pagan** cultus, perhaps representing an older hero-god or sun-god.[2] As guardian of Britain, Arthur may be identified with **Bran** the Blessed, a Celtic god who in the Mabinogion tale 'Branwen Daughter of Llŷr' appears as an ancient king of Britain. Due to a wound he receives in the foot (or loins), Britain falls into waste. The mysterious **Fisher King** in the Grail Castle is likewise wounded.[3]

Later writers such as Chrétien de Troyes, Wolfram von Eschenbach and the unknown author of *Sir Gawain and the Green Knight* elaborated the magical and chivalric aspects of the Arthurian 'Matter of Britain' and of the 'Quest for the Holy Grail'. By the time Malory introduced the Round Table theme, the cycle had become a vehicle for ideas which, though christianised, were pagan at root. The sword Excalibur derives from the Irish sword Caliburn; the original Celtic Arthur raids **Annwn**, Land of the Dead, to steal a magic **cauldron** (grail) once owned by Bran (or by the Irish **Dagda**); the tale of Arthur hunting the boar Twrch Trwyth predates AD 800.

Malory was first to identify the Isle of Avalon (whence Arthur was borne after his final battle) as **Glastonbury** (Ynys Witrin: 'The Isle of Glass') where, in 1191, monks claimed the discovery of the coffin of Arthur and Guinevere: a claim that brought the monastery good pilgrim trade! Yet more likely Avalon derives from Celtic tales of the Isles of the Blest (Mag Mell, **Tir nan Og**, etc.) mythically located in the Western ocean.

The Arthurian mythos thus provided a bridge between pagan Celtic and Christian imagination, tapping sources so deep that it has fired European imagination for a millennium. But did a 'real' Arthur live? Was there a Romano-Celtic war-leader, son of Ambrosius Aurelianus, who *c.*AD 516 defeated Anglo-Saxon invaders at Mount Badon? Was there a poet-shaman, Myrrdin (**Merlin**), driven mad after the defeat of his king at Arderwydd, thereafter roaming the Forest of Celydon in Scotland?

1. *Religion and the Decline of Magic*, Keith Thomas, Peregrine Books, London, 1978, p.508.

2. *The Magic Arts in Celtic Britain*, Lewis Spence, Rider, London, 1946.
3. *King Arthur and the Grail*, Richard Cavendish, Paladin, London, 1980.

ARYAN CONTROVERSY (*See* INDIAN MYTH, JEWS, NAZI MYTH)

In Europe during the 1930s Adolf Hitler and his Nazi followers claimed that they belonged to an Aryan 'master-race' – white-skinned, blond, blue-eyed, inherently superior to all other racial stock, especially Semitic and Negroid peoples. So, who were the Aryans?

Arya is a Sanskrit term, implying nobility, in opposition to *anarya*, meaning 'unworthy' or 'vile'. In the ancient Indian *Rig Veda* it was used to designate tribes invading from the northwest *c.*1700 BC, horse-tamers who held themselves superior to the people they defeated, whom they called *Dasa*, 'Fiends'. The Dasa being reduced to slavery as the fourth caste, the term *Arya* ceased to connote a tribe or nation, being thereafter applied to a social or ethical condition. Yet in Persia it retained its ethnic meaning. The Greek historian Herodotus (fifth century BC) records that the Medes were once known as Arii, and Persia as Aria – thus the modern name for Persia, Iran.

The modern use of the term was introduced by the German ethnologist Max Müller in the nineteenth century to describe the racial family formerly known as 'Indo-Germanic'. Ironically, he was motivated by dislike of the racist implications of 'Indo-Germanic'. Müller initially accepted the theory of an Aryan race, but later concluded there was no evidence that such a race had ever existed. 'Aryans', he wrote, 'are those who speak Aryan languages, whatever their colour, whatever their blood.'[1] So 'Indo-European' became the preferred reference – at least until the Nazis seized on the Aryan myth to justify their murderous theory of a 'master-race'.

1. *Indian Myth and Legend*, Donald A. Mackenzie, Gresham, London, 1910, p.xxiii.

ASCLEPIUS (*See* GREEK MYTH, HEALING, MEDUSA, PERSEUS)

After a lifetime devoted to healing, this legendary doctor (his father was **Apollo**, his mother perhaps **Athene**, or the **nymph** Coronis) raised Glaucus, son of **Sisyphus**, from the dead. For this **Zeus**, fearing he would make men immortal, blasted him to cinders with a thunderbolt. Or perhaps it was not just this assumption of godlike power that enraged the Olympian father, but other acts of *lèse-majesté*. For Asclepius had slept with fifty amorous women in one night (more than Zeus ever managed), and had also employed the blood of the Medusa (after Perseus slew her) to cure mortal illnesses, even as Athene took the rest of the blood to stimulate murder, dissension and war. Thus as a patron of healing he had many shrines in which sick people slept, it being supposed that he cured or prescribed remedies in **dreams**. Many festivals were held in his honour. He was usually portrayed standing bare-breasted beneath a long cloak, holding a staff with a **serpent** coiled round it. This emblem is the only true symbol of medicine: the **caduceus**, or magical wand of **Hermes**, has no medicinal relevance.

His cult as a god was a late development, **Homer** referring to him only as a clever physician. It is said the **centaur** Cheiron taught him his art.

ASGARD (*See* AESIR, NORSE MYTH, ODIN)

ASH (*See* HORSE, NORSE MYTH, ROWAN, TREES, YGGDRASIL)

In Norse myth the **world-tree**, Askr-**Yggdrasil** ('The ash tree that is the horse of Yggr'), signifies the life-force. **Odin** (Yggr being among his titles) made Ask, the first man, from the ash, and Embla, the first woman, from the elder. From this tough wood men made spears, oars and coracle-slats; thus it was the tree of sea-power, vital to the Norsemen.

In Wales, the ash-god **Gwydion** used the ash as his steed, as did Odin. In the Celtic Beth-Luis-Nion **tree alphabet** the ash represents the third letter N, *nion*. It was thought a cruel tree, as grass or corn cannot easily grow in its shade. In Ireland the Tree of Tortu, the Tree of Dathi and the Branching Tree of Usnech (three of the five magic trees whose fall in AD 665 symbolised the triumph of **Christianity** over **paganism**) were all ash trees. At Killura in the nineteenth century a descendant of the Sacred Tree of Creevna still stood. Pieces of its wood were carried to America by Irish emigrants after the Great Famine as **charms** against drowning.[1]

In British folklore the ash is a tree of rebirth. It was thought that a sick child passed through the cleft of an ash would be cured, and that the burning of ash logs would drive evil spirits out of a room. A **Druid** wand, found in Anglesey and dated to the early first century AD, was of ash.

In Greece the ash was sacred to **Poseidon**, patron of **horses** before he became a sea-god: the ash-spirits called Mĕliai (said by Hesiod to have sprung from the blood of **Uranus**) were popularly worshipped.[1]

1. *The White Goddess*, Robert Graves, Faber & Faber, London, 1961, pp.168–9.

ASHANTI (*See* AFRICAN MYTH)

This West African folk hold that the **ancestors**, *nsamanfo*, are always close to the world of the living, and that everyone has a *sunsum*, 'ego', and a *kra*, 'life-force'. They worship a supreme god, Nyame, who has no priest, since he lives close to every human being. But Nyame has many children, all of them gods, each with their temple or shrine. The greatest of these are the rivers Tano and Bea, also Lake Bosomtwe and the Ocean in the South. These gods choose their own priests, as in the case of the man, Di Amono, who, seeing a stone in the forest aflame, recognised the presence of a divinity. Such people, receiving revelation, return to society after forest seclusion to be initiated by existing priests, and may thereafter receive worshippers, who come with offerings, requesting good health or children. Especially venerated is the earth-goddess Asase Yaa.

They also speak of *ntoro*, 'inherited spirit'. Once they divided their society into twelve *ntoro* groups. Each epitomised a different psychological type – the audacious, the eccentric, the fanatic, the chaste, the liberal, the fastidious and so on. Today the idea of *ntoro* is interpreted more individually than formerly.

ASHOKA (273–232 BC) (*See* INDIAN MYTH)

As with and fifty years after **Alexander the Great**, myth and history converge in this Indian emperor. Bringing almost all the Indian subcontinent under one rule for the first time, this philosopher-king, the greatest of the Maurya dynasty, regarded his subjects as his children and insisted on gentle government. It was he who erected the original Seven Pillars of Wisdom (in fact, there were nine). These metal posts, set up across India, carried inscriptions making known his laws and convictions, which included the need to honour one's parents, respect all living things, speak truth, treat servants well, preserve bodily health, tolerate the belief of others and to study the works of the **Buddha**. Condemning animal **sacrifices**, he favoured vegetarianism, self-examination and hard work. Yet, though willing to forgive rebels and wrongdoers, he reminded all that he was powerful, and would execute those who did not repent. For also he supported *ahimsa*, love of duty, and the *dharma*.

ASHTAROTH (*See* ASTARTE, DEMONS)

ASHUR (*See* ASSYRIA)

ASMODEUS (*See* DEMONS)

ASSYRIAN MYTH (*See* CONCORDANCE)
About 2500 BC Babylonian colonists moved northwest up the course of the River Tigris into the mountains of Mesopotamia, carrying their civilisation, religion and mythology, all originally from the earlier Sumerian culture. A millennium later, from their cities of Nineveh and Ashur these 'Assyrians' began imperial expansion under Tukulti-Ninurta I (1244–1208 BC). At its height the Assyrian empire ran from Sinai and Tarsus in the west to the Persian Gulf in the east. Under Ashurbanipal (668–627 BC) the Scythians and Medes brought ruin: Nineveh was sacked in 612 BC, by 605 BC Assyria was destroyed. Few were sorry. Assyrian hegemony had been characterised by cruelty, sadism and lack of invention. Even their gods were borrowed.

The name 'Assyria' came from the native Assur or (Hebrew version) Ashur, the patron god of the land, derived from the ancient Babylonian god Anshar. Additionally assuming the roles of the Babylonian gods **Marduk** and **Enlil**, Ashur was also (inevitably) god of war. Shown as a winged disc enclosing a drawn bow, or mounted on a **bull**, he accompanied Assyrian armies into war, claiming the vanquished as his subjects. His consort **Ishtar**, elsewhere renowned as a love-goddess, was 'Lady of Battles' to the Assyrians. Riding a chariot drawn by **seven lions**, she had a beard falling to her breasts.

What was wrong with them? Did they glory in cruelty because they lost touch with the gods? In 1230 BC Tukulti-Ninurta I, who began the expansion, had a stone altar erected, showing him kneeling before an empty throne: the throne of the god. No former king had ever been shown kneeling. A cuneiform tablet of the time says: 'One who has no god, as he walks along the street, Headache envelops him like a garment.' A century later, King Tiglath-Pileser abandoned the old custom of hyphenating his name with the god. These were a people who lost all spiritual connection, and as a result for 600 years ran riot, displaying a sadism typifying the modern, not the ancient, world.[1]

1. *Starseekers*, Colin Wilson, Hodder & Stoughton, London, 1980, p.74.

ASTARTE (*See* BAAL, DEMONS, PHOENICIAN MYTH)
Wife and sister of Baal, this Phoenician-Syrian mother-goddess was not only the equivalent of **Ishtar** and **Venus**, but also appears in other guises. The Ras Shamra texts portray her as Anat, the 'Maiden', the 'Virgin' and 'Lady of the Mountain'. Despite these tender epithets Anat was warlike, portrayed with helmet, axe and spear, wading in the blood of her victims. Introduced to Egypt by the invading Hyksos (*c.* eighteenth century BC), her cult (identified with that of cow-horned **Hathor**) endured after the invaders were expelled. As with **Inanna** and Ishtar, temple prostitution was a feature of this cult. As late as the fifth century BC the Hebrew community still saw her as consort of **Yahweh**. She was also a **moon** and **fertility**-goddess, while as Asherat, 'Lady

of the Sea', she was 'Mother of the Gods' with seventy children, and in this form the wife of **El**, the Canaanite Yahweh, and mother of Baal.

Thus as Ashtart (Greek Astarte) she appears as a conflation of older goddesses. In this guise she was worshipped as the planet Venus, not only beautiful but dangerous, **bull**-horned, 'mistress of **horses** and chariots'.

She is also the same as 'Ashtaroth the abomination of the Zidonians' (2 Kings xxiii:13), and as such underwent a final transformation, being reckoned in medieval demonologies as a male demon pied black and white, beautiful yet foul of breath, though capable of revealing the future.

ASTRONOMY AND MYTH (*See* CONCORDANCE)

Astronomy may be a cold science, denying its older sister, astrology – yet still the heavens are a tapestry of myth, a screen on which we project our ancient imaginings. Most of us know our 'star-sign' – one of the twelve constellations of the zodiac (Greek, 'Circle of Animals'): a narrow band of sky against which sun, moon and planets wheel. These signs are Aries (Ram), Taurus (Bull), Gemini (Twins), Cancer (Crab), Leo (Lion), Virgo (Virgin), Libra (Scales), Sagittarius (Archer), Scorpio (Scorpion), Capricorn (Sea-Goat), Aquarius (Water Carrier), and Pisces (Fishes).

Yet they constitute but twelve of the eighty-eight identified constellations, almost every one characterised as giant beasts, heroes or artefacts of ancient Greek and Roman mythology. There is a **Unicorn**, a **Dragon**, a **Peacock** and a **Phoenix**. On a clear night many mythic dramas are eternally re-enacted in the sky. **Perseus** forever rescues Andromeda from the sea-monster Cetus, her mother Cassiopeia looking on distraught. The hunter **Orion** brandishes his club at the snorting bull, Taurus, his dogs (Canis Major and Canis Minor) at his heels – but they cannot stop the **Scorpion** stinging him to death, so that every night as Orion sets Scorpio rises. **Hercules**, one foot on Draco the **Dragon**, perpetually slays Leo the Lion as nearby the otherworld castle of **Arianrhod**, Corona Borealis, welcomes the dead. The severed tresses of Queen Berenice of Egypt (Coma Berenice) float between Virgo and the Great Bear, called Arth Vawr in Welsh, alias King Arthur.

These mythical beings remain constant, but against them the Wanderers, the planets of our solar system, forever chase each other round the zodiac, every one of them a Roman god: **Mercury, Venus, Mars, Jupiter, Saturn, Uranus, Neptune** and **Pluto**. And all of them we watch from our own planet, which some now call **Gaia**, after the Greek earth-goddess, while by day the **sun**-god rises and by night the **moon**-goddess endures her periods.

Yet this imaginative projection began at least 2,000 years before the Romans, when the Chaldean astronomers (or astrologers: no distinction then) nightly observed the sky for **omens** of human fate. They saw the planets, wandering amid the fixed, sheep-like stars, as *bibbus*, 'goats': each a god governing different aspects of human life. Their identifications persist. When Nergal (Mars) dominated the sky, war was near. **Ishtar** (Venus) shone after sunset, the time of love. As for Nabu (Mercury), so fast and hard to see, he was obviously a sharp-witted **trickster**. **Marduk** (Jupiter) in his bright, reliable course was as remote as the god-king on the throne. And slow heavy Saturn warned of death.

The Chaldeans were doubtless not the first to characterise the heavens, but their records are the earliest to survive. How did those mysterious builders of northern European megaliths (*c*.3000 BC–*c*.1500 BC) see the sky? They left no records, yet their preoccupations are apparent from the lunar, solar and stellar alignments of their monuments. It seems unlikely that they denied the universal ancient perception: 'As above: so below.'

This hermetic epigram sums up astrology's basic principle: the cosmos is a unity; our human fate is writ in the stars.

Modern denial of such belief has not ended mythic identification with the heavenly bodies. The outer planets, unknown until recent times, bear the names of Roman gods – Uranus (discovered 1781 by Herschel); Neptune (1846; Leverrier and Adams); and Pluto (1930: Tombaugh). Yet why Roman gods? Why not Greek? For while Roman deities characterise the planets, minor Greek deities identify their moons. The moons of Mars are Phobos ('Fright') and Deimos ('Fear') – sons of **Ares**, Greek predecessor of Roman Mars. The four largest of Jupiter's sixteen moons, known since the seventeenth century, are Io, Europa, Ganymede and Callisto: Greek, as are Saturn's nine moons: Mimas, Enceladus, Tethys, Dione, Rhea, **Titan**, **Hyperion**, Iapetus and Phoebe.

Yet round Uranus whirl Miranda, Ariel, Umbriel, Titania and Oberon – more **Shakespearian** than Classic, yet mythic all the same. Neptune (Roman sea-god) is circled by **Triton** and **Nereid**, both mythic Grecian sea-monsters serving the Greek **Proteus**, who preceded Neptune. As for Pluto (Greek **Hades**), he seems to be moonless and all alone.

So too the constellations represent a cultural mix. Orion, Perseus, Cassiopeia and Andromeda come from Greek myth. Ursa Major, Canis Major, Leo and others with Latin titles represent beasts, not tales.

Of the stars, the greatest, the Dog-Star **Sirius** (Greek for 'Sparkling' or 'Scorching'), was called Sothis in Egypt, its annual rising presaging the Nile flood. Thought the home of **Isis** and **Osiris**, to occultists, Sirius is 'the sun behind the Sun', radiating evolutionary power into our solar system. The **Dogon** of Mali hold a celebrated myth about Sirius. Yet few other great stars – Canopus, Arcturus, Vega, Rigel, Spica, Betelgeuse and so on – have any mythic associations. Many were named by Arab astronomers. Others bear only a Latin or Greek alphabetical reference (e.g., Alpha Centauri, for the brightest star in Centaurus). As for even remoter stellar objects, myth fails almost entirely. Two star-clusters in the constellation Taurus are named the Hyades (Greek for 'Daughters of **Atlas** and Aethra'), and their half-sisters, the famed **Pleiades**, or 'Seven Sisters'. This nursery of new stars (only seven visible to the naked eye, but the cluster includes hundreds) has been mythologised as the 'Seven Sisters' from Greece to Australia. The **Aborigines** (who claim that their **ancestors**, the Wondjina, returned to the sky to become lights seen moving in the night sky), also recognise the Pleiades as 'Seven Sisters'.

We always have and always will project our myths on to the sky. **Science fiction** movies like *Star Wars* and tv series like *Star Trek* maintain this ancient process.

ASURAS (*See* DEMONS, INDIAN MYTH)

Just as the *daemon* ('genius') of **Socrates** later transformed into the image of the 'demon', or negative spiritual entity, so the Asuras of the oldest Vedic texts were likewise transformed by historical process. The original Vedic gods (**Agni**, **Indra** and **Varuna**) were Asuras; only later demonised by new cultures who imposed their own morality on those they conquered. Thus 'asura' came first to mean 'non-god', then, later, 'demon'.

ATHENE (*See* APHRODITE, GREEK MYTH, HOMER)

Variously a goddess of war, peace and wisdom, this complex Greek divinity is said to have sprung fully formed (and armed) from the brow (intellect) of **Zeus**. The smith-god **Hephaestus** aided this odd caesarian birth with his axe.

In origin a storm-goddess, in Classical Greece she came to assume the dual roles of Promachos ('Front-rank Warrior'), and Ergane ('Working Woman'). Patron of architects, sculptors, spinners and weavers, she also protected **horses** and oxen, yet her emblem was the **owl**. Never happy in her love-life, she resented Aphrodite, who married Hephaestus after she had rejected him. With **Hera** and Aphrodite contesting the Judgement of **Paris**, after she lost this contest she remained energetic, supporting **Ulysses** on his long homeward voyage. Though belligerent and cruel, she protected the brave, including **Perseus** in his battle with the Gorgons, guiding his arm and giving him a mirror shield so that he could slay the **Medusa** without having to view the monster's petrifying face and **serpent**-locks directly.

ATLANTIS (See FLOOD, GREEK MYTH (1), LOST WORLDS, PLATO, THEOSOPHY)

In 'a single day and night' 10,000 years ago, the isle of Atlantis is said to have been destroyed by earthquake and flood. Some claim Atlantis really existed; that its empire embraced parts of the Americas, Africa, Europe and Asia; that the abuse by its people of a crystal-based technology led to the disaster, and that **Stonehenge** and the pyramids were built by survivors.

The tale first appears in the *Timaeus* by **Plato** (427–347 BC), in which Critias tells **Socrates** how, visiting the Egyptian capital, Saïs (Plato's) ancestor Solon (*c*.640–569 BC) was told by a priest: 'You Greeks are all children . . . You have no belief rooted in old tradition . . . And the reason is this. There have been and will be many different calamities to destroy mankind, the greatest of them by fire and water.' From 'an island larger than Libya and Asia combined' that lay 'opposite the strait . . . you call the Pillars of Heracles', a great empire had invaded Europe, to be defeated by the ancient Greeks. Later 'in a single dreadful day and night' earthquake and flood had swallowed the Greek armies: 'and the island of Atlantis was similarly swallowed up by the sea and vanished . . .'[1]

Plato claims that ten kings ruled Atlantis, and that the capital city lay within three circular canals guarded by metal-clad walls. The largest temple on the central island was dedicated to **Poseidon** and Cleito. The royal palace had hot and cold running water; wild **bulls** were kept in its grounds. Some say such detail excludes mere invention, yet Aristotle said Plato invented it to moralise on the consequences of overweening ambition.

Yet many long considered the tale to be true. Fifteenth-century Portuguese charts show Antilia, a mythic isle. Francis Bacon's *The New Atlantis* (1624) depicts an ideal society, or **utopia**. In 1882 the US Congressman Ignatius Donnelly published his *Atlantis: The Antediluvian World*. Siting Atlantis in the Azores, he argued that ancient European and pre-Columbian American societies were influenced by diffusion of Atlantean culture.[2] Occultists like Blavatsky and Steiner later took up and developed the myth.

Another approach is that Plato mythologised a real event. K.T. Frost's theory (1909) that the myth describes the damage caused to the Cretan civilisation by the eruption of Thera *c*.1470 BC was later taken up by J.V. Luce and others. On the face of it this theory assumes that Plato (or Solon or the priests of Saïs) could not distinguish (1) between 10,000 BC and 1500 BC; (2) between the Atlantic and the Mediterranean. Neither was Cretan culture wholly destroyed by Thera.

Yet perhaps these 'flaws' are explained by the geoarchaeologist Eberhard Zangger, who claims that the myth refers to the destruction of Troy by the Achaeans, *c*.1300 BC. He points out that: (1) Poseidon was the patron of Troy; (2) the Dardanelles entry to the Black Sea was called the

Pillars of Hercules long before the Greeks knew of the Straits of Gibraltar; (3) the Achaeans certainly overthrew the militant empire of Troy; (4) Plato's description of the canal-ringed city fits Troy; (5) the Trojans were 'sons of **Atlas**', and thus were known as 'Atlanteans'; (6) earthquake and flood later destroyed Achaean society *c*.1200 BC, leading to illiteracy and the Greek 'Dark Ages'; (7) the landlocked Egyptians tended to refer to external lands as 'islands'; (8) the Egyptian reference to a period 8,000 years in the past makes sense if not solar but lunar 'years' (months) are counted – 8,000 months from 560 BC gives a date of 1337 BC; (9) the Saïtian priests may have (mis)interpreted earlier (mis)translations of Achaean records.[3]

1. *Timaeus and Critias*, Plato (trans. Desmond Lee), Penguin, London, 1971.
2. *Atlantis, The Antediluvian World*, Ignatius Donnelly, Sidgwick & Jackson, London, 1970.
3. *The Flood from Heaven*, Eberhard Zangger, Sidgwick & Jackson, London, 1992.

ATLAS (*See* ASTRONOMY AND MYTH, GIANTS, GREEK MYTH)

Son of the **Titan** Iapetus and the Oceanid Clymene, the older brother of **Prometheus**, Menoetius and Epimetheus, Atlas was condemned by **Zeus** for his part in the revolt of the Titans to stand on the edge of the Western world before his daughters the **Hesperides**, bearing the vault of the heavens on his shoulders for ever. The Atlas Mountains in Morocco are named after him.

Among his other children were the Hyades ('Rain-Makers'), seven sisters translated to the heavens as stars at their deaths, and the **Pleiades** (*plei*, 'to sail'), also seven sisters (amorously pursued by Zeus) who also became stars after killing themselves in despair at the deaths of the Hyades.

ATMAN (*See* INDIAN MYTH, *UPANISHADS*)

A word originally meaning 'breath', thus by derivation '**spirit**' (as in the Latin *spirare*, 'to breathe'). In **Hindu** mythology atman has come to mean 'world-spirit' as well as the **soul** of the individual. This may be seen as contradictory, yet is no more so than the Hindu insistence that the One God may be worshipped in a multitude of lesser forms, or gods. The atman means our inner self, hidden so deep that most of us never realise it: the primal essence that both underlies yet informs all individual consciousness.

Thus too the **pagan** philosophies see beyond the many forms (gods) of Nature to the One God: the one underlying inspiration, or 'breathing in'.

ATTIS (*See* CASTRATION, CORN-GODS, CYBELE, DYING GODS, EASTER)

Fulfilling the same function as **Adonis** and **Tammuz**, in ancient Phrygia (in Asia Minor) the spring festival honoured the self-castrated **fertility**-god Attis. Son of the mother-goddess Cybele (equated with **Inanna** or **Ishtar**), Attis was usually portrayed as an effeminate youth or eunuch, killed and annually reborn. Cybele's festival was violent: the blood of sacrificed rams was used to baptise self-castrated initiates even as already unmanned eunuchs cut their flesh in holy delirium. Reaching Rome *c*.200 BC, this cult celebrated its 'Day of Blood' on 25 March. Early **Christians** celebrated **Easter** on this day: in Russia the Christian Skoptsky cult practised ritual self-castration at least as late as the eighteenth century.

ATUM (or **ATON, ATUN, TUM**) (*See* **EGYPTIAN MYTH, RA**)
This ancient Egyptian god of Heliopolis was the primeval 'spirit, still formless, who bore within him the sum of all existence'. Thus similar to the primeval essence of **Hindu** creation myth, **Brahma**, he was early characterised by attachment to the **sun**-god Ra, as Atum-Ra, in which form he was at least psychologically visible. Seen as **ancestor** of the human race, he is not so much a god as a philosophical principle. By masturbation he created the first divine couple, unaided, though later authorities allowed him a wife.

AUSTRALIA (*See* **ABORIGINES, ARANDA, LIZARD MEN, YURLUNGUR**)

AVALOKITESHVARA (*See* **BODHISATTVA, BUDDHISM, TIBET**)
This most popular of the Buddhist **bodhisattvas** exemplifies compassion. He attained **Nirvana** yet chose to remain on earth to aid suffering humanity. Represented in public parades as a handsome young man holding a lotus blossom in his left hand, in Buddhist lands he is called 'Bhagavan', the Lord, who looks around (*avalokita*, 'looking around') to gain happiness for mortals and to teach them the way to enlightenment. Worshipped as a god since the third century AD, some say he has reincarnated 333 times since **Gautama Buddha** entered Nirvana 2,500 years ago. He is often depicted with the goddess Tara, who is likewise devoted to alleviating human suffering. He has vowed not to accept the peace of Nirvana until all human souls find enlightenment, for their misery is his: no joy lies in a selfish freedom.
   In Tibet called Chenresi, he reincarnates as the Dalai Lama. In China he is venerated as a goddess, after his consort Tara, and called Kwan Yin, who since before 1000 AD has guaranteed the rice-harvest that keeps people alive. His 'thousand' arms are insufficient for all the work he must do.

AVALON (*See* **APPLE, ARTHURIAN MYTH, ATLANTIS, EARTHLY PARADISE**)

AVATAR (*See* **ATMAN, INDIAN MYTH**)
From the Sanskrit word, 'descent', this term applies to the descent of the divine spirit from heaven to earth to incarnate in human or other material form. Used especially of Hindu deities such as **Brahma, Shiva** and **Vishnu**, the latter being said to be represented by ten avatars, including **Krishna** and **Rama**, while himself not stirring from endless sleep in the unlimited ocean of the uncreated universe. This concept is connected to that of the Atman, the indivisible spirit of the One God which none the less may be manifest in many differentiated mortal forms, each inspired by the first cause.

AVESTA (*See* **ZEND-AVESTA, ZOROASTRIANISM**)

AWONAWILONA (*See* **CREATION MYTH, NATIVE AMERICAN MYTH, TWINS**)
The **creation** myth of the cliff-dwelling Pueblo Zuni of the desert in the southwest USA tells how this androgynous deity preceded and created all else, including the **sun** and the primeval sea. From these two sprang the Earth Mother, Awitelin Tsta, and the Sky Father, Apoyan Tachi. They generated all things via four worlds or wombs, one including Poshaiyangkyo, the Zuni **Adam**. Escaping to the light, he begged the sun to free the beasts still locked up in Awitelin Tsta's womb. Awonawilona sent the divine **twins** down on **spider**-web threads to cleave her womb with thunderbolts. They

told her creatures to prepare for birth. Many reached the light, but others emerged only as monsters or fools. Even the first men, seeing their first sunrise, were more beast than human, with tails, scales, webbed feet, huge ears and the eyes of **owls**. They wailed in terror at their birth. So they do still.

AXIS MUNDI (See **OMPHALOS, TREES, YGGDRASIL**)

An axis in general is an imaginary line about which any solid body rotates. The *axis mundi* ('world axis') is thus literally a line running through the globe from pole to pole. In myth the *axis mundi* is a symbolic point about which the world and universe revolve. In a medieval *mappa mundi* Jerusalem is often found at the world-centre, equating to the **New Jerusalem** of Christian mystics. The Great Pyramid, sited at the exact geographical centre of the earth's land-mass including the Americas and Antarctica, is an *axis mundi*, as are all pyramids, ziggurats and holy mountains. In **Hindu** myth Mount Meru is the vertical axis of the universe, as with the **ash Yggdrasil** of **Norse myth**. *Axis mundi* and **omphalos**, 'world navel', are similar concepts.

AZAZEL (See **ANGELS, DEMONS, DJINNS, ENOCH**)

In Genesis vi:2 it is said 'That the sons of God saw the daughters of men, that they were fair; and they took them wives of all which they chose.' So the **giants** were born, evil proliferated and **Yahweh** sent the **Flood**.

The Book of Enoch expands on this. Two hundred 'sons of God' (Watchers) led by Shemyaza descended to Mount Hermon in Syria to guide human society. But Azazel persuaded some to take human wives and teach banned arts, from weapon-making to the use of cosmetics. The giants were born, evil spread; God condemned the Watchers to rot in the Valleys of Fire for ever. Shemyaza and Azazel were buried alive much deeper. Later, Azazel came to designate the **goat** chosen to bear Israelite sins on the Day of Atonement: thus the 'scapegoat' (Leviticus xvi:7). In Arabic myth he was Iblis, the **djinn** taken to and educated in heaven who, escaping back to earth to become king of those djinns surviving heavenly wrath, took the name Azazel.

AZRAEL (See **AFRICAN MYTH, ANGELS, ISLAMIC MYTH**)

In Genesis it is said that the first people, like **Methuselah**, lived many centuries. So how was our span reduced? A Tunisian tale is that a virgin, 500 years old at death, resurrected by Allah at the behest of **Moses**, said she was sick of life. So Allah told Azrael, Angel of Death (who figures in Jewish myth as early as the reign of **Solomon**), to free folk from mortal care after a mere threescore years and ten.

AZTEC MYTH (See **CONCORDANCE**)

Taking their name from Aztlan, the fabulous land of the 'Seven Caves' or 'Seven Cities of **Cibola**', the Aztecs emigrated south to Mexico some three centuries before Cortes 'discovered' them in 1519. Overthrowing the Nahua folk, who in turn had overwhelmed the earlier Toltecs and **Mayas**, they set up a warrior culture based on their own polytheistic religion.

This involved horrors eclipsing even **Assyrian** sadism. Continuous war, not for conquest but to seize victims for **sacrifice** and **cannibalism**, was the order. The dedication of the Temple of the Sun in Tenochtitlán (now Mexico City), just before the Spanish invasion, demanded the ceremonial murder of 70,000 victims. Over three days their hearts were torn out on black basalt altars on top of the pyramid. After their conquest the Spaniards, well used to cruelty, were amazed to find towers of lime-cemented skulls. In the Xocotlan plaza they found over 100,000 skulls; in Tenochtitlán, 136,000 skulls on racks. The American anthropologist Marvin Harris explains this Aztec obsession as arising from a need for protein, due to a lack of domesticated beasts in the New World. Living bodies taken up the pyramid were rolled down the other side, then butchered, roasted and stuffed with peppers and other delicacies.[1]

What could stop these people but their own guilt? The inedible skulls were displayed to the hungry gods. So when the tiny band of Spaniards arrived, the Aztecs were so obsessed with the myth, common to Mexico and lands to the north, that one day the 'white' god or 'Feathered Serpent' **Quetzalcoatl** (**Kukulcán** to the Maya) would return from the east to reclaim his kingdom as anciently promised, that they abandoned their bloody kingdom to the bearded white *conquistadores*. **Prophecy** said Quetzalcoatl would return in the very year Cortes landed, and that after their defeat, the 'Nine Hells' would begin – nine epochs of fifty-two years each, from 1519 until 1987, after which the spirit of the land would again walk tall. A long time to wait!

This myth has proved so potent that in 1987 the so-called 'Harmonic Convergence' was celebrated by the mystically-minded across North America and in other lands as establishing the true beginning of a 'New Age'.

But what of the Aztec deities who in the first place, quite apart from the subsequent genocidal excesses of European 'Christians', had established a reign of terror not only over all Middle America but over the Aztec mind?

These are described elsewhere. In short, Ah Puch, Mayan god of death, inherited by the Aztecs, still feared today. **Coatlicue, 'Serpent** Lady', earth-goddess; mother of **Huitzilopochtli**, god of war, the daily reborn **sun**-god, who flayed corpses for food. Ometucuhtli, source of life, above earthly duality and war. **Tezcatlipoca**, 'Smoking Mirror', **trickster**-god of **witches** and thieves, to whom a youth was sacrificed each spring, having ruled for a year in his name. **Tlaloc**, a rain-god, originally Toltec. **Xipetotec**, 'The Flayed Lord', corn-god and lord of penitential torture who sends illnesses. **Xiuhtecuhtli**, the fire-god, the great pillar, *axis mundi*, helping the dead in their return to the earth. **Xochiquetzal**, 'Most Precious Flower', the Aztec **Persephone**, an **underworld** goddess who in the **Golden Age** of Quetzalcoatl brought flowers and beauty to the world, and was also associated with childbirth.

1. *Cannibals and Kings*, Marvin Harris, Random House, New York, 1977, pp.161–5.

B

BA (*See* **EGYPTIAN MYTH, KA**)

BAAL (*See* **DYING GODS, PHOENICIAN MYTH**)
Many Canaanite fertility-gods were called Baal ('Lord') before *the* Baal, Lord
of Thunder and Rain, assumed their roles *c.*1350 BC. The **name** *Baal* hid the
true names of this god which, as with the **Hebrew** deity **Yahweh**, could be
pronounced only by initiates and under exceptional circumstances.

With his chief temple at Tyre, his worship entered Israel via **Jezebel**
(Jeze-baal), Ahab's wife, but Elijah had all 'the prophets of Baal' slain:
Yahweh triumphed. Temples to Baal-Hammon, 'Lord of the altar of
incense', were popular from Carthage to Palmyra. The **Babylonian** Bel-
Marduk may be associated, or may be a masculinisation of the Sumerian
goddess Belili. Connection with the British **Bel** (or Belinus), is unsure,
though the Celtic May Day festival of **Beltane**, 'Fire of Bel', is suggestive.

Baal's father was **El**, or **Dagon**. His wife (and mother) was Anat, later
Astarte. Defeating the sea-god Yam, Baal denied the authority of Mot, his
brother, lord of the arid desert, also spirit of the harvest. Mot invited Baal to
the Land of the Dead, and would not revive him. Anat killed Mot; burning,
grinding and scattering his members over the fields. Baal and Mot were duly
resurrected, fighting an annual stalemate ended only when El dismissed Mot,
leaving Baal in sole authority; the fecund god of rainfall and vegetation
overcoming the parched, harvested plains.

BABEL, TOWER OF (*See* **NIMROD**)
Genesis xi:1–9 tells how men tried to build the tower of Babel, so high that
from its summit they could assault heaven itself. The work went well, for all
men spoke the same language. To confound it, **Yahweh** cursed them so all
began babbling in different tongues, and split into seventy hostile nations,
scattering over the face of the earth. The name Babel is commonly derived
from the Aramaic *balbel*, 'confound', but it may be that it comes from
Bâb-îli, 'Gate of God'. The biblical account says this tower was built 'in the
land of Shinar': the prophet Micah calls Assyria 'the land of Nimrod' – in
Hebrew lore the name of the evil king who ordered the tower to be built.
Others have identified it with the ziggurat Esagilla in **Babylon** itself. The
myth seeks to account for the dispersal of humanity into different nations and
languages: similarly a **Sumerian** legend tells how the god **Ea** diversified
language, so ending the **Golden Age**.

BABYLONIAN MYTH (*See* **CONCORDANCE**)
About 3500 BC or earlier the **Sumerian** culture developed in the Mesopotamian desert and marshlands adjacent to the Persian Gulf – land fertilised by
the Rivers Tigris and Euphrates. Here arose the first city states – Lagash,
Kish and Eridu; Sippar and Uruk. Here too writing developed. Pictographs
impressed on tablets of baked clay led to the wedge-shaped cuneiform script.

Babylon (Bâb-îli, 'Gate of God', or 'Gate of the Gods': see **Babel**) was one such city state, though prominent only after the accession *c*.2200 BC of the first dynasty. By the era of Hammurabi (1792–1750 BC: famed for his code of civil law) 'Babylon' epitomised a new culture, amid the waves of Semitic invasion. Yet Sumerian texts survived, being now interweaved with Akkadian translation. Thus Babylonian (and Assyrian) myths remained much as first expressed by the Sumerians, not least as all Mesopotamian culture relied – whatever the era – on the fertility of the land between the two rivers.

Yet shifts in attitude arose from the historical conflicts shaping the politics of the region. The Babylonian creation epic *Enuma Elish* (from its opening words: 'When on high . . .') agrees with the Sumerians that the gods created man to serve them, in return for which service they renew the world each day – but the nature and status of the earlier gods changed.

The Sumerian **Ea**, lord of the deep, creator of all things, is known in Babylon, but now bows to Babylon's champion, **Marduk** (Bel-Marduk), slayer of the **dragon Tiamat**. **Enlil**, city-god of Nippur and a powerful Sumerian deity, retains his name and status in the Assyrio-Babylonian pantheon, but the fearful aspect of his elemental nature is emphasised.

Yet the names of **Shamash** (**sun-god**), **Sin** (**moon-god**), **Nergal** (god of death and the **underworld**), **Ishtar** (love-goddess, consort of **Tammuz** and the Babylonian version of Sumerian **Inanna**) are not Semitic, but Sumerian.

And though the *Epic of Gilgamesh* was found in the library of the Assyrian emperor Ashurbanipal (668–627 BC), the tale remains Sumerian, from the third millennium BC. The cultural continuity remains. Our problem is that we deal not with centuries but millennia. Between the earliest Sumerian city-states and Hammurabi's Babylon lie at least 1,200 years: and again 1,200 years from Hammurabi to the Jewish captivity. In Europe, 1,200 years ago, **Charlemagne** was crowned. Before the birth of **Alexander the Great**, 'Babylon the Great' was already a memory, 2,400 years ago. King Nebuchadnezzar (d. 562 BC) and Belshazzar his son (d. 539 BC), to whom Daniel interpreted the Writing on the Wall just before Cyrus the Persian seized Babylon, precede Alexander by as many years as Napoleon precedes the last decade of the twentieth century.

But mythic memory endures. Before the Gulf War, Saddam Hussein of Iraq was attempting to restore this city and its empire, rebuilding the walls of ancient Babylon.

BACCHUS (*See* DIONYSUS)

BADB (*See* BANSHEE, CROW, IRISH MYTH, TRIPLE GODDESS)
In Gaelic folklore the badb (meaning 'rage, fury, violence') is the generic title of a crow-goddess who rules over carnage and battle. In old Ireland, this goddess (as elsewhere) has a triple aspect. Neman brings madness, Machan drinks the blood of the slain, the **Morrigan** makes men brave. Connected to the banshee, keening for the dead, it was the badb in her triple aspect who confronted the Irish hero **Cuchulainn** before his last battle and made him break his vows (*geasa*) and thus lose his strength – and his life – by feeding him **dog**-meat. So in *Macbeth* the three **witches** are this same crow-goddess, whom **Shakespeare** associates with **Hecate**.

BALDUR (*See* ACHILLES HEEL, DYING GODS, MISTLETOE, NORSE MYTH)
Called the 'Beautiful' or the 'Bleeding God', this son of **Odin** and **Frigga** is a northern European version of died-and-reborn **Adonis**, **Attis**, **Tammuz**, even the crucified **Christ**. Frigga made all things on earth swear not to harm

him, but never approached the **mistletoe**. The **trickster Loki** got Baldur's blind brother Hodur to hurl the mistletoe dart that killed him, so sending him to the prison of the queen of the **underworld, Hel**. Odin sent the god Hermod on his eight-legged stallion, Sleipnir, down to Hel to plead for Baldur's release from death. Hel, who tortured all those sent to her who had not died in honourable battle, agreed to release the beloved god – so long as all created things wept for him. But Loki failed to do so, and for it was bound by the other gods of **Asgard**. Yet it is said that, after the awful day of **Ragnorak**, Baldur the Beautiful will be resurrected.

Christianity has no monopoly on the myths it borrowed.

BALLARD, J.G. (1930–) (*See* SCIENCE FICTION)

This English writer, mythologer of the atomic age, was born in Shanghai and during World War II was interned in a Japanese civilian POW camp, as described in his autobiographical novel *Empire of the Sun* (1984), which clarified the themes of his earlier **surreal** and (to many) 'difficult' novels and short stories.

First published in 1956, in 1962 he coined the term 'inner space' to describe his area of concern. Later short stories like 'The Assassination of **John F. Kennedy** Considered as a Downhill Car Race' eschewed conventional narrative structure, creating his reputation as an experimentalist in form as well as theme. His obsession with ruined technology and global disaster (nuclear, environmental, or surreal) led in 1973 to the novel *Crash*. This exploration of the connection between sexuality and the modern cult of fast cars enraged those unsympathetic to the psycho-mythic connections he highlighted; the book was labelled 'pornographic'; but by others, this and similar works typically dealing with landscapes of urban ruin (*Concrete Island*, 1974) were said to penetrate deep into the psyche of a sick post-atomic world. Yet only when *Empire of the Sun* appeared were his obsessions (seemingly) explained. In this 'novel' he describes seeing the overglow of the Hiroshima bomb against the sky.

His wartime experience, later RAF service and medical training all contributed to his subsequent literary career, in which he balances mythic imagination against the horrors of ordinary, everyday, human atrocity.

BALOR (*See* IRISH MYTH, CYCLOPES, LUG)

In the Irish *Lebor Gabála* (*Book of Invasions*) it is told how the giant king of the demonic Fomorians, Balor of the Baleful Eye, was killed by **Lug** the Long-Handed, solar hero of the magical **Tuatha dé Danaan**. Of this terrible cyclopean **giant** it is said that four men were needed to lift the lid of his single eye. Once opened, it killed all it looked upon. But Balor had an **Achilles heel**: the prophecy that his grandson would kill him. So he kept his only child, the beautiful Eithne, imprisoned in an island cave. Yet, disguised as a woman, the Danaan hero Cian macCainte gained entry, seducing Eithne and her twelve guardian-women. All bore children, and Eithne, triplets. Balor had all the babes drowned in the sea, to become the ancestors of the **seals**, but one, Lug, escaped. Aged twenty-one he claimed his place in the Danaan court at Tara, and later led the Danaan against the Fomorians at the second Battle of Moytura. Balor's Baleful Eye was opened and many Danaan warriors were shrivelled. But Lug stayed out of range until the weary Eyelid fell, then just as it began to open again, like David he cast a stone from his sling. The stone burst through the Baleful Eye into Balor's brain, slaying him instantly. Thus the prophecy came true, and the Danaan won the day.

BAMBARA (*See* AFRICAN MYTH, CREATION MYTH)

BANOI (*See* **OCEANIC MYTH, UNDERWORLD**)

BANSHEE (*See* **BADB, CELTIC MYTH**)
A Gaelic name meaning 'supernatural woman', referring to a Celtic spirit of the dead whose dismal wailing foretold death. Called *cointeach* or 'keener' in southwest Scotland and the Hebrides, where she was seen as bloodless and boneless – 'a little white thing, soft as wool' – the banshee was usually envisaged with a sunken nose, scraggy white hair and huge hollow eyesockets, a tattered white sheet flapping about her. She would squat wailing outside the door of the dying, or follow those she met on the road, keening and clapping her hands, continually repeating the name of the doomed one.

She might also appear (from Brittany to Scotland and Ireland) as the *bean-nighe* ('washerwoman'), crouched by a ford washing bloody garments, her feet webbed like those of a duck or **goose**. It was fatal for a traveller not to see her before she saw him, though in parts of the Scottish Highlands it was thought that only those about to die could see her at all.

She was also related to the glaistig, a gruesome and dolorous ghost, once mistress of the house she now haunted. Yet, unlike the banshee, the glaistig could be propitiated with offerings of milk, or kept at bay with a drawn dirk made of **iron**, the metal feared by all the fairy folk or *sidhe* (Gaelic, pron. 'shee' as in 'banshee').

Originating in the ancient Irish crow-goddess of battle and slaughter, the badb, the banshee suited the Celtic soul. All the best Scottish and Irish clans had their private banshee, keening for them alone. Lesser folk had to make do with the raucous 'hoody' or royston crow.[1]

1. *The Magic Arts in Celtic Britain*, Lewis Spence, Rider, London, 1970, p.81.

BAPHOMET (*See* **GREEN MAN, HEAD, KNIGHTS TEMPLAR**)

BARBAROSSA (1123–90) (*See* **ARTHURIAN MYTH, SLEEPING EMPEROR**)
Named 'Barbarossa' for his red beard, the Holy Roman Emperor Frederick I became virtual master of Germany and Italy, led the Third Crusade, but then perished in a stream in Cilicia. Elevated in the nineteenth century as a mythic symbol of German unity, as early as the fourteenth century it was believed that he had not died, but lies sleeping under a hill, or in the imperial castle of Kyffhäusen. It is said that one day (like King Arthur and other heroes) he will return in the hour of Germany's greatest need.

BARDO THÖDOL (*See* *TIBETAN BOOK OF THE DEAD*)

BARDS (*See* **CELTIC MYTH, DRUIDS**)
The bards (composers, memorisers and chanters of hymns, sacred tales and – if insulted – deadly satires) were one of three orders in the old Celtic priesthood. The other two were the **Druids** (moral philosophers) and Vates (diviners and natural philosophers).

Everywhere, ancient myth survives either in writing or via the 'oral tradition'. In pre-literate cultures, or where (as with the Celts) it was forbidden to write down sacred tales or philosophical knowledge, the 'art of memory' was crucial. That it (and other arts largely forgotten today) was well developed in the ancient world is clear from what was demanded of all would-be bards (*cyfarwydd* in Welsh) or ollaves ('master-poets').

An Irish ollave's twelve-year course involved memorising 500 prescribed tales and poems, study of advanced prosody and metrical composition, and mastery of Old Goidelic. The Irish *Book of Ollaves* (bound up with the fourteenth-century *Book of Ballymote*) says the lower status of bard followed a minimum seven-year course: more severe than in the poetic schools of Wales, where bardic status was lower. The Welsh Penkerdd (Chief Bard) was but the tenth court dignitary, equal to the Chief Smith. His main function was to flatter his patron. He was forbidden to employ dangerous satire or to **curse**. Why?

The ollave was feared. In the *Book of Invasions* it is said the ollave Cairbre, insulted by King Bres of the **Tuatha dé Danaan**, satirised him so fiercely that boils burst out on his face, thus forcing him to abdicate, as no Danaan king was permitted any physical defect. Even after **Christianity** came to Ireland, poetic satire was thought capable of driving men mad.

The ollave (as likely to call on **Ogma**, the Eloquent God, as on **Brigit** the **Muse**) sat next to the king and (like the queen alone) could wear six colours in his clothes. When armies fought, the poets of either side would discuss the carnage from a convenient hillside. If displeased, they might stop the fight by wading in barehanded. In the *Gododdin*, a sixth-century Welsh poem relating an attack by men of Edinburgh on those of Catterick (in Yorkshire), it is said: 'the poets of the world assess the men of valour'.[1]

Is it futile today to dream that poets could again be so well thought of as to restrain the modern 'men of valour' with their satires?

1. *The White Goddess*, Robert Graves, Faber & Faber, London, 1961, p.22

BARRIE, J.M. (1860–1937) (*See* FAIRIES, NEVERLAND, PAN)

Son of a weaver, this Scottish author of the romance *Peter Pan* (the boy who refused to grow up), went to Edinburgh University, then spent two years with the *Nottingham Journal* and in 1885 moved to London as a freelance writer.

In 1897 he met a 'little mother', Sylvia Llewellyn Davies. To her children he told tales that led in 1904 to a play, *Peter Pan*, and in 1911 to a book, *Peter and Wendy*. His other plays include *The Admirable Crichton* (1902), and he was publicly honoured (baronetcy 1913, Order of Merit 1922). In *Peter Pan*, still popular, he trivialised the true Pan-myth to assert a cosy modern fantasy in which nobody ever need grow up; it also diminishes fairy-lore into gauzy-winged Tinkerbell. From their middle-class London home the Darling children fly to the **Neverland**, where Captain Hook leads his pirates against the lost children in their womb-like burrow.

Yet Barrie wrote his womb-myth well. The tale survives. In 1991 the American movie director Steven Spielberg made *Hook*, a modern Peter Pan tale of an American male who remains tied to childhood.

BARROW-WIGHTS (*See* EARTH MOUNDS)

BASILISK (*See* FABULOUS BEASTS)

From the Greek, 'little king', in Classical times this imaginary beast was envisaged as a serpent with deadly stare and venom, sprung from the blood of the **Medusa**. By the Middle Ages it had become a yellow-feathered, four-legged cock with a crown, thorny wings and a serpent's tail ending in a hook or another cock's head. Thus Chaucer in *The Parson's Tale* speaks of the 'basilicok': it also became known as the cockatrice. Other accounts say it had scales, not feathers, and eight legs. Dwelling in the desert, its glance killed birds, split rocks, burned grass and rotted fruit. Any stream from which it drank stayed poisoned for centuries. A useful weapon against it was a mirror: the sight of its own image would make it drop dead. Though both Pliny and Lucan attested to it, by the seventeenth century few believed in it. As Quevedo points out in his romance *The Basilisk*: 'If the man who saw you is still alive, your whole story is a lie, since if he has not died he cannot have seen you, and if he has died, he cannot tell what he saw.'[1]

1. *The Book of Imaginary Beings*, Jorge Luis Borges, Penguin, London, 1974.

BASTET (*See* **CAT, EGYPTIAN MYTH**)

BAT (*See* **BATMAN, VAMPIRISM**)
The symbolism attached to this nocturnal rat-like flying mammal has always been ambivalent. Haunting dark caves or melancholy ruins it suggests the restless **souls** of the unquiet dead; its ambiguous nature, neither bird nor beast, arouses instinctive unease. In **Christian** myth this 'bird of the Devil' is an incarnation of Satan, who is depicted with bat's wings: this imagery and the habits of the blood-drinking vampire bat (*Desmodus rufus*) make association of the bat with the lore of vampirism, **black magic** and **witchcraft** inevitable. In Hebrew lore the bat represents impurity; to the Japanese it implies unhappy chaos. Yet not every connection is negative. In Africa, though representing obscurity and darkness, it also represents wisdom, due perhaps to its radar-like sensitivity; among the Amerindians it was valued as a rain-bringer; in China a group of five bats represents the five blessings of health, wealth, long life, peace and happiness. In southeastern Australia the Wotjobaluk people held that the life of Ngünügünüt (the bat) is the life of a man: if a bat is killed, the life of some man is thus shortened. Dracula does not have it all his own way!

BATMAN (*See* **BAT, COMICS, SUPERMAN**)
Following the first appearance and instant success of the omnipotent comic-strip hero Superman (Action Comics, 1938), many imitations appeared. Among the most enduring is Batman, the 'Caped Crusader' of Gotham City, a bizarre masked figure who with his side-kick Robin the Boy Wonder forever battles even more bizarre evil-doers (the Penguin, the Riddler, the Joker). Most if not all such 'superheroes' are presented as ordinary mortals whose transformation to superhero status is involuntary or in response to the needs of justice. Batman would not be worth mention but for the continuing success of tv and movie versions.

BEAN-NIGHE (*See* **BANSHEE, CELTIC MYTH**)

BEAR (*See* **AINU, ANIMALS, ARTHURIAN MYTH**)
As one of the great beasts, the bear is identified in many myth systems as tribal **totem**, creator god (as with the Ainu of Japan), or epitome of the hero (as with King Arthur: Arth Vawr, 'Great Bear'). Why, is clear enough. Since early times hunters have feared and respected this potent adversary, fighting it for food and the shelter of caves. The Lapps thought it the height of glory to kill this King of Beasts, but all men involved in the slaughter were thought unclean, and had to remain apart for three days in a special tent while they butchered and cooked the carcass. In Canada, men of the Ottawa tribe's Bear

Clan made the slain bear a feast of his own flesh while explaining their need to eat him, thus propitiating its ghost.

The bear's habit of hibernation, emerging from its winter cave with a new-born cub each spring, early suggested it as an image of **resurrection**. Sacred to **Thor** among Scandinavian and Teutonic peoples, the she-bear Atla represented the feminine principle: the he-bear Atli the masculine. In **hero myth** (as with King Arthur) the bear is solar, or masculine (an old Gaelic proverb, 'Art an neart', describes a hero as a bear in heat); but in **flood myth** it is lunar, or feminine. In Greece the goddess **Artemis** was worshipped by *arktoi*, 'bear virgins', wearing yellow robes and imitating bears at their rites. **Zeus**, to shield the nymph Callisto from the rage of Artemis after he had taken the form of the goddess to seduce the virgin, turned her into a bear, but Artemis shot her with an arrow: whereupon Zeus transformed her into the constellation, the Great Bear. In **Indian myth** Jambavat, King of the Bears, fought **Krishna** for three weeks for possession of a jewel; on surrendering, to learn his opponent was a god to whom the jewel rightly belonged, he gave Krishna his only precious possession, Jambavati his daughter. Later his bear-army aided **Rama** in the war against Ravana.

In myth the bear is usually noble. Yet in Christianity it represents (yet again) the Devil, being the image of greed and carnal desire. It is odd, or maybe not, how implacably Christianity has demonised nature.

BEATLES (*See* ORPHEUS, ROCK'N'ROLL MYTH)
The process of myth-creation is continual. Modern parallels of old myths continually emerge. The power of music to excite mass hysteria is ancient; just as Orpheus was torn to pieces by women in **Dionysiac** enthusiasm, popular musicians today run a similar risk, as seen in the career of the rock group the Beatles and the fate of their singer John Lennon. The Beatles served their musical apprenticeship in Hamburg and in Liverpool's Cavern Club; a 1962 recording contract led to the release of *Love Me Do*. Breaking with tradition by writing their own songs and by their publicised involvement with drugs and eastern religion, the success of later releases led to mass hysteria among the youth first of Britain and then (in 1964) the USA. Dubbed 'Beatlemania' by the London *Daily Mirror*, this hysteria became a phenomenon guaranteeing the Beatles demi-god status among sections of the Western public. The abandonment of live appearances (which had become dangerous due to the frenzy unleashed among female fans) soon led to mythic speculations. When on a record sleeve the bass guitarist McCartney was shown barefoot, the myth grew that he was dead. Formally splitting up after the release of the album *Let It Be* in 1970, the Beatles never regrouped. On 8 December 1980 Lennon was shot dead in New York by a 'fan', who seemingly by this wanton act hoped to immortalise himself as part of the myth of the Beatles.

BEATRICE (*See* DANTE)

BEDIVERE (*See* ARTHURIAN MYTH)
Bedivere is to King Arthur as Doubting Thomas is to Christ. This knight of the **Round Table** alone survived the carnage of the final battle of Camlan. With Arthur's son and enemy Mordred dead and Arthur himself badly wounded, Bedivere and another knight, Lucan, carried the king from the battlefield. Lucan having collapsed and died, Arthur told Bedivere to throw his **sword Excalibur** into a nearby lake. Instead, Bedivere hid it behind a tree. On his return, Arthur asked what he had seen. 'Nothing,' said

Bedivere. So Arthur knew his order had been disobeyed. Again Bedivere tried deception: again he was told to go back and do as ordered. This third time he hurled the sword out as far as he could . . . and saw emerge from the lake an arm and a hand, which caught Excalibur, brandished it thrice, then disappeared with the sword under the water. These were the arm and hand of the Lady of the Lake. The **otherworld** sword had returned to its home.

Bedivere told Arthur what he had seen. The king was satisfied. Then Bedivere hoisted Arthur on to his back and took him to the water, lowering him into a black barge crewed by three black-clad queens. These included **Morgan Le Fay** and the Lady of the Lake: aspects of the three-fold goddess.

As they rowed the king away, Bedivere cried out: 'What shall become of me?' Arthur told the knight, 'Pray for my soul.'

Weeping, Bedivere came to a hermitage at **Glastonbury**. The hermit told him a company of ladies had brought the king's dead body there at midnight, and that Arthur now lay buried in the chapel. Then Bedivere vowed to stay at the hermitage and spend the rest of his life praying for Arthur.[1]

1. *King Arthur and the Grail*, Richard Cavendish, Paladin, London, 1980.

BEE

Greek myth tells how the mortal Anchises slept with the goddess **Aphrodite**, and was stung to death by bees. Why? Because bees signified **virginity**, since it was believed that they were parthenogenetic – reproducing without sexual union – and Aphrodite was 'virgin' (Greek *parthenos*): i.e. unmarried. Being famously busy, they were also regarded as messengers carrying news to the spirits or the **otherworld**. They produce honey, like nectar a food of the gods, always acceptable as an offering. They also signify **immortality**.

In all traditions the bee has a good name for diligence, industry, thrift, purity, sweetness, courage and economy. Even **Christian** myth, usually antagonistic to the natural world, views the bee with approval. Regarded as unsleeping, it is vigilance and zeal; also the flying **soul** in its entry to **heaven**; while the beehive symbolises the Church.

The emblem of the Pharaoh of Lower Egypt, in **Egyptian myth** it was said that the tears of the **sun-god Ra**, falling to the ground, became working bees. In India, bees are associated with **Vishnu** and **Krishna**. The Greek corn-goddess **Demeter** was 'the pure Mother Bee'; the **mother-goddess** the 'Queen Bee'. It was also an emblem of the goddesses **Cybele** and **Diana**. Bestowing song and eloquence, bees were regarded as 'the birds of the **Muses**'.

BEHEADING GAME (*See* GAWAIN, GREEN KNIGHT)

BEHEMOTH (*See* FABULOUS BEASTS)

As described in the Bible (Job xl:15–24), the bones of this magnificent imaginary beast 'are as strong pieces of brass'; he 'moveth his tail like a cedar'; while he 'lieth under the shady trees' and 'drinketh up a river'.

The word is the plural of the Hebrew *b'hemah*, 'beast'. It is generally thought to refer to the **hippopotamus**, the **elephant**, or both.

BEL, BELINUS (*See* BAAL, BELTANE, CELTIC MYTH, WILLOW)

The name Bel appears in the title of the **Babylonian** god Bel-Marduk – perhaps from the older Sumerian goddess Belili. There was also an Irish-British Bel (or Beli, or Belinus). Said to be son of the Irish goddess **Danu** (thus the **Tuatha dé Danaan**: 'the Children of Danu'), his connection with Bel-Marduk is possible. The root *bel* is found in the Slavonic *beli*, 'white',

Latin *bellus*, 'beautiful' and Goidelic *bile*, 'sacred tree'.[1]

Indeed, though he was Beli or Belinus in Britain, in Ireland he was called Bile. Some texts say he came from Spain. Graves identifies him as a **willow**-god, a divinatory son of Belili, who supplanted the *alder*-god **Bran**. As god of light he patronised the Celtic **fire-festival**, **Beltane**.

Geoffrey of Monmouth records Beli as the brother of Bran (Brennius), king of Britain. The brothers quarrelled, but were reconciled, together sacking Rome. A road-builder, his capital was at Caer Usk. He also gave his name to Billingsgate in London, where he was buried in a golden urn.

Lewis Spence writes that in Welsh poetry Beli, son of Benlli the Great, was associated with a great spear and was buried in the 'Great Plain', Maes Mawr. Suggesting connection with the Irish **cyclops Balor**, also with **Cernunnos** and **Herne the Hunter**, he quotes Welsh scholar Sir John Rhys in suggesting that Beli represents 'the King of the Brythons in the golden age of their history'.[2]

These traditions are too various to cast a sure light.

1. *The White Goddess*, Robert Graves, Faber & Faber, London, 1961, pp.58–9.
2. *The Magic Arts in Celtic Britain*, Lewis Spence, Rider, London, 1970, pp.139–40.

BELLEROPHON (See GREEK MYTH, PEGASUS, SISYPHUS)

Hipponous, a grandson of **Sisyphus** and son of Glaucus (fatally trampled by his own **horses** for offending **Aphrodite**), murdered Bellerus, a fellow-Corinthian, and was renamed Bellerophon. Fleeing the city, he sought refuge with Proetus, king of Tiryns, whose queen, Anteia, fell in love with him. Scorned, she accused him of trying to rape her (as Phaedra accused Hippolytus: see **Theseus**). Fearing the wrath of the **Furies** if he slew a guest, Tiryns sent him to his father-in-law, Iobates, with a death-sentence in a sealed letter. Iobates, equally fearing the Furies, imposed on Bellerophon tasks he hoped would prove fatal. The first was to slay the monstrous **Chimera**. Mounted on the winged horse **Pegasus**, which he tamed with a golden bridle given him by **Athene**, he flew over the Chimera, shot it with arrows, then poured lead into its fiery jaws. The molten lead killed the beast.

Next, Iobates sent him to fight the savage Solymians and their allies, the **Amazons**. He defeated them by dropping rocks from the back of Pegasus, then defeated the pirate Cheimarrhus on the Lycian plain of Xanthus. On his return Iobates sent men to ambush him, so he prayed to **Poseidon** to flood the plain behind him. Dismounting, he neared the palace on foot, the waves following. Hoisting their skirts, the Xanthian women ran to him, offering their favours if he would relent. He turned and fled, the waves with him.

At last persuaded of his daughter's false accusation, Iobates begged Bellerophon's forgiveness, offering his daughter Philonoë in marriage. Yet Bellerophon fell foul of the gods, trying to ride Pegasus to Olympus. **Zeus** sent a gadfly to sting the winged horse. Bellerophon fell back to earth, to end his days a lame, blind, cursed wanderer, his two children being slain by the gods: one, Laodameia, by **Artemis**; the other, Isandrus, by **Ares**.

BELTANE (See AGNI, BEL, FIRE-FESTIVALS, HALLOWE'EN)

One of the four annual Celtic festivals (Imbolc, Lugnasad and Samhain are the others) this **May Day** fire-festival (Gaelic: Beallteinn) was celebrated in Highland Scotland until late in the eighteenth century, though lacking the human **sacrifices** of earlier times. Central to the celebration of 'the Fire of Bel' was the kindling of the *tein eigin*, 'forced-fire', which, carried into every house, would be sustained as the hearth-fire throughout the coming year: the old year's fires having been extinguished the previous night.

Many reports survive. At night, following extinction of the old fires, folk climbed the local holy hill, playing music to keep evil **spirits** away. At dawn the unwed girls (hair loose, all **knots** undone) washed their faces in the dew as, three by three, the young men took turns to whirl a spindle in an oak-log until the new fire came; preferably at sunrise. The bonfires (*bone*-fires) being lit, the young danced round them, crying 'Fire! Fire! Burn the witches!' In Scotland and Wales it was said that to leap thrice through the fires, or run thrice between them, ensured a good harvest.

Then the Beltane cake was broken and eaten, pieces being flung away in offering to spirits said to preserve horses, sheep and cattle. In some areas the pieces were drawn from a bonnet by blindfold celebrants; whoever drew the charcoal-blackened piece was sacrificed to Bel – at one time, literally.

This done, the new fire was carried into houses bearing above the door crosses of **rowan** and juniper put up to keep out evil during the hours when the hearth had been cold. Cheese and butter, made at dawn by the old women to keep the **fairies** away, were distributed: later more fires were lit and the cattle driven between them to prevent the murrain.[1]

Such fire-festivals, usually but not always held on May Day, were once common throughout the world.

1. *The Golden Bough*, Sir James Frazer, Macmillan, 1963, pp.617–22.

BENU BIRD (*See* EGYPTIAN MYTH, PHOENIX)

BEOWULF (*See* DRAGON, HERO MYTH)

Written in the West Saxon dialect of Old English, the earliest surviving example of 'English literature', the action of this eighth-century poem takes place in Denmark and Sweden. Beowulf, a hero embodying bravery, loyalty and desire for fame, crosses the sea to the Danish court of King Hrothgar, which is tyrannised by a man-eating monster, Grendel. Maiming the monster after an epic wrestling-match, Beowulf pursues Grendel's hideous mother, a **water-troll** who lives deep under a lake. Vanquishing her and her son and thus gaining glory, he becomes King of the Geats (a south Swedish tribe), whom he rules in peace for fifty years until his people are attacked by a dragon. Though aged, he goes out to fight the monster, helped only by his kinsman, Wiglaf, the other Geats hiding terrified in the forest. Braving the venomous fumes of the dragon, Beowulf attacks, but his **sword** snaps: he struck too hard. Seeing Beowulf wounded, Wiglaf attacks the beast even as the king, dragon-poison boiling in him, despatches it. Dying, he tells Wiglaf to seize the dragon-hoard of **gold** so, seeing it, he may find death easy. This done, with Wiglaf his royal heir, he is cremated on a vast pyre, his heroism exalted.

BERMUDA TRIANGLE (*See* ATLANTIS, DIMENSIONS)

This is allegedly a western Atlantic area between Bermuda, Puerto Rico and the Florida coast, also called the 'Devil's Triangle', notorious for the many ships and planes lost in it leaving no wreckage or survivors, the loss sometimes preceded by garbled radio reports of strange fogs, electronic failures, power-loss, the sea looking odd, and so on. The myth peaked in the 1970s, despite official insistence that unexplained losses were due to heavy traffic, sudden violent weather or the Gulf Stream, which can rapidly carry a disabled ship off course, dispersing all wreckage. Yet speculation persisted that an unknown force had destroyed the lost vessels, or removed them to another **dimension** via some electromagnetic anomaly or in invisible **UFOs**. Some claimed submarine Atlantean crystal generators were responsible; others that official denial proved cover-up, out of either ignorance or complicity.

The myth of the Bermuda Triangle (so named in 1964 by Vincent Gaddis) began on 5 December 1945. Training Flight 19 of five US Navy Grumman TBM-3 torpedo-bombers from Fort Lauderdale was lost after odd radio messages from the flight: 'We seem to be off course. We cannot see land . . . We don't know which way is west. Everything is wrong . . . even the ocean doesn't look as it should.' Fading inter-flight messages said magnetic compasses and gyros in the planes were 'going crazy'. A thirteen-crew Martin Mariner went out and was also lost. A search party found nothing. 'They vanished as completely as if they had flown to Mars,' said a Naval Board member. The myth thus begun grew with each new 'unexplained' loss. Documentaries, novels, movies, even a board game came out. It was a great story – while it lasted.

Yet Flight 19 involved an inexperienced crew, rough weather, poor radio conditions, a flight-leader uncorrected when wrongly thinking he was off-course. A storm blew up, night fell, the planes ran out of fuel and ditched in heavy seas which tore them apart. The radio messages cannot be traced beyond a 1962 magazine article. And in 1991 the remains of the flight were located on the sea-bed. Other reports appear to be similarly mythic – in the negative sense.[1]

1. *The Bermuda Triangle*, Charles Berlitz, Granada, London, 1975.

BEROSSUS (*See* BABYLONIAN MYTH, DOGON, SIRIUS)

In his lost *Babylonian History* this Chaldean priest (*c*.300 BC) seems to say that (**Sumerian**) civilisation was founded by amphibious beings led by one Oannes (later **Dagon**). Collectively called Annedoti ('Repulsive Ones'), they were physically abominable. Berossus (via Apollodorus and Alexander Polyhistor) writes: 'The whole body of the animal was like that of a fish; and had under a fish's head another head, and also feet below, subjoined to the fish's tail. His voice too, and language, was articulate and human . . . When the sun set, it was the custom of this Being to plunge again into the sea, and abide all night in the deep, for he was amphibious.'

This myth has lately been employed to suggest alien intervention in the earliest affairs of human society by beings from the star-system **Sirius**.[1]

1. *The Sirius Mystery*, Robert K.G. Temple, Futura, London, 1977, pp.200–5.

BERSERKERS (*See AMANITA MUSCARIA*, NORSE MYTH, WEREWOLF)

The name of these demented **Odin**-worshipping warriors derives from the Old Norse *berserkr*, meaning 'bearskin'. Hiring themselves out throughout pre-medieval Europe and the Near East, when these mercenaries did not rush into battle naked they wore bear- or wolf-skins, thus by their ferocity helping to develop the **werewolf** legend of blood-lusting men who raped and murdered at will. It is said that to incite their bloodlust and bravery further they would, before battle, eat the hallucinogenic toadstool *Amanita muscaria*.

BESTIARY (*See* FABULOUS BEASTS)

Lacking modern media, our ancestors enjoyed bestiaries: collected tales of fabulous beasts. The fourteenth-century *Travels* of Sir John Mandeville, abounding in accounts of dog-headed men and other marvels, was a best-seller for two centuries. The **Basilisk, Chimera** and other imaginings satisfied public need for fantasy long before **Hollywood**. A good modern bestiary is *The Book of Imaginary Beings* by the Argentian writer **Jorge Luis Borges** (1899–1986).[1]

1. *The Book of Imaginary Beings*, Jorge Luis Borges, Penguin, London, 1974.

BHAGAVAD GITA (*See* **ARJUNA, INDIAN MYTH, KRISHNA** *MAHABHARATA*)

Meaning 'The Song of God', this famous religious dialogue (perhaps first century BC: author(s) unknown) is found in the Bhishma Parva section of the vast Indian epic, the *Mahabharata*. Comprising 606 verses arranged in 18 cantos, the action occurs on the dawn of the first day of the epic war between the Pandavas and Kauravas. With the (disguised) god **Krishna** as his charioteer, the famed archer **Arjuna** rides out between the opposing armies. Seeing his teachers and cousins on one side, and his brothers on the other, he grows utterly dejected about the carnage to come, and doubts his duty as a warrior. Krishna, revealing his true identity, inspires and persuades Arjuna that the war must be fought. The dialogue, miraculously overheard by the sage Sanjaya from a nearby hill, is reported by him to the blind king Dhritarāshtra. This report forms the text of the poem.

In his argument Krishna employs existing doctrines from the *Upanishads* and **Buddhism**, but adds the notion of *bhakti*, 'loving devotion', as a true devotional route to God as distinct from the ways of 'knowledge' (*gnosis* in the West), and 'action' (**karma**). So that even if the man (Arjuna) must go to war through caste duty (as God himself always works to keep the world in being), he must deny attachment to the immediate goals – conquest, victory and glory – of his action. All he does in battle is to carry out what the gods have already established as necessary. None of the prizes (or blame) won (or endured) by such action ultimately prevail. What matters is that God (the **Atman**, 'inner self') should be actively loved – even though this ultimate spiritual condition remains beyond conscious reach.

Doubts dispelled, Arjuna submits to Krishna and is ready to fight. 'I have already killed them,' Krishna insists before the battle begins.

BHARATA (*See* **INDIAN MYTH**, *MAHABHARATA*, **RAMA**)

In Indian myth there are four different, unconnected, characters with this name. The earliest is a legendary king of the Bharatas, the 'Lunar Race', who worshipped the goddess Bharati, associated with the **Saraswati** River and a wife of **Brahma** in **Vedic** times. They may represent a late invasion by people who displaced the **Aryans** of Hindustan.

Another Bharata was a hermit, meditating by a river. One day a pregnant doe fell into the river and drowned while giving birth. Bharata rescued the fawn and brought it up so lovingly that, as he died, his thoughts were not of his god, **Vishnu**, but of the **deer**. Thus he was reborn as a stag, but in a later incarnation was allowed to recall this life. On dying again, he had passed beyond the cycle of rebirth.

A second King Bharata is found in the *Ramayana*. Son of Queen Kaikeyi, he renounced the throne in favour of his elder half-brother **Rama**, exiled by Kaikeyi who wanted Bharata to rule. He followed Rama into the forest but Rama sent him back. For fourteen years Bharata ruled in Rama's name, then later welcomed him back and gave up the kingdom without complaint.

The third King Bharata was the son of King Dushyanta and Shakuntala, daughter of a celestial nymph. A mighty warrior, he conquered widely and gave his name to his kingdom: Bharatavarsha (India). He was the ancestor of Kuru and Pandu, and thus of the Kauravas and Pandavas, the conflicting families in the great war who were collectively known as the Bharatas – thus the title of the epic *Mahabharata*.

BHIMA (*See* BHISHMA, INDIAN MYTH, *MAHABHARATA*)
Bhima, 'The Terrible', one of the names of **Shiva**; the second of the five Pandava brothers and son of the wind-god **Vayu**; coarse, jovial, fierce and greedy, this **giant** was also called Vrikodara, 'Wolf's Belly'. Poisoned by a cousin and thrown dead into the **Ganges**, his body was found and revived by the **water-serpents**. Like **Beowulf** or **Finn MacCool** he was a mighty slayer of **demons**, especially the gorilla-like man-eaters, the **Rakshasas**. Tearing one of them to pieces with his bare hands, he slew so many others that they agreed to leave humanity alone. One was his wife, who carried him through the sky to a celestial retreat. Later he went forth to obtain for her the flowers of paradise: celestial thousand-petalled **lotuses** which prolong life and renew beauty. As he crashed through the demon-haunted forest like a hurricane he awoke the monkey-god **Hanuman**, also Vayu's son, who stopped him in his tracks to lecture him concerning the Four Ages, the **Yugas**. In time allowed to continue, he slew many **Yakshas** (**shape-shifting** forest deities: usually benign, sometimes not) who resisted him. Then he gathered the lotuses for his queen. Later, during the great war of the *Mahabharata*, he proved among the most potent of the Pandava warriors. On the first day of the great Battle of Eighteen Days, he fought Bhishma. Subsequent **blood**-drinking victories only increased his terrible status.

BHISHMA (*See* BHIMA, INDIAN MYTH, *MAHABHARATA*)
Bhishma, also 'The Terrible'. Son of the river-goddess Ganga (**Ganges**) and King Shantanu, he always kept his word. Denying his claim to the throne in favour of his younger half-brother Vichitra-virya, when the latter died he asked Vyasa, hermit son of his father's second wife (supposedly the poet-composer of the *Mahabharata*) to 'raise seed' on his behalf. Shantanu's two wives accepted Vyasa's embraces unwillingly. One shut her eyes, so her son was born blind. The other went pale with fright: her son was born pale. But both had to lie with their dead husband's brother to bear a legal heir. This was the custom, from India to Israel. Bhishma educated their sons, Dhritarashtra and Pandu, and their sons, the Kauravas and Pandavas. When war arose between these families, he failed to keep the peace. Siding with the Kauravas as their commander, he was mortally wounded by the arrows of **Arjuna**. Able to decide the day of his own death, for fifty-eight days he lectured on moral philosophy, offering up all the knowledge of his long and altruistic life. Then he passed away.

BIBLE (*See* CHRISTIANITY, HEBREW MYTH, PHOENICIAN MYTH)
One of the world's great books of religious revelation, divided into two distinct books, the Old and the New Testaments. The Old Testament deals (1) with the **creation myths** and early mythic history of the Hebrew people; (2) the Hebrew captivity in Egypt and their escape into the wilderness led by **Moses**; (3) their entry to Israel and covenant with **Yahweh**; (4) their wars with Canaanite tribes and establishment of monarchy at Jerusalem under

David and **Solomon** (tenth century BC); (5) the Books of Psalms, Proverbs and Song of Solomon; and (6) the Books of the Prophets, from Isaiah, Jeremiah, Ezekiel and Daniel to Haggai, Zachariah and Malachi. These cover a period from the fall of Jerusalem and the captivity in Babylon to the rise of the Persian empire (eighth to sixth century BC), and also foretell the coming of the **Messiah** (Hebrew: *Mashiahh*, 'the Anointed One').

Of the initial five books (the Pentateuch: Genesis, Exodus, Leviticus, Numbers, Deuteronomy), the first two are the richest in myth. Genesis takes the creation tale from **Eden** and the **Flood** to the death of the patriarch Abraham and the emigration to Egypt. Exodus describes the Ten Plagues, the Parting of the Red Sea, the Pillar of Fire and the Ten Commandments given to Moses on Mount Sinai. The Genesis creation and flood myths echo earlier **Sumerian myths**: it may be that they did not take their final, present form until the time of the Babylonish captivity (597–538 BC).

Yet many other tales from later Old Testament books, while essentially historical, are mythically potent: **Samson** pulling the temple down on the Philistines; David slaying the **giant** Goliath; **Solomon** meeting the **Queen of Sheba**; the visions of Ezekiel; Jonah in the **whale**; Daniel unharmed in the **lion**'s den with the **angels**, and so on.

In Hebraic belief, the Old Testament and associated esoteric texts (such as the Midrash) retain an authenticity denied to the New Testament.

The New Testament consists (1) of the four synoptic gospels (Matthew, Mark, Luke and John), telling of the virgin birth, teachings, miracles, death and resurrection of Jesus Christ; (2) the Acts of the Apostles: how Christ's disciples suffered persecution yet spread the Christian message from the Jewish to the Gentile (non-Jewish) world; (3) the Epistles, being letters written, typically by **St Paul**, to new Christian congregations in Asia Minor and Greece; and (4) the Revelation or Apocalypse of St John.

Of mythic interest is the concordance between the life of Christ and the former died-and-reborn **corn-gods** and **avatars** (**virgin birth**, baptism, miraculous mission, death on the (**world**)-**tree**, **resurrection**, ascent to heaven, promise to return). The basic Christian myth differs little from many others then popular (**Mithra, Adonis, Dionysus**), save perhaps in its central message: 'Love thy neighbour as thyself', also in its substitution (in the rite of communion) of symbolic for actual **blood** sacrifice.

Also of interest is how the Gospels were selected and edited. Twentieth-century discoveries of **Gnostic** texts of the earliest Christian times at Qumrun and Nag Hammadi establish that there were not just four 'gospels' describing, explaining, or interpreting the life of Christ, but more like 140. These others were suppressed. Those, like Mark, which became part of the official myth, were scrupulously edited (by such as Clement, Bishop of Alexandria *c*.AD 130) to exclude contentious material. The New Testament we know today is the final result of choices made by the early Church fathers as to 'acceptable dogma': a process more or less completed by the time of the Council of Nicaea (AD 325). **Gnostic** gospels like Pistis Sophia (which suggests that the disciple Jesus loved most was Mary Magdalene), or the Thomas Gospel, paint a very different picture of Christ, his life and his teachings, to the version which has been accepted for nigh on 2,000 years.

The use of myth as propaganda is nothing new. Perhaps what is of most interest in the Bible is not what is in it, but what was left out, from the apocryphal Book of **Enoch** to the long-lost Gnostic texts.

BIGFOOT (*See* FABULOUS BEASTS, YETI)

Reports of this giant hairy man-ape (also called sasquatch) still emerge from

the forested mountain wilderness from northern California to British Columbia. Originating in Amerindian lore, Bigfoot is reminiscent of the Himalayan
Yeti (Abominable Snowman), the Australian Yowie and many other 'Big
Hairy Monsters' reported the world over, in that no specimens have ever
been captured or killed so as to lead to positive proof of their existence.
Persisting tales of the abduction of humans or attacks on isolated camps by
this wary and elusive giant should therefore continue to be regarded as
mythic.

BILIBIN, IVAN (1876–1942) (*See* **ART AND MYTH, SLAVONIC
MYTH**)
Born near St Petersburg, working from 1899 until his death during the Nazi
siege of that city then called Leningrad, this extraordinary artist remains
largely unknown in the West. Drawing on a rich heritage of Slavonic myth,
his colourful stage-designs for ballets on mythic subjects by Stravinsky and
Rimsky-Korsakov (among others) and his book-illustrations express a unique
style marrying Art Nouveau to the lush style of Russian iconography as well
as to the broad humour of Russian folklore. A master of imaginative
depiction of fantastic scenes and beings, his work deserves recognition among
those interested in world mythology. Perhaps more than any other 'modern'
artist working in the often-denigrated field of book-illustration, he succeeded
in marrying the dramatic context of the tale to exact visual imagery.

To enter into one or another of his magical paintings of Russian **fairy-tales**
and byliny (old Russian epic poems), or of the *Arabian Nights* can be as
revealing as to read the tales themselves: the capture of detail is remarkable,
stimulating the imagination with lush oriental elaboration and cinematic
precision of dramatic detail.[1]

1. *Ivan Bilibin* (text: Sergei Golynets), Aurora/Pan, Leningrad/London,
   1981.

BILLY THE KID (*See* **WILD WEST**)

BIRCH (*See* **NORSE MYTH, SHAMANISM**)
In Norse myth it is said that **Ragnorak**, the final battle of the gods, will be
fought round a birch tree. In some shamanistic traditions the birch is the
world-tree; the ascent of it (via seven or nine notches cut in its trunk)
symbolising the climb from the lowest to the highest world of **spirit**.

BIRDS (*See* **CONCORDANCE**)

BLACK ART (*See* **BLACK MAGIC**)
As distinct from black magic, the 'black art' was that of alchemy, derived
from the ancient name for Egypt, Khem, 'Black Earth', thus: 'The art of the
Land of the Black Earth'. Perhaps inevitably, given the suspicion attached to
alchemy, the term became confused in its usage.

BLACK CAT (*See* **CAT, WITCHCRAFT**)

BLACK DOG (*See* **ANUBIS, CERBERUS, COYOTE, DOG**)

BLACK MAGIC (*See* **AGRIPPA, EVIL, MAGIC**)
Means magic undertaken for destructive or selfish purposes; to dominate or
harm others; to gain power, wealth or knowledge by **necromancy** or **sorcery**,

traditionally by calling up **demons** or by **blood**-sacrifice. The rites of inverted **cross**, Black Mass, black **cock** and so on constitute an inversion of Christian dogma: black magic as defined above is much more ancient and (probably) more widespread. Throughout Africa it is thought that the basic urge of all **witches** (male or female) is to cause harm by black magic, or to 'eat' people by devouring their **souls**. The Haitian **voodoo** priest who turns his victims into 'undead' zombies employs black magic by implication, though the art may rely primarily on the use of a nerve-poison, tetradotoxin.

Circe, the enchantress who in *The Odyssey* turns men into beasts; and **Morgan Le Fay**, taking the form of her half-brother King **Arthur**'s wife to seduce him, exemplify the black magician: the powers of a **Merlin** and many another **shaman** are at least ambiguous. The 'blackness' of the magic lies in the intent to harm, not in the ritual. **Qabalists** claim that a distorted reflection of the **Tree of Life** exists, and that powers employed in magical workings may be summoned for evil as well as good purposes. Such purposes belong to the inverse Tree, known by the term *qliphoth*, meaning 'harlots' or 'shells'. The results of such focus, conscious or not, may be found: 'in the nearest hospital, lunatic asylum, prison, brothel, or slum.'[1]

1. *A Practical Guide to Qabalistic Symbolism*, Gareth Knight, Helios, Cheltenham, 1965, vol. 1, p.232.

BLACK VIRGIN (*See* ISIS, MOON, MOTHER-GODDESS, VIRGIN MARY)

Discreetly in many churches across France and Western Europe stand images of the Virgin with a black or dark face – matriarchal symbols hearkening back to the **pagan** goddesses. In St Germain des Prés, built in 542 AD on the site of a temple of Isis and the oldest church in Paris (Par-isis = Grove of Isis), a black statue of Isis was worshipped as the Virgin until destroyed in 1514. Of two black madonnas at Chartres Cathedral, Notre-Dame de Sous-Terre (Our Lady Underground) in the crypt maintains the pre-Christian Chartres tradition of a virgin birth. The wooden statue stands near the 'Puits des Saints Forts' well in the oldest part of Chartres, which tradition claims as the ancient **Druid** capital. In Toulouse, the church of La Daurade was a troubadour centre in **Cathar** times (twelfth century) when the Pays d'Oc all but escaped Church control. Initiates courted 'La Reine Pédauque' (**Goose-Foot Queen**): a goddess of many disguises (**Lilith** to the **Queen of Sheba**) today half-remembered as **Mother Goose**. The present Notre-Dame la Noire in La Daurade is the latest of several such images in the church, the first being a statue of **Athene**(?) found in a drained lake in 109 BC. Today, though over 400 black Virgins are known worldwide, the Church remains reticent about the matriarchal and pagan origins of these potent images.[1]

1. *The Cult of the Black Virgin*, Ean Begg, Arkana, London, 1985.

BLAKE, WILLIAM (1757–1827) (*See* ALBION, ART AND MYTH)

Visionary, radical prophet and poet of the 'dark satanic mills', a Londoner all his life, for many years this gifted son of a hosier earned a bare living as an engraver. Today he is remembered as a poet and artist of extraordinary insight: author of the hymn 'Jerusalem', the poem 'The Tyger', and many potent aphorisms: 'Energy is eternal delight', 'Everything possible to be believ'd is an image of truth', 'Damn braces. Bless relaxes.'

Known initially for his popular *Songs of Innocence* (1789) and *Songs of Experience* (1794), his complex later epics 'Jerusalem' and 'Milton' baffled his contemporaries much as **Joyce**'s *Finnegans Wake* baffles people today. Illustrated, engraved and published by Blake himself, these 'Prophetic Books' remain hard to penetrate but worth the effort.

Claiming that 'All deities reside in the human breast', in these books he dramatises the war in the human soul by characterising Reason, Feeling, Intuition and Sense as the **archetypal** four Zoas – Urizen, Luvah, Urthona (Earth-Owner?) and Tharmas. Each Zoa (Greek, pl, 'living creatures') has a negative counterpart (spectre), plus sons, daughters and an 'emanation' (**avatar**). The villain is Urizen (Your Reason; also horizon from the Greek, 'to limit'). Born of Los (Divine Imagination: Sol the Sun backwards), he enchains the other three, like **Yahweh** insisting on the singular male rule of Intellect alone. One of Blake's best-known etchings, *Urizen Creating the Universe*, shows the bearded Yahweh-Urizen leaning down from heaven to measure the earth's circle with scientific compasses.

What Blake deplores is not Christ (forgiveness) but **Yahweh's** pride and intellectual wrath. Denouncing 'All Bibles or sacred codes' for demonising human energies as **Devil**-born, like Gurdjieff a century later he sees humanity as lost 'in Deadly sleep', bound down by materialism, which he characterises as 'Single vision and Newton's sleep'. His poetic answer is to invoke the return of the old free spirit of Britain, **Albion**. But this giant soul lies buried, both in the land and deep in our minds, by 'Reasonings like vast serpents' that 'infold around my limbs'.

He opposes not Reason as such but its tyranny over the other human faculties. Urizen, denying love and stifling all energy with iron rules, is miserable, makes everyone else miserable, but won't give up or learn. He will destroy the world unless Albion, the ancient wholesome holy spirit of primordial man awakens in us all. For, as he wrote in 1793, 'He who binds to himself a joy/Doth the winged life destroy.'[1]

1. *Poems and Prophecies*, William Blake, Dent Everyman, London, 1972.

BLODEUWEDD (See *MABINOGION*, ORESTES, OWL, WELSH MYTH)

The name means 'Flower-Face'. In the Welsh *Mabinogion* ('Math Son of Mathonry'), it is told how, to circumvent the *geis* laid on **Arianrhod**'s inadvertently born son **Llew Llaw Gyffes** (that he live nameless, weaponless and without wife), Math and his foster-father **Gwydion** create Blodeuwedd out of flower-blossom and nine other elements. As she is not human, he may safely wed her. But she hates Llew, and falling for the hunter Gronw Pebr, plots Llew's death with him. Feigning love, she inveigles Llew into admitting that he may be killed only by a spear a year in the making, made on Sundays alone, and then neither inside nor outside, nor on horseback, nor on foot. Only if a bath be made by a river, a thatched roof over it; and only if he stand with one foot on the edge of the bath and the other on the back of a roebuck, can he be slain. A year later she persuades him to prove these unlikely conditions true. He does, and Gronw Pebr slays him, whereupon his **soul** ascends as an **eagle**. But Gwydion returns him to human form and then transforms Blodeuwedd into an **owl**, the shameful night-bird that other birds mob. Llew kills Gronw Pebr, and thereafter rules Gwynedd.

In this died-and-reborn myth, like **Adonis** or **Christ** Llew connives at his own death, flies off as an eagle (holy spirit), then is **resurrected**. Blodeuwedd's owl-transformation reminds us of the Greek myth of how **Apollo** overthrew Pytho at **Delphi**, dismissing the **mother-goddess** into the night, far from the light of male solar wisdom. **Guinevere**, the 'White One', the wife of **Arthur**, was also originally an owl-goddess.

BLOOD (*See* CIRCUMCISION, HEART, MENSTRUATION, SACRIFICE)

Hedged about with superstition the world around. **Taboos** relating to the **menstruation** of women were early imposed by primitive man or his gods: today folk still refer to the 'curse', just as we speak of holy blood, blue blood, the blood royal and of personality traits as 'being in the blood'. The words 'blossom' and 'blessing' come from 'blood'. By mixing blood, former enemies become blood brothers. The **Nazis** extolled their 'pure' or '**Aryan**' blood while reviving the ancient blood libel (*see* **Jews and Anti-Semitism**), that the **Jews** drank the blood of **Christian** children, as in the myth that **vampires** need to drink the blood of the living.

Royal blood must not be spilt on the ground. The Mongol emperor Kublai Khan executed his uncle Nayan by having him tossed in a carpet until he was dead, so that the Imperial blood be neither spilt nor exposed to the **sun**. In Siam (Thailand) princes of the blood were executed by being pounded in a **cauldron** of **iron**. In Sussex, England, it was said that ground on which blood had been spilt would always be barren. In **Aboriginal circumcision** rites, blood from the wound was caught on a platform made of the bodies of the men. In West Africa, if blood fell on the ground, it had to be covered up, so that **sorcerers** should not get hold of it; the belief being that the **soul** resides in the blood. Thus the Celts of Gaul and Ireland drank their enemies' blood and painted their bodies with it, to take on the strength of it. In Greek myth, the winged **horse Pegasus** sprang from the severed neck of the **Medusa**; from one side of her body, **Asclepius** took blood to concoct cures; from the other, **Athene** took blood to make poisons.

Blood-sacrifice, actual or symbolic, was found in many cults. **Adonis** gored by the **boar**, **Orpheus** torn to pieces by the **Maenads**; such rites are paralleled by the symbolism of Christian Communion, **cannibalised** body and blood being replaced by bread and red wine. In one Indian state, at the end of his reign the sacred king ascended a pyre and sliced off his body-parts until he fainted and died through loss of blood. And though **hearts** are not now ripped out atop **Aztec** pyramids, blood-sacrifice still persists on the battlefield in the name of patriotism, race or economics.

BLUEBEARD (*See* FAIRY-TALES, PERRAULT)

The theme of the murderous husband trying to slay his younger wife who wishes to penetrate his guilty secret beyond a locked door is epitomised by 'La Barbe Bleue' ('Bluebeard'), one of the fables by Charles **Perrault** in his 1697 collection: *Contes de ma Mère l'Oye* (*Tales of Mother Goose*). This is based on the life and trial of a fifteenth-century marshal of France, Gilles de Rais (1404–40). Accused of murdering 140 children, rather than endure torture he confessed and was executed. Given that medieval torture was usually worse than a quick death, the charge must be considered unproved.

Another source for Perrault's tale was a legendary sixth-century Breton chief renowned for his cruelty, Comorre the Cursed. A variant (locked room, wife's fatal curiosity, eleventh-hour release) is found in 'Featherbed', in the collection by the Brothers **Grimm** (1812–15).

BO-TREE (*See* BUDDHA, TREES)

BOAR (*See* ADONIS, PIG)

BOAT (*See* **BEDIVERE, BRAN, JASON**)
Boat-symbolism is universal. The earth itself is a boat, floating on the primordial cosmic **ocean**, while how else are **sun** and **moon** carried through the sky save in celestial boats? In Egyptian myth, **Isis** cries out to the sky to stop the Boat of the Sun (also the Boat of Millions of Years), so that **Thoth** may disembark and descend to cure her son **Horus**, poisoned by the **serpent** of Set. This Thoth does quickly; the Sun-Boat (pushed by the scarab-headed dung-beetle Khepera, an aspect of **Ra**) cannot wait long.

The dead are ferried to the **underworld** over **river** or **ocean** in **boats**, as by Charon, or as by the Triple Goddess, taking King Arthur to **Avalon** in a black barge. More ambiguous in **Celtic**, **Greek** and other tradition is the nature of boats manned by **heroes** like **Bran MacFebal**, **Maelduin** or **Jason**. While seemingly ordinary craft, such boats metaphorically bridge the gulf between the living and the dead, this world and the **otherworld**. They may even be built (Teutonic) out of the nail-parings of dead men, or (Finnish: *see Kalevala*) from pieces of the **spindle** of the fate-goddess. The crescent **moon** on its back is such a boat (*see* **Noah**). In **Hindu myth** the moon is said to be a boat carrying the souls of the dead over the waters to the sun, there to be redeemed. **Buddhists** speak of the Ship of the Law as helping man cross the Ocean of Existence to the further shore. In **Christian** symbolism, the Church is such a boat, the **cross** its mast. The mast is also the *axis mundi*, or world-tree; phallic where the boat is the protective womb. This is perhaps why boats traditionally bear feminine names, and why once many sported carved female figureheads, representing the protective **mother-goddess**. Ships with a **horse**-figurehead are, on the contrary, protected by the sun-god in his solar **chariot** (sky-boat).

BODACH (*See* **CAILLEACH, SCOTTISH MYTH**)
Scots Gaelic: means 'old man', referring to Highland belief in a spirit who would creep down the chimney and, like the Daoine Sidhe or **fairies**, steal away naughty children. His female counterpart was the **Cailleach**, the 'old woman', or 'hag', about whom there is a much wider body of folklore. In some parts the bodach, like the **banshee**, was considered to be a spirit who came to warn of imminent death.

BODHIDHARMA (*See* **BUDDHISM**, *DHARMA*, **ZEN BUDDHISM**)
Founder of the Ch'an Tsung ('inner light') Buddhist school, in China called Ta-mo and in Japan Daruma, the teachings of this mysterious man led to the development of **Zen** philosophy. Reaching Nanking in China from South India *c.*AD 520, when the emperor described how he had promoted the Mahayana and asked what merit he had gained, Bodhidharma said: 'None whatsoever.' Asked by the dumbfounded emperor about Buddhism's first principle, the sage said it did not exist – all being emptiness, how can anything be holy? Leaving for the north, he spent the rest of his life in a monastery, gazing at the wall. Once falling asleep while meditating, he was so angry he cut off his eyelids. The tale is that these, planted, produced the first tea-bushes.

His successor, a Chinese monk called Hui-k'o, was so long refused by the master that he cut off his left hand and sent it in to Bodhidharma, who at last asked him what he wanted. 'Peace of mind,' said Hui-k'o, but could not find his mind when asked to do so. 'You see,' said Bodhidharma, 'I've pacified your mind.' At this, Hui-k'o experienced *satori*, the state of sudden inspiration, all dogma and preconceptions dismissed.

BODHISATTVA (See AVALOKITESHVARA, BUDDHISM, MAITREYA)

In Buddhism, this is a person who, achieving total enlightenment (bodhi), can abandon worldly rebirth to enter *Nirvana*, but who decides to remain in this suffering world to guide others towards the goal he has reached. In accord with the **Mahayana** principle that ordinary folk need the help of the past masters to gain salvation, the bodhisattvas fulfil the same function as **Christian** saints, their temple images (in bronze, wood or stone) being worshipped by prayer. Saviours of humanity on account of their charity and merit which they transfer to lesser beings by means of the flow of **karma** to those in need of it, the chief bodhisattvas are known by many names from India through China to Japan. Avalokiteshvara is described elsewhere: the others include Ratnapani, Samantabhadra, Vajrapani and Vishvapani.

The last bodhisattva, Maitreya, is a Buddhist equivalent of **Christ** in that he will not descend to earth again until the coming of the End Times, when he will lead all humanity to salvation.

The title of bodhisattva is also given to Gautama the Buddha.

BOGATYRI (See BILIBIN, HERO MYTH, SLAVONIC MYTH)

As given in the byliny ('tales of that which has been'), the epic heroic poems of the Russians, the bogatyri are demi-gods and heroes (as **Hercules** or **Cuchulainn**) of the Slavonic mythic age. The name means 'elder valiant champions'. The byliny recount numerous hero myths equivalent to those of other cultures . . . with subtle differences. Thus the poem about the bogatyr Svyatogor describes the Slav **Atlas**: a being so strong he boasted he could support the weight of the world. But on riding about the steppe he found a small bag lying on the ground. His staff did not shift it, leaning down he could not move it, dismounting, he raised it as high as his knees – only to realise that he had sunk knee-deep into the earth. Tears of blood rolled down his face as he fought but failed to lift himself up from the hole into which he had sunk. So Svyatogor perished, punished for his pride.

The bogatyr Volkh or Volga could **shape-shift** into falcon, grey **wolf**, white golden-horned **bull**, tiny ant, pike or wild ox.

The earlier cycle of byliny describes the exploits of older heroes: the later deals with younger champions. Ilya-Muromyets, the 'peasant's son', is prominent among the latter. Derived from Pyerun, the lightning-god, his **horse** like **Pegasus** flies through the air, while the arrows shot from his wonderful bow split buildings and forests asunder. Born weak, for some years he could not even stand, until one day two passing **bards** gave him a honey drink (**soma?**). Then (only after he was blessed in **Christ** by his aged parents) he found his strength, defending Russia against the infidels. Before dying he built a cathedral at Kiev, then turned to stone, in which form his body is said to be preserved.

Later tales of the bogatyri include that of Sadko, a rich merchant of Novgorod. At sea his ship suddenly stopped. Realising he had never paid tribute to the Tsar of the Sea, he put out cupfuls of silver, gold and pearls on a plank. When the plank did not sink he concluded that the God wanted not money, but a human head. Lots being drawn, it was Sadko who descended on to the plank. Falling asleep, he awoke in a white stone palace, and played his *gusli* (a stringed instrument) so furiously that the sea-god's dance caused a tempest that drowned Sadko's sailors. Breaking the *gusli*'s strings, he made the storm subside and returned to Russia. Later he plied his trade on the River Volga. Wishing to return to Novgorod, he offered the river salted bread. Thanking him, the Volga suggested that he give offering to his brother, the Lake of Ilmen. In response the Lake advised Sadko to cast three great nets into its water. These immediately filled with fish which, taken to Sadko's warehouses, miraculously became silver.

Thus the transition from the heroic to the mercantile age. In time, the bogatyri all fell in battle against a foreign army whose numbers kept on doubling. The survivors fled into dark mountain caves where every one was turned into stone. After that there were no more bogatyri in Russia.

BONNIE PRINCE CHARLIE (1721–88) (*See* **HERO MYTH**)

The ignominious career of Charles Edward Stuart (the 'Young Pretender' or 'Bonnie Prince Charlie') shows how romantic myth can replace hard fact.

Grandson of the Catholic King James II (deposed and exiled from England by the 'Glorious Revolution' of 1688) in 1745 this headstrong youth attempted to restore the Jacobite monarchy in Britain by fostering rebellion in Scotland against the Hanoverians. Most Highland chiefs refused to help him, but his **charm** won such support that soon he had seized Edinburgh and routed a weak English army. With 6,500 men he invaded England and in December reached Derby. Amid general panic King George II prepared to flee the country. But here the bubble burst. Charles's men were deserting: there were no new recruits. The retreat thus begun ended on 16 April 1746 at Culloden Muir near Inverness. His Highland army was slaughtered. The victorious general, William Duke of Cumberland (ever since known in Scotland as 'the Butcher') had a weed named after him, 'Stinking Willie', while in England his name was given to a flower, 'Sweet William'.

The subjugation of the culture followed, and the carrying of arms was forbidden. Later, thousands of people were forced to emigrate, yet despite a huge sum on his head, his followers stayed loyal. 'Bonnie Prince Charlie' fled to France after months of wandering. Yet this pathetic man, latterly a drunken wife-beater, who had destroyed not only his own cause but the culture he fled, became the heart of an enduring myth. How?

Essentially it arose through nostalgia for a vanished past, as in Lady Nairne's 'Skye Boat Song'. The tale of how Flora Macdonald rowed the fugitive from the mainland to the Isle of Skye remains potent. Yet by all accounts she thoroughly disliked him: later she and many of her clan had to emigrate to America as a result of the catastrophe he had brought upon them.

'Will ye no come back again?' is still the sentimental refrain of those who find hard fact less palatable than romantic myth.

BOOK OF INVASIONS (*See* **IRISH MYTH**)

BOONE, DANIEL (*See* **WILD WEST**)

BORGES, JORGE LUIS (1899–1986)

This 'greatest living writer in the Spanish language today' (*Time Magazine*) specialised in short, paradoxical narratives characterised by mathematical precision of language and an erudition drawing on a vast range of Classical scholarship compounded by mythic inventiveness. Born in Buenos Aires and educated in Europe, he returned to Argentina where he worked for the rest of his life. His physical blindness did nothing to obstruct the clarity of his inner vision. Attracted by fables, absurd paradoxes and metaphysical speculations, he specialised in the invention of imaginary worlds, adopting the grave tone of an academic, analysing and dissecting books that never existed save in his own imagination. Famously, he questioned the need to write lengthy novels, the essence of which may be stated in a few pages.

The best-known of his metaphysical fictions are found in his collection *Labyrinths*. These include 'Tlön, Uqbar, Orbis Tertius': his report on the history of an unknown world, in which only the inner life exists, as set down by a secret society of astronomers, metaphysicians and geometers; and 'The Library of Babel', in which the narrator wanders the library (alias the universe) in futile quest for the Book of Books that explains all.

'The impious maintain that nonsense is normal in the Library and that the reasonable (and even humble and pure coherence) is an almost miraculous exception.'[1]

The importance of Borges in any study of mythology is that he found a new way to relate just those paradoxes in which mythology always dealt.

1. *Labyrinths*, Jorge Luis Borges, Penguin, London, 1970, p.84.

BORI (*See* AFRICAN MYTH, SPIRITS, VOODOO)

Among the Hausa of West Africa, the Bori are spirits possessing those subject to trances. Illness or bad luck are said to be caused by specific spirits placated by dances performed by those possessed by the spirit concerned. The dances are led by drum-rhythms specific to each particular spirit. The victim of any spirit-disorder is protected by a Bori cult-member, but such spirits cannot be permanently dismissed: the sufferer must join the Bori cult, so that the possession is limited to (and controlled by) the big dance.[1]

The names of 178 different spirits have been listed. During the dance, each will 'ride' their human 'mounts' until the latter collapse, exhausted.

1. *African Mythology*, Jan Knappert, Aquarian Press, Wellingborough, 1990.

BRAHAN SEER (*See* CURSES, PROPHECY)

BRAHMA (*See* CREATION MYTH, INDIAN MYTH, YUGA)

One of the primary **Hindu** triad of deities, with **Vishnu** the Preserver and **Shiva** the Destroyer, Brahma is God the Creator, not in the Western sense of a deity consciously organising the world, but as the creative principle, Universal Self or **Atman**. The root of the word brahma is from the Sanskrit, *brih*, 'expansion': the Days and Nights of Brahma, each 4,320,000,000 years long, refer in the **Vedas** to an unending cosmic cycle. When Brahma awakens and 'breathes out', the universe (Day of Brahma) comes into being. When he falls asleep, 'breathing in', the universe ceases to be until a new waking cycle begins. Each such cycle is one *kalpa*: seven of them (a week) form a *solar kalpa*, while one year of Brahma equals 360 Divine Days, said to be the duration of a planet's life.

In later texts it is said he created the cosmic ocean and in it laid a golden egg (the 'Egg of Brahma'), which hatched **Purusha**, the primordial or cosmic **Adam**: also how one day he awoke to find himself seated on a white lotus which, afloat on the ocean, grew from the navel of Vishnu, asleep at the bottom of the sea, his head on the coils of the **serpent Ananta**. Both began arguing as to who had created the other, when suddenly a huge pillar of light (or *lingam*: 'phallus') speared from the bottom of the ocean to the top of the sky. As **Varaha** the **boar**, Vishnu dug for the base of the pillar; as Hansa the **goose** (or **swan**), Brahma flew up to find the top. Even as each returned unsuccessful the pillar burst apart to reveal the god Shiva – for all three are the creative One, however many forms and names they take.

It is said Brahma fell in love with Vishnu's consort, **Lakshmi**, his daughter, and from their union humanity was born. Otherwise his consort is **Saraswati**, goddess of learning and music. He created **Soma** (moon), and Surya (sun), and put them in the sky. He created **Agni** (fire), **Vayu** (wind) and **Varuna** (water). Brahma is not only every being, he is in every being.

BRAHMANISM (*See* **BRAHMA, HINDUISM, INDIAN MYTH**)

Following the **Aryan** conquest and early (*c*.1000 BC) Vedic era of Indian history, and before the rise (fifth century BC) of **Buddhism**, a rigid caste system developed. Caste (Varna) signifies colour: the four castes were Brahmans (priests), Kshatriyas (warrior aristocrats); Vaisyas (commoners and free traders), and Sudras (slaves and aborigines). The three upper castes consisted of Aryans only: the Sudras were denied knowledge of the Vedas and were otherwise severely restricted. The Brahmans were first in caste importance, the most renowned being the **rishis** (poets), composers of new songs to the gods and seen as divinely inspired. Their hymns, memorised over centuries, were chanted at ceremonies by the Hotri priests. Others specialised in the correct performance of **sacrificial** rites; the Purohitas acted as court philosophers and teachers. In time an organised priesthood came into being: the creation of new hymns ended, those already created being thought enough for all purposes. Ritual became more complex: no rite could be performed save by the now hereditary caste of Brahmans.

Yet their ideals were high. Their faith survived the rise of Buddhism, their scriptures (**Vedas**) remain the basis of modern **Hinduism**. Pantheistic in origin, neither idolatry nor human sacrifice had any place in Brahmanic belief. Their lives were strictly ordered into four periods: Brahmachari, the student phase, studying with and serving a guru; Grihastha, the stage of married life; Vanastha, in which, with his eldest son old enough to take over family responsibilities, the Brahman retires to a forest hermitage to meditate and study with others more advanced on the yogic path; Sannyasa, being by now wholly detached from worldly need and desire, the old Brahman returns to the world to wander and teach until at last wholly absorbed by the divine. Brahmanism remains (after 3,000 years) a surviving doctrine.

BRAN THE BLESSED (BENDIGEIDFRAN) (*See* **ALDER, GIANT, HEAD,** *MABINOGION*)

In the Welsh story, 'Branwen Daughter of Llŷr' (see *Mabinogion*) it is told how the giant Bran gives up his life-restoring **cauldron** to the Irish, in recompense for insults his brother Efnisien has winged their way. It is also a wedding gift: his sister Branwen marrying Matholwch, the king of Ireland. But in Ireland Branwen is mistreated and locked up in Matholwch's kitchen. Bran wades the Irish Sea in leading the British attack. Defeated, Matholwch is deposed by the Irish in favour of Branwen's son *Gwern*. At the amnesty feast, Efnisien throws Gwern into the fire and fighting erupts again, the Irish reviving their dead in the cauldron. Only seven Britons (including **Pryderi** and **Taliesin**) escape, with Bran mortally wounded by a poisoned spear in the heel. He tells them to cut off his **head** and bury it facing France at the White Tower in London, but that this will take many years. So they come with his head to Harlech. For seven years they feast, the **birds** of **Rhiannon** singing to them, then move onto Gwales in Penfro (Pembrokeshire), to a hall with three doors, two open but that facing Cornwall shut. Told never to open that door, they pass eighty years in amnesiac delight, talking to the Head, without sense of time or worldly sorrow. Yet one day Heilyn son of Gwyn opens the door: immediately their sense of time and loss returns. So they come to London and bury the head: it was said no plague should ever visit the Island of the

Mighty so long as the head is buried there.[1]

Bran means 'raven'. It is said that should the ravens leave the Tower of London, Britain will be invaded, so their wings are kept clipped. The name also refers to the **alder**: Bran's son, Gwern, is alder, which may be why Efnisien threw him on the fire. The Bran cult may have originated in the Greek cult of **Asclepius**, whose mother was *Coronis*, 'Crow': the crow was also sacred to his father, **Apollo**. Bran is wounded in the heel like **Achilles**: beheaded, he continues to sing (is resurrected).

Bran's wound is reflected in the **Fisher King** of **Arthurian** lore: the myth of the **wasteland** originates here (so far as we know). As Brons, he appears in **Grail** myth as guardian of the Grail (cauldron). It may be that after the withdrawal of Rome from Britain (fifth century), a revived cult of Bran stimulated the growth of the original Arthurian mythos. **Geoffrey of Monmouth** calls him Brennius, king of Britain, brother of **Bel** (Belinus).

1. *The Mabinogion*, trans. Gwyn Jones and Thomas Jones, Dent Everyman, London, 1974.

BRAN MACFEBAL (*See* BRENDAN, IRISH MYTH, MAEL DUIN, OISIN)

Like Oisin, this Irish rover met an **otherworld** woman. Invited to sail west to find the Land of Women (Tir na mBan) amid the supernatural Isles of the Blessed, en route he meets the sea-god **Manannan MacLir,** who tells him of further delights to be found in Mag Mell and other magical isles. Reaching the Land of Women, like Oisin he rejects **immortality** to return to Ireland, the land of the living – to find that centuries, not months, have passed, so that when one crew-member wades ashore, he falls immediately to dust.

Due to similar name and circumstance, this Bran is as easily confused with **Bran the Blessed** as with two other Irish navigators: Mael Duin and **St Brendan**.

SAINT BRENDAN (*c.*489–583) (See **BRAN MACFEBAL, MAEL DUIN, OISIN**)

Born in Co. Kerry, this Irish navigator is remembered for his voyage in an ox-skin boat to the Promised Land of Saints. With seventeen monks he spent years exploring the Isles in the West. Landing on a **whale** (*see* **Zaratan**), he said Mass while his monks tried to heat a **cauldron**. It seems that Brendan is to Bran MacFebal as Brennius is to Bran the Blessed: a Christian revision of the older pagan hero. The Brendan voyage closely parallels the voyage of Mael Duin.

The modern British explorer Tim Severin built an ox-hide boat according to specifications given in the account of Brendan's journey, and in it crossed the Atlantic. Though failing to land on a whale to cook a meal, his journey (like Thor Heyerdahl's *Kon-Tiki* expedition) suggests that Irish stories of voyages to fabulous Western Isles (West Indies?) may have a factual basis.

BRICRIU (*See* CUCHULAINN, IRISH MYTH)

BRIDGE (*See* RAINBOW, SWORD-BRIDGE)

In mythology there are many bridges between heaven and earth; between the gods and men; between lower and higer understandings. Such bridges are always dangerous or evanescent, the crossing sometimes involving a death to the self that results in rebirth at a higher level. Even those who keep their balance above the frightful depth meet the **giant** guardian who will not step aside. One or the other must fall. In **Islamic** myth the bridge is 'narrower than a hair', demanding cool balance and swift reaction on the part of those who would cross it. Below in the abyss await the open jaws of the greedy **demons** of sin and ignorance. This is the Bridge Perilous: there is no other crossing over the gulf separating humanity from the otherworld. It is Death, the Final Frontier; yet also it is Bifrost, in **Norse myth** the beautiful **rainbow** bridge separating the land of the **Aesir** from that of ordinary mortals. When sun shines through falling rain, we see it, and remember the promise that treasure of **gold** lies at the other end.

BRIGIT (*See* **IRISH MYTH, TRIPLE GODDESS**)
Daughter of the **Dagda** (father-god of the **Tuatha dé Danaan**, a pot-bellied old man whose miraculous **cauldron** was never empty however much his heroes ate and drank from it), Brigit survived her pagan 'sisters' **Anu** and **Danu** to become the Brigid (or Bride) of Christian times. Yet in her also survived her 'sisters': all three are One, as in the Christian Trinity. As the Irish **Muse** (her name means 'The High One'), she was overtaken by the masculine **Ogma** ('Eloquence') – but she has never yet given up her hold on Irish poets.

Why were Beckett, **Joyce**, O'Brien, Stephens and **Yeats** so potent in their passion? Because they knew that the true poet is a **fool**, distracted from any local commonsense by the **siren**-call of the subconscious goddess, knowing that to deny her is to die – in the spirit.

BROWNIES (*See* **DOMOVOI, FAIRIES, KIRK**)
It was long thought that these shy domestic sprites would by night clean up the kitchen and hearths, so long as a bowl of milk was left out for them. Though brownies were said to be friendly, they were fickle. Woe betide the wife who forgot the bowl of milk – an insulted brownie might get up to all sorts of mischief. In his exposition on St Matthew (1518), the English author John Major calls them Fauni or brobne, saying they can thresh as much grain in one night as twenty men, and may throw stones at people sitting by the fire. The **Rev. Robert Kirk** in *The Secret Commonwealth* calls them members of the Sleagh Maith ('good people': the fairies).[1] The nineteenth-century folklorist **Andrew Lang** compares them with the Russian household spirit, the **Domovoi**, also to the hearth-sprites the ancient Romans called Lares. The Welsh bwbach is a similar entity.

Sir Walter Scott and others argued that brownies, as with other fairy-folk, were the remnants of a neolithic race; small, dark, broad-shouldered folk literally driven underground by iron-weaponed invaders. Kirk denies this, holding that such beings were insubstantial, visible only to those blessed (or cursed) with the **second sight**.

1. *The Secret Commonwealth of Elves, Fauns and Fairies*, Robert Kirk, Observer Press, Stirling, 1933 (1691).

BRUTUS THE TROJAN (*See* **AENEAS, GEOFFREY OF MONMOUTH**)
Accidentally slaying his father, this great-grandson of Aeneas fled from Italy to Greece, whence, directed by a dream while sleeping in the Temple of Diana, he led the enslaved Trojans to Britain. Founding Troia Nova (New Troy: Trinovantium) on the banks of the Thames, he defeated an army of **giants** led by Gog and Magog, whom he enslaved to serve him – or alternatively, as Geoffrey of Monmouth claimed, the singular giant Gogmagog was hurled into the sea by

his lieutenant Corineus. Cited as the ancestor of the Britons, he may have affinities with Partholan, leader of one of the Irish invasions (*see* **Irish myth**), who had also been banished from his native land for parricide.

BUDDHA (*See* BODHISATTVA, BUDDHISM, INDIAN MYTH)

BUDDHISM (*See* CONCORDANCE)

Major religious philosophy, influential in the Far East since its inception in India 2,500 years ago. The word *buddha* (from the **Sanskrit** *budh*, meaning 'to perceive', 'to awaken') signifies a spiritually enlightened being who, on attaining **Nirvana**, has no further need of the world but may choose to **reincarnate** as a **bodhisattva**. Siddhartha Gautama, founder of Buddhism, is but the best-remembered of many such 'buddhas'. Born in Nepal *c*.563 BC, he belonged to the warrior Kshatriva caste. Raised in closeted luxury and married at sixteen, he felt no religious calling until, it is said, aged twenty-nine he visited the outside world for the first time. Shocked to realise that all humanity suffers, he resolved on the 'great renunciation'. Giving up all he had to become a wandering monk, he fasted by a river for six years. Near death, he realised his austerities were futile. Abandoned by his five disciples, he came (*c*.530 BC) to the bo-tree. Seated under it, he swore not to move until he gained Enlightenment. **Demon**-tempted all day (like **Christ** in the Wilderness), as night fell Enlightenment dawned. He saw the cause of rebirth, recalled his former lives, and grasped the meaning of **karma**. By dawn, it is said, he knew how worlds begin and end. Thus in Benares *c*.530 BC he 'set in motion the wheel of the Law' (**Dharma**).

Being moved to reform **Hinduism**, which he saw as having become corrupt, he taught avoidance of extremes: austerity or hedonism, by pursuing the Four Noble Truths: all life is suffering; the cause of suffering is desire; suffering ceases when desire ceases; and the Noble Eightfold Path leads to cessation of desire. Right Views, Right Intent, Right Speech, Right Action, Right Livelihood, Right Effort, Right Mindfulness and Right Concentration.

Proclaiming the essential equality of all humankind, he declared that we live to escape the Wheel of Rebirth and attain non-being (**Nirvana**) by self-sacrifice, meditation and the suppression of desire. Entwined with this belief in reincarnation was the moral doctrine of karma, or cause and effect: whatever we do or think affects our fate. When we die in one life, we are the sum of what we have done in that and in former lives, and so must return to try again. Only by abandoning worldly desire (ego) can we hope to escape the cycle of rebirth and gain the relief of non-existence.

Buddhism began to spread only after the death of its founder (*c*.483 BC). Councils held to decide questions of faith and order led to a distinction between Theravādins and Mahāyānists: the former being traditionalists who interpreted the new Way in terms of existing Brahmanic doctrine; the latter revolutionaries, claiming their understanding of Gautama's philosophy to be the purest. Since both parties emerged after Gautama's death, it is hard to say which, initially, was correct. Gautama left nothing in writing.

The Theravāda emphasises external rules of social morality, regulating life by reference to the *Jakata* (myths) of Gautama's rebirths. Patronised by **Ashoka** (third century BC), it remains dominant in south India, Sri Lanka and southeast Asia. The aim is to attain the aloof state of the *Arhat* who, gaining the spiritual peak, is not expected to descend to the world again.

The more intellectual Mahāyāna school emerged later, between *c*.200 BC and *c*.200 AD. Scriptures claiming to be Gautama's true teachings came from self-styled followers of the Greater Vehicle (Mahāyāna) as opposed to what they termed the Lesser Vehicle (Hinayāna). Rejecting the self-concern of the Theravāda, these schools idealised the **bodhisattva**, or enlightened one, who out of compassion abandons Nirvana to help less-developed beings. This school – influential in China, Korea and Japan – has not wholly avoided the cult of personality. **Avalokiteshvara**, the bodhisattva of compassion and mercy, remains popular throughout the East: **Bodhidharma** (sixth century AD) initiated Japanese **Zen Buddhism**. Images and statues of the Buddha are as common as the venerated relics and assumed personal belongings of Gautama and his early followers. Ideally these images promote meditation.

Buddhism, of whatever school, remains vastly influential.

BUFFALO (*See* BULL, SHAPE-SHIFTING)

The buffalo or bison bears similar symbolic meaning to the ox or bull: strength, fortitude, supernatural power. In **Taoist** myth **Lao Tsu** rode a green buffalo (implying mastery over his animal nature) as he departed the world of men. The Indian goddess Chamunda rode a buffalo when fighting **demons**: so too **Yama**, the Indian god of death, rides a buffalo. In African idiom 'buffalo' (*mbogo* or *nyati* in Bantu) means a man of great strength, bravery and endurance. But white hunters slaughtered the African buffalo as in North America they wiped out the bison. In Amerindian lore the bison represented supernatural strength. In both Africa and in North America there are tales of buffalo cows becoming human women. An African tale from Lake Chad relates how a hunter saw women bathing naked in the river and, on the bank, a row of buffalo hides. He took the finest. Emerging from the river, the women put on the hides and became buffaloes – all but for the one whose hide he had stolen. He married her, and they had a son, but when they visited his parents-in-law, he asked them to turn him into a buffalo, as he was tired of the wicked human world. An Amerindian tale tells how a man hit his buffalo-wife: she and her child vanished, and a buffalo cow and calf were seen running from the camp. He went to where the buffalo herd were dancing to get her back, but was trampled to pieces. Only one tiny bone of him could be found, with which the buffalo bull restored him to life. Returning to human form, the calf-boy and his mother went back with him into human society.[1]

1. *Tales of the North American Indians*, Stith Thompson (1929), Indiana University Press, 1966, pp.150–2.

BUFFALO BILL (*See* WILD WEST)

BUGANDA (*See* AFRICAN MYTH)

Before the advent of **Islam** and **Christianity** the chief god of the Buganda tribe (Uganda) was Mukasa. Kind, he wanted no human offerings, giving his people cattle, children and food. Of his many temples, only one was sacred to the king alone. This, at Bubembe, was built round a **moon-stone** fallen from heaven. Here Mukasa drank the **blood** and ate the **hearts** and livers of **sacrificed** animals: the meat went to his human children, who used the hides to make thongs to bind hut-poles together. In the annual ceremony the blood of the sacrificed animals flowed down a canal into the lake. As soon as the red met the white, the priests posted there cried out: 'He has drunk it.' The departed god left a medium, Mandwa, to interpret his pleasure or displeasure at the success of the sacrifice.[1]

1. *African Mythology*, Jan Knappert, Aquarian Press, Wellingborough, 1990.

BULFINCH, THOMAS (1796–1867)

Viewing Classical myth through the references of the Romantic poets, from Keats and Tennyson to Longfellow, this wealthy Bostonian wrote *The Age of Fable* (1855), a hugely popular introduction to ancient myth. Compressing over a thousand fables and tales into forty-one compact chapters, his 'little windows into the antique world' remains in print.[1]

1. *The Age of Fable*, Thomas Bulfinch, J.M. Dent, London, 1973.

BULL (*See* ANIMALS, APIS, COW, DAEDALUS, THESEUS)

In general this potent beast symbolises the male principle in nature: its roaring is thunder, rain and fertility; it is ridden by or sacred to sun- or sky-gods (**Ashur, Jupiter, Marduk, Ra, Thor, Shiva, Zeus**). Ridden by moon-goddesses (**Astarte**, Europa), it signifies the taming of the animal or masculine nature. In **Celtic** lore bull-gods imply divine power: the **Druids** held that the **sun** is a bull and the **moon** a cow, while the best-known epic of pre-Christian Ireland, the '*Táin Bó Cualnge*' ('*Cattle Raid of Cooley*') concerns a war between Connaught and Ulster fought for possession of the great Brown Bull of Cooley. The Hebrews called **Yahweh** the 'Bull of Heaven': in Egypt the bull **Apis** was avatar of **Osiris** and also considered a reincarnation of **Ptah**; elsewhere it was thought that earthquakes were caused by the celestial bull tossing the earth on its horns. In Christian myth the bull is emblem of St Eustace, martyred in a brass bull: in the French city of Toulouse the oldest church is dedicated to St Taur (from the Latin *taurus*, 'bull'), and probably commemorates an older bull-cult.

Bull-cults were once widespread and in certain forms (the annual bull-run at Pamplona in Spain, bull-fighting) survive. Bull-sacrifice occurred in the rites of **Attis** and **Mithra**. In the former a garlanded bull, driven on to a grating over a pit, was stabbed to death with a consecrated **spear**, its baptismal blood drenching the devotee in the pit below, so that when he emerged, scarlet from head to toe, he was adored by his fellow-worshippers as one born again, his sins washed clean in the blood of the bull.[1]

In the biennial Cretan festival sacred to **Dionysus**, the worshippers of this slain god (sometimes represented as horned and bull-headed) are said to have torn a live bull to pieces with their teeth.[2] The slaying of a bull at New Year symbolised the death of winter and the regeneration of Nature. The bull-man, found from Sumeria to Europe, was usually a guardian who protected **treasure** (like the **dragon**), or **door**. The **labyrinth** in the palace grounds of King Minos of Crete contained the best-known bull-man: the Minotaur, slain by the hero **Theseus**.

The constellation Taurus the Bull (the star Aldebaran its gleaming red eye) has everywhere been known as such since earliest times. The 'Age of Taurus' spanned the period between 4000 and 2000 BC; Taurus is the second sign of the zodiac, assigned the element Earth. Taureans are said to be sensuous, home-loving and placid – unless angered, in which case they may turn into the proverbial 'bull in a china-shop'.

1. *The Golden Bough*, Sir James Frazer, Macmillan, London, 1963, p.351.
2. *Ibid.*, p.389

BULWER-LYTTON, EDWARD (1803–73) (*See* HOLLOW EARTH, NAZI MYTH)

In *The Coming Race* (1871) this English novelist describes how his hero enters an underground world inhabited by nasty beings who control 'Vril fluid', a magical energy that strikes over distances. This novel inspired occult groups such as the 'Luminous Lodge' or Vril Society in Nazi Germany, whose members thought that Bulwer-Lytton had described an **Aryan** super-race inhabiting the **lost world** of Thule. Bulwer-Lytton is also said to have known the Comte de St Germain, widely believed by modern romantics to have survived his reported death in 1784 and to be still alive.

BUNYIP (See **LAKE MONSTERS**)

BUNYORO (See **AFRICAN MYTH, BUGANDA**)

This Ugandan people had an elaborate pantheon of deities, each served by trained priests who conducted rituals and received and interpreted their god's **oracles** via mediums. Each of the forty-six clans had its own **totem** name and protective deity. Ruhanga, the supreme Creator, was too remote to be approached. The goddess Mulindwa protected the royal clan. Muhingo, god of war, demanded **sacrifice** before battle, and a sacrifice of sheep if the battle was won. The god of epidemics, Ndaula, had his temple on the border; offerings were made to him to keep out disease. Those wishing to cross Lake Albert safely by boat made offerings to the lake-god, Mugizi. The cattle god was Kigare; Kaikara was goddess of the harvest; Lubanga, god of health, was said to enjoy beer. Amid flood or drought the king sacrificed an ox to Munume, god of weather; Wamala, god of plenty, also appreciated offerings of cows or bull-calves when asked to increase children, calves or crops.

Sacred **pythons** were fed on milk in a special temple.[1]

1. *African Mythology*, Jan Knappert, Aquarian Press, Wellingborough, 1990.

BURIAL

The disposal of the bodies of the dead has always been hedged about with ritual and myth. Typically, this has been done by burial, cremation or exposure of the body on towers or platforms for scavenging birds to consume.

The latter was once practised by Persian **fire**-worshippers, as today by **Parsees** and in Tibet. Cremation, now as common in the West as among Hindus inheriting **Agni** fire-worship, may always have been preferred by nomadic peoples. Yet most common was and is burial; typically accompanied by rites suggesting that physical death is but a transition of the **spirit** to another plane. Burial also symbolises return to the mother-womb; from early times corpses were buried caked in red ochre (known as '**blood** of the earth'). The body of a child buried in Border Cave, Swaziland, 80,000 years ago had been dusted with ash and ochre. That of a Neanderthal man buried 46,000 years ago in the south of France was packed about with it.[1]

Found with neolithic burials are beakers, food, drink, weapons, horse-gear and armour: all to help the **soul** to cross the Great Divide. Often the dead are buried crouching, as if ready for new action. Later, from Sumeria to China, kings were buried not only with their gold but with their living servants, even their wives, who thus went to the **otherworld** with them.

The most elaborate burials were of Egyptian pharaohs and aristocrats, their mummified bodies placed within a succession of gilded wooden shells, then within the stone sarcophagus, and this within a hollowed underground chamber, secured by **curse** and blocked doors against the depredations of grave-robbers, so that the bird-soul or *ka* of the dead one might ascend.

Almost as elaborate were the prehistoric British long barrows: **earth mounds** in which the burial chamber occupies only one small corner.

The Buriats (Mongols settled by Lake Baikal in Siberia) cremated their dead. But if a man died in autumn or winter, his body was put on a sled drawn by his favourite **horse** to a hidden place in the forest and put in a rough house built of fallen trees and boughs. The horse was slain. When in early May the **cuckoo** called, his kin would come to burn the house down.

In cases of burial alone, the corpse was set before a living man on horseback and taken to its grave. The saddle was broken up and put under the corpse, set facing the south-east. Again, the horse was sacrificed: its master was thus well prepared for his journey to the Spirit-Land.

1. *Lifetide*, Lyall Watson, Coronet, London, 1983, p.60.

BURIAL MOUNDS (*See* **BURIAL, EARTH MOUNDS**)

BURIED TREASURE (*See* **DRAGONS, EARTH MOUNDS, JUNG, TREASURE**)

BURNING BUSH (*See* **FIRE-CULTS, SACRIFICE**)

BURROUGHS, EDGAR RICE (1875–1950) (*See* **SCIENCE FICTION**)
Chicago-born, this author created one of the most enduring mythic heroes of the twentieth century. The novel *Tarzan of the Apes*, first published 1914 (the original tale a 1912 short story) led to twenty-three sequels (translated into many languages), plus films and literary imitations playing on the theme Burroughs made his own: rediscovery of the 'noble savage'.

Infant son of English aristocrats (John Lord Greystoke and Lady Alice) who die stranded on the jungle shores of West Africa, Tarzan grows up amid a tribe of 'great apes' (species non-existent). Before ever he meets another human being he has become a superb athlete and warrior, Lord of the Apes. Despite lacking the realism of **H. Rider Haggard** and **Rudyard Kipling** (both influential), and though clearly dated (as in its racial attitudes), the Tarzan saga still delights many.

Even less plausible than Tarzan, Burroughs' tales relating the doings of his hero John Carter on Barsoom (**Mars**) present an exotic and gorgeous never-never land, the atmosphere of which has influenced many later **science fiction** authors, particularly the prolific Michael Moorcock.

One town in California and another in Texas are named Tarzana after his principal hero. Tarzan has also attracted accomplished **comic**-strip artists – notably Hal Foster and Burne Hogarth.

BURROUGHS WILLIAM S. (1914–) (*See* **SCIENCE FICTION**)
Grandson of the inventor of the Burroughs adding machine, this St Louis-born author has lived a life as nightmarishly mythic as his novels. After experimenting in Amazonia with hallucinogenic drugs, in 1953 he published *Junky* (later *Junkie*), a confessional novel describing the addict's life. While living in Tangier in Morocco, though still an addict, he developed a literary power first widely recognised on the Paris publication of his novel *The Naked Lunch* (1959). This owed much to his satirical, scatological and wildly vivid literary style and insights.

In *The Naked Lunch* his preoccupations with an underworld of drug use, homosexuality and police persecution are so explicit that only his humour and deep insight into 'control mechanisms' save it and subsequent 'novels' from futility. Using drug-addiction as a total metaphor for the control of our lives by capitalising politicians (dealers), his gallery of grotesques, though derived from the **comics, science fiction**, movies and other modern mass media sources, is original. His myth comes not from **Olympus** but **Hades**: his main achievement is to make hell so funny while reminding us that it *is* hell, lacking any redeeming features whatsoever. He has remarked that in the twentieth century the paranoid is the only sane person.

In public readings of pieces like 'Ah Pook Was Here' his contempt for material Western culture is matched only by his horrific rendering of what it may have meant to live in pagan agrarian societies where the **corn-god** died annually; where human **sacrifice** was actual, not symbolic.

BUSHMEN (*See* **AFRICAN MYTH, HOTTENTOT**)
Otherwise known in the Khoi tongue as the San, or by themselves as the Ju ('People'), these nomads of the Kalahari desert in Botswana and adjacent territories were named 'Bosjesmannen' by the Afrikaaners because they hid in the bushes. Distinct from the *Khoikhoin* (Hottentot) people, today numbering some 70,000 people divided into many groups or clans, the Ju are expert at finding water and have 'words in their bodies' (premonitive dreams), and so are often consulted as diviners. They say animals are descended from folk who preferred a wild life in the bush, and that they were the first people who ever lived on earth. They say the remote **sky-god** Kaang made the world but met such opposition that he sent death and destruction, then went away. Mankind had even rejected his sons, Cogaz and Gewi, who had descended to earth as educators. Yet he remains manifest as the invisible spirit in all natural phenomena. When wind blows up and a sudden rain falls, it is his doing. He is also the died-and-reborn god. Once he was eaten by an ogre, then vomited up. Again, killed by thorns and with his bones picked clean by the ants, he reassembled his skeleton, **resurrecting** himself. When his daughter married a **snake**, the snakes became 'Kaang's people'. He is always opposed by the mischief of Gauna, chief of the spirits of the dead, who can escape their dark underworld only if the living break **taboos**. The living also avoid graves for fear of being dragged off by the dead.

Though no longer an independent culture, at one time the Ju expanded from the Cape to Kenya, leaving everywhere their rock-paintings.

BYELUN (*See* **SLAVONIC MYTH**)
Byelobog (the 'White God') and Chernobog (the 'Black God') – one the good god of light and daytime, the other the evil god of darkness and night – epitomise an old **dualism** once favoured by the Western Slavs from Ukraine to White Russia (Byelorussia), where many once believed in the existence of the god Byelun. Popularly represented as an old man dressed in white with a flowing white beard, Byelun appeared only during daytime and was always benevolent, helping those overburdened or who had lost their way.

C

CABBALA (*See* **QABALAH, TREE OF LIFE**)

CADMUS (*See* **EUROPA, GREEK MYTH, OGMA, TREE ALPHABET**)
One of five sons of Agenor, king of Tyre, sent to recover their abducted sister Europa from **Zeus**. Failing, and told not to return unless they had succeeded, they settled in Greece, Cadmus founding the city of Thebes. To get fresh water to a spring he had to slay a **dragon**. **Athene** advised him to sow its teeth, from which sprang an army of warriors. He set them against each other: the Theban aristocracy was said to have descended from the five who survived. Cadmus was also credited with the introduction of a sixteen-letter alphabet from Phoenicia, replacing the old thirteen-letter 'Pelasgian alphabet'. The name Cadmus itself means 'of the east'.

CADUCEUS (*See* **DUALISM, HERMES, MERCURY**)
This magical winged **serpent**-wand as held by Hermes or Mercury represents power, the *axis mundi*, the Middle Pillar in the **Qabalistic Tree of Life**. It is the royal road, Jacob's Ladder between heaven and earth, up and down which messenger-gods and **angels** arise and descend. The wings symbolise the transcendence of lower by higher. Coiling round about and up the **wand** itself the two serpents, eternally opposed, are complementary and finally united in their **dualism**: sickness and health, fire and water, good and evil, night and day, male and female. It is also carried by the Egyptian **Anubis** and sometimes by **Isis**, the Phoenician **Baal** and the Babylonian **Ishtar**.

CAILLEACH (*See* **BADB, BANSHEE, CERRIDWEN**)
Gaelic: 'old woman' or 'hag', a term rich in supernatural implication. The *cailleach* may turn out to be the banshee, or the washerwoman by the ford, or the Welsh goddess Cerridwen whose rage is unforgiving when Gwion Bach accidentally drinks from her **cauldron** of inspiration. She may be the **crow**-goddess lapping up battle-blood, or the *tricoteuses* knitting under the guillotine, blood-spattered and calling for more heads. In triple form she appears as the three **witches** of **Shakespeare**'s *Macbeth*, identified by Shakespeare as **Hecate**: also the three crones who, waylaying **Cuchulainn** en route to his final battle, doom the **hero** by inviting him to eat **dog**-meat.

CAIN (*See* **ADAM, BIBLE, EDEN, EVE, YAHWEH**)
In Genesis iv:1–17 it is told how, expelled from Eden, Adam and Eve had two sons, Cain and Abel, the elder a farmer, the younger a shepherd. When Cain brought the Lord God an offering of the fruits of the soil, **Yahweh** showed no pleasure. Then Abel offered the 'firstlings of his flock and of the fat thereof', and Yahweh was pleased. In jealousy, Cain murdered Abel, then in guilt denied the act. Yahweh cursed him, as he had already cursed Adam, 'to be a fugitive and wanderer on the earth'. So Cain went out of the presence of the Lord and lived east of Eden in the Land of Nod ('Wandering').

Behind this tale lies political intrigue. The Canaanites ('Cain') were farmers, settled in the land. The newly-arrived Hebrews were shepherds. No surprise that in **Hebrew myth** Yahweh prefers the offering of the young nomad to that of the settled older brother. Abel is slain, but Yahweh denounces ritual human **sacrifice** as murder. Cursed, Cain is driven from his land, and from his loins spring generations of good and evil: human history. A mark is set on his brow (worry-lines?) so that all may know him and none kill him. So he is condemned to life on earth. As to the original territorial war implied by the myth, that continues.

CALYPSO (*See* ATLAS, GREEK MYTH, ODYSSEY)
This daughter of Atlas and Tethys ruled the enchanted isle of Ogygia in the Ionian Sea. Odysseus being cast up on her shores, she kept him **seven** years, and offered him immortality, but **Zeus** ordered her to let him go. Her isle and his captivity remind us of the celestial castle of **Arianrhod**, or **Morgan Le Fay**'s **Avalon**, or the Celtic Blessed Isles. Like **Aphrodite**, her original realm lay amid the sea: her name, from a Greek root 'to hide', implies the depths. **Alder**, white poplar and cypress (the three **trees** of resurrection) surrounded her cave; in them nested sea-**crows**, **falcons** and **owls**.

CAMELOT (*See* ARTHURIAN MYTH, KENNEDY)

CAMPBELL, JOSEPH (1904–87)
'Religions, philosophies, arts, the social forms of primitive and historic man, the very dreams that blister sleep,' wrote this great modern American mythologist, 'boil up from the basic, magic ring of myth . . . the flavour of the ocean is contained in a droplet . . . the whole mystery of life within the egg of a flea.'[1]

Born in New York City, early fascinated by **Native American myth**, his MA course in English Literature led him to **Arthurian** parallels with Native American lore. Concluding that these are **archetypal**, not cultural, he began to elucidate the common psychology of global myth and, in particular, the worldwide image of the **hero**. *The Hero with a Thousand Faces* (1949), which compared and analysed global hero myths in terms of contemporary psychology, was followed by his four-volume masterpiece, *The Masks of God*. In face-to-face interviews he related the hero-ideal to everyday life. 'We have not even to risk the adventure, for the heroes of all time have gone before us. The labyrinth is thoroughly known, we have only to follow the thread of the hero path.'

By hero Campbell meant not just **Achilles** or **Cuchulainn**, but Leopold Bloom, the cuckolded, self-effacing Dublin Jew whose experience and reverie during one day and night provide the adventure of the modern *Ulysses* by **James Joyce**. The hero, Campbell and Joyce both knew, is Everyman.[2]

1. *The Hero with a Thousand Faces*, Joseph Campbell, Abacus, London, 1975, p.13.
2. *The Masks of God* (4 vols), Joseph Campbell, Penguin, London, 1976.

CANNIBALISM (*See* BLOOD, KINGSHIP, SACRIFICE)
The very image of savagery is of people who eat people: cannibals. What merit can there be in such feral activity? Tales of survivors of crashed planes or lost Arctic expeditions resorting to cannibalism make our own living flesh shudder. Yet cannibalistic metaphor still pervades religious symbolism, as in the Christian rite of Communion; and once, the world over, cannibal

consumption of the sacrificed god-king was more than metaphor. So too in warrior cultures everywhere it was customary to consume the bodies and blood of enemies slain in battle, to take on their bravery and wisdom.

In southeast Africa, when a brave enemy was slain, it was customary to burn his liver (seat of valour), ears (seat of intelligence), testicles (seat of strength) and other vital organs. The ash was mixed into a paste. Carefully stored, this was eaten at **circumcision** ceremonies. When in West Africa Sir Charles M'Carthy was slain by the **Ashanti**, it is said his heart was eaten by the Ashanti chiefs, so as to take on his courage.[1] The Hurons, Iroquois and other forest tribes in eastern North America ceremonially tortured captured enemies to death, then ate them. This was considered no insult to the brave enemy, but the height of honour. Similar rites existed in the Amazonian rain-forest and elsewhere. To eat the body of the defeated enemy was both to do him honour and to gain his strength.

So too the **sacrifice** and consumption of the body of the god-king was intended not only to propitiate the gods responsible for drought or flood, but to perpetuate the holy power invested in that body. In ancient Greece the king called the **Hercules** was, at the end of his half-year reign, made drunk on mead, tied to a T-shaped **oak**, beaten, flayed, blinded, **castrated**, impaled with a **mistletoe** stake, then hacked to pieces, roasted and eaten by the tribe. His tanist succeeded him as king until midwinter, when a new Hercules killed him. A similar rite was reported from China by the Arab merchant Suleyman in AD 851.[2] The Pelasgian Lycaon, son of the **bear**-goddess Callisto and himself an oak-god, practised cannibalism, the choice of a new king every nine years being settled by a cannibal feast.[3]

But the greatest cannibal ritualists were the **Aztecs** of Mexico. Their gods **Tlaloc** and **Huitzilopochtli** had an unquenchable appetite for human flesh. Wars were fought purely to seize captives for sacrifice and feast. At the dedication of the Temple of the Sun in Tenochtitlán (*c*.AD 1516), it took the priests three days and nights to slaughter and butcher 70,000 captives. The most beautiful Aztec youths and maidens, beloved as the personification of specific gods and goddesses during a year-long reign, had their hearts torn out and offered to the **sun**. Then their corpses were rolled down the other side of the pyramid to the kitchens.[4]

It has been suggested that this Aztec obsession was based on a lack of protein from other sources. This fails to explain the similar ceremonies of the sacrifice and ritual feast of the god-king the world about. For it is found in **Christianity** too. 'This is my body and my blood.' The rite of Communion is implicitly cannibalistic: by eating the flesh and drinking the blood of the crucified Christ, sin is redeemed, **immortality** conferred.

So, flesh and blood become bread and wine. Yet some 30 million lives were sacrificed during the Thirty Years War (1618–48), in part due to a theological dispute as to whether the Communion bread and wine were *actually* or only *symbolically* the real body and blood of **Christ**.

Today, rumours of ritual killings and the cannibalism of serial killers such as Dennis Nilsen suggest that the human urge to eat human meat, though now shorn of religious approval, is not yet exorcised.

1. *The Golden Bough*, Sir James Frazer, Macmillan, London, 1963, p.497.
2. *The White Goddess*, Robert Graves, Faber & Faber, London, 1961, pp.125–6.
3. Frazer, *op.cit.*, p.367.
4. *Cannibals and Kings*, Marvin Harris, Random House, New York, 1977, pp.147–66.

CARGO CULT (*See* **FIJI, GHOST- DANCE, NEW AGE, OCEANIC MYTH**)
In Papua about 1919, and in response to European colonial exploitation, arose an ecstatic cult, *Iki-haveve* ('Belly Don't Know'), led by an old man, Evara. He prophesied the coming of a steamship, on which the spirits of their **ancestors** would bring the 'cargo', including rifles to drive out the white settlers. Later he said an aeroplane would land, bringing the promised cargo. That this cult was an effort by distressed people to make a new myth to explain their collapsing society in the face of technological invasion is clear. The new god *Ihova* ('Jehovah'?) dressed like a European businessman: imitation radios were used to contact the ancestors; ancient beliefs were abandoned. Though over by 1923, it led to the 'cargo cult' stimulated by World War II; the Americans' establishment of airfields, supply depots and Coca-Cola causing wide fascination and bewilderment.

CARROLL, LEWIS (1832–98) (*See* **CAT, FAIRY-TALES**)
The pseudonym of the English mathematician and novelist, Charles Dodgson, author of *Alice's Adventures in Wonderland* (1865), and a sequel, *Through the Looking-Glass* (1871). He began inventing tales for the three children of the dean of Christ Church, Oxford, Henry George Liddell. One of them, Alice, in 1932 recalled how Dodgson would tell 'fantastic tales, which he made up as he told them, drawing busily on a large sheet of paper all the time.' On 4 July 1862, rowing the Liddell children up the Thames, he invented *Alice's Adventures Underground*. The real Alice implored him to write it down. So he did. On reading it to his own children, the Scots fantasist George Macdonald (author of *Lilith*) was told by his son Greville (aged six) that he 'wished there were 60,000 volumes of it'. Persuaded to publish, Dodgson went to John Tenniel, the *Punch* artist, who illustrated the first edition. By the time Dodgson died, it and its sequel had become the best-loved children's book in the world. Dodgson had invented (adapted?) the Cheshire **Cat**, the March **Hare**, the White Rabbit and the Mad Hatter's **riddle** ('The riddle, as originally invented, had no answer at all').

CASSIOPEIA (*See* **PERSEUS**)

CASTLE (*See* **BRIDGE, CAVE, TREASURE**)
A walled defensible enclosure, typically reached by a bridge over a circular moat of water: an ambivalent symbol in that it both includes and excludes. It may protect its inhabitants against monsters, ogres or foreign armies or it may be a stronghold of evil powers, depending which side of its walls you stand. In myth, castles typically contain a treasure (**Holy Grail**) or royal prisoner (true self), neither won nor saved until the evil guardian of the ego is overcome. An extension of the treasure-cave guarded by a **dragon** or a **loathly worm**, such a castle represents **Camelot**, a realm of spiritual aspiration and attainment; occultly the human body, its treasure the mind, its mystery our ignorance as to our own true human nature.

CASTRATION (*See* **CANNIBALISM, CIRCUMCISION, CORN-GODS**)
In mythic terms the reaping of the harvest is castration of the corn-god, followed by his death: thus the fate of **Adonis**, **Attis** and others, whose human representatives (god-kings reigning for a given span of time defined by the passage of the seasons) were castrated by themselves or by others; this rite often followed by ritual murder and cannibal feast. The Egyptian **Set** was

castrated by **Horus**; the Greek love-goddess **Aphrodite** was born from the white foam produced when **Cronus** threw the severed phallus of his father **Ouranos** into the sea. So too the **sun** is 'castrated' as it enters the realm of winter, while in **Arthurian** myth the wound suffered by the **Fisher King** (**Bran**), which leads to the land turning into an infertile **wasteland**, is associated with a **spear**-thrust through the loins. It may also be that the centurion's spear-thrust into the side of **Christ** while crucified implies this same rite of castration.

CAT (*See* **DOG, SHAPE-SHIFTING, WITCHCRAFT**)

Human attitudes swing between extremes. In Christian Europe cats were long associated with the **Devil**. Lonely old women with cats as pets risked being burned as **witches** – some were even accused of changing into cats, and cats themselves were often tortured to death in baskets suspended above fires.

Yet once cats were venerated. In ancient Egypt, anyone who killed a cat, even by accident, was executed. The Roman author Diodorus Siculus, born *c.*100 BC, tells how in Egypt he saw the lynching of a Roman citizen who had accidentally killed a cat. 'The populace crowded to the house of the Roman, who had committed the "murder"; and neither the efforts of the magistrates sent by the King to protect him nor the universal fear inspired by the might of Rome, could avail to save the man's life, though what he had done was admitted to be accidental. This is not an incident which I report from hearsay, but something I saw myself during my sojourn in Egypt.'[1]

The Egyptian goddess Bast was shown as a giant cat, or as a woman with a cat's head. A **sun-goddess** with (oddly) no connection to **moon**-worship, her cult-centre, Bubastis, was once Egypt's capital. Here, during the fourth century BC, as goddess of music, dance and pleasure, she gained her greatest popularity. Her worshippers enjoyed licentious revelry – perhaps another reason for later demonisation of the cat. And though Bast was said to be benevolent, cat-killers were lynched. Cat-goddesses were always fearful. In **Norse myth** the cat is sacred to **Freya** who, though a fertility-goddess and patroness of lovers, was also (like **Kali** or the Irish Morrigan) the goddess of those slain in battle. When not riding her **horse** into battle, she used a chariot drawn by cats. Pagan British cat-goddesses demanded human sacrifice. These included the *cailleach* Bheur (Blue Hag of Winter) in Scotland, and Black Annis of the Dane Hills in Leicestershire. Derived from the Celtic goddess **Danu**, Black Annis is said 'to have been a savage woman with great teeth and long nails', who ate human victims, and went out only at night.[2]

So the connection between witch and cat grows plain. Folk belief claims the cat as the witch's familiar: her demonic agent appointed by the **Devil** to aid the war against **Christ**, the new male (sun)-god. A black cat (black as night, death or sin) was said to be the witch's favourite familiar. As late as the 1800s an old woman was thrown into a pit in Suffolk, because she had a black cat. Other creatures, like the moon-mad **hare**, were also seen as familiars, but the cat remained primary. Witches might ride cats through the air, or even change into cats (or any other beast, save the Christian **dove** or **lamb**). In Ireland and in Britain, the King of the Cats was thought malevolent, given to appearing in human form, identifiable only if a little bit of his ear were cut off. **Satan** himself was said to take the form of a cat. Yet nowadays the black cat signifies good luck.

In China and Japan the cat signifies powers of transformation, without evil overtones as in Europe. Yet everywhere the cat signifies stealth and mystery, as with the Cheshire Cat of **Lewis Carroll**'s *Alice's Adventures in Wonderland* (disappearing, leaving only its grin), or Ireland's Kilkenny Cats, arguing so fiercely they ate each other, leaving only their tails.

In recent years mysterious big cats are said to prowl rural areas in Britain. The 'Surrey puma' is an all-embracing term covering such reports in southern England from August 1962 onward.[3] In Scotland, local newspapers thrive on tales of the 'wangie' seen slinking through towns by night.

There is nothing occult about this smart feral cat, but in popular belief the supernatural element of the mystery prevails.

Where the **dog** early became the servile friend of Man the Hunter, cats cannot be trained, but walk their own way, by night. When male religion took over, cats were out in the cold – despite their legendary nine lives.

1. *Nine Lives: Cats in Folklore*, Katherine M. Briggs, Routledge & Kegan Paul, London, 1980, p.2.
2. *Ibid.*, p.5.
3. *Alien Animals*, Janet and Colin Bord, Granada, London, 1980, pp.49–80.

CATHARS (*See* DUALISM, GNOSTIC MYTH, HOLY GRAIL, REINCARNATION)

Exterminated by Church and state in the thirteenth century, the **dualist** Cathars (also called Albigensians) of Provence (southern France) denied that **Christ** ever lived as a man, considered the crucifixion fictitious, believed in **reincarnation**, the equality of good and evil as a universal principle, and that the physical world was created by the **Devil**, alias the Old Testament **Yahweh**. Their priests (*parfaits*, 'perfect ones', were vegetarian, chaste and espoused non-violence. Because they travelled in pairs of the same sex they were calumnised as homosexual – 'buggers', from '*bougres*' (Bulgarians) – their faith being derived from the Bogomils of Bulgaria. This arose also from their rejection of marriage and sexuality as causing the birth of more poor souls into hell – so they saw earthly life. In fact such abstinence was asked only of the *parfaits* who had undertaken the *consolamentum*: a rite which most undertook only on their deathbed. The faith, though mystic in its attitude to Christ, was practical in terms of human psychology: asking nothing of those unable to overcome their human nature.

As such, it became so charismatic that it threatened the power of the Church. A crusade against Catharism was declared in 1208 by Pope Innocent III. The resulting forty-year war led to the establishment of the Dominican Inquisition, the destruction of over 400 villages and the death of all Cathars refusing to recant. At the fall of Montségur, the last important Cathar stronghold, over 200 Cathars were burned alive (1244).

Their interest today arises from (1) a rebirth of interest in **Gnostic** beliefs; (2) their apparent connection with esoteric movements such as the troubadours and **Knights Templar**; (3) the association of Montségur with the legend of the **Holy Grail**; and (4) the strange events recorded by the English psychiatrist Arthur Guirdham in the 1960s, suggesting that some of his patients, disturbed by recurrent dreams, were reincarnated Cathars who had lived and died in the years preceding the fall of Montségur.[1]

1. *The Medieval Manichee*, Steven Runciman, Cambridge University Press, 1982; *The Great Heresy*, Arthur Guirdham, Spearman, Sudbury, 1977.

CAULDRON (*See* BRAN, CERRIDWEN, DAGDA, HOLY GRAIL)

The magical cauldron of pagan **Celtic** lore signifies nourishment, rebirth, abundance, transformation. In Irish myth the cauldron of the **Dagda** cannot be exhausted, no matter how much is eaten and drunk from it. The cauldron of the **giant Bran** in the Welsh *Mabinogion* resurrects dead warriors thrown into it at dusk. The cauldron of the Welsh hag **Cerridwen** contains a brew of inspiration and enlightenment; accidentally drinking from it, Gwion Bach gains knowledge much as the Teutonic hero **Siegfried** does by drinking **dragon**'s blood. Just as the Irish **sword** Caliburn is the model for **Excalibur**, so the pagan symbol of the cauldron gives rise to the **Christian Holy Grail**.

CAVE (*See* AGHARTI, DRAGON, HOLLOW EARTH, UNDERWORLD, WELL)

Like **castles** and **cauldrons**, caves are symbolically ambiguous. The womb is a cave; so is the grave. Taken down from the **cross** dead, **Christ** was laid in the womb-tomb of the sepulchre, a cave, blocked from the light of day by a great stone. Yet by the morning of the third day the stone had been set aside and the resurrected Christ had departed from the grave-womb.

The earliest surviving human art is found in **graves** (caves in the body of Mother Earth), or as painted by ancient hunter-magicians on the walls of cave-systems (Lascaux, France). The **Mysteries** at **Delphi** were conducted in caves, the pythoness (oracular priestess) seated on a tripod straddling an abyss from which arose entrancing fumes from the (literal) **underworld**.

Descent into underworld (afterlife) cave-systems is a staple feature in tales of sacrificed **corn-gods** or **fertility-goddesses** who, with the summer gone, go down to the Land of the Dead. When spring comes, they emerge to renew the world with fresh growth and hope.

The up-pointing triangle of the **mountain** is a male symbol, the down-pointing triangle of the cave is female. Yet both are complementary: both belong to the *axis mundi*. The cave (and its **treasure**) is often guarded by a **dragon**. Positively this symbolises fertility; negatively it symbolises the greed of the ego, guarding what it cannot use.

CELTIC MYTH (*See* CONCORDANCE)

Who were the Celts? About 1400 BC in eastern Europe emerged a culture marked by new forms of decoration of weapons, ornaments, pottery and tools, and by **earth-mound** burial. Yet perhaps this culture originated as far east as the Himalayas. Celtic place-names (*nemeton*, 'grove') are found from Turkey to Ireland: poetic conventions, marriage laws, craft techniques and beliefs (as in **reincarnation**) all suggest **Brahmanic** or Indian influence.

Defined by common social organisation, religion, dress, language and battle-technique, these flamboyant peoples settled Europe from Denmark to Spain. Raiding Rome in 386 BC, in 278 BC a Celtic army sacked **Delphi** in Greece. The Goidels (Gaels) invaded Britain and Ireland. Later came the Brythons, their language the basis of Welsh, Cornish and Breton.

They left no written record, their **Druid** priesthood relying on trained memory. 'Celtic' literature dates from a Christian era (*c*.AD 700–1400).

Classical writers describe Celts as warlike, quarrelsome, boastful and vain, also as poetic, imaginative, generous, profound. Aristotle (*c*.350 BC) wrote: 'It is not bravery to withstand danger through recklessness, as when the Celts take up arms to attack the waves.'[1] Polybius (third century BC) and Strabo say they fought naked and beheaded slain enemies, the women as wild as the men. Inheritance was matrilinear: a man's uncle (mother's brother) preceded his father. Diodorus calls the Celtic Gauls 'terrifying in appearance, with deep sounding and very harsh voices. In conversation they use few words and speak in riddles, for the most part hinting at things and leaving a great deal to be understood. They are boasters given to bombastic self-dramatization, and yet they are quick of mind and with a good natural ability for learning'.[2]

Honouring their warriors, **bards** (poets), Vates (diviners) and Druids (philosophers), they held the human soul to be indestructible. At feasts, warriors fought to the death for the champion's portion of meat. Kings and champions were bound by magical prohibitions (*geasa*), involving impossibly contradictory demands leading to death. Heroism lay in accepting this fate serenely. Druids would stab men to read auguries from the death-convulsion: the bard's resonant curse was feared by kings. Celts believed in a spirit-world and in **shape-shifting, divination** and **second sight** (Gaelic *an-da-shealladh*, 'two sights'). The wailing wind was the **banshee**'s death-cry; a shoulder-blade of mutton picked clean reflected the future; grain was sowed in the moon's increase; cattle-disease was cured by forcing new **fire** and burning juniper; the mounds of the Sidhe (**fairies**) were best avoided. In rivers lurked **kelpies**, swelling the flood to drown travellers; on mountain peaks spirits waited to kill the unwary and carry them west, though not to blessed **Tir nan Og** (Avalon), the Land of Youth reserved for heroes like **Cuchulainn** or **King Arthur**. The Celtic love of the word persists in the flair of modern Irish authors: **Joyce**, Stephens, O'Brien and **Yeats**.

No written versions of Celtic myths survive from Gaul or the continent. Even the first Irish writings came long after the origin of tales recorded orally for generations. Irish tales (*Book of Invasions, Book of Leinster, Book of Ballymote, Book of the Dun Cow, Yellow Book of Lecan* from the eighth century on) are openly pagan and without any obvious heavy hand of Christian dogma. Welsh tales (*White Book of Rhydderch, Red Book of Hergest* (fourteenth century)) as collected in the *Mabinogion* are more Christianised.[3]

1. *Celtic Myths and Legends*, T.W. Rolleston, Studio Press, London, p.17.
2. *Ibid.*, p.42.
3. *The Magic Arts in Celtic Britain*, Lewis Spence, Rider, London, 1970; *The Celts*, Nora Chadwick, Pelican, London, 1970.

CENTAUR (*See* FABULOUS BEASTS, GREEK MYTH, HORSE)

The first sight of horsemen bewildered the **Aztecs**, who had never seen a horse. A text quoted by Prescott, historian of the Spanish invasion of Mexico, tells how when a Spanish rider fell off his horse: 'the Indians, seeing the animal fall asunder, up to now having deemed the beast all one, were so filled with terror that they turned and fled, crying out to their comrades that the animal had made itself into two.'

Yet the Greeks knew all about the horse. The beast they called centaur (head and torso human, the rest of the body equine) was probably deliberate invention, an archetype taking centuries to gain final form. Early images of centaurs show them as hairy giants: the elegant final version of man-horse dates from Phidias and the Parthenon carvings in Athens (438 BC).

The centaurs were descendants of the Thessalonian King Ixion (son of **Ares**; bound to a fiery wheel in Tartarus for embracing a cloud formed by **Zeus** in the shape of **Hera**; or of Centaurus, son of **Apollo** and Stilbia; or of Centaurus and the mares of Magnesium. Whatever their origin, some say the word 'centaur' comes from the Vedic **Gandharvas** (minor gods who drive the horses of the sun). More likely the original 'centaurs' were Thessalonian cowboys, infamous for their rude, drunken lechery. The best-known centaur tale is of their battle with the (likewise fabulous) Lapiths at a marriage feast. Unused to wine (though followers of **Dionysus**), they began the fight by insulting the bride. Defeated, they were driven out of Thessaly. Later destroyed by **Hercules**, their revenge came when he put on a shirt soaked (unknown to him) in the poisoned blood of Nessus, a centaur he had slain.

Not all centaurs were louts. Chiron, educated by **Artemis** and **Apollo**, taught **Achilles** and **Asclepius** the arts of medicine, music, hunting and war. Killed by Hercules, he was placed by Zeus (as was Sagittarius, another centaur) among the stars as the constellation Centaurus.

CERBERUS (*See* CHARON, DOG, GREEK MYTH, HADES, UNDERWORLD)

This feral hound who guarded the underworld gates is said in the *Theogony* of the Greek poet Hesiod (*c.*750 BC) to have fifty heads, later reduced to three, each infernal and terrific, each perhaps representing past, present and future. Strangled bare-handed by **Hercules**, Cerberus is imbued by **Dante** with human characteristics: filthy black beard and clawed hands tearing the souls of the damned. His tail is that of a **serpent**: to appease his wrath a honey-cake was put in the coffin of the newly dead. More ferocious than the Egyptian **Anubis**, he is similar to the blood-spattered hell-hound Garm of **Norse myth**, who guards the underworld and who will fight the gods when at **Ragnorak** the hell-wolves swallow both **sun** and **moon**, so ending this world.

CERES (*See* DEMETER, ROMAN MYTH)

Tutelary goddess of ancient Sicily, this Roman version of Demeter (Greek goddess of fruits and fields), survives as a name given to cereals – white-straw crops; also fruit, corn or nut-based breakfast foods), and as given in 1801 by the astronomer Guiseppe Piazzi to the first-discovered asteroid.

CERNUNNOS (*See* GREEN MAN, HERNE, HORNED GODS, ROBIN HOOD)

The name of this **pagan** Gaulish/British stag-god ('Horned One') is found in many localities. At Cerne Abbas in Dorset, England, a fertility-**giant** is carved in the chalk hillside, portrayed naked with erect phallus and club raised in his right hand. The local legend is that a barren woman sleeping for one night on the giant's body will become fertile. The lord of horned and hoofed animals, Cernunnos is associated with the '**Wild Hunt**', by which the souls of the dead are swept into the **otherworld**. Shown with **ram**-headed **serpents**, he is a **fertility-god** in the broad sense: death and sexuality go hand-in-hand, as in other British myths of **Herne the Hunter**, the **Green Man** and Robin Goodfellow, the sprite later transformed into **Robin Hood**.

CERRIDWEN (*See* CAULDRON, SHAPE-SHIFTING, TALIESIN, WELSH MYTH)

In Welsh myth the hag Cerridwen ('Old White Sow'), who lived on an isle in Lake Tegid, set young Gwion Bach to stir a cauldron in which bubbled a Brew of Inspiration meant for her husband Tegid Foel, or maybe for her hideously ugly son, Afagddu, to compensate him for his looks. Gwion is warned never to taste the brew. Yet one dark night, with Cerridwen absent, the boiling pot spits out three drops, burning his thumb. Thrusting it into his mouth, he is thus inspired, he sees all things – including the fact that Cerridwen means to kill him. Pursued by her, he changes himself into a **hare**: she changes into a greyhound. Desperately he turns into a fish, but she turns into an otter: he becomes a bird, she becomes a hawk. At length he hides as a grain of corn on the threshing-floor, but as a hen she swallows him. Yet this is not the end. In seasonal myth, as in modern physics, there is no 'end':

transformation is continual. Cerridwen is also fertility: having eaten him, nine months later she gives birth to him again. Unable to kill him, she puts him in a leather bag and throws him into Cardigan Bay. He drifts into a fish-weir to be found and renamed Taliesin, 'Radiant Brow', the **wonder-child** who makes fools of all the poets at King Gwyddno's court.

CHANGELINGS (*See* CHILDREN, FAIRIES)

Throughout the **Celtic** world, especially Highland Scotland, it was thought that the **fairy**-folk were always anxious to steal new-born human children, in their place substituting wizened changelings (fairy infants), or a broom with rugs wrapped round it. Likewise women might be seized from child-bed, as **Kirk** reports, and 'a lingering image of herself substituted'.[1] Abducted into the fairy-realm, such women were made to nurse the children of their kidnappers. These tales might be rationalised as factual reports of the theft of children by an embattled aboriginal people so as to interbreed with their conquerors and thus survive. Yet the theme is found not in Europe alone, but from China to North America, and today persists in tales of **UFO** kidnappings of and sexual interference with human beings. Furthermore, the myth may have been used as excuse by disappointed parents for mistreatment of children with congenital defects. A London *Daily Telegraph* report of 17 May 1884 tells of the arrest of two women of Clonmel, Ireland, for cruelty to a three-year-old child. Claiming he was a changeling, they said that by mistreating him they hoped to get the real child back from the elves. So too it may be that some women, traumatised by childbirth and never restored to their former health, might easily have been seen by distraught husbands and neighbours as having been stolen away, leaving but 'a lingering image'.

1. *The Secret Commonwealth of Elves, Fauns and Fairies*, Rev. Robert Kirk, Observer Press, Stirling, 1933 (1691).

CHARIOT

In the Katha Upanishad (III: 3–4) it is written: 'Know that the Self is the lord of the chariot, the body verily is the chariot; know that the soul is the charioteer, and emotion the reins. They say that the bodily powers are the **horses**, and that the external world is their field.'

In myth, chariots are drawn by many different creatures according to the nature of the charioteer. The solar chariot of **Apollo** is drawn by white horses; solar chariots may also be drawn by **griffons** or **swans**; the solar chariot in **Buddhism** is the Great Vehicle. The chariot of the **Norse** Thor is drawn by solar **rams**; the lunar chariot of Norse **Freya** by **cats**; that of the **Celtic** Flidass, goddess of wild things, by **deer**; that of **Cybele** by **lions**; that of Venus by **doves**; that of **Eros** and **Dionysus** by goats or leopards; that of **Pluto** by black horses. The chariot of the Greek war-god **Ares** is also horse-drawn, as are the chariots of many battle-heroes.

Chariot symbolism survives in the seventh card of the Major Arcana of the **Tarot** – the Chariot. It portrays (in the Rider-Waite version) a spear-carrying prince erect in his chariot. He holds no reins: the chariot is drawn not by horses but by two **sphinxes**: a variation introduced by the French occultist Eliphas Lévi (1810–75) so as to imply the charioteer was one who has answered the riddle of the Sphinx and thus triumphed on all planes of human endeavour – physical, emotional, mental and spiritual.

When in 1968 Erich von Daniken published his bestseller, *Chariots of the Gods*, the choice of title was astute, though his theory of alien intervention in human affairs is dubious.

CHARLEMAGNE (AD 742–814) (*See* **ARTHURIAN MYTH, SLEEPING EMPEROR**)
The reign of this Merovingian king of the Franks (son of Pepin the Short, grandson of Charles Martel) was so memorable that not only did he gain the title of Charlemagne ('Charles the Great') but after his death he was elevated to mythic status in European folklore. Like King Arthur and the emperor Frederick **Barbarossa** it is said of Charlemagne that he is not dead but sleeps with his knights under a mountain, awaiting recall in time of need. Even in his own lifetime his mythic status was such that few armies dared face him.

CHARMS (*See* **AMULETS, MAGIC, SPELLS, TALISMAN**)
In magical belief a charm consists of any object believed to be charged with power so as to gain a desired end or ward off evil. Yet whereas an amulet is said to work solely as a shield against evil, a charm is said to exercise direct influence against an animal or another person. All over the world since early times folk have used charms to gain success in love, hunting or business; to prevent theft of property, or wife or husband from straying. Some love-charms are aphrodisiacs, made to be eaten or drunk; others are written down and hidden in places where the desired one may sit or sleep. In India, a neglected woman might prepare a love-potion with 'salve, sweet wood, and spikenard', while a languishing man might seek the favour of the beloved by reciting a spell from the Atharva-veda (i:34):

> Honey be mine at the tip of my tongue,
> May sweetness of honey pervade my speech,
> So that my love may come under my spell –
> So that my lady may yield to my will.[1]

So too in India warriors were charmed against spells, cattle and sheep against wild beasts, houses against ghosts. Throughout pagan Europe **iron** was used as a charm against **fairies**, **witches** and other dark powers. In Africa, charms remain widespread, verses from the Koran often being used. '*Nkondi*' is the Kikongo word for a charm returning stolen property: *kapiangu* is a charm that in Zaïre is said to pursue thieves until they drop dead.

In human terms, charm is a suspect quality, often associated with psychological manipulation, or with a person of superficial attraction but no real depth. In this it is cognate with **glamour** in its original sense: the spell-binding magic of illusion practised by the **fairy**-race whereby rags may seem riches, a dirty cave a sumptuous palace, an old hag a lovely young woman. The victim is charmed into seeing what does not exist.

1. Quoted in *Indian Myth and Legend*, Donald A. Mackenzie, Gresham, London, 1910, p.86.

CHARON (*See* **CERBERUS, GREEK MYTH, HADES, UNDERWORLD**)
Son of Erebus, in Greek myth the ferryman who conveyed the souls of the dead over the River Styx into the underworld. He was perceived as an old man of squalid appearance. A coin was put in the mouths of the dead to meet his fee for the crossing.

CHARYBDIS (*See* **CLASHING ROCKS**)

CHASTITY

The self-denial of sexual relationship in any form so as to concentrate the bodily energies toward the attainment of higher goals, real or imagined, is a common theme in many **religions**. Chastity is typically required of monks and nuns in various sects of prominent world religions. The Roman Christian Church demands chastity of its priests (though only since medieval times) – yet it remains unclear if this arose through rejection of sexuality *per se* or from male fear of female influence – understandable in a religion which has downgraded Woman for 2,000 years. The demand for lifelong chastity is not commonly regarded as healthy. The *parfaits*, 'perfected ones' of the **Cathar** 'heresy' in southern Europe (eleventh–thirteenth centuries) embraced chastity, but only after they had already lived in the world and raised families. In this they agreed with Indian **Brahmans** and the rabbis of Israel: there is no good reason to reject the world before experiencing it, and those who do so are not necessarily the best teachers for others. Yet the Western flight from former matriarchal or **pagan** religions in favour of the new patriarchy that created our modern scientific and rational world made chastity a main plank of its enforced demand: elevating virgin birth and the asexuality of **Christ** as the epitome of right behaviour. **Gnostic** gospels insisting that Christ married the Magdalene were ruthlessly suppressed as unfit in a war to win over brutal, sexual humanity to higher standards.

Nor has this manipulation of human nature offered any understanding as to the higher value of chastity: i.e., not in terms of sexual conduct, but as the epitome of a state of mind leading to clear thought and individual decision as a source of common social, intellectual and spiritual growth.

CHERUBIM (*See* ANGELS)

CHILDREN (*See* CHANGELINGS, MOSES, TALIESIN, WONDER-CHILD)

Children are the hope of the future, epitome of innocence and simplicity. The mythic role of miraculous children is described elsewhere: here it is enough to state the obvious, that the child is proof of rebirth, himself or herself growing to sexual maturity to repeat the same proof in terms of a new generation. The infant **Christ** is born in a manger; a symbolic scene affecting millions of Christians every year. The Welsh boy Gwion is reborn as **Taliesin**, who as an infant confounds his superiors. The mystery of our childhood is that we remember so little of it.

CHILDREN OF DON (*See MABINOGION*)

CHILDREN OF LLŶR (*See MABINOGION*)

CHILEAN FAUNA (*See* FABULOUS BEASTS)

Borges mentions the work of the Chilean author Julio Vicuña Cifuentes, in whose *Myths and Superstitions* appear beings as fantastic as any invented elsewhere. Chief among these is the Alicanto, a night-bird unable to fly due to its taste for gold and silver – when gorged it can scarcely crawl. Yet any prospector following an Alicanto in search of hidden ore must be careful: if the bird suspects it is followed it dims the gold or silver light shining from its wings, and may lure its pursuer over a cliff.

The Chonchón is equally odd. Shaped like a human head, its huge ears serve as wings when it flies on moonless nights. Possessing magic powers, it is dangerous and should never be molested. The Huallepén is a fierce yet shy amphibian with head of a calf and body of a sheep. Able to mate with cows or ewes, its progeny are known by their twisted hooves and muzzles. A pregnant woman seeing or hearing a Huallepén, or dreaming of it three nights in a row, gives birth to a deformed child.

CHIMERA (*See* BELLEROPHON, FABULOUS BEASTS, GREEK MYTH)

From a Greek noun meaning 'she-goat', this fantastic creature first appears in Book 6 of *The Odyssey*. **Homer** tells us it had a **lion**'s head, **goat**'s body, and **serpent**'s tail, that it vomited fire, and that it was slain by Bellerophon. **Hesiod** says it had three heads, as in the Arezzo bronze (fifth century BC). At Carchemish, a chimera was found carved on the walls of a Hittite temple. **Graves** considers that, as with other composite beasts (**basilisk**, **sphinx**, **unicorn**), it was initially a calendrical symbol, each part representing a different season in the sacred year.[1] Certainly its reality was always doubted – the Greek biographer Plutarch (born *c*.AD 40) suggested that 'Chimera' was the name of a pirate captain, the figureheads of his ships being a lion, goat and a snake. In the sixteenth century, Rabelais asks: 'Can a chimera, swinging in the void, swallow second intentions?'[2] Today the sole trace of its existence attests to its impossibility: the adjective 'chimerical' refers to vain, fanciful or foolish notions.

1. *The Greek Myths*, Robert Graves, Penguin, London, 1960.
2. Quoted in *The Book of Imaginary Beings*, Jorge Luis Borges, Penguin, London, 1974.

CHINESE DRAGON (*See* CHINESE MYTH, DRAGON)

CHINESE MYTH (*See* CONCORDANCE)

In one form or another the culture of imperial China endured from the era of the feudal Hia (2205–1766 BC), Shang (1766–1122 BC) and Chou dynasties (1122–255 BC) until 1912. An old **curse**: 'May you live in interesting times', suggests how deeply the long, turbulent history of the land bred a desire for stability, sought as much in the imperial divinity as in the teachings of and legends accruing round three major religions: **Buddhism**, **Taoism** and **Confucianism**.

None of these was initially a repository of supernatural myth, instead offering pragmatic moral and philosophical codes, but myth developed about them none the less, especially given the prevailing **animism** and **ancestor-worship** of the great mass of the rural populations.

Confucius (551–479 BC) taught ethical behaviour based on veneration of the ancestors, but the development of the imperial cult of his teachings began only in the second century BC. The founder of Taoism, **Lao Tsu** (*b*. 604 BC, author of the celebrated *Tao Te Ching*, was popularly deified, though his teachings ('The Tao that can be told is not the eternal Tao') likewise invoked no supernaturalism. Popular Taoism was founded in the second century AD by Chang Tao-Ling, deified in the eighth century. Buddhism, the most popular though despised of pre-revolutionary Chinese religions, reached China in the first century AD. These religions, plus the animism of the rural populace, dictated the forms of Chinese myth, which may be divided into official and popular.

Chinese cosmogony tells us that the Ten Thousand Beings are born through the ever-shifting interplay of two eternal principles, *yin* and *yang*. The oracular *I Ching* ('Book of Changes'), dating from *c*.1150 BC and later elaborated by Confucius, remains the most profound exposition of yin-yang **dualism**, and perhaps the most important exposition of Chinese philosophy. Yet this belongs to a study of philosophy rather than myth.

The official imperial Chinese pantheon is a vast bureaucracy in which heaven reflects earthly values, not vice versa. Function matters more than individuality. Even the supreme god (supervising a **heaven** of nine or thrity-three administrative levels) has no name, only a title: The August Personage of Jade. This father-god (or managing director) created humanity by modelling us in clay. It is he who tells the four celestial Dragon-Kings when to distribute rain to each given region of the land. Yet he is only Number Two in the hierarchy, below the Celestial Master of the First Origin – the title claimed for Lao Tsu by some. Below him waits the Heavenly Master of the Dawn of Jade of the Golden Door, who will one day succeed him: the third part of the trinity.

Women play little part in this hierarchy. The August Personage has a wife and daughters, but no sons – sons tend to plot to seize the throne. His wife, the Queen Mother Wang, presides at banquets at which guests are served the Peaches of Immortality. Though old, she appears beautiful and youthful beside her wispily bearded, middle-aged husband.

Popular Chinese myth was always more vital. Elemental gods and goddesses – **sun, moon, rain, thunder, fire, wind** – remained the primary concern of most folk in the many different provinces during frequent invasions and turmoil. The sun, they say, at first took the form of a **cockerel**, but by following the Way he gained a human face. The moon-festival, at the full moon of the autumn equinox, was devoted to women and children. The moon-goddess, Ch'ang-o, was married to I, the Excellent Archer, who shot down nine suns. She drank his drug of immortality and fled to the moon, where the **hare** protected her by fighting I as he came after her. He abandoned his desire for revenge: she remained in the moon. Also renowned was the thunder-god, Lei-Kung, repulsively ugly, his blue body winged and clawed, who punished undetected criminals, often with human aid. Gods of happiness were also honoured, especially Shou-hsing, the god of long life, identified with the star Canopus. Shown as bald and leaning on a stick, he decides the date of everyone's death, but may change this date if he pleases.

Yet most respected were the Dragon-Kings – not the celestial four, but elemental fertility deities presiding over every stream, river or well. In time this preoccupation with fertility and harmonious ordering of the land led to the the art of geomacy, or *feng shui*, 'wind and water'. Basic to this art is a belief that land (like human body) has nerve-points (acupuncture), and that fertility and social harmony arise by learning to harness opposed natural principles: light and dark (yang and yin) as manifest in nature. *Lung mei* ('dragon currents') were believed to course the land, either yin or yang, negative or positive, the former a white tiger, the latter a blue dragon. Nineteenth-century European businessmen were amazed to hear they could not site factories as economic sense dictated: railway tunnels could not be put through 'dragon hills'. The Chinese were equally amazed when Europeans sited a port at Hong Kong – geomantically a disaster area.

The Chinese **dragon** is very different to its greedy Western counterpart. One of the four magic animals (the others are the **unicorn**, **phoenix** and **tortoise**), it is divine, riding the wind and reaching heaven. It is said a dragon crawled out of the Yellow River with the alphabet inscribed on its back. With horns, claws and scales, this expansive beast remains at the centre of New Year festivals in Chinese communities everywhere.

Chinese myth did not end with the overthrow of the emperors. Mao-Tse

Tung took power in 1949 in the name of the People's Republic . . . yet later in his life relied ever more upon the myth of his own personality cult to maintain control. Thus supposedly he swam twenty miles of the Yangtse River at the age of seventy.

CHRIST, JESUS (*See* BIBLE, CHRISTIANITY, MESSIAH)

CHRISTIANITY (*See* CONCORDANCE)

One of the world's four major **religions** (**Buddhism**, **Hinduism**, and **Islam** the others), Christianity was a primary influence on European culture after the collapse of the Roman Empire, and later globally militant via missionary activity. Though now divided into many churches that vary in interpretation of the original teachings as given in the New Testament, Christians generally hold that Jesus Christ (*c*.4 BC – *c*.AD 29) was the true Son of God, born to redeem humanity's sinful nature (*see* **Original Sin**) by his suffering and death.

Originating in Roman-occupied Palestine during the reign of the Emperor Tiberius (AD 14–37), Christianity's source myths remain as ambiguous as the true nature and purpose of Christ himself. For ages there had existed in Israel the hope of a prophet, the **Messiah**, who would come to deliver the Jews from oppression. It is said the historical Jesus of Nazareth claimed this role as he claimed the title 'Christ'. 'Jesus' may derive from Yeshua, a common Aramaic name; but 'Christ' is the Greek *christos* (the 'Anointed One') referring to the unction of a **Mystery** initiate. The Hebrew word *māshīahh* (messiah) refers to the unction of a Jewish king or high priest.

Thus, to his early followers, Jesus the Christ or Messiah embraced the offices of priest, king and prophet. Was the original Jesus a prophet, an **Essene** or militant Zealot, seeking to free Judaea from Roman rule? The Gospels certainly imply Zealot connections. 'Simon Zelotes' is Simon the Zealot; 'Iscariot' may refer to the sicarius, a dagger used by Zealots for assassination. 'Nazarene' may refer not to a village but to a militant Judaic sect, the Nazareans. And he was crucified as 'King of the Jews'.[1]

If this is so, the real Jesus is not as given in the New Testament's synoptic gospels (Matthew, Mark, Luke and John) – all written years after the events described. The supernaturalism (virgin birth, Star of Bethlehem, miracles, resurrection, ascension) was seemingly invented by Saul of Tarsus, the man who persecuted the early Christians then, as a convert, rewrote and sold their ideals to a Gentile (non-Jew) audience. Saul, later St Paul, was both a Jew and Roman citizen – and a man who remains as mysterious as Christ.

In time, Paul's sales campaign created a theocracy: the Roman Catholic Church. To spread the new faith, he promoted Christ in terms of popular myths already well known to Graeco-Roman society. It is said he was married, yet his fear or mistrust of women is plain. At any rate, the misogynistic assertions in the Epistles attributed to his name have deeply influenced two millennia of Christian patriarchy. His version of the new religion described how, born to a virgin (like **Horus** to **Isis**?), Jesus escapes death at the hands of a tyrant (Herod = **Set**?). Rejecting Satan's temptations (as Buddha rejects **Mara**), he begins to teach aged thirty. Choosing twelve Apostles, he embraces 'thieves and sinners'. He performs miracles, changing water into wine (like **Dionysus**?), walking on water and raising the dead. Like other died-and-reborn gods (**Adonis**, **Attis**, **Mithra**), he is slain, yet after three days (dark of the **moon**) is reborn in the flesh. **Resurrected**, he ascends to **heaven**. Preaching love, he also comes with a sword. He promises eternal salvation and eternal retribution, meaning in his name the Church promised all things to all men. Following Paul, Christianity borrowed from the older cults it dispossessed. Saturday is the Jewish holy day, whereas Sunday as the Christian holy day was borrowed from the popular Roman cult of Mithras; so too 25 December as Christ's birthday and the rite of Communion. The feast of **Easter** (from a pagan fertility-goddess, Oestre) was originally synchronised with the Jewish Passover. Only in the sixth century AD did Rome decree that Easter Day must fall on the Sunday between the fifteenth and twenty-first days of the moon in the first month of the Jewish lunar year.

At the Council of Nicaea (AD 325), it was declared heresy to assert Christ's mortality. Newly dominant, the Church began to flex its muscle. When the Roman Empire collapsed, the Church alone offered continuity. By then the historical Jesus was wholly lost in the Pauline myth expanded by Irenaeus, Tertullian and Augustine. Generations of martyrs had given the new religion a moral authority guaranteed more by their courage than by the original message (whatever it had been). The myth of Christ had prevailed, absorbing old beliefs into a new body of ideas with supernatural sanction. Hermits in the desert as much as Popes in the Vatican lent reality to the myth: all 'Christendom' (as the new European order knew itself) conspired to believe in the unifying ideal of Holy War against the 'infidel' when in 1095 the First Crusade was declared.

Meanwhile, a trade in relics supposedly connected with Christ or his saints developed. Pieces of the True Cross, the bones of saints and, most of all, the cup from which Christ supposedly drank at his Last Supper (the **Holy Grail**) became venerated, bringing cash from pilgrims to the monasteries or churches possessing them. Thus the twelfth-century tale of the Holy Grail, which was supposedly brought to Britain by **Joseph of Arimathea** and later became the core of the esoteric Christianity of **Arthurian** lore. The tale that Christ himself visited Britain still survives in **Blake**'s 'Jerusalem' (begun 1804): 'And did those feet in ancient time/Walk upon England's mountains green . . .'

Today, Christian myth persists in apocalyptic forms, not least in the USA where fundamentalists await the Rapture, the End Times, when they will leave the sinful world to be raised up into 'the middle of the air', where Jesus Christ himself will meet them and bear them away to heaven.

1. *The Armageddon Script*, Peter Lemesurier, Element Books, Shaftesbury, 1981.

CHUANG TSU (*c.*350 BC) (*See* **CHINESE MYTH, TAOISM**)
Author of a fanciful collection of tales bearing his name, this Chinese Taoist of the fourth century BC satirised serious philosophers and pedantic scholars with such brilliance that, along with the *Tao Te Ching* of *Lao Tsu* (sixth century BC), his work survives of early Taoist writings.

Famously he comments: 'I did not know whether I was Chuang Tsu dreaming I was butterfly, or a butterfly dreaming I was Chuang Tsu.' He also tells the tale of a sage out walking who sees a great tree that towers over all the rest, its branches broad enough to shelter a thousand horses. 'What kind of tree is this?' he asked himself. 'Its timber must be extraordinary.' But, looking up, he noted that the higher branches were too gnarled for use as floorboards or rafters. Further down, the trunk was too soft and pitted to make coffins. He licked a leaf: it left a burning taste in his mouth. The bark smelled so pungent he lost his appetite for three days. 'This tree is totally useless,' he exclaimed, 'which is why it has grown so big – it is exactly the kind of uselessness the holy man uses!'

CIBOLA (*See* AZTEC MYTH, EL DORADO, HOPI, LOST WORLDS)

The 'Seven Cities of Cibola' were legendary cities of wealth and splendour sought in North America by sixteenth-century Spanish *conquistadores*. While maybe related to Aztlan, the fabulous land of 'Seven Caves' from which the Aztecs had emigrated to Mexico, they were first reported by Alvar Nuñez Cabeza de Vaca. Shipwrecked off Florida in 1528, he wandered west into Mexico before in 1536 meeting fellow-Spaniards again. En route he had heard of Cibola: his tale led Antonio de Mendoza, Viceroy of New Spain, to send an expedition in 1539 to find these marvellous cities. Led by Esteban, a slave shipwrecked with de Vaca, a friar, Marcos de Niza, claimed to have seen the shining cities in the distance – a desert mirage? In 1540 a second expedition, led by Francisco Vásquez de Coronado, came to the villages of the **Hopi** people in present-day Arizona. Attacking them, the Spaniards were told the Hopi had awaited the return of the White Brother, Pahana, for centuries. However, there was no gold. Coronado searched as far as Kansas, but found nothing.

This legend is on a par with that of El Dorado, the Land of Gold that the Spaniards and others sought in the Orinoco region of South America – a myth that led Sir Walter Raleigh to the execution block in 1616.

CID CAMPEADOR (1040–99)

A Spanish warlord, historically legendary as El Cid, his real name was Ruy Diaz de Bivar, originally a Castilian noble and soldier of fortune, his title compounded of the Arabic *saiyid*, 'lord', and the Spanish *campeador*, meaning 'challenger' or 'champion'. He survives in European legend, as in the 1961 **Hollywood**-Italian movie *El Cid*, as the epitome of the noble liberator of his land, yet the truth (as so often) is otherwise. He began his career as a standard-bearer in the army of Sancho II of Castile. When in 1071 Sancho met his brother, Alfonso VI of Leon, for a final battle to decide which of them should retire to a monastery and which should rule both realms, Alfonso won the battle, but while his army rested after the fight, Ruy Diaz attacked and overwhelmed him. Alfonso escaped to Moorish Toledo: when in 1072 Sancho was murdered, Alfonso gained both thrones, and in 1081 banished Ruy Diaz from Castile. Taking service with the Moorish king of Saragossa, in 1083 the Cid led the Moslems to victory over the Christian king of Aragon, and in 1085 conquered the northern part of Moorish Valencia. As a mercenary available for hire, in subsequent years he overran Spain with his army of 7,000 chosen desperadoes, exacting tribute and ransom on his own account, playing one kingdom off against another. At length in 1094, having burned, slaughtered and plundered his way through Castile, he took the city of Valencia, and there ruled as an independent king until he died in 1099. Rapacious, greedy and boastful, the Cid was none the less brave, characterised by a code of rough yet generous chivalry ensuring his mythic survival as Spain's national hero from that day to this. The famous *Poem of the Cid*, the first great epic in the Spanish tongue, was modelled on the French *chanson de geste*, being written some forty years after his death. Yet again, the discrepancy between history and legend: what in fact happened versus whatever we prefer to believe.

CINDERELLA (*See* FAIRY-TALES, PERRAULT)

The tale of the beautiful youngest daughter with sneering stepsisters, a jealous stepmother and cruel or absent father, who with supernatural aid attends a masked ball and wins the love of a prince, is found in Europe alone in over five hundred versions. The earliest known version comes from China in the ninth century. The pantomime version popular today, complete with Fairy Godmother, pumpkin turning into a coach and the glass slipper, originates in 'Cendrillon', in Charles Perrault's 1697 collection, *Contes de ma Mère l'Oye* (English translation 1729: *Tales of Mother Goose*).

Perrault's Fairy Godmother is as untypical of the theme as his choice of a glass slipper as the test of recognition. Usually the helper is the girl's dead mother or a supernatural animal; likewise the test by which the prince recognises her is generally a golden or silver slipper, or a **ring**.

The pumpkin that turns into a coach is likewise Perrault's invention.

CINEMA (*See* COCTEAU, DEAN, DISNEY, GARBO, HOLLYWOOD, MONROE)

CIRCE (*See* GREEK MYTH, PIG)

In **Homer**'s *Odyssey* this daughter of the Greek sun-god **Helios** lived on the fabulous isle of Aeaea, though only after she had poisoned her husband, king of the Sarmatians. Known for her evil **spells**, it was the bad luck of Ulysses and his companions to land on her enchanted isle. All his men were turned into swine by her enchantment: he alone escaped, having eaten a herb given him by the god **Hermes**. Though forcing her to restore them to human form, he was not so immune to her charms that he failed to spend a year with her, meanwhile forgetting his wife and patriotic duty. Yet it was by her advice that he learned how to escape the **sirens**, and to navigate the deadly water between the **clashing rocks**, Scylla and Charybdis – the Strait of Messina.

Aeaea means 'wailing' (an onomatopoeic term). **Trees** sacred to Circe were **alder** and **willow**. Later, after **Jason** and the Argonauts came to her isle, it is said she was slain by the hero Telemachus. She is defined by some as a **moon-goddess** and by others as a goddess of carnal love.

CIRCLE (*See* RING, WHEEL)

This universal symbol (evident shape of **moon** and **sun**, less evidently the shape of the earth) implies totality, perfection, the unity of the Self. It is said: 'God is a circle whose centre is everywhere and circumference nowhere.' The eastern meditational designs called mandalas are usually circular designs within an inscribed square, possessing a centre, symmetry, cardinal points and the harmonious balance of all elements. **Megalithic** stone circles (though more often elliptical than circular) mark a cosmic round as does the face of a clock: what has gone round before comes round again. The heavens wheel round the earth, human life wheels from birth to death, and then – claim **Buddhists** and **Hindus** – wheels round again, if we cannot overcome the cycle of rebirth. The circular Native American tipi and Asian yurt are sacred dwellings: in Amerindian lore the circle is the Great Hoop of Life. In **Norse myth** the **world-serpent**, or serpent of Midgard, encircles the world, biting its own tail. The circle is also the wheel, essential basis of all modern land transport-systems: the wheels are the third rank of **angels** after the Seraphim and Cherubim.

The circle is both reassuring and tyrannical. As an image of defence it implies unbreachable walls: conversely it implies fixed thinking. Ptolemaic astronomy saw the universe in terms of fixed spheres (circles); the astronomer Johannes Kepler (1571–1630) long denied evidence of elliptical planetary orbits, desiring to believe circular motion perfect, therefore necessary. In time he acknowledged scientific truth even as contemporaries were obsessed with how to square the circle: i.e., how to harmonise worldly truths (the square) with celestial philosophy (the circle). This search, like that for the

Philosopher's Stone, remains as mythic now as ever it was.

CIRCUMCISION (*See* BLOOD, CASTRATION, DOGON, INITIATION, SACRIFICE)

The rite of male circumcision (removal of the foreskin of the penis) is practised in many cultures. Among Christians, it occurs (if at all) soon after birth: its purpose today is unclear, being performed too early to possess initiatory meaning. It may be but a simple inheritance of the rite practised by the Jews on the eighth day after birth: perhaps initially as sacrifice to **Yahweh**. The explanation that it affords sanitary protection against disease remains unsatisfactory, though plausible in hot lands.

Carried out at puberty as a rite of initiation into manhood, it was practised by the early Egyptians; later by the **Aztecs** and Bantu: it survives in cultures such as those of the **Masai** of Kenya and Australian **Aborigines**, the purpose being literally to 'cut' the boy away from his mother.

The Masai rite at one time required the candidate to sit with pellets of goat-excreta balanced on his knees and on the back of his hands. If he trembled so badly during the operation that any of the pellets fell, he was killed. Those surviving such a rite were unlikely to return to mother.

When a boy of the Murngin tribe in Australia was to be circumcised, the old men would say: 'Great Father **Snake** smells your foreskin, he is calling for it.' He would run to his mother. When the men came for him, the women pretended to fight for him. Amid fearful ceremony he was put on a platform made of the bodies of the men so that his blood would not touch the ground. The operation over, he was congratulated for not crying out. In New Guinea it was said the boy-child had been swallowed by a monster who had then to be persuaded to disgorge him. Following the act, the youth stayed in seclusion 'in the monster's belly' – a long hut, far from the sight of women. When brought back 'from the dead' as an initiated man, he kept his eyes tightly shut, or sealed with a plaster of chalk, until slowly awakening, reborn.

Among the Murngin, the second operation of subincision was performed a year after circumcision – the underside of the penis being slit open: this opening being called the 'penis-womb': a symbolic male vagina.[1]

Such operations were also found among devotees of **moon-goddesses** like **Astarte** and **Cybele** in Asia Minor in Classical times. In these instances the purpose was not so much initiation into the male cult, but a form of mitigated or lesser castration in service of the dark face of the goddess.

Where performed by poor hunter-gatherer societies, this harsh rite is not without logic. Less excusable is its Christian survival, as performed on new-born children. The corresponding rite of clitorectomy – excision of the female clitoris – has no religious or even initiatory purpose. This practice remains widespread in parts of Africa.

1. *The Hero with a Thousand Faces*, Joseph Campbell, Abacus, London, 1975, pp.118–19, 129.

CLARKE, ARTHUR C. (1917–) (*See* HOLLYWOOD, SCIENCE FICTION)

Somerset-born, resident of Sri Lanka since 1956, this English author has created some of the best-known myths of the future, including the novels *Childhood's End* (1953), *The City and the Stars* (1956) and a short story, *The Sentinel* (1951) which led to the movie *2001: A Space Odyssey* (1968). This tells of the discovery on the **moon** of an enigmatic monolith left millennia ago by an advanced alien race to stimulate human evolution. Discovered, it departs to a pre-programmed orbit round the planet **Jupiter**. The astronauts sent after it die when Hal, the on-board computer of the spaceship *Discovery*, malfunctions. One of the crew, Bowman, escapes in a 'pod' (space lifeboat) to follow the monolith through the 'Stargate' to a surreal extraterrestrial world. As the tale ends, he is reborn to hover above the earth as a cosmic infant – the hope of the future: implicitly a god: a **Christ** or **Horus**.

Trained as physicist and mathematician, Clarke's interest in religious myth was always manifest. *Childhood's End* describes the transformation of humanity from an earthbound species into a godlike group mind. *The City and the Stars* tells how in a sterile future culture is born a 'Unique', Alvin, who discovers an alien spaceship left millennia ago. Visiting the stars, he gains the cosmic perspective needed to liberate his ailing culture.

Clarke elevates technology, yet typically it proves futile before godlike races from other star-systems. Like **Bellerophon** riding **Pegasus** to **Olympus**, his heroes leave the familiar earth in their space-**chariots** only to learn that humanity is still in the larval stage of cosmic growth.

CLASHING ROCKS (*See* GREEK MYTH, JASON)

The motif of the clashing rocks (Symplegades), between which only heroic sailors like Jason safely pass, is found the world over. In Greek myth they were named Scylla and Charybdis, and associated with two rocky isles in the Sicilian sea. A lovely nymph, Scylla was changed by **Circe** into a monster lurking in an undersea cave, from which her six heads would leap to snap mariners from the deck of passing ships. Charybdis, daughter of **Poseidon**, was turned by **Zeus** into a whirlpool that swallowed ships.

In **Navaho** myth (Arizona, far from any sea) **Spider** Woman warns the Twin Heroes of a similar obstacle. The clashing rocks represent psychic opposites which travellers on the Path of Life must overcome and integrate.

CLEOPATRA (68–30 BC) (*See* HELEN OF TROY)

This queen of Egypt, epitome of the *femme fatale*, was the third daughter of King Ptolemy Auletes. At his death (51 BC), with Ptolemy her brother she was made co-ruler. Denied, she intrigued to regain her throne. In 48 BC Julius Caesar arrived in Alexandria: a year later she bore him a son and followed him to Rome, where he was killed by assassins. Back in Egypt she aided the Roman triumvirs (Augustus, Lepidus, Mark Antony), gaining such ascendancy over the latter that he abandoned the Roman cause for her. She bore him three children before she and her forces fled his sea-battle at Actium in 31 BC against Augustus. Spreading rumour of her death, she learned how the besotted Antony had stabbed himself only when he was brought to die in her arms. Failing to seduce Augustus, who meant to take her captive to Rome, she killed herself with the bite of an asp. Popularly thought to be Egyptian, she was in fact Macedonian: thus as foreign as the Romans. Yet the myth of Cleopatra, queen of the Nile, whose beauty infatuated great men, persists.

Cleopatra's Needles – two obelisks of red syrenite brought in 14 BC from Heliopolis to Alexandria – had nothing to do with Cleopatra. In 1878 one was removed by Sir Erasmus Wilson to the Thames Embankment in London, the other was later erected in Central Park, New York.

COATLICUE (*See* AZTEC MYTH, SERPENT)

This Aztec earth-goddess, the 'serpent-lady', bore **Huitzilopochtli**, sun-god and god of war. Known for her piety and already the mother of 400 sons and a daughter, one day, as she prayed, a crown of feathers fell on her from heaven. She put it in her bosom and afterwards it could not be found, but soon it was seen that she was pregnant. Her daughter, claiming that she was dishonoured, urged the 400 sons (Centzon-Huitznahuas) to kill her, but Huitzilopochtli emerged armed from her womb and slew them all.

Another version says she had many daughters, one of whom, Coyolxauhqui ('Golden Bells'), had tried to warn her, rushing ahead of the sons as they came to kill her. Killing her first, Huitzilopochtli later learned how good she was. Decapitating her, he threw her head into the sky, where it became the **moon**, and where nightly the golden bells of her cheeks still gleam.

This myth may be an Aztec justification for their ferocious love of human **sacrifice**. Coatlicue was even more hideous than other Aztec deities, with skirt of writhing snakes, necklace of human hearts, clawed feet and hands and diet of human corpses – a taste shared by Huitzilopochtli. Like **Kali** in India and the Celtic **Cerridwen**, she was the devouring mother; both womb and grave, but also the fertility of the soil. As such, nobody could hope to own her (Aztec land was held in common), or cultivate any part of her in perpetuity – after two or three years her fields had to be left fallow.

COCK (*See* BIRDS)

Pre-eminently a symbol of strutting masculinity ('cock' remains among the most commonly used slang terms for the penis), the cockerel is also a solar bird in many cultures, its raucous cry greeting the new day and the rising of the **sun**. To the Chinese the golden-plumed Heavenly Cock is a lordly bird that crows thrice daily – at sunrise, noon and sunset. Also known as the Bird of Dawn, this magnificent three-legged fowl perches in the gigantic fu-sang **tree**, and is the father of all earthly roosters. In some Chinese initiation ceremonies a white cock was killed, signifying the death of the old life and birth of the new; also in China the red cock was the original form of the sun, while in its aggression it was a war symbol. To **Christians**, in its vigilance the golden, solar cock is the weathervane on the steeple of the church, turning in all directions on the watch for evil during the dark hours: it also symbolises the rising of Christ in the east. Yet the black cock symbolises the Christian **Devil**, while **Buddhists** associate the cock with carnal pride. In **Norse myth** it is an **underworld** bird whose crowing awakens the heroes of Valhalla for the final battle, **Ragnorak**.

Throughout Europe the cock is also a **corn**-spirit. In Austria children were told not to stray in the corn-fields, or the corn-cock would peck out their eyes: in North Germany it was said that 'the cock sits in the last sheaf.' Cutting the last corn the reapers would cry: 'Now we will chase out the Cock.' From Poland to Picardy to Transylvania a cock was buried up to its neck and then decapitated with a sickle as the last sheaf was cut; or bound into the last sheaf and killed, its flesh being thrown away, its feathers mixed with the seed-corn of the last sheaf, to be sown in spring.

In British and **Celtic** folklore it is the bird whose crowing dispels night-terrors. Should a dead lover visit his woman's bed by night, his ghost is dismissed by the cock crowing at the break of day.[1]

1. *The Golden Bough*, Sir James Frazer, Macmillan, London, 1963 (1922).

COCKATRICE (*See* BASILISK, FABULOUS BEASTS)

COCTEAU, JEAN (1889–1963) (*See* FAIRY-TALES, ORPHEUS)

French poet, novelist, film director, painter and occultist, Cocteau grew up in Paris in a prominent family. Established in bohemian artistic circles by

1908, he was associated with Proust, Gide, Debussy and Diaghilev, and later with the prodigy Raymond Radiguet (1901–23). His pain at Radiguet's death led to opium addiction. This, his homosexuality and other eccentricities led many to dismiss him. Yet a play, *Orphée* (1926) and a novel, *Les Enfants terribles* (1929) established him as an artist of deep and shocking mythic power. His first film, *Le Sang d'un Poète* (1930) and his play, *La Machine infernale* (1934), increased his reputation. Two later films, *La Belle et la Bête* (1946: based on the fairy-tale 'Beauty and the Beast'), and *Orphée* (1950), put him beyond reach of criticism based on his eccentricity alone, as did his work as a graphic artist. Already legendary, during his later years he painted frescoes in a number of churches: his self-admitted desire for recognition by now resulting in membership of the Académie Française (1955), and an honorary degree from Oxford (1956).

La Belle et la Bête remains perhaps the most deeply moving, frightening and enchantingly surreal of all modern filmed versions of medieval fairy-tales, its dream-logic surpassed only by *Orphée*: a modern retelling of how the poet, his love seized by the goddess of death and her black-leathered motor-cycle agents, follows her through mirrors into an **underworld** as odd as anything depicted by **Salvador Dali** or imagined by **Homer**.

Even more remarkably, Cocteau has been posthumously associated with a rumoured organisation, the Prieuré de Sion, said to have existed since the eighth-century demise of Europe's Merovingian dynasty in order to maintain the bloodline of **Christ**, supposedly the founder of that dynasty. He is said to have been Grand Master of this Order, following (among others) Leonardo da Vinci, Robert Fludd, Isaac Newton, Victor Hugo and Claude Debussy. If this be but myth, we cannot tell.[1]

1. *The Holy Blood and the Holy Grail*, Michael Baigent, Richard Leigh and Henry Lincoln, Corgi, London, 1983.

COLERIDGE, SAMUEL TAYLOR (1772–1834) (*See* **SHELLEY**)
The ninth son of a Devon vicar, in 1790 this English visionary caught rheumatic fever. Given opium to alleviate his 'seas of pain', like **Cocteau** he became an addict. Embracing the difficult life of freelance poet, in 1797–8 he wrote the works for which he is chiefly remembered: 'The Rime of the Ancient Mariner', and 'Kubla Khan'. The former, among the most popular narrative poems in English, tells of the fate befalling a sailor who shoots an albatross (a sacred **bird**): he alone of the crew survives to return home, a cursed man, his 'glittering eye' avoided by all. As for 'Kubla Khan', the tale of its composition is as famous as the surviving fragment of the poem itself.

It is said that Coleridge awoke from an opium dream with the entire poem, some three hundred lines, vivid in his mind. But after writing some forty lines, he was called out on business by the infamous visitor from Porlock. He returned an hour later only to find that 'with the exception of some eight or ten scattered lines and images, all the rest had passed away.'

Is this true? Though the opening lines: ('In Xanadu did Kubla Khan/A stately pleasure-dome decree') seem the product of pure fancy, those that follow show every evidence of sure conscious work. Maybe he simply could not carry the vision further. Over the next twenty years he sank ever deeper into addiction. Only towards the end of his life did he recover his reputation.

1. *Samuel Taylor Coleridge: A Bondage of Opium*, Molly Lefebure, Quartet, London, 1977.

COLLECTIVE UNCONSCIOUS (*See* ARCHETYPES, DREAMS, JUNG)

Why do myths affect us so deeply? Why are they so often similar or the same from one culture or continent to another? The Swiss psychologist C.G. Jung (1875–1961) proposed (from his discovery in dreams and myths of recurrent patterns suggesting the existence of unconscious archetypes) the existence of the collective unconscious: a substratum of every individual human psyche, underlying the conscious ego yet common to all. From it wells the same archetypal symbols whatever the culture or historical era. We experience these symbols personally, yet they derive from the collective experience of the entire human species. Thus in **fairy-tales** the **hero**, his **quest**, the wicked **witch**, the **giant** or ogre, the supernatural **helper**, the **three** wishes and a multitude of other basic themes recur time and again as *spontaneous* productions of this collective substratum of mind.

Unlike the personal unconscious, it does not owe its existence to personal experience. Its contents have never been in consciousness, but owe their existence exclusively to heredity.

Jung regarded the collective unconscious as common to all humanity but also as differentiated between racial types. His disciple Marie-Louise von Franz thought that below the personal unconscious is a 'group unconscious' (families, tribes); below that, a 'common unconscious' of national units and, below that, 'the sum of those universal psychic archetypal structures that we share with the whole of mankind'.[1]

More simply, as John Donne put it: 'No man is an island.'

1. Quoted in *The Presence of the Past*, Rupert Sheldrake, Vintage, 1989, p.253; *Essays on a Science of Mythology*, C.G. Jung and C. Kerényi, Harper & Row, New York, 1963, p.74.

COLOURS

The effect of different colours on our perception and judgement is evident yet often confusing and unfortunate, as in the continuing common prejudice held by people of one skin-colour against those of another. Yet apart from such superficial differentiations, all primary and secondary colours carry specific symbolic or **archetypal** meanings which tend to be similar whatever the culture. Such meanings are usually derived from collective experience.

Thus black and white in the first place refer to night and day, dark and light, passive and active, negative and positive, and also bear secondary associations. The blackness of night is dangerous, therefore black often symbolises evil (black **cock**, black art, **black magic**, death and hell), or that which is hidden, obscure, underground (**black virgin**; the chthonic or dark aspect of the great mother).

At the other end of the scale, white symbolises light, love, chastity, holiness, transcendence or pure consciousness, as in the 'white light' to which the soul is taught to aspire in the *Bardo Thodol* (**Tibetan Book of the Dead**). In the **Qabalistic** Tree of Life, the colours of Kether, the primal source of manifestation, are pure brilliance, shading down to white flecked with gold. White is the colour of the wedding-gown, signifying death of the old life and birth of the new: likewise white burial-shrouds symbolise passage from one world to another. In **China** the 'white tiger' represents the yin or negative '**dragon** current'. The white flag denotes truce; the white feather, cowardice.

Neither black nor white are colours, but absence of colour. Of the colours of the spectrum in between these extremes, those reflecting light (orange, yellow, red) are active and positive: those absorbing it (violet, blue) are passive and negative; while green, the colour of growing things, synthesises the interaction of the others. Taking them alphabetically:

Blue is the sea and the sky, the colour of the Great Deep and of the Great Mother, Queen of Heaven (**Hera, Isis, Juno, Virgin Mary**). It is also the colour of **sky-gods** (**Zeus, Jupiter**); of the Celtic **bard**, and of the Chinese Azure Dragon. It implies truth, wisdom, loyalty, piety, peace, meditation, coolness ('blue with cold'), also conservatism and aristocracy, as in 'blue blood' or the symbolic colour of Britain's Conservative Party.

Brown is the colour of the earth, of renunciation and penitence.

Gold is the divine splendour of the sun, **immortality**; the colour of **corn-gods** and goddesses and the ripened harvest. In alchemy, to turn lead into gold is to transmute the consciousness: a gold medal at the Olympic Games or other sporting competitions is the prize of the most excellent competitors.

Green is springtime, the abundance of nature, resurrection and renewal of life. Green turning to gold is the young **corn-god**; the **Green Knight** is decapitated but always reborn. Green is the colour of Ireland, of the **Celtic** muse-goddess Brigit, and is the name given to political activists, 'the Greens', who favour ecological awareness. Yet to be 'green' is also to be inexperienced or undeveloped, or to be 'green with envy'.

Grey is neutral: dust and ashes; to be 'grey with pain'; or old, as in 'greybeard'; or an unseen power behind the throne (*éminence grise*).

Orange is the leaping flame; the rising sun; luxury, or (in China and Japan) love and happiness, or the colour of the robes of **Buddhist** monks.

Purple symbolises ('imperial purple') power, pomp and pride; the colour of the Roman **sky-god Jupiter**.

Red is fire, the sun and all war-gods: thus the colour of **Mars**, the masculine principle: also as activity, excitement and sexual ardour it is the colour of Priapus. The colour of **blood**, it signifies bloodlust and fury ('red with rage'). It also means embarrassment, as in 'to blush'. Saints' days are written in red, thus 'red-letter days'. It is the colour of martyrdom and the shedding or sacrifice of blood.

Silver is the **moon**, the feminine principle, **virginity**. Linked to gold, it is one of two aspects of the same cosmic reality. The value-relationship between silver and gold (approx. 13:1; as months in the solar year) offered the ancient world the basis of stable currencies.

Violet, as in the amethyst, is sobriety, sanctity, sorrow, old age, nostalgia, mourning and grief. It is the colour of St Mary Magdalene.

SAINT COLUMBA (521–97) (*See* LAKE MONSTERS, SCOTTISH MYTH)

An Irish prince of Donegal, educated for the Church, but who in 561 was exiled for causing the bloody battle of Culdrevny. With twelve followers he founded a monastery on Iona off the west coast of Scotland and began his life work as 'Apostle of the Highlands'. Apart from his ecclesiastical mission his chief mythic interest comes from the report in Adamnan's seventh-century *Life of St Columba* of how this redoubtable soldier of Christ, en route from Iona to Inverness to convert the Pictish King Brude, encountered the Loch Ness Monster. It rose from the loch 'with a great roar and open mouth', but Columba's prayers were sufficient to dismiss it back to the depths.[1]

1. *The Loch Ness Story*, Nicholas Witchell, Corgi, London, 1989.

COMEDY (*See* COMICS, GREEK DRAMA)

COMETS (*See* **ASTRONOMY AND MYTH**)
Comets, unexpected fiery-tailed visitors moving even more independently
through the night sky than the planets, were anciently regarded as signs of
unexpected change or ill-omen. **Noah**'s **Flood** was blamed on a comet. More
recently the English astronomer Sir Fred Hoyle speculated that comets seed
the earthly atmosphere with organisms that bring new strains of influenza.
More common opinion is that these heavenly snowballs, whirling round the
sun in irregular orbit, do not influence earthly life, and that the only damage
is caused by 'self-fulfilling superstition'.[1] Yet traditionally a comet is bad
news, at least for the eminent. Of a comet appearing *c*.AD 60, Tacitus wrote
of the Roman emperor: 'As if Nero were already dethroned, men began to
ask who might be his successor.' The astrologer Balbillus told Nero he could
deflect heavenly wrath by 'using his most prominent subjects as omen-
conductors and letting the message in the sky be fulfilled in their deaths
rather than his.' So Nero 'resolved on a wholesale massacre of the nobility . . . all children of the condemned men were banished from Rome, and
then starved to death or poisoned' (Suetonius). Nero survived: even a visit in
AD 66 by Halley's comet failed to destroy him, though soon he died. Yet
public expectation had been gratified: powerful and hated folk had perished
due to the comet. As for Halley's comet, one of its subsequent appearances
was in 1066, when the Normans conquered England. When it appeared in
1910, Oklahoma sheriffs arrived just in time to prevent the sacrifice of a
virgin by crazed Americans called the Sacred Followers: many committed
suicide to escape the celestial wrath, and King Edward VII of England
perished promptly, 'from the comet complicated by bronchitis'.

Yet when in 814 no comet appeared to herald the death of **Charlemagne**,
the chroniclers duly recorded that a comet had come. The **Incas** saw comets
as a death-threat from their sun god Inti: one appeared in 1531 before the
conquistador Pizarro arrived. Recently it was claimed that in 1963 President
Kennedy's assassination in Dallas, Texas, was prefigured by the comet
Pereyra. Yet those foretelling this event were not decapitated – the legendary
fate befalling Chinese imperial astronomers Hi and Ho, too drunk to notice
and warn of a coming solar eclipse.

1. *The Comet is Coming*, Nigel Calder, BBC, London, 1980.

COMICS (*See* **ART AND MYTH**)
Pictures precede writing. Long before the Sumerians invented cuneiform,
paleolithic hunters painted bison and **deer** on cave walls. Early versions of
the comic strip may be found in Egyptian funerary paintings, Assyrian
bas-reliefs, on Greek vase-friezes and the Parthenon, and particularly on the
Column of Trajan (second century AD) which depicts the military triumphs
of this Roman emperor in a dramatic relief winding up the column in a strip
over 600 feet long. Nine centuries later, after the Battle of Hastings (1066),
the Bayeux Tapestry was woven. This narrates the entire detail of the
Norman invasion of England in continuous images occupying a strip of fabric
230 feet long and 20 inches wide. Thereafter writing became the norm.
Painted drama was fixed in a single frame, save in the stained glass windows
of medieval churches; another form of 'comic strip' where dramatic action
moves from one window to the next.

In eighteenth-century England, cartoonists like Hogarth and Gillray
developed the art of telling a tale in related dramatic images running from one
frame to the next, with words in balloons. But it was in the late nineteenth-
century USA that the comic tradition really took off, gaining huge popularity

in papers owned by William Randolph Hearst (1863–1951). The phrase 'Yellow Journalism' came from a comic-strip character, 'The Yellow Kid', stolen by Hearst from the rival *New York World* in 1896. This led to characters like Buster Brown, the Katzenjammer Kids (1897) and (most surreal of all) Krazy Kat, by artist George Herriman. Yet a mythic dimension developed only with the 1929 birth of a Tarzan comic strip (*see* **E.R. Burroughs**), followed by **Disney** cartoon versions of popular **fairy-tales** and in 1938 by the first comic strip superhero – **Superman** – invented by writer Jerry Siegel. The success of Superman led to many imitations – **Batman**, Captain America and others – all possessing god-like super powers while maintaining an ordinary daily identity. These comic-strip heroes are Everyman writ large, as bold in their fight for Truth, Justice, the American Way, etc., as ancient mythic heroes like **Hercules**, **Arthur** or **Cuchulainn**. This suggests that, in a new culture, myth has to be reinvented; the past has already been rejected. Such myths have never caught on to the same extent in Europe. The old world naturally dotes on older myths.

Yet latterly the US comic-strip superhero has invaded the rest of the world via popular images as commercialised as the gods of ancient Rome (if not those of Greece). A positive aspect of this invasion is a rebirth of respect for the visual portrayal of myth as a popular rather than elitist process. The negative aspect lies perhaps in the typically black-and-white morality of images easily exploited for propaganda purposes.

Yet true myth, expressed in popular terms, works either through heroes or anti-heroes. Lately the simplistic morality of early superhero myths has led to a more ambivalent, complex art. The growing popularity in the 1980s of 'graphic novels' suggests not only a culture ever more attuned by tv and video to visual rather than literary media, but to mounting public doubt as to conventionally expressed values of right and wrong, as in the bizarre adventures of English writer Neil Gaiman's *The Sandman*.[1]

1. *The Penguin Book of Comics*, George Perry and Alan Aldridge, Penguin, London, 1989, (1971).

CONCHOBAR MACNESSA (*See* IRISH MYTH, TÁIN BÓ CUALNGE)

This king of Ulster and uncle of the hero **Cuchulainn** was said to have been born the same day as Christ. Infatuated with his beautiful ward, Deirdre, he tried to marry her, but she fled to Scotland with Naoise and the other sons of Uisnech. Promised forgiveness, they returned, but Conchobar betrayed them and had them killed then possessed Deirdre, who committed suicide.

Later, when a sling-shot became lodged in his brain, the doctors could not remove it lest he die. But on hearing of the crucifixion of Christ he so over-exerted himself trying to avenge him that the sling-shot fell out of his head and he died.

CONFUCIUS (551–479 BC) (*See* CHINESE MYTH, LAO TSU)

The name given to this Chinese sage is a western corruption of 'K'ung fu-tsze', meaning 'Philosopher of the Family K'ung'. His mother's death when he was twenty-four required him to withdraw for three years from public service as a grain distributor. Visiting the imperial court, he met the keeper of the archives, the mystic **Lao Tsu**. Unconvinced by him, he set up his own 'school of thought', on 'how to get through life like a courteous gentleman'.

Fleeing to avoid embroilment in politics, he later returned to accept public office under a new duke. His administration was successful, but the subsequent intrigues led to a thirteen-year exile. On return he wrote a history of Lu – the first known Chinese attempt at systematic history. Collecting and editing folklore, poems, songs and rites, he produced 'the classics': *The Book of History*, *The Book of Odes*, *The Book of Rites* and his commentary on *The Book of Changes (I Ching)*. His last words were to regret that no rulers existed who were wise enough to appreciate his teachings.

Pleading for truth, justice, moderation and public duty, he created not a religion but an ethical system for public and private conduct, based on veneration of the **ancestors**. Unhonoured at his death, in 195 BC the emperor visited his tomb. Subsequent Chinese dynasties honoured his teachings, his memory and descendants. Into the twentieth century, his direct descendant of the seventy-seventh generation ruled a city enclave, much like the Pope in the Vatican. Yet in 1949 the People's Republic under Mao Tse-Tung was the final break with the traditions Confucius himself had always espoused.

COPPER WOMAN (*See* NATIVE AMERICAN MYTH)

A myth among Native Americans of the northwestern USA tells how before people came to the Pacific coast Copper Woman lived alone in a house on the shore, harvesting sea urchins, clams, crabs and **salmon**, eating **seal**-meat and wearing sealskins. She was lonely. But one day several magic women came and taught her how to improve her life. When they left, she cried so much that her face swelled up and mucus dripped from her nose on to the beach. Ashamed, she tried but failed to hide or bury the mucus. The magic women came back and told her not to be ashamed, but to cherish it as evidence of her mortality. Also they said her **menstrual** time was sacred.

Placing the mucus-stained sand in a shell, a few days later she saw an 'incomplete thing' writhing in the sand. Steadily it grew, until too large for the shell. She put it in a sea-urchin shell, then into a crab shell. Soon it took her hands and would not let go, so she let it sleep with her. It grew whiskers like a sealion; its chest and belly grew soft fur; its voice grew deep and soon it wailed jealously if ever she left it alone.

One night 'mucus boy' tried to make love to her. Feeling sorry for him and for herself too, she let him. They coupled; he shrieked like a gull. He was only, after all, a collection of different sea-creatures. And though thereafter they often coupled, she never entirely lost her loneliness.[2]

1. *Native American Mythology*, Page Bryant, Aquarian Press, London, 1991.

CORD (*See* KNIGHTS TEMPLAR, KNOT)

In the first place, the cord is the placenta, broken away from the mother at birth so that individual life is established; in the second place, it is the life of the individual, broken at death. In occult descriptions of astral travel (out-of-the-body experiences) it is often told how the astral body is attached to the sleeping physical body by a silver cord of light which must remain unbroken so that the **soul** may return to the body.

The cord is an ambivalent symbol: both that which binds, attaches and limits, and that which leads those able to climb it to spiritual freedom. The knotted cord of a **Hindu** saint depicts the number of acts of devotion performed. The cord circling the waist of a **Christian** monk reminds him of his commitment to celibacy. So, too, in the form of girdle or locked belt, the cord is the chastity belt. More ambiguous still is the meaning of the cords or girdles said to be worn round the waist and under the clothing of **witches**, medieval **Knights Templar** and the *parfaits* ('perfect ones') of the heretical **Cathar** sect in Languedoc.

One of nine charges made by the Inquisition against arrested Templars when in 1307 the French branch of the Order was suppressed was that they wore a heretical cord or girdle. The contemporary *Chronicle of St Denis* states: 'In these girdles was their mahommerie.' This means not that they were secret Mohammedans (some may well have been), but 'having to do with idols' – the term 'Mammot' then being used to denote a doll or idol. They were said to use these cords to bind the skull or head (Baphomet) they were accused of worshipping. But what was the purpose? The tale is told of how when a Templar learned his servant had stolen his cord, he instantly slew the servant with his sword. Also how an outsider heard a Templar tell his novices to guard and conceal their cords, from which prosperity arose.

As for the Cathar cord or golden girdle, this relates to that which the prophet Daniel saw round the waist of an **angel** he met on the banks of the River Tigris: a cord conferring strength on those who wore it.

Witches of the time were accused of 'Raising Storms, Human Sacrifice and Wearing Girdles'. Women in the Wicca movement today wear consecrated cords, usually coloured red. Even Gerald Gardner (1884–1964), who in other respects was more than willing to reveal old witchcraft secrets, remained reticent about the meaning of the witch's cord.[1]

1. *Witchcraft Today*, Gerald B. Gardner, Rider, London, 1954.

CORMAC MACAIRT (*See* HOLY GRAIL, IRISH MYTH, SILVER BOUGH)
Stolen (like **Romulus** and Remus) by a she-**wolf** and raised as one of her cubs, this wise Irish king (reign perhaps AD 226–66) restored the realm of Tara to its former greatness, so much so that he became known as the Irish **Solomon**. A contemporary of the **giant** warrior **Finn MacCool** and father of Finn's wife Grainne, it is said his wisdom came from a wonderful golden Cup of Truth. If three lies were spoken over it, it shattered into three pieces. If three truths were told, it became whole again. This cup (which seems a precursor of the Holy Grail) was a gift from the sea-god **Manannan MacLir**, as was Cormac's **silver bough**, on which three golden apples hung. When he shook it, the sick, the wounded and women in childbed fell asleep until the next day. Both these gifts vanished with him when he died.

CORN-GODS (*See* CANNIBALISM, SACRIFICE)
Genesis iv:2 tells us: 'Now Abel was a keeper of sheep, and Cain a tiller of the ground.' Early folk subsisted by hunting wild animals and by gathering wild nuts, berries and seeds. In time the hunters domesticated the beasts they hunted and became herdsmen. The gatherers learned how to till soil and plant seeds, so becoming settled farmers able to build houses, raise their families, and ultimately to create cities and states. The crops most vital to the latter were developed via selective cross-breeding of seed-bearing wild grasses to produce corn: barley, oats, maize and wheat.

Yet despite the skills developed, the process was never certain. A rich harvest assured survival, a poor harvest meant famine. By and large, this is as true today as ever. Yet while modern city-dwellers may take the annual agricultural miracle for granted, our ancestors held the fate of the harvest to be at the disposal of the gods. Personifying every aspect of nature, to them the corn itself was a god. In spring they sowed, in summer they reaped – if the corn-god willed. Offspring of earth-goddess and sky-god, he was literally the 'son of the earth', yearly reborn. Men nourished him, then decapitated him and ate him. This required payment. How else to guarantee her bounty and his annual return save by invocation, thanksgiving and sacrifice?

In many cultures the myth of the slain corn-god was literally enacted by killing his human or animal representative, typically as the last sheaf was reaped, his or its blood being mixed with the seed-corn. In some lands the age and stature of the victim representing the corn-god was adapted to that of the crop. Passing strangers might be seen as the corn-god escaping, and so were seized and slain: or the victim might be the unlucky reaper tricked by his fellows into cutting the last sheaf. They would kill him, or pretend to do so, by beating him to death with hoes and spades, as the corn-spirit was said to lurk in the corn until the final cut, and then fly into the reaper.

The god might also be seen as a **cat, cock, hare** or other beast. In parts of France as the last sheaf was cut it was said, 'They are going to kill the cat', a live cat being put under the last bundle then flailed to death, roasted and eaten on Sunday. In much of Europe a cock would be buried up to its neck then decapitated with a sickle as the last sheaf was cut. In Galloway, Scotland, the last cut was called 'cutting the hare' – the 'hare' being the final cut plaited, its ears tied in a knot and the reapers throwing sickles until the stalks below the knot were cut. (Hares lurk in the crop until the last moment.) In Scotland and Styria the corn-god might be called the maiden, so the last sheaf was cut by a maiden; or by an old woman where it was seen as the corn-mother, as in Lorraine.[1]

In India, a sacrificial cake of the new barley or rice was offered to **Indra** and **Agni**, these having won a dispute among the gods as to which of them should be offered the first fruits. In Greece, corn was offered to **Artemis**. In the cult of **Cybele**, the slain god **Attis** was 'the reaped yellow ear of corn'. In Mesopotamia, **Tammuz** was identified as the died-and-reborn corn-god, as was **Adonis** in Phoenicia. In every culture the vision is the same: the earth-mother gives up the body and blood of her son to be eaten and drunk. The **Christian** rite of Communion commemorates this. Thus all corn-gods and their annual sacrifice of human representatives; thus annual growth, death and rebirth, immaculate conception, **resurrection**.

1. *The Golden Bough*, Sir James Frazer, Macmillan, London, 1963, pp.437–53.

CORNUCOPIA (*See* **CAULDRON, HOLY GRAIL**)
The Horn of Amaltheia, 'giver of wealth', like the cauldron of the **Dagda** in Irish myth, giving forth in endless abundance. Phallic as a horn, it was carried by **Priapus**; receptive and hollow it was also an attribute of the **mother-goddesses Demeter, Ceres** and **Fortuna**.

COSMIC DANCE (*See* **DANCE**)

COSMIC EGG (*See* **EGG**)

COW (*See* **ANIMALS, BULL**)
As provider of milk the world over, the cow is the great **mother** in her nourishing, maternal, productive aspect. As such she was worshipped in ancient Egypt as the goddess **Hathor**, the divine **sun**-disc between the crescent moons of her horns, sometimes shown as double-headed. **Nuit**, the Egyptian Lady of Heaven, was also depicted as a cow, legs the four quarters of the earth, the stars of heaven on her underbelly. **Isis**, too, is depicted with

the cow's horns, again with the disc between them. In India, Prithivi, the Hindu earth mother and source of all vegetation may be depicted as a cow. In **Celtic** Britain the cow was protected by **Brigit**, invoked to keep cows healthy and increase their milk yield. The medieval Irish manuscripts recording old myths includes the *Book of the Dun Cow*: the monks wrote down the ancient tales on vellum made from bleached cow-hide.

COYOTE (*See* DOG, NATIVE AMERICAN MYTH, TRICKSTERS)
As with Reynard the **Fox** in Europe, this North American wild dog appears in numerous Native American myths as epitome of the trickster. Unreliable, amoral, greedy, sly, too clever by half, on occasion the Coyote is portrayed as a culture-**hero** or **flood**-bringer. But most of the time he is simply out for himself. Thus a myth of the Jicarilla Apache (southwest USA) tells how one night Coyote meets **Owl**, who has arrows and a club to kill and eat men.

Says Owl: 'The one who vomits human flesh will kill men.' Coyote says: 'Shut your eyes.' Owl does so and vomits flesh and grasshoppers. Coyote takes the meat, but gives Owl the grasshoppers. 'Open your eyes,' he says, and shows Owl the meat. 'What did I tell you?' he grins. 'This is the meat I threw up.' Owl is confused, wondering why there are only grasshoppers in his hand. 'Where did I drink these?' he asks.

'Because I run fast I can eat people,' said Coyote, running round him. 'Your legs are too big to run. Shut your eyes, and I'll fix them.' So Owl again shuts his eyes. Coyote breaks his leg with a stone, takes the arrows and runs away, leaving Owl only his club. Crippled, Owl hurls his club at Coyote, and calls it back again and again, until at last he hits Coyote, who curses him, saying: 'Wherever a stick falls when one throws it, there it will lie.' So that the club does not return to Owl. Coyote shoots him with his own arrows, and thereafter is feared by everyone.[1]

For other Coyote tales, see **Wind** and **Wishpoosh**.

1. *Tales of the North American Indians* (ed. Stith Thompson), Indiana University Press, 1966 (1929), pp.70–1.

CREATION MYTH (*See* CONCORDANCE)
Four questions underlie attempts to explain our human origins: (1) how being arises from non-being; (2) how the universe emerges from primal being; (3) how this world with its land and seas was created; and (4) how the natural order of mineral, plant, bird, fish, animal and human kingdoms came to be.

Creation myth (its corollary: myths of **apocalypse** or Last Days) has several basic patterns. Describing not so much ancient events as an ever-renewing process, it models our deepest intuitions about reality, its path from spiritual abstraction (the One) to materiality (the Many), and relates as much to individual experience as to broader collective **archetypes**.

Current theories of cosmic creation ('Big Bang'; 'Steady State') belong as much to the general field of 'creation myth' as do older theories based on **Greek, Judaic, Vedic** and other ancient modes of perception.

Such theories tend to fall into four models or patterns. Creation manifests directionally out of the void or abyss; or anthropomorphically, the universe being perceived as emanating from a primal cosmic man or woman (Adam Kadmon, **Purusha**); or by vibration ('In the beginning was the Word'), whereby an all-pervasive sound generates creative deity out of itself; or serially, as by a **ladder** (*axis mundi*, **Tree of Life**) from high to low, on which the descending and ascending spirit manifests at progressively denser or more ethereal levels (as Jacob's **dream** of the **angels** on the ladder).

The initial problem is how to describe not only what happened 'In the Beginning', but *before* it. The Indian *Rig Veda* (X, 129) states it thus:

> There was neither existence, nor non-existence,
> The kingdom of air, nor the sky beyond.
> What was there to contain, to cover in –
> Was it but vast, unfathomed depths of water?
> There was no death there, nor Immortality.
> No sun was there, dividing day from night.
>
> There was there only THAT, resting within itself.
> Apart from it, there was not anything.[1]

The Bible (Genesis 1) describes the primeval Earth as formless and void, engulfed in darkness, covered in raging ocean. Greek myth tells how in the beginning **Gaia** (Mother Earth) and **Eros** (the generative force) emerged from Chaos – Chaos being a state of utter emptiness. The Bambara of Mali also tell of a primal emptiness, *fu*, from which arose *glan*, 'movement', then *zo nyami*, 'breath', then *yo* ('voice', Creative Word), then *yereyereli* ('vibration', the effect of creative thought), then *yalan*, *fayan*, *sani* and *yeren* (air, wind, fire and earth) to work on each other via *mana* ('power' or 'magnetic attraction'). In **Babylonian Myth** two primal watery principles are the creative agents: **Tiamat** (salt water: chaotic procreative force) and Apsu (sweet water: a watery abyss surrounding a discoid earth). From their commingling, Mummu (waves) births other beings. Scandinavian myth (*see* **Eddas**) also speaks of an endless abyss, Ginnungagap, pervaded by the primal All-Father. From it first formed the icy northern world, Nifleim, then (to the south) the fire-world, Muspelheim, home of Surtur the Fire-Giant, present at the beginning and ending of creation. Between these two realms was formed the human world, Midgard (*see* **Aesir**): and through these three worlds grows the world tree **Yggdrasil**.

This theme of the world tree (*axis mundi*) linking the various created worlds is common. In Africa, the **Swahili** say God made the Lotus Tree of the End. Rooted in Paradise, from it springs unending rains that water the Nile. Our names are written on its leaves: when our leaf falls we die. In Tonga (Oceania) it is said Eitumatupua the creator god climbed down to earth from heaven on a giant tree to create the human race from worms. (*See* **Ahoeitu**.)

The most developed tree-model is Judaic, as in the complex **Qabalistic** Tree of Life. Fusing the tree emblem with the concept of ten interlinked **dimensions** (*sephiroth*), it depicts Being's emergence from *Ain Soph Aur* – 'limitless space' – into a supernal triad of sephiroth, from which creative energy pours over the Abyss into a second triad. In these, nothing is yet manifest: only the idea of form exists. The energy pours into ever-denser spheres, culminating in *Malkuth*, the physical realm. The creative process is continual, worlds and lives forever coming in and out of being.[2]

As common is the idea of four world ages, each destroyed and succeeded by the next, each typically darker than the former. The **Hopi** Indians (Arizona, USA) widely agree with **Hindu** (Indian) belief in four world ages (*Yugas*), declining successively from **gold** through **silver** and bronze ages into our present *Kali Yuga*, the age of iron. The Irish *Book of Invasions* (*see* **Irish Myth**) speaks of four invading races, each changing the land before the arrival of the Sons of Mil, the modern Irish. Hörbiger (1860–1931: *see* **Nazi Myth**) impressed Adolf **Hitler** with his tale of four worlds, each ended by a **moon** crashing into the earth, the last destroying **Atlantis** 13,000 years ago.

More subtle creation myth implies that there is neither beginning nor end: creation and destruction are in balance. Indian myth tells how the gods **Brahma**, **Vishnu** and **Shiva** each claimed to be the creator, only to realise that all Three are One, however many their forms and names. The *Upanishads* also tell how the **Vedic** god **Indra**, having slain the drought-**demon** Vritra, built himself a huge palace on Mount **Meru**. The architect Vishwakarman went to Brahma, complaining that the work was as vast as Indra's ego. Brahma sent to Indra the god-child **Krishna**, who said (as **Campbell** describes it): 'I hear you build a palace such as no Indra before you ever built.' Indra asked: 'What do you mean, no Indra before me?' Krishna replied: 'Indras before you? I have seen them come and go, come and go. Just think: Vishnu sleeps in the cosmic ocean; from his navel the **lotus** grows; on the **lotus** Brahma sits. Brahma opens his eyes – a world comes into being, governed by an Indra. He closes his eyes, an Indra goes out of being. There are uncountable Brahmas and Indras.' Just then an army of ants marched over the floor. Krishna laughed. When asked why, he said: 'Former Indras all.' On realising what Krishna meant, Indra was so disillusioned he decided to become a yogi. Yet finally he was persuaded to remain the king, the egoless representative on earth of Eternal Truth.[3]

1. *Rig Veda* (Griffith translation), *Indian Myth and Legend*, Donald A. Mackenzie, Gresham, London, 1910.
2. *Creation Myth*, R.J. Stewart, Element Books, Shaftesbury, 1989.
3. 'Joseph Campbell and the Power of Myth', six-part tv series, BBC 2, UK, 1990.

CRESCENT (*See* MOON)

CROCKETT, DAVY (*See* WILD WEST)

CROCODILE (*See* AFRICAN MYTH, ANIMALS, EGYPTIAN MYTH)

In many African myths this large, carnivorous, armoured reptile is said to be an evil spirit, lecherous and greedy. The Bakongo of Zaïre tell of an old voyeur who, watching girls bathing in the river, wanted them so much he bought a crocodile-**fetish**. Out of porridge he made a porridge-man shaped like himself in his bed while he **shape-shifted** into a crocodile and ate all the girls. But a *nganga* (**medicine** man) provided a more potent fetish, forcing the crocodile to resume human shape.

In Lesotho it is told how the maiden Selekana, thrown into the river by others who hated her goodness, on the bottom of it met the River Woman, who had but one hand and one leg. Made to clean the palace of the River King, a giant crocodile, Selekana was released by the old woman with a gift of jewels. The chief's daughter, jealous at Selekana's rich return, dived into the river, seeking jewels herself. Asked to clean the palace, she refused, and was eaten by the River King: here the guardian of justice.

In early Egyptian myth the crocodile signified the brutal, evil side of the god **Set**. Lurking in the reeds he tore to pieces his brother **Osiris**. The crocodile-headed Sebek symbolised treachery, deceit and hypocrisy: on swallowing the **moon** he wept 'crocodile tears'.

In general, to be swallowed by a crocodile signifies the descent into **hell**.

CROESUS (See DELPHI, ORACLE)

Noted for his great wealth (to be 'as rich as Croesus' remains a byword) and for his reverence for the oracle at Delphi in Greece, this king of Lydia (560–546 BC) extended his empire all over Asia Minor. Making many gifts to the oracle, at last he asked it if he should declare war on Persia to the east. The oracle said that if he crossed the River Halys he would destroy a great empire. So he marched on Cyrus, king of Persia – only to be utterly defeated and to learn too late that the 'great empire' he had destroyed was his own. This example of oracular ambiguity remains perhaps the most famous of all.

CRONUS (See CANNIBALISM, GREEK MYTH, TITANS, ZEUS)

The painting by Goya (1746–1828), Cronus Devouring his Children, is among the most horrific images in art. Son of **Ouranos** (sky) and **Gaia** (earth), this eldest Titan **castrated** his father and threw the phallus into the sea, leading to the birth of **Aphrodite**. With Ouranos impotent, Cronus liberated his brother Titans, save for the three **Cyclopes** (storm-gods) and the three Hecatoncheires (the 'hundred-handed'; also elemental forces). Then (according to **Hesiod's** Theogony) he ruled over a Golden Age during which the work of terrestrial creation continued. Night gave birth to Doom and Death, Sleep and Dreams, also Gaiety, Misery, the **Hesperides**, the **Fates**, Nemesis and many other supernal beings. **Rhea**, sister of Cronus, bore him three daughters: **Hestia, Demeter** and **Hera**, and three sons: **Hades, Poseidon** and **Zeus**. Fearing one of them would supplant him, he swallowed each as it was born, except Zeus, for instead of her last-born Rhea presented to Cronus a stone wrapped in swaddling-clothes, which he gobbled up. So Zeus survived to make Cronus vomit up his brothers and sisters. Cronus himself was chained in the depths of the universe (claimed **Homer**); or was imprisoned asleep in the remote isle of Thule or Ogygia, guarded by his brother Titan, the 'hundred-handed' (or 'hundred-headed') Briareus.

The latter legend became amalgamated with **Celtic** traditions of the Blessed Isles of the West, a realm of otherworldly bliss. Cronus is also associated with **Bran the Blessed** and with **Saturn**, and all three with the crow: the root of Cronus being not chronos, 'time', but more likely cron or corn, giving the Greek and Latin words for crow: corone, cornix.

Statues of the Latin Cronus, **Saturn**, bear a pruning-knife shaped like a crow's bill; perhaps referring to the **castration** of Ouranos and to the crow's reputation for long life. The tale of castration may refer to the overthrow of a (sacrificial) **oak**-cult by a (sacrificial) barley-cult; the overthrow of Cronus by Zeus to the overthrow by invading Achaean herdsmen of the Pelasgian barley-cultists formerly dominant in northern Greece.

Yet in **Orphic** cosmogony (Greek: c. seventh century BC), Cronus is not a personified being but a principle, time, from which came chaos, infinite space, and ether, finite creation. Via the action of these two, surrounded by night, cosmic matter slowly developed in the form of an **egg**, night its shell. Amid the egg was formed Phanes the light who, matting with night, created heaven and earth. The Orphics also claimed that it was Phanes, not Cronus, who created Zeus.

CROSS (See CHRISTIANITY, TREES, YGGDRASIL)

Though most commonly associated with the crucifixion of Christ, the cross is perhaps the oldest and most universal of all cosmic symbols. It is the Tree of Life or world-tree, reaching between and uniting heaven and earth. It is the very image of the cosmic androgyne, the union of opposites. Its vertical arm is all that is spiritual, active, male; its horizontal arm is all that is earthly, passive and female. The Egyptian 'ankh' (*crux ansata*) unifies the male and female symbols. The *Tau* (or T-cross, from which in the **Tarot** the Hanged Man hangs upside down bound by an ankle, one leg crossing the other) is also the Tree of Life and Nourishment to the **Maya** of Yucatan, while in **Norse myth** it represents the hammer of the storm-god **Thor**. Set in a square it is the Chinese symbol of the stable earth: set in a **circle** it is typically the ground-plan of a Christian church within its circular churchyard, or (within square or circle) of the meditative mandala device.

The Nazi **swastika** (however perverse its use) likewise implied (via its shorter peripheral arms) the cross within a circle, the peripheral arms in wheeling motion: thus the **sun**. Shown with a crescent (as in **Babylon**) the cross implied lunar gods or the **moon**-boat, a female receptive symbol.

In **Native American** lore the north arm of the cross is the north wind (cold intellect); the east, the east wind (heart-source of life and love); the south the seat of heat, passion and burning; the west the spirit-wind, the going-out from bodily life. At the centre is earth and man.

The cross on which Christ died is represented with a shorter horizontal arm set higher up the longer vertical arm, maybe representing the triumph of spirit over matter. St Andrew (patron saint of Scotland) died on an X-shaped, equal-armed cross; the cross of St George (patron saint of England and **dragon**-slayer) is also equal-armed, the vertical and horizontal arms suggesting the four cardinal directions, or winds, as above.

The crucifixion (of Christ as with other deities, including the **Norse** god **Odin**, hanging self-impaled by his own spear from the **ash Yggdrasil**) not only implies the common sacrifice of humanity, stretched between spirit and matter, but also reminds us of the ancient ritual **sacrifice**, **castration**, and **cannibal** feast of the slain god-king in pagan fertility cults.

Everywhere, the junction of the arms of the cross symbolises the centre of things, the heart of man, the hearth fire at the heart of the house, the axis of the wheel of **Buddhist** law and of the Eternal Round, the earth as centre of the universe, and the cycle of the seasons.

CROSSROADS (*See* **CROSS, ROCK'N'ROLL MYTH**)

As manifestations on earth of the symbol of the cross as well as junctions between different choices of direction, crossroads invariably imply meaning beyond their merely mundane function. Traditionally suicides and **vampires** are buried at crossroads to confuse them and prevent their return to haunt the living. **Dogs** were sacrificed to **Hecate** at crossroads, which are also associated with **Janus**, the double-headed Roman god of **doors** or openings.

The song 'Crossroads' by the US blues pioneer Robert Johnson (d. 1938) has entered modern pop mythology, as in the movie of the same name (USA 1986), in which a young white New York guitarist follows an old black bluesman ('Blind Boy Fulton') back to the Mississippi crossroads where in the 1930s he had sold his soul to Scratch, the **Devil**, in return for musical talent . . . as, it is claimed, did Robert Johnson, who died in a mysterious fight. At the crossroads Scratch reappears: Eugene the guitarist barters his own soul (like **Orpheus**) in musical duel with Scratch's man to buy back Blind Boy Fulton's hellish contract. Eugene succeeds, the Devil, as good as his word, tears up both contracts, whereupon the arena vanishes and both men, old and young, find themselves alone, back at the crossroads.

CROW (*See* **BADB, BANSHEE, BIRDS, BRAN, CRONUS, RAVEN**)

CROWN (*See* **KINGSHIP**)

Whether crown of thorns or crown of pomp, the crown or diadem set on the head (crown of the body) of king, victor or sacrifical victim symbolises sovereignty, victory or great attainment. As Queen of Heaven the **Virgin Mary** is commonly shown with a crown of stars; the Pope in Rome wears the triple crown of the **Christian** Trinity – heavier but no doubt less painful than the mocking crown of thorns (a parody of the Roman emperor's crown of roses) placed on Christ *en route* to Calvary. The crowns of worldly kings are typically of gold, encrusted with jewels and pearls, a statement not only of worldly but symbolic wealth. In **Qabalism** one of the titles given to the first sephirah of the **Tree of Life**, Kether, is crown of creation, meaning godhead: that from which all else springs.

CRUCIFIXION (*See* **CHRISTIANITY, CROSS**)

CUCHULAINN (*See* **BADB, BULL, CONCHOBAR,** *GEIS,* **IRISH MYTH,** *TÁIN BÓ CUALNGE*)

The **Achilles** or **Hercules** of Irish myth, this hero of the *Táin Bó Cualnge* ('Cattle Raid of Cooley', perhaps first century AD) was the son of **Lug**, the god of all arts who had slain his own grandfather, **Balor**. Aged five, this Irish **wonder-child** overcame 150 other boys attacking him with spears: as he fought his hair stood up and caught fire; one eye shut as the other rolled wide in its socket (memory of the one-eyed **Balor**?).

He got his name ('Hound of Chulainn') when, still a boy, bare-handed he killed the ferocious hound belonging to Chulainn, smith of King Conchobar (his uncle), and so agreed to take its place until another could be found.

Later, as a man, his battle-fury was such that only 150 naked women (as with **Bellerophon**) sent out to meet his **chariot** could distract him. Each carried a tub of cold water. They put him in the first: it burst apart with his heat. They put him into the second: it only boiled. The third only got hot as Cuchulainn cooled down. The fort he had attacked was spared.

At the feast of the troublemaker Bricriu he was the only hero present brave enough to accept the challenge of the beheading **game** later known in the **Arthurian** tale, *Gawain and the Green Knight*: chopping off the head of the **giant** in return for his promise that he would offer his own head in response, when called upon to do so.

Fostered and trained by the greatest Red Branch Knights of Ulster, he wooed the lovely Emer, but her father demanded that he train further with the warrior-queen Scathach in Alba (Scotland). Through her enemy, Aoife, he had a son, Conlaoch, whom years later he killed ignorantly, for Conlaoch was bound by Aoife never to refuse a challenge nor to tell his name. When Conlaoch landed in Ireland and found his father, they fought: Conlaoch knew his father but Cuchulainn did not know his son, who was bound by the *geis* never to reveal his name. Conlaoch refused to strike a fatal blow: only after killing him did Cuchulainn see on Conlaoch's finger the **ring** he had left as a gift for his abandoned infant son, so realising his crime.

Then, despite his great skills (the **salmon**-leap that let him jump over any obstacle); his weapons (the *gae-bolg*, an invincible **spear**), and the battle-fury that protected Ulster when Maeve of Connaught came to seize the great Brown **Bull** of Cooley and all Ulster's other warriors were cursed by a magical weakness), he knew he was doomed. No more could he break the *geasa* set on him than his son had been able to do. After a single combat lasting many days and nights against his foster-brother Ferdiad, whom Maeve had sent against him and whom at last he slew in sorrow, en route to his final battle he met the

Morrigan, who invited him to share a feast of roasted **dog**-meat. The **badb** or **crow**-goddess, Triple Goddess of the **Fates**, sealed his doom.

So in his final battle he was mortally wounded. Binding himself to a pillar-stone (stone **tree**), he fought until he fell. His head was no doubt taken: his body was probably roasted and eaten, though with great respect and humility, by those who had survived the final battle of the great hero whose name has survived another two millennia of human history. An old belief is: why give the earth brave meat that might fortify those still living?

CUCKOO (*See* BIRDS, CELTIC MYTH)

In traditional Gaelic Celtic lore the cuckoo is connected with the Blessed Isles, or Isles of Earthly **Paradise**, the **otherworldly** home of heroes. A belief at Callanish, a **megalithic** henge on the Isle of Lewis in the Outer Hebrides, is that at sunrise on Midsummer Day the 'Shining One' walks along the avenue, his arrival heralded by the cuckoo's call. In **Greek myth** the cuckoo was one of the transformations undertaken by **Zeus** to win **Hera**.

CULHWCH AND OLWEN (*See* ARTHURIAN MYTH, GIANT, LABOURS, *MABINOGION*)

One of the Four Independent Native Tales in the Welsh *Mabinogion* (perhaps tenth century) 'Culhwch and Olwen' tells how Culhwch, nephew of Arthur and son of Celyddon Wledig, got his name ('Pig-Run') when his mother, Goleudydd, bore him prematurely in a pig-run when terrified by the sight of **pigs** (**otherworld** beasts). On her death his father remarried: his stepmother laid a *geis* on Culhwch that he should marry only Olwen, the daughter of Ysbaddaden the Chief **Giant**.

At Arthur's court (many fantastic heroes there) Culhwch demanded help. Ysbaddaden gave him thirty-nine *anoethu* (impossible tasks) to carry out, including the hunting of the giant **boar** Twrch Trwyth, and the descent of Arthur to the **underworld** to obtain the Thirteen Treasures of Britain (as also related in the 'Preiddu Annwfyn' (ninth century: found in the thirteenth-century *Book of Taliesin*). Culhwch completes fewer than half the tasks: three he does complete do not figure on Ysbaddaden's list. Yet Ysbaddaden is overcome, decapitated by one of Culhwch's companions, and Culhwch marries Olwen.

This fragment of a greater original conception remains one of the great native British sagas, charging full-tilt through many basic mythic themes – jealous stepmother, destiny sworn, boon asked, the magical helping animal, **otherworld** journey and the fight with the giant. Crucial to a study of the sources of Arthurian lore (Arthur is here a Welsh chieftain, not the noble king of later myth), it is, despite its incompleteness, the only Independent Native Tale which is irreplaceable.[1]

1. *The Mabinogion*, trans. Gwyn Jones and Thomas Jones, Dent, London, 1984.

CUP (*See* HOLY GRAIL)

CUPID (*See* GREEK MYTH, LABOURS, ROMAN MYTH, VENUS)

Eros son of **Aphrodite** was the Greek god of love: Cupid son of Venus was the Roman imitation, visualised as a beautiful boy, his golden quiver full of 'arrowed desires'. It is told how his mother, envying the beauty of a princess, Psyche ('Soul'), told Eros-Cupid to punish her. Condemned to be eaten by a monster and set on a rock to await her fate, Psyche was taken by the wind

Zephyrus to a wonderful palace. To her dark room that night came a mysterious visitor. He said he was her destined husband, but that she must never try to see his face. Nightly he visited her and all went well, until her envious sisters said he would not let her see his face because he was hideous. So next time he slept by her she lit a lamp and saw he was Eros-Cupid who had fallen in love with her. But oil from the lamp scalded his shoulder and woke him. Reproaching her, he vanished, as did the palace.

Back on the lonely rock, she threw herself into a river, but the waters refused to drown her. Pursued by Aphrodite-Venus, she underwent many hard trials in seeking her lover, even descending to the **underworld**. At last **Jupiter-Zeus** heard the pleas of Cupid (who had secretly helped her all along) and made Psyche immortal. So the lovers were reunited and married.

This tale is best known via the version told by **Apuleius** (*c.*AD 130–180) in *The Golden Ass*. Notably, it reverses the themes of **quest** and **labours** or 'difficult tasks' in that, in this case, the bride seeks the husband.[1]

1. *The Golden Ass*, Apuleius (trans. Robert Graves), Penguin, London, 1985.

CURSES (*See* EVIL EYE, MAGIC, PROPHECY)

The first kind of curse or ill-wishing is cast by the gods on humanity or on individuals defying the gods; the second by a priest, witch-doctor or wronged person on another person or group. Either way, harm or death is intended. Today it is often said that a curse works, if at all, only if the victim believes in it. Belief in the 'evil eye' is dismissed, as is the theory that curses involve highly concentrated will-power. Celtic **Druids** chanted curses in verse, standing on the left foot, right eye shut, left arm pointing at the victim. In Irish lore, even kings feared a **bard**'s curse. When the Danaan king Bres insulted the bard Cairbre, the bard cursed him so fiercely that his face broke out in boils so that he had to abdicate, no blemished man being able to remain king (*see* **Irish Myth**).

The most famous curse of all is found in the **Bible** (Genesis III:13–19), when **Yahweh** curses the **Serpent**, then **Adam** and **Eve**. For tempting Eve to eat forbidden fruit, the Serpent is: '. . . cursed above all cattle, and above every beast of the field: upon thy belly shalt thou go, and dust shalt thou eat all the days of thy life.' As for Eve: 'I will greatly multiply thy sorrow and thy conception: in sorrow thou shalt bring forth children, and thy desire shall be to thy husband, and he shall rule over thee.' To Adam he said: '. . . cursed is the ground for thy sake: in sorrow shalt thou eat of it all the days of thy life.' So Adam and Eve are expelled from Eden; their **Original Sin** damning all later generations (from **Cain** on), until Christ comes to redeem mankind (*see* **Christianity**).

In **Greek myth** mortals are frequently cursed by the gods for hubris, or overweening pride. **Bellerophon** rides the winged horse **Pegasus** to **Olympus** but is cast down to become a despised outcast. **Icarus** flies too close to the sun: his wings of wax melt and he falls to his death. **Prometheus** steals **fire** from the gods: in retribution **Zeus** sends Pandora and her Vase down to earth; when the Vase is opened all humanity is cursed by the afflictions that fly out of it. Such myths suggest that mortality itself is the curse, and that efforts to improve our situation ('rebel against the gods'; 'eat of the Tree') only increases the suffering. Yet in most Eastern belief the curse is our inability to see through illusion. It is our self-delusion, not a supernatural imposition. Either way, the theological 'curse' is, in effect, self-consciousness. Adam and Eve ate the **apple** and knew they were naked: they had lost their animal consciousness – innocence.

Female **menstruation** is still known as 'the curse'. In 'primitive' culture, menstruation is hedged about by **taboo**: women typically being sequestered in dark silence at this time, and kept far from growing crops or milking cows for fear that 'the curse' will blight the corn or curdle the milk. Odd? Yet such belief is found throughout the world. Why?

The 'magical' curse, delivered by man against man, is another matter. Those claiming that such curses work only on those who believe in them fail to consider cases of curses working where the victim either does not know of or believe in the curse; or in which the curse seems not to have been cast by any individual at all, or is aimed not at one person but at anyone who inherits a cursed object, or is born to a cursed family.

A legendary Scottish curse was imposed in the seventeenth century by Coinneach Odhar Flosaiche ('Swarthy Kenneth the Enchanter'). Condemned to die for his sorcery by Lady Isabella Mackenzie of Brahan in Ross, he cursed her family, the Seaforth Mackenzies, predicting their extinction in a time when four sons would predecease their deaf and dumb father, the lands to be inherited by a 'white-hooded lassie from the East' who 'is to kill her sister', all in a time of four great lairds; one buck-toothed, another hare-lipped, a third half-witted, the fourth a stammerer. In 1816, all this came to pass when the deaf-and-dumb Francis Humberston Mackenzie followed his four sons to the grave. His daughter, widow of the lately deceased Admiral Hood, came back from India to inherit. In 1823 she was driving a pony trap when the pony bolted and her sister was killed. This prophetic curse was known to many at the time, including Sir Walter Scott and Sir Humphry Davy. The odd thing is that, while the curse existed, there is no evidence that Coinneach did.

CYBELE (*See* ATTIS)

This Phrygian fertility-goddess, also goddess of **caves** and the **underworld**, was literally worshipped as a Queen **Bee**, underground and on mountain tops, with wild beasts in her retinue. She retained her archaic nature even when introduced to Greece and Rome with her emasculated god-son Attis and her priests, the Galli, who sought ecstatic union with her by self-castration.

Her cult reached Rome in 204 BC, towards the end of the long war against Hannibal of Carthage. The streets were filled with her chanting eunuchs, on whom citizens threw showers of roses. The emperor Claudius (AD 41–54) incorporated the great spring festival of Cybele and Attis as part of official Roman worship 250 years later. Early Christians may have learned from this how to assume the existing mythology of died-and-reborn gods in their own cult, the better to gain popular support.

CYCLOPES (*See* BALOR, CRONUS, GIANTS, GREEK MYTH)

The Cyclopes were Greek storm-gods, epitomes of elemental force. **Hesiod** in his *Theogony* (*c*.750 BC) described them as **Titans** or **giants**, rejected and thrown into **Tartarus** by **Ouranos** their father. They were released, but Cronus, after castrating Ouranos, had them thrown back again. Later, released by **Zeus**, they were set to work as **horse**-smiths and builders of cyclopean walls. In time **Apollo** killed them in revenge for the death of **Asclepius**. Three in number – Brontes (Thunder), Steropes (Lightning) and Arges (Thunderbolt) – they gained no great fame until, as told by **Homer**, **Odysseus** in his wanderings reached an isle ruled by Polyphemus, a typical cyclopes not only in that he had but one eye, set amid his forehead, but in having degenerated into **cannibalism**. Unaware that he existed, the Greeks made merry. When the giant appeared he casually murdered several of them, then shut the door of the cave with a stone, locking the heroes inside. On his return he got drunk. Odysseus drove an olive-wood stake into his single eye, then tied up his companions and himself under the bellies of the flock of sheep that Polyphemus let out to graze each dawn. So they escaped back to sea despite the rocks that Polyphemus threw after them.

The myth of the one-eyed giant (strong, but stupid or hideously ugly) is found in other cultures. Sedna, the hideous sea-goddess of **Eskimo** mythology, is one-eyed. The tale of how **Irish Lug** slays his one-eyed grandfather **Balor** (or David, Goliath) is similar. Two-eyed human cunning beats one-eyed elemental force, however invincible the latter appears.

The original Greek 'cyclopes' (the word means 'circle-eyed') may have been cannibalistic herdsmen, but they remain entirely mysterious.

D

DAEDALUS (*See* **BULL, GREEK MYTH, LABYRINTH, THESEUS**)
In Greek myth, King Minos of Crete sought from **Poseidon** the sea-god a
white bull to sacrifice in Poseidon's honour, but on receiving it added it to his
own herds. In revenge, Poseidon made Pasiphäe, wife of Minos, fall in love
with the bull. To help her satisfy this odd passion, the legendary Greek
craftsman Daedalus (meaning 'cunningly wrought', or 'bright'), built a
hollow **cow** of wood (or bronze), in which she hid as the bull mounted it.

Thus she gave birth to the **Minotaur**, a monster with bull's head and man's
body. In his shame Minos asked Daedalus to build him a **labyrinth**, at the
heart of which he hid Pasiphäe and the Minotaur. Daedalus revealed the
secret of it and was jailed by Minos, but escaped Crete by making wings for
himself and his son Icarus. Despite all warnings, the boy flew too close to the
sun, so that the wax binding his wings melted and he fell to his death in the
sea. Daedalus reached Sicily safely.

Later, many Greeks preferred to believe Pasiphäe had mated not with a
bull but with a man called Taurus ('Bull'). As for the labyrinth, the myth
perhaps arose from the mazy architecture of the palace at Cnossus, the word
itself from *labrys*: a double-headed axe emblematic of Cretan sovereignty.

Before fleeing Crete, Daedalus gave Ariadne, daughter of Minos, a magic
ball of thread which later she gave the hero **Theseus** when he entered the
labyrinth to slay the Minotaur. It is also said he built her a dancing-floor
marked with a maze pattern. A Cypriot account is that Minos pursued him
with warships, but Poseidon raised a storm, driving Minos to his death in
Sicily, whereupon Theseus invaded Crete. This is not the common tale.

DAGDA (*See* **CAULDRON, IRISH MYTH, TUATHA DÉ DANAAN**)
Chief deity of the **Tuatha dé Danaan** of Irish myth, this 'good god' was a
coarse, pot-bellied old peasant who owned an inexhaustible **cauldron** of
plenty; also a club so heavy that eight men were needed to carry it, so that it
was mounted on wheels. With one end he could kill nine men, with the other
he could revive them. He also had fruit trees whose fruit never failed, and
two marvellous **pigs** – one always roasting, the other always fattening. As a
fertility-god with many lovers he fathered the **muse**-goddess **Brigit** and (with
the river-goddess Boann) the 'young god' **Angus Mac Og**. He also slept with
the fearful Morrigan. Famed as a builder of forts, he was a pillar of strength
at the second Battle of Moytura (Mag Tuired), where **Lug** slew the one-eyed
Fomorian king **Balor**. Also a god of **Druidry** and magic, his titles included
Eochaid Ollathair, 'All-father'; Aed, 'Fire'; and Ruad Rofessa, 'Lord of
Great Knowledge'; while as a fine harpist he was able to evoke the seasons of
the Celtic year.

DAGON (*See* **BAAL, BEROSSUS, EL, PHOENICIAN MYTH**)
The Bible tells how the Philistines conquered the Israelites in war and carried
off the **Ark of the Covenant**, which they placed before the phallic, fish-tailed
statue of their god Dagon in his temple; but **Yahweh** in the Ark wrestled with

Dagon and broke his statue into pieces. This **shape-shifting** marine deity may once have been the Sumerian **Oannes** who, though repulsive to human eyes, emerged from the **ocean** to educate mankind.

DAKINI (*See* INDIAN MYTH, KALI)
Servants of Kali the black goddess, these female **demons** enjoy human flesh, and thus are also called Ashrapa, 'drinkers of blood'.

DAKSHA (*See* BRAHMA, INDIAN MYTH, REINCARNATION, RISHIS)
An Indian **rishi** or demigod (his name means 'brilliant') who sprang from the right thumb of **Brahma**. Told to create all creatures that move, with his wife Prasuti (from Brahma's left thumb), he fathered twenty-four daughters. These mothered all living beings, including the gods, **demons**, men, **birds** and reptiles. One of them, Sati, married the god **Shiva**. When Daksha insulted Shiva, she threw herself onto the sacrificial **fire**, to be reborn as Uma, 'Light', the epitome of divine wisdom. So in India (cases persist), widows voluntarily immolating themselves on the pyres of their dead husbands are called Sati, or suttee, and are said to exemplify ideal wifely devotion.

In revenge for Sati's death, Shiva cut off Daksha's head and replaced it with that of a **goat**. In his next life Daksha had seven sons, including Krodha, 'anger'; and Tamas, 'darkness'. His incarnations continued. Some say it was his son-in-law Shiva who condemned him never to escape rebirth, because of their original argument which led to Sati's death; others, that **Vishnu** was incarnated through him to create all living beings. It is also said that he was the first man who, re-creating himself as the first woman, loved her so much that he married her, and who keeps returning to the world via his endless generations of offspring.

DALAI LAMA (*See* TIBET)

DALI, SALVADOR (1904–89) (*See* ART AND MYTH)
As a youth this Catalan painter learned that, by once throwing himself down a flight of stairs at school, thereafter he held attention just by standing at the top of them. In 1920s Paris his discovery of **Freud**'s writings on the erotic meaning of subconscious imagery, and his affiliation with the Surrealists (artists exalting the superiority of subconscious expression), led him to work in states of self-induced hallucination. During the 1930s he produced a flood of extraordinary paintings.

Typically these explore arid desert landscapes amid which modern images and artefacts are juxtaposed with vast, amorphous creatures and shapes as fluid as **dream** – famously, limp watches draped over bare branches, or his *Soft Construction with Cooked Beans – Premonition of Civil War* (1936), in which the deformed limbs of an agonised giant stamp on and grapple with each other. Completed and titled six months before the Spanish Civil War erupted, he claimed it as 'a typical example of Dalian prophecy'.

Living in New York from 1940 until 1948, in 1941 he decided to 'become classic', designing theatre sets, commercial interiors and jewellery. He signed blank canvases, aware that his now mythic status guaranteed them a value simply by his signature. Notoriously he endorsed fake paintings signed 'Dali' while disowning his own works. On returning to Spain, he produced perhaps his greatest work: *The Crucifixion of St John of the Cross* (1951), startling in its downward perspective of the earth from black heavens above the head of the crucified man. *The Last Supper* (1955) likewise demonstrates classical mastery of technique allied to surreal esoteric vision.

Equally master of pagan, Christian, esoteric or technological imagery, his work belonged to no school or fashion but his own. An exhibitionist obsessed with death, his last years as a recluse in the castle of Pubol in Spain further inflated his myth. At his death-parade 20,000 people filed past his embalmed, white-robed corpse.

Dali also worked with the surrealist Spanish film director Luis Buñuel on two short films of continuing influence on new artists seeking original mythic input: *Un Chien andalou* (1928) and *L'Age d'Or* (1930).

DAMAYANTI (*See* INDIAN MYTH, *MAHABHARATA*)
Wife of King Nala, subject of a subsidiary tale in the *Mahabharata*, famed for her loyalty and devotion to her **demon**-possessed husband who, ashamed at losing all his wealth and at the spell of deformity put on him, deserts her, despite which she remains faithful until by ruse she gains his return.

DAMBALLAH (*See* FON, VOODOO)

DANAË (*See* GREEK MYTH, PERSEUS, ZEUS)

DANCE (*See* CIRCLE, GHOST DANCE)
In origin dances imitate cosmic or seasonal processes, or by sympathetic magical identification with such processes ensure their continuity, or are a means of ecstatic consciousness-raising. Round dances imitate the course of **sun**, **moon** and other heavenly bodies, also the cycle of the seasons: the round also creating a magic circle about a sacred space, object or person, implying the protection, strengthening or worship of whatever or whoever is in the middle. Thus the moon dances round the earth; the earth round the sun; the twelve Apostles round **Christ**; **angels** round the throne of God. The fertility dance round the phallic Maypole, with each dancer attached to the pole by a long coloured ribbon, leads all to weave a **labyrinthine** path that results in common union at the centre. Chain dances imply the union of male and female, heaven and earth. Morris dances and **sword** dances began as magical rites designed to ensure that the sun stayed in its course, as did the Sun Dance of the Amerindians of the Great Plains. The latter, as with sword dances and other rites involving ordeal or danger, had an **initiatory** function; the initiate at its centre enduring a form of crucifixion, being suspended from a pole by skewers thrust through the flesh. In a delirium of pain he sought ecstatic vision as the dance proceeded about him. Other Amerindian dances, especially in the southwest deserts, were held to invoke rain, ensure fertility or protect against evil spirits. So too war dances built courage before battle; hunters invoked success by dances in which they wore the hides of the animals they hoped to slay.

Among the **Sufi** mystics called **dervishes**, the Mevlevi sect of 'Whirling Dervishes' dance to gain union with God, the power descending through the dancer's uplifted arm to pass through his body and soul before grounding in the earth via his other, downward-pointing arm. The 'whirling' is the whirling of the planet.

In **Hinduism** the Dance of **Shiva** is the eternal rhythm of the universe. Lord of the Dance, he dances on the defeated demon of chaos and ignorance; dancing on a child, his feet are so light no harm is done; with a woman his dance is graceful and kind; dancing on his own round the world, self-accompanied on a **drum**, he dances so violently that the whole world shakes.

The dance of his bride, blood-smeared **Kali**, is a dance of death: she dances on the battlefield and on Shiva's prostrate body. In the orgiastic European rites of Bacchus or **Dionysus**, the dance often turned into a frenzy, an emotional chaos leading to blood-letting and death, and (at least this was the intention) new life.

DANTE ALIGHIERI (1265–1321) (*See* HEAVEN, HELL, PURGATORY)

Author of the *Divine Comedy*, commonly regarded as one of the world's great poets, Dante was born in Florence to a noble (Guelph) family. Aged nine, he met Beatrice, the eight-year-old daughter of Folco Portinari. In love with her at first sight, she inspired his life-work, though his love was never returned. In 1302 his opposition to those in power in Florence sent him into exile under threat of death. Refused permission to return in 1311, again in 1315 denounced and in his absence sentenced to death, in 1316 he refused an offer to return as dishonourable. In 1321 he died and was buried at Ravenna in Italy.

Involved with the Fideli d'Amore, a heretical sect respecting **Gnostic**, **Cathar** and troubadour lore, in his writing he allowed no inspiration but that of Beatrice. This inspiration is found not in the *Commedia* alone, but in the lyrics of the *Vita Nuova* (1290–5) and the *Canzoniere* (1290–1300). He also wrote urgent contemporary political tracts. But his fame rests on the three books of his *Commedia*, or (later title) *Divine Comedy*.

Composition of the *Inferno*, *Purgatorio* and *Paradiso* occupied the two decades before his death. He feigns that in Easter Week of the year 1300 he was let into the **otherworld** through the intercession of Beatrice. The Roman poet **Virgil** (earthly wisdom) guides him through Hell and Purgatory, while Beatrice (heavenly wisdom) leads him through the realms of Paradise. The complexity of the mythic landscape is compounded by its satire on the contemporary Italian politics causing his exile. In short: passing three wild beasts (Lust, Pride and Avarice: Florence, France and Rome), he passes the Gate of Hell to the Ante-Hell, inhabited by those who have lived 'without praise and without blame'. Crossing the River Acheron, he enters the first of the nine concentric circles of Hell, conceived as a giant funnel-shaped abyss.

At every level of Hell he encounters the damned: those guilty in their lives of varying degrees of sin and injustice, from the unbaptised children and virtuous heathen who inhabit Limbo (First Circle), through the hells of those who in life were lustful, gluttonous, avaricious, wrathful or sullen, heretical, violent and bestial, fraudulent or malicious, until, on reaching the Ninth Circle (inhabited by malicious traitors), he is at the bottom of Hell, which is the centre of the earth. Returning through the other half of these bowels of **Hades** he sees light again in Jerusalem, at the foot of the Mount of Purgatory. Here, seven terraces circling the mount from the bottom up are inhabited by spirits atoning for their vices while alive. Now at the Earthly Paradise, he is led by Beatrice up through the ten Heavens of Paradise. The first nine constitute the Heavens of Space, in which spirit is manifested: the tenth is the Heaven of Light and Love, beyond space-time (perhaps derived from **Qabalistic** doctrine) in which Spirit abides. The seven lower Heavens are the planetary spheres of: the **moon** (inconstancy); **Mercury** (intellectual ambition); **Venus** (earthly love); the **sun** (prudence); **Mars** (fortitude); **Jupiter** (justice); **Saturn** (temperance). In the eighth heaven, of the Fixed Stars, are manifested the redeemed souls; in the ninth, or *Primum Mobile*, the **angelic** hierarchies, while in the empyrean tenth dwells God, his angels and the redeemed.

Throughout this tour of worlds inhabited by spirits lost, expiating themselves or redeemed, the poet never fails, but at every point reacts with love, hate, tenderness, fury or terror to what he experiences, doing so in rhythmic and sublime language. So, though Dante called his work no more than *Commedia*, 'comedy', posterity added to his title the world *divina*, or 'divine', as an indication of respect.

DANU (*See* INDIAN MYTH, IRISH MYTH, TUATHA DÉ DANAAN)

Also known as Anu or Danaan, this supreme divine mother in Irish lore (the Tuatha dé Danaan, the magical race, are the 'Children of Danaan'), is so old that no myths about her have survived. Yet as embodiment of the forces of the lands and the waters fertilising it, her name and its variants have survived far to the east. In Indian myth, the **Asuras** (**Vedic** gods later regarded as **demons**), were descended from the chaos-hag Danu, whose name means the 'Waters of Heaven' (implying a generic connection with the Babylonian **Tiamat**). In Greek myth, **Zeus** took the form of a shower of gold (as in the famous painting by Titian) to visit and seduce Danaë – not a goddess, but a mortal princess. However it seems likely that Danaë was originally a fertility-goddess of the pre-Achaean peoples, who by **Homer**'s time had been masculinised as 'Danäus, son of Belus'.[1] The root also survives in the names of the European rivers Dnieper, Dniester and Don, while the name of the Danes of Denmark adds weight to the possibility of historical truth in the legend that the Tuatha dé Danaan reached Ireland from Greece via Denmark. And as in Greece, so in Britain: Danu was eventually masculinised as Don, father of the Children of Don in the Welsh *Mabinogion*. There is also a river called Don in Scotland. Yet her original nature may survive in the myth of the howling hag, 'Black Annis', a **cat**- or **owl**-goddess, as found in Leicestershire, England. A devourer of children, in Christian times she became a saintly veiled nun, Agnes. Death, after all, is always veiled.

1. *The White Goddess*, Robert Graves, Faber, London, 1961, p.64.

DAZHBOG (*See* SLAVONIC MYTH, SUN-GODS)

This Slav sun-god came into being only after the people of the steppes and forests that later became Rus ceased to address the sky directly, instead adopting the personification of it as a god, Svarog ('Bright', 'Clear'; of a Sanskrit root). After that they told how Svarog, the father of all gods, had two children: the Sun, Dazhbog, and Fire, Svarogich.

Yet in time Dazhbog himself was identified as the Creator, Father of Sun and Fire. The fire of his younger brother Svarogich (also known as Ogon: perhaps cognate with **Agni** the **Vedic** fire-god) vanished in his own radiant splendour. It was said that far in the East, in a land of eternal summer, he had built a golden palace from which every dawn he emerged in a chariot drawn by fire-breathing white **horses**, which took him shining over the celestial vault. He owned twelve kingdoms – the twelve signs of the zodiac. He lived in the sun; his children lived in the stars. Every day he is reborn; every noon he is the king; every night he dies. Yet each new summer he marries Myesyats, the **moon**, and they generate the stars.

DEAN, JAMES (1931–55) (*See* HOLLYWOOD)

Born in Indiana, USA, this stage and television actor was chosen by the film director Elia Kazan as the hero of *East of Eden* (1955). The anguished persona Dean portrayed in this and two later films, *Rebel Without a Cause* and *Giant* (1956), quickly established him as the idol of rebellious US youth in a decade which saw the rise of the 'Beat Generation'. His car-crash death in 1955 led to a posthumous cult.

Though man and myth were far apart (it seems he was a homosexual sado-masochist) his hypnotic screen presence left its mark. Tales persist of a jinx on the red Porsche in which he died. Unloaded from a breakdown truck, it slipped and broke a mechanic's legs. Its engine was put in another car which crashed in a race, killing the driver. Another car in the same race, with the Porsche's drive-shaft, overturned and injured its driver. Two of its tyres on a third car burst simultaneously without apparent cause.

Used in a Highway Safety display, the shell of the Porsche fell off its mounting and broke a teenager's hip. The truck carrying it to another display crashed, killing the driver. Another truck carrying it slipped its handbrake and crashed into a store. At last, in New Orleans in 1959, it broke into eleven pieces while on stationary supports. So it is said.

DEER (*See* ACTAEON, STAG, TRANSFORMATION)

Never domesticated, always hunted, the deer features in myths of **shape-shifting** or transformation. In **Greek myth** the hunter **Actaeon** sees the goddess **Artemis** bathing naked: she turns him into a stag torn to pieces by his own hounds – apparently a memory of pagan rites whereby a man garbed as stag was chased, killed and eaten. The theme is also common in **Celtic myth**. A Scots tale tells how a forester with the Duke of Argyll in a seventeenth-century military campaign was told to shoot a hind following the army. 'It will be the last shot I ever fire,' he said. Firing, he dropped dead even as the deer – his sweetheart – reassumed human form and, with an awful wail, 'rose like a cloud of mist up the shoulder of the neighbouring mountain'.[1]

Such tales, found worldwide, may arise from the propensity of deer-cult priestesses to wear deer-skins, discarding or reassuming them at will, also from the 'primitive' identification of hunters with his prey. So **shamans** in ritual **dance** the world over wore horned deer-masks to promote success in the hunt, creating the lore of stag-gods like **Cernunnos**, and no doubt too the sacrificial rites leading to myths like that of Actaeon.

Fleet and elusive, the deer was often represented (especially in the form of white doe or white stag) as an epitome of the soul, or as a **fairy** messenger, leading hunters deep into the wild wood to unknown adventures.

1. *The Magic Arts in Celtic Britain*, Lewis Spence, Rider, London, 1970.

DEIRDRE (*See* CONCHOBAR MACNESSA, IRISH MYTH)

DELILAH (*See* SAMSON)

DELPHI (*See* APOLLO, CROESUS, ORACLE, PROPHECY)

Sited 2,130 feet up the southern slope of Mount **Parnassus** in Greece, the **oracle** at Delphi (from *delphyne*, 'womb-like'), was the most famed of four great oracles of the ancient world, the others being those of Trophonius, Latona and the 'talking oaks' of Dodona. Anciently sacred to the earth-goddess, later annexed by Dorian immigrants who worshipped **Apollo**, this oracle caused frequent sacred war among those seeking to seize its wealth. That of 339–338 BC led to Philip of Macedon, father of **Alexander the Great**, conquering Greece. In 278 BC the **Celts** sacked Delphi; in 86 BC the Roman general Sulla plundered the temple; as did Nero a century and a half later. Only during the reign of Theodosius (AD 379–395) was the cult of the oracle finally suppressed.

It is said the oracle was first found by shepherds who, observing their goats acting oddly near a chasm on the slopes of Parnassus, located a vent from which toxic fumes arose. Inhaling these, they began to prophesy in ecstasy. Later, virgin priestesses were chosen to prophesy, being thought more susceptible to 'the fumes of enthusiasm' (*enthousiasmos*: 'inside the god'). Originally known as Pytho ('to rot', from the rotten smell of the fumes), the oracle retained its character after Apollo took it over. The pythoness (trance priestess) sat on a tripod above the subterranean fissure from which the fumes arose, breathing them in. At first she would tear her clothes, struggle and cry, then grow calm, as if seized by another mind. Uttering cryptic prophecies of the sort that doomed **Croesus**, her every sound and movement were carefully recorded. When the ecstasy (*ekstasis*, 'outside the body') passed, she was carried away to sleep and recover.

The **Neoplatonist** Iamblichus (third–fourth century AD) tells how the Delphic pythoness 'entirely gives herself up to a divine spirit'. When the first-century magus Apollonius of Tyana asked if his name would be remembered, he was told that it would, but in calumny. He left angrily. Later the Church declared his name to be synonymous with the **Antichrist**.

DELUGE (*See* FLOOD MYTH)

DEMETER (*See* ELEUSIS, GREEK MYTH, HORSES, PERSEPHONE)

Daughter of **Cronus** and Rhea, this Greek corn- and **mother-goddess** was originally portrayed as **horse**-headed. She fled **Poseidon** as a mare, but as a stallion he mated with her. Bearing the horse-man Arion and a mysterious daughter, in rage she left **Olympus** and became a **Fury**. After **Zeus** took **bull**-form to seduce her, she bore Kore, whom she loved. One day the girl bent to pluck a **narcissus**; the earth opened and **Hades** kidnapped her. When Demeter learned Zeus had given Kore to Hades, in her rage she wandered the world disguised as a hag, carrying two torches (intuition and reason) in search of Kore. Welcomed by Celeus in **Eleusis**, she revealed herself, teaching Triptolemus, Celeus' eldest son, the arts of agriculture but, saying she would not let the earth bear fruit until she saw Kore again, inflicted a 'cruel and terrible year'. Zeus sent **Hermes** to Hades to return **Persephone** (as Kore was now called) to the world. But Hades got her to eat pomegranate seeds, making their marriage indissoluble. It was agreed that Persephone would spend four months of each year with Hades and eight with her mother. So the earth became fruitful again. This annual abduction and return of Persephone formed the heart of the Mysteries of Eleusis. Demeter's forest temples, Megara, were the heart of a mysterious, orgiastic cult. Always in contact with mortals to whom she gave many civilised arts, her name means 'earth mother'.

DEMONS (*See* ANGELS, BORI, DEVAS, DEVIL, INCUBI)

Demon, from Greek *daimon*, is a morally neutral **elemental** force. The daimon of **Socrates** was his genius. Early Hebrew belief held that **Yahweh** created all things, including evil. Later **Christian** belief (influenced by Persian **dualism**) said good could not create evil. So evil was ascribed to rebel angels who, led by **Lucifer**, had been hurled from **heaven** to **hell**. To the medieval mind, bad luck, bad habits, thoughts and deeds were all caused by demons. Such belief was widespread. Called **Oni** in Japan, **Rakshasa** in

India, **Djinn** in Arabia, they were thought to be malicious, yet also knowing and potent. Many were said to exist. One medieval estimate states that of 399,920,004 angels, 133,306,668 fell with Lucifer. All demonologies blame demons for human vices; all say black magicians can summon them to do evil and that demons take bodily form as **incubi** or succubi to enjoy carnal pleasure with human beings. Such beliefs once led to witch hunts. Some historians say all belief in witches or demons arose from a mass neurosis imposed by the Church and the impossibly high moral standards it demanded.[1] But belief in demons also exists in non-Christian lands.

The **Hindu Rakshasas** are explicitly evil, though diverse in species – some are **giants** who (like Greek **Titans**) attack the gods; others are **ghosts** that haunt cemeteries (like the Arabian **ghoul**); or they are **Yakshas**, lesser nature spirits, not evil at all, perhaps even friendly . . . to the innocent.

The horned, triple-eyed Japanese Oni have three talons on each hand, to seize the souls of evil men about to die. The **Buddhist** sect of Nichiren (1222–82) still holds retreats for exorcising demons. Nichiren, in a time of Mongol invasion, saw the Oni at work all about. 'Demon est Deus inversus,' claims an old tag – 'The Demon is God reversed.'[2]

1. *The Powers of Evil*, Richard Cavendish, Routledge & Kegan Paul, London, 1975, pp.234ff.
2. *The Magical Arts*, Richard Cavendish, Arkana, London, 1984, p.260.

DERVISHES (*See* DANCE, SUFIS)
These Sufi mystics form independent orders and schools, linked by a force called *baraka*, each practising distinct techniques to produce the perfected human being. 'Dervish' implies an Islamic holy man, though there have been Christian Sufi schools. The 'whirling dervishes' belong to the Mevlevi sect alone; 'howling dervishes' are associated with the Rufai sect.

DEUCALION AND PYRRHA (*See* FLOOD MYTH, NOAH, PROMETHEUS)
Enraged by human evil, and by the theft of sacred **fire** by Prometheus, the Greek god **Zeus** sent Pandora and her vase (not a box) to earth. From it escaped all human affliction. He decided to destroy humanity by flood. Prometheus, chained in the Caucausus, told Deucalion his son to build an ark. With his wife Pyrrha (daughter of Epimetheus and Pandora), Deucalion did so. In it for nine days and nights they floated, and on the tenth day (having sent out a **dove**) they disembarked on Mount **Parnassus** (or Etna), then **sacrificed** to Zeus Phyxias ('Protector of Fugitives'). Zeus, touched by their piety, granted Deucalion's first wish: to renew humanity. Or it was to Themis, goddess of justice, they prayed. 'Shroud your heads and throw your mother's bones behind you,' the goddess ordered. So they threw rocks (bones of **Gaia**) behind them, which turned into men and women.[1]

1. *The Greek Myths*, Robert Graves, Penguin, London, 1960.

DEVA (*See* AHRIMAN, AHURA MAZDA, ASURAS, INDIAN MYTH, PERSIAN MYTH)
Sanskrit term meaning 'shining one' or 'celestial being'; from it derives Latin *deus*, (god), also probably the word '**devil**'. To Persian **Zoroastrians** it implied evil entities, created by Ahriman the Destroyer. The name Ahura Mazda, the Persian Lord of Light, is from the Sanskrit *Asuras* ('air of life'). Yet **Vedic** references suggest that originally the Asuras were synonymous

with the Devas: gods of an earlier epoch, including **Agni, Indra**, and **Varuna**.

At some point the Persian **demons** became Indian gods and vice versa. Why and how? In the Brahmanas (texts attached to Vedic hymns) it is said: 'The Devas gave up lies and adopted truth, while the Asuras gave up truth and adopted lies', and that the Devas mastered the Asuras. Yet later both Asuras and Devas became identified with darkness, drought and evil. Both were demonised. A tradition of the Devas as 'shining ones' survived, as in worship of the **Hindu** goddess **Devi**. Gypsies in their Romany tongue (Indo-European) call God 'Duvel'. Scotland's **'New Age'** Findhorn Community in the 1960s identified **elemental** powers as 'devas' which, sympathetically invoked, aid fertility. Again: 'Demon est Deus inversus' ('The Demon is God reversed'). Like the Elohim of **Hebrew** myth (also 'shining ones'), the origin and nature of the Devas remains obscure.

DEVA-RISHIS (*See* INDIAN MYTH, RISHIS)

DEVI (*See* DEVA, INDIAN MYTH, MATRIKA, MOTHER-GODDESS, TANTRAS)

Also known as Mahadevi, this great **Hindu** goddess, wife of **Shiva**, is worshipped in two aspects, fierce or kind. Fierce, she is Durga (the 'Inaccessible') and **Kali** (the 'Black'). Kind, she is Uma ('Light'). As Sati she gave herself up to **fire** when **Daksha** insulted Shiva. Also she is Jaganmata ('Mother of the World', 'source of heavenly milk from which the gods must drink'). With Shiva as her male **avatar** she personifies **Brahma**. She was never defined in one form alone. Her worship peaked in the seventh century AD, when the rite of *mithuna*, 'the state of being a couple', was legitimate practice. Licentious as a fertility-goddess and as terrible as Kali, Devi remains supreme as the Hindu Divine Mother, who: 'holds the universe in her womb', and, 'lights the lamp of wisdom'. Her name, 'Devi', is the feminine of deva. The poem called 'Devi-Mahatmya' ('The Greatness of Devi'), constitutes thirteen chapters (700 verses) of the ancient Markandeva Purana, celebrating Devi-Uma's victories over the **demons**. This textbook is recited daily in her temples.'

1. *Indian Mythology*, Jan Knappert, Aquarian Press, London, 1991.

DEVIL (*See* ANGELS, CHRISTIANITY, DEMONS, DEVAS, EVIL)

The idea of personified **evil** ruling the world and called Satan, Lucifer, or the Devil, remains deeply rooted in the **Christian** West. Christ named Satan 'prince of this world'; **St Paul** named him 'god of this world' – admissions later used by **Gnostics** to favour their **dualist** claim that evil not only rules the world but created it. But this belief, and even orthodox Catholic belief in Satan as the rebellious fallen angel causing all worldly ills, has always been contradicted by Isaiah XLV:7: 'I form the light, and create darkness: I make peace, and create evil: I the Lord do all these things.'

Satan means 'adversary' (Hebrew), implying (as in the Book of Job) an accuser of men. The satan, God's prosecution lawyer, gradually became Satan, the source of all evil in later Jewish and early Christian writings.

Lucifer (Hebrew *Helel ben-Shahar*, 'Day-star, Son of the Dawn', lovely morning star who walked in **Eden**) is Latin for the planet **Venus** meaning 'light-bearer'. The passage in Isaiah: 'How art thou fallen from heaven, O Lucifer, son of the morning', predicts doom for Babylon, oppressor of the Jews, employing as metaphor the daily eclipse of this brightest planet by the greater light of the rising sun. The passage was later used, like the **Enochian** myth of the fall of the Watchers, to demonise Lucifer as the proud angel fallen to earth, there in darkness to oppose God (the sun) in eternal contest for human souls.

Thus arose the myth that Satan and his angels fell from heaven for refusing to worship **Adam**, and that, as the **Serpent**, he tempted **Eve** to make Adam eat the **apple** and so gain knowledge of good and evil (self-consciousness). It is not said in Genesis that (proving **Yahweh** a liar) he is the Devil. This came later, as did St Paul's dogma of '**Original Sin**', so that only Christ could redeem them. This was convenient, as was later association of the serpent, or **dragon** (originally a symbol of natural energy fertilising Eve, the Mother Goddess Earth, or **Gaia**) with the by now demonised 'Satan', or Devil.

The Book of Revelation completes the link: 'And the great dragon was cast out, that old serpent, called the Devil, and Satan, which deceiveth the whole world: he was cast out into the earth, and his angels were cast out with him.' Meanwhile in the unchristianised East the dragon retained its beneficient image of life-fertilising energy.

So the young Church tried to tame the wild, impulsive gods of the old nature religions of wild human nature. Horny, cloven-footed **Pan** was yoked to the Devil, or 'Old Nick' (Nik being the pagan god Woden). Fire was used to fight fire, and lies to birth truth – a devilish strategy? Yet despite every effort by the Church to damn energetic human nature, the Devil-image remains darkly attractive.[1]

1. *The Magical Arts*, Richard Cavendish, Arkana, London, 1984, pp.286–7; *An ABC of Witchcraft Past and Present*, Doreen Valiente, Hale, London, 1971, p.85.

DHARMA (*See* BUDDHISM, INDIAN MYTH, KARMA)
Dharma is (1) an abstract **Sanskrit** term referring to the moral obligations of each person in life, and (2) a **Hindu** personification of moral duty or law in the form of Dharma-rajah, both God of Death and Lord of Justice.

In its abstract sense the term implies 'natural law', or 'that which is right', referring not to divine decree or personal wish but to social duty arising from the position in which one finds himself by birth into a class, race, sex or era. Men are men, women are women, nobody can go back to the (falsely remembered) innocence of childhood: it is as futile to want to be what one is not as to want to stop the sun rising. This is dharma. There is no escape from it: it is simply the way things are.

DIANA (*See* ARTEMIS, FRAZER, ROMAN MYTH)
Roman equivalent of the Greek Artemis, fertile goddess of the woods associated with the forest-god Silvanus. Among her many sanctuaries found in groves, her chief temple was on the shores of Lake Nemi, its priest traditionally an escaped slave. To gain this office he had to kill his predecessor in single combat, then he too became the target for anyone wishing to kill him. Patroness and owner of the wild beasts, she required sacrificial offerings from hunters killing her beasts, and was also the yellow harvest **moon**. She was especially worshipped as a goddess of childbirth, bestowing offspring and hearing the prayers of women in labour.

DIANCECHT (*See* HEALING, IRISH MYTH, TUATHA DÉ DANAAN)
Physician of the Irish Tuatha dé Danaan. By his art he restored **Nuadu**, deposed as king on losing his hand (no man with any physical blemish

could be king), to the throne by making him a silver hand. Or Diancecht's son made the hand grow back on the stump. Diancecht also slew a giant **serpent** which had been killing cattle throughout the land. Given this connection with healing and serpents, Diancecht's role is similar to that performed in Greek myth by **Asclepius** (who used the **Medusa**'s blood to make healing potions) and **Apollo** (who slew the dragon of Pytho, later **Delphi**).

DIARMUID (*See* **FINN, IRISH MYTH**)

DIMENSIONS (*See* **ABDUCTIONS, FAIRIES, KIRK, UFOs**)
Many myths tell of folk entering or abducted into other dimensions. King **Arthur** to **Avalon**, **Bran MacFebal** or **Oisin** to the Isles of the Blessed, **True Thomas** or **Tamlin** into the **fairy** world, Barney and Betty Hill into the UFO: all enter topsy-turvy realms inhabited by beings more aware of us than we are of them. Typically there are specific times (twilight or after midnight, solstices and equinoxes) when the way between the worlds is open. Those returning suffer amnesia, or find their few hours in the other world has seen a year, or seven years, or centuries, pass in this. Nor in doubt is the congruity between the worlds. One need merely step over a threshold or, as in the *Narnia* books by **C.S. Lewis**, through the back of a wardrobe.

In magic lore, dwellers of such dimensions may be called 'inner plane' or 'inner world' beings, which does not mean they are merely imaginary. The **Rev. Robert Kirk** of Aberfoyle, Scotland, author of *The Secret Commonwealth of Elves, Fauns and Fairies* (1691), affirmed their physical nature. When in 1692 he was found dead on a known fairy knowe it was assumed that he was not dead, but had been taken by the fairies into their realm – part of what today might be called the 'multiverse'.

Modern physicists, faced by the odd behaviour of elementary particles that deny Newtonian rules by insisting on being in two places at once or by arriving before they start, now speculate about 'superstrings' and multiple dimensions in a way that would be familiar to ancient Norse *skalds* who told of a nine-dimensional universe of congruent but separate worlds, each with its own intelligent inhabitants and physical laws.

DIONYSUS (*See* **GREEK MYTH (2), MAENADS, ORPHEUS, SATYRS**)
Greek god of wine, born to Semele, daughter of King **Cadmus** of Thebes, son of the sky-god **Zeus**, whose jealous wife **Hera** persuaded Semele to ask her mysterious lover to show his true form. Zeus refused and burned Semele to ashes. **Hermes** sewed up the unborn son in the thigh of Zeus. So Dionysus ('twice-born' or 'child of the double **door**') was born, **horned** and crowned with serpents. Or he was a son of Zeus and **Persephone**. He was cut up and boiled in a **cauldron** by **Titans** sent by Hera. Resurrected by **Rhea**, Persephone then gave him to King Athamas and Queen Ino of Orchomenus, who raised him as a girl, but Hera drove them mad. Zeus changed him into a kid, reared by Mount Nysa's nymphs, who later became a star-cluster, the Hyades. The **Muses**, **Satyrs**, and **Maenads** educated him and he learned to make wine. But Hera drove him mad. Cured by the **oracle** at Dodona, with an army of Satyrs and Maenads he travelled, spreading wine. On Naxos he married Ariadne, the daughter of Minos of Crete, abandoned by **Theseus**. In Egypt he defeated the Titans and restored King Ammon. He flayed King Damascus alive for uprooting vines he had planted, and made laws and built

cities in India. Returning, at Ephesus he slew the **Amazons** and was initiated into **Cybele**'s orgiastic **Mysteries**.

Back in Greece his drunken, effeminate rites led Lycurgus of Thrace to jail his followers. He cursed the land with drought and maddened Lycurgus, who killed his own son, mistaking him for a vine. When the Thracians had Lycurgus torn to pieces by wild **horses**, Dionysus ended the drought. When Pentheus of Thebes jailed him, Dionysus maddened his mother Agave and the other Theban women, who held Maenad orgies on Mount Cithaeron. Pentheus was torn to pieces by Agave. The folk of Argos also denied Dionysus: the women, driven mad, ate their children. **Orpheus** denied him, so Dionysus sent the Maenads to tear him apart. After further drunken slaughters, none denied him.

This complex myth describes the orgiastic spread of wine-making. Hera's opposition reflects conservative hate of the wine-cult, rejected until the late seventh century BC; seven centuries after Dionysus was deified. As late as 186 BC Rome's Senate banned the cult and its god (Bacchus in Italy). Many Bacchantes were slain before the cult took hold. Yet Bacchus was solely a god of wine: Dionysus was also a vegetation deity: born in winter as a **serpent**, transformed into a **lion** in spring and dismembered and eaten as a **bull** at midsummer. Thus too the fate of Orpheus, in origin Dionysus.

DIOSCURI (*See* GREEK MYTH, HELEN OF TROY, THESEUS, TWINS)

Twin sons of **Zeus**, Castor and Polydeuces (Roman: Pollux), born to the mortal Leda, whom the amorous god visited in the form of a **swan**. Each hatched with a sister from one of two eggs: Polydeuces and **Helen** from one; Castor and Clytemnestra from the other. The first two were viewed as children of Zeus; the second pair of Tyndareus. Devoted to each other, when **Theseus** abducted Helen to Athens they rescued her, and later joined **Jason** on the voyage of the *Argo*. When storm struck, **Orpheus** called on the gods, and twin flames came to hover above the twins: the origin of St Elmo's Fire. Later they abducted and married the two daughters of Leucippus but, fighting the Aphareids, Castor was mortally wounded. Zeus authorised Polydeuces to share his **immortality** with his brother: thus each continued to live on alternate days. Later they became the constellation Gemini, 'the twins'. Their cult was important to the Spartans (who had a tradition of dual kingship), and later (fifth century BC on) to the Romans. Their semi-divinity arises from the superstitious awe that in many cultures surrounds the birth of twins.

DISNEY, WALT (1901–66) (*See* COMICS, FAIRY-TALES, HOLLYWOOD)

Born in Chicago and brought up on a Missouri farm, this American film and tv producer is famed as pioneer of animated cartoon films with a strong mythic or fairy-tale content, and as creator of Mickey Mouse and Donald Duck.

In 1929 he launched a series, 'Silly Symphonies'. The first, to the music of Saint-Säens' *Danse Macabre*, portrayed a skeleton rising from the grave to perform a grotesque dance. This idea, though shelved due to the cost of such complex animation, led to the masterpiece *Fantasia* (1940).

By then Disney had gained world-wide popularity through the creation of cartoons featuring talking animals; happy fantasies that soothed many amid the trials of the Great Depression. *The Three Little Pigs* (1933), with its **fairy-tale** of the hard-working pig who builds a house of brick against the **wolf** ('Who's Afraid of the Big Bad Wolf') increased his popularity (and profits). In 1935 he began work on his first feature-length cartoon film – *Snow White and the Seven Dwarfs*. The success of this funny, sentimental, mythic romance led to other feature-length cartoon films still loved by children of all ages: *Pinocchio* (1940: from the folk-tale of a wooden puppet-boy whose nose sprouts every time he tells a lie), *Dumbo* (1941: the tale of a flying elephant), *Cinderella* (1950) and *Peter Pan* (1953). In 1955 outside Los Angeles he opened the first Disneyland: an amusement park retailing Disney cartoon characters amid medieval cities and mythic landscapes.

DIVINATION (*See* PROPHECY)

Implies any system for enquiry into hidden matters other than by use of the five senses. Inspiration, magical ritual, intuition, **dream** or trance may be employed in conjunction with or boosted by 'mechanical' aids such as (in dowsing for water or other hidden matter) rods, wands or pendulums or (in seeking information on the future or other obscured matters) systems based on what **Jung** called an 'acausal connecting principle' like the I Ching or **Tarot**. In the past and in primitive cultures such systems have included divination of **omens** by crystal-gazing, by the state of entrails and liver or by marks on the shoulder-blades (*scapulimancy*) of slaughtered animals; or by the casting of bones or 'omen-sticks'. It is said the **Druids** divined from the appearance of tree-roots or clouds, by the howling of **dogs** and the way smoke rose from a fire, and sometimes by stabbing a man and observing his death-convulsions. Another Druid technique involved incantation and the trance-process called 'illumination of rhymes'.[1]

Modern divination takes many forms, from Tarot or *I Ching* (Chinese *Book of Changes*) to the interpretation by astrologers of birth-charts, said to provide an accurate blueprint not so much of the individual's preordained fate as of his or her characteristic psychological tendencies.

Many divinatory techniques exist round the world. More than sixty are practised in Africa alone. These include astromancy (reading the stars for the right time to sow); cleromancy (throwing lots, or short sticks, as with the I Ching); geomancy (by studying lines made in sand by those ignorant of the system); haematomancy (seeing how blood flows from a stabbed victim); and ornithomancy (observation of the flight-patterns of birds, and where and how they perch). The flight of **birds** was also used by Roman augurs.

All such systems are ancient, and are found (in one form or another) in every culture. Whether sought by tossing sandals (among the Kenyan **Kikuyu**) and trancing on the pattern made by their fall, or by reading tea-leaves left in a cup, each method is based on the belief that there is meaning in every seemingly accidental event: i.e., nothing is accidental.

1. *The Magic Arts in Celtic Britain*, Lewis Spence, Rider, London, 1970.

DJINNS (*See ARABIAN NIGHTS*, DEMONS, IFRIT, INCUBI, ISLAMIC MYTH, SHAITAN)

Belief in djinns (the word from the Arabic *jinn, jann, jinnee* or *genie*; plural *junun*) is or was common throughout Arabia and in Africa north of the Equator. Moslem tradition tells how Allah created four species of sapient spirits: **angels**, made of light; **shaitans**, made of the fire of God's wrath; *djinns*, created from the Simoon, the searing Saharan wind; and man, made of earth. The first djinn was called Taranushi, to whom Allah taught the laws binding his kind. Yet just as **Adam** and his descendants disobeyed God, who punished Man with the **Flood**; so the djinns, likewise deluded by their own pride, were destroyed by an army of angels. One, called Iblis, was brought to

heaven and educated, but later joined the other surviving djinns, who had reassembled on an isle in the Indian Ocean. Becoming their king, he was renamed **Azazel**, who in the apocryphal Book of **Enoch** is identified as the Watcher, or 'Son of God', who led the rebellion against heaven.

Evil djinns tend to be identified with shaitans, but even good djinns may be unreliable and tricksy. The Arab cosmographer al-Qaswini says: 'the Jinn are aerial animals, with transparent bodies, which can assume various forms.' These forms, once solidified, are generally monstrous due to their miscegenation with beasts of different kinds. Thus they may appear as man, jackal, **lion**, **scorpion** or **wolf**; with horns, snouts, hooves or scales. If taking human form, they are usually gigantic; if good, they are of great beauty; if evil, they are hideous beyond the imagination of **Hollywood**.

Able to attain the lower heavens and to overhear angels prophesy, they have great magical power over humanity. They can put us to sleep, transport us instantly to distant lands and show us miracles, then return us to our beds. They can make us fall in love with them and marry them: the children of such unions can walk through walls, fly, and age very slowly. Egyptians say that desert whirlwinds of sand mark the flight of evil djinns, and that shooting stars are arrows hurled by Allah against them. They love to throw stones at passers-by from rooftops, abduct beautiful women, steal food and delude folk with base illusions. Invoking Allah's name is usually enough to prevent such trouble. The **ghoul**, haunting graveyards to feed on human corpses, is generally reckoned to be an inferior order of djinn.

DOG (*See* CONCORDANCE)

Just as the world over the dog, or tamed wolf, guards the domestic **door** or gateway, so in the mythology of many cultures the dog guards the door to the secrets of the **underworld**. Jackal-headed **Anubis**, the dog that attends Melkarth (the **Phoenician Hercules**), three-headed **Cerberus** in Greek myth, the dog with **Asclepius** – all symbolise entry to the underworld. In England spectral black dogs presage illness or death, in Scotland tales of the *cu sith*, or 'fairy hound', persist. The Irish hero **Cuchulainn**, the 'Hound of Chulainn', was forbidden to eat dog-meat, the dog being his **totem**. Tricked by the Morrigan into doing so, his strength was lost and he went to his fatal battle. The **Aztec** god Xoltl, god of death and the setting sun, had a dog's head: likewise in **Buddhist** lore the dog is an attribute of **Yama**, god of the dead; elsewhere it is a messenger or intercessor with the gods.

The Greek hero Hercules overcomes Cerberus by feeding him a drugged cake: the Finnish hero **Väinamöinen** steals the magical *sampo* from Queen Louhi of Pohja by playing his *kantele* (harp) so wondrously that the guard-dogs Halli and Lukki fall asleep. Yet in other tales the dog (as the wild beast) is not so easily fooled. It may be an inventor and bringer of fire, as in Africa; or it may symbolise the **trickster**, as in **Native American** myths of the **coyote**, or again as in the **Norse myth** of **Loki** the trickster in dog-form. The **fox** is a wild dog everywhere renowned for its sly cunning. In **Christian** symbolism the tamed dog is a faithful guardian of the flock, but the fox, feigning death to trap its prey, is as deceitful as Satan. In China, the fox is considered a bad **omen**, a potent beast able to foretell the future, which only has to strike the ground with its tail to start a fire, and which can **transform** itself into old men, young women and scholars. It loves causing pranks and misfortune, it lives near graves, and when men die they may transmigrate into the body of a fox. So too, in sixteenth-century France, thousands of people were executed in the belief that at full moon they had transformed into murderous **werewolves**: wolf- or dog-men.

Other mythic wild dogs are capable of destroying worlds. The **Fenrir** wolf (or his cubs) in Norse myth chases the sun, and at last, at **Ragnorak**, devours it. Garm, another terrible dog, howls furiously, calling all men to war.

So too the dog is guardian of the 'sun behind the sun' – **Sirius**, the Dog-star, in the constellation Canis Major, occult repository of secrets known only to **Isis, Osiris** – and, perhaps, to **Anubis,** the jackal-god who can scent water far over the empty desert that separates death from life . . .

DOGON (*See* AFRICAN MYTH, BEROSSUS, CREATION MYTH, SIRIUS)

In 1950 the French anthropologists Marcel Griaule and Germaine Dieterlen published their twenty-year investigation into the cosmological lore of the Dogon people of Mali. In *The Sirius Mystery* (1976), Robert Temple argued that this lore suggests a visit to earth by beings from the star-system of **Sirius** five millennia ago. Telling of a secret star they call po, after the tiniest seed they know, Dogon priests draw in sand an apparently accurate diagram of the eccentric fifty-year orbit round Sirius A of the white dwarf star, Sirius B. They say Sirius B is made of a non-terrestrial material, *sagala*, 'strong', heavier than all the iron on earth. They also say that there is a third Sirian star: the emme ya, 'sun of women', orbiting Sirius A also in fifty years and in the same way as Sirius B, but at right angles to the dwarf; and that the emme ya nurtures a satellite, the 'star of women'.

Sirius B, a cubic inch of which weighs about a ton, invisible to the naked eye, was unknown to Western astronomy until 1862 and not photographed until 1970. Yet the Dogon claim to have known about it for centuries, also about Saturn's rings and Jupiter's four large moons. Their sand-drawings show the descent to earth of the '**ark**' carrying a god Nommo (fish-tailed, like the **Oannes** of **Sumerian creation myth**). Temple's thesis, that this suggests alien intervention, convinced many, but is debunked by the astronomer Carl Sagan and the author Ronald Story, who claims the Dogon heard of Sirius B from local French schools before Griaule and Dieterlen began recording their beliefs in 1931. The case remains unproved, though Temple traced the cosmology of the (apparently) far-travelled Dogon back some 4,000 years to the myth of Oannes as told by **Berossus**.[1]

The Dogon say that Amma, the creator-god, made the **sun** as a clay pot, fired white hot, about which he wound a spiral of red copper eight times. He made the **moon** likewise but smaller, winding about it a spiral of brass. He made the black people out of sunlight, white people out of moonlight. With more clay he created the earth as a female body, head to the north, legs to the south, her *mons veneris* an anthill, her clitoris a termite hill, which he circumcised. Mating with him, she gave birth to the first animal, the Golden Jackal. Again he fertilised her, with rain: she bore twins, half human, with forked tongues and **serpent** tails. They were named Nummo ('Nommo'), meaning 'Water'. They became the grass, plants and trees, then joined Amma in the sky. Looking down to see their mother naked, they began clothing her with reeds and shrubs. Their movements caused the first wind to stir the leaves and branches; language was born even as Amma made the stars by scattering bits of the sun across the sky. Then, modelling the first man and woman out of clay, he **circumcised** both. The man's foreskin became a black and white lizard; the woman's clitoris a **scorpion**. Mating, they made four sets of twins, from whom descended all the Dogon.[2]

1. *The Sirius Mystery*, Robert K.G. Temple, Sidgwick & Jackson, London, 1976.

2. *African Mythology*, Jan Knappert, Aquarian Press, Wellingborough, 1990.

DOLPHIN (*See* **WHALE**)
Descendant (as with the **whale**) of a warm-blooded mammal which some seventy million years ago returned from the land to the sea, the friendliness of the dolphin to human beings has always been noted, as by the Roman writers Plutarch and Oppian two thousand years ago. From age to age tales persist of the dolphin, King of Fishes (which they are not), rescuing drowning or shipwrecked mariners by guiding or towing them safely to shore. In return, humanity has usually acknowledged the dolphin as divine or semi-divine. In **Celtic myth** it was associated with **well**-worship and the power of the sea; in Egypt it was an attribute of the goddess **Isis**. In Greece, where it was viewed as capable of guiding **souls** to the Isles of the Blessed, it was also erotically associated with the love-goddess **Aphrodite** (who rose from the waves), and with the sea-goddess **Thetis** (who rode naked on a dolphin).

Here the dolphin's association with the feminine principle and with the womb may arise from the assonance between *delphis* (dolphin) and *delphys* (womb): equally, it may be, such assonance was not accidental, the dolphin springing like a newborn, playful child from the womb of the sea. It was also an attribute of the Greek gods **Poseidon** (sea-power), **Dionysus** (wine and merriment), and **Apollo** Delphinos, the light of the sun. To the Romans it represented the soul's journey over the sea of death; more anciently the Sumerians regarded it as an alternative to the fish in their imagination of the being **Oannes**, said to have emerged from the **ocean** bringing the gifts of civilisation to humanity (and also associated with the fish-tailed Nommo ('Water'), a god of the **Dogon** in landlocked Saharan Mali).[1] Further east, in the **Hindu** *Shrimad Bhagavatum*, the dolphin's body is recognised as one well suited to spiritual pleasures: elsewhere in this same text the sphere of the heavens is said to represent the shape of a dolphin.[2]

It is worth recalling that in ancient Greece, the slaying of a dolphin, by accident or design, was considered murder, and was punished as such.

1. *An Illustrated Encyclopaedia of Traditional Symbols*, J.C. Cooper, Thames & Hudson, London, 1978.
2. *The Phoenix Returns*, Kristina Gale-Kumar, Cardinal Enterprises, Hawaii, 1983, pp.181–4.

DOMOVOI (*See* **BROWNIES, RUSALKA, SLAVONIC MYTH**)
From the Slav term *dom* ('house', as in Latin *domus*, whence the English words 'domain', 'domestic', etc.), the Domovoi was the spirit or 'brownie' of the Russian household, though rarely referred to by his proper name for reasons of superstitious respect. Just as in **Celtic** Britain and Ireland the **fairies** were usually called the 'good folk' or the 'gentry', so the Domovoi was typically referred to as 'grandfather', or as 'Himself'.

It was hard to see him exactly, not least as to see him was dangerous. Said to be hairy and human-shaped, he might be covered with silky fur, or might even (after **Christianity** attacked Slav myth) bear horns and a tail. He might take the form of a domestic animal or bundle of hay. Yet though not easily seen, he was often heard: groaning, weeping or speaking softly.

He had reason to be sad. He and other 'little gods' had once revolted against the sky-god and had been cast down from sky to earth. Those falling into peoples' houses or yards, rather than into wild woods or rivers, had grown friendly with folk, each so loving his own human house that he hated to leave it. When a peasant family moved, the wife put bread by the stove in the new house to persuade their Domovoi to come along. Himself liked to live near the stove, while his wife Domovikha preferred the dark cellar.

If well-fed, Himself would warn his hosts of dangers at their door, by pulling the wife's hair if her husband was about to beat her, or sobbing if a death was nigh. He was certainly friendlier than his relations living outside. These included the Dvorovoi, spirits of the farmyard who loathed white-furred creatures but protected white hens, especially if appeased by bread and friendly talk; the Bannik (from *banya*, 'bath'), who lived in the outside bath-house and liked water left in the tub so that he could bathe. (If interrupted during his turn he might even strangle the intruder or at least pour boiling water over him, but if properly respected he would tell you about the future.) The Ovinnik (from *ovin*, 'barn') inhabited a corner of the barn; he most often resembled a large black **cat**, dishevelled and half-wild. He was so unreliable as to burn down the barn if displeased.

Yet all these household and farmyard spirits were more dependable than those who, having fallen into the wilderness beyond human settlement, owed humanity nothing. These included Leshy, from *les* ('forest'), the Russian **Green Man** who, though good-natured, led travellers astray and was angry in springtime when, reborn out of winter, his anguish at knowing he would die again in the autumn made him nasty with flood and storm. Polevik (*pole*, 'field') enjoyed strangling drunkards falling asleep on him instead of tilling him. Vodyanoi, the dangerous water-sprite, would, like the Gaelic **kelpie**, lure imprudent travellers into the river or mill-spate and drown them. If it was a virgin girl who drowned, she became a **rusalka**, a Slavonic **siren** who sang songs luring men to death in her watery arms.

DON, CHILDREN OF (*See* DANU, *MABINOGION*, WELSH MYTH)

DONAR (*See* TEUTONIC MYTH, THOR)

DOOR (*See* KNOT)
'If the doors of perception were cleansed, everything will appear to man as it is, infinite' (**William Blake**). So Aldous Huxley (1894–1963) titled an essay 'The Doors of Perception' (1954), arguing in it that the human brain is a 'reducing valve' excluding excess information flooding in from 'mind at large': i.e., the brain-door is almost but not quite entirely shut.

Doors imply passage from one domain or state to another, thus (if open) birth, death, **initiation**, liberation or (if shut) imprisonment, denial, restriction. Doors into temples or churches imply passage from the mundane to the spiritual world. A cathedral's three doors symbolise faith, hope and charity. In the **Tarot** card the High Priestess, the pillars Boaz and Jachin, between which sits the High Priestess (**Isis**), symbolise entry to the cosmic temple. In **Hindu** temples, gods carved on the door-jambs signify the deity through which man enters the Supreme Mystery. On the outer doors of some Chinese houses two guardian warriors are painted, one red-faced, the other white. These door-gods originated in two mythical beings, Shen-t'u and Yü-lü, who guarded the Ghost's Door to stop the spirits of the dead escaping from **hell** to plague the living. In Chinese **Buddhist** temples huge grimacing figures guarded the entry. In Assyria winged human-headed bulls, *lamassu*, guarded temple gates or doors. The two-faced Roman god Janus guarded public gates and private doors. He bore a key, and a stick to hit the unwelcome. His two faces let him watch both ways at once. In parts of Scotland, Germany, India, Sumatra and elsewhere, when birth took place in a house, every door was unlocked to aid the birth, including cupboard doors, and the lids of chests, boxes and pans. Conversely, in parts of England as late as the mid-nineteenth century, when a person was dying hard, all doors were opened to let the soul escape more easily.

DOVE (*See* BIRDS, HOLY GHOST)

In **Christianity** epitomising the descent of the Holy Spirit, the white dove is sacred to **mother-goddesses** as personifying femininity and maternity: it also represents the lunar wisdom associated with **moon**-goddesses. Doves and pigeons were prominent in the shrines of **Aphrodite**; the dove with an olive branch was an emblem of **Athene**; the dove was also sacred to **Adonis** and to **Bacchus**. In *The Aeneid* **Virgil** describes how two doves led **Aeneas** to the gloomy vale where grows the **Golden Bough**, alighting on a tree 'whence shone a flickering gleam of gold'. In Babylonian **flood-myth**, the goddess **Ishtar** chooses a dove as her messenger: this detail appears in the Hebrew version of **Noah** and his ark, in which the dove, sent to see if the waters recede, returns to the ark with an olive leaf, indicating life renewed. **Sophia**, the epitome of **Gnostic** wisdom, Light of the Heavenly Mother, is the Holy Dove of the Spirit. In medieval paintings the Conception of the Virgin Mary is depicted as a ravishment by the Holy Dove. Seven doves refer to the seven gifts of the spirit. A flock of doves, like a flock of sheep or lambs, depicts the faithful. The dove with a palm branch is victory over death.

In a modern Greek tale the life of a magician is bound up with three doves in the belly of a wild **boar**. When the first is killed, he grows ill; when the second dies, he gets worse; at the death of the third he dies. In this tale the dove represents the magician's external **soul**.

The dove is the purified soul, even as the **raven** is sin.

DRACULA (*See* DRAGON, VAMPIRISM)

DRAGON (*See* CONCORDANCE)

This most famed of all fabulous beasts is found in myth the world around as winged **serpent**, a fire-breathing and beneficent fertility-bringer, or as the '**loathly worm**' guarding treasure it cannot enjoy, kidnapping maidens and wreaking havoc on the land until slain by a **hero** like **St George** or **St Michael**. In the dragon-image, myth and symbol coincide not only with mysteries of earth-energy but with variant human perceptions and religious requirements. In general, in **Christian** or other monotheistic cultures the dragon is a symbol of chaotic evil, a fallen **angel** or the very **Devil**, as described in the Book of Revelation and numerous European legends, while in the east, especially China, traditionally the 'dragon-energy' is precisely that power which guarantees the fertility of the land.

But the two images are not so opposed as may at first seem. The dragon initially epitomises life-giving energies; the fertilisation of earth/water (**serpent**) by air/fire (**bird, phoenix**). Such energies may be chaotic and beyond human control, devastating the land with thunder, lightning, drought or flood. Thus, long before Christian demonisation of the dragon, the myth of the evil female dragon slain by the solar hero existed; as with **Tiamat** slain by **Bel-Marduk** in **Babylonian myth**, or Pytho (dragon of the rotten-smelling hallucinatory fumes arising from the caves at Delphi) by **Apollo** in Greek myth. The myth of the **vampire** rising from the midnight grave to feast on human **blood** is likewise a myth of the chaotic, chthonic dragon – the name 'Dracula' originates in the Latin word for the dragon, *draco*. As for the common European tale of the virgin (Andromeda in Greek myth: many variants since) sacrificed to the voracious dragon of lake or sea, this is found not in Europe alone, but in every land where threat of drought (death) vies with hope of fertility (life).

An African tale from Mali tells of a town by a vast lake, its folk so terrorised by a dragon in it that they could draw its water only one day a year, and then only by sacrificing a virgin. One year the only virgin left was the king's lovely daughter, Fatouma. A foreign prince, Hammadi, heard of her beauty and came to marry her. Arriving, he found all in mourning, for Fatouma was already tied up by the lake, awaiting her fate. But Hammadi (like **Perseus**) was unafraid. Untying her, he promised her his protection. Thunder rolled and rain poured down, but when the fiery dragon emerged from the lake, he killed it, whereupon the two married. A familiar tale?

So too in India the god **Indra** slew **Vritra**, the **demon** or dragon of drought; as in **Hebrew myth Yahweh** slays **Leviathan** – even though in the oldest Jewish texts Yahweh is portrayed as a serpent-god. The ambiguity is perpetual. The battle between dragon and hero is between chaotic natural fertility and the human need to channel and direct it – as expressed in the **Welsh myth** of how, when as a **wonder-child** asked why the tower of King Vortigern kept falling each time it was built, the magician **Merlin** said it was because two dragons fought under the foundations. The implication was that the virility (dragon-energy) of the land could be harnessed only by a true ruler – which Vortigern was not. Today the red dragon is the national symbol of the Welsh, while as symbol of lightning, mountain-tops and high places (as at **Glastonbury**) it is mythically controlled by St Michael, a solar dragon-slayer.

In **Chinese** symbolism dragon and serpent are one, representing wisdom, benevolent heavenly power and the fertilising earth-currents (*lung mei*: in the West identified with 'ley lines'). The four dragon-kings, seen in the clouds, gave rain to each region of the land as needed: local dragon-kings were said to preside over every stream, river or **well**. It became the imperial emblem: the earliest Chinese emperors were said to be dragons. The two 'contending dragons', are the *yin-yang* forces of **dualism**, as are the Egyptian **Set** and **Osiris** – twin powers whose contention leads to creation.

The persistent Western perception of the dragon not as winged fertility symbol but '**loathly worm**', Devil or sterile guardian of buried treasure remains ambiguous. To 'slay the dragon' means to overcome one's own fears, ignorance and dark or evil side. The treasure it guards is the gold of the soul, unreleased save by heroic struggle, just as the lovely maiden to be rescued is (in **Jungian** terms) the anima: the sleeping female aspect of every masculine mind. Dragon-slaying heroes are thus individuals with the courage and resources to seek out and slay or redeem within themselves those psychological elements resisting illumination.

DRAGON-KINGS (*See* CHINESE MYTH, DRAGON)

DRAUPADI (*See* BHIMA, HELEN OF TROY, INDIAN MYTH, *MAHABHARATA*)

The epic **Indian** *Mahabharata* tells of the part played by this beautiful daughter of Drupada, king of Panchala, in the war between the Pandavas and Kauravas. Sprung full-grown from a sacrificial fire, she married all five Pandava brothers simultaneously. Spending two nights with each in turn, to each she bore a son and a daughter. One day Yuddhisthira the eldest diced with his Kaurava cousins and lost all, including Draupadi and his brothers. Enslaved and told to sweep the floor by the Kaurava leader, Duryodhana, she protested. Duryodhana's brother Duhsasana pulled her hair and tore off her clothes. She demanded revenge, but Yuddhisthira reminded her that they were slaves. Bhima swore to drink Duhsasana's blood before he died.

Exiled thirteen years in the forest, one day her husbands were hunting when her cousin Jayadratha came and abducted her. Bhima would have killed him, but Yudhisthira said a cousin must not be killed. Instead, she took his jewels. Later, her husbands served the king of Virata. As lady-in-waiting to his queen she would not wash the feet of others, saying the **Gandharvas** protected her. When the queen's brother Kichaka tried to seduce her, Bhima killed him. She was sentenced to die, but Bhima rescued her.

Exile over, the Pandavas went to war. On the eighteenth night of battle they invaded the Kaurava camp. Alone in the Pandava camp, she was attacked by Ashvatthaman, the last Kaurava general, who decapitated her five sons. Bhima and **Arjuna** would have killed him, but Yudhisthira reminded them that he was a Brahman, whom only **Vishnu** could punish. So they took the jewel in his hair and gave it to her, but she gave it to Yudhisthira who, though the cause of all their ills, remained the family head. Then, all worldly joy lost, she followed the Pandavas to meditate in the Himalayas. One by one they died, first Draupadi, then Sahadeva, Nakula, Arjuna and Bhima. Finally Yudhisthira was left alone with his faithful hound which, when he asked if it might be taken to heaven with him, transformed into **Dharma**, the god of justice. Entering Swarga, the celestial city of **Indra**, he was reunited by **Indra** and **Krishna** with his brothers, and with Draupadi.

DREAMS (*See* FREUD, JUNG)

In the first of many dreams recorded in the **Bible** it is told how Jacob saw a **ladder** from earth to heaven, 'the **angels** of God ascending and descending it', and above it God telling him 'I am with thee.' It has been said that this dream meant that from then on humanity and the source of its meaning (God) would forever be in communication, creator and created in perpetual partnership. So too in myths the world over the power of dreams to elicit knowledge beyond conscious reach is acknowledged. In dreams occur primeval **archetypes** providing the stuff of myth – the perils and obstacles of the hero-journey; bizarre events, beings and transformations; the meetings with messengers from the gods; dreams of flying like Icarus; or of challenging the Dweller at the Threshold before descending to the **underworld**, or of being swallowed by the monstrous sea-**dragon**. In dream, one meets spirits.

Since the pioneering work of **Sigmund Freud** and **Carl Jung**, the mythic content of dreams has been widely acknowledged. Both saw dreaming as a road to the unconscious mind. But where Freud saw dreaming in terms of personal (sexual) conflict alone, Jung saw it as an autonomous, primordial process with its own laws and language. 'The dream is a little hidden door in the innermost and most secret recesses of the psyche, opening into that cosmic night which was psyche long before there was any ego consciousness.'[1]

Also he wrote: 'Usually a dream is . . . distinguished by . . . lack of logic, questionable morality, uncouth form, and apparent absurdity or nonsense.'[2]

That such 'absurdity' does make sense (to those able to penetrate it) is borne out by the experience of many so-called 'primitive' cultures. In the 1930s the anthropologist Kilton Stewart reported how the Senoi of Malaysia practised daily dream-analysis to maintain a healthy society. The Senoi claimed to have had no crime, murder or intercommunal conflict in over 300 years. They say sexual dreams should move through to orgasm; that in falling dreams the dreamer should let himself fall (a rapid way to contact the spirit-world); and that a dreamer endangered in a dream should advance and attack, calling friends for help if needed. The enemy thus killed or overcome will become the dreamer's friend or ally. In the Andaman Islands, the word *oko-jumu* ('one who speaks from dreams') refers to highly respected and feared individuals able to contact the spirit-world in dream. Likewise the Dreamtime of the Australian **Aborigines** refers to that era when **spirits** walked and shaped the earth. The Dreamtime is not in the past, in the historical sense: it is eternally present. 'You know,' a Kalahari hunter told Laurens van der Post, 'there is a dream dreaming us.'[3]

Typically, the dream is understood as the actual experience of the **soul** of the sleeper, wandering away from the body to visit the places, see the people and perform the acts he dreams about. On awakening, a Macusi man in South America, having dreamt his employer made him drag a canoe up a series of cataracts, was bitterly reproachful. A Bororo village panicked, with all fleeing, when someone dreamed of enemies approaching it. A Fijian man, suddenly awakened by someone who trod on his foot, was heard imploring his soul to return, for he had dreamed he was far away in Tonga. Awakening, he was sure he must die unless his soul could be brought back immediately.[4]

In Irish myth the god **Angus Mac Og** fell in love with a supernatural woman who visited him in dream: he fell ill until he found her in fact. Two tales in the Welsh *Mabinogion* concern dreams: 'The Dream of Rhonabwy', and 'The Dream of Macsen Wledig'; in each case, the dream is the tale.

Art and science profit by dream. **Coleridge** composed *Kubla Khan* in a dream. Stevenson's *Dr Jekyll and Mr Hyde* began in a dream. The nineteenth-century chemist Friedrich von Kekulé, seeking the molecular structure of benzene, dreamed (in 1865) of snakelike chains of atoms swallowing their own tail (like **Ourobouros**). He awoke knowing the structure of benzene to be a closed carbon ring. Elias Howe invented the sewing machine following a dream in which **cannibals**, giving him twenty-four hours to invent the machine or else provide them with their supper, danced round him with spears which, he saw, had eye-shaped holes near their tips . . .

1. *Civilisation in Transition*, C.G. Jung, Collected Works, Vol.10.
2. *Dreams*, C.G. Jung, Ark Books, London, 1985, p.68.
3. *Jung and the Story of our Times*, Laurens van der Post, Penguin, London, 1978.
4. *The Golden Bough*, Sir James Frazer, Macmillan, London, 1963, p.182.

DREAMTIME (*See* **ABORIGINES, DREAMS**)

DRUIDS (*See* **BARDS, CELTIC MYTH, OAK**)
'It is especially the object of the Druids to inculcate this,' wrote Julius Caesar in *De Bello Gallico*, speaking of the Celtic priesthood, 'that souls do not perish, but after death pass into other bodies, and they consider that by this belief more than anything else men may be led to cast away the fear of death, and become courageous. They discuss many points concerning heavenly bodies and their motion, the extent of the universe and the world, the nature of things, the influence and ability of the immortal gods; and they instruct the youth in these things.'

The Druids are often falsely associated with the **megaliths** and **earth mounds** found throughout Western Europe. In fact the Celts reached Britain over a millennium after megalithic culture failed. Yet Druid lore was well respected: some Romans sent their children to Irish Druid colleges. Even so, their ban on writing means that little is now known of their beliefs and ceremonies. The name 'Druid' may come from *drus*, or the Welsh *derw*, both meaning '**oak**'; thus they were 'men of the oak'. It may be that they revered the oak for its connection with lightning (growing above water, it attracts lightning); and also **mistletoe** (which Pliny says they named all-healing), which grows on the oak, the fire-tree, as a visible manifestation of celestial fire. Moreover, in that mistletoe never touches the earth, it symbolises Man, who exists between heaven and earth. Pliny says that, when found, mistletoe 'was gathered with due religious ceremony, if possible on the sixth day of the moon'. Cut with a golden sickle and caught as it fell on a white cloak, the rite involved the sacrifice of two white **bulls**.

The Druids practised human sacrifice, of condemned criminals or war captives. The greater the number of victims, the greater was thought to be the fertility of the land. The victims might be impaled, speared, drowned, or shut and burned alive in huge wickerwork cages shaped like a **giant** or god: perhaps **Bel**, as such sacrifices often occurred at the spring festival of **Beltane**. Ritual **cannibalism** was also practised while, claims Tacitus, the Druids 'consult the gods in the palpitating entrails of men'. Strabo adds that they stabbed their human victim in the back and drew **omens** from the convulsions of his death-struggle.

They were said to be able to cast dense fogs, raise storms, take animal form and create illusion by 'glamouring' the eye. By the rite of *taghairm*, wrapped up all night in a newly-flayed bull-skin, they would emerge at dawn prophesying. By the 'fith-fath' spell, standing on one leg, pointing with one finger with one eye shut, they made themselves **invisible**. They were said to carry a 'serpent's egg': a crystal ball that could defuse **curses**; and to carry magical yew-staffs. It is said that Irish Druid Mog Ruith, a student in Rome of **Simon Magus**, built a stone flying-machine and fought an aerial battle over Ireland with a rival Druid – before, like Simon, falling to his doom. The archetypal Druid was later personified in the form and myth of the wizard **Merlin** – **demon**-born seer, commander of **dragon** powers, and, though finally defeated by female wiles, never killed but suspended in a crystal cave to return in a future time.

Such a myth not only reflects Druid beliefs in **reincarnation** but the way **Christianity** superseded them. The tale of **St Patrick**'s magical battle with the Irish Druids is as well known as the Druid prophecy of **Christ**'s coming. Perhaps the latter was invented by an Irish monk *c*.AD 700: after all, the monks of the Celtic Church inherited Druid tradition. Even after the Synod of Whitby (AD 664), many maintained not the Roman but the Druid tonsure (shaving not the crown but the forehead in an ear-to-ear line), and refused celibacy or hierarchic rule. Descendants of Druids who had turned Christian hermit, alias *culdee* (Gaelic *cil*, 'cell', *dee*, *deus*, 'god'), they recorded what by then was already all but lost in the mists of the past.[1]

1. *The Magic Arts in Celtic Britain*, Lewis Spence, Rider, London, 1970; *The Golden Bough*, Sir James Frazer, Macmillan, London, 1963.

DRUM (*See* SHAMANISM)

The sound of the drum is primordial speech (as in 'talking drums'), its rhythm the heart-beat of the universe, its function to induce ecstasy in sacred dance or orgy (as in the rites of **Cybele** or **Dionysus**) and to call the spirits. Among the **Bori** of West Africa every spirit has its own drum-rhythm; among other African peoples the drum itself is believed to be or to contain a spirit. In Swahili, *tari* is the name of a drum, also that of the dance played on it and danced with it, and that of the spirit summoned by it to possess the dancers.

In Zaïre the drum-maker, selecting his tree, begs forgiveness of the tree-spirit for cutting it down, and also asks the spirit to remain in the drum to be carved. When the drum is first struck, the sound it gives is the voice of the spirit. **Taboo** surrounds all such drums: they are not to be touched or played by the wrong person for fear of offending their spirits. In Burundi, after the king dies, his drum (called the king's voice) can no longer be touched.

Elsewhere the rolling of drums implies the voices of the **thunder**-gods such as **Indra**, **Zeus** and **Thor**. In **Buddhism** the drum of the **dharma** awakens the ignorant; in **Hinduism** it is an attribute of **Shiva** and **Kali** as destroyers. To **Native Americans** the roundness of the drum is the wholeness of the cosmos: its medicine is that of the dance.

DRYADS (*See* ELEMENTALS)

DUALISM (*See* AHRIMAN, AHURA MAZDA, CATHARS, ZOROASTRIANISM)

Insisting on the existence of two co-equal universal powers of good and evil, alias light and dark, dualists regard the material world as created by the dark, or evil, power, and thus all fleshly appetite as a distraction from spiritual life. Initially a natural consequence of observations on the alternation of night and day, winter and summer, elements of dualism pervaded early **Vedic** thought in India, and also the Chinese perception of *yin* and *yang*. But whereas in these cultures a basic unity was seen to underlie the duality, in Zoroastrian Persia (seventh century BC on), dualism became a dogma in itself, later permeating Western thought from **Pythagoras** (sixth century BC) to the Cathars (twelfth century AD), en route influencing Essenes, **Neoplatonists**, **Gnostics** and **Manichaeans**. Though persecuting dualism fiercely for centuries, **Christianity** itself was never wholly free of the tendency, insisting that God does not cause the world's evil, this being solely the **Devil**'s work. Nor can dualism be said to be dead, being in the first place a spontaneous human response to the *natural* dualism of day and night, life and death and other obvious elemental oppositions.

DUMUZI (*See* INANNA, SUMERIAN MYTH, TAMMUZ)

DURGA (*See* DEVI, INDIAN MYTH, KALI, TANTRAS)

DWARVES (*See* ELEMENTALS, FAIRIES, LEPRECHAUN)

Are traditional tales of human interaction with dwarf races any more than fantasy? Pygmies still inhabit tropical Africa, yet, in Africa, dwarves are not identified with pygmies. Pygmies are small human beings; dwarves are not thought to be human, but semi-simian, or evil spirits in disguise – possibly envious spirits of the dead. The vicious Biloko of Zaïre live in hollow trees, wearing only leaves, with grass instead of hair, sharp long claws and mouths which can gape wide enough to swallow a human body. Dwarves in East Africa may steadily disappear as you talk to them: the South African dwarf Uhlakanyana, though born of a human mother, is an evil **trickster** reminiscent of the **gnome**, **leprechaun** or wizened **changeling** of **Celtic myth** – an unconscious, amoral or **elemental** force of nature.

The Dasyus ('dark folk') of **Indian myth** appear to be spirit-creatures, though some argue that they refer to dark-skinned aborigines displaced by the **Aryans** and later demonised.[1] The same argument is found in Europe. The eleventh-century Adam of Bremen describes a race of dwarves inhabiting Northern Europe before the Celtic invasions, as having 'large heads, flat faces, flat noses, and large mouths'.[2] They were also described as 'black people', living underground and emerging only at night. This is a reasonable way to survive if you fear for your life: the description might also fit primeval mining communities. Yet these 'black dwarves' of **Teutonic myth** are matched by the 'white **elves**' of air and ocean. Is there anything here but a human tendency to symbolise every aspect of nature in supernatural terms?

It seems not impossible that, in the warmer paleolithic climate, the descendants of folk now found only in Africa ranged further north, before being driven south by chill weather and invasion. The problem in accepting such a thesis (as in accepting the tales of elves and **pixies** as distorted historical memory of earlier peoples) lies in how oral or unwritten history merges with **fairy-tale**, magic romance or folklore of a sort hard to take literally. Aboriginal inhabitants no doubt lived in every land; maybe they were stunted (poor diet) and secretive – and no doubt they were despised by those conquering them as 'evil spirits' or 'dwarves'. But human imagination needs no 'evidence' to invent dwarves – or **giants**.

1. *Indian Myth and Legend*, Donald A. Mackenzie, Gresham, London, 1910, pp.67–70.
2. *Dimensions*, Jacques Vallée, Sphere, London, 1990, p.97.

DYAUS-PITA (*See* ARYANS, INDIAN MYTH)

Husband of the vaguely-perceived earth-goddess Prithivi, the name of this **Vedic Aryan** sky-god derives from the root *div*, 'to shine'. (Dyaus rhymes with mouse.) Thus the name, Dyaus-pita ('Sky-Father'), seems phonetically to be reflected in the Greek **Zeus**-(*pater*) and the Roman *Ju-piter*.

Sometimes referred to as a ruddy **bull** bellowing thunder; as the night sky he is depicted as a pearl-bedecked black **horse**, the pearls being the stars. In that he is a sky-father slain by his son **Indra**, he may loosely be associated with the Greek **Ouranos** (sky), likewise slain by his son, **Cronus**. Having done the deed, Indra is reproached by his earth-mother Prithivi. She, though source of all vegetation, was never as vital to the pastoral, patriarchal Aryans as the powerful **mother-goddesses** were to the peoples of the Middle East and Europe. She was sometimes perceived, like the Egyptian **Hathor**, as a **cow**, and may also be identified with the Greek **Gaia**. Regarded as the parents of all gods and human beings, it remains unclear which was born first.

A Vedic hymn tells how, when their son the fire-god **Agni** was born, Dyaus and Prithivi fled him, but 'returned to embrace the lion'.[1]

1. *Indian Myth and Legend*, Donald A. Mackenzie, Gresham, London, 1910.

DYING GODS (*See* CONCORDANCE)

These typically are the deities of fertility religions, their annual death and rebirth symbolising the annual death and rebirth of vegetation. Often perceived as effiminate (**Attis**) or beautiful (**Adonis**), and as beloved by their Great Mother the earth, they combine male and female characteristics, and annually (through their sacrificial human representatives) were slain, typically while bound to or crucified on a **tree**; their flayed, **castrated**, dismembered remains being then eaten by their worshippers, or reduced to ash and mixed into the seed-corn for the new season, or scattered on the land. That **Christ** fits the pattern is clear from the characteristics of this **archetype**: the (**virgin**) birth of dying gods is announced by a star; as children they teach their teachers; they predict their death and return, then die on a tree while still young; they descend into the **underworld** for three days (dark of the **moon**), a winter, or an age before resurrection. Christ, like the Norse **Baldur**, does not return annually, but only at the end of the old world (Last Days, **Ragnorak**) and beginning of the new; the Egyptian **Osiris**, dismembered by Set and magically revived by **Isis**, chooses not to return but to remain below as the Lord of the Underworld. In **Arthurian myth** Galahad (the most godly knight of the **Round Table**) is transported to **heaven** on attaining the secret of the **Holy Grail**: a variant on the theme.

As slain fertility-goddesses (**Inanna, Ishtar, Isis, Persephone, Eurydice**) descended to the underworld are sought out and restored to life by consort or mother, likewise Middle Eastern dying gods are sought out and restored by wife or sister. Where not directly sacrificial, all such cults are initiatory: the candidate for initiation must 'die' to the world before he or she is 'reborn'. This symbolism is apparent in modern fundamentalist Christian cults of the 'born-again' or 'twice-born': the archetype figures also in popular modern cults built up around the early death of media stars (gods) such as **James Dean** or John Lennon of the **Beatles**. Thus too it is still said that 'Those whom the gods love die young.'

DYLAN (*See* **LLEW LLAW GYFFES**, *MABINOGION*, **WELSH MYTH**)

This son of **Arianrhod** and brother of **Llew Llaw Gyffes** was nicknamed 'Dylan' ('Son of the Wave') because he swam off to sea after baptism. It is said that this son of the sea, who swam as well as the best of the fishes, and beneath whom no wave ever broke, became Llew, on being slain by his uncle, the smith-god Gofannon (Welsh equivalent of Irish **Goibniu**, Saxon-Teutonic **Wayland Smith**). In British myth, this crime was called one of the Three Unfortunate Blows.

DYLAN, BOB (*See* **ROCK'N'ROLL MYTH**)

E

EA (*See* **ENKI, SUMERIAN MYTH**)

EAGLE (*See* **BIRDS, HAWK, PHOENIX**)
This highest-flying and most regal of birds was thought able to reach and identify with the sun; hence it symbolises **sky-gods, sun-gods** and the spiritual principle in man. **Hermetic** symbol of sulphur, one of the three symbols of the zodiacal sign of Scorpio, shown double-headed it represents twin gods, also omniscient political power, as in the crest of the Habsburg dynasty, rulers of the Holy Roman Empire (AD 1273–1914). It was sacred to the **Norse** god **Odin**, the **Greek** sky-god **Zeus** (and **Pan** before him), and to **Roman Jupiter**: Roman legions were led by an eagle standard. In **Hindu myth** it is an emblem of **Indra** and the solar **Garuda** Bird that **Vishnu** rode. As bird of stormcloud and lightning, it was the most sacred of all animals to the Native Americans, and the source of their Thunderbird; a divine being living above the clouds, its flashing eyes the lightning, its beating wings the thunder: thus represented by the eagle-feathered head-dress. The eagle **dance** of the Pueblo peoples of the southwestern USA dramatises the relationship between humanity and the sky powers. The bald-headed eagle is the symbol of the USA: should a mythic inference be drawn from the fact that it has been hunted virtually into extinction?

In **Celtic** lore the eagle was thought among the oldest of the animals. **Mael Dúin** and his companions saw an eagle renew itself, **phoenix**-like, by a lake. In some occult traditions the phoenix represents the celestial sun, the eagle the mundane. A Celtic myth says that **Adam** and **Eve** survive as eagles: the Celtic heroes Fintan and Tuan macCarill spent a lifetime as eagles before changing into the oldest, wisest, animal of all, the **salmon**. This may derive from belief that the eagle renewed its plumage by flying up to the sun before plunging into the sea: hence **resurrection** and baptismal rebirth, as in **Christian** belief, in which **Christ** is variously identified with the eagle. Grasping the **serpent** between its talons it symbolises the war between good and evil: their conjunction in battle symbolises the ultimate union of spirit and matter. It also has affinities with the **Egyptian hawk**-god **Horus**.

EARTH MOTHER (*See* **BURIAL, EARTH MOUNDS, FERTILITY-GODS, GAIA, MOTHER-GODDESS**)
'The earth is not a dead body,' declared the medieval alchemist Basilius Valentinus, 'but is inhabited by a spirit that is its life and soul. All created things, minerals included, draw their strength from the earth spirit. This spirit is life, it is nourished by the stars'.[1]

Danu, Gaia, Nerthus, Lakshmi and Prithivi are names by which the earth was honoured as **archetypal** mother, nurse and nourisher of all life – one aspect of the Great Goddess from whom we come and to whom we return. The first known paintings are found deep in her womb-caves, at Lascaux or Altamira; the first known human sculptures are of the pot-bellied, full-breasted, broad-hipped Earth Mother; the first myths are of the Sky Father mating with her to create Nature's fruits and humankind – the name '**Adam**' means 'earth'. She was not always kind: early folk feared her displeasure or withdrawal of fecundity via drought or other natural disaster. To mine or otherwise violate her was dangerous. When mines were dug to acquire red ochre (haematite: blood of the earth), to cake the bodies of the dead when buried (born in her **blood**, buried in her blood), they were later filled in to heal the wound, as at the world's oldest known mine (Swaziland's Lion Cavern, dated 100,000 BC.)[2] To do otherwise was thought to court disaster by upsetting the spirit energies pervading matter.

'You ask me to plough the ground. Shall I take a knife and tear my mother's breast?' asked the nineteenth-century **Native American** prophet Smohalla. Such a view no longer seems odd, as environmental pollution leads to deadly ecological and climatic imbalance. But how did we forget her and let this happen? Sky-god-worshipping patriarchal folk (insisting that Adam created **Eve**, not vice versa) founded cities, denying natural cycles and the older rural wisdom as **fairy-tale**. Whatever could not be weighed and measured was rejected. The process was gradual. Catholic *conquistadores* rededicated the holy places of those they slew, guided partly by the image of the **Virgin**, but Protestants in North America scorned Earth Mother notions as **pagan**, fey or silly. Now we inherit an 'energy crisis' even as old Earth Mother ideas of power-places, holy **wells** and spirit-paths revive. Rural folk from Ireland to China perceived the seasonal flow of earth-energy as fairy- or **dragon**-paths; so too England's 'green ways' and 'old straight tracks' seem to follow fertilising, seasonal geomagnetic currents. The properties of streams, lakes and rivers are seasonal, says **Ovid** in the *Metamorphoses*. Shrines, oracular sites like **Delphi**, and other centres holy to the Earth Mother (as Chartres in France is holy to the Virgin) have a specific season of power when the 'god' or fertilising spirit is in residence. Grotesque open-thighed **sheela-na-gig** images found in some medieval Celtic and English churches (as at Kilpeck in Hereford) suggest ancient acknowledgement of her sexuality as essential to the fertility of Nature and humanity.

The earth lives, not in an anthropomorphic sense, but as a complex and energetic organism. Our health is intimately bound up with it. We despise the image of the earth as mother at our peril. She may not always be kind. Like **Cerridwen** or **Kali, Cybele** or Nerthus, she will pursue, destroy and consume us unless we mend our ways. The '**New Age**' movement celebrates Gaia as the epitome of a 'new consciousness' – but does 'Gaia' celebrate us?

1. *The Earth Spirit*, John Michell, Avon Books, New York, 1975, p.4.
2. *Lifetide*, Lyall Watson, Coronet Books, London, 1980, p.62.

EARTH MOUNDS (*See* DRAGON, EARTH MOTHER, FAIRIES, MEGALITHIC MYTHS)

The myths connected with the mysterious neolithic earth mounds (*c.*4,000–2,000 BC) found the world over (some 40,000 in Britain alone) typically involve buried **giants**, 'barrow-wights' (guardian ghosts), **dragon**-guarded buried treasure or association with **fairies**. Many long barrows (some over 300 feet) are said to have giants buried in them: skeletons over eight feet tall are said to have been unearthed. Yet even those in which stone burial chambers are found consist mostly of earth alone.[1] Burial does not seem to have been their primary purpose. Then what were they for?

Tales of dragons protecting 'treasure' suggest vague folk memory of such mounds being erected on sites of known geomagnetic properties – the 'dragon' being associated, in West as well as East, with the flow of such fertilising energies. Early churches were often sited either on or near such mounds (Bleddfa or Cascob in Wales), and are associated with dragon-slaying myths. Such mound-churches in Wales are often called Llanfihangel, 'Church of the Chief Angel' (**St Michael**, the dragon-slaying patron saint of high places and lightning). So, were such mounds erected to increase the land's fertility? The **serpent** symbology associated with many suggests so. At New Grange in Ireland (pre-4,000 BC) the main stone passageway, oriented to midwinter sunrise, is carved with spirals. The Ohio serpent mound in the USA, snaking over hundreds of yards, is one of many American animal effigy mounds invoking fertility symbolism of **egg** and serpent. So too in China earth mounds were erected on *lung mei* – 'dragon-paths'.[2]

Silbury Hill near Avebury in Wiltshire, may represent the pregnant **earth mother**. This largest of European man-made mounds, 130 feet high, covering 5 acres, its flat top 100 feet across, is dated *c*.2750 BC. No chambers have been found in it, yet it stands amid proven alignments of standing stones and straight tracks – *lung mei*.

Elsewhere, hills of artificial appearance (Butthouse Knapp in Hereford) or capped by prominent earthworks (the Wrekin in Shropshire) are said to have been built by the **Devil**. **Glastonbury** Tor also appears too regular to be natural: some say the paths winding up it form an **initiatory** maze.

Many conical British tumuli are identified as fairy hills or knowes. Into such mounds mortals were abducted, there to remain, oblivious of time. Some, like **True Thomas**, escaped, only to find (like **Oisin** or **Mael Dúin** on return from the Isles of the Blest) their loved ones long dead. In his 1691 treatise on the fairies, the **Rev. Robert Kirk** (who died *c*.1692 on a fairy knowe) remarks that Scots Highlanders 'superstitiously believe the souls of their predecessors to dwell' in fairy hills.[3] This identifies fairies as the spirits of the mound-builders. In an apocryphal case, excavation of a Welsh mound said to possess treasure guarded by a ghost-king revealed the grave of a neolithic king, buried with gear including torcs of gold. Oral tradition had maintained the memory of an event some four thousand years old. Or so it is said. No wonder that, in fairy hills, time is said to stand still. You may enter them . . . but you may never emerge.

1. *Mysterious Britain*, Janet and Colin Bord, Paladin, London, 1974, pp.69ff.
2. *The New View over Atlantis*, John Michell, Thames & Hudson, London, 1983.
3. *The Secret Commonwealth of Elves, Fauns and Fairies*, Rev. Robert Kirk, Observer Press, Stirling, 1933 (1691).

EARTHLY PARADISE (*See* AGHARTI, ATLANTIS, EDEN, HESPERIDES, HY-BRASIL, LYONESSE, SHAMBHALA, TIR NAN OG)

The earthly paradise is a supernatural land which only heroes may enter, to enjoy eternal youth amid sparkling fountains and ever-flowering gardens. It is **Eden** brought full circle: the innocence of creation restored. It differs from the **Christian heaven** or **Buddhist** enlightenment in that it is usually found over the Western sea in the land of the sunset (land of the dead). The idea persists in modern forms (as in: 'Go west, young man').

The belief is ancient. In **Egyptian myth** the land of the *Ka* (spirit-double) lies to the west. The **Greek** Garden of the Hesperides (daughters of Atlas and Hesperus) lies beyond the river-ocean at the western edge of the world: here grew the wondrous golden **apples** seized by **Hercules**. The **Celts** described how beyond the Atlantic sunset lay the Isles of the Blest – Emhain, Findargad, Argadnel and Mag Mell, Emhnae and Magh Mon. Irish manuscripts (seventh to ninth centuries AD) describe thrice fifty such isles. There, where golden gulls swoop through sparkling skies, death is unknown; music, drinking, dancing and love-making are continual. Beautiful Emhain stands out of the amethyst sea on its four great pillars of brass, the sun shining even in the shadow beneath it. Sweet rain falls at dusk and dawn; amid bright days and glowing nights silver **moon** and golden **sun** make love.

Thus **Avalon**, whence King **Arthur** was taken; thus the original 'Utopia' of Sir Thomas More (sixteenth century), and Sir Francis Bacon's 'New Atlantis' a century later. The myth of **Atlantis** itself, and other drowned or mythic lands in the West from Ys and Lyonesse to **Hy-Brasil** (thus Brazil), also arise from this archetype, or drowned memory.

Yet not every earthly paradise is located in the West. Other versions of it are hidden, like **Shambhala** in the Himalayas, or underground, like **Agharti**. All are mythic states of mind, not geographical locations. Even so, belief in the actual existence of an 'earthly paradise' persisted into historical times. The Spanish *conquistadores* did not easily abandon their search for **Cibola** or **El Dorado** in America, while the lure of the New World over the Atlantic drew millions of European emigrants from the seventeenth century on. Seeking an earthly paradise, they founded the USA.

EASTER (*See* ATTIS, CHRISTIANITY)
The pagan aspects of Easter, the main festival of the Christian Church year celebrating the resurrection of **Christ,** persist even today. The name of the festival itself is derived from Oestre, a **Teutonic** goddess of spring's fertility (thus oestrus?), while the movable date, originally synchronised with the Jewish Passover, may also at one time have been connected with the death and resurrection of **Attis**, officially celebrated in ancient Rome on 24 and 25 March. According to an ancient tradition, Christ was crucified on 25 March: for centuries many Christians celebrated the festival on that date without regard to the phase of the moon, which by the sixth century had come to determine the movable date. As late as the fourth century many worshippers of Attis contended that Christ was an imitation or mere counterfeit of their own, older god.

As for the Easter **egg**, this too is a pre-Christian symbol of rebirth and renewal at the time of the vernal equinox, while the Easter rabbit was probably in origin the **hare**, a lunar animal sacred not only to Oestre but to all **moon**-goddesses.

EASTWOOD, CLINT (*See* HOLLYWOOD, WILD WEST)

EDDA (*See* NORSE MYTH)
From the same linguistic root as the Sanskrit Veda, 'knowledge', this term refers to two collections of old Norse literature, known respectively as the *Edda Snorri Sturlusonar*, or 'Prose Edda', and the *Edda Soemundar*, or 'Elder Edda'. The *Prose Edda* comprises the Scandinavian myths as collated and set down in his native Icelandic by Snorri Sturluson (1179–1241). Because of his wit, scholarship and artistry, today we know many Norse myths which, had he not collected them, might well have been lost. Yet, as much of his material came from poets themselves working in a Christian age, it is hard to know how accurately he represented a pagan faith even then all but lost. The first part consists of mythical tales told by **Odin** to a Swedish king, the second treats of the art of poetry, the third is a system of prosody.

The Elder Edda (late ninth century), consists of thirty-three lays in verse, discovered in 1643 by an Icelandic bishop, Brynjulf Sveinsson.

EDEN (*See* ADAM, BIBLE, EARTHLY PARADISE, EVE)

That Eden and its primal garden is but a metaphorical paradise without real historical or geographic reference goes without saying. Or does it?

Certainly this wondrous garden, in which Adam and Eve were created by the Lord God before being corrupted by the **serpent** and expelled from it, is on one level but a charming stage on which the drama of emerging human self-consciousness (**original sin**) is enacted. Also it is clear that the Biblical Eden is derived from the older Sumerian Garden of **Immortality**, though in the latter the **earth mother Eve** is the bride of the serpent (celestial fertilising principle). No jealous god, guilt or original sin is involved in the Sumerian version, in which there is only one **tree**, the Tree of Life. The biblical garden was created by **Hebrew** patriarchs.

Yet where, if anywhere, was the site of an actual physical 'Eden'? It lay in the East (from the viewpoint of the narrator, a Hebrew), and from it flowed a river which divided into four, called Pishon, Gihon, Tigris and Euphrates. It appears too that Edin was a Sumerian name for the plain of Babylonia, at the south end of which, near Eridu, was a beautiful garden in which the gods dwelled, and in which stood the Tree of Life. Perhaps there was indeed a Garden of Eden on which the later Hebraic myth was based.

EDSHU (*See* AFRICAN MYTH, TRICKSTERS, YORUBA)

EGG

The cosmic egg is the universal womb of space-time, all creative potential in it, hatching all life. The image of the world as hatched from an egg is found from Fiji and the Far East to Egypt, Greece, Finland and Central America. In **Hindu myth** the cosmic egg was laid on the primeval waters by the Divine **Bird**, and **Brahma** hatched from it; in Egypt, laid by the Nile **goose**, it hatched the **sun-god Ra**, also **Ptah**; and Kneph the **serpent** produced it from his mouth, symbolising the Word. In **Druid** lore it was the 'egg of the serpent'; in **Orphic** belief it symbolised life, death and **resurrection**: the world-serpent **Ourobouros** surrounded it.

EGYPTIAN MYTH (*See* CONCORDANCE)

It is not only Egyptian myth that fascinates, but Egypt itself. The name Egypt is from the Greek Aigyptos, a transcription of Haikuptah, the name of the temple of the god **Ptah** at Memphis. Ancient Egyptians called their land Kemit or Khem ('the black one', from the colour of Nilotic soil); also the Two Lands (Upper and Lower Egypt); and Ta meri (the 'beloved' or 'magnetic earth'); and Ta nutri ('Land of the Neters', meaning 'Land of the Gods').

Ancient Egypt has fascinated younger cultures for over three millennia. The **Sphinx**, the **pyramids**, the obsession with the **afterlife**, the pantheon of animal-headed gods and goddesses, the Israelite Exodus and the drowning of Pharaoh's host in the Red Sea, legends of magical initiations and secret sciences, and the very origins of Egypt itself, remain as mysterious now as to **Plato** and Herodotus 2,500 years ago. Egyptian society has excited more bizarre speculation than any other. The **Sumerian** culture may be as old, but Sumerians never built a Great Pyramid, or ever were rumoured to be the survivors of **Atlantis**: a tale **Plato** (427–347 BC) recorded (or invented) in the *Timaeus*. In this dialogue, an Egyptian priest tells the Greek statesman Solon that the Greeks are but children; that the Greek myth of **Phäethon** refers to an ancient global destruction by **fire**, and that 'the age of our institutions is given in our sacred books as eight thousand years'.[1]

Though many in Plato's time (Aristotle included) thought his tale only a moral fiction, even then the Great Pyramid was ancient, and perplexing. Today dated as built by the pharaoh Khufu (Cheops) *c.*2600 BC, age-old occult rumour dates it 8,000 years earlier. Visit a museum with a representative selection of the huge statues of animal-headed deities, or of the pharaohs, then examine the bas-reliefs carved on funerary stelae or sarcophagi and the hieroglyphs painted on mummy-cases or illuminating the papyri of *The Book of the Dead*, and it is hard to suppress awe – not least at their sheer alien quality. It is not just that ancient Egyptians are remote in time, but that their cosmogony is so hard to grasp – especially given the many millennia over which cults rose and fell, different deities prevailing at one time or another, and the vast number of such gods. Those listed in the tomb of the pharaoh Thuthmoses III number 740. The nature and myths of the most important (**Amon, Anubis, Apis, Atum, Geb, Hathor, Horus, Isis, Nepthys, Nuit, Osiris, Ptah, Ra, Set, Thoth**) are described under their own entries.

Such deities were conceived by or before the fifth millennium BC. The accepted view is that they began as tribal **fetishes** prior to the uniting of the Upper and Lower Kingdoms. Some Egyptologists claim to have perceived, in accounts from the prehistoric period, histories of kings fighting for the crowns of Upper and Lower Egypt. But such tales may refer not to human but to divine dynasties, symbolising cosmic principles, finally materialised in the form of the man-king Menes, a manifestation of the falcon-god Horus.

From this era until the Alexandrine and Roman conquests three (or five) millennia later, Egyptian history is defined in terms of seven historical periods and eighteen dynasties. Throughout this lengthy period, at one time or another the great cult-centres flourished. In each a particular deity was worshipped as supreme: each held power in different eras. Yet, apart from the chaotic epoch (eighteenth century BC) when the Hyksos (shepherd-kings) conquered Egypt, and the period in the fourteenth century BC when Akhenaton broke with the past and proclaimed monotheistic worship of the solar disc Aton (a period ended by the suspicious death of the boy-king Tutankhamun), Egyptian theology and myth remain internally consistent.

Changes that were made were deliberate. The beginning of each greater epoch is marked by grammatical modifications; by the further development of some part of the overall myth in connection with a specific centre; and by the dominance of the cult of one specific deity. Innovations occurred by the imposition of an overall will. Thus differing cosmogonies as taught in different eras at different centres are complementary.

Thus at Memphis, it was taught that from Ptah, creator of all on earth, arose the eight primordial neters. At Thebes and Hermopolis, variants on this scheme were taught. Each centre emphasised a different stage in a continuing creative process which the entire society manifested. To select one or another of the variant cosmogonies as the true myth is as false as to attempt to define the entire zodiac from one sign alone.

Yet the popular myth remains that was taught at Heliopolis. Briefly: **Lotus**-enclosed amid primal chaos (**Nun**), Atum the self-created emerged from creative battle with the cosmic **serpent** Apep as Atum-Ra, the **sun**. Atum-Ra 'emitted' Shu (who holds up the sky) and Tefnut (rain-goddess). He created dry land. From his tears sprang men and other living beings. Shu and Tefnut bore Geb (Earth) and Nuit (Sky), who in turn bore Osiris (Fertility, later God of the Dead), **Isis** (the Great Goddess of the ancient world), **Set** (murderer of Osiris, barren desert), and Nepthys (identified by Greeks with **Aphrodite**). Thus, again, eight primal neters, after Atum-Ra.

The mythic drama is not consistent. Different versions combine.

1. *Timaeus and Critias*, Plato (trans. Desmond Lee), Penguin, London, 1971, pp.35–6.

EL (*See* BAAL, DAGON, ELVES, PHOENICIAN MYTH)

Dating from the fourteenth century BC, the cuneiform tablets discovered in 1929 at Ras Shamrah in Lebanon reveal an ancient Canaanite mythology based on a cult of the elements and natural phenomena. Heading the pantheon of gods was El, 'father of years', 'master of time', 'merciful lord'. It was he who made rivers flow into the abyss of **ocean**, thus assuring fertility. Father of **Baal**, he dwelt on Mount Saphon or by the sea. Always portrayed as seated, his omnipotence was represented by the **bull** -horns he wore.

Yet the word or root *el* is significant in many ancient languages. In Sumerian it means 'brightness' or 'shining'; in Old Cornish 'an angel'. The Babylonian *ellu* meant 'the shining one'; the Old Welsh *ellyl* is 'a shining being', as is the Anglo-Saxon *Aelf* (**elf**). Even more perplexing, in the Old Testament the supreme god **Yahweh** is also named El, or its feminine plural derivation, Elohim; a term first appearing in Genesis i:1, reading (1966 Jerusalem Bible) 'In the beginning, God created the heavens and the earth.' Or in Genesis i:26: 'God said, "Let us make man in our image, in the likeness of ourselves . . ." '

This is odd. If El means 'God' or 'shining one', then Elohim (plural) must mean 'the Gods' or 'the shining ones'. Thus: 'In the beginning, the Shining Ones created the heavens and the earth'; or, 'The Shining Ones said, "Let us make man in our image, in the likeness of ourselves . . ." '

This anomaly (the term 'Elohim' appears some thirty times in the Pentateuch) remains unexplained – and thought-provoking.

EL CID (*See* CID CAMPEADOR)

EL DORADO (*See* CIBOLA, INCA, LOST WORLDS)

Invading Mexico in the early sixteenth century, the Spanish heard rumours of a mysterious people whose cities were paved with gold and who were ruled by a priest-king called 'El Dorado', 'the gilded king', whose body was covered in powdered gold. Even as the similar myth of **Cibola** later drove Coronado north through Arizona in search of fabulous wealth, the myth of El Dorado stimulated Francisco Pizarro's invasion (1532–41) of Peru. Overwhelming the **Inca** civilization by guile, murder and treachery, he did indeed find gold, not that it did him much good: in 1541 he was assassinated. (Note that King **Midas** starved to death after achieving his wish that all he touched should turn to gold.) However, the myth of El Dorado survived: for centuries thereafter, anxious Europeans plundered the New World and killed its inhabitants in search of gold.

ELEMENTALS (*See* BROWNIES, DJINNS, DOMOVOI, DWARVES, ELVES, FAUNUS, FAIRIES, GNOMES, INCUBI, NYMPHS, SALAMANDER)

Medieval occultists hypothesised four categories of invisible beings: **angels**, devils or **demons**, the souls of the dead and nature's elemental spirits. Once the physical world was seen as the visible manifestation of the earth spirit, its activity springing from the interplay of the four elements: earth, air, fire and water. This interplay and events arising from it, from the wave bursting on the shore to the wind in the woods, was thought to be orchestrated by the appropriate elementals or nature spirits – natural forces personified as intelligent entities, existing in several orders, and occupying a realm between man and God. Lacking free will, they maintained seasonal processes and the systems of wind, wave, earth and fire that bore them. Thus, deep in the earth dwelt slow, dark **gnomes** (from the Greek *gnoma*, knowledge); temperamental sylphs (Greek *sylpha*, butterfly) rode the air; in the sea the *Undine* (Latin *unda*, wave) surged; in the fire the salamander (perhaps from Greek *salambe*, fireplace) flamed. The latter, visualised as a lizard, or little dragon, was also called the fire-drake.

Dwarves, elves and other such near-human beings have been defined as the folklorish memory of aboriginal races driven to hide in the forests or underground to escape invading races who later wove myths about them. Maybe so, but as with the **brownies, djinns, Domovoi** and other such sprites it seems likely that they, as with the **nymphs** and dryads (woodland nymphs) of **Greek myth**, also originate in human personification of natural forces. A whirl of autumn leaves may be seen as a dryad, dancing about the trees it protects. **Bestiaries** and other medieval romances are full of such beings: bugaboos, puckles, imps, urchins, hags, sprites and hellwains, Boneless and Hobgoblin, **fauns** and **satyrs, incubi**, succubi and other imaginings. The English forest imp Robin Goodfellow lies between the **Green Man** and **Robin Hood**. Such imaginings cannot be pinned down: in each generation they take on new forms according to local social requirements.

Yet the Renaissance magus **Paracelsus** (1493–1541) declared elementals to be 'of an elastic semi-material essence, etherial enough so as not to be detected by the physical sight, and they may change their forms according to certain laws.'[1] In Celtic lore, **fairies** were 'spirits who could make themselves seen or not seen at will. And when they took people they took body and soul together.'[2] **Robert Kirk** largely agreed with this.

The human relationship with these forces was both intimate and remote. If well treated, they would help people, but they were capricious, to be respected, as in the Highland Scots tradition of referring to the fairies as the 'good folk'. The plough broken by a rock, the ship lost at sea, the house burned down: such events were seen not as 'accidents' but as caused by human failure to placate the elementals. Woe betide the housewife who forgot to leave out milk at night for the household **brownie**.

In **theosophical** usage the term refers to beings starting evolutionary growth, thus in an elemental stage. Men too were once elemental beings, entering the created universe on the lowest plane of being to begin their climb up the stairway of life: from elemental to human to god.

1. *Dimensions*, Jacques Vallée, Sphere, London, 1990, p.90.
2. *Ibid.*, Evans-Wentz, *The Fairy Faith in Celtic Countries* (1909).

ELEPHANT (*See* ANIMALS, BEHEMOTH)

The size and supposed wisdom and memory of the elephant makes it a source of mythic lore not only in the lands (India and Africa) where it lives, but (anciently) in European cultures to which this fabulous beast was reported before anyone had seen or could believe in such a fabulous creature. Thus the **biblical** myth of **Behemoth** is widely thought to refer to the elephant.

African myth portrays it as too noble for its own good. The Wachaga of Tanzania say it was a man cheated out of all his limbs save the right arm, now its trunk. The **Ashanti** of Ghana say it is a human chief from the past.

In Indian myth, the great white elephant Airavata, born of the churning primal sea and 'furnished with four tusks', was given as a gift to the god **Indra**. The god **Shiva** sometimes wore the skin of an elephant: the god of wisdom, **Ganesa**, is shown four-armed and elephant-headed.

There is also the tale of how in Nepal long ago Queen Maya dreamed one night of a six-tusked white elephant entering her body. The king's sages interpreted this to mean that she would bear a son who either would rule the world or save mankind. The son she bore was Gautama the Buddha.

Another tale involves five blindfold sages who, to establish their wisdom, were tested by an elephant. Asked to tell by touch what it was, one touched the tusks, another the tail, a third the legs, the fourth the belly. Each falsely identified the beast in terms of the part they had touched. Only one was wise enough not to trust identification of one part or another but, by feeling his way all about, correctly identified the whole beast.

ELEUSIS (*See* DEMETER, GREEK MYTH, MYSTERIES, PERSEPHONE)

The site of a **Mystery** teaching mythically established near Athens by the goddess **Demeter** during her grief among mortals after the abduction of her daughter **Persephone**. Among the best-known initiatory rites of the ancient world, the priests of the Eleusinian Mysteries taught that most people are ruled not by living spirit but animal personality, which is unintelligent, thus dead. They taught **reincarnation** and said that souls slip into the body at the midnight hour. Thus their chief ceremonies (derived from the older **Egyptian** rites of **Isis** and **Osiris**, and sacred to Demeter and Persephone) were performed at midnight. Candidates underwent a complex, terrifying subterranean drama or ordeal, requiring them to overcome animal terror by negotiating deadly pitfalls and passages involving many real or illusory obstacles. Those unable to tell one from the other died or were rejected. **Apuleius** was an initiate: Strabo says that the temple at Eleusis held over 20,000 people. These Mysteries survived until the late fourth century AD, when they were suppressed by the Roman emperor Theodosius. The Roman poet Cicero (106–43 BC) said the Eleusinian Mysteries taught men not only how to live but how to die. For, once entering the initiatory maze, there was no turning back. Initiates staked their lives on getting every answer right. A wrong move (alone in darkness underground) meant death. The symbolic journey into the **underworld** too easily became literal. In Athens, the dead were called 'Demeter's people'. The drama also symbolised the annual death and rebirth of fertility, as in the myth of **Persephone** seized into the underworld, yet released each spring.

ELIADE, MIRCEA (1907–)

Born in Bucharest, this historian of religion studied Indian philosophy in Calcutta (1928–31). Returning to Romania for his Ph.D., he moved to Paris (the Sorbonne), then (1956) to the University of Chicago as professor of the history of religions. His subsequent writings expressed ancient and contemporary religious phenomena as 'hierophanies': manifestations in the world of sacred power, interpreted in his myth of the 'eternal return' as a process whereby mythic global **archetypes** continually replay themselves throughout the generations. His major works are *Patterns of Comparative Religion* (1958), *The Myth of the Eternal Return* (1949: English edition 1954) and *Shamanism: Archaic Techniques of Ecstasy* (1951: English edition 1964).

ELOHIM (*See* EL, YAHWEH)

ELPHIN (*See* TALIESIN, WELSH MYTH)

ELVES (*See* **DWARVES, EL, ELEMENTALS, FAIRIES**)
The most exalted of many orders of **fairy** beings. The root of the name, *el*, infers 'brightness', or 'shining one' from ancient **Sumeria** to Britain and Iceland. The name of the Irish king of Connaught, Ailill (whose white **bull** caused the cattle-raid of Cooley: *see* **Irish Myth, Táin**), is philologically identical to the Welsh word *ellyl*, 'elf', or 'shining being'. In **Norse myth**, the elves inhabited Alfheim, a world beyond Asgard. In **Teutonic myth**, 'white elves' are the spirits of air and ocean: the *Prose Edda* also distinguishes between Light and Dark Elves. Though, as in **Tolkien**'s *Lord of the Rings*, the Light Elves are generally depicted as tall, slender, fair beings, the Dark Elves are black as night – the German word for nightmare '*alp*', derives from elf, it being thought once that elves caused bad dreams by leaning on the breast of sleepers. In Scandinavia they are depicted with huge heads, tiny legs and long arms. In Denmark they are said to cause the bright green circles called *elf-dans*, sometimes seen on lawns, these being where they dance at night. Like other fairies they inhabited burial or **earth mounds**. **Tricksters**, they stole cattle and children, but were sometimes helpful if respected. In the Icelandic *Kormáks* Saga a spae-wife tells a wounded man to take a sacrificed bull to an elf mound, smear the mound with its blood, and make the elves a feast of the flesh, whereupon they would heal him. Elves could also be dangerous. Leroux de Lincy, in his *Livre des Légendes*, says they can kill mortals with their poisonous breath. Likewise the tiny fairy arrows called 'elfshot' had only to prick human flesh to kill.

ELYSIUM (*See* **EARTHLY PARADISE, GREEK MYTH**)
Like many another **earthly paradise**, this enchanted isle of the **afterlife** was located in the Atlantic West. Here, to the Elysian Fields, went many a valiant hero, like Menelaus, husband of **Helen of Troy**, whose abduction from his court by Paris triggered the Trojan War. The name (it may derive from 'Alys', an old name for the Great Goddess) came to be applied to any island paradise to which the souls of the heroic dead were borne.

EMERALD TABLET (*See* **HERMES TRISMEGISTUS**)

EMPEDOCLES (*c*.490–430 BC) (*See* **GREEK MYTH**)
This Greek disciple of **Pythagoras** described himself as a god condemned by sin 'to wander thrice ten thousand seasons [far] from the abodes of the blessed'. A renowned healer who along with his teacher believed that human souls can inhabit beans, he told his followers: 'wretches, utter wretches, keep your hands from beans.'[1] When he vanished suddenly, some said he had been abducted into the heavens, but cynics claimed he had jumped into the fiery crater of Mount Etna so that, his death being a mystery, he might pass for a god. Unfortunately for his reputation, amid an eruption the volcano spewed out one of his bronze slippers . . . or so it is said.

1. *Survival?*, David Lorimer, Routledge & Kegan Paul, London, 1984.

END DAYS (*See* **ANTICHRIST, APOCALYPSE, ARMAGEDDON**)

ENKI (*See* **BEROSSUS, ENLIL, NINKHURSAG, SUMERIAN MYTH**)
Also called Ea, this Sumerian creator deity, 'lord of the house of water', ruled the Apsu, the ocean of sweet water on which the world floated. With his

daughter Nanshe, goddess of springs and canals, he was honoured in the holy city of Eridu, his priests wearing garments in the form of a fish. It is said, one day in the earliest times, he appeared from the sea, part fish and part man, to civilise rude humanity. This seems to be the origin of the **Babylonian** tale (recorded by **Berossus**) of how the annedoti, 'repulsive ones', came from the sea, led by the double-headed fish-man Oannes, to do likewise. The Philistine god **Dagon** may also derive from Enki.

It is also said he lived in the **earthly paradise** of Dilmun with the **earth mother Ninkhursag**, providing the sweet water to fertilise the isle. But he ate eight plants she had grown. She cursed him with death. Sickness attacked eight parts of him: not even **Enlil** could help. The **fox** persuaded her to relent, so she created eight deities to cure his eight afflictions.

By union with his wife Damkina he fathered the solar god, **Marduk**, who vanquished **Tiamat, dragon** of chaos, before consigning **Anu, Enlil** and his father to their various abodes – heaven, earth and the abyss. When Enlil sent the **flood**, it was Enki who advised the good King Ziusudra to build an **ark**, though in the Babylonian **Gilgamesh** epic it was Utnapishtim whom he warned.

ENKIDU (*See* GILGAMESH, WILD MEN)

ENLIGHTENMENT (*See* BUDDHISM)

ENLIL (*See* BABYLONIAN MYTH, SUMERIAN MYTH)
Symbolising the forces of nature, this hurricane-god was born of the union between **Anu** (remote heavens) and Ki (the earth). These two were in fact one, the undivided cosmic mountain Anki, the lower part female; the upper, male. Enlil then separated them into two, so creating the temporal world (as with **Adam**'s separation into Adam and **Eve** before Eve ate the **apple**). He mated with his mother, who begat humanity. In time perceived not only as storm-god but as master of all human fate, his attitude to humanity was ambivalent at best: he sent the **flood** and also created the monster Lahmu, 'the raging one', to devastate the world. Yet as holder of the *tupsimati* ('tablets of destiny'), he ordered earthly affairs, and gave men the pickaxe, to help them build cities, including his own centre at Nippur. He had his own home in the heavens ('Enlil's Way') but usually lived on the Great Mountain of the East, where anciently he was associated with **Ninkhursag** ('Lady of the Great Mountain'). Later his wife was said to be Ninlil. Raping her, he was banished to the **underworld**, but she followed him and bore their child, the moon-god Nanna.

Assimilated by the Babylonians as Ellil, he also acquired the name of **Bel** ('Lord'), becoming associated with **Marduk** as Bel-Marduk, his consort now taking the name 'Belit' (the 'Lady'), who with her sacred milk nourished those he chose to be kings among men. In the **Gilgamesh** epic, not Enlil alone but the gods *en masse* decide to destroy humanity with the Flood.

ENOCH (*See* ANGELS, EL)
Father of Methuselah, who 'walked with God (Elohim: 'shining ones') and he was not, for God took him' (Genesis v:18–24), in the apocryphal Book of Enoch this obscure Hebrew prophet expands on the event described in Genesis vi:2 – 'That the sons of God saw the daughters of men that they were fair; and they took them wives of all which they chose.' The text (possibly second century BC but derived from older material) tells how two hundred **angels** called Nephilim or Watchers 'descended on' Mount Hermon (border-

ing modern Syria, Lebanon and Israel). They too were Elohim: shining so brightly few men could face them. Against their leader Shemyaza's advice, led by Azazel (in Arabian lore the king of the **djinns**), they taught forbidden arts, many taking human wives who bore '**giants**'. Then God sent the scribe Enoch to 'tell the Watchers of heaven, who have deserted the lofty sky [and] been polluted with women' that their children must die and that they were denied mercy.[1] Sent by the Watchers to plead for them, Enoch, driven by 'agitated stars and flashes of lightning', reaches heaven: a crystal wall surrounded by 'vibrating flame'. Through this he passes into a 'spacious habitation', also of crystal. Here One in a robe 'brighter than the sun' orders him to tell the Watchers: 'You ought to pray for men, and not men for you . . . [for] you from the beginning were made spiritual, possessing a life which is eternal, and not subject to death for ever. Therefore I made not wives for you, because, being spiritual, your dwelling is in heaven.'[2] The Lord's judgement is duly carried out by his satans (prosecutors) on earth. The Watchers are imprisoned to await the Day of Judgement; their progeny is destroyed, but from the corpses issue evil spirits that plague us still.

The Church suppressed the text so thoroughly that *c.*AD 325 St Jerome declared it apocryphal. Talk of sexual relations between men and 'angels' was out of order. However, the book was rediscovered in an Ethiopian Coptic monastery early in the nineteenth century (just as author Graham Hancock claimed that the **Ark of the Covenant** was also anciently hidden and protected in Ethiopia).

1. 1 Enoch xii:5–6 (trans. Richard Laurence).
2. 1 Enoch xv:2–7.

ENUMA ELISH (*See* SUMERIAN MYTH)

EPONA (*See* CELTIC MYTH, HORSE)
This **Celtic** mare-goddess was widely worshipped throughout Europe. Usually depicted semi-naked, seated on a **horse** or on a throne, two foals feeding from her lap, she has affinity with the **Greek** goddess **Demeter**. Adopted by the Romans and favoured by cavalry regiments, her feast was celebrated on 18 December, her shrines being decorated with **roses**. Her cult survived into the twelfth century. *The Topography of Ireland* by Giraldus Cambrensis (1146–1230) tells how, as a preliminary to his enthronement, a minor Irish king had to crawl naked on all fours towards a white mare as if he were her foal. The mare being slaughtered, butchered and boiled in a **cauldron**, the king-to-be bathed in the broth, drinking it and eating the flesh.

ER (*See* GREEK MYTH, PLATO, REINCARNATION)
The Greek philospher Plato (427–347 BC) tells the tale of a brave man, Er. Apparently slain in battle, his body did not putrefy. On his funeral pyre twelve days after his 'death', he revived to describe his experiences in the other world. He had seen travel-stained **souls** from the earth in tears tell of their wordly experience to souls descended from heaven, the latter in ecstasy describing marvellous enjoyments. Yet many of the earthly souls were not destined for heaven: their fate was to **reincarnate**.

Even so they had a choice. 'Your destiny shall not be allotted to you,' their instructor declared, 'but you shall choose it for yourselves. The responsibility lies with the chooser. Heaven is guiltless.'

It was wonderful, ludicrous and strange, said Er, to see how each soul chose its new life; typically on the basis of past experience. It happened that the soul of **Odysseus** (Ulysses) drew the final lot. After Odysseus' former sufferings he now sought only a quiet, retiring life, which in due course he found lying about, contemptuously discarded by everyone else. When at last he found it, he embraced it gladly, saying he would have done the same even had his been the first choice.

All the souls having chosen their new lives, they went to the Plain of Forgetfulness, taking up their station by the River of Indifference. Each drank of the waters and forgot everything. At midnight, after they had all fallen asleep, there was a clap of thunder, then an earthquake; in a moment all the souls were carried like shooting stars to their birth. Er, who had been prevented from drinking the waters, knew only that suddenly he opened his eyes at dawn to find himself upon his funeral pyre.

ERESHKIGAL (*See* INANNA, SUMERIAN MYTH, UNDERWORLD)

'Princess of the Great Earth', originally this Sumerian goddess was sole ruler of the **underworld**. Then **Nergal**, until then god of destruction and war, invaded with an army of fourteen **demons** which he posted at different gates. Ereshkigal was forced to accept him as her husband and as the new overlord of the dead. The myth appears to belong to the process by which, over millennia, patriarchal rule replaced matriarchy.

ERINNYES (*See* GREEK MYTH, FURIES)

ERLIK (*See* ADAM, SLAVONIC MYTH)

From Siberia to Lapland this spirit of evil was sometimes seen, like Adam, as primal man fallen from grace. A Tartar myth of his origin tells how the sky-god Ulgan saw floating on the ocean a piece of mud with human features. Inspiring it with life, he named it Erlik, and Erlik became the father of mankind, but due to his pride was banished to the depths, to become Lord of the Dead. Later, when Ulgan ordered him to bring earth up from the depths, hoping to create his own world, Erlik hid a piece in his mouth. When Ulgan threw the earth Erlik had brought on to the primal ocean, it began to grow. The piece in Erlik's mouth likewise began to expand, nearly choking him to death. Ordered to spit it out, he did: the mud he vomited became all the marshlands and unpleasant places of the earth.

EROS (*See* APHRODITE, CUPID, GREEK MYTH)

This male companion of **Aphrodite**, Greek goddess of love, first appears in **Hesiod**'s *Theogony* as son of Erebus and the Night. Others say he was the son of Aphrodite by **Ares**, **Hermes** or **Zeus**, or that he was hatched from the world-egg. A mere abstraction to Hesiod, he came to epitomise sexual passion. Early Greeks doubted his value, uncontrolled lust being a danger to social order: later poets delighted in his trickery, so that in time he was sentimentalised as a beautiful, irresponsible youth. As Roman **Cupid** the tale of his amatory adventure with Psyche was immortalised by Lucius **Apuleius**. Cruel, charming and gracious, malicious and rebellious, he took delight in torturing men with the prick of his arrows, respecting not even his own mother. Forever young, he was never thought responsible enough to be counted among the twelve ruling **Olympian** gods. The tale of his affair with Psyche appears to be a late invention: the early Eros was little more than an abstract personification of fertilising cosmic forces.

ERZULIE (*See* VOODOO)

ESKIMO MYTH (*See* CONCORDANCE)

Inhabiting a vast Arctic region from the west of Greenland through Canada and Alaska (including the Aleutian Isles) to the eastern edge of Siberia, this sub-group of the Mongoloid racial stock was once part of an Ice Age migration from Asia into America via the Bering Strait. Adapting to the harsh northern climate of the tundra even as others moved south through North America to Mexico and beyond, their name for themselves is not 'Eskimo' (a European term) but 'Inuit'. Originally most of the Inuit lived in wooden earth-covered houses along the seashore: the igloos (made of snow or ice) were specific to those in northern Canada.

Their culture and mythology (before they were persuaded into American society) related particularly to their climate and sources of food: **fish**, walrus, **seal, whale**, caribou, reindeer and **bear**. Living in a land which is dark six months of the year, traditionally they respected the **moon**-god Igaluk, the **crow**-father Tulungusaq and Sedna, the one-eyed sea-goddess.

Igaluk is the supreme god among the Eskimo of Alaska. In Greenland the tale is told of how, long ago one night in the dark, men and women played together inside. Going outside, they lit lamps to find out who had slept with whom. To their horror, **Moon** Man and **Sun** Woman – brother and sister – discovered that they had lain with each other. Tearing off her breasts and throwing them down before the moon, the sun rose into the sky, carrying a torch. The moon followed her, but his torch went out. This is why, even now, he lacks the brilliance of the sun.

In Alaska it is said that Tulungusaq made the world with the help of a **swallow**. Yet there is no real idea of creation: how could there be, so far north, where so little grows? The closest Eskimo equivalent to terms like 'create' or 'make' is 'to work upon', reflecting their marginal existence.

Perhaps the most potent mythic image is that of Sedna, a sinister sea-goddess, her one-eyed glare and vicious temper so evil that only a **shaman** (*angakoq*) can withstand it. Controlling over-population by drowning men, she rules the dead – *adlivun*, 'those below us'.

According to one legend, she was an unruly child who ate any flesh she could seize. One night she began to eat her mother and father as they slept. Horrified, they took her to sea and threw her overboard, but she held on to the boat until her father cut off her fingers one by one. Each severed finger turned into whales, seals and fish. Sinking to the bottom, now she guards sea-life, but – not surprisingly – she detests people.

Another version is that she was beautiful, but denied all her suitors. Her father (needing a young man to help him hunt) insisted that she accept the next to appear. Soon a fur-dressed hunter landed in a kayak, his face concealed by snow-goggles, saying he had heard of her beauty and wished to marry her. Reluctantly, promised warmth and wealth, she joined him. But, landing on a bleak isle, he removed hood and goggles to reveal himself as hideously ugly, while the promised house turned out to be ramshackle. At that point he turned into a black bird – a storm-petrel in disguise.

Her father recaptured her, but the petrel pursued. Terrified by its storm, her father tried to give her back by throwing her overboard. She clung on, but he beat her hands loose with his paddle. Her frozen fingers broke off, turning into seals. Still she clung on. Severed, the second joints of her fingers turned into the first walrus. Still she clung. Her father cut the remaining joints, which became the whales. Then she sank.

Sedna still lies under the sea, guarding her creatures. Fingerless, she cannot brush her matted hair. Hating men, she raises storms to stop men fishing. Shamans must visit her to beg forgiveness and comb her hair to make her happy, so that she will release sea creatures to be caught.

ESUS (See CELTIC MYTH, TEUTATES)

EURIPEDES (See GREEK MYTH (1))

EUROPA (See CADMUS, GREEK MYTH, ZEUS)

Yet another target for the amorous Greek god **Zeus**, this daughter of Agenor, king of Tyre, was one day gathering flowers by the seaside when she saw a **bull** browsing amid her father's herds. The beast was so majestic yet gentle that she approached it, garlanded its horns and climbed on its back – whereupon it sprang into the sea and carried her to Crete. It was Zeus in disguise. Wading ashore, he turned into an **eagle** and raped her. She bore him three sons – Minos, Rhadamanthys and Sarpedon. Her father sent her brothers, including **Cadmus**, to find her, but they had no idea where to look. Europa later married Asterius, king of Crete, who adopted the sons of Zeus and in reward received from the god the miraculous bronze **giant, Talos**.

EURYDICE (See GREEK MYTH, ORPHEUS, UNDERWORLD)

EVE (See ADAM, BIBLE, EARTH MOTHER, EDEN, FALL, LILITH)

Anomalies in the Biblical creation myth of Adam's wife, Eve, are explored in the entry on **Adam**. Formed from his rib, she heeded the **serpent**, who said if she and Adam ate the forbidden fruit of the **tree**, they would not die, as **Yahweh** warned, but would become wise. Eating, she persuaded Adam to eat. For this Yahweh cursed Eve, making her subject to the Man for ever. Cursing Adam for listening to her, he expelled them from Eden.

This myth of the 'Fall of Man' was later exploited by the patriarchal **Christian** Church to control its believers (only through Christ could they be redeemed, for Christ alone had overcome the Fall, also called '**Original Sin**'), and to assert male authority by blaming Woman for everything.

Yet who was Eve? Adam named his wife Eve, 'because she was the mother of all living' (Genesis iii:20). If so, she must have been the **earth mother** or mother-goddess. So Adam was her son as well as her husband. The tale that she was born of his rib was a patriarchal inversion. In an earlier **Sumerian** account of the primordial garden, the husband of the earth mother is the serpent, the cosmic fertilising principle. Oddly, there is evidence that Yahweh, the Lord God himself, was himself originally an aspect of this serpent power.[1] The tale of the Fall, caused by the Woman, is as fine an example of the Big Lie as may be found anywhere in religious history.

A further aspect of the myth of Eve concerns her rival **Lilith**, Adam's mistress or first wife, of whom little mention is made in orthodox texts.

1. *Occidental Mythology*, Joseph Campbell, Penguin, London, 1976, pp.28–30.

EVIL EYE (See EYE)

EXCALIBUR (See ARTHURIAN MYTH, SWORD)

This famous magical sword guaranteed King **Arthur**'s invincibility until its scabbard was stolen by his vengeful half-sister, the enchantress **Morgan Le Fay**. Derived from the earlier **Irish myth** of the sword Caliburn, it is not the same as the sword by which, pulling it from the **stone** in which his dying father **Uther** had plunged it, Arthur proved his kingship. That sword broke in battle: the Lady of the Lake gave him Excalibur to replace it and, after his final battle, took it back again, despite **Bedivere**'s reluctance to return it to the waters of its origin.

EYE

The eye, the 'window of the soul', invariably represents power of one sort or another: the omniscient eye of the all-seeing god; the 'third eye' of **Buddha** or **Shiva** (a pearl set amid the forehead: the eye of the mind) as awakened in **Buddhist** and **Hindu** ascetics by long spiritual discipline; the 'Eye in the Triangle' is likewise the omniscient all-seeing eye.

The **Egyptian** creator-god **Atum** had a detachable eye, an agent of both his creative power (humanity was formed from its tears) and his fury. It is said that when he grew old, mankind plotted against him. In fury he sent out his eye in the form of the goddess **Hathor**. Her slaughter was such that she would have destroyed humanity had not Atum made her drunk. The power of his eye was inherited by the god **Horus**. A spell from one of the Coffin Texts reads: 'I am the all-seeing Eye of Horus, whose appearance strikes terror'.[1] The glyph called 'The Eye of Horus', with detached eyebrow and two lower horns or wings, may represent a cross-section of the human brain, the 'eye' itself being the limbic system or mid-brain.

The single withering eye of monsters like **Balor** or the **Cyclopes**, or the **Eskimo** sea-goddess Sedna, represents destructiveness or brute elemental force. The gaze of the **Medusa** in **Greek myth** turned men to stone.

The 'hundred eyes' in the **peacock**'s tail are those of the all-seeing Church in **Christian** symbol; conversely they are connected with Satan. In occult tradition the **Devil** is linked to the Hebrew letter *ayin*, said to represent an eye. The 'thousand eyes' or 'ten thousand eyes' of sky-gods are the stars of the night; unsleeping, always watchful; or, again, they are the eyes of Satan, a leader of stars and **angels**.

In the West, the right eye is the sun, the day and the future; the left eye is the moon, the night and the past: in the East, the symbolism is reversed. In Egyptian lore, the right eye represented **Osiris**, and **Ra** the sun-god; the left eye belonged to **Isis** and the **moon**.

As for the globally common belief in the 'evil eye', by which a stare leads to misfortune; the **Celts** thought it arose from envy or malice. Its owner might be unaware of possessing the power. It was usually attributed to old women: suspected **witches** were often accused of it, especially if their eyes were differently coloured. If a child (the prettiest) or beast (the finest) fell suddenly ill, the evil eye was blamed. Horses afflicted would sweat, tremble and grow weak. It turned ale or milk instantly sour. Charms against it included **rowan**, juniper and **iron**. The power (it could be cast at great distance) was regarded not as an instrument of deliberate **sorcery** so much as the effect of pure malice.[2]

In Africa the evil eye is believed to be heritable. Those born with it cannot remove it. It can cause abortion, make spears break, make rats eat the corn, or sicken cows. In many areas, prolonged staring may cause suspicion of witchcraft. That the same fear persists in modern cultures is easily proved. Try staring at someone opposite you in an Underground train.[3]

1. *The Powers of Evil*, Richard Cavendish, Routledge & Kegan Paul, London, 1975, pp.166–7.
2. *The Magic Arts in Celtic Britain*, Lewis Spence, Rider, London, 1970.
3. *The Evil Eye*, Frederick Elworthy, Collier Books, New York, 1970 (1895).

F

FABULOUS BEASTS (*See* **CONCORDANCE**)

FAERY (*See* **FAIRIES**)

FAFNIR (*See* **DRAGON, LOKI, NORSE MYTH, ODIN, SIGURD**)
Out with Odin one day, the Norse **trickster**-god **Loki** killed an otter. It was
the son in animal form of a man, Hreidmar. To repay him for this loss the
two gods made the **dwarf** Andvari give up his golden hoard, down to the last
golden **ring**, and pile it over the otter. But Hreidmar's sons Fafnir and Regin
killed Andvari for the **gold** and Fafnir turned into a dragon to guard it. Regin
urged the hero Sigurd to kill Fafnir. Slaying not only Fafnir but Regin too,
Sigurd took the hoard, including the ring, which later led to his own death.
This tale symbolises the sterility of ill-gotten gains.

FAIRIES (*See* **DWARVES, EARTH MOUNDS, ELVES, INCUBI,
KIRK, UFOs**)
Belief in an unseen world, peopled by unseen beings, is universal. Such
beings – **asuras, demons, devas, djinns**, fairies, **fauns, rakshasas** and so on
– all share certain characteristics: magical powers, tricksiness, association
with earlier cultures or the dead. The English name for these beings is
Fairies, from 'fays' – Fatae or **Fates**. Said to be fallen **angels** or children of
Adam by **Lilith**, these immortals, neither human nor divine, live in Faery, a
realm adjacent to the mortal world and impinging on it at 'in-between' times
(twilight) and places (fairy hills: earth mounds). Belief in them persisted in
rural areas until recent times.

Were they but personified elemental forces? Or did the belief involve
folk-memory of earlier cultures killed, banished or absorbed by conquering
iron age tribes? Were they the feared **ghosts** of neolithic mound-builders? Or
are they beings from an alternate **dimension**, today manifesting not as
'fairies' but as UFO entities? Descriptions change but the mystery persists.

Fairies (**brownies, dwarves, elves** and so on) vary in stature, are physically
strong, have no towns, iron tools or weapons, but inhabit mazy earth-houses
under grassy mounds. Shy, sly and quick, they are elusive and demand
respect. Their 'elfshot' is deadly: the tiny arrow need only prick to kill. They
can (like **Druids**) raise storms and mists. They steal human babies, leaving a
wizened '**changeling**' or 'halfling'. They cause mischief but are friendly if
approached with sympathy. If a man taking a fairy bride speaks of her origin
he loses her. The wise Gael always placated them by calling them *Daoine Sith*
('Men of Peace'), or *Sleagh Maith* ('Good Folk').

Poison arrows, hidden earth houses, nocturnal excursions, baby-theft,
intermarriage, shyness – it all suggests an older folk fighting to survive, being
in time so genetically absorbed (save for giveaway signs like green eyes) that
their independent existence became a remote, romantic memory.

Yet belief in intelligent beings from a realm coincident with our own is
found the world over. The fairies are masters of magic. They can make

human eyes see old hags as beautiful girls, dross as gold, shabby caves as palaces. So 'fairy gold' came to mean evanescent wealth; to be 'away with the fairies' means one who lives in a dreamworld; a 'fey' person is dreamy and strange. That in medieval times many folk were executed for sexual and other association with **incubi** suggests long-held fearful belief in the reality of fairies. As late as 1846–7 some blamed the Irish potato famine on disturbance in the fairy world. One man claimed that before the disaster he saw: 'the Good People and hundreds like me saw them fighting in the sky over Knock Magh and on towards Galway.'[1]

In 1691 the **Rev. Robert Kirk**, in his *The Secret Commonwealth of Elves, Fauns and Fairies*, wrote that fairies: (1) have a nature between man and angels; (2) have light, fluid bodies, and can appear or vanish at will; (3) are intelligent and curious; (4) can steal whatever they like; (5) live in caves reached by any gap where air passes; (6) once had their own society and agriculture; (7) cannot stay in one place but travel constantly (i.e., are nomads); (8) are physically immaterial; (9) belong to tribes, and have children, marriages and burials; (10) have houses invisible to human eyes; (11) speak with a whistling sound; (12) have habits and language that to humans seem human; (13) say nothing dies, that all evolves and is forever renewed; (14) have chiefs but no organised religion; (15) have books for pleasure and philosophy; (16) may be commanded to appear at our will.[2][3]

Folklorist J.Y. Evans-Wentz maintained that 'fairies actually exist as invisible beings or intelligences', and held that our own visible world is immersed like an island in an unknown ocean peopled by species of living beings beyond our comprehension. Today, with UFO reports to add to fairy-tales through the ages, scientific evidence from relativity to chaos theory increasingly suggests we inhabit a universe in which material explanations of things are not entirely reliable.

1. *Dimensions*, Jacques Vallée, Sphere, London, 1990, p.83.
2. *The Secret Commonwealth of Elves, Fauns and Fairies*, Rev. Robert Kirk, Observer Press, Stirling, 1933 (1691) (introduction by Andrew **Lang**).
3. *Robert Kirk: Walker between Worlds*, R.J. Stewart, Element Books, Shaftesbury, 1989.

FAIRY-TALES (*See* **CONCORDANCE**)

Everywhere fairy-tales well up from ancient sources, their origin lost in time, their themes **archetypal**. Jack forever climbs a Beanstalk (**Tree of Life**) to kill the **giant**; princes forever defeat evil **witches** to wake and win Sleeping Beauties; princesses forever meet talking frogs who seek love, not money. As recorded in Europe for 300 years by **Perrault**, the Brothers **Grimm**, **Andersen**, **Lang**, **Cocteau** and others, their cautionary element is plain. Hansel and Gretel stray in the Wild Wood; Beauty meets the Beast and, denying appearances, humanises him. Such tales may be older than we know. The earliest version of **Cinderella** is Chinese, from the ninth century AD.

From ancient **Irish myth** of **Cuchulainn** to **Frankenstein** or the latest Schwarzenegger movie of robot violence, the major themes are universal. Take **transformation** – the shape-shifting Siberian **shaman** Morgon-Kara; the Welsh myth of Gwion Bach's shape-shifting flight from the angry goddess **Cerridwen**; **Zeus** deluding Leda in swan form; the **Yoruba trickster**-god Edshu who causes conflict by seeming black to one man and white to another; the shock to *Star Wars* hero Luke Skywalker on learning that the evil-masked Darth Vader is his father. All are variants of the same tale, recasting basic mythic truths into currently comprehensible form.

Fairy-tale advises, warns, encourages and educates. A chief theme is of the simple man or woman (**Perceval**) who accepts a challenge to journey into magic domains. En route, realising his own latent strengths and aided by an ambiguous supernatural helper (the two may be the same), he overcomes all obstacles to defeat a supernatural foe. Ogre, evil magician, wicked witch, **dragon** or another monster is slain, defeated or transformed into nobler guise. A **curse** is lifted, treasure is won, the hero returns to his own world, time and kind; Nature flowers.[1]

Such tales inhabit a dreamland in which a toad may talk, where people may really be **deer, seals** or **wolves**. Nothing is as it seems. Penalties, dangers and possible gains invoked by crossing into the fairy realms are emphasised, as is need of a stout heart and shrewd mind. Magical helpers, threats, **omens**, prohibitions and marvels abound. Some entities in this magical multiverse are benevolent: none may be taken for granted. They are, after all, the gods and **demons** of pagan belief, thinly disguised.

Fairy-tales are often bowdlerised due to the pagan or sexual content of the original, or due to horrors thought too scary for the infant mind, or because the original meaning is lost. Thus Mother **Goose** of the nursery rhyme was once La Reine Pédauque (La Reine du Pays d'Oc), or Goose-foot Queen, the inspiration of troubadours in twelfth-century Provence. This Queen of many disguises goes back to Queen Sibylla, ancestress of all magicians; to the **Queen of Sheba** who entranced King **Solomon**; but she is ultimately derived from the shadowy ancient **Lilith, Adam**'s first wife.[2]

1. *The Hero with a Thousand Faces*, Joseph Campbell, Abacus, London, 1975.
2. *The Cult of the Black Virgin*, Ean Begg, Arkana, London, 1985, pp.32ff.

FALCON (*See* **HAWK, HORUS**)

FALL (*See* **ADAM, AFRICAN MYTH, DUALISM, EDEN, EVE**)

The myth of mankind's Fall from innocence into sin tries to explain why evil and death exist. Two main religious views persist in the West. **Dualism** claims that evil pre-exists human disobedience, the latter resulting from spirit's fatal fall into matter. Christian tradition insists that human disobedience caused the Fall. Hebrew prophets concluded that, if God is One, then evil cannot come from Him (if so, Creation is flawed), but is caused by evil persons – even if God created them. Yet the doctrine of the Fall, central to **Christianity**, is absent from Hebrew belief, the solution having emerged when Moses brought God's law down **Sinai**. The Christian argument is that only via Christ's Passion (God taking on the guilt of **Original Sin**) may we be redeemed. Advanced by **St Paul**, this dogma has persisted to cause misery in every generation. 'Allas, allas, that ever love was sinne!' cries Chaucer's Wife of Bath in the fourteenth century.

The Baganda of Uganda tell how God sent Kintu, the first man, and Nambi, the first woman, down to the still-barren earth, warning them of disaster if they tried to return to heaven. Nambi, carrying a chicken, realised she had forgotten the corn to feed it. Despite Kintu's warnings, she went back to heaven for it and duly returned with it in a basket. They settled, and while Kintu built a hut she fed her chicken and planted the heavenly seed. Yet at the bottom of the basket lurked a **serpent**, which was death.

FATES (*See* **GREEK MYTH, NORNS**)

Homer speaks of the Moerae (Fates) as the destiny of every mortal. **Hesiod**

in the *Theogony* later personifies them as goddesses; the three Daughters of Night: Clotho, Lachesis and Atropos. Clotho spins life's thread, Lachesis is Chance or Luck, Atropos the inescapable fate of every incarnate being. Associated with this moral notion turned into a triple goddess is the idea of nemesis – at first a concept of moral equilibrium. A man might displease the gods either by offending moral law or by doing too well in life. By the first he made them angry, by the second he made them jealous. In either case they sent Nemesis (later personified as a goddess) to hound him to death or disaster. At heart lies the age-old notion of balance. 'Pride comes before a **fall**', but the innocent deserve better. The **Norns** of **Norse myth** served a similar function and the term **'Fairy'** comes from 'Fay' or 'Fate'.

FATHER CHRISTMAS (*See* SANTA CLAUS)

FATHER-GODS (*See* CONCORDANCE)

In the early life of most children the father is the one who looms above and makes the loud, threatening noise. Offering unexpected approval, he still punishes any transgression of his loud-voiced rules, even as the mother tries to dissuade him, protecting the fearful child. Thus it is no surprise if, in the myths of the global family, father is associated with the fearful empty sky, and mother with the comforting friendly earth.

Father-gods are typically the gods of the sky and the stormy elements associated with it: thunder, lightning and rain. They are unpredictable and frightening. You never know where you are with them: their love, if it exists at all, is remote, and they are often not there when you want them. They demand propitiation and sacrifice. (So does mother, but of another sort.) They may be jovial one moment and violent the next: rarely (at least in myth) are they calm, reliable or philosophic. Philosophic fathers are no more reliable than growlers, roarers or drinkers: they are liable to be stern moralists, like the Jewish **Yahweh**, demanding impossible moral standards of his offspring – furious if the son disobeys him; outraged if the grown-up daughter prefers another man to him.

All father-gods are autocrats: in myth their son may be the sun itself, or **Christ**, or any number of other **sacrificed** children – the father never apologises. Often the only way through is for the son to slay or mutilate him (with the aid of mother, as **Ouranos** by **Cronus**); the son then turns into the new father-tyrant, in turn slain by his own rebellious son.

Thus history (*his*-story), up till this present day: father-gods are transformed from gods into industrialists and the dictators of nations.

It seems they cannot and will not change. They lay down the law, and fight to the death to do so.

Yet still there is the myth of the Prodigal Son, welcomed home by the anxious father, a man wise enough to see that youthful rebellion had led the son to that same (female) wisdom by which he himself was conceived.

FATHERLESS CHILD (*See* PERCEVAL)

FAUNUS (*See* PAN, ROMAN MYTH, SILVANUS, WOLF)

Grandson of **Saturn**, this Roman fertility-god (equivalent of the Greek god **Pan**) was (mythically) an early king and law-maker of Latium. He invented the rustic pipe and could prophesy the future, but would do so only if he was caught and tied up, as he was by King Numa Pompilius. Also called the Chief Wolf, Lupercus, his temple on the Palatine, the Lupercal, was the grotto where the she-wolf Mother of Rome had suckled **Romulus** and **Remus**.

His purificatory festival, the Lupercalia, celebrated on 15 February, involved goat-sacrifices by priests wearing only goat-skins. It is said that, once finding **Hercules** and Omphale asleep, he tried to have his way with Omphale, in the dark not seeing that the lovers had changed clothes. Embracing Hercules, he was lucky to escape in one piece, so that thereafter he demanded that his priests be naked or semi-naked so that he could tell the difference. The cult of his wife (or daughter) Fauna or Bona Dea was celebrated by women in an orgiastic festival forbidden to men. More generally, the name 'faun' was given to images of any rural divinity.

FAUST (*See* MAGICIANS, MEPHISTOPHELES)

Also called Faustus or Doctor Faustus, this most persistent of European legends concerns the archetypal magus who sells his soul to the **Devil** in exchange for knowledge and power. Though a composite of many figures from **Simon Magus** to **Agrippa** and **Paracelsus**, there was indeed a historical Dr Johannes Faustus who died *c*.1540 and who called the Devil his crony. In a letter dated 1507 the Abbot Trithemius calls him a swindler and quack: his reputation was evil, yet Luther and Melanchthon took him seriously.

The legend began with the first *Faustbuch* (1587: printer Johann Spies). The unknown author depicts Faust as a magus who, via magical powers gained by a pact with **Mephistopheles**, conjures up **Helen of Troy**, who bears him a son. After twenty-four years, he is taken to hell by the Devil. Translated into English (1592), this coarse drama led to a play, *The Tragicall History of D. Faustus* (1604) by Christopher Marlowe. Its tragic boisterousness (as in the mysterious fate of Marlowe himself) increased the demand for Faust dramas and puppet plays in which the damnation of Faust was never in doubt.

But in an unfinished play the German writer G.E. Lessing (1729–81), who saw Faust's quest for knowledge as noble, undertook Faust's salvation: a theme adopted by the German visionary J.W. von Goethe (1749–1832), the first part of whose dramatic poem *Faust* appeared in 1808; the second part after his death. No subsequent treatment (notably Berlioz's cantata, *The Damnation of Faust* (1846), Gounod's opera *Faust* (1859) and Mann's 1947 novel *Doktor Faustus*) has emulated Goethe's grand vision of Faust as tragic hero: maybe the definitive commentary on the conflict to which modern man remains prey:

> . . . Two souls contend
> In me, and both souls strive for masterdom,
> which from the other shall the sceptre rend.
> The first soul is a lover, clasping close
> To this world tentacles of corporeal flame,
> The other seeks to rise with mighty throes
> To those ancestral meadows whence it came.

FEATHERED SERPENT (*See* QUETZALCOATL)

FEMMES FATALES (*See* CONCORDANCE)

The theme of the *femme fatale*, the woman whose beauty leads men or nations to disaster, is as potent today as ever. Goddess, mortal, **swan**-maiden, **siren** or **Lorelei** luring sailors on to the rocks, *La Belle Dame sans Merci* or Mata Hari, the image of mysterious, alluring, wanton femininity seeking its own way whatever the consequences is as much with us today as in the biblical tale of **Salome**, daughter of Herod, who demanded (and got) the **head** of John the

Baptist on a plate; or as in the tale of **Cleopatra**, queen of the Nile, who, ousted from the Egyptian throne, seized it by seducing Rome's most powerful men: Julius Caesar, then Mark Antony, so causing catastrophic war. Or she is no schemer, but her helplessness, if abducted like **Helen of Troy** or enslaved like **Draupadi**, leads men to fight, die and tear empires apart for her; they blame her for bewitching them, burning her at the stake – or exalting her.

The *femme fatale* is the destructive, vengeful aspect of the goddess: what Swiss psychologist **Carl Jung** called the negative anima. The anima is the unconscious female side of every man, as the animus is the unconscious male side of every woman. When men reject their own female side, either as individuals, or (collectively and historically) by imposing intellectual (sky-god) rule over feeling (earth-goddess) they invoke their negative anima, and become easy meat for the *femme fatale*. So, too, women fall prey to the animus: **Zeus** and Casanova, or Heathcliff in *Wuthering Heights*.

FENIANS/FIANNA (*See* FINN, IRISH MYTH)

FENRIR (*See* AESIR, ARMAGEDDON, NORSE MYTH, RAGNORAK, WOLF)

This monstrous offspring of **Loki** and the giantess Angrboda took the form of a giant **wolf**. It is said that for season after season he or one of the cubs chases the sun, and at last, at **Ragnorak**, devours it. For seven years winter envelops the world. With all light extinguished, brother will slay brother, and children their parents. Amid this terrible time of Ragnorak the world we know will end. Fenrir, chained up by the **Aesir**, escapes. The earth and the world-ash **Yggdrasil** tremble. Fenrir's slavering upper jaw touches the sky, his lower, the earth. **Odin** attacks him: Fenrir swallows the god and Odin's son Vidar stabs him to the heart. So Fenrir dies amid the climactic battle amid which all the old gods also perish. Stars fall into the sea; the earth flames.

At last, from the global carnage, a new world is born.

FERTILITY MYTHS (*See* BELTANE, CORN-GODS, DYING GODS, MAY DAY)

FETISH (*See* AFRICAN MYTH, HOPI, VOODOO)

This is any inanimate object in which a **spirit** is said to live, or which is said to possess magical powers. Fetishism refers to the veneration of such objects. Reliance on good luck **charms** or belief that inherent virtue lies in the bones of saints constitute fetishism: which is thus not limited to West Central Africa, though most developed there. It is thought the spirit inhabiting a fetish may be an **ancestor** of its owner or maker, or an alien spirit magically trapped and lured into its container by the fetish-master, or (as with the **zombie** of Haitian **voodoo** lore) the spirit of a dead man or woman exhumed from the grave and revived. Objects housing the spirits range from statues or wooden carvings to gourds, boxes, skulls, or pouches made from the skin of magically potent animals. Though mainly to protect their owner against misfortune – illness, the evil **eye**, theft or assault – they may also be used to do evil: their owner sending the fetish-spirit to harm neighbours, or using it to enter houses invisibly, or lie with another man's wife by magically convincing her (as **Uther Pendragon** did with Ygraine to conceive King **Arthur**) that it is her own husband making love to her. Such fetishes are always eager for human flesh and blood: the more they are required to do evil, the more voracious they become, in time destroying not only the owner's family but himself as well. Fetishism is also native to the Pueblo peoples of the southwestern United States (*see* **Hopi Lore**); and is found in the East Indies, particularly in parts of Timor.

FIG (*See* **ADAM, BUDDHISM, EVE**)
Sometimes used in place of the **apple** in the myth of the **Tree** of Knowledge from which **Eve** persuaded **Adam** to eat, it was after eating either apple or fig that they knew they were naked, and covered themselves with fig-leaves. Symbolically the fig-leaf is the male organ and the fig itself the female. The bo-tree beneath which Gautama the Buddha sat to attain enlightenment is a species of fig-tree. *Ficus religiosa*, its fruit naturally rich in the nerve-hormone serotonin which, associated with hallucinogenic or visionary experience, is produced by the pineal gland – anciently identified as the 'third **eye**' of wisdom. This may perhaps be why the fig-tree is viewed as the Tree of Knowledge, or (**Islamic** lore) the Tree of Heaven, or (**Oceanic** lore) the Tree of Life.

FIJI (*See* **CARGO CULT**)
Synthesising **Christianity** with Fijian lore, the hereditary priest Ndugomoi in 1876 led the Tuka heresy, teaching that there had been two gods, Ndengai (a local **serpent**-god) and **Jehovah**. Challenged by Jehovah to create man, Ndengai had failed and been expelled. Seeing clouds full of flying chariots and inciting revolt against British rule, Ndugomoi was arrested and jailed, yet his version of Christianity (forerunner of the **cargo cults**) prevailed in Fiji. He also associated Rokola the carpenter-god, builder of the canoes by which the Fijians had reached their islands, with **Noah**.

FIMBULWINTER (*See* **NORSE MYTH, RAGNORAK**)

FINN MACCOOL/FIONN MACCUMHAL/FINGAL (*See* **IRISH MYTH, OISIN**)
Fostered by the **Druidess** Bodhmall, this third-century Irish hero is said to have acquired prevision by burning and sucking his thumb while cooking the **Salmon** of Knowledge, or by sucking it after trapping it in the door of a **fairy** mound. His two hounds, Bran and Sceolan, were really his nephews in canine form. His son Oisin lived three centuries in the Land of Youth, **Tir nan Og**. He led the Fianna or Fenians, a war-band admitting only those who passed stern tests of their bravery, learning and athletic ability. His pursuit of Grainne when she eloped with Diarmuid led to the latter's death – the prototype for the tale of **Tristan** and **Iseult**. Able to step over mountains in his seven-league boots, he built the Giant's Causeway. His Fenians being routed at the Battle of Gabhra, he was taken to the otherworld where, like King **Arthur**, he sleeps. Mendelssohn's overture *Fingal's Cave* commemorates his name.

FINNEGANS WAKE (*See* **JOYCE, JAMES**)

FINNISH MYTH (*See* **CONCORDANCE**)

FINTAN (*See* **FISH, IRISH MYTH**)

FIR BOLG (*See* **IRISH MYTH**)

FIRE (*See* CONCORDANCE, FIRE-FESTIVALS)

The harnessing of this elemental, transformative force was a step perhaps more vital than any other in the growth of human culture, as is implied by the **Greek myth** of **Prometheus**, the **Titan** who stole fire from the gods to benefit mankind. The gods punished him brutally for giving away such power.

With fire, early man could cook, see by night, venture into underground places, settle cold climes and ward off wild beasts. Declared by the Greek philosopher Heraclitus (*c.*576–480 BC) to be the cause and first principle of all life; with **water** the chief agent of the destruction of **Atlantis**, in **Norse myth** the union of fire and water is both source of life and cause of the world's final destruction. In alchemical symbolism the *Schamayim*, 'Divine Fiery Water', is the first outflow of the Word of God, the flaming river pouring from the presence of the Eternal. 'The operation begins with fire and ends with fire,' wrote the Arabic alchemist ibn Bishrun.[1] It is said that no material world existed until **Lucifer**, trying to perform the cosmic alchemy, misused the *Schamayim*. For this and other sins he and his rebel angels were flung into the fiery pit of **hell**, also said to be the fate of all sinners. Yet righteous men, like Shadrach, Meshech and Abednego, thrown bound by the **Babylonian** king Nebuchadnezzar into a fiery furnace for refusing to worship his golden idol, are not even singed.

For this ambiguous yet most potent of all religio-philosophic symbols is also the life-giving generative power of the **sun**, rising each day to light and warm the world, dying in winter, majestically reborn each spring. Thus at spring **fire-festivals** the old fire, kept alight all year, was put out, and a new fire was lit. In parts of Australia and Arabia fire was used to stop or drive away rain, by throwing fire-sticks in the air, or sprinkling a burning brand with water. In New Caledonia the sunshine was invoked by a **shaman** who, climbing to a mountain-top with a bundle of charms, set fire to the bundle as the sun rose from the sea. In Cambodia lived two strange kings, the Fire-King and the Water-King who, if falling ill, were stabbed to death and cremated. In India cases of the practice of suttee, of the widowed wife immolating herself alive on the pyre of her dead husband, are still reported. Less brutally, disposal of the bodies of the dead by fire remains the most common alternative to their **burial** in the **earth mother**.

Symbolically, fire on an altar is the spirit, the breath of life; fire resting on the head or surrounding it is the halo or nimbus; a rekindled fire is rebirth; baptism by fire restores purity by burning away the dross; the 'tongues of fire' visiting the Apostles at Pentecost were the advent of the Holy Spirit; the Burning Bush in the Old Testament signifies the Lord's presence. The domestic hearth-fire, at the centre of every house, is the feminine or earth aspect of fire, as symbolised by **Vesta**, Roman goddess of the hearth (thus the name of a British brand of matches: Swan Vestas).

In Native American culture the fire at the centre of the Medicine Lodge was the home of the Great Spirit: Grandfather Fire. Fire was worshipped as a god in pre-**Zoroastrian** Persia: in **Vedic** India the god **Agni** (thus the Latin word *ignis*, 'fire'?) personified solar fire, lightning and the fire by which men burned forests to clear ground. As destructive fire he was identified with **Rudra**, the roaring god: **Kali** too depicted this destructive aspect. The **Babylonian Marduk** was also a fire-god; so too all volcanic or smith-gods: **Hephaestus**, **Vulcan**, **Wayland Smith** or red-bearded **Thor**. The stone images of the **Mayan** fire-god Huehuetlotl portrayed him with a brazier on his head, in which his divinity was kindled and fed. The

Hawaiian volcanic fire-goddess **Pele** remains likely to burn to death anyone displeasing her.

Fire was also associated with **Thoth, Hermes** and **Mercury** as the very flame of intellectual inspiration.

1. *The Secret Teachings of All Ages*, Manly P. Hall, Philosophical Research Society, Los Angeles, 1989 (1928).

FIRE-FESTIVALS (*See* CONCORDANCE, FIRE)

Throughout Europe and elsewhere since early times folk held fire-festivals, kindling bonfires (*bone*-fires) on set days, and dancing round or leaping through them. Often, as still found in Britain on Guy Fawkes Night (5 November), effigies were burned – a reminder not only of medieval **witch**-fires but of the **Druid** rites in which victims were shut into a vast wicker man and immolated. Typically lit at spring or midsummer, such fires were also lit on Hallowe'en, Christmas Day and the Eve of Twelfth Day.

Spring fire-festivals occurred on the first Sunday of Lent, Easter Eve or May Day. Lenten fires were lit in Belgium, France and Germany, where Easter fires were also common. A strawman, the Judas, was burned in the churchyard on Easter Saturday in some areas; in Bavaria the Easter Man was burned on a height. The Scottish **May Day** ceremony of the **Beltane** fire is described elsewhere; so too the custom of kindling it by friction, and the belief that leaping through the flames guaranteed a good harvest.

Notable among fire-festivals enduring in Scotland is the Burning of the Clavie at Burghead on the Moray Firth coast. This ancient fort was held by the Picts, then the Norse; the ceremony may be pre-Christian. Every 11 January (New Year by the old Julian calendar), a team of fishermen carry the flaming clavie – a barrel filled with tar and staves – round the town. Folk scramble to grab the blazing pieces falling from it to gain good luck for the next year. Finally set on a stone altar atop a steep mound on the ramparts of the old fort, fuel is hurled onto it until the entire mound is ablaze. While marking the town boundaries and the sun's rebirth, the main reason for the festival is to have fun at the darkest, direst point of the northern year. Maybe this is why fire-festivals were always held. In every heart there is a secret arsonist (or fire-god)!

FISH (*See* CONCORDANCE)

Fish represent the teeming, fecund life of the ocean, the womb giving birth to all life on land. Thus it is a common Middle Eastern myth that civilised arts came to humanity via fish-headed gods (Sumerian **Enki**, Babylonian **Oannes**, Phoenician **Dagon**) who emerged from the deep to teach by day, returning to the ocean by night. The fish head-dress of the priests of Enki-Oannes became the mitres of Christian bishops. **Moon**-goddesses were often shown as half-fish (**mermaids**), signifying the unconscious aspect of female nature. **Ishtar**, in the form of the whale-**dragon** Derketo (like **Aphrodite** born from the sea-foam), caused the **Flood**, lamenting that her children were now like the fishes of the sea. Sacred to all love/fertility-goddesses (**Isis, Venus, Frigga**), fish was eaten on their day, Friday, and (along with bread and wine) was the sacramental meal of the **Mystery** cults. In **Egyptian myth**, the son of King Malek fell from the boat of Isis and drowned, to become known as the Fisher, a title given to **Orpheus** and later by **Gnostics** and Christians (though not by the Greek Orthodox Church) to **Christ**: *Ichthyos*, the fish, whose mission occurred at the dawn of the astrological age of Pisces, 'The Fishes'. A medieval hymn calls Christ the 'Little Fish which the Virgin caught in the fountain', making him both fisher and fish.[1]

Christ's apostles were called 'fishers of men': one of his miracles was to feed a multitude with five loaves and two little fishes. Again, clearly Christianity took over the symbols of religions later persecuted as **pagan**.

In **Roman myth** the constellation Pisces is identified with **Venus** and her son **Cupid**, who turned into fishes to escape the monster **Typhon**. The southern constellation, Piscis Austrinus, is anciently identified with the Babylonian fish-god Oannes, and is said to be the parent of Pisces.

In **Hindu** flood-myth the ark of **Manu**, the **Vedic Noah**, is towed over the raging sea by a giant fish which, at last beaching the ark on a high peak, Naubandhana (the harbour), reveals itself as **Brahma**, or **Vishnu**.

In **Celtic** lore, Fintan survived the Flood by turning into a **salmon**, associated with the Salmon of Knowledge that lived in the **well** of Segais under a hazel-tree, the sacred nuts of which sustained it. While roasting this salmon **Finn** burned his thumb and sucked it, so gaining wisdom, as did **Gwion Bach** when three drops from **Cerridwen**'s **cauldron** hit and burned his thumb. Gwion Bach also turned into a fish during his flight from Cerridwen. In Scotland, as late as the seventeenth century, holy wells situated under hazel-trees and containing mystical fishes were maintained; to kill or eat such fish was regarded as a crime sure to bring down celestial punishment.[2]

1. *Woman's Mysteries*, M. Esther Harding, Rider, London, 1982, p.54.
2. *The Magic Arts in Celtic Britain*, Lewis Spence, Rider, London, 1970, p.96.

FISHER KING (*See* ARTHURIAN MYTH, BRAN, FISH, HOLY GRAIL, PERCEVAL, WASTELAND)

In **Arthurian** lore the Fisher King, **guardian** of the **Holy Grail**, lies in the Grail Castle neither dead nor alive, wounded by the Dolorous Blow. His wound, maybe in the loins, has made the land infertile, the health of king and land being one. Until a true knight overcomes all obstacles to gain the Grail Castle and ask the questions that revive him, the land is waste.

The Fisher King, Bron or Brons, began as the Celtic **giant Bran**, whose wound likewise made the land infertile. Or he is *Pelles*, father of Elaine, mother of **Galahad** (the true Grail-knight) by **Lancelot**. The name 'Pelles' may be from the Cornish Peller, 'Wise Man', or from **Pwyll**, the **otherworld** king of the Welsh *Mabinogion*. The term 'Fisher King' may be a pun on the French *pêcheur* ('fisherman'), and *pécheur* ('sinner'); the waste of the land being caused by the king's sin, wound or blemish (as in the old Irish law that no man with a physical defect could be High King). Yet also it refers to his feeding a multitude with one small **fish** from the Grail.

Is **Christ** the Fisher King, wounded on the **cross** by Longinus thrusting a spear into his side? Yet why should the right questions ('Whom does the Grail serve?') free him and revive the land? The mystery incorporates pagan symbols in that esoteric post-Crusades **Christianity** involved **Catharism**, **troubadour** romance and the enigmatic fall of the **Knights Templar**. Some ideas could be expressed only obliquely: open talk led to the stake. Today, what was hidden behind metaphoric castle walls remains hidden: the meaning of the Fisher King remains a tantalising mystery.[1]

1. *From Ritual to Romance*, Jessie L. Weston (1920), Anchor Books, USA, 1957; *King Arthur and the Grail*, Richard Cavendish, Paladin, London, 1980.

FLIGHT (*See* **CONCORDANCE, UFOs**)

Tales of magical flight embrace many categories. One involves supernatural winged entities: **angels**, **demons** or **elemental** spirits now anomalously manifesting as **Unidentified Flying Objects** (UFOs). Such entities, as with the Arabian **djinn**, may snatch sleepers on dream-journeys, depositing them in seconds in a far-off land before returning them, bewildered and amnesiac, to their point of origin. Or the supernatural flight may be that of the **Wild Hunt**: a spectral god of the dead leading his red-eyed white hounds through the stormy night sky, seeking the **souls** of the newly dead.

Another involves human levitation, as by **Simon Magus** in his magical battle with the Apostle Peter in Rome. He perished when Peter shot him down with a well-aimed prayer. A third involves human flight by artificial means: flying carpets; the wings **Daedalus** made to escape Crete; the stone flying-machine in which the **Druid** Mog Ruith (student of Simon Magus) came to grief during a magical battle over Ireland. The stone flying-machine reminds us of tales of a now-lost art by which huge blocks of stone could be levitated: so, it is said, the magician **Merlin** brought the 'Giant's Dance' from Ireland to Stonehenge. More remarkable still are the 'celestial cars' (*vimanas*) as described in the Indian *Ramayana* and *Mahabharata*. Such cars were 'made of light wood looking like a great bird with a durable and well-formed body having mercury inside and fire at the bottom'.[1]

Then there is flight courtesy of **fabulous beasts**: Sinbad hitching a ride on the giant **roc**, **Bellerophon** riding the winged horse **Pegasus**, or **Santa Claus** winging his way through the Christmas sky on a sleigh drawn by flying reindeer. Or the hero may **shape-shift** into a bird; Gwion Bach in flight from **Cerridwen**; the Russian **bogatyr** Volga, changing into a hawk; both suggesting shamanic flight, by which in trance (perhaps induced by a hallucinogen like fly agaric), the **shaman** 'flies' to the spirit-world.

The **Sioux** shaman Black Elk (*c*.1862–1950) would sit by a tree, symbol of the *axis mundi*, and up it in trance rise through a tunnel-like aperture, led by a spirit-bird, to a 'flaming rainbow tepee' in the sky, there to speak with his **ancestors**, the 'grandfathers'.

Such shamanic flight is internal; 'flying' in the sense that drug-users speak of 'tripping' or being 'high'. So too the image of the witch on her broomstick implies trance-flight, perhaps aided both by narcotic herbs and by sexual excitement – the broomstick is phallic. Such flight reminds us of the sexual rites of **Tantric** cultists, undertaken to raise the kundalini **serpent** power and thus gain enlightenment, longevity and other powers.

But flight is dangerous. Many such tales warn of hubris (pride comes before a fall). **Bellerophon** riding the winged horse **Pegasus** too close to **Olympus**, **Icarus** flying too close to the sun: both are hurled down to be crippled or die, as are Simon Magus and Mog Ruith.

1. *War in Ancient India*, Ramachandra Dikshitar, Macmillan, London, 1945.

FLOOD MYTH (*See* **CONCORDANCE**)

Versions of the myth of a universal Flood or deluge are found the world over. Typically they agree that the entire world was inundated, that the event (though foreseen) was sudden, and that the few survivors built arks, rafts or other vessels having been warned by God or the gods. The best-known account is the biblical story (Genesis vi–viii) of Noah. Yet this is based on the Sumerian epic of **Gilgamesh** (pre-2000 BC), itself based on an earlier tale in which **Enlil**, angered by human evil, sends the Flood.

Gilgamesh is told by the **immortal** Utnapishtim how the god **Ea** told him to build a **boat** and on it load: 'all that I had of gold and of living things, my family, my kin, the beast of the field both wild and tame.'[1] This **ark** is a **seven**-decked cube, 120 cubits (about 175 feet) a side. Noah's ark is 300 cubits long, 50 broad and 30 high. Otherwise the Sumerian account is clearly the original. For six days and nights the storm rages and on the seventh day the boat grounds on Mount Nisir. Utnapishtim sends out a **dove** which returns, then a **swallow** which returns, then a **raven** which does not.

One account derives 'arc' from Latin *arca* ('a chest'), another from the Hindu *argha* ('crescent', or 'arc' of a circle). Harding suggests that the ark is a **moon** boat and that 'Noah' is from *Nuah*, a Babylonian moon goddess. While accepting that Flood-myth may refer to a genuine event, as recorded worldwide, she says the ark or 'moon boat' refers to psychological events in which living men are ferried from one world to another.[2] Thus Egyptian **Osiris** ferries dead initiates to the **Otherworld**, **Charon** ferries the dead over the Styx and King **Arthur** is ferried to **Avalon**.

In **Greek myth**, Deucalion and Pyrrha escape the Flood in an ark. In the Indian *Rig Veda* the ark of Manu is towed to safety by a giant **fish**. The Norse *Edda* tells how the **giant** Ymir is slain, his blood causing a Flood in which all Frost Giants drown but for Bergelmir and his wife, who escape in the boat Lodr. The Irish *Lebor Gabala* (Book of Invasions) says Ireland's first invaders all died in the Flood but for Fintan, who changed himself into a **salmon** then, as the waters fell, into an **eagle**.[3]

So too the theme of arks built on high ground is global, found in the myths of the Choctaw of Louisiana, the Marquesans and New Hebrideans of the Pacific, and the Votyaks of Western Siberia. Where shipbuilding skills are scarce, the ark is a raft. The Hopi of Arizona, describing three former world ages (*see Yugas*), tell how city-building Third World folk attacked each other with **flying** machines (*patuwvotas*). The creator-god Sotuknang sent the Flood to destroy them all. The Hopi survived on rafts of hollow reed, sending out birds which returned exhausted, until in time **Spider** Woman brought them to the Fourth World, *Tuwagachi*, landing them on the west coast of the USA.[4]

Rafts also feature in the Flood myths of other North American folks, the Karens of Burma and New Zealand's **Maori**. The Maori tell how the god Tawaki, angered by human sin, broke the crystal floor of heaven so that through it poured the waters of the upper world, to submerge the entire earth.[5]

Even more fanciful 'arks' are reported. Trow, **ancestor** of the Dyaks of Borneo, survived the Flood in a trough; Rock of the Arapahoe in North America in a boat made of fungi and spider's webs; the ancestors of the Chane of Bolivia in an earthenware pot; and Lithuanians in a nutshell.[6]

Hawaiian lore tells how the Flood, *Kaiakahinalii*, destroyed all living beings but for a man, Nuu, who built a huge vessel with a house on top. He survived with his wife, his three sons and their wives. The ark in time landed on top of Mauna Kea, Hawaii's highest mountain.[7]

Carved symbols and animal images are found high up a Venezuelan cliff (Tepumereme means 'Picture Rock'). The local explanation is that they were carved during the 'Time of the Great Water' by artists in canoes. The cliff-face rocks involved remain clearly wave-hollowed.[8]

Just as odd is wide agreement about the specifics of the catastrophe: the size of the raindrops, the heat of the deluge. The Sacs and Fox tribes of North America say every drop of the falling rain was as large as a wigwam. St John's Revelation describes hailstones each weighing a hundredweight. The Persian *Zend-Avesta* speaks of saucer-sized raindrops, of raindrops the size of a man's head. Such rain was also boiling hot, as is claimed by the Makah tribe of Washington State (northwest USA) and by the Voguls of Finland, who say a flood of hot water followed global fire which had raged for seven years. The 'fiery waters' were so hot that even their rafts burned. A Jewish Flood myth tells how: 'The Lord made every drop boiling hot in hell before he let it fall on the Earth.' The Ipurinas of Brazil, also speaking of a flood of hot water, say this was because the sun, a **cauldron** of boiling water, once tipped over.

Other tales say the Flood began with underground water overflowing. A Jewish tale says: 'The fountains of the deep broke up first. Then came the flood from above. Then fire fell also, and rain, boiling hot.' A Syrian tradition tells how suddenly huge volumes of water burst from the earth, then the rain began to fall. The rivers left their beds and the seas so flooded the land that everyone drowned. The Koran mentions how an 'oven' suddenly threw out vast masses of water, followed by Flood from the sky. This account is found throughout the Americas. Likewise it is a common belief that sin caused the Flood. The *Prose Edda* tells how: 'Brothers lift hands against one another; the ties of kinship are torn; full of hate is the world and of shameless adultery; axe-time, this is, and sword-time, shields are cloven; storm-time this is, and wolf-time; the end of the Earth.'[9]

That a sense of impending doom gripped pre-Flood societies is plain from the many myths of 'righteous men' (Manu, Deucalion, Noah, etc.) who, with god-warned foresight, built arks. Many myths tell of how, long before the actual Flood, the seas began to rise. The coming catastrophe was obvious, but few wished to know. Does this sound familiar?

Modern catastrophe theorists like Velikovsky remain widely derided for collating such myths in their effort to suggest that the global Flood was not a mythic but an historical event, one so terrible that few survivors could later relate it accurately.[10]

1. *The Epic of Gilgamesh* (ed. N.K. Sandars), Penguin, London, 1972.
2. *Woman's Mysteries*, M. Esther Harding, Rider, London, 1982 (1955).
3. *Moons, Myths and Man*, H.S. Bellamy, Faber & Faber, London, 1936, p.109.
4. *Book of the Hopi*, Frank Waters, Penguin, London, 1977, p.20.
5. *op.cit.* Bellamy, p.109.
6. *Ibid.*, pp.121–30.
7. *Hawaiian Folk Tales*, Thomas G. Thrum, McClurg, Chicago, 1912, p.20.
8. *op.cit.* Bellamy, p.112.
9. *Prose Edda* (*Völuspá; Gylfaginning*), quoted in Bellamy, *op.cit.*, p.113.
10. *Mankind in Amnesia*, Immanuel Velikovsky, Abacus, London, 1983.

FLORA (*See* CONCORDANCE)

FLYING DUTCHMAN (*See* GAMES, WANDERING JEW)

In European seafaring lore the appearance of this spectral ship, doomed to sail for ever, signifies imminent disaster. It is said that Captain Vanderdecken bartered his soul to round the Cape of Good Hope in a storm, and was thus condemned to sail that course eternally. This version of the myth was used by the German composer **Richard Wagner** (1813–83) in his 1843 opera *Der fliegende Holländer*. Another version has a Captain Falkenberg sailing through the North Sea, dicing for his soul with the **Devil**: a motif used by **Samuel Taylor Coleridge** in his 'Rime of the Ancient Mariner' (1798), in which the mariner sights a ghost-ship on which Death and Life in Death dice for him.

FOMORIANS (*See* **BALOR, IRISH MYTH, LUG**)

FON (*See* **AFRICAN MYTH, AWONAWILONA, PYTHON, VOODOO**)

The dual or androgynous creator-god of this people of Dahomey is Mawu-Lisa: Mawu male and Lisa female. They are *xoso*, 'twins', and it is through their union that the world exists. This concept reminds us of the creator-god of the Zuni of North America, Awonawilona, also androgynous. Their offspring are the *vodu*, meaning 'gods', 'spirits', 'sacred object', a term from which the name of the Haitian spirit-religion, **voodoo**, may be derived. The Fon see the earth as floating on water (an idea reminiscent of the Sumerian Apsu, the subterranean ocean of sweet water ruled by **Ea/Enki**), and the heavens as rotating on the inside of a gourd. The **serpent**-god Da, child of Mawu-Lisa, is likewise androgynous, and supports creation with his 3,500 coils above the earth and a similar number below. His name may provide the root of the Voodoo serpent-god Damballah. Other twinned or androgynous deities or *vodu* governing secondary aspects of creation include Heyveso ('thunder') the sky; Sakpata the earth; Agbe-Naete the seas and all waters, and Age the deserts and wastelands.

FOOD OF THE GODS (*See AMANITA MUSCARIA*, **HAOMA**, **NECTAR, SOMA**)

FOOL (*See* **PERCEVAL, TAROT**)

In the Major Arcana of the **Tarot**, the unnumbered or zero card depicts (in the Rider-Waite pack) a gaily-dressed youth ignorant of the abyss at his feet. His gaze is fixed on the heavens, and he seems not to hear the **dog** (instinct) barking warning at his heels. This is the Fool: naive spirit in search of experience, character unformed. Yet out of this primal empty zero arises all worldly experience. The **Arthurian** Grail-knight **Perceval** is so unworldly he becomes known as 'Perfect Fool', 'Pure Fool' or 'Holy Fool'. Yet his innocence protects him, leading some to associate him with Christ.

In many cultures the simpleminded are associated with holiness: the English word 'silly' comes from the German *selig*, 'holy'.

Other aspects of the Fool are less innocent. As clown or court jester the Fool evades laws binding everyone else; he may say or do as he pleases, for nobody holds him responsible. He may tell the king truths nobody else dare utter: on one day a year (Feast of Fools) he may play the king (Order) while the king plays the Fool (Chaos). Yet in ritual **sacrifice** he might take the king's place as scapegoat. In medieval carnivals derived from the Roman Saturnalia the Bishop of Fools, Abbot of Unreason or Lord of Misrule were burlesque figures who, after a brief, dissipated reign, were actually or symbolically burned to death or otherwise sacrificed.

FORTUNA (*See* **FATES, ROMAN MYTH**)

Originally called Fors, then Fors Fortuna, and said to be the daughter of **Jupiter** (and his nurse), from the earliest times this Italian goddess of chance or fate was worshipped as one bringing good crops and rich flocks. Introduced to Rome in 204 BC as Fortuna Primigenia, she was combined with an already-existing Roman Fortuna, invoked to explain the amazing good luck of Servius Tullius, the slave who became king, and who was said to be either her son or her lover. Thus her festival, held in June, was open to slaves as well as citizens – who could say whom she would bless or deny? Chance personified, the worship of Fortune's Wheel survived the Middle Ages. Those who play at roulette or bet on the horses are among her current devotees.

FOX (See COYOTE, DOG, SHAPE-SHIFTING, TRICKSTERS, WOLF)

Many fables concern the cunning of the common fox (*Canis vulpis*), Europe's last surviving wild dog. The best-known in Europe, 'Reynard the Fox' (tenth century; many versions since) tells how Reynard defeats every enemy by his wit. **Witches** were thought to **shape-shift** into foxes (especially in Wales and Germany): foxes were thus burned alive at midsummer **fire-festivals**.

Labrador **Eskimos** tell of a bachelor hunter who returned home to find everything put in order as if by a dutiful wife. Pretending to go hunting, he hid nearby and saw a fox enter his hut. Following it, he saw a lovely woman wearing fine-cut skins. Hanging on a line was a fox-skin. She said she was his wife; but after they had lived together a while he complained about a musky odour. Taking umbrage, she threw off her clothing, reassumed the fox-skin and slipped away. Since then she has never visited any man.

The magical Chinese fox (see **dog**) was said to live a thousand years. A story by the ninth-century poet Niui Chiao tells how the hero, Wang, met two foxes on their hind legs, laughing at a sheet of paper. Shooting in the eye the one who held it, Wang fled with the paper, which was covered with indecipherable script. As he told his tale to other guests in the inn that night, a man with a bandaged eye asked to see the page. Wang was about to show it when the innkeeper saw the man had a tail. 'He's a fox!' he cried. The man turned into a fox and fled. Deciding to return home, Wang met his family walking to the city. His mother said he had written telling them to sell their home and join him there. She produced the letter, but the page was blank. So they returned, though now homeless. One day a brother they thought dead reappeared. When Wang, telling the tale of their ruin, came to the part about the foxes, the brother said: 'Ah! That's the root of the problem!' Wang showed him the page. The brother snatched it. 'At last I have back what I wanted!' he said, changing into a fox and escaping.[1]

1. *The Book of Imaginary Beings*, Jorge Luis Borges, Penguin, London, 1974, p.44.

FRANKENSTEIN (See FAUST, GOLEM, ROBOTS, SHELLEY)

The tale of Baron von Frankenstein, a Swiss scientist or magus slain by an artificial monster he created out of spare parts stolen from dead bodies, originated one night in Switzerland in 1816 with a story-telling contest between the poets Byron and **Shelley**, Doctor Polidori and Shelley's second wife, Mary Wollstonecraft Shelley (1797–1851). Mary's tale, *Frankenstein; or, the Modern Prometheus* (1818) was an immediate and continuing success.

The first movie version was by Thomas Alva Edison in 1910. *The Golem* (1910) and *The Homunculus* (1914: both German) explored similar themes from Jewish myth. The 1931 **Hollywood** remake of *Frankenstein* (Boris Karloff as the monster) remains the classic, despite many versions since.

The theme was not original to Mary Shelley: the myths of the **Golem** and of **Faust** already existed, expressing the unease of many who felt that the untrammelled pursuit of knowledge and scientific power leads to damnation or disaster. That the script of the Karloff film has little to do with the original novel matters little: the theme has become **archetypal**.

FRAZER, SIR JAMES (1854–1941) (*See* **DIANA, GOLDEN BOUGH**)
Born in Glasgow, this Scots anthropologist and folklorist, author of *The Golden Bough*, was a fellow of Trinity College, Cambridge, from 1879 until the end of his life (save for a brief spell at Liverpool University).

In *The Golden Bough; a Study in Magic and Religion* (1890; reissued in twelve volumes, 1907–15; abridged edition 1922), Frazer argued that human culture develops from **magic** (defined as an attempt to control phenomena by methods based on faulty reasoning) via religion (the appeal to spiritual beings for help) to science. This evolutionary sequence is now dismissed, but his vast synthesis of global folklore remains valuable. He argued that all social and rural health was once held to depend on the vitality of the king, who was thus killed and replaced when his powers began to fail, as in the rites of Roman goddess **Diana** at her temple-grove by Lake Nemi, each high priest succeeding by slaying his predecessor. Knighted in 1914, he also wrote *Totemism and Exogamy* (1910) and *Folk-Lore in the Old Testament* (1918).

FREEMASONRY (*See* **HIRAM ABIFF, KNIGHTS TEMPLAR, ROSICRUCIANS**)
The obscure origins and rites of this exclusive male order all aid its mystique. Variously associated with Knights Templar, Rosicrucians and other secret societies, Freemasonry is said to date back to Hiram Abiff, the legendary builder of **Solomon**'s Temple, and to have begun as a guild of itinerant medieval masons using secret signs for mutual recognition. Yet recent research suggests that the order began in the flight from torture of the Knights Templar after their overthrow in France (1307), and that its initiatory oaths originated in their fugitive need for secrecy.[1] This may explain the continuing hatred of the order by the Catholic Church which helped destroy the Templars, and also its connection with Scotland, where fleeing Templars perhaps aided Robert the Bruce (and gained his protection) during his war against England. A later, Rosicrucian connection (perhaps only wishful thinking) is offered in a poem (*c.*1638) by Henry Adamson of Perth:

> For we be brethren of the Rosie Crosse;
> We have the Mason word, and second sight,
> Things for to come we can tell aright[2]

Certainly by the late seventeenth century, functional or 'Operative' Masonry had become 'Speculative' Masonry; as evolved in Scotland (Scotch Rite). Such lodges may have maintained Templar lore, and certainly required loyalty to Jacobitism. The English Grand Lodge (1717) was formed as a Whig/Hanoverian attempt to break this Jacobite monopoly: by 1723 the original four English lodges had grown to fifty-two. In 1733 in Massachusetts the first American lodge was formed, and in 1776 masons played a prominent role in establishing the US constitution. Masonic symbols like the Eye in the Triangle remain conspicuous on the dollar bill to the present day.

This new order let Europe's new trading gentry (middle classes) meet in exclusive clubs to further their business secretly. Such secrecy even now causes alarm, both through fear of social subversion and 'insider dealing' by lodge members as through the mystique of the Craft itself. Insisting on the brotherhood of man, it requires the purification of its members via the 'seven steps of Solomon's Temple': discretion, obedience, morality, love of man-kind, courage, generosity and love of death. The last requirement makes sense if the first masons were not builders but warrior monks – Templars. A third aim is to work to regenerate mankind. Freemasonry is divided into three 'Craft' degrees – Entered Apprentice, Fellow Craft and Master Mason.

1. *Born in Blood*, John J. Robinson, Random Century, London, 1989.
2. *The Temple and the Lodge*, Michael Baigent and Richard Leigh, Corgi, London, 1990, p.168.

FREUD, SIGMUND (1856–1939) (*See* AKHENATON, DREAMS, INCEST, JUNG, MOSES, OEDIPUS)

Author of *The Interpretation of Dreams* (1900) and founder of psychoanalytic theory, Freud elucidated the hidden psychology behind basic mythic themes. Interpreting dream **symbols** as masked allegorical reference to shocks arising during the dreamer's infancy, he diagnosed mythologies as symptomatic of similar shocks in the infancy of peoples. Stressing the importance of symbols in folklore, legends, myths and jokes, he saw human behaviour as arising from suppressed desire and inner conflict. 'We base everything upon the assumption of a psyche of the mass in which psychic processes occur as in the life of the individual,' he wrote (1913). 'Moreover, we let the sense of guilt for a deed survive for thousands of years, remaining effective in generations which could not have known anything of the deed.'[1]

His core-theory of the Oedipus complex as cause of adult irrationality suggests that every male infant desires its mother but hates its father as a rival (vice versa for females). Claiming that all men forever slay their father and marry their mother (symbolically and unconsciously), he defined two conflicting hidden impulses in every human psyche: **eros** (love: libido) and *thanatos* (death: destrudo). From the **Greek myth** of the King of Thebes, he argued: 'King Oedipus, who slew his father Laïus and married his mother Jocasta, merely shows us the fulfilment of our own childhood wishes'.[2]

Analysing patriarchal cosmogonies, where the myth of divine motherhood is assumed by the father (thus **Eve** born from **Adam**'s rib, or **Athene** from the brow of **Zeus**), he defined a process: 'displacement of accent', whereby the original event is hidden by introducing a distracting secondary theme, the elements of the original condition being reordered or omitted. Thus, whether in individual dream or in collective mythology: '. . . the manifest content [of the original situation] is made so unlike the latent thoughts that nobody would suspect the presence of the latter behind the former.'[3]

He also described the processes of 'sublimation' and 'transference': as the mother (**Gaia**) gives birth from the womb, so does the father (Zeus), but from the brain. The power of the Word ('In the beginning was the Word') is given as another example: mouth as vagina, the Word as birth. (The wounding of Christ in the side by the spear has been interpreted by some Freudians as transference to the male of female **menstruation**.)

In his last major work, *Moses and Monotheism* (1939), Freud argued that **Moses** was an Egyptian noble serving the heretical pharaoh Akhenaton (1377–1358 BC). When Akhenaton's monotheistic cult collapsed, Moses led a band of Semitic settlers out of Egypt. He tried to impose monotheism on them but they killed him (again: murder of the father), instead adopting as leader the Midianite priest of an Arabian volcano god, **Yahweh**. So they came to the Promised Land (re-entering the mother). Yet Moses's teachings persisted until at length Yahweh became the Mosaic god. Freud said this accounted for the neuroticism of biblical religion; its myths hiding a repressed guilt at the murder of Moses. Also he insisted that his theory accounted for the dual nature of Yahweh: on the one hand a crude Midianite volcano-deity and **serpent**-god; on the other hand, the righteous One God of Akhenaton and Moses. This theory has been attacked ever since.[4]

Joseph Campbell believes that Freud's interpretation of this and other myths is over-literal; imaginative events being cast as historical truths.[5] Today, the approach to myth of Freud's one-time disciple **Carl Jung** is generally considered more fruitful.

1. *Totem and Tabu*, Sigmund Freud (1913), quoted in *Creative Mythology*, Joseph Cambell, Penguin, London, 1976, p.652.
2. *The Interpretation of Dreams* (trans. James Strachey), Sigmund Freud, Hogarth Press, London, 1953, p.262.
3. *A General Introduction to Psychoanalysis*, Sigmund Freud, Garden City, New York, 1935, p.125.
4. *Moses and Monotheism*, Sigmund Freud (trans. Katherine Jones), Knopf, New York, 1939.
5. *Occidental Mythology*, Joseph Campbell, Penguin, London, 1976, p.140.

FREY AND FREYA (*See* AESIR, FRIGGA, NERTHUS, NORSE MYTH, TWINS, VANIR)

In Norse myth as given by Snorri in the *Prose Edda*, the warlike Aesir are balanced by the Vanir: peaceful fertility-deities whose chiefs were Frey and Freya, twin children of **sea-god** Njord and the **earth mother Nerthus**.

Inhabiting the **elf**-realm Alfheim, Frey ruled the Light Elves, the Lios Alfar. God of fertility, sunshine and growth, his marriage to the maiden Gerd, who lived in the **underworld** with the **giants**, is interpreted as the fruitful harvest-union of the sky-god with the earth-goddess. Adam of Bremen (eleventh century) says Frey's image in his temple at Uppsala in Sweden was phallic, and that human **sacrifice** was made to him at a festival called the Fröblod. Ritual marriage was part of his cult which, popular in Viking times, had replaced the earlier worship of his 'mother' Nerthus. Frey was also associated with the **horse** cult, and (with Freya) the boar cult. It is said the **dwarves** made then gave him the golden boar Gullinbursti, able to run faster than a galloping horse and even to fly through the air. In Viking and Anglo-Saxon times the boar was seen as protector of warriors.

He also owned *Skidbladnir*, a magic ship able to travel at will in any direction. Big enough to hold all the gods, when not in use he could fold it up into his pocket. This tale may derive from the association of Frey with death and **burial**: dead Viking chieftains were commonly placed in their longboat which, fired, was sent out to sea to sink in flames.[1]

As for Freya, Snorri (thirteenth century) declares that she alone of the gods still lived in his time. Many surviving place-names in southern Norway and Sweden support his claim. Known as goddess or bride of the Vanir, she was associated with love-affairs. The **trickster Loki** accused her of having an affair with Frey, and of taking all the gods and elves for lovers. In the *Flateyjarbók* it is said she won her necklace by sleeping one night with the four dwarves who forged it. Ritual marriage was part of her cult. As for her own marriage to Odur (sunshine), by whom she had two daughters, it is said that when he left her (or was stolen away to the underworld like **Osiris** or **Adonis**) she wept tears of amber and gold. Able to fly and take falcon-shape at will, she was also Syr, the boar-sow. Associated with the underworld and with divinatory trance-ecstasies as practised by **shamans** and spae-wives, she rode in a carriage drawn by **cats**. It may be that the seeresses who once travelled between isolated farms in Norway and Iceland were the last representatives of this popular fertility-goddess.[2]

1. *Gods and Myths of Northern Europe*, H.R. Ellis Davidson, Penguin, London, 1964, pp.92–103.
2. *Ibid.*, pp.114–25.

FRIGGA (*See* **AESIR, FREYA, NORSE MYTH, TEUTONIC MYTH**)
Confusingly similar in name and function to Freya, this **Teutonic/Norse** fertility-goddess, wife of **Odin**, was also known as Frija or Frya, giving her name to the sixth day of the week: Friday. Queen of Heaven among the Aesir in Asgard, she often successfully resisted Odin's will. Yet, though able to foresee the future, she could not change it. Her failure to get a promise from the **mistletoe** not to harm her son **Baldur** led to his death via the trickery of **Loki,** who jeeringly accused her (as he did **Freya**) of sexual misconduct. Again like Freya, she slept with four dwarves in a night to obtain a golden necklace they had made. Loki told Odin about this: Odin told Loki to steal the necklace. Her door being locked, he turned into a fly and entered through a hole in the roof and found Frigga asleep. To get her to change position so he could unclasp the necklace, he became a flea and bit her. Then he took the necklace to Odin, who refused to return it unless she provoked a war in which, each night, all the heroes that fell by day were to be resuscitated to continue the fight next day. This reminds us of the tale of **Bran**'s cauldron in the Welsh *Mabinogion.* The war would not end until a **Christian** knight came to vanquish all the pagans, whereupon the dead would find rest. Agreeing, Frigga regained her necklace.

The assimilation here of different mythologies is clear enough. The latter tale shows clear Christian insertion, while similarities between Freya and Frigga are not coincidental. The likelihood is that the Aesir and Vanir were the deities of successive waves of Teutonic folk colonising Scandinavia, and that in time these deities merged. The *Eddas* speak of a war between the two, followed by mutual assimilation.

FRODO (*See* **TOLKIEN**)

FROST GIANTS (*See* **GIANTS, JOTUNHEIM, NORSE MYTH**)

FRUIT (*See* **APPLE, FIG**)

FURIES (*See* **GREEK MYTH**)
The three Erinnyes (the 'Angry Ones', or Furies), sprang from the union of air and mother earth **Gaia**, along with lies, strife, terror, vengeance, pride, battle, oblivion and other unfortunate personifications of human conduct and emotion. Another myth is that drops of blood from the **castrated** Ouranos fell on mother earth, so that she bore the Furies: Alecto, Tisiphone and Megaera. The Meliae, **ash**-nymphs, also sprang from that blood.

The Furies avenged crimes of parricide and perjury. Older than any **Olympian** god, **Zeus** included, they are **snake**-haired, **dog**-headed, **bat**-winged hags who pursue evildoers relentlessly with brass-tipped scourges from city to city, land to land. When they catch up, they show no mercy. Their victims die in hideous torment.

It was thought unwise to speak their name openly: so they were usually called the Eumenides, the 'Kindly Ones'. The love-goddess **Aphrodite** was said to be their sister, via association with Nemesis. The complex tale of this association is told by Robert Graves.[1]

1. *The Greek Myths*, Robert Graves, Penguin, London, 1960, vol.1, 32.1–32.4.

G

GAIA (*See* CRONUS, GREEK MYTH, OURANOS)

In the beginning, claimed **Hesiod**, Gaia the deep-breasted earth emerged out the darkness of Chaos. Bearing Ouranos (Uranus), the star-crowned sky, she made him 'her equal in grandeur, so that he entirely covered her'. Creating the mountains and Pontus, 'the sterile sea', she mated with Ouranos to bear the twelve **Titans**, the three one-eyed **Cyclopes** and three monsters: Cottus, Briareus and Gyges, each hundred-armed and fifty-headed – so they were called the Hecatoncheires or Centimanes. Horrified by such charming offspring, Ouranos locked them up deep in the earth. Vowing revenge, Gaia made a sharp sickle. She told her children her plan, but only the oldest, **Cronus**, agreed to help. When Ouranos next slept with her, Cronus castrated him with the sickle. So the **Furies**, the Meliae, and **Aphrodite** were born.

Portrayed as a giant, this great **earth mother** of the early Greeks not only created the universe and the gods, but bore humanity, drawing Erichthonius (Attica's first inhabitant) out of her bosom. Presiding over marriages and said to be the first prophetess, she possessed the **Delphic** oracle before **Apollo** took it over. Though later her fame dwindled, as Gé her name persisted as the root of terms like *ge*-ology, *ge*-ometry and *ge*-ography. In 1969 the English earth-scientist James Lovelock, defining planet earth as a self-regulating system, named this system 'Gaia'. The concept of Gaia as a single living organism is today a core idea of **New Age** thought.[1]

1. *Gaia*, James Lovelock, OUP, 1979.

GALAHAD (*See* ARTHURIAN MYTH, HOLY GRAIL, KNIGHT, ROUND TABLE)

The only knight to penetrate the Grail-mystery, this son of **Lancelot** (the best knight in the world) and Elaine (Grail-Bearer and daughter of Pelles the **Fisher King**), was conceived when Lancelot, spellbound, slept with Elaine, thinking her **Guinevere**, **Arthur**'s wife. Raised fatherless (like **Perceval** and Lancelot), he remained in a nunnery until, one Pentecost, a slab of red marble floated downriver to Camelot, in it a sword that only the world's best knight might draw. **Gawain** and Perceval tried but failed: Lancelot declined even to try. The company returned to the **Round Table**; all the palace doors and windows shut of their own accord. A white-robed old man entered with a swordless young knight in red armour: Galahad. When the young knight sat safely on the Siege Perilous (representing **Christ**'s seat at the Last Supper), all knew him as the champion to break the spell on the land. Arthur took him to the river, where he drew the sword from the stone. That evening at the Round Table, the Grail appeared amid a clap of thunder and a bright light, borne by no mortal hand and obscure in form. When it vanished, the dumbstruck knights regained speech. Gawain vowed to seek the Grail and return only if he saw it plain: the other knights vowed likewise. But only four realised the quest was spiritual, not worldly – of these four, only Galahad was perfect in his godly chastity. Lancelot the adulterer was allowed only a distant vision of the Grail; Bors repented, having once slept with a woman; Perceval, though chaste, relied not on God but on himself.

Together, Galahad, Bors and Perceval came to the Castle of Corbenic to be welcomed by King Pelles. When the old Maimed King was brought in on a litter, they saw the Holy Lance and the Grail borne by **angels**, the lance dripping **blood** into the Grail. From it appeared Christ, naked and bleeding. He told them the Grail must leave the sinful land of **Logres**, whereupon the spell on the land would be broken. Christ vanished. Galahad touched the legs of the Maimed King with blood from the Grail: the old man was healed.

That night the three knights rode to the sea, to join the Grail and the Lance on a ship that sailed itself to Sarras (Jerusalem), where Galahad was made king. A year later, looking into the Grail, Galahad learned its innermost mystery. No longer desiring earthly life, his **soul** was carried by angels to heaven, from which a hand descended to take up the Grail and the Lance, neither ever seen again. Perceval died a year later; Bors returned to Camelot.

Perfect from the start, without any failings, Galahad is not a human character but a symbol whose inevitable triumph rewards nobody but himself. The adulterous Lancelot represents **Adam**, imperfect man; the virgin Galahad represents **Christ**, the second Adam, man perfected, destined to be greater than his father, and like Christ raised to heaven.[1]

1. *King Arthur and the Grail*, Richard Cavendish, Paladin, London, 1980.

GAMES (*See* **CONCORDANCE**)
Mythic games are either contested between mortal heroes, as with the ancient Olympic Games of Greece, or involve tests or riddling duels against supernatural enemies to gain knowledge; freedom from **curse**, enchantment or imprisonment; the right to safe passage; or to save one's life or **soul**.

Terrorising the Greek city of Thebes, the **Sphinx** devoured all failing to answer the **riddle** taught her by the Three **Muses**: 'What being, with only one voice, has sometimes two feet, sometimes three, sometimes four, and is weakest when it has the most?' **Oedipus** answered: 'Man, because he crawls on all fours as an infant, stands firmly on his two feet in his youth, and leans upon a staff in his old age.' Whereupon the Sphinx threw herself to her death from Mount Phicium, and Oedipus was made king of Thebes.

The Welsh child-poet **Taliesin** rescued Elphin from captivity by posing King Maelgwyn's twenty-four court bards a riddle they could not answer:

> Discover what it is:
> The strong creature from before the Flood
> Without flesh, without bone,
> Without vein, without blood,
> Without head, without feet . . .
> It is also as wide
> As the surface of the earth,
> And it was not born,
> Nor was it seen . . .

The answer, 'The wind', he gave by raising a violent storm which frightened the king into freeing Elphin from the dungeon.[1]

Lancelot, riding in the Lost Forest, found a tower where spellbound knights and ladies danced endlessly, and in which was a magic chessboard on which the pieces, moving by themselves, could be checkmated only by the best knight in the world. Lancelot won: all were released.

In Bricriu's Feast (*see* **Irish myth**) the **giant** Uath strides into **Conchobar's** court and offers his head to be struck off on condition that next night the hero who strikes offers his own head in turn. Leary the Triumphant and Conall of the Victories both strike off Uath's head; each time the giant picks up his head and stalks out, but next night neither Leary nor Conall is to be seen. Only **Cuchulainn**, smashing Uath's head into a pulp, has the courage to return next night and offer his own head: Uath brings down his axe on the stones and transforms into Curoi, wizard-king of Munster, to tell the company that there is no doubt: Cuchulainn is the only honourable hero. This tale was later adapted as the **Arthurian** legend of *Sir Gawain and the Green Knight*.

'To dice with the Devil' is a cliché: the **Flying Dutchman**, the Ancient Mariner and many another unfortunate has lost his soul by gaming with Old Nick, just as **Draupadi** and her Pandava brothers were enslaved when their eldest brother Yuddhisthira diced with the Kauravas and lost.

As for merely mortal sporting contests, the epitome of all, the Grecian Olympic Games, began in ancient times. In the ninth century BC (the age of **Homer**), Iphitus of Elis reorganised them. Peace between all warring states prevailed during the festival. The traditional list of victors was begun in 776 BC. Held every four years at the first full moon after the summer solstice, the festival lasted five days. The site, at Olympia, contained temples to **Zeus** and **Hera**. The glory of Olympic victory was great: **Jason** chose many of the Argonauts from the Olympic victors, including Castor the wrestler and Polydeuces the boxer (the **Dioscuri**), Euphemus the swimmer, and Herakles (**Hercules**), the strongest man who ever lived. Abandoned in the fourth century AD, the modern Olympics were inaugurated in Athens in 1896.

In old Ireland, versions of chess and draughts (*fidcheall* and *branfad*) were popular. The hero Cuchulainn was (naturally) an expert hurley-player. Round Table knights like **Galahad** and Lancelot were peerless at the joust, while **Robin Hood**, attending the great tournament at Nottingham Castle in disguise, gave himself away (as the rascally sheriff intended) by splitting in two the bull's-eye arrow of his chief opponent in the archery contest.

1. *The White Goddess*, Robert Graves, Faber & Faber, London, 1961, p.29.

GANDALF (*See* TOLKIEN, WIZARD)

GANDHARVAS (*See* FAIRIES, INDIAN MYTH, RAKSHASAS, YAKSHAS)

Said to number 6,333, these minor male deities haunted the air, forests and mountains of India. Empowered like the **Rakshasas** to work illusions during the twilight hour, anciently they often fought with human warriors. Those overcoming them received wisdom; those defeated were carried off into their own realm, like Western mortals by **elves** and **fairies**. Their music made the voluptuous Apsaras, inspirers of love in paradise and on earth, dance merrily. They were irresistibly handsome: 'Gandharva marriage' means love at first sight. Yet all these spirit-tribes appear to have arisen from one original couple. The *Rig Veda* describes a water-nymph, *Apsaras*, the wife of *Gandharva*, a spirit of the air who reveals divine truth to mortals and also prepares the celestial wine, **soma**, for the gods. Perhaps equivalent to the elf-king and fairy-queen of Western folklore, these two are submerged in the later **Vedas**, which deal with the Gandharvas as a group of tribes.

Some authorities have identified them as tribes displaced by the **Aryan** invasions, much as in the West fairies have been identified with aboriginal

European tribes. Yet again, such interpretation seems over-literal.

In the *Mahabharata,* when the Pandavas were exiled in the forest (*see* **Draupadi**), the enemy Kaurava king, Duryodhana, tried to enter the forest to spy on their misery, but a dancing band of Gandharvas and Apsaras stopped him. Threatened, they fought, defeated and captured him with his courtiers and ladies. Hearing of this, the Pandava brothers **Arjuna** and **Bhima** came to fight the Gandharvas, making them release Duryodhana, thus humiliating him. Then Arjuna was taken in a chariot over Suravithi, the Milky Way, where, enchanted by Gandharva music, he saw the lovely Apsaras 'with their fair round hips and slim waists . . . perform various evolutions, shaking their deep bosoms and casting their glances around'.

The Indian paradise seems more lively than the Christian version.

GANESA (*See* ELEPHANT, INDIAN MYTH)

This four-armed, **elephant**-headed Indian god of wisdom, son of **Shiva** and Parvati, was patron of learning and brought good luck. Lord of the Ganas (**dwarf-demons**), his long-trunked, pot-bellied statue is still found in most Indian towns. Traditionally, poets invoke him at the start of a book, architects place his image where a new house is to be built, he is honoured whenever a journey or new business begins. He has an elephant head because the elephant is anciently thought wise due to its long life, huge size and ability to push through the thickest jungle – as can the tiny mouse, which rides on Ganesa's back. A myth in the **Puranas** tells how the cursed planet Saturn cut off his original human head just by looking at him. Flying the man-**eagle Garuda**, **Vishnu** cut off the head of **Indra**'s elephant and set it on Ganesa's neck.

Another tale is that Shiva's wife Parvati (praise-name of **Devi**-Uma as high goddess of the Himalayas) wanted a guard to stop Shiva spying on her as she bathed. So from her bath-oil and other materials she formed a pot-bellied man. Sprinkling her bathwater (the **Ganges**) over him, he came to life as Ganesa. When Shiva approached, Ganesa held him off. Enraged, Shiva decapitated him then, looking about, saw an elephant. He cut off its head and put it on Ganesa's shoulders, perhaps hoping Parvati would not notice the difference.

Elsewhere it is said Parvati gave birth to a fat man with four arms and an elephant's head – a lazy beast obstructing spiritual development. Yet it was to Ganesa, the first scribe, that Vyasa dictated the epic *Mahabharata.*

A god of huge appetite, Ganesa enjoys offerings of fruit and vegetables. He won his two wives Siddhi ('achievement') and Buddhi ('intelligence') by his intellect. Challenged by his brother **Kartikeya** to race him round the world to win them both, he sat idly while Kartikeya rounded the world. When Kartikeya returned, Ganesa described all he had seen from the books he had read. So this original armchair traveller won his wives.

GANGES (*See* INDIAN MYTH, RIVER MYTH)

Rising in a Himalayan ice-cave (Bhagirathi), this great Indian river flows 1,557 miles east past Allahabad and Benares to Bengal. It unites with the Brahmaputra to form the world's most dangerous delta. Throughout its long journey its waters and those of its sister rivers keep India alive. So 'Mother Ganges' is a goddess in her own right: Ganga, daughter of the mountain god Himavan, the 'Owner of Snow'; sister of Parvati, **Shiva**'s mountain-wife. It is said that once the gods refused to share her with mortals, for she was too precious and lovely. The pious prince Bhagiratha prayed to **Brahma** that Ganga be let down to earth. Brahma agreed, but only if the god Shiva let

Ganga flow through his hair. When Shiva agreed, Ganga came roaring down from the mountains. She would have drowned the land, but the forests of Shiva's hair tamed and slowed her, so that she became gentle, fertilising the land via the many canals that run from her. As important to Indian civilisation as is the Nile to **Egypt**, the waters of Ganga remain holy to millions, no matter what is carried in her flow. To bathe in her means purification from sin; to die in her is blessedness; to be cast into her after death ensures peace.

GANYMEDE (*See* GREEK MYTH)
Cup-bearer of the Grecian gods of **Olympus**, this beautiful youth originated as a rain-god, anciently identified with the zodiacal constellation of the Water-Carrier, Aquarius. Said to be the mortal son of King Tros of Phrygia, his good looks so charmed **Zeus** that the king of the gods took **eagle**-form and swept the youth up to immortal Olympus.

GARBO, GRETA (1905–90) (*See FEMMES FATALES*, HOLLYWOOD)
One of the most glamorous Hollywood stars of the 1920s and 1930s and later a famous recluse, when Stockholm-born Greta Lovisa Gustafsson met director Mauritz Stiller, he named her Greta Garbo, and in 1925 he got her a contract with MGM in Hollywood. She made twenty-four films before in 1941 withdrawing into New York seclusion. Her low voice, remote beauty, capacity to respond instinctively to the camera and total indifference to public opinion ensured her mythic status during her own lifetime. Garbo epitomised the mysterious rather than the overtly destructive aspect of the *femme fatale*: her allure lay in what is hidden, not in what is revealed.

GARM (*See* CERBERUS, DOG, FENRIR, NORSE MYTH)

GARUDA (*See* ANANTA, INDIAN MYTH, VISHNU)
The **Hindu** god **Vishnu** is usually portrayed as riding the **serpent Ananta** or the bird-man Garuda. With scarlet wings and eagle talons, the body of a golden man, and white-headed like a bald eagle or vulture, this demigod is also sometimes represented as a long-tailed peacock. Son of Kasyapa and Vinata, at birth he shone so brightly that folk thought him an incarnation of **Agni** the fire-god. In a seventh-century drama, the *Mirth of the Snakes*, each day he kills and devours a snake until a **Buddhist** prince, preaching abstinence, persuades him to restore to life the bones of the generations of serpents he has eaten. This may be a **Brahman** satire on Buddhism.

Garuda may once have been the lightning, as he is still called Taraswin – the 'swift one'. Once he stole **Indra**'s thunderbolt and the god had to fight him to get it back. In soaring up to the sky he symbolises the human spirit and intellect: in the *Garuda Purana* he expounds on the birth of the universe, the solar essence of Vishnu, the rites of his cult, the plot of the *Ramayana* and on the crafts of verse, grammar and medicine. Recently he has found modern employment as the symbol of Indonesian Airlines.

GAUTAMA (*See* BUDDHISM)

GAWAIN (*See* ARTHURIAN MYTH, GALAHAD, GAMES, GREEN KNIGHT, KNIGHT)
Eldest son of King Arthur's sister Morgause and Lot of Orkney (or Lothian), this early Arthurian knight was called Gwalchmai (Hawk of May) in **Welsh**

tales, and may derive from the Irish hero **Cuchulainn**, also nephew (sister's son) of a king: **Conchobar** of Ulster. Cuchulainn's father was the sun-god **Lug**: Lot may be a corruption of Lug. Gawain's solar connection is shown by the tale that his powers grew in the morning, peaked at noon and waned in the afternoon. Also, the '**beheading game**' Cuchulainn played with Uath is the source of Gawain's contest with the **Green Knight**.

It is said Morgause and Lot hid his bastard birth by abandoning him at sea in a barrel with a letter explaining his origin. A **fisherman** found him and took him to Rome, where the Pope brought him up until he was able to return home. In *Le Conte del Graal* (*c*.1180), Chrétien de Troyes tells how in a garden he espied the beautiful Orgueilleuse admiring herself in a mirror. Disdained by this *femme fatale*, he followed her to a Castle of Wonders, a woman's face in each of its five hundred windows – widows robbed of land, and **fatherless** girls. **Spell**-bound, they were guarded by five hundred magic bows. Though warned he would die, he entered, and sat on a bed which shrieked at him. Arrows sped at him; a **lion** attacked, but he beheaded it and cut off its paws, so breaking the spell, to learn that the queen of the castle was Ygraine, Arthur's mother, and that her daughter was his mother. They tried to keep him there, but he returned to the world of action to win Orgueilleuse. Here his nobility is unquestioned, but later he was depicted as a rapist and evil killer, perhaps as his role as leading Round Table knight was usurped by **Lancelot**, also because of the infamy of his mother Morgause and half-brother **Mordred**, and his connection with the harsh Viking north. Though he initiated the **Grail**-quest, on reaching Corbenic he was more interested in Elaine, the Grail-Bearer, than in the Grail, and was driven out in disgrace. Yet in the north he remained a noble figure, as in the medieval poem, *Sir Gawain and the Green Knight*.[1]

1. *King Arthur and the Grail*, Richard Cavendish, Paladin, London, 1980.

GEB (*See* **EGYPTIAN MYTH, NUIT**)

GEIS (*See* **BLODEUWEDD, CELTIC MYTH, CUCHULAINN, LLEW LLAW GYFFES, TABOO**)

Celtic kings and heroes were bound by magical prohibitions called *geis* or *geas* (singular), *geasa* (plural); from *guidh*, 'to entreat'. Such taboos were partly designed to rein in the mighty and stop them mistreating those they ruled, but, in addition, involved the king's individual destiny: break his word, or fail to conduct ceremonies on which the health of land and people depended, and he died. The **Arthurian wasteland** arises from the sin (broken oath; moral incompetence) of its king. The wasteland is symbolic of the barbarism bred by ignorance.

Many *geasa* are fantastic. The Welsh sun-god **Llew Llaw Gyffes** could be slain only by a spear a year in the making on Sundays, and only if he stood with one foot on the back of a **goat** and the other on the edge of a bath. Prompted to do so by his faithless wife **Blodeuwedd**, he died. Cormac, son of **Conchobar**, could not yoke his horses with **ash**-poles, or hunt a stag with golden horns, or listen to the harp-music of the **bard** Craptine. He died by neglecting his *geasa*. **Cuchulainn** could not give his name to any other warrior, or refuse combat (so he had to kill his son who challenged him without knowing who he was), or swerve from his path before joining in combat, or enter a meeting without permission, or refuse an invitation to a feast or eat **dog**-meat. He met three hags (the **badb**) by a ford, who invited him to feast on roasted dog, which he accepted. Such *geasa* reflected his

An Aboriginal rock painting. These figures at Nourlangie Rock are an example of the rich Aboriginal art heritage of the Alligator Rivers region of the Northern Territory. (Australian Overseas Information Service, London)

The painted wooden mask worn by Yoruba tribesmen to invoke ancestral spirits and convey messages to the living. (Michael Holford)

Alexander the Great, who
sought to emulate the mythic
heroes Achilles and Hercules.
(Michael Holford)

"Well, then," the Cat
went on, "you see a dog
growls when it's angry,
and wags its tail when it's
pleased. Now *I* growl when
I'm pleased, and wag my
tail when I'm angry. Therefore I'm mad."

"*I* call it purring, not
growling," said Alice.

"Call it what you like,"
said the Cat.

Alice and the Cheshire Cat,
from Lewis Carroll's *Alice's
Adventures in Wonderland.*
(e.t. archive)

In Greek myth, the Amazons were a race of female warriors, the name meaning 'woman without breast'. It is said that they cut off their right breast to enable them to draw their bowstrings. (C.M. Dixon)

Aladdin and the genie, characters from one of the most popular tales known collectively as the *Arabian Nights*. (Aldus Archive)

A detail from Sir Edward
Burne-Jones's painting
*The Last Sleep of Arthur
in Avalon*. (Bridgeman
Art Library)

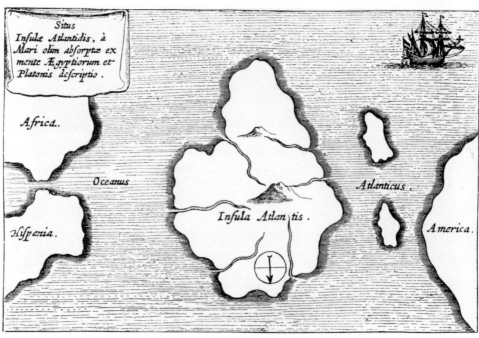

The mythical island of Atlantis is said to have been destroyed by an
earthquake some 10,000 years ago. (Mary Evans)

Christ on the cross – one of the most powerful symbols of the Christian faith. (Michael Holford)

Noah's Ark as depicted in the Nuremberg Bible (1483). (Bridgeman Art Library)

The temptation of Adam and
Eve in the Garden of Eden.
(Aldus Archive)

Buddha teaching his disciples. (Michael Holford)

Since its foundation in India 2,500 years ago, the Buddhist religion has spread throughout the Far East. This is one of the many temples found in Bangkok, Thailand. (Zefa)

Kuanyin, the Chinese Buddhist goddess of mercy. (Aldus Archive)

This emperor's embroidered robe shows the dragon – held as divine in Chinese mythology – and the hare of the moon pounding the elixir of life and immortality. (Michael Holford)

The portentous 1066 appearance of Halley's comet is reported to King Harold in the Bayeux Tapestry. (Michael Holford)

Christopher Lee as Count Dracula in the 1972 film recounting the popular vampire-myth. (Kobal)

The Sphinx and pyramid of Cheops at Giza in Egypt. (Bridgeman Art Library)

The Egyptian mother-goddess Isis with her brother and husband Osiris. (Aldus Archive)

A detail from the Egyptian *Book of the Dead*. This papyrus shows Hunefer adoring the phoenix. (Michael Holford)

This Eskimo mask, with the salmon as its central symbol, was worn by the shaman to impart magical powers to the hunters. (Michael Holford)

'Shui Rhys often met the fairies in the woods, and one day she never returned . . .' From *British Goblins*, Wirt Sikes (1880). (Fortean Picture Library)

Sigmund Freud, author of *The Interpretation of Dreams*. He elucidated the hidden psychology behind basic mythic themes. (Mary Evans)

A medieval Spanish altarpiece depicting St George slaying the dragon. (Michael Holford)

Left Zeus, chief of all Greek deities and ruler of Olympus, hurling a thunderbolt. Paramount among his many functions was that of procreation. He seduced goddesses and mortal women alike, often appearing in animal form. When he visited Leda it was in the guise of a swan (*below*). (Aldus Archive)

This fifth century BC vase depicts Herakles, the greatest of Greek mythic heroes, killing the Nemean lion with his bare hands. (Michael Holford)

The bronze head of Aphrodite, Greek goddess of love. (Michael Holford)

The head of the Gorgon
Medusa by Caravaggio.
(Aldus Archive)

The mythical griffon,
with the head and
wings of an eagle and
the body of a lion.
(Fortean Picture
Library)

Blake's Devil, from *Visions of the Daughters of Albion* (1793). (Michael Holford)

Rama and his wife Sita with the monkey-god Hanuman. (Bridgeman Art Library)

sun-god status (the sun cannot leave its course).

But also involved was a moral conception seemingly forgotten today: that those in power must serve not only those they rule but the laws of the gods. Thus heroism lay in the calm, willing acceptance of fate.

Likewise, conquering Roman generals granted a public triumph had at their shoulder a priest to whisper in their ear, 'You are only mortal.'

GENII (*See* DJINNS)

GENIUS (*See* ROMAN MYTH)

In Roman belief, the Genius was the creative force or tutelary spirit that watched over the growth, marriage, life and death of every man. It appeared in the hour of birth and formed his personality. As *genialis* it presided over the nuptial bed: thus its association with the English words 'genial' (genera-tive, thus enlivening, cheerful), and 'genital'. The female equivalent of the Genius was **Juno**, watching over every girl-child. Genius and Juno, aided by many spirit-helpers, fostered every aspect of human growth. The modern use of 'genius' to mean 'exalted creative power' is a corruption.

GENTRY (*See* FAIRIES)

When Irish folk spoke aloud of the fairies they would, just in case one of these sometimes malevolent and tricksy sprites was listening invisibly nearby, refer to them as the 'gentry'. Other such titles of deference or appeasement included 'good folk' or 'men of peace'.

GEOFFREY OF MONMOUTH (*c*.1100–54) (*See* ARTHURIAN MYTH, MERLIN)

The *Historia Regum Britanniae* (*History of the Kings of Britain*: *c*.1135) by this Welsh monk and chronicler was not only a great best-seller in its time (still in print) but created the impetus for the development of the Arthurian literary cycle. Chaplain till 1128 of William, Count of Normandy, and later Bishop of St Asaph (1151), Geoffrey begins his history *c*.1170 BC with the arrival in Britain of **Brutus**, great-grandson of **Aeneas**. Having conquered the **giants** led by Gogmagog, Brutus establishes a dynasty at New Troy, later Kaerlud (London). A millennium later, the Romans arrive, but the independent British kings shake off the oppressor's yoke. Next he tells of the Saxon conquests, Vortigern's treacheries, **Merlin**'s prophecies, and of the seduction of Ygraine by **Uther Pendragon** leading to the birth of King Arthur who, after a glorious reign, is slain by his treacherous nephew **Mordred** at the battle of Camblan in Cornwall in AD 542, then taken to Avalon.

Ending with the inheritance of the kingdom by Athelstane the Saxon, and offering what appeared at the time to be reliable history, his account took cultured Europe by storm. There had been nothing like it before. Within a dozen years of its appearance, children were being christened 'Arthur' and 'Merlin'. Out of the subsequent cult arose all later developments in the Arthurian mythos, culminating in **Malory**'s *Le Morte d'Arthur* (1470).

Geoffrey claimed that his history came from a book brought to him from Normandy by Walter Mapes, Archdeacon of Oxford. However, internal evidence shows the source to be the *Historia Brittonum*, apparently by a Welsh monk, Nennius (eighth–ninth century). By the twelfth century this text had been so often edited that the identity of the real author remains obscure. Even so, it contains the Arthurian source-material that Geoffrey so ably exploited.

Geoffrey enlarged on the legend of the wizard **Merlin** in two texts, the

Prophetia Anglicana Merlini (*Prophecies of Merlin*), and the *Vita Merlini* (*Life of Merlin*: *c*.1150). Both have received attention in recent years. The latter in particular is a beautifully told drama. Unlike the **bards** before him, Geoffrey mastered the art of converting oral tales into lucid written narrative. His success was no accident.[1]

1. *History of the Kings of Britain*, Geoffrey of Monmouth, various modern translations (Penguin Classics, London); *The Prophetic Vision of Merlin*, R.J. Stewart, Arkana, London, 1986; *The Quest for Merlin*, Nikolai Tolstoy, Sceptre, London, 1988 (1985).

SAINT GEORGE (d. AD 303) (*See* DRAGON)

This dragon-slaying patron saint not only of England but of Portugal and Aragon is said to have been a Cappadocian who, driven by the harsh anti-Christian policy of Diocletian to confess his faith before this Roman emperor, was tortured to death at Nicomedia in Asia Minor on 23 April 303, the day on which he is still honoured by the Roman Catholic Church. Other accounts say his martyrdom occurred at Lydda in Palestine, and that he was shod in red-hot shoes, broken on a spiked wheel, then buried in quicklime.

His festival in England took on national characteristics following the decree of the Council of Oxford (1222): the English King Richard I (the Lionheart: 1188–99) apparently had a vision of him during the Crusades and restored his tomb at Lydda. Recognised as patron saint of England in 1349 (during the Black Death), this status was confirmed when in 1415 the English army under Henry V won the Battle of Agincourt against the French.

The origin of the legend that by slaying a dragon he rescued a king's daughter and so converted her people to Christianity is obscure, but became central to his myth.

GERMANIC MYTH (*See* TEUTONIC MYTH)

GHEDE (*See* VOODOO)

GHOST DANCE (*See* CARGO CULT, FIJI, NATIVE AMERICAN MYTH)

In 1890, during the final military destruction of ancient Native American cultures by European immigrants, a Paiute **prophet** called Wovoka declared the religion of the Ghost Dance: the dance of all who had been slain. He said Christ had been mistreated by the white men, and had returned to heaven, but had come back to earth as an Indian. Soon the **buffalo** and wild **horses** would also return, along with green grass and sweet water, and new soil would bury all the white men, and those who danced the Ghost Dance would be raised in the air and safely held there while a cataclysm visited the earth below. Afterwards they would be set down on a new earth amid their **ancestors**, to live and hunt in peace again.

Many of the Plains people learned this dance. Amid its slow, circular course they would fall into trance and enter the spirit world. By mid-November the dance was so popular among the Sioux of South Dakota that all other activities ceased. 'Indians are dancing in the snow and are wild and crazy,' a frightened agent telegraphed Washington. 'We need protection and we need it now.' So the US army was sent in. On 28 December 1890, at Wounded Knee Creek in south Dakota, the army opened fire with machine-guns.

Over 300 women, children and old people were slain. The Ghost Dancers themselves became ghosts, haunting the American conscience still.[1]

1. *Bury My Heart at Wounded Knee*, Dee Brown, Bantam, New York, 1973.

GHOST WIFE (*See* NATIVE AMERICAN MYTH)

This legend of the Brule **Sioux** (North American Plains) tells of a hunter whose wife died giving birth to their third child. Later outside his tipi he met her ghost, like a white fog. She invited him and the children to join her in the Milky Way, but he said they were not yet ready to die, and that she should rejoin the living. Vanishing, she returned four days later and said this could be arranged if he made a curtain of **buffalo** hides for her to hide behind and did not look at or touch her for four days, or she would remain dead. So she came back to life. Years later he took a second wife who jealously told the first she was only a ghost. The first wife vanished, taking husband and children with her. The second wife regretted her harsh words, but her sorrow did not bring any of them back.

GHOSTS (*See* CONCORDANCE)

GHOUL (*See* AFRICAN MYTH, DJINNS)

In Eastern lore the ghoul (Arabic *ghūl*: an inferior type of djinn) haunts graveyards to eat newly buried corpses. In Africa it is said that ghouls (*ghuli* in Swahili) were **giants** who, cannibalising corpses, were condemned by God to be as ugly and black as the carrion they ate. Intelligent but evil, they are dark, hairy and sharp-tusked. Inhabiting the deep forests, their females may carry away lost human hunters to their caves to make love with them. Likewise their males abduct human females and seduce them with precious stones and ornaments. The Saharan ghoul is one-eyed like the **cyclopes**. It has the legs, body and stubby wings of an ostrich. The word 'ghoul' mispronounced as *ghrool* or *ghorool* led to the name 'gorilla'.

In Western lore a ghoul may be a vampiric **elemental** preying on human energies, or may haunt a site where tragedy occurred, imposing a suicidal depression on visitors, negative emotion remaining imprinted there.

GIANTS (*See* CONCORDANCE)

Giants personify **elemental** forces or ancestral races. In **Greek myth** the **Titans**, the first divine race and humanity's ancestors, warred against the new gods of **Olympus** so violently that the forests flamed and everything melted and boiled, until in time the Titans were defeated and chained under the earth. Later Olympus was attacked by a new race of giants, sprung from the blood of castrated **Ouranos**, causing fresh chaos. In **Vedic** myth the **Asuras**, once **Aryan** gods, also attacked heaven and also were cast down and buried, but will be loosed to fight in the final battle. **Norse** myth tells how the giant Ymir emerged from melting northern ice, the Frost Giants springing from his feet. His grandson Borr mated with his daughter Bestia, giving birth to the first three **Aesir** (gods), who slew him. His **blood** flooded the world, drowning every Frost Giant but Bergelmir, whose descendants will fight the Aesir at **Ragnorak** – the final battle. In Irish myth the awful Fomorians, beaten by the **Tuatha dé Danaan**, are hurled into the depths. In **Geoffrey**'s *History of the Kings of Britain*, **Brutus** invades Britain and defeats an army of giants, hurling its leader, Gogmagog, into the sea.

So too the **Bible** (Genesis vi:4) tells of 'giants in the earth in those days' – beings so evil that God sent the **Flood**. **Enoch** tells how they were born to mortal women as the 'impious offspring' of **angels** called Watchers who, overthrown, were chained deep underground. The fate of the giants was to become 'evil spirits . . . like clouds, which shall oppress, corrupt, fall, contend, and bruise upon earth . . . no food shall they eat: and they shall be thirsty; they shall be concealed.'[1]

The tale is everywhere the same: 'giants' epitomise forces of nature in chaotic conflict. Only later did the giant become the traditional cannibal ogre in an Otherworld castle, as in the tale of Jack climbing the beanstalk (**Tree of Life**) to face and defeat the ogre who, like the **dragon**, may also be Giant Hold-Fast – guarding **treasure** or the fair maiden for the sole sake of sterile possession. To win the daughter of Ysbaddaden Chief-Giant, **Culhwch** has to perform thirty-nine impossible tasks, before at length Ysbaddaden is beheaded (as **Ouranos** is castrated), and Olwen is his.

The giant is not always evil. He may lie asleep in the landscape like **Blake**'s **Albion**, or like the giant fertility-figures cut in south English chalk hills (Cerne Abbas Giant, Long Man of Wilmington, the Gogmagog giant at Wandlebury Camp). Or he may be Másaw in **Hopi** myth, arrogant caretaker of the Third World who, demoted when that world died to become Lord of the Dead, is made caretaker of the new, Fourth World.[2] Or he is **Finn McCool** with his seven-league boots, striding from Ireland to Scotland with one bound. It is said poets seeking inspiration by spending a night alone on the Giant's Seat high up Cader Idris in Wales infallibly go mad by dawn. This may only mean they find what they seek.

Giantism involves passage beyond local physical boundaries into what others call madness. Giantism also refers to amazing cultural achievement. **Stonehenge** was anciently known as 'the Giants' Dance. The assumption was not only that the **megaliths** themselves are frozen giants (in Gaelic, *fir chreig*, 'false men'), but that only giants could erect such huge structures. So too giant **ghouls** are said to have erected the dolmens of North Africa. Likewise the Baalbek platform in Syria, the cyclopean Peruvian city of Tiahuanaco and the Great Pyramid *must* have been built by giants. Who else could have cut, moved and placed such huge stones?

1. Enoch i: XV (Laurence translation).
2. *The Book of the Hopi*, Frank Waters, Penguin, London, 1977.

GILGAMESH (*See* BABYLONIAN MYTH, FLOOD MYTH, SUMERIAN MYTH)

Excavation of the library at Nineveh of **Assyrian** king Ashurbanipal (668–627 BC) led, in 1853, to the discovery of baked clay tablets recording the world's oldest known tale: *The Epic of Gilgamesh*. Comprising twelve cantos of about 300 verses each, a Babylonian fragment dates back to *c*.2000 BC, perhaps even older. It describes the Flood and a quest for **immortality** by Gilgamesh, the legendary Sumerian king of Uruk (Erech). It tells how he was so lusty that no woman of Uruk was safe so, to distract him, the goddess Aruru made from clay and spittle an hairy grass-eating wild man, Enkidu. Living in the desert, Enkidu protected the wild beasts from hunters and terrorised the region. Gilgamesh sent a woman to seduce him so that the wild beasts avoided him, meanwhile dreaming he fought a strong man he could not defeat. Enkidu came to Uruk, wrestled the king and was thrown. The two men became friends, but one night Enkidu dreamed of his own death. Afraid, Gilgamesh approached the sun-god **Shamash** who told him to fight the **giant** Khumbaba the Strong to affirm the immortality of his **name**. Gilgamesh and Enkidu slew Khumbaba and the goddess **Ishtar** offered herself to Gilgamesh. When he rejected her, she persuaded the sky-god **Anu** to send a celestial **bull** to cause havoc. Gilgamesh and Enkidu slew it, but Ishtar made Enkidu ill, so that after thirteen days he died.

Mad with grief, Gilgamesh left Uruk to learn the secret of immortality from his ancestor Utnapishtim, the sole survivor of the Flood. In a garden by the sea the goddess Siduri Sabitu told him to give up, mortality being the lot of man. Refusing her advice, he crossed the Waters of Death and so came to Utnapishtim, who challenged him to stay awake six days and seven nights, sleep being the image of death. As soon as Gilgamesh sat, he fell asleep, but Utnapishtim told him of a prickly plant on the sea-bed, called 'The Old Man Grows Young'. The hero dived deep and obtained the plant, but while returning to Uruk he drank from a spring of fresh water and slept. A **serpent** crept up and ate the plant, so gaining the power to slough its skin. Awakening, Gilgamesh now knew he must die like all men, but the god **Enlil** told him not to grieve, for he had done great deeds. So he died.[1]

1. *The Epic of Gilgamesh* (trans. N.K. Sandars), Penguin, London, 1972.

GINNUNGAGAP (*See* CREATION MYTH, NORSE MYTH, YMIR)

GIRDLE (*See* CORD)

GLAMOUR (*See* FAIRIES, HOLLYWOOD, MAGIC, SHAPE-SHIFTING, SPELLS)

Originally the power of fairies or **wizards** to hypnotise suggestible folk into perceiving illusion as reality. Thus in many a **fairy-tale** the hero, entering the **otherworld**, must rub a magic ointment on one eye so as not to see a pile of rags as gorgeous raiment; a crone as a lovely maiden; a hovel as a palace. Considered to be a power owned by gypsies, Scottish author Sir Walter Scott (1771–1832) said it was possessed by 'a particular sect of mathematicians, so called by Saxo Grammaticus', and that '**Merlin**, the son of Ambrose, was particularly skilled in this art', and that the jongleurs of medieval Europe 'were also great professors of this mystery, which has in some degree descended with their name, on the modern jugglers'. So too the famed Indian Rope Trick, in which the fakir sends a boy up an imaginary rope, seems to involve the same process – the fakir wills the victim to see what in fact does not exist. Nowadays the term is applied to the lurid life of movie stars or royalty whose every act or word is said to be glamorous; larger than life.

GLASTONBURY (*See* ARTHURIAN MYTH, CHRISTIANITY, JOSEPH OF ARIMATHEA)

'The holyest erthe in Englande' – Glastonbury, alias the Celtic Ynys Witrin ('Isle of Glass') or Ynys Avallon ('Isle of Apples'), is a sleepy town located in Somerset. The first pre-Roman village was built under Glastonbury Tor (hill) amid a marsh undrained until the Middle Ages. On top of the Tor **Gwynn ap Nudd**, the Welsh God of **Annwn** (**otherworld**) was said of old to maintain a palace. Here, in the seventh century, the Welsh hermit St Collen, refusing to be **englamoured** by the **fairy**-feast he was offered, sprinkled holy water so that the castle and its inhabitants vanished. In its place was built a chapel dedicated to **St Michael**. Some claim that the Tor is artificial, like Silbury Hill in Wiltshire, and that the earth-courses snaking up its sides once formed an initiatory maze. Others claim that a vast zodiac, thirty miles round, was anciently sculpted in the landscape round the Tor, its giant figures 'discovered' in 1929 by sculptress Katherine Maltwood.[1]

Yet chiefly Glastonbury is associated with Christianity's arrival in Britain. It is said **Joseph of Arimathea** brought the **Holy Grail** here and that here he planted his staff, which immediately flowered as a thorn tree. Its descendant, despite Cromwellian desecration *c.*1650, still flowers every January.

In 1191 Glastonbury monks claimed to have found the graves of Arthur and **Guinevere** in the Abbey grounds. Later myth states that the Holy Grail lies in the depths of the Chalice Well; and that invisible 'Watchers from the Other Side' (long-dead monks) led archaeologist Bligh Bond to uncover the Abbey's lost original foundations between 1907 and 1918.

1. *A Guide to Glastonbury's Temple of the Stars*, K.E. Maltwood, Clarke, UK, 1929.

GLOOSCAP (*See* NATIVE AMERICAN MYTH)
Algonquin tribes of the eastern USA tell how this first man, conquering a race of **giants**, a host of fiends and many **magicians** and **sorcerers**, boasted to his wife that there was nothing left to conquer. She pointed out that their infant son Wasis remained unconquered. Glooscap beckoned the child, who refused to come. Glooscap turned himself into a songbird, but Wasis ignored his song. In a rage Glooscap ordered Wasis to come at once, but Wasis just wailed. Finally he recited his most potent **spells** – but Wasis just looked bored. Himself conquered, Glooscap left the house in despair while the child cried 'Goo, goo!' The Algonquin say, when a baby makes this sound, it is remembering how it beat Glooscap.

GLUSCAP (*See* NATIVE AMERICAN MYTH)
This legendary hero of the Micmac people of Nova Scotia came to the shores of the earth in a stone canoe. It turned into an island still to be seen off the coast. From his stone bow he shot his arrows into the trees, and human beings evolved from the bark. His evil brother Malsum, friend of all the forces of darkness, came to the earth with him but constantly fought him, making the poisonous plants and giving the animals teeth and claws so that they could resist being killed for food. The Micmac say the battle between these two demonstrates the continual war between good and evil.

GNOMES (*See* BROWNIES, DWARVES, ELVES, FAIRIES)
Though the name 'gnome' is Greek (from *gnosis*, 'knowledge'), it was unknown to the ancients, being coined by the Swiss alchemist **Paracelsus** (1493–1541), apparently because gnomes were said to know the exact location of precious metals. An alternative derivation is *genomus*, Greek for 'earth-dweller'. Popularly envisaged as grotesque bearded **dwarves** wearing tight-fitting brown clothes with monastic hoods, like the **griffon** and **dragon** they were said to guard buried **treasure** and to live in deep caves. Paracelsus said they built houses of material like alabaster, marble and cement. In **Wagner**'s opera cycle, *The Ring of the Nibelungen*, Alberich forces them to give up their treasure. They are of various sizes, and perhaps have no physical essence at all, being **elementals** like **brownies**, **elves** and other members of the **fairy** realm. They are hard-working and many appear to be very old. In the woods, they may vanish from human sight by dissolving into the trunk of a tree. Their king is called Gob, so sometimes they are referred to as 'goblins', although goblins are often considered to be malevolent cousins of the essentially good-natured, industrious and reliable gnome. However, as elemental rulers of the cold North, some gnomes tend to be melancholy.

GNOSTIC MYTH (*See* CHRISTIANITY, DUALISM, NEOPLATONISM, SOPHIA)

The name 'Gnostic' (Greek *gnosis*, 'knowledge'), was applied to any early Christian insisting on the primacy of individual revelation, and rejecting the authority of the Church as sole intermediary between God and man.

It is said that **Simon Magus**, the magician of New Testament fame who supposedly died in magic battle with the Apostle **Peter**, founded Gnosticism. Though vilified by Christians, his philosophy survives in his statement of Gnostic principle, as preserved by Hippolytus:[1]

> Of the universal aeons there are two shoots, without beginning or end, springing from one Root, which is the power invisible, inapprehensible silence. Of these shoots one is manifested from above, which is the Great Power, the Universal Mind ordering all things, male, and the other from below, the Great Thought, female, producing all things. Hence pairing with each other, they unite and manifest the Middle Distance, incomprehensible Air, without beginning or end. In this is the Father who sustains all things, and nourishes those things which have a beginning and end.

Thus, in Gnostic belief, manifestation arises through the interaction of a positive and a negative principle, and occurs in the middle plane, the pleroma, from which emerges the Demiurge, the immortal mortal, the cause of our physical being. From this Eternal One emanate three pairs of opposites (Syzygies). These primal six are Mind (Nous) and Thought (Epinoia); Voice (Phone) and Name (Onoma); Reason (Logismos) and Reflection (Enthumesis). From these, united with the Eternal Flame, come forth the Aeons (Angels), who form the lower worlds as directed by the Demiurge.

The two major Gnostic schools were the Alexandrian and the Syrian; the former dualistic and Simonian, the latter pantheistic and inspired by an Egyptian Christian philosopher, Basilides, who taught *c.*AD 125–40. Seeking to incorporate **Egyptian, Pythagorean,** Chaldean and **pagan Mysteries** into Christianity, he formed a concept of deity known by the seven-lettered name Abraxas, the number of which, by gematria, is 365 (as with the name Mithras). Signifying the seven creative powers or planetary angels, this deity was portrayed with a **cockerel**-head, man's body and **serpent**-legs.

The German novelist Hermann Hesse 1,800 years later revived the concept of Abraxas in *Demian* (1919), even as the Swiss psychologist **C.G. Jung** also explored this image in his oddest book – *Septem Sermones ad Mortuous* (*Seven Sermons to the Dead*: 1917), a treatise he attributed to Basilides himself. 'The unlikely likely one, who is powerful in the realm of unreality', he called Abraxas, later concluding that the Gnostics had practised a form of depth psychology.[2]

Viewing **Christ** as the personification of Nous, the Divine Mind, which had entered a mortal body at the baptism and left it before the Crucifixion, Gnostics divided humanity into savages, who worshipped only visible nature, those who worshipped the Demiurge (**Yahweh**) and those like themselves who worshipped Nous (Christ), and the true spiritual light of the higher Aeons.

But Gnosticism embraced many beliefs. The Ophites worshipped Christ as a serpent. Others interpreted the Christian *agape* (love-feast) in terms of Dionysian orgy.[3] Increasingly the Demiurge, ruler of this world, was seen as a false creator, cause of all suffering. Such views led to mounting persecution, as did growing Gnostic **dualism** and heterodox interpretation of the Christian message. Gnostic texts buried during the persecutions and rediscovered at

Nag Hammadi in Egypt in 1945 show how varied and radical were such interpretations. They include gospels, poems, astrological treatises, mythical exegesis and instructions in magical practice. The Thomas Gospel (starting 'Whoever finds the interpretation of these sayings will not experience death'), and the oddly-named 'Thunder, Perfect Mind' reveal dogmas far from orthodox. Typically, Woman is exalted. 'I am the whore and the holy one,' cries Thunder, Perfect Mind. 'I am the wife and the virgin'. The *Pistis Sophia* claims that the disciple Jesus loved best was the Magdalene, and that Peter and the other Apostles hated her. So too the Gnostic image of Wisdom is female: **Sophia**.[4] This hearkening back to the Great Goddess (**Isis**) was another cause of persecution. Irenaeus, Tertullian and other early Churchmen decry Gnosticism for attracting 'many foolish women'.[5]

Yet, though bloodily suppressed by the third century, Gnosticism kept returning in the beliefs of **Manichaeans**, Bogomils and the Provençal **Cathars**. The extermination of the Cathars (thirteenth century) seemed to mark the end. Wholly dualistic, they said Christ never existed as a man: he was literally a **Holy Ghost**, a manifestation of Nous. They held that the Aeons, or spirits of light, had been lured into matter by Satan (**Yahweh**); falling through a hole in heaven down to the dark, fiery, time-trapped, flesh-bound earth. God noticed, and put his foot over the hole, but too late: many spirits were already corrupted in bodies, and forced to **reincarnate** over and over again, the worst as snakes or insects, the not-so-bad as **horses** and **pigs**, the better ones as people, the best of all as Cathars (pure ones) who would ascend to heaven. Only when everyone recalled the truth would the world end. The sky would fall, the **sun** and **moon** go out, fire and water consume each other, and Satan be left with nothing but a lake of sulphur and pitch to rule.

The Inquisition did its best to prove them right, burning thousands in mass bonfires, as at Montségur in the French Pyrenees (1244).

1. *Simon Magus: An Essay*, G.R.S. Mead, London, 1892.
2. *Demian*, Hermann Hesse, Granada, London, 1969 (1919); *The Gnostic Jung and the Seven Sermons to the Dead*, Stephen A. Hoeller, Quest Books, Wheaton, Illinois, 1982, pp.7ff.
3. *Creative Mythology*, Joseph Campbell, Penguin, London, 1976, pp.145–71.
4. *The Nag Hammadi Library* (ed. James M. Robinson), Harper & Row, New York, 1981.
5. *The Gnostic Gospels*, Elaine Pagels, Pelican, London, 1982, p.80.

GOAT (*See* **ANIMALS**)

Like **serpent**, **cat**, **hare** and many another beast, the goat has had a bad press in **Christian** myth. In the goat's case this is due to its supposed carnal lust. The horrific image of the bat-winged, shaggy-thighed, female-breasted, phallic Goat of Mendes as the very epitome of the **Devil** suggests that the goat has indeed become a scapegoat for our own moral shortcomings. In fact the original Goat of Mendes is a composite, **hermaphroditic** beast, perhaps identical with the Arabian Baphomet, formulated (like the **Gnostic** Abraxas) to symbolise specific transcendental doctrines. The denial of such doctrines by the medieval Church led to the demonisation of the goat and its association with **black magic**. Thus in France in 1307 arrested **Knights Templar** were accused by the Inquisition of worshipping Baphomet: i.e., they were accused of practising 'black magic', of worshipping the 'Devil'.

If one abandons Christian moral superimposition, the goat remains a symbol of phallic energy (as when we speak of being 'horny'), and is also an emblem of courage or aspiration because of its sure-footed ability to scale the highest peaks. Thus it symbolises masculine vitality, virility and creative energy. In **Greek myth** it is sacred to **Artemis** and also to **Zeus** as Dictynnos, suckled by the goat Amalthea, her horn the **cornucopia**, source of abundant gifts. Likewise the first sign of the zodiac, Aries, was once the ram whose **golden fleece** was sought by **Jason** and the Argonauts.

Aries is a **fire**-sign: the **Vedic** fire-god **Agni** rides a goat. The chariot of **Thor**, **Norse** god of thunder and fertility, is drawn by goats. To the alchemists, the goat's head symbolised sulphur.

GODODDIN (*See* WELSH MYTH)

Attributed to the poet Aneirin (*c.*AD 600), this heroic elegy is the oldest surviving piece of Welsh literature. Yet its action occurs not in modern Wales but between Scotland and Yorkshire. Gododdin was a kingdom comprising eastern Scotland south of the River Forth and part of northeast England. When the poem was written, the Irish Gaels had only just begun to settle Scotland; the Angles and Saxons had not yet conquered what is now called 'England'. Welsh was spoken in what is now Scotland. The poem describes an attack by the men of Gododdin, led by King Mynyddawg, on the enemy Angles of Catraeth (Catterick in Yorkshire). Though they slew many, none returned alive. The poem is an elegy for those who never went back to Dun Eidinn (Edinburgh).

GOGMAGOG (*See* BRUTUS, GEOFFREY OF MONMOUTH, GIANTS)

GOIBNIU (*See* IRISH MYTH, SMITH-GODS, TUATHA DÉ DANAAN)

The divine smith of the Irish **Tuatha dé Danaan**, Goibniu was assisted by Creidhne, god of metal-working, and Luchtaine, the divine wheelwright. So, as in much other Celtic lore, the god is defined as triple. It was the job of Goibniu and his associates to make weapons for **Lug** and the other Danaan heroes at the second Battle of Moytura (Magh Tuiredh), at which **Balor** was slain and the Fomorians defeated. Like other smith-gods associated with the **otherworld**, he hosted a feast at which his guests were made immortal by a magical intoxicating drink – a theme also found in **Greek** and **Indian** lore. In later Irish tradition Goibniu becomes a master mason, or great builder, like **Wayland Smith**, the Teutonic/Saxon smith-god. He was called Gowanan in Scotland, and Gofannon in Wales, where an old law declared that in the chief's court the smith should have the first drink of any feast.

GOLD (*See* MIDAS, JEWELS, SILVER)

This metallic element, found free and unalterable in rock formations or in alluvial deposits in many parts of the world, has always cast a spell over the human mind. As with certain precious stones, its value is symbolic, not practical. In colour representing the **sun**, as **silver** represents the **moon**, it implies self-illumination, superiority, nobility, wealth, while its incorruptibility leads to its association with purity of soul. In **Qabalistic** symbology, the inner nature of Man is potential gold (Aphar Min Haadamah): this gold is his deathless spiritual body; and gold is also the masculine symbol of the universe. Yet from King **Midas** to the Californian Gold Rush of 1849, gold has also represented material greed. The Golden Calf, made by the Israelites while **Moses** was on Mount **Sinai**, symbolises idolatry and spiritual blindness. The alchemical quest to transmute lead into gold was primarily a metaphor for the spiritual transformation of the alchemist himself, via the Great Work. 'The philosopher's gold resembles common gold neither in colour nor in substance' (*The Golden Tract*).

Yet tales of actual transformation persist. Helvetius, the seventeenth-century doctor to the Prince of Orange, tells (in *Of a Transmutation*) how a stranger showed him three sulphur-coloured lumps of stone: apparently the famed **Philosopher's Stone**. Stealing a piece, he heated it with six drams of old lead. A goldsmith declared the product pure gold. The philosopher Spinoza affirmed the reality of the transmutation. So too the seventeenth-century Scots alchemist Alexander Seton owned a lemon-yellow powder with which he produced gold before witnesses. Jailed and tortured by the Elector of Saxony, he refused to reveal the secret. A student, Sendigovius, helped him escape, and when Seton died soon after, was given the remaining powder – but not the secret. Lewis Spence claims (*Dictionary of Occultism*): 'it was impossible for him as an adept to reveal the terms of the awful mystery.'[1]

1. *The Occult*, Colin Wilson, Grafton Books, London, 1979, pp.317ff.

GOLDEN AGE (*See* BRAHMA, GOLD, OTHERWORLD)

Refers to a legendary era usually located at the dawn of the world, a time of titanic joy and natural innocence when the **lion** lay down with the **lamb** and there was no sin in the world – in short, the Garden of **Eden**: a realm as fabulous as the **otherworld**, the **Celtic** Isles of Paradise, the **utopian** realms located by modern **science-fiction** writers in the remote future, or on distant planets inhabited by god-like beings. The initial reference may be to nostalgia for the safety of the womb as much as to an ethical state of idealised beauty, harmony and proportion . . .

Hindu cosmology counts four world ages, each of 12,000 'divine years' (each 360 human years), totalling 4,320,000,000 years – a 'Day of Brahma': one cosmic cycle. These world ages are *Krita Yuga* (gold); *Treta Yuga* (silver); *Dvapara Yuga* (bronze) and *Kali Yuga* (**iron**). Stuck deep in *Kali Yuga*, we are now as far from the Golden Age as it is possible to get . . .

GOLDEN ASS (*See* APULEIUS)

GOLDEN BOUGH (*See* AENEAS, FRAZER, GREEK MYTH, MISTLETOE, SILVER BOUGH)

In *The Aeneid*, the Roman poet **Virgil** (70–19 BC) tells how **Aeneas** entered the land of shades armed with the Golden Bough, a passport to the **otherworld** that lit up the vast, gloomy wood he traversed. Virgil compares it to the **mistletoe**, the plant which, growing on the lightning-struck **oak**, was said to lose its healing virtue if ever it touched the ground.

The priest of **Diana**'s sacred grove had to kill his predecessor by breaking the Golden Bough and probably, as in the **Norse myth** of **Baldur**, throwing it at him as a dart. In *The Golden Bough* (1890), **Sir James Frazer** argues that the soul of the priest, or King of the Wood (personification of the oak) was thought to inhabit the mistletoe. Overcome or slain by arms, part of the ritual of his execution or cremation by **fire** thus involved his conqueror (successor) hurling the Golden Bough at his living or dead body.

Yet why was the mistletoe called the Golden Bough? Virgil says both the bough's stem and leaves were golden: mistletoe berries are whitish-yellow. Yet a mistletoe bough cut and kept over several months gains a rich golden colour. Frazer points out that a century ago Breton peasants would hang up bunches of mistletoe before their cottages, which by June glowed bright gold. Thus again (perhaps) the mythic association of fire, sun and gold.[1]

1. *The Golden Bough*, Sir James Frazer, Macmillan, London, 1963.

GOLDEN FLEECE (*See* GOAT, GREEK MYTH, JASON, RAM)

It was to obtain the legendary Golden Fleece from Colchis that the Greek hero **Jason** and his Argonauts underwent many adventures before succeeding, so that Jason could assume the kingship. The quest itself symbolises the search for spiritual illumination and the conquest of nature's dark side. The Golden Fleece is solar; so is the **ram**, on which **Zeus** flew to the sky. As for the tale itself: Phrixus and Helle, children of the Boeotian King Athamas, were hated by their stepmother Ino. Secretly she engineered a cataclysmic crop-failure. Athamas asked the **Delphic oracle** what caused it: Ino bribed the oracle's messenger to say that the famine would not end until Phrixus and Helle were sacrificed to Zeus. But the god **Hermes** sent a supernatural ram with a golden fleece. Able to talk, and to fly, it warned Phrixus and Helle of their danger, then carried them over the sea. During the journey Helle fell to her death: thus the Hellespont. Reaching Colchis on the Black Sea, Phrixus offered the ram to Zeus, and gave its fleece to Aeëtes the local king, who hung it from a **dragon**-guarded **tree**. Meanwhile Athamas, maddened, slew Ino's son Learchus. Ino threw herself and her other son, Melicertes, into the sea. Athamas was condemned to die for the land as a sin-offering, but fled into the wilderness, where even the beasts avoided him. His remaining family were condemned in his place: many fled, but some returned later, only to be seized and sacrificed. (For the rest, see **Jason**.)

GOLEM (*See* FABULOUS BEASTS, FRANKENSTEIN, ROBOTS)

It is said that in the city of Prague in the seventeenth century, a Jewish rabbi named Judah Loew ben Bezabel made an artificial man, the Golem, to ring the bells and perform the menial tasks of the synagogue. The creature was made by combining holy letters: the word 'golem' means a shapeless, lifeless clod of earth. As told in the dream novel *Der Golem* (1915) by the Austrian writer Gustav Meyrink, this sad creation had only a dim, half-conscious existence, controlled by the daily placement under its tongue of a magic tablet, and by writing on its forehead the Hebrew word *Ameth*, 'Truth' (almost the word *Meth*, 'Death'). Meyrink tells how, one night before evening prayer, Rabbi Loew forgot to remove the tablet from the Golem's mouth. The Golem ran amuck in the night, knocking down everyone it met, until the rabbi caught it and removed the tablet. The Golem fell lifeless, leaving behind it only the sad clay dwarf now in a Prague museum, *Meth* inscribed on its forehead so that it should not return to life. Later came the myth of **Frankenstein** and other tales of artificial men or **robots**, notably those by the American author Isaac Asimov (1920–92). The tomb of Rabbi Loew remains in Prague.

GOMMATESVARA (*See* INDIAN MYTH, JAINISM)

Son of Rishabha, first saviour of the Jain religion which became popular in India in the sixth century BC, he fought his brother Bharata for his father's empire and won, but, disillusioned, handed over the worldly kingdom to his brother, and retreated into the forest to do penance. For a year he stood in *samadhi*. To commemorate this feat, made in imitation of their father's renunciation, Bharata raised a statue five hundred bows'-lengths in height. Even Ravana, **demon**-king of Sri Lanka, made a pilgrimage to the site. In AD 983 at Sravana Belgola in South India a statue of Gommatesvara, 56 feet high, was erected. This colossal statue survives today.

GOOSE (*See* **BIRDS, SOLOMON**)
Like the **swan**, a solar bird, the Christmas goose represents the transition
between the death of the old year and the birth of the new. Yet, as Mother
Goose, the bird has a more elevated mythic ancestry. In **Egyptian myth** the
Nile Goose, 'the Great Chatterer', created the world and laid the cosmic **egg**
(**golden** egg) which hatched the sun-god, **Amun-Ra**. In medieval Provence,
when troubadour romance prevailed, the image of the 'Goose-Foot Queen',
La Reine Pédauque (a pun on *La Reine du Pays d'Oc*: 'Queen of the Land of
Oc') inspired poets. La Reine Pédauque was said to have built the viaduct
that brought Toulouse its water. Connected with a Black Virgin now in the
church of La Daurade, she was identified with the mother of **Charlemagne**,
Bertha of the Big Foot, and linked to the **Greek** goddess Pallas **Athene**, who
in turn was linked to the **Phoenician Astarte** (Anat), wife and sister of **Baal**.
As the Roman Venus Anate this goddess of fertilising waters is said to have
been turned into a duck. Virginal, whorish, destructive and maternal, she
seems to be the origin of the **fairy-tale** nanny, Mother Goose. Other web-foot
connections are with Queen Sibylla, mythical ancestress of magicians, the
African **Queen of Sheba** who entranced king **Solomon**, and the **Celtic**
bean-nighe (washerwoman), who crouched by fords from Brittany to Scotland
washing the bloody garments of those slain in battle.[1]
  In Greece the goose was revered as an attribute of **Hera**, Queen of Heaven,
and of the sun-god **Apollo**; in Rome as the symbol of the fertility of **Priapus**
and of **Juno**; in India as a vehicle of **Brahma**.

1. *The Cult of the Black Virgin*, Ean Begg, Arkana, London, 1985, pp.44–6.

GORGON (*See* **GREEK MYTH, MEDUSA, PERSEUS**)

GRACES (*See* **GREEK MYTH**)
Completing **Aphrodite**'s retinue, these smiling divinities ruled budding
plant-life and ripening fruit. Daughters of **Zeus** by the Oceanid Eurynome,
their number and names varied. In time it was agreed that there were three:
Aglaia, Euphrosyne and Thalia. Bringers of joy to every heart, in spring they
danced with the nymphs. In **Roman** lore, they were depicted naked, as 'they
must be free of deceit' (Servius), or barely-clad, as 'benefits want to be seen'
(Seneca). To **Neoplatonists** symbolising the threefold aspect of love, in
medieval times they epitomised Beauty, Charity and Love.

GRAIL (*See* **CAULDRON, HOLY GRAIL**)

GRAVES, ROBERT (1895–1985) (*See* **MOTHER-GODDESS, TREE
ALPHABET**)
Poet, novelist and authoritative student of myth, Graves was born of Irish–
German parentage and served in World War I with the Royal Welsh
Fusiliers, when he was badly wounded. The publication in 1929 of *Goodbye
to All That*, his autobiographical account of the war, established his name.
His historical novels, *I, Claudius* and *Claudius the God* (both 1934), *Count
Belisarius* (1938) and *The Golden Fleece* (1944) deepened his interest in
mythology as a repository of (coded) factual revelation about the structures of
pagan religion. In what he considered his most important prose work, *The
White Goddess* (1946: subtitled 'A Historical Grammar of Poetic Myth') he
argued for the existence of an ancient global religion rooted in the worship of
a goddess of many names and triple aspect.
  The circumstances of its publication are as odd as the book itself. In 1944

his work on *The Golden Fleece* was interrupted by a sudden desire to write about a mysterious 'Battle of the Trees', fought in ancient Britain. In three weeks he completed 'The Roebuck in the Thicket' – the first draft of *The White Goddess*. What had prompted this obsession? He owned a brass box with an intricate lid, on which he kept the brass figure of a hump-backed man playing a flute. Later he learned that the lid-design represented Ngame, an African moon-goddess, and that the hump-backed flute-player was the herald of an African queen-mother who claimed descent from Ngame. Other items connected with the goddess kept turning up, and he felt driven to complete the book. The first publisher to reject it died of heart failure. The next, rejecting it rudely, hanged himself in female underwear. The third (the poet T.S. Eliot) accepted it, and was awarded the Order of Merit that same year. Graves implies that all these events were meaningful.[1]

Though dauntingly complex in its scholarship, *The White Goddess* remains essential reading to all wishing to penetrate the deeper levels of myth.

In 1955 he published *The Greek Myths*, a complete retelling of the Greek tales of gods and heroes.[2] Professor of Poetry at Oxford University in 1961–6, he openly despised all aspiring to the profession of poet who failed to address the goddess as **muse**: 'how you come to terms with the Goddess is no concern of mine,' he concludes his foreword to *The White Goddess*. 'I do not even know that you are serious in your poetic profession.'

1. *The White Goddess*, Robert Graves, Faber & Faber, London, 1961 (1946).
2. *The Greek Myths*, Robert Graves, Penguin, London, 1960.

GREAT GODDESS (*See* CONCORDANCE)

GREEK MYTH (1): FROM MYTH TO DRAMA (*See* CONCORDANCE, HOMER)

Greek philosophy and myth have influenced Western culture for the last two millennia. This first of two essays outlines an evolution from vague myth to tragedy and satire: the second describes how out of **Mystery** teachings grew philosophical and scientific thinking.

Greek history begins *c*.7000 BC after the last Ice Age, when a farming culture settled the region. By 3000 BC, ox-drawn ploughs and bronze and copper alloys were in use and soil erosion and deforestation were advanced. About 2000 BC Minoan Crete was the dominant regional power, with Troy on the east side of the Aegean also prosperous. Mainland Greece remained 'barbaric'. Trade records were made in the (still undeciphered) script called Linear A.

The eruption of Thera (*c*.1500 BC) disturbed Crete, but only *c*.1400 BC did mainland Achaeans gain control of Knossos (as in the myth of **Theseus**). The chief Cretan deity was the Great Goddess. Portrayed as bare-breasted and clutching **serpents, Hesiod** (*c*.800 BC) names her as Rhea, the mother of the Greek sky-god **Zeus**. Originally she had no husband. Hesiod later describes her as married to her brother, **Cronus**. The myth of how Cronus swallows all his children before being overthrown by his son Zeus implies an anarchic era in which the Achaeans, **horse**-riding Indo-Europeans from the steppes north of the Black Sea, invaded Greece, each group with its own quarrelsome **totemic** deities. These in time became the quarrelsome **gods** of **Olympus**. Supreme among them was the sky-god Zeus, equivalent of the **Vedic Dyaus**.

The Achaeans arrived with horse-drawn chariots, pottery, metal-working skills and a willingness to adopt new ways, including sea travel. Thus

Poseidon, originally a horse-god, became the Olympian god of the sea.

These energetic invaders seized the region, founding cities at Tiryns, Athens and particularly Mycenae. Dominant from *c.*1550–1150 BC, the Mycenaeans forced the Minoan goddess (now **Hera**, the 'Lady') to 'marry' Zeus. Cretan resistance is suggested by tales of Hera's angry nature, of how Zeus was born in Crete, and how **Apollo** sent Cretan priests to guard **Delphi**.

The new deities took on so many forms that it remains hard to know what history their changes describe. At first arrogantly viewing humanity from Olympus, later they became but personifications of human nature. 'Of one race,' writes Pindar (fifth century BC), 'are men and gods. Born of one mother we draw our breath, though in strength are gods and men far divided.'

But in the thirteenth century BC, after the Trojan War, natural cataclysm and self-inflicted ecological problems (deforestation leading to flash floods) devastated Achaean society. Nearly a millennium later, **Plato** describes how soil erosion causes political disaster followed by social collapse.[1]

A dark age followed. By the time of **Homer** (*c.*850 BC), Mycenaean history and the tale of the war with Troy had assumed mythic lustre. Oral tradition alone survived. Yet Homer distinguishes between two historical epochs: (1) the *Iliad*, and (2) the *Odyssey*.[2] The first was the war between ancient god-like heroes; the second was a man's fight to survive a world turned upside down, in which aristocracy is lost and swineherds prevail over kings. Yet the hiatus was brief. By *c.*1000 BC new city-states had developed. The Olympic **Games** had begun; the **Mysteries** of **Demeter, Dionysus, Orpheus** and **Eleusis** attracted thinkers. The *rhapsodes* (**bards**) were at work. The 'blind' poet Homer tied lost history into an enduring myth, and Hesiod related and named the gods and their doings, in the process creating vast new mythic genealogies.[3]

Then the first democrats of Athens overthrew not only the gods, but the human tyrants ruling them. The expulsion of the last tyrant (510 BC) and his defeat (and that of the Persians) by the free men of Athens at the Battle of Marathon (490 BC) led, among other things, to the birth of modern drama. The new intellectual freedom was so potent that within a generation old mythic forms were transformed into the new art of theatre (*theos*; 'god').

The rhapsodes had recited the myths at feasts or religious festivals. Now, for the first time, storytelling and religious festival were combined to fix specific themes in written texts ('plays') that survive. The purpose of these plays was catharsis: to purify those involved via experience of pity, terror or laughter. Actors representing the gods wore masks (*persona*) to protect spectators from the naked god-power flooding through the actor. Dramatic contests came to be valued as much as contests of athletic prowess. Four great playwrights soon emerged: the tragedians Aeschylus, Euripedes and Sophocles; and Aristophanes, the comedic writer.

Aeschylus (525–456 BC) was born at Eleusis, fought at Marathon and died in Sicily. This first great tragedian developed Attic drama (then monologues divided by the chorus) by introducing the second actor, scenery and stage appliances. His seven surviving plays (out of seventy) include the *Oresteian Trilogy*. Unsurpassed for tragic force, these endorse traditional reliance on the **Fates** and **Furies** as arbiters of human destiny. The first deals with the murder of Agamemnon by his wife, Clytemnestra, sister of **Helen of Troy**. The sequels deal with her murder by Agamemnon's son, **Orestes**, who, chased by the Furies, is later acquitted by **Athene**. A conservative, he broke down traditional doors, was exhausted in so doing and was later denounced by lesser spirits for lacking the radicalism he stimulated.[4]

First appearing in the tragic contests in 468 BC, Sophocles (497–406 BC) invented the third actor, scene-painting and brought tragedy down to the human level. His characters suffer due to their own errors; thus he abandons the gods. A master dramatist (as in *Antigone, Ajax, Oedipus Tyrannus* and *Electra*), he was thought greater than both Aeschylus and Euripedes.[5]

Euripedes (*c.*485–406 BC) was a sceptic whose use of current slang made him unpopular: he won first prize in the tragic contests just four times. His noblest characters are women (Medea, Iphigenia): other plays include *Hippolytus, Alcestis* and the *Bacchae*. He died pathetically at the court of Archelaus, king of Macedonia: dogs were set on him in his old age.[6]

Aristophanes (*c.*444–380 BC) mocked everyone. Of his plays, *The Birds* (origin of 'Cloud-cuckoo-land': a satire on Athenian ambitions) is thought the best. *Women in Parliament* mocks Plato's argument that the sexes are equal; *The Wasps* mocks Athenian litigiousness. His originality, wit and lyrical power mark him as a comic genius. Writing barely a generation after Aeschylus, in his work the ancient identification with the gods as powers working on levels beyond human comprehension has all but vanished. His concerns are political, satirical and individualistic, i.e., modern.[7]

1. *The Flood from Heaven*, Eberhard Zangger, Sidgwick & Jackson, London, 1992.
2. *Iliad*, Homer, trans. Robert Fitzgerald, OUP; *Odyssey*, trans. Walter Shewring, OUP, 1980.
3. *Theogony*, Hesiod, ed. F. Solansen, OUP, 1990.
4. *Oresteian Trilogy*, Aeschylus, trans. P. Vellacott, Penguin, London, 1956.
5. *Electra and Other Plays*, Sophocles, trans. E.F. Watling, Penguin, London, 1969.
6. *Works*, Euripedes, OUP, 1984.
7. *The Wasps and Other Plays*, Aristophanes, Penguin, London, 1970.

GREEK MYTH (2): THE SOUL (*See* CONCORDANCE, DIONYSUS, GNOSTIC MYTH, NEOPLATONISM, PLATO, SOUL)

Greek ideas about the soul (**psyche**) went through many stages. Centuries before Plato, **Homer** saw man as embodying three distinct entities: body (*soma*); *psyche* and *thumos* – the latter being the diaphragm or midriff, seen as the seat of will and feeling. A fourth part, the *eidolon* (image), appeared in dreams and was thought to survive death. But the early Greeks did not venerate their dead. **Tartarus**, as punishment for earthly sin (as in the torments of **Tantalus** and **Sisyphus**), was a land of shades condemned to a 'restless purposeless fluttering to and fro.'[1]

The Corn-**Mysteries** of **Demeter** and **Persephone** (perhaps pre-1500 BC) encouraged the idea that what dies underground must sprout again into new life every year. The Mysteries of **Dionysus** (*c.*1300 BC) offered new life via wine. His drunken acolytes, enjoying *enthousiasmos* (inside the god) and *ekstasis* (outside the body), thought they knew immortal bliss. The soul seemed free of the body. But hangover and memory of bloody acts committed while drunk led these cultists to demand soul-purification by denying bodily impulses, leading to the elevation of Dionysus as god of the **Orphic** Mysteries.

The Orphics abstained from meat, beans and eggs, and practised rites to gain deliverance from rebirth. Their beliefs parallel those in the Indian *Upanishads*. Orphic ideas of sin, salvation by asceticism, and initiation by sacrament influenced **Christianity. Pythagoras** (sixth century BC) holds that the divine human soul is embodied as punishment for sin and condemned to many incarnations, animal or human. Abstinence from meat and beans (in which human souls may live) aids deliverance from the circle of necessity.

The soul is 'a harmony of contrary elements united together in the body.'

Empedocles (*c*.490–430 BC) described himself as a god condemned by sin 'to wander thrice ten thousand seasons [far] from the abodes of the blessed.' He told his followers, 'wretches, utter wretches, keep your hands from beans.' The tall tale of his low fate is told elsewhere.

For Plato, the soul ('psyche') is 'one of the first creations, born long before all physical things, and is the chief cause of all their alterations and transformations.'² In the *Timaeus* he describes its three parts as reason, emotions and appetite. Plants have appetite and animals have appetite and emotions, but only man has a rational soul – located in the head, immortal and divine. Yet reason finds it hard to control emotion and appetite. In the *Phaedrus* he compares the rational soul to a charioteer of two horses (as in the **Tarot** trump, the Chariot). He described how at death, 'Our real self – our immortal soul as it is called – departs . . . to the gods below to give an account of itself. To the wicked, this is a terrifying doctrine, but a good man will welcome it.'²

Later, the material atomists endlessly disputed the nature of the world's basic substance. Thales (sixth century BC) thought it was water while Anaximenes (*c*.500 BC) thought it was air. Heraclitus said it was fire, and that the world endures continual transformation from which the soul, being a mixture of the four elements, is not exempt. Only the pure soul, resisting transformation into water, could hope to join the cosmic fire. Parmenides said there is but one Being – eternal, indivisible and homogeneous – and that Heraclitus' doctrine of flux arises from sensory deception; the mind being similar in nature to the body. Empedocles likewise taught that the basic constant is matter, not the migrating soul. Anaxagoras (*c*.500–432 BC) said that all living things contain mind (*nous*), a self-contained unity present in varying degrees in all life's manifestations, and that in death the soul is extinguished for how can there be independent survival of souls if all animated being derives from the single mind? Democritus (born *c*.460 BC) said that soul and mind are of the same atomic substance. Aristotle (384–322 BC) defines the soul as the 'form' of the body, inseparable from it and perishing with it, while Epicurus (342–270 BC) considered body and soul to be interdependent – 'Neither can be itself without the other.'³

1. *Survival?*, David Lorimer, Routledge & Kegan Paul, London, 1984, pp.39–59.
2. *Laws*, Plato, Penguin, London, 1982, No. 959 (pp.512–13).
3. *Op.cit.* Lorimer, p.57.

GREEN KNIGHT (*See* ARTHURIAN MYTH, GAWAIN, GREEN MAN)

Composed *c*.1400 AD by an unknown author, the Middle English poem *Sir Gawain and the Green Knight* takes the theme of the **beheading game** from the Irish tale of Bricriu's Feast. Into **Arthur's** Camelot one New Year's Day strode a green-clad, green-skinned **giant**, in one hand holding a **holly** branch, in the other a razor-sharp battle-axe. He offered his head to any knight who would accept a return blow a year hence. Only Gawain agreed, beheading the giant with one blow. Picking up his head, the giant turned it to Gawain. Its mouth told him to be at the Green Chapel a year hence. Then the giant left.

A year later Gawain rode north through a wintry land on his **otherworld** warhorse, Gringolet. On Christmas Eve he came to a castle in a wild wood. The lord, Sir Bercilak, told him the Green Chapel was near and invited him to stay until New Year's Day. Also here lived Bercilak's lovely wife and an old hag, her companion. Bercilak went hunting each day while Gawain stayed indoors: Bercilak agreed to give Gawain whatever he caught in the hunt, and Gawain agreed to give Bercilak whatever he received in the castle.

Each day Bercilak's wife tried to seduce Gawain, kissing him fervently: each evening when Bercilak returned, Gawain kissed him. But the lady had also given Gawain a magical green **girdle**, saying it would protect him at the Green Chapel. This, fearing for his life, he kept secret.

On New Year's Day he rode to the Green Chapel – a hollow mound in a valley by a waterfall. The Green Knight appeared: Gawain bowed his head, but flinched. Rebuked, the second time he kept still. Down came the axe – just nicking his neck. Then the giant revealed himself as Bercilak, saying he was spellbound by the old hag, in fact the enchantress **Morgan Le Fay**, who had devised the entire test to discredit the **Round Table**. Gawain was spared for honourably denying Lady Bercilak's advances, but his neck had been nicked for concealing the girdle. Though free to leave, Gawain felt disgraced. He returned to Camelot wearing the girdle tied round his arm as a badge of shame. But then every knight also agreed to wear a green baldric in his honour, for he had brought renown to the Round Table.[1]

1. *Sir Gawain and the Green Knight* (ed. J.A. Burrow), Penguin, London, 1972.

GREEN MAN (*See* CERNUNNOS, CORN-GODS, GREEN KNIGHT, HEAD, ROBIN HOOD)

As grotesque as the **sheela-na-gig** (images of a pagan fertility-goddess), bizarre images of an ancient vegetation-god today called the 'Green Man' (a name coined in 1939 by Lady Raglan) may be found carved in many churches. Typically a leering face with bulging eyes, bulbous nose and fanged mouth from which foliage sprouts, or peering sadly through a tracery of leaves, the severed head of the Green Man may have originated as an architectural motif in Rome in the first century AD.[1] Though ugly, tricksy, mysterious and perhaps malignant, his popularity spread widely. In the sixth century, when the cathedral at Trier in Germany was being built, a mason found an effigy of the Green Man in a ruined Roman temple, and incorporated it into the cathedral. The image endured in Christian iconography during medieval times, returning in seventeenth-century Scotland. Carved on tombstones, it was often associated with an epitaph from Job xix:26: 'Though after my skin worms destroy this body, yet in my flesh shall I see God.'

The persistence of the severed **head** theme, as in the early Irish tale Bricriu's Feast, or the Welsh myth of **Bran**'s head, or the medieval English *Sir Gawain and the Green Knight*, reflects the enduring power of the Green Man as a modern version of ancient died-and-reborn **corn-gods** or of forest gods like **Cernunnos**. The legend of **Robin Hood** ('Robin Goodfellow'), in his 'Lincoln Green' deep in Sherwood Forest, epitomises old fertility rites ruled by the Green Man and celebrated on May Day with orgy and laughter.

When in 1307 the **Knights Templar** were accused of worshipping a 'head', Baphomet, they were charged with claiming that the head 'made the trees flower', and that it made 'the land germinate'.[2] So yet again we encounter the **Arthurian** mystery of the **wasteland**, the wounded **Fisher King**, and the quest for the **Holy Grail**, the vessel of sustenance and fertility.

Recently the Green Man has again returned as a personification of the annual natural cycle, and as an emblem (to some) of the Green movement.

1. *The Green Man*, Kathleen Basford, Ipswich, 1978.

2. *The Temple and the Lodge*, Michael Baigent and Richard Leigh, Corgi, London, 1990, p.119.

GRENDEL (*See* BEOWULF, DRAGON)

GRIFFON (GRYPHON) (*See* FABULOUS BEASTS)

With an **eagle's head** and **lion's** body, griffons are said by Herodotus (fifth century BC) to be winged monsters always fighting the one-eyed Arimaspians. Pliny (AD 23–79), calling them 'mere fables', mentions their long ears and hooked bills. The medieval English fabulist **Sir John Mandeville** says in his *Travels* that they inhabit Bactria, and that:

the Griffen hath a body greater than viii Lyons and stall worthier than a hundred eagles. For certainly he wyl beare to his nest flying, a horse and a man upon his back, or two Oxen yoked togither as they go at plowgh, for he hath large nayles on hys fete, as great as it were hornes of Oxen, and of those they make cups there to drynke of, and of his rybes they make bows to shoote with.'[1]

This interesting beast is said by Marco Polo to live in Madagascar; by **Dante** is seen to draw a triumphal chariot (the Church); while in *Alice in Wonderland* **Lewis Carroll** tells how with the Mock Turtle it demonstrates the Lobster Quadrille to a bemused Alice.

1. *The Book of Imaginary Beings*, Jorge Luis Borges, Penguin, London, 1974.

BROTHERS GRIMM (*See* FAIRY-TALES)

German brothers Jacob (1785–1863) and Wilhelm (1786–1859), Grimm remain famous for a collection of folk-tales, *Kinder und Hausmärchen*, better known as *Grimm's Fairy Tales* (1812–22). The original title means the tales are for children and adults alike. Born at Hanau, both led careers studying linguistics and literature, and laid the foundations of folklore as science. After serving as Hessian ambassador in Paris (1814–15), Jacob joined Wilhelm in work at the Elector's library in Kassel. There they researched the past, finding in antiquity all the modern social institutions. Holding folk poetry to be the true poetry, they published the 200 tales forming their famed collection. Drawing primarily on oral sources, they aimed to convey not only the original teller's beliefs and speech, but popular imagination and beliefs throughout the ages; Wilhelm being able to make such tales readable without changing their basic nature. Following the success of *Kinder und Hausmärchen*, they published many other collections of legends and ancient texts from German, **Norse**, **Irish** and other sources. In later years, despite political trials that took them from Kassel to Göttingen (1829), and then to Berlin (1840), they published philological works, dictionaries and grammars, all influential and ground-breaking in scientific approach.

Yet it is for their early collection of fairy-tales that they remain popularly remembered. *Hansel and Gretel, The Frog-Prince, Rumpelstiltskin, The Golden Goose* and others remain a delight to children of all ages whose tastes are not so sophisticated that their imagination has withered.

GUEST, LADY CHARLOTTE (*See MABINOGION*)

GUINEVERE (*See* ARTHURIAN MYTH, LANCELOT, OWL)

Unlucky Queen of King Arthur who fell in adulterous love with Lancelot, 'the best knight in the world'. In **Welsh** origin Gwenhwyfar, the 'White One', is associated with the owl and with the **Triple Goddess** as manifested in the Irish **Morrigan**. Thus she was long the image of British sovereignty (later epitomised as Britannia) before being reduced to Arthur's wife.

As such she is not (by medieval writers) seen as noble. Every effort is made to display her as a weak, silly woman whose unbridled desire causes the ruin of the land and her king. Notably, her marriage to Arthur (the **Bear**) is fruitless, while her love for Lancelot causes the destruction of the **Round Table**. Men blame her (like **Eve**) for their failure to control their own passions. **Malory** tells how **Mordred**, born of Arthur's ignorantly **incestuous** union with **Morgause**, revealed Guinevere's adulterous love, so setting in motion a law that she should die at the stake. (An older myth tells how Mordred abducts and marries her so he may seize the kingship of Britain.) Condemned by Arthur to be burned, 'because a queen who was guilty of treachery could die in no other way, given that she was sacred' (so admitting her older, goddess-status), she was rescued by Lancelot (in May, the chaste month) who carried her to his French seat, Joyous Garde, which Arthur then besieged. Lancelot declared that he loved her but his loyalty to Arthur mattered more. So he gave her up, the political solution being that she should abandon all her pretensions to queenhood (or divinity) by becoming a good **Christian** nun at Amesbury. Lancelot, banished from Britain, attended her deathbed after the death of Arthur.

As with the reduction of **Isis** into the humble **Virgin Mary**, the myth of the fall of Guinevere describes the long process whereby goddess-worship was first demonised then overwhelmed by newer male gods and their power.

GWION BACH (*See* CERRIDWEN, TALIESIN, WELSH MYTH)

GWYDION (*See MABINOGION*, MATH, PRYDERI, WELSH MYTH)

In *Math Son of Mathonwy* (Fourth Branch of the Mabinogi), it is told how Gwydion, son of the wizard Don and steward to his uncle Math (king of Gwynedd in north Wales) caused a war with neighbouring Dyfed. This happened when, in support of his brother Gilfaethwy's lust for the maiden Goewin (Math's footholder), he went to the court of Pryderi, king of Dyfed, and exchanged Pryderi's domesticated **pigs** (gifted by **Arawn**, king of the underworld) for magical **horses** and greyhounds which, made of (hallucinogenic?) mushrooms, reverted next day to their original, worthless form. Pryderi and his men chased the **trickster**; but Gwydion killed Pryderi and his brother raped Goewin. Math rejected them both. When at last Gwydion gave himself up, Math turned him successively into a **stag**, a sow and a **wolf**. Forgiven after three years and back in human form, Gwydion suggested his sister **Arianrhod** become Math's new footholder. Asked to prove her virginity by stepping without mishap over Math's **wand**, Arianrhod immediately delivered two children, **Dylan** and **Llew**. The latter Gwydion raised himself, creating Llew's wife **Blodeuwedd** out of flowers to evade the *geis* that the boy never marry a (mortal) wife. When she betrayed and killed Llew, he cursed her and changed her into the shape of an **owl** forever. Yet, as with the other owl-goddess, **Guinevere**, her tale may contain other elements forgotten, rejected or buried.

GWYNN AP NUDD (*See* NUADU, WILD HUNT)

H

HADES (*See* **GREEK MYTH, PERSEPHONE, UNDERWORLD**)
Son of Rhea and **Cronus**, eaten by his father like his brothers and sisters, when saved by brother **Zeus** this Greek god became lord of the underworld, **Poseidon** taking the sea, and Zeus the sky. Ruling this realm as its dread overlord, he was seen to leave it only twice; once to abduct **Persephone**, later to seek cure for a wound inflicted by **Hercules**. Yet nobody knew how often he entered the upper world: his helmet made him invisible. Among his names was Polydegmon, 'receiver of many guests' (no visitor was ever turned away), and **Pluto**, 'giver of wealth'. As Pluto he received buried treasure; from Pluto's subterranean realm emerged the blessings of the earth: crops, minerals, sweet water. All fearing to speak the dread name of Hades called him Pluto. To pray to him, one struck the ground with rods or bare hands. Appropriate offerings were black rams or black ewes; plants sacred to him were cypress, narcissus and mint – the latter due to his affair with the nymph Minthe. When his wife Persephone trod her underfoot, Hades turned her into mint. His one other affair was with Leuce, a daughter of **Oceanus**, who on dying became a white poplar, the tree of the **Elysian** Fields.

HAGGARD, SIR HENRY RIDER (1856–1925) (*See* **AFRICAN MYTH, LOST WORLDS**)
Civil servant, lawyer and novelist, Haggard spent six years in the British colonial service in South Africa. Called to the bar in 1884, in 1885 he enjoyed the huge success of his first African romance, *King Solomon's Mines*. This was followed in 1887 by *She*, *Jess* and *Allan Quatermain*, and thereafter by many other tales typified by storytelling power aided by supernatural imagining.

Mostly set in the mythic past or **lost worlds**, Haggard's tales combine his interest in **immortality, reincarnation**, spiritualism and primitive customs with realistic detail, especially in the African novels. In *Nada the Lily* (1892), he recounted the early life of his **Zulu** hero Umslopogaas, who had appeared in *Allan Quatermain*, the first of many linked tales about this white hunter, Haggard's main hero. In *Allan and the Ice Gods* (1927), a drug throws Allan back in time into the body of a paleolithic man. *She and Allan* (1921) linked the Quatermain series with perhaps his most remarkable character.

She (1887), immortal queen of a lost African kingdom, tries to persuade an English explorer that he is a reincarnation of her ancient lover, Kallikrates. She bathes once more in the flame of life but crumbles to dust, only to be reborn in Tibet in a later novel, *Ayesha* (1905).

Other tales explored different cultures. *The World's Desire* (with **Andrew Lang**, 1890) is a fantastic sequel to *The Odyssey*. *Eric Brighteyes* (1891) enters the world of **Norse** saga, while *When the World Shook* (1919, written in collaboration with **Rudyard Kipling**) is a tale of **Atlantis**.

HAIR (*See* **HEAD, SAMSON**)
Hair is the life-force, energy, the virility of the head. Flowing loose it is freedom, convention rejected; cut short it is marriage or enslavement; shorn

or tonsured it is worldly renunciation, the ascetic life; dishevelled or torn it signifies grief or (among **Hindus**) the ascetic. The **Buddha**'s coiled hair is peace of mind; long loose hair in **Christians** is penitence; hair standing on end is terror, or divine possession. **Serpent** locks, as with the **Medusa**, are the dark or deadly side of the feminine power.

In many societies to cut the hair was thought perilous – one could anger the spirit of the **head** – and led to the problem of disposing of the shorn locks, it being widely thought that harm done to severed body-parts (hair or nail-parings), would harm their owner. Such dangers especially affected sacred persons. The Frankish Merovingian kings (AD 448–754) lost all right to rule if they cut their hair. Coveting the throne of their dead brother Clodomir, Clotaire and Childebert abducted his two young sons and sent their mother a messenger, bearing scissors and a sword, to ask her if they should be shorn and live, or remain unshorn and die. She chose that they should die, and they did. The priests of the Hos of West Africa were forbidden to cut their hair on pain of death, as their god dwelt in the hair. In Kenya, if Masai rainmakers plucked their beards they lost their supernatural gift, just as **Samson** lost his strength when Delilah cut his hair. In the Marquesas Islands, men taking vows of vengeance left their hair uncut until the vow was fulfilled. Youths of the Chatti in pagan Germany would not cut their hair until they had slain their first enemy.

If hair *had* to be cut, precautions were taken. The chief of Namosi in **Fiji** had to eat a man to avert the risks involved. New Zealand **Maori** were **taboo** for several days after a hair-cut, and dared not touch their food, so had to be fed by another: the barber was also taboo. As to disposing of shorn locks, precautions were taken the world round, to avoid the danger of bewitchment or **black magic**. In the Carpathians it was said that if mice made a nest of shorn hair, its owner would suffer headaches or go mad. The same was said of birds in Germany and in Sussex in England. In the Tyrol, it was said that witches used cut or combed-out hair to cause storms. The Tlingit Indians (northwest USA) attributed storms to girls who rashly combed their hair outside. In Scotland, girls with a brother at sea never combed their hair at night. So, cut hair (or nail-parings) were buried, hidden or (as by the **Inca**) kept, for the owner to recover them when **resurrected**.[1]

1. *The Golden Bough*, Sir James Frazer, Macmillan, London, 1963, pp.231–7.

HAITI (*See* VOODOO)

HALLOWE'EN (*See* BELTANE, FIRE-FESTIVALS, MAY DAY)
Allhallow Even (Hallowe'en) falls annually on 31 October, the day before All Saints' or Allhallows' Day, and marks one of the two great turning-points of the year. But where the other, **May Day**, celebrates the promise of summer, Hallowe'en recognises the return of winter, the time of darkness, death and chaos. Though superficially **Christianised**, the **pagan** origins of both festivals remain explicit. The paraphernalia of Hallowe'en includes children dressed as **witches** who go 'trick-or-treating', the **game** of ducking for **apples** and carving turnip-lanterns as grotesque **heads**.

For Hallowe'en was originally the Celtic festival of the dead, Samhain, equivalent to the Roman Saturnalia, the opposite of the May Day festival of **Beltane**. Marking the start of the Celtic year, it was then that herdsmen drove their beasts back to the safety of the byre. Only a century ago, 1 November was regarded in the Isle of Man (in the Irish Sea) as the date of

New Year. In ancient Ireland on this Eve of Samhain a new **fire** was kindled, from which all other fires in the land were relit. In Wales and in Scotland bonfires were widely lit, as at Beltane. The celebration today in Britain of Guy Fawkes Night on 5 November, when an effigy of the man who tried to blow up the Houses of Parliament in 1605 is burned on *bone*-fires throughout the land, is a survival of the Samhain fires.

Hallowe'en was also the night to cast auguries and divine the fate of the coming year. It was the night when the **ghosts** of dead **ancestors** came shivering inside to enjoy the warmth at the hearth. As on May Eve, on this night witches, **fairies** and every sort of sprite were set mischievously loose. Yet, maybe because of the darkness approaching, Hallowe'en always was the year's most merry festival.

HAMMER (*See* THUNDER)

All thunder-gods, sky-gods and **smith-gods** (**Hephaestus, Vulcan**) carry a hammer which, with the anvil as its feminine receptacle, epitomises the male formative force, and which, in origin, is the thunderbolt: the hammer from the sky. The hammer of the **Norse** god **Thor**, the 'Destroyer', never missed its mark when hurled, and always returned to his hand, like **Indra**'s *vajra* or the thunderbolts of **Zeus** and **Jupiter**. The hammer as gavel is a symbol of justice, authority or final decision, as used by judge, chairman or auctioneer. A team badly defeated in a sporting contest is said to have 'taken a hammering': when opponents in a fight lose self-control, they go at it 'hammer and tongs': these being the smith's implements, also the Tau cross; in **Egyptian myth** it is the emblem of **Ptah** as 'Avenger' or 'Grinder'; and in the **Tarot** pack the **Tree** from which The Hanged Man is suspended upside down (card XII, Major Arcana). The English king Edward I (1239–1307) was called 'Hammer of the Scots'. More recently the symbol of the hammer was revived (crossed with the sickle) as the state symbol of the USSR (1917–1991); the hammer representing industry, and the sickle, agriculture.

HANUMAN (*See* BHIMA, INDIAN MYTH, RAKSHASA, RAMA, TRICKSTERS)

In **Hindu** myth this divine king of the monkeys, son of **Vayu** the wind-god, helped the hero **Rama** in his battle to recover his wife Sita from Ravana, the Sri Lankan **demon**-king. He did this by shifting his **shape** in such versatile fashion that first, assuming gigantic form, he leapt across the sea from the mainland to Sri Lanka. But the demonic **Naga**-hag Surasa rose up with gaping mouth to swallow him, whereupon he shrank to the size of a thumb, in which form he leapt into her mouth and out again. Then he met the she-**dragon** Sinhika, and again leapt into her mouth, where he dealt a mortal blow. So he landed in Lanka where, in the form of a **cat**, he crept through Ravana's jewelled palace until he found Sita, guarded by hideous **rakshasas**. He offered to carry her away, but she would not touch any male body but that of Rama. Assuming his **giant** form, Hanuman uprooted trees to use as clubs and with them destroyed half the city. Magically captured by Ravana's son Indrajit, Ravana set his tail on fire. But, shifting his shape yet again, he escaped, and leapt away over Ravana's city, his flaming tail burning it down. He returned to Rama, whose army then invaded Lanka with the aid of Hanuman's monkey-battalions. Ravana and his rakshasa demons fought hard, awakening Kumbha-karna, the greatest demon of all. Many men and apes were slain, but Hanuman the wind-god's son flew to the Himalayas for healing herbs to resurrect the dead. So the battle was won, and Sita was restored to Rama, who rewarded Hanuman with eternal life and youth.

HAOMA (See *AMANITA MUSCARIA*, DIONYSUS, PERSIAN MYTH, SOMA)

The ancient reference to a divine elixir, named soma in India, nectar or ambrosia in Greece, remains obscure. It may imply the discovery of alcoholic intoxication via fermented grain or grape, or the more ancient use of toxic mushrooms like *Amanita muscaria*, or to some combination of the two. In **Greek myth, Dionysus** spread viniculture as far east as India, perhaps *c.*1300 BC, while some have argued that the Western European success of the mysterious Beaker People was due less to the beakers (jugs) they made than to what they sold in those jugs. Either way, the Persian equivalent of the Indian **soma** was haoma, the ritual of which was condemned by **Zoroaster** (seventh century BC) for its 'filthy drunkenness'. Acknowledged as a god, haoma was declared to be 'correct in faith and the adversary of death', and so in time it became the central sacrament of the Zoroastrian liturgy.

But what was it? It is tempting to believe that few involved in the haoma rite were ever sober enough to remember. Certainly haoma seems to have been connected with the honey-wine called mead (Persian *mada*): while there is also an ironic poem of the Indian *Rig Veda* comparing soma-drinking Indian sages with croaking frogs that 'shout aloud like Brahmans drunk with Soma . . .' (*Rig Veda*, vii, 103).

HARE (See ANIMALS, CORN-GODS)

Connected with the **moon** and fertility throughout the world, the hare's odd behaviour in spring has brought about its association with madness ('mad as a March hare'). Like the **cat** it was a beast into which **witches** were said to transform themselves at will, presumably due to its lunar connection. It is said in China (where the ordinary hare is said to live for a thousand years) that the **Buddha** was hungry in one of his former lives: to feed him, a hare leapt into the fire. In gratitude the Buddha sent the hare's soul to the moon where, under an acacia tree, the hare pounds in a magical mortar the herbs that make up the elixir of life. A similar tale is told in India of the hare jumping into the fire for **Indra**: the impressed god painted the figure of a hare on the face of the moon. In **Native American** lore Manabozho the Great Hare lives in the moon with his grandmother and is 'provider of all waters, master of winds and brother of the snow'; he is hero, saviour and the **trickster** invariably able to outwit brute force. In parts of Scotland, Germany and Norway the hare was regarded as embodying the **corn-spirit**. In the Greek isle of Lesbos reapers in neighbouring fields would try to finish first to drive the hare into the other field, believing this guaranteed a better crop next year. In **Christian myth** it is negative as fecundity and lust, though at the feet of the **Virgin** it is triumph over lust. Even so, it is the **Easter** hare that lays the Easter **egg**.

HARPIES (See GREEK MYTH, JASON)

Like the **chimera, Cerberus** and the **Hydra**, the Harpies were monsters born to **Typhon** (Greek hurricane-spirit) and Echidna, whose upper body was **nymph**-like, the rest a scaly **serpent**. **Homer** names one as Podarge, **Hesiod** names two: Aello and Ocypete. These storm-goddesses, 'the ravagers', winged monsters with long loose hair and swifter than birds or winds, were an early version of **Athene** in her role as destroyer. In *The Aeneid*, **Virgil** pictures them as hag-faced vultures with sharp curved claws. Invulnerable, yet weak with unappeased hunger, they swooped down on feasts, screeching, devouring everything, emitting a foul stink, soiling the table. By order of **Zeus** they snatched the three daughters of Pandareus and delivered them to the **Erinnyes**, who made them suffer for their father's sins. Later, **Jason** and

the **Argonauts** met King Phineus of Thrace, blinded by Zeus for prophesying too accurately, and plagued by the Harpies. When Phineus gave a
banquet, the Harpies swooped. Calais and Zetes, winged sons of Boreas,
chased them over the sea to the Strophadic isles, but spared them when Iris,
messenger of **Hera**, promised that they would never again molest Phineus.
Ocypete accepted; but Aello flew on, to drown in the Peloponnesian river
Tigris, renamed Harpys after her. Of the fate of Podarge, nothing is known.

HASSAN IBN SABBAH (1054–1124) (See ISLAM)
Known as 'The Old Man of the Mountains', in 1090 this Shi'ite warlord took
the Persian fortress of Alamut and began a reign of terror with the sect to
which he gave his name, the Assassins. These agents, when selected for a
mission, were intoxicated with hashish (also from Hassan). After Hassan
died, the Assassins endured until 1266, when a Mongol army massacred
12,000 of them.

HATHOR (See COW, EGYPTIAN MYTH, EYE)
Worshipped at Dendera, later identified by the Greeks with **Aphrodite**, this
Egyptian fertility-goddess was the celestial **cow** who had created the world
and all within it, including the **sun**. She was depicted as a cow, solar disc
between its horns, or as a woman with cow's horns, or as a woman with cow's
ears. Said to be daughter of **Atum** and wife of **Horus**, in other texts she was
called mother of Horus (and so identified with **Isis**). Her name means 'the
dwelling of Horus'. As cow-goddess she ruled love, joy, merriment, music
and dance, and nourished the living with her milk, suckling Pharaoh and all
others. As 'Queen of the West' and 'Lady of the Sycamore' she welcomed the
dead into the **otherworld**, offering bread and water, holding the **ladder** by
which they could climb to **heaven**. Latterly a dead person, once an '**Osiris**',
became a 'Hathor'. Her **fetish**, the *sistrum*, was a musical instrument that
drove away evil spirits. Yet she had a dark side, like Indian **Kali**. It is said
that Atum, convinced that men plotted against him, sent his **eye** in the form
of Hathor to destroy all humanity. Repenting of the slaughter, to stop her he
made her drunk with beer dyed red to resemble **blood**, so mankind was
spared.

HAWAII (See ADAM, FIRE, FLOOD, OCEANIC MYTH)
In the Pacific 2,700 miles southwest of San Francisco, geographically as
isolated as any culture on earth before their European 'discovery' (1549), the
myths of the Hawaiian Islands none the less display many parallels with
legends found elsewhere. The **Creation** account tells how Kane, Ku and
Lono (Sunlight, Substance and Sound) form a basic triad existing from all
eternity. By act of will these gods shattered chaos. Light entered space. The
gods created three heavens, and the earth as their footstool, then the **sun**,
moon, stars and ministering spirits. Last, out of red earth and spit, they
made Man in the likeness of Kane, and Woman out of his rib as he slept.
Another tale says Kane destroyed the first world by **fire** because of the evil of
its folk, then re-created humanity, as above. So too their myth of the **flood**,
Kaiakahinalii, tells how all beings died but for a man, Nuu (or Nana-nuu,
pronounced *lana*, 'floating'). In the **ark** he built he survived with his family to
land on Mauna Kea, Hawaii's highest peak.
    Another story tells how the **fire**-goddess Pele, deserted by her husband
Wahieloa, wandered far from Hapakuela northeast to Hawaii, which then had
no sea about it. In her misery she wept so much that her tears caused the
flood, only the highest peaks remaining visible. Later the waters receded to

their present level, and Pele and her family settled in Hawaii.

These legends 'were told to the missionaries before the Bible was translated into the Hawaiian tongue'.[1]

Kane demanded no human **sacrifices**, as 'life is sacred to him'. Like **Zeus**, **Indra** or **Thor**, he was the 'Thunderer'; 'Lightning flashing in the heavens'. Other gods were less particular. Offerings to the wizard-god Kahoali included the eyeball of a fish and of a man. The evil-smelling squid-god Kanaloa (an aspect of Kane) became associated with the **Christian Devil** and the land of the dead. But most unpredictable was Pele, goddess of volcanoes and lava-flow. After the flood she settled at Kilauea, on Hawaii itself, by the volcano Mauna Loa. Though beautiful, she was totally unreliable. The only hero ever to best her was Kamapua, a **pig**-god who used his snout to defeat his enemies and build great forts. He tried to woo her. She insulted him, and her family poured fire on him, but his friends almost put out her volcano with rain, so that she yielded.

Kahawali, king of Puna, was less fortunate. With his friends he was sledging down a steep hill. Alerted by the laughter, Pele came out of her volcano and challenged him to a race. Losing, she asked to use his sledge, but he refused. In fury she stamped her foot, causing the earth to quake and lava to pour from Mauna Loa. It overwhelmed everyone but Kahawali, who fled over the sea to escape her, and never dared return.

Again, she married a chief called Lohiau, but after three nights left him to prepare his house. This took so long that he died of grief. Her helpers and attendants restored his spirit to his body, and with him started back to her. The journey took so long, and her sisters so admired the handsome man, that again she lost her temper and overwhelmed them all with fire. As a result of this quarrel her family dispersed.

Today, tourists are warned that to take stones from Mauna Loa makes Pele angry. She will **curse** them.

1. *Hawaiian Folk Tales*, Thomas G. Thrum, McClurg & Co., Chicago, 1912, p.25.

HAWK (*See* BIRDS, EAGLE, HORUS)

Like the **eagle** thought able to eye the **sun** unflinchingly, the hawk also represents the heavens, royal power, nobility. All hawk-gods are solar. The **Aztecs** of Mexico regarded the hawk as a messenger of the gods. The **Ainu** of Japan kept hawks in cages and **sacrificed** them with this prayer: 'O divine hawk, thou art an expert hunter, please cause thy cleverness to descend on me.' In **Arthurian** myth the knight **Gawain** was once Gwalchmai, the 'Hawk of May'. In ancient **Egypt** the hawk is the royal bird of the **soul** (*ba*), associated with **Ra** the sun-god and especially with **Horus**, who was conceived by **Isis** while she fluttered over her dead husband **Osiris** in hawk-form. The **Sphinx** is sometimes shown as hawk-headed. In **Hindu** lore Gayatri the hawk brought **soma** from heaven. The hawk is also a vehicle of **Indra**, and in Persia symbolised **Ahura Mazda** as the principle of light.

HAWTHORN (*See* TREE ALPHABET, TREES)

The flower of the hawthorn symbolises virginity, chastity, **virgin** birth. Representing the sixth letter (*Uath*) in the old Celtic **tree alphabet**, it also represents May, when it flowers, and like May was thought unlucky. To marry in May was thought disastrous: no children would result. Prickly and spiky, in **Welsh myth** the hawthorn is the unpleasant **giant** Ysbaddaden, resisting the marriage of his daughter Olwen to **Culhwch**. In Ireland, to destroy an old hawthorn tree was thought to cause the death of cattle and children, and loss of money. The **Glastonbury** thorn, supposedly planted by **Joseph of Arimathea** in the first century AD, was a hawthorn. The inventors of this myth may have introduced it to combat the orgiastic use of hawthorn blossom as maypole decoration, following its introduction (first century BC) to Britain as part of the cult of the **Roman** fertility-goddess Flora.[1]

1. *The White Goddess*, Robert Graves, Faber & Faber, London, 1961, pp.174–6.

HAZEL (*See* SALMON, TREE ALPHABET, TREES)
The nuts of the hazel (*Coll*, the ninth letter in the Celtic tree alphabet) symbolise wisdom (thus, 'in a nutshell'). The **Salmon** of Knowledge became wise by eating nuts from the nine hazels of poetic art (*see* **Muses**) that overhung its pool or **well**. In Ireland it was the Bile Ratha, 'holy tree of the rath': death was the price for wantonly felling it, as with the **apple**-tree. The Ancient Dripping Hazel of Fenian lore, dripping poisonous milk (destructive wisdom) split in two when the **head** of **Balor** was placed in its fork. Hazel-rods remain preferred by water diviners; once it was also used to divine **treasure**, and guilt in cases of murder or theft.

HEAD (*See* BRAN, CELTIC MYTH, GREEN MAN, HAIR)
Along with the **heart** widely seen as seat of the life-force, the head was widely thought magically potent. In many warrior cultures the 'taking of heads' was regarded as the proof of manhood: severed heads were preserved from Borneo to Africa to South America. Many **Celtic myths** attest to the power of the severed head, notably that of the Welsh god **Bran the Blessed** which, buried outside London, face turned towards France, warded off attack and ensured the fertility of the land – a function later attributed to the **Holy Grail**. The early Irish tale of **Cuchulainn**, Bricriu's Feast, and its late medieval variant, *Sir Gawain and the Green Knight*, exemplify the same fascination with the severed head. Celtic divinatory heads sunk in **wells** were said to speak to those able to listen. The **Green Man** images found in medieval churches are of grimacing, foliage-sprouting heads. The medieval **Knights Templar** were accused of worshipping Baphomet, a mysterious severed head promoting fertility. When agents of the French king broke into the Paris Temple on 13 October 1307 they found a head-shaped silver reliquary containing a woman's skull and labelled 'Caput LVIIIm' – 'Head 58m.'[1]

Two-headed gods (**Janus**) symbolise past and future, and other dualities; the head atop a pillar is phallic. **Cernunnos** is sometimes shown as triple-headed. The 'head' of the **corn** was a symbol in the **Eleusinian Mysteries** of Greece. In the **Qabalistic Tree of Life**, the first sefirah, Kether, the primal source from which all else proceeds, is the Crown of Creation. Among its other titles are the Vast Countenance, the White Head and the Head which is Not. Relating in modern cosmological terms to the moment of the Big Bang and also known as the Primordial Point, Kether may be visualised as a vast white head rising from the limitless ocean of eternity – 'God'.[2]

1. *The Temple and the Lodge*, Michael Baigent and Richard Leigh, Corgi, London, 1990, p.119.
2. *A Practical Guide to Qabalistic Symbolism*, Gareth Knight, Helios, Cheltenham, 1965, vol.1, pp.65ff.

HEALING (See CONCORDANCE)

All mortals are subject not only to sickness but in time to death. Myths of healing belong to two main types: that which restores the halt, blind, mad or possessed to the use of their limbs, organs or mental faculties; and that which heals the disease of mortality itself, by restoring the dead to life, or by conferring **immortality**.

Most great religious teachers are recorded capable of miraculous cures in cases where ordinary medicine fails, such cures being prosaically seen as evidence of their spiritual authority. In the **Christian** New Testament, Jesus is portrayed not only as healing Man in the sense of being the Son of God sent to redeem **Original Sin**, but as a **shaman** able to cure leprosy and other evils by touch (as English kings were said to cure scrofula, 'The King's Evil', as late as the seventeenth century), and also as able to heal at a distance, given the faith of either the sufferer or an intermediary (the centurion and his slave); to cast out evil spirits (Gadarene **swine**); and even to raise the dead (Lazarus). Yet the Gospels insist that such 'miracles' arise only via faith in God. Healed body or mind results from healed spirit or soul. Spiritual faith reliant on such physical evidence is deplored ('Oh ye of little faith . . .'). Faith is the ultimate healer.

Yet in this worldly context Christ and other teachers function like the shaman or witchdoctor, healing physical or mental ills by treating a spirit sickened by disbelief in its innately divine condition. But five centuries before Christ, **Indian** texts describe techniques for channelling the vital energy they call *prana*, and which the Chinese call *ch'i*. The Greek doctor Hippocrates (born *c*.460 BC: the 'Father of Medicine') was the first Western healer (unlike **Asclepius** before him) not to be mythologised as a god.

He wrote: 'It has often appeared [to me], when I have been soothing my patients, as if there was a singular property in my hands to pull and draw away from the affected parts aches and diverse impurities'.[1]

Such techniques, between myth and science, are now derided by sceptics as 'spiritual' healing, and as such widely dimissed by those in the medical profession who still regard the human body as a mere machine.

As to the healing of mortality itself, this is first found in the epic of **Gilgamesh** who, told by Utnapishtim of a herb on the sea-bed that cures old age and prevents death, gains it, only to lose it to the **serpent**. The message in this old tale, as in **Haggard**'s novel *She* (1887), is that death is unconquerable. In other myths, death is not so much conquered as seen as a transformation. So in **Greek myth Zeus** often raises already semi-mythical beings (**Pleiades, Hyades**, etc.) to the status of constellations or stars – hardly a mortal immortality. Yet all mythic and other evidence that mortal life remains subject to death has not prevented the lasting search for bodily immortality. Adherents of the modern myth of cryogenics hold that, by freezing the body of the deceased soon after death, the disease that killed it may later be solved by superior future science, restoring its occupant to life. **Walt Disney** is said to be among those who in recent times have been so treated.

1. *The Power to Heal*, David Harvey, Aquarian Press, Wellingborough, 1983, p.35.

HEART (See BLOOD, HEAD)

Where the **head** represents the centre of reason or Crown of Creation, the heart is the centre of being, both spiritual and physical, as represented on the **Qabalistic Tree of Life** by the sefirah Tiphareth. Also centre of the wisdom of feeling, it mediates between selfless consciousness (God) and selfish egotism (Devil). As easily pierced by **Cupid** as by cupidity, we are perpetually torn between idealism and personal desire. To be 'great-hearted' is to be courageous. If someone is cruel we call them 'heartless' or beg them to 'have a heart'; the opposite is to be 'kind-hearted'. In some cultures the hearts of sacrificial victims were offered to the **sun**, said to rule the heart: **Aztec** priests slew their victims by tearing out the heart. Elsewhere, the hearts of slain enemies were eaten to gain their courage. African **Bushmen** would not let children eat a jackal's heart, fearing it made them cowardly; to eat the heart of the leopard conferred courage. In **Hindu myth** the 'eye of the heart' is the third eye of **Shiva**; in **Buddhism** the Diamond Heart is indestructible purity; in **Christianity**, the heart symbolises love, joy, compassion and understanding. In **Greek myth** it is said of **Dionysus** that he was slain and eaten by the **Titans**, but for his heart, which **Zeus** swallowed so that Semele might bear him anew.

HEAVEN (*See* ANGELS, HELL)

Prosaically, the 'heavens' are the skies above and all that lies beyond reach of mortal, earthbound humanity. Mythically, 'heaven' refers to the spiritual realm as 'earth' refers to the material: heaven is thus the abode of God or the gods, to which the risen **Christ** ascended bodily. Heaven thus implies a perfected state entered by those few mortals whose life on earth has been impeccable. But heaven is not invariably associated with a land beyond the sky. In **Egyptian** and **Teutonic** symbolism, the abode of the blessed lies under the earth; in **Celtic** and other traditions paradise is associated with mythic isles said to lie far out in the Western ocean.

In literature, many attempts have been made to depict heaven, among the first in the apocryphal Book of **Enoch**, in which, driven by 'agitated stars and flashes of lightning', Enoch reaches a realm surrounded by 'vibrating flame', beyond it a habitation containing an exalted throne impossible to face, on which sat 'One great in glory'.[1]

In *The Divine Comedy* by **Dante**, ten heavens of paradise are described. The first nine are the heavens of space, in which spirit is manifested; the tenth is the heaven of light and love, beyond human conception. Yet where Dante succeeded, others failed. *Paradise Lost* by John Milton is greater than his *Paradise Regained*, the hell on earth portrayed in *Dead Souls* by Nikolai Gogol (1809–52) succeeds, but his attempt to portray heaven in Part II of *Dead Souls* caused him such despair that he burned it uncompleted.

Why should this be? In *The Marriage of Heaven and Hell*, **William Blake** remarks of Milton that: 'The reason Milton wrote in fetters when he wrote of Angels & God, and at liberty when of Devils & Hell, is because he was a true Poet and of the Devil's Party without knowing it'.[2]

1. 1 Enoch xiv:9–22.
2. *Poems and Prophecies*, William Blake, Dent Everyman, London, 1972, p.44.

HEBREW MYTH (*See* ADAM, ARK, CHRISTIANITY, ENOCH, EVE, JEWS AND ANTI-SEMITISM, MOSES)

HECATE (*See* DOG, GREEK MYTH, MOON, UNDERWORLD)

This Thracian moon-goddess was said by **Hesiod** to be daughter of the **Titan** Perses and the Titaness Asteria (symbols of shining light). With **Helios** she witnessed the abduction by **Hades** of **Persephone**. Later named daughter of **Hera** and **Zeus**, she stole Hera's make-up and gave it to **Europa**, then fled from Hera to hide in the house of a mortal woman in childbirth. Contact with the child defiled her; plunged into the River Acheron to be purified, she became a powerful underworld goddess. Thereafter called the Invincible Queen, or Prytania of the Dead (thus maybe Prytain, 'Britain', the Land in the West), this blood-drinking, excrement-eating virgin goddess of **charms** and enchantments sent **demons** to torment humanity. She was associated with suicides and those dying before their time. With her **serpent**-hair and pack of baying hell-hounds she appeared at night by tombs, the scenes of crimes, or at crossroads, where stood her triple-faced statues (representing the three phases of the **moon**).[1] In this guise as queen of the witches she makes a brief, late appearance in **Shakespeare**'s *Macbeth* (1605), to commend the Three Witches for their good work in brewing up a **hell**-broth.

1. *The Powers of Evil*, Richard Cavendish, Routledge & Kegan Paul, London, 1975, pp.97–8.

HEEL (*See* ACHILLES HEEL)

HEIMDALL (*See* AESIR, NORSE MYTH, TEUTONIC MYTH)
The name of this Teutonic–Norse sentinel-god of the dawn may mean 'he who casts bright rays'. Son of **Odin** and the nine daughters of the sea-god Ran, he was thus also a 'son of the waters'. Clad in silver armour and wearing a burnished helm with ram's horns, his hearing so sharp he could hear grass grow, his sight so acute he could see a hundred miles by night or day, the **Aesir** sent him to guard the **bridge** Bifrost against an invasion of Asgard by the Frost Giants (return of the Ice Age?). There on his horse Gulltop he watches unsleeping, his magic horn Gjallarhorn to hand, its blast audible throughout every realm, mortal and immortal. At the dawn of **Ragnorak** it will be this horn that summons the gods to their final battle. Also called Gullintani because his teeth were gold, and loved both by men and the gods, this tall handsome god spent his youth on Midgard (Middle Earth: the human realm) and as Scef grew up as a teacher among men. Scef is identified as the patriarch Scyld in *Beowulf*: humanity is descended from Heimdall-Scef via his three sons – Thrall, from whom slaves descend; Churl, father of free men, and Jarl, ancestor of all noblemen. The sworn enemy of **Loki** the trickster-god, at the end of time he and Loki will slay each other.

HEL (*See* HELL, NORSE MYTH, TEUTONIC MYTH, UNDERWORLD)

HELEN OF TROY (*See FEMMES FATALES*, GREEK MYTH, HOMER, *ILIAD*, PARIS)
This legendary beautiful Spartan sister of Castor and Pollux (the **Dioscuri**) was said to have been born when the god **Zeus** took **swan**-form to seduce her mother Leda. Aged ten she was abducted by **Theseus**, but her brothers rescued her. Tyndareus her earthly father made each of her princely suitors swear to back the man he chose for her – Menelaus, son of King Atreus of Mycenae. So when **Aphrodite** caused **Paris** (son of King Priam of Troy) to kidnap her, the oathbound Greek princes under Agamemnon (also a son of Atreus) besieged Troy for ten years until at last they took the city and restored Helen to Menelaus. (The tale may refer to a war fought between Achaeans and Trojans *c*.1300 BC: *see* **Atlantis**.) Yet worse was to come. Her sister Clytemnestra, Agamemnon's wife, slew him and in revenge her nephew **Orestes** slew his mother. Condemned for matricide by Tyndareus and Menelaus, Orestes tried to murder Helen too, but the god **Apollo** took her to

Olympus, where she joined the Dioscuri as an **immortal**. Another tale is that, driven from Sparta, she was hanged on Rhodes, to be venerated as Helena Dendritus (Helen of the Trees). This latter Helen may be a variant of **Artemis** or **Ariadne**.

HELIOS (*See* GREEK MYTH, HYPERION, PHAETHON, SUN-GODS)

In ancient Greece the cult of the sun personified as Helios was widespread. Said to have been drowned by his uncles, the **Titans**, then raised to the sky, this god daily harnessed his eight winged horses to the sun-chariot and took off from Ethiopia to course the sky and at night seem to plunge into the ocean by the land of the **Hesperides**. Here his family awaited him in a barque, in which nightly he sailed back to his point of daily departure.

On the isle of Rhodes, sacred to him, stood a statue of Helios thirty yards high, through the legs of which full-sailed ships could sail. When the gods divided up the world, he had been absent and was forgotten, so **Zeus** gave him this island which had just begun to emerge from the sea.

As god of light, like the Indian **Agni** or Babylonian **Shamash**, he saw and knew everything, including people's most secret thoughts. Deep-breasted **Gaia**, Mother Earth herself, was among his many wives.

HELL (*See* DEVIL, HADES, HEAVEN, NORSE MYTH, UNDERWORLD)

In orthodox **Christian** belief, the awful destination of all who live sinful earthly lives, ruled by **Satan**, alias the **Devil**. Belief in this realm of eternal punishment grew in medieval Europe out of earlier notions that the dead inhabit an underworld as ghosts or restless shades. But earlier there had been no sense that the dead were punished by descent to the underworld – it was simply the Land of the Dead.

The name derives from the Scandinavian word *Hel*, at first meaning only the abode of the dead, later personified as the goddess who ruled **Nifleim** ('Mist-World'). Once conceived as the land north of the abyss from which the world was born, 'Hel' was a place of ice, snow, mist and gloom, maybe derived from folk-memory of an era when glaciers at last retreated from bleak regions that remain essentially 'Hel'-ish even today. Later **Norse myth** (influenced by the Greeks: *see* **Hades**) pictured the worlds of gods, men and the dead as stacked on top of each other. As for the goddess Hel, she was more a poetic creation than the object of a popular cult, and remained a vague figure: it was left to Christians to appropriate her name and terrify generations with the threat of eternal fiery torture. Daughter of **Loki** and Angrboda, said to be sister of the **wolf Fenrir** and the Serpent of Midgard, Hel was envisaged as half-black and half-white. Into her realm – inhabited by **giants** and **dwarves**, and guarded by the terrible **dog** Garm – she received all who died of old age or disease.

Yet the idea of hell as a fiery pit full of **demons** employed to torture the wicked for ever was not solely a product of medieval European masochism, nor simply a control device used by the Church to make folk behave, but is found in other cultures. In **Jain** cosmology, the underworld consists of seven hells. In each a special torture is applied by specific gods. The Ambas scrape nerves, the Ambaras carve flesh from bones, the Sama beat with sticks, the Rudra spear the flesh, the Kara roast sinners on a griddle, the Maharudra grind the flesh, the Sabala tear it out with hot pincers, the Kumbha rub hot chili into their wounds – and so on.

The **Hindu** *Bhagabata* lists twenty-eight hells; each as imaginatively horrible as anything Hieronymous Bosch ever depicted.

Old African lore says nothing of a place where sinners are punished on dying, but **Islamic** tradition offers many more tales about the horrors of hell than the blessings of heaven. **Swahili** accounts say that hell exists under the earth as a vast seven-floored building. The worst sinners (as in **Dante**'s *Divine Comedy* and in Jain belief) occupy the icy seventh level: they are those who denied the existence of God while alive. On the first floor are the drinkers, who after a while may be paroled into purgatory; on the second, the misers; on the third, hypocrites and liars; on the fourth, embezzlers; on the fifth, adulterous women, sorcerers and cannibals; on the sixth, idolaters; on the seventh, Hawiya, the atheists.

So the Christian idea of hell is in fact widespread. Yet of interest is how it has persisted despite the rise of 'Rationalism'. John Bunyan, the seventeenth-century author of *The Pilgrim's Progress*, was so terrified by nightmares of hell that he wished he was a **demon** – one of the torturers, rather than one of the tortured. 'I carry my hell about me,' wrote the Methodist evangelist John Wesley. Later, **William Blake** wrote of the 'dark satanic mills' of the Industrial Revolution; and at the start of the twentieth century, in *A Portrait of the Artist as a Young Man*, **James Joyce** wrote perhaps the most vicious hell-fire sermon ever committed to print, in describing his own Anglo-Catholic upbringing in Ireland. Even today the fear of hell is strong, especially in the seemingly wholly materialistic USA, where many fundamentalist cults interpret heaven and hell as literally real domains.

Yet it is worth remembering that **Gnostics**, **Cathars** and other **dualist** sects were exterminated by the Church not least for insisting that the only real hell exists here and now, in our life on earth. They endangered Church control by insisting that there is nothing to fear after death; all we have to fear is life on earth itself.

HELPERS (*See* CINDERELLA, FAIRY-TALES, HERO)

HEPHAESTUS (*See* APHRODITE, FIRE, GREEK MYTH, SMITH-GODS, VULCAN)

From early times the Greek personification of terrestrial fire, the cult of this lame metal-working god arose on the volcanic isle of Lemnos. It seems he interfered in a quarrel between his parents, **Zeus** and **Hera**, and that one or the other threw him out of **Olympus** down to Lemnos. His lameness may have come from this fall. **Homer**'s account is that he was lame from birth and that Hera, ashamed of his ugliness, threw him down to earth because of it. Falling into the sea, he would have drowned, but **Thetis** and her sea-nymphs rescued him. For nine years he lived underwater, not only learning his metal-working skills but planning revenge. So in time he sent Hera a wonderful golden throne; when she sat on it, invisible hands gripped her.

Only **Dionysus**, making him drunk, could get him to leave the **ocean** and ascend to Olympus: on arrival, as the price of Hera's release, he demanded **Aphrodite** as his bride. The marriage was no success: Aphrodite slept with **Ares**, **Hermes** and the gods knew who else. But Hephaestus, now at peace with Hera, netted Aphrodite and Ares as they slept together. The Olympians were delighted by the scandal – especially as, now restored to godhood, he built marvellous palaces for them, and for himself a 'sparkling palace of glittering and incorruptible bronze', amid which he had his workshop.

Here he made many marvels, including the armour worn by **Achilles**, and two living golden statues of young girls who helped him to walk – for under the rough, hairy, unprepossessing exterior was a subtle but fiery creative spirit: progenitor of **Vulcan, Goibniu, Wayland Smith** and all other Western gods of the smithy and of subterranean fire. It may be that in his origin he was the Vedic fire-god **Agni**. Later he became the god of all craftsmen using fire for their trade, his workshop being located within the volcanic Mount Etna on Sicily – adopted by the Romans as the home of **Vulcan**.

HERA (*See* GREEK MYTH, JUNO, ZEUS)

This quarrelsome Greek goddess ('Lady' is given as one meaning of her name: another derivation is from *svar*, the sky, a Sanskrit term) began life as the earth-goddess of Argos in pre-Classical times. Daughter of **Cronus** and **Rhea**, sister of the father-god **Zeus**, it seems that her forced marriage to Zeus led to her famous vindictiveness. In other words, the cult-followers of Hera resisted assimilation into the cult of Zeus. Another interpretation of the continual marital strife between these two is that it represents the continual climatic war between sky and earth: storms and other bad weather.

In any case, losing her cosmic attributes, Hera came to represent woman in all her phases – virgin, wife and crone: the 'Triple Goddess' eulogised by **Graves**. Primarily the goddess of marriage and maternity, she was shown as a young woman of severe and chaste beauty, diadem-crowned, veiled and wearing a long robe. Yet most Greek myth depicts her as a jealous harridan, obsessed with the extra-marital affairs of her husband, and using any means to kill or cast down his numerous lovers, and persecuting his children.

Outraged by his amours, once she managed to tie him up, and was stopped from killing him only by the arrival of hundred-handed Briareus. Equally outraged by his giving **hermaphroditic** birth to Pallas **Athene**, the goddess of wisdom, she too gave birth, without his insemination, to the **monster Typhon**. When Zeus hit her, and her son **Hephaestus** tried to stop him, Zeus seized Hephaestus by one foot and threw him down to Lemnos: another version of how the smith-god was lamed.

Her fury was famous. It led to the destruction of **Troy**, the death of **Hercules**, the destruction of Semele (mother of **Dionysus**) and many another murder. And all because she hated but wanted to hang on to her husband. Yet, despite endless vicious quarrels, they stayed married. Maybe, already on **Olympus**, they had nowhere better to go.

HERAKLES (*See* HERCULES)

HERCULES (*See* GREEK MYTH, HERO MYTH, THESEUS)

The name 'Hercules' is the latinised form of the Greek Herakles or Heracles. To this greatest of Greek mythic heroes is ascribed the foundation of the Olympic **Games**: he remains a popular personification of physical strength.

Fathered by **Zeus** after the latter yet again used trickery to seduce a mortal (in this case the Theban Alcmene, by taking the form of her husband Amphitryon; *see* **Arthurian myth**), Hercules was thereafter pursued by the hatred of **Hera**, wife of Zeus. First she sent two serpents to attack the infant. He strangled them with his bare hands: the start of his heroic career. But later Hera drove him mad. He killed his own family, mistaking them for that of his enemy, King Eurystheus of Argolis. To expiate this sin he undertook the famous twelve labours, imposed by the **Delphic oracle** via Eurystheus, on whose mercy he had to throw himself.

These successfully concluded labours were: to kill the Nemean lion and bring back its hide (from which, having strangled the lion, he made a coat that rendered him **invulnerable**); to slay the Lernean Hydra, a nine-headed **dragon** or **serpent** sacred to Hera; to capture the Erymanthian boar – when he brought it to Eurystheus, the king was so scared he hid himself deep in a bronze jar; the destruction of the iron-clawed Stymphalian birds, which he frightened with cymbals then slew with arrows; the capture of the hind of Mount Ceryneia – he spent a year chasing this golden-horned and bronze-hoofed deer before he caught it; the cleansing of the stables of Augeias, which contained 3,000 oxen – a task concluded in one day by his diversion of two rivers through the manure-fouled cow-sheds; the capture of the **bull** which **Poseidon** had sent to **King Minos** and which now terrorised the isle of Crete; the capture of the man-eating **horses** owned by King Diomedes of Thrace (he gave Diomedes to them for their supper); the theft of the girdle of Hippolyte, queen of the **Amazons**, whom he slaughtered in order to seize it; the capture of the cattle of Geryon, a three-bodied Iberian (Spanish) **monster**. This tenth labour also required him to go to Sicily to recapture an ox which had escaped the herd. Then Eurystheus ordered him to bring the golden **apples** kept by the **Hesperides** in their garden at the western edge of the world. En route, he defeated the **giant** Antaeus, son of **Gaia**, by holding him off the ground so long that he lost his strength, then strangling him. After other feats in Egypt and Ethiopia he crossed the sea to seize the Golden Apples. These he gave to the king, who gave them back; Hercules presented them to the goddess **Athene**, who returned them to the Hesperides.

For the last labour, Eurystheus (now certain that no mortal peril could defeat him) sent Hercules to **Hades** to seize **Cerberus**, the three-headed **dog** guarding the underworld. Guided by **Hermes** following his initiation into the **Mysteries** of **Eleusis**, Hercules wounded **Hades** himself, then mastered Cerberus by strangulation. Showing the brute to Eurystheus, he sent it back to Hades again. So his labours were accomplished.

After many other adventures, Hercules died when persuaded by Deianeira, daughter of the Aetolian king, to wear a white tunic she had soaked in the blood of Nessus, a **centaur** he had killed for (as he saw) trying to rape her. Dying, Nessus had told her his blood would guarantee the love of her husband. She got the wrong idea. For when Hercules put on the tunic, he was immediately poisoned and maddened with pain. Making himself a funeral pyre, he put himself on it and told his companions to light it. All refused but for Poeas, to whom Hercules gave his bow and arrows. Then in flame the hero ascended to **Olympus**, and also became a constellation, adjacent to Draco the **dragon**. This constellation was also once identified with the Sumerian hero **Gilgamesh**. The epithet 'herculean' remains in common usage.

HERMAPHRODITES (*See* GREEK MYTH, HERMES)
Hermaphroditism refers to any organism in which the two sexes are united, as in flowers, which typically contain both stamens and pistil, or in many parasites and simple animal forms. The term derives from the Greek myth of Hermaphroditus, the son of **Hermes** and **Aphrodite**. Reared in the forests of Mount Ida, he grew up a wild youth. One day the nymph Salmacis saw him bathing and fell in love with him. He tried to reject her, but she asked the gods that they should never be separated, whereupon their two bodies were immediately united into one, of neither sex, yet of both.

This myth is not unusual. The concept of a primal hermaphroditism or androgyny is found in many **creation** accounts. In particular the idea of a divine androgyne (such as **Adam** before **Eve** is created from his rib) arises from the notion that Ultimate Being is a unity in which all potential pairs of opposites, including the sexes, are contained. Ancient myth abounds in tales of a time when the eternal male (father sky) and the eternal female (mother earth) were locked in unending embrace. There was neither duality nor multiplicity: only one androgynous condition. Later, the cosmic **egg** being broken, creation took place. The sexes were separated, and have ever since longed to be reunited, each in the other. The myth also refers to the desire for conjunction of masculine and feminine elements within each individual human being: a state explored especially in the psychology of **C.G. Jung** (1875–1961), who referred to androgyny as an **archetype** inherent in the human psyche. This condition has also been explored in **Hinduism** (the god **Shiva** is shown as physically half-male, half-female), **Buddhism**, **Taoism** (the Chinese god of night and day is androgynous, like the Chinese **dragon** and **phoenix**), Platonic lore (in the *Symposium* **Plato** relates the fable that originally humanity was of one sex, four-armed and four-legged), and in alchemy (the great work consists in producing the perfect androgyne, the whole human being). In Greek myth, **Zeus** and **Hercules** often dress as women; **Dionysus** has feminine features; in Cyprus, Aphrodite was depicted as bearded. The Phoenician **Baal** and **Astarte** were androgynous; the Phrygian **Attis**, who emasculated himself, was not. In patriarchal Christianity the concept has been all but expunged as threatening the dogma of male dominance.[1]

1. *Androgyny*, June Singer, Anchor Books, New York, 1977.

HERMES (*See* GREEK MYTH, HERMES TRISMEGISTUS, MERCURY, THOTH)

Another son of **Zeus**, this important Greek god (the etymology of his name is obscure) was born to the **nymph** Maia in a cave in Arcadia. Legend says he was only a few hours old when he stole the cattle of **Apollo**, his half-brother, which he did with the aid of his winged sandals, while his quick wit (winged thoughts) spared him Apollo's wrath, for in return he offered Apollo one of his many inventions, the lyre. His ingenuity also led him to be regarded as the inventor of the alphabet, numbers, weights and measures, and gymnastics. As Hermes Psychopompus (leader of souls) he conducted the dead to the **underworld**. As Diactoros (messenger) of **Zeus**, he was always moving between **Olympus** and earth, bringing messages, carrying out delicate missions. As patron of roads and travellers, statues of him called Hermae were set up on roads and at **doors**. He was honoured by athletes, especially gymnasts, who named him Agonios – 'he who presides over contests' – and was said to have invented pugilism and racing. As patron of good luck, games of chance and commerce (thus patron both of thieves and merchants), he was called Logios, god of eloquence – every salesman needs a nimble tongue and a quick wit. Depicted as a graceful, athletic youth (as in the statue by Praxiteles at Olympia), he wore a broad-brimmed cap and the winged sandals that bore him on his journeys, and carried the herald's staff or **caduceus**.

His predecessor was the Egyptian **Thoth**, his successor the Roman **Mercury** or Mercurius, who adopted many of his roles, including that of psychopomp.

HERMES TRISMEGISTUS (*See* PHILOSOPHER'S STONE)
'That which is above is like that which is below . . . And as all things have been derived from one . . . so all things are born from this thing.'

This, the core statement of hermetic philosophy, comes from an obscure and enigmatic text called the Emerald Tablet, said by Renaissance scholars to be by 'Thrice-Great' Hermes (Greek name for **Thoth**, the Egyptian scribe-god and mythic inventor of writing and all arts). He was said, variously, to be

Adam's grandson who built Egypt's **pyramids**; or an Egyptian magus living three generations after **Moses**; or a Babylonian magus who instructed **Pythagoras**. It was claimed that the Emerald Tablet had been found (with his corpse) in a cave by Sara, Abraham's wife, or by **Alexander the Great**, or by the magician Apollonius of Tyana (first century AD). Works attributed to this mythic figure included (says Bishop Clement of Alexandria, c.AD 180) forty-two books – thirty-six containing all Egyptian philosophy and six being on medicine. St Augustine (AD 354–430) attacked one book, *The Asclepius*, as containing demonic magic. In Florence a millennium later, c.AD 1460, Cosimo de' Medici received a copy of the *Corpus Hermeticum*, said to be by Hermes. Translated by Ficino as the *Pimander*, this and other hermetic texts deeply influenced the growth of European alchemy, **astrology** and magic studies, conferring on such research (frowned on by the Church) an aura of antique authority. The *Pimander* (first printed 1471) went through sixteen editions by the end of the sixteenth century. More recently the psychologist **C.G. Jung** found much of value in these texts in his attempt to establish Renaissance alchemy as an early form of depth psychology. Historian Frances Yates lately established that the works attributed to Hermes in fact date from **Gnostic** and post-Christian Graeco-Roman sources.[1] Even so, their rediscovery and translation helped stimulate the explosive intellectual climate of the Renaissance. As for 'Hermes Trismegistus' himself, he remains as cryptic as his Tablet.

1. *Giordano Bruno and the Hermetic Tradition*, Frances Yates, Routledge & Kegan Paul, London, 1964.

HERNE THE HUNTER (*See* CERNUNNOS, GREEN MAN, ROBIN HOOD, WILD HUNT)

An antler-horned **pagan** British stag-god is said to haunt Windsor Great Park, especially at midnight near where Herne's Oak (reckoned to be 650 years old) fell in 1863, and where Queen Victoria planted a new, young oak. In his book *Windsor Castle*, author W. Harrison Ainsworth described this ghost as, 'a wild, spectral object . . . clad in the skin of a deer and wearing on its head a sort of helmet, formed of the skull of a stag, from which branched a large pair of antlers. It was surrounded by a blue phosphoric light.'

Like Arawn, Cernunnos or **Gwynn ap Nudd**, Herne was said to lead the Wild Hunt through the night sky. Like Hermes, he led the souls of the dead to the **underworld**. The name 'Herne' is also implied in British place names like 'Cerne', as at Cerne Abbas in Dorset where in the chalk hillside is carved a giant figure portrayed with erect phallus and upraised club.

Herne, Cerne or Cernunnos all refer to the Horned God, later demonised as **Satan**. The cult perhaps arose from sympathetic magical identification between hunter and hunted, man and stag. The Horn Dance, still conducted every 4 September at Abbots Bromley in Staffordshire, may be a survival of such a cult, once intended to promote fertility.

HERO MYTH (*See* CONCORDANCE)

As defined by **Joseph Campbell** in *The Hero with a Thousand Faces*, the structure of hero myth world-wide is as follows:

Leaving hovel, house or castle, the potential hero is carried away, lured to, or voluntarily seeks, the threshold of adventure. Here he meets a shadowy presence guarding entry to the unknown world beyond any ordinary experience. Defeating (brother-battle, **dragon**-battle), or conciliating this power (offering or **charm**), he enters the **underworld** alive, or else reaches it by being slain and dismembered (crucifixion, self-**sacrifice**).

Either way, he abandons the daily world to enter a realm of strange yet oddly intimate forces (his own unconscious?). Some of these forces threaten him with tests and trials; others (helpers) offer magical aid. At the nadir of this journey (**Hercules** fighting **Cerberus**, or **Gilgamesh** confounded by Utnapishtim), he undergoes a supreme ordeal. Triumphing (mastering himself), he gains his reward. This may be sacred marriage with the goddess-mother, his recognition by the father-creator (atonement), his divinisation (apotheosis), or (if the chthonic powers remain unfriendly) his successful theft of the treasure he came for: **fire**, knowledge or otherworld bride.

The theme is expansion of consciousness, thus of the boundaries of our being (illumination, transfiguration, freedom from ignorance).

The final act is the hero's return. If the otherworld powers have given their blessing, he now sets forth under their protection as an emissary. If not, he flees with stolen treasure, and is pursued (like Gwion Bach by **Cerridwen**) through transformations by which he is further evolved.

Winning back to the threshold of day (the ordinary world, at the dawn of which all supernatural pursuit must end), he returns (**resurrection**) into society with his otherworld treasure. This may restore a **wasteland** to life (**Holy Grail**, Elixir of Life), rid the land of a tyrant, or lead to marriage with the princess who formerly rejected him. So he founds a new dynasty under which the land prospers.[1]

Yet the term 'hero' is feminine, derived from the Greek goddess **Hera**: thus the name of **Hercules** (Herakles). The first 'heroes' thus may have been representatives of **Zeus** dedicated to the service of Hera. In Greek myth, Hero was a priestess of **Aphrodite** at Sestos on the Hellespont. The youth Leander of Abydos so loved her that nightly he swam the strait to visit her, guided by the lighthouse of Sestos. One stormy night the light failed and he drowned. When his body was cast up on the shore, Hero saw it and drowned herself in the sea to join him.

1. *The Hero with a Thousand Faces*, Joseph Campbell, Abacus, London, 1975.

HESIOD (*See* GREEK MYTH, HOMER)

The best-known early Greek poet after **Homer**, probably eighth century BC. Herodotus (fifth century BC) dates him *c.*860 BC. The tale that he and Homer contested the poetry prize is untrue as Homer lived earlier. Born in Boeotia, Hesiod is said to have lived and died in Orchomenus, where his tomb was later shown. Thucydides says he was slain in the temple of Nemean Zeus in Locris by local people. The two surviving poems certainly attributable to him are the *Works and Days* and the *Theogony*. The former, mostly concerned with husbandry, education and household management, contains some mythic material, notably the fable of **Prometheus** and **Pandora**, and an account of the different ages of the world. The *Theogony* describes the creation of the world, the ocean, heaven, earth, stars and gods, and offers a genealogy of the gods. A third work sometimes attributed to him, the *Shield of Heracles*, displays none of his vigour.[1]

1. *Theogony*, Hesiod, Penguin, 1989.

HESPERIDES (*See* GREEK MYTH, HERCULES)

Variously cited as the daughters of Night and Erebus, or **Zeus** and Themis, or Phorcys and Ceto, these Greek sea-**nymphs** were widely seen as offspring of **Atlas** and the evening star Hesperus (Roman **Venus**, also associated with Lucifer: 'Daystar, Son of Dawn'). Three or four in number and named Hespere, Aegle, Erytheis and Hestia or Arethusa, they inhabited a wondrous garden beyond the river-ocean at the extreme western edge of the world. Here they protected the golden **apples** which the mother goddess **Gaia** gave **Hera** when Hera married Zeus. Theft of these apples was the eleventh labour imposed on **Hercules** by King Eurystheus: the apples were returned after the labour was accomplished. Later associated with Mount Atlas in Morocco and at other sites variously seen as the furthest point west, these sweet-singing nymphs also epitomised clouds made gold by the setting sun. As in Greek the words for 'apple' and 'flock of sheep' are identical (*melon*), some surmise that in fact the Hesperides guarded not golden apples but the golden clouds of sunset – in Indo-European myth described as 'celestial flocks'.

HESTIA (*See* AGNI, BELTANE, FIRE, GREEK MYTH, VESTA)
In Greek, *hestia* means 'hearth'. This goddess, personifying the domestic fire, source of light, warmth and cookery, was venerated throughout Greece – every town had its *prytaneum* or public hearth – but especially in Delphi, its hearth not just the centre of Greece but of the world. Cognate with the **Vedic** fire-god **Agni** and later called **Vesta** by the Romans and seen as the oldest daughter of **Cronos** and **Rhea**, Hestia was said to preside over all **sacrifices** (the *hestia*-fire being also a place of sacrifice). The first part of every sacrifice was offered to her. Should this fire ever go out, it might not be rekindled by ordinary fire, but only by the sun's rays or by friction of two pieces of wood (*see* **Beltane**).

As chaste as **Athene** and **Artemis**, she ignored the **Olympian** squabbles. There are as few legends about her as there are statues. Surviving statues show her as immobile, dignified, hooded and serene.

HIAWATHA (*See* NATIVE AMERICAN MYTH)
In 1855, US poet Henry Wadsworth Longfellow (1807–82) published a version of a legend of the Iroquois peoples of northeast America. Written in the same lilting (some call it monotonous) measure as the Finnish *Kalevala*, the tale of Hiawatha went through thirty editions in one year, and remains the work by which Longfellow is best remembered. Hiawatha, a person of divine or miraculous descent, is said in the tradition on which Longfellow drew to have been sent to earth to teach men the arts of peace and civilisation – like the **Aztec Quetzalcoatl** or the **Mayan Kukulcán**. He is said to have taught navigation, medicine and the husbandry of maize. When the white man seized the land, he ascended to Ponemah, Kingdom of the Hereafter.

Longfellow makes him an Algonquin chief. But the historical Hiawatha was a Mohawk who in the sixteenth century with the Huron **prophet** Degandawidah founded the original Five Nations Confederacy of the Iroquois – Seneca, Mohawks, Oneidas, Onondagas and Cayugas. This league was later joined by the Tuscaroras. Having led an evil life after an Onondagan had murdered his wife and children, on meeting Degandawidah he reformed, persuading all he met that the prophet was holy and that they should heed his advice as to how to lead a moral life. As for Degandawidah, it is said that, after the League was formed, he headed east in a sacred canoe and (again like Quetzalcoatl) was never to be seen again.

HINAYANA (*See* BUDDHISM, INDOCHINA)

HINDUISM (*See* BRAHMA, BRAHMANISM, INDIAN MYTH, SHIVA, VISHNU)

Polytheistic Indian religion, evolved from the monotheistic **Vedic** worship of the one supreme being, Brahma, and out of conflict between devotees of folk religion and those pursuing the philosophy of the Aran'yakas ('Forest Books') and *Upanishads* ('the sittings down': teachings wherein pupils sat at their master's feet). Using popular myths to illustrate deeper ideas, the authors of the 'Forest Books' found their tales taken up literally: so Hindu teachings are often found cloaked in supernaturalism.

The doctrine of the **Trimurti** embraces a triple godhead: Brahma the Creator, Vishnu the Preserver and Shiva the Destroyer. There are many other manifestations or **avatars** of the chief deity, but Hindus generally recognise that there is but one god or creative principle behind the many lesser forms. Even so, the worship of Brahma is now confined to a few. Shiva the Destroyer is widely seen as Mahá-Devi (the Great God), Hindus holding that destruction leads to regeneration via the transmigration of souls. This doctrine of metempsychosis or **reincarnation** has long been insisted upon as a necessary element of orthodox Hindu belief.

In the old *Satapatha Brahmana* the teacher says that those neglecting sacrificial rites decline through successive existences until death claims them, while those who perform such rites ultimately attain **immortality**. Austere and devoted to duty, Shiva is less popular with ordinary Hindus than Vishnu the Preserver, a kind and gentle god who, identified with human cares, inspires confidence and love. The worship of the one or the other of these gods represents not opposite or incompatible creeds, but different lines of religious thought. Also, as the deities of the Trimurti are co-equal, interchangeable and multiplex, and as they often manifest as lesser deities (thus **Krishna** as avatar of Vishnu), the complications are endless, not least due to the recognition of the female element. Every incarnation of the deity has a female counterpart or wife (*sakti*), leading to further division between those following the 'right-hand path' (male and cerebral) and those following the 'left-hand path' (devotees of goddesses and thus of the feeling or emotional side of life).

HIPPOPOTAMUS (*See* AFRICAN MYTH, ANIMALS)

This ungainly yet impressive African beast has been the subject of human worship and myth, usually as a goddess. In Ancient Egypt the hippopotamus-goddess Tawaret protected pregnant women and women in childbirth: faience images of her were used as **amulets** to give protection against demons. The Ronga of Mozambique tell of a mother who, her child's life threatened by a jealous rival, gave her baby to the hippopotamus-goddess for protection. Nightly, Mother Hippo emerged from the river with the infant for its mother to suckle, so the boy grew strong and rapidly. Yet male hippopotami could be seen as **shape-shifting** monsters. One such, in Mali, ate all the rice in the fields until the **hero** Fara Maka decided to destroy it. He threw all his spears, but the blades melted as they struck its hot body. The hunter Karadigi sent his 120 **horse**-sized black hounds against it, but it ate them all. Fara Maka went home to sleep with his wife, Nana Miriam, who next day put a spell on the beast, so paralysing and defeating it.

HIRAM ABIFF (*See* FREEMASONRY, PHOENICIAN MYTH, SOLOMON)

Initiation of a Master Mason involves miming the murder of Hiram Abiff, legendary architect of Solomon's Temple in Jerusalem *c*.955 BC. Brief Old Testament accounts (I Kings and II Chronicles) tell how Hiram, King of Tyre ('Abiff' means 'father'?) was hired by Solomon to build a Temple like those in Phoenicia dedicated to **Astarte** (later worshipped by Solomon). The Bible says he went home safely. Masons claim otherwise. Deriving their tradition from Talmudic legend and Judaic apocrypha, they say that Hiram's workforce (of over 150,000 men) was of three grades: apprentices (called 'Boaz' after one of the brass pillars supporting the Temple porch); fellows ('Jachin', after the second pillar); and masters ('Jehovah'). With each name went a particular secret sign and handshake. On pay-day, each worker had to give Hiram the appropriate word, sign and grip, so as to get his wage.

One day, three fellows – Jubela, Jubelo and Jubelum – decided to make Hiram tell them the master's password. At noon they awaited him at the main gates of the unfinished Temple as he prayed within. At the south gate he denied Jubela, who hit him on the throat with a ruler; at the west gate Jubelo hit him on the breast with a square; and finally, at the east gate, still refusing to speak, he was struck dead by Jubelum's mallet. They buried him on a nearby hillside, a sprig of acacia on the grave, then fled but were caught and executed. Seven days later, nine subordinate masters found Hiram's body and reburied it in the Temple, all wearing aprons and gloves of white hide to show none had stained his hands with his blood.

Is this a veiled account of a human **sacrifice**? The consecration in **blood** of new buildings was common in biblical times. Hiram may be a type of the dying god, similar to Egyptian **Osiris**, whose death and resurrection portrayed man's spiritual death and rebirth via initiation. Osirian myth tells how the chest containing his dead body was washed ashore near Byblos and lodged in the roots of an acacia tree: thus maybe the connection of acacia with Hiram, who in Masonry also represents Christ, slain by Caesar (the state), Sanhedrin (religious establishment) and by the incited populace (the mob). Thus he symbolises man's higher nature (Right Thought, Right Feeling and Right Action: the Three Gates to the Temple) murdered by Wrong Thought, Wrong Feeling and Wrong Action, by fear, ignorance and superstition (Jubela, Jubelo and Jubelum).[1,2]

Yet the Temple was built and the Bible says Hiram went safely home. Why does Masonic myth differ? Who were Jubela, Jubelo and Jubelum? A recent author, asserting that the first Freemasons were Knights Templar in hiding, finds that the medieval French word 'jube' means the rood screen in a church, before which sinners were publicly punished, and that Hiram Abiff is not a name but a designation – Hiram a Biffe, 'Hiram who was eliminated' – as in 1307 the Templars were all but eliminated by King Philippe le Bel (state), Pope Clement V (religious establishment) and by the rival order of Knights Hospitaller. Thus Jubela, Jubelo and Jubelum? As for the Temple, the Knights Templar were first established on its site (thus their name) while its unfinished state in Masonic myth refers not to the physical temple but to the Temple of Mind, to civilisation, with the fate of Hiram an allegory for the fate of all who seek the Light in the face of persecution.[3]

1. *The Temple and the Lodge*, Michael Baigent and Richard Leigh, Corgi, London, 1990, p.176.
2. *The Secret Teachings of All Ages*, Manly P. Hall, Philosophical Research Society, Los Angeles, 1989 (1928), p.78.
3. *Born in Blood*, John J. Robinson, Century, London, 1989, p.227ff.

HITLER, ADOLF (*See* NAZI MYTH)

HOLLOW EARTH (*See* AGHARTI, HELL, LOST WORLDS, NAZI MYTH, SHAMBHALA)

The ideas that under the earth exists a kingdom inhabited by intelligent but subhuman or superhuman beings derives from old **underworld** myths, also from the existence of old cave dwellings, catacombs, earth houses and mines. So Egyptian pharaohs were said to be able to reach the underworld via secret tunnels under the pyramids; **Greek myth** tells how **Orpheus** tried to rescue his wife Eurydice back from **Hades**; the **Norse Hel**, at first conceived as a northern land of mist and snow, in time became an underworld realm in which, in **Christian** myth, sinners are eternally punished. Yet, though in most tales this underworld is clearly metaphoric (**Dante**'s journey through the seven circles of hell describes human self-torment, not a physical geography), literal belief in a magical underworld kingdom persists.

In the eighteenth century, mathematician Leonard Euler and Dr Edmund Halley (of Halley's comet) held that the hollow earth contains three planets. A century later American Civil War hero John Cleves Symmes sought backing for an expedition to prove the earth hollow: Cyrus Read Teed founded a religion (Koreshism) on this basis. The Victorian novelist **Bulwer-Lytton** used the idea (as did Verne, **Poe** and **E.R. Burroughs**) in a novel, *The Coming Race*, telling of an evil race inhabiting caves under the earth. In 1913 American Marshall B. Gardner published a book 'proving' that the sun is inside the earth; a later claim was that the centre of the earth is a vacuum, where lies sun, moon and a phantom universe (a globe of bluish gas pierced by bright points of light: the stars). In March 1945 in *Amazing Stories* (an American science fiction magazine), Richard S. Shaver published *I Remember Lemuria*, claiming the earth's interior to be inhabited by subhumans (deros) who, once slaves of a **Lemurian** master race, now cause all our troubles. When in 1947 **UFO** mania began, Shaver claimed that the UFOs were sent by an advanced subterrene race via huge holes at the North and South Poles.

In June 1970 Ray Palmer, editor of *Flying Saucers* magazine, reproduced North Pole photos taken by the ESSA-7 satellite. One showed a huge round black hole at the Pole. Palmer claimed it as proof of the existence of the subterrene super race, quoting the controversy over the polar expeditions of Rear-Admiral Richard E. Byrd (1888–1957). Byrd's reported comments prior to his 1947 flight over the South Pole that: 'I'd like to see that land beyond the Pole. That area beyond the Pole is the centre of the Great Unknown' – were exploited by Palmer and others to suggest that he had flown not over the Pole but into an 'enchanted continent', a 'land of everlasting mystery', where lay a 'Rainbow City', lush vegetation, lakes, rivers, etc.

Byrd being dead, he could not deny this misuse of his actual words, nor were Hollow Earth fans upset by the fact that the image of a 'hole' at the Pole came from a mosaic of satellite tv images taken amid the continuous North Polar night, resulting in a central 'hole of darkness'.

The myth persists: a good example of the persistent human desire to literalise enduring psychological belief in the underworld.[1]

1. *The Morning of the Magicians*, Pauwels and Bergier, Mayflower, London, 1979, pp.187ff.; 'Is the Earth hollow?' W.A. Harbinson, in *The Unexplained* (Orbis partwork, London, 1983), pp.530–33; *The Subterranean*

Kingdom, Nigel Pennick, Turnstone Press, Wellingborough, 1980.

HOLLY

In ancient Rome, sacred to **Saturn** and used in the annual winter festival of the Saturnalia as a symbol of health and happiness (its blood-red berries emerging just when most other growth is dormant or dead), the spiky, shiny bright holly foliage today remains familiar in its seasonal symbolism. With the **mistletoe** and the Christmas tree, the holly-spray still reminds us of our pre-**Christian, pagan** origins. In Christian terms its spiked leaves may signify the crown of thorns, its red berries the blood of Christ.

HOLLYWOOD (*See* DEAN, GARBO, MONROE, WILD WEST)

A district in Los Angeles, California, USA, synonymous with the production of 'motion pictures' or 'movies', Hollywood is the world centre of a modern industry devoted to the sale of celluloid fantasy, dream and drama. Founded by Horace Wilcox, a Kansas Prohibitionist who in 1887 laid it out as a real-estate subdivision, meaning to create a community based on his own sober religious principles, Hollywood (also known as 'Tinseltown') did not turn out as he planned. For in 1908 one of the first storytelling movies, *The Count of Monte Cristo*, begun in Chicago, was completed in Hollywood. Soon many producers and directors, such as Cecil B. de Mille and D.W. Griffith, moved to this former desert, attracted by the low costs, and created movie myths even as Hollywood itself became a myth, attracting those wishing to become 'film stars' or 'film idols'. A glamorous, extravagant culture developed, decried by moralists as a modern version of Babylon. Meanwhile studio managers like Samuel Goldwyn, William Fox, Darryl F. Zanuck and Louis B. Mayer ensured that most Hollywood movies were so tuned to public taste as to turn a good profit.

Yet many aspiring Hollywood 'stars' found that success demanded that they live their private lives in public. Many found such pressure hard to endure. Some, like Garbo and Dietrich, became recluses. Others, like Errol Flynn or James Dean, burned themselves out in excess, or, like Marilyn Monroe, became psychologically unstable. Unlike former European royal families or Greek demi-gods, they could not simply retreat from their public. They were expected to serve the Hollywood myth, while their owners and paymasters (like Howard Hughes) remained as remote as **Olympian** gods.

Though now its Golden Age is gone, Hollywood remains synonymous with the creation of modern myths. Ambitious would-be 'stars' still head west towards Los Angeles in the hope of wealth and fame. Mythical longing retains an allure more potent than daily reality.

HOLY CITY (*See* NEW JERUSALEM)

HOLY GHOST (*See* CHRISTIANITY, DOVE, SPIRIT, THREE)

Also referred to as the Holy Spirit. In Christian theology the third person of the **Trinity** (as in 'God the Father, God the Son and God the Holy Ghost'), foreshadowed in the Old Testament, in which the spirit of **Yahweh** is the active divine principle in nature (Genesis i:2) and source of the higher energies of the soul (I Samuel xvi:13). Later prophets foresaw its full manifestation in the **Messianic** age, but the doctrine is developed chiefly in the New Testament. Acts ii describes how on the Day of Pentecost the Holy Spirit descended on the Apostles as tongues of fire, so that all began to speak in languages formerly unknown to them. In John xiv:16–26, Christ promises the Apostles that God the Father will send it to help and teach them after he is gone. Yet the doctrine of the Trinity and of the Holy Ghost was not fully formed until the divinity of Christ was formally recognised. It may be viewed as the agency which, proceeding from Christ, informs his Church as its witness and power, or as an energy implying the presence of the deity. The question as to whether it proceeds from the Father alone, or from the Father and Son, ultimately caused the Greek and Roman Churches to separate.

HOLY GRAIL (*See* ARTHURIAN MYTH, CAULDRON, FISHER KING, GALAHAD, PERCEVAL, PHILOSOPHER'S STONE)

Cup, dish, stone or symbol? First mentioned in twelfth-century Europe, this mysterious relic of **Arthurian** myth was the dish (or a cup) used by Christ at the Last Supper, or a vessel containing his blood and sweat brought by **Joseph of Arimathea** to **Glastonbury**. Or it was a **stone**, the **Ark of the Covenant**, the Magdalene's womb, or **initiatory** vision of Christ. Which?

The word 'grail' may be from Greek *krater*, a mixing bowl. Latin *cratus* (or 'crater') gives the low Latin *craticula* or *gradella* (a 'grid' or 'grill'), or (medieval French) *greil*. Latin *cratis* also gives *gradalis*, in medieval French *calice* ('chalice') alias 'cauldron' or 'bowl'. Certainly, one strand of Grail-myth lies in older Celtic tales of a magic **cauldron** offering food without end (the **Dagda**'s cauldron), or a Brew of Inspiration (**Cerridwen**'s cauldron), or rebirth for dead warriors (**Bran**'s cauldron). So too the myth of Bran, whose decapitated head ensures fertility, originates the Arthurian tale of the wounded Fisher King who guards the Grail and whose unhealed wound means a sterile land ('Land and King are One'). The theme of the bowl that fertilises is also found much further afield, in the Indian myth of Amrita Surabhi, the Buddha's begging bowl which feeds the starving, heals those who touch it, and makes rain fall so that crops grow.[1]

Where, when, how, and why did the medieval theme originate? As the Saracens took Jerusalem, *c.*1180, Chrétien de Troyes penned the first Grail story: *Le Roman de Perceval* (*Le Conte del Graal*). Of the Court of Champagne (like Hugues de Payens, founder of the **Knights Templar**), he got his theme from Philippe d'Alsace, Count of Flanders. Set in the age of Arthur popularised by **Geoffrey of Monmouth**, it tells how Perceval (Son of the Widow Lady: a **Gnostic**, later **Freemason** term) leaves his widow mother to win his knighthood. The Fisher King offers him refuge in his castle. That night the Grail (golden, gem-studded, carried by a damsel) appears. Failing to ask who one serves with it, he awakes next day to find the castle empty and the land blighted by his omission. He learns he is of the Grail family and that the Fisher King, 'sustained' by the Grail, is his uncle. Christ is not mentioned (nor, in this or other versions of the time, is Galahad).

In *Le Roman de l'Estoire dou Saint Graal* (1190–1199), Robert de Boron calls the Grail the Cup of the Last Supper. In it Christ's blood is caught by Joseph of Arimathea, whose brother-in-law Brons takes it to England and becomes the Fisher King, Perceval's grandfather.

In the *Periesvaus* (1206–12: its unknown author perhaps a Templar), Sir **Gawain** enters a castle housing two masters and thirty-three other men 'clad in white garments' with red crosses on the breast: Templar garb. One master claims to have seen the Grail. The poem abounds in magical and Gnostic references – a good reason for anonymity. The crusade against the **Cathars** had begun, and the Templars too were suspect. Here the Grail is a set of visions: of a chalice ('calice') or candle ('chandoile') seemingly in the Grail; the **Holy Lance** from which blood flows; two **angels** carrying a gold candelabra with lighted candles; then three angels and the image of a child, again in the Grail; then a man on a cross, speared in his side – Christ crucified.[2]

The best-known Grail romance is *Parzival* (*c.*1195–1216), by the Bavarian Knight Wolfram von Eschenbach. He says Chrétien's account is false and that his version comes from Kyot de Provence (troubadour Guiot de Provins?), who got it from Spanish Moslem sources. He writes, 'The Grail is unknown save to those who have been called by name.' It is said to be a 'stone' (*lapsit exillas*: *see* **Philosopher's Stone**). He hints at the crucifixion and at a mission set for those called to serve it. A specific bloodline is involved. As in the *Perlesvaus*, it is knowledge, not an object. He speaks in riddles.

Some say that secretly Wolfram was a Cathar. These Provençal **dualists** remain popularly linked with Grail-myth. Montségur, their Pyrenean citadel which fell in 1244 to French and Papal forces, has been identified as the Grail Castle, Munsalvaesche (safe or wooded mountain). Yet so too has the unlocated Corbenic (in Britain?) and the Persian palace of Takt-i-Taqqis, built (seventh century) by Chosroes II on a site used for seasonal fertility rites. The mystery endures. It is said the Cathars had a treasure which was hidden and never found again. Was it what they called *pecuniam infinitam*, treasure both infinite and invisible – i.e., the Grail as an initiatory process?

Other tales involve Mary Magdalene. Gnostic texts (like *Pistis Sophia*) say that she was 'the disciple Jesus loved most'. Islamic lore says Jesus survived the crucifixion and lately it is claimed he came to Provence with the Magdalene, that the 'Grail' was her womb (cup) and its fruit the 'magical' Merovingian dynasty. Is *Sangraal* (womb; Holy Grail) also *sang raal* (royal blood of Jesus) and the Grail-bearer the Magdalene?[3]

Some say that the Grail was a casket containing something that cured or inspired – perhaps the 'severed head' the Knights Templar were said to worship? In the *Mabinogion*, Peredur (Welsh Perceval) sees two maidens enter a hall, 'bearing a large platter with a man's head covered with blood on it.' In the *Perlesvaus* (see above), Gawain sees a 'chalice' (*un calice*) or a 'candle' (*une chandoile*) within the Grail. If the Grail is a chalice, why is a second chalice in it? Others say that the Grail (casket) contained an image of Christ's head (see **Shroud of Turin**), that the Templars possessed both Shroud and Grail, and that the image was what they venerated.[4]

Another recent claim is that the Grail was (is) the Jewish Ark of the Covenant, that potent casket containing the stone tablets on which the Ten Commandments were inscribed, long-lost yet now said to be held in the city of Axum in Ethiopia.[5] The mystery will doubtless persist.

1. *Indian Mythology*, Jan Knappert, Aquarian Press, London, 1991.
2. *King Arthur and the Grail*, Richard Cavendish, Paladin, London, 1980.
3. *The Holy Blood and the Holy Grail*, Michael Baigent, Richard Leigh and Henry Lincoln, Corgi, London, 1983.
4. *The Shroud and the Grail*, Noel Currer-Briggs, Weidenfeld & Nicolson, London, 1987.
5. *The Sign and the Seal*, Graham Hancock, Heinemann, London, 1992.

HOLY LANCE (*See* CHRISTIANITY, GALAHAD, HOLY GRAIL, LUG)

Closely associated with the Holy Grail, the Holy **Lance** appears in origin to have been the lightning spear of the **Irish** sun-god Lug, famed for its destructiveness. The older myth is that Lug sent three heroes to seize it from its owner, King Pisear. They found it with its head in a **cauldron** of water, boiling and hissing because of its heat. (The sexual connotation is obvious.)

In other old Irish accounts what appears to be the same blazing spear (lightning flash) stands in a cauldron of blood. This weapon appears cognate with the thunderbolt, hammer or 'sky-axe' wielded by storm- and sky-gods from **Thor** to **Indra** and **Zeus**. Until lately it was popularly said in Greece that lightning flashes are caused by the blows of the 'sky-axe'.

In **Christian** Grail tradition the Holy Lance, dripping blood into the Grail, is identified as the spear the Roman soldier Longinus thrust into the side of Christ as he hung on the cross, 'and at once there came out blood and water'. This relic was said to have been miraculously found at Antioch in 1098, during the First Crusade. Its discovery in the Church of St Peter followed a priestly vision and so heartened the besieged Crusaders that they stormed from the city to rout the Saracens. So it is said.[1]

It may also be this lance which, thrust through both his thighs, led to the wounding of the **Fisher King** and to the death of **Perceval**'s father.

Much complex mythology was more recently woven about this 'Spear of Destiny' by the German composer Richard **Wagner** and later by the **Nazis**.[2]

1. *King Arthur and the Grail*, Richard Cavendish, Paladin, London, 1980.
2. *The Spear of Destiny*, Trevor Ravenscroft.

HOMER (*See* GREEK MYTH, HESIOD, *ILIAD*, *ODYSSEY*, SHAKESPEARE)

Who was Homer? When did he live? The problem is like that faced by those scholars who try to decide if Shakespeare was Shakespeare or someone else. Yet in both cases the author's original identity matters less than the fact that Shakespearean drama and Homeric epic both exist. Somebody wrote them. That is what counts. Yet the myth of an author's identity can be as potent as the work: so here we explore not Homer's work but the myth of Homer himself, the myth of the 'blind' poet who birthed the modern world.

Homer is the name given by the ancient Greeks themselves to the author not only of *The Iliad* and *The Odyssey* but of many other works. Yet as early as the fourth century BC these two poems alone were considered as Homeric, i.e., as incorporating the moral, poetic, practical and heroic themes that formed the basis of Classical Greek culture. Their power is such that they have retained their impact ever since. Homer, whoever he was, is not only one of the world's great literary artists, but among the most influential.

Relating events dated thirteenth century BC, just before pre-Greek Mycenaean society collapsed, *The Iliad* tells of the decade-long siege of Troy by the (Mycenaean) Greeks after the abduction of **Helen**. *The Odyssey* concerns the long homeward journey, after the war, of the **hero Odysseus** (Ulysses).

It is now thought unlikely that Homer lived during or even soon after the events he described: the consensus is that he was a professional **bard** or *rhapsode* who composed his epics *c*.850 BC, maybe a century before **Hesiod**. The historian Herodotus, writing *c*.450 BC, claims that neither of these poets could have lived more than 400 years before his own lifetime.

Yet, given that, before Heinrich Schliemann excavated Troy (1870–2), few thought Homeric epic historical at all, and given that one age's dates are usually dismissed by the next, it is hard to assign any firm date. Grammatical structure and other internal evidence suggests a date between 1000 BC (earliest) and 800 BC (latest), but who is to say that the original oral epics were not later grammatically restyled when first written down?

Likewise, the description of Homer as 'blind' (about all we know of him) may also be unreliable, or purely metaphoric, given that 'blindness' in the context of poets, prophets or seers (*see* **Tiresias**) is often used to mean that those possessing poetic vision are 'blind' to the outer world.

References to Homer go back to the mid-seventh century BC, but information about the man himself is absent. The dialect of the poems suggests he came from Ionia (the central part of Turkey's western coast), but even in classical times no authentic local memory survived of him. This is odd. Though he may have worked orally as a *rhapsode* or *aiodos* (singer), the complexity and length of his epics implies that, despite the greater skill in the art of memory possessed by preliterate folk, somebody (if not Homer himself) must have written them down. There is too much internal consistency to suggest a group effort, though given differences in genre between the two epics (*Iliad* martial and heroic; *Odyssey* picaresque and fantastic), doubts were raised early as to whether the same author composed both poems. In the fourth century Aristotle suggested that *The Iliad* was a product of Homer's earlier or middle life, *The Odyssey* of his late life. Despite all the scholarship on the subject, nobody has resolved these questions. The fact is that Homer remains known only through the power of Homeric epic.

Thus the man remains as mythical (and as fascinating) as his work.

HOPI LORE (*See* CREATION MYTH, FETISH, NATIVE AMERICAN MYTH)

The westernmost of the Pueblo (village-dwelling) tribes of North America, this deeply religious people (the name 'Hopi' means 'peace') have inhabited the desert region of Arizona since early times. Even their neighbours, the **Navaho**, are relative newcomers, said to have entered the continent via the 'Back Door' (Bering Strait).

The Hopi **creation myth** tells of three worlds before this, the Fourth World (as in **Hindu** cosmology: *see* **Golden Age**). In the beginning Taiowa the Unmanifest made Sótuknang to create the material universe. He created **Spider** Woman, **Mother Earth**, who gave birth to the people of the First World (Tokpela, 'Endless Space'). The door in the top of their heads was open to wisdom; they knew no sickness. But language was invented; the animals drew away from them and they from each other. So Sótuknang destroyed Tokpela with fire, but the people survived underground with the ants. Entering the Second World, Tokpa (Dark Midnight), they found it not so lovely, nor was the door atop their heads so open. They began to trade; evil spread, so Sótuknang told the Twins of the North and South Poles to leave their posts. The earth rolled over twice: the sea invaded the land. Again the folk survived with the ants, to enter the Third World (Kuskurza). Building cities, they became materialistic. There was a great war. Flying machines (*pátuwvotas*) attacked enemy cities. So Sótuknang sent the **flood**. Continents sank, but the folk survived in hollow reeds floating on the seas. Seeking land, they sent out birds which returned, exhausted. But Spider Woman brought them to the Fourth World, Túwaqachi (World Complete): they landed on the Pacific coast. The **giant** Másaw, guardian of the lands, said they could stay, but must make a pilgrimage. Másaw broke in four pieces a tablet of stone. Each piece sent the white, black, yellow and red races in different directions, one day to reunite. So they went their ways. First to return and find the desert homeland, the Hopi awaited the **prophecy**'s fulfilment. But when the White Brother (Pahana) returned, he had forgotten. He brought fire, sword and cruelty. He had forgotten everything. This too was in the prophecy.

The Hopi have long foretold a war begun by 'old countries, which first received the light of knowledge' (Middle Eastern nations?). This will be 'a spiritual conflict with material matters'. A 'Gourd of Ashes', dropped from the sky, will boil the oceans and burn the lands. Then Hopi ceremonial will cease. Yet in the dire time of the Great Purification, marked by the appearance of a 'blue star', Pahana will return, bringing the dawn of the Fifth World to the 'safe' lands of the Southwest.

The Hopi prophecies are carved on Black Mesa in the Four Corners area. The petroglyphs are dated to at least 2,000 years ago. Three signs – **swastika, sun** and the colour red – were given to signal the approach of the Great Purification. Then the Hopi would release their prophecies and teachings in a final effort to avert disaster. This has now been done.

The basis of Hopi religion is the cult of the kachinas, 'Cloud People', beings embodying the spirits of living things and those of Hopi **ancestors**. Ensuring soil-fertility and said to possess powers over the weather, over 500 have been identified. Carved kachina dolls are used to teach children about these spirits, invoked by **dances** in which those impersonating the kachinas are said to become the kachina involved. **Fetishism?** This depends on whether or not the kachina dolls are seen to be imbued with the kachina-spirits, or merely as representing them – perhaps academic.[1]

1. *Book of the Hopi*, Frank Waters, Penguin, London, 1977.

HORAE (*See* GREEK MYTH)
Greek climatic divinities (their name signifies a period of time; either the year, the seasons or the hours of the day) initially symbolising the fertilising rain showering the earth, so that fruit blossomed and ripened. So they symbolised spring and summer, but later governed the seasons as a whole. Depicted as maidens holding the fruits of the earth, they numbered three – Dike, Irene and Eunomia – and came to guard not only the natural but the moral order. **Hesiod** says that they 'mellowed the behaviour of men'. Daughters of **Zeus** and Themis, as protectors of children they nurtured **Hera**, swaddled **Hermes** and received **Dionysus** from the thigh of Zeus.

HÖRBIGER, HANS (1860–1931) (*See* NAZI MYTH)

HORNED GODS (*See* CONCORDANCE)
Horns as such represent masculine virility (phallus; as in the slang term 'horny'); or, if receptive and hollow, feminine or lunar fertility (horns are attributes of all mother-goddesses: **Hathor, Isis, Nuit**). The Horn of Plenty or **cornucopia** carried by **Priapus** implies both attributes. Worn on helmets or the head (as by **Amon, Anu, Ashur, Bel**), horns once implied both the manifestation of divine spirit and the royal power and generosity of the wearer. **Pagan** horned gods (**Cernunnos, Herne**) represent warriors, fecundity and the lordship of animals – typically **bull, goat, ram** or **stag** – and as such were demonised by the **Christian** Church, which adapted the horned god into the lustful, bestial Goat of Mendes, alias the **Devil** – a symbol perhaps chiefly derived from horned **Pan** and his **satyrs**.

So in England, by the Middle Ages, horns no longer signified generosity or virility, but disgrace, contempt and cuckoldry.

HORSE (*See* CONCORDANCE)
Early empires were won by nomadic tribes who, mastering the art of taming and riding the horse, then of fighting from horseback, were unstoppable. They could cover distance faster than their pedestrian opponents, remain stronger and strike from greater height. On settling their conquered land, the horse aided both the hunt and the cultivation of land.

Thus no surprise that the mythic importance of the horse is vast and ambiguous. In its fleetness and power, anciently represented as drawing the sun's chariot (**Helios**), or as the steed of the **sea-gods**, the horse is in one context a symbol of animal power controlled by superior intelligence.

Thus Buddha left his home on a white horse; in the *Bhagavad Gita* the central dialogue is between the warrior **Arjuna** and the god **Krishna**, his charioteer. Mastery of the 'horse' implies human mastery of emotion.

Yet the horse also symbolises death or chthonic forces when ridden by the **Devil** or by the **Wild Hunt**. A team of horses out-running their driver (**Phaethon**), or leading their rider to disaster (**Bellerophon**) symbolises the unyoked powers of the mind, or the immature pride or ambition of any mortal reaching too high. The four horses of the **Apocalypse** are famine, pestilence, death and war. The 'Nightmare' survives as the term for a bad **dream** over which the sleeping conscious mind has no control. The black horse, used to draw the funeral cortège, symbolises death and chaos.

Replacing the **bull** as a **sacrificial** animal from India to Ireland, the horse was also worshipped in the form of Celtic goddesses like **Rhiannon** or **Epona**. Well into **Christian** times, Irish coronations required the new king first to crawl naked towards a white mare as if he were her foal, then to bathe in and drink the broth of that mare and eat her flesh. Many similar fertility rites were practised in ancient India, Greece, Persia and Rome. A horse was offered to **Diana** at the August harvest festival: another Roman horse sacrifice occurred on 15 October as an offering to **Mars**, the blood being preserved until April when, mixed by virgins with calves' blood, it was given to shepherds to increase their flocks. The Scythians offered horses to their gods of fertility and the dead. The Patagonians sacrificed horses to **tree** spirits; similar rites were found elsewhere.

HORUS (*See* EGYPTIAN MYTH, HAWK, ISIS, OSIRIS, SET)

Egyptian falcon-god. When her jealous brother Set killed her husband and brother Osiris and scattered his dismembered body throughout Egypt, Isis found every piece but for the phallus (swallowed by a **crocodile**), yet from the dead god she conceived Horus. She bore him while hiding from Set in the Nile delta swamps. Forced to leave him to go about the Two Lands disguised as a beggar-woman, she returned to find him bitten by a **snake** (which was Set). She asked the sky to stop the Boat of the Sun, from which **Thoth** came down in a hurry as the Boat could not wait long. Cured by Thoth, Horus grew up and fought Set. He wrenched off Set's testicles, and Set tore out Horus' left **eye** and threw it into outer darkness, but wise Thoth turned it into the full **moon**. Alternatively, the other gods made Set return Horus his eye, but Horus gave it to Osiris, himself adopting the divine serpent that became emblematic of Egyptian royalty. So this falcon-headed **sky-** or **sun-god** (his other eye representing the sun) succeeded Osiris, the older vegetation deity.

This myth and its variants appear to be pre-dynastic – at least 3000 BC. It suggests ancient identification of the high-flying falcon with the sky (the Egyptian name 'Hor' resembles the word for 'sky'). But the attributes of Horus vary confusingly. The Horus of this tale (Greek Harsiesis, 'Horus son of Isis', infant avenger of his father, Osiris the dead god) is Horus the Younger. Horus the Elder (Har Wer: Greek Haroeris), an older sky-god, was reckoned as the son of (so the same as) **Ra** the sun-god, not Osiris.

In Greek myth identified with **Apollo**, and shown as a youth born with a finger to his lips as a sign of **Mystery**, Horus survived via **Neoplatonic** mysticism to become a potent **hermetic** symbol: falcon-god of youth, his piercing eye (the Eye of Ra) epitomising searching intelligence.

HOTTENTOTS (*See* AFRICAN MYTH, BUSHMEN)

Ex-nomads of the Namibian desert in south-west Africa, the Khoi (their own name) are distinct from the San, or Bushmen. Their supreme god Tsunigoam ('Wounded Knee', now pronounced 'Tsuigoab') got his name when warring against the black god Gaunab. Each time Gaunab threw him to the ground, like the **giant** Antaeus (*see* **Hercules**) he arose strengthened by the contact. Gaunab was expelled to the Black Heaven, but first wounded Tsuigoab in the knee. So, like the Greek **Hephaestus**, Tsuigoab has since walked with a limp.

Or his name may come from *tsu* ('red' or 'bleeding') and *goa* ('dawn') thus making him 'Red Dawn': the God of Light who daily defeats Gaunab, God of Night, after a fierce, bloody struggle. Another benevolent sky-god was thunder-voiced Utixo, who sent rain for the crops.[1]

Of many fearsome **monsters**, Hai-uri is one-legged, one-armed, one-sided and semi-**invisible**, leaping over bushes to catch his human prey. With eyes in their insteps, the cannibal Aigamuxa have to get down on hands and knees and hold up one foot to see anything.

Ga-gorib, 'thrower-down', sat on the edge of a pit daring men to throw stones at him. These rebounded to hit the thrower and cast him into the pit. Ga-gorib was defeated only by the **hero** Heitsi-eibib. Born of a **cow** which had eaten miraculous grass, this great magician refused combat until, distracting the monster, he threw his stone and tumbled Ga-gorib into the pit.

Though often killed, Heitsi-eibib was always reborn. The Hottentots say all early men arose again from the dead until one day the **moon** sent **Hare** to tell men they would live forever. Confused, Hare told men the opposite, whereupon the furious moon split its lip with a fierce blow. Since then, mortality has prevailed, save for heroes like Heitsi-eibib.

1. *African Mythology*, Jan Knappert, Aquarian Press, Wellingborough, 1990.

HOUND (*See* DOG, WILD HUNT)

HSI WANG MU (*See* BUDDHISM, CHINESE MYTH, HEAVEN)

In Chinese mythology as elsewhere, the realm of the dead is located in the west, the Land of the Setting Sun. The souls of the just, if not returned to life immediately, go either to the K'un-Lun mountain where the Immortals dwell, or to the Amitabha Buddha in the Land of Extreme Felicity in the west. Yet K'un Lun also lies in the west, and is ruled by Hsi Wang Mu, the Lady Queen of the West. As wife of the august personage of **Jade**, she is the Queen Mother of Heaven.

Her nine-storeyed palace of jade dominates the summit of the mountain, with wonderful gardens about it, in which grows the Peach Tree of Immortality. Here live the Immortals, banqueting forever. As for the Land of Extreme Felicity in the West, this (like the **Celtic** Land of Youth or the **Greek** Garden of the **Hesperides**) is almost as entrancing – ever-flowering, offering all delights.

HSIEN (*See* CHINESE MYTH, IMMORTALITY, SOMA, TAOISM)

In the fourth century BC tales of a drug-plant (Soma) conferring immortality or longevity reached China from India or perhaps Mesopotamia, where in the early *Epic of Gilgamesh* the hero found on the sea-bed such a plant, called 'The Old Man grows Young'. Alchemical experimentation followed, leading to popular belief in the existence of *Hsien* ('Immortals') who in early texts were depicted as feathered men and were said to have found the elixir of life, thus surviving in material but 'lightened' form.

Just as, today, some seek longevity via scientific or pseudo-scientific means ('cryogenics'), so the Chinese approach was not so much 'religious' as pragmatic and technical. In the third century, the **Taoist** alchemist Ho Kung speaks of two types of elixir. One restrains the flight of the *pho* ('**soul**'; animating principle of the body which, being *yin*, or of earth, perishes when the body dies); the other recalls the *hun* ('**spirit**', *yang*, sky-descended, and returning to the sky when the body dies). Those who mastered the *hun* elixir, he wrote, might raise their embodied souls to a state of celestial immortality, or *t'ien hsien*; while those mastering the lesser *pho* elixir would become *ti hsien*, terrestrial immortals.

It is said Ho Kung succeeded in preparing the elixir and tested it on a dog, which dropped dead. Unbelievably self-confident, he then took it himself. He too dropped dead. Yet amid the funeral preparations both he and the dog returned to life. So says the myth.

Subsequent popular Taoist belief in the *t'ien hsien* led to a mythology dominated by the *San Ch'in*, or 'Three Purities'. First is Yuan-shih, son of P'an-ku, the primeval man, and T'ai-yuan, the holy woman. Second is Wu Wang, who in 1027 BC overthrew the tyrant Chou Hsin. Third is **Lao Tsu**, the legendary founder of Taoism. These are joined by other legendary men and women who, by strict preparation, succeeded in overcoming death.

HUANG-TI (*See* CHINESE MYTH, *HSIEN*, LAO TSU, TAOISM)

Legendary for his benevolent rule and the quest that made him a *hsien* ('Immortal'), the myth of Huang Ti ('Yellow Emperor') grew in the fourth century BC. *The Book of Lieh-tzu* (second century BC?) tells how thirty years of his kind but dissipated rule led the land to disorder and himself into stupefaction. Realising this, he left state affairs to his ministers and dismissed his attendants. Fasting in a hut in his courtyard, one day while asleep he dreamed of the **otherworld** kingdom of Hua-hsu, mother of Fu Hsi, the legendary emperor. This kingdom of the soul needed no ruler, its populace being without sensual desires, cravings or attachments.

Awakening, he told his ministers that The Way, Tao, 'cannot be sought through the senses. I know it, I have found it, but I cannot tell it to you.' Thus enlightened, he brought order to the land, ruling for another twenty-eight years before rising into the sky as a *hsien*. He is said not only to have been a great teacher and innovator, inventing the compass and the coining of money, but also to have been a great hero, defeating rebels and monsters alike. Here again we meet the **Grail** proposition that 'land and king are One.' For, once the emperor regained his higher senses, the society prospered. After his death, he was mourned for two centuries.

HUITZILOPOCHTLI (*See* AZTEC MYTH, COATLICUE, SUN-GODS)

This bloodthirsty Aztec war-god, son of the hideous **Coatlicue**, was born fully armed in blue armour, a blue javelin in his left hand, humming-bird feathers decorating his head (thus his name: 'Blue Humming-bird on the Left'). Immediately he slew his sister, Coyolxauhqui, and the Centzon-Huitznahuas, his four hundred brothers, for plotting against Coatlicue.

Huitzilopochtli had two sides. One was that of Xochipilli, lord of flowers and guardian of souls, requiring flowers, incense and food for his sacrificial offerings. Yet as the young solar warrior reborn each day in **blood** and **fire**, his appetite for human flesh was equalled only by his mother. 'My mission and my task is war,' he told the Aztecs as they began their conquest of Mexico. After that conquest, with the island capital of Teotihuacan (now Mexico City) established (1325), the Aztecs embarked on further wars solely to seize victims to feed their hungry god. Scant years before Cortes arrived (1519), the dedication of Teotihuacan's new Temple of the Sun required the sacrifice to Huitzilopochtli of an estimated 70,000 victims. Each, led up the Temple pyramid, had their heart torn out at the top. The killings took three short days. The priests at the sacrificial stone atop the new pyramid had to work overtime; so too did the butchers as the meat was rolled down to them.

The Spaniards, conquering by means hardly less appalling, were shocked by what they found. What were good European Christians to do, but rid the land of such evil by fire and sword? Which they proceeded to do. Thus was Huitzilopochtli defeated. Or was he?[1]

1. *Cannibals and Kings*, Marvin Harris, Random House, New York, 1977.

HUNAB KU (*See* **FLOOD, MAYAN MYTH**)

HUVEANE (*See* **AFRICAN MYTH**)
The **creator**-deity of the Bapedi and Bavendu peoples in Lesotho, South Africa, ensured his privacy in a novel manner. Having finished making both sky and earth, he climbed into the sky by driving pegs in it to give him footholds, then pulled out each behind him to stop human beings from following. He still lives up there. In some tales he is the first man, and in others he is a **trickster**-god with magical powers.

HY-BRASIL (*See* **LOST WORLDS**)
From **Atlantis** to **Ys** or **Tir nan Og**, the idea of a land beyond the Western Ocean long attracted the European imagination. Whether this idea was purely mythic (in the sense of imaginary: referring to the Land of the Dead beyond the Sunset, the Land of Immortality) or had some basis in ancient records remains unclear. The **Phoenicians** may have reached South America over two millennia ago: medieval sea-charts (*portolans*) and maps like that ascribed to the sixteenth-century Turkish admiral Piri ibn-Haji Memmed (Piri Re'is) indicate an ancient knowledge of global geography. Claiming that some of his source maps had been drawn in the time of **Alexander the Great**, Piri Re'is drew Antarctica as an unglaciated river-rift land, even though Antarctica was not officially discovered until 1818, three centuries later.

The name given to one such 'imaginary' western land, 'Hy-Brasil', led to the naming of what is today South America's largest state, Brazil (though when 'discovered' in AD 1500 by Cabral he named it Tierra da Vera Cruz).

1. *Maps of the Ancient Sea Kings*, Charles Hapgood, Chilton, USA, 1966.

HYADES (*See* **ASTRONOMY AND MYTH, DIONYSUS, GREEK MYTH**)

HYDRA (*See* **FABULOUS BEASTS, DRAGON, GREEK MYTH, HERCULES**)
With **Cerberus** and the **chimera** said to have been part of the monstrous brood that the sea-nymph Echidna bore to **Typhon**, in Greek myth it is said

that the Hydra of Lerna was a water-beast with a dog-like body and eight or nine heads (some say fifty, a hundred, or even ten thousand), its breath so venomous as to kill any who sniffed it. Perhaps originally a metaphor for underground rivers bursting forth to inundate the land, the destruction of this monster, which terrorised the region, was the task set **Hercules** as his second labour. Forcing it out of its lair by firing burning arrows at it, he held his breath while trying to strangle it, but it kept tripping him up. Every time he cut off one of its heads, two more grew. A huge crab nipped his heel, he crushed it: the goddess **Juno** (who had reared the Hydra to menace Hercules) later put it in the heavens as the constellation Cancer. Meanwhile the charioteer Iolaus set the forest ablaze: Hercules triumphed by searing each neck after decapitation with burning brands. The last, immortal, head he buried under a great boulder, where it remains. Then he soaked his arrows in the hydra's poisonous blood. Later, he too was slain by poisoned blood.

The ambiguous nature of **dragon blood** that both kills and cures is a common motif in **hero myth**, from the tale of **Siegfried** to that of the **Medusa**. **Sun-gods** are forever slaying watery chaos-**serpents**: neither ever quite conquers the other; each has its annual or cosmic season of power. The motif of the malign water-spirit is equally common. The **kelpie** (water-**horse**) of **Celtic** folklore is one equivalent, requiring offerings if it is not to flood land or drown people. The Waterlord of Mali in south Saharan Africa is a dragon that destroys yet fertilises. Seven-headed, he claims the child of a woman who comes to him for protection against her enemies, dragging this child when born down to the bottom of the river to live with him. Yet when the girl, Jinde Sirende (the 'One Whom the Water Spirit will Claim') begs him to let her go for one last day to see the sun, he lets her. Both her mother and her mother's new husband refuse to admit her – but her lover fights for her, destroying the monster, slashing off all its **seven** heads and thus releasing her.

Another myth of regeneration: of youth claiming its birthright in spite of the dragon of tradition and tribal conformity.

HYENA (*See* AFRICAN MYTH, SHAPE-SHIFTING)

Three species of this powerful dog-like African carnivore are scavengers; the fourth, the spotted hyena, hunts in packs and is bold enough to attack travellers at night. The Sudanese say that **sorcerers** use hyenas to hunt down their enemies. Some in East Africa say the glowing spirits of the dead may be seen in the luminous eyes of the hyena that ate them: others claim that their **ancestors** ride hyenas by night to visit living relatives. Zimbabwean witches are also said to ride the hyena: Zambian sorcerers take hyena form to devour their victims. In Mali, evil spirits called Hyena men take human or hyena form at will to hunt and eat people and their animals. Few hunters can escape the hyena men who, protected by **talismans**, are too wary to be ambushed. One way to kill a hyena man is by persuading a lovely woman to lie down naked before him, so hypnotising him that he may be shot. Few hyena men are other than wicked, but the tale is told in Mali of a poor man who, to feed his large family, nightly changed into a hyena and went hunting. Growing old, he changed his eldest son into a hyena, telling him to do the hunting. But then he died, leaving the boy without the magic formula to regain human form. This innocent new hyena man howled so sadly by night that the villagers took pity on him and started feeding him.[1]

1. *African Mythology*, Jan Knappert, Aquarian Press, Wellingborough, 1990.

HYPERBOREA (*See* **ABAROS**)

HYPERION (*See* **GREEK MYTH, HELIOS,** *ODYSSEY*)
Father of the Greek **sun-god Helios** and rosy-fingered Eos of the dawn, with
his wife Theia placed in charge of the sun by **Gaia**, it was said that Hyperion
('Dweller on High') was every night blinded by his enemies but at dawn
restored to sight. Later absorbed by or identified with his son, as Hyperion
he kept seven large herds of cattle on Sicily. When during his wanderings the
hero Odysseus landed on Sicily, he made his men swear not to steal a single
cow. But when after thirty days the south wind still refused to let them go
and their provisions had run out, several of them, with Odysseus asleep,
slaughtered a number of cows and had a feast. Hyperion complained to **Zeus**
who, when he saw that Odysseus' ship was at sea again, sent a storm in which
the ship sank, all but Odysseus being drowned.

HYPNOS (*See* **DREAMS, GREEK MYTH, HADES, UNDERWORLD**)
Son of Night, Hypnos ('Sleep') lived with his brother Thanatos ('Death') in
Hades, whence he issued forth to put men to rest by touching them with his
magic **wand** or by fanning them with his dark wings. **Homer** in *The Iliad*
describes him as originally being a man who, to escape the wrath of **Zeus**,
turned himself into a bird and fled the daylight to seek refuge with Night.
His three sons, Morpheus, Phobetor and Phantasos, sent dreams to human
beings, animals and inanimate forms respectively. As the bringer of sleep,
Hypnos was regarded as comforting rather than terrible: Thanatos, though
more fearful, was also commonly seen as a bringer of comfort.

I

IBIS (*See* **EGYPTIAN MYTH**)
In ancient Egypt this long-billed water-bird, sacred to **Thoth** the scribe-god (who was represented with the head of an ibis), symbolised the winged dawn, the flight of the **soul**. As a destroyer of reptiles, the crested ibis symbolised the **sun** in the boat ('The Boat of Millions of Years') on which Thoth daily rode the heavens. Yet as a water-bird it was also lunar, and was sometimes shown with the crescent moon on its head.

ICARUS (*See* **DAEDALUS, GREEK MYTH, SUN**)

ICON (*See* **ART AND MYTH, BLACK VIRGIN, IDOL**)
Refers to any image, statue, painting or mosaic which, depicting saint or god, is itself regarded as sacred or supernaturally potent. From the Greek *eikon* ('image'), icons are mainly associated with the Eastern **Christian** Church (Greek and Russian Orthodox), but are also found in Catholic churches, usually in the form of images of the **Virgin Mary**. Images of the Black Virgin, usually discreetly placed, are prayed to by pregnant women.

Icons have long been rejected by those (like Protestant reformers or orthodox Muslims) who insist that deity must never be depicted. Thus the term 'iconoclast' – one who breaks images – originally from a movement in the Eastern Church (eighth–ninth centuries) to destroy all such images. More broadly, an iconoclast is one who attacks cherished beliefs.

IDOL (*See* **FETISH, ICON**)
From the Greek *eidolon*, 'phantom', an idol is any image of deity used as an object of worship. The **Bible** (Exodus xxxii) tells how, with **Moses** up Mount **Sinai**, the Israelites demanded of his brother Aaron that he 'make us gods, which shall go before us'. So Aaron had them melt down their **gold** to make a golden calf, an idol, which they worshipped. Moses persuaded **Yahweh** not to destroy 'this stiffnecked people', but on descending his own wrath waxed hot when he saw the orgiastic revelry. Destroying the calf, he called on the Levites (the tribe of Yahweh's **mysteries**) to slaughter the idolators; 'and there fell of the people that day about three thousand men'.[1]

In **Hebrew** and **Christian** tradition thereafter, contempt was heaped on all idol-worship. Though in AD 601 Pope Gregory told Abbot Mellitus (about to evangelise **pagan** Britain) that the idols must be smashed, but that the temples should be sprinkled with holy water and converted to Christian use, in later times Christian missionaries smashed not just idols but temples too, even as idolatry persisted in Christianity itself. **Icons** are idols, but to see every carving of a god as implying literal belief in the carving as the god depicted is to suggest that Church art from Giotto onwards is 'idolatrous'.

1. Holy Bible (Revised Standard Edition), Exodus xxxii:28.

IFRIT (*See* **DEMONS, DJINNS, FAIRIES, ISLAM**)
Arabian evil spirit, associated with the djinns, from the word *nifrit* ('wicked').
The Koran (Sura 27, The Ant), tells how **Solomon**, desiring the throne of the
Queen of Sheba, was visited by 'an efreet of the jinns' who promised to
'bring it to thee . . . I have strength for it and I am trusty.'[1] Ifrits are
magically strong, but unreliable – why else would this Ifrit have insisted that
'I am trusty'? No Ifrit works for any man unprotected by Solomon's Seal
which, with God's secret name engraved on it, subdues all **demons** but Iblis
(**Azazel**, the **Devil**) himself. Like Gaelic **fairies**, they can not only marry and
have children but, taking human form, can mate with human beings. With
batlike wings, they rise from the ground amid black smoke. They kidnap
girls who sleep alone on the rooftop on hot nights. They are vengeful, easily
insulted and quick to wrath, but may be compassionate to human children.
The **Swahili** of southeast Africa, of mixed Arab–Bantu descent, speak of the
afriti as spirits inhabiting rivers where children swim, liable to seize
swimmers by the legs and drag them down (cramp).

1. Koran (trans. Arthur J. Arberry), OUP, 1964.

IGALUK (*See* **ESKIMO MYTH**)

ILIAD (*See* **GREEK MYTH, HOMER,** *ODYSSEY*)
Dramatising the last year of the decade-long Greek siege of Troy (now dated
thirteenth century BC), Homer drew his themes for *The Iliad* and its
successor, *The Odyssey*, from a body of epic tales then well known throughout
Greece (ninth century BC?). These included the *Argonautika*, the *Herakleia*
and the Trojan Cycle. The latter contains The Sack of Ilion, the Homecom-
ings and other tales, all thought mythic before Schliemann excavated Troy
(1870–82).
   In *The Iliad*, Homer tells how **Helen** is abducted by **Paris**, son of Priam,
King of Troy. The Greeks raise an army which, as *The Iliad* begins, has
besieged Troy for nine years. Having attacked a Trojan ally, the Greek
commander Agamemnon seizes a girl, Chryseis, refusing to release her when
her father, a priest of **Apollo**, tries to ransom her. Apollo sends a plague on
the Greeks who force Agamemnon to release Chryseis without ransom. But
Agamemnon seizes another girl, Bryseis, prize of **Achilles** who, outraged,
withdraws his men from the Greek army. Single combat between Paris and
Helen's husband, Menelaus, fails to resolve the war. The battle resumes.
Without Achilles, the Greeks find their own camp and ships besieged. The
Trojan commander, Hector, breaks through the defences and fires a Greek
ship. Persuaded to let his friend Patroclus rejoin the war, Achilles is outraged
when Hector kills Patroclus. Making up with Agamemnon, Achilles kills
Hector and drags the corpse behind his chariot in front of Troy. Priam, King
of Troy and Hector's father, begs back his son's body. *The Iliad* ends with an
uneasy truce for the funeral of Hector.[1]

1. *The Iliad*, Homer (trans. Robert Fitzgerald), OUP.

ILLUSION (*See* **FAIRIES, FAIRY-TALES, GLAMOUR,
SHAPE-SHIFTING**)

IMANA (*See* **AFRICAN MYTH**)
Meaning 'almighty', this supreme god of the Burundi in central Africa made
Kihanga, the first man. Zebra-striped black and white, he came from **heaven**

to earth like a spider down its thread, landing so hard that he bounced up and down: even today an earthquake is said to be 'Kihanga bouncing'. His children created the nations of Burundi: grandfather Imana often visited his people shaped as a young **ram** or a lamb. The Burundi hold the universe to be three-storeyed: beyond the rock of the visible sky is the realm of *ijuru*; below the earth is that called *ikuzimu*. This universe is gradually degenerating, and would collapse entirely without Imana to hold it up.

IMMORTALITY (*See* **CONCORDANCE**)
Belief in eternal life falls under four heads: (1) spiritual immortality; (2) immortality via reincarnation; (3) the immortality of culture heroes 'who are not dead but sleepeth'; (4) bodily immortality here on earth.

Most cultures hold that physical death is survived by the **'soul'** or **'spirit'**, and that our fate after death is decided by our acts during life. Egyptians believed that **Osiris** judged the spirits of the dead in the **underworld** – their cult of mummification implies an expectation that the soul (*see* **ka**) would in time reunite with the body. **Pythagoreans** believed in transmigration of souls. The **Celts** believed that heroes lived forever in the Isles of the Blessed. The Babylonians and Assyrians held that true immortality began with the **resurrection** of the body, the dead inhabiting a city called Sualu – analogous to the Hebrew **Sheol**. Hebrew lore also tells of immortality: the prophet **Enoch** 'walked with God and was not, for God took him'. The Greeks, though denying bodily resurrection, spoke of heroes gaining a place in the heavens as constellations. Christians believe in the resurrection of the spiritual body; **heaven** for the good, **hell** for the bad. So too Moslems envisage Paradise as reward for the righteous.

Buddhists and **Hindus** assert the doctrine of **reincarnation**, by which all mortals are continuously reborn until, attaining enlightenment, they abandon form and attain **samadhi**, union with the divine source.

Medieval heroes like King **Arthur** or **Charlemagne** were thought not to have died, but to be asleep, typically under a magic mountain.

Also, ancient myth tells how **Golden Age** folk lived longer, but that human evil led to a reduced lifespan. But it seems likely that **Methuselah** lived not 969 years, but 969 months (lunar years), i.e., eighty solar years. Yet the lack of evidence that immortality or even extended life is possible never stopped the search. From the tale of **Gilgamesh**, to that of the eighteenth-century Comte de Saint-Germain, the myth of immortals among us persists.

In 1926 rumour swept Paris that the alchemist Fulcanelli (author of *Le mystère des cathédrales*) had attained immortality. It was said that day by day he grew visibly younger. Nobody saw him, then or now. Now in the USA some folk pay vast sums so, when they die, their bodies may be frozen so that in the future a more sophisticated science will revive them.

Immortality is often seen not as boon but curse, as the **Wandering Jew** and the **Flying Dutchman** learned. Writers from Charles Maturin (*Melmoth the Wanderer*, 1820), **Rider Haggard** (*She*, 1887) and George Bernard Shaw (*Back to Methuselah*, 1921), to **Arthur C. Clarke** (*The City and the Stars*, 1956), typically conclude that, while the desire for immortality is natural enough, the condition itself must inevitably lead to boredom, sterility and despair.

INANNA (*See* **MOTHER-GODDESS, MYSTERIES, SUMERIAN MYTH**)
Queen of Heaven and Earth in early Sumerian myth, this mother-goddess (the daughter of **Enlil**) was identified with the planet **Venus** and as such with

fertility and love. The Babylonian **Ishtar** and Egyptian **Isis** both derive from her, while the descent of the Greek **Persephone** into **Hades** echoes the descent by Inanna into 'the land without return', ruled by **Ereshkigal**, 'mistress of death', her hostile sister. Leaving behind her servant Ninshubur to rescue her should she not return, obliged at each of the seven gates leading into the **underworld** to take off an ornament or garment, at last she comes naked before Ereshkigal and the Seven Judges of the Dead. She is slain and hung on a stake. After three days and nights Ninshibur beseeches the gods for help. The water-god **Enki** creates two sexless beings which, entering the sexless Land of the Dead, restore Inanna to the world. But **demons** go with her, refusing to leave unless a substitute is found. In Uruk she finds her husband Dumuzi: demon-seized, he takes her place in the underworld.

INCA MYTH (*See* SOUTH AMERICAN MYTH)

Dominating Peru from the twelfth century until Pizarro's conquest (1531), the Inca dynasty was founded by the legendary Manco Capac. One myth tells how the sun-god Inti, taking pity on humanity, sent down to an isle in Lake Titicaca his son Manco Capac and his daughter Mama Ocilo, ordering them north with a wedge of gold, to settle wherever this sank into the ground. The event occurred at what became the city of Cuzco.

Another tale is of four brothers and four sisters wandering the land, seeking a place to settle. The eldest brother claimed all the land for himself. The youngest, Manco Capac, decided to kill the other three. He walled the eldest into a mountain cave then, pretending to search for him, lured the next eldest up the mountain, threw him over a cliff and turned him into a stone. The third fled in terror. Manco Capac built Cuzco with his sisters, one of whom he married.

The Incas replaced the land's old **totemism** with worship of **sun** and **moon**, and the stars as lesser deities. They believed that above the earth lie four heavens inhabited by gods. The sun-god Inti, their **ancestor** who had sent them to earth to create society, was portrayed in human form, his face a gold disc with rays and flames about it. Daily, crossing the sky, he would plunge into the sea, partly drying it up with his heat, then return east by swimming under the earth to rise again refreshed. As kind and generous as his moon-wife, Mama Quilla (protectress of married women, portrayed as a silver disc with human features), solar eclipses indicated his rage. His sacred **fire** was kept by the Aclla, 'Virgins of the Sun', who were buried alive if convicted of relations with men. But if they could prove that they were pregnant, this was supposedly Inti's doing and they were spared.

No Inca deity was as vicious as the **Aztec** gods, but human sacrifice occurred annually at festivals honouring Inti, Pachacamac and Viracocha; two or three children and many animals being slain. Children were also offered to Catequil, the storm-god, who carried a sling and a mace. **Venus** was worshipped as Chasca, the long-haired star, protectress of flowers and girls. Other planets and stars were regarded as maids-in-waiting to the moon: the **Pleiades** protected cereals. Also revered were the fire-god Nina and the earth-goddess Pachamama, today identified with the **Virgin Mary**.

Two older gods annexed by the Incas were Pachacamac ('Earth-Maker') and Viracocha. Considered supreme by Peru's coastal population and so once a sea-god, Pachacamac became a fire-god, teaching arts and crafts to the men made by Viracocha. Said to be **invisible**, he could not be represented in any form. Viracocha, the rain-god said to live in Lake Titicaca, became the supreme being who made the earth, sky, stars and mankind. Angered by the first men (probably **giants**) he sent a deluge to destroy them – again, the **flood myth**. Wandering the earth as a beggar weeping at the plight of his children, his sister-wife was Mama Cocha (rain and water).

Inca cosmology describes five world ages. First was that of Viracocha, when the gods ruled and there was no death; second, the age of giants who worshipped Viracocha; third, of primitive men; fourth, of the *auca runa* ('warriors') who preceded the Inca; and fifth, of the Inca, ruling from the city of Cuzco and ended by the Spanish conquest. Viracocha is said to have disappeared west over the Pacific.

INCEST

Carnal intercourse between close kindred – brother and sister, or child and parent – was once a capital offence in England. The forbidden degrees of relationship as given in the Bible (Leviticus xviii) include relatives with whom there is no actual consanguinity, such as an uncle's wife. Incest has everywhere been condemned for weakening the blood and destroying social relations. Yet many **creation myths** involve incest, if only due to the problems inherent in explaining the initial generation of things. From **Adam** in **Eden** to the Tahitian creator 'Mighty Ta'aroa', primeval being procreates with itself. Dividing into male and female to procreate, its first generation necessarily mates incestuously. Thus Egyptian **Isis** marries her brother **Osiris**, Phoenician **Baal** marries his mother Anat (**Astarte**), Greek **Gaia** mates with **Ouranos** her son to bear the twelve **Titans**, and so on.

Yet the human revulsion commonly felt against incest is expressed in the Greek tale of Oedipus, after whom **Sigmund Freud**, proposing that all children secretly desire the parent of the opposite sex and hate the parent (competitor) of the same sex, named his so-called Oedipus complex.

As an infant exposed to die on a mountainside by Laius his father, king of Thebes, Oedipus ('Swollen Foot') is saved by a shepherd and brought to Corinth. Ignorant of his true parents, he asks the **Delphic Oracle** about his future. 'Away from the shrine, wretch!' the Pythoness cries. 'You will kill your father and marry your mother!' To avoid this disaster, he leaves Corinth for Thebes, en route slaying Laius in a fight. Still unaware that Laius was his father, he reaches Thebes where, freeing the city from the tyranny of the **Sphinx**, he is made king, and innocently marries the widowed Jocasta, his mother. When the blind seer **Tiresias** reveals the truth, Jocasta hangs herself: Oedipus blinds himself with a pin taken from her garments, and is later hounded to death by the **Furies** – conscience.

In *The Greek Myths* **Robert Graves** opines that Oedipus was a foreigner who took Thebes by storm, and was entirely unrelated to Laius and Jocasta, but that Theban patriots preferred to consider him the lost heir to the kingdom, later invaders misrepresenting the event as patricide and incest.

Either way, the horror felt by Oedipus at his own (innocent) crime is later paralleled by the legend of Pope Gregory the Great (590–604), born of incest, living in incest. Horrified at learning the truth, he flees to a rock in the sea to live thereafter as a penitential hermit.

INCUBI AND SUCCUBI (*See* ABDUCTIONS, DEMONS, FAIRIES)

The Latin-derived *incubus* means 'that which lies upon'. *Succubus* means 'that which lies beneath'. These terms were used by the medieval Church to refer to demons said to engage in sexual intercourse with mortals.

Tales of amorous contact between humans and gods, demons, **spirits** or fairies are ancient. Greek god **Zeus** seduced many mortal women, assuming many shapes to do so. 'In our Scotland,' wrote the **Rev. Robert Kirk** in his *The Secret Commonwealth* (1691), 'there are numerous and beautiful creatures of that aerial order, who frequently assign meetings to lascivious young men as succubi, or as joyous mistresses and prostitutes, who are called Leannain Sith or familiar spirits.'[1] Christian myth speaks of the **Holy Ghost** visiting a 'virgin'. Accounts of affairs between men, women and **angels** are given by St Augustine, St Ambrose, Tertullian and many others. Yet **Enochian** belief in angels as physical beings capable of mating with humans (Genesis vi:2: 'the sons of God saw the daughters of men that they were fair; and they took them wives') was condemned. Later opinion was that all such contact, real or imagined, was the **Devil**'s work, to be punished as such. St Augustine wrote:

> It is a widespread opinion, confirmed by direct or indirect testimony of trustworthy persons, that the Sylvans and Fauns, commonly called Incubi, have often tormented women, solicited and obtained intercourse with them.

The medieval scholar Isodore Lisieux asked: (1) is such intercourse physically possible? (2) how does demoniality differ from bestiality? (3) what sin is committed by those engaged in such acts? (4) what should their punishment be? Another medieval scholar, Sinistrari, argued that the Devil, lacking a body, has intercourse with mortals by borrowing the corpse of a human being, or by forming with other materials a new body. He was referring to real physical intercourse, as testified in books such as the *Compendium Maleficarum*. He said two kinds of people may be carnally contacted: sorcerers making a pact with demons, or ordinary folk possessed by them. He says incubi are not the same as common devils: they ignore exorcists and laugh at holy relics. The father of the magician **Merlin** was said to have been an incubus, while the eminent Cardinal Bellarmin claimed that **Antichrist** would be born of a woman mating with an incubus.[2]

Many of those accused of sexual contact with the 'Devil' hastened to assert the truth of the claim, even if it meant their death. Accounts like that of Isobel Gowdie (Auldearn, Scotland, 1662), suggest a mental tyranny so vast that even its victims embraced it. Giving herself up, she said the Devil ('a meikle, blak, roch man') was as 'cold within me as spring-well-water'.[3] Her fate is unknown, but death by fire was a common solution. Medieval hysteria? Reports of such contacts continue today, incubi and succubi being replaced by the inhabitants of **UFOs**. (For the experiences of the Hills and of Whitley Streiber, *see* **Abductions**). British psychologist Stan Gooch tells how an ex-policeman, Martyn Pryer, was 'attacked' in bed by an invisible entity which lay on top of him. Paralysed, he realised it was a woman wanting to make love to him. Eventually it faded away. Gooch himself claims to have made love to a succubus – a composite of various ex-girlfriends. Concluding that such creatures are mental creations, Gooch's testimony suggests that, imaginary or not, such entities are as active now as ever in the past.[4]

1. *Dimensions*, Jacques Vallée, Sphere, London, 1990, p.141.
2. *Ibid.*, p.147.
3. *An ABC of Witchcraft Past and Present*, Doreen Valiente, Hale, London, 1984, p.201.
4. *Creatures from Inner Space*, Stan Gooch, Rider, London, 1984.

INDIAN MYTH (*See* CONCORDANCE)
Populated by some 800 million people speaking some 745 distinct languages

(fourteen officially taught), the Indian subcontinent hosts more major religions than any other land on earth – **Hinduism, Islam, Buddhism** and **Christianity**, the Sikh and **Jain** faiths. Christianity and Islam entered India late. Buddhism, though native to India, never fully engaged popular imagination. But Hinduism, practised by some 83 per cent of the population, has sustained a wide popular appeal for over two millennia.

India's religious history may be divided into four ages: (1) the Vedic Age; (2) the Brahmanical Age; (3) the Buddhist Age; and (4) the revival of and transformation of Brahmanism. (Jain belief is considered separately.)

While Dravidian languages were perhaps spoken in India by 10,000 BC, the first archaeological record is of the Indus civilisation, over twenty sites along the Indus and Ghaghar rivers having been excavated. The cities of Harappa and Mohenjodaro, built by sophisticated agriculturalists, prospered after *c*.2500 BC. **Shiva** and **Devi** were already worshipped. Yet by *c*.1500 BC this civilisation was being absorbed by waves of horse-riding **Aryan** nomads from the west (Persia: Iran), worshippers of a sky-god, **Indra**. The caste system developed, descendants of the Aryans being in control by 1000 BC. The first inhabitants (now named Dasa: 'fiends') were reduced to slavery as the fourth caste, the Sudras, under the Brahmans (priests), Kshatriyas (warrior aristocrats) and Vaisvas (free traders).

With culture shifting east to the **Ganges** valley, between 1500 BC and 1000 BC (i.e., before **Homer**) the first **Vedic**, then **Sanskrit** literature appeared. The hymns of the *Rig Veda* (perhaps 1400 BC), marked the first of the four Ages. Indra, **Agni** and **Varuna** were the great gods.

By 1000 BC the Brahmanic Age had begun, the Aryan influx being by now absorbed and Indra by now inferior to the triad of **Brahma**, **Vishnu** and Shiva. The *Upanishads* (philosophical treatises) and *Puranas* (verse narratives of the **creation** and the lives of the gods) were being composed.

Brahma was metaphysical conception, not personal deity: cosmic day and night and source of the world-ages (**yugas**). Brahmanic intellectualism also developed the idea of the physical universe as **maya** (illusion), a doctrine propounded as early as the ninth century BC by Sankara. Yet this austerity helped the Brahmans to survive the rise of Buddhism (third Age), its tenets first preached by Prince Siddhartha Gautama in Benares in 530 BC. There arose a complex mythology eventually synthesised into Hinduism.

So Brahmanism was revived (fourth Age), with Shiva and Vishnu paramount, their **avatars** (manifestations, like **Krishna**) and their **shaktis** (female aspects, like **Kali**) answering many popular needs. Behind the polytheism, Brahma, the One God, remained remote.

From the fourth century BC dates the *Mahabharata*, one of the world's great epics. A century later, under the Buddhist emperor **Ashoka** (273–232 BC), Indian history, philosophy and myth converged. Ruling most of the subcontinent, Ashoka established law and denied religious persecution. Those unattracted by Buddhist or Jain austerity developed the paths of Hinduism and **Tantric** Buddhism. No legal or religious prohibitions distorted the quest: thus the erotic sculptures of the temples at Khajuraho and Bhubaneswar. The mother goddess **Devi** regained her earlier supremacy. Later arguments led to the Mahayana and Hinayana schools of Buddhism. This religious ferment deeply influenced surrounding lands, from Sri Lanka to **Tibet**, Cambodia, **China** and **Japan**. Long before Christianity reached the East, Hindu tolerance and Buddhist metaphysics had spread throughout south, central and eastern Asia. India remains a crucible of myth and religion.

INDOCHINA AND INDONESIA (See BUDDHISM, HINDUISM, ISLAM)

Indochina comprises the modern states of Vietnam, Laos, Cambodia, Thailand, Burma and Malaysia. As the old regional name suggests, the traditions both of India and China influenced the culture of this peninsula south of China, as later did **Islam** and, to a lesser extent, **Christianity**. Likewise with Indonesia, an island chain to the south and east consisting of Sumatra, Java, Borneo, the Celebes, the Philippines and western part of New Guinea.

Though the Vietnamese accepted **Confucianism**, nowhere else did Chinese beliefs gain a hold. Much of the region early became **Hindu**, Indian spice-traders being followed by **Brahmans** who converted local chieftains and set up kingdoms after the Indian model. Cambodian lore tells of Kaundinya, a Brahman who (first century AD), married a princess said to have been a *nagini*, a **serpent**-girl, and made himself king. The temples of the ruined city of Angkor Wat (abandoned 1540) still bear witness to Hindu influence.

Later **Buddhist** monks, threatened in India by Hindu resurgence, brought to Indochina and Indonesia the monastic ideal of individual salvation as in the Hinayana, Buddhism's 'Lesser Vehicle'. This survives mainly in Burma and Thailand. Their welcome by the Sailendra kings is commemorated by the building of a Buddhist shrine in Java (AD 778); the construction on the same isle of the enormous *stupa* of Borobudur (ninth century) indicates the eclipse of the Hinayana by the tradition of the Mahayana ('Greater Vehicle').

The coming of Islam to Sumatra (thirteenth century) led to many conversions, particularly in western Indonesia. Christianity spread more slowly, though the annexation in 1521 of the Philippines by Spain gave it added impetus. Here older animistic beliefs survive in the popularity of occult Christian cults such as Spiritism. Indigenous beliefs survived throughout the region in a mythology of **ghosts, elementals** and **shamanic** practices; of the **soul** as a bird (Malaysia); of binding a woman's body to stop her soul escaping in childbirth (Sumatra); of refusing men venison lest it make them timid as a deer; of expelling sickness by setting adrift an image of the sick person in a boat (Borneo); and of the belief (as among Australian **Aborigines**) in New Guinea that the **initiation** and **circumcision** of youths involves them in being swallowed, then disgorged by a dreadful supernatural monster.

INDRA (See INDIAN MYTH, SKY-GODS, VEDAS)

Sky-god of the **Aryan** invaders of India, son of the **earth-goddess** Prithivi and killer of his father **Dyaus**, portrayed in **Vedic** hymns as a handsome, ruddy man, who loved 'sweet, intoxicating **Soma**', this ruler of thunder and lightning (and thus fertility) was the Vedic equivalent of **Zeus**, **Jupiter** or **Thor**. Riding a golden chariot, with his sky-spanning arms he hurled his disc-like, lightning-emitting *vajra* (thunderbolt) so that rain fell as and where he chose. Before the Aryans left the north, he made ice melt and glaciers retreat. He reached India to find the land's seven great rivers dried up (imprisoned) by the drought-demon Vritra. He slew Vritra, freeing the seven rivers and the cloud-cattle imprisoned in Vritra's mountain fort. Also he slew Vala, thief of the heavenly **cows** (rain-clouds), and fought the evil **Asuras**. Yet in the oldest texts Indra and his brothers **Agni** and **Varuna** are themselves Asuras, a term only later demonised. A millennium later in the *Mahabharata* (fourth century BC), Vritra is described as *atman* (spirit) of the universe, the cosmic **dragon**, his murder by Indra a crime: meaning that the Aryans have been assimilated and their gods downgraded.

As amorous as Zeus, Indra loved his wife Indrani, the Queen of Heaven, who lived with him in Svarga, the Good Kingdom, at the top of cosmic Mount **Meru**. Also called Sahasraksha, 'thousand eyes', he could see all creation at a glance. His capacity for love was shown when his son **Arjuna** visited him, 'seated on one seat, the father and son enhanced the beauty of the assembly, like the sun and moon beautifying the firmament together.'

In early times attended by a **dog**, as befitting the god of a hunting people, later he gave up his chariot and travelled on the great four-tusked white **elephant** Airavata, 'the handsome and ever-victorious'.

1. *Mahabharata*, Vana Parva, section xliii.

INITIATION (*See* MYSTERIES)

Any rite stimulating a person's transition from one stage of life to the next. Such rites, especially as connected with puberty, were conducted by most cultures until recent, 'civilised' times. Boys might undergo symbolic death via ordeal (entombment, scarification, **circumcision**), from which they emerged as men. **Native American** boys would fast alone, seeking a dream to reveal their **totem** beast and their future path. Female pubertal initiation usually involved seclusion at the time of first **menstruation**. Girls were not usually asked to formulate their initiatory dream consciously.[1]

Initiation rites persist among secret societies (like the **Freemasons**) to mark transition from 'outer world' to 'inner'. Ordination of a priest into the Church constitutes initiation, as does the first Communion of a **Christian** or the Jewish Bar/Bar Mitzvah. Secular initiation – as in 'hazing' ordeals required of children or students new to a gang, school or college – persists, the purpose, conscious or not, being the same. The child is father to the man: the man cannot thrive until the child dies.

In the mysteries of the ancient world up to ten stages of initiation were common. The first three involved teachings alone – a discipline the Greeks called *katharsis* (cleansing). The fourth degree required direct participation in the deeper mysteries. In higher degrees the powers of the candidates evolved to a point at which they were considered 'reborn'. In India, such men were called *Dvijas*, a Sanskrit word meaning 'twice-born'.[2]

Labyrinths were often part of the procedure. The passages under the temple of the Alexandrian god Serapis (*see* **Apis**) hid mechanical devices controlling pitfalls and other terrors designed to test the candidate to the limit. **Druid** candidates in Celtic lands were initiated only deep in caves or deep in forests: the oath of secrecy being so fearsome that little then or now has ever been learned about Druidry's core doctrines.

1. *Woman's Mysteries*, M. Esther Harding, Rider, London, 1982 (1955).
2. *An Occult Glossary*, G. de Purucker, Theosophical University Press, Pasadena, California, 1969 (1933), pp.65–6.

INSPIRATION

The Latin *spirare* means 'to breathe'. 'Inspiration' is thus a 'breathing-in' of sudden revelation, energy, purpose or knowledge from an unexpected, unseen or magical source. Thus the process has about it the implicit aura of the divine or supernatural. There are many tales of prophetic or poetic inspiration arising through trance induced by eating the hallucinogenic *Amanita Muscaria* toadstool (Food of the Gods); or by drinking a magic brew distilled in a **cauldron** (**Cerridwen**); or by breathing in fumes from an underground vent (**Delphic oracle**); or by bathing in **dragon**'s blood (**Siegfried**) and thus becoming **invulnerable**, and/or instantly learning the secret language of beasts and birds. The state may come about by accident. Only when one of three hot drops spat out by Cerridwen's bubbling cauldron hit Gwion Bach on the thumb, which automatically he licked, was he inspired with prophetic power. Or 'inspiration' may also refer to knowledge induced by listening in trance to the wind playing in the trees of the sacred grove, 'breathing in' its message, as was done at the oracle of Dodona in Greece. It is said the **Druids** of Gaul used a similar technique. Likewise in the Bible (I Chronicles xiv:15), the Lord God advises King David to listen to the wind in the mulberry trees, and to march against the enemy when he hears the sound of marching in the tops of the trees.[1]

1. *The White Goddess*, Robert Graves, Faber & Faber, London, 1961, pp.439–40.

INUIT (*See* ESKIMO MYTH, NORTH AMERICAN MYTH)

INVISIBILITY (*See* IMMORTALITY, INVULNERABILITY)
That supernatural beings (usually both immortal and invulnerable) can move invisibly among men is a common theme. The Irish god **Angus MacOg** owned a magic cloak conferring invisibility. He was a son of the otherworld tribe, the **Tuatha dé Danaan**, to whom as a whole **Manannan** the sea-god (master of sight-cloaking fog) had granted this power. So too many an **angel, demon, incubus and succubus** has approached mortals invisibly, being known only by their disturbing presence. The **Holy Spirit** is as invisible as the wind. The ghosts and spirits of the dead are generally invisible or semi-visible. A movie cliché is that you see through the phantom. This makes it fearfully powerful. The invisible adversary symbolises fear and insecurity.

But to be invisible is to do as we wish. The state implies undetected mischief. Only by night are we 'invisible' or not easily seen, and so dark hours hide dark deeds. The honest man is visible to all, and acts openly. Only the guilty hide, though few of us have not sometimes wished we were 'invisible', or that we could 'vanish' to escape some social embarrassment.

This old dream of power without responsibility has led to many a quest – alchemic, magical or scientific – for invisibility. Certain **spells** were often said to confer the power, like the 'fith-fath' rhyme used by Gaelic poachers to leave river or forest unseen. The US Air Force has developed radar-invisible 'Stealth' bombers the more easily to cause destruction. Yet what good can invisibility do, even if attainable? In *The Invisible Man* (1897) by **H.G. Wells**, the hero is not freed but bound (literally: he is seen only by the bandages and clothes that reveal his vanished form) after attaining invisibility which turns out to be a murderous **curse**.

INVISIBLE COLLEGE (*See* ROSICRUCIANS)

INVULNERABILITY (*See* ACHILLES HEEL, IMMORTALITY, INVISIBILITY)
The myth of the invulnerable god or hero with one weak spot by which he may be overcome or slain is universal. **Baldur, Siegfried, Cuchulainn** and Achilles are well-known examples in European legend. Typically the power is gained by bathing in a sacred river, or in **dragon**'s blood, or by drinking a magical herbal decoction. Another species of mythic invulnerability arises in the primitive belief that a man's **soul** or **name** may be hidden in a secret place and that, so long as it remains hidden (or, in the case of his name, unknown),

no harm may befall him. From India to Ireland the common tale is of the **immortal**, invulnerable **giant** or warlock who betrays his secret to the maiden fair, whereupon the hero, seeking out his soul or heart, destroys him. A variant, common in Africa, is that the wizard deposits his soul in a wild beast, his familiar, and is invulnerable until the beast should die. Yet another variant consists in the wearing of magical armour that deflects all darts, arrows or spears. But, yet again, such armour invariably proves to have a chink somewhere in it.

IRISH MYTH (*See* CONCORDANCE)

Few records of pre-Christian Celtic folklore, mythology or beliefs survive. The Celts of the European mainland, subjugated by Roman imperial power, relied on oral and not written tradition, while later the Roman Church frowned on transcription of oral pagan lore. Likewise the Celts of the British mainland, though not wholly subjugated, were heavily influenced first by Roman power then by Christian evangelisation. Only in Ireland (never even visited, far less subjugated, by the Romans) did an indigenous Celtic civilisation survive into the Christian era. The Irish Celtic Church inherited many of the older pagan traditions. Its clerics were sufficiently independent and sympathetic to the old traditions to transcribe much of the old nature poetry and narrative cycles in texts such as Books of *Leinster*, *Ballymote*, *Lecan* and the *Dun Cow*.

These texts, for the most part written down *c*.AD 700–1300, long after their original oral composition, offer a unique body of information about ancient Irish Celtic society, its beliefs, myths and organisation. They depict a late Iron Age culture distinct from that of Roman Britain and Europe as a whole – aristocratic, warlike, brutal, extravagant, upholding clan loyalty, prowess in battle, poetry and boasting – and describe the ubiquity of **fate**. The supernatural is omnipresent, yet the protagonists are (for the most part) human. No Christian elements are apparent save in later tales. Preserved by the *filidh* (**bards**) before being written down, nevertheless they contain little or no cosmological element. Nothing is known of **Druid** teachings save via the commentaries of Roman authors like Julius Caesar.

The three major Irish narrative cycles are: (1) mythic prehistory as in the *Lebor Gabala* (Book of Invasions); (2) the Ulster Cycle (first century AD?); and (3) the Fenian Cycle, perhaps third century in origin.

The *Lebor Gabala* tells of five prehistoric invasions of Ireland. The followers of Partholon came from the west, fought the Fomorians (sea-demons), then all died of plague save Partholon's nephew Tuan. Next, the Nemedians continued to clear the land until, also decimated by plague and the Fomorians, they fled to the next isle, Britan. Third, from Europe, came the Fir Bolg (Belgae?), Fir Gaileoin (Gauls?) and Fir Domnann (Dumnonii?) – warriors who set up regional kingships: Meath (centre) Munster (south), Leinster (east), Ulster (north) and Connaught (west). Fourth came the mysterious **Tuatha dé Danaan** (Children of **Danu**) with their four great possessions: the Lia Fail (Stone of Destiny) which cried out when the true king touched it; the spear of their warrior-god **Lug**; the sword of **Nuadu**, seeking out all enemies; and the inexhaustible **cauldron** of the Good God, the **Dagda**. This mythical race, said to have wafted into Ireland on a magical cloud, defeated the Fir Bolg and fought the Fomorians until, armed with the smith-god **Goibniu**'s magical weapons, Lug and the Danaan slew one-eyed **Balor** their king and drove the demons into the sea.

Centuries later a new tribe landed – the Milesians from Spain, armed with **iron**. Defeated, the Danaan were driven underground, to live on as the

invisible fairy-folk. The Milesians may be seen as the Goidelic ancestors of the modern Irish, entering the land sometime between the eighth and fourth centuries BC.

The Ulster Cycle (first century AD?) is based round the epic *Táin Bó Cualnge* ('Cattle Raid of Cooley'). Related tales (Deirdre and the Sons of Uisnech and Bricriu's Feast) involve the same characters (**Cuchulainn**; Ailill and Maeve, king and queen of Connaught; **Conchobar**, king of Ulster). The *Táin* describes a war fought by Connaught to seize Ulster's Brown Bull of Cooley to satisfy Queen Maeve's greed to own a **bull** as potent as the White Bull owned by Ailill her husband. It consitutes western Europe's longest continuous mythic narrative, outside **Homer**.

The tragedy of Deirdre (*see* **Conchobar**) predates the *Táin*; while the raucously humorous Bricriu's Feast (*see* **Cuchulainn, Games**) is the original of the Middle English poem '*Sir Gawain and the Green Knight*'.

The Fenian cycle concerns **Finn MacCool** (Fionn mac Cumhal) and his warband, the Fianna. Dating perhaps from the third century, written down after the seventh century, it is celebrated only after the twelfth and not in prose but poetry, or as ballads said to be by Finn or his son **Oisin** (Ossian) (round whose name eighteenth-century Scot, **James Macpherson**, wove one of history's more celebrated literary frauds). The tales are set mostly in Leinster and Munster. The *Toraigheacht Dhiarmuda agus Ghrainne* (The Pursuit of Diarmuid and Grainne: fourteenth-century) tells how the aging Finn, losing his wife, wishes to marry Grainne, daughter of **Cormac MacAirt**. Appalled, she drugs the wedding banquet wine. With the guests asleep, she offers herself first to Oisin, then Diarmuid, laying a *geis* on Diarmuid to carry her away before Finn awakes. In time Finn slays Diarmuid. This tale and that of Deirdre may have inspired the later romance. **Tristan** and Iseult.

Showing Christian influence, the twelfth-century Colloquy of the Old Men tells how the surviving Fianna told **St Patrick** the ancient tales of pre-Christian Ireland. Of Oisin it is said that, returning from the Land of Youth (**Tir nan Og**), he set foot in Ireland and began crumbling into dust – but not before St Patrick met him and recorded his tale.

So perished the last Irish mythical hero. Yet St Patrick himself used magic powers to overcome the Druids: that magic has persisted in Irish myth ever since, to be taken up later by **Joyce**, **Yeats** and James Stephens.

IRON (*See* BANSHEE, SMITH-GODS)

Iron was first obtained from meteoric stones (and known as 'the metal of heaven'), later by smelting from its compounds. Those mastering the art of working this hard metal gained a crucial advantage in war, manufacture and trade. Thus the Iron Age succeeded the Bronze Age, bronze being a softer metal. The mythology of iron thus relates directly to its success as a means of enforcing new social orders. **Smith-gods** like **Hephaestus**, **Vulcan** and **Wayland** epitomised the new iron power. **Fairies**, **witches** and **vampires** (demonised remnants of older social orders) are said in most lands to be terrified of cold iron. In **Celtic** lands, iron was sewn into the clothes of children; they wore iron brooches in their caps; women in childbed were protected by a row of iron nails; iron horseshoes (the crescent shape has lunar significance) are still often nailed by the door of stable or house (points upward) to keep out evil influence and bring good luck.[1]

The Scots minister **Robert Kirk** is said after his funeral to have appeared to a cousin. Saying he was captive in fairyland, he promised to appear at the baptism of his posthumously born son. Should the cousin hurl an iron dirk over his head, he would be restored to life. The cousin was so shocked at the apparition that he forgot to throw the dirk.

In **Eskimo** lore, for four days after the killing of a white **whale** the use of iron implements was forbidden, and it was said that anyone cutting a whale's body with an iron axe would die. In Korea, no iron was allowed to touch the king's body. When in 1800 King Tieng-tsong-tai-oang died of a tumour in the back, nobody dreamed of using a lancet which might have saved his life. Iron was banned from most Greek sanctuaries. Roman and Sabine priests could be shaved only by bronze, never with iron. The **Jews** used no iron tools in building the Temple at Jerusalem. **Hottentot** priests always used quartz, never iron, for **sacrifice** or **circumcision**.[2]

In **Brahmanic** cosmology, the worst of the four world ages or *yugas* is *Kali Yuga*, the Black or Iron Age (following the Ages of **Gold**, **Silver** and **Bronze**). The Greek poet **Hesiod** defined the ages similarly, adding an Age of the Heroes as the fourth age, the fifth age being the Iron (black) Age – an era of sin, disease, affliction, warfare and violent change.

1. *The Magic Arts in Celtic Britain*, Lewis Spence, Rider, London, 1970.
2. *The Golden Bough*, Sir James Frazer, Macmillan, London, 1963, pp.224–5.

ISEULT (*See* TRISTAN)

ISHTAR (*See* BABYLONIAN MYTH, MOTHER-GODDESS, TAMMUZ, VIRGINITY)

As the Sumerian **Inanna** pursued her slain lover the **corn-god** Dumuzi to the **underworld**, this Babylonian fertility-goddess likewise pursued **Tammuz**, to beg his release from **Enki** (Ea). Daughter of **Anu** and sister of **Shamash** the sun-god, as wife of the **moon-god Sin** she was known as the Holy Virgin or Virgin Mother. As goddess of sexual love she presided over a cult of sacred prostitution: her city Erech was the 'town of sacred courtesans'. In her name every woman of Babylon was required, once in her life, to sit in Ishtar's temple and couple with the first stranger to cast coins into her lap. They, like she, were called 'virgin', meaning unmarried. Herodotus called this 'the foulest Babylonian custom'. Irritable and violent, her love was fatal even for the gods. She lamented only the death of Tammuz. As consort of **Ashur**, she was celebrated as the **Assyrian** 'Lady of Battles', riding a chariot drawn by seven **lions** and sporting a full beard falling to her breasts. Yet, though fickle and cruel, she was said to be capable of tenderness – on rare occasions.

ISIS (*See* BLACK VIRGIN, EGYPTIAN MYTH, HORUS, OSIRIS, SET)

This great Egyptian mother-goddess was initially a deity of the Nile Delta, daughter of Geb (earth) and **Nuit** (sky), wife of her older brother **Osiris**. As Plutarch tells it, they ruled Egypt jointly, she helping Osiris civilise the land, teaching women to grind corn, spin and weave, ruling as regent when he went abroad to civilise the world. But their brother Set murdered Osiris, launching his body on the Nile in a coffer which Isis found at Byblos (**Phoenicia**) enclosed in an acacia (or tamarisk) tree. She hid his body in the swamps at Buto but Set found it, cutting it up in fourteen pieces which he scattered through Egypt. Finding every piece but the phallus, magically she revived Osiris and (even more magically) conceived their son **Horus**.

To gain power over the **sun-god Amon**-Ra she made a **serpent** by mixing earth with his spit. When it bit him she withheld the cure until he told her his secret **name**. She became associated not only with earth but heaven and the star Sothis (**Sirius**), its annual rise preceding the annual Nile flood. She was thus Egypt's fertility: the Nile being Osiris and the desert being Set.

Portrayed as a woman bearing on her head a throne (later a disc between **cow**'s horns: *see* **Hathor**), she was worshipped into **Christian** times, her temple at Philae closing as late as the reign of Justinian (AD 483–565). Yet her cult persisted. The name 'Paris' is from Par-Isis, the 'Grove of Isis'. The city's oldest church, St Germain-des-Prés, built AD 542 over a former temple of Isis, held a black statue of Isis worshipped as the **Virgin Mary** until 1514. Many 'black virgins' originate with Isis: her immaculate conception of Horus prefiguring Christ's birth.

Representing the archetypal virginity of the feminine side of God, and of Nature's receptivity as mirrored by the **moon**'s reflection of the sun, Isis endures as one of the great transformative forces. As such, she is intuitively recognised by each new generation, even if her characteristics are absorbed in the passive image of the Christian Madonna. The **Tarot** High Priestess, blue-robed, seated between the pillars Boaz and Jachin, scroll of the Law in her lap, and crowned by the horned disc (Sirius), is Isis. Madame Blavatsky named her **Theosophical** 'bible' *Isis Unveiled* (1877). In 1920s England occultist Dion Fortune founded the Fraternity of the Inner Light to re-establish Isis as an image of dynamic womanhood.

In the *Golden Ass*, **Apuleius** tells how in a dream Isis tells him:[1]

I am Nature, the universal Mother, mistress of all the elements, primordial child of time, sovereign of all things spiritual, queen of the dead, queen also of the immortals, the single manifestation of all gods and goddesses that are. My nod governs the shining heights of Heaven, the wholesome seabreezes, the lamentable silences of the world below. Though I am worshipped in many aspects, known by countless names, and propitiated with all manner of different rites, yet the whole round earth venerates me.

1. *The Golden Ass*, Lucius Apuleius (trans. Robert Graves), Penguin, 1985 (1950), p.228.

ISLAM (*See* CONCORDANCE)

A major religion, founded by the Prophet Mohammed (AD 571–632), Islam (named from Arab *aslama*, 'be surrendered': thus too the word 'Moslem') derives from the same roots as **Judaism**. So **Adam** is the first of twenty-four prophets before Mohammed. Abraham, the Hebrew patriarch, is also the Arab patriarch. Ishmael, his first-born by his second wife Hagar, fathered the Arabs: Isaac, his second-born by his first wife Sarah, fathered the Hebrews. Christ is recognised as Mohammed's divine predecessor, though not as the Son of God.

Formerly the Arabs peopled the universe with good and evil **djinns** and **ifrit,** and worshipped **trees** and **stones**. The Kaaba, the Islamic sanctuary at Mecca, still holds a black meteoric stone. Rejecting **Christian** and Judaic evangelisation as well as their existing **animism**, many Arabs sought to renew old **Mystery** doctrines. This was done via revelations received by Mohammed from the **angel** Gabriel during meditations in a cave on Mount Hira near Mecca from *c.*AD 610 until just before his death. A merchant who had married into wealth, Mohammed gave up riches and status to pursue divine truth, supported by Khadijah his wife. Well-schooled in Christian theology and older teachings, he may have been taught by an unknown holy man during the revelation of the 114 Suras (chapters) of the Koran. An epileptic, he dictated these Suras to friends while in ecstatic trance. Later they were assembled from 'scraps of parchment and leather, tablets of stone, ribs of palm branches, camels' shoulder-blades and ribs, pieces of board, and the breasts of men.'

The definitive canon was established by a panel of editors in the reign of the third caliph 'Uthmān (644–54). They placed the Suras in order of length – longest first, shortest last. Non-believers find the text random, without order. Moslems venerate the Koran as comprehensible only in the original Arabic, to be grasped as a whole and not merely as the sum of its scattered parts. It seems likely that many Suras did not originate with Mohammed, but were created after his death to fit emerging requirements.[1]

Teaching that, 'There is no God but God (Allah), and Mohammed is his Prophet; that Allah rules with love and mercy; that He alone is to be worshipped'; Mohammed did not preach fatalism. He repudiated all atonement, insisting that each believer must work out his own fate.

Fearing assassination, in AD 622 he fled from Mecca with his followers – the *hejira* ('departure'). From Medina his guerrilla war against Mecca led, eight years later, to its capture and the triumph of the new faith throughout Arabia. The original philanthropic message was rejected. Fast-days were announced; the value of pilgrimage to Mecca stressed; holy war (*jihad*) declared against infidels (unbelievers); usury and intoxicants banned; polygamy encouraged. Mohammed himself took ten wives. Yet the Koran insists that Woman is fully equal to Man. Friday, the Moslem Holy Day, is sacred to the planet **Venus**; green, the Prophet's colour, is associated with the World Mother.

Believing in the immaculate conception, divine character and miracles of Christ, Moslems deny that he is Son of God the Father or that he died on the Cross, saying another died in his place. They claim these lines have been deleted from the Christian Gospels:

And when Jesus, the Son of Mary, said, O children of Israel, verily I am the apostle of God sent unto you, confirming the law which was delivered before me, and bringing good tidings of an apostle who shall come after me, and whose name shall be AHMED.

In 632 Mohammed died without male issue, leaving the land to the rule of the caliphs. In 654 the third caliph, 'Uthmān, was assassinated. The murder divided Islam into two factions: the Sunni and the Shi-ites. The former recognised no divine right of succession; the latter saw the caliphs as usurpers. Power reverted to Mohammed's son-in-law, Ali, who was assassinated in 660. Ali's eldest son Hasan was poisoned (by his own wife); his youngest son Hosain (and 3,000 of his men) were slaughtered by a Sunni army. Meanwhile Islamic armies swept east to China, northwest to Constantinople and west through North Africa to Spain and France, being halted by Charles Martel at Tours (AD 732). Later conflict with Christian Europe led to the Crusades (Wars of the Cross: 1095–1291) and to Islamic control of the Middle East, Asia Minor, North Africa and parts of Spain and the Balkans. Constantinople fell in 1452; Suleiman the Magnificent later besieged Vienna. Defeat of the Turks at the sea-battle of Lepanto in the Mediterranean in 1571 led, after renewed siege of Vienna in 1683, to their decline under the Ottomans.

Out of this expansion also arose a culture long ranking higher than any in Christendom. Astronomy, algebra, mathematics, geometry, chemistry and other disciplines owe their origin to Moslem genius even as Europe endured the Dark Ages. Islamic poetry and philosophy was of a high order, schools like the **Sufis** and Mevlevi ('Whirling') Dervishes guarded the esoteric lore of the Faith; and Islamic sailors rounded Africa before Vasco da Gama.

Islam denied all anthropomorphic depictions, images of gods, symbols and fables. To ensure pure monotheism, it confined all art to geometric representation, the Law (Shari'a) being the sole legitimate expression of truth. No idolatrous representations of God were permitted. Yet (as in every other major religion) many myths and superstitions endured within the orthodox canon. Thus there is continuing Islamic veneration of the Kaaba and of Fatima, the daughter of Mohammed and one of the 'four perfect women', while the vast anthology of interlinked, fabulous tales known as the *Arabian Nights* has entranced generations.

1. *The Koran* (trans. Arthur J. Arberry), OUP, 1964, Introduction, p.ix.

ITZAMNA/IXCHEL/IXTAB (*See* **MAYAN MYTH**)

IZANAGI/IZANAMI (*See* **JAPANESE MYTH, SHINTO**)

J

JACKAL (*See* **ANUBIS**)

JADE (*See* **CHINESE MYTH, JEWELS**)
Throughout the Far East and particularly in China the symbolic status of this translucent precious stone was higher even than **gold** or diamonds. Thus the supreme father-god of the official imperial Chinese pantheon was the August Personage of Jade (Yü-ti), or the August Supreme Emperor of Jade (Yü-huang-shang-ti). Yü means any precious stone in general, but jade in particular. Jade is the Jewel of Heaven, product of the interaction of mountain and water, symbolising 'All that is supremely excellent', and the unified powers of *yin* and *yang*. Jade was said to unite the five cardinal virtues: charity, modesty, courage, justice and wisdom. Khivan Ghung in the seventh century AD enumerated the nine qualities of jade as reflecting man's best attainments: its smoothness suggests benevolence, its polish, knowledge, its firmness, righteousness, its harmlessness, virtuous action, its spotlessness, purity, its imperishability, endurance, its power to pass unsullied from hand to hand, morality and its clear bell-like note when struck, music. Invariably symbolising good fortune, as used in healing it was thought to cure all diseases of the kidneys, while its various colours are *wan*, the Ten Thousand Things, or infinity.

JAGANNATH (JUGGERNAUT) (*See* **HINDUISM, INDIAN MYTH, VISHNU**)
Means Lord ('Nath', 'Naut') of the World ('Jagan'), referring to a triple form of the god **Vishnu** as worshipped at a temple at Puri in the Indian state of Orissa. The first form is that of the dark **Krishna**; the second, of the fair Balarama; the third, of their sister, Subhadra. Once a year (during the festival of Snana-Yantra) the **idol** or statue is bathed in milk, in honour of Krishna. During the festival of Ratha-yatra ('car-feast'), the statue is put on a huge wheeled vehicle (juggernaut), which, weighing many tons, is pulled through the city streets by the god's worshippers. Desiring to view the god, who cannot be seen by living mortals, some throw themselves under the wheels to be crushed, thus dying wholly sinless.

JAGUAR (*See* **CAT, SOUTH AMERICAN MYTH**)
In pre-Columbian South America, where this big **cat** roamed the jungle, many statues of gods with staring eyes and double fangs exist from early times. In **shamanistic** lore the jaguar may be the familiar spirit of, or the form taken by, the magician. Personifying fertility, as in statues of jaguars coupling with women, it is also the chthonic power which the adept must master, or (in Bolivia) the beast that a man must kill single-handed while armed only with a wooden spear in order to be called a warrior. In Mexico generally it was seen as messenger of the forest spirits; to the **Aztecs** it represented the powers of darkness at war with the solar **eagle**. In Mochica culture the creator-god of the mountain was shown as jaguar-faced.

JAINISM (See INDIAN MYTH, REINCARNATION)

This Indian religion was founded by Mahavira (the 'Great Man'). Jain myth claims he lived peacefully in **heaven** before incarnating on earth to save humanity. On being born, he received the name Vardhamana ('He who grows and develops'). Some thirty years after Siddhartha Gautama first preached the **Buddhist** Way at Benares in 530 BC, this prince of Bihar (c.540–468 BC), equally dissatisfied with life, became a wandering ascetic, until he gained enlightenment and the title of Jina ('Victor'). He preached until one night, in the small hours, all his followers had fallen asleep. So he died. When his followers awoke, they brought lamps, but his soul had returned to heaven.

Claiming the world to be disc-shaped and eternal, the holy Mount **Meru** at its centre; the Jains deny the existence of a creator. They say that the gods are great but not immortal, being subject to the laws of **karma** and **reincarnation**; and that beyond the worlds both of men and gods lies the realm of those now exempt from rebirth. They say that if control of desire is achieved, the enlightened ascetic may end his life by ceasing to eat; when he dies, his liberated soul ascends the world-mountain, there to live for ever. However this practice of systematic self-starvation (also once practised by French **Cathars**) is now obsolete.

Vegetarians, the Jains take such care to harm no living creature that some carry brooms to sweep from their path any insects they might otherwise crush. Today, the sect numbers no more than four million. The twelve Jain holy books, written in the Prakrit language, are called Angas, the last being lost; some members use the so-called 'Secondary Canon'.[1]

1. *Indian Mythology*, Jan Knappert, Aquarian Press, London, 1991.

JANUS (See DOOR)

JAPANESE MYTH (See CONCORDANCE)

Called Nippon ('sun-origin' or 'eastern land') by its inhabitants, Japan consists of a chain of volcanic islands in the Pacific Ocean immediately east of Siberia and Korea: Hokkaido to the north, the main isle of Honshu in the middle and the lesser isles of Kyushu and Shikoku to the south. The isle of Sakhalin is north of Hokkaido.

Japan's main religious systems have long been **Shinto** (the 'Way of the Gods': an indigenous system of folk-belief offering respect to local **pagan spirits**, the **ancestors**, and the imperial family), **Confucianism**, reaching Japan after the third century AD and introducing Chinese philosophy, ethics and rationality, and **Buddhist** schools which, from the Mahayana ('Greater Vehicle') to the Ch'an Tsung ('Inner Light': later **Zen**), reaching Japan in AD 522, deeply affected the later development of Japanese mythology.

Prince Shokutu (572–621) compared these three ethical systems to the roots, stem, branches, fruit and flowers of a **tree**.

The first Japanese apparently came from Korea. Driving the indigenous **Ainu** north to Hokkaido, they absorbed other tribes while retaining Asiatic contacts; an important factor in their later acceptance of foreign ethical and religious systems. Tribal, their chiefs were often women. **Animists** like other pagan peoples they deified the elements and natural features of the land as Kami ('Beings More Highly Placed'). Embodying their gods with human attributes, good and bad, they regarded none as omniscient, dividing them into gods of **heaven** (Ama-Tsu-Kami) and gods of earth (Kuni-Tsu-Kami). Heaven was not remote, being linked to earth by a bridge which let the gods go to and fro. Below earth lay the Land of Darkness, the Japanese **hell**, a bottomless abyss into which on the day of purification all sins and impurities will be swept down by the ocean waters overlying it. Every spring, well and river had its god; there were gods of wind, storm and thunder, while the volcanic instability of the land led naturally to veneration of the mountains, especially of the extinct volcano Fujiyama, the sanctuary of the goddess Sengen-Sama being later built on it. Other sacred mountains had shrines dedicated to different gods, and the chief god of mountains as a whole was O-Yama-Tsu-Mi.

Early Japanese history is so interlaced with local and foreign legends that it is hard to know what really happened, not least as these myths were associated with the origins of the Japanese Imperial family, making it dangerous for native scholars to rationalise them too closely.

Even so, history is said to begin with the enthronement (660 BC) of the Mikado (Emperor) Jimmu-Tenno. It is said that in 3 AD human **sacrifice** at the death of the Mikado was abolished.

In the fifth and sixth centuries growing Chinese influence led to the introduction (AD 522) of Buddhism, adopted as the official religion during the reign of the Mikado Yomei (585–87). Later, to prevent powerful families altering old legends to their advantage by claiming descent from Shinto gods, the Mikado Temmu (672–86) sponsored the conversion of Shinto myths from the oral tradition (as preserved by the 'reciters' or **bards**) into written history. This led first to the 'Kojiki' ('Book of Ancient Things': AD 712), the 'Nihongi' ('Chronicles of Japan': 720); the 'Jindaiki' ('Records of the Age of the Gods': 720) and the 'Kogoshui' ('Gleanings of Ancient Words': 807). Other anthologies of mythic lore followed, formalising the old tales sequentially from the **creation** to within decades of the contemporary era.

The Kojiki tells of three deities, self-born, who hid in high **heaven**. Later, 'when the earth was young and like floating oil', two more hidden divinities were born. From seven more mythic generations arose the **ancestor**-deities, Izanagi and Izanami, who gave birth to the islands of Japan and to many gods. Last came the god of fire, whose birth so burned Izanami that she died in agony and descended to hell. Inconsolable, Izanagi followed her, but she refused to return with him. Later, she swore 'every day to strangle to death one thousand of the people of your land'. He retorted: 'If you do thus, I will every day cause one thousand five hundred women to bear children.'[1]

Leaving Izanami in the Land of the Dead, Izanagi went to purify himself in the River Tachibana. As he washed his left eye there appeared **Amaterasu**, the sun-goddess; as he washed his right, Tsukiyomi, the moon-god (note: in **Egyptian myth**, the left eye of **Horus** becomes the moon; his right becomes the sun); and as he washed his nose, the storm-god Susanowo was born.

Then Amaterasu and Susanowo between them created eight children, the ancestors of the Emperors. Susanowo (*see* **Amaterasu**), was expelled from heaven. Yet, though impetuous, this fertility god was not really evil. Associated with **serpents**, water and thunder, he slew an eight-headed serpent (*see* **Hydra**). In its tail he found the wonderful sword Kusanagi, which he gave to Amaterasu, and which today, kept in the temple of Atsutsa near Nagoya, is one of the three emblems of Imperial Japanese power.

Susanowo's son, O-Kuni-Nashi, master of sorcerous medicine, cured the white **hare** of Inaba, which his brothers had rejected in its suffering, but was then murdered by his jealous brothers. Resurrected, he become strong again. To save him from his angry brothers his mother sent him to the underworld.

Next, Amaterasu sent her grandson Ninigi down to earth with the sword

Kusunagi, the heavenly **jewels** and a mirror. He landed on Kyushu and built a palace from which he developed his power. It may be that the mythologers made him land here, and not in Honshu, as a means of bringing the hostile tribes of this southern island under Imperial control. He married the daughter of the mountain-god O-Yama-Tsu-Mi. A descendant married the daughter of the sea-god, from which union a generation later came Jimmu, the legendary founder of the Imperial family.

Ancient Japanese texts speak of 'the eight hundred myriads of gods', and every local village owned a Kami and its attendants, of which many were mythologised in terms of oddly-shaped rocks and stones. The Japanese mind was always in imaginative ferment. The arrival first of Confucianism then of Buddhism brought some order to the original mythic exuberance.

1. *Oriental Mythology*, Joseph Campbell, Viking, New York, 1972, pp.461–504.

JASON (*See* GOLDEN FLEECE, GREEK MYTH)

A pre-Homeric Greek ballad cycle, the Argonautika, tells how Pelias, son of **Poseidon**, usurped the Iolcan throne from his half-brother Aeson, whose son Diomedes was smuggled to safety. Educated by the **centaur** Chiron, the youth, renamed Jason, set out to reclaim the kingdom, en route losing a sandal as he carried a hag over the River Anaurus. The hag was the goddess **Hera** who meant to punish Pelias for denying her **sacrifice**. Warned to beware a one-sandalled man, when Jason arrived and revealed himself Pelias promised to abdicate if Jason could steal back from far-off Colchis the ghost of Phrixus who haunted him and the fleece of the golden **ram** on which Phrixus had fled Iolcus to avoid sacrifice to **Zeus**.

Persuading Argus the Thespian to build a fifty-oared ship, the *Argo*, Jason mustered a crew including Argus, Atalanta the virgin huntress, Castor and Pollux the **Dioscuri, Hercules, Theseus** and **Orpheus**. Outwitting the **Harpies**, risking the **Clashing Rocks** and fighting off predatory birds, the 'Argonauts' crossed the Black Sea to Colchis, where King Aeëtes agreed to give up the Golden Fleece if Jason could harness two wild **bulls** to a plough and sow a field with **dragon**'s teeth. Aeëtes' daughter **Medea** fell in love with Jason and with her magic helped him subdue the bulls. As he sowed the dragon's teeth, armed men sprang up, but he made them fight each other and killed the wounded survivors. Aeëtes broke his word and meant to slay the Argonauts, but Medea helped Jason seize the Fleece from the **oak** where it hung by magically pacifying the thousand-coiled guardian dragon. Regaining the *Argo*, the heroes left in haste, Medea delaying the pursuit by killing her brother Apsyrtus (aided by Jason) and scattering his remains on the sea, forcing the Colchians to stop and give Apsyrtus the decent burial that Phrixus had been denied. This occurred near the mouth of the Danube.

Jason and Medea left the *Argo* and returned to Greece via Aeaea, island home of Medea's aunt, the witch **Circe**, who purified them of the murder. Back in Iolcus they found that Pelias had slain Aeson. Medea persuaded the daughters of Pelias to dismember Pelias and cook him in a **cauldron** so she could restore him to youth, which she did not. This may imply a fertility rite involving the killing and eating of the king, his remains being stewed in a cauldron of rebirth. Medea was originally a lunar **serpent-goddess**.

Made king of Corinth after Medea poisoned the usurper Corinthus, Jason deserted Medea for Glauce ('**Owl**'). Medea sent her a robe that consumed her and all others present in fire, her father King Creon included. Only Jason escaped, leaping from a window. Then either Medea cut the throats of her fourteen children by Jason, or they were stoned to death by the enraged Corinthians. Medea fled to Hercules, curing him of his madness, then to Athens, where she tried to poison Theseus. Returning to Colchis, she was reconciled to Aeëtes. Jason died when a beam of the now-rotting *Argo* fell on his head. Another version is that he tired of life and killed himself.

JEHOVAH (*See* **JUDAISM, YAHWEH**)

JESUS CHRIST (*See* **CHRISTIANITY**)

JEWELS (*See* **GOLD, JADE, SILVER, STONE, TREASURE**)

Anciently valued not only as ornaments implying wealth, status and (set in crowns) royalty, jewels have long been used as **amulets** to ward off evil, for **divination** (lithomancy) and to heal. The Egyptians inscribed spells on blue lapis lazuli. Sumerians, Babylonians and Persians employed agate, amethyst, jade, carnelian, jasper, onyx and other stones as amulets.

Diamond was said to neutralise poison; agate to invigorate the wearer; jasper to aid pregnant women and protect against witchcraft. Sapphire cured sweats, sore eyes and ulcers; emerald restrained passion; ruby banished evil spirits. If engraved with the head of **Bacchus**, god of wine, chastity-promoting amethyst prevented intoxication. Topaz and chalcedony were said to dispel lunacy; hyacinth, says Marbodius (1037–1125) dispels suspicion, beryl cures belching; pearls dissolved then drunk fortify the heart.

Dragon-guarded jewels symbolised hidden treasure (knowledge or truth), also lust, greed and transient wealth. Cut jewels represent the soul shaped into a state capable of reflecting divinity: thus the alchemical quest for the **Philosopher's Stone**, the purified soul. The Chinese called jade the Jewel of Heaven, curing all kidney diseases. The Three Jewels of **Jainism** are right belief, right knowledge and right conduct. In **Buddhism**, jewels signify wisdom. In the *Mahabharata*, a magic jewel stolen from the **Naga** king Vasuka restores **Arjuna**'s life. The wisdom of **Hermes Trismegistus** was engraved on an Emerald Tablet. The Ten Commandments were said to be carved on sapphire, and the twelve stones in the High Priest's breastplate represented (in **Judaism**) the twelve sons of Jacob and the twelve tribes. The twelve stones of the Mystic City of St John's **Apocalypse** are the twelve apostles, also the **zodiac**.

The stone of **Minerva** was sard (Aries); of **Venus**, carnelian (Taurus); of **Apollo**, topaz (Gemini); of **Mercury**, chalcedony (Cancer); of **Jupiter**, jasper (Leo); of **Ceres**, emerald (Virgo); of **Vulcan**, beryl (Libra); of **Mars**, amethyst (Scorpio); of **Diana**, hyacinth (Sagittarius); of **Vesta**, chrysopase (Capricorn); of **Juno**, rock crystal (Aquarius); and of **Neptune**, sapphire (Pisces). In medieval **Christianity**, the church altar was adorned with seven kinds of jewels symbolising the seven planets, also the seven gifts of the **Holy Ghost**. Diamond (Saturn) symbolised fortitude; sapphire (Jupiter) wisdom; ruby (Mars) devotion or piety; topaz (sun) enlightenment; emerald (Venus) sympathy or understanding; amethyst (Mercury) good counsel; and chalcedony or selenite (**moon**), fear of the Lord.

The **Holy Grail** is said once to have been a huge ruby or emerald worn by **Satan** which, when **Michael** struck Satan, fell meteor-like to earth, to become a chalice acquired by **Solomon**, then used at the Last Supper, then by **Joseph of Arimathea** to catch Christ's **blood** after the crucifixion.

JEWS AND ANTI-SEMITISM (See JUDAISM, NAZI MYTH, WANDERING JEW)

A Jew (Hebrew *Yehudi*) is a member of *Judah*, meaning of the tribe of Judah, one of the twelve claiming the Promised Land, or of the later kingdom of Judah (as opposed to the northern kingdom of Israel). Initially called Hebrews (*Ivrim*), the Jews were called Israelites (*Isre'elim*) until the end of their exile in Babylon (538 BC). Thereafter the term, 'Yehudi' was used to describe all adherents of Judaism, Israel's ten tribes being dispersed.

In 333 BC **Alexander the Great** seized Judaea. Greek influence then Roman rule led from revolt by the Maccabees (*c.*167 BC) to the Zealot uprising that ended in their mass suicide at Masada (AD 74). Simeon bar Kochba's revolt (AD 132) failed to recapture the land. Jews were enslaved and scattered. After Roman emperor Constantine (AD 279–337) embraced **Christianity** as the state religion, the sole civil right granted a Jew was to be baptised as a Christian . . . or to lend money at interest (usury: banned to Christians). As usurers the Jews were condemned and yet were found useful. Briefly (*c.*AD 900–1200) their scholastic talents flowered in **Islamic** Spain. But, prohibited by Judaic law from marrying Gentiles (non-Jews), those living in North Europe were denied racial assimilation. This separatism, and crusading hysteria, led to fantastic myths. **Antichrist** would be a Jew of the tribe of Dan; Christ-denying Jews ritually slaughtered Christian children to get blood for use in the Passover rites. This infamous 'blood libel' (attributed to 'Hugh of Lincoln': England 1255) was used to justify atrocity. Jews under torture vainly pointed out that they could not consume blood in any form, while neurotic Christian imagination developed the reverse fantasy of the 'demonic' Jew.

The slaughter began in the twelfth century. In 1290 the Jews were expelled from England, in 1395 from France, and in 1492 from Spain. Forced into ghettoes throughout north Europe, they were blamed for the Black Death which (1348–50) killed a third of Europe's population. They were said to poison the wells. In 1349 the folk of Brussels, Frankfurt, Mainz and Cologne killed every Jew they found, 'because they thought to please God in that way'.[1]

The myth of the demonic Jew endured. Late in the nineteenth century, men like **Richard Wagner** and Houston Stewart Chamberlain fanned the flames. In 1903 in Russia a text appeared: *The Protocols of the Elders of Zion*, apparently proof of an 'international Jewish conspiracy' for world conquest, said to be issued by the Judaic Congress at Basle in 1897. Anti-Semites eagerly believed the fraud. In 1919 the White Russian army slaughtered some 60,000 Jews, blaming them for the 1917 Revolution. Even in 1921 the London *Times* called the *Protocols* genuine. In his *Mein Kampf*, Nazi leader Adolf Hitler used the *Protocols* to justify his own anti-Semitism (though he too may have had Jewish blood). When in 1933 he took over Germany he began a pogrom that led to the 'Final Solution': an attempt to exterminate all Jews. Some six million Jews died, many in the gas chambers of Auschwitz and Belsen.

Today, though the Jews have regained their old homeland, Israel, the *Protocols* (long dismissed as a total forgery) remain in circulation, while apocalyptic Christian sects continue to insist that **Armageddon**, the final battle between the forces of good and evil, Christ and Antichrist, will take place in what some still call the Holy Land.

1. *The Pursuit of the Millennium*, Norman Cohn, Paladin, London, 1970, p.139.

JEZEBEL (*See* **BAAL**, *FEMMES FATALES*, **YAHWEH**)
This daughter of the Phoenician priest-king Ethbaal married the Hebrew King Ahab (ruled *c*.874-*c*.853 BC) and persuaded him to deny the Hebrew god **Yahweh** (Jehovah) in favour of the Tyrian **Baal**. When she had the prophets of Yahweh slain, the prophet Elijah (I Kings xvii) accurately prophesied severe drought as divine retribution, then had Baal's priests slain when they lost a contest with him to see which god would ignite a **bull**-offering. Jezebel forced Elijah to flee for his life. When her false accusations led to the death by stoning of Naboth of Jezreel, Elijah told Ahab that he and all his heirs would be destroyed, and that Jezebel would be devoured by the dogs of Jezreel. Surviving Ahab's death in battle with the Syrians, Jezebel defied the prophet Elisha and perished, whereupon dogs ate most of her body (*c*.843 BC). Her name survives as the epitome of the wicked woman.

JOSEPH OF ARIMATHEA (*See* **CHRISTIANITY**, **GLASTONBURY**, **HOLY GRAIL**)
About AD 1200 Robert de Boron (author of *Le Roman de l'Estoire dou Saint Graal*) wrote a poem, 'Joseph d'Arimathie', telling how this wealthy **Jew**, a secret follower of **Christ**, came to be the first keeper of the **Holy Grail**. The New Testament tells how, with Pilate's permission, Joseph took down Christ from the **cross** and with Nicodemus, another secret follower, buried him in his own tomb, from which the risen Christ then vanished. A fourth-century tale says the Jews, furious with him, locked him up in a windowless room, meaning to kill him, but that Christ appeared to lead him safely home.
Robert de Boron (claiming he had seen a 'great book' containing all he tells) said the vessel in which Christ celebrated the Last Supper was given by Pilate to Joseph who, preparing Christ for burial, in it gathered blood from Christ's wounds. Entombing the body, he hid the vessel in his house. In prison he was visited by the risen Christ who, bearing this 'great and precious vessel', told him only three men would ever guard it and that all who saw it would be forever in Christ's presence. Joseph remained in jail, but the chalice sustained him. Later freed, with his sister Enygeus and her husband Bron (**Bran**, the **Fisher King**) he left Palestine. Later Bron carried the Grail to the West, Joseph being left behind.[1]
A later account says Joseph himself brought the Grail to Britain, and that at Wearyall Hill, **Glastonbury**, he planted his staff. This flowered as a thorn tree – its descendent is said still to flower every January. The first mention of the Glastonbury Thorn is *c*.1500. It is ambiguous, as the original legend says nothing of the Grail. The monks claimed that in AD 63 the apostle Philip had sent twelve disciples from France to Britain, led by Joseph, who brought two silver vessels, one containing Christ's sweat, the other his blood. Later popular demand converted these vessels into the Grail. To preserve it from profanity, Joseph buried the Grail at the foot of Glastonbury Tor, perhaps in the Chalice Well – a recent myth. Either way, Joseph is credited with the introduction of Christianity to Britain.[2]
Other spurious accounts claim him as Christ's uncle, and say that, because of his connection with the Cornish tin trade, he brought the young Jesus to Britain.

1. *King Arthur and the Grail*, Richard Cavendish, Paladin, London, 1980, p.147.
2. *Ibid.*, p.181.

JOTUNHEIM (*See* AESIR, NORSE MYTH, THOR)

Norse land of the Frost **Giants**, who were constantly trying to kidnap the goddess **Freya**. Once the giant Thrymr stole **Thor**'s **hammer** 'Mjollnir' and refused to return it unless Freya married him. **Heimdall** persuaded Thor to take her place, disguised by a bridal veil, with **Loki** disguised as his handmaid. Received in Jotunheim, Thor almost gave the game away by eating eight salmon and an entire ox. Loki said the bride was ravenous because her desire to wed had kept her fasting eight nights. Thrymr tried to kiss 'Freyja' but saw glaring eyes under the veil: Loki said this was because 'she' had been unable to sleep for eight nights. When the hammer was laid in the bride's lap to hallow the marriage, Thor threw off his disguise to slay Thrymr and every other giant, as is told in the Elder **Edda**.

JOVE (*See* JUPITER, ROMAN MYTH)

JOYCE, JAMES (1882–1941) (*See* IRISH MYTH, YEATS)

Irish author famed for the novels *Ulysses* (1922) and *Finnegans Wake* (1939). Jesuit-educated, on graduating from University College, Dublin, he went to Paris in 1902 then with his lover, Nora Barnacle (whom he married in 1931), to Trieste, where two children were born, then to Rome, then Zurich (1915) then Paris (1920–40), then back to Zurich where he died in 1941.

An early autobiographical novel, *Stephen Hero* (1904), was rewritten as *A Portrait of the Artist as a Young Man* (1916), following *Dubliners* (1914) a short story collection, and preceding *Exiles* (1918), a play. *Portrait* shows that he rejected Catholicism but not myth and theology, as developed in *Ulysses* and *Finnegans Wake*: both experimental in theme and structure.

He made **Homer**'s **Ulysses** (his boyhood hero) a modern Dubliner. Begun 1914, *Ulysses* (1922) describes a day in the life of middle-aged Jew, Leopold Bloom, and his young friend, Stephen Dedalus (*see* **Daedalus**). Both are Joyce: father seeks son and vice versa. Bloom's wanderings round Dublin follow Homer. The **Sirens** are two barmaids; the one-eyed **Cyclopes** a mad Irish nationalist; **Circe**, who turned men into swine, a brothel madam; Bloom himself a resilient cuckold who turns humiliation into wit. His Dublin day (Bloomsday, 16 June, when Joyce met Nora) is mythic in the breadth of its allusion. In the brothel scene, the Voice of Elijah delivers its message, Celtic sea-god **Manannan MacLir** rises from behind a coal-skuttle, right hand holding a bicycle pump (*pneuma*, breath of life), his left a crayfish glowing with the twelve signs of the zodiac. Joyce calls him 'Mananaun', 'aun' being both the Sanskrit holy syllable AUM and the Irish *aun*, 'one'.

Finnegans Wake (unreadable as an ordinary novel), begins with the end of a sentence: 'riverrun, past Eve and Adam's', its start ending the book, to demonstrate Vico's theory of cyclic history (Italian: eighteenth century). Telling of Dublin publican Humphrey Chimpden Earwicker (alias 'Here Comes Everybody'), his wife (Anna Livia Plurabelle) and their children (Shem, Shaun and Isabel), or, on another level, of Dublin and the River Liffey, it portrays humanity's dream-life. Languages, words, events and characters merge. Thus four tavern cronies are the four evangelists, the world's four quarters or the four posts of the bed in which the dreamer lies, endlessly confusing (or elucidating?) the apparitions of reality, any of which may or may not be true, as echoed throughout as St Augustine's oxymoron: *O felix culpa!* ('O happy fault!'). 'Poor Felix Culapert!' cries a voice in this nightmare vision, or, as Joyce has Elijah cry in *Ulysses*, 'It's up to you to sense that cosmic force. You have something within, the higher self.'

JUDAISM (*See* **JEWS AND ANTI-SEMITISM, YAHWEH**)
Monotheistic Jewish religion holds that the presence of God (Yahweh) is
manifest in human history; that He confronted the early Jews to establish a
'covenant' (*berit*) between God and Man, with the Jews as witness of it for all.
God is source of the *Torah* (Hebrew Scriptures), the *Mishna* and *Talmud* (oral
tradition), and all other moral and ceremonial demands as interpreted
through the texts of the *Midrash*. Abraham (twentieth century BC?) is viewed
as Judaism's founder. God's covenant with him preceded the migration of his
descendents, the twelve Tribes, to **Egypt**, and was fulfilled via **Moses** who
led the Hebrews out of Egypt (*c*. fourteenth century BC), new obligations
being laid on them when Moses brought the Ten Commandments down
Mount **Sinai**. The Mosaic claim, that humanity has a dual nature, is defined
by the ability to choose between obedience ('good') and disobedience ('evil').
To sin is to disobey the Law, *Torah*, return to which must be deliberate. This
ethical capacity involves establishing a just society.

Jewish belief that Yahweh rules all humanity ensured them the power to
survive the persecutions marking their history. Assyrian conquest of Judah
(eighth century BC) led the **prophets** Isaiah and Micah to foretell an ideal
future society on earth under the **Messiah** and the conversion of the world to
Yahweh. Messianic hopes remained unfulfilled by the fall of Babylon and
restoration of the Kingdom of Judah (538 BC). Further conquests of Judah
by **Alexander** and the Romans led to revolt by the Maccabees and to the rise
of the Pharisees, holding to the Oral Law, and the Sadducees, insisting on the
written word of the *Torah*. Christ was rejected as a false Messiah.

Jews scattered by the diaspora (Dispersal) developed the *Talmud* (Oral
Law), maintaining their calendar and the authority of the rabbis (teachers of
the Law) to ensure Judaism's survival despite new beliefs: Sephardic Judaism
in Moslem Spain and Ashkenazic Judaism in North Europe. Conflict was
averted by the need to resist anti-Semitism in Europe as a whole. Hasidism
and **Qabalah** also arose in the medieval era. Later nationalistic Zionism,
reacting to twentieth-century anti-Semitism, asserted a militant programme
of resettlement in Palestine which, in 1948, following the **Nazi** holocaust of
World War II, led to the establishment of the state of Israel.

JUDAS ISCARIOT (*See* **CHRISTIANITY**)

JUJU (*See* **AFRICAN MYTH, FETISH, SORCERY**)
African term for a magical fetish, from the creole French *joujou*, 'toy',
something to play with – thus worry-beads or **amulets** worn against evil
spirits – or from the **Koran** (xxi, 96), speaking of Doomsday brought by two
demons, Yajuju and Majuju. Either way, juju implies a rite or object that
protects against evil, typically involving **blood** sacrifice of man or beast to
make it work. A West African derivation is from the Hausa **Bori** spirit jigo or
jugu, 'father of the hunters'.

JUMALA (*See* **KALEVALA**)

JUNG, CARL GUSTAV (1875–1961) (*See* **DREAMS, FREUD,
GNOSTIC MYTH, NAZI MYTH**)
As this great Swiss seer died, his favourite tree in his garden at Küsnacht near
Zurich was struck by lightning. His distant friend Laurens van der Post
dreamed Jung waved and said, 'I'll be seeing you', and next day learned Jung
was dead. Years later, making a film about Jung at Küsnacht, van der Post
saw lightning strike again as he described Jung's death to camera.[1]

A clergyman's son, Jung's **dreams** fascinated him. In one, aged twelve, he saw Basle Cathedral shattered by excrement from a throne in the sky. Later he interpreted this to mean that traditional Christianity was exhausted. As a psychiatry student at Zurich he denounced the 'lack of ordinary, healthy curiosity' on the part of 'men in command of religious, and scientific and philosophic heights.'[2] Early work led him to conclude that madness arises from the arrested development of an individual's personal myth. Insisting that 'healer' and 'patient' must enjoy a sacred relationship of mutual quest, he commented, 'In the end only the wounded physician heals.'[3]

An early supporter of **Freud**, Jung aimed to reconcile opposites which to Freud were permanent and fixed. Nor could he support Freud's insistence on sexuality as the main subconscious driving force. They parted company. Jung published *Psychology of the Unconscious* then suffered a period of personal crisis. In 1913 he resigned his professorship amid a flood of terrifying dreams. In one he saw a bloody tide flood Europe from the north, carrying mangled corpses to the rim of the Alps. Dreaming of the land of the dead, he met a black **serpent**, a whitebearded man and a blind girl. The serpent he identified as his instinctual self; the old man as Elijah (archetype of the 'wise old man'), and the blind girl (Salome) as his *anima* (female element in the male subconscious). Yet why was she blind? Painting and writing down his dreams, Gnostic and alchemical studies led him to the ancient **Mysteries**. He saw restoration of this despised body of knowledge as vital to global mental health.

In 1916–17 he wrote a bizarre book – *Septem Sermones ad Mortuos* (Seven Sermons to the Dead) – its origin as weird as its Gnostic language. He and his three children sensed ghostly entities in the house, the doorbell rang with no visible cause, a crowd of 'spirits' seemed to fill the hallway, and when he cried 'For God's sake, what in the world is this?' the answer came 'in a chorus of ghostly voices': 'We have come back from Jerusalem where we found not what we sought.'[4]

Thereafter in his work (*The Psychology of Type; Roots of the Conscious; Archetypes and the Collective Unconscious; Psychology and Religion; Modern Man in Search of a Soul*, etc.) he tried to establish the objective validity of the collective unconscious: a primal energy-field which carries mythic archetypes and underlies the personal unconscious. In 1921 he proposed the theory of extroversion and introversion. Extroverts seek meaning via outer forms; introverts, via inner quest. He claimed that modern Western man, by rejecting natural feeling, has embraced an 'intellectual barbarism'.

Studying astrology as a projected form of human psychology, in 1928 he read Wilhelm's translation of the Chinese alchemical classic, *The Secret of the Golden Flower*. This led to study of Eastern mandala patterns as images of wholeness in nature (and in humanity). His research into the Mysteries led to rediscovery of the 'Shadow' – the mass of unconscious forces rejected by the conscious mind, thus always accumulating and ready to break out. As early as 1918 he foresaw the coming **Nazi** eruption of suppressed Germanic **archetypes**, later calling Hitler 'The loudspeaker that makes audible all the inaudible mutterings of the German soul'.[5] His solution was to accept the hated opposite as an integral part of the hitherto divided self, thus transforming and redeeming it (i.e., 'Love your enemy as yourself').

His ground-breaking researches into the 'dark wood' of myths and dreams complemented the similar journey undertaken by many contemporary writers, poets and artists (**Dali**, **Joyce**, Klee, Magritte, **Yeats**, Picasso, etc.). Combining scientific rigour with the intuition of the mystic, over and over again he warned of the consequences of rejecting the inner, mythic life. 'I am convinced,' he wrote, 'that the growing impoverishment of symbols has a meaning. Everything that we have not thought about, and that has therefore been deprived of a meaningful connection with our developing consciousness, has got lost . . . We have inherited this poverty from our fathers.'[6]

1. *Jung and the Story of our Time*, Laurens van der Post, Penguin, London, 1978, pp.263ff.
2. *Ibid.*, p.104.
3. *Ibid.*, p.128.
4. *The Gnostic Jung and the Seven Sermons to the Dead*, Stephan A. Hoeller, Quest Books, Wheaton, Illinois, 1982, pp.7ff.
5. *op.cit.* Jung, pp.263ff.
6. *The Archetypes of the Collective Unconscious*, C.G. Jung, pp.13–15

JUNO (*See* **JUPITER, MOTHER-GODDESS, ROMAN MYTH**)

Roman queen of heaven, sister and wife of the god Jupiter, this great goddess dates from early times as the mother deity of pre-Roman tribes including the Sabines and Etruscans. As Goddess of Light (Juno Lucina), she also became the goddess of childbirth (Juno Sospita), the new-born child being brought forth into the light, and as such she also ruled fecundity and marriage (Juno Pronuba) – the month of June, once Junonius, was anciently thought the most favourable for marriages. She was invoked by barren women and as Juno Lucina saved the Sabine women from the curse of sterility that struck them after their abduction and rape. As Martialis she was mother of the war-god **Mars**, giving birth to him by means of mystic union with a fabulous flower. As Juno Moneta (Latin *monere*, 'to warn'), she advised the Romans. Her sacred bird was the **goose**. When the Gauls tried to scale the walls of the Capitol, her geese warned the defenders of the danger. Later, when the mint where money was coined was installed near her temple, the term 'moneta' changed its meaning. The Matronalia, the festivals of Juno Lucina (represented with a child in her arms and two more at her feet), were celebrated by Roman matrons at the Kalends of March. Her Greek equivalent, more tempestuous by half, was the goddess **Hera**.

JUPITER (*See* **DYAUS-PITA, JUNO, ROMAN MYTH**)

The root of the name of this Roman sky-god of light is identical to that of the **Vedic Dyaus-pita**, from *div*, 'to shine'. Jupiter is thus in origin 'Di-Pater' or 'Zeus-Pater' – 'Sky-Father'. As the Etruscan god Tinia (*Tonans*, 'Thunderer') his role was to warn men and, if necessary, punish them. Of his three thunderbolts, he could hurl the first whenever he liked, as a warning, but to hurl the second, which was also to warn, he required the permission of twelve gods called *consentes* or *complices*. The third, which did the punishing, could be released only by permission of the superior or hidden gods – *dii superiores* or *dii involuti*.

Forming a triad with **Juno** and **Minerva**, he was worshipped throughout Italy as the god controlling all celestial phenomena, thus he was the deity of agricultural fertility. As Jupiter Elicius he made the rain fall. As Jupiter Dapalis he presided over sowing and as Jupiter Terminus guarded the boundary-stones of fields. Later his rural functions were subsumed in his more important roles as warrior-protector of the Roman city and state and as tutelary deity of the Empire. As such he was called *Imperator* ('Supreme

General'); *Invictus* ('Invincible'); and *Triumphator* ('Triumphant'). As Jupiter Capitolinus (with his temple on the Capitoline Hill in Rome, where he was also known as Optimus Maximus: 'Best and Greatest') he presided over the *ludi romani*, the annual Roman games, and also over all declarations of war. Victorious generals offered him a crown of gold and a share of the booty (thus he was called *Praedator*, 'Booty-Snatcher'). As Prodigialis he revealed the future by **omens** and portents; as upholder of justice he had oath-breakers hurled from the Tarpeian Rock on the Capitoline Hill.

Reduced in function and power by the introduction (first century BC) of emperor worship, he became more remote, directing human destiny from afar. Cicero, executed in 43 BC for advocating a return to republicanism, equated Jupiter with 'the awful presence of a supreme mind'. His representations came chiefly from Greek art: his functions were similar to those of the Greek god **Zeus**. Yet, as with other Roman deities, Jupiter remains oddly abstract and without personality compared with other **hammer** or **thunderbolt**-hurling sky-gods – libidinous Zeus, **soma**-drinking **Indra**, or roaring lusty **Thor**. Only if referred to as Jupiter Jovis (*Jove*, thus 'jovial'), does any sense of character emerge.

K

KA (See EGYPTIAN MYTH, IMMORTALITY)

In ancient Egyptian belief the *ka* (double) reflects the *khat* (perishable physical body) and dwells with the mummy in the tomb. The *ba* (**soul**) is a **bird**, symbolising the bodily animating principle *khu* (the imperishable soul) which is part of the spiritual body (*sahu*), seen as material in an early view of the resurrection. *Sahu, ba, ka, khaibit* (shadow) and *ikhu* (vital force) were said to recombine after 3,000 years, leading to a rebirth germinated from the physical body. To ensure rebirth the body had to be preserved by mummification. This Egyptian concept retains a potent emotional force.

Egyptologist Wallis Budge called the *ka* 'an abstract individuality or personality which possessed the form and attributes of the man to whom it belonged, and, though its normal dwelling place was in the tomb with the body, it could wander about at will; it was independent of the man and could go and dwell in any statue of him.'[1] Entombed, it needed food and drink or would seek wider sustenance. Flinders Petrie cites the tale of the *ka* of Ahura, buried at Koptos, visiting the tomb of her husband in Memphis. He says the *ka* contains 'the inner mental consciousness and hereditary powers of thought, as apart from the influence of the senses, and continued without the use of the bodily actions'.[2]

1. *The Egyptian Book of the Dead*, E.A. Wallis Budge, Routledge & Kegan Paul, London, 1969, p.lix.
2. *Religious Life in Ancient Egypt*, Sir Flinders Petrie, Constable, London, 1924, p.113.

KABBALAH (See QABALAH)

KACHINAS (See HOPI LORE)

KALEVALA (See RUNES, SIBELIUS)

National epic of Finland. The native name, *Suomi*, means 'Land of Waters', one-ninth of the land consisting of lakes or marshes, the rest being fir and pine forest. There are no mountains and few hills. Lapland (land of the Lapps, reindeer-herders once famed as magicians), north of the Arctic Circle, is called Pohjola in the *Kalevala*. The Finnish language, Suomi, is related to the Magyar of Hungary, people of Finno-Ugric stock being found from the upper Volga and western Siberia to Hungary and Finland itself.

The epic consists of older oral materials organised by Elias Lönnrot, who *c*.1828 began gathering the popular songs or *runot* (runes) of the land. In 1835 he published these as the *Kalevala* ('Fatherland of Heroes'), an epic poem of 12,000 verses. His final 1849 version, 22,800 verses long, gained European fame and later stimulated Finnish nationalism, especially through its musical interpretation by Sibelius. Written in eight-syllabled trochaic verse (copied by Longfellow in *Hiawatha*), it encapsulates Finnish myth just as Snorri's *Prose Edda* (thirteenth century) encapsulated **Norse** myth.

It tells how the once-supreme god Jumala fell to Ukko, 'ancient father who reigns in the heavens', who gathered clouds and made the rain fall. His wife was Akka, or Rauni, the **rowan**. Other primeval deities were Päivä the **sun**, Kuu the **moon**, Otava the Great Bear, and Ilma, goddess of the air.

The tale begins with Ilma's daughter Luonnotar ('Daughter of Nature') who, tired of her celestial virginity, fell from the sky to the unformed **ocean**. Fertilised by the ocean, for seven centuries she floated, pregnant but unable to give birth or find a place to rest. At last an **eagle** (or duck), seeing her knee emerge from the water, built its nest on her knee, laid its **eggs**, and for three days sat on them. But Luonnotar threw off the bird's heat. The eggs sank into the abyss. From them came the material universe.

From the lower shells came the earth, from the upper shells the skies, from the yolk the sun, from the white the moon. White spots in the eggs formed the stars; dark spots, the clouds. Then Luonnotar made the coastline and the ocean bed, setting up rocks as pillars for the sky.

So the earth came into being. Luonnotar's son Väinamöinen spent thirty years fully grown in her womb then escaped her. Already old, he fell into the sea, but struggled ashore to clear then sow the bare land of Kalevala. Joukahainen 'the thin son of Lapland' (*see* **Jotunheim**: the Frost Giants of the Ice Age were ever-terrible to folk clearing the north) challenged him. So he sang magic songs that made swamps roar, the earth tremble, the copper mountains sway. They also turned Joukahainen's **sword** into lightning, his bow into a **rainbow**, his arrows into **hawks** and his **dog** into stone.

Trapping the Laplander ear-deep in a bog, Väinamöinen made him pledge his sister Aino in marriage to him. Aino, aghast, threw herself into the sea and became a water-sprite rather than marry the newcomer.

To get a wife, Väinamöinen was told to go north to Pohja (Pohjola: the 'back country' of ice and darkness). Ambushed by Joukahainen and thrown in the sea, he swam for eight days. An eagle carried him to the dismal land where the Maid of Pohja heard him weep. Her mother, the sorceress Louhi (the original Wicked Witch of the North) promised him the Maid, but only if he could forge the sampo: a magical mill that could grind flour, salt and gold endlessly. This, he said, only Ilmarinen the **smith-god** (his brother) could do. Declaring that only the sampo's maker could have the Maid, Louhi dismissed him. Leaving, he saw the Maid on a rainbow, weaving golden cloth. He asked her to be his wife. She said yes, but only if first he split a horsehair with a blunt knife, tied an egg in knots, peeled a stone, cut a pile of ice without splinters and, last, built a ship from pieces of her spindle and shuttle. All these impossible tasks he did. But as he began the final task the **demons** Lempo, Paha, and Hisi made him axe his own knee. Healed by an old man, he built the ship by singing a magic song for each part. Yet when he came to join the planks, he had forgotten the necessary three magic words. Going down to Tuonela (the **underworld**) to find them, he met the sleeping **giant**, Antero Vipunen, from whose body trees grew.

Felling the trees, Väinamöinen plunged his **iron** staff into the giant's throat. Vipunen swallowed him, but in his belly Väinamöinen made a forge, bellows, anvil and hammer. Then Antero Vipunen 'opened the coffer full of words, the coffer full of songs.' So Väinamöinen returned to life to complete his ship, then sent Ilmarinen his brother to Pohjola to forge the sampo. This Ilmarinen did. Firing barley grain and milk of a barren heifer with **swan's** feathers and fine wool, he won Louhi's daughter, returning to Kalevala even as Väinamöinen set out to woo her. Ilmarinen tried to cut him off. Väinamöinen got there, but the Maid still preferred Ilmarinen.

Väinamöinen gave up. Odd that, after his defeat of Vipunen by using the blacksmith's magic iron-working power, Väinamöinen gave Ilmarinen the advantage. Perhaps he and Ilmarinen were originally one and the same?

But then the Maid was eaten by the evil **bears** of Kullervo. Ilmarinen asked Louhi for her second daughter. Rejected, he abducted the girl, who slept with another man so he turned her into a seagull. Then back in Kalevala he told Väinamöinen how the sampo made Pohjola rich. The two heroes, deciding to steal it, were joined by the hero Lemminkäinen (see below). Their ship hit an island, in fact a huge pike. Slain by Ilmarinen's iron sword, from the pike's bones Väinamöinen made the *kantele* – a five-stringed harp. Reaching Louhi's now rich court, he played it so wondrously that all – even Halli and Lukki, the **dogs** guarding the sampo in a room with seven locks – fell asleep.

The heroes stole the sampo, but Lemminkäinen's victory song awoke the Pohjolans. Sailing south, the three heroes were pursued by Louhi's raging magical storm. The kantele was lost and the sampo broken, but Väinamöinen's recovery of its fragments ensured Karelia's wealth. Louhi loosed scourges on Karelia, locking up sun and moon in the cave of northern night. Yet Väinamöinen, declaring his mission complete, sailed off (like King **Arthur,Bran** or **Frodo**) into the west, never again to be seen by mortal man.

As for the seducer Lemminkäinen, son of Lempi ('Love'), he first came to Pohjola to woo the Maid that Ilmarinen later married. Reaching Louhi's palace in the dark, he drove out all other men save for the blind cowherd Märkhättu, whom he pitied. Asking Louhi for the hand of her daughter, he was set three tasks: one, to catch the Elk of Hiisi; two, to catch Hiisi's fire-breathing **horse**; three, to shoot a swan on the underworld river of Tuonela. As he neared the river, Markhättu (furious at being pitied) sent a water **serpent** to attack him. Not knowing the magic words of protection, he perished. The son of Tuoni, God of the Dead, hacked his body into five pieces (so Egyptian **Set** hacked up **Osiris**). But Lemminkäinen's mother Kyllikki went down to Tuonela and, collecting the scraps of his body, she rejoined them (*see* **Isis**). She sent a **bee** to heaven for honey to anoint his body, so that, like many another fertility god, he was revived.

The tests set on Väinamöinen are like those imposed on **Hercules** or **Gilgamesh**. Mythic heroes are invariably set upon by angry goddesses who resent the male takeover of former female preserves. Myth is an historical shorthand.

Later, angry at not being invited to the wedding of Ilmarinen with Louhi's daughter, Väinamöinen laid Pohjola waste, but Louhi unleashed the cold. Ice held fast his ship as he tried to escape south. But this time Lemminkäinen knew the magic words he needed to melt the ice and escape.

The *Kalevala* closely details the magical element in Finnish myth. Once the Finns and Lapps were feared for their **shamanic** powers. In the sixteenth and seventeenth centuries the Swedish authorities searched out and seized the *quodbas* (magic **drums**) of the Lapps. Certainly, the long dark nights of the north concentrate the mind. Here, the Snow-Queen has her lair.

KALI (*See* DEVI, HINDUISM, INDIAN MYTH, TANTRAS)

Like Durga (the 'Inaccessible') an emanation of Devi, this fierce Hindu death-goddess (her name means the 'Black') is voluptuous but terrifying. She destroys everything since nothing lasts forever. Human blood drips from her three blazing eyes, her tongue hangs out to lap the blood of her victims, **snakes** writhe about her neck, her black body is festooned with chains of human skulls, and there are weapons in each of her ten hands. Victims (including, some say, human beings) are sacrificed in her rites, the Durga-puja. Like Egyptian **Hathor** she glories in killing, ignoring every plea to stop.

When her husband **Shiva** lay down among her victims, she decapitated him then danced on his dead body, his head in one hand and a sword in the other. Her **Celtic** equivalents are the Scottish *Cailleach* (hag) and the Irish **Morrigan**.

KALI YUGA (*See* BRAHMA, IRON, *KALPA*, YUGA)

KALPA (*See* BRAHMA, JAINISM, YUGA)
In Brahmanic cosmology a kalpa is one day of the god Brahma, equating to a mere 4,320,000,000 years, and consists of four world ages (yugas). The day (universe) begins when Brahma opens his eye and ends when he closes it. Then he sleeps for an equal period, before opening his eye to generate a new universe. The Buddha said that when a piece of cloth has rubbed away a mountain sixteen miles long, high and broad, then one second of kalpa is past.

In **Jain** cosmology, kalpa and kalpathitha are the universe's two highest levels. The kalpa region consists of sixteen devalokas or heavens, the kalpathitha of fourteen abodes for the gods.

KALUNGA (*See* AFRICAN MYTH, UNDERWORLD)
This supreme god of the Ndonga in northern Namibia may assume human form but is so vast that those claiming to see him never see more than a part of him, the rest being hidden by mist and cloud as he strides above the hills.

Kalunga is also an **underworld** kingdom where the dead live. The Mbundu of Angola tell how when his head wife Muhungo died, chief Kitambe told his people not to speak or eat until she was restored to life. So a medicine-man built a grave in the fireplace of his house, descended into it with his son, told his wife to water the grave daily, then ordered the men to entomb him. At the bottom of the grave was a road. Following it, he and his son met Muhungo weaving a basket. She indicated a man nearby – Kalungangombe, Lord of the Underworld – and also a shadowy figure in chains, the spirit of Kitambe, also destined soon to die. Giving the medicine-man a bracelet as proof of his visit, Muhungo said he must tell Kitambe that none who entered Kalunga could ever leave. Yet he must not mention seeing Kitambe's spirit, nor should he or his son eat while in Kalunga, or they too would have to stay. So one day, watering the grave, the medicine-man's wife saw the earth crack. Her husband reappeared, pulling their son after him. He showed Kitambe Muhungo's bracelet, which Kitambe recognised. Soon after, Kitambe died.

KAMADEVA (*See* CUPID, INDIAN MYTH, SHIVA)
The **Hindu** God of Love (Kama means 'desire'). The **Vedas** say that desire caused life by making the first being move. Like **Aphrodite**, Kamadeva's mother **Lakshmi** arose from the ocean waves. Kamadeva rides a parrot, the wisest bird, or a peacock, symbol of impatient desire.

KAMI (*See* JAPANESE MYTH)

KANE (*See* HAWAII)

KARINA (*See* EGYPTIAN MYTH, ISLAM, OWL, SOLOMON)
King **Solomon**, hunting in the Egyptian desert, met a beautiful naked woman who asked why he hunted on her land. She said no man could defeat her. He asked who could. She said (not knowing who he was) the **archangel Michael**. Solomon invoked Michael, whose shining armour so scared her

that, instantly becoming old and grey, she identified herself as the **demon** Karina, feared in all **Islamic** lands, often appearing as an **owl**, a **snake** or a **dog**. Mother of Dead Children, Sender of the Evil **Eye**, Bird of Illness, her look stopped cows calving, ewes lambing, withered crops, and dried up the seed of husbands. She was once human but ate her children to gain magic power. God condemned her to bear only dead children. Any woman to whom she showed her bloody pudenda would bear only dead children thereafter. Any human at all who set eyes on her fell sick. That, she told Solomon, was **fate**.

KARMA (*See* BUDDHISM, HINDUISM, REINCARNATION)
Central to **Buddhism** and **Hinduism**, the doctrine of karma ('act', 'deed': Sanskrit) asserts that every act and thought creates consequences. Over a lifetime, each individual accumulates karma, either positive (via good deeds) or negative (via evil deeds), a metaphysical reckoning being made at the end of each life. Likewise, the **Christian** doctrine that the good go to **heaven**, the bad, to **hell**. In each case, a type of spiritual accountancy is involved. But the Eastern perspective differs in two ways.

One: Karmic doctrine is tied to belief in **reincarnation**. There is no easy escape from the world. The **atman** ('soul') is reborn, bearing the sins accumulated from its former incarnations. Good karma earned in one earthly incarnation leads to a higher social status or a happier life in the next. Bad karma leads to rebirth in a lower order of existence – as a debased person, or worse, as an animal, or even reptile or fish. The acts and thoughts of one life immutably create the conditions of the next. There is no escaping the cycle of rebirth save by living many good lives.

Two: Western science asserts cause and effect, but Christianity exempts believers from such natural law. The doctrine of the Redemption of Christ implies salvation for all who believe in Christ. A repentant murderer may be 'saved', but not a virtuous 'pagan'. To Buddhists, this is delusion.

Studying murder-rates among different religious groups in India during the 1880s, a British Royal Commission found that murder among Christian and Moslem populations (both without a theory of karma) was three times higher than among Hindus, and six times higher than among Buddhists, and decided that belief in karma explained the difference. Both Christians and Moslems killed more readily, believing such crimes might be forgiven. Buddhists killed reluctantly, believing that such acts might rebound against them in future lives. Whichever belief is of greater social utility (whatever the basic metaphysical reality of either) may be left to impartial judges.

KARTIKEYA (*See* GANESA, GANGES, INDIAN MYTH)
One day the Indian god **Shiva** drenched the **fire** with his seed; the fire went out, the River **Ganges** received the seed and bore the war-god Kartikeya. Another tale is that he was son of Devasena ('God's Army') and **Agni** the fire-god. Either way, like **Mars**, he was also god of fire and of the destruction fire causes in war. This celestial general and **demon**-slayer rides the peacock Paravani, holding a bow and arrow.

KELPIE (*See* CELTIC MYTH, FABULOUS BEASTS, LAKE MONSTERS, RIVER MYTH)
This fierce Scottish river-**sprite** usually appeared as a black, wild-eyed **horse** haunting fords. Seeing it browsing by the water, wayfarers would mount it in hope of a dry crossing, then be thrown and drowned. Or it might appear as a fine young man, its **fairy** origin betrayed by the water-weed or rushes caught

in its hair. If caught in equine form, it could be harnessed with a bridle on which the sign of the **cross** had been made, and thus made to drag stone to build a dyke or steading. But usually it fled.[1]

Deadly in flood, the River Conan in Easter Ross was noted for kelpies and other river-sprites, including a tall, scowling woman dressed in green, who would leap out of the river at travellers and urge them to their doom – a version of the *bean-nighe*. Some 300 years ago, harvesters by the Conan heard a voice cry: 'The hour is come, but not the man.' Then they saw the kelpie in the 'false ford' under the old kirk. It vanished into a lower pool as a man rode up to the ford. They warned him, but he rode on. To save him, they shut him in the kirk until the danger-hour was past. But on returning they found him dead, face down in an old stone trough. He had had a fit and had died of drowning, as fated and foretold by the kelpie.

A version of this tale is told *c*.AD 1212 by Gervase of Tilbury in his *Otia Imperialia*, of a pool in the Rhône near Arles in Provence.[2]

It is easy to see how in the foaming peaty water of a Highland river folk would see the black tossing mane of the kelpie, and how in riverbank **alder** or **willow** with their trailing fronds they'd see the beckoning arms of the green-clad river-demon, inviting them to death.

1. *The Magic Arts in Celtic Britain*, Lewis Spence, Rider, London, 1970, p.91.
2. *Albion*, Jennifer Westwood, Granada, London, 1985.

KENNEDY, JOHN FITZGERALD (1917–63) (*See* ARTHURIAN MYTH, CURSES)

Still potent is the myth of President John Kennedy, assassinated on 22 November 1963 in Dallas, Texas. Ever since, ill-luck on a scale suggesting pursuit by the **Furies** of Greek myth has dogged the rich, prominent Irish Catholic family to which he belonged.

Entering politics as Democratic candidate in the 1960 Presidential campaign, Kennedy won by under 100,000 votes nationwide, to become the country's youngest-ever President. The White House became known as 'Camelot', as if he were a new King **Arthur**. While riding through Dallas in an open limousine on 22 November 1963 he was shot dead by one or more snipers. The murder seemed to be that of a god, of the hope of the future. His wife Jackie, drenched in his blood, became the tragic heroine of the West.

In 1968, there were rumours of a high-level conspiracy when his brother, the Presidential candidate Robert Kennedy, was killed in Los Angeles soon after the similar gun-murder of the black leader Martin Luther King. In 1969 Edward Kennedy drove off a bridge while drunk, leaving a secretary to drown, yet twenty years later was still a likely Presidential candidate. The 'Kennedy myth' still gripped America, and it persists.

KHADIR (*See* AFRICAN MYTH, GREEN MAN, IMMORTALITY)

Arabic name of a pre-**Islamic** deity, 'the Green One'. Immortal, since long ago he drank from the **Well** of Life, Khadir wanders the earth, visiting the same spot every 500 years. When local people tell him their land has always been a desert, he remembers forests, orchards and green fields. Identified with the vegetation-god **Adonis**, annually killed then born again in spring, Khadir is also identified with the Hebrew prophet Elijah, who never died. It is said he entered Africa with **Alexander the Great**. They reached a city guarded by a bronze horseman holding a sword, on it inscribed: 'This sword is for none but him who rules the world.' Khadir, speaking all languages on earth, deciphered the inscription, whereupon Alexander claimed the sword.

KICI MANITOU (*See* GLOOSCAP, HIAWATHA, NATIVE AMERICAN MYTH)

Or Gitche Manitou ('Great Spirit'). This supreme god of the Algonquins of eastern North America created heaven, earth, animals and plants. Uncreated and eternal, master of light and breath of life, manifest in the **sun** and fountainhead of all that is good, the Arapahoe tribe tell how at the start of the world this 'ancestor with the sacred pipe' wandered over the watery waste which alone existed, seeking a place where earth would rise. Calling together all water-birds and reptiles, which already existed, he asked them to help him. The turtle knew where to find earth; the birds brought it to him in their bills. Drying the clay on his pipe, he made the world and admired its beauty. Mankind he made from earth, breathing spirit into the body. Even the emergence of Bitter Man (disease, old age and death) could not destroy his achievement. The rite of smoking the pipe of peace he instituted when the northern tribes decided to exterminate the Delaware people. A white bird came to hover above the great chief's one daughter. She heard an inner voice tell her that Kici Manitou was sad and angry, and that to appease him all the warriors must wash their hands in the blood of a fawn, then, bearing gifts and their pipes, go to their elders and smoke with them the great pipe of peace, to unite them for ever.

KIKUYU (*See* AFRICAN MYTH, NGAI)

This numerous Kenyan people claim descent from Kikuyu (*kuyu*, 'fig'), whose nine daughters became the ancestral mothers of their nine clans. They call God *Ngai*, the Apportioner, the spirit of Mount Kenya, who at the **creation** gave his gifts to all folk on earth. To the Kikuyu he gave the knowledge of and tools for agriculture. Ngai is a **sky-god** who, like **Jupiter**, strikes oath-breakers with lightning. They say that a man's character and life is predestined by Ngai. They say that everyone has a spirit, *ngoma*, which at death becomes a ghost. They were at the core of Mau-Mau rebellion against British colonialism (1946–56). Mau-Mau may derive from the cry: '*Uma, Uma*' ('Out, Out'). Many Kikuyu, unwilling to join this war to expel Europeans, joined Mau-Mau for fear of being butchered, strangled or buried alive. The secret 'oathing chapels', at which recruits agreed to kill, cut and burn, were decorated with intestines and the gouged-out eyes of **goats**. Mau-Mau **initiation** was said to involve intercourse with dead goats and the eating of human brains. Such degradation was designed to so shame the initiate that any desire to return to Western ways was rooted out. Some 2,000 Kikuyu were killed by the Mau-Mau activists, and 11,000 by the British. About one hundred European settlers died during the conflict. 'History is the lie commonly agreed upon.' The British account is that the Mau-Mau activists were bestial, yet over a hundred Africans died for every white.

KING LEAR (*See* FISHER KING, LLŶR, SHAKESPEARE, WASTELAND)

William **Shakespeare** (1564–1616) based one of his four famous tragedies (*Hamlet, Macbeth* and *Othello* the others) on the myth of a British king originally called **Llŷr** ('of the sea': *see* **Manannan**).

KINGSHIP (*See* CANNIBALISM, FISHER KING, KING LEAR)

'Long live the king; the king must die' – as must all men. But in the case of the king, a man elevated to dominion and power (actual or symbolic) over others by personal achievement, or by birth into a hereditary royal family, such life and death assumes a potency distinct from the personality of the anointed individual. Epitomising the male principle, the king represents the deity and mediates God's powers on earth. **Head** of the body politic as the queen is its **heart**, in many traditions his vitality is held to reflect that of his people and the land itself (thus **Arthurian myth** of the wounded **Fisher King** and the sterility of the land). So in some old societies the king (or a scapegoat) was ritually slain when his vitality waned; or he was appointed for a season only, then **sacrificed** to propitiate the deities on whose good-will the society's health was said to rely. The **Aztecs** elected the most beautiful youth and loveliest maiden to reign for a year, then cut out their hearts and offered these to the **sun**. The king's sacrificed body might even be eaten, to perpetuate the holy power invested in it.

Kings were always hedged about by strict rules and **taboos**. As the very symbols of tribal or national coherence and prosperity, they were not free to act as they chose. Ancient kings might be scourged before their coronation to remind them of their duties. Irish coronations required the new king to crawl naked towards a white mare as if he were her foal, then bathe in and drink the broth of that mare, and eat her flesh (*see* **horse**). They might be forbidden to eat and drink in public (gods need not eat or drink), be protected by elaborate magic rituals, their **names** might not be spoken aloud, (as with the Merovingians) they might be forbidden ever to cut their **hair**, or no portraits might be made of them lest part of their **soul** (and thus vitality) be lost. They might be seen as divine by descent and thus possessed of miraculous powers: medieval French and English kings were said to be able to cure scrofula ('King's Evil') by touch alone – as late as 1745 **Bonnie Prince Charlie** held healing sessions in Edinburgh.

But always about them were ambitious men, thus: 'Uneasy lies the head that wears a crown.' Not surprisingly, some tried to advance the idea of the 'divine right of kings', justifying themselves as 'absolute' rulers with divine dispensation to do as they chose. The French 'Sun King', Louis XIV (1638–1715), promulgated this doctrine: in Britain the execution (1649) of the Stuart King Charles I and the deposition (1688) of his son, James II, led to the constitutional shackling of the monarchy.

KIPLING, (JOSEPH) RUDYARD (1865–1936)
This Indian-born English novelist, short-story writer and poet, though still vilified for celebrating British imperialism, is remembered mostly for his animal fables, of which in particular *The Jungle Books* (1894, 1895) and *Just So Stories* (1902) are generally (and rightly) regarded as classics.

His study of British colonial life and Indian folklore led to six volumes of short stories. While in the USA, he wrote (among other works) *The Jungle Books* – Indian fables of the wild boy Mowgli and his jungle life with humanised animals ('Shere Khan the Tiger', 'Baloo the Bear') which still enchant many. Later books – *Puck of Pook's Hill* (1906) and *Rewards and Fairies* (1910) – were set in Sussex.

KIRK, ROBERT (*c.*1641–92) (*See* CELTIC MYTH, FAIRIES)
This **seventh** son of James Kirk, a minister in Scotland, studied theology then also took the cloth. In 1685 he succeeded to his father's old ministry at Aberfoyle, a Highland region then rife with **fairy**-belief. Far from denouncing such belief, in 1691, a year before his seeming death, he completed a sympathetic study of the subject: *The Secret Commonwealth of Elves, Fauns and Fairies* (first published 1815).[1] A believer in his own psychic power as a

seventh son; in 'some secret virtue in the womb of the parent, which increaseth until the seventh son be borne, and decreaseth by the same degree afterwards,' Kirk's own fate is bound up with fairy-lore. It is said that in 1692, his text complete, he was out walking on a *dun-shi* (fairy-hill), and 'sunk down in a swoon, which was taken for death'.

'After the ceremony of a seeming funeral,' wrote Sir Walter Scott in his *Demonology and Witchcraft* (1830), quoting Kirk's successor, the Rev. Dr Grahame, 'the form of the Rev. Robert Kirk appeared to a relation, and commanded him to go to Grahame of Duchray. "Say to Duchray, who is my cousin as well as your own, that I am not dead, but a captive in Fairyland; and that only one chance remains for my liberation. When the posthumous child, of which my wife has been delivered since my disappearance, shall be brought to baptism, I will appear in the room, when, if Duchray shall throw over my head the knife or dirk which he holds in his hand, I may be restored to society; but if this is neglected, I am lost forever."

'True to his tryst' (Scott continued), 'Mr Kirk did appear at the christening, and "was visibly seen" but . . . to society Mr Kirk has not yet been restored.'

When Kirk's tomb at the east end of Aberfoyle churchyard was opened in Scott's time, no remains were found. Lately a new twist was given to the mystery by R.J. Stewart, author of a commentary on Kirk and his text.[2] In a later book on fairy lore, Stewart describes how in 1982, meditating on top of the fairy hill at Aberfoyle, he found himself 'communing with . . . a short man, fairly plump, who declared himself to be Robert Kirk, fully alive in the faery realm.' He claims Kirk told him of a group of men (the 'Justified Men') from many ages and sources who, like himself, had physically entered the fairy realm. Invited by Kirk to join them, Stewart sensed a doorway opening from one world to another, through which he could physically step, but just then a distant car-horn summoned him back to the everyday world.[3]

1. *The Secret Commonwealth of Elves, Fauns and Fairies*, Rev. Robert Kirk, Observer Press, Stirling, 1933 (1691). From the Comment by **Andrew Lang** (1893 edition), quoting Scott quoting Grahame.
2. *Robert Kirk: Walker between Worlds*, R.J. Stewart, Element Books, Shaftesbury, 1989.
3. *Earth Light*, R.J. Stewart, Element Books, Shaftesbury, 1992, pp.25–6.

KNIGHT (*See* **ARTHURIAN MYTH, KNIGHTS TEMPLAR**)

From Anglo-Saxon *cniht* (servant-boy), and Dutch-German *knecht* (soldier), in feudal England after 1066 a knight was any man with £20-worth of land who thus owed the king military service on demand: an obligation made explicit by the Oath of Salisbury (1086). The knight was required to own his own **horse**, armour and other war-gear; thus he was also a *caballarius* (Latin: 'horseman'), leading to the term 'chivalry' (Old French *chevalerie*) – the knightly code of honour. This code, representing the mythic aura about the medieval knight, embraced the religious nature of his investment, and the idea that honour mattered more than life ('Death before Dishonour'). The troubadours encouraged knightly respect for women (ideally the knight offered platonic love to some haughty married lady who despised him), and cultivated song, dance and poetry as well as the arts of war.

Arthurian mythologers encouraged the theme of the knightly **quest**, as in the **Grail** myth. The knight (spirit) guides his horse (body) through the trials (quest) of the world, overcoming all obstacles to prove his character and attain perfection. Knightly grades in secular society corresponded to the images purveyed by the romancers. Only the perfect knight, both pure and chaste (**Galahad**), might attain the Holy Grail, vanishing from the world in its attainment. Lesser knights, admirable by ordinary standards, all failed the final test because of one weakness or another. So **Lancelot**, 'the best knight in the world', could not subdue lust; **Bedivere** doubted; **Gawain** told the **Green Knight** a lie (by omission), and so on.

Symbolically, the Green Knight typifies the neophyte ('green behind the ears') or, if a **giant**, the forces of nature; the Red Knight the conqueror, **blood**-baptised; the White Knight innocence and purity; the Black Knight the powers of evil, expiation and sacrifice.

The concept of knighthood, a civilising force in the Middle Ages, was later devalued. Where once a knight-errant rode the land demonstrating his prowess and generosity, in eighteenth-century Britain a 'knight of the road' meant a mere footpad or mugger.

KNIGHTS TEMPLAR (*See* FREEMASONRY, HEAD, HOLY GRAIL, ISLAM, KNIGHT)

Ever since their overthrow (in France 1307), fantastic theories have persisted as to the true beliefs and fate of this order of warrior monks. Even their origin is obscure. Guillaume of Tyre claimed *c.*1180 that the crusading Order of the Poor Knights of Christ and the Temple of Solomon began when Hugues de Payens, a knight of Champagne, reached Jerusalem with eight companions in 1118. Baudouin I, king of Jerusalem, chartered them to 'keep the roads and highways safe . . . with especial regard for the protection of pilgrims', and quartered them in his palace, said to be built on the foundations of **Solomon**'s Temple. Thus, Knights Templar. Sworn to poverty, chastity and obedience, they were supposedly so poor they shared horses while policing pilgrim routes (thus the Templar seal). Yet there is no evidence that they ever guarded any routes at all.

In 1128 St Bernard of Clairvaux (Europe's most powerful churchman) drew up their Rule. In 1130, de Payens returned to Europe with 300 knights, and in 1139 Pope Innocent II absolved them of loyalty to any power but the Pope. Their wealth grew even as construction of the first Gothic cathedrals began. With their own ports and fleets, they were exempt from tithes, but imposed their own. Monopolising new technology and influencing politics from England to Persia, they banked for the kings of Europe, but also became known for drunkenness and arrogance. In war, they had to fight to the death. The order, attracting men whose main skill was fighting, prospered while the Crusades against Islam (1095–1291) lasted.

Yet when in 1291 they were driven out of the Holy Land after the fall of Acre, they were already doomed. In 1307 King Philippe le Bel of France, desiring their income (in 1306 he had expelled the Jews and seized their wealth) arrested the French Templars. Those caught were accused of denying Christ, defiling the **Cross**, perverting the Mass, adoring an idol (a head called Baphomet), also of **ritual** murder, immorality, obscene kissing and of wearing a heretical **cord**.[1] Many died under torture or at the stake. The last Grand Master, Jacques de Molay, died at the stake in Paris in 1314, calling (so it is said) King Philippe and Pope Clement V to join him before God's throne within the year. Both perished as cursed.

Yet many escaped, along with their fleet and treasure, finding safety in Portugal, England and Scotland. Some fought with the Scots against the English at Bannockburn in 1314. Later they may have originated Scotch Rite Freemasonry. Viscount Dundee, killed at Killiecrankie in 1689, was found after his death to be wearing a Templar cross under his armour.[2]

Their mystique proliferated before and after their dissolution. The **grail** myth suggests Templar involvement, as in the *Perlesvaus*, while in *Parzival*, Wolfram von Eschenbach describes the Grail knights as 'Templeisen'. In early texts the Grail is not a cup but a plate bearing a severed, bleeding head. Under torture, some Templars described this head as bearded, long-haired, and existing as paintings or carvings – presumably copies of the original – shown only at the order's general chapters (assemblies). They were accused of venerating such heads, which could save them, make them rich, fertilise the land – all charges reminiscent of the power attributed to pagan heads. Yet confession wrung by torture is unreliable and Philippe had to demonise them to justify seizing their wealth. Still, it has been argued that this 'head' was the image of that imprinted on the **Shroud of Turin**; that the Shroud was kept by the Templars, and that its casket was the Grail itself.[3]

Another recent, related claim is that the Grail was in fact the **Ark of the Covenant**, kept at Axum in Ethiopia and that the Templars had tried but failed to snatch it away, yet that their secret knowledge of its nature both led Wolfram to write *Parzival*, and stimulated the growth of the Gothic architectural movement in Europe.[4]

Again, it is suggested that (as a now secret order dedicated to the overthrow of the medieval Church and feudal monarchies which had overthrown them) they were the 'great society' behind the Peasants' Revolt in England in 1381 and that subsequently, as Masons, they worked through the centuries to establish democratic movements.[5]

1. *Witchcraft Today*, Gerald B. Gardner, Rider, London, 1975 (1954).
2. *The Temple and the Lodge*, Michael Baigent and Richard Leigh, Corgi, London, 1990, p.233.
3. *The Shroud and the Grail*, Noel Currer-Briggs, Weidenfeld & Nicolson, London, 1987, pp.78–100.
4. *The Sign and the Seal*, Graham Hancock, Heinemann, London, 1992.
5. *Born in Blood*, John J. Robinson, Random Century, London, 1989.

KNOT (*See* DOOR, RING, TABOO)

Implies restraint, binding and loosing, continuity, unity. To 'tie the knot' is to get married. The three knots in the **girdle** of Christian monks denote the three vows of poverty, chastity and obedience. The harder the knot is pulled, the firmer the union. Loosening it is freedom or salvation. Yet it may be so tangled that, as **Alexander the Great** did with the Gordian knot, it can only be cut. Magically, to tie a knot is to weave a spell. Finnish wizards sold wind to becalmed sailors, enclosing it in three knots. Untying the first was said to bring a moderate wind, the second a half-gale and the third a hurricane. **Witches** tied knots to ill-wish or obstruct an enemy. In ancient Rome the priest of **Jupiter** (the Flamen Dialis) wore no rings and had no knots on his clothes. Moslem pilgrims to Mecca may wear neither knots nor rings. Just as doors were opened to ease childbirth, so too in Transylvania knots on the clothes of women in labour were untied. In the East Indies pregnant women tied no knots nor braided their hair lest they too be 'tied up' when their time came. At difficult births among the Hos of West Africa a magician would tie the woman's hands and feet, then cut the bonds, supposedly releasing the child from her womb. To sit by a pregnant woman or sick person with clasped hands or crossed legs, or for a pregnant woman to sit likewise, was widely thought to be dangerous. A European belief was that an ill-wisher could stop consummation of marriage by hiding a knotted cord: it had to be found and untied to make union possible. Yet the tying of knots might also be used to win lovers. In parts of Russia brides had nets thrown over them to protect against sorcery. A woman taken to be burned alive at St Andrews in Scotland in 1572 was found to wear a knotted collar, believing it would protect her against the fire.[1]

1. *The Golden Bough*, Sir James Frazer, Macmillan, London, 1963, pp.238–43.

KORAN (*See* ISLAM)

KORE (*See* GREEK MYTH, PERSEPHONE, UNDERWORLD)

KOSHCHEI THE DEATHLESS (*See* SLAVONIC MYTH, SOUL)

Imprisoning a princess in his golden castle, this Russian sorcerer thought he had her secure. But one day in the castle garden she met a prince who cheered her with hope of escape, and so she flattered Koshchei to learn how to kill him. He told her his death lay in the broom under the threshold. She threw it on the fire but he remained unharmed. Next he said that under three oaks in a nearby field lay a **worm**. If this were crushed, he would die. Her lover found and crushed the worm, but still Koshchei lived. A third time she tried, and this time he told the truth. His death lay far away on an isle in the ocean, in a chest under an oak, and in the chest a basket, in the basket a **hare**, in the hare a duck, in the duck an **egg**. Whoever broke this egg would kill him. The prince found the egg and came back with it. Koshchei would have killed him, but the prince squeezed the egg. Howling in pain, Koshchei turned to the princess. 'Was it not out of love for you,' he demanded, 'that I told you where my death was? And this is how you repay me?' He reached for his sword, but the prince squeezed the egg and Koshchei the Deathless died – a victim of misconceived love. As for the prince and princess, presumably they lived happily ever after.

KRAKEN (*See* FABULOUS BEASTS)

Tales of this fabulous Scandinavian sea-monster may originate in distorted accounts of the octopus. In his *Natural History of Norway* (1754), Erik Pontopiddan, Bishop of Bergen, asserted that its tentacles can seize the largest ship; that its back, rising from the sea like a floating isle, is a mile and a half long, and that its discharges turn the sea murky.

'Far, far beneath the abysmal sea,' wrote the poet Alfred Lord Tennyson (1809–92) in a piece of juvenilia, 'The Kraken sleepeth . . .'

> There hath he lain for ages, and will lie
> Battening upon huge sea-worms in his sleep,
> Until the latter fire shall heat the deep:
> Then once by men and angels to be seen,
> In roaring he shall rise and on the surface die.

This theme was used by the English author John Wyndham (1903–69) in a science fiction novel, *The Kraken Wakes* (1953), in which the beast, an elemental force of nature, erupts from the deeps with disastrous effect.

KRISHNA (*See* BHAGAVAD GITA, HINDUISM, INDIAN MYTH, VISHNU)

It is said of this dancing, flute-playing **Hindu** god that he was Vishnu's eighth **avatar** and that he and his brother, Balarama, were princes of the kingdom of

Dwaraka. He was born when Vishnu put one of his **hairs** in the womb of Devaka, wife of Vasudeva, where it became Krishna (or 'Kesava', from *kesa*, 'hair'). Devaka and Vasudeva were locked up by the tyrant Kansa who feared a prophecy that this, her eighth, child would kill him. When she bore this blue child, the gods put the palace guards to sleep. She fled with Krishna and came to Nanda, a cowherd whose wife Yasoda had just borne a daughter. The infants were exchanged as Vishnu ordered. Vasudeva returned to the prison with the girl-child, whose cries awoke the guards. Kansa came to kill the baby, but the child flew away, crying out that Kansa's killer had been born and was safely hidden.

With Kansa hiding in his palace, Nanda took the infant Krishna to rural safety. But Kansa sent **demons** to murder Krishna. First Putana gave him her poisoned breast, but he sucked the life out of her. Then the flying demon Sakta-Sura made the cart under which Krishna slept collapse, but the young god kicked it away so that it crushed Sakta-Sura. Four other demons came to kill him, but he destroyed all of them. At length Krishna killed Kansa, then founded the city of Dvaraka, where he lived with his parents while enjoying numerous love affairs with the *gopis* (cow-girls). Whenever he played his flute by night they left their husbands to dance with him in the forest, each believing that she alone was his lover. As a god, Krishna divides himself into as many men as there are women desiring him.

Krishna especially loved Radha, an avatar of **Lakshmi**, wife of Vishnu. Her love, though illicit in patriarchal terms, is expressed by the poets not as wanton adultery but as devout worship of the Beloved, who is God, not a man. Later he fell for Rukmini: also an incarnation of Lakshmi. She, betrothed by her brother to Sisupala (avatar of the demon-king **Ravana**), smuggled him a message for help; he arrived on the wedding day and eloped with her. Sisupala's demon-army pursued them: Krishna and Balarama slew all but Rukmini's brother Rukma, spared when Rukmini begged for his life. Marrying many more wives and slaying many more demons, Krishna appears in the *Bhagavad Gita* as **Arjuna**'s charioteer and counsellor, revealing himself as god of love and as Vishnu, and teaching that the salvation of sinful man lies in knowledge through works.

KRONOS (*See* CRONUS)

KUJATA (*See* FABULOUS BEASTS)
In **Islamic** myth, this huge **bull** (with four thousand eyes, ears, nostrils and mouths) stands on a fish called Bahamut. On the back of Kujata is a rock of ruby, on it an **angel**; and on the angel's shoulders the body of the earth-planet. Under Bahamut lies an ocean; under the ocean an abyss of air; under that realm, **fire**; under that a **serpent** so omnipotent that, but for its fear of Allah (God), it would swallow all creation.

KUKULCÁN (*See* MAYAN MYTH, QUETZALCOATL)

KUPALA (*See* SLAVONIC MYTH, YARILO)
From the root *kupati*, 'to bathe'. The festivals of this Russian water-god were celebrated widely among **pagan** Slavs, whose folk-tales told of 'dead water' and 'live water', each with its own miraculous properties. On the holy night of Kupala, floral crowns were thrown into the water and **fires** were lit. As in Celtic **Beltane** festivals, the worshippers danced round the fires then jumped through them to be purified. The straw idol of Kupala bedecked with

ribbons and necklaces was then carried in procession to the holy river to be drowned, or to the holy fire to be burned.

L

LABOURS (*See* **GILGAMESH, HERCULES, HERO MYTH, TASK, THESEUS**)

The labours (difficult tasks) imposed on mythic heroes represent Everyman's struggle to win self-realisation by overcoming his animal nature (slaying the **dragon**, etc.). The twelve labours of **Hercules** may represent the **sun** passing through the twelve signs of the **zodiac**. **Culhwch** the Welsh hero undertook thirty-nine *anoethu* (impossible tasks) in order to win the hand of Olwen.

LABYRINTH (*See* **CAVE, DAEDALUS, THESEUS**)

Often situated underground or in darkness, a labyrinth (Greek *laburinthos;* etymology obscure, but from the maze built on Crete by **Daedalus** to house the Minotaur, so perhaps from *labrys*, a double-headed axe emblematic of Cretan sovereignty) may be a structure, a design, a **dance** or an open path, or a path enclosed by hedges, banks or walls. It consists of intricate winding passages doubling back on each other but leading to a centre. Labyrinths are unicursal (a single route to the centre and out again without choice or confusion, covering maximum ground without treading the same path twice); or multicursal (many confusing routes and blind paths, demanding knowledge of the key to the route). Symbolising the perplexities of the human journey through life, the labyrinth creates and protects the hidden centre, which variously represents the womb of the **Earth Mother**, attainment after trial or ordeal of self-knowledge, **initiation**, the depths of inner being, death and rebirth. To reach the centre is to find the true self. By confronting and slaying the Minotaur in the labyrinth of Minos, **Theseus** overcame the beast in himself. This **bull**-man at the centre may also be the solar male force; the spiral passages about it the lunar female power. In Christian symbolism the beast at the centre is the **Devil**, the centre itself **hell**. Labyrinths share **cave** symbolism, entry to the **underworld** and the mystery **quest** (for the **Holy Grail**), and may be connected with funerary rites (journey to the otherworld). The Lord of the Labyrinth is Judge of the Dead. So too **knot** symbolism, both binding and loosing; also the symbolism of the coiled **serpent**. It allows entry (initiatory step on the path of knowledge) only to those with knowledge who may find the centre. Those entering ignorantly are lost. As important is the return from the centre to the outside world (rebirth). Theseus, having slain the Minotaur, found his way out of the Cretan labyrinth aided by the ball of golden thread (divine instinct) given him by Ariadne: unwinding it as he penetrated the maze, he wound it up again on return, and so reached the exit.

LADDER (*See* **AXIS MUNDI, BRIDGE, DREAMS, TREE OF LIFE**)

A means of ascending or descending from one level to another, thus a symbol of access, transition and **initiation**. In the first of many dreams recorded in the **Bible**, Jacob saw a ladder stretch from **heaven** to the earth, God's **angels** upon it, and God at the top telling him, 'I am with thee'. It is said that once there was free communication between God and man via such a ladder, lost at the **Fall**. The rungs of the ladder represent degrees of self-realisation and in symbology usually number seven or twelve. The two sides of the ladder are the pillars of the Temple: Boaz and Jachin. Laid horizontally, the ladder **bridges** the abyss, and is thus associated with **rites of passage** and the idea of the 'Narrow Way'. The ladder may also be seen as the *axis mundi* and as the Tree of Life.

LAKE MONSTERS (*See* DRAGON, FABULOUS BEASTS, KELPIE, LOATHLY WORM)

Scotland's Loch Ness Monster is but the best known of many such mysterious beasts said to inhabit lakes around the world. The usual view is that folk who see or make contact with such beasts are hallucinating, are mistaken in what they see, or are hoaxers seeking media attention or to boost the local tourist trade. Thus when in April 1933 the modern spate of sightings at Loch Ness began, sceptics noted that the two people who saw an 'enormous animal rolling and plunging' in the loch were both local hoteliers'.[1] By October, with over twenty sightings reported, the story was international news. Most sightings suggested an unknown beast with long neck, tiny head and a huge black body, as indicated by the famous photographs taken in April 1934 by London surgeon R.K. Wilson. Since then, despite many efforts to track down or identify the creatures in Loch Ness (nobody suggests there is only one), they have remained so elusive (no body, floating or beached, has ever been found) that most zoologists still assert that 'Nessie' is entirely imaginary. Sonar recordings indicating the presence (in 1972) of a large moving body were dismissed by zoologists of London's Natural History Museum as being of 'small gas bubbles', produced by 'the larvae of phantom midges'.[2] Yet reports of the Monster date back to St **Columba**'s encounter with it (AD 565).

Some 300 lakes the world around are said to host similar beasts; from Canada (Okanagan Lake, Lake Champlain) and the USA (Flathead Lake, Lake Elsinore) to Russia (Lake Labynkyr, Lake Vorota) and Australia, where in Lake Modewarre lurks the dreaded Bunyip. Irish loughs, especially in Galway (over twenty) and Connemara appear to be full of them; likewise over twenty Scottish lochs other than Loch Ness are implicated. One Scottish close encounter occurred in August 1969 to two men fishing Loch Morar, a West Coast trench over 1,000 feet deep. A humped creature some 25 feet long and with a rough dirty skin struck their motor cruiser. One man broke an oar fending it off, the other fired a rifle at it and saw it sink slowly away. Some thirty-three sightings of 'Morag' have been reported over the last century.

Revulsion and dread often accompany sightings. Connemara librarian Georgina Carberry and others saw the *peiste* (Irish water-monster) in Lough Fadda in 1954. Its body had 'movement all over it', it was 'wormy' and 'creepy', and for weeks after she had recurring nightmares.[3] A woman and her twelve-year-old son who saw Nessie at close range felt 'paralysed by fear'. Another witness said of Nessie, 'It was horrible – an abomination.' This reminds one of the mythic 'loathly worm' or of the Welsh wyvern (two-legged **dragon**) of Cynwch Lake, which (says an anonymous legend, translated 1921) would creep onto the land with 'hateful, stealthy movements . . . jerking its cumbersome form into uncanny humps . . . and leaving a slimy trail behind it.'

'Ogopogo', the monster of Okanagan Lake in British Columbia, has been seen almost as often as Nessie, being described as 30 to 70 feet long with a dark, sleek body and a horse-like head. 'Champ', the monster of Lake Champlain on the Quebec-Vermont border, first sighted by a white man in

1609, has likewise been described as dark, sleek, serpentine, as thick as a barrel and with a head like a horse. In Australia, lake monsters are called 'Bunyip' after an aboriginal word meaning 'devil' or 'spirit'. In the early nineteenth century William Buckley, an escaped convict who had lived with the Aborigines by Lake Modewarre told his biographer John Morgan how in the lake existed 'extraordinary animals . . . about the size of a full-grown calf and sometimes larger [which only appeared] when the weather is very calm and the water smooth . . . the natives had a great dread of them, believing them to have some supernatural power over human beings, so as to occasion death, sickness, disease, and such like misfortunes.'[4]

Throughout the world the mystery of these beasts is compounded by the apparent lack of food available in many lakes where they are seen or said to exist, and by the lack of bodily evidence. That commonly they seem to be oddly immaterial; that sightings of them often rely on the mental state of the observer; and that typically they cause feelings of repulsion and dread, has been noted. It is theorised (especially of 'Nessie') that such beasts are surviving prehistoric reptiles, giant eels or even giant cat-fish. Yet, to date, nobody can prove their existence – or lack of it.

1. *The Loch Ness Story*, Nicholas Witchell, Corgi, London, 1989, p.29.
2. *Alien Animals*, Janet and Colin Bord, Granada, London, 1980, p.30.
3. *The Dragon and the Disc*, F.W. Holiday, Sidgwick & Jackson, London, 1973.
4. *op. cit.* Witchell, p.46, quoting John Morgan, *Life and Adventures of William Buckley*, Hobart, 1852.

LAKSHMI (*See* HINDUISM, INDIAN MYTH, KRISHNA, VISHNU)

Hindu goddess of fortune and vegetation, wife of Vishnu the Preserver in each incarnation, among her **avatars** are Radha and Rukmini, lovers of Krishna. Born (like **Aphrodite**) from the primal **ocean**, she rose to her **lotus** throne, where she sits, a lotus in her left hand. Benevolent and magnanimous, she is Vriddhi, goddess of growth; Matrirupa, mother of living things; Ambika, goddess of the mango and all other fruits; Devi Sri, rice-goddess annually reborn with the new crop; Dakshina, the cow transforming herself into many daughters, her full breasts a source of unending succour. She is Bhu, the creation; Sadana, dark ocean, waves and moonlight; and Jaladhi-ja, 'ocean-born', and empress of the sea, to whom fishermen make sacrifice to ensure good catches and safe voyages. It is told how, at the start of every new *kalpa* or world-age, the primal ocean sprouts a thousand-petalled lotus of gold, and from it is born **Brahma**, whose mother is Lakshmi as Loka-mata, 'mother of the world'. Together she and Vishnu fly through the sky on the back of **Garuda**, the man-bird, symbol of the **sun**.

LAMB

Symbol of innocence, gentleness, purity. The lamb is Christ crucified for the sins of the world; Christ carrying a lamb is the Good Shepherd caring for his flock; the apocalyptic lamb with seven horns and seven eyes denotes the seven gifts of the **spirit**; with the book and seven seals is Christ as Judge at the Second Coming. In the temple of **Apollo** at Argos in Greece, a lamb was sacrificed by night once a month, a chaste priestess drinking its **blood** to gain **prophetic** inspiration. An Argive (Greek) tradition of the death in and **resurrection** of **Dionysus** from the Alcyonian lake was annually celebrated by summoning the god from the waters with trumpet blasts while throwing a lamb into the lake as offering to the god of the dead. Frazer relates how the

Moru of Central Africa annually sacrificed the choicest of their lambs as a sacramental offering. First a boy would fetch the lamb, then lead it four times round the assembled people, who would pluck bits of its fleece, putting these in their hair. Then on the altar the lamb was slain by the priest. Taking the blood, he sprinkled it four times over the people, then applied it individually to each person, smearing the children below the breast-bone, the women above the breast and men on the shoulder. Then he exhorted the people to be kind to one another. The blood of the lamb is thus a form of communion not peculiar to **Christianity** alone.[1]

1. *The Golden Bough*, Sir James Frazer, Macmillan, 1963, p.534.

LAMIA (*See* FABULOUS BEASTS, *FEMMES FATALES*, GLAMOUR, SIRENS)

From the waist up a beautiful woman, from waist down a **serpent**. The ancient Greeks and Romans held that these **witches** or evil monsters lived in the African desert. Unable to speak, they issued a whistling sound to beguile and devour travellers, enchanting their victims with **glamour** and illusion. Robert Burton in *The Anatomy of Melancholy* (1621), dealing with the power of love, cites a tale by the Greek writer Philostratus (*c*.AD 170–250), of how a young man, Menippus Lycius, near Corinth met a lovely lady who told him she was a Phoenician. She took him home and so besotted him that he married her, but to the wedding came the philosopher Apollonius (third century BC), who unmasked her as a lamia despite her begging him to keep quiet. Then she, her house and everything in it instantly vanished.

   This account led English poet John Keats (1795–1821) to write his poem, 'Lamia'.

LANCE (*See* HOLY LANCE)

LANCELOT (*See* ARTHURIAN MYTH, GUINEVERE, HOLY GRAIL, KNIGHT, LUG)

In **Arthurian** legend the 'best knight in the world', the supreme hero of the **Round Table**, the father of **Galahad** who alone beat him, both in arms and spirit. Son of King Ban of Benoic in France, when he was only a year old, his father died in battle, and he was kidnapped to the **otherworld** by a powerful **fairy**, the Lady of the Lake: thus 'Lancelot du Lac'. She brought him up fatherless, initiating him into female **mysteries**, and preparing him to support Arthur and the ideal of the Round Table. So from the start he is an ambiguous figure. He represents both **pagan** (female) and Christian (male) belief. In origin he may derive from the **Irish** sun-god **Lug**, who slew the Fomorian **Balor** with a sling-stone, as David slew Goliath. King Ban was said to be descended from David: in Lancelot is thus harnessed both **Christian** and **Celtic** myth, as expressed in his conflict between his love for Arthur's wife **Guinevere** and his sense of duty to Arthur. Because of this fatal inner conflict he remains perhaps the most attractive character in the Arthurian mythos. A brave warrior, decisive and loyal, kind and thoughtful yet highly strung, generous and always respectful of others, he stands out in **Malory** and other accounts as a believable character – whereas Galahad, too perfect and pure, is not. Compelled by his sense to honour to give up Guinevere, his affair with her robs him of the **Grail**; he gets only a glimpse of it. Banished from Britain to his castle of Joyous Garde in France due to his affair with Guinevere, he hurries to England to fight for Arthur against **Mordred**, but arrives too late. After Arthur falls at Camlann, he again meets Guinevere in her nunnery; then he too forsakes the world. After six years at **Glastonbury**, now an ordained priest, when she dies he buries her at Glastonbury beside Arthur. Losing all will to live, he dies, and is buried at Joyous Garde.[1]

1. *King Arthur and the Grail*, Richard Cavendish, Paladin, London, 1980.

LANG, ANDREW (1844–1912) (*See* FAIRY-TALES, HAGGARD, KIRK)

A Fellow of Merton College, Oxford, in 1875 this Scots scholar, folklorist and author moved to London, to become famed for his translations of **Homer** and his twelve-volume **fairy-tale** collection, from *The Blue Fairy Book* (1889) to *The Lilac Fairy Book* (1910). Collaborating with **H. Rider Haggard** on a novel, *The World's Desire* (1890), his own fairy-tales (*Prince Prigio*, 1889) became children's classics. An accomplished poet, historian of Scotland and author of historical mysteries, he contributed to the study of comparative mythology in works such as *Custom and Myth* (1884), and *Magic and Religion* (1901). His devotion to Homer led to translations of *The Odyssey* (1879) and *The Iliad* (1883). His *World of Homer* remains an important study: his 1893 essay introducing a new edition of *The Secret Commonwealth of Elves, Fauns and Fairies* by **Robert Kirk** remains among the most lucid expositions on Celtic **fairy**-lore, **second sight** and related topics. Today his novels and fairy-tales are less known than those by his fellow Scot George MacDonald, but perhaps his range was broader.

LAO TSU (b. 604 BC) (*See* CHINESE MYTH, TAOISM)

Said to have founded **Taoism** and to have written the *Tao Te Ching* (*Book of the Way*, a text of eighty-one laconic epigrams expressing the core philosophy of Taoism, translated more often than any other work save the Bible), Lao Tsu remains venerated by many **Confucianists** and worshipped as a god by some Chinese. Little is known of his life. He is said to have been keeper of the archives at the imperial Chou court, in which post he may have met **Confucius**. This meeting is probably as fictional as the tale of how he composed the *Tao Te Ching*. Apparently sick of corrupt human life, he rode west into the desert (on a green **buffalo**) to die. A gatekeeper at a pass in northwestern China persuaded him to write down his teachings. So he wrote a book of 5,000 characters, containing his ideas about the *Tao* ('Way', or 'Supreme Principle'), and the *Te* (the Tao's 'Virtue'). Then he rode off into the west, and was never seen again. His biographer Ssu-ma Ch'ien (*c.*100 BC), claims nothing is known of his life because he was a gentleman recluse who believed in non-action, the cultivation of inner calm and purity of mind. The *Tao Te Ching*, dated *c.*300 BC, is not considered the work of one man: the name 'Lao Tsu' may represent a certain type of reclusive sage who typically chose to leave no trace of his life. By *c.*200 BC, 'Lao Tsu' had already become a myth. He was said to be the **Buddha**, and to adopt different personalities in his many incarnations. Whatever the truth, Lao Tsu has always been venerated.[1]

1. *Tao Te Ching* (trans. Gia-Fu Feng and Jane English), Wildwood House, Aldershot, 1973.

LEAR (*See* KING LEAR, LLŶR)

LEGBA (*See* VOODOO)

LEMMINKÄINEN (*See KALEVALA*)

LEMURES (*See* **ROMAN MYTH**)
The ancient Romans held that after death human souls wandered the world, disturbing the living. The good spirits they called *Lares familiares*; the evil ones, who haunted the wicked, *Larvae* or *Lemures*. Festivals in honour of the latter were held annually in May. Called Lemuria or Lemuralia, they were instituted by **Romulus** to appease the ghost of his brother Remus, and originally called Remuria. For three nights all temples would be shut and marriages prohibited. Folk threw black beans on the graves of the dead, or burned the beans, it being said that the dead hated the smell, and banged kettles or drums to scare the ghosts away.

LEMURIA (*See* **ATLANTIS, HOLLOW EARTH, THEOSOPHY**)
As if the myth of one drowned continent (**Atlantis**) were not enough, since the late nineteenth century some occultists have promoted the legend of a second, called Lemuria or Mu, and said to be lost under the Indian or the Pacific Ocean. In *Isis Unveiled* (1888), the **Theosophist** Madame Blavatsky claimed that the Lemurians were anthropoid telepathic **giants** who flourished a million years ago before the Indian Ocean overwhelmed their island continent. In 1926 an ex-British army officer, Colonel James Churchward, claimed (in *The Lost Continent of Mu*) that man first appeared on Mu, which extended from north of Hawaii to Fiji and Easter Island, and which was destroyed some 12,000 years ago by earthquake and submersion. Today the Stelle group of Illinois, USA, claims descent from Lemuria which, they say, was destroyed 26,000 years ago, its wise inhabitants escaping the planet and since then invisibly guiding the destiny of chosen groups like themselves. A similar myth, combined with **hollow earth** theory, was promoted by the horror novelist **H.P. Lovecraft** in *The Shadow out of Time* (1936).

LEPRECHAUN (*See* **FAIRIES, IRISH MYTH**)
Also known as the *cluricane* or *luricane*, this diminutive Irish sprite lived in caves or nooks, cobbling tiny shoes, sometimes guarding treasure. Like the brownie, he was fond of playing practical jokes on mortals, who rarely got the better of him. The *fir larrig*, or 'red man', was a sprite wearing a sugarloaf hat, scarlet coat, corduroy breeches and woollen stockings. He had a long yellow face and grey hair, and announced his presence to mortals he visited by thrusting his arm through the keyhole of their door. If they did not open it, harm would befall their cattle.

LESHY (*See* **DOMOVOI, SLAVONIC MYTH**)

LEVIATHAN (*See* **DRAGON, SERPENT, TIAMAT, YAHWEH**)
The **Hebrew** equivalent of the **Sumerian** chaos-**dragon** or cosmic **serpent** **Tiamat**, the seven-headed Phoenician monster Lotan, the Greek **Typhon** or Vedic **Vritra**, the name means 'coiled'. As Tiamat is vanquished by **Marduk**, Lotan by Anat/**Astarte**, Typhon by **Zeus** and Vritra by Indra, so Leviathan is conquered by **Yahweh**, who boasts (Job xli): 'Canst thou draw out Leviathan with an hook, or his tongue with a cord which thou lettest down? None is so fierce that dare stir him up: who then is able to stand against me?'
    Yet, though defeating the ancient cosmic serpent, Yahweh himself is an aspect of the serpent power. The priestly tribe of Levi, protagonists of the worship of Yahweh, derived their name from Leviathan. When images of the unpicturable god did appear in the Hellenic period (after Alexander's

conquest in 331 BC), Yahweh (Jehovah) is portrayed with serpent legs.[1]

The apocryphal Book of **Enoch** mentions a companion beast, **Behemoth**, a male. Leviathan is female. In the last days Leviathan will repulse every angelic attack before finally Behemoth slays her.

1. *Occidental Mythology*, Joseph Campbell, Penguin, London, 1976, pp.22, 30.

LEWIS, C.S. (1898–1963) (*See* **ARTHURIAN MYTH, MERLIN, TOLKIEN**)

British scholar, novelist and **Christian** apologist, Professor of Medieval and Renaissance English at Cambridge 1954–63, Clive Staples Lewis is remembered for his children's fairy-tales, the *Chronicles of Narnia* (1950–6); also for his theological apologetics and the best-selling *The Screwtape Letters* (1942), supposedly written by an elderly devil to educate his junior in the arts of corrupting mortals. Yet perhaps his best work is his **science fiction** trilogy: *Out of the Silent Planet* (1938), *Perelandra or Voyage to Venus* (1943) and *That Hideous Strength* (1945).

The hero of the trilogy is the linguist, Ransom, like **Christ** offered as a ransom for humanity. The premise of the first novel, set on Mars, is that earth is a 'silent planet', cut off by human evil from the rest of the universe. The second novel explores the **Eden** myth on the ocean planet of Venus; an evil scientist playing Satanic tempter to the **Eve**-like ruler of that world. In the third book, he attacks modern science as 'that hideous strength', a totalitarian force threatening all humanity, resisted by the rediscovery of **Logres** – the ancient **Grail**-kingdom of Britain, the secret land of the heart; by the reawakening of the magician **Merlin**, and by the descent of the celestial powers, tutelary rulers of the planets described in the earlier books. When he wrote these now classic fantasies, Lewis was closely associated with the novelists Charles Williams and **J.R.R. Tolkien**.

LILITH (*See* **ADAM, BLACK VIRGIN, EVE, LAMIA**)

This shadowy figure, an apparition of the night haunting those who sleep or travel alone and described in early Hebrew texts as Adam's first wife, was in origin a **Sumerian** storm-**demon**; a **vampiric** succubus, her nest in the Huluppu tree, a **dragon** at its base and a bird perching atop it. The hero **Gilgamesh** slew the dragon and cut down the tree, forcing her to flee into the wilderness. She was also 'the hand of **Inanna**', taking the men of Erech from the streets to the temple of the goddess. She is associated with the **Queen of Sheba** and the concubine of Abraham, Hagar the Egyptian. Victor Hugo (1802–85) made her **Satan**'s eldest daughter, the great woman of the shadow, the black soul of the world. The name, derived from the Hebrew *layil*, 'night', appears just once in the Bible, translated as 'screech-owl' (Isaiah xxxiv:14). In the first known portrait (the terracotta Burney relief in the British Museum, *c*.1850 BC), she is a beautiful, winged, naked woman with the feet of a bird, standing on two **lions** and flanked by a pair of **owls** – the bird of **Blodeuwedd** and **Guinevere**. Like **Isis**, she knows the secret **name** of God; she is woman rebelling against patriarchy, rejected by **Adam** for refusing to lie under him. Invoking **Yahweh**'s name, she was granted wings and fled from **Eden**. Sentenced to bear innumerable children of whom one hundred would die each day, she cast herself into the Red Sea. The **angels**, pitying her, gave her power over new-born infants, children born out of wedlock being forever at her mercy. As described by the English poet Dante Gabriel Rossetti (1828–82) she is the **serpent** or **lamia** who urged **Eve** to eat the forbidden fruit and conceive **Cain**, brother and murderer of Abel. After Abel died, Adam abstained from Eve for 130 years, during which time he slept secretly with Lilith.

In **Jewish** and **Gnostic** lore, Lilith is sometimes viewed favourably. By the mid-thirteenth century, with the **black virgin** cult well established, the vindication of Lilith reached the point where a Spanish Qabalist called her 'a ladder on which one can ascend to the rungs of prophecy'.[1]

1. *The Cult of the Black Virgin*, Ean Begg, Arkana, London, 1985, pp.32ff.

LILY

Sacred to all virgin goddesses, the lily represents purity, resurrection, peace; also the fertility of the earth-goddess. It shares many of the symbolic characteristics of the **lotus**. As chastity, it is the flower of Easter, called by **Dante** the 'lily of faith'.

LINGA (LINGAM) (*See* HINDUISM, SHIVA, TANTRAS, YONI)

The most prominent of the twelve emblems of the **Hindu** god **Shiva**, *lingam* is usually translated as 'phallus', though some scholars deny that it ever represented the male organ. It is often seen in India as a pillar with a hemispherical top, standing in a basin called a *yoni* ('vagina' or 'womb'). Offerings are brought to it by supplicants hoping for children and for abundant crops. Elsewhere, the pillar is an abstract cylinder, implying the god's essential shapelessness. Shiva's followers may carry a *linga*, often a round object such as a soapstone globe, representing the god's universal formlessness – as a god, he needs no genitals, procreating by will alone. Thus the symbol represents cosmic creation, the renewal of vitality, the **omphalos**, the self-existing, and is not merely an expression of male sexuality. It is the masculine generative principle, just as the *yoni* is the feminine principle.

LION (*See* ANIMALS, CAT)

The 'king of the beasts': to be 'leonine' or 'lion-hearted' implies regal (solar) power, courage, majesty and strength. Yet the lion also represents cruelty, ferocity, war and various lunar attributes. In the latter sense it is the lioness accompanying the Great Mother or drawing her chariot, or as depicted with **virgin** warrior-goddesses. The eighth card of the **Tarot** Major Arcana shows a young woman forcing or drawing open a lion's jaws: the triumph of human will over the beast. The demoness **Lilith** stands on the backs of two lions. Lion and **unicorn** shown together depict warring solar-lunar forces: in alchemy the red lion, sulphur, is the male principle; the unicorn, quicksilver, the female. Lion and **dragon** eating each other means union with no loss of identity. The lion lying down with the **lamb** depicts rediscovery of primordial innocence and the **Golden Age**. In **Greek myth**, lions accompany **Artemis**, **Cybele**, **Dionysus**, **Phoebus** and the Gorgons: the lion-skin worn by **Hercules** after he kills the Nemean lion symbolises the solar hero overcoming death. In **Buddhism** a lion cub represents a newly initiated **bodhisattva**. **Buddha** is sometimes shown as seated on a lion throne. **Christ** is said to be the 'Lion of Judah'. The Hebrew tale of Daniel in the lions' den symbolises **Yahweh**'s redemption.

Lion-myth is best developed in **Africa**, the lion being widely revered as a god, or as the physical shape taken by a god. The **Egyptian** god Tefnut is lion-headed; the lioness-goddess Sekhmet loved eating men. The famed lions of Tsavo, killing many people before being shot, were locally thought to be an ancient king and queen reappearing as lions to defend their territory. It was said lions lay with mortal women and sired human sons to whom they taught the arts of hunting and of spell-binding game: such sons could also change themselves into lions and back again, and often became chiefs or kings, being loved by women and feared yet respected by men. These lion-men possessed great physical and spiritual strength, also the art of healing by magic. So too there are said to be lion-women, of great beauty but highly dangerous, some being said to enjoy eating their husbands.[1]

1. *African Mythology*, Jan Knappert, Aquarian Press, Wellingborough, 1990.

LITTLE PEOPLE (*See* FAIRIES, LEPRECHAUN)

LIZARD MEN (*See* ABORIGINES)

The Wati-kutjara, 'Lizard Men', are the two totemic ancestors of legend to many Australian Aboriginal peoples; one called Kurukadi, his **totem** the iguana; the other Mumba, his totem the black iguana. The Mandjindja of Western Australia say these Lizard Men came down from the mountains during the Dreamtime, making ceremonial instruments like the inma board, and that the dark patches of the Milky Way are such boards that they placed in the sky. Others say they gave to mortals a means of contacting the **ancestors**. The Lizard Men caused the first death, that of Kulu the **moon**-man, for when he tried to rape the first women, they struck him with their magic boomerang. The molested women fled to the sky, and turned into the star-cluster called the **Pleiades**.

LLEW LLAW GYFFES (*See* ARIANRHOD, BLODEUWEDD, LUG, *MABINOGION*)

For the odd birth and even odder death-and-rebirth of this pagan **Welsh** god ('The Lion with the Steady Hand'), see **Arianrhod** (his mother) and **Blodeuwedd** (the flower-maiden: his faithless wife transformed into an **owl** for her sin). As with other Welsh deities, he seems to derive from an earlier Irish model: in this case the sun-god **Lug** – also apparently a prototype for the later **Arthurian** Sir **Lancelot**.

The identities of Llew and of **Lludd** and **Llŷr** suggest a confusion caused by the recasting of older oral traditions by newcomers to Britain, each reordering existing beliefs to their own advantage or scheme.

So **Irish myth** becomes Welsh/British myth becomes Christianised **Grail**-lore, the same basic themes (and gods) being adapted in each new era to suit new requirements, even as older versions survive alongside the new.

LLUDD (*See* BEL, LLŶR)

This Welsh god-king, son of sun-god **Bel**, also known as Lludd Llaw Ereint ('Lludd of the Silver Hand') is a **Welsh** version of the **Irish** king of the **Tuatha dé Danaan**, **Nuadu**. King of Britain, Lludd rebuilt London, which is named after him. In the *Mabinogion* tale 'Lludd and Llefelys', it is said that in his reign three plagues visited Britain: the first a race called the Coranians who heard on the wind every word anyone said; the second a scream heard on May Eve, blighting the crops, making women barren, robbing men of their strength and killing children and animals; the third the vanishing of the king's annual provisions save those consumed the very first night. Lludd's brother Llefelys, king of France, told him that the Coranians could be destroyed by making them drink insects mashed in water; that the scream was caused by **dragons** buried at Britain's very centre and that they could be overcome by strong mead buried there; and that the third plague was caused by a magician who, casting sleep on the court, stole all the food and drink. Overcoming the first two plagues as advised, Lludd took the advice of Llefelys on the third count, too, taking a cold bath when he felt sleep come upon him, then rose out of it to overthrow the enemy.[1]

1. *Mabinogion* (trans. Gwyn Jones and Thomas Jones), Dent Everyman, London, 1984.

LLŶR (See BEL, KING LEAR, LLUDD, *MABINOGION*, MANANNAN MAC LIR)

Meaning 'of the sea', cognate with the Irish Lir and **King Lear** as given by **Geoffrey of Monmouth** and **Shakespeare**, also with **Lludd** and thus with **Nuadu**. In the *Mabinogion* ('Branwen, Daughter of Llŷr') he is the father of Manawyddan (see **Manannan MacLir**); **Bran the Blessed**, Branwen, Efnissien and Nissien. The English city, Leicester, is named after him ('Leircester'), **Geoffrey of Monmouth** claiming that his grave there was in a vault built in Roman times in honour of Janus, the two-headed Roman god of **doors**. Yet in origin he was probably the god of a seafaring pre-Roman Bronze Age people.

LOATHLY LADY (See BANSHEE, CAILLEACH, COATLICUE, KALI, LAMIA, LILITH)

In **Celtic** literature the figure of the keening hag, **banshee**, washerwoman by the ford, of **Cerridwen**, crow-goddess or **Morrigan**, carries precisely the same horrific charge as is found from India (**Kali**) to Egypt (**Hathor** as Destroyer) and **Aztec** Mexico (**Coatlicue**). The Loathly Lady is the dark aspect of the **mother-goddess**, who bears life but must also destroy it, so that new life is born. Typically in **Arthurian** myth she appears to the new king as an ugly hag: if he overcomes his disgust and fear and kisses her as she demands, she turns into a desirable maiden and becomes his wife. The theme is that she is the sovereignty (fertility: *see* **Fisher King**) of the land, and that any ruler unwilling to embrace her ugly as well as her lovely aspect is incapable of ensuring the good of the land and its folk, being too weak or ignorant to understand the nature of his task.

LOATHLY WORM (See DRAGON, LAKE MONSTERS, SERPENT, STOORWORM)

This concerns the same theme. Where Eastern myth (Chinese-Indian) embraces the idea of the **dragon** as the fertiliser of the land, beyond human ideals of good or evil conduct; Western ideas (developed or regressed by **Judaic**-Pauline **Christianity** and by Persian **dualism**) insist on viewing all life as a moral conflict between Good and Evil. Thus **Christ** and **Antichrist** – opposites, black and white, with no compromise. The Loathly Worm is a Christian expression of disgust about the dragon of natural instinct. Notably, it lacks wings, it cannot fly, but crawls, spreading devastation. The Lambton Worm of Northumberland in England, ravaging the country, could join together if cut in two. The Loch Ness Monster, first recorded in the time of **St Columba** (sixth century), who did battle with it and defeated it by prayer, is often reported as a species of giant worm, causing disgust and revulsion. No good is ascribed to such demonic creatures . . .

LOCH NESS MONSTER (See COLUMBA, LAKE MONSTERS)

LOGRES (See ARTHURIAN MYTH, HOLY GRAIL, LEWIS)

From Lloegr, the Welsh name for England, this enchanted land of later

Arthurian myth invokes the magical atmosphere of early **Celtic** legend, its inhabitants moving from natural to supernatural realms without any sense of incongruity. In Logres there are enchanted castles and forests, ships that sail by themselves, knights who ride from England to France without having to cross the English Channel – all such phenomena caused, the romancers explained, by the hidden presence in Castle Corbenic somewhere in Logres of the **Holy Grail**, brought thence by **Joseph of Arimathea**. The castle itself (perhaps from *cor benoit*, 'blessed body') has the eerie habit of appearing and disappearing. When the Grail is removed from it and from Logres (for the people did not honour it) by **Galahad**, **Perceval** and Bors, the spell on the land is broken, but this is a punishment, not a blessing.

LOHENGRIN (*See* **PERCEVAL, TEUTONIC MYTH, WAGNER**)

LOKA (*See* **HINDUISM, INDIAN MYTH, KALPA, YUGA**)
Hindu cosmology holds the universe to be divided into three or seven worlds. The Tri-Loka (three-world model) consists of earth, **heaven** and the **underworld**. The Sapta-Loka (seven-world model) consists of: (1) Bhur-Loka, the earth; (2) Bhuvar-Loka, a realm between earth and sun where the sages live; (3) Svar-Loka, **Indra's** realm, between the sun and Pole Star; (4) Mara-Loka, where the *rishi* (high priest) Bhrigu lives with the other saints; (5) Jana-Loka, the home of **Brahma's** children; (6) Tapa-Loka, the realm of the Vairagis (the spirits of those who have become **immortal** by their own merits and who need not **reincarnate**); (7) Satya-Loka or Brahma-Loka, the 'Abode of Truth', where Brahma dwells for a hundred years of his time, during which many kalpas (the cosmic days of his awakening before he sleeps again) come and go. The first three of these seven worlds suffer destruction at the end of each kalpa. At the end of a hundred years of Brahma, all seven worlds are destroyed, leading to an entirely new creation peopled by unknown beings and forces. There are also other lokas where many other deities are said to live: **Soma**-Loka for the **moon** and planets, Indra-Loka for demigods, **Rakshasa**-Loka for the **demons**, and so on.

LOKI (*See* **ASGARD, BALDUR, NORSE MYTH, TRICKSTERS**)
Among the best-known gods of Asgard in Norse myth, this mischievous, sly, destructive, yet sociable and sometimes helpful deity remains a mystery. A purely Scandinavian creation, he is a trickster, satiric scandal-monger and master-thief. Yet, while often embarrassing or inconveniencing his fellow-gods, sometimes he rescues them by his wit, as when **Thor** loses his **hammer** to the Frost **Giants** (*see* **Jotunheim**). Handsome and wittier than his fellow-gods, the Viking *skalds* made him out to be more naughty than evil. His chief talents were **shape-shifting** and theft, as when he took the form of a flea to steal **Freya's** necklace. When the walls of Asgard were being built by a giant, he became a mare to lure away the giant's **horse**, then bore Sleipnir, **Odin's** eight-legged horse. He took bird-form to steal the **apples** of youth and later, to escape the wrath of the gods, he became a **salmon**. He also fathered monsters, including the wolf **Fenrir** and the **world-serpent**. So, while the *skalds* presented him as an amusing prankster tolerated by the other gods despite his misdeeds, the **Christians** later identified him as the very **Devil**. In the *Prose Edda*, Snorri (1179–1241) portrays him as causing the murder of the Christ-like **Baldur** – a process similar to the blackening of **Gawain** in **Arthurian myth**. Images of Loki bound in chains and about to be executed, as on the twelfth-century Gosforth Cross (Cumberland, England) explicitly identify him with the bound Devil of apocalyptic lore. Yet it may

be that, in origin, Loki was conceived not so much as the enemy of the gods but as a parody of them – a jester and clown, or what today would be called an anti-hero.[1]

1. *Gods and Myths of Northern Europe*, H.R. Ellis Davidson, Penguin, London, 1964, pp.176–82.

LONGFELLOW, HENRY WADSWORTH (1807–92) (*See* **HIAWATHA**)

LORD OF THE RINGS (*See* **RING, TOLKIEN**)

LORELEI (*See* **SIREN, TEUTONIC MYTH**)
The Lorelei is a rock above the River Rhine in Germany from which a maiden, in despair at a faithless lover, is said to have thrown herself, to become a **siren** whose singing lured sailors to their doom.

LOST WORLDS (*See* **CONCORDANCE**)
Legends of lost worlds or kingdoms unknown to civilisation persist even today. The heyday of such romance was the late nineteenth and early twentieth century, a period when the known world rapidly grew even as unknown territories as rapidly vanished. Earlier tales of fabulous voyages to unknown cultures came from an era when they seemed plausible. From **Plato**'s dissertation on **Atlantis**, to **Mandeville**'s tall tales of unknown lands and **dog**-headed men (fourteenth century), to More's *Utopia* (1516) and Bacon's *New Atlantis* (1617), there was no essential reason for disbelief. Even as late as 1726, when **Swift** published *Gulliver's Travels*, Australia was unknown to Europeans; Africa, South America and large parts of Asia remained *terrae incognitae*.
  Yet by the mid-nineteenth century it was clear that fabulous unknown lands did not exist. So it was exactly then that 'lost world' romance exploded, via the tales of **Verne, Haggard, Wells, E.R. Burroughs**, Conan Doyle, John Buchan and others. Haggard in particular exploited public desire for unknown realms in tales of African discovery; Conan Doyle's *The Lost World* (1912) explored a South American plateau where dinosaurs survived. Other authors explored the romance of drowned continents (**Atlantis, Lemuria**), often presenting their romances as fact. Ignatius Donnelly's *Atlantis: the Antediluvian World* (1882) spawned many successors; as did Verne's *Journey to the Centre of the Earth* (1864) (see also **Hollow Earth**). Secret Tibetan kingdoms (**Shambhala, Agharti**) were also popular.
  Yet by the 1930s, the mystery of such remote 'lost worlds' had begun to evaporate. Recent romancers have tended to locate 'lost worlds' in outer space, or in other dimensions, or in the human mind itself (*see* **Science Fiction**).

LOT'S WIFE (*See* **ANGELS, BIBLE**)
It is told in Genesis xix how **Yahweh** decided to destroy the cities of Sodom and Gomorrah, their people being evil, but, begged by the patriarch Abraham, agreed to stay his hand if there were but ten righteous men in Sodom. So he sent two **angels** there to seek. At the city gate the good man Lot recognised them and offered hospitality, but the Sodomites besieged his house, demanding their surrender. Lot offered his two virgin daughters instead. The Sodomites still insisted on 'knowing' the angels, who then struck them blind, telling Lot to remove his family before Yahweh destroyed

the city, and not to look behind as they fled, 'lest thou be consumed'. So Lot and his family fled to the hills; and as the sun rose Yahweh 'rained upon Sodom and Gomorrah brimstone and fire from the Lord out of heaven'. But Lot's wife (unnamed) looked back, and turned into a pillar of salt. Hiding with Lot in a mountain cave, his daughters feared they would never know a man. Making Lot drunk so that he did not know who they were, first one then the other slept with him. Both got pregnant, bearing the progenitors of the races of Moab and Ammon. So even Lot, the righteous man, was compromised. Yet the real mystery is: who was Lot's wife?

LOTUS (*See* ROSE)

As with the **lily** or **rose** in the West, in the East the lotus is widely used as a symbol of the divine presence in human life, the expanded flower forming the rosette or sun-wheel of the cycles of existence, also the receptive cup of the feminine principle; its root signifying the indissoluble, its stem the umbilical cord, its seed-pod the fecundity of creation. The Flower of Light, born of interaction between fiery **sun** and watery **moon**, it appears with **Egyptian** and **Hindu** sun-gods and with the Great Mother as goddess of the moon. A symbol of divine birth from the muddy waters, in Graeco-Roman and other ancient traditions it also had a funerary meaning, implying death and **resurrection**. The Thousand-Petalled Lotus is the sun, also the seat of human intelligence (the skull or brain). In yogic systems the chakras (psychic centres) are shown as lotuses, each with a different number of petals. To obtain this Flower of Paradise for his queen, **Bhima**, a hero in the Indian *Mahabharata*, went on a dangerous quest. The **Hindu** god **Vishnu** reclines on Shesha, the cosmic **serpent**, a lotus flower sprouting from his navel, on it seated **Brahma** the Creator. The **Vedic fire-god Agni** also rises from a lotus. In **Buddhism** the lotus stem is the world axis (spine; **Tree of Life**) supporting the flowering lotus throne, which represents the spiritual peak, perfect harmony, the centre of the flower being Mount Meru. The **Buddha** is depicted as the heart of the Jewel in the Lotus, as in the mantram (repetitive prayer) '*Aum Mani Padme Hum*': 'All Hail the Jewel in the Lotus'. **Bodhisattvas** stand on the unopened flower: in Chinese Buddhism the lotus is one of the Eight Treasures. In ancient **Egypt** the lotus was sacred to **Horus**, whose four sons stand on a lotus before **Osiris**, Lord of the Dead. Attributed to **Isis**, it is fecundity but also virginity: later it was an emblem of the Graeco-Roman **Aphrodite/Venus**.

LOUHI (*See KALEVALA*)

LOVECRAFT, HOWARD PHILLIPS (1890–1937) (*See* POE, SUPERNATURAL BEINGS)

An American author of supernatural fiction, a recluse who lived his life in Providence, Rhode Island. Originally influenced by Lord Dunsany, during his last years he wrote a set of tales with a common background, the Cthulhu Mythos, created by his fascination with 'the thought of some curious interruption in the prosaic laws of nature, or some monstrous intrusions on our familiar world by unknown things from the limitless outside'.

Fusing traditional supernaturalism with modern **science-fiction** themes (other **dimensions**, alien invasion), his dense, adjectival style was well suited to the build-up of horror in tales like *At the Mountains of Madness* (1936), in which **demonic** entities lie buried deep beneath the cyclopean ruins of a lost civilisation. Absorbing into his personal mythos entities like the fish-tailed **Phoenician** god **Dagon**, he also invented many horrific deities of his own, such as *Cthulhu* and *Yug Suggoth*, their dark wisdom and the knowledge of how to conjure them contained in an ancient grimoire, the *Necronomicon*, supposedly penned by 'the mad Arab' Abdul Alhazred, which since Lovecraft's death has taken on a mythic life of its own.

LUCIFER (*See* ANGELS, DEVIL)

LUG (LUGH) (*See* BALOR, IRISH MYTH, LANCELOT, TUATHA DÉ DANAAN)

Known as Lugh Lamhfhada, 'Long-Handed' or as Samildanach, 'God of All Arts', the name of this important Irish deity, grandson and slayer of the Fomorian demon-king **Balor** is cognate with Welsh god **Llew Llaw Gyffes**, and later with **Lancelot**. Born to Ethniu and Cian, surviving all Balor's attempts to kill him due to a prophecy that he would kill Balor, he was fostered by **Manannan** and Tailtiu, then came to the court of the Danaan king **Nuadu**. At first refused entry because every skill he had was already possessed by some other Danaan hero, in time he was admitted as he combined all these skills in one person (thus: 'God of all Arts'). Later leading the Danaan against the Fomorians, he slew Balor by putting out the latter's 'baleful eye' with a slingshot (thus: 'Long-Handed'). The mythic father of the hero **Cuchulainn**, this **Celtic** sun-god wore a **golden** helmet and armour, and as god of all arts (abilities) is also **Hermes/Mercury**. As such, in some tales he is said to have come 'from overseas'. His name is remembered in place-names like Lyons (France), Leiden (Holland) and Carlisle (England). One of the four great annual Celtic festivals, the Lugnasad ('Marriage of Lug', in which he took the whole land of Ireland as his bride), held every 1 August, was celebrated in his honour. It is said he established it in remembrance of his foster-mother Tailtiu, who died on that day. The festival, once consisting of month-long **games** (they survived into recent times) at Tailtiu in Ireland, had close connection with the widespread cult of the dying **corn**- or sun-god, being enacted to ensure his return the next year. Many marriages were celebrated at Lug's festival, its proper observance being held to have a direct bearing on the annual yield of corn, fruit, milk and fish. Later, the Lugnasad became the **Christian** Lammas-Day; today, it persists as the Harvest Festival. The name 'Lug' means 'light' or 'shining': he is the triumph of light over darkness.

LYCANTHROPY (*See* SHAPE-SHIFTING, WEREWOLF)

M

MAAT (*See* **EGYPTIAN MYTH**)
Daughter of **Ra** and one of the underworld retinue of **Osiris**, in Egyptian myth this wife of the scribe-god **Thoth** wore on her head a single ostrich feather, the ideogram of her name – truth or justice. When the soul of a newly deceased person arrived in the vast 'Hall of Double Justice', this feather was placed in one pan of the scales, the heart of the dead one in the other pan, so testing the soul's worth. The 'Hall of Double Justice' was so called because Maat (pure abstraction, deified and personified) was often doubled into two identical goddesses standing at either end of it.

MABINOGION (*See* **CELTIC MYTH, WELSH MYTH**)
First collected, translated and published (1838–49) under this title by Lady Charlotte Guest (1812–95), these eleven Welsh tales were originally preserved in two medieval collections, *The White Book of Rhydderch* (*c*.1300–25) and *The Red Book of Hergest* (*c*.1375–1425). A number were composed up to four centuries earlier, but much of the material dates from the early Celtic world. Consisting of the Four Branches of the Mabinogi ('the four parts of the tale'), the Four Independent Native Tales and the Three Romances, the core of the work is the Four Branches. The term 'Mabinogion' was thought by Lady Charlotte to be the plural of 'Mabinogi'. Yet *mabynnogyon* occurs only once in the manuscripts, and is probably a scribal error.

The Four Branches outline a mythic history of Britain in which, as in the earlier **Irish** *Lebor Gabala* ('Book of Invasions'), older gods or magic races are dispossessed. These tales are: 'Pwyll Prince of Dyfed', 'Branwen Daughter of Llŷr', 'Manawydan Son of Llŷr' and 'Math Son of Mathonwy'. All four may originally have dealt with the birth, exploits and death of the hero **Pryderi**, yet later accretions led to domination of the second and third branches by the Children of Llŷr, and of the fourth by the Children of Dôn: British/Welsh versions of the Irish **Tuatha dé Danaan**. So Manawydan ab Llŷr derives from the Irish sea-god **Manannan Mac Lir**; Govannan the **smith**-god from the Irish **Goibniu**; **Lludd** Llaw Ereint ('Lludd of the Silver Hand') the Irish god-king **Nuadu** ('of the Silver Hand'), etc. These parallels imply an Irish infiltration of Wales – the Children of Llŷr and the Children of Dôn may represent two successive pantheons reconciled by intermarriage. Yet **Christian** influence on the later Welsh tales makes it hard to reconstruct the original nature of the British/Welsh deities as described here, while centuries of sifting and alteration of original material by the *cyfarwydd* (**bards**) led to considerable electicism in the final, written versions. The exploits of **Arianrhod, Blodeuwedd, Gwydion, Llew, Manawyddan**, Pryderi, **Math, Rhiannon** and others are described under their own heads.

The Four Independent Native Tales ('The Dream of Macsen Wledig', 'Lludd and Llefelys', 'Culhwch and Olwen' and 'The Dream of Rhonabwy' do not compare either in length or stature with the Four Branches save for the unique tale of **Culhwch**, the earliest **Arthurian** tale in Welsh (perhaps tenth century). The Three Romances ('The Lady of the Fountain', 'Peredur' and 'Gereint Son of Erbin'), are full of Norman-French influence and, in their early exposition of Arthurian myth, bridge the older **pagan** world of the Four Branches and the medieval romance of Arthur, the **Holy Grail**, and the 'Matter of Britain'.

In its diversity, moral grandeur and imaginative power, the Mabinogion remains a primary source of insight into the magical world of the ancient Celts, and survives as a template for much later myth-making.[1]

1. *The Mabinogion* (trans. Gwyn Jones and Thomas Jones), Dent Everyman, London, 1984.

MABON (*See* ANGUS MAC OG, APOLLO, BEL, CELTIC MYTH, *MABINOGION*, MERLIN, WELSH MYTH)

Before 'mabinogi' meant 'tale', it meant 'tale of a hero'. Before that, it meant 'tale of a youth'. Earlier still, it meant simply 'youth' (*mab*). The Celtic god Mabon, often identified with **Apollo**, **Angus Mac Og**, **Bel** and even **Christ**, is 'Son of Light', son of the mysterious **Mother** of All, mediating between humanity and the deeper or higher powers. Sacrificed for humanity, shut in the **underworld**, Mabon epitomises the died-and-reborn **corn-god**, as later did Christ. One of the tasks undertaken by the early **Arthur** is to liberate him. Later the magician **Merlin**, driven insane after the Battle of Arderydd in the Welsh poem 'Peiryan Vaban' (sixth century?), exhorts Mabon to avenge the defeat of his king and his own exile in the otherworld Forest of Celydon. Merlin is a late version of Mabon – a 'Son of Light' who, though driven into darkness, will rise again, like the sun, like Christ.[1]

1. *Celtic Gods, Celtic Goddesses*, R.J. Stewart, Blandford, London, 1990; *The Quest for Merlin*, Nikolai Tolstoy, Sceptre, London, 1988.

MACPHERSON, JAMES (1723–96) (*See* FINN MACCOOL, OISIN)

In 1762 and 1763 respectively, Scots scholar James Macpherson published 'translations' of two manuscripts, 'Fingal' and 'Temora', claiming both to be by a third-century Gaelic **bard**, Ossian (Irish **Oisin**), son of the mythic hero Finn MacCool, or Fingal. These florid, hugely popular romances (it was less than twenty years since the Jacobite rebellion led by **Bonnie Prince Charlie** in 1745), caused violent argument. None of those denouncing Macpherson as a fraud (including David Hume and Dr Samuel Johnson) spoke Gaelic. Yet his talk of third-century texts was too ambitious: the earliest-known Scots Gaelic text is tenth century. Though based on fragments of genuine Gaelic myths, Macpherson was certainly the author. He was buried in Westminster Abbey in London.

MADONNA (*See* BLACK VIRGIN, MOTHER-GODDESS, VIRGIN MARY)

MAEL DÚIN (*See* BRAN, BRENDAN, IRISH MYTH, OISIN)

Some Irish tales of voyages over the western ocean (**Bran**, Oisin) focus more on the magical destination than the voyage. In others (Brendan), the *imrana* ('journey') matters more. Yet this 'Navigatio Brendani', influential since the Middle Ages as a signpost to real Western lands, may be based on the 'Immram Curaig Maile Dúin' ('The Voyage of Mael Dúin's Boat': *c.*AD 700).

Ostensibly **Christian** (Mael Dúin's mother is a nun), he voyages to find his father's killer, visiting many isles as fantastic as anything in **Homer**. On one a

horse-like beast with **dog**'s claws tries to eat the crew. On the next, a branch sprouts three **apples**, each enough to feed the crew for forty nights. On the third is a giant beast, the skin on which whirls round the flesh and bones, then vice versa. With the apples eaten they reach a fourth isle, on it a rich fort empty but for a **cat**, and a meal of meat and ale. They eat and drink, but when they try to take the food away, the cat leaps through one of Mael Dúin's three foster-brothers, burning him to a cinder. Next, an isle of wailing black-clad black men; then an isle with a glass bridge at its door, a woman taking water from the well. **Siren**-music puts the crew to sleep. On the fourth day the queen-like woman comes, knowing the name of every man, offering every pleasure. They awake to find their boat wrecked on a rock, the lovely isle and the woman vanished. At length they find the killer of Mael Dúin's father but are told to spare him, as God has spared them. They get back to Ireland by following a **falcon**-hawk.

MAENADS (*See* DIONYSUS, GREEK MYTH, ORPHEUS, PAN)
Lovers of the goat-god Pan, acolytes of the wine-god Dionysus, these wild women held drunken orgies on the Arcadian mountains, tearing animals and sometimes people to shreds. They slew Orpheus for not honouring Dionysus. When they tried to wash off his blood in the River Helicon, the river-god vanished underground to re-emerge elsewhere with a new name, the Baphyra, to avoid association with the crime. They tore Pentheus king of Thrace to pieces, led by his wife Agave (once a **moon**-goddess, ruler of the beer revels). In an ancient rite, mare-headed Maenads annually tore to pieces and ate raw a boy. Later, in the Dionysian revels, a foal replaced the boy.

MAEVE/MEDB (*See* IRISH MYTH, TAIN)

MAGDALENE (*See* CHRISTIANITY, GNOSTIC MYTH, SOPHIA, VIRGINITY)

MAGI (*See* AHURA MAZDA, ZOROASTRIANISM)
Initially a sect of **fire**-worshipping Median philosopher-priests hostile to Persian rule, until the Persian prophet Zoroaster (*c*.660–583 BC) reconciled their cult with that of the kings. Under the Sassanian dynasty (*c*.224 BC–AD 651) they became the official priesthood of Ahura Mazda. Later the term (especially in the singular: magus) was applied to 'wise men' in general, particularly those involved in **hermetic** or occult practices. The terms 'magic', 'magician' and 'imagination' also derive from this root.

MAGIC (*See* CONCORDANCE)
Inherent in myth is the power of sorcerers, often supernatural beings, who by magical **charm**, rite or **spell** work good or evil. They englamour human eyes, **shape-shift** into animal form, brew potions to confer **immortality**, **invulnerability**, the power of **flight** or **prophecy**. They may change men into **pigs** (**Circe**), sow **dragon**'s teeth that spring up as warriors, or create beautiful women from flowers (**Gwydion**).

There are two main principles behind magical practice. One, that like produces like. Two, that objects or things once in contact with each other continue to influence each other even at a distance. Also inherent is the belief that the outer world reflects the inner, and that invoking spirit forces (guardian **angels**, **demons**, **fairies**, etc.) has outer effects.

Imitative magic consists in the idea that imitating the desired effect produces it, as in **dances** or rites to bring rain, maintain a food supply, or ease labour (as by undoing **knots** or opening **doors**). Or a hunter might abstain from certain acts (**taboos**) to avoid spoiling his luck, just as today many refuse to walk under a **ladder**.

The notion that objects once in contact forever influence one another (contagious magic) is equally ancient and universal. Thus the common fear of letting an enemy get hold of one's **hair**, nail-parings or secret **name**: when **Isis** learned the secret name of **Ra**, she gained power over him.

Much 'magic' is a matter of suggestion and will, as when a victim who believes in curses knows he has been cursed. The magician's will defeats that of the victim. Poet **Robert Graves** once said that men unconsciously employ magic as an aid to seduction: they focus their will and imagination on overcoming the will of the desired one to gain sexual union.[1]

1. *The Occult*, Colin Wilson, Grafton Collins, London 1979, p.197.

MAGICAL CONTESTS (*See* GAMES, GNOSTIC MYTH, RIDDLES)

MAHABHARATA (*See BHAGAVAD GITA*, DRAUPADI, INDIAN MYTH)

From the **Sanskrit**, 'Great Epic of the **Bharata** Dynasty', and one of the two great epics of India (the *Ramayana* the other), this huge work of 220,000 lines is said to be based on actual events occurring perhaps between 1400 and 1000 BC and to be the work of the mythical author, 'Vyasa the Compiler'. Certainly it was composed over many centuries, reaching its final form *c.*AD 400.

Built round a war between the related Pandava and Kaurava families, the tale begins with the death of Queen Satyavati's two young sons. She invites the demigod **Krishna**-Dvaipayana (her son by an earlier affair) to lie with the two widows. But at his approach the older widow shuts her eyes, so her son Dritarashtra is born blind. The younger widow turns pale with fright, so her son Pandu is born pale. A blind man being considered unfit to rule, Pandu becomes king of Hastinapura, fathering two daughters and five sons: Yudhisthira, **Bhima**, **Arjuna**, Nakula and Sahadeva (Pandavas). Dritarashtra has a hundred sons (Kauravas) by favour of Krishna-Dvaipayana. Accused of leprosy, Pandu gives up the throne to Dritarashtra and becomes a hermit. Followed by his two wives, he dies with his sons still young. Dritarashtra takes them into his court and brings them up with the Kauravas, but when he appoints Yudhisthira as heir apparent, the jealousy of his own sons forces the Pandavas to flee. But on hearing of a competition for the hand of the beautiful Princess Draupadi, they return to compete with the Kauravas, and defeat them. Draupadi falls in love with Arjuna, but marries all five of the Pandavas, their mother ordering them to share her.

Dritarashtra now divides his kingdom into two, shared between Pandavas and Kauravas but, tricked into a game of dice with Duryodhana, the eldest Kaurava brother, Yudhisthira, loses his kingdom and is enslaved along with his brothers and Draupadi. A final losing throw leads to their sentence, of twelve years in exile, and a thirteenth year in a king's service. With this term completed, they decide to reconquer their kingdom. Krishna, the cousin of both sides, offers Arjuna and Duryodhana a choice: one can have his army, the other, himself. Duryodhana chooses the army, Arjuna chooses Krishna – wisely, for as **avatar** of **Vishnu**, Krishna wins the war for the Pandavas. Arjuna, the Pandava commander, approaches battle with Krishna as his charioteer, yet is reluctant to attack his cousins. To reconcile him to the war, Krishna recites the famous poem, the *Bhagavad Gita* (*The Song of God*). Only three Kauravas survive, to sneak into the Pandava camp and kill

Draupadi's five sleeping sons. After the accidental death of Krishna, shot by a hunter who mistakes him for a deer, the five Pandavas and Draupadi set out for **Indra**'s heaven, joined en route by a dog (the god **Dharma**, justice, in disguise). One by one they fall and die, victims of their own moral defects. Only Yudhisthira reaches **heaven**, there to be tested and then reunited with his brothers, and with Draupadi.

Interwoven with this main tale are myths of the gods, legends of the saints, heroic sagas and expositions on codes of conduct (*dharma*), history (worldly and divine), philosophy, morality and politics.

MAHAVIRA (*See* JAINISM)

MAHAYANA (*See* BUDDHISM, INDOCHINA)

MAHDI (*See* ISLAM)

In Islamic belief this 'divinely guided one' (Arabic) will bring justice and restore true religion, ushering in a brief **golden age** before the end of the world. Not found in the Koran, Mahdism is doubted by the orthodox Sunni sect, but is central to Shi'ite faith. Arising during the wars in early Islam (seventh and eighth centuries), it tends to revive during crises as a title claimed by revolutionaries who aim to restore Islam's political power and religious purity. In the Sudan in 1881 a Nubian, Muhammad Ahmad (1844–85), proclaimed himself Mahdi. Expelling Ottomon Turks and other foreign influences, he established an Islamic empire from the Red Sea to Central Africa. His capture of Khartoum from the British and the death there of General Gordon made him a mythic bugbear in the West. Yet his death soon after made it clear that he was not, after all, *the* Mahdi.

MAITREYA (*See* BUDDHISM)

The last of the five great **bodhisattvas**, the Buddha yet to come at the end of the world, said to live in a limbo state in the **heaven** called Tushita, which as Gautama the **Buddha** he entered having completed 550 former lives as animal, man and god. He will pass up to 5,000 years in Tushita before returning to bring justice and liberation to all in a time when the oceans have dried up, the mountains are plains and there is but one kingdom on earth, ruled by the righteous King Shankha.

Many Buddhists commune with Maitreya and ask his advice about their future deeds, as he is said still to be alive and concerned for humanity. Maitreya statues have been found from Pakistan to Java: he is called Mila-Fu in China, Miroku in Japan, Maitri in Tibet, Maidari in Manchuria. His original name is Mitri, 'the one who has friendship' (*see* **Mithra**).

MALORY, SIR THOMAS (*c*.1410–71) (*See* ARTHURIAN MYTH)

The identity of the author of *Le Morte d'Arthur*, the first prose account in English of the myth of **King Arthur** and the knights of the **Round Table**, remains doubtful. In a colophon to the text he calls himself 'Syr Thomas Maleore knyght', says he ended the work in the ninth year of the reign of Edward IV (March 1469–March 1470), and prays for 'good delyueraunce' from prison. This suggests Sir Thomas Malory of Newbold Revell in Warwickshire, who in 1450 began a career of violent crime. Cattle-rustling, rape, theft, looting and extortion were among his unchivalrous specialities. First he fought on the Yorkist side in the Wars of the Roses, then switched to the Lancastrians. For this misjudgement, in 1469 he was imprisoned in Newgate, in London. Here it seems he wrote the last words of 'the whole book of King Arthur and his noble knights of the Round Table', being buried in Greyfriars church by the jail. In 1485 William Caxton edited and printed his masterpiece. It is ironic that the author of this famous romance was an aggressive ne'er-do-well – or is it? Arthurian myth is not all sweetness and light: villains may be even more attracted by the heroic ideal than deskbound clerks or monks.

MANANNAN MAC LIR (*See* IRISH MYTH, JOYCE, SEA-GODS)

This ancient **Irish** sea-god is usually associated with the magical race, the **Tuatha dé Danaan,** but appears to predate them. He fostered many gods, including **Lug,** and lost his wife, Fand, to **Cuchulainn.** His name remains extant in that of the Isle of Man in the Irish Sea, his chief home, about which he cast dense mists. By his magic (he was a famous **shape-shifter**), he could make one object seem like a hundred; chips of wood he threw into the sea assumed the size of great ships of war. In the coat of arms of the Isle of Man he is portrayed as three-legged: some have seen in this a form of the **swastika.** He owned a marvellous **silver bough** or branch, on which three **golden apples** hung. This, giving forth sweet music and providing favoured wayfarers (like **Mael Dúin**) with magical sustenance during their journey to the otherworld, he gave to the legendary Irish king, **Cormac MacAirt.** He also gave Cormac his magic Cup of Truth, a precursor of the **Holy Grail.** Amorous, he would visit women by night in the shape of a heron.

He is said to have incarnated as a **Druid,** Manannan MacOirbsen, who travelled in a magical copper boat, the 'Wave-Sweeper', which required no oars or rudder. He owned a famous magic cloak (fog?) which, if shaken between two persons, meant neither could ever meet again. He is analogous with Manawyddan ab Llŷr who, in the Welsh *Mabinogion,* left landless on the death of **Bran,** becomes **Rhiannon**'s husband, thus stepfather of the hero **Pryderi.** As Manawyddan he is a wise craftsman, teacher and man of power. Yet ultimately he is robbed of his lands and sovereignty by the British hero, Caswallan, wearer of a magic tartan cloak that confers **invisibility.**

So the son robs the father of the father's powers. Yet Manannan Mac Lir (if only for the euphony of his name, or the stride of the waves) remains potent even today, at least along the Celtic seaboard.[1]

1. *The Magic Arts in Celtic Britain*, Lewis Spence, Rider, London, 1970.

MANAWYDDAN (*See MABINOGION*, MANANNAN MAC LIR)

MANCO CAPAC (*See* INCA MYTH)

MANDEVILLE, SIR JOHN (*fl.* 1356) (*See* FABULOUS BEASTS, LOST WORLDS)

Though in his time famous as the greatest traveller in the Middle Ages, by the sixteenth century Sir John Mandeville of St Albans in Hertfordshire had acquired a new reputation: as the greatest liar of the medieval era. Not that this stopped folk reading his account of global discoveries, widely known as 'The Travels of Sir John Mandeville', first published as *The Voyage and Travels of Sir John Mandeville, Knight,* in which, *c.*1356, this unknown author tells how between 1322 and 1356 he travelled the world, discovering many marvels, including isles inhabited by dog-headed men, the realm of **Prester John,** the Land of Darkness and the abode of the ten Lost Tribes of Israel (locked up by **Alexander the Great** in the Caspian

Mountains). Mandeville probably never left England, but selected his fantastic tales from the travel books and encyclopedias already available, offering them as personal experience. As such, he stands as the precursor not so such of **science fiction** writers as of authors like Erich Von Däniken (*Chariots of the Gods*), who seize upon popular myths and retail them as fact.

MANDRAKE (*See* FABULOUS BEASTS)
This plant, the root of which looks like a man, is said to cry when torn out of the ground, a cry driving those who hear it mad, as **Shakespeare** reported in *Romeo and Juliet* IV:iii. Anciently, to uproot the mandrake was thought to invite terrible calamity. The Roman author Flavius Josephus advised use of a trained dog to dig it up – the dog dies, but the mandrake's leaves may be used as a narcotic, a laxative or for magical purposes.

MANGU (*See* AFRICAN MYTH, SORCERY, WITCHCRAFT, WITCHDOCTOR)
A term used in Zaïre and Sudan for **witchcraft** or a witchcraft substance that kills, either an organ or a liquid, sometimes translated as 'stomach' or 'bile', or 'witches' extra organ' meaning a part of the body that kills by non-physical means, i.e., by **magic**. There is no English word for this African concept.

MANICHAEISM (*See* DUALISM, GNOSTIC MYTH)
Persian dualist cult named after Mani, born in Babylonia *c.*AD 216. Claiming supernatural revelations, he visited India and China, won royal recognition in Persia, but in AD 276 was crucified and flayed to death by Bahram I.

He preached the eternal co-existence of two realms, Light and Dark. In the former dwells God, in the latter the Dark Lord and his brood. Evil began when Dark invaded Light. God evoked the Mother of All, who evoked the Primal Man to ward off the attack. Clad in the Five Bright Elements (Light, Wind, Fire, Water, Ether), the Primal Man was beaten. The Archons, Princes of Darkness, consumed the Five Bright Elements but were captured, a wall being built to stop Darkness spreading. Light was disgorged to form **sun**, **moon** and stars, and the sky and earth were made from dismembered Archons. God evoked the Messenger, attracting the lustful Archons to give out stolen light to form the vegetable world. The Dark Lord begot of his wife a new being, **Adam**, in whom he put sparks of light. God sent Jesus to make Adam eat from the Tree of Knowledge. Adam cursed the creation and denied **Eve**, who then bore Cain and Abel to the Archons. At last Adam lay with her and Seth was conceived: so humanity endures, particles of light still imprisoned in it.

To Mani, all great religious leaders were Messengers. Christ, he said, was pure spirit, his body a phantom. Mani claimed to be the last Messenger, sent to continue separating Light from Dark. His followers, the initiated Elect and lay Hearers, would at world's end enter the realm of light, but meantime must purify themselves. The Elect might not marry, own property, eat meat, drink wine or even break bread. They wandered alone but for the company of a Hearer, who (unbound by taboos) broke bread for them.

The movement became widespread, briefly embracing even **St Augustine** (AD 373–382), but by the sixth century had failed. Rulers persecuted wanderers who refused to work and relied on charity. Though wiped out, the church had caused such alarm that later the word 'Manichaean' became synonymous with heresy, being applied to Bogomils, **Cathars** and all **Gnostics**.[1]

1. *The Medieval Manichee*, Steven Runciman, Cambridge University Press, 1982 (1947), p.12–18.

MANITOU (*See* KICI MANITOU, NATIVE AMERICAN MYTH)

MANU (*See* FLOOD MYTH, INDIAN MYTH, NOAH)

First Indian lawgiver, eponymous ancestor of mankind. Manu is also the title of any one of seven or fourteen patriarchs who have ruled the earth. The first Manu (an emanation of **Brahma**, Svayam-bhuva, 'Existing by his own power') founded **sacrifices** and gave his name to the best-known code of Brahman law, the Laws of Manu. The Manu of our age is the seventh, Manu-sanhita, the Indian Noah. The **Hindu** *Rig Veda* tells how one day in his washing water he found a tiny fish. 'Spare my life, and I will spare yours,' begged the fish, and foretold a Flood. Manu put the fish in a pot, but it grew so fast he had to put it in a tank, a lake, then in the sea. Told that the Flood was imminent, Manu built an ark which, when the waters rose, the fish towed by a cable. When the waters fell Manu prayed for and was granted a wife. From their union came the generations of Manu, or mankind.

MAORI MYTH (*See* OCEANIC MYTH)

The Maori of New Zealand originate from Polynesian conquest and assimilation of Melanesians already on the two islands. They say Oceania's many isles – from **Hawaii** to Easter Island and New Zealand itself – were once one land, broken into pieces by the war between the sky-god Rangi and his children. In the beginning, they say, from Te Kore (primal void) emerged night, day and space, from which sprang two formless beings, male and female, who bore Rangi and Papa, the divine parents. But Rangi's close embrace of Papa the earth crushed the gods she had borne. There was no light, nothing ripened or bore fruit. Tu-matauenga, one of the desperate divine children, advised killing both Rangi and Papa. Tane-mahuta the forest-god said it would be better to tear them apart, setting Rangi far away, but keeping Papa close. Tane-mahuta forced Rangi up into the sky. At last light came to the earth: many beings sprang out of the earth-womb to multiply. But Tawhiri-ma-tea the storm-god supported Rangi and threatened to destroy the new land. Only Tu-matauenga, god of fierce men, could resist his rage. Their drawn battle, the Maori claim, caused the **Flood** that formed the Pacific Ocean. Or it happened when the god Tawaki, enraged by human evil, broke heaven's crystal floor by stamping on it, so that down poured the waters of the Upper World.

The Maori also tell of a magic wooden **head** that destroyed all daring to approach the fort of two **sorcerers**, Puarata and Tautohito. Determined to conquer the evil head, the wizard Hakawau set out with a companion, constantly working magic to ward off evil spirits. They passed piles of rotting corpses, but Hakawau and his good spirits pressed on to overwhelm the fort. Puarata appealed to the head, but it could only moan. Hakawau scaled the gateway unharmed and clapped his hands, whereupon everyone inside the fort died immediately.

MAPONUS (*See* APOLLO, CELTIC MYTH, MABON)

Closely linked with and perhaps identical to the Celtic 'Son of Light', Mabon, this 'Divine Youth' was worshipped in northern Britain during the Roman period and was probably associated with music and poetry.

MARA (*See* **BUDDHISM, INDIAN MYTH**)
Buddhist god of death, lust and temptation, originally a **demon** skilled in creating **illusion**, thus the enemy of the Buddha. As Christ in the wilderness was tempted by **Satan** so, as Gautama sat under the bo-tree, Mara tried to destroy the sage's meditation, sending his voluptuous daughters to dance enticingly. Gautama, unwavering, simply touched the earth with his finger-tips. Though defeated, Mara still haunts the world, seeking to snatch the souls of the dying. Originally he may also have been one of the four avatars of **Kamadeva**, **Hindu** god of love, son of **Vishnu** and **Lakshmi**.

MARDUK (*See* **BAAL, BABYLONIAN MYTH, SUN-GODS**)
Or Bel-Marduk (Bel, 'Lord': *Marduk*, 'Bull-Calf of the Sun'). This son of **Sumerian**/Babylonian sun-god **Enki/Ea** epitomised agricultural growth via the fertility of the waters. Before slaying the chaos-monster **Tiamat** he demanded of the other gods that victory should gain him supreme authority and the power to determine **fates**. Vanquishing her, he fixed the tablets of destiny to his chest and created a new world order, humanity included in it. The gods granted him fifty titles, including: 'He who created grain and plants and made green things to grow', 'The Lord of pure incantation, making the dead to live', and 'Guardian of justice and law'. Later, when evil **djinn**, aided by **Ishtar** and **Shamash**, occluded the **moon**-god **Sin** whose cold eye pursued nocturnal criminals, he routed the rebels and restored Sin to his proper brilliance. Thus he absorbed all other gods, set planets and stars in their courses, governed all magic and incantation, and decided human fate at his spring festival, the *zagmuk*, at which he was annually resurrected, his statue being carried from the temple called Esagil and out of the city to a country temple, the Akitu. Here, **mystery** rites celebrated his death, resurrection and marriage to the goddess Zarpanit.

His defeat of Tiamat is ambiguous. Though slain and dismembered, she remained manifest in all her children who paid Marduk homage. The myth may imply the taming of the Tigris and Euphrates via irrigation to fertilise the desert. If so, 'Marduk' is not only the light of the sun but the power of reason to overcome natural chaos and organise it into a functional city-state. His fifty titles imply the amalgamation of and co-operation between many different groups of people, without which no state can be founded, far less prosper. Thus the gods of fifty tribes become the common god, or the aim of one city-state based on the taming of the waters.

MARS (*See* **ROMAN MYTH**)
Father of **Romulus**, this most Roman of Roman gods was an agricultural deity before he became god of war. The name, from the root *mar*, may mean 'to shine'. Thus like **Marduk** he was originally the sun, ripening the corn. Son of the union of **Juno** with a mystic flower, his early rustic qualities were taken over by his warrior aspect. Sacrifices were offered to him before battle and after victory he got his share of the booty. *Mars Gradivus* 'to grow' became *Mars Gradivus* 'to march': soil became spoil. The sacred spears and shields of his cult were kept on the Palatine Hill in Rome. He is shown as bearded, with cuirass and helmet.

MARUTS (*See* **INDIAN MYTH, INDRA, RUDRA**)
Spirits of tempest, these forty-nine terrible sons of the **Vedic** storm-god **Rudra** (who later developed into **Shiva**) were also called Rudras. Their mother Diti (or Rudrani) bore them in one lump which Rudra-Shiva shaped into handsome boys. Another tale is that Shiva as a **bull** begat them on

Prithivi, a **cow**. Armed with lightning-spears and thunder-**hammers**, riding **chariots** each drawn by two spotted deer and by one never-tiring red deer, in golden armour and wearing bright skins, these stalwart 'cloud-shakers' went into battle for the sky-god **Indra**. When Indra came to attack the drought-demon **Vritra**, first the Maruts freed the cows (rain-clouds) that Vritra had imprisoned and 'chased them aloft', then advanced, roaring, on Vritra himself as Indra hurled the *vajra* and slew him. They also accompanied Indra to happier events, like the **horse sacrifice** King Dasaratha performed to persuade the gods to grant him an heir (they gave him four), and in Indra's heaven attended the sky-god's throne brilliantly.

MARY (*See* MOTHER-GODDESS, VIRGIN MARY)

MASKS
Either a means of concealment or of identification with supernatural forces or gods. In Sri Lanka when a man was dangerously ill and the doctors could do nothing, a devil-**dancer** was called in, wearing masks appropriate to each of the demons of disease and drawing them out of the sick man into himself. In Mali, West Africa, annually the Komo society celebrate in mask dance the river-god, Faro, who put fish in the Niger. Each year a new mask is carved, of a specific animal, bird, or human, or with a combination of animal features. To frighten the worshippers and remind them of the power of the god, the outside of the mask is painted red, white and black; inside the mask is the skull of a man or **hyena**. The mask has huge eyes, ears and nose the better to see, hear and sniff out evildoing. Inside the mask, the dancer becomes the god. The Australian **Aboriginal** 'bush soul' masks identity the wearer with the soul of the animal, bird or plant represented. In North America masks are worn by members of secret **medicine** societies and by dancers. Carved from wood by the Iroquois of the northeast and by the **Hopi** in Arizona, they are worn while curing the sick, to alleviate pain, and for exorcisms. Membership of the False Face Societies of the Iroquois can be gained by dreaming of a specific mask.

In sacred plays masks not only portray the supernatural forces of the deities represented, but were once thought to protect the audience from the sheer power of such forces. In secular plays masks symbolise the way that inner characteristics are hidden by outer personality. Thus the Latin term '*persona*' means mask, as does the word '*larva*'. '*Larvatus*', 'masked', implies a personality possessed or imprisoned, as with *The Man in the Iron Mask*. The *larva* metamorphoses into a *pupa*, 'pupil'; the eye is opened, the mask removed, the child initiated. 'The Masks of God' (title of **Campbell**'s four-volume exposition on the inner meanings of myth) are the illusions of the material world, **Maya**. The set face of the newly-dead person is called the death-mask; carved, hideous death-masks are worn in ritual or at winter festivals like **Hallowe'en** to transform fear of dying into acceptance of death as a process of change. Oracles wore masks with their clients, the mask denoting the transpersonal source of prophetic authority. In Greece the mask symbolised either the petrifying power of **Medusa** the Gorgon, or the tragic or comic nature of the character in plays.

MATH (*See* ARIANRHOD, BLODEUWEDD, GWYDION, *MABINOGION*, WELSH MYTH)
The tale of this ancient Welsh monarch or demi-god is told in the Fourth Branch of the *Mabinogion*, 'Math Son of Mathonwy'. Lord of Gwynedd in the north while **Pryderi** reigned in the south, though omniscient and wise, he

could live only 'while his two feet were in the fold of a maiden's lap, unless the turmoil of war prevented him'.[1] His footholder Gowein is raped by his nephew Gilfaethly (brother of **Gwydion** and **Arianrhod**). In shame he marries her, punishing Gilfaethly and Gwydion (who had pursued Gilfaethly's cause at Pryderi's court) by turning them one year into stag and hind, the next into **boar** and sow, the third into **wolf** and she-wolf. When Arianrhod applies as his new footholder, he makes her step over his **wand** to prove her **virginity**, but she bears two infants, **Dylan** and **Llew**. Their tales, and those of Arianrhod and **Blodeuwedd**, are given separately.

1. *The Mabinogion* (trans. Gwyn and Thomas Jones), Dent Everyman, London, 1984.

MATI-SYRA-ZEMLYA (*See* EARTH-MOTHER, MOTHER-GODDESS, SLAVONIC MYTH)

Means 'Mother-Earth-Moist'. The pagan Slavs regarded the earth as a supreme being; conscious, wise, just and prophetic. In parts of Russia folk would dig a hole in the ground with stick or finger, then put their ear to the hole to hear what the earth said. A sound like that of a well-filled sleigh gliding over the snow meant the crop would be good. That of an empty sleigh meant otherwise. Legal disputes over landed property were settled by calling on Mati-Syra-Zemlya as witness. Oaths were sworn with a clod of earth on the head. Until the 1917 Revolution, if plague or cholera struck a village, at midnight the old women would secretly summon out all the other women. Nine virgins and three widows were chosen. A widow was hitched to a plough driven by another. With the widows clutching skulls and the virgins scythes, they ploughed a furrow round the village to let out the earth-spirit so that it might destroy the illness. Any man meeting this shrieking procession was cut down on the spot.

MATRIKA (*See* DEVI, INDIAN MYTH, MOTHER-GODDESS)

The **Hindu** divine mother, an amalgamation of seven original divine mothers who protected human morality. In another version, there are eight. It is told how the **demon**-king desired the lovely Parvati. One of his servants took elephant-form, to kill the god **Shiva** (knowledge). But Shiva's son slew the elephant-demon, while Shiva's arrow made the demon-king bleed so heavily that drops of his blood fell to earth. Each drop took the form of an andhakasura (spirit of ignorance). To counter this, each of the eight gods present created a *shakti*, or female aspect of themselves, each as an antidote to the evil spirits created: these being desire, anger, illusion, covetousness, pride, fault-finding, tale-bearing and envy. So the demon army was defeated and no new evils emerged.

MAUI (*See* OCEANIC MYTH, TRICKSTERS)

This Polynesian **trickster**-god and culture hero performed many remarkable feats. With the sharp jawbone of his ancestress, Muri-ranga-whenua, he drew land from the sea, but his brothers cut it up, leaving only islands amid the ocean. He lassooed the **sun** with a rope of coconut-cord to make it go slower, so that his mother Hina had enough time each day to do all her domestic work. Like the **Maori** god Tane-Mahatu, he lifted the sky to give men more room. To do this, say the Tongans, he used a poker. As he prepared an earth-oven, this poker got jammed in the sky. In his struggle to get it out, he pushed the sky up. By the Hawaiian account (one of the main Hawaiian isles is named after him) he was the son of Hina-lau-ae: his **incestuous** marriage to

Hina bore four sons, all fishermen. It was while out fishing with them that he came on the isle where the mud-hens guarded the secret of fire, which he tricked them into giving up. In the Tuamoto Archipelago (east of Tahiti), the tale is that Hina, wife of the monster eel *Te Tuna*, fled him in search of a new lover. Nobody dared take her for fear of Te Tuna, until Maui was sent to her by his own mother. Amid world-shaking storm Maui confronted Te Tuna, and with enormous phallus in hand clubbed down three of the eel-god's frightful cronies. Subduing Te Tuna, he claimed Hina. When Te Tuna again attacked Maui, he was pulled to pieces by Maui's magic . . . yet from his buried head grew the first coconut tree.

MAY DAY (*See* BELTANE, DANCE, HALLOWE'EN, TREES, YARILO)

Until discouraged by the Puritans, celebration of the ancient **pagan** fertility festival of May Day was widespread. From Cornwall to Russia folk greeted the coming of spring by decking their doors with green boughs adorned with flowers, or by planting a tree adorned with multicoloured ribbons before each house, or by cutting down a maytree and taking it door to door before setting it up in the middle of the village. Meanwhile the young folk of both sexes had, as English Puritan Philip Stubbes wrote with disgust (in *Anatomie of Abuses*, 1583), 'run gadding over night to the woods, groves, hils, and mountains, where they spend all the night in plesant pastimes . . . for there is a great Lord present amongst them . . . namely Sathan, prince of hel.'

Thus too the association of May Eve with one of the two great annual festivals of **witches**, the other being **Hallowe'en**, at the other end of the year. Yet in origin there are no such evil associations. Where Hallowe'en (Celtic Samhain) recognises the return of winter; May Day (**Beltane**) is a celebration of the rebirth of the sun, of fertility; its most potent symbol (especially loathed by Puritans) the Maypole. Stubbes tells how, drawn by yoked oxen, the horns of each decorated with flowers, and with great crowds following it, the Maypole – bound with strings, painted many colours, with flowers and ribbons tied to it – was brought into the village and erected. Dancing and feasting would commence round what Stubbes called 'this stynkyng ydol'. A May King, or Queen of the May, or both, would be elected, perhaps by winning a race to the pole. Wearing boughs or leaves (like the English Jack-in-the-Green), this representative of the vegetation spirits led the dance round the pole then proceeded round the village, blessing each house. From Ireland to Hungary the prettiest girl was chosen as May Queen, decked in flowers and carried singing through the streets.

Stripped of foliage and erected as the Maypole, the tree is the *axis mundi* about which the world revolves. The pole is phallus or *lingam*, the disc at the top the feminine symbol, and the seven ribbons are the colours of the rainbow. Once it was the sacred pine of **Attis**, taken in procession to the temple of **Cybele**, where **dances** took place round it.

Usually in Europe it was customary to erect a new maytree each year, but in England the village maypole tended to become permanent, the meaning of the custom by then being forgotten. Today, in many industrialised parts of the world, May Day is celebrated as the traditional working-class holiday.

MAYA (*See* BUDDHISM, INDIAN MYTH, MARA)

Also called **Kali**-Durga, goddess of magic and spells; or Maha-Devi, 'the great goddess': identified with **Cybele** by the Greeks and by them called Maia, this Indian goddess represents all false appearances. She personifies the ancient conviction that what we see is not real, that physical reality is treacherously seductive: false. As such, she is the *shakti* of **Mara**, the **Buddhist** god of death and **illusion** whose daughters tempted Gautama the **Buddha** under the bo-tree.

MAYAN MYTH (*See* CONCORDANCE)

Chief branch of the Maya-Quiché family, between AD 300 and AD 900 the Maya of Yucatán were the greatest astronomers and mathematicians of pre-Columbian America, also fine architects, building at least eighty-three ceremonial centres in the Petén, a dense jungle region. These included complex buildings grouped round plazas, ball-courts, stelae, altars and statues of the Mayan gods, all dominated by steep truncated pyramids, with stone temples on top. At Tikal (its ninth-century population perhaps 40,000) the pyramids rise 190 feet above the plaza. But by then slash-and-burn agriculture had exhausted the soil. One by one the centres failed; the great civilisation degenerated into village tribalism. Today, many in Yucatán remain of Mayan stock, and still speak the old tongue.

Heading their mythological pantheon was Hunab Ku, the 'One God', also called Kinebahan ('Mouth and Eyes of the Sun'). He renewed the world after the first three **floods** poured from the mouth of the sky-**serpent**.

His wife Ixazaluoh (water) created weaving. Their son Itzamna invented drawing and letters, restored the dead to life and guaranteed fertility in return for pilgrimages, gifts and sacrifice of squirrels. He was a kind old man with a big nose and no teeth. Yet his wife *Ixchel* had helped the sky-serpent to drown the earth. A storm-goddess, she required frequent sacrifice. With writhing serpents on her head and crossbones on her skirts, she was as terrible as Ixtab, Mayan goddess of suicide. Shown as hanging from heaven, a rope round her neck, Ixtab took into paradise the souls of sacrificial victims, women who had died in childbirth, men killed in battle, suicides by hanging and priests.

They also recognised four wind-gods, the Bacabs; a god of life, Acat, who shaped children in the womb; Akna, goddess of birth; Echua, god of travellers; Chin, god of vice, and many others, of whom the two most important were Ah Puch and Kukulcán.

Ah Puch, god of death, was shown as a skeleton or bloated corpse. As Hunhau, Demon-Lord, he ruled the ninth, lowest **hell**, Mitnal. Inherited by the **Aztecs**, Ah Puch remains feared in modern Yucatán and Mexico as Yum Cimil, haunting the sick and dying. Like many other Amerindian tribes the Mayans practised ritual human **sacrifice** and **cannibalism**, though fearing death more than their neighbours.

The god or culture-hero Kukulcán, basis of the Aztec god **Quetzalcoatl**, the 'Plumed Serpent', is said to have come from the west with nineteen companions including two fish-gods, two gods of agriculture and a thunder-god. Like the **Sumerian** fish-god Oannes he educated and made law, then after ten years departed into the east, promising to return. Like the **Hopi** Pahana ('White Brother') or Quetzalcoatl, Kukulcán is said to have been white, or a white man. One such 'Kukulcán' is said to have conquered from the sea, *c.*AD 987. Yet this same culture-hero was known to the earlier Toltecs as Huemac. The 'Kukulcán' of AD 987 may have been but the last of several.

Who was the first? One tale (perhaps sourced in **Atlantean** longings) claims that Naram-Sin, son of Menes who united Egypt and founded the First Dynasty (*c.*3100 BC or earlier), sailed west, returning when his father died, and that he brought to the Americas the knowledge of number and proportion, as found in Mayan architecture and mathematics. Thus, the 'Winged Serpent' may be but a metaphor for the power of the enlightened, reasoning mind.

The Mayan calculations of time are more involved and vast than any but those of the **Brahmans** and modern physicists. Their mathematician-priests posited a universe millions of years old even as **Christians** claimed there had been but 5,500 years since the Creation. They had two calendars: one, tzolkin, with 260 days; the other, haab, with 365. Oddly, the year 1519, a New Year, was widely foretold as the year of Kukulcán/Quetzalcoatl's return. Belief that Cortés was Kukulcán greatly aided his 1519 conquest of Mexico.

According to reported ancient Mayan **prophecy**, a new world order would begin in 1987. Thus on 16 and 17 August 1987, in many countries, 'New Age' believers celebrated the 'Harmonic Convergence', supposedly (and hopefully) marking the dawn of a new and better era in world history.

MECCA (*See* **ISLAM**)

MEDEA (*See* **GREEK MYTH, JASON, THESEUS**)

MEDICINE (*See* **AFRICAN MYTH, NATIVE AMERICAN MYTH, SHAMANISM**)
Especially in Africa and North America, all words translated as 'medicine' refer not to cough-drops but to all that is sacred, supernatural, magical or holy. In North America medicine people are holy men or women who act as **prophets**, soothsayers, moral leaders and healers. Their medicine is their essential psychic power; their capacity to interpret good and evil omens, to offer protection against evil spirits or psychic assault, and to gain power from animals, plants, stars and ceremonies. People carried sacred or prized objects in a medicine bag. The Mandans of the Upper Missouri used medicine poles as the northwestern tribes used **totem** poles, as a symbol of the totem animals of the tribes. Medicine wheels refer to the enigmatic stone circles (*see* **Megalithic myths**) anciently constructed by nomads of the Great Plains and western Canada. These, as with Stonehenge and other well-known European henges, appear to have served ceremonial and calendric purposes, marking summer solstice and the midsummer rise of certain stars.

Similarly in Africa, medicine may mean 'magic antidote', 'spirit' or 'fetish'. In both Nilotic and **Zulu,** the word for 'medicine' is the same as for 'tree'. The Malagasy **charm** *ody tandroka*, 'horn medicine', prevents attacks by **bulls**; *ody basa*, 'gun medicine', is an **amulet** said to prevent soldiers being hit by bullets. Yet *ody andoha* is a herb to cure headache. No distinction is made in the word *ody* between ordinary medicine and magic charms. The African medicine man, like his North American counterpart, is a **shaman**, receiving spirit-messages, providing charms to protect their wearers against evil; 'sniffing out' **witches**, those with the evil **eye**, and those said to be able to **shape-shift** into beasts of prey by night.

MEDUSA (*See* **EYE, GREEK MYTH, HAIR, PERSEUS, SERPENT**)
From the same root as **Medea** ('Cunning'), one of the three Gorgons ('Grim Ones') fathered by the sea-deity Phorcys. Medusa and her sisters, Stheino ('Strong') and Euryale ('Wide-roaming'), were beautiful. But one night Medusa slept with **Poseidon** in **Athene**'s temple. Enraged, Athene turned her into a winged monster with **serpent** locks, brazen claws and glaring **eyes**, the gaze of which turned men into stone. The hero **Perseus** agreed with the tyrant Polydectes that, if he slew Medusa, Polydectes would stop trying to

marry his mother, Danaë. Aided by Athene and **Hermes**, Persues stole the single eye and tooth shared by the Gorgons' three sisters, the **swan**-like Graeae, making them tell him where the Stygian **nymphs** lived. The nymphs gave him winged sandals, a helmet of **invisibility** and a magic pouch. Thus armed, he found the Gorgons in the **Hyperborean** land, asleep amid the rain-worn shapes of men and beasts petrified by Medusa's glare. Eyeing her reflection in Athene's polished shield, with Athene guiding his arm, he decapitated Medusa with the sickle Hermes had given him. From her gouting neck sprang the winged horse **Pegasus** and the warrior Chrysaor, fully-grown and armed, both begotten on her by Poseidon. Putting her head in the pouch, he fled Stheino and Euryale with the aid of the helmet.

This may tell how Hellenic invaders, sky-god worshippers, usurped the powers of the **moon**-goddess. Likewise it was from the back of Pegasus that **Bellerophon** slew the hideous **chimera**. Later, the physician **Asclepius** obtained the Medusa's blood to cure illness: Athene took the rest to cause destruction. In **Homer**'s time only one Gorgon was known: the three appear to represent the triple moon-goddess, their awful faces meant to terrify strangers unfit to enter her **Mysteries**. In short, these petrifying faces were **masks**. **Graves** adds that Greek bakers painted Gorgon masks on their ovens to stop the curious from peering in and spoiling the bread.[1]

1. *The Greek Myths*, Robert Graves, Penguin, London, 1960.

MEGALITHIC MYTHS (*See* DRAGON, EARTH MOTHER, EARTH MOUNDS, STONE, UFOs)

Erected *c*.4000–*c*.1500 BC by pre-literate cultures who left no explanation of their purposes or other record of their lives, megaliths ('big stones') are found the world over, either singly (menhirs, standing stones), in circles (Stonehenge), rows (Carnac) or as dolmens (two uprights and a lintel). In whatever form, they are often aligned directly with a number of other such sites locally or even internationally distant. Typically they stand over underground water-crossings, near geological faults or tectonic intrusions where the geomagnetic field exhibits measurable anomalies, and consist of stones with high crystal content, capable of generating piezoelectricity.

Megalithic myth comes in two forms: (1) myths about the magical powers of the builders, (2) myths about the magical properties of the stones.

Brittany and Britain are especially rich in these remains, which employ Pythagorean geometry 2,000 years before **Pythagoras** who, it is said, was taught by **Abaros**, priest of a winged temple in **Hyperborea**. Some say this temple was Stonehenge, others that it was Callanish in the Outer Hebrides. Yet, to have known Pythagoras, Abaros must have lived a millennium after the collapse of megalithic culture *c*.1500 BC. When the **Celts** reached Britain, the megalith-builders were already mythic, as in **Irish** tales of the magic race, the **Tuatha dé Danaan**. Legends of **giants** and **dragons** abounded; the stones were said to be alive (Gaelic: *fir chreig*, 'false men'), 'walking' or 'dancing' by night, or (as with Oxfordshire's Rollright Stones) going to nearby rivers to 'drink'. Odd lights and will-o'-the-wisps (spirits of the dead?) hovered above them. The early Church found it hard to keep folk away from these 'sacred' sites. Saints trying to found a church elsewhere would find that the 'Devil' nightly removed the stones from the new site back to the old pagan mound. Many churches, especially in Wales, ended up within stone circles, on old earthworks or on alignments of standing stones.

That megaliths were associated with fertility and healing is clear from folk-myth and made explicit by **Geoffrey of Monmouth** in his *History of the*

Kings of Britain. Of the Giant's Dance (Stonehenge), he has **Merlin** (who traditionally was said to have 'flown' or 'sung' the stones from Ireland to England) say: 'the stones possess mystical power and are useful for many healing purposes. The giants [who] brought them from Africa and placed them in Ireland . . . designed to take baths among them whenever they were stricken with illness. For they washed the stones and placed their sick in the water, which invariably cured them.' So too cromlechs (stones with hollow centres) were widely said to refertilise barren women.

As to myths of foreign origin, of the Callanish Circle on Lewis (Outer Hebrides) it is said that a priest-king and his acolytes, wearing bird-feather robes, came in ships with the stones and gangs of black men to erect them. Another local legend is that they came from China.

Puritanically regarded as satanic, many megaliths were broken up. Much of the great circle at Avebury was thus destroyed in the seventeenth century, even as antiquarians like Aubrey and Stukeley declared the stones to be Druidic in origin. **Blake** refers to 'Britain's ancient rocky Druid shore', and to the 'giant Albion', which he saw hidden in the ancient landscape.[1]

Then science stepped in. In the 1890s Lockyer proposed the purpose of circles like Stonehenge and Callanish to be calendrical, with individual stones marking the motions of sun and moon. In the 1960s, the Boston astronomer Gerald Hawkins showed Stonehenge to be a sophisticated calendar. Professor Alexander Thom's surveys of many British circles and megaliths later proved the precision of the system. Also he deduced the common use of the 'megalithic yard' (2.72 feet), not only in Europe but also in North America.[2]

The scientific evidence encouraged renewed mythologising. Occultists began claiming such sites as central nodes in a system of 'sacred' science devoted to the amplification and distribution of 'earth-energies'. In 1923 Katherine Maltwood claimed to have discerned a giant zodiac carved into the landscape round **Glastonbury** Tor. In 1936, the occultist Dion Fortune described 'sacred sites' as 'power centres' radiating 'lines of force'. Such claims flouted scientific, archaeological and historical orthodoxy. 1960s claims linking megalithic sites with **UFOs** only widened the gap, as did the claim by the dowser Guy Underwood that standing stones marked sites of exceptional magnetic force, anciently associated with healing. Yet research since the 1970s suggests that myths of 'giants' dances' and 'walking stones' are not entirely nonsensical. Photographs of the Kingstone at Rollright, taken on three separate dawns in 1979 as part of the Dragon Project (a collaboration between dowsers and scientists) showed a hazy glow round the upper part of the monolith, a 'streamer' effect rising at an angle from it. Photographs taken earlier or later (on the same reels of film) showed no such effect. They showed no processing faults, no ordinary explanation was found and attempts to reproduce the effects failed.

The Carnac complex in Brittany is on an intrusion surrounded by fault lines, its rows delineating magnetic field changes.[3] Devereux speculates that **UFOs** are terrestrial emanations connected with faults and the megalithic system; being electromagnetic, they may influence the brain directly. It may be that the megalith-builders knew of such processes and used them to stimulate visionary or altered states of mind.

1. *The New View over Atlantis*, John Michell, Thames & Hudson, London, 1983.
2. *Megalithic Sites in Britain*, Alexander Thom, OUP, 1967.
3. *Earthlights*, Paul Devereux, Turnstone Press, Wellingborough, 1982.

MELANESIA (*See* **OCEANIC MYTH**)

MELANGELL (*See* **HARE, WELSH MYTH**)
Fleeing the advances of Brochwel Ysgythrog (a sixth-century king of Powys in Wales), this maiden hid in the valley of Pennant, where she befriended the wild animals, especially the hares. One day the king's hounds put up a **hare**, which fled straight to Melangell, hiding under her skirts. The hounds would not attack either her or the hare, so that the king knew she was a saint and, forgiving her for fleeing him, gave her land to build a church – Pennant Melangell. There, from then till now, hares have been regarded as sacrosanct, and are called 'Melangell's little lambs'.

MEN IN BLACK (*See* **DEMONS, FAIRIES, UFOs**)
A modern myth: some people claiming **UFO** sightings or contact subsequently report threatening visits by sinister beings termed 'Men in Black'. Typically such visits occur so soon after the encounter that the subject (usually alone at home) has had no time to contact anyone. The visitors (usually three of them) arrive in a large black car. They are said to wear dark suits, hats, ties, shoes and socks but white shirts; are dark-complexioned, perhaps oriental, and frail. They may claim to be government agents or produce false identity cards. They move stiffly, are formal and cold, their speech is stilted. They interrogate the contactee, then give a warning not to speak about the UFO encounter, or to abandon the enquiry.

This composite description is not invariable. The men may masquerade as journalists, insurance salesmen or (in America) USAF personnel; sometimes no threat is offered or there is no personal visit, only a phone call; or there is no black car, only an abrupt appearance and disappearance.

No such men have ever been caught or interrogated. All the reports are by individuals alone at the time. John Keel suggests that their behaviour is reminiscent of 'fairy hoaxes . . . of an earlier epoch'.

Two points emerge: (1) in all reports the men have access to information known only to the 'victim', (2) such visits are not limited to the modern UFO phenomenon but have been reported for centuries, and have usually been seen as diabolical. They seem to be a new version of an old tale.[1]

1. *Operation Trojan Horse*, John A. Keel, Abacus, London, 1973.

MENSTRUATION (*See* **BLOOD, INITIATION, MOON, TABOO**)
A mysterious connection between woman and **moon** is acknowledged from early times, not least due to her monthly bleeding (menstruation) in obedience to the lunar cycle. This event, long associated not only with female fertility but with female temperament, led early man to see the waning moon, like the menstrual woman, as 'sick' or 'cursed'. In Germany, the menstrual period was simply called 'the moon'; in French, '*le moment de la lune*'. The **Maori** call menstruation '*mata marama*', meaning 'moon sickness'. They say a girl's first menstruation comes only when the moon sleeps with her. From India to North America the old words for moon and menstrual blood were similar or identical. Throughout the ancient world, menstruating women were considered **taboo** – meaning unclean, holy or set apart from normal life. They were secluded in the menstrual lodge. Their touch might cause illness. Their presence in the house might put out the hearth-**fire**. Their bleeding was supernatural, not an earthly wound. They were dangerous. Food brought for them was left at a distance. No menstruating woman walked round ripening crops for fear of blighting them. An Australian **Aborigine**,

learning that his wife had lain on his blanket while menstruating, would kill her, then himself die of fright within the fortnight. Where adolescent youths were **initiated** into adulthood by strenuous rites to test their courage and separate them from mother, the initiation rite for pubescent girls was the natural rite of their first menstrual seclusion.

The word 'Sabbath', since applied by Christians to the holy day of rest, Sunday (also to the sabbat of **witches**), comes from the Babylonian *sabattu*, or *Sa-bat*, meaning 'Heart-Rest'. On this Day of Rest, or Evil Day, when the moon was full, it was said that **Ishtar** the moon-goddess was menstruating. On this day it was said to be unlucky to work, eat cooked food or go on a journey. This monthly day later became a weekly day, religiously observed, on which, until recent times, nobody was allowed to do anything that went against the ancient taboo of menstrual inaction. This taboo, Esther Harding suggests, arose out of necessity. Human tribal and social organisation could not develop without it. Every **dog** follows a 'bitch on heat': if that had been the case in developing human society, no human society could have developed. The taboo against menstruation was in the first place an attempt by men, everywhere, 'to protect themselves by segregating the dangerous female, and in this way protect themselves from the devastating effect of their own sexuality.'[1]

1. *Woman's Mysteries*, M. Esther Harding, Rider, London, 1982 (1955), p.60.

MEPHISTOPHELES (*See* DEVIL, FAUST, SATAN)
This Satanic personage as found in the literature of Renaissance Europe is usually associated with the **Faust** myth. In earlier forms of this legend, he is but a familiar **spirit** ordered to obey Faust's commands according to the terms by which Faust had sold the Devil his soul. Marlowe's version of the legend (1604) individualised Mephistopheles, allowed him a melancholy dignity. But, much later, Goethe in his version (1808) portrays him as a sneering cynic, embodying all that is worst in man's intellectual nature.

MERCURY (*See* HERMES, LUG, ROMAN MYTH, THOTH)
The name of this Roman version of the Greek **Hermes** and Egyptian **Thoth** derives from the roots *merx*, 'merchandise', and *mercari*, 'trade'. Unknown before *c*.500 BC (his first temple in Rome is dated 495 BC), his main function was initially that of god of merchants and messages. Like Hermes depicted as a beardless youth with **caduceus**, winged sandals and pouch, his attributes were later assumed by the Celtic **Lug**. As messenger of the gods he gave his name to the planet Mercury, closest to the **sun** and fastest to orbit; also to the element quicksilver, liquid at ordinary temperatures. Viewed by alchemists as a solvent, mercury has affinity with the Persian **Mithra**, harmonising the celestial opposites (**Ahura Mazda** vs. **Ahriman**; salt vs. sulphur). In this context he is Mercurius, alias **Hermes Trismegistus**, the divine **Androgyne** inhabiting a mythic terrain between man and **angel**; also Azoth, the river of fiery living water flowing from the throne of God, identified by some occultists as the astral light.

MERLIN (*See* ARTHURIAN MYTH, MEGALITHIC MYTHS, MORGAN LE FAY, PROPHECY)
Did this **archetypal** British magus and prophet ever exist? There may have been a sixth-century bard, Myrrdin, who fled into madness and exile in the Forest of Celydon (north of the Solway Firth) following the defeat of his king

Gwenddolau in AD 573 at the Battle of Arderydd.[1] This historic Merlin, born of earthly mother and father, was perhaps an influential seer. But the Merlin of **Arthurian** lore is an archetype, not a person: the British prophet par excellence, personifying earlier magical themes as introduced by **Geoffrey of Monmouth** in his *History of the Kings of Britain* (1135).

Merlin first appears in Geoffrey's elaboration of the myth of the semi-historical fifth-century King Vortigern who collaborated with invading Anglo-Saxons. Usurping the British throne but driven back to Wales by the Saxons, his magicians told him to build a tower. When it collapsed, they told him to seek a fatherless youth, kill him and use his **blood** to cement the weak foundations. Merlin, a boy born of union between a **virgin** and an **incubus**, was brought to Vortigern, and told him his magicians were liars, and that under the tower was a pond into which the foundations had sunk. This pond was duly found. 'Command the pond to be drained,' said Merlin, 'and at the bottom you will see two hollow stones, and in them two **dragons** asleep.'

This was done. The red and white dragons, released, fought. And so Vortigern listened to Merlin, the true prophet, who then began to prophesy even as the contending dragon-powers (fertility denied) found release.

The myth of Merlin combines earlier traditions. 'Merlin' is a means of knowledge and transformation. In Arthurian myth he often retreats from the action (the waking mind), only to return from the (unconscious) wilderness with insight that creates the **Round Table**, or sets **Grail**-quest in motion. His absence is thus more important than his presence. Hidden deep in forest or 'hollow hills', ultimately tricked into crystalline suspended animation by **Nimüe** (or **Morgan Le Fay**), he represents magic processes informing all mundane human life and death. His appearances are the flash of intuition – mysterious, illogical, yet potent. His daemon-father is the **serpent**, the fertilising spirit, his mother is the earth. Like **Mercury/Hermes** he moves easily between the conscious and unconscious worlds, fertilising one with the other. Neither dead nor alive, he expresses the power creating both life and death, each relying on the other. He is not dead because he never lived in any form that dies. As such, he (and other such archetypes in other cultures) is reborn whenever called upon. Merlin lives in the mind.[2]

1. *The Quest for Merlin*, Nikolai Tolstoy, Sceptre, London, 1988.
2. *The Prophetic Vision of Merlin*, R.J. Stewart, Arkana, London, 1986.

MERMAIDS (*See* OCEAN, SELKIE, SIRENS)

Voluptuously naked from waist up, fish-scaled and fish-tailed from waist down, forever combing her tresses on some sea-rock, since time immemorial this semi-human marine enchantress has captured masculine imagination with promise of orgiastic pleasure. Yet a thousand tales warn how those who pursue the mermaid are lured to their doom, to be shipwrecked and drowned.

In origin the mermaid is the **undine** or water-spirit, inhabiting not only the sea but also rivers, waterfalls and streams. Little in Classical myth is said of male undines, though the Fomorians of **Irish myth** appear to have been a race of sea-**demons**, while the fish-tailed **Babylonian** god **Oannes**, rising daily from the deep to impart knowledge to humanity before returning to the sea every night, appears to belong to the same elemental species. Folk have always preferred to regard (and desire, and fear) such elementals in female form. So, according to ancient myth, every fountain has its **nymph**; every Scottish river its **kelpie** (water-horse). For a **Celt**, to meet the *bean-nighe* (washerwoman) by the ford was a sign of doom approaching. The **Lorelei** of the Rhine were as beautiful but deadly as the Greek **sirens** (once bird-women derived from the Egyptian bird-soul, or *ba*), their song luring men to disaster.

But the mermaid on her rock remains among the most potent symbols of the fate awaiting those who lose their way and follow desire alone. The **mirror** in which she views herself as she combs her **hair** (the Greek and Roman words for comb, *kteis* and *pecten*, also mean the female pudenda) was anciently a symbol of **Aphrodite**, or, in astrological lore, of **Venus**, the cloud-mirrored planet. The ocean itself, the deep womb, is naturally the source of all biological desire, tempting the weak spirit. The medieval Church made the most of this, embodying in the image of the mermaid-siren the lure of lust, to be utterly denied by those fearing God the Father.

Yet **Plato** calls siren song 'music of the spheres'; an irresistible heavenly harmony.[1]

1. *Mermaids*, Beatrice Philpotts, Russell Ash/Windward, Leicester, 1980.

MEROVINGIANS (*See* CHRISTIANITY, HAIR, HOLY GRAIL, KNIGHTS TEMPLAR)

MERU (*See* *AXIS MUNDI*, INDRA, MOUNTAINS)
Like the Greek **Olympus**, this is the holy **mountain** of **Hindu** lore, upon which **Indra** built his heavenly court, Swarga, to which Yudhisthira the Pandava king alone gained access at the end of the *Mahabharata*. It is the city of eternal bliss, the **New Jerusalem**, triple-peaked, luminous, the abode of all celestial spirits and noble souls. Some occultists claim that the image of Mount Meru, Mount **Olympus**, the New Jerusalem and the **Norse** Asgard all derive from the legend (reported by **Plato**) of **Atlantis**, from the central isle of which arose a mountain so high that its summit touched heaven.

MESSIAH (*See* CHRISTIANITY, JUDAISM)
From the Hebraic *Māshīahh* ('Anointed One'), in Christian theology applied to one individual, Jesus Christ, and taken to mean the supernatural world-saviour. But in Judaic origin the term applies not to the Christian 'Son of God' but to the anticipation of the coming of two priest-kings, one of the stock of Aaron, the other from the regal line of Israel: i.e., from David and **Solomon**. Solomon was anointed as '*Māshīahh*', as was the High Priest and his successors who did the anointing. Thus, since *c*.1000 BC, Israel had been governed by two parallel lines of 'Messiahs': the kings (ruling worldly affairs) and the priests (spiritual affairs). Later, first under Hellenic then under Roman occupation, the Jews 'grew zealous' (as the historian Flavius Josephus described) for a Messiah who would combine the two functions (kingly and priestly). Messianic desire thus stimulated the militant Jewish resistance to foreign occupation, from the revolt of the Maccabees (*c*.167 BC), to the final revolt of Simeon bar Kochba (AD 132). The life of 'Christ the Messiah' falls amid this long nationalistic tumult – he too was 'zealous for the law', and the image we have of him today ('Gentle Jesus, meek and mild') is probably a **Pauline** invention. The original *Yeshua* (Jesus) came perhaps not to bring peace on earth, but as a militant priest-king of Essene/Zealot background, to restore the ancient law with a sword.

METAMORPHOSES (*See* OVID, SHAPE-SHIFTING)

METEMPSYCHOSIS (*See* PYTHAGORAS, REINCARNATION)
Popularly associated with the Greek philosopher **Pythagoras** (*c*. 582–507

BC), the doctrine that after death the human **soul** transmigrates into a living human body as yet unsouled, into animal form or even into plants like beans. If Pythagoras ever held such a view (he left no writings) is unclear, but certainly the belief is ancient and widespread. It was part of **Orphic** theology long before Pythagoras, being obtained by them (claims Herodotus) from Egypt. Until lately it was also found among the Zuni of Arizona in North America, among the South American Piros and Chiriguanos, in West Africa, where huge **bats** haunting the Tanoe River were said to be the souls of the dead, and on the Upper Zambezi, where folk believed not only that after death their souls entered an animal, but that, by certain rites, while still alive they could choose the animal. A similar belief was held by the Chams of Indo-China. The Igorrots of the Philippines held that river eels were animated by the souls of their **ancestors**. The Batta of Sumatra believed that by **witchcraft** the souls of living persons might be transferred into animals. The list may be extended indefinitely, yet still the doctrine remains primarily associated with Pythagoras, as in Marlowe's *Doctor Faustus* (1604):

> Ah, Pythagoras' metempsychosis! were that true,
> This soul should fly from me and I be changed
> Into some brutish beast! all beasts are happy,
> For when they die,
> Their souls are soon dissolved in elements;
> But mine must live, still to be plagued in hell.

Of another order is belief in the transmigration of a divine soul into man (incarnation), or that after death the human soul returns into a newly-born human body (**reincarnation**).

METHUSELAH (*See* BIBLE)
Genesis v:27 tells how this son of **Enoch** and grandfather of **Noah** lived to the ripe old age of 969 years. So too Enoch's father Jared was said to have lived 962 years; other descendants of Adam (930 years) routinely lasted for 900 years. Yet when mankind grew wicked, the Lord said (Genesis vi, Good News Bible), 'I will not allow people to live forever; they are mortal. From now on they will live no longer than a hundred and twenty years.'

Yet what if Methuselah's 969 'years' were lunar years; i.e., months, of which there are twelve (solar calendar) or thirteen (lunar calendar) in a solar year? Division of 969 by 12 gives a reasonable lifespan of 80 years and 9 months. The only problem with this is that a number of these ancients are said to have begotten their first-born relatively young.

MEXICO (*See* AZTEC MYTH, MAYAN MYTH)

SAINT MICHAEL (*See* ANGELS, DRAGON)
One of the four great archangels (Gabriel, Raphael and Uriel the others), patron of Israel, Brittany and Cornwall, patron of the Nile whose feast is celebrated the day the river rises, counterpart of the Persian **sun**-god **Mithra** and the German **Woden**, Michael as chief of the heavenly hosts led the war to hurl Lucifer and the rebel angels out of **heaven**. He is said to be merciful and long-suffering, and to raise departed **souls** to heaven. From the Middle East to the **Celtic** West he is best known as a **dragon**-slayer and patron saint of high places; a solar hero who prevails (like **Marduk**) against the lunar, watery, reptilian night.

Yet to 'slay' the dragon is to tame, not kill it. The dragon is vital spirit, but chaotic and destructive if not ordered by intellect. At first, St Michael and **St George** (Michael's **avatar**) guarded the dragon hills of the old religion as heirs: thus Michael's association with high places and lightning. The high place is a temple; the temple is the head, but also the lightning is the cosmic dragon, fertilising **Eve**. In Michael's defeat of the dragon the Church saw only **paganism**'s defeat by **Christianity**. This selective view ignored the dragon's wider significance. Yet the evidence that Michael and the dragon are one remains – on the ground. In Wales, a common church dedication is Llanfihangel, 'Church of the Chief Angel', i.e. Michael. Such churches are typically found on old pagan mounds. A Michael-chapel surmounts **Glastonbury** Tor, which may or may not be a natural hill; aligned with it are other Michael hills and sites terminating in Cornwall at St Michael's Mount, all sites where once the spirit was worshipped as the fertilising **serpent** or dragon. Dragon and dragon-slayer are one.

This is another instance of original myth changed to mean something else altogether, the old wisdom being lost, corrupted or demonised.[1]

1. *Angels*, Peter Lamborn Wilson, Thames & Hudson, London, 1980; *The New View Over Atlantis*, John Michell, Thames & Hudson, London, 1983.

MIDAS (*See* GOLD, GREEK MYTH)

When this legendary Phrygian king helped a drunken **satyr**, **Dionysus** offered him whatever he wanted as a reward. Midas asked that whatever he touched should turn to **gold**, but when he found that this applied even to his food, he begged the god to revoke the gift. Known as 'the Midas touch', this tale probably alludes to the renowned wealth of Phrygia, which issued the first coinage known to the Greeks. Another tale is that, when the gods **Pan** and **Apollo** engaged in a contest on flute and lyre, Midas was appointed to choose the victor. When he selected Pan, Apollo changed his ears into those of an ass and, though he hid his shame under his Phrygian cap, a rustling reed whispered the secret abroad.

MIDGARD (*See* AESIR, NORSE MYTH)

MILESIANS (*See* IRISH MYTH)

In the Irish *Lebor Gabala* (*Book of Invasions*), it is said that this race came from Scythia and Egypt via Spain to overthrow the **Tuatha dé Danaan** and take Ireland for themselves. Reckoned as ancestors of the Gaels, they were named after their own ancestor, Mile or Miled, who may be the same as Bile, the Irish name for the British god **Beli**. He invaded Ireland to avenge the death of his uncle (or brother), Ith, and defeated the Danaan despite their swathing the isle in a magical mist.

MIMIR (*See* AESIR, HEAD, JOTUNHEIM, NORSE MYTH, YGGDRASIL)

Considered the wisest of the **Aesir**, in the *Prose Edda* this **Norse** god is described as guardian of the fountain under the world-tree **Yggdrasil**, in the land of the Frost **Giants**. Thus he was probably a giant himself. From this **well** all wisdom flowed: even **Odin** wanted to drink from it, though the price was the loss of one **eye**. It is also said Mimir was given as a hostage to the **Vanir**, who killed him, but that Odin preserved his **head** and consulted it for advice. Again, the tale of the prophetic head. Mimir may thus be derived from **Bran the Blessed** of Welsh myth. One lives in a giant land guarding a well of inspiration. The other is a giant owning a **cauldron** of rebirth. Both are decapitated, but in each case the miraculous head (like that of **Orpheus**) continues to speak and prophesy.

MINERVA (*See* ATHENE, ROMAN MYTH)
Identified with the Greek **Athene**, the name of this Roman goddess of wisdom and the arts derives from the roots *manas* or *mens* ('thought', 'mind'). In origin she was Etruscan, represented with wings, a screech-**owl** held in her hand (*see* **Lilith**). Her image, seized by the Romans when they took the town of Falerii in 241 BC, was put in a temple built for her at the foot of Mount Coelius. At first a protectress of commerce, industry and education, later (with the expansion of imperial Rome) she became a warrior-goddess, shown with helmet, shield and armour. Spoils of war were dedicated to her as to **Mars**, with whom she was honoured in a five-day festival, the Quinquatrus, held during the spring equinox. In Roman Britain her chief temple was at Bath (Aquae Sulis), where she was twinned with the local goddess, Sulis.

MINOS/MINOTAUR (*See* ARIADNE, BULL, DAEDALUS, LABYRINTH, THESEUS)

MIRROR
'Mirror, mirror on the wall/Who is the fairest of them all?' The theme of the magic mirror, and of the otherworld the far side of its glassy surface, remains as potent today as ever. In **Jean Cocteau**'s *Orphée* (1950), it is by donning magic gloves given him by the goddess of death that the doomed hero steps through the everyday mirror into the land of the dead. In one of Magritte's best-known paintings, a man portrayed from the back is gazing into a mirror – but the painted reflection is not of his face; it is of the back of his head. While living in Paris in 1959, **William Burroughs** experimented with mirror-gazing, the idea being that continued staring would reveal the face of his previous incarnation. Another American caught him at it, and later swore he had seen the face of another man altogether in the mirror.[1]

Symbol of the **Japanese** sun-goddess **Amaterasu** (who emerged from the cave of night to restore sunlight to the world only when she saw herself reflected in the mirror held up by the good gods); the 'shining' (solar) and 'smoking' (lunar) mirrors were twin attributes of Texcatlipoca, the **Aztec** trickster-god. In **Chinese Taoist** belief the mirror represents self-realisation: looking into one's own nature one sees the horror of it, and so evil is killed.

1. *Literary Outlaw*, Ted Morgan, Pimlico, London, 1991, pp. 306–7.

MISTLETOE (*See* AENEAS, BALDUR, DRUIDS, GOLDEN BOUGH, OAK)
The Golden Bough of **Aeneas**, this parastic plant grows not on the ground, only on several trees, more commonly on the **apple** than on the **oak** with which it is associated. Belonging to neither sky nor earth, anciently it was venerated, especially when found on the oak, a tree seen to be struck more often than any other by lightning (divine fire) – this perhaps due to its propensity to grow above underground streams. So the mistletoe itself came to be seen as a divine or heavenly gift. Pliny tells how, on finding a mistletoe-infested oak, the **Druids** would, on the sixth day of the **moon**, send one of their number up the tree to harvest the plant with a **golden** sickle. He would drop it into a white cloth held up so that the plant did not touch the ground, then two white **bulls** were sacrificed. Thus gathered without touch

of **iron** or earth, it was thought to cure epilepsy, to make the barren fertile, to protect against poison and to heal ulcers. Until recent times, in Celtic lands mistletoe was called the 'all-healer'. Nor was this belief local. The **Ainu** of Japan regarded mistletoe as a divine cure for many ills, though preferring to harvest mistletoe from the **willow** tree, which they considered most sacred. In Africa too it was thought that this plant with no roots on earth possessed a supernatural virtue, offering protection against **sorcery**. Welsh farmers said: 'No mistletoe, no luck.' In Sweden it was thought that a sprig of mistletoe in house or byre would stop the **trolls** harming man or beast.

Yet in **Norse myth, Baldur** the Good is slain by a mistletoe dart. His mother **Frigga** made all things on earth swear not to harm him, but forgot the mistletoe, which does not grow on earth. So **Loki** used mistletoe to ill effect. This may be the one time mistletoe was ill used, yet the tale may be but a folkloric explanation of ancient ceremony: the died-and-reborn god-king, slain by the supernatural power from heaven.[1]

1. *The Golden Bough*, Sir James Frazer, Macmillan, London, 1963, pp.658–67.

MITHRA/MITRA (*See* AHRIMAN, AHURA MAZDA, DUALISM)

Worshipped in one guise or another in several different cultures spanning some two millennia, in Indian origin the **Aryan/Vedic sun**-god Mitra is brother of **Varuna**, the **moon**. They maintained universal order, *rita*; Mitra governing friendship and the ratification of contracts, Varuna the sanctity of oaths. The term *mitra*, in origin meaning 'sun' or 'sky', came to mean 'world' then 'community' or 'village', then 'friend' or 'peace' (as in Russian *mir*, 'peace'). It also meant 'contract' or 'covenant' implying the essence of what lets people live together without fighting.

Declining in importance in India, in neighbouring Persia he became popular as Mithra, the dawn, son of **Ahura Mazda** (Ormuzd), the 'Wise Lord'. Mithra-Ahura of the Zend **Avesta** thus equates to Mitra-Varuna. When the **dualism** of **Zoroaster** gained acceptance, with Ahura in eternal conflict with **Ahriman**, the 'Destructive Spirit', Mithra still epitomised the need of social compromise. A **bull** being sacrificed to him, enemies could sit down and talk. Yet while the friend of all who honoured right conduct, he was also a terrible war god, merciless to all contract-breakers.

Later he became a self-sacrificing deity, 'the Mediator', a precursor of **Christ**, the sun-bull slaughtering himself for the sake of collective peace and harmony. Later still he became the **Mystery**-deity, Mithras, his cult so popular among Roman soldiers that it rivalled early **Christianity**. Central to it was bull-**sacrifice**, said to guarantee prosperity, fertility and survival of the **soul** after death. As late as AD 362 the Roman Emperor Julian (the Apostate) had in his Constantinople palace a *mithraeum*, a cave-sanctuary, in which he sat in a trench to be drenched in the **blood** of a bull slaughtered above him. This may be the origin of Christian Communion: bread and wine, body and blood. So too Sunday as Christian holy day is in origin Mithraic; while the mitre worn by the Christian bishop was once the mitra; a headcloth, epitomising binding agreement, contract or friendship.

MOHAMMED (*See* ISLAM)

MOKELE (*See* AFRICAN MYTH, TRICKSTERS)

In Zaïre it is said the first man, Wai, left his pregnant wife Moluka to go hunting, saying he wanted to see the baby born when he returned. Weeks went by but Moluka's belly grew no bigger. In despair she prayed to the

Mother. One evening by the river she met an old woman, who touched Moluka's belly – and out came an **egg**! Taking the egg and telling Moluka to bring food next day, the old woman vanished. When Moluka returned, the old woman held a fine baby. Moluka suckled the child but, having eaten, the old woman took back the baby. Telling Moluka to return next day, she vanished. Moluka returned to find the little boy walking by the old woman. 'Take him now,' said the old woman. 'Your husband returns today. But don't show your son to anyone. Keep him in your hut.' So Wai returned. Next day all his wives, meeting with their children to greet him, laughed when Moluka came without a child. Wai was about to divorce her when a voice rang from her hut: 'Door, open thyself.' It did. A tall handsome youth appeared. 'Grass, disappear,' he commanded. Invisible hands swept a path clear between him and Wai's hut. 'Mats, unroll yourselves.' Invisible hands laid down mats. Over them the youth strode to greet his father, introducing himself as Mokele. Wai was so overjoyed that he made Moluka his chief wife.

Yet then there was no sunshine, only moonlight. 'Father, does the sun not rise here?' asked Mokele. Wai didn't know what he meant. 'I will go and buy the sun for you,' said Mokele. As he dug a canoe from a big tree, he invited the wasps along to sting the sun's owners if they would not give it up, and the tortoise Nkulu as his sorcerer, and the kite Nkombe, to fly off with the sun if need be. So all the animals joined him. After a long voyage they reached the land of ancient Mokulaka, where the sun was hidden. 'Mokulaka, can I buy the sun?' Mokulaka agreed but told Mokele to wait, then told his daughter Molumbu to brew poison to kill the strangers. The wasps overheard him and told Mokele. So Mokele seduced Molumbu: she threw away the brew. Meanwhile the tortoise found the sun hiding in a cave and the kite carried it up into the sky. Mokele and his crew fled to their boat, chased by Mokulaka's son, Yakalaki, and his men. Stung by the wasps, they gave up the chase, so Yakalaki went to the *elokos*, evil forest dwarves, who stole Mokele's boat. But Mokele got home safe with his bride Molumbu. Wai and his people were overjoyed by this **Promethean** triumph.[1]

1. *African Mythology*, Jan Knappert, Aquarian Press, Wellingborough, 1990.

MOLOCH (*See* BAAL, PHOENICIAN MYTH)

Or Molech. Once thought to have been Melqart, Melek or Milcom ('King'), a god worshipped in Tyre and in its colony, Carthage, and associated with the fiery **sacrifice** of children. A Roman author mentions that in Carthage was a bronze **idol** on the outstretched hands of which children were placed, to fall into the fire below. Yet the Phoenician Ras Shamrah tablets (*c*. fourteenth century BC) make no mention of child sacrifice: the view now is that Moloch was not a god but rather the term used for this gruesome rite. So Abraham was told by **Yahweh** to take his only son Isaac to Moriah, and there offer him up as a burnt sacrifice. Abraham was about to obey, but Yahweh spared Isaac, providing a ram instead. Introducing the cult to Israel, **Solomon** erected an altar to Milcom, 'the disgusting god of Ammon', on the Mount of Olives (I Kings xi:5). Under Ahaz and Manasseh, children were burned alive at Tophet in the Valley of Hinnom (Jeremiah vii:31), seemingly as sacrifices to **Baal**, a rite introduced to Israel by **Jezebel**. Some hold that Molech was an epithet of Yahweh, and that the reproaches of the prophets were really directed against this savage custom (Jeremiah xix:5).

MONKEY (*See* HANUMAN)

MONROE, MARILYN (1926–62) (*See FEMMES FATALES*, **HOLLYWOOD, KENNEDY**)
Born Norma Jean Mortensen, later Norma Jean Baker, the affairs of this
Hollywood 'love-goddess' with President John F. **Kennedy** and his brother
Robert were little publicised. Her reputation as an insecure, unreliable
woman pressurised by the demands of the 'star system' did not lessen
worldwide shock when on 5 August 1962 she died at her Los Angeles home
by drug overdose, apparently in depression at being dismissed from the set of
a movie. Later it emerged that the studio had secretly re-hired her, doubling
her salary; also that both Kennedy brothers, fearing she might damage their
careers, had rejected her. This, it was said, was the reason for her suicide.
Yet darker rumours persisted; that she had threatened to 'go public' about
her Kennedy affairs, and that she had been murdered. Whatever the truth,
she remains very much part of the 'myth' of the Kennedy era; in her own
right as a woman able at will to project a **glamorous** image, sexy yet
vulnerable, and as one tragically involved in the Kennedy mystique.

MONSTERS (*See* **DRAGON, FABULOUS BEASTS**)

MOON (*See* **CONCORDANCE**)
Dominating the night sky, every twenty-eight days the earth's satellite goes
through a cycle of phases from new (unilluminated), through waxing to full.
Then it wanes, and so back to the three nights (dark of the moon) when it
reflects no sunlight and is invisible, or 'dead'. Repeating this cycle thirteen
times annually, the moon has always influenced not only human imagination
but the motion of seas, the growth of plants and women's ovulation. Since
early times central to the religious myths of every culture on earth, it has long
been personified or deified, though not always as feminine or as a goddess. In
Iran 4,500 years ago it was venerated as the Great Man, able to incarnate on
Earth as a powerful king. Ancient Celtic, Egyptian and Assyrian kings wore
horned head-dresses symbolising the 'horned moon'. The Mongol emperor
Genghis Khan (thirteenth century) traced his ancestry to a king whose
mother was impregnated by a moonbeam. The **Maori** held that the moon is
husband to all women, fertilising and protecting them.
    A common tale was that the moon-man began to grow by defeating the
dark **dragon** which had swallowed his father, the old moon. Full, he reigned
in triumph, just and wise, teaching folk when to sow and to reap. Waning, he
was chased and swallowed by the old dragon, to die and be replaced by his
son. Belief in the immortal moon-god came later.
    The city of Ur of the Chaldees was named after the moon-god Hur. Above
Babylon (second millennium BC) the moon-god **Sin** (thus Mount **Sinai**)
nightly sailed his moon-barge, dispensing justice and wisdom. At the end of
each month he descended for three nights to the **underworld**, during this
period sending storm, **flood** and death. He was triune, three persons, each
ruling one segment of the moon's bright period. Later his daughter, the
goddess **Ishtar**, superseded him as 'Mother of the Moon'. Many early
cultures came to assume that the moon-god, protectress of women, was a
woman in disguise. Yet even after feminisation, the moon retained masculine
characteristics. **Noah** in his ark (Sanskrit argha, 'crescent'), began as 'Nuah',
a Sumerian moon-goddess. So the moon came to be seen both as goddess and
as her son or lover, who dies and is reborn. **Adonis, Attis, Osiris, Tammuz**
and **Christ** (who on the third day rose again) reflect this phase of belief.
    The moon goddess (**Isis, Inanna, Ishtar, Astarte, Demeter, Selene,
Aphrodite, Diana**, Ch'ang O, Maja Jotma, Tsuki-Yomi, **Brigit, Hecate**, the

Badb and others) is immortal, the eternal feminine, goddess of **fate**, All Giver, Great Mother: as mysterious as **menstruation**, fertility, birth and death. Also triple in aspect (virgin, mother, crone), she too must descend to the underworld for a season, pursuing her dismembered or kidnapped lover or husband before returning to fertilise the world (new moon, spring). As Moon Mother she is also Mother Earth, Magna Mater, the Great Goddess, both moon and earth being born from the primal **World Egg** which split into two.

Yet even as moon-worship flowered, a new principle arose. To men the moon rules the night (unconscious) alone. Goddess-worship was in decline even before **Christianity** arose. **Orpheus** was slain by the **Maenads**, but only at the behest of **Dionysus**. **Apollo, Indra, Mithra, Zeus, Jupiter, Thor, Yahweh** and many other sun- or sky-gods came to represent the male viewpoint of warrior cultures 'mastering' first the **horse**, then the art of working bronze and **iron**, the building of cities, the reorganisation of the world via conquest, trade and priestly control of the Word. Apollo seized **Delphi**, Indra, **Marduk**, and Yahweh subdued **Vritra**, **Tiamat** and **Leviathan**. Christian St **Michael** and St **George** continued the dragon-slaying work. Now apparently cowed, the moon-goddess became the **Virgin Mary**, meek and mild, mother and wife, without a life of her own, burned at the stake if she dared challenge the power of the sun (son). Yet she survived as Magdalene, **Black Virgin**, as houri, strumpet and whore. Her son had rejected her but she was in his blood, in his unconscious language and culture. In love, he mooned about. Married, he went on a honeymoon (from Teutonic custom: for a month after a wedding his kin drank honey mead). If mentally disturbed he was lunatic, especially at full moon. Fishermen had to watch the tides; farmer or gardener planted in the waxing moon to gain the best growth.

The moon's power, both mythic and actual, is obvious. It controls the tides of the oceans and our bodies; the phases of conception and growth. Words like 'man', 'mania', 'mantic', 'memory', 'menstruation', 'menopause', 'menhir', 'meniscus' and 'mental' all derive from moon. Human 'prehistory' was ruled by the moon and its ever-shifting effect on the mind. When four-billion-year-old rock was found on the moon by the US 'Apollo' mission, it was named 'Genesis Rock'.[1]

1. *Woman's Mysteries*, M. Esther Harding, Rider, London, 1982 (1955); *Moon, Moon*, Anne Kent Rush, Random House, New York, 1976.

MORDRED (*See* ARTHURIAN MYTH, INCEST, MORGAN LE FAY, MORGAUSE)

Arthurian legend tells how, having subdued all opponents including King Lot of Orkney, Arthur received Lot's wife Morgause as a peace envoy. Unaware that she was his half-sister, he slept with her, whereupon **Merlin** warned that on **May Day** she would bear a son, Mordred, who would destroy him and all his knights. The medieval *Suite de Merlin* (though not **Malory**) implies that Morgause knew he was her half-brother. Arthur set every child born on May Day adrift in a boat, but Mordred was cast ashore, to be fostered by a peasant, or (another version) with his Orcadian half-brothers, including **Gawain**. Vowing revenge, he grew up playing a waiting game, so that when Arthur went to France to fight **Lancelot**, he offered to stay in England to guard **Guinevere**. Inexplicably, Arthur agreed. Mordred forged a letter from Arthur saying Arthur was mortally wounded, his knights dead, the war lost, and that he should be king and Guinevere his wife. Horrified, she hid in the Tower of London, where Mordred besieged her. Her messenger found Arthur, who vowed to kill his son. Supported by most of the English lords, Mordred raised a great army. Before battle Arthur dreamed that Gawain, now dead, warned him that to fight Mordred meant his own death. Seeking truce, he met Mordred, each with fourteen knights. A viper bit a knight, who drew his sword to kill it. Both armies, seeing a drawn sword, joined battle. After terrible slaughter, Arthur speared Mordred through. Mordred dragged himself up the spear, struck Arthur a mortal blow, then fell dead himself.

This Battle of Camlann, in which 'Arthur and Medraut fell', is recorded in the Welsh Annals as occurring twenty-one years after the Battle of Badon Hill, perhaps *c*.AD 520. Though Mordred is usually portrayed as the villain, at the heart of the tragedy is his incestuous birth and the **taboo** on it.

MORGAN LE FAY (*See* ARTHURIAN MYTH, MERLIN)

Half-sister and implacable enemy of **King Arthur**, feminine counterpart and opposite of **Merlin, Geoffrey of Monmouth** says she had healing powers and could fly, and lived with eight sisters on the isle of **Avalon**. In origin she may be the Irish **Morrigan** ('Great Queen'; an aspect of the **badb**, or crow-goddess; the carrion-crow her favoured disguise). Hating **Cuchulainn** for rejecting her advances, the Morrigan tried to destroy him, yet retained her affection for him. Likewise Morgan tries to kill Arthur, but finally saves him from death by taking him with her (in her triple form) to Avalon. The Morrigan could appear either as a beauty or as a hag: so could Morgan. Thus in *Sir Gawain and the Green Knight*, she is the hag in the castle of the Green Knight who plans the overthrow of the **Round Table**, but also the Green Knight's beautiful wife who tries to seduce Gawain.

Morgan was also the Welsh goddess Modron, daughter of Avallach the ruler of Avalon, and like Morgan the wife of Urien and mother of Owain.

Her (unexplained) hatred of Arthur extended to **Guinevere**. Originally one of the queen's ladies-in-waiting, Guinevere caught Morgan with her lover, the knight Guiomar, and persuaded Guiomar to give her up. Vowing revenge, Morgan went to Merlin, offering herself to him if he taught her magic. He did, but she broke her promise. Using her new arts, she created the magical Valley of No Return, from which no knight unfaithful in love could escape, being trapped in a carnal web. Only a true knight could break the spell; when **Lancelot** did so, she had to release her captives. She stole the sword **Excalibur**: it was recovered, but its scabbard, which protected its wearer from all wounds, was lost for ever. Usually portrayed as evil, as a healer she is an ambivalent figure (at least to **Christian** writers), in origin also being the benevolent Lady of the Lake who fostered Lancelot. In later medieval romances such as 'Huon of Bordeaux' she is Fata Morgana, the Queen of Faery, **abducting** mortal men to be her lovers. Later still her name became synonymous with **witchcraft**.[1]

1. *King Arthur and the Grail*, Richard Cavendish, Paladin, London, 1980.

MORGAUSE (*See* ARTHURIAN MYTH, MORDRED)

Like **Morgan Le Fay** a daughter of King Gorlois of Cornwall. To King Lot of Orkney she bore **Gawain**, Gaheris, Agravaine and Gareth. Her **incestuous** union with King Arthur led to the birth of **Mordred**. When her son Gaheris found her sleeping with Lamorack, son of Pellinore, the Orkney clan's arch-enemy, he cut off her head but let Lamorack go since he was unarmed.

Later four of the brothers pursued and slew him. It is said Mordred finished him by stabbing him in the back.

MORRIGAN (*See* **BADB, CUCHULAINN, IRISH MYTH, MORGAN LE FAY**)

MOSES (*See* **AKHENATON, BIBLE, EGYPTIAN MYTH, FREUD, JUDAISM, SINAI, WONDER-CHILD**)
The Book of Exodus tells how, when the Hebrews were enslaved in Egypt, they so multiplied that Pharaoh ordered the death of all new-born boys. Moses, born of the tribe of Levi, was hidden by his despairing mother in a basket amid bulrushes at the edge of the Nile. Finding him, an Egyptian princess brought him up as her own. Learning of his origin, he slew an Egyptian for killing a Hebrew. Fleeing to Midian, he came to the holy Mount **Sinai** where from a burning bush **Yahweh** told him to lead the Hebrews out of Egypt. When Pharaoh would not free them, Moses, armed with Yahweh's power, visited the Ten Plagues upon Egypt, culminating in the death of all Egypt's first-born sons. Pharaoh let them go (the Exodus), then pursued them to the Red Sea. With Yahweh's aid Moses opened a dry path through the waters. The Hebrews crossed safely, then the sea fell on the pursuing army. Starving in the wilderness, the Hebrews complained. Yahweh rained manna from heaven, which fed them forty years until they reached Canaan. Also Moses brought water from a rock by striking it with his staff. At Mount Sinai he ascended to receive from Yahweh the Ten Commandments. Descending, he found the Hebrews worshipping an **idol**, a golden calf, and destroyed the idolators.

The Books of Leviticus, Numbers and Deuteronomy tell of the Hebrews' further wanderings and of the laws and customs laid down for worship of Yahweh. At last within sight of the Promised Land of Canaan, Moses died.

Who was Moses? **Freud** argued in *Moses and Monotheism* (1939) that he was an Egyptian noble serving the heretical pharaoh Akhenaton (ruled 1377–1358 BC, who tried to impose monotheistic worship of the **sun**-god **Atum-Ra**). This failing, Moses left Egypt with a band of Semitic settlers on whom he imposed Akhenaton's monotheism. In the wilderness his oppressed followers killed him, but their guilt at this deed later transformed the Midianite volcano-god Yahweh into the stern God the Father.

Joseph Campbell pointed out that the myth of his birth derives from the Mesopotamian tale of Sargon of Agade (*c.*2350 BC), whose mother put him as an infant into a basket which she hid among riverbank reeds, to be discovered by a 'princess'. This tale dates from a document composed in Israel in the eighth century BC. He notes that the name Moses is Egyptian, meaning 'child', and that there was good mythic precedent for portraying the Future Saviour as living within the house of the tyrant-monarch (pharaoh).

This 'history' was probably composed up to 500 years after the events it purports to describe, or even later, during the Babylonish captivity of the **Jews**.[1]

1. *Occidental Mythology*, Joseph Campbell, Penguin, London, 1976, pp.125–33.

MOTHER-GODDESS (*See* **EARTH MOTHER, GAIA, MOON**)
The **archetypal** feminine, origin of all life, universally identified since earliest times as guardian of hearth and home, keeper of the **mysteries** of fertility, keeper of the keys of birth, death and rebirth; the weaver or spinner of

human **fate**. Perceived as triple or multiple, with terrestrial (**earth mother**) and celestial (**moon**-goddess; **Queen of Heaven**) aspects, typically she is Magna Mater, the Great Mother, married to (**Frigga, Hera**) or fertilised (**Eve, Gaia**) by the **sky** father or celestial **serpent**. She has many functions and guises inexplicable in masculine 'either-or' terms. Governing both life and death, she is nourishing mother (**Cybele, Hathor, Inanna, Ishtar, Lakshmi, Parvati, Mary**), and hag of death (**Astarte, Circe, Kali, Lilith**, the **Medusa, Morgan Le Fay**, the **Morrigan**). She is **Leviathan, Tiamat** and **Typhon**; cosmic **dragon** of chaotic fertility tamed but never entirely conquered by the **sky**- or **sun-god**. She is **Kore** abducted to the **underworld**, as **Persephone** returning annually to the world above to renew its fertility. She is **virgin** fertilised by **Holy Ghost** and thus the Mother of God; also the **black virgin** in Catholic churches to whom pregnant women pray; also the virgin huntress of the wild woods (**Artemis, Diana**) and lady of the wild beasts; also the mad **Maenads** who tear men to pieces. As Mother of Wisdom (**Athene, Sophia**) she is *yin* (dark, lunar, passive and watery) as opposed to *yang* (bright, solar, active and fiery). Her symbols include crescent moon, crown of stars, horns of the **cow**, the evil sow; fountains, **wells, labyrinths, cornucopia, cauldron** or **Grail, earth mound, dolphin, unicorn; lotus, lily** and **rose**.

MOTHER GOOSE (*See* **GOOSE**)

MOUNDS (*See* **EARTH MOUNDS, MEGALITHIC MYTHS**)

MOUNTAINS (*See* **CONCORDANCE**)
High places the world over are seen as 'holy', as the abode of supernatural beings or gods, their moods expressed in the wild elements associated with such heights. Thus Mount Kenya in Africa is home to **Ngai**; Mount **Olympus** hosted the Greek pantheon; the Gaelic 'Great Men' dwelt on the heights; the 'Watchers' (**Enoch**) landed on Mount Hermon in Syria; **Indra**'s heaven Swarga is located on mythic Mount **Meru; Moses** came down Mount **Sinai** with the Ten Commandments; Abraham was sent up to a high place to sacrifice Isaac; on a high place the **Devil** tempted **Christ** with the promise of earthly kingdom.

Holy mountains are often volcanic (California's Mount Shasta, Fujiyama in **Japan, Pele in Hawaii**), associated with fiery **dragons** or dragon-slayers (**St George, St Michael**), regarded as the *axis mundi* (world axis) or **omphalos** (world navel), or as junctions between heaven and earth, offering passage from one plane to another. They also symbolise constancy and eternity. Pilgrimages up sacred peaks symbolise wordly renunciation, aspiration, ascent from the partial to the whole. The accounts by modern mountaineers suggest that many seek not 'conquest' but the attainment of a state in which earthly values fall away and the sublime is encountered.

Human attempts to imitate the sacred mountain are found in ziggurat, **pyramid** and **earth mound**. Such constructions are concerned not with height alone but with proportion, **number** and harmony, reflecting on earth a human perception of the cosmic order.

MU (*See* **LEMURIA**)

MUSES (*See* **APOLLO, ART AND MYTH, GREEK MYTH, MUSIC**)
The 'artist's muse' is a modern cliché, implying the otherworldly source of inspiration on which poet, painter or composer draws. In origin the Muses

accompany the Greek deity **Apollo** in his aspect as god of **music**. Three in number (Melete, Mneme and Aiode), they seem once to have been regarded as minor divinities of springs. Later they became goddesses of memory, then of poetic inspiration. In pre-literate eras a good memory was essential to the **bard**, responsible for transmitting the sagas, laws and heroic tales of his culture. In Classical Greece nine Muses were in time defined: Clio (history), Euterpe (flute-playing), Thalia (comedy), Melpomene (tragedy), Terpsichore (lyric poetry and dance), Erato (love poetry), Polyhymnia (mimic art), Urania (astronomy) and Calliope (epic poetry and eloquence).

MUSIC AND MYTH (*See* CONCORDANCE)

From early times people imitated and organised natural sounds (birdsong, waves crashing, wind in trees, growl of feral beast, wail of grief, shout of joy) and rhythms (heartbeat, marching feet) to induce altered states of mind. Plucking a taut string, blowing through a hollowed ram's-horn or beating on a **drum** all induce different emotional states. Frantic drumbeat or wild **Pan**-piping stimulates ecstasy, excess, **dance**. The soothing harp or lyre creates serenity. Horn-blasts fire the blood, calling men to assembly or to battle, the skirl of bagpipes likewise. And where Gregorian chant and other holy music elevates the mind, certain chords, progressions and rhythms were banned by the **Christian** Church as **Devil**'s music, said to lead to 'immoral' behaviour, a belief with which **Pythagoras** and **Plato** would have agreed.

It is said that the Egyptian god **Thoth** (later **Hermes Trismegistus**) founded the art of music, constructing the first lyre by stretching strings over the concavity of a turtle-shell. In Greece, the invention of music and song was ascribed to **Apollo**, said to be father of **Orpheus**, who with his seven-stringed lyre charmed wild beasts, arrested the **clashing rocks**, made trees follow him, defeated the **sirens** and entranced even the deities of **Hades**. And though Orpheus was slain by the **Maenads** (**Dionysiac** orgiasts), they could not destroy his **head** (inner doctrines of the Orphic cult), or his lyre (seven strings: seven divine truths). Lodged in a temple on Lesbos, it is said that when Neanthos, son of the tyrant of Lesbos, tried to play it, he was devoured by **dogs** attracted by the sweetness of the sound. Orpheus may represent Mystery doctrines revealed as music through the **Muse** Calliope.

Steeped in Orphism, the Greek philosopher Pythagoras (sixth century BC) taught occult mathematics, music and **astronomy** as the triple foundation of all knowledge. Though other cultures had long used both instrumental and vocal music in their religious ceremonies, he demonstrated the mathematical foundation of music and (probably) discovered the diatonic scale. Though Chaldean astrologers had earlier conceived of the heavenly bodies joined in cosmic chant as they moved across the sky, and though the Book of Job describes how 'the stars of the morning sang together', it was Pythagoras who first taught a theory of celestial harmonics or 'music of the spheres', whereby harmonic intervals between the earth, the seven known planets and the sphere of the fixed stars correspond to half-tones or their multiples up to one and one-half tones, the sum of these intervals equalling the six whole tones of the octave. Each of the planetary spheres, rushing through space, was thought to sound a continuous tone specific to itself. Saturn, the most distant, sounded the gravest note; the **moon**, closest to *terra firma*, the sharpest. The universe he conceived of as an immense monochord, its single string connected above to absolute spirit and below to absolute matter.

Recognising music's therapeutic power, he prepared specific harmonies for various diseases, and warned his followers against the sound of flute or cymbal. It is said one night he met a drunken young man who, mad with jealousy, was about to burn down the house of his unfaithful mistress, his fury made worse by a flutist nearby playing a tune in the stirring Phrygian mode. Pythagoras got the musician to change his air to the calmer Spondaic mode and the youth came to his senses. The **Neoplatonist** Iamblichus described 'certain melodies devised as remedies against the passions of the soul, and also against despondency and lamentation, which Pythagoras invented as things that afford the greatest assistance in these maladies.'

Plato (*c*.427–347 BC) said that nothing more strongly influences man's inner feelings than melody and rhythm; that music should be played to develop a love of whatever is noble, and hatred of whatever is mean; and that the casual alteration of even a key could shake society itself. This sense of the relationship between music and form pervaded the **Mysteries**: thus the construction of new buildings necessarily involved an understanding of the mathematical requirements of harmonic intervals. This theory of the 'Golden Mean', largely ignored or forgotten today, led Goethe (1749–1832) to state that 'architecture is crystallised music'.[1]

More obviously, the influence of mythology on musical composition is apparent in many works by Romantic composers, some of whom drew on mythic texts of their own cultures in creating their best-known compositions, while the use by the Nazis of **Wagner**'s music to inflame German nationalism during the 1930s demonstrates, darkly but precisely, just how potent is the allure of myth allied with music.

1. *The Secret Teachings of All Ages*, Manly P. Hall, Philosophical Research Society, Los Angeles, 1989 (1928), pp.81–4.

MUSPELHEIM (*See* AESIR, NORSE MYTH)

MWUETSI (*See* AFRICAN MYTH, CREATION MYTH)
The Makoni of Zimbabwe tell how the **sky-god** Maori created Mwuetsi, the first man, who is also the **moon**, and set him down on a lake-bed. Seeking dry land, when he got there Mwuetsi wept to find no trees, grasses or animals. To comfort him, Maori created the maiden Massassi, the morning star, but told him she could stay with him only two years. He gave Mwuetsi a **horn** (crescent moon, phallus) filled with ngona oil (lightning), and to Massassi a fire-maker. Aided by the horn, Massassi birthed trees, bushes and grasses. With the fire-maker they warmed themselves. But when Massassi left, Mwuetsi was so sad Maori gave him another woman, Morongo, the evening star, who bore sheep, goats, chickens, cattle and children. Warned that he was due to die and must not produce more children, Mwuetsi went on sleeping with Morongo, who now bore **lions**, leopards, **snakes** and **scorpions**. Morongo turned to the snake for her pleasure and Mwuetsi to his daughters for his. But one day he raped her, the snake bit him so that he fell sick and drought struck the world, slaying animals, plants and people. Throwing the 'sacred dice' (*hakata*), Mwuetsi's children learned that he had to go back to the primeval lake. They strangled and buried him, then chose a new king.

The parallels here with **Arthurian myth** of the wounded **Fisher King** and the **wasteland** ('The Land and the King are One'), and with biblical myth of **Adam** and **Eve** suggest how widely separated cultures evolve similar tales to explain what (after all) are similar circumstances the world over.

MYRRDIN (*See* MERLIN)

MYSTERIES (*See* **CONCORDANCE**)
Since early times the riddle of human existence and destiny has led to the establishment in most cultures not only of public or exoteric religions and cults, but of secretive philosophic schools devoted to the understanding of Nature and her laws. In Classical times the latter, to which only a chosen few were admitted after severe initiation rites whereby they proved their courage, intelligence and devotion (or died), were called the Mysteries.

Derived from the Sumerian cult of **Inanna** and more directly from that in Egypt of **Isis** and **Osiris**, the Graeco-Roman cults of **Cybele**, **Orpheus**, Sabazius/**Dionysus**, **Eleusis** and (later) **Mithras** put initiates (via three, seven or ten stages of instruction) through fearful tests (*see* **Initiation**) before imparting their inner doctrines. Secrecy was enjoined at every level, with severe penalties for whoever revealed the secrets of his grade not only to outsiders but even to lower-grade initiates. This secrecy was necessary on several counts. First, Mystery knowledge was (by definition) beyond ordinary understanding and thus open to abuse in the wrong hands. (A modern example is in the abuse of nuclear power, first employed by politicians not for peaceful purposes but to make the A-bomb.) Second, Mystery teachings often contradicted the politico/religious worldview then in power and thus risked being seen as heretical or subversive; especially after the rise of the Christian church. Third, prosaically, was the need to maintain monopoly control over the secrets of profitable new technology, from viniculture (Dionysus) to the manufacture of iron or the maintenance of a money-spinning oracular establishment (*see* **Delphi**).

As epitomised by initiates like **Pythagoras** and later openly revealed (in part) by **Plato** and others, the inner Mystery teachings were typically of the One God, **resurrection, reincarnation**, the dignity of the **soul**, and the truths of morality and virtue. Marking a vital stage in the growth of intellectual culture, they aimed to develop the 'reborn' or 'twice-born' individual who has overcome all fear, while also teaching the understanding of and obedience to natural law on which social order relies. Thus, above the entry to the temple at Delphi was inscribed: *Gnosce Teipsum* ('Know thyself'), an injunction implied by Mystery teachings the world over.

From Siberia to Central America (*see* **Popol Vuh**), from Ireland to Australia and India, the would-be initiate had first to confront his fear of death via strenuous ordeal. To survive – to die to the self, then to be 'reborn' to the daily world – was to gain knowledge and power the hard way.

Though Mystery ceremonies were typically performed in secret, usually at night and often in subterranean grottoes or **labyrinths**, sacred dramas for the uninitiated were publicly performed at stated occasions during the year, notably in Greece at Eleusis, the temple at which is said to have held over 20,000 people. Dedicated to **Demeter** and **Persephone** and to the latter's descent into the **underworld**, these reflected the older Egyptian rites of Isis and Osiris, which in turn paralleled the early Mystery of the Sumerian goddess **Inanna**. Said to descend annually to the underworld, abandoning wealth and beauty, Inanna strips herself naked before the Lord of the Dead, imploring the release of her lover Dumuzi (springtime, the **corn-god**, fertility) from winter's clutch. Embracing death, she asks only that she be mourned. Yet if the goddess must die, what of the rest of us?

The enactment of such dramas at the great seasonal festivals explained the meaning of winter and summer in terms of annual death and rebirth, and exalted the need for virtue and integrity as requisites for salvation.

For this reason, arguing that faith alone is insufficient, Mystery initiates opposed not the early Christian Church, in which many Mystery traditions were embodied, but the form it took on becoming the Roman state religion (fourth century). They perceived Christ as the successor of Dumuzi, **Tammuz**, Osiris, Orpheus and Mithra; a Mystery deity, slain by the Evil One, resurrected as the Christos, the divine man in man. Such beliefs soon met with persecution. The patriarchal Church brooked no pagan opposition. The Eleusinian Mysteries were banned by Theodosius (AD 346–395); the Isis temple at Philae was closed in the reign of Justinian (AD 483–565). In part this may have been justified: by then the Mysteries had become corrupt, with much of the older teachings lost.

Yet some of these teachings were known to and preserved by **Gnostics**, **Neoplatonists**, Essenes, Mithraics and other groups inheriting the older lore. Though adulterated and distorted, they survived in hiding, to rise again among **Cathars, Knights Templar** and other sects denounced by the Inquisition. Ficino's translations of the *Asclepius* and *Pimander c.*1460, texts ascribed to **Hermes Trismegistus**, led to a new interest in alchemy, astrology and magic throughout Europe. Later German publication (1614–15) of the first two **Rosicrucian** manifestos caused a furore by claiming the revival of an ancient Mystery fraternity, the 'Invisible College'.

This school may never have existed (as such), but belief that it did and the traditions on which it drew had a powerful effect. The founder-members of England's Royal Society, including Boyle, Hooke and Newton, were immersed in hermetic or Mystery doctrines; while the establishment by the end of the seventeenth century of Scotch Rite Freemasonry also owed much to this surviving underground current of Mystery lore.

Later occult groups such as the Theosophical Society (founded by Madame Blavatsky in New York in 1875) and the Hermetic Order of the Golden Dawn (founded in London in 1887) drew heavily on the ancient Mystery tradition that enlightenment is gained not through faith but via constant conscious effort and step-by-step initiation into the hidden truths. Due not least to the influence of these two orders, today the Mysteries persist, taught in many forms by many 'New Age' sects. How far they represent the original Mysteries is impossible to say. The 'Mysteries' are 'mysterious' not in that they are the jealously guarded secrets of private groups, but in that they represent our age-old human desire to uncover those natural laws that govern not just the material world but the origin, destiny and wondrous mystery of the nature of the human soul.

N

NAGA (*See* INDIAN MYTH, SERPENT)

In Indian myth the Nagas are dangerous demons – human down to the waist and serpentine below. Dwelling in the glittering **underworld** realm of Patala and regarded as demigods by the **Aryans**, their statues (always set under a **tree**) are still worshipped in southern India, where it is said these venomous **tricksters** are friendly to men if allowed their own domain. To those they favour they offer potent **soma**, giving the drinker great strength. Their lovely daughters, like Ulupi who married the hero **Arjuna**, may seem wholly human. Descendants of Kadru, wife of the Vedic sage Yasyapa, their king is the great seven- or thousand-headed serpent **Ananta**-Shesha who protects the god **Vishnu** during epochs of cosmic rest, and who in the *Ramayana* is also Ravana, demon lord of the evil **Rakshasas** of Sri Lanka. Among these is the Naga-hag Surasa, defeated by the monkey-god **Hanuman**. The term 'Naga' also describes the snake (cobra capella) or **elephants** (because of their serpentine trunks) or an historical dynasty of kings who ruled Naga-Dwipa.

NAMES

Magical belief holds that the name of a thing contains its essence. To know its name is to control it. Once it was thought a man might be harmed by an enemy writing his name on a piece of lead, wax or pottery, adding a **curse** and burying it. This led to the concept of the 'real' or 'secret' name. In ancient or primitive societies a man had two names – one for daily use, the other his real name whispered into his ear by his mother at birth, and so secret that not even he always knew it. Misuse of it could, after all, kill him. Likewise the names of supernatural beings were secret: medieval magicians sought the secret names of **demons** to gain power over them. In the Testament of Solomon it is said an **angel** gave **Solomon** a magic ring enabling him to make demons reveal their secret names. Egyptian myth tells how **Isis** tricked the sun-god **Ra** into telling his secret name. Collecting his spittle, she mixed it with earth to make a **serpent** that bit him, so that in his agony he let Isis know his name. Thus she stole his power.[1]

In **Judaism** the hidden name of God is literally God: to know it is to control all things. In the **Bible**, God has many names – **El** ('God' in Assyrian, Phoenician and Hebrew); **Elohim** ('Shining Ones'); Sabaoth ('Lord of Hosts'), Shaddai (the 'Almighty'); Adonai (the 'Lord') – all 'ordinary' names. Jehovah (**Yahweh**) are assumed pronunciations of the four letters forming the Hebrew Tetragrammaton, YHVH (*yod he vau he*; 'he is' or 'he exists'). The **Jews** held this name in awe, speaking it, if at all, inaudibly so that it could not be put to evil use. By the time of Christ the High Priest spoke it only on the Day of Atonement, in the Holy of Holies. For centuries now nobody has known how YHVH is really pronounced – which perhaps means only that nobody has yet understood or deciphered the universe![2]

1. *The Magical Arts*, Richard Cavendish, Arkana, London, 1984, pp.43–5.

2. *Ibid.*, pp.124–5.

NARCISSUS (*See* GREEK MYTH)

This handsome son of the **nymph** Leiriope so loved himself that he rejected many lovers, including the unfortunate nymph Echo, deprived of her voice by the vengeful goddess **Hera** as punishment for distracting Hera with endless chattering while Hera's husband **Zeus** seduced the other nymphs. Able only to repeat the last syllable of anything said to her, she fell in love with Narcissus, but could not speak first or declare her love. When Narcissus spurned her she wasted away in grief, leaving only the echo of her voice. Then this nasty youth sent a sword to another suitor, Ameinius, who took the hint and killed himself on Narcissus's doorstep, but called on the gods to avenge him. So **Artemis** made Narcissus fall in love with his own image in a clear pool of water. Unable to look away from his reflection, yet unable to embrace it, in his torment he killed himself, so fulfilling the prediction of **Tiresias**, that he would live only so long as he never knew himself. Soaking the earth, his blood became the flower bearing his name, which contains a narcotic oil. Thus the terms 'narcotic' and 'narcissism'.

In origin, both narcissus and hyacinthus seem to have been names given to the Cretan spring-flower hero, elsewhere called Antheus.

NARNIA (*See* LEWIS)

NASRUDDIN (*See* ISLAM, RUMI, SUFIS, TRICKSTERS)

Popular in **Islamic** lands are the tales told about a mythical trickster, the Mullah Nasruddin. These tales were originally Sufi teaching devices designed, **Zen**-like, to jolt the mind into lateral thought. So it is told how, day by day for a year or more, Nasruddin crossed a certain frontier, his donkey laden with bags bulging with straw. With every trip he grew obviously wealthier, but the puzzled customs official, though sure he was a smuggler, never found anything in the bags but straw. At length Nasruddin retired in luxury. Years later the official, also now retired, met him and asked him what he had been smuggling.

'Donkeys,' said Nasruddin.

Or again: one day the Mullah's friend finds Nasruddin on his hands and knees in the street peering under the stalls. 'What are you looking for?' he asks. 'My key,' says Nasruddin, 'I've lost it.' So his friend joins him, scrabbling about in the dust, but no key.

'Are you sure you lost it here?' asks his friend.

'Of course not,' says Nasruddin. 'I lost it in my house.'

'Then why are we looking out here if you know it's inside?'

'It's *dark* inside,' says Nasruddin patiently. 'It's *light* out here.'[1]

1. *The Exploits of the Incomparable Mullah Nasruddin*, Idries Shah, Picador, London, 1970.

NATIVE AMERICAN MYTH (*See* CONCORDANCE)

The pre-Columbian inhabitants of North America ('Red Indians') form many ethnic groups, with a huge variety of languages and social, spiritual and climatic backgrounds. Ancestors of Asian immigrants who crossed the frozen Bering Strait up to 35,000 years ago then spread from Alaska through the two Americas (*see* **Aztec, Eskimo, Inca, Mayan**), those remaining in North America formed tribes which settled to farm, or went on roaming as hunters, gatherers or raiders – patterns of life persisting until the arrival of European immigrants from the sixteenth century onwards.

These cultures occupied four main regions: (1) the forested Eastern seaboard from Hudson Bay in the North (Iroquois, Algonquin, Mohawk) down to the Gulf of Mexico (Cherokee, Creek, Huron, Seminole); (2) the Plains, from the Mississippi to west of the Rockies and north into Canada (Blackfeet, Comanche, Cheyenne, Crow, Kiowa, Mandans, **Sioux**); the barren southwest (Pueblo-dwellers and others; Apache, **Hopi, Navaho**, Zuni) and (4) the West and northwest Pacific coast (Nez Percé, Yuki and many others).

Despite such diversity, common beliefs persisted as to the formation and structure of the universe, the ruin of former worlds by **flood** and **fire**, the power of the **ancestors**, in elemental forces as manifested via **totems**, and in the former existence of magical **heroes** who conquered the monsters of chaos and brought law. Everywhere, the woods, plains, rivers and sky were thought to be peopled by unseen beings, benign or malevolent, to be placated if not to be magically controlled.

The earth, venerated as the great mother, was an intermediate realm, bounded above by the realm of **Kici Manitou**, the Great Spirit, and below by a frightful **underworld**, the abode of shades and infernal deities. Yet the Land of the Dead was not necessarily seen as under ground but (variously) as in the heavens above, across the ocean or across (as in the Greek **Styx**) a wide river. As in Egypt, Greece and Rome, **Mystery** cults abounded, their purpose to gain the **initiate** the power to pass in and out of the physical body and visit the Shadow Land, there to commune with the spirits at will. Such **shamanistic** communion brought good medicine, good hunting or crops, many strong children, social wealth, peace and harmony.

Everywhere the **number** four was regarded as sacred, perhaps because the Great Spirit created the universe within a square frame. The **sun** was not worshipped, save as a symbol of the Great Spirit. The Thunderbird, also called the Fird Bird and akin to the **Phoenix**, was sacred to many tribes; its work being to fertilise the earth. Likewise most tribes attributed special powers to the snake. The great Serpent Mound in Adams County, Ohio, indicates, as in **megalithic** Europe, a preoccupation with the symbol of **serpent** or **dragon** as a fertilising power (see **Quetzalcoatl**).

Also found from coast to coast was the use of the *calumet* (sacred pipe, or peace-pipe), the pipe itself an altar, its smoke the proper offering to **heaven**. Everywhere it was believed that the pipe was a divine gift. Grey clouds hanging over the horizon were the smoke from the pipes of the gods, who could use comets like matches to light their pipes.

Indian perception of nature was inherently mystical, philosophical and (in modern terms) cruelly unsentimental. To die young in honourable battle was a fine fate. To torture a brave captured enemy to death then ritually to eat his body was not regarded as sadism but as a mark of respect. The Spanish spoke of the Indians as 'the bronze race that knew how to die'.

Belief in **reincarnation** and transmigration was common, many children being given the name supposedly their own in a former life. The difference between the ghost or shade of a dead person, and his **soul**, was commonly recognised, as was the **Platonic** ideal of an **archetypal** sphere in which reside the patterns of all forms manifesting physically on earth. Guardian **spirits** protecting entire tribes manifested as **totems**; either a mental image or (in the Pacific northwest) a wooden pole carved with figures of the gods. Argument as to whether such poles are **fetishes** (inhabited by the god) or but symbolic representation may be set against the argument in Reformation Europe over transubstantiation: is Communion wafer and wine actually or only symbolically the body and **blood** of Christ?

Yet increasingly, as white European settlers penetrated further west, the native peoples were subdued, herded onto reservations or exterminated by war, disease and alcohol. In the process they were demonised ('the only good Indian's a dead Indian'), or mythologised as 'noble savages' who attacked wagon-trains and took scalps (a custom learned from white bounty-hunters). The brief popularity among Plains tribes in 1890 of the **Ghost Dance** was born in desperation and died in machine-gun fire.[1]

1. *Native American Mythology*, Page Bryant, Aquarian Press, London, 1991.

NATURE SPIRITS (*See* ELEMENTALS, FAIRIES)

NAVAHO (*See* HOPI, NATIVE AMERICAN MYTH)

Calling themselves Dineh, 'the People', this largest native American tribe (among the few to have kept their land) inhabits the desert of northern Arizona and New Mexico. Their territory surrounds that of the Hopi, who say the Navaho are (relatively speaking) newcomers to America, arriving via the 'back door' (the Bering Strait): a claim supported by anthropologists.

Navaho **creation myth** tells how **Flood** drove their ancestors (the Holy People) from the **underworld** onto a sunless earth. There they fashioned a quartz slab into two discs. The first (the **sun**) they gave a **mask** of blue turquoise to radiate heat and light, with red coral about it and feathers on it to spread heat in all Four Directions. Pinning it to the eastern sky with lightning bolts, then they set the second disc up in the sky. This, made of ice with a rainbow about it, was the **moon**. Does this describe a time of global warming, ice-melt and long decades of cloud cover?

They tell of two heroes: Nayenezgani ('Slayer of Alien Gods') and his brother Tobadzistsini ('Child of the Water'), born to Tsohanoai the sun-god and Estsan Atlehi ('Changing Woman': the moon). One is a god of light, the other of darkness. One day, on their way to visit Tsohanoai, seeing smoke rising from the ground they descended a **ladder** into the underground house of Naste Estsan ('**Spider Woman**'). She warned them of four dangers en route: rocks that crushed, reeds that cut men to pieces, sharp cacti, and boiling sands. Armed with her two magical feathers (one to subdue enemies, the other to preserve life) they reached Tsohanoai's square house. Two young women wrapped them in a bundle and put them on a shelf. When the sun-god returned, he threw them onto sharp spikes, but they clutched the feathers; then he tried to steam them; then made them smoke a poison-pipe. Each test they survived. Acknowledging them as his sons, he asked why they had come. They told him of the *anaye* ('evil gods') plaguing the Navaho, and asked for help. Admitting that Yeitso, the **giant** chief anaye, was also his son, he gave them arrows of sunbeam, of rainbow, of sheet- and chain-lightning.

Returning to earth via the sky-hole down shining cliffs they met and slew the scaly **demon** Yeitso. Nayenezgami next slew the monster Teelget with an arrow of chain-lightning, then with his sheet-lightning arrow slew the huge **eagle**-like Tsenahale, whose plucked feathers turned into wrens and warblers; their offspring became eagles. Later he rid the world of the Binaye Ahani, 'the people who slay with their eyes', and other mischievous forces that oppressed the Navaho.

The Navaho Black God arranged the constellations in the sky in a time when both sky and earth lay on his floor. The **Pleiades** (Seven Sisters) got on his foot. He stamped it, they jumped to his knee. He slapped it, they jumped to his shoulder. He swatted that, and they jumped on to his temple, where they have remained ever since. Later, as he placed the 'star rocks' from his pouch in the heavens, along came **Coyote**, wanting to help. When Black God refused, Coyote snatched the pouch, in which only one star rock remained. This Coyote placed as the star **Sirius**, which the Navaho still call 'Coyote Star'. Finding only dust left in his bag, Black God threw it into the sky, so forming the Milky Way.

NAVEL (See *AXIS MUNDI*, MOUNTAINS, OMPHALOS)

NAZI MYTH (See CONCORDANCE)

'I go the way fate has pointed me like a man walking in his sleep,' said Adolf Hitler (1889–1945). Leader of the National Socialist Workers (or Nazi) Party, in January 1933 he became Chancellor of Germany and began to put his violent mythic fantasies into effect. Backed by the Nazi terror in a time of economic depression and national demoralisation, he reawoke old **pagan** beliefs in the collective German mind, succeeding in this by virtue of his primacy as **shaman** and medium of the order he initiated. This order was characterised by mythic ceremonial on a vast scale, as at the Nuremberg rallies. These, held by night, with flags dipped in **blood** and searchlights spearing the sky like the pillars of cosmic temples, were implicitly and deliberately ritualistic, staged to drown individual conscience in a flood of primitive impulse. Hijacking **Wagner**, **Nietzsche**'s Superman theory and any other potent Germanic mythology he could find, he hypnotised millions into abandoning rationality and embracing the old **Teutonic** gods of blood and revenge. Claiming that Germans were of pure-blooded **Aryan** stock and so constituted a 'master race' mystically privileged to rule the world and having founded the Third Reich (German kingdom) to last a thousand years, he began to pursue a policy of international military aggression which combined with first the suppression and then extermination in Germany and elsewhere of the **Jews**.

The thousand-year Third Reich lasted a mere twelve years, but those twelve years saw an unparalleled Terror characterised by a set of magical, mystical and mythic propositions in which not only Hitler but most senior members of the Nazi hierarchy believed. Many were current at the time, embracing elements of **Theosophy** and other occult beliefs as promoted by groups such as the Order of New Templars, and the Thulegesellschaft (Thule Society). These beliefs were usually racist and supremacist, justifying anti-Semitism by insisting on the authenticity of the 'International Jewish Conspiracy' to dominate the world as proposed in the spurious 'Protocols of the Elders of Zion'. They would be merely absurd if not for the fact that they dominated Nazi theory.

They included not only belief in the supremacy of the Aryan master race and the demonic nature of the Jew, but (typically) belief that the earth is **hollow** and that Hitler's rise to power had been predicted by Nostradamus (1503–66). Hitler also believed the cosmology of Hans Hörbiger (1860–1931), 'proving' that four moons once circled the world, the last falling 13,000 years ago to destroy **Atlantis**, the original Aryan homeland.

In effect, while employing science for military ends, the Nazis denied both reason and science, instead substituting an apocalyptic theology based on grandiose racial self-assertion, little of which was original. The idea of the 'Third Reich' was itself borrowed from the medieval system of three ages as developed by Joachim of Fiore (1145–1202). The phrase itself was coined in 1923 by the publicist Moeller van den Bruck, and later adopted as a name for the 'new order' which, as in many former millennial fantasies, would last a thousand years. Yet such beliefs affected Hitler's military decisions and influenced the outcome of the war, not least in his final apocalyptic wish to condemn the entire German nation to annihilation.

Hitler and the Nazis did not create but only exploited old resentments. **Carl Jung**, whose 1913 dream of a 'sea of blood' flooding Europe presaged World War I, had in 1918 warned against the breakout of 'a blonde beast from an underworld prison'. Later he referred to Hitler as 'The loudspeaker that makes audible all the inaudible mutterings of the German soul'.[1]

1. *Jung and the Story of our Time*, Laurens van der Post, Penguin, London, 1978.

NECROMANCY (*See* MAGIC, SORCERY, WITCHCRAFT)

Necromancy ('divination by the dead'), involves invocation of the spirits of the dead, typically to discover the future, find buried **treasure** or commune with **demons**. There is said to be high risk of possession.

Tradition states that for nine days before the rite the necromancer inculcates death's aura. He dons grave-clothes stolen from corpses while reciting the funeral service over himself. Avoiding the sight of women he eats **dog**-flesh, black bread baked without salt or leaven, and drinks unfermented grape-juice. The dog belongs to **Hecate**, goddess of death; the lack of salt infers putrefaction; no leaven or fermentation means matter without spirit and parodies **Christian** Communion. The necessary rapport thus induced, he approaches the grave of the chosen corpse at sunset, or immediately after midnight. A circle is drawn about the grave; a mixture of henbane, aloe wood, hemlock, saffron, opium and mandrake is burned. With coffin opened, he touches the corpse thrice with his wand and tells it to rise. The body, disinterred, is arranged head to the east and arms and legs in the position of Christ crucified; thrice the spirit is told to enter its old body and answer all questions put to it or else suffer 'torment and wandering thrice seven years'. Slowly the body rises upright and in a faint, hollow voice answers the questions. The magician then rewards the spirit by destroying the body (via fire or quicklime) so that it can never again be so abused.[1]

This 'art', an undercurrent in every magical tradition, has often been charged against those known to 'dabble in spirits'. The Roman author Lucan tells in the *Pharsalia* how Sextus Pompey, son of Pompey the Great, sought to learn the future by consulting the dead through the witch Erichtho, who 'kept on good terms with the infernal powers by squatting in tombs'. She insisted that the operation be conducted with the aid of a recent carcass with sound lungs, as older corpses 'only squeak incoherently'.[2]

The Elizabethan magus John Dee was popularly thought to be a necromancer; certainly his scryer Edward Kelley was pilloried in Lancashire for digging up and using new-buried corpses. Whether he had done so or not is unclear. Oxford dons of the time, influenced by **Neoplatonists** and **Paracelsians**, thought it possible that the dead might be made to walk. Others lamented such belief as 'still in the mouth and faith of credulous superstition at this day'.[3] Yet as late as 1854 the French occultist Eliphas Lévi tried to evoke the spirit of Apollonius of Tyana, a renowned magus of the first century AD, and concluded that such practices lead to 'exhaustion, and frequently a shock sufficient to occasion illness'. In his 1920s novel *Moonchild* the English occultist Aleister Crowley describes this dangerous operation in gory and excremental detail. Today the practice persists in Haitian **voodoo**.

1. *The Magical Arts*, Richard Cavendish, Arkana, London, 1984, pp.267-8.
2. *Ibid.*, p.269.
3. *Religion and the Decline of Magic*, Keith Thomas, Peregrine, London, 1978, p.706.

NECTAR (*See AMANITA MUSCARIA*, **HAOMA, SOMA**)

NEMESIS (*See* **FATES**)

NEOPLATONISM (*See* **GNOSTIC MYTH, MYSTERIES, ORIGEN, PLATO, PLOTINUS**)

Founded in Alexandria *c.*AD 193 by Ammonius Saccas or perhaps by **Plotinus** (AD 204–*c.*269), the influence of this school of mystical philosophy endured despite being banned in AD 529 by the emperor Justinian. Also known as the Philalethians, Lovers of Truth, the school had little to do with **Plato** but sought to reconcile all religions and philosophies. This task it held to be the real purpose of **Christ**. It embraced **reincarnation** and the idea that all manifestation emanates from one transcendent source. Its students sought to apprehend divinity via intuition or ecstatic states transcending intellectual knowledge, and held that the ground of being (ultimate source of existence) cannot be identified with its emanations. The first of these emanations was said to be reason (nous); the second, the **soul** or world-soul; the third, matter, said to be devoid of real being, thus evil.

Yet though superficially similar to the **Gnostic** teachings of the same era, the Neoplatonists dissociated themselves from Gnosticism, Plotinus complaining that the Gnostics 'say only: "Look to God", but they do not tell anyone how or where to look.'[1]

Origen was an early disciple; the emperor Julian was among later initiates. At first there was no conflict with **Christianity**, **Judaism** or the older **Mystery** schools. The school gained its height of popularity under Hypatia, an Athenian lecturer whose youth, eloquence and beauty proved so potent that in AD 414 the Bishop of Alexandria had her murdered. Monks led by Peter the Reader slew her on a church altar, dragged her body through the streets and scraped the flesh from her bones. This Christian terrorism destroyed Alexandrian Neoplatonism. But, as Plotinus wrote:[2]

> Murder, death in all its guises, the reduction and sacking of cities, all must be to us just such a spectacle as the changing scenes of a play; all is but the varied incident of a plot, costume on and off, acted grief and lament. For on earth, in all the succession of life, it is not the Soul within but the Shadow outside of the authentic man, that grieves and complains and acts out the plot on this world stage which men have dotted with stages of their own constructing . . .

Macrobius (fourth–fifth century) adds:[3]

> But all, indeed, in descending, drink of oblivion; though some more, and others less. On this account, though truth is not apparent to all men on the earth, yet all exercise their opinions about it; because a defect of memory is the origin of opinion. But those discover most who have drunk least of oblivion, because they easily remember what they had known before in the heavens.

1. *The Gnostic Gospels*, Elaine Pagels, Pelican, London, 1982, p.142.

2. *Selection from The Enneads*, Plotinus (trans. Stephen MacKenna)
3. *Commentary on the Dream of Scipio*, Macrobius, footnote in *Select Works of Porphyry* (trans. Thomas Taylor), 1821.

NEPTHYS (*See* EGYPTIAN MYTH, ISIS, OSIRIS, SET)
Younger sister of **Isis**, also sister of **Osiris** and **Set**, in Egyptian myth this daughter of Geb and **Nuit** was taken to wife by Set but remained barren. Seeking to seduce Osiris she made him drunk, and so bore **Anubis**. When Set murdered Osiris she deserted him and helped Isis to embalm the corpse of the slain god. Given that she was barren, then became fruitful, she may have represented the lands at the edge of the Egyptian desert; lands fruitful only when the Nile (Osiris) floods.

NEPTUNE (*See* ASTRONOMY AND MYTH, MANANNAN MAC LIR, POSEIDON, SEA-GODS)
Once perhaps a water-god or protector against drought (during the festival of the Neptunalia every 23 July, Italian countryfolk made huts of branches for shelter against the sun), this obscure Roman deity in time assumed the attributes of the Greek sea-god **Poseidon**. When in 1846 the eighth planet from the sun was discovered simultaneously (and independently) by John Adams in England and Urbain Leverrier in France it was named Neptune. Modern astrologers associate the planet with the influence of magic and mysticism.

NEREIDS (*See* ACHILLES, GREEK MYTH, MERMAIDS, NYMPHS)
Fifty in number, in Greek lore these **mermaids** are daughters of the **nymph** Doris and of Nereus, a **shape-shifting** marine deity known as the 'Old Man of the Sea'. Son of Pontus and **Gaia**, he was said to be kind and helpful, leaving his submarine Aegean home only to help shipwrecked or distressed sailors. To the Trojan hero **Paris** he prophesied the destruction of Troy.

Fair golden-haired virgins, the Nereids (their name means 'Wet Ones') lived under the sea with their father (who had originally been the goddess Nereis), but sometimes were seen to frolic on the surface of the water.

The three best known were Arethusa, Galatea and Thetis. The latter was so beautiful that both **Zeus** and **Poseidon** desired her. But on hearing a prophecy that she would bear a son more powerful than his father, Zeus tried to wed her to Peleus, king of Thessaly. Outraged by the affront of union with a mortal, Thetis tried to escape by changing herself into a fish, an animal, a wave, a flame. But Peleus, advised by the wise **centaur** Chiron, seized her, and from their union was born the hero **Achilles**.

In origin, Thetis (also Nereis and Amphitrite) is one of many different local Aegean titles of the threefold **moon-goddess** as ruler of the sea.

NERGAL (*See* ERESHKIGAL, SUMERIAN MYTH, UNDERWORLD)
Aided by fourteen demons this Sumerian god of destruction and war invaded the **underworld** and seized lordship of it from the goddess **Ereshkigal**. His name means 'Lord of the Great Dwelling'; his symbols, a **lion**'s head or a sword. He gained his greatest authority in **Babylon**, where he was feared and zealously propitiated. As Irra he was plague, pestilence, war, **fire** and the desert. He was the killing power of the **sun**, thus also an aspect of the sun-god **Shamash**.

NERTHUS (*See* EARTH MOTHER, MOTHER-GODDESS, NORSE MYTH, VANIR)

In his *Germania*, the Roman author Tacitus (*c*.AD 55–120) described how the **pagan** Danes worshipped this mother- or earth-goddess. She visited them in a sacred wagon (usually kept in a grove on an isle) which only the priests could touch or look inside. She was warmly welcomed everywhere; during her flower-bedecked procession there was no fighting or war. Though associated by some with the similar processions of **Cybele** in southeastern Europe, it seems that worship of Nerthus was particular to the folk of the north, who later identified her with the **Norse** fertility-god **Frey**, the 'bringer of peace' in whose temples weapons were banned, and claimed her as his mother.

Thus the role of Nerthus and Frey was similar to that of **Mithra/Mitra** (the 'friend') in Persia/India.

NEVERLAND (*See* BARRIE, PAN)

Or Never-Never-Land – a modern myth of mischievous childhood innocence retained, as told by **J.M. Barrie** in his play *Peter Pan* (1904) and his novel *Peter and Wendy* (1911). Barrie portrays the Neverland as an isle populated by 'lost boys', 'redskins', 'pirates' and 'beasts', ruled by Peter Pan yet threatened by evil Captain Hook and the equally villainous **crocodile**. Though reminiscent of **Celtic otherworld** tales of the Isles of Immortality in the West (**Tir nan Og**, etc.), the Neverland is myth reduced via fairy-tale into moralistic nursery sentiment, playing on the sense of a lost world of magic (childhood) which cannot be regained. Pagan themes of once frightful imaginative potency (the goat-god **Pan**, the **fairies** in their original sense) are diminished into mere post-Victorian cuteness.

NEW AGE (*See* APOCALYPSE, NEW JERUSALEM)

Belief in a 'New Age' about to dawn connected with the astrological concept that the 2,100-year-old age of Pisces has given way to the era of Aquarius which, supposedly, will see a global renewal of spiritual idealism. Such belief is found in esoteric traditions; among 'twice-born' **Christians** who await the Second Coming, and among cults expecting supernatural or otherwordly intervention, typically amid global cataclysm. The belief implies a 'Great Purification' (**Native American** lore), the salvation of the self-elected elect into a new world or higher spiritual plane and the damnation or extinction of 'non-believers'. The prophecies of seers are invoked in justification.

Yet the idea of imminent spiritual renewal of the evil material world is **archetypal**, going back at least to Jewish expectation of a **Messiah**. Persecuted by Rome, early Christians awaited the imminent return of Christ to overthrow Babylon and establish the **New Jerusalem**, the perfect kingdom, as in the Revelation of St John, xxi: 'And I saw a new heaven and a new earth: for the first heaven and the first earth were passed away, and there was no more sea. And I John saw the holy city, new Jerusalem, coming down, from God out of heaven, prepared as a bride adorned for her husband.'

In AD 999 millennarian expectation consumed Dark Age Europe with panic. The End was thought imminent. Yet fear of (or desire for) it was based not on chronological expectation alone, but persists.

The Calabrian hermit *Joachim of Fiore* (1145–1202) claimed that in the Bible he had found a key to historical pattern. The first Age, he said, was that of the Law (God the Father; the past); the second was that of the Gospel (God the Son: the present); and the third that of the Spirit (Holy Ghost: a future age of love and freedom). His trinitarian system remained influential. Every new calamity threw up sects (Brethren of the Free Spirit, **Rosicrucians**) proclaiming the birth of a new age. It influenced the German Idealists (Lessing, Fichte, Hegel) and Marx, whose dialectic of primitive communism, class society and a final realm of freedom unconsciously evoked Joachite thinking. The Nazi Third Reich relied on this same pattern to justify itself. American Transcendentalists like Emerson (1803–82) invoked New Age imagery, as did nineteenth-century occult groups (Society of the Golden Dawn).

New Age myth (Death of Old World: Birth of New) equates with the death of every old generation and its rebirth in the new; also with an extension through historic time of the symbology of the annual died-and-reborn **corn-god**. On the larger scale, **Brahmanic** cosmology deals in universal death and rebirth in terms of multi-billion-year cycles (*see* ***kalpa***).[1]

1. *The Pursuit of the Millennium*, Norman Cohn, Paladin, London, 1970.

NEW JERUSALEM (*See* NEW AGE, NUMBER, SACRED GEOMETRY)

St John's vision in Revelation of the holy city, the New Jerusalem, is not solely poetic or visionary, but expresses an ancient canon of geometry and **number**, whereby written knowledge is so coded that, even if the meaning is lost via translation, alteration or degradation, it remains clear in terms of **sacred geometry**, expressing the known proportions of the planet itself. Here we have not myth but mathematics disguised as myth. The proportions of the New Jerusalem express the relationship between heaven, earth and man himself as the 'cosmic temple'. The now acknowledged sophistication of edifices such as Stonehenge and the Great Pyramid shows that the 'ancients' routinely encoded their esoteric ('scientific') knowledge in constructions (real or symbolic) and texts offering multiple levels of meaning. Thus the art of gematria, whereby sacred texts were written in accord with a number-code. By conversion, a hidden meaning underlies the surface text.

Today, interpreting ancient myth, we may deduce one level of the tale, or another, but rarely all levels at once. We tend to deny multiple levels of meaning, insisting that our forebears may have been clever, but not that clever. Nor does a materialist outlook aid penetration of the value system ('As above, so below') underlying the visionary science expressed in the plan of the New Jerusalem, and in the Book of Revelation as a whole.

The book of Revelation is 'an arrangement of symbols, each having a precise meaning in terms of the others, by reference to which various groups of symbols could be placed together in geometric or harmonic order, the total sum of all amounting to the complete structure of the Temple itself'.[1] These symbols are not arbitrary. Thus the nucleus of the New Jerusalem may be identified as a cube containing a sphere that models the earth on the scale 1 foot: 1 mile; the diameter of the sphere being 7,920 feet, the mean diameter of the earth being 7,920 miles. So we have no more the plan for an earthly city than for a spiritual kingdom alone. The New Jerusalem is both: a measuring-out of heaven on earth via observation of natural law (objective science) revealed by prophetic inspiration. Every number in its groundplan relates to a corresponding principle in Nature: its architecture is not arbitrary, but sacred; i.e., it expresses the laws of harmony and proportion as revealed in Nature and the human heart. If these laws are disobeyed wilfully or in ignorance, chaos results. To St John, true science, morality, and spirituality are one and the same.

1. *City of Revelation*, John Michell, Abacus, London, 1973.

NGAI (*See* AFRICAN MYTH, KIKUYU)

Supreme god of the Masai and **Kikuyu** tribes of Kenya, the creator of the universe who dwells on the twin peaks of Mount Kenya. It is said by the Masai that at birth Ngai places a guardian **angel** beside each of them, to defend them against all dangers, and at death to carry them off into the next world. Ngai means 'the Apportioner', the one who, during the creation, apportioned his gifts to all the tribes and nations of earth. Thus to the Kikuyu he gave the knowledge of, and tools for, agriculture; to the Masai he gave cattle, and lands on which to graze them. The Masai believe in a future life, rewards and punishments being granted according to one's just deserts. The wicked wander for ever in an arid desert; the blessed enjoy fruitful meadows amid which range vast herds of cattle. Ngai punishes those who deny oaths sworn in his name by striking them with lightning.

NIBELUNGENLIED (*See* EDDA, TEUTONIC MYTH, SIEGFRIED, SIGURD, WAGNER)

The generally accepted title (*Lay of the Nibelungs*) of an epic poem, the greatest in Middle High German, its final version written *c.*AD 1200 by an unknown Austrian from the Danube area and preserved in three thirteenth-century manuscripts. In two parts, it contains much antique material. Various of the deeds of the hero of the first part, **Siegfried**, derive from earlier tales of his namesake **Sigurd** in the **Norse** Thidriks Saga, also from the 'Elder Edda' and *Völsunga Saga*. Yet the author of the final version wrote the individual tales into a meaningful whole. The term 'Nibelung' appears in the first part as the name of Siegfried's lands, peoples and treasure, but throughout the second part is used as a name for the Burgundians.

The tale is as follows: despite parental warning, lured by reports of her beauty, Siegfried, a prince of the Lower Rhine, goes to woo Kriemhild, a Burgundian princess of Worms and sister of King Gunther. On arrival he is identified by Hagen, Gunther's henchman, who tells how Siegfried had won a **dragon**-guarded treasure. Slaying the dragon (*see* **Fafnir**), he had bathed in its blood and become **invulnerable**, all but for one spot on his back to which a leaf had stuck as he bathed.

Leading the men of Burgundy against invading Danes and Saxons, Siegfried distinguishes himself in battle, and on return to Worms meets Kriemhild for the first time. They fall in love even as news reaches Gunther of Brunhild, an Icelandic queen of great beauty and strength, sworn to give herself only to the man who can defeat her in three contests. Whoever loses to her must also lose his head. Undeterred, Gunther decides to woo her with Siegfried's aid, promising him Kriemhild in marriage if successful.

Presenting himself as Gunther's vassal, Siegfried wraps himself in his Tarnkappe ('cloak of darkness'). **Invisible**, he performs the deeds that defeat Brunhild while Gunther acts them through. Brunhild accepts Gunther as her husband, but remains suspicious. Siegfried and Kriemhild marry. Taunting Kriemhild for marrying below her station, Brunhild gets her to reveal the deception. Hagen, secretly siding with Brunhild, makes Kriemhild betray the spot on Siegfried's back to which the leaf clung – his **Achilles heel**. Catching him unawares, Hagen murders him. After his funeral, apparently reconciled with Gunther and Hagen, Kriemhild starts giving out Siegfried's dragon-hoard among potential followers. But Hagen, fearing her growing influence, sinks and loses it in the Rhine.

The second part describes Kriemhild's vengeance against Hagen and the

Burgundians, until she herself is slain by Hildebrand. First on the scene, she is the last to depart.

Die Klage (*The Lament of the Survivors*), a continuation of the tale, dates from the same era, but it is based on an older Latin work. As for the *Nibelungelied*, many variations have since appeared in Germanic art, most notably **Richard Wagner**'s opera cycle *Der Ring des Nibelungen* (1853–74).

The tales of Sigurd, Siegfried's progenitor, are described elsewhere.

NIETZSCHE, FRIEDRICH (1844–1900) (*See* NAZI MYTH)

German classical scholar, philosopher and passionate critic of the ethos of his time, he became a Swiss subject and professor of classics at Basel in 1869, where he wrote *The Birth of Tragedy* (1872). Resigning his post in 1879, he gave himself up to increasingly passionate condemnations of modern **Christianity**, conformity and nationalism in works such as *Thus Spake Zarathustra* (1883–4); *Beyond Good and Evil* (1886) and *On the Genealogy of Morals* (1887). Schopenhauer in philosophy and **Wagner** in music were his initial guides: both later fell prey to his sweeping condemnations.

He taught that there are two basic human types: weak-minded slaves who favour 'virtues' that suit their weakness and who deprecate the virtues of the powerful; or the strong and masterful, above the common herd, who hate all base or utilitarian virtues. Numbering Christians as among the weak, his statement that 'God is dead' had received lasting attention from moralists and social commentators throughout the twentieth century.

NIFLEIM (*See* AESIR, NORSE MYTH)

NIMROD (*See* BABEL, BIBLE)

Described in Genesis x:8–10 as a 'mighty hunter' and as the world's first great conqueror, this mythical ruler of Babylonia is also said in the Bible to have founded the Assyrian city of Nineveh. Genesis xi describes the building of the **tower of Babel** and its destruction by **Yahweh**, but does not attribute the building to Nimrod. Elsewhere in Hebrew tradition, however, it was the godless iniquity of Nimrod that led to this architectural attack on **heaven**. He had already acquired world dominion by wearing the garments once owned by **Adam** and **Eve**, which in every battle secured him victory, so that both animals and people worshipped him. But this was not enough. So he ordered the building of the tower in the time when all men spoke the one language. So Yahweh threw it down by confusing human tongues into the many languages we have inherited. The myth may derive from Hebrew resentment at their captivity first in Egypt (land of the pyramids) then in Babylon (land of ziggurats, or stepped towers).

NIMÜE (*See* ARTHURIAN MYTH, MERLIN, MORGAN LE FAY)

It is said that the magician **Merlin** saw this wood-**nymph** making merry and was so captivated that, when she begged him to show her how to make a tower out of air, he did it, whereupon she imprisoned him in it. In Breton tradition this happened in the Forest of Broceliande. Also called Niniane or Vivienne, Nimüe is analogous to the Lady of the Lake, and thus to **Morgan Le Fay**, Merlin's deadly enemy yet also the source of his (and of **Arthur**'s) survival after death. The castle of air is also described as a glass or spiral tower; a **fairy** edifice to which the poet-magician retires to learn the mysteries of life and death. Thus it seems to be a version of Caer Sidi, the **otherworld** tower of the Welsh goddess **Arianrhod**, in which the dead were received between incarnations, and with which the Welsh poet **Taliesin** was well acquainted.

NINKHURSAG (*See* **ENLIL, SUMERIAN MYTH**)
Also called Ninlil or Bêlit, this 'Lady of the Great Mountain' symbolised fertility as reaped even from stony soil. As Ninkhursag, the earliest wife or consort of her younger brother **Enlil**, she was among the chief Sumerian deities, her sacred milk nourishing those chosen by him to be kings on earth, thus allowing them to claim divine descent.

NINURTA (*See* **SUMERIAN MYTH**)
'God of fields and canals, who brings fertility.' The name of this son of the Sumerian god **Enlil** may mean 'Lord Plough'. Yet, as with **Mars**, his plough later became a sword. He became 'the strong one who destroys the wicked'. When war broke out against him, even Nature joined in, including the stones. After his victory he rewarded those supporting him (amethyst, lapis lazuli) with glittering brilliance, so they were valued thereafter. The rest remain trodden underfoot. He married Bau, daughter of the **sky-god Anu**; the lady who breathes life into men.

NIRVANA (*See* **BODHISATTVA, BUDDHISM**)
Buddhist: refers to a state in which all opposites, desires and illusions have been eliminated; 'a state of neither being nor not-being', in which, attaining enlightenment (bodhi), the individual gains liberation (moksha) from the limitations of personality and bodily existence. Being no longer self-limited, the consciousness grows to include all other conscious minds, resulting in communion with and compassion for all other living beings. Nirvana is gained by pursuing the Noble Eightfold Path and by acknowledging the Four Truths that underlie it. The transition is voluntary.

NJORD (*See* **AESIR, NORSE MYTH, VANIR**)

NOAH (*See* **BIBLE, FLOOD MYTH, GILGAMESH, MANU**)
The best-known (but not the earliest) account of the Flood is the biblical tale of Noah (grandson of **Methuselah**), the only godly man in a sinful age. Deciding to destroy humanity and start again, **Yahweh** saved Noah, his wife, his sons Shem, Ham and Japheth, and their wives. They built an ark as he ordered and in it put two of every creature. Seven days after they entered and sealed it, the Flood came, lasting forty days and nights. All life on earth died, save in the ark. After 150 days the Flood began to recede. The ark grounded on Mount Ararat, but not until the first day of the tenth month did the tops of other mountains appear. After forty days Noah sent out a **raven** which did not come back, then a dove, which did. A week later he sent it out again and it returned with an olive leaf. Again he sent it out: this time it did not return. Later, the waters gone, Noah's family repopulated the earth. Noah may be Nuah, a **Babylonian moon-goddess**. The dove (**Ishtar**'s messenger in Babylonian Flood myth) is connected with lunar deities. The ark (**Sanskrit** *argha*, 'Crescent') may be the new moon. Later, planting the first vineyard, Noah got drunk and (Genesis ix:18) lay naked in his tent. His sons, holding a robe, walked backward into the tent to cover him up. Apocryphal texts say his drunkenness arose from a partnership with **Satan**, who poured on the vine-roots the **blood** of a **lamb, lion, pig** and monkey, implying wine's effects. Before drink, man is as quiet as a lamb; after a little he feels as

strong as a lion; too much, he behaves like a pig; wholly drunk, he acts like a monkey.

NODENS (*See* **NUADU**)

NOMMO (*See* **DOGON**)

NORNS (*See* **FATES, NORSE MYTH, TEUTONIC MYTH**)
Spinners of the threads of human destiny, these three wise mistresses of fate (*wurd* in Low German; *urdr* in Old Norse, *wyrd* in Anglo-Saxon: thus the English word 'weird') were called Norns by Germanic and Scandinavian peoples. Judging gods as well as men, they guarded the Well of Urdr, the Spring of Fate below the world-ash **Yggdrasil**. Their names were Urdr, Verdandi and Skuldr (Fate, Being and Necessity; Past, Present and Future). Once there was only one Norn, Urdr, who soon had many sisters, prefiguring the good or wicked **fairies** who, at the birth of heroes, offer gifts or malediction. That they increased (or were reduced) to three suggests Greek influence. There were three Fates, so there had to be three Norns.

NORSE MYTH (*See* **CONCORDANCE**)
Germanic, Anglo-Saxon and Norse myth reflects a common tradition. Norse **Sigurd** is Germanic **Siegfried**; Germanic **Woden** is Norse **Odin**. Centuries before Christ the Teutons, an Indo-European or **Aryan** people, colonised the Baltic, north Germany and Scandinavia. Though not politically united and often at war, their shared language, customs and beliefs diverged only gradually as each tribe settled its particular region. Remote kin of other Aryan stock (Latins, Celts, Greeks, Slavs), they separated into three main groups: the Goths, who settled east by the Black Sea; the west Germans, ancestors of modern Germans and English; and the northern Teutons, taking over Scandinavia (save for Finland, occupied by folk of Finno-Ugric stock).

Geographical isolation led the northern folk to resist **Christianity** longer than their southern cousins, the Swedes resisting conversion until *c*.AD 1200. So pagan Teutonic myths were best preserved in the Norse **sagas**, and in the *Prose Edda* by Snorri Sturluson (Iceland: thirteenth century). The Icelandic 'Elder Edda' (ninth century: author anonymous), dates from a pre-Christianised era, while other sources include the *Codex Regius*, a small collection of Icelandic poems about the pagan gods and the *Gesta Danorum*, tales collected by Saxo Grammaticus, a twelfth-century Dane. The Anglo-Saxon poem **Beowulf** also reflects the pagan Teutonic spirit, while Roman writers like Tacitus offer useful documentary and historical background.

Yet the authenticity (i.e., originality) of particular Norse/Teutonic myths remain in doubt. Similarities between extant texts and Graeco-Roman or Celtic stories *may* arise in common Indo-European ancestry, but later cross-cultural influence seems more likely. The tale of **Mimir**'s prophetic **head**, for example, reminds us of the Celtic-Welsh tale of **Bran the Blessed**: neither the literary tradition nor archaeological evidence suggesting that decapitation or mutilation played any part in Norse sacrificial rites.

NUADU (*See* **DIANCECHT, IRISH MYTH, LLUDD, LLŶR**)
King of the magical Irish race, the **Tuatha dé Danaan,** Nuadu abdicated on losing an arm fighting the Fir Bolg (no physically blemished man could remain king), but regained his throne when Diancecht made him a silver arm. Thereafter he was called Nuadu argat lámh ('Nuadu of the Silver Hand'). Later he died fighting the Fomorians. After the Milesians defeated

the Tuatha dé Danaan, he lived in an **otherworld** mound. 'Nuadu' may mean 'Cloud-Maker', as may 'Nodens', the name of his British counterpart. His Welsh counterpart was Gwynn ap Nudd, Lord of the Dead and leader of the **Wild Hunt**, who in the medieval legend of St Collen inhabits an otherworld kingdom entered via **Glastonbury** Tor. Another Welsh counterpart was Llŷr, or Lludd Llaw Ereint ('Lludd of the Silver Hand').

NUIT (*See* EGYPTIAN MYTH)
Or Nut. Egyptian sky-goddess who secretly married her twin brother Geb, so enraging the sun-god **Ra**, who sent Shu (supporter of the sky) to tear them apart. Geb, left vainly struggling under the feet of Shu, represented the mountains and the undulating terrestrial crust. He and Nuit were reputedly the parents of **Osiris, Isis, Set** and **Nepthys** and perhaps **Horus**. Ra had decreed that she could not bear a child in any month of any year, but **Thoth** pitied her. Playing draughts with the **moon,** he won a seventy-second part of its light, with it creating five new intercalary days to add to the official year of 360 days. On these days Nuit was able to bear her five children. Usually depicted as a giant, naked woman with elongated body and arched back, her toes and fingertips touching the earth, her star-spangled belly (supported by Shu) forming the arch of the heavens, she was also the **cow** that bore Ra up to the sky when he decided to abandon wicked humanity. The sun was said to be a child who entered her mouth in the evening, passed through her body by night, and in the morning was born again from her womb.

NUM (*See* SLAVONIC MYTH)
Sky-god of the Samoyeds, a Ural-Altaic people inhabiting the Yalmal Peninsula by the Kara Sea in northern Russia. They tell how, when the world began, Num sent birds to explore the watery chaos below, and created dry land from the mud that one bird brought back in its beak.

NUMBER (*See* CONCORDANCE)
In the ancient world numbers were seen as symbolic entities that generate and order the outer world, as in the claim by **Pythagoras** that, 'Everything is disposed according to numbers'. Plutarch (first century AD) writes in *Isis and Osiris,* 'The Pythagoreans . . . honour even numbers and geometrical diagrams with the names and titles of the gods . . . the number thirty-six, their Tetraktys, or sacred Quaternion, being composed of the first four odd numbers added to the first four even ones . . . is looked upon by them as the most solemn oath they can take, and called Kosmos.'

Some sense of the complex Pythagorean number-system may be gleaned from the art of gematria, whereby every letter of the Hebrew and classic Greek alphabets had a specific number-value so that hidden meaning might be coded in words or names. Thus in Greek the name of the **Gnostic** deity Abraxas is 'Αβραξασ, where A = 1, β = 2, ρ = 100, α = 1, ξ = 60, α = 1, σ = 200. The sum is 365, the number of days in a year. Abraxas thus symbolises the 365 Aeons, or Spirits of the Days. He also symbolises five creatures. As the circle of the year contains 360 degrees, each of these deities has a number value one-fifth of this power: 72, a number sacred in **Qabalah** and in the Old Testament (also *see* **Nuit**).[1]

Also, by adding their digits, all numbers over ten may be reduced to a single digit and 10 itself to 1 (1+0 = 1), so creating yet another level of coded meanings. Thus the 'Number of the Beast' as given in Revelation xiii:18, is 666 ('Here is wisdom. Let him that hath understanding count the number of the beast: for it is the number of a man, and his number is six hundred threescore and six') which is 6+6+6 = 18, hence 1+8 = 9. Revelation also says 144,000 will be saved – 1+4+4+0+0+0 also equals 9, symbolically the number of Man. So both the Beast and the number of the saved refer to Man himself. Another number reducing to 9 is 1080. Whereas 666 is positive, masculine, active, *yang*, solar; 1080 is negative, feminine, receptive, *yin*, lunar. Greek phrases giving 1080 include those for the Holy Spirit, the Spirit of the Earth, fountain of wisdom, Tartaros, the abyss, etc. Adding 666+1080 = 1746, in Greek equivalent to a grain of mustard seed – the number of fusion and fertile union of the two opposite principles. (Note: 1+7+4+6 = 1+8 = 9).[2]

So the combination of words and number equivalents can literally speak volumes. Yet such a system is open to superstitious misinterpretation. The number 666 especially remains a source of fear – and insult. Over the centuries this 'Number of the Beast' has been applied (by their enemies) to Nero, Luther, Napoleon and Hitler. On retiring in 1988, ex-US President Reagan refused to move into a house numbered 666: it had to be changed to 667!

The ancient Chinese considered odd numbers as *yang* – male, celestial and auspicious; even numbers as *yin* – female, terrestrial, inauspicious. Today in the West the odd number 13 is still thought unlucky, being not only indivisible but lunar (13 × 28 = 364: the true number of months in a year). Even today our basic approach to numbers remains symbolic, specific values being ascribed, as in the past, to particular numbers. Thus: Zero, 0, is non-being, the Void. The **Tarot** card 'The Fool' is usually numbered Zero. It is the empty circle, total abstraction, the Cosmic **Egg**. One is a point, primal unity, the centre. '**Tao** begets One.' Two is duality, opposition: sun and moon, light and dark, *yang* and *yin*, male and female; also line, tower, phallus. Three is the trinity, 'three-in-one' (*See* **three**). Four is the four-square, physical world. The 'four-gated city' is the balanced soul: guarded, static, total, whole, square. There are four cardinal points, seasons, elements, limbs of the body. Five is da Vinci's spreadeagled human form: two arms, two legs plus head. A five-pointed star or pentagram is a human microcosm. Six is the number of Christ and reason; 666 is the Number of the Beast, alias Man (head, arms, legs and phallus), also the number of the **Sun** and of intellect. The symbolic world was created in six days. Seven is the magical number (*see* **seven**). Eight is double-four, the octagon, a new beginning. Nine, thrice three, the Hebrews thought too holy to include in their numerology.[3]

1. *The Secret Teachings of All Ages*, Manly P. Hall, Philosophical Research Society, Los Angeles, 1989 (1928), pp.69ff.
2. *The New View Over Atlantis*, John Michell, Thames & Hudson, London, 1983.
3. *The Magical Arts*, Richard Cavendish, Arkana, London, 1984; *An Illustrated Encyclopaedia of Traditional Symbols*, J.C. Cooper, Thames & Hudson, London, 1978, pp.113–20.

NUN (*See* EGYPTIAN MYTH)

Represents primeval watery chaos or the ocean in which before creation lay the germs of all life. Called 'father of the gods' and sometimes shown as a man standing waist-deep in water who holds up his arms to support the gods issuing from him, he remained an intellectual concept, without either temples or a cult. Notably, there is no **flood myth** in Egyptian lore.

NYMPHS (*See* ELEMENTALS, GREEK MYTH, NEREIDS)

Semi-divine elemental forces personified as beautiful, graceful maidens in Greek myth, of several classes, and their names varying according to the element they represented. The Oreads (like Echo, who pined away for love of **Narcissus**) belonged to the mountains and caves. Crowned with **oak**-leaves, the Dryads guarded trees, especially the sacred oak, about which they danced. The Hamadryads formed an integral part of the trees themselves. The Napaeae, Auloniads, Hylaeorae and Alseids haunted the woods and valleys. Others rode the air (Sylphs), inhabited the seas (**Nereids**, Undines), rivers or fountains, or formed part of the retinue of superior deities: **Apollo**, **Artemis** and **Dionysus**. The lecherous sky-god **Zeus** was much given to chasing and abducting nymphs, including Aegina and Antiope, daughters of the river-god Asopus. Even lovelier was the nymph Calliope, to whom the infatuated Zeus presented himself in the form of Artemis. Too late she realised her mistake and tried to hide her shame. To shield her from Artemis, Zeus changed her into a bear, but the enraged goddess killed her even as she bore a son, Arcas, ancestor of the Arcadians. Placed in the heavens, Callisto became the Great Bear. Artemis likewise slew the nymph Mera for giving herself to Zeus.

O

OAK (*See* DRUIDS, GOLDEN BOUGH, MISTLETOE, THUNDER, TREES)

If the **lion** is King of Beasts, the oak is the King of Trees. Pre-eminently the sacred tree of all branches of **Aryan** stock in Europe, emblem of sky- and fertility-gods, widely associated with **thunder**-gods and with lightning (which strikes it with greater frequency than other trees, perhaps because of the oak's tendency to grow above water), the oak is also associated with the 'all-healer', **mistletoe**, and thus with the **Golden Bough**. At one time it was widely thought that the oak's life resides in the mistletoe, which in winter remains green while the oak itself is leafless. Sacred to **Zeus**, who was revered in the **oracular** oaks at Dodona in Greece, it was also the tree of his wife Hera; likewise the tree of the Roman **Juno** and **Jupiter**, their annual marriage celebrated in an oak grove by worshippers wearing crowns of oak leaves. It was also an emblem of **Cybele** and of **Silvanus**. In Greek myth, the dryads were **nymphs** of the oak. Celtic **Druids** conducted their rituals in oak groves, thus perhaps their name (Welsh *derw*, 'oak'). One of the 'Seven Chieftain Trees' of the Celtic Beth-Luis-Nion tree alphabet (as the letter D, or *dair*), oak wood was preferred for kindling the **Beltane** fires of **May Day**, also the sacrificial fires lit on Midsummer Eve. 'The Celts,' says Maximus of Tyre (second century AD: *Logio* VIII.8), 'worship Zeus, and the Celtic image of Zeus is a tall oak.' When in the *Mabinogion* the Welsh god **Llew Llaw Gyffes** is slain by the trickery of **Blodeuwedd**, with a shriek he transforms into an **eagle** that alights in a magical oak. In Asia Minor, as Strabo (*c.*55 BC–AD 25) reports, the Galatian senate met in a place with the pure Celtic name Drunemeton, 'temple of the oak', or 'sacred oak grove'. **Grimm** claims the oak as the chief sacred tree of the Teutons, especially dedicated to the thunder-god Donar, equivalent to the Norse **Thor** or (again) to Jupiter and Zeus: so too among the Slavs it was sacred to the thunder-god Pyerun. The oak also represented durability, courage and strength; thus was adopted as a symbol of **Christ**: oak, **holly** and aspen being variously claimed as the tree of the cross. Sacred to the **Earth Mother** in **Native American** lore; to the Chinese it symbolised not only strength but also the weakness of strength that resists and breaks in the storm, even as the weak willow bends and survives.

OANNES (*See* BEROSSUS, DOGON, ENKI)

OCEAN (*See* FLOOD MYTH, RIVER MYTH, WATER)

Common to many cultures is the myth of a primeval ocean, or watery chaos, out of which all life swam or crawled, often associated with she-monsters or **dragons** (Leviathan, Tiamat, Typhon) to be overcome, slain or tamed by the solar hero or god (**Yahweh, Marduk, Zeus**) so that civilised order may be established. Among the river civilisations of Mesopotamia and Egypt the world was viewed as a raft floating on this primal ocean (the **Sumerian** Apsu). It was from this ocean that the fish-headed god **Enki** (Ea) arose to educate the Sumerians, likewise **Oannes**, and from the ocean that the Plumed Serpent

Quetzalcoatl or **Kukulcán** came sailing to educate the **Aztec** and **Mayan** cultures. Another idea is of a river circling the world, source of all waters, also sometimes viewed as a **serpent** or dragon (**Ourobouros,** or the serpent of Midgard that in **Norse** myth encircles the world, swallowing its own tail). Thus the Greek **Titan** Oceanus was conceived as an immense river girdling the universe, lying beyond the sea but not mingling with it. Said to be son of **Ouranos** and **Gaia,** Oceanus was regarded by **Homer** (who refers to him as 'begetter of all') as superior to all gods but Zeus. He was husband and brother of Tethys, who bore the three thousand Oceanids and the three thousand rivers, including the **Styx** that separates the land of the living from the **underworld.** From him arose all the stars, except the Great Bear, only to plunge back into him every dawn. On his furthest shores lay the fabled lands of Ethiopians, Cimmerians and Pygmies.

OCEANIC MYTH (*See* CONCORDANCE)

Four thousand miles of ocean lie between Hawaii in the northeast Pacific to the Australian coast in the southwest. Embracing Polynesia, Melanesia, Micronesia, New Zealand and Australia, 'Oceania' covers a vast region, in it many scattered islands and archipelagos, each with their own cultures and beliefs. Yet there are resemblances between the beliefs of people inhabiting these four main Oceanic regions. Many gods with the same or similar names and attributes are found in widely separated island cultures. Often, migratory myths explain such similarities, but there are many variations. The term 'Oceania' is an academic convenience, and, though in general use, it should be used with care.

The largest region is Polynesia, embracing a 4,000-mile triangular area from New Zealand to Easter Island and **Hawaii.** Supernaturalism prevailed throughout. Deities were thought able to manifest in human or other visible (animal, bird, fish) form. They might also live in stones, appear as meteors or take fantastic form, as ogres, **demons,** multi-limbed or many-headed monsters. Typically they ruled only one aspect of nature: the Hawaiian volcano-goddess Pele; the Maori storm-god Tawhiri-ma-tea. The creation of the world could be ascribed to a single god (i.e., **Tangaroa** in Polynesia, variously named and with many different attributes throughout Oceania), but nowhere was he considered omnipotent. Animism prevailed. Gods belonged to particular places or elements, or were deified culture-heroes, sometimes (it seems) derived from Christian missionary activity. Thus the Hawaiian gods made Man in the likeness of Kane, and Woman from his rib as he slept. But the **trickster**-god **Maui** enlivened the myths of the entire region.

The souls of the dead might survive in spirit-bodies and remain linked with their old home or burial-place, reaching the next world only after arduous struggle. **Reincarnation** was possible, but just as likely was the soul's destruction by **demons** or other hungry, malevolent forces.

As elsewhere, magical **taboo** was common. In the Marquesas, nobody might step over the **head** of another, not even a father over that of his sleeping child. In Tahiti, whoever passed his hands over the head of the king might be executed. The head of a Maori chief was so sacred that, if even he touched it himself, he had to make ritual amends. Thus too with **hair**: when a Fijian chief had his hair cut, first he ate a man by way of magical precaution against **witchcraft.** Similar beliefs prevailed through the entire Pacific region. **Cannibalism** was common. Captured enemies were eaten to gain their strength and knowledge.

Polynesian myth is rich in tales of **hero**-journeys to the **sun** or to the

underworld. Hawaiian **flood-myth** tells how men died but for one, Nuu, who survived with his family in an **ark**. In New Zealand, the Maori tell how the god Tawaki caused the flood by stamping on heaven's crystal floor and breaking it, so that the waters poured down.

In one form or another, many of these 'Polynesian' deities, beliefs and customs prevailed; differences between the regions lay in specific local custom rather than in overall belief.

Melanesia, the central Oceanic area from Papua to Fiji, includes the Solomon Islands, New Hebrides, New Britain and New Caledonia. Unlike the Polynesians and other Oceanic folk, Melanesians deny supernatural beings or gods, being given instead to the concept of *mana*, an impersonal power or quality beyond reach of human or natural influence. Everywhere present, *mana* may attach itself to an individual, who may channel and use it, yet at the risk of its bursting out in some new, unexpected form. Creator spirits like **Quat** are essentially human, deriving power from their control of *mana*. In New Britain the notion persists that ill-luck arises from human folly, not from any conscious or hostile supernatural agencies. Good and evil are explained by the actions of two brothers, To-Kabinana and To-Karvuvu, the latter a halfwit whose attempts to imitate his brother's magic created the shark and other evils. Perhaps **Buddhist** and **Islamic** beliefs, influencing neighbouring Indonesia (see **Indochina and Indonesia**) had some effect on this region during the last two millennia (*see also* **Cargo Cult**).

Inhabitants of the scattered isles of Micronesia north of Melanesia (the Caroline, Gilbert, Marshall and Mariana archipelagos) worshipped the *ani* (deified ancestors) in the forms of the bird, animal, fish or tree in which they were said to live. Christian missionary activity later led to an idea that death entered the world after the first people damaged a sacred **tree**. In Micronesian belief, the virtuous dead went to an undersea heaven called pachet, the evil dead to a gloomy hell, pueliko. Yet again, the cause of human misfortune and evil was blamed on a trickster brother, the god of fire, Olofat, whose **shape-shifting** antics upset the balance of the world.

For the indigenous myths of the fourth Oceanic region, Australia, *see* **Aborigines, Aranda, Yurlungur**.

OCEANUS (*See* OCEAN)

ODIN (*See* AESIR, NORSE MYTH, TEUTONIC MYTH)

Or (among the pagan Germans and Anglo-Saxons) Wotan, Woden, whence the English Wednesday, also the German word *wüten*, 'to rage'. Odin is the Norse name for this furious Teutonic sky-god, supernatural magician, giver of law and poetic inspiration, god of war and chief of the **Aesir**. Compared by the Latins with **Mercury** in his role of decider of the fate of men and Lord of the Dead, once he may have led the supernatural '**Wild Hunt**', whereby on stormy nights folk heard a phantom army of dead warriors rampaging over the sky. Seen as one-eyed, with a flowing mantle and wide-brimmed hat, or with gold breastplate and horned golden helm, armed with the **dwarf**-forged spear Gungnir he rode the eight-hooved **horse** Sleipnir, inspiring *Amanita*-crazed **berserkers** with battle-fury. To **Valhalla** ('Hall of the Slain') he invited heroes slain in combat, presiding over festive war-games with two **ravens** Hugin ('Thought') and Munin ('Memory') perched on his shoulder. These he sent out daily to question the living and the dead: each night before dawn they returned with news of the world. He was also served by the **Valkyries**, supernatural warrior-women who served his guests and took part in every mortal battle, deciding who should die and which side should win.

Odin was also the **shaman**-magician, Lord of the Otherworld, sometimes (like Mercury-Hermes) a psychopomp guiding the newly-dead, and also (like **Mithra-Christ**) a **sacrificial** victim himself. In the poem *Hávamál* he is described as hanging on the world-tree **Yggdrasil** for nine days and nights, self-impaled on his own spear. But there is no suggestion that he suffers to save others. His purpose is to win the secret of the **runes** via ritual death-and-rebirth: an **initiatory** process once common from Scandinavia to Siberia and North America. It may also imply the once-common Scandinavian practice of stabbing victims to death and hanging their bodies from trees. The shamanic aspect is underlined by frequent reference to Odin as shape-**shifter**: throughout the world the shaman was thought able to take the form of specific animals at will (*see* **Vampirism, Werewolf**).

Odin often mingled with men, disguised as a simple wayfarer, favouring especially the Volsungs, a family founded by one of his sons, Sigi, whose great-grandson was the **hero** Sigmund. One night Sigmund and his warriors feasted in their hall when a tall old man entered. Blind in one eye, he wore a cloak and a wide-brimmed hat, and carried a **sword**. This he thrust up to the hilt into the tree-trunk that supported the centre of the hall. Declaring the sword belonged to the man who could pull it out, he vanished. Like **King Arthur**, Sigmund was the man. Thereafter he won many victories with this sword, which was later wielded by his son, the hero **Sigurd** (**Siegfried**).

No more faithful to his wife **Frigga** than **Zeus** was to **Hera**, Odin enjoyed many amorous exploits with mortal women as well as goddesses. He was also a renowned healer, and the god of poetry, having stolen 'the mead of the poets' from the Frost **Giants**. This inspirational beverage he dispensed to those mortals who pleased him. He had only one **eye**, having plucked out and thrown the other into the **well** of **Mimir**, so as to earn the right to drink from the well and gain immortal wisdom.

ODYSSEY (*See* **GREEK MYTH, HOMER,** *ILIAD*, **TELEMACHUS**)

Called Ulysses by the Romans, the legendary Greek hero Odysseus gave his name to the second of **Homer**'s great narratives, *The Odyssey*, which tells how this resourceful king of Ithaca (a small isle in the Ionian Sea) made his way home at the end of the siege of Troy, as described by Homer in *The Iliad*. Yet where *The Iliad* is chronologically tied to a single year, and geographically to a specific place (Troy), *The Odyssey* ranges over a decade and through a multitude of different myths and encounters.

The tale begins ten years after the fall of Troy. All the Greeks have returned home except Odysseus. His stratagem of the wooden horse took Troy, yet he remained captive to and reluctant lover of the demi-goddess **Calypso**, daughter of **Atlas**. At home in Ithaca, his wife Penelope has not seen him for twenty years; her son **Telemachus** cannot expel her vicious suitors.

Zeus now proposes that Odysseus be allowed to return home, though not easily. The distance to be covered is minimal in geographical terms, but in metaphoric or mythical terms it is vast. What should take under a month takes much longer. As told by Homer, the physical journey is continually interrupted by **otherworld** episodes (meetings with the **Cyclopes**, **sirens**, **Circle**, Scylla and Charybdis and other fantastic beings). At last, tardily reaching the land of King Alcinous, he is begged by the king to tell his tale.

Thus, as Homer presents it, we have only the word of Odysseus himself that his story of wandering is true. Not everyone believes him. When at last he returns to Ithaca, the goddess of wisdom, Pallas **Athene** (disguised as a shepherd boy), though she helps him, rejects his tale. 'Shameless and all too subtle man, never surfeited with your trickeries – not even here, in your own land, will you lay aside the deceitfulness and the wily words that you love in every fibre of you.'[1]

Is Odysseus a liar, a hero only in his own imagination? Certainly the gods give him a hard time all the way back home. Was Homer, himself perhaps born in Asia Minor, not far south of Troy itself, making a moral point? Why should Odysseus, whose wooden horse trick had doomed Troy, be allowed an easy return home, or the Greeks be persuaded that their culture was so superior?

1. *The Odyssey*, Homer (trans. Walter Shewring), OUP, 1980.

OEDIPUS (*See* FREUD, GAMES, INCEST, RIDDLES, SPHINX)

OENGHUS (*See* ANGUS MAC OG, IRISH MYTH)

OGMA (*See* CADMUS, IRISH MYTH, RUNES, TREE ALPHABET)
A son of the **Dagda** and warrior of the **Tuatha dé Danaan**, this Irish god was said to have invented the Celtic ogham alphabet: a system of writing that consisted of horizontal or slanting strokes cut in a vertical column on to wood or stone and used for inscriptions. A 'strong man', Ogma later became the Romano-Gaulish Ogmios, equated with **Hercules**. As described by Lucian of Samosata (Greek, second century AD), Ogmios carried the club and bow of Hercules, but was portrayed as a bald old man, followed by men with golden chains linking their ears to his tongue, meaning that his strength lay in his eloquence. He was also portrayed with hair raying out like a **sun-god**, suggesting connection with the cult of **Maponus/Apollo**.

OGRES (*See* CANNIBALISM, GIANTS)

OGYGIA (*See* CRONUS, OTHERWORLD)

OISIN (OSSIAN) (*See* FAIRIES, FINN MACCOOL, IRISH MYTH, TIR NAN OG, YEATS)
Son of the Irish hero **Finn MacCool**, Oisin ('Little Fawn') jumped, ran and versified better than all Finn's other warriors (the Fianna). One day, chasing a stag by Loch Lene in Kerry, they saw a white-crowned, red-mantled woman on a white horse riding over the loch. Naming herself as Niav of the Golden Hair, she declared love for Oisin, then bewitched him by describing a golden Land of Youth without illness, death or pain. So he joined her on her **fairy** horse. Invisible to all they passed, they reached the sea. A mist fell, bringing Oisin strange visions: a deer pursued by a bear, then a turreted castle from which stately riders rode, then another deer, chased by a hound, one ear red, the other white. 'Prepare for the Land of Youth,' Niav said, and the mists cleared to show white beaches. Smiling riders led them to a vast round castle, silken rainbow banners hanging from its walls. Before they dismounted, Niav told Oisin that once his feet touched the ground, all he saw was his and he would never age, for he had come to the Land of Youth, **Tir nan Og**. But should he try to return to the world of man, dreadful old age would immediately seize and destroy him.

Seduced by the wonder of all he saw, he dismounted and instantly grew younger. So he ruled Tir nan Og, yet in time yearned to see Ireland again. Niav lent him her white horse, but warned him not to dismount if he wished to return. He rode over the sea to Ireland, but found everything changed. A new folk ruled the land. Finn and the Fianna were gone. The castle of his youth was in ruins. As he rode the shore he met men who told him that the Fianna were three centuries dead. In shock, he pulled away his horse so hard that it threw him on to the sands. Immediately he began crumbling with age. **St Patrick**, who was busily fighting the **Druids** and converting folk to a new god, **Christ**, came before Oisin died and recorded his tale.[1]

In the eighteenth century, **James Macpherson** published what he claimed as his translation of old Gaelic texts recording the poems of Ossian, alias Oisin.

1. *Legends of the Celts*, Frank Delaney, Hodder & Stoughton, London, 1989.

OLORUN (*See* AFRICAN MYTH, YORUBA)

OLWEN (*See* CULHWCH, *MABINOGION*)

OLYMPUS (*See* GREEK MYTH, MOUNTAINS)
Bordering Macedonia and Thessaly by the Aegean Sea, Mount Olympus was early viewed by the Greeks as the seat of their gods. Higher than any other peak in the region, its cloud-bound upper tiers resemble gigantic seats. Here they built their palaces, had their quarrels and affairs and viewed the mortal world far below. Here, the twelve great gods and goddesses (**Aphrodite, Apollo, Ares, Artemis, Athene, Demeter, Hephaestus, Hera, Hermes, Hestia, Poseidon** and **Zeus**) were served by many lesser deities. Feasting on nectar and ambrosia at golden tables while **Apollo** played his lyre and the **Muses** sang, they passed their days in merriment, nightly retiring to the houses Hephaestus built for them. For even the gods, though **immortal** and **invulnerable** (*ichor*, not blood, ran in their veins), needed their rest.

Only **Hades**, along with **Persephone** and **Hecate**, spurned the delights of Olympus, preferring their own dark **underworld** abode.

OM (*See* BUDDHISM, HINDUISM)
Spoken aloud or breathed silently, to **Buddhists** and **Hindus** alike this sacred syllable represents the essence and power of God, much as in **Hebrew** belief the letters YHVH (*Yod He Vau He:* **Yahweh**) incorporate the ultimate, unpronounceable holy mystery. Though sounded as 'OM', the syllable is in essence threefold: AUM. A represents **Brahma**'s creation; U is the balance of things by which **Vishnu** preserves this world; M is the disintegration of the universe. For when Vishnu falls asleep, Brahma breathes in, and **Shiva** the Great Lord oversees the undoing of things. Uttered together, the A and the U produce the sound of the long O. Here too is the trinity. It is said by the Brahmans that in an earlier era, before the Ages of Bronze and Iron, people were so perfect that no religious ceremony was needed; they had only to utter the word 'OM' to gain full connection with all that is holy.

OMAR KHAYYAM (1048–1122) (*See* ISLAM)
Persian poet, astronomer and mathematician, remembered for his *Rubáiyát* ('quatrains'), especially via the free English translation first published 1859 by Edward Fitzgerald (1809–83). It may be that, without this version, Omar Khayyam ('Omar the Tentmaker') would be no better known in the West than probably greater **Islamic** poets like Jalaluddin **Rumi**. Yet Omar's passionate and impulsive verses, characterised by rapid transitions from

love-minstrelsy to mystical argument, from grave fatalism to ribald tavern song, indicate a mind steeped in **Sufi** lore. Contemporaries disregarded his poetry, which contains elements of the ancient **Mystery** tradition of both West and East. It is notable that he lived and worked during the time of the First Crusade when, via religious war, Europe was reinvigorated by the insemination of precisely those themes that Omar explores. Fitzgerald did not invent Omar, any more than **Malory** invented **King Arthur**. After all:

> We are no more than a moving row
> Of magic Shadow-shapes that come and go. (LXVIII)

OMENS (*See* **DIVINATION, PROPHECY**)

Any events or objects said to portend good or evil, their meaning interpreted by **divination**. Omens occur spontaneously or are sought. Celtic **Druids** and Roman augurers sought omens in the flight of birds, marking out a given space and seeking answers to their questions by observing the flight pattern, species, and other behaviour of birds impinging on that space. In Ireland, each sound, position and movement of domesticated wrens or **ravens** has its significance. If the bird called from the door, strangers or soldiers were on the way; if it called with 'a small voice', sickness was expected.

'I heard the **cuckoo** while fasting,' remarked a Scot, 'and I knew the year would not go well with me.'[1] In 1814 a minister at Dornoch in Scotland fell ill. A cormorant settled on the church steeple; his rapid death was seen to fulfil the fatal omen. Thirty-five years later, the event recurred and the incumbent also died. Likewise in Scotland a **raven** settling on the roof was an omen of approaching death within the house. A **dove** that flew round a person's head was also ominous. In Devon a swarm of **bees** alighting in a dead tree was taken as an omen of death, but a strange swarm alighting in the garden was an omen of wealth to come. **Druids** derived omens from the chirping of wrens. Before joining battle with the Romans, Queen Boadicea let loose a **hare**, which ran off in what the Iceni considered the auspicious direction, so that they 'shouted with pleasure, seeing victory within their grasp', as Dio Cassius reports.

Omens were also drawn from the direction taken by the smoke and flames of sacred **fires**, from the apperance of clouds, by the howling of **dogs**, by the shape of tree-roots, by the death-throes of a stabbed man; from **dreams**; the state of the entrails, liver or shoulder-blades of slaughtered animals, and by many other means. In Kenya a *murogi* (**shaman**) of the **Kikuyu** would toss his sandals and derive omens from the way they fell. So too the throw of dice, coins or yarrow sticks (as in the I Ching system of divination) has been universally employed to generate omens.

Underlying such systems is the belief that all events interconnect; the meaning in apparently chance events may be divined by intuition. Jungian speculation that the collective **unconscious** knows all things implies that this approach may not be so absurd as rationality alone supposes.

1. *The Magic Arts in Celtic Britain*, Lewis Spence, Rider, London, 1970.

OMPHALOS (*See AXIS MUNDI*, **MOUNTAINS**)

Greek, meaning 'navel', or the boss of a shield; also originally a conical stone at **Delphi** which supposedly marked the exact centre or navel of the earth: thus often used to refer to the Cosmic Centre or World Navel, and widely represented as a holy **mountain** or island rising from the primeval **ocean** or waters of chaos – **Olympus**, Sinai or the mythical Mount **Meru** – the dwelling-place of the gods where earth and heaven meet.

ONI (*See* DEMONS, JAPANESE MYTH, SHINTO)

Associated with disease and disaster, these Japanese **demons** of ill-**omen** derived relatively late from Indian and Chinese ideas and are conceived of in two classes: the Oni of **Hell** and those haunting earth. Basically human in appearance, but with red or green bodies and the heads of oxen or **horse**, the former may also be horned, three-eyed and have three sharp talons both on hands and feet. With these they seize the souls of evil folk about to die and, in a chariot of fire, carry them off to eternal torment. In their birdlike aspect they may derive from the **Hindu** man-eagle **Garuda**. The earthbound Oni can take the shape of living beings or inanimate objects. Other **invisible** demons may be detected by their singing, whistling or chattering. Some of the Oni are women changed into demons by jealousy or grief. Though maleficent, the Oni are susceptible to **Buddhist** exorcism and may even be converted. The Buddhist sect founded by Nichiren (1222–82) holds periodic retreats to drive out the Oni and other evil spirits. Not unlike **Christian** Puritans, Nichiren saw the Oni at work everywhere, and called the **Zen** sect, 'the work of the devil'. The **Shinto** Oni-yarahi (demon-expelling) ceremonial drama occurs on the last day of every year, the Oni as personifications of every kind of mischance being forcibly expelled during the drama.

ORACLE (*See* DELPHI, PROPHECY, TREES)

From Latin *orare*, 'to speak'; thus a place, person, or both, at and from which prophetic advice is given. The great classical oracle at **Delphi** on the slopes of Mount **Parnassus** in Greece is described elsewhere. Originally governed by **Gaia** the **Earth Mother**, it passed into the hands of **Apollo**, yet the mouthpiece of the oracle remained the pythoness, a priestess seated on a serpent-legged tripod in a cave above a subterranean fissure emitting trance-inducing fumes. Overwhelmed by these, she would prophesy, usually with that famous ambiguity that doomed King **Croesus**.

Other renowned oracles were found at Dodona and Trophonius. Dodona (a city in Epirus) was the oldest, mythically founded by **Deucalion**, the Greek survivor of the **Flood**. There, **Zeus** prophesied via 'talking' **oak**-trees, **birds** and brass vases. The 'talking' trees formed a sacred grove, as in **Druidic** rites. From their branches the famed oracular **dove** of Dodona was said to answer the queries of supplicants. Probably the 'dove' was a priestess: in Thessaly both prophetesses and doves were called Peleiadas. The talking vases, or kettles, were so made that, when struck, they sounded a note lasting hours. Some authors describe a row of such vases. One being struck, its vibrations went through all the others. Another tale is of one vase in an open hall, alongside it the statue of a child holding a whip tipped with many swinging cords, each ending in a small metal ball. These, wind-blown, continually rang against the vase, creating reverberations interpreted by the priests.

The oracle at Trophonius was in a tiny hillside cave, its entrance so small it seemed impossible to enter, with two fountains nearby, from which those about to enter drank. The first contained the water of forgetfulness and the second that of remembrance. Lowering his legs into the cave-mouth, the supplicant was rudely dragged downward, later to be ejected feet first, usually delirious. The prophecies were given as dreams and visions: the supplicants experienced severe headaches and traumatic after-effects. On departure, the confused supplicants were required to leave an account of their experience while in the cave at a neighbouring temple: this account the priests interpreted as the oracle.

ORAL TRADITION (*See* BARDS, MUSES)

For generation after generation, the myths, tales, history and genealogical information important to every people on earth have been handed down through the 'oral tradition'. Before the **Muses** were goddesses of art they were goddesses of memory. In every generation and culture, specialists trained in this art transmitted the core knowledge of their culture to students who, after years of rigorous training, themselves in turn became bardic custodians of it. Knowledge survived – and evolved – without writing. Written information was not even necessarily respected. Whatever is written down in a sense becomes 'dead': like an **idol**, it takes a fixed, material form. Thus little is known of **Druid** metaphysics because they deliberately refused to commit their knowledge to writing.

ORESTES (*See* GREEK MYTH)

This son of King Agamemnon of Argos (Greek leader at Troy) slew his mother Clytemnestra, who had beheaded Agamemnon after her lover Aegisthus (who had also killed Atreus, Agamemnon's father) cut him down. Agamemnon himself had slain Clytemnestra's former husband Tantalus (not the **Tantalus** punished in Tartarus) and a new-born child at her breast. She had no reason to love Orestes and he had none to love her. Reared in exile, he asked the **Delphic Oracle** if he should kill his father's murderers. **Apollo** told him he would become an outcast if he did not: yet the Pythoness warned that the **Furies** would not forgive matricide. Returning to Mycenae, he entered the palace in disguise, killed Aegisthus, then beheaded his mother. For this act of retributive matricide he was chased by the Furies before being acquitted by **Athene**, goddess of wisdom and agent of **Zeus**. So the chain of retribution ended; the family feud with it. The Furies retired: good sense and 'holy Persuasion' won the day, as Aeschylus describes in *The Oresteian Trilogy*.

It is also said Orestes went mad, or that he did not kill Clytemnestra, but had her tried and refused to intercede when she was condemned to death.

Agamemnon's fate parallels that of Welsh god **Llew Llaw Gyffes**. He dies in a bath-house, a net over his head, one foot in the bath but the other on the floor – neither clad nor unclad, on dry land or in water, in his palace or out of it. Yet again the myth of the sacred king slain at midsummer when waxing turns to waning; the tanist or dark brother (Aegisthus) taking over from the sacrificed king (Agamemnon), himself to be slain in due season.

1. *The Greek Myths*, Robert Graves, Penguin, London, 1960.

ORIGEN (*c*.185–254) (*See* CHRISTIANITY, NEOPLATONISM, PLOTINUS)

Early Christian patriarch, held that all that is true in Greek metaphysics is completed in biblical scripture. Surnamed Adamantius and born probably in Alexandria, he was influenced by the Neoplatonism of Ammonius Saccas. He saw Christ as a ladder of divine ascent to beatific vision of God who, in his overflowing love, had created all rational and spiritual beings via the Logos (Word). Incarnated as Christ, the Logos restored the original unity between divinity and humanity. This implied self-limitation by God, who is transcendent yet also immanent in his Creation. Origen taught that God created the material world as a means of discipline, but that it is not man's ultimate destination. He held that pre-existing **souls** fell varying distances, some to become **angels**, some, human beings and some, **devils**. Yet not even **Satan** is beyond hope of redemption, the climax of which is incarnation of the one soul, the Son, which never fell but remained united with the Father. Joined to this soul, the Logos incarnated via the **Virgin Mary** as Christ. Influenced by **Gnostic** ideas, Origen said Jesus appeared differently to men according to their spiritual capacity; that redemption restores fallen souls from matter to spirit, image to reality; and that the Church is a 'school of souls'. He denied the theory of **transmigration** or the idea that rational souls can incarnate in animal bodies, but speculated on the theory of world cycles (as found in **Brahmanic** cosmology).

His world-denying influence was considerable during his life and later. Attacked as a pagan who denied **hell** and the **resurrection** of the body, opposition to his ideas mounted after he died. Eusebius of Caesarea (264–340) alleged that as a youth he had castrated himself – perhaps but hostile gossip. Attacks by Epiphanius (375) and Jerome (393–402) damaged his name, yet his influence persisted, especially in the growth of monasticism.

ORIGINAL SIN (*See* ADAM, CHRISTIANITY, EVE, FALL, ST PAUL, SIN-EATING)

Christian dogma that mankind is innately evil and doomed because (Genesis iii) Adam ate of the Tree of the Knowledge of Good and Evil. This sin ('Ye shall not eat of it, neither shall ye touch it, lest ye die', **Yahweh** had warned) led to the **Fall** and to later generations inheriting Adam's guilt. So claimed St Paul, stating that Adam's act brought sin and death into the world, but that grace and eternal life came in greater wealth via Christ (Romans v:12–19). Yet the Old Testament says nothing of hereditary guilt and the Gospels are vague, while Genesis implies that the **Serpent**, persuading Eve to eat the Forbidden Fruit ('Ye shall not surely die') before offering it to Adam, proves Yahweh a liar for they do not die, save to Eden, the state of primal innocence. It is implied that the condition of sin (disobedience to divine law) is connected with the creation of man as a being with the capacity for choice, or free will. If the 'sin' is 'original', i.e. pre-existing, what room is there for free will? Paul's answer is that free will lies in submission to Christ (i.e., to the Church as representative of Christ).

ORION (*See* ASTRONOMY AND MYTH, GREEK MYTH)

Associated in ancient Egypt with **Osiris**, this prominent constellation is named after a hunter of Greek myth, a son of **Poseidon** who desired Merope, daughter of Oenopion and granddaughter of **Dionysus**. Oenopion promised her in marriage if Orion rid the isle of Chios of its wild beasts. This Orion did but Oenopion, himself in love with Merope, broke his word. In disgust Orion got drunk and raped her. Oenopion blinded him. An **oracle** told him his sight would be restored if he turned his empty eye-sockets to the rising sun. He reached the easternmost sea and **Helios** restored his sight. Seeking revenge on Oenopion, on Crete he met **Artemis**, who persuaded him to hunt with her. Her brother **Apollo**, fearing she would fall for this handsome man, sent a giant **scorpion** which stung him to death. Artemis begged **Asclepius** to revive him, but **Zeus** blasted Asclepius to ashes (or Apollo tricked Artemis into shooting Orion with an arrow). Either way, she set his image in the sky as a constellation, eternally pursued by the scorpion.

Orion, Egyptian **Horus** and Sumerian **Gilgamesh** (all solar heroes) are all attacked by scorpions; the zodiacal sign of Scorpio being associated with autumn, the onset of winter and the annual death of the sun.

ORMUZD (*See* **AHURA MAZDA**)

ORPHEUS (*See* **DIONYSUS, GREEK MYTH, JASON, MUSIC AND MYTH, MYSTERIES**)

Legendary Thracian bard, initiator of the early Greeks into the Mysteries bearing his name. He may have been an initiate of the Egyptian Mysteries, living some centuries before Homer. It is said that he was the son of **Apollo** and the **Muse** Calliope (i.e., that Orpheus is the secret doctrine Apollo, revealed through music, Calliope) and that the Muses taught him to play his seven-stringed lyre (a gift from Apollo: the lyre itself the secret teaching, seven strings for seven divine truths) so entrancingly that wild beasts and even rocks and trees danced after the sound of it.

Leaving Egypt, he joined Jason and the Argonauts to seek the **Golden Fleece**. His singing persuaded the ship *Argo*, stranded high on a beach, to descend back to the sea; made the **Clashing Rocks** let the *Argo* pass safely; entranced the **dragon** guarding the Golden Fleece, and lulled the **Sirens**.

He married the **nymph** Eurydice who, pursued by Aristaeus, a would-be rapist, was bitten to death by a snake in the grass. Following her to the **underworld**, his music charmed the ferryman **Charon**, the dog **Cerberus** and even **Hades** himself. Releasing Eurydice, Hades warned that if he looked back at her before she was safely in sunlight, she was lost forever. He led her back to the Land of the Living but, on reaching sunlight himself, looked back – and she, still in the shadow, was lost.

One tale says that in his misery he killed himself. Another, that Zeus slew him for divulging divine secrets. The common tale is that, denying the wine-god **Dionysus**, he continued praising Apollo and avowing homosexuality, so angering **Aphrodite**. His condemnation of sacrificial murder and **Maenad** promiscuity led Dionysus to set these mad women on him. They burst into the Temple of Apollo where he was priest, murdered their husbands and tore him to pieces, casting his **head** and lyre into the River Hebrus. Both floated, singing, to the isle of Lesbos (meaning his body, the cult itself, could be destroyed but not its inner doctrines). His head became an **oracle** (*see* **Bran**) kept in a cave sacred to Dionysus, where it prophesied until Apollo, finding his own oracles deserted, told it to shut up. His lyre became so venerated that to touch it was sacrilege. Neanthos, son of the Tyrant of Lesbos, tried to play it, but was torn to pieces by dogs. It is also said he reincarnated as a white **swan**, signifying the survival of the spiritual truths he promulgated. That he was torn to pieces by the Maenads just as the infant Dionysus was dismembered by the **Titans** suggests that he and Dionysus were one and the same, as does the lodging of his head in a cave sacred to Dionysus. His fate, like that of Persian **Mithra**, also seems to presage the Passion of Christ: 'I am the fruit of the vine.'

ORWELL, GEORGE (1903–50)

Pseudonym of Eric Blair, English novelist, essayist and critic famed for his fable *Animal Farm* and his grim satire *Nineteen Eighty-Four*. Born in Bengal, in 1922 he joined the Indian Imperial Police in Burma, but soon regretted his collusion with imperialism. Resigning in 1928, he lived among the poor in London and Paris, and later among unemployed miners in northern England. In Spain in 1937 he reported on the Civil War from the Republican side. In 1945 he published *Animal Farm*, a political fable describing the Russian Revolution in terms of the animals taking over the farm, declaring all to be equal, only to be betrayed by the tyrannical **pigs**. This was followed by *Nineteen Eighty-Four* (1948), a bleak futuristic satire of global tyranny maintained by perpetual war between three equally repressive world states, each systematically distorting the truth and rewriting history. This ominous totalitarian myth describes the future as a boot crushing the human face for ever; the novel remains influential. Orwell died of tuberculosis in 1950.

OSIRIS (*See* EGYPTIAN MYTH, HORUS, ISIS, NEPTHYS, SET)

The most prominent Egyptian deity after **Ra**, said to be first son of Geb and **Nuit** and brother of Isis, Nepthys and Set. Originally a vegetation god, annually slain and reborn, Osiris represented corn, vine, trees and the fertilising power of the Nile as opposed to the arid desert (Set). Yet he enjoyed his greatest popularity as god of the dead. At Abydos he was identified with Khenti Amenti, the wolf-god, as Osiris Khenti Amenti, 'Lord of the Westerners', meaning Lord of the Dead, who dwell in the west, land of the setting sun. Here, it was said, his **head** lay buried. Also sacred to him was the town of Zedu, where his mummy was displayed.

Euhemerised by some as an ancient culture-hero only later deified, it is said he was born in Thebes and grew up handsome, taller than other men, and dark of skin. When his father Geb retired to the heavens, he became king of Egypt, taking his sister Isis as his wife and queen. Abolishing **cannibalism**, he instituted agriculture, crafts, wine-making, religious ceremonial and the worship of the gods, and invented the two kinds of flute that accompanied ceremonial song. He journeyed the world on a civilising mission, his musical talent (as with **Orpheus**) and gentleness disarming all he met. He returned to find Isis ruling wisely in his place. But the 'good' Osiris was later assassinated by conspirators led by Set, his jealous brother. Set adrift in a coffer, his body floated down the Nile, eventually reaching Byblos in Phoenicia. Here it came to rest at the base of an acacia (or tamarisk) tree, which grew so fast as to enclose the coffer entirely within its trunk. Recovering his body, Isis hid it in the swamps of the Nile delta near Buto. Set regained it and cut it into fourteen pieces which he scattered throughout the land. But Isis recovered all these save the phallus, swallowed by fishes, or by a crab, or a **crocodile** (symbolising Set's brutal side). Magically rejoining the body, she performed the rites of embalmment for the first time. Assisted by **Nepthys**, **Anubis** and **Thoth**, she restored Osiris to life and (such was her power) conceived a child (**Horus**) by him, despite his lost phallus.

Thus resurrected, Osiris decided not to retain the throne and continue to rule the living, but retired to the halls of the **underworld**. Here, in the 'Hall of Double Justice', he welcomed the souls of the dead, presiding over their judgement and attended by **Maat**, Anubis, Thoth and the forty-two assessors. Those whose souls tipped in the balance against the feather of truth in the other pan went to Am-mut, 'Eater of the Dead', a monster part-**lion**, part-**crocodile** and part-**hippopotamus**. Yet the souls of the just enjoyed an eternally happy life under his benevolent rule.

Osiris was depicted as bearded, green of face and tightly swathed in white mummy wrappings, wearing the crown of Upper Egypt and in his hands (folded over his breast) holding a flail and a crook.

OSSIAN (*See* MACPHERSON, OISIN)

OTHERWORLD (*See* CONCORDANCE)

Generic term applied to supernatural realms or **dimensions** distinct from the daily world of the living, typically the land of the dead inhabited by spirits, fairies or other magical beings; typically reached by entry into a fairy knowe (*see* **earth mounds**) or located in the West (land of the setting sun, thus of death), and associated with the **earthly paradise** or Isles of the Blessed to which dead heroes and kings are borne, there to enjoy eternal youth and happiness. The otherworld may also be an underworld, but enjoys more pleasant connotations, except that mortals abducted into it (**Oisin, True Thomas**) may find that they cannot return from it or, if they do return, find that centuries have passed and that their families and everything familiar are long gone.

OURANOS (*See* APHRODITE, CRONUS, GAIA, GREEK MYTH)

Or Uranus, in Greek myth the star-crowned sky, son of **Gaia**, the 'deep-breasted' **Earth Mother**, who took him as her husband and bore the twelve **Titans**, the eldest of whom, **Cronus**, castrated Ouranos and threw the severed genitals into the sea, leading to **Aphrodite**'s birth. Thus castrated, as in Western Asian and **Oceanic** myth, the sky was separated from earth and pushed up on high. Ouranos had no cult in Greece and was said to have passed into oblivion. In due course Cronus himself was deposed by his own son, **Zeus**, as described in **Hesiod**'s *Theogony*. Later the name Uranus was given to the seventh planet from the sun, discovered in 1781 by Sir William Herschel.

OUROBOUROS (*See* OCEAN, PYTHON, SERPENT)

Early Greek cosmology conceived of the world as circled by a never-ending river, the **Titan** Oceanus. The Greek philosopher Heraclitus of Ephesus (*c*.576–*c*.480 BC) said that in the circumference of a **circle** the beginning and the end are a single point. This led to the image of the **serpent** eating its own tail, the cycle of disintegration and reintegration, life and death and rebirth, in **Orphic** cosmology encircling the cosmic **egg**; in Egyptian lore the path of the sun-god. Thus from the Greek *uroboros* ('the one that devours its tail') arose one of the basic mandalas of medieval **alchemy**. 'Ourobouros' is a variant spelling, as used by the English fantasist E.R. Eddison (1882–1945) in his 1922 novel, *The Worm Ourobouros*. In **Norse myth** the serpent of Midgard, or world-serpent, born to **Loki** and flung into the sea by Odin, lies round the world, biting its tail. At **Ragnorak**, when the gods must die, it will emerge from the sea to devour the earth even as the wolf **Fenrir** swallows the sun. **Thor** will slay it, but not before its venom wounds him fatally.

OVID (43 BC–AD 17) (*See* ROMAN MYTH, VIRGIL)

Roman poet. Born Publius Ovidius Naso, he turned to the literary life with great success, enjoying imperial favour. Yet in AD 8 he was exiled to Tomis on the Black Sea, where he died – in part because of the subversive mockery of his *Ars Amatoria*, a treatise on the arts of seduction and intrigue, and also because the emperor Augustus took offence at some indiscretion. In exile he continued to work, yet is best remembered for his *Metamorphoses*, completed the year of his exile. Written (unlike his other work) in hexameters, this poem of fifteen books offers a mythic history, in chronological order, via a series of transformations, from the Creation (chaos into order) to the death and deification of Julius Caesar (the culminating metamorphosis, from civil war to Augustan peace). His supple, broadminded and exuberant style has been criticised as too smooth and lacking the heroic gravity of **Virgil**, whose unfinished epic *The Aeneid* had, on its recent appearance, immediately been hailed as the national Roman epic. Yet Ovid's erotic imagination commended his work to a wide public: no previous poet had portrayed the doings of the gods and goddesses of myth in quite so human (or scandalous) a fashion.

OWL (*See* ATHENE, BLODEUWEDD, GUINEVERE, LILITH)
Bird of the night with haunting cry, thus symbol of darkness and death, yet also (with its large, shining eyes) a symbol of female wisdom, sacred to **Athene** in Greek myth, also to **Minerva, Hecate** and **Persephone**, the last two being goddesses of night or the **underworld**; also in **Native American** lore the bird of wisdom and **divination**. Yet commonly the owl, especially the screech-owl, was feared. The Chinese associated it with evil, crime and death. So did Mexicans, Japanese, Egyptians and Etruscans. **Christian** symbolism associates it with **Satan**: its call is the 'song of death'; it was used to slander Jews rejecting the Light of the Gospel – they were 'owls'.

   Ovid claimed that the screech-owl (*striges*) attacked children by night, tearing their flesh and drinking their **blood**, being descendants of the **Harpies**. They may be real birds or old hags changed into owls by **curse** or **spell**. In *The Golden Ass* of **Apuleius**, the nymphomaniac **witch** Pamphile turns herself into an owl to fly in at the bedroom window of the youth she desires. Shadowy **Lilith**, said to be **Adam**'s first wife and by the Middle Ages regarded as a **demonic succubus** haunting the dreams of lonesome men, was also identified with the owl, which in Scots Gaelic was called 'night hag', or in parts of England Annis, the Blue Hag, who also sucked the blood of children (as 'celebrated' by Milton in *Paradise Lost* and *Comus*).

   For her part in killing her husband **Llew Llaw Gyffes**, the Welsh flower-maid **Blodeuwedd** was turned into an owl, the bird that other birds attack. King **Arthur**'s wife, **Guinevere**, was originally called Gwenhwyfar, the 'White One', associated with the owl and with the dark side of the Celtic Triple Goddess (the Irish **Morrigan**). Like Lilith, both Blodeuwedd and Gwenhwyfar were 'owls' long before their 'crimes' (murder, adultery) were invented (by **Christian** patriarchal propagandists) to justify condemning them. Gwenhwyfar became Guinevere the repentant nun; likewise Black Annis became Agnes the repentant nun: likewise the fate of the **Virgin Mary** and other older **moon**-goddesses who ruled not only fertility but death – all derived from a time when folk knew that death guarantees life.

P

PACHACAMAC/PACHAMAMA (*See* INCA MYTH)

PAGANISM (*See* ELEMENTALS)

Latin *paganus*, 'countryman', gives the term paganism, implying 'heathen' (of the heath or moor) nature-worship, whereby the elements, trees, earth, rivers, sea and sky are perceived as alive, each with their own indwelling spirits or deities. More specifically or negatively, in **Christian** terms a pagan is one who has no religion or who denies Christian beliefs, so being defined as barbarous or unenlightened. Conflict between Christianity and paganism arose not only via the Christian assertion that any belief-system other than Christianity is 'pagan' or 'heathen', but via the doctrine that nature (including human nature) is corrupt and to be corrected (*see* **Fall, Original Sin**). This negative definition offered apparent justification for medieval Church persecution of **witchcraft** and other beliefs.

PAN (*See* DIONYSUS, GREEK MYTH)

Born with the legs, **horns** and beard of a **goat**, often confused with the **satyrs**, the origin of this Greek deity (said to be son of **Hermes**) remains obscure. Above all a god of shepherds, woods and pastures, it is said he haunted the groves of Arcadia, amusing himself by playing on pipes cut from reeds (Pan-pipes, the syrinx) and by inducing in travellers terror without apparent cause (thus the word 'panic'). He chased nymphs, especially Echo, who loved **Narcissus**. He promised the Athenians aid against the Persians if they would worship him. Victorious, they built him a sanctuary on the Acropolis in Athens. His cult spread through Greece; in time he symbolised the universal god. His name means 'everything', 'all'. Yet his death was reported (by Plutarch) in the reign of Roman emperor Tiberius (AD14–37). It is said that sailors on a ship sailing from Greece to Italy (about the time **Christ** was born), becalmed off Paxos, heard a voice from the shore cry out thrice: 'Tell them that great Pan is dead.' Probably what they heard was a ritual seasonal lamentation honouring **Adonis** or **Tammuz**.

Marrying Autononoë, daughter of **Cadmus**, Pan had a son, **Actaeon**, and then fell in love with Eurydice, wife of **Orpheus**. In other parts of Asia Minor he was venerated as **Priapus**. His mother was perhaps **Aphrodite**, his father **Dionysus, Adonis, Hermes**, or even himself. Pan is universal.

It is said that a vision of Pan in the Princes Street Gardens of Edinburgh in the 1960s aided the creation of the **New Age** Findhorn Community, in the north of Scotland.

The twentieth-century image (as created by **J.M. Barrie**) of 'Peter Pan', the boy who never grows up, marked perhaps the nadir of his fortunes. Yet even in *Peter Pan* there is strangeness, if not the original terror or panic.

PANDORA (*See* GREEK MYTH, PROMETHEUS)

PARACELSUS (1493–1541) (*See* **AGRIPPA, ELEMENTALS**)
A legendary Renaissance **alchemist**. Philippus Aureolus Theophrastus Bombastus von Hohenheim called himself Paracelsus, 'Greater than Celsus' – an ancient Roman physician. Arrogant and aggressive, he over-reacted to imagined slights, making enemies everywhere. His name gives us the word 'bombastic'.

Born near Zürich, he studied at Basel and Würzburg, then worked in the Tyrolese silver mines before travelling Europe, in time becoming the chief physician in Basel. Like **Agrippa** seeking the Elixir of Life, he loathed theoretical alchemists for carrying 'golden mountains in their heads before they had put their hands to the fire'. He asserted that the duty of alchemists was to make not gold but healing drugs. Dropping the 'al' from 'chemy', he coined the term 'chemistry', also applying the Arab word for black eye-paint, *al-kohl*, to the spirits of wine ('alcohol'), and making advances in using alcohol bases to extract the oils of healing herbs.[1]

Yet like John Dee and others, he was caught between **magic** and science: thus the mythic aspect of his reputation. Though advising the cleansing of wounds, he used arsenic and mercury in often-fatal 'cures'. Viewing illness as caused by spiritual imbalance, he emphasised that man is the microcosm of nature.

Teaching that each of the four elements has a dual nature – one gross and corporeal, the other subtle and vaporous – he said that two different worlds interwine: that of men, animals, plants and minerals, and the **elemental** kingdom. 'The elementals are not spirits . . . they have flesh, blood and bones; they live and propagate offspring; they eat and talk, act and sleep, etc., and consequently they cannot properly be called "spirits". They are beings occupying a place between men and spirits . . . [though] resembling spirits in the rapidity of their locomotion.'

In this he was in agreement with the Scots minister **Robert Kirk**.

Magic he defined as a 'power that comes direct from God', adding that 'Magic is a Great Hidden Wisdom – Reason is a Great Open Folly.' Certainly he made no effort to be reasonable. At Basel he began by burning the books of Galen and other old masters, claiming they were all less gifted than the hairs of his beard. 'You are nothing but teachers and masters combing lice and scratching,' he told his colleagues. 'You are not worthy that a dog should lift his hind leg against you.'[2] No surprise that, despite his many cures (including the gout of Erasmus), he was expelled. In April 1541 he gained refuge at Salzburg, but died mysteriously five months later. Some say he was poisoned, others that he was pushed from the top of a cliff. Later his tomb was found empty. Rumours of resurrection spread. But in a time when grave-robbery for medical purposes was common, such a famous body would have been worth money for dissection.

1. *The Alchemists*, Ronald Pearsall, Weidenfeld & Nicolson, London, 1976, p.85.
2. *The Occult*, Colin Wilson, Grafton/Collins, London, 1979, p.312.

PARIS (*See* **APHRODITE, GREEK MYTH, HELEN OF TROY**)
Before his birth it was prophesied that this brave, handsome, intelligent son of King Priam of Troy would be the ruin of the land. Yet Priam spared him, sending him away to be fostered by a shepherd. While herding cattle he was called upon by **Hermes** to judge which **Olympian** goddess was fairest: **Athene, Aphrodite** or **Hera**. He rewarded Aphrodite with the apple, and so got Helen as his wife; but the vengeance of Athene and Hera led to the Trojan

War, and to the prophesied destruction of Troy.

Paris is also the name of France's chief city, derived maybe from *Par-Isis*, 'the Grove of **Isis**'. A temple to this Egyptian goddess stood on the banks of the Seine since **pagan** times.

PARNASSUS (*See* GREEK MYTH, MOUNTAINS)

After **Olympus**, the next most holy mountain in **Greek myth**, on the heights of which **Zeus** the sky-god was worshipped. Overlooking the Gulf of Corinth, it was sacred to **Dionysus** and the **Maenads**, and later to **Apollo** and the **Muses**, annual revels being held on one of its peaks. From the slopes of this and other sacred Greek heights gushed prophetic springs and sacred **wells**, and **nymphs** and **satyrs** played, though not always innocently, nor without bloody intention. These were awesome places of **oracle** and **sacrifice**.

PARSEES (*See* ISLAM, ZOROASTER)

From the Indian word for Persian, referring to the only modern survivors of the once-powerful **Zorastrian** community formerly dominating Iran and Iraq. Originally fleeing **Islamic** invasion of Persia in the late seventh century, the Parsees found refuge on the west coast of India, especially in Bombay and throughout Gujerat. As surviving Zoroastrians, in India their beliefs early became coloured by those who gave them asylum and a safe existence. Today numbering some 100,000 they call themselves Zaradushtri, followers of (Old Persian) Zarathustra (the Greek Zoroaster), who still follow the Word of **Ahura Mazda**, god of light, denying **Ahriman**, Spirit of Darkness and Lies. Their belief remains optimistic. They worship only Ahura Mazda, and claim that one day Soshyant, a **virgin**-born saviour, will restore truth on earth. **Fire** (as in the ancient **Aryan** worship of **Agni**) remains prominent in Parsee ritual as a purifying element or symbol, but is not (as Islamic critics claim) worshipped as a god. Ahura Mazda remains the One God of the Parsees.

PARVATI (*See* DEVI, INDIAN MYTH, MATRIKA, SHIVA)

PARZIVAL (*See* HOLY GRAIL, PERCEVAL)

SAINT PATRICK (*c*.373–*c*.463)

Irish patron saint, born in Dumbarton (Scotland) of a Romanised family, aged sixteen he was kidnapped by Irish raiders and enslaved as a herdsman in the north of Ireland. After six years, sustained by his Christian faith and hearing in a dream that the ship of his escape was ready, he fled back to Britain, later visiting Europe. In his spiritual autobiography, the *Confessio*, he tells of a dream in which he was handed a letter headed 'The Voice of the Irish'. As he read it, he heard Irish voices requesting his return. Though doubting his fitness, in time, consecrated bishop, he landed at Strangford Lough. From his initial settlement near Armagh he embarked on his mission. Often at risk of martyrdom, he dealt fairly with those he came to convert and within two centuries of his death had become a mythic figure. It is said he met the dying **Oisin** who, crumbling of sudden old age on his return to Ireland from the **otherworld**, told Patrick his tale; also that he drove the **snakes** of Ireland into the sea; also that he sanctified the shamrock by using its three leaves on one stalk to illustrate the Trinity.

SAINT PAUL (*See* BIBLE, CHRISTIANITY, ORIGINAL SIN)

Born at Tarsus in Cilicia (Turkey), his father a Jewish citizen of Rome, this leading early Christian received the tribal name Saul, also the Roman name

Paul. Studying Judaic law in Jerusalem, he persecuted the Christians. Sent to Damascus to stamp out the fledgling Church, en route he underwent a sudden conversion (Acts ix:3). Now calling himself Paul, he began preaching Jesus as the Son of God. Those he had persecuted understandably doubted his good faith. His preaching in Antioch *c.* AD 43 led the Jerusalem Christian community under James (brother of Jesus) to accuse him of denying **Judaic** law. He promoted Christ as a died-and-reborn god like **Adonis**, **Attis** or **Tammuz**. He spoke of **virgin** birth, miracles, **resurrection** from the dead, and the doctrine of **original sin** – all at odds with **Judaism**. He began to preach to Jews and Gentiles abroad. Writing to his congregations (AD 50–58), he denounced his Jerusalem opponents, like James and **Peter** who had known Jesus, as he had not, insisting he was not a liar (suggesting that many said he was). In AD 58 his return to Jerusalem caused a riot (Acts xxi:28). His lynching by angry Jews (Zealots?) was prevented by the Romans. Under arrest, he was escorted to Caesarea. Jewish leaders demanded his death but, invoking his Roman citizenship, he demanded to be heard in Rome, where after AD 60 he was imprisoned for two years before his trial. He may have died a martyr under Nero, but this is as unclear as the date of his death.

The account of his life and work by the unknown author of Acts remains perplexing. Why did the Romans rescue a man who exalted a 'criminal' whom they had executed? Why did the Jews hate him so fiercely? There are clues. The Dead Sea Scrolls found in 1947 suggest that Jesus sought to restore Judaic law and authority in Palestine. Was Paul the 'Liar' described in the Scrolls? Was he the outsider who, admitted to the community of the 'Teacher of Righteousness', turned renegade, 'flouted the Law', 'led many astray', and founded his own congregations on 'deceit'? Is this why in his Epistles he insists he is not a liar? Whatever the truth, his supernatural myth of Christ was crucial to the growth of 'Christianity', being ratified at the Council of Nicaea (AD 325) and leading to dogmas that survive today.[1]

1. *The Dead Sea Scrolls*, Michael Baigent and Richard Leigh, Corgi, London, 1992.

PEACOCK (*See* PHOENIX)
This gorgeous bird with its 'hundred eyed' tail is widely associated with love and the stars in the sky. Its restless spiral dance before rainfall associates it with storm. In **Christian myth** its renewal of its plumage associates it with **immortality** and **resurrection**. Associated by Romans with the goddess **Juno**, earlier it was an attribute of the Greek god **Pan**, who gave it up to **Hera**, who scattered its hundred starry eyes over its tail. An emblem of the Chinese Ming dynasty, in **Indian myth** it is sometimes the mount of **Brahma**, **Lakshmi**, or of **Kama**, god of love. It is also the emblem of **Sarasvati**, Indian goddess of wisdom, music and poetry. Its association with worldly pride and vanity is more recent. It also denotes royalty, as in the 'Peacock Throne' of the Shahs of Persia.

PEARL
Once thought to be the product of lightning penetrating the oyster, widely prized as a gem, it was anciently regarded as a union of **fire** and **water**, both fertilising forces, thus denoting birth and rebirth. As a crystallization of light in the East it represents the Third Eye of **Shiva** and of **Buddha**, implying spiritual wisdom or enlightenment. **Aphrodite** is the 'Lady of the Pearls'; in **Christian** symbol, Christ is the 'Pearl of Great Price', the gaining of whom

involves diving into the uncharted waters of baptism. In China it is associated with the **moon**, swallowed by the cosmic **dragon**, and also, more widely, with the spiritual essence of the cosmos. It also symbolises innocence, purity, virginity and secrecy.

PEGASUS (*See* BELLEROPHON, HORSE, MEDUSA)

PELE (*See* FIRE, HAWAII, MOUNTAINS)

PELLES (*See* ARTHURIAN MYTH, FISHER KING, HOLY GRAIL, PERCEVAL)

PERCEVAL (*See* ARTHURIAN MYTH, FOOL, GALAHAD, HOLY GRAIL)

Also Perlesvaus, Peredur or Parzival. Tales of this **Arthurian** knight and **Grail**-seeker are as various as his names. He appears first in the Welsh tale 'Peredur Son of Efrawg' (*see Mabinogion*), then *c*.1180 in *Le Roman de Perceval* (*Le Conte del Graal*) by Chrétien de Troyes. In both tales he is reared by his mother deep in a Welsh forest, his father having rejected the world after (*see* **Fisher King**) being wounded through the thighs. His mother has kept him ignorant of sex, society, chivalry, **Christ** and even of his own name. Though comically naive, he is handsome, sturdy and cheerful.

One day meeting five of Arthur's shining knights, he concludes they are **angels**. They explain who they really are; he decides to follow them, and at Arthur's court he tries to prove himself. Yet, though a brave fighter, he is so simple that many call him a 'pure **fool**'. He is knighted by a lord, Gornemant, who tells him to learn to hold his tongue. Returning to his mother, a crippled fisherman invites him to his castle for the night, he gives him a sword, then confronts him with mysteries: a young man carrying a lance down which runs a drop of **blood**; two more young men carrying golden candelabra, with them a lovely girl holding a shining golden grail; then another maiden carrying a silver dish. Though curious, he is so shy that, recalling Gornemant's advice, he asks no questions. Awakening next day to find himself alone in the empty castle, he rides off, but in the forest meets a girl cradling her lover's corpse. She tells him he had slept in the Grail Castle, that the fisherman was the **Fisher King**, and that by not asking the correct questions ('Why does the lance bleed? Whom does the Grail serve?') he has failed to heal the Fisher King, so dooming the land to continued sterility and himself to misfortune. Yet now at last he recalls his name: Perceval of Wales.

He is welcomed at Arthur's court, but a crone on a mule bursts in and berates him for his failure at the Fisher King's castle. Much misery must result. He vows never to spend two nights in the same place, nor to shirk any danger until he learns why the lance bleeds and whom the Grail serves. Five years later, no closer to solving the mystery, having never entered a church nor thought of God, he meets a hermit, his mother's brother, who explains that all his woes arise from the grief he caused his mother, which killed her. There, Chrétien's tale breaks off unfinished.

In the *Perlesvaus* (1206–12), he is son of a king who has lost his lands ('perd les vals' – 'lost the valleys'). Here, his crime in not asking the question occurs before the tale begins. The land is waste, Perceval ill, and King Arthur deserted by his knights. The Fisher King dies, his castle is seized by his brother, King of Castle Mortal – lord of sin and death. Insisting that he is the true heir, Perceval visits another of his mother's brothers, King Pelles, with whose help he storms and takes the Grail Castle. The Grail reappears and, once Arthur introduces it into the rite of Mass, prosperity is at last restored. So Perlesvaus becomes Grail King himself.

As *Parzival*, by Wolfram von Eschenbach (same period), on restoring the Grail he is incorporated as Grail guardian into the Templeisen (Knights of the Grail). Members of this family, preserving a blood-link with Christ, serve the Grail. Both the *Perlesvaus* and *Parzival* imply that the **Knights Templar** were involved in this esoteric duty. In both texts the hero is son of the Fisher King's sister with hereditary right to Grail kingship. There is no **wasteland** in *Parzival*; the question he must ask is not: 'Whom does the Grail serve?' but 'Sir, why do you suffer so?' – meaning that he has learned not just humility but compassion.[1]

In later Grail-myth, Perceval's role as chief Grail-knight is taken over by the much too perfect and altogether less attractive **Galahad**.

1. *King Arthur and the Grail*, Richard Cavendish, Paladin, London, 1980.

PERRAULT, CHARLES (1628–1703) (*See* ANDERSEN, FAIRY-TALES, GRIMM)

French poet and storyteller, born in Paris and admitted to the Académie Française in 1761, remembered for his collection of fairy-tales, *Contes de Ma Mère l'Oye* (1697; published in English as *Tales of Mother Goose*, 1729). His rescue and simple recitation of (even then) almost forgotten tales like 'Little Red Riding-Hood', **'Sleeping Beauty'**, 'Puss in Boots', **'Bluebeard'** and **'Cinderella'** makes him a worthy precursor of the Brothers **Grimm** and **Hans Christian Andersen**. Yet he held 'modern' literature superior to anything produced formerly: in his view, Molière and Malherbe were greater than **Apuleius, Homer** or **Virgil**. A lawyer by training, his fairy-tales were written to amuse his children. They stand the test of time, still amusing children of all ages, especially through modern interpretations by **Cocteau** and **Disney**.

PERSEPHONE (*See* DEMETER, ELEUSIS, GREEK MYTH, HADES, UNDERWORLD)

Queen of the Greek underworld, the original name of this goddess of death and regeneration (her Roman equivalent Proserpine), is Kore. Daughter of **Zeus**, with her mother Demeter Kore lived on earth until one day, playing with the daughters of **Oceanus**, she bent to pick a **narcissus**. The earth opened, Hades burst out and snatched her down to his realm. Enraged that Zeus had consented to this crime, Demeter inflicted death, sterility and drought on the world, so that Zeus demanded that Hades give Kore up unless by word or deed she had consented to the abduction. As she had eaten a pomegranate seed (fertility symbol) at Hades' behest, it was ruled that henceforth she must spend four months (winter) of each year with Hades and eight (spring to autumn) with her mother. So she took the name Persephone: 'She who Destroys the Light', or perhaps 'Dazzling Brilliance'.

Though faithful to Hades (despite her passion for **Adonis**), she had no children by him, preferring the company of **Hecate**, queen of witches. Yet **Orphic** initiates made out that she had mothered **Dionysus**. As Kore, 'the maiden', she and her mother Demeter are in origin one and the same, a corn-goddess whose cult lay at the heart of the **Mysteries** of **Eleusis**.

PERSEUS (*See* GREEK MYTH, MEDUSA)

Greek hero, grandson of King Acrisius who, told at **Delphi** he would have no sons yet that his grandson would kill him, imprisoned his daughter Danaë (as in **Irish myth Balor** imprisons Eithne) in a dungeon guarded by savage dogs.

Yet **Zeus** came to her as a shower of gold and she bore a son, Perseus ('Destroyer of Light' or 'Brilliance': *see* **Persephone**). Acrisius believed the true father to be his hated **twin** brother Proetus, who had once seduced Danaë. Fearing the wrath of Zeus if he killed mother and child, he set both afloat at sea in a chest (*see* **Dionysus**). Washed ashore at Seriphos, they were protected by King Polydectes who, as Perseus grew up, wished to marry Danaë. Perseus made a bargain: if he slew the hideous Medusa, Polydectes would leave Danaë alone. The goddess **Athene** helped him to succeed. Carrying the deadly **head**, Perseus flew back from **Hyperborea** on **Hermes'** winged sandals. Denied hospitality by the **Titan Atlas**, he showed the head. Atlas, petrified, became Mount Atlas. Continuing to Egypt, the hero rested on the Nilotic isle of Chemmis (where **Isis** bore **Horus**). Then, flying up the Phoenician coast, he saw a beautiful naked woman chained to a rock under a sea-cliff and immediately fell in love with her.

She was Andromeda, daughter of Cepheus and Cassiopeia, whose boast that she and Andromeda were lovelier than the **Nereids** had so enraged **Poseidon** that the sea-god had sent a **flood** to drown the land and a sea-monster to devour its people. The Oracle of Ammon (*see* **Amon**) said the only solution was to sacrifice Andromeda to the monster. Petrifying the beast with the Gorgon's head, Perseus married Andromeda, but the king and queen summoned another suitor (Agenor) with his army. Perseus petrified them all, set Cepheus and Cassiopeia in the sky as constellations, then back at Seriphos found Danaë besieged by Polydectes, to whom (with all his men) he showed the head: they became a circle of rocks. Then with Andromeda he went back to Argos. Acrisius fled, but one day, unknown to each other, both were at funeral games at Larissa. Perseus threw a discus which, carried by the wind, killed Acrisius, so fulfilling the prophecy. Ashamed to rule in Argos, he took the throne of Tiryns, founding Mycenae (*mycos*, 'mushroom') and the Perseids, a family which later bore **Hercules**. The constellations of Perseus and Andromeda now stand hard by those of Cassiopeia and Cepheus.

Many myths intertwine here. The rivalry between royal twins (Acrisius and Proetus) speaks of a time when sacrificial kings (slain at midsummer) and their tanists ('brothers': slain at midwinter) altered the system to their own advantage, each in turn ruling, neither threatened with sacred slaughter, yet each still at war to possess the **moon**-priestess (Danaë), without whom royal legitimacy was impossible. Perseus and **Bellerophon** are related – one slays the Medusa aided by winged sandals, the other slays the **Chimera**, aided by **Pegasus** the winged **horse**. Both myths suggest the new 'winged' power of reason, defeating the older, instinctual power of the moon-cults. The sea-monster is Babylonian **Tiamat**, the watery she-**dragon** 'slain' by solar **Marduk**; Andromeda may be Phoenician **Astarte**.[1]

1. *The Greek Myths*, Robert Graves, Penguin, London, 1960.

PERSIAN MYTH (*See* CONCORDANCE)

With the Caspian Sea to the north, Persian Gulf to the south, Mesopotamia to the west and India to the east, the Persian plateau forms a gateway between east and west. Persia is the Greek name for Iran. Iran is Aria, 'home of the **Aryans**', horse-riding nomads who *c*.1700 BC settled the land. 'Persians' were but one of many Aryan tribes, first mentioned 837 BC in connection with an expedition of the **Assyrian** king Shalmaneser III.

Before the rise of **Zoroastrianism** (seventh century BC), the Aryans of Iran and of India shared common language and pantheon. Grammar and vocabulary in the Gathas (earliest part of the Iranian *Zend Avesta*, or sacred books), closely matches the **Sanskrit** of the *Rig Veda*. Indian Mitra and Persian **Mithra** are much the same; Indian **Agni's fire**-cult was in Persia that of **Atar**, fire personified, who became **Ahura Mazda**, Zoroastrian 'Wise Lord' (**Asura** in the Vedas). The **haoma** of the *Zend-Avesta* is the Vedic **soma**: an intoxicant said to heighten spirituality. Yet where Vedic belief grew into distinct Indian forms (**Brahmanism, Hinduism**), by the eighth century BC Iran had fallen to **Ashur**-worshipping Assyrians. About this time Iranian gods (Ahuras) became Indian **demons** (Asuras). Likewise Indian Devas (gods, 'shining ones') became Iranian **devils**.

Other early Iranian gods were heavenly bodies: Hvare-Khshaeta the **sun**; Mah the **moon**; Anahita, Venus; Tishtriya, Sirius the Dog-Star. Yet Ahura Mazda eclipsed them all. This followed Median-**Babylonian** destruction of Assyria (605 BC), the rise of the Persian empire under Cyrus the Great (sixth century BC), and of Zoroastrianism, which became official only with the advent of the Sassanian dynasty (AD 224–651). During the intervening eight centuries other religions held sway, especially Mithraism.

Zoroastrianism endured until the **Islamic** conquest of Persia in the mid-seventh century AD: a splinter-group (**Parsees**, 'Persians'), fleeing to Gujerat (India) and surviving there still. Under Islam original thought for a time suffered, but the later growth of **Sufism** helped impart a typically Persian quality to Islamic belief, especially in the works of the great poets, who include **Omar Khayyam**, Hafiz (*d*. AD 1398) and **Jalaludin Rumi**, and also in the subtle teaching tales attributed to the mythical Mullah **Nasruddin**.

SAINT PETER (d.*c*.AD 64) (*See* **CHRISTIANITY, SAINT PAUL**)
Simeon (Greek Simon), Christ's first apostle and by Christ surnamed Peter (Latin *Petra*, Greek *Cephas*, Aramaic *Kepha*, a 'rock'). On this rock, Christ said, he would build his church. Peter would hold the keys of the kingdom of **heaven**. A fisherman on the Sea of Galilee, with Andrew his brother and James and John, sons of Zebedee, he obeyed Christ's call to, 'Follow me, and I will make you fishers of men' (Matthew iii:19). The Gospels portray him as loyal yet impetuous. He denied Christ in the Garden of Gethsemane but later (with James, brother of Jesus) led the early Christian community. Leaving Jerusalem after being imprisoned by Herod, he became a missionary, effecting miracle cures in Christ's name, like St **Paul** breaching **Judaic** law by eating with Gentiles. This led to a compromise (Galatians ii:7–8): Paul preaching to the Gentiles; Peter to the Jews. Legend tells how in Rome he defeated Simon Magus (*see* **Gnostic Myth**) in magical contest, casting him down from the sky with a prayer. By the end of the first century it was said he died in Rome *c*.AD 62. John xxi:18–19 alludes prophetically to his death: one tale says he lived in Rome thirty years, was martyred and buried near the Vatican. Later he was recognised as the first Roman Catholic Pope, Father of the Church, and founder of the 'Apostolic Succession'.

PETER PAN (*See* **BARRIE, NEVERLAND, PAN**)

PHAETHON (*See* **APOLLO, GREEK MYTH, HELIOS, HYPERION, SUN**)
Ancient Greek sun-god, son of Helios..His divinity doubted by a rival, he begged Helios to let him prove it. Helios agreed, swearing by the **Styx** (an irrevocable oath) and Phaethon insisted on driving the sun's chariot for a day. Appalled, but oath-bound, Helios gave over the reins of the sun's wild **horses** to Phaethon, who lost control of them, so that they seared the earth. Rivers dried up and the Sahara Desert was created. **Zeus** struck Phaethon with a

thunderbolt and the luckless youth fell into the River Eridanus (Po). Buried by the **nymphs**, the Heliads (his sisters) mourned by his tomb and were turned into poplar trees.

In **Plato**'s *Timaeus* it is said this tale refers to a periodic variation in the course of the heavenly bodies causing fiery destruction on earth. It may also imply **sacrificial** rites held in Thrace and Corinth, whereby the sacred king (Helios) pretended to die at sunset of the shortest day. A day later the victim set in his place would be dragged by mad horses behind a (sun)-chariot (*phaëton*) to his death. The wily old king would reappear to continue his rule . . . until the rite was repeated a year later.

PHANTOM HITCH-HIKERS (*See* MEN IN BLACK, UFOs)

A modern myth. Motorists pick up hitch-hikers who offer prophetic messages then vanish en route. As with Men in Black, there is rarely a witness of such encounters. Most appear to fit the old pattern of lonely travellers, exhausted or despairing, who generate imaginary or visionary companions.

Of his historic thirty-four-hour solo Atlantic flight in 1927, Charles Lindbergh later wrote how he fought to stay awake. In mid-Atlantic, he fell asleep, and a new 'extraordinary mind' thereafter flew the plane. In this state, with his skull become 'one great eye, seeing everywhere at once', he sensed the fuselage behind him crowded with ghostly human presences, appearing and disappearing at will, passing through the walls of the plane, advising him with messages from beyond his walls of bone, bringing up 'old associations, bygone friendships, voices from ancestrally distant times.'[1]

Solo Everest climbers and Arctic explorers also report ancestral voices or spirits accompanying them. Typically, the visitant delivers a message, then vanishes. **Angels** (messengers) act similarly in mythic tradition, as do gods, **demons**, or **trickster** spirits delivering messages (true or false) from the unconscious. The hitch-hiker is often said to be Christ promising the **Second Coming**, or a UFO entity threatening global disaster.[2]

1. *Reincarnation: The Phoenix Fire Mystery*, S.L. Cranston and Joseph Head, Julian Press, New York, 1977, pp.390–1.
2. *The Evidence for Phantom Hitch-Hikers*, Michael Goss, Aquarian Press, Wellingborough, 1984.

PHILADELPHIA EXPERIMENT (*See* ROSWELL INCIDENT, UFOs)

Another modern myth – of Project Rainbow, an odd experiment in 'electronic camouflage' allegedly undertaken in October 1943 by the US Office of Naval Research at the Philadelphia Naval Yard, and conducted on a destroyer, the USS *Eldridge*. The purpose was to render ship and crew invisible within an electromagnetic 'force field' by applying Einstein's Unified Field Theory.

Allegedly the *Eldridge* vanished, appeared in the harbour at Norfolk, Virginia, then rematerialised at Philadelphia. Not just invisibility but teleportation had been achieved. Many of the crew reportedly went mad, fell ill and died, burst into flames, walked through walls or vanished.

The evidence? In 1956 UFOlogist Morris K. Jessup received two letters from a man calling himself Carl M. Allen or Carlos Miguel Allende, claiming that, crewing the SS *Andrew Furuseth* out of Norfolk, he had seen it occur and knew the fate of the *Eldridge's* crew. Allende remains a mystery: Jessup committed suicide in 1959. Allende's main evidence was a newspaper article he said he read in 1943. Berlitz and Moore claim to own a photocopy of it.[1]

Received anonymously, it is undated and the newspaper unidentified. Under the headline 'Strange Circumstances Surround Tavern Brawl', it tells how the Philadelphia police, answering a call from the Navy Shore Patrol to break up a bar fight, arrived to find the bar empty. Two frightened waitresses said the Shore Patrol had already cleared the bar, but not before two of the sailors involved 'just sort of vanished into thin air . . . right there', as one of the waitresses claimed.

This story has survived half a century, but Einstein, said to have been party to this test of his theories, is no longer available for questioning.

1. *The Philadelphia Mystery*, Charles Berlitz and William Moore, Granada, London, 1980.

PHILOSOPHER'S STONE (*See* HOLY GRAIL, JEWELS, PERCEVAL, STONE)

In the alchemical Great Work, a potent, mysterious catalyst said to turn whatever it touched to **gold**, cure all ills and confer youth eternal; also a spiritual process whereby 'lead' (base animal **soul**) is transmuted into 'gold' (enlightened consciousness).

The quest for it, instrumental in the growth of modern science and philosophy, may have originated in Egypt and may be connected with the Emerald Tablet of **Hermes Trismegistus**. The core statement of this perhaps **Gnostic** text is: 'That which is above is like that which is below'. In *Parzival* (*c*.1195–1216), Wolfram von Eschenbach describes the Holy Grail not as a cup but as 'a stone of the purest kind . . . called *lapsit exillas*', a meaningless phrase recalling a myth of **Alexander the Great**, sent the *lapis exilis* ('paltry stone') from the Earthly Paradise. Resembling a human eye, heavier than any amount of gold, if dust was sprinkled on it, it became lighter than a feather. It taught Alexander humility, a virtue Perceval also had to acquire. The 'paltry stone' also had **Christian** significance as 'the stone which the builders rejected'. Wolfram may have meant *lapsis lapsus ex caelis*, 'the stone fallen from heaven'. Elsewhere in *Parzival* he says this stone was a jewel, an emerald fallen from Lucifer's brow during the war in heaven, and brought to earth by neutral **angels**. Some link this with the **pearl** in the brow of the Indian god **Shiva**, representing his Third Eye of inner wisdom. Without the emerald, Lucifer must inhabit the earth as a manifestation of evil: the stone itself can be redeemed only in the act of healing performed by the Grail-knight.

Other associations are with the stone vomited out by **Cronus** when **Gaia** tricked him into swallowing it in place of his infant son **Zeus**: this fell from **heaven** to the sacred Mount Helicon in Greece. Again, the Black Stone in the Kaaba at Mecca, sacred to **Islam**, is said to have been a meteorite, fallen out of the sky, while Thomas Aquinas (*c*.1226–74) says that the stone is an allegory for the soul of the **Virgin Mary**, rightly called 'the stone of chastity' – which brings us back to Wolfram's 'pure stone', generally accepted as referring to the *lapis philosophorum*, or Philosopher's Stone.

About the same time as Wolfram, the alchemist Arnold of Villanova wrote, 'Hic lapis exilis extat precio quoque vilis/ Spernitur a stultis, amatur plus ab edoctis' ('This insignificant stone is indeed of trifling value/ It is despised by fools, the more cherished by the wise.'[1]

1. *The Grail*, John Matthews, Thames & Hudson, London, 1981, pp.17–19.

PHOEBUS (*See* APOLLO, GREEK MYTH)

PHOENICIAN MYTH (See CONCORDANCE)

Semites from the Persian Gulf who settled the eastern Mediterranean coast from the river Orontes (north) to Jaffa (south), the sea-faring Phoenicians named themselves Canaanites, after a dye-producing shellfish. Their cities were Sidon and Tyre, the latter long under Egyptian rule, later independent under **Hiram Abiff**, builder of **Solomon**'s Temple (*c*.955 BC). Conquests by Assyrians, Babylonians, **Alexander the Great** and Romans led their trading empire to fall to the Greeks and to their own colony of Carthage on the North African coast. The Romans coined the name Phoenician (*Poeni*) to distinguish Canaan from Carthage (into **Christian** times Carthaginians called themselves Canaanite). By then the names and characteristics of Phoenician deities were so widespread that Philo of Byblos claimed (in his *Cosmogony*: first century AD) that all Greek myth was Phoenician in origin.

The oldest Canaanite seals, found at Byblos (Lebanon), dated *c*.3000 BC, show the chief deity, Ba'alat (the 'Lady') with **hair** dressed in the Egyptian style and crowned by a disc set between two **horns**, like Egyptian **Hathor**, with whom later she was identified. Her consort was identified with **Ra**, the Egyptian **sun**-god, being called 'Ra, of Foreign Lands'. Their son, the **lion**-headed god of Byblos, had an Egyptian name, Ruti ('He who resembles a lion'). A fourth deity, Hay-Tau of Nega, was a forest-spirit, prototype of Adonis. Said to have become a **tree**, the Egyptians identified him with **Osiris** (perhaps why, when slain and set adrift by **Set**, the body of Osiris was said to have landed at Byblos, to become a tamarisk tree).

Cuneiform tablets found in 1929 at Ras Shamrah (fourteenth century BC) reveal a fertility cult, its chief god El, a name found in the names of foreign deities (*Elohim*) and nature spirits (**elves**). So too the name of his son **Baal** ('Lord') is found from Babylonia (**Bel-Marduk**) to Britain (**Belinus**). The epithet Baal hid or prefixed the true names (not to be spoken, as with Hebrew **Yahweh**) of local fertility gods: Hadad the storm-god, Baal Tsaphon (Lord of the North), Baal-Hammon, god of Carthage, where the great goddess was Tanit, 'face of Baal'. Also Carthaginian was the pot-bellied **dwarf**-god Bes, his bow-legged image set in the prows of ships. Also a statue of **Moloch** (perhaps from *Melqart*: 'king') was worshipped in Hiram's Tyre, and associated with the propitiatory sacrificial death by fire of children.

Baal's mother Asherat-of-the-Sea (said to have borne seventy children) appeared as Anat, 'Lady of the Mountain', later (as Baal's sister-wife) as Ashtaroth (Astarte: thus, Greek **Aphrodite**). His brother Mot, a desert-spirit, parallels Egyptian **Set** (*see* **Baal**). The texts tell how annually, Mot being slain, Baal's son Aleyin ruled, and the rains fell. Aleyin is also a 'Baal'. There is no clear distinction between these deities: each conjoin or oppose aspects of the others, as do the seasons (*see* **Adonis**).

PHOENIX (See FABULOUS BEASTS, QUETZALCOATL, ROC, SIMURGH)

Every 500 years, claimed Egyptian myth, this unique Arabian bird built a nest of myrrh then died, its decaying flesh producing a worm which sprouted feathers. Carrying its parent's bones in a ball of myrrh to the temple of **Ra** at Heliopolis, the new phoenix then returned to Arabia. Identified with the Benu Bird (an aspect of Ra), its myth was elaborated by Greek **Mystery** initiates as a standard measure of the motion of the heavenly bodies, also by medieval alchemists as a symbol of **immortality** and transmutation. Pliny claimed that multiples of its lifespan symbolise the Great Year, given by Tacitus as 12,994 common years. Chinese

peacock, Persian roc and Mayan quetzal-bird share the symbolism. Sacred to the sun, portrayed as **eagle**-like on a nest of flaming incense, by the fourth century AD it was celebrated as consuming itself in flame then rising from its ashes the third day after its death (as did Christ). The 'eagle' on the Great Seal of the USA (a compendium of **Masonic** symbols) is in origin a phoenix.

PIED PIPER (See **BEATLES, ORPHEUS**)

Medieval German tale describing how the wealthy trading city of Hamelin was swamped by rats enjoying the full granaries and storehouses. One day a man in a pied (patchwork) cloak appeared at the Town Hall, declaring himself a rat-catcher. Demanding a thousand gold crowns to get rid of the rats, next day he walked the streets, playing a haunting melody on his pipe. The rats followed him to the sea, where they all drowned. But when he asked for his thousand gold crowns, Hamelin's governors dismissed him with only a hundred gold coins, jeering at his talk of revenge. But when next night he returned and again played his tune, this time it was not rats that followed him, but the children of Hamelin. He led them into the sea, where they all drowned, himself too. Another version says he led them to a hill, in which a door opened up, only to close as the last child vanished inside: a **fairy** hill?

The tale reminds of how **Orpheus** charmed all who heard his music.

PIG (See **CORN-GODS**)

Symbolises fertility and prosperity, also gluttony, ignorance and all that is unclean. The wild boar, a natural war symbol, was respected, feared and hunted by all early societies. In Indian myth, the boar Varáha was an incarnation of **Brahma** later of **Vishnu**. In Egypt, malefic **Set** was depicted as a boar; in **Celtic** Britain the boar was regarded as the **Devil**. The Canaanite vegetation-god **Adonis**, like Phrygian **Attis**, was annually gored to death by a wild boar; each god may once have been identified as a boar. The sow, associated with **mother-goddesses**, death and the **underworld**, was sacred to the Egyptian **Isis** and Babylonian **Tiamat**. In Tibetan **Buddhism**, Vajtavarahi, the Queen of Heaven, is the Diamond or Adamantine Sow. Epitomising the **corn**-spirit in Europe, in Rome sows were sacrificed to **Ceres** (corn-goddess) and to **Mars** as god of agriculture. Greek **Zeus** was said to have been suckled by a sow: sows were sacrificed to **Demeter**, being thrown into 'the chasms of Demeter and **Persephone**', after the myth that, when **Hades** kidnapped Persephone, a herd of pigs plunged into the chasm down which the pair vanished. Demeter-Persephone was once a sow, like Welsh **Cerridwen**, the 'Old White Sow'.

The underworld connection is emphasised by the name of the Greek 'Old Man of the Sea', Phorcys, reputedly father of the Gorgon **Medusa**. This is a masculine form of Phorcis, corpse-eating sow-goddess. This name appears in Latin as Orcus, a title of Hades, and as *porcus*, 'hog'. Orc is 'pig' in Irish, thus the Orcades, or Orkneys, abode of the death-goddess.

To eat pork (flesh of pig), is **taboo** to **Jews** and Muslims. In Egypt (where even to touch a pig was said to cause leprosy) the taboo was broken only at the midwinter feast of the Boar's Head. A similar taboo survived until recently in Wales and Scotland. Yet Celtic Gauls, Indian **Aryans**, Greeks and Teutons all ate pork. Roast pig is eaten in **Valhalla**, and at Bricriu's Feast (*see* **Irish Myth**). Every *bruidhen* (**otherworld** hostel) served pork, the pigs (sacred to **Manannan** as to Phorcys) being killed and eaten then, magically reborn, killed and eaten again.

Supernatural boars abound in Celtic lore, as in the *Mabinogion* tale of Culhwch and Olwen, in which Twrch Trwyth is an evil king transformed into a giant boar. So too in *The Odyssey* the witch **Circe** (daughter of **Hecate**, the death-goddess) transforms Odysseus's men into pigs. In **Christian** myth the pig, associated with **Satan** and with sensuality, is the emblem of St Anthony, who overcame the **demon** of gluttony and is famously associated with the unfortunate Gadarene swine which, possessed by the devils cast into them by Jesus, went charging over a cliff to their doom. This use of pigs as a decoy for demons is also reported elsewhere.

PIXIES (*See* ANCESTOR-WORSHIP, BROWNIES, DOMOVOI, DWARVES, ELVES, FAIRIES)

Elemental or fairy spirits of British folklore, usually represented as dwarf- or elf-like. The unclear etymology suggests the medieval Pech or Pecht, which may imply the Picts, a highland Scottish people conquered and absorbed by invading Ulster Gaels (Scots) by the ninth century AD.

Little is known of the Picts save via missionary **Christian** myth (*see* **Columba**). That they left no record but carved standing stones ('symbol stones'), has led to much romantic speculation. Can pixies be euhemerised as Picts? The tale of the last Pecht dying rather than tell the secret of 'heather ale' (whisky, *usquebaugh*, the 'water of life'?) is also found in the **Norse** Volsunga Saga and the German *Nibelungenlied*. So too the tale of the breaking by this last Pecht of a bar of iron (an arm?) is also found in Greece, though there connected with the Drakos (**dragon**) or the one-eyed **Cyclopes**. The legend that Pechts built Glasgow Cathedral (twelfth century) parallels the Greek myth that the Cyclopes built Mycenae.

Perhaps such mythic races are a composite of distorted memory, poetic invention and fearful propitiatory reverence based on a guilty dread of the slain former race, now become the fairy-folk, inhabiting ancestral grave mounds (*see* **Earth Mounds**).

PLANETS (*See* ASTRONOMY AND MYTH, JUPITER, MARS, MERCURY, MOON, NEPTUNE, OURANOS/URANUS, SATURN, VENUS)

PLATO (*c*.427–347 BC) (*See* ATLANTIS, GREEK MYTH (2))

'Out of Plato come all things that are still written and debated among men of thought', wrote the transcendentalist Ralph Waldo Emerson (1803–82). With **Socrates** and Aristotle one of the great shapers of Western intellectual traditions, he was born of an Athenian political family but, revolted by political corruption and by the execution of his teacher Socrates in 399, he sought a cure for human ills in philosophy instead. Concluding that no society could ever prosper were its rulers not also philosophers ('lovers of wisdom'), on return to Athens *c*.388 after ten years of travelling, he founded the Academy, prototype of all later Western universities, to train such philosophers. Aristotle (*c*.384–322 BC) was an early graduate.

His persisting influence is due not only to the survival of so many of his writings, but also to the dramatic form in which he cast them, as dialogues dominated by the figure of Socrates, to whom Plato attributed his wisdom. In the later ones (in which the **Atlantis** myth is introduced), the speculative interest is paramount. Using farce to satirise Sophist quibbling he is equally able to deal with the most elevated themes of human yearning for a life, love and existence beyond the senses. Yet the greatest dialogue is *The Republic*, a discussion in ten books of the nature and organisation of human society, in it the famous allegory of men who, shut in a cave with no sight of the sun, mistake the shadows flickering on the wall of the cave for sunlight (reality) itself.

He taught the **immortality** and **reincarnation** of the **soul** (for a fuller account see **Greek Myth (2)**), and in this context, in the *Phaedrus*, retails the myth of **Er**, a warrior apparently killed in battle who, with his body about to be cremated twelve days later, returns to life to describe his otherworldly experiences.

Adapted by the **Neoplatonists** of Alexandria during the early Christian era, Plato's teachings (rediscovered and translated into Latin by the Italian scholar Marsilio Ficino) profoundly influenced the growth of the Italian Renaissance, following centuries of medieval scholasticism dominated by the teachings of his more pragmatic pupil, Aristotle.

PLEIADES (*See* ASTRONOMY AND MYTH, GREEK MYTH)

A prominent star cluster located in the constellation Taurus (the **Bull**), known (seven of its approximately 250 stars being visible to the naked eye) as the Seven Sisters. The name Pleiades comes from a Greek root, *plei*, 'to sail'. The tale is that they were **nymphs**, virgin daughters of the **Titan Atlas**, and sisters of the Hyades and **Hesperides**, pursued so strenuously by the hunter **Orion** that the gods first changed them into **doves**, then set their images among the stars. Yet (it is said) three of them had already slept with **Zeus**, two with **Poseidon** and one with **Ares**, while the seventh (Merope) married **Sisyphus** of Corinth, a mere mortal, and subsequently (at least in Greek myth) vanished from the sky, leaving only six sisters. (Did the eruption of Santorini *c*.1470 BC so obscure the sky that only six Pleiads were left visible?) Their heliacal rising in May marked the start of the Greek navigational year; their setting its end.

Other cultures, from Australia to North America, have also seen Seven Sisters in this lovely cluster, which in fact is a 'stellar nursery' of young stars, some only two million years old – mere nymphs, indeed.

PLOTINUS (*c*.AD 204–*c*.269) (*See* NEOPLATONISM)

Egyptian by birth but probably of Roman descent, this great philosopher of the Alexandrian Neoplatonic school (and perhaps founder of it) in his philosophy held that the **soul** is the one source of knowledge, that the nature of deity may be grasped by intuition alone and that this absolute godhood is the sole productive cause of all existence. From primal deity emanates universal spirit (nous), from which develops the practical or individual soul, able to fend for itself amid the trials of its incarnation in the lowest principle, matter. Insisting too on the existence of divine providence and of free will, he stressed that it is the use of intellect that leads to truth, so that his followers inclined more to meditative trance than to observation of nature. The chief work by which he remains known, *The Enneads*, was arranged by his pupil Porphyry:

'Every man has his place, a place that fits the good man, a place that fits the bad: each . . . makes his way, naturally, reasonably, to the place, good or bad, that suits him, and takes the position he has made his own. There he talks and acts, in blasphemy and crime or in all goodness: for the actors bring to this play what they were before it was ever staged . . .'[1]

1. Selection from *The Enneads*, Plotinus (trans. Stephen MacKenna).

PLUTO (*See* HADES, ROMAN MYTH, UNDERWORLD)

POE, EDGAR ALLAN (1809–49) (*See* **LOVECRAFT, SCIENCE FICTION**)

Boston-born, this American author published many poems ('The Raven', 'The Bells', 'Annabel Lee') and short stories or novellas (*The Fall of the House of Usher*, *The Murders in the Rue Morgue*, *The Masque of the Red Death*), which showed him to be a literary stylist haunted by the sense that the fabric of 'reality' is a 'grotesque' illusion (*see* **Maya**) imposed by the limitations of human reason and the material world we inhabit. In his work he tried to penetrate this illusion; an effort attracting little attention during his life, save in France. In 1847, already worn out by failure both commercially and personally, he wrote *Eureka*, an intuitive account of the creation and destruction of the universe. 'No other author ever flung such an intensity of feeling, or ever believed more steadfastly in the truth of his work, than did Edgar Allan Poe in this attempted unriddling of the secret of the universe', wrote his first biographer.[1]

In this forgotten work, Poe asserted that space and time are identical; that the universe began as a single ball of matter, exploded outward, and that in time it will collapse on itself and then begin again – assertions predating Einstein by fifty years and 'Big Bang' and 'Black Hole' theory by a century. 'What I propound here is true', he stated in his preface.

1. *The Works of Edgar Allan Poe*, John H. Ingram, London, 1880.

POLYNESIAN MYTH (*See* **HAWAII, MAORI MYTH, MAUI, OCEANIC MYTH**)

POLYPHEMUS (*See* **CYCLOPES, EYE, GREEK MYTH**)

POPOL VUH (*See* **MAYAN MYTH, MYSTERIES, VIRGINITY**)

Sacred book of the **Mayans** of Yucatan. Discovered by the Jesuit Father Ximinez (seventeenth century), translated into French and published in 1861, it contains the initiatory rites of a mystical school, compiled from older records by a Christianised Mayan who called them 'The Tale of Human Existence in the Land of Shadows, and, How Man saw Light and Life'. Its name may mean 'The Collection of Written Leaves', *Popol* meaning the 'prepared bark' and *Vuh* 'book', from *uoach*, 'to write'. Other interpretations are 'The Book of the Holy Assembly', or 'The Book of the Azure Veil'.

It tells how the princes of the **Mysteries** of subterranean Xibalba sent four **owl**-messengers to the brothers Hunhun-ahpu and Vukub-hunhun-ahpu, ordering them to an **initiatory** trial. Slain for their failure, they were buried together, but Hunhun-ahpu's **head** was set in a calabash tree by the road to Xibalba. The tree fruited; the head became one with the fruit. Desiring the fruit, the **virgin** Xquiq reached for it. Saliva from the head fell on her hand; she became pregnant. Disbelieving her tale, her father demanded her death, but her executioners spared her, substituting for her heart the fruit of the rubber plant, its sap as red and as thick as blood. When the sorcerers of Xibalba burned this 'heart' on their altar, perfume arose.

Xquiq bore two sons, Hunahpu and Xbalanque, who grew up determined to avenge their father and uncle. Hearing of their prowess, the sorcerer-princes sent for them, meaning to kill them during the seven days of the Mysteries. Crossing first a river of mud then one of blood, the brothers reached Xibalba, first having magically learned the names of each of the twelve princes. Told to worship the king, they laughed, knowing the 'king' was a lifeless wooden **idol**. Invited to sit on a stone bench, they refused, knowing it was heated and would burn them to death. So they survived the first trial. The second took place in the House of Shadows. Each brother had to keep a pine torch and a cigar alight all night. Succeeding in this by putting fireflies on the tips of cigars and by burning feathers in place of the pine splinters, at dawn they were brought to the House of Spears for the third test. After fending off spearmen hour upon hour, they were next required to produce four vases of rare flowers without leaving the temple, but got the ants to gather the flowers. Now afraid, the princes put them in the House of Cold for the fourth ordeal, which they survived by making fires of pine-cones. The fifth ordeal was to survive a night in a pit full of **jaguars**. Tossing bones to the big cats, at dawn they emerged unharmed. The sixth test was to survive from sunset to sunrise in the House of **Fire**. This they did. Now the twelve princes, fearing for Xibalba's secrets, cast them into the House of **Bats**, an underground **labyrinth** ruled by Camazotz, god of bats, human in body but with the head and wings of a bat. Soaring through the gloom, he decapitated Hunahpu while Xbalanque passed safely through. Yet, with Hunahpu magically restored to life, the brothers had passed even this seventh and last ordeal.

Now, so as better to gain revenge, they let themselves be burned on a funeral pyre. Cast into a river, their cremated bones became two great man-fishes. Turning into two old wanderers, they wrought such miracles that the princes of Xibalba (who thought them dead) called these old men to entertain them. The brothers slew the **dog** of the princes, then restored it, burned the royal palace and instantly rebuilt it. Then the Xibalban king asked them to slay, then revive, him. Willingly they slew him, and the other princes, then left them all dead.

These Mysteries offer parallels with many other initiation rites, from Egypt to **Eleusis**. The twelve princes of Xibalba govern the lower universe as Lords of the Dead (**Gnostic** archons). The two brothers are the sons of the died-and-reborn vegetation god; their ordeal is that of spirit emerging from matter. To reach the **underworld** realm they must cross two rivers of death; to begin the trial they must know the names of their judges and also refuse to worship the false idol. They play the game of life and win, their final victory over the Lords of Death representing the ascent of spiritual consciousness from the lower nature, wholly consumed by the purifying fire.

POSEIDON (*See* GREEK MYTH, MANANNAN MAC LIR, NEPTUNE, SEA-GODS)

Greek **sea-god**, anciently a Pelasgian deity governing a celestial dominion. His name, also spelt 'Potidan' may imply 'drink', 'river', or may be from a root meaning 'to be master'. His emblem, the trident, was in origin the thunderbolt. Supplanted by Zeus, he remained god of earthquakes (**Homer** calls him Enosichthon, 'Earth-shaker'). As told by **Hesiod**, he was second son of **Cronus** and **Rhea**. Like his brothers (**Hades** and **Zeus**) and sisters (**Hestia, Demeter** and **Hera**) he was swallowed at birth by his father, then vomited up due to the wiles of Zeus. Deposing their father, the brothers shook lots for the lordship of sky, sea and underworld. Gaining the sea, Poseidon built his submarine palace, then married the **Nereid** Amphitrite ('the sea', as in 'third element'), who was reluctant. Bearing him three children, she loathed his affairs with goddesses, **nymphs** and mortals; especially his infatuation with Scylla, daughter of Phorcys, whom she changed into a monster.

Surly and quarrelsome, he rode the deep in a chariot drawn by golden-maned steeds, whipping up storms with his trident. Equal to Zeus by birth and dignity, he hated his brother's sovereignty (implying defeat of the Pelasgians by Zeus-worshipping Achaeans). Conspiring with Hera and **Athene** to dethrone Zeus, he was punished by being forced to spend a year building the walls of Troy. Homer calls him the enemy of **Odysseus**, who had blinded his son, the **Cyclops** Polyphemus. Greedy for land, he claimed Athens by thrusting his trident into the Acropolis; a well of sea-water gushed out. Athene supplanted him by planting the first olive-tree by this well. When the **Olympians** decided that she, having given the better gift, should own the land, he angrily flooded the Thriasian plain. Though he owned all rivers and lakes, and could make the earth shake, he kept trying to seize lands owned by other deities. Continually rejected, forbidden to carry on flooding such lands in revenge, he began causing droughts instead.

It was his boast that he created the **horse**, which is sacred to him, perhaps due to his seduction of the mare-goddess Demeter in the form of a stallion. This myth also seems to imply the Hellenic invasion of Greece, the invaders introducing a larger breed of horse and taking over the pre-Hellenic horse-cult, their warrior-kings forcibly marrying the priestesses of the cult and so gaining title to the land.

PRECIOUS STONES (See JEWELS)

PRESLEY, ELVIS (1935–77) (See ROCK'N'ROLL MYTH)
The huge success of this American rock'n'roll singer led to his mythologisation during his lifetime and, after his death, to a widespread belief that he was still alive.

Only child of a poor white family, born in Memphis, Tennessee, and raised on Pentecostal church music, white country music and the 'blues' (rural black music), in 1954 he recorded the first of fifteen songs for Sam Phillips, a producer looking for a white singer who sounded black. These and his wild stage performances – his sexy hip gyrations earned him the nickname of 'Elvis the Pelvis' – led to his adulation, especially by female fans, while moralists condemned him for corrupting youth. Drafted into the US Army, after discharge in 1960 he resumed his career, making 'teen movies' and moderating his style to suit an ageing but growing audience. Latterly in seclusion in his mansion at Graceland in Memphis, he suffered a decline involving drug dependence and obesity, then suddenly died. Such was his myth that many denied his death: for others, Graceland has become a shrine for those who still call Presley 'The King'.

PRESTER JOHN (See ARK OF THE COVENANT, HOLY GRAIL, PERCEVAL)
Or Presbyter John: mythic priest-king of a Far Eastern Christian kingdom, popularly identified with the Apostle John, held to have escaped death as a fulfilment of John xxi:22. Evidence for his existence lay in the testimony of a Syrian bishop visiting Rome in 1145, and in a letter to Emperor Manuel at Constantinople *c*.1165, supposedly from John himself, King of the Indias. Yet no Christian potentate ruled in Asia during the twelfth century. Did the tale arise from crusading Europe's desire to believe in Christian kingdoms beyond **Islam**? No European at the time was quite sure where 'India' lay: the term was equally applied to Ethiopia. Certainly, after *c*.1300 'Prester John' was said to be an Ethiopian (Coptic Christian) emperor. Wolfram von Eschenbach in *Parzival* (*c*.1195–1216) calls him son of the Grail princess, Repanse de Joye and Feirefitz; later tradition makes him Grail guardian.

Yet again, were Holy Grail and Ark of the Covenant one and the same?

PRIAM (*See* **HOMER,** *ILIAD*, **PARIS**)

PRIAPUS (*See* **GREEK MYTH, PAN**)
Originally worshipped by Greek colonists at Lampsacus in Asia Minor, this local version of Pan was portrayed as a grotesque **gnome** with a huge erect phallus. His mother was **Aphrodite** or Chione, his father **Adonis, Hermes, Dionysus** or Pan. It is said that **Hera,** disapproving of Aphrodite, caused his deformity. Abandoned by his mother and taken in by shepherds, he ruled the fecundity of flock and field, **bee**-keeping, viniculture and fishing. He originated in the wooden phallic images presiding over Dionysian orgies; images also placed in gardens and orchards. It is said that once, when at a rustic feast all the gods had fallen asleep from over-indulgence, he tried drunkenly to rape **Hestia**. Awakening, her screams sent him packing. Even the ass, a symbol of lust, proclaimed the folly of this sacrilegious violation of a woman guest. His cult spread to Greece after the death of **Alexander the Great** (323 BC), then to Italy where his image was thought effective against the **evil eye**.

PRITHIVI (*See* **DYAUS-PITA, INDIAN MYTH**)

PROCRUSTES (*See* **GREEK MYTH, THESEUS**)
Or Polypemon, in Greek myth a criminal **giant** with two beds in his house, one large, the other small. Offering travellers lodging, he laid short men on the large bed and racked them to fit it, and tall men on the small bed, sawing off their overlapping legs. The youthful hero **Theseus** did the same to him, having already killed his son, Sinis, called Pityocamptes ('pine-bender') from his habit of tearing passers-by to pieces by tying them to sprung pine-trees. **Ovid** says Procrustes was but another name for Sinis.

PROMETHEUS (*See* **FIRE, GREEK MYTH, TITANS**)
Greek, son of the **Titan** Eurymedon, or of Iapetus by the **nymph** Clymene, brother of Epimethius, **Atlas** and Menoetius. Defeating the Titans, **Zeus** cast Menoetius into Tartarus and condemned Atlas to bear the weight of the heavens on his shoulders forever. The fate of Prometheus ('forethought') and Epimetheus ('afterthought' or 'reflection') was otherwise. Neutral during the revolt, Prometheus was admitted to **Olympus**, but secretly hated Zeus for destroying his race. Aiding the birth of **Athene** ('wisdom') from the brow of Zeus, she taught him many useful arts and crafts which he gave to mankind, so angering Zeus. Arbitrating a dispute between men and gods as to which part of a sacrificial ox the gods should be offered, Prometheus cut up the ox. Hiding the flesh under the unwanted stomach and the bones under tempting fat, he tricked Zeus into choosing the bones. Enraged, Zeus refused mankind use of fire. Prometheus thrust a torch at the chariot of the sun, hid the fire in a hollow stalk and brought it to men. Or he stole it from the forges of **Hephaestus** on Lemnos. So Zeus had Hephaestus create Pandora ('all-gifted') out of clay and water. All the Olympians gave this maiden their gifts: **Hermes** put lies in her mouth and treachery in her heart. Zeus gave her to Epimetheus who, warned by his brother, refused her.

Zeus now chained Prometheus to a rock in the Caucasian mountains, with a vulture to tear at his liver all day long – an endless torture, as nightly his liver grew whole again. Now Epimetheus accepted Pandora, who opened the vase she carried (not a box). From it sprang out every disease and affliction to curse humanity since. Only hope did not fly away. His rage unabated, Zeus sent the **Flood** to destroy humanity. But Prometheus warned his son

Deucalion who, with his wife Pyrrha (daughter of Epimetheus and Pandora), built an ark and in it survived. Zeus then let humanity renew itself. Prometheus was tortured for thirty years (or 30,000), before Zeus sent **Hercules** to free him. Then he warned Zeus to abandon his pursuit of the **Nereid Thetis**, or risk the birth of a son who would kill him. Zeus gave up Thetis to the mortal Peleus, to whom she bore **Achilles**. As for Prometheus, he gained immortality when the **centaur** Chiron, suffering the poisoned wound inflicted by Hercules, begged to descend to **Hades** in his place. Zeus agreed, and so Prometheus became a permanent Olympian.

Though a divine benefactor of mankind, the gifts of Prometheus had two sides. His theft of fire (arising from his teaching men to cheat the gods out of their due sacrifices) led to technological advances, but also to the opening of Pandora's box, causing the miseries that endure on earth today.

PROPHECY (*See* CONCORDANCE)

Interest in prophecy is as common now as ever it was. Foretellings (usually dire, always ambiguous) ascribed to semi-mythic seers like Nostradamus, Merlin, Mother Shipton or St Malachy, command as much popular attention as ever was paid to Hebrew prophets or to Classical oracles as at **Delphi** or Dodona. Few now seek to see the future by stabbing a victim to interpret his death-throes (as did the **Druids**), or by studying the shoulder-bone of a sheep (scapulimancy), or by seeking **omens** in the flight of **birds**; yet divination, fortune-telling, palmistry and so on still flourish.

The prophet has one function – to perceive and reveal spiritual truth by whatever means (vision, fasting, drugs) and at whatever personal cost. Like the **shaman**, he is beyond ordinary human life. He may be the Greek **Tiresias**, who has been both man and woman, or Welsh **Taliesin**, who as an infant turns the wise men of the king's court into blethering idiots, or **Merlin**, son of an **incubus**, or Scotland's Brahan Seer, feared and executed for telling the truths that nobody wants to hear. Or she may be the **pythoness** of Delphi, an entranced or intoxicated medium uttering ambiguous predictions.

Prophetic utterances are moulded by the traditions and expectations of a land or people. The prophet tries to get people to transform themselves, aiming to set them into new courses, defusing the predicted misfortune in advance. If misfortune is inevitable, he aims to minimise it. Prophecy may appear false because, due to it, people act to avoid the prophesied fate. Prophecy is **Prometheus**, 'foresight', born of **Athene**, 'wisdom'.

Prophecies may also lead to deliberate or 'participatory' fulfilment. Some say Christ intended to fulfil Old Testament prophecies of a **Messiah** who would restore the law. He entered Jerusalem on an ass (Psalms cxviii:25-26) having been anointed as prescribed in Leviticus (Messiah: 'Anointed One'). His Last Supper, betrayal, trial and crucifixion were preordained acts in a symbolic, ritualistic drama.[1]

The 965 ambiguous quatrains of the *Centuries* by Nostradamus (1503–66) encouraged both Napoleon and Hitler to believe that he had prophesied their triumph. So encouraged, they pursued their historic courses. Their belief influenced the fate of nations. As famous is the misinterpretation by King **Croesus** of the message given him by the Delphic Oracle. Asking if he should declare war on Persia, he was told if he crossed the River Halys he would destroy a great empire. So he did – his own.

Any well-known prophecy breeds change by its very existence, and by its legitimisation of radical action. In late fifteenth-century England the upstart Tudor dynasty hijacked **Arthurian myth**, basing its right to rule on ancient prophecy of 'the return of the king'. During the English Civil War, radical

The Merciful Lord Vishnu surrounded by his ten avatars. (Bridgeman Art Library)

The Japanese sun-goddess Amaterasu hiding in a cave. (Michael Holford)

This ivory carving shows Shoki, a Japanese god, wrestling with two Oni, or demons. (Michael Holford)

A fertility symbol relating to the Maori god Tane, this jade Tiki was worn as an amulet. (Michael Holford)

A seventeenth-century drawing of Jason and the Argonauts, having captured the Golden Fleece. (Aldus Archive)

'Nessie', the famous Scottish legend which has parallels the world over. (Fortean Picture Library)

Hans Christian Andersen's Little Mermaid. (Bridgeman Art Library)

This turquoise mask with teeth and eyes of white shell is thought to represent the Aztec god Quetzalcoatl. (Michael Holford)

Mictlantecuhtli, the Aztec god of death and ruler of the underworld. (Aldus Archive)

Andy Warhol's *Triple Elvis* (1962). Idolised by millions and dubbed 'The King of Rock'n'Roll', Elvis Presley's mansion at Graceland has become a shrine since his death in 1977. (Bridgeman Art Library)

Comic-strip hero Superman brought to life by actor Christopher Reeve in *Superman: The Movie*. (Kobal)

Hollywood 'sex goddess' Marilyn Monroe, whose relationship with the Kennedy brothers caused some to question the official version of her death. (Kobal)

James Dean in *East of Eden*. The original 'rebel without a cause', Dean became the symbol of a generation, and tales persist of a jinx on the red Porsche in which he died. (Syndication International)

A bronze statuette of the Norse god Thor with his hammer. (Aldus Archive)

Baldur the Beautiful dies pierced by a branch of mistletoe. According to Norse legend, he will be resurrected after the awful day of Ragnorak. (Aldus Archive)

Heimdall blows his horn to summon the gods to their final battle at the dawn of Ragnorak. (C.M. Dixon)

The statue of Odin at the National Museum, Copenhagen. (Aldus Archive)

Red Indian chief Hiawatha, immortalised by American poet Henry Wadsworth Longfellow. (Peter Newark's Western Americana)

Totem poles carved with animal crests were originally used by North American Indians as grave-posts. (Zefa)

This woodcut from the *Roxburghe Ballads* shows English outlaw hero Robin Hood robbing the rich – in this case a wealthy bishop – to give to the poor. (Peter Newark's Historical Pictures)

Botticelli's *The Birth of Venus*. (Bridgeman Art Library)

Romulus, the legendary
founder of Rome, is said to
have been suckled by a she-
wolf together with his twin
brother Remus.
(C.M. Dixon)

Bernini's sculpture of Roman
sea-god Neptune and Triton.
(Michael Holford)

In Greek myth, the Titans were the first divine race. (Mary Evans)

An unidentified flying object (UFO) photographed in 1981 over Vancouver Island, Canada. But reports of 'flying saucers' are centuries old. (Fortean Picture Library)

A fifteenth-century woodcut of unicorn and virgin. It was said that only a virgin's touch could tame the fabulous beast. (Peter Newark's Historical Pictures)

Belief in lycanthropy was widespread in the fifteenth and sixteenth centuries. Today, the image of the werewolf, like that of the vampire, remains potent. (Kobal)

The frontispiece of Matthew Hopkins' *Discovery of Witches* (1647), showing witch-finder general, witches and familiars. (Fortean Picture Library)

A Cameroon witchdoctor wearing a lion mask to share in the animal's psychic identity. (Syndication International)

Bigfoot captured on film in 1967 at Bluff Creek, northern California, USA, and the cast of its footprint made following the sighting. (René Dahinden/ Fortean Picture Library)

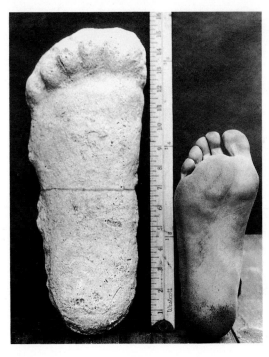

The yeti commemorated in a series of stamps issued in Bhutan in 1966. (Aldus Archive)

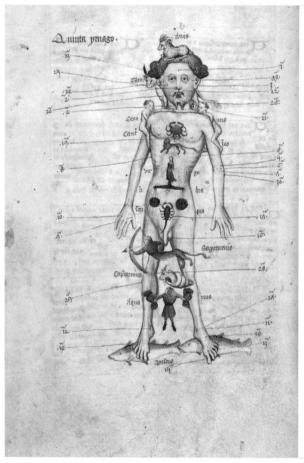

A fifteenth-century manuscript showing astrological man: the twelve signs of the zodiac are said to rule different parts of the body. (e.t. archive)

acts (the execution of King Charles I in 1649) were justified by 'ancient' prophecies, no other authority being available. 'Prophecies (were) many times the principal cause of the event foretold,' wrote Hobbes.[2]

The tradition most influencing the West is that of the 'end times' of Judaeo-Christian lore. Belief in the **Second Coming** of Christ peaked in AD 999, again during the Black Death in 1348 and again today. Apocalyptic sects quote 'prophecies of doom' as evidence of imminent cataclysm. Dates of approaching catastrophe as given by Nostradamus (1999), Mother Shipton and others remain influential, even when his (Nostradamus') dating derives from a **Christian** eschatology well-established in his own era, or (Mother Shipton) all 'modern' prophecies attributed to this shadowy seeress are nineteenth-century inventions dramatised by modern writers.[3]

Spurious interpretation of biblical text as prophesying imminent global doom led in 1970 to US publication of Hal Lindsay's *The Late Great Planet Earth* which, 'proving' the EEC to be the ten-horned Beast of Revelation, forecast Armageddon via world war starting in Israel, with Russia ('Gog') and China aiding the Antichrist. This thesis is said to have sold some twenty million copies, mostly in the USA. Misinterpretation of prophetic texts originating in the Middle East 2,000 years ago and which refer to then-current events in that region suggests a certain degree of confusion.[4]

1. *The Armageddon Script*, Peter Lemesurier, Element Books, Shaftesbury, 1981.
2. *Religion and the Decline of Magic*, Keith Thomas, Peregrine, London, 1978, p.501–5.
3. *Patterns of Prophecy*, Alan Vaughan, Dell, New York, 1976, p.20.
4. *The Late Great Planet Earth*, Hal Lindsay, Zondervan, Michigan, 1970; *Prophecy*, R.J. Stewart, Element Books, Shaftesbury, 1990.

PROSERPINE (*See* PERSEPHONE, ROMAN MYTH, UNDERWORLD)

PROTEUS (*See* GREEK MYTH, POSEIDON, SEA-GODS, SHAPE-SHIFTING)

Like Nereus (*see* **Nereids**) another 'Old Man of the Sea', the duty of this son of Oceanus and the **nymph** Tethys was to guard Poseidon's **seal**-flock. Daily at noon he emerged from the waves to rest beneath a rock on the isle of Pharos. This was the time to get him to **prophesy** the future, for he was wise and always truthful. But, able to shape-shift at will, he was hard to catch. He could appear as a **dragon** or as a **lion**, or as water, **fire** or a **tree**. Those not terrified by his changes would get their way. Ben:gn by nature, he would admit defeat and give the required advice.

This god was commonly confused with a fabled king of Egypt of the same name, who welcomed **Helen** and **Paris** when they fled Sparta, but kept Helen to return her to her legitimate husband, Menelaus.

PROTOCOLS OF THE ELDERS OF ZION (*See* JEWS AND ANTI-SEMITISM)

PRYDERI (*See* MABINOGION, PWYLL, RHIANNON, WASTELAND, WELSH MYTH)

The First Branch of the Mabinogi tells how, the night he is born, Pryderi son of **Pwyll**, lord of Dyfed (southwest Wales), and of the **horse**-goddess **Rhiannon**, disappears mysteriously as his mother and the six women set to watch over him sleep. Awakening, to save their own skins the women smear Rhiannon's face with the **blood** of stag-hound puppies and throw the bones before her, claiming she slew her own child. Three days later, on May Eve, in the house of Teyrnon Twrf Liant, lord of Gwent, an odd event occurs. Every May Eve past his mare has foaled, but the foal vanishes. This night he watches his mare. As she casts a colt, a huge claw bursts through the stable window and seizes it. Hacking off the arm to save the colt, he hears a scream and a commotion, then finds an infant boy wrapped in silk brocade on his doorstep. He and his wife foster this child, who grows so fast in size and intelligence that, when he is four, they recognise his resemblance to Pwyll, lord of Dyfed, and so return the boy to his parents.

When Pwyll dies, Pryderi becomes lord of Dyfed. But, to avenge Gwawl, Rhiannon's original suitor whom Pwyll had tricked and beaten to win her, Llwyd son of Cil Coed casts a spell on Dyfed. The Third Branch tells how with **Manawyddan** (now his stepfather) Pryderi goes hunting, but is trapped in the **otherworld**, from which Manawyddan rescues him. With Dyfed **waste**, he and Manawyddan wander in Lloegyr (England), before in time the spell is lifted. The Fourth Branch tells how the magician **Gwydion** steals Pryderi's **pigs** then slays him by magical force. Elements in this tale suggest the identification of Pryderi with the Divine Youth, **Mabon**.[1]

1. *The Mabinogion* (trans. Gwyn Jones and Thomas Jones), Dent Everyman, London, 1984.

PSYCHE (*See* CUPID, NARCISSUS, NYMPHS)

PTAH (*See* EGYPTIAN MYTH)
Worshipped from early times at Memphis, once capital of northern Egypt where pharaohs were crowned, this god was said in the beginning to have been **Nun**, the primeval waters, and by speech or kneading mud to have created the world. The Memphis priests claimed also that he created the great gods Tatenen, **Atum**, **Horus**, **Thoth** and four others nameless ones. Venerated by the pharaohs Set I and Rameses II of the 19th dynasty (1328–1203 BC), he attained his greatest prominence after the eleventh century BC, superseded only by **Amon** and **Ra**. He was worshipped with his consort, the **lion**-headed Sekhmet, and Nefertum their son, later succeeded by Imhotep (deified architect of the Step Pyramid at Sakkara). Depicted as a deformed **dwarf** with twisted legs, huge shaved head and always holding the *ankh*, the sacred symbol of life and generative force, in his aspect of protector of artisans he was identified by the Greeks with **Hephaestus**, the crippled **smith-god**. In Memphis too was celebrated the cult of the **bull Apis**, sacred to Ptah.

PUCK (*See* BROWNIES, ELEMENTALS, FAIRIES, SHAKESPEARE)
Or Robin Goodfellow, in Anglo-Saxon lore a merry domestic sprite famed for playing pranks and practical jokes. Employed in *A Midsummer Night's Dream* by **Shakespeare** as jester to the **Fairy King**, Oberon, he is said to have come to England with the **Norse** settlers, his Danish name being Pokker. In Cornwall he was associated by the tin-miners with Bucca, one of a race of fairy miners called 'knockers' from the sounds of their labour, and said to be the remnants of a pre-**Celtic** people, neither good enough for **heaven** nor bad enough for **hell**. Bucca and his relations could lead a miner to a rich lode of tin, but could be vindictive if upset.

PURANAS (*See* **BRAHMANISM, HINDUISM, INDIAN MYTH,** *MAHABHARATA*)
'Ancient traditions'; a specific category of **Sanskrit** religious literature in thirty-six books, including the Upa ('additional') Puranas, each containing the praise-name of a god or of one of his incarnations in the title, including **Brahma, Vishnu, Shiva, Garuda, Agni** and Bhagavata (**Krishna**). Full of wild speculations as to the creation and dissolution of the universe, they abound in heroic, grotesque legends of ancient kings, patriarchs and the gods themselves, especially Vishnu. Dating perhaps from the eighth to the sixth centuries BC, their authors aimed to perpetuate older **Brahmanic** teachings in a popular form, effecting a compromise between folklore and the higher religious conceptions to which they wished to elevate people. The older gods like **Indra** and Agni were not excluded, but portrayed as subject to Brahma-as-Vishnu. Many of the tales deal with the incarnations of Vishnu.

PURGATORY (*See* **CHRISTIANITY, DANTE, HEAVEN, HELL**)
Roman Christian doctrine derived from early Church belief in the existence of an afterlife state between **heaven** and **hell**, by which all those newly dead (save for a few sainted **souls**) must pass through torturing fires of **purification** before earning the right (via penance, privation and prayers of aid sent by the still living) to ascend the Mountain of Purgatory and be greeted by **St Peter** at the Gates of Heaven. Inhabited by those who have lived 'without praise and without blame' (**Dante**, *Purgatorio*), belief in this nasty half-world became official Catholic dogma in 1245, and persists.

PURIFICATION (*See* **PURGATORY, TABOO**)
Belief in the need to purify or cleanse the soul of an individual so as to free it from sin, guilt or pollution is found the world over. Takers of life, whether animal or human, **menstruating** women or those giving birth and priests or magicians preparing ceremonies to invoke spiritual powers are typical candidates for such purification.

In Timor (East Indies), the returning leader of a successful **head**-hunting expedition had to spend two months in a special hut, avoiding his home and his wife, and not feeding himself, to appease the spirits of the slain. In New Guinea a killer could not be approached, could only eat the central portion of toasted bananas, and had to undergo many other rites to purify himself. After killing, a Nandi warrior of East Africa was unclean and could not return home for four days. Young braves of the Natchez tribe of North America had to observe similar rites of abstinence for six months after taking their first scalp. Among the Omaha of North America, should a murderer by spared by the dead person's relatives, for four years he had to walk barefoot, eat no warm food, never raise his voice, look round, nor comb his hair. Ancient Greeks insisted even in cases of involuntary killing that the killer leave the land for a year and not return until the **ghost** of the slain person had been appeased by sacrifice and purification. Thus the myth of **Orestes**, pursued by the **Furies** of his slain mother. Many societies also imposed similar taboos on returning hunters or fishermen; again, to appease the ghost of the slain animal.[1]

Even natural death requires purification. In East Africa the death of a Bantu man, especially a chief, requires that all his relatives purify themselves of the contagion of his death. The Tsonga of Mozambique would invite a stranger to sleep with the widow, so as to remove the 'ill-luck'. Evil **spirits** thought to be the cause of death, disease or ill-luck might be cast on to a **goat**, **pig** or other animal, then abandoned elsewhere, in hope that someone else would find it and possess it – and the spirits causing the misfortune. Certain animals are regarded as impure in many cultures. In Egypt, a man touching a pig would step into a river fully clothed to wash off the taint; swineherds could not enter any temple. The pig, especially its meat, remains impure to Moslems and Jews.

Yet the 'impurity' is in many cases ambiguous: ritual cleansing is also associated with the handling of sacred objects. Jews must wash their hands after reading the holy books. Christian baptism is a purification ritual; childbirth, like menstruation, being surrounded by taboos. The ducking in water of **witches** was in one sense a purification ceremony, likewise death by **fire** at the stake. Less savage were the purifying fires of **Easter** or **May Day** (see **Beltane**), burning away the old year. All ascetic disciplines are likewise a form of purification, ridding the **soul** of worldly dross by prayer, fasting or by beating, as with medieval flagellants during the Black Death (1347–50), who by flogging themselves hoped to avert the evil, or as with submission by King Henry II (1133–89) to flogging when his rage led to the death of Thomas à Becket, Archbishop of Canterbury.

1. *The Golden Bough*, Sir James Frazer, Macmillan, London, 1963, pp.212–16.

PURUSHA (*See* ADAM, INDIAN MYTH)

In **Indian** lore the cosmic **giant**, the first man, his limbs and body the different parts of the universe, all his parts continually **sacrificed** to the others, the original continually dying-and-reborn god from whose agony arose all that is, including the gods. 'From his navel arose the air, from his head the sky, from his ears the four quarters; in this manner [the gods] formed the world', claims a late *Rig-Vedic* hymn.

This resembles the **Norse** myth of the giant **Ymir**, his body chopped up by the gods to become the parts of the physical world.

PWYLL (*See MABINOGION*, OTHERWORLD, PRYDERI, RHIANNON)

At the start of the First Branch of the Mabinogi ('Pwyll Prince of Dyfed'), this Welsh lord, out hunting, sees a pack of red-eared white hounds bring down a stag. Driving them off, he sets his own hounds on the stag. Their owner, Arawn, king of **Annwn** (the **otherworld**), appears and condemns such discourtesy. To redeem himself, Pryderi changes places with Arawn for a year, each taking the shape, identity and kingdom of the other. At the end of the year (having never taken advantage of Arawn's wife while in Arawn's form), Pryderi kills Arawn's enemy, Hafgan, another king of the otherworld. He and Arawn meet again as friends, each returning to their own realm.

Thereafter called Head of Annwn, years later, seated on a **mound**, Pwyll sees a silk-clad woman ride past on a white **horse**. He pursues but cannot catch her, though she seems to ride slowly. Challenged, she stops. She is **Rhiannon**, who wishes to marry him, not Gwawl, her official suitor. They marry, but ill-luck dogs them. Years pass before Pryderi their son is born, and many more before the **curse** put on Dyfed by Gwawl's kinsmen is lifted.

Gwawl means 'light'; Rhiannon is cognate with **Epona**, a Celtic mare-goddess with underworld associations, as shared by Pwyll himself. Their conflict with Gwawl epitomises the ancient rite of seasonal combat between fertility (spring-summer) and death (winter).[1]

1. *The Mabinogion* (trans. Gwyn Jones and Thomas Jones), Dent Everyman, London, 1984.

PYERUN (*See* BOGATYRI, SLAVONIC MYTH)

PYRAMIDS (*See* EGYPTIAN MYTH, MOUNTAINS, SACRED GEOMETRY, SPHINX)

Belief that gods inhabit holy **mountains** led early man to imitate nature by building artificial hills, up which **Mystery** candidates might climb to be tested. Earth mounds (Silbury Hill in England) gave way to stone pyramids (Greek πυρ, 'fire', signifying the Divine Flame). The biblical tower of **Babel** was probably a Sumerian ziggurat or stepped pyramid. The typical ziggurat had seven levels, each for a different plane of consciousness, its peak the height of spiritual attainment. Four-sided like the mythic Mount **Meru**, the pyramid's square base symbolises material life or (**Plato**) the earth element. As found in Egypt, pyramids are thus not only physical but symbolic constructions, knowledge coded in their very dimensions.

Egyptian pyramids developed by trial and error from the Sakkara Step Pyramid, via the 'Bent Pyramid' to the Great Pyramid. Dated *c*.2600 BC, this remains the world's most controversial building. Orthodox belief, that it was the tomb of the pharaoh Khufu (Cheops), originates with Greek historian **Herodotus** (*c*.440 BC) who, as a **Mystery** initiate, may have concocted this tale to hide the Pyramid's true age and purpose. Nothing proves that it was ever used or intended as a tomb. When in AD 820 the Caliph Al-Mamoun broke in and by accident found its formerly unknown upper passages, no body was found in the granite coffer in the so-called King's Chamber.

The pyramid itself is the prize. The side of its designed base square measures 365.242 sacred cubits: the exact length of the solar year. Other measured values match the eccentricity of the earth's orbit (0.004 minimum, 0.019 maximum); its distance from the sun (92,992,270 miles); and the length of the cycle of the precession of the equinoxes (25,826.4 years). Quite as marvellous as its geometric precision are the myths about its supposed age and properties. An Arab claim is that it was built as a defence against the **Flood**. American seer Edgar Cayce (1877–1945) claimed that building began in 10,490 BC, after the destruction of **Atlantis**. It is said that its huge stones (some 70 tons) were moved by magical song (as **Merlin** is said to have moved the 'Giant's Dance' (**Stonehenge**) from Ireland to England), and that its internal passages and features constitute a coded **prophecy** – a spiritual blueprint for human progress, a time-chart of future events from the date of construction, measured by distance from the entry and counting one pyramid inch (1/25th of the sacred cubit) per year.[1]

1. *The Great Pyramid Decoded*, Peter Lemesurier, Element Books, Shaftesbury, 1977; *The Secrets of the Great Pyramid*, Peter Tompkins, Allen Lane, London, 1973.

PYTHAGORAS (*c*.590–*c*.520 BC) (*See* GREEK MYTH, MUSIC AND MYTH, NUMBER)

Early Greek philosopher, a myth in his lifetime, said like **Christ** to be **virgin**-born, his mother Parthenis (Greek *parthenos*, 'virgin') bearing him to the god **Apollo**. She and Mnesarchus his father (a ring-merchant from Samos) consulted the **Delphic Oracle**, which said her son would be born in Sidon in **Phoenicia** to benefit mankind. Mnesarchus changed his wife's name to Pythasis to honour the oracle and named the child Pythagoras: a **name** consisting of specially arranged letters of sacred meaning. Later, he was known as 'Son of God'. It is said he travelled widely and was initiated into the **Orphic, Judaic, Egyptian,** Chaldean and other **Mysteries**; and that he was taught by **Zoroaster** and the **Brahmans.** He is said to have been the first man to call himself a 'philosopher' (in his definition, 'One trying to find out'), as opposed to the older term 'sage', 'One who knows'.

Establishing a school at Crotona in southern Italy, he instructed his disciples (selected only from the self-disciplined) in the basics of music, mathematics and astronomy, delivering his enigmatic, allegorical lectures from behind a curtain, denying personal contact until students had passed through a series of initiatory degrees to attain the higher grades. In so doing, he obeyed his own teachers' injunctions to secrecy.

He taught that all knowledge is related to number, and discovered that musical scales may be numerically expressed, also that the arrangement of the heavenly bodies depends on intervals regulated by musical harmony (thus 'Music of the Spheres') (*see* **Music and Myth,** and **Number**). Teaching that the **soul** is 'a harmony of contrary elements united together in the body', he taught the doctrine of **transmigration** of souls and that souls may live again in animals, even in beans, so leading his followers to vegetarianism.

Aged about 60, he married a disciple who bore him seven children. It is said he died after refusing Cylon, a would-be discipline, entry to his school due to Cylon's temper. Infuriated, Cylon brought the mob to burn down the house where Pythagoras and forty followers were assembled. Pythagoras died. Another account says he escaped, but died of grief at what seemed an empty attempt to illuminate humanity. Though persecuted, his disciples persisted. It is said one of them, when sick, was taken in by an innkeeper. Before dying, he traced a sign on the door, saying, 'Rest assured, one of my brothers will pay my debt.' A year later a stranger saw the sign and told the host, 'I am a Pythagorean; one of my brothers died here; tell me what I owe you for him.'[1] The order lasted some 250 years and had a profound regenerative influence on Greek thought. The **Neoplatonist** Iamblichus (fourth century AD) lists 218 men and 17 women as the most famous of Pythagorean philosophers.

1. *The Great Initiates*, Edouard Schuré, Harper & Row, New York, 1980 (1889).

PYTHIA (*See* PYTHON)

PYTHON (*See* APOLLO, DELPHI, GREEK MYTH, SERPENT)
A mythic female serpent slain at Delphi in Greece by the infant Apollo. This tale refers to takeover of the famed **oracle** by a new male priesthood. The serpent was said to have been generated from the mud left on the earth after **Deucalion**'s Deluge. Delphi's original name was Pytho ('to rot') from the stench of the fumes which, arising from a subterranean chasm, were breathed by the pythoness, or trance-priestess, who would then prophesy. The name survived in the Pythian festival and games celebrated at Delphi every four years. Said to have been established by Apollo, its main event was re-enactment of his victory over Python. In **Indian myth** a corollary is found in the tale of the **demon** Putana, which means 'stinking'. She tried to kill the infant god **Krishna** by offering him her poisoned breast, but he blew into it instead of sucking, so killing her with her own poison.

Today the name is applied to a genus of large, non-poisonous snakes. Widely found in tropical lands, they kill by crushing prey in their coils. A

Zulu (African) myth tells how, long ago, a pregnant queen grew huge, but could not give birth. At last a python's head emerged. All the women fled. For hours the python kept emerging. The king and his household also fled, leaving the queen alone with her awful offspring. She grew corn to feed herself and the python, which made its home in the river. Months later its skin peeled, revealing the head of a baby boy, then that of a baby girl and so on until there were five of each. She called the first boy Uhlathu Yesiziba, 'Python of the Pool'. As they grew up, he became chief of the village. At last, hearing of it, the king came to visit and was glad to find ten fine children. The clan of Uhlathu Yesiziba still lives there.

In Senegambia it is said a python will visit every child of the Python clan within eight days of birth. In Tanzania, whenever Nyamwezi folk meet a python in the fields, they address it with respect, clapping their hands as if greeting a king. If it enters a house, the chief orders a **goat** to be sacrificed to it. To kill a python is to court disaster, not only for the killer but his whole family. The perpetrator is stiffly fined, the dead python being addressed as 'our king'. Likewise, after killing Python at Delphi, Apollo had to **purify** himself by a period of exile and expiation.

Also in West Africa is found the common myth of the world-**serpent** with its tail in its mouth (*see* **Ourobouros**). There the world is said (by the **Fon** and others) to have been created by co-operation between Mawu, the supreme being, and Da, or Dan Ayido Hwedo, the divine python or Rainbow Snake. The first created being, Dan Ayido Hwedo carried Mawu all over the world. Wherever they stopped for the night, mountains were formed from the snake's excrement. To stop the world sinking from the weight of all they had created, Mawu asked the python to support the earth, tail in mouth. The Rainbow Snake agreed and, though for most of the time he lies still, sometimes he wriggles, causing earthquakes. It is also said that he holds the earth in his coils: 3,500 above, the same number below. If they were loosened, the world would fall apart. Their revolution above keeps the stars and planets in motion. He arches in the **rainbow** and flashes in the lightning. He is perhaps the origin of the **Voodoo** serpent-god Damballah.

PYTHONESS (*See* **PYTHON**)

Q

QABALAH (*See* **QLIPHOTH, TAROT, TREES**)
A body of esoteric teaching, its name meaning 'the received', from a Hebrew root *QBL*, 'to receive'. Rabbinic tradition claims Qabalah was taught to **Adam** by the **archangel** Gabriel and thereon passed orally 'from mouth to ear'. **Judaic** in origin, it absorbed Persian, Egyptian, Greek, **Neoplatonic** and **Gnostic** elements. About AD 1280 the Spanish Qabalist Moses ben Shemtob de Leon issued the *Zepher ha Zohar* (*Book of Splendour*), a vast commentary on the Pentateuch (the Bible's first five books), claiming it as the work of the mythic Rabbi Simeon bar Yohai, said to have died in ecstatic trance 1,200 years earlier. Deviating from orthodox Judaism, it initiated the growth of Qabalah into a flexible, sophisticated symbolic system which offers many techniques for training the mind, evoking spiritual powers and correlating different disciplines, philosophies, mythologies and pantheons. Central to the system is the Tree of Life; a glyph, symbol or psychic map which has been called 'a ground plan of the universe and the soul of man'.

Qabalah claims that positive existence emanates from a negative state of limitless undifferentiated being (Ain Soph), from which emanates the Tree, on it the ten sephiroth (spheres: states of being) which, connected by twenty-two Paths, embrace creation in all its forms, from Kether to Malkuth, high to low, a process visualised as Divine Energy plunging from one sephirah to the next in a zigzag: the 'Lightning Flash'. The Tree is divided into three Pillars: Passive (left), Active (right), and Middle. To seek the 'Middle Way' is to seek progress by uniting extremes without surrendering to them. So the purely intellectual life of the sephirah Hod (**Mercury**) is as poorly balanced if pursued as an end in itself as is the sensual life of Netzach (**Venus**): both are better served by marriage of the faculties involved at the '**Christ**'-level of Tiphareth at the very centre of the Middle Pillar.

The sephiroth or spheres are (1) Kether, the Crown, fount of creation, the universal point where vital energy pours in from the unmanifest. These energies activate in (2) Chokmah, Wisdom, powerhouse of force, symbolised by phallus, straight line, tower. Initiating action, Chokmah stands under Kether at the head of the Pillar of Mercy (Right). Through it the energy flashes to (3) Binah, Understanding, Great Mother, primal ocean at the head of the Pillar of Severity (Left). Fertilised by and taking in the pure energy of Kether and Chokmah, Binah manifests the idea of form.

This supernal trinity stands above the Abyss separating Idea from Form. Straddling the Abyss (Middle Pillar) is the hidden, numberless sephirah, Daath, associated with **Sirius** and with confidence in the future.

From Binah through Daath the energy powers (4) Chesed, Mercy, the four-square principle of organisation and worldly rule (**Jupiter**). Here it forms subtle material blueprints, then crosses to (5) Geburah, Severity, **Mars**, where Chesed's forms are destroyed, assessed and refracted down to (6) Tiphareth, Beauty, Christ-consciousness. This, the Tree's central sephirah, mediates what is above with what is below. From it, the energy pours on to (7) Netzach, **Venus**, its symbol a beautiful naked woman. Here Tiphareth's coherent love rays out into Nature in all her forms, creating natural forces perceived by human imagination as gods and goddesses.

From Netzach the lightning flashes over to (8) Hod, Glory, **Mercury**, **hermaphroditic** Intellect. Here, formless truths descend from the higher sephiroth into the mind. From Hod the energy plunges transversely to the Middle Pillar, to (9) *Yesod*, **Moon, etheric** foundation of physical being, its forces co-ordinating the emergence of physical form, source of psychic, unconscious and reproductive energies. And so on down to (10) Malkuth, the kingdom of earth, the nadir of creation. This is no damnation. Qabalah, unlike some other philosophies, holds that spirit must descend into deepest matter, that our destiny must be realised in Malkuth, or further progress is impossible. In this, Qabalah agrees with **Christianity**, though reaching its conclusions not through faith but gnosis (knowledge).[1]

1. *A Practical Guide to Qabalistic Symbolism*, Gareth Knight, Helios, Cheltenham, 1965.

QLIPHOTH (*See* DEMONS, EVIL, QABALAH)

Qabalists say that a distorted reflection of the Tree of Life also exists, and that magical powers may be summoned not only for good but for evil or selfish purposes. In Qabalistic terminology the latter intention, and the **demons** thus summoned, belong to the inverse Tree, associated with the word *Qliphoth*, meaning 'harlots' or 'shells'. This state requires no romancing: the consequences of focus upon it, conscious or unconscious, may be found 'in the nearest hospital, lunatic asylum, prison, brothel or slum'. In all cases where the negative aspect of a sephirah is invoked, the result is confusion, disorder and misery arising through a denial of unity.[1]

1. *A Practical Guide to Qabalistic Symbolism*, Gareth Knight, Helios, Cheltenham, 1965, vol.1, p.232.

QUAT (*See* OCEANIC MYTH, SPIDER, TANGAROA)

One of the eleven brothers of **Tangaroa** (the 'Wise One'), this Melanesian creator-spirit was born of Qatgoro, a stone that burst apart, then made **pigs, trees** and human beings; the latter with the aid of the **spider** spirit Marawa. For six days Quat carved the bodies of the first men and women from a tree, hid them for three days, then for three days brought them to life by **dancing** and **drumming**. But Marawa buried these animated wooden people for six days in a pit, then dug them up and found them all rotting. So death came to the world. Yet Marawa and Quat were not enemies, Marawa often rescuing Quat from traps set by his brothers. Once, having tried to drown Quat, they kidnapped his wife Ro Lei and took her off to another island. Making himself small, he followed them in a coconut-shell bottle. Eating a banana, he discarded the skin in the sea. They saw it, but disbelieved Tangaroa when he insisted that Quat had left it as evidence of his pursuit. When they landed, they found him waiting. He smashed their canoe, then demanded that henceforth they all live in friendship. Later, when the **demon** Quasavara ate all his brothers, he slew Quasavara, then revived them by blowing through a reed on to their bones and making them laugh. Alternately or simultaneously regarded as a god, a spirit (*vui*) or a hero, Quat then left the New Hebrides, the people of which until recently still hoped for his return.

QUEEN OF SHEBA (See BLACK VIRGIN, DJINNS, LILITH, SOLOMON, SOPHIA)

1 Kings x tells how this mysterious queen heard of **Solomon**'s fame and came to Jerusalem to **test** him with hard questions. Impressed by his wisdom, she gave him **gold, jewels** and spices, then returned to Sheba. Solomon's most famous lover, she inspired him to write the erotic *Song of Songs*. In Matthew xii:42, Jesus says that on Judgement Day she will judge the unbelievers. He even implies that she is greater than Solomon. Why?

Today, Sheba or Saba is the Yemen (southern Arabia). The Sabaeans were famed astrologers, later associated with the **Gnostics**. Sheba can mean 'seven', i.e. the planets, or 'oath', a solemn vow witnessed and enforced by the heavenly powers. Sura 27 of the Koran tells how her father, the hoopoe-bird, having taught Solomon the language of the birds, tells him of a land ruled by a virtuous woman who worships the **sun**. When she visits Solomon he greets her in a room with a glass floor, so he can look up her skirts to learn if she has a **djinn**'s hairy legs. In another version, he sits at the far side of a stream to see if she will use a bridge made of the wood of the true cross. Instead she hoists her skirts and wades across, revealing her hairy legs. Having rejected **Yahweh** for other gods, Solomon is undisturbed, and they become lovers.

In Ethiopia she was called Eteye Azeba ('Queen of the South'). Tied to a tree as a **dragon-sacrifice**, she was rescued by seven Coptic saints who slew the dragon. But its **blood** touched her heel, changing it into that of an ass. Solomon cured this deformity and she bore him Menelek ('Son of the Wise'). To this legendary founder of a dynasty lately ending with Haile Selassie, he is said to have entrusted the **Ark of the Covenant**.

Like **Lilith**, **Sophia** or the **black virgins** in Catholic churches, this Queen of the South is an **archetype** of feminine wisdom. Christianised by Honorious of Autun (twelfth century) as the queen and concubine of **Christ**, she was revered by the troubadours of twelfth-century Provence as La Reine de Saba, *reino saba* ('wise queen'), and by them associated with Queen Sibylla, the web-footed ancestress of all magicians, likewise with Le Reine Pédauque ('**Goose**-foot Queen'). Gérard de Nerval (1808–55) writes in *Aurélia* of 'the queen of the south, crowned with stars, in a turban sparkling with the colours of the rainbow . . . her face is olive-tinted'.[1]

1. *The Cult of the Black Virgin*, Ean Begg, Arkana, London, 1985, pp.30–4.

QUEST (See HERO MYTH, HOLY GRAIL, TASK, TEST)

Found the world over is the theme of **heroic** quest for a prize, treasure or knowledge of benefit not only to the hero but his people. Imposed by a supernatural power, or undertaken voluntarily, the quest (as for the **Holy Grail** or **dragon**-treasure, or to win a princess) requires the would-be hero to overcome not only hostile powers but also his own fears and inner divisions. As metaphor of Everyman's life-journey, its goal is the healing or integration of the **soul** by seeing through illusion (**maya**) to reality. So **Gilgamesh** sought **immortality**; his triumph came in recognising the need to accept death. In Grail-myth, **Lancelot**, **Perceval**, **Galahad**, **Gawain** and others all seek the Grail, but even those who find it may not know what to do with it or what to ask it. The **otherworld** powers (our unconscious mind?) fight to keep their secrets and must be defeated, tricked, seduced or persuaded to give up their prizes. Even if the boon is granted, the hero's successful return to the world and triumph thereafter is uncertain. **Orpheus** seduced **Hades** with his music and freed Eurydice, but lost her because he looked back; **Perceval** reached the Grail castle but did not ask the right question; **Siegfried** slew the dragon and became almost invulnerable by bathing in its **blood**. The powers of darkness may be overcome, but rarely in worldly terms of wealth or fame. The goal is not worldly, but philosophical.

QUESTING BEAST (*See* ARTHURIAN MYTH, FABULOUS BEASTS, MALORY)

With a **serpent**'s head, leopard's body, **lion**'s hindquarters and **deer**'s hooves (or **hare**'s paws), its belly emitting the sound of a pack of hounds in full cry, this perverse beast runs continually, seeking water to slake its thirst. A symbol of incest and anarchy, it was begotten by the Devil on a princess who, when her brother rejected her advances, accused him of rape, so that he was condemned to be eaten alive by dogs. In **Malory**'s *Le Morte d'Arthur*, King Arthur meets it by a fountain soon after making love to his half-sister **Morgause**. In one tale, Palomides the Saracen knight caught it by a lake where it had stopped to drink. Speared through, with a frightful cry it sank beneath the lake, which was whipped up by a demonic storm.

QUETZALCOATL (*See* AZTEC MYTH, MAYAN MYTH, PHOENIX, SERPENT)

When in 1519 the Spanish *conquistador* Hernando Cortes and his men invaded Central America, they were aided in their conquest by **Aztec** belief that Cortes was the god Quetzalcoatl, the 'Plumed Serpent', his return from the eastern ocean that very year foretold by ancient **Mayan** prophecy.

Called Kukulcan by the Mayans, and Huemac by the earlier Toltecs, in origin this **sun-god** was the creator, giver of breath and bringer of rain. He went down to the land of the dead, then returned. Sprinkling the bones of the dead with his own sacrificed **blood**, he formed human beings. Human **sacrifices** were not made to him, even by the Aztecs. *Quetzal* means 'bird of paradise'; *coatl* is '**serpent**'. Thus, 'the serpent veiled in the plumes of the bird of paradise'. The serpent is mind raised from chthonic night to self-awareness via the light of the sun (Quetzal-bird, **phoenix**).

Later this abstract deity was euhemerised as an ancient king who, like the Babylonian **Oannes**, emerged from the sea to civilise the region, perhaps *c*.AD 987 (*see* **Mayan myth**). He taught agriculture, weaving, religion, arts and crafts, the measuring of time, annual ceremonies, prayers and hatred of war and animal sacrifice. Bernardino de Sahagun (sixteenth century) writes in *History of Things of New Spain*: 'In the city of Tollan (Chololan) reigned many years a king called Quetzalcoatl . . . the place of this king among these natives is like King Arthur among the English.' The Aztecs, invading the region in the thirteenth century, took over this earlier Toltec and Mayan deity, ignoring the original abstract philosophy. Their version of his departure is that the **trickster** and warrior-god **Tezcatlipoca** ('Smoking Mirror', meaning the obsidian mirror used by Aztec priests to look into the future) drove him out, having tempted him to drunkenness and promiscuity. In grief he burned his palace built of silver and shells, underwent a mock death, buried his treasure, donned his insignia of feathers, then (preceded by his attendants, all transformed into bright-feathered birds) sailed east on a raft of serpents, promising to return one day.

Either that, or he immolated himself on a pyre, from which (again, as with the **phoenix**) arose the Quetzal-bird).

Traditionally represented as a white-haired old man with long beard, wearing a long robe, his face and body painted black, he was said to have been 'white' or a 'white man': perhaps meaning blinding white, like the **sun**.

Thus when the sentries posted on the east coast to watch for his return saw the bright breastplates of the Spaniards, they assumed that their god had come back. So they gave themselves up to Cortes and his men. Likewise in 1540 the **Hopi** of Arizona confused the Spaniards of Coronado's expedition with Pahana, their lost 'White Brother'. Such misunderstanding did much to aid the Spanish conquest of the 'New World'.

R

RA (*See* **AMON, ATUM, EGYPTIAN MYTH, SUN-GODS**)
Or *Re*, probably meaning 'Creator', Egyptian sun-god and lord of the sky, his main cult centre Heliopolis, where, it is said, he first manifested in the form of the stone obelisk called *ben-ben* (erected during the 12th dynasty by Senusert I, still standing). He was said also to manifest as the Benu-bird (see **Phoenix**) or the **bull** Merwer. Revered in Egypt as world creator and ruler, whenever a new Pharaoh was conceived, Ra was said to have lain with the queen.

In origin he was the formless god **Atum**, enclosed in a **lotus**-bud in the bosom of **Nun**, primeval **ocean**. Alone, by act of will he arose from the depths and appeared in splendour as Ra the sun. By masturbation or by use of spittle he bore Shu (air) and Tefnut (moisture), who bore Geb and **Nuit**, from whom issued **Osiris**, **Isis**, **Set** and **Nepthys**. He created dry land, on which he put man and all living creatures, formed from his tears. Nightly he was swallowed by the cosmic **serpent** Apep (Apophis), who even in daytime dared to raise storm-clouds that obscured Ra's glory.

In time, say the Pyramid texts, he grew old and decrepit. In this state Isis tricked him into revealing his secret **name**, so gaining power over him. When even men plotted against him, in his fury he hurled his divine **eye** against them in the form of the goddess **Hathor**. Though ending the carnage before all men were slain, he left the world he hated, riding Nuit high into the heavens. So the present world was created. Yet still daily he rode his boat through the sky; nightly, grown old, he was swallowed by Apep, to pass through the **underworld**, worshipped by the dead, to be reborn each dawn as an infant. His lordship of the dead was later assumed by Osiris.

Depicted as a child seated on the lotus; as a man crowned by the solar disc entwined with the flame-spitting sacred asp, the Uraeus, or as a man with the head of a **ram**, even in his dotage Ra retained his power. The pharaoh Chephren (third millennium BC) was first to call himself 'Son of Ra'. The heretical pharaoh Amenophis IV (1377–1358 BC), known as Ikhnaton or **Akhenaton** ('Devotee of Aton'), rejected all other gods and instituted monotheistic worship of the solar disc, Aton. This cult soon collapsed (*see* **Freud** for the claim that **Moses** served Akhenaton, and that Israelite monotheism was derived from the cult of Aton).

RADHA (*See* **INDIAN MYTH, KRISHNA**)

RAGNORAK (*See* **AESIR, ARMAGEDDON, FENRIR, NORSE MYTH, OUROBOUROS**)
As paraphrased from the old Norse Voluspá by Snorri Sturlusson (*see* **Edda**) and popularised by **Wagner**'s *Götterdämerung*, this 'Doom of the Gods' or 'Destruction of the Power' tells of a final terrible battle in which all creation, including the gods, will perish. The doom will be preceded by self-destructive anarchy, war and crime among men, and by the wolf **Fenrir** swallowing the **sun**, causing the three-year Fimbulwinter. Amid earthquakes

and falling stars the monsters chained in the deep escape. The serpent of Midgard leaves the sea; its waters **flood** the earth, and on the flood comes the ship Naglfar, made of dead men's nails, crewed by Frost **Giants**, **Loki** at its helm. The fire-fiend Surtur and his army join the war against the gods, en route shattering the **rainbow bridge** Bifrost. Summoned by the horn-blast of **Heimdall**, the guardian of Bifrost, the **Aesir** and **Vanir** ride out behind **Odin** and his host, each to slay and be slain by their mortal foe: Odin by Fenrir; **Thor** by the Midgard serpent; **Tyr** by the hell-hound Garm; **Heimdall** by **Loki**. All die but Surtur who, the battle done, torches the world. The blazing, lifeless earth sinks under the raging sea. All is done, yet a new heaven and a new earth emerge. A new sun shines down. New gods appear to renew the world. **Baldur** is resurrected to take the place of Odin as father of the gods. Men also emerge, some having survived the storm within the world-tree **Yggdrasil**, where they lived by feeding on the morning dew.

Some claim this potent myth to be but a rendering of the **Armageddon** theme familiar in **Christian** eschatology from the Revelation of St John onward. Yet belief in a ship made of dead men's nails, in the swallowing of the sun by a **wolf**, in the image of a bound giant breaking loose to destroy the world is widely found in **pagan** Norse folklore. Christianity has no monopoly on **archetypal** fears. The myth of global death and destruction by **fire** and flood, followed by renewal, is worldwide and pre-Christian, as with **Plato**'s tale of **Atlantis**, or in **Brahmanic** accounts of world cycles.

RAIN-BIRD (*See* CHINESE MYTH, FABULOUS BEASTS)
When rain fails, Chinese farmers may call not only on the **dragon** to help them but also on a one-legged bird, the shang yung, said to draw water from the rivers with its beak and blow it out over the fields. **Borges** tells how children would hop up and down on one foot, repeating: 'It will thunder, it will rain, 'cause the shang yung's here again.' It is said an ancient magus carried a tame rain-bird perched on his sleeve, and how the Prince of Ch'i, alarmed when a rain-bird came hopping before him, consulted **Confucius**, who advised the immediate construction of dykes and channels. In his wisdom the prince heeded this advice: when the rains came, disaster was avoided.

RAIN-MAKING (*See* WATER, WOODPECKER)
The need of rain at the right time to fertilise crops and ensure survival led in many societies to a special class of magician – the 'rain-maker' – who usually employed imitative magic, as by **dancing** while sprinkling water on the ground, **drumming** to imitate thunder or striking sparks to imitate lightning. Black **pigs**, sheep, fowl, cattle or **horses** might be sacrificed (rain-clouds being black). Bathing ceremonies, or processions round the drought-starved village by naked women, were common from Europe to India. In the Caucasus, the women would drag a plough into a river, hoping thus to draw the rain. The Chinese would make a huge paper **dragon** to represent the rain-god and carry it about; if no rain came, the dragon was beaten, threatened or torn to pieces. Elsewhere, corpses might be dug up and sunk in water, or appeals made by the living to their **ancestors**, or (Christian Europe) prayers offered up to the saints. If no rain fell, as in Sicily in 1893, the images of the recalcitrant saints were stripped of their robes, ducked in horse-ponds, insulted and threatened. Breton peasants would draw water from a fountain called Barenton (associated with **Merlin**) and throw it on a slab, or dip a cross in the fountain. Variations on such rites were and are found the whole world over.

Likewise, if too much rain threatened flood, **fire** rites were thought to be the answer, fire being contrary to water. In wet lands, rain-doctors concerned not to produce but to stop rain would (as in Java) begin a fast. Neither drinking nor bathing, whatever they ate had to be eaten dry.

In Indian myth, the defeat by the sky-god **Indra** of the demonic **Vritra** is the defeat of drought by the fertilising (rain-making) power. Vritra has kidnapped and imprisoned the sky-cattle (rain-clouds): his defeat and their release by the good god leads to fertilising rainfall, and thus survival.

So too the Egyptian **Set** is the arid desert; **Isis** and **Osiris** represent the annual flooding of the Nile, bringing fertility and prosperity. On the other hand, the Babylonian **Tiamat** is watery chaos or flood out of control, to be channelled into irrigation courses by the rational power of the sun-god **Marduk**.

RAIN-QUEENS (*See* AFRICAN MYTH, HAGGARD)
The Lovedu people of eastern Transvaal (South Africa) were ruled by queens said to be incarnations of the rain-goddess, the Mujaji, who protected them against the **Zulu** invasion of the early nineteenth century. Just to mention their name caused such magical fear of drought and disease that the Zulu warriors of Chaka left these people well alone. Famed for their wisdom and cunning, they were thought able to send storm to destroy their enemies, or gentle rain to nourish their friends. They inhabited the northern slopes of the Drakensberg (**Dragon**) Mountains (the dragon being widely associated with the fertility of rain, or the chaos of flood). They never showed themselves to white men, but had other women impersonate them. Their reputation gave **Rider Haggard** the inspiration for *She* (1887), his romance about the **immortal** queen of a lost African kingdom.

RAINBOW (*See* FLOOD MYTH, PYTHON, SERPENT)
Genesis ix:8–17 tells how, after the **Flood**, **Yahweh** promised never again to destroy mankind by deluge, and as evidence of his 'covenant' set his rainbow in the sky. The rainbow has many other symbolic meanings. To the **Norse** it was the **bridge** Bifrost, joining the human world with that of the gods. In Africa and India it was viewed as a **serpent**, quenching its thirst in the sea; in China as the sky-**dragon** joining **heaven** and earth; in North America as a **ladder** up to the spirit-realms. In **Hindu** lore the 'rainbow body' is the highest yogic state attainable to those who remain in the realm of **samsara**, illusion, and is the bow of **Indra**. To the Bakongo of Zaïre in Africa it is a giant protector, the god Lubangala, who guards the sea, the village and the graves of the **ancestors**. In European folklore, there is said to be a pot of **gold** at the other end of the rainbow. This assertion cannot be disproved, the rainbow being so physically elusive, yet also implies its role as an image of psychological transformation between one state of consciousness and another.

RAINBOW SNAKE (*See* PYTHON)

RAKSHASA (*See* ASURAS, BHIMA, DEMONS, HANUMAN, INDIAN MYTH, YAKSHA)
As the **Asuras** of Indian myth are enemies of the gods, the Rakshasas are enemies of man. Sometimes identified with the Asuras, these hideous **demons** are night prowlers, able to fly faster than the wind and to change their shape. Servants of **Kali**, their name means 'harmers' or 'destroyers'. In the *Ramayana* the monkey-god **Hanuman** penetrates the Sri Lankan palace of their leader, Ravana, and sees them in their true shapes: some hideously

deformed, with **dwarf** bodies and long arms, some **elephantine**, some ugly, snaggle-toothed **giants**, some with the heads of **horses** or **serpents**, some with one eye or one leg, or three eyes or three legs. In the *Mahabharata*, they resemble gorillas, with arrow-shaped ears, big red eyes, red hair and red beards. With their poisonous nails and cavernous mouths they feast on human flesh and **blood**. Of their several clans, the repulsive black Dasyus stole the cloud-cows for the demon **Vritra**, which **Indra** recovered; the Pisachas are disease-bringing **ghouls** who devour corpses in cemeteries; the Darbas ('tearers') are blood-vomiting fiends of ill-omen; the aerial Panis inspire slander and foolishness. Though impervious to weapons, the hero **Bhima** slew so many that they agreed to leave people alone. They are not all vicious. The Yakshas are forest spirits and usually benign, while female Rakshasas sometimes fall in love with human beings and transform into lovely women. Bhima married one of these; **Rama** denied one, with unfortunate consequences.

RAM (*See* ANIMALS, GOLDEN FLEECE)

Symbolises virility, aggression, procreative power. The first sign of the zodiac, Aries the Ram, represents spring's annual renewal of solar power. The ram's spiral horns, suggesting the crescent, may be connected with the **moon**, but are more usually associated with sun-, sky- and war-gods. The **Phoenician** god **Baal** is usually shown with ram's horns. In Egypt, the ram personified **Amon-Ra**; while in Greece the ram was sacred to **Zeus**, **Dionysus**, **Pan** and to **Hermes/ Mercury**. In India the ram was sacred to **Indra**; in Norse myth, the chariot of **Thor** is drawn by rams. In Celtic belief, the ram-headed **serpent** associated with the horned god **Cernunnos** yokes the fertility of the ram with the regeneration imagery of the serpent: some northern British war-gods are depicted with ram's horns. Yet first and foremost the ram is a **sacrificial** beast. So in Genesis xx Abraham is about to obey **Yahweh**'s command by sacrificing Isaac, but instead Yahweh supplies a ram, its horns caught in a bush. The **Golden Fleece** of Greek myth came from a supernatural ram, able to talk, fly and prophesy the future. Sent by Hermes to save Phrixus and Helle from being sacrificed to Zeus by their stepmother Ino, it carries them over the sea. Helle falls and dies, but Phrixus reaches Colchis, where he sacrifices the ram. At Thebes in Egypt a sacred ram was killed annually at the festival of the god **Amon**. Its fleece being placed on the statue of the god, it was then mourned and buried in a sacred tomb. The implication is that it was not a ram that was sacrificed, but Amon himself. Likewise in **Christian** symbolism the ram is Christ as leader of the flock, but it is also Christ crucified, as prefigured by the ram substituted for Isaac.

RAMA (*See* BHARATA, HANUMAN, INDIAN MYTH)

The life of this Indian hero is the subject of the *Ramayana*, the greatest epic of **Sanskrit** literature after the *Mahabharata*. Composed by the poet Valmiki *c.*300 BC, differing versions are found throughout India, where it is said that even to read it will remove all the reader's sins. Emphasising the values of conjugal affection and domesticity, its seven books each deal with a different episode in Rama's life.

An incarnation of the god **Vishnu** and eldest of four sons born to the three wives of King Dasaratha of Ayodhya, Rama the divine man was born to defeat the **Rakshasa** king Ravana, against whom neither god nor demon could prevail. In a contest at the court of King Janaka, only Rama could bend a bow which had belonged to the god **Shiva**. So he won his wife, Sita, but the intrigues of his stepmother Kaikeyi led Dasaratha to exile him for fourteen years. Sita and his brother Lakshmana insisted on joining him. Dasaratha died of a broken heart, whereupon Kaikeyi's son Bharata sought out Rama and offered him the throne. Rama insisted on completing his exile, so Bharata returned to rule in his place. Rama, Sita and Lakshmana wandered in lands subject to Ravana, whose sister, the Rakshasi Surpa-nakha, rejected in love by Rama, attacked Sita but was wounded by Lakshmana. Surpa-nakha appealed to Ravana, who kidnapped Sita and imprisoned her in his palace in Sri Lanka. Rama gained the aid of **Hanuman**, the monkey-god, who flew to Sri Lanka. Infiltrating Ravana's palace to find Sita, he returned to Rama and advised the building of a bridge over the sea to Sri Lanka. Crossing this bridge, Rama with Lakshmana and Hanuman's army fought bravely to defeat the demons. Yet, like **Hercules** with the Hydra, whenever Rama cut off one of Ravana's ten **heads**, a new head sprang up. At last a sacred arrow slew the demon king. With every Rakshasa dead, Sita was freed, but Rama refused to receive her, fearing Ravana had dishonoured her. Wishing to die, Sita had a pyre built and lit. She entered the flames, but **Agni** the **fire**-god would not burn her. Another version is that the fire could not even be lit. Then Rama, insisting he had merely wished to prove her innocence to the world, joyfully embraced her. Asking **Indra** to resurrect his fallen companions, he returned with them to Ayodhya in *Pushpaka*, a magical flying vessel. On arrival, Bharata willingly gave up the throne and Rama ruled at last.

The seventh book, perhaps a later addition, tells how his people still complained that Sita was impure. Heeding them as foolishly as his father had heeded Kaikeyi, he sent Sita into exile. She bore **twins**. Some sixteen years later he met and recognised them, but too late. She called on the **earth mother** to testify to her purity. The earth opened and (like **Persephone**) Sita sank into it, never to return. Grieving, Rama followed her by walking into the River Sarayu, where he disappeared. In another version, the manbird **Garuda** took him to heaven, where he was reunited with Sita (now the goddess **Lakshmi**), and they lived happily ever after.

Still worshipped in many parts of India, Rama symbolises the man who remains faithful to his wife. His tragedy is his jealous disbelief that she could possibly remain faithful to him.

RAMAYANA (*See* RAMA)

RANGI (*See* MAORI MYTH)

RAPTURE (*See* APOCALYPSE, ARMAGEDDON)
Apocalyptic belief held by modern Christian fundamentalists, chiefly in the USA, that the End Times are at hand and that, following a global purgation of war and suffering (the Tribulation), true believers will experience the Rapture, whereby **Christ** resurrected will raise them 'in the middle of the air' to **heaven**, the rest of humanity being condemned to perdition.

RAS SHAMRAH (*See* PHOENICIAN MYTH)

RAVANA (*See* HANUMAN, RAKSHASA, RAMA)

RAVEN (*See* DIVINATION, ESKIMO MYTH, TRICKSTERS, WHALE)
Symbol of darkness and death, this large black carrion bird is also known as a 'talking' bird, and thus associated with prophecy, usually of ill-omen or

destruction, as in **Poe**'s 'Quoth the raven; Nevermore', or as in Irish myth, where two ravens warn the god **Lug** that the Fomorians approach. The hero **Cuchulainn** is linked with magical ravens, as is the giant **Bran**. The fearful **Badb**, the triple goddess ruling carnage and battle, is the 'Raven of Battle'. In **Christian** symbolism the raven is **Satan**, pecking out the eyes of sinners and feeding on corruption; a symbol of evil as opposed to the innocence of the white **dove**, and also associated with the **Fall**. In Egypt it was associated with malevolent destruction; in **Judaic** belief it is unclean; in alchemy it symbolises dying to the world. It also depicts the solitude of hermit saints. In the Welsh *Mabinogion*, it is the benevolent **otherworld** creature of **Rhiannon**; in the 'Dream of Rhonabwy' the raven army of Owein ap Urien regains human form when Owein's standard is raised. In Norse myth, **Odin** has two ravens perched on his shoulder, which he sends out daily to question the living and dead; nightly before dawn they return with news of the world. In North America the raven was widely respected as a **trickster** and culture hero.

The **Eskimos** say Raven was born of the darkness when the world began. Realising he was Tulugaukuk, Raven Father, Creator of Life, he vitalised the world and covered it with growing things. When the first man fell out of a giant peapod, Raven fed him, created the musk-ox and caribou for him to eat, and created woman to be his companion. He taught them how to sew skins and make canoes and houses. Soon there were many people, but they ignored Raven, killing more animals than they needed. So he returned to the Sky Land, causing darkness to cover the world again. Yet from time to time he let the **sun** peep through so that the people could see to hunt. In Sky Land he took a snow **goose** as his wife, and she bore Raven Boy, who one day stole the sun from the chest where Raven kept it, and soared into the dark sky. Raven begged him to put the sun back in its place. Raven Boy did so, and with a flip of his wing sent the sky spinning round the earth, creating day and night, so that people would not forget the evils of darkness.

In Ireland, ravens were domesticated for purposes of **divination**. If the raven cried from above the bed in a house, a distinguished grey-haired guest would visit. If it cried 'bach', the visitor would be a monk; if '*gradh, gradh*', a member of the clergy. If it called from the northeast corner of the house, robbers would raid; if from the door, strangers or soldiers. If it chirped '*err, err*', sickness would come.[1]

1. *The Magic Arts in Celtic Britain*, Lewis Spence, Rider, London, 1970.

REBIRTH (*See* REINCARNATION, RESURRECTION)

REINCARNATION (*See* ER, KARMA, PHOENIX, RESURRECTION, TIBET)

Asserting that we live not once but many times on earth, **Buddhists** and **Hindus** hold that in each life we accumulate karma, positive or negative, and that we cannot escape the cycle of rebirths save by leading many good lives. The evil will be reborn to a lower order of existence as a debased person or as animal, reptile or fish. Texts like the *Tibetan Book of the Dead* teach how to avoid rebirth. Belief that we can escape incarnation after just one life is seen as wishful thinking, a denial of karmic law, which holds us responsible for our every thought, word or deed.

Pythagoreans, Platonists, Qabalists, Neoplatonists, Gnostics and **Sufis**, Essenes and **Christian** patriarchs have also promoted reincarnation. The Koran (Sura Nahel) says, 'Those who doubt are dead and they do not know when they will be born again.' The African **Abakulu-Bantu** are

Perfect Men for whom rebirth has ceased. Australian **Aborigines**, Balinese, **Eskimos**, Iroquois and **Hopis** in North America, early Teutons and **Celts** all hold or held such belief; so too many modern Western thinkers. Leonardo ('Read me, O Reader . . . because very seldom shall I come back into this world'). Bruno, **Paracelsus**, Donne, Spinoza, Leibnitz, Voltaire, Hume, Franklin, Fielding, Goethe, **Blake**, Schiller, Hegel, Wordsworth, Coleridge, **Shelley**, Schopenhauer, Carlyle, Balzac, Emerson, Thoreau, Whitman, Tolstoy and Dostoevsky, **W.B. Yeats**, Aldous Huxley, William James, **Freud, Jung** and others all spoke of reincarnation as a theory commanding respect.[1]

Sceptics ask, if rebirth occurs, why do we not recall our former lives? Or, if amnesia is involved, then surely rebirth is essentially the same as the death of one person followed by the birth of another? But amnesia does not disprove the reality of rebirth (**Pythagoras** was surnamed Mnesarchides, 'one who remembers his origins'), while the karmic hypothesis suggests that in any case not our memory but our actions are the issue.

The objection (made by Tertullian 1,800 years ago as by sceptics now) to reincarnation as inconsistent with population increases is likewise flawed. It assumes the proportion of discarnate to incarnate beings as roughly one-to-one. Yet in the *Phaedo*, **Plato** suggests that 'many revolutions of ages' ensue between lives and in the *Republic*, he mentions a 1,000-year cycle between rebirths – as does **Virgil** in *The Aeneid*. The *Bhagavad Gita* speaks of an 'immensity of years'. The objection that reincarnation cannot occur as there is no life without the body asserts a belief, no more. More easily denied is the theory of **metempsychosis**, that human souls may be reborn in animals, or even in beans. Associated with Pythagoras, there is no evidence that he taught such belief. In the *Phaedrus*, Plato states that the reborn soul descends into savage life, but not into savage or bestial body, i.e., an evil-doer may be reborn ape-like, which is not to say, in the body of an ape. Yet the idea that evil-doers take on animal form via enchantment or rebirth is found in folklore the world over, as is the theme that magicians or supernatural beings can **shape-shift** into animal form at will.

In essence, this doctrine demands that each incarnated soul make the choices that lead it downward or upward in succeeding lives, as in Plato's myth of **Er**. Without a theory of karma, reincarnation is senseless.

1. *Reincarnation: The Phoenix Fire Mystery* (ed. S.L. Cranston and Joseph Head), Julian Press, New York, 1977.

RELIGION (*See* CONCORDANCE)
From Latin *religare*, 'to reconnect' or 'bind back', although Roman poet Cicero (106–43 BC) offered a root to 'select' or 'choose'. The term came into general use in the West during the Renaissance as an attempt by Christian scholars to define true religion (i.e. in their terms, **Christianity**). Hebrew, Arabic, Chinese and **Sanskrit** have no such general term. It may be taken to cover any belief-system invoking faith in and worship of a supernatural entity or powers. Many classifications have been attempted, few satisfactory. The German philosopher Hegel (1770–1831) divided religions into (1) natural (humanity's childhood); (2) spiritual (humanity's youth); and (3) the absolute religion, Christianity (humanity's manhood). His bias here is evident: among the **pagan** or nature religions he included **Confucianism** and **Buddhism**, neither of which possess any supernatural elements. Others have distinguished between (1) nature religions, involving **fetishism, magic, shamanism** and polytheism; and (2) ethical religions, in which a race or nation is

bonded by law under divine sanction (**Jainism, Brahmanism, Judaism, Taoism,** etc.), or in which the religious community is global while still relying on an assumed supernatural sanction (Christianity, **Islam**). Yet the basic religious impulse seems everywhere to be the same; i.e. the desire to reconnect with the source of being and to seek meaning (redemption, salvation); to penetrate the mysteries of life and death and thus gain power or knowledge by alliance with wisdom (gnosis), or with the spirit-world, or with the deity (however understood).

REMUS (*See* ROMAN MYTH, ROMULUS)

RESURRECTION (*See* CHRISTIANITY, JUDAISM, *KA*, REINCARNATION)

Christian doctrine of the body rising from the grave, as with Christ on the third day after crucifixion. Resurrection is a belief going back to Egyptian obsession with the preservation via mummification of the body so that the departed 'subtle bodies' might in time return to reanimate the corpse (*see ka*). Later Greek conception of the **immortality** of the **soul** denied bodily revival: yet in the Old Testament the belief ripens. Daniel xii:2 states that, in the end times, many who 'sleep in the dust of the earth shall awake', some to eternal life, others to eternal disgrace. Whether such resurrection is of the body is unclear; but various apocryphal books (**Enoch**) are more explicit. Among the Judaic priesthood the Sadducees had doubts, but in Matthew xxii:23–33, Jesus affirms Pharisaic belief in bodily resurrection. Thereafter, with Jesus himself said physically to have risen again (so even Doubting Thomas was ultimately convinced), the truth of bodily resurrection was proclaimed as universal. It is said by fundamentalists today (*see* **Rapture**) that on Judgement Day the bodies both of believers and unbelievers will be revived to be judged. Yet the implication, as in I Corinthians xv, is that the resurrected body is not physical but spiritual – more appropriate not only to older Judaic but also to Classical Greek and eastern belief.

REVELATION (*See* APOCALYPSE, ARMAGEDDON, CHRISTIANITY, NUMBER)

REYNARD (*See* FOX)

RHEA (*See* CRONUS, EARTH MOTHER, GREEK MYTH)

In Greek myth, the daughter of **Ouranos** and **Gaia,** sister and wife of Cronus, to whom she bore **Hestia, Demeter, Hera, Hades, Poseidon** and **Zeus.** Cronus swallowed every one as they were born, fearing dethronement, but when Zeus was born Rhea tricked him into swallowing a stone instead, then helped her youngest son to trick Cronus into vomiting up the others, who became the greatest **Olympian** gods. Worship of this earth-goddess, to whom the **oak** was sacred, probably originated in Crete: the Greeks also identified her with Phrygian **Cybele.** As such, her rites became orgiastic, connected with those of **Dionysus.** Her chariot, like that of Cybele, was drawn by **lions.**

RHIANNON (*See* HORSE, *MABINOGION*, PRYDERI, PWYLL, WELSH MYTH)

Maybe from Rigantona ('Great Queen' or 'Divine Queen'), this Welsh goddess appears in the *Mabinogion* (*see* **Pwyll** and **Pryderi**). In penance for a crime she did not commit she sat seven years outside Pwyll's palace by the horse-mounting block, offering to carry any visitor into the palace on her back. After Pryderl was returned and Pwyll died, she married Manawyddan, son of Llŷr (*see* **Manannan Mac Lir**), who undid the **curse** cast on Dyfed by the kinsmen of Gwawl, the suitor from whom Pwyll had won her. At first a fertility-goddess associated with the **otherworld** (as were Pwyll and Pryderi), in the romance of Branwen, and in the tale of 'Culhwch and Olwen' (both also *Mabinogion*), the sweet singing of her three 'magic birds', heard over the sea, could wake the dead and lull the living to sleep (like the song of the **Sirens**). Her later association with the horse-cult led her to be identified with **Epona**. She was therefore both **Muse** and (night)-mare: thus the charge that she slew her own son. She has also been identified with **Nimüe**, mistress of **Merlin**.

RIDDLES (*See* **GAMES, NUMBER, SPHINX, TRICKSTERS, WIND**)
At the heart of mythic **quest** lies the riddle as asked by the **Queen of Sheba** of **Solomon**, or by the guardian of **Mysteries** of a hero, who must prove he has brains as well as brawn, or die. The riddle may lie in asking the right question, as when **Perceval** saw the **Holy Grail** but failed to ask, 'Whom does the Grail serve?' His failure doomed the land to continued sterility. The **Sphinx** of Thebes asked **Oedipus**, 'What being, with only one voice, has sometimes two feet, sometimes three, sometimes four, and is weakest when it has the most?' All about were the bones of those who had given the wrong answers and been throttled. Oedipus answered, 'Man' (who crawls on all fours as an infant, walks on two legs as an adult, but needs a stick – third leg – when old). Vanquished, the Sphinx (herself a riddle, a creature of many unrelated parts) leapt to her doom.
   Riddling language may hide esoteric doctrines (as with gematria: *see* **Number**) in tales offering different levels of meaning. The verbose Celts loved asking riddles, preceded (in Wales) by the phrase 'Dychymig Dychymg' ('Riddle me this riddle'). So **Taliesin** confounded the court bards of King Maelgwyn with the riddle of a 'strong creature' without flesh, bone, blood, hand, foot, head or feet, unborn and invisible, from before the **Flood** and as wide as the surface of the earth. The answer, 'the wind', he gives by raising a violent storm that frightens the king into releasing **Elphin**.
   In an old Welsh poem, 'Cad Goddeu' ('The Battle of the Trees'), Robert Graves found a 237-line riddle so complex it led him to write a 500-page book to untangle the layers of meaning and lost history involved: a text itself so riddling that still it infuriates but fascinates many.[1]

1. *The White Goddess*, Robert Graves, Faber & Faber, London, 1961.

RIG VEDA (*See* **INDIAN MYTH, RISHIS, VEDAS**)

RING (*See* **CIRCLE, CORD, KNOT, SIGURD, TOLKIEN, WHEEL**)
Like the circle, it represents wholeness, eternity and cyclic time. It is also a binding symbol, as in a wedding ring, or as protection against evil. The medieval magus stood in a protective ring or circle when conjuring spirits. From Thailand to Scotland, children were protected from evil by encircling their wrists with thread or cord. In the Tyrol women in labour were told never to remove their wedding rings lest **witches** and **demons** gain power over them. In Lapland, one about to place a corpse in the coffin received from a relative of the deceased a brass ring, to be worn tied to his right arm as an **amulet** against any harm the ghost might do him. Many **taboos** against knots applied to rings. On Carpathus (a Greek island) all rings were removed

from the newly dead to free the soul. Moslem pilgrims to Mecca wear no knots or rings; likewise the Flamen Dialis (priest of **Jupiter**) in Rome, unless the ring were broken, so as not to hinder the movement of the spirit embodied in him. A ring sent by the Chinese emperor was a summons to return to court; a broken or half-ring signified banishment.

In folklore, rings are often endowed with magical power. The spirit dwelling in Aladdin's ring (*Arabian Nights*) is found in many tales. Likewise is the magic ring that confers **invisibility**, from **Plato**'s story of Gyges to the Ring of Power in **Tolkien**'s modern fantasy, *Lord of the Rings*. As in Tolkien's tale, such rings are found by accident, their finders being at first ignorant of their properties. Magical or not, the efficacy of the finger-ring remains widely respected, especially as a symbol of marriage.

RISHIS (*See* BRAHMA, DAKSHA, INDIAN MYTH, VEDAS)

Mythic Indian priest-poets who wrote the Vedas, the symbolic hymns of the **Aryans** of India. Founders of **Brahmanism**, they were known as prajapatis, 'the mind-born sons' of Brahma. Deified as Maha- or Deva-rishis who took **swan**-form to visit humanity, later Brahman lore claimed they were created before gods or **demons**. They were named: Gorama, Bharadwaja, Jamadagni, Vasishtha, Kasyapa, Atri and Visvamitra (the original seven), also Daksha, Bhrigu, Angiras, Pulaha, Kratu, Marichi and Pulastya. Of them it is said Bharadwaja lived three lives and then ascended to **immortal** union with the **sun**. Jamadagni's wife Renuka bore five sons and shared his ascetic life but one day saw two lovers and was filled with desire. Jamadagni ordered his sons to behead her. Only Parasurama, the fifth, would obey, Jamadagni cursing the others with idiocy. Parasurama asked that Renuka be restored to purity and his brothers to their wits, and Jamadagni agreed. Vasishtha ('most wealthy') had a sacred **cow** that gave him all he desired. Failing to steal it, Visvamitra, son of a kshatriya (warrior aristocrat), told the River **Saraswati** to bring Vasishtha to him for execution. The river would not: Visvamitra turned its waters to blood, but after that practised such austerities that he became a rishi too. This may refer to a contest between the brahman and kshatriya castes for power. Atri ('eater') was father of **Soma**, the **moon**; Gorama wrote a book of law; Kasyapa ('tortoise') was an avatar of **Vishnu**. These original seven came to be represented in the sky by the seven stars of the Great Bear, and their wives by the **Pleiades**.

Of two later added to make the 'nine brahma-rishis', Daksha and his quarrel with **Shiva** is described elsewhere; while Bhrigu, son of **Manu**, married a daughter of Daksha and fathered **Lakshmi**, Vishnu's wife who arose from the ocean of milk. Five other rishis were added still later: Angiras, Kratu, and Pulaha (the latter a famed slayer of **Rakshasas**) were deva-rishis who also married daughters of Daksha. Marichi was grandfather of the dwarf-incarnation of Vishnu, while Pulastya was a famous slayer of Rakshasas.

RITES OF PASSAGE (*See* CONCORDANCE)

RIVER MYTH (*See* GANGES, OCEAN, SARASWATI, STYX, WATER)

Rivers have long been venerated as sources of life and fertility. Sumerian civilisation arose by the Rivers Tigris and Euphrates, the Egyptian by the Nile and the Chinese by the Huang-Ho or Yellow River from which, it is said, crawled a **dragon** with the ideograms of the alphabet inscribed on its back. Rivers are typically associated with **serpent** or dragon imagery, or personified as a god or goddess, especially the latter, with power not only to fertilise but to purify. To bathe in 'Mother Ganges' (India) is to be purified; John the Baptist baptised Christ in the Jordan; the Greek **Maenads** tried to cleanse themselves of the **blood** of **Orpheus**, but the Helicon dived underground to avoid them. When the Roman emperor Elagabalus was assassinated in AD 222, his body was thrown into the Tiber which, it is said, promptly rejected him.

Many European river-names are those of **pagan** goddesses. Russia's Don and its Scottish namesake are from **Danu** ('Waters of Heaven'), likewise the Danube, Dnieper and Dneister. France's Marne derives from Matrona; the Saône from Souconna; the Seine from Sequana. England's Thames is Tämēsa; the Severn is Sabrina; the Brent, Brigantia. Ireland's Boyne is the goddess Boann. Scotland's Clyde is Clōta, the death-hag; the Dee is **Deva** – again, the eastern connection. Indeed, from China to Britain not only every river but every stream, spring or **well** was associated with its own particular divinity, dryad or **elemental** spirit (*see* **Water Cults**).

Cosmic rivers energise many **creation** myths. **Oceanus**, conceived as an immense river girdling the universe, and regarded by **Homer** as 'begetter of all', is also the world-serpent, **Ourobouros**. The four biblical Rivers of Paradise flow from **Eden** in the four cardinal directions to the ends of the earth, their source in a spring below the **Tree of Life**. They represent the creative power flowing from the unmanifest (highest plane) to the limit of the material (lowest), as in the lightning flash of the **Qabalistic** Tree. So too in **Hindu** myth four rivers flow from sacred Mount **Meru**; in **Norse myth**, four rivers of milk flow from Asgard. Another universal symbol, the River of Life, metaphorically describes the macrocosm, while to 'return to the source' is to return to Eden, the pristine, innocent state. The River of Death, on the other hand, is this transient world of change, or the **Styx**, separating the living from the dead, its crossing an **initiation**.

ROBIN (*See* WREN)

ROBIN GOODFELLOW (*See* PUCK, ROBIN HOOD)

ROBIN HOOD (*See* CERNUNNOS, FAIRIES, GREEN MAN)

Legendary English outlaw hero who, with his Merry Men, roamed Sherwood Forest robbing the (Norman) rich to give to the (Saxon) poor. Associated with the absentee reign of Plantagenet king, Richard I (1188–99) and with the county of Nottinghamshire, the first Robin Hood ballads originated in fourteenth-century Yorkshire in a time of agrarian revolt and plague, expressing a discontent that led to the Peasants' Revolt (1381). The ballads deal with restriction of hunting rights, rejection of tyranny and the theme of a local nobleman turned outlaw who respects women and the poor. Evil is personified by the Sheriff of Nottingham, Guy de Gisbourne, greedy agent of King Richard's grasping brother, John (king from 1199 to 1216). Robin Hood's association with this era may stem from a fake pedigree invented by Richard Stukeley, an eighteenth-century antiquarian. The original Robin was perhaps a disinherited follower of Simon de Montfort (founder of the English Parliament) after the latter's defeat in 1265. Or he may be but the romantic euhemerisation of a **pagan** woodland sprite like the Green Man or Cernunnos. Some of his band, like Friar Tuck, date from the original ballads. Others, like Maid Marian, are post-medieval. That they wear green allies them with **fairy**-lore. Certainly Robin and Marian became popularly associated with images of the Fairy King and Queen. Today, just as **Walt Disney** recast ancient fairy-tales like Snow White so that few now remember the original tales, so Hollywood portrayals of Robin Hood have fixed the image of the hero who 'robs the rich to give to the poor'.

ROBOTS (*See* FRANKENSTEIN, GOLEM, SCIENCE FICTION)
The tale of the mechanical **giant, invulnerable** but for one weak spot (*see* **Achilles Heel**), begins with the Greek myth of how **Jason** and the Argonauts meet the bronze giant Talos, who pelts them with rocks. But the witch Medea tricks him to sleep and removes the bronze nail that stoppers the vein that runs from his neck to his feet. Out pours the divine ichor, and Talos dies.

The theme re-emerges with the Golem, an artificial man who escaped his creator (Rabbi Judah Loew ben Bezabel, said to have lived in Prague in the seventeenth century), and again in the novel *Frankenstein* by **Mary Shelley**. The word 'robot', first used in *R.U.R.* (1921), a play by the Czech writer Karel Čapek (1890–1938), is from the Czech word *robota* (statute labour). Čapek's robots are artificial men of organic origin.

In 1940, American **science fiction** author Isaac Asimov took up the theme in tales collected (1950) as *I, Robot*. Developing ethical systems of conduct in his fictional robots, he posited 'Three Laws of Robotics'. In Asimov's tales, the robot attains quasihuman status. Other authors of the period, like Clifford D. Simak and C.L. Moore, were equally optimistic. Yet the explosion of the A-bomb at Hiroshima in 1945 bred doubts. Later robot stories more typically explore the sense of threat or sin engendered by creating such ambiguous beings (as in the original Golem and Frankenstein tales). Later writers, like Philip K. Dick, explored the theme of the man-machine hybrid, the cyborg or android.

ROC (*See* EAGLE, FABULOUS BEASTS, PHOENIX, SIMURGH)
This fabulous **bird** of Arabian myth is so vast that when Sinbad the Sailor, having been stranded by his shipmates on an island and needing a means of escape (*see Arabian Nights*) first encounters it in the Valley of Diamonds (on his second voyage), he walks round a vast white dome which turns out to be its **egg**. A huge cloud covers the sun: this turns out to be the Roc (or Rukh) itself. Lashing himself to its leg with his turban, he is carried away to a distant mountaintop and there set down, without the bird even noticing him. Venetian traveller Marco Polo (1254–1353) reported that every year Madagascar folk saw this bird, like an eagle but so much larger that with its talons it could lift an **elephant** from the ground, in order to drop the beast to its death then prey on its carcass.

ROCK'N'ROLL MYTH (*See* BEATLES, CROSSROADS, PRESLEY)
Fusing black rhythm'n'blues with white country music, and characterised by electrically amplified guitar played over bass and drums, the rise in 1950s USA of this popular music form coincided with the invention of 'teenagers' as a new economic market. Self-consciously rebellious and explicitly sexual in style and delivery, the first rock 'hit' ('Rock Around the Clock': 1955) by Bill Haley and the Comets led to the rise of 'stars' like Buddy Holly, Jerry Lee Lewis and Elvis Presley (known as 'Elvis the Pelvis' for his suggestive on-stage gyrations). Black singers like Chuck Berry and Little Richard made a mark, but most rock musicians and their 'fans' were white. Presley in particular was adulated yet when he was drafted into the US army (1960), rock'n'roll lost its way. In 1963 (1964 in the USA) a British group from Liverpool, the Beatles, excited public hysteria exploited by other British groups (Rolling Stones, the Who). Their bizarre appearance and behaviour was matched by a growing complexity in the music, as in the work of

guitarists Eric Clapton and Jimi Hendrix and of US singer-songwriter Bob Dylan (*b*. Robert Zimmerman: 1941). In 1965 Dylan, formerly a folksinger, 'went electric', outraging many fans. But his move, amid a growing popular use of psychedelic drugs and the new association of rock music with social causes (pioneered by Dylan in songs like 'The Times They Are A-Changin' '), was crucial. His influence and that of the Beatles presaged the rise of the 'hippies' and 1967's 'Summer of Love'. Briefly, many hoped youthful idealism might improve the world, yet rock's self-mythologisation soon became absurdly pompous. The dawning of the Age of Aquarius was announced even as fortunes were made. Hit songs like 'Eight Miles High' by the Byrds and 'White Rabbit' by Jefferson Airplane (both from California) glamorised psychedelic drugs. Author Tom Wolfe, in 'The Electric Kool-Aid Acid Test', promoted San Francisco band the Grateful Dead as standard-bearers of LSD-induced ecstasy: the Beatles publicly abandoned drugs for Transcendental Meditation, stimulating wide interest in Eastern philosophies. Millions of young people believed in an imminent **New Age** heralded by rock gurus.

Yet a darker side of rock-myth was first expressed by the Who in their 1963 hit 'My Generation' as 'Hope I die before I get old'. Rock had gained its first martyr in 1959 when Buddy Holly (*b*. 1936) died in a plane crash. A year-long retirement in 1966 by Bob Dylan after a motorbike crash caused as much query as his surreal, myth-laden lyrics: was he dead or alive? The drug-related deaths (1969–70) of Rolling Stone Brian Jones, Doors singer Jim Morrison, guitarist Jimi Hendrix and blues-shouter Janis Joplin all suggested that the 'Golden Age' was over. The unromantic demise of Elvis Presley (1977) reinforced this sensation, while for many the murder of ex-Beatle John Lennon in New York in December 1980 by fan Mark Chapman, who like Herostratus sought fame via crime, truly marked the end of the myth.

Yet the end had already been proclaimed in the early 1970s by 'glam-rock' and the self-mythologisation of stars like David Bowie, and in the late 1970s by nihilistic 'punk-rock' parody of rock's pretensions. 'I am an anarchist,' sang Johnny Rotten (John Lydon) of the Sex Pistols, 'I am the **Antichrist**.' He wasn't, but by then it hardly mattered.

By the 1990s, **narcissistic** rock myth was heavily exploited by singers like Madonna and Michael Jackson and via resale of 'golden oldies' playing on mythic nostalgia – a process also testifying to rock's loss of vitality.

ROMAN MYTH (*See* CONCORDANCE)

Founded 753 BC by **Romulus** (with his brother Remus said to have been suckled by a **wolf**, early Rome was affected by Greek culture and colonies in southern Italy. With the Republic established and Italy conquered (509 BC), Rome now spread into neighbouring lands, finally destroying the rival trading empire of Carthage in 146 BC. By 31 BC, with the Republic now the Empire, Rome ruled or was soon to rule lands from Britain and Spain to North Africa and the Near and Middle East. Yet while Roman arms were invincible, Romans were without any defence against foreign religion. Importing and renaming Greek gods, they assimilated other deities both local (Alban, Etruscan, Sabine) and distant (Carthaginian, Egyptian, Syrian, Persian). Practically minded, they lacked tradition and got their historians to invent it. By the third century BC it was accepted that Rome had been founded by the Trojan warrior **Aeneas** after the fall of Troy: a myth taking its final form in *The Aeneid* by **Virgil**.

The Romans saw the gods as abstract guardians of state and family, to be respected only if offerings to them produced results. Gods who failed were easily replaced by others. After Augustus, they deified even their emperors. They borrowed every deity of every culture they conquered, from Greek gods to **Adonis**, **Cybele**, **Mithra** and **Christ**. Yet Janus, the two-headed god of **doors**, his cult established supposedly by Romulus, is purely Roman, as is **Mars**, though in part derived from the Greek **Ares**. Of all Roman gods taken from the Greeks, Mars alone has a nobler character than his Greek original.

Jupiter, **Juno**, **Minerva**, **Diana**, **Mercury**, **Vulcan**, **Venus**, **Cupid**, **Neptune**, **Vesta**, **Ceres**, **Bacchus**, **Pluto**, **Proserpine**, etc., are abstract shadows of their Greek originals (**Zeus**, **Hera**, **Athene**, **Artemis**, **Hermes**, **Hephaestus**, **Aphrodite**, **Eros**, **Poseidon**, **Hestia**, **Demeter**, **Dionysus**, **Hades** and **Persephone**). The Romans did not even change **Apollo**'s name. Administering an empire left no time for imagination. Yet Rome became and remains the centre of the oldest, most powerful Christian Church.

ROMULUS (See ROMAN MYTH, TWINS, WOLF)
Mythical founder of Rome in 753 BC, twin brother of Remus and son of **Mars**, who raped the vestal virgin Rhea Silvia. Cast into the Tiber, she became a goddess, the twins being washed ashore by the grotto Lupercal, where a she-wolf suckled them. Protected by the shepherd Faustulus and his wife Acca Larentia, growing up they decided to found a city. Seeking an **omen** in the flight of **birds**, in his part of the sky Romulus saw twelve vultures, but in his part Remus saw only six. Romulus ploughed a furrow to mark the city boundary, but Remus jumped it, jeering. Murdering him, Romulus made the Capitol an asylum for homicides and runaway slaves. No women would marry them, so Romulus held sacred games, during which the Romans seized the Sabine maidens. War followed, ended by the mediation of the Sabine women. Romans and Sabines became one community, jointly ruled by Romulus and the Sabine king, Titus Tatius. After the murder of the latter, Romulus ruled alone until his mysterious death and disappearance in 715 BC. It is said he was carried up to heaven in a fiery chariot by his father, Mars.

ROSE (See LOTUS, ROSICRUCIANS)
Lovely flower guarded by cruel thorns, the rose symbolises both heavenly perfection and earthly passion; fertility and virginity; the centre of the **Cross** (so Rose Cross: Rosicrucian); also voluptuousness and sensuality, especially the red rose, flower of **Aphrodite**, goddess of love; associated also with wine and with the **blood** of **sacrificed** gods (**Adonis**, **Christ**). The white rose is the flower of light, innocence, chastity and the **Virgin Mary**. Red and white roses together unite opposites. The rose's thorns are the sins that led to the **Fall**. Like the lotus in the East, in the West the Mystic Rose (without thorns) symbolises **resurrection**, eternal spring. Its centre is the sun, its petals the diverse harmony of nature.

ROSICRUCIANS (See CROSS, FREEMASONRY, ROSE)
Secret society supposedly founded in the seventeenth century, its name from 'Rose Cross' or 'Christian Rosencreutz', originating in anonymous publication at Cassel in Germany of two pamphlets, the *Fama Fraternitatis* (1614) and the *Confessio Fraternitatis R.C.* (1615). The *Fama* claims that 'Father C.R.C.' founded an ancient Fraternity, now revived, its purpose to develop new wisdom opposed by old authority still tied to Galen and Aristotle. It tells how Christian Rosencreutz (1378–1484) travelled in the East. Working to reform knowledge, he returned to his native Germany, where he initiated the Fraternity of the Rosy Cross to aid the sick and to gain and spread

knowledge. He is said to lie in a vault, rediscovery of which will signal a reformation. The *Fama* claims to herald new learning via old alchemical and hermetic truths, and via the growth of new mechanical ('scientific') knowledge. A year later the *Confessio* appeared. Written in Latin, seemingly aimed at an educated international audience, it announced thirty-seven aims, including an end to sectarian and political strife, also an end to hunger, poverty, disease and old age.

The furore these pamphlets caused (the *Fama* reprinted thrice in 1615) grew in 1616 with publication in Strasbourg of an alchemical romance: *The Chemical Wedding of Christian Rosencreutz*, the tale of a husband and wife living in a magical castle. Divided into seven days, it describes the mystic marriage of the **soul** via vision, theatrical performance, **initiation** rite, and the ritual of life in the castle (echo of the **Holy Grail** Castle).

Invited to a royal wedding, Christian dons a white linen tunic with a red sash and with four roses in his hat, and sets out. Reaching the castle gate, he enters past a roaring **lion** to meet guests who boast of all they know, yet who fall silent when sweet music begins. A **virgin** enters to say that the bride and groom are not far away. Next day, as in Egyptian myth of the Hall of the Dead, souls are weighed. Christian bears himself humbly, and is given a high place at the banqueting table. On the fourth day, six people are beheaded and put in coffins and next day they are resurrected. On the sixth day the alchemical **bird** (*see* **phoenix**) is created. The seventh and last day sees the guests leave, gathering on the shore by twelve ships, each flying flags showing the signs of the **zodiac**.

This symbolic romance and the pamphlets preceding it had huge influence in Europe. The mood was dangerous, especially after the outbreak (1618) of the Thirty Years War. In 1623 in Paris, placards announced the presence of the Brotherhood RC and their Invisible College. It was said that thirty-six of these invisible adepts had sworn before **Satan** to abjure **Christianity**, in return gaining magical powers of flight, **invisibility** and ever-full purses. The philosopher Descartes (1596–1650) was accused of involvement. Now it seems there never was any organised movement, it was all a serious jest.

The pamphlets were probably written by Württemburg theologian Johann Valentin Andraeae. Born *c*.1586, *c*.1602 he wrote a tract, *Chemical Wedding*, which he called a *ludibrium* (jest) of little worth. His refusal to admit to writing the RC manifestos suggests common sense. The immediate furore died. Yet the jest of the Invisible College led to the foundation of the Royal Society in England by men like Boyle, Hooke, Isaac Newton and Thomas Vaughan – all so tempted by the serious joke of the Invisible College that they created it. So older **gnostic, hermetic** and alchemical traditions survived via Rosicrucian mystery. Later, in the nineteenth century emerged the Order of the Golden Dawn and other occult groups. Andraeae's mythic jest also influenced the development of modern science.[1]

1. *The Rosicrucian Enlightenment*, Frances A. Yates, Routledge & Kegan Paul, London, 1972.

ROSWELL INCIDENT (*See* **PHILADELPHIA EXPERIMENT, UFOs**)
A persistent modern myth: that an alien spacecraft crashed near the USAF nuclear bomber air base at Roswell, New Mexico, in July 1947, dead aliens being found in the wreckage, but that the US military and fledgeling CIA mounted a cover-up ('Operation Majestic') – though not before the Roswell Army Air Field issued a press release confirming the discovery on the remote ranch of William 'Mac' Brazel, who had informed the military authorities.

In his (fictionalised) account of the event, Whitley Streiber claims that while researching it forty years later he met and spoke with Walter Haut, who wrote the press report as published in the Roswell *Daily Record*; also with Dr Jesse Marcel Jr, son of Colonel (then Major) Jesse Marcel, the intelligence officer who recovered the debris before being ordered by General Ramey, commander of the 8th Air Force, to accept the assertion that he and other trained intelligence officers had mistaken a radar target (or weather balloon) for the remains of an unknown craft. Mac Brazel was held in illegal isolation for a week but refused to deny what he'd found.

In 1979, soon before he died, Colonel Marcel insisted in videotaped interviews that the USAF had covered up the truth. He described finding beams about a half-inch square: 'with some sort of hieroglyphics on them that nobody could decipher'. They resembled flexible, light balsa wood but were hard and would not burn. There was also a metal similar to but stronger than tin-foil, and a strong, brown papery substance which Mac Brazel's daughter Bessie described as having flowers pressed into it. Marcel showed this material to his son, then aged eleven, who later described it to Streiber. Marcel was then transferred to Washington DC to continue his intelligence career. Yet the cover-up infuriated him and others. In the *New York Times* (28 February 1960) Admiral Roscoe H. Hillenkoetter (first CIA Director), stated: 'Through official secrecy and ridicule, many citizens are led to believe that unidentified flying objects are nonsense. To hide the facts the Air Force has silenced its personnel.' Later he joined a UFO organisation, stating: 'I know the UFOs are not US or Soviet devices.'[1]

1. *Majestic*, Whitley Streiber, Macdonald, London, 1990.

ROUND TABLE (*See* ARTHURIAN MYTH, CIRCLE, GALAHAD, RING)

Constructed (one tale has it) for King Arthur by a Cornish carpenter, the Round Table was made round to avoid disputes over precedence among his many ambitious **knights**. It could be disassembled, so Arthur could take it with him wherever he wished. A better-known account, largely derived from Robert de Boron (*see* **Holy Grail**), is that **Joseph of Arimathea**, first Keeper of the Holy Grail, set up a Grail Table to commemorate the Last Supper, with one seat always left empty to represent that of the traitor, Judas Iscariot. This was the model for the Round Table, made on **Merlin**'s advice for Arthur's father, **Uther Pendragon**. Again, at it one seat (the 'dangerous seat', Siege Perilous) was always left empty, now representing the seat not of Judas but of **Christ** himself. Only the perfect knight who would win the Grail might safely occupy it. Thus when **Galahad** sat on it unharmed, all knew that he would redeem the land. This Round Table came to Camelot as **Guinevere**'s dowry when she married Arthur, whereupon Merlin chose the knights to sit at it and predicted the **Grail-quest**. In this version the Round Table has become a cosmic symbol of wholeness, the Grail its mystic centre and the twelve (equal) knights the signs of the **zodiac**. Yet with one seat empty it remains not quite perfect until the arrival of Galahad.

ROWAN (MOUNTAIN ASH) (*See* RUNES, WITCHCRAFT)

Often planted in churchyards or outside houses to ward off evil, the rowan (mountain ash, or quicken) is named from the Norse word *runa*, 'a charm'. On **May Day**, a rowan-spray was hung over doors to repel evil, and **wells** were dressed with rowan to repel **witches**. In Britain it was thought to prevent lightning, and that only a rowan whip could control a bewitched

horse. The 'witch-wand', used to divine metals, was of rowan; in Ireland a rowan-stake hammered into a corpse was thought to 'lay' its ghost and prevent **vampirism**. The death of the hero **Cuchulainn** was caused by three old crones spitting his taboo animal, a dog, on rowan-twigs and tricking him into eating it. Sometimes used in place of **yew** in making long-bows, it was the second tree of the Irish-Welsh Beth-Luis-Nion **tree alphabet**. Its round wattles, spread with newly-flayed bull-hides, were used by **Druids** to make evil spirits answer hard questions; thus a proverbial Irish expression, 'to go on the wattles of knowledge'. **Graves** claimed that this **oracular** usage explains the presence of rowan-thickets by **megalithic** stone circles. Also in Ireland, the Druids of opposing armies lit rowan-fires, over them chanting incantations to summon helpful spirits. In the romance of Diarmuid and Grainne, the rowan berry, with the apple and red nut, is called 'food of the **gods**' and is taboo, being as red as the hallucinogenic, deadly scarlet toadstool *Amanita muscaria*.[1] Likewise in Greece all red foods were taboo, save at feasts honouring the dead; the colour red being associated with death and with grave-rites the world over since earliest times, as witnessed by the discovery of Neanderthal burials in which the dead were painted with red ochre, the 'blood of the earth'.

1. *The White Goddess*, Robert Graves, Faber & Faber, London, 1961, pp.167-8.

RUDRA (*See* INDIAN MYTH, MARUTS, SHIVA, VEDAS)
Terrible **Vedic** god of wind, storms, time and death who rides a wild boar, this 'Howler' or 'Roaring One' was invested with both good and evil qualities. Dreaded as the furious god of drunken behaviour, sudden hurricane and disease, he was also revered as a destroyer of evil, hatred and disease, and as a guarantor of long life. Father of the tempestuous Rudras and **Maruts**, as Lord of Time the year was his bow, his shadow the bowstring. Early on he was sometimes identified with the Vedic **fire**-god **Agni**, but later Shiva ('the friendly one': *see* **Mithra**) absorbed both Agni and Rudra.

RUMI, JALALUDDIN (1207-73) (*See* ISLAM, NASRUDDIN, PERSIAN MYTH, SUFIS)
The most famed of medieval Persia's philosophical poet-teachers, he was a semi-mythical figure to whom later generations attributed miracles. Tales about and anecdotes attributed to him are used in **Sufi** schools to develop insights beyond ordinary perception, as with the **Nasruddin** tales. Author of the pantheistic *Masnavi*, it is said that as a child prone to visions he was with playmates on the roof of his house when suddenly he vanished from view. A hue and cry was raised, whereupon as suddenly he reappeared, pale and shaken, describing how men in green mantles had carried him to heaven. Later, as a student in Aleppo, reports of his nocturnal disappearances one night led Kamaluddin, the governor of the seminary, to follow Moulana (as Rumi was called). They reached the city gate, which opened itself: beyond was a white-domed building full of unearthly green-mantled figures, who greeted Moulana. Fainting, next afternoon Kamaluddin awoke to find himself alone in the empty desert. There was neither building nor human presence. For two days and nights he roamed, lost. A search-party rode out and found Moulana, who told them where to look, so Kamaluddin was found, near death. This event attracting publicity, Moulana moved on to Damascus. *En route* his caravan camped in a place of **sorcerers** who, to impress him, sent a boy up into the air. Moulana prayed. The boy cried out:

'I cannot descend. I feel as if I am nailed here.' Nothing the sorcerers did would bring him down, until Moulana persuaded them to accept the power of Allah (God) and the Prophet Mohammed. Once they did this, the boy was allowed to descend to earth: thereafter the sorcerers devoted themselves to good deeds.

Many such tales are told about the saintly Jalaluddin Rumi.[1]

1. *The Hundred Tales of Wisdom*, Idries Shah, Octagon Press, London, 1978.

RUNES (*See* NORSE MYTH, OGMA, TEUTONIC MYTH)

The Gothic word *rūna* or *rūn* originally implied anything cryptic, and so early became a synonym for hidden wisdom or knowledge. Thus in Northern European **pagan** lore, any oracular saying was a 'rune'; the magic **drum** of the Lapps was the 'rune drum'. Later the term came to denote a northern alphabet, its letters modified from the old Greek alphabet and introduced to the North perhaps as early as the seventh or sixth century BC. Displaced by Latin even as Norse pagan religion was displaced by Roman **Christianity**, runic characters resemble the **Celtic** script called Ogham (*see* **Ogma**). The two systems, though of different origin, are approximate. Ogham, like runic script, is carved in vertical columns on stones. Both use a **tree alphabet** whereby the 'letters' come from tree- or branch-shapes (like semaphore?).

From Norway to Ireland, runic inscriptions, as also found on ornaments like brooches, were in their very making seen as magical. Not surprising, given the power attributed in every ancient culture to 'The Word'. Without parchment, paper or wide dissemination of Greek learning, the few wise men of the old pagan northlands who mastered not only the art of writing runes but the intellectual abstraction involved in learning how to write were (of course, and rightly) regarded as magicians. The signs they left carved in stones inevitably assumed a 'magical' aura. Not until literate Christian monks penetrated northwestern Europe did 'writing' become simply a means of recording mundane as well as supernatural events, in the process losing its supernatural aura. Until then, the power of setting down 'memory' or 'knowledge' as signs carved in rock or brass was inherently 'magical', if only because of the huge individual effort required in learning such skill.

Thus the Norse god **Odin** hangs self-impaled by his own spear from the world-tree not (as in Judaeo-**Christian** mythology) to liberate mankind, but to gain the magic of the runes.

RUSALKA (*See* DOMOVOI, LORELEI, NYMPHS, SIREN, SLAVONIC MYTH)

Throughout Russian and Slavonic lands it was said that if a girl or young woman drowned, either accidentally or by suicide, she became a rusalka, a water-**nymph**; possibly friendly (in the south), but probably not (if in the north). The rusalki (plural) of the Danube and Dnieper in the south were gracious and bewitching, beautiful and sweet-singing, mist-clad **sirens** who like the **Lorelei** of the Rhine lured men to death. But to drown in their arms was much more attractive than to suffer the same fate at the hands of their Siberian cousins. More like the Celtic **banshee** or *bean-nighe* (the washer-woman at the ford), the northern rusalki were cadaverous and ugly, crude and dishevelled, without art or song, naked hags who simply grabbed their prey (men or women) and tortured them before drowning them. When not murderous, they were mischievous, damaging nets and breaking millstones, sending flood and storm, stealing linen or thread from nearby houses.

Yet whether of north or south, they had not only a dryad (water) but a sylvan (woodland) nature. At the start of summer these souls of the dead would leave river or lake for the green woods about, choosing as a nest the branches of a **willow** or **birch** where it overhung the water, green **trees** being thought the abode of the dead. On moonlight nights they would dance in the clearing, their presence leaving thicker grass or barley. They were not all nasty.

RUSSIAN MYTH (*See* SLAVONIC MYTH)

S

SABBAT (*See* MENSTRUATION, WITCHCRAFT)

SACRED GEOMETRY (*See* NUMBER, PYRAMIDS, PYTHAGORAS)
Pythagoras said, 'Everything is disposed according to number'. Protagoras (fifth century BC) wrote, 'Man is the measure of all things'. In *Nature* (12 April 1979), B.J. Carr and M.J. Rees discuss microphysical constants that govern proportional relationships between galaxy, star, planet, man and microcosmos. A planet's size is the geometric mean between that of atom and of galaxy; a human's mass lies between that of planet and proton. These harmonic relationships inform the proportions of much ancient architecture. The Great **Pyramid** may be the best example of 'sacred geometry', but the knowledge was widely applied elsewhere. Chinese geomancy, **Aboriginal** 'Songlines', the Nazca lines and sacred peaks all express it. **Megalithic** circles, henges and dolmens were measured and laid out with precision.

At the core of the **Mysteries**, this knowledge arose from reflection on basic geometric forms found in nature. **Sun** and **moon** are circular, the square implies solidity, hexagons are found in honeycombs, triangles focus elemental dynamism, and the Vesica Piscis (produced by drawing two circles of equal size through each other's centres) was seen to form the genitals of the **mother** of all things. So, the vesica formed the basis of all holy structures from stone circles to Gothic cathedrals. At sunrise on a set day, the site geomantically chosen, the oriented vesica was measured out and from it, as from the goddess, other structural forms were generated.

Proportional relationships were ruled by the dynamic symmetry of the Golden Mean (Golden Section), a ratio derived from a set of root rectangles produced by compass from a double square and its diagonals, so generating a series of terms in which each number equals the sum of the two preceding. Today known as the Fibonacci Series, this generates a progression: 1, 2, 3, 5, 8, 13, 21, 34, 55, 89, 144, etc., governing forms from the pads on a cat's feet to the spirals in microscopic shells.

Considered by **Plato** to be the key to cosmology, the system survived in the Gothic cathedrals, though the masons rejected the traditional *ad quadratum* (square based) system in favour of the newer *ad triangulum*. But the rise of 'scientific method' led the system to be denied, forgotten and all but replaced by what **Blake** called 'single vision and Newton's sleep'. In the twentieth century Steiner used it in the Goetheaneum, Corbusier in his 'modular' system and Gaudi in his Sagradia Familia in Barcelona.

Geometry means 'measuring of the earth'. Of itself a 'sacred' art, to call a branch of it 'sacred geometry' implies that there is also 'profane geometry'. What is that but false measure?[1]

1. *Sacred Geometry*, Nigel Pennick, Turnstone, Wellingborough, 1980, pp.104–6; *City of Revelation*, John Michell, Abacus, London, 1973.

SACRED KINGSHIP (*See* KINGSHIP)

SACRIFICE (*See* CONCORDANCE)
The custom of offering gifts to a god to propitiate divine wrath, or in hopes of personal or social benefit, or in thanksgiving, or to renew relationship between the human and the divine, or (if the deity is an animal) simply to feed it. A devout **Hindu** brings grass to the holy **cow**; in ancient Egypt living men were fed to the sacred **crocodile**. For though in most **religions** now sacrifice is symbolic only, in many ancient societies animals and human victims were ritually slain and offered up as **blood** sacrifices. Central to such rites is the magical nature of the act: properly performed, it brings benefits, maintains social stability or prevents disaster by pleasing the gods or by showing them that man knows his proper place.

Sacrifices were made typically on a regular annual basis, on a god's feast-day, or at harvest time to ensure future fertility (*see* **corn-god**); or in times of anxiety due to drought, flood, war or other disaster; or to commemorate and renew a mythic cycle; or to appease the **ancestors** (as by placing food and goods in a grave to aid the dead man on his journey). In various cultures from China to Africa, the wives, servants and slaves of a newly dead king might be buried alive with him in a hecatomb (a Greek term for the sacrifice of a hundred oxen, applied to any mass sacrifice).

Human sacrifice might also involve cannibalism. The Aztecs of Mexico went to war specifically to capture sacrificial victims, killing them by tearing out their hearts, then eating them. Cannibalistic sacrifice also took place to mark the seasonal round by slaying and eating the old king, or to take on the courage of a slain enemy, as in 1824 the heart of English soldier Sir Charles M'Carthy was eaten by **Ashanti** chiefs in West Africa.

Another Ashanti king killed 200 young girls to mix their blood with the mortar of his new palace. This belief, that new buildings demand a blood-sacrifice, is explored by English novelist Peter Ackroyd in his *Hawksmoor* (1984), in which an eighteenth-century London architect buries a murdered victim in the foundations of each new church he builds. **St Columba** is said to have buried a disciple alive at Iona to 'consecrate' the soil.

Human sacrifice was also performed to divine the future. Celtic **Druids** stabbed victims to **divine** from their death-throes. Julius Caesar says (*De Bello Gallico* VI, 16) the Druids believed the supernatural powers could only be controlled if one human life was exchanged for another. They also held that the more captured victims were burned alive in a 'Wicker Man' at the **Beltane** festival, the more providential would be the coming harvest.

Yet that a **goat** replaced Abraham's son Isaac (Genesis xxii) as a burnt offering suggests how animals came to replace people as sacrificial victims. In time the killing even of animals became unacceptable – sacrifices became symbolic, with no real blood shed or lives taken.

SAGA (*See* AESIR, *EDDAS*, NORSE MYTH)
A term used of the traditional tales of the ancient Norse and Vikings, associated especially with old Icelandic literature and as following the earlier mythic song-cycles and poetry of the *skalds* or **bards**. Written in prose, they may be divided into those with historical foundation such as *Njal's Saga*, or the description of Erik the Red's 'discovery' of Vinland (North America), or those that are essentially heroic-mythic (*Völsungasaga, Ragnar Lodbrok, Hrolf Kraka*).

SALAMANDER (*See* ELEMENTALS, FIRE)

SALMON (*See* **FINN MACCOOL, FISH, HAZEL**)
In Celtic lore this silver fish, the largest found in British rivers, is a symbol of wisdom and knowledge. Fintan, a mythical Irish survivor of the **Flood**, escaped it in the form of a salmon. Later the poet Finegas, who lived by the River Boyne (goddess Boann), sought the Salmon of Knowledge (*Eo Feasa*) for **seven** years. This mysterious fish had gained its wisdom by eating nuts fallen from the divine hazel-tree growing above its pool. The nuts of the hazel are red, the colour associated with **blood**, death and the 'Food of the Gods' (*see* **Rowan**). At last Finegas caught it and roasted it, and his pupil Demne (Fionn MacCumhal: Finn MacCool in disguise) gained universal knowledge when, struck on the thumb by the hot juices, he sucked it. Thus what in Ireland is known as 'the thumb of knowledge'. So too the Welsh Gwion Bach, stirring **Cerridwen**'s **Cauldron** of Inspiration is struck on the thumb and enlightened. Fleeing Cerridwen, the salmon is one of the forms he takes before Cerridwen swallows him, to bear him as **Taliesin**.
Why should the salmon have gained such status? Maybe due to its size, silvery colour, sweet pink flesh and complex life-cycle involving both sea and river, but maybe most of all because of its ability to *leap*.

SALOME (*See* **FEMMES FATALES**, **HEAD**)
The Gospel of Mark (vi:16–29) tells how John the Baptist died through the wiles of Salome, daughter of Herodias, wife of Herod (Roman puppet king of Judaea) having already been married to Herod's brother Philip. Though imprisoning John for causing disturbances, including the baptism of Christ, Herod both listened to and feared him. Herodias hated John for calling her marriage unlawful, but Herod would not harm him. Thus at his birthday feast Herodias brought in the voluptuous Salome to dance before the king. Salome so pleased him that he vowed to give her whatever she wanted. Herodias told her to ask for the head of John. This Herod could not refuse, having made a vow before all his guests. The guard sent to decapitate John returned with the prophet's head on a dish, which Salome gave to her mother.

SAMĀDHI (*See* **BUDDHISM, YOGA**)
A Sanskrit term meaning 'to direct towards', signifying meditative focus on the ultimate unity of things; Samādhi is the eighth and final stage of **yoga**. The highest form of self-possession, it involves the abstraction of consciousness from mental as well as worldly concerns, total control of every faculty and complete conscious union with the divine source.

SAMHAIN (*See* **BELTANE, HALLOWE'EN**)

SAMSARA (*See* **BUDDHISM**)
In Buddhism, the illusory realm of worldly phenomena and existence, of attraction and repulsion, inhabited by incarnate beings who seek freedom from it via enlightenment. Though it is said that in time normal process of human evolution will reveal the unreality of the Samsara, it is the aim of all **yoga** to accelerate escape from this Ocean of Misery, this quagmire into which unenlightened lost souls **reincarnate** again and again, to become attached to Samsaric phenomena. Again, it is said of this state:[1]

> Indeed, all these are like dreams, like hallucinations, like echoes, like the cities of the Odour-eaters, like mirage, like mirrored forms, like phantasmagoria, like the moon seen in water – not real, even for a moment. In truth, they are unreal; they are false.

1. *The Tibetan Book of the Dead* (ed. W.Y. Evans-Wentz), OUP, 1960, p.181.

SAMSON (*See* BIBLE, HAIR)

The Old Testament tells (Judges xiii–xvi) how this semi-mythical Hebrew leader and strong man fought when the Hebrews were driven back by the Philistines. To start with, he caught 300 **foxes**, tied their tails together, torched the knots, then set them loose in the enemy cornfields. When they came for him and his own people handed him over, the power of the Lord made him strong. But then he fell for Delilah. The five Philistine kings bribed her to trick Samson into revealing the source of his strength. When she asked, he said he could be bound by **seven** new still-wet bowstrings. So she bound him and, with men in another room, cried that the Philistines were coming. Samson snapped the bowstrings. She tried again. He said he would be weak if she wove his seven locks of hair into the loom. This too failed. Finally he admitted that to have his hair cut would make him weak. So she lulled him to sleep and a man cut off his hair. Captured and blinded, he was taken to Gaza and set to work as a slave. For their entertainment during a sacrificial feast to **Dagon**, the kings called him to the temple to mock him, They did not notice his hair had begun to grow again. So he took hold of the middle pillars of the temple and pulled it down, killing not only himself and the kings but about 3,000 people on the roof.

SANSKRIT (*See* INDIAN MYTH, RISHIS, SARASWATI)

The ancient holy language of India and oldest known member of the Indo-European or **Aryan** family; the poetic language of the *Vedas*, *Upanishads*, *Puranas*, *Ramayana* and *Mahabharata*. Its alphabet and grammar were developed and elaborated by the semi-legendary Rishi priest-poets during the early **Brahmanic** period *c*.1000 BC. Mythically, Sanskrit is said to have been invented by Saraswati, goddess of eloquence and the arts.

SANTA CLAUS

Originally St Nicolas (*d.* AD 326), Russian patron saint, bishop of Myra in Lycia (Turkish Mediterranean coast), also patron of merchants, travellers by land or sea, and young people and scholars. At one time English schools celebrated his festival. Later (from the Dutch Sint Klaas) he became Santa Claus, alias Father Christmas – a fat, jolly, white-whiskered old man in red who, every Christmas, leaves his North Pole cavern to bring children gifts prepacked by willing **pixies** and **elves**. He travels on a flying sleigh drawn by red-nosed reindeer and brings his gifts down the chimney. All of which suggests a convergence of St Nicolas with an old Teutonic or Norse spirit of winter or the dead. His red garb and the flying reindeer suggest the old **shamanic** cult of the scarlet hallucinogenic toadstool *Amanita muscaria*.

SARASWATI (*See* BHARATA, INDIAN MYTH, RISHIS, RIVER MYTH)

Or Sarasvati ('waters'); a river now disappeared into the Tharr (Indian Desert), once flowing from the Himalayas to the Indian Ocean and deified by the **Vedic** Bharata people (the 'Lunar Race') who lived on its banks, by which the Vedic poets recited their verses. In **Puranic** times Saraswati became wife of **Brahma** and goddess of the arts and was credited with inventing **Sanskrit**. Identical with Vach (goddess of eloquence and 'Mother of the Vedas'), she was also associated with Viraj, the female form of the cosmic **giant**, **Purusha**. Paintings show her smiling in a gold-embroidered sari, holding a book and a *vina* (stringed instrument). She rides a **swan** (her control of passion) floating on a calm pond (her serenity of mind). Yet it is said that when Brahma took a second wife, she cursed him, so he could be worshipped only once a year. The **Buddhists** call her Vajravina, wife of Manjushri, **bodhisattva** of Wisdom. In Tibet she is (or was) worshipped in **Tantric** form, bright red and belligerent with three faces and six arms.

SASQUATCH (*See* BIGFOOT, YETI)

SATAN (*See* DEVIL, SHAITAN)

SATI (*See* DAKSHA, DEVA, INDIAN MYTH, RISHIS)

SATURN (*See* CRONUS, GOLDEN AGE, ROMAN MYTH)

From *satur* ('gorged') or *sator* ('sower'), an ancient Latin **corn-god** equal to **Janus** and **Jupiter**. Identified by the Romans with Greek **Cronus**, it is said he ruled Italy during the Golden Age after Jupiter drove him from the sky down to Latium. The prosperity he brought was celebrated in his annual festival, the Saturnalia (17 to 23 December). During this week of orgy and merriment a mock-king, the Lord of Misrule, governed Rome in memory of the Golden Age; masters served slaves, who could behave as they liked, and vast open-air banquets took place in the Forum. Schools, shops and law-courts were shut, gifts given and received, and military operations suspended. In his temple near the Capitol, the god's effigy, its hands usually bound with woollen strips to stop him leaving Rome, was untied for the week. At first a series of rural festivals, the feast became important after 217 BC when military defeats led to a religious revival in Rome. Today it finds a dim modern echo in Christmas, though **Hallowe'en** may be closer to its spirit. Later his name was given to the planet Saturn, the outermost of the anciently known **seven** and alchemically identified with lead. Thus the modern perception of a saturnine person as gloomy or sluggish, as in symptoms of lead poisoning which, some historians believe, was a central cause of the downfall of Rome due to wide domestic use of this metal.

SATYRS (*See* DIONYSUS, GREEK MYTH, NYMPHS)

Rude, bestial, mischievous **elementals** of Greek forest and mountain, these attendants of Dionysus loved drinking, chasing nymphs and terrifying shepherds or travellers by suddenly appearing and playing tricks. They had the **goat**'s pointed ears, hairy body, tail and cloven hooves, but in time lost these attributes but for the pointed ears and two small horns on the brow. Acquiring skill in **music** and **dance**, they played a chief role in the festivals of Dionysus. In Greek drama from the sixth century BC on, the satyr-play (satire) took place after each group of three tragedies.

Also in the retinue of Dionysus was Silenus, a fat, bald old drunkard swaying precariously on an ass. Able to see both past and future, he could be made to reveal the fate of anyone managing to tie him up as he lay in a drunken stupor. His name derives from the Sileni, similar to the Satyrs, but with the tails, hooves and ears of **horses**, and native to Phrygia, not Greece. In the satyr-plays they were represented as comic drunks.

SAVIOUR (*See* CHRISTIANITY, MESSIAH)

SCANDINAVIAN MYTH (*See KALEVALA*, NORSE MYTH)

SCAPEGOATS (*See* **GOAT, SIN-EATING**)

SCHEHERAZADE (*See ARABIAN NIGHTS*)

SCIENCE FICTION (*See* **CONCORDANCE**)
Also sci-fi or SF: speculative literary genre rooted in fantastic romances or 'tales of wonder' going back to Lucian of Samosata (*c*.AD 120–180) whose *True History* involves space-war and other marvels. Later came More's *Utopia* (1516), describing the ideal state; Kepler's *Somnium* (1634), and the comic histories of Cyrano de Bergerac (1619–1655). **Swift's** *Gulliver's Travels* (1726), Gothic romances like *Frankenstein* (1818) and **Poe**'s dark dreams preceded the romances of **Jules Verne. H.G. Wells** established the genre's staple themes: time-travel, invasion from outer space, genetic mutations, **invisibility**, etc. Fantasists like Bulwer-Lytton, Conan Doyle, **H. Rider Haggard**, M.P. Shiel, and **E.R. Burroughs** were also popular before World War I.
Yet SF is basically American. In 1926 Luxembourg emigré Hugo Gernsback (1884–1967) introduced *Amazing Stories*, 'the magazine of scientifiction', publishing predictive tales of supposed scientific accuracy. During the Depression, millions read 'scientifiction' monthlies full of 'space opera', bug-eyed monsters, death-rays, mad scientists, etc. In 1937 author John W. Campbell became editor of the magazine *Astounding Stories*. Nurturing new writers like Asimov, Heinlein, Sturgeon, Simak and Van Vogt, and demanding rigorous extrapolation from an original idea, his belief that science could solve all human ills led to the '**Golden Age**' of 'hard' SF (see below).
Post World War II anxieties (the bomb, communism) led to a satirical pessimism. A new magazine, *Galaxy* (1950) promoted the 'dystopias' (anti-utopias) of Sheckley, Gunn, Pohl and Kornbluth, etc., typically extrapolating existing social trends into an awful near future tyrannised by advertising, overpopulation or atomic pollution. **Hollywood** films like *Red Planet Mars* (1952) or *Invasion of the Body Snatchers* (1955) mythologised paranoia about communism as an alien invasion from outer space. English authors Aldous Huxley (*Brave New World*: 1932) and **George Orwell** (*Nineteen Eighty-Four*: 1948) had explored such fears, yet few British or European authors entered the American SF market. Among the few were **Arthur C. Clarke**, John Wyndham (*Day of the Triffids*) and later Brian Aldiss. SF remained as American as **Superman** or apple pie.
In 1964 English fantasy author Michael Moorcock took over the ailing British magazine *New Worlds*. Renaming 'science fiction' as 'speculative fiction', he encouraged writers like **J.G. Ballard** to reinvent SF, even as in the USA authors like Samuel Delany, Roger Zelazny, Robert Silverberg and Philip K. Dick gave the genre new authority – Dick in particular by his exploration of the nature of reality in tales typically denying any fixed reality at all.
SF now became popular among young people also interested in mysticism and the '**New Age**'. The first episode (1966) of the *Star Trek* tv series presaged Stanley Kubrick's movie *2001: A Space Odyssey* (1968) – a portrayal of human evolution as guided by enigmatic alien intelligence. The success in 1977 of two films: *Close Encounters of the Third Kind* (director Steven Spielberg) and *Star Wars* (George Lucas), showed that standard SF themes were now part of the mythic landscape of the late twentieth century.
Star Wars, a 'space opera', employs old mythic themes. Fatherless hero Luke Skywalker (**Perceval**) is fostered on a desert planet (**wasteland**). Educated and magically armed by a wise old man (**Merlin**), he rescues the princess (**Sleeping Beauty**) from villainous Darth Vader (evil **giant**) who, at the end of the Star Wars trilogy (*Return of the Jedi*: 1982), is revealed as

Luke's worm-like, impotent father (**Ouranos** castrated).

Yet where old myth is unchangeably set in the past, or in an **Olympian** realm of all-potent gods, SF is **Promethean**. Human know-how (science) will defeat or at least fight to a draw with alien invaders or natural catastrophe.

Concern with science is most evident in so-called 'hard SF', less so in the other main sub-category of the genre, science fantasy, which derives from the older tradition of fantastic romance. **Tolkien**'s *Lord of the Rings* (1954–55) remains the best-known modern example. In his *Perelandra* trilogy (1939–45), **C.S. Lewis** re-enacts the myth of **Eve**'s temptation. In *Seven Days in New Crete* (1949), Robert **Graves** explores the myth of the **king sacrificed** to ensure fertility. *Star Maker* (1937) by **Olaf Stapledon** remains perhaps the best modern example of pure speculation as to humanity's ultimate goal.

Others have adapted ancient myths – thus, characters like 'Jack **Odin**', or the **comics** hero, 'The Mighty **Thor**'. In *Creatures of Light and Darkness* (1969), American author Roger Zelazny rebirths the Egyptian pantheon. Philip José Farmer has explored the theme of the doomed **horned** god. Rationalised myth is exemplified by English author Robert Holdstock's *Mythago Wood*, in which depth psychology is applied to explain the hero's haunted involvement with the mythic **elemental** denizens of an old English wood (1984).[1]

1. *The Encyclopedia of Science Fiction* (ed. Peter Nicholls), Granada, London, 1981.

SCORPION (*See* GILGAMESH, ORION, SERPENT, SPIDER)

Found in all hot lands, the scorpion eats insects and its fellow arachnid, the **spider**. Sheltering in daytime and easily trodden upon, its poisonous sting can prove fatal. So like the **serpent** it represents destruction, the treachery of Judas, or death. The Egyptian god **Set** murdered **Osiris** in the month of Athyr with the sun in Scorpio (21 October – 20 November). When **Isis** fled him to hide in the Nile delta, **seven** scorpions followed her. She gave birth to **Horus**, but Set's scorpion killed him. So too the Greek sun-god **Apollo** sent a scorpion to sting **Orion** to death. Yet while **Thoth** taught Isis a spell to counteract the poison, Orion had no such luck.

Also an attribute of the Phrygian beer-god Sabazius and the Babylonian **Ishtar**, in the Sumerian epic, Gilgamesh has to pass through caves under Mount Mashu. These are guarded by scorpion-men created by the chaos-hag **Tiamat**, symbolising the setting sun, the onset of winter and dark cold night.

SCOTTISH MYTH (*See* BELTANE, IRISH MYTH, CURSES, KIRK, SECOND SIGHT)

Though as rich in folklore as the nearby Celtic lands Wales and Ireland, no major native Scots mythic tradition survives, the Scots being Ulster Gaels who began entering 'Scotland' *c*.AD 500, so assimilating the indigenous Picts that all earlier lore was lost. Yet the presence of earlier cultures since at least *c*.3500 BC is revealed by **megalithic** circles from Callanish (Lewis) to Stenness (Orkney) and by the many knowes (**earth mounds**: 'fairy hills') found throughout the land. The Picts left 'symbol' stones throughout the north, all rich in zoomorphic carvings, yet their beliefs remain as unknown as those of the Britons of southern Scotland. But any attempt at definition via modern national boundaries only confuses the issue.

The earliest surviving Welsh epic, the *Gododdin*, describes war between Gododdin (Edinburgh) and Catraeth (Catterick, Yorkshire) in the sixth century AD. The Battle of Arderydd (*c*.AD 573), from which the poet

Myrrdin (**Merlin**) fled insane to the Forest of Celydon, was probably fought north of Carlisle (modern Anglo-Scottish border): 'Celydon' was Scotland's Caledonian Forest. In **Arthurian myth**, Arthur's stepsister **Morgause** and son **Mordred** live in the Orkneys, north of Scotland. This is believable. Beehive towers called 'brochs', found throughout northwest Scotland, were built to resist persistent Norse invasion.

Even as Anglo-Saxons drove back the Welsh, the Scots seized Pictland, bringing their myths with them. The Irish Ulster Cycle tale of **Deirdre** is set as much in Scotland's Argyll ('Coast of the Gael') as in Ulster. Fionn mac Cumhal (**Finn MacCool**) and **Oisin** become Fingal and Ossian, as in the eighteenth-century hoax by **Macpherson**. This led to many secondary legends, as in the tale of how Fingal stepped from the vitrified fort of Knockfarrel (Easter Ross) to the opposing heights of Ben Wyvis in one giant bound.

Native myth or import? It's hard to tell. In Ireland the myths were written down from the eighth century on (in Wales later) by Celtic monks. This did not happen in Scotland, a composite 'nation' of Gaels, Norse, Picts and Anglo-Saxons, their co-existence uneasy even today. Little in Gaelic or in Old Scots was written down before the fourteenth century. Not just the mythology but even the history of pre-Gaelic Scotland remains obscure.

Yet certain Scots traditions suggest older myths, notably the survival into recent times of **fire-festivals** like **Beltane** (Bealltuin), as well as belief in **witchcraft**, **fairy**-lore and dangerous **elemental** beings (*bean-nighe*), **kelpie**, **selkie**, the Loch Ness Monster or the Big Grey Man (Fear Liath Mhór) said to haunt Ben Macdhui and lead climbers astray amid the swirling grey mists. Highland Scotland also has many tales of **curse** and **second sight**.

SCYLLA (*See* CLASHING ROCKS, GREEK MYTH)

SEA (*See* FLOOD MYTH, OCEAN, SERPENT)
About every land, forever changing the shape of shores, bringing life and death to those living by it and especially to those upon it, the sea was always seen as the birthplace of life – as the River Oceanus engirdling the known world, or as the home of awful monsters tamed by **Marduk**, **Yahweh** or **Zeus**: Tiamat, **Leviathan**, **Typhon**, the **kraken**, the **serpent** of Midgard, the **whale** that swallowed Jonah. It is the home of **mermaids**, **sirens** and **selkies** whose sweet songs lure mariners to their death by drowning, but also of the giant fish that towed **Manu**'s ark to safety, or of friendly **dolphins** rescuing shipwrecked mariners. The sea is **Ananta**, the cosmic serpent protecting the sleeping **Vishnu** as he dreams new worlds into being. In the sea were thought to be **Janus**-headed **hermaphrodites**, man-headed **bulls**, four-headed **dogs** with one body. Everything ever born on the fixed earth has a **protean** origin in the sea.

SEA-GODS/GODDESSES (*See* CONCORDANCE)

SEA MONSTERS (*See* CONCORDANCE, KRAKEN, LEVIATHAN, SEA, TYPHON)

SEALS (*See* BALOR, ESKIMO MYTH)
The Irish *Lebor Gabala* (*Book of Invasions*) tells how the demonic **Balor** drowned all the infants born to his daughter Eithne and her guardian-women. These infants became seals. In Caithness in the north of Scotland it

was said seals are fallen angels, and also found here are tales of selkies: seal-people taking human form, leaving their seal-skins well hidden when doing so. If a man found and hid the skin, he could get a selkie to marry him, but if she found her skin again she would abandon husband, children and home for the sea. Folk with webbed hands or feet were said to be selkie-born.

SEASONAL FESTIVALS (*See* CONCORDANCE)

SECOND COMING (*See* ANTICHRIST, APOCALYPSE, CHRISTIANITY, SLEEPING EMPEROR)

Christian dogma that after the Battle of **Armageddon** the risen Christ will descend to the world to slay the wicked with the sharp sword of the Last Judgement, then raise believers up to **heaven**. This will lead to 'a new heaven and a new earth'. The saints will rule for a millennium, then this world will pass away. In early Christian times it was widely thought that this event would happen during the lifetimes of those who had known Christ. In AD 999 believers throughout Europe feared that midnight of the New Year 1000 would see the end of the world. Even bankers gave away their wealth to buy salvation. Now the Christian year AD 1999 is near and apocalyptic movements once again grow stronger.

SECOND SIGHT (*See* CURSES, OMENS, PROPHECY, SCOTTISH MYTH)

'The Second Sight is a singular faculty of seeing an otherwise invisible object,' wrote Martin Martin in *A Description of the Western Isles of Scotland* (1703), 'without any previous means used by the person that sees it for that end; the vision makes such a lively impression upon the Seers, that they neither see nor think of anything else, except the vision, as long as it continues: and then they appear pensive or jovial, according to the object which was represented to them.'

So firmly associated with Scottish Highlanders that it may be seen as specific to them, *an da shealladh* ('the two sights') consists of unsought vision, omens of impending disaster, physical changes affecting the seer, and perception of specific symbols that denote specific events so systematic as to suggest that second sight may derive from a once consciously directed precognitive art. Well into historical times it was a part of everyday Highland life and taken for granted. Seers like the Petty Seer, Thomas the Rhymer and (best-known) Coinneach Odhar, the Brahan Seer (*see* **curses**), were thought not to be blessed but cursed with a malady. Martin, factor to the Laird of Macleod in the Outer Isles early in the eighteenth century, wrote:[1]

> At the sight of a vision, the eye-lids of the person are erected, and the eyes continue staring until the object vanish . . . There is one in Skye, [who] when he sees a vision, the inner part of his eyelids turn so far upwards, that after the object disappears, he must draw them down with his fingers . . . This faculty of the Second Sight does not descend lineally in a family . . . neither is it acquired by any previous compact. And . . . I could never learn . . . that this faculty was communicable any way whatsoever.
>
> The Seer knows neither the object, time, nor place of a vision; and the same object is often seen by different persons, living at a considerable distance from one another. The true way of judging as to the time and circumstance of an object, is by observation . . . If an object is seen early in the morning . . . it will be accomplished in a few hours afterwards. If at noon, it will commonly be accomplished that very day. If in the evening,

perhaps that night . . . When a shroud is perceived about one, it is a sure prognostic of death: the time is judged according to the height of it about the person; for . . . as it is frequently seen to ascend higher towards the head, death is concluded to be at hand within a few days, if not hours . . . If a woman is seen standing at a man's left hand, it is a presage that she will be his wife . . . To see a spark of fire fall upon one's arm or breast, is a forerunner of a dead child to be seen in the arms of those persons . . . To see a seat empty at the time of one's sitting in it, is a presage of that person's death quickly after.

All those who have the Second Sight do not always see these visions at once, though they be together at the time. But if one who has this faculty, designedly touch his fellow-seer at the instant of a vision's appearing, then the second sees it as well as the first . . .

A Treatise on the Second Sight, Dreams and Apparitions (by 'Theophilus Insulanis': 1763) catalogues many hundreds of cases, all matter-of-factly. The pseudonymous author (perhaps the Rev. John Macpherson of Skye) accepts that 'deists and freethinkers, who deny all revelation', refuse to credit Second Sight and 'raise what dust they can to cloud and discredit it'. Yet he finds it 'lamentable' that the Church, being based on 'Sacred Oracles', should also deny the truth of revelation.[2]

1. *A Description of the Western Isles of Scotland*, Martin Martin, 1703.
2. *A Treatise on the Second Sight, Dreams and Apparitions*, Theophilus Insulanis, Edinburgh, 1763; *Ravens and Black Rain*, Elizabeth Sutherland, Corgi, London, 1987.

SECRET DOCTRINE (*See* **THEOSOPHY**)

SECRET SOCIETIES (*See* **CONCORDANCE**)

SEERS (*See* **CURSES, OMENS, PROPHECY, SECOND SIGHT**)

SELKIE (*See* **SEALS**)

SEPHIROTH (*See* **QABALAH**)

SERPENT (*See* **CONCORDANCE**)
Denounced in the **Bible** as the **Devil**, tempting **Eve** to tempt **Adam** to deny **Yahweh** by eating the fruit of the Tree of the Knowledge of Good and Evil, the serpent has had a bad press in Judaeo-Christian lore, becoming 'that old **dragon**', source of all evil and temptation. Yet the mythic history of the serpent/dragon is complex. It has always symbolised fertilising power, the cosmic **river**, the lightning flash from the heavens, chthonic currents snaking through the earth. The Garden of **Eden** myth is adapted from the Sumerian Garden of Immortality, with crucial alterations. In the latter, **Mother Earth** (Eve) is wife of the Serpent (lightning flash). No jealous God exists. All may enter the Garden to seek **immortality**, like **Gilgamesh** who, having gained it, fell asleep, only for a serpent to eat the plant of everlasting life, so gaining the power to slough its skin. Then Gilgamesh knew that he, like all men, must die, while the serpent lived.

The mythical serpent is androgynous: male, female or self-created. As a killer by crushing or poison, it is death and destruction. By renewing its skin, it is life and resurrection. Its coils represent the cosmic cycles, the river circling the world (Oceanus, Ourobouros), or the very support of the world itself, as in **Fon** (African) myth that the 3,500 coils of the serpent-god Da below the world support it, and the 3,500 above it support the heavens. Norse myth tells how at **Ragnorak** the serpent of Midgard will surge up out of the depths of the **sea** where it has been chained to flood the world. In this case, as 'Master of the bowels of the Earth', it is the dark side of the human mind, the chaotic aspect of nature, forever at war (**Leviathan, Set, Tiamat, Typhon, Vritra**) with the sky-power of reason and conscious insight (**Yahweh, Osiris, Marduk, Zeus, Indra**).

In such myths, the **sky**- or **sun**-god slays the dragon/serpent or brings it under social control. The serpent is naturally dangerous, like **flood** or sexual desire. Mythically it may be demonised as evil, but its potency as a fertility symbol gave even the authors of Genesis some difficulty in establishing it as such without ambiguity. Not only does it prove Yahweh a liar ('Thou shalt not surely die', it assures both Adam and Eve), but the Old Testament scribes could not conceal the serpent origin of Yahweh himself, as when Yahweh gives **Moses** a serpent-rod to scare the Egyptians, a rod that later drew (dowsed?) water from the desert. Later Yahweh sent serpents against the Israelites, then told Moses to 'Make a fiery serpent, and set it on a pole; and every one who is bitten, when he sees it, shall live.' So Moses set a bronze serpent on a pole, as in the *caduceus*, sign of **Mercury, Asclepius,** Hippocrates and of all **healing**.

So too, it was the Tribe of Levi (Leviathan) who recorded Yahweh's doings: when Hebraic images did in time appear of the God who-must-not-be-pictured, they were of a god with serpent legs.[2]

1. Numbers xxi:5–9
2. *Occidental Mythology*, Joseph Campbell, Penguin, London, 1976, pp.9–15, 30.

SET (*See* EGYPTIAN MYTH, HORUS, ISIS, OSIRIS)

Also Seth, Sutekh, in Egyptian myth the evil brother of Osiris, Isis and **Nepthys**, his wife. Tearing himself prematurely from his mother's womb, he was violent, cruel and jealous, his white skin covered by red hair giving him a donkey-like appearance. Identified by the Greeks with **Typhon**, he personified the barren desert. His childless wife Nepthys seduced Osiris (the fertilising Nile) and bore **Anubis**. Hating Osiris and desiring the throne, Set tricked his brother into a coffer which he threw into the Nile. Isis recovered the body, but Set hacked it into fourteen pieces, scattering them far and wide. Recovering them, Isis remade Osiris and bore Horus. Set sent a **scorpion** to slay Horus, but **Thoth** helped Isis to revive him. Later Horus avenged Osiris by castrating Set. This refers to the overthrow of Set, originally Lord of Upper Egypt, by the followers of Horus. The Hyksos invaders identified Set with their warrior-god Sutekh. Later the great Pharaoh Rameses II (thirteenth century BC), whose father was called Seti, proclaimed himself the 'Beloved of Set'. This infuriated the Osirians who broke Set's statues and erased his inscriptions. Made a god of the unclean, this one-time Lord of Upper Egypt ended up the enemy of all the gods.

SEVEN (*See* NUMBER, THREE, TWELVE)

A mystical number since early times, being the union of three (the trinity, the heavens, **spirit**) and four (the earth, material creation, body). Pythagoreans called it the number of religion. The Jewish Elohim ('Shining Ones') were seven in number and ruled the seven anciently known planets. In Daniel ix:24, seven times seventy years are appointed 'to bring in everlasting righteousness'; in Revelation xiii:5 the rule of the Beast will last forty-two (six times seven) months; the Lamb of God's seven horns symbolise his power. Seven golden candlesticks represent the Church Universal and Triumphant; the Jewish Menorah has seven branches; the lyre of **Orpheus/Apollo** has seven strings; **Pan** has seven pipes; in Greek lore there are Seven Wise Men. The cave of **Mithras** has seven doors, seven altars and a seven-runged **ladder** for seven grades of **initiation**. **Noah**'s Ark landed during the seventh month: the **dove** was sent out on the seventh day. There are seven heavens, seven hells, seven deadly sins, seven pillars of wisdom, seven sacraments, seven days in a week, seven wonders of the world, seven ages of man; the seventh son of a seventh son has magical gifts. The Great Bear's seven visible stars are 'indestructible'; i.e. visible (northern hemisphere) all year round; the seven visible stars in the **Pleiades** are the Seven Sisters. Other uses of seven, alias the heptad, follow:

SEVEN AGAINST THEBES (*See* **GREEK MYTH, INCEST**)
Born of incest, cursed by their disgraced father **Oedipus**, king of Thebes, his **twin** sons Polyneices and Eteocles agreed to reign alternately. With Eteocles ruling first, Polyneices went to Argos to marry Argeia, daughter of King Adrastus. Another daughter, Deipyle, wed Tydeus, son of the exiled king of Calydon. At the year's end Eteocles kept the throne, so Adrastus mobilised an army, Polyneices and Tydeus among its seven chiefs who died attacking Thebes. Eteocles and Polyneices killed each other, fulfilling the **curse**. When the sons of the Seven grew up, Adrastus at last captured the city, but died on his homeward journey. This tale was the subject of the plays *Seven Against Thebes* by Aeschylus and *Phoenician Women* by Euripedes.

SEVEN SLEEPERS OF EPHESUS (*See* **BARBAROSSA, SLEEPING EMPEROR**)
It is said that seven **Christian** soldiers hid in a cave during the persecution by Roman emperor Decius (*c*.AD 250). Tracked down and walled in to die, they fell into a miraculous trance, awakening when the cave was opened two centuries later during the reign of Theodosius II. Convincing the emperor of the reality of bodily **resurrection**, they died, or, according to another account, returned into a trance which will last until the **Second Coming**. In medieval times this tale was popular throughout Christendom and **Islam**.

SEVEN WISE MASTERS (*See* *ARABIAN NIGHTS*)
Or *Sindbadnameh* (Book of Sindbad), a collection of tales that came west from India via Persia in the eleventh century. Having a son in his old age, King Kûrush is warned that danger will threaten the youth at the age of twenty. The king asks the sage Sindbad (not Sinbad the Sailor) to educate the boy. When the critical year arrives, Sindbad declares that the prince must keep quiet for a week, or die. During the week, the youth's stepmother tries to seduce him. Failing, she accuses him before his father and tells seven lying tales meant to bring about his death. Each in turn is confuted by seven wise viziers, who tell tales about the deceits of women. At the end of the week the prince, spared execution, can speak again. He tells what actually happened and all ends well . . . save for his stepmother.

SHAITAN (*See* **DEVIL, DJINNS**)
Or Shetan. In **Islamic** belief, shaitans are evil spirits related to the djinns,

created by God from **hell**-fire to punish folk for their sins, given to possessing women and tempting them to disobey their husbands. They may take the form of a **serpent** living in the woman's body, making her act against her will. Their names must be known before they can be expelled. Shaitans are known and feared from India to Africa, where many versions are recognised. Some were djinns inadvertently released from bottles by Moroccan fishermen who foolishly removed King **Solomon**'s seal. Some are whirlwinds or seductive voices in the desert, or voluptuous apparitions driving the traveller mad. Others appear as serpents, leopards, **scorpions** or **owls**, or as hideous flesh-eating ogres, or malicious **elementals**.

SHAKESPEARE, WILLIAM (1564–1616) (*See* KING LEAR, PUCK)

Did William Shakespeare, an obscure actor from Stratford-on-Avon, write the dramas bearing his name? Some cannot believe that the author of *Macbeth, Hamlet, King Lear*, etc., could have been this son of an illiterate rural yeoman, pointing out that the author knew modern and classical languages, was versed in esoteric philosophy, also that playwright Ben Jonson claimed that the actor from Stratford had 'small Latin and less Greek'; that his will says nothing of the disposal of a library or manuscripts; that none of his heirs were involved in printing the *First Folio* and none benefited financially from it; that no autographed manuscripts of his plays and sonnets are known; that the six known examples of his handwriting are all unsure signatures, suggesting one unused to the pen. All supposed portraits are dissimilar: the best-known, the Droeshaut, prefacing the *Great Folio* (1623) is odd, the head seemingly unattached to the body and half its coat is on backwards. Conspiracy theorists have made much of this. Cryptographers perceive in Shakespearian texts veiled messages suggesting another author. Who?

One candidate is the philosopher and statesman Francis Bacon (1561–1626?), Lord High Chancellor under King James 1. A Renaissance man of the first order, he certainly had the learning the plays demonstrate. Rumours persist that his death in 1626 (after disgrace and downfall from public office) was faked; that he was the secret son of Elizabeth I and the Earl of Leicester and that (writing plays being a despised activity) he engaged the Stratford actor as 'mask' for his work, in it revealing his authorship via acrostic, cipher and other hints. In *Henry IV Part I* the name 'Francis' appears thirty-three times on one page; in *The Tempest* (Act I: Scene 2: 'Begun to tell me what I am, but stopt/ And left me to a bootelesse Inquisition,/ Concluding, stay: not yet'), the first letters of the first two lines and the first three of the third spell *BACon*. Superimposition of his portrait (as printed in the 1640 edition of his *The Advancement of Learning*) on the Droeshout portrait of the Bard of Avon reveals an exact equivalence of the two faces in terms of bone structure, facial shape and other features.

The argument that Bacon was Shakespeare has endured with sufficient intensity still to outrage those insisting that a Warwickshire yeoman's thespian son wrote what many regard as the greatest works in the English language. Given that 'there's no smoke without a fire', the case remains open. Either way, someone wrote Shakespeare's plays.[1]

1. *The Secret Teachings of All Ages*, Manly P. Hall, Philosophical Research Society, Los Angeles, 1989 (1928), pp.165–8; *Francis Bacon's Personal Life Story*, Alfred Dodd, Rider, London, 1986 (1949).

SHAKTISM (*See* HINDUISM, KALI, TANTRAS)

SHAMANISM (*See* INITIATION, MEDICINE)

A term (originally Siberian) used to describe the practices of those who in primary or 'primitive' cultures function (or functioned) as medicine men, healers, witch-doctors, **trance**-experts and prophets, via their power to contact the **spirit**-world and utilise its energies.

Male or female, the shaman may inherit the role from mother, father or other relative, being trained by them. Usually seen as superior is the shaman spontaneously 'called' by the spirits, typically in late childhood or at puberty, via a psychological crisis of a sort which in modern society is treated as mental illness alone. Yet in many older cultures the process, once recognised, is encouraged, the troubled child being taught that these inner events are initiatory, that the spirits have called him, yet that to develop on this path he must 'die to the world'. Ordeals are imposed which he may or may not survive. He may be plunged into icy water, left out on the ice to fast for a month alone, walled up in a cave or slashed with quartz knives, so attaining intimacy with the spirits by visions of death.

Candidates among the Apaches of the American Southwest jumped over a cliff, the survivors gaining spirit-knowledge. The **Sioux sun-dance** required braves to dance with skewers through their flesh, these attached to heavy **buffalo**-skins, pain opening the door to shamanic knowledge. In Norse myth the god **Odin** hung self-impaled by his own spear for nine days and nine nights from the world-tree **Yggdrasil**, so gaining shamanic powers to raise the dead, **prophesy** the future, fly and **shape-shift** at will.

Hallucinogenic drugs were widely used. The scarlet toadstool, *Amanita muscaria*, was employed from Siberia to Norway. In the Americas, peyote, jimson weed, psilocybin and other drugs stimulated visionary communication with supernatural forces or 'allies' (as they are called in the *Don Juan* tales of shamanic initiation by Carlos Castaneda).[1]

In another procedure the candidate follows his **totem** animal into the wilderness, there in trance to visit the **underworld** or a celestial realm. The Oglala Sioux shaman Black Elk induced visions by sitting under a **tree**, symbol of the cosmic pillar. Led by a spirit-guide in **bird** form, he would rise up it in trance through a tunnel-like aperture to a 'flaming rainbow tepee' to 'communicate with the grandfathers'. The process, involving painful apparent dismemberment, brought him spiritual rebirth and renewed energy. He would return to earth on a 'little cloud'. Another version of this technique (as in 'Jack and the Beanstalk') involves climbing a cosmic rope to kill the **giant** at the top, returning to earth with his power. The more violent the encounter, the more power the shaman gains – if he lives. Ritual dismemberment may precede the encounter, the shaman uniting himself with a higher order of being beyond the limits of the physical body. In some ancient rites sacramental dismemberment also occurred, the king being tortured to death, dismembered, then eaten (as in the Christian Communion, Christ's body and blood being symbolically **cannibalised**).

Returning to the daily world, the shaman thereafter is both feared and respected as healer, prophet and sage, though remaining forever apart from his fellows who have not died and been reborn as he has.[2]

1. *The Teachings of Don Juan*, Carlos Castaneda, Penguin, London, 1970.
2. *The Shaman's Doorway*, Stephen Larsen, Harper Colophon, New York, 1977.

SHAMASH (*See* BABYLONIAN MYTH, SUN-GODS)

Son of the Babylonian **moon**-god **Sin**, daily this **sun**-god emerges through a great door opened by the **scorpion**-men in the mountains of the east. He climbs the mountain then mounts the sky in his chariot, guiding it over the zenith down to the great mountain of the west into which, as evening falls, he vanishes. With his light banishing night and scaring away evil-doers, he is the all-seeing God of Justice, his rays a net catching criminals. He was also the god of **divination**, via soothsayers revealing the future. At Sippar, a divinatory centre, he was especially venerated, there ruling with his wife Aya and their children, Kittu ('Justice') and Misharu ('Law').

SHAMBHALA (*See* AGHARTI, HOLLOW EARTH, LOST WORLDS)

Sanskrit name for a mystic land amid snowy mountains, a golden city at its centre. Associated with the subterranean cultures of Agharti and Shangri-La, here amid the hot springs of its hidden valleys live superhuman beings. It has been sought but never found in the Gobi Desert, **Tibet**, Afghanistan and in China's Kun Lun Mountains: a 1923 Russian expedition seeking it vanished beyond the Kokushi Mountains. Rumours that tunnels connect it with Lhasa's Potola Palace persist. It has been claimed that 'aeroplanes might fly over the place without "seeing" it, for its frontiers are very carefully guarded and protected against invasion.'[1] En route from Mongolia to India, Nicholas Roerich (1874–1947: designer of Stravinsky's *Rite of Spring* ballet) was, in 1928, told by a lama that Shambhala is of another **dimension**, and that only the spiritually prepared may find it, for it is lost and found in the mind. Roerich also met a mysterious lama on the Darjeeling-Ghum road. Later the monks of Ghum said this lama was from Shambhala.[2]

1. *An Occult Glossary*, G. de Purucker, Theosophical University Press, California, 1969.
2. *Alta-Himalaya*, Nicholas Roerich, Jarrolds, London, 1930.

SHANGRI-LA (*See* AGHARTI, HOLLOW EARTH, LOST WORLDS, SHAMBHALA)

SHAPE-SHIFTING (*See* CONCORDANCE)

Belief in the power of wizards, **witches** and supernatural beings to take the shape of animal, bird or fish (or of **trees**, waves, storms and other phenomena) is global. It may date back to ancient hunting rites (as shown on the walls of Lascaux) in which men wore the skins of animals they wished to slay, dancing as **deer, bear, boar** or **buffalo**. Thus the many **Scots** tales of enchantresses who turn themselves into deer suggest a deer-cult, its priestesses wearing the skins of hinds. So too the assumption by tribes of particular animals as **totems** would encourage neighbours to believe that (for example) the 'Bear People' actually became bears. Also influential was the idea that immaterial **spirits** can take any form they want. Then again, natural transformations (egg to bird, chrysalis to butterfly, day to night, summer to winter) and nature's sudden changes (**sun** emerging after a storm to turn the sea **gold**) would encourage belief that certain beings can take new forms at will, either physically or by casting glamour on the senses.

So **Merlin** helps **Uther** deceive Ygraine that he is her husband Gorlois, a deception leading to the birth of King **Arthur**, himself later likewise deceived by his half-sister **Morgause**, leading to the birth of **Mordred**.

Another factor (as in **werewolf** legend) may well have been the attempt to explain violent (bestial) behaviour, especially at full **moon**. It is easy to believe that someone acting like a beast has become that beast.

The theme, especially common in Greek and Celtic myths, is widespread:

buffalo-women in Africa and North American lore; **lion**-men in Africa; the **avatars** of **Hindu** gods, etc. Yet if imposed on an unwilling victim such changes are defined not as shape-shifting (voluntary) but transformations. Thus in the Welsh tale 'Culhwch and Olwen', the giant boar Twrch Trwyth was a human king, transformed for his evil-doing; in *The Odyssey*, Ulysses' men are changed into swine by **Circe's** spells. Giraldus Cambrensis (*c.*1146–1230) tells in his *Topography of Ireland* how a priest met a **wolf** able to speak. It led him to its mate, in agony under a tree. They told him the witch Natalis had changed them into wolves for **seven** years, after which time they would recover human form and two others be substituted for them. Greek seer **Tiresias**, seeing two **serpents** couple, kills the female and is changed into a woman. Seven years later she encounters the same event and kills the male serpent, so regaining manhood. In the Welsh *Mabinogion*, to punish **Gwydion** and Gilfaethly, **Math** turns them into a stag and a hind, then after a year into a sow and a boar, changing their sexes, then into a wolf and she-wolf. They and their bestial offspring are all later returned to human form. In Scots lore, all such tales, whether involving man or woman, involve transformation into the female sex, typically hind or mare.

Shape-shifting in Greek myth is endless. To seduce mortal women Zeus becomes a shower of **gold** to Danaë, a **bull** to **Europa**, a **swan** to Leda. **Demeter** flees **Poseidon** as a mare but he turns into a stallion and rapes her. When **Actaeon** peeps at **Artemis** bathing naked, she turns him into a **stag**. To evade Peleus, **Thetis** becomes a fish, an animal, a wave and a flame.

To escape Welsh hag **Cerridwen**, Gwion Bach becomes a **hare**, a **fish**, a bird, a grain of corn: she becomes a greyhound, a **hawk**, an otter and a hen. Swallowing him, nine months later she bears **Taliesin**.

Such tales symbolise seasonal transformation, just as shape-shifting sea-gods like Poseidon, **Proteus** and **Manannan Mac Lir** represent the dangerous changeability of the sea. Proteus could appear as **dragon**, lion, water, **fire** or tree. The Celtic god Manannan Mac Lir was just as fluid, mantling the Isle of Man in fogs, and by his magic making one object seem a hundred, or tiny chips of wood seem the size of great ships.[1]

1. *The Magic Arts in Celtic Britain*, Lewis Spence, Rider, London, 1970 (1946).

SHEBA (*See* QUEEN OF SHEBA)

SHEELA-NA-GIG (*See* BADB, BANSHEE, GREEN MAN, KALI, MORGAN LE FAY)

Odd carvings of leering naked hags with exaggerated genitalia found in more than a few Irish and British churches, as at Kilpeck in Herefordshire. As with the Green Man, they are a pagan survival of the old Triple Goddess in her crone-like or crow-aspect, their revolting ugliness (as with Hindu Kali) a reminder that death and destruction guarantee life and creation.

SHELLEY, MARY WOLLSTONECRAFT (1797–1851) (*See* FRANKENSTEIN, SHELLEY, P.B.)

Second wife of the poet Shelley, daughter of philosopher William Godwin and feminist Mary Wollstonecraft Godwin, remembered less for her life with Shelley or her editing of his works after his death but for writing perhaps the world's favourite horror novel, *Frankenstein, or the Modern Prometheus* (1818). Her second, historical novel, *Valperga* (1823) is considered her most stylish work, while *The Last Man* (1826) was long regarded as her best.

SHELLEY, PERCY BYSSHE (1792–1822) (See COLERIDGE, SHELLEY, M.W.)

With Wordsworth, Byron, Keats and S.T. Coleridge, the best-known of English Romantic poets, this eccentric man drew on the myths of Greece and Rome for inspiration in works like *Prometheus Unbound*, *Hymn of Apollo*, *Hymn of Pan* and others. Yet as a range of mythic reference was common among educated people in an era when education meant the classics, Shelley is cited here rather for the way his life was subjected to mythic inflation after his early death. Rejecting conventional morality, his anarchic beliefs, repudiation of his wife Harriet, elopement with Mary Wollstonecraft Godwin and marriage to her after Harriet's suicide all aided scandal. His friendship with the equally notorious George Lord Byron (1788–1824); the famous story-telling contest which led Mary to create *Frankenstein*; their peripatetic life in Italy; his own excitable yet melancholic nature and most of all his early death by drowning when caught in a storm in the Gulf of Spezia (8 July 1822), all ensured that Shelley the mythologer himself became a myth.

SHEMYAZA (See AZAZEL, ENOCH)

SHEOL (See HELL, JUDAISM, UNDERWORLD)

A dreary Jewish underworld, also called Abaddon, 'destruction' or 'the pit'. Judaism being monotheistic, Sheol had no god, but was a realm of inertia to which the dead were abandoned. Only the living could carry out **Yahweh**'s historical purposes: national and not individual destiny was what mattered. Yet concern with personal fate (why do the good suffer and the wicked do well?) led to changes in Sheol. Psalm 49 says the wicked will be herded to Sheol like sheep, but God will save the good. **Enoch** describes this new Sheol as a high mountain in the west with four hollow places. One with a spring of bright water is for the good, the others are for the wicked, who suffer pain (perhaps from thirst) – the good and the wicked being separated immediately after death. To this hell, which offered 'a deep valley of burning fire', were introduced the **angels** of punishment, who in later **Christian** belief became the **Devil** and his **demons**. Agents of Yahweh perhaps, but their grotesque forms and function suggest that in fact these angels were exactly the same underworld deities as found in other myths.[1]

1. *The Powers of Evil*, Richard Cavendish, Routledge & Kegan Paul, London, 1975, pp.142–5.

SHESHA (See ANANTA, SERPENT, VISHNU)

SHINTO (See AMATERASU, JAPANESE MYTH)

'The way of the gods', this indigenous Japanese folk-belief preceded the import of **Confucianism** (third century AD) then of **Buddhism** (fifth century). Though government-supported and with shrines throughout the land, it was not so much an organised religion or church as a means of offering respect to local **spirits** (*Kami*: the **ancestors**) and the Royal House, which was said to be descended from Amaterasu the **sun**-goddess. The nature of these folk-beliefs is described more fully in Japanese Myth.

SHIVA (See BRAHMA, GANGES, HINDUISM, INDIAN MYTH, VISHNU)

Or Siva. With **Brahma** and **Vishnu** one of the Hindu **trimurti** manifesting the godhead, Shiva the Destroyer, 'he who takes away', is an ascetic who destroys not to punish but to wipe out illusion and regenerate reality. Though worshipped in the form of the **lingam** (phallus), he so ignores pleasure while meditating the world into being that, it is said, his wife Parvati, unable to distract him, sent Kama (love) to seduce him. Kama aimed his arrow of love, but Shiva opened his third eye and burned him to ashes. Though reborn as Rukmini, 'Son of Delusion', Kama is bodiless (*ananga*), reimbodied only when a man and woman unite in true love. Shiva and Parvati, creative male and female principles, are usually sculpted in the act of physical love. The **elephant**-god **Ganesa** and war-god **Kartikeya** are among their offspring.

Absorbing the **Vedic** storm-god **Rudra**, in ancient effigies he carries a trident (as **river**-god) and other weapons (as hunter- and forest-god). As Himalayan **moon**-god, he holds the moon in his matted hair, which diverts the flow of Ganga (Ganges) into many streams which, lower down, become the divine river itself. He sits on Mount Kailasa teaching the **rishis** and sages. Depicted as a fair, four-armed man, his upper two hands hold a **drum** and a doe, the lower two make gestures of giving and receiving. He has three eyes in each of his four faces – the third eye in his forehead is fiery. He wears a snake-belted tiger-skin. Round his neck coils the cobra Vasuki who, once used as a rope pulled one end by the **Asuras** (demons) and the other by the gods, vomited venom on the earth. To save humanity, Shiva took the venom into his mouth. He cannot swallow it or it would kill him, so he holds it in his throat, which is why his throat is blue. His other ornaments he got when teaching 10,000 heretical rishis truth. Cursing him, they sent a **tiger** and snakes to attack him. He defeated these, so they sent a **demon dwarf**, symbol of ignorance. He threw it down and danced on its back with such energy that the awestruck rishis threw themselves at his feet.

Shiva's **dance** destroys and recreates the world of appearances. Clad in a **fire**-fringed halo, he dances before Parvati as Nataraja, 'King of the Dancers'. Dancing in graveyards with a necklace of skulls, he is Bhairava, 'joyous devourer'. The graveyard is also the disciple's heart, from which all must vanish save the divine Dancer, the **soul**.

Shiva has three qualities: Sattva, Rajas and Tamas (truth, energy and darkness). The first two create light, leading us to justice, but the last two create crime, prospering only in darkness. He embodies the universal contradictions as found in every human soul. Western theology says **spirit** creates matter but remains outside it, whereas Hindus regard spirit and matter as inseparable. The withdrawal of spirit (destruction) is but a change of shape and activity. Shiva creates to destroy; destroys to create.

SHROUD OF TURIN (*See* CHRISTIANITY, HOLY GRAIL, KNIGHTS TEMPLAR)

Claimed as the winding-sheet in which Christ was laid after crucifixion, the Santa Sindone, or Holy Shroud of Turin, is a linen strip, 14 feet 3 inches long by 3 feet 7 inches wide. On it (front and back) is the faint image of a tall man and what appear to be bloodstains consonant with the wounds said to have been suffered by Christ. Associated with the Mandylion (a wrapped cloth bearing the image of Christ's face) of early Church history, it is first recorded as owned by French nobleman Geoffrey de Charny, whose Templar name-sake and ancestor died at the stake in 1314. When de Charny died at Poitiers in 1356, his widow exhibited it for profit. She was accused of fraud. Growing acceptance that it was genuine brought it in 1578 to Turin.

In 1989 radiocarbon dating established it as a medieval fraud. But how was the image produced? What happened to the Mandylion? Apparently hidden in Edessa (an early Christian city) since AD 57, its sixth-century rediscovery led to wide belief that the image on it was not 'made by hands'. 'How can we with mortal eyes contemplate this image whose celestial splendour the host of heaven presumes not to behold?' asks a Byzantine hymn. In AD 943 it came to Byzantium (Constantinople), but in 1204 vanished when a Christian army looted the city. Some say the Knights Templar took it, that the **head** on it (Christ's or not) was the head they worshipped as Baphomet, for which the Inquisition condemned them in 1307. Among the Templars executed was the ancestor of the man whose widow revealed the Shroud after 1356. There have been claims that the Holy Grail was no cup but a casket, 'containing traces of Christ's blood and sweat' as on the Shroud, and that in Byzantium there were two such cloths: the original, and a copy for public display.

Might it be the copy which is dated as medieval?[1]

1. *The Turin Shroud*, Ian Wilson, Penguin, London, 1979; *The Shroud and the Grail*, Noel Currer-Briggs, Weidenfeld & Nicolson, London, 1987.

SHU (*See* EGYPTIAN MYTH)

SIBELIUS, JEAN (1865–1957) (*See KALEVALA*, MUSIC AND MYTH)

Twentieth-century Finnish composer. His love of the north and of the *Kalevala* lend his work a melancholy yet stirring grandeur. Early musical studies in Helsinki led him to Berlin then Vienna. First performance of his Kullervo Symphony (1892) established him as the leading Finnish composer of his day. Evocative patriotic works (Karelia Suite; Finlandia) led in 1897 to a grant by the Finnish senate of a life pension even before his Symphony No. 1 in E Minor (1899). In later works he rejected his earlier Romantic technique for a more austere, complex classical discipline, leading not only to a growing international popularity but also to greater intellectual concentration. No one of his symphonies is like another in structure: with each he seems able to generate a new musical viewpoint. Yet, as in his tone poems (Pohjola's Daughter: 1906; Tapiola: 1925) his mythic vision persisted and developed.

Appreciation of his music is enriched by knowledge of the legends on which they draw. Yet his own melancholic search for perfection silenced him. By 1929 he had completed an eighth symphony, which he destroyed. In the last three decades of his life he published nothing.

SIBYL (*See* AENEAS, GOLDEN BOUGH, ORACLE, PROPHECY, ROMAN MYTH)

Roman equivalent of **Delphi**'s trance-priestesses, also owned by **Apollo**. Virgil in *The Aeneid* tells how the Sibyl of Cumae armed Aeneas with the Golden Bough before he descended to the **underworld**, also how at Cumae **Daedalus** built a temple to Apollo – a **labyrinthine** network of caves with many entrances, through which the Sibyl's utterances poured up to the outer world. From Cumae in the fifth century BC the Sibyl came to the Etruscan king Tarquin in Rome, offering him nine books of prophecy (the Sibylline Books) at a price he found too high. She threw three on the fire and offered the remaining six at the same price. Again he refused. She burned three more and offered the last three, again at the same price. Convinced by now that he was losing a bargain, he bought them for the price of nine. These, kept in the Capitol and consulted only by order of the Senate, told how to win the favour of foreign gods. The books vanished in AD 410 when the Vandals sacked Rome, but by then the Romans had profited by Tarquin's investment, having adopted every foreign god (and country) they could lay hands on.

SIDDHARTHA (*See* **BUDDHISM**)

SIDHE (*See* **EARTH MOUNDS, FAIRIES, IRISH MYTH**)
Refers to the Hollow Hills (earth mounds) found throughout Celtic Britain.
This Irish word implies the dwelling-place of the fairies or spirits of the dead.
They are associated with the mythical race, the **Tuatha dé Danaan** who,
when defeated by the Children of Mil (Goidels: Gaels) retired underground,
each to their own peaceful **otherworld** home. Each such sidhe forms part of a
happy land where there is no pain, disease or old age, but perpetual food,
drink, hunting and revelry; the original **Neverland**.

SIEGFRIED (*See* **ACHILLES HEEL,** *NIBELUNGENLIED*,
SIGURD)

SIGMUND (*See* **NORSE MYTH, ODIN, SIGURD**)

SIGURD (*See* **DRAGON, FAFNIR, NORSE MYTH, RING**)
The Norse Völsunga Saga tells how Sigmund, great-grandson of Sigi (son of
the god **Odin** and founder of the Volsung family), like King **Arthur** drew a
sword (from a tree-post, not a stone) into which Odin (disguised as a
wayfarer) had stuck it. With it he was victorious, until it was shattered by
Odin, again in disguise. Later it was reforged for his son, Sigurd – the Norse
version of the Teutonic hero, Siegfried.
    Born posthumously (a fatherless son), Sigurd is fostered by the smith
Regin, who persuades him to kill the dragon Fafnir (Regin's transformed
brother) to win the **gold** Fafnir guards; a hoard stolen from the **dwarf**
Andvari. Slaying Fafnir and bathing in his **blood**, Sigurd gains not only the
gold but **invulnerability**, but for a spot on his back to which a leaf clings as he
bathes. Learning bird-language by eating Fafnir's **heart**, he realises Regin
means to swindle him and kills Regin. But in the hoard is a magic ring, with
a **curse** (set by the slain dwarf Andvari) on all who own it. Unaware of this,
Sigurd comes to a hill where in a ring of **fire** he finds Brynhild, a beautiful
valkyrie condemned by Odin to sleep until awoken by a hero who will dare
the fire. Awakening her, he gives her the ring, then goes south to the land of
the Nibelungs (Burgundians?). Given an enchanted drink, he forgets Brynhild and marries the Nibelung Gudrunn (Kriemhild). He persuades his
brother Gunnarr to seek out Brynhild. Gunnarr cannot penetrate the fiery
circle, so Sigurd takes his place (as Siegfried takes the place of Gunther: *see
Nibelungenlied*). Exchanging rings with Brynhild, he gets back the cursed
ring of Andvari, but gives it to Gunnarr. Mocked by Gudrunn even as she
weds Sigurd, Brynhild decides on revenge. She persuades her brother-in-law
Guttormr (Hagen in the *Nibelungenlied*) to kill Sigurd as he sleeps. In
remorse she kills herself and shares Sigurd's funeral pyre. Sigurd's widow
marries Atli (Attila), king of the Huns.
    Compare this account with that of Siegfried in the *Nibelungenlied*.

SILENUS (*See* **GREEK MYTH, SATYRS**)

SILVANUS (*See* **FAUNUS, PAN, ROMAN MYTH, VENUS**)
Popular since early times, this Roman woodland deity was said to be the son
of a shepherd and a she-**goat**. Watching over the work of clearing land and
creating rough pasturage in woodlands, he also guarded cattle and those who

tilled the soil. Unpredictable, he required those seeking his protection to **sacrifice** domestic cattle to him. He was often confused with the Greek goat-god **Pan**. The Gauls associated him with the **hammer**-god; representing him with hammer, pot and leaf crown; elsewhere with a billhook, implying the pruning and taming of wild nature. The British linked him with various local deities, including the healing god Nodens (**Nuadu**).

Other Roman agricultural deities included **Faunus**; Pales (protectress of flocks who gave her name to the Palatine Hill in Rome); Liber Pater (god of fecundity, the fertility of the fields, and later of the vine); Tellus Mater (an ancient goddess of fecundity, protecting the soil and the seed sown in it); and Flora, goddess of cereals, fruit-trees, the vine, flowers and all that buds in springtime. Her licentious festival at which all had fun, the Floralia, lasted from 28 April to 3 May (*see* **May Day**). A **rose** festival was also held in her honour, on 23 May.

SILVER (*See* GOLD, JEWELS, TREASURE)

A white lustrous metal used chiefly with alloys of harder metals for use in coin, plate and ornaments, valued as precious since antiquity, silver is to **gold** as the **moon** is to the **sun**, its value in regard to gold anciently reckoned in proportion 13:1, as in the **number** of lunar months in the year. Silver represents feminity as gold represents masculinity. In alchemy it represents the **virgin** state of the *prima materia*; silver symbolises virginity *per se*, also chastity, purity and eloquence. Of the four world ages in **Hindu** cosmology, the Silver Age (Treta Yuga) is the second, after gold, followed by bronze and **iron**.

SILVER BOUGH (*See* CORMAC, GOLDEN BOUGH, MANANNAN MAC LIR, MISTLETOE)

Irish myth tells of a marvellous silver branch or bough owned by the sea-god **Manannan**, and used by him to lure favoured mortals to the **otherworld**. Cut from a mystical **apple**-tree, it gave out irresistible music when it was shaken; its nine golden apples provided the traveller with all the food and drink he needed while in the Land of the Gods. It could also lull folk into magical trance. When Cormac MacAirt, High King of Ireland, met a young man who carried it and he heard its music, happily he exchanged wife, son and daughter for it. When they heard its music, willingly they went with the youth. After a year he longed to see them. Enveloped in a magic cloud, he came to a fine house, in it a supernatural pair whom he recognised as the god Manannan and his wife. Bringing to him his wife, son and daughter, the god admitted that the youth had been himself, Manannan, and that he had wished to lure Cormac to his realm. Cormac and his family duly returned to the world with this and other gifts. Another hero lured by Manannan to the Land of the Gods in this way was **Bran MacFebal**. The Silver Bough, a link with or **talisman** leading to the unseen world, seems to have no direct link with the **Golden Bough** of Classical myth, though some authorities have associated it with the 'all-healer', mistletoe.[1]

1. *The Magic Arts in Celtic Britain*, Lewis Spence, Rider, London, 1970.

SIMON MAGUS (*See* FLIGHT, GNOSTIC MYTH)

SIMURGH (*See* BIRDS, FABULOUS BEASTS, PERSIAN MYTH, PHOENIX)

In ancient Persian belief this **immortal** king of all **birds** nests in the branches of the **Tree** of Knowledge. In the 'Mantiq al-Tayr' ('Parliament of Birds'), the twelfth-century **Sufi** poet Farid al-Din Attar tells how far away in China the Simurgh drops one glorious feather; hearing of this, all other birds, tired of anarchy, decide to seek him out to rule them. They know only that his name means 'thirty birds', that his castle lies in the Kaf, a range of **mountains** girdling the earth, and that the journey will be hard. But, fearful, the nightingale will not leave the **rose**, the parrot his cage, the partridge his hills, the heron his marsh, the **owl** his ruins.

The rest set out. They cross seven valleys or seas; Bewilderment and Annihilation among their names. Many desert, until only thirty are left to reach the peak of the Simurgh, whereupon they realise that they are it, and that it is each and all of them. The cosmographer al-Qaswini said that the Simorg Anka lived 1,700 years, then (like the **phoenix**), cremates itself on a pyre when its son grows up. The French author Flaubert (1821–80) spoke of it as an attendant to the **Queen of Sheba**, and described it as possessing metallic, orange-coloured feathers, a vulture's talons, four wings, a **peacock**'s tail and a small silver head with a human face.

SIN (See **BABYLONIAN MYTH, MOON**)
Eldest son of the Sumerian god **Enlil**, in **Babylonian myth** father of both **Shamash** the **sun**-god and Ishtar the love-goddess, nightly this **moon**-god of Ur (birthplace of the patriarch Abraham) sailed his barge across the sky. Depicted as a turbaned old man, his beard the colour of lapis-lazuli, he was regarded as triune, each aspect ruling one phase of the moon. Just as Shamash lit up the day and banished evil-doing, so by illuminating the night did Sin. Yet at the end of each month he descended for three days and nights into the **underworld**. Then came storm, **flood**, death and crime. The regularity of his phases also established him as lord of the calendar, as the measurer of time. Also known as Suen and Nannar, his worship spread to Arabia. It seems likely that he gave his name to Mount **Sinai**. Later his daughter **Ishtar** took over his role, becoming the moon-goddess.

SIN-EATING (See **SACRIFICE**)
An Irish custom whereby the sins of the newly-dead, for which retribution might be expected in the hereafter, were passed to a hereditary scapegoat family. Food left out for the dead person to aid his journey beyond was eaten by the 'sin-eater', who thus accumulated the sins of many before, his own time come, all the sins he had eaten were eaten in turn by his son or successor. Such techniques for transferring evil exist worldwide. Singalese devil-dancers cured the sick by drawing the possessing devils into their own bodies then, shamming death on a bier, were carried outside the village to recover. The **Maori** of New Zealand transferred the tribe's collective sins to one person by tying a fern-stalk to his leg; he would jump into the river, untie it, then let the river carry the sins away. As for the origin of the term 'scapegoat', on the Jewish Day of Atonement, the High Priest laid hands on the head of a **goat**, confessed over it the sins of the Jews, then drove it into the wilderness. In the Himalayas folk would intoxicate and feed a dog, chase it out of the village, and stone it to death in the belief that no disease or ill-luck would visit them for another year. So too in parts of Nigeria two human victims were annually killed to remove the sins of all who paid a required sum of money towards the **sacrifice**, the victims being brutally dragged away, then killed. In Thailand once a year a woman taken in adultery would be driven out of the city, thrown on a dunghill to attract all the evil spirits, and forbidden ever to return. So too in many ancient cultures

the periodic torture, murder and **cannibal** eating of the divine **king** or elected **corn-god**, to placate the gods and ensure fertility. Such scapegoat rites persist: Christians still claim that Christ died for their sins; while in any group there is invariably an individual made the 'butt' of the jokes of others, such jokes all the more cruel due to the jokers' relief that someone else is suffering, not they.[1]

1. *The Golden Bough*, Sir James Frazer, Macmillan, London, 1963.

SINAI (*See* MOSES, MOUNTAINS, NEW JERUSALEM, YAHWEH)

Named after the Chaldean **moon**-god **Sin** and itself probably connected with moon-worship, this 'Mount of the Lawgiving' is first mentioned in Hebrew texts *c.*1000 BC. Located in the Sinai peninsula between the Gulf of Suez and that of Aqaba, it was here that the Israelites camped for a year following their Exodus from Egypt, and from its heights that **Moses** (who had here earlier encountered **Yahweh** in the form of a burning bush) descended with the Law. In fact there are several peaks in the area, any one of which might be the biblical Mount Sinai, which (Deuteronomy iv:11) 'burned with fire unto the midst of heaven, with darkness, clouds, and thick darkness', and where (Exodus xix:16,18) 'there were thunders and lightnings, and a thick cloud upon the mount . . . and the smoke thereof ascended as the smoke of a furnace, and the whole mount quaked greatly'.

The Hebrew Talmud and Midrash describe this quaking as so great that the Israelites could not stand secure, but felt an invisible force lifting them up. Was the Law delivered amid an earthquake, or worse?

Authors like Velikovsky have suggested that the lawgiving occurred amid global catastrophe caused by the near approach to earth of the proto-planet Venus, ejected from Jupiter and causing gravitational havoc before taking up its present stable orbit. Sinai breeds myths both ancient and modern.[1]

1. *Worlds in Collision*, Immanuel Velikovsky, Abacus, London, 1972.

SIOUX (*See* DANCE, GHOST DANCE, GHOST WIFE, NATIVE AMERICAN MYTH, SHAMANISM, WILD WEST)

This warrior-people of North America's Great Plains provided the very image of the war-bonneted, war-painted, **horse**-riding, **buffalo**-hunting redskin, savage but noble, as offered in **Hollywood** myths of the **Wild West**. After they defeated the US army under General George Armstrong Custer (Little Big Horn 1876), the names of their warriors (Crazy Horse) and **medicine**-men (Sitting Bull) epitomised all that the whites both feared and respected in the New World's ancestral dwellers. Though courageous to the point of utter folly, they were deeply religious, worshipping Wakan Tanka (*see* **Kici Manitou**) the Great Spirit, his light on earth the full moon, under which in June or July they celebrated the Sun Dance (*see* **Shamanism**), by which ordeal braves contacted the spirit-realm. They ate the powdered hearts of brave enemies, hoping to acquire their valour. The 'Indian Wars' followed the arrival of European settlers in this vast area after 1840; by 1890 the Sioux and all other native peoples had been subjugated (*see* **Ghost Dance**).

SIRENS (*See* GREEK MYTH, HARPIES, LORELEI, MERMAIDS)

Named from a Greek root, 'to bind', these mythical Greek sea-monsters had not only the bodies of birds and the heads of women, but voices so sweet that all hearing them were seduced to destruction. When (*see* **Odyssey**) Ulysses left the enchantress **Circe** on his homeward journey, she warned him to get his men to tie him to the mast, and to stop their ears with wax as they rowed past the rocky islet where these creatures roosted amid the bodies of their victims. This was done, and though the sirens begged him to stop and come to them, the danger was averted.

In origin the sirens were daughters of the **river**-deity Achelous. They numbered from two to eleven, according to the author, with names meaning beautiful face, beautiful voice, white being, shrill, music, maiden face, persuading the mind, improvement, perfect, soothing words, persuasive face.

It is said they had challenged the **Muses** to a musical duel but were beaten, and so abandoned their riverbank forests for the rocky shoreline of southern Italy, perching there and luring sailors to death by their song.

Ulysses escaped, but did not defeat them. It was left for **Orpheus** to do that; for when the Argonauts sailed past and they tried to seduce them with their song, he tuned his lyre and sang back, turning them into rocks.

In origin they were funerary deities derived from the Egyptian image of the bird-**soul**, the *ba*, invoked at the moment of death, their **blood**-hungry images often found on Greek tombs. Later their bird-bodies were transformed into the fish-tails of the traditional but equally deadly **mermaid**.

SIRIUS (*See* ASTRONOMY AND MYTH, DOGON, ISIS, OSIRIS, SUN)

This brightest star in the night sky, named from the Greek for 'scorching' or 'sparkling', lies in the constellation Canis Major (the Great Dog, one of the hunter **Orion**'s two hounds), and is itself known as the 'Dog-star'. Inevitably, its brilliance makes it a star of mystery. In Egypt, where its annual rise presages the annual Nile flood at the height of summer (thus lethargic 'Dog Days'), it was called Sothis, and so anciently associated with **Isis** and **Osiris**: deities epitomising the fertility of the flood. So Sothis came to be seen as the home of Osiris and of the Cosmic or Winged Isis. Later occult myth claims Sirius as the centre from which power is distributed throughout the local galactic neighbourhood: it is said to be 'the **Sun** behind the Sun'. Others claim it as the sun of a planetary system birthing superior beings who anciently manifested on earth to direct the growth of human civilisation: (*see* **Oannes**). This legend is explored by Doris Lessing in her *Shikasta* sequence of novels.[1] Other recent claims – that the **Dogon** people of Mali in Africa have a precise ancestral knowledge of other stellar bodies in the Sirius system, a knowledge since established by scientific observation – remain controversial. Yet it would be surprising if the brightest star in the sky stimulated no myths at all.

1. *Shikasta*, Doris Lessing, Cape, London, 1979.

SISYPHUS (*See* BELLEROPHON, GREEK MYTH)

In Greek myth the grandfather of Bellerophon, who tried to ride the winged horse **Pegasus** to **Olympus** and was thrown down by **Zeus** for his pride, this 'craftiest of men' enraged the gods with his cunning. When he told Asopus the river-god that his daughter Aegina had been abducted by Zeus, Zeus sent Thanatos, god of death, to pursue him. Sisyphus won free, but not for long. Destined to die, he told his wife to pay him no funeral honours. Arriving in the **underworld**, he complained to **Hades** that his wife was negligent. He asked permission to return to life to punish her. Hades let him go back, but then he refused to return to the Land of the Dead. Hades had to ensure that no other men followed his rebellious example, and so punished Sisyphus for his bad faith by condemning him forever to roll up a mountain slope a huge boulder which, whenever he gets it near the summit, slips and rolls on down again. So the god of the dead makes sure that we all still obey him.

SITA (*See* INDIAN MYTH, RAMA)

SKY (*See* ASTRONOMY AND MYTH, CREATION MYTH, FATHER-GODS, MOTHER-GODDESS)

While the earth is invariably perceived as female ('Mother Earth'), as the womb bearing all physical life, the sky is a masculine domain, abstract and infinite; home of a remote, invisible creative power as mysterious as the phenomena manifesting through it: alternation of night and day, rise and set of **sun**, **moon** and stars; the wanderings of planets; eclipses, comets and meteors; all as awesome to the adult as is the father to the child.

Worship of Earth Mother necessarily preceded that of Sky Father. We have but lately (in evolutionary time) 'progressed' from four legs to two. Four legs means nose to the ground. Standing on two, we have 'left' the ground. The sky is closer; easier to see. Its very nature as an infinite open question invites the growth of self-awareness and abstract thought.

Myth everywhere suggests that early folk found it hard to determine the precise difference between earth and sky. Typically, the two are seen as a primeval husband and wife so closely united that nothing can prosper unless they are separated. The **Maori** tell how Rangi and Papa, the divine parents, were so conjoined that there was no light; nothing could bear fruit until one of their desperate children, Tane-mahuta, banished Rangi into the sky. Then at last there was light. In Greek myth, **Ouranos** crushes **Gaia** and their children; **Cronus** castrates him and forces him up into the sky.

'Sky, thou seeest me! Sky, thou hearest me!' the pagan **Slav** prayed to Svarog, the sky-god. Contemplation of the infinite developed the power of abstract philosophy as in the hermetic statement: 'As Above, So Below.'

SKY-GODS (*See* CONCORDANCE)

SLAVONIC MYTH (*See* CONCORDANCE)

Of Indo-European origin, *c.*AD 500 Slavonic tribes began to disperse from the Carpathians to colonise a vast territory from the Balkans to the Elbe in the west, and northeast over the steppes to Siberia. Though characterised by different dialects, these eastern (Russian), southern (Serbs, Croats, Bulgarians, Slovenes), and western (Czechs, Poles, Bohemians, Silesians) groups for the most part developed a common mythology.

Slav culture evolved late due to the utter remoteness of their vast new land, one defined only by forests, lakes, marshes and rivers. Settling in small groups, hunting, fishing and raising cattle in forest clearings or on natural meadows, even after the Russian court at Kiev was Christianised (AD 988), the outlook remained **pagan**. Subject to nature's whims, the Slavs personified her manifestations, and by worship tried to moderate their evil effects. They sensed an all-pervading life force in each rock, tree, lake, river, forest, ravine, field, stable or house; each such domain epitomised by a wide range of divinities, spirits and demons. Even after Christianity at last penetrated their remote world and drove out the old gods, belief in lesser **elemental** beings persisted in folk custom and magical practice.

Modified only by contact with other races in the Baltic west and Kievan south, this mythology was as vague as the land itself. Early accounts of it come not from Slavs but from travellers and Christian chroniclers. Much can be reconstructed from folk customs existing until the 1917 Revolution, yet though many names of Slavonic gods and spirits survive, it is rarely clear which myths were native, or even where which gods were worshipped. Nothing at all is known of the gods of the Czechs, Serbs and Bulgarians: available information relates to the eastern and to the western (Baltic) Slavs.

The basic belief was a **Persian**-derived **dualism**, as in the term *divu* (*see* **deva**) for **demons**, or as in *miru* (see **Mithra**) for 'peace agreement'. The twelfth-century chronicler Helmold asserts that the Elbe Slavs prayed to two gods: Byelobog (the 'white god' of daylight, thus good: also known as **Byelun**) and Chernobog (the 'black god' of night, thus evil). To one they prayed for good luck, to the other to avert ill-luck. This simple dualism failing to explain all phenomena, a more complex vision developed. Helmold adds that they also worshipped one god, all other divinities having 'sprung from his blood'. This Supreme Being resided in heaven and cared solely for things celestial. His name is not known, but he may have been related to the **sky**-god Svarog (from svar, 'bright', a **Sanskrit**-related term).

Creator of celestial **fire** who daily kindled the **sun**, Svarog had two children to whom in time he transferred his powers. These were **Dazhbog** (the sun) and Svarogich ('son of Svarog', the fire-god, also called ogon, comparable with the Vedic fire-god **Agni**). Svarogich epitomised the divine gift of terrestrial fire, brought to earth by lightning (*see* **Prometheus**).

Another fire-god was Perunu (from *per*, to 'strike', or 'splinter', as by lightning). Place-names in Bohemia, Bulgaria and Poland testify to his former popularity. Though derived from a native cult, he has parallels with the Norse **Thor**. Armed with a great bow, he fired bolts of lightning down from heaven to strike the **oak**, also part of his cult. Shown as a man with silver **head** and gold moustache, a **rain-making** rite invoking him had a naked flower-decked maiden whirling ecstatically amid a ring. In time he became the bogatyr Ilya Muromyets (*see* **Bogatyri**); this was after AD 988 when Prince Vladimir, converted to Christianity, had Perunu's **idols** in Kiev and Novgorod torn down.

Arising out of the Slavonic worship of the hearth, in time the 'holy fire' became part of Orthodox ritual. Until recently, every **Easter** the old fires were put out and 'new' fire produced (*see* **Beltane**, **Fire-Festivals**).

Other deities included the Earth Mother, **Mati-Syra-Zemlya**, and Veles, protector of cattle. In south Russian harvest festivals the last sheaf was plaited into a knot: 'the beard of Veles' (*see* **Corn-God**). His worship was later transferred to St Blaize, a Caesarean martyr called 'guardian of the flocks' by the Byzantines (also *see* **Kupala**, **Yarilo**).

Yet though in time the old gods died, belief in **elemental** deities of forest (Leshy), river (**Rusalka**), field (Polevik), barn (Ovinnik), bath-house (Bannik) and house (**Domovoi**) persisted, while modern Russian music like Moussorgsky's *A Night on the Bare Mountain*, Stravinsky's *Rite of Spring* and Prokofiev's *Alexander Nevsky* suggest that the old Slav spirit survives.

SLEEPING BEAUTY (*See* FAIRY-TALES, GRIMM, NORNS)

The common version of this widespread European folk-myth, presented by the Brothers **Grimm** as 'Little Briar Rose', tells how a childless king and queen are at last blessed with a beautiful daughter. In gratitude the king gives a feast to all in the realm, including its Wise Women. There are thirteen of these but, as he has only **twelve gold** plates, he invites but twelve. At the feast eleven bestow their gifts, but then in stalks the thirteenth, to prophesy that when she is fifteen the child will prick her finger on a spindle and die. Whereupon the twelfth says: 'She shall not die, but sleep a hundred years.'

The king burns every spindle in the land, but on her fifteenth birthday the princess finds a tower room in the castle where an old woman sits spinning. Pricking her finger, she falls asleep. This magical sleep seizes the entire palace, about which grows up a hedge of thorns. Many years pass, and many princes die trying to breach the barrier. At length after a century comes one who gets through the hedge, enters the castle and awakens the Sleeping Beauty with a kiss. The whole palace wakes up, and the two are married, to live happily ever after.

The theme of the slighted, spiteful goddess or **fairy** is ancient, as in the tale of the Greek goddess Eris who, uninvited to the **Olympian** wedding of Peleus and Thetis, interrupted it by throwing the Apple of Discord into the midst of the happy company (*see* **Aphrodite, Paris**). The Wise Women are the **Fates** or **Norns**. However many blessings they bestow, a **curse** always lies somewhere in the baggage of human destiny, to be overcome only by the devoted and wilful bravery of the **hero** whose action cancels it, so winning not only the beautiful princess but restoring the land to life.

SLEEPING EMPEROR (*See* APOCALYPSE, PROPHECY, SECOND COMING)

Medieval apocalyptic fantasy of the Sleeping Emperor or Emperor of the Last Days. The murder in AD 350 of the Roman emperor Constans led to the Tiburtina, a **Sibylline prophecy** predicting his return to unite Christendom, convert the heathen and **Jews**, and prepare all for the **Second Coming**. The seventh-century Pseudo-Methodius, ascribed to a fourth-century martyr, predicted a mighty emperor rising from miraculous sleep to slay the heathen and prepare for the End Days. In the Middle Ages such prophecies (and tales like the **Seven Sleepers**) grew in popularity, being applied to several historical figures. **Charlemagne** (742–814) was said to live on asleep under a hill, awaiting recall to defeat **Islam**.

Baldwin IX, Count of Flanders, was murdered soon after his installation as Emperor of Constantinople (1204), but the tale spread that he had become a penitential beggar. In 1224 an unknown hermit claimed to be Baldwin, was crowned as such, but lost his nerve, was unmasked and hanged. In 1250 the Emperor Frederick II died, but was said to have entered the bowels of Etna, the Sicilian volcano, long thought an abode of departed heroes, including King **Arthur**. The fabulous eastern monarch **Prester John** was said to have given him an asbestos robe (against **fire**), a magic **ring** of invisibility and a magic drink of **immortality**. Even a century later his return was expected, especially during the Black Death (1348–50).

Such fantasies reflected the fears of a brutal age with little to hope for but the return of an imperial father-figure who would slay all enemies and prepare the world for the triumphant return of **Christ** himself.[1]

1. *The Pursuit of the Millennium*, Norman Cohn, Paladin, London, 1970.

SLEIPNIR (*See* HORSE, ODIN)

SMITH-GODS (*See* CONCORDANCE)

SNAKES (*See* DRAGON, SERPENT)

SOCRATES (469–399 BC) (*See* **GREEK MYTH, PLATO**)
An Athenian philosopher who left no writings of his own, known chiefly through the use of his character and style of dialogue by his disciple Plato in the latter's many surviving texts. He presented himself as ignorant and, by asking searching and ironic intellectual questions, first made his victims admit their own incoherence, then, by further questioning, led them to state truth. 'Virtue is knowledge,' he said. 'No man willingly chooses what is evil.' Rejecting wealth or office, stirring young people to think for themselves, insisting on the supremacy of knowledge and rejecting the democratic notion that all citizens were equally fit to govern and rule, he fell foul of the Athenian political establishment. Tried as a corrupter of youth, he was condemned to death. Refusing escape, he insisted on obeying the law, and serenely drank a decoction of the poison hemlock. Surrounded by his disciples, he continued his final discourse until the poison reached and stopped his heart. Or so Plato has it. His calm acceptance of death remains an inspiration to all seeking knowledge that flies in the face of worldly power.

SODOM (*See* **LOT'S WIFE**)

SOLOMON (ruled *c.*970–930 BC) (*See* **HIRAM ABIFF, QUEEN OF SHEBA, SOPHIA**)
Second son of David and Bathsheba, third king of Israel. Choosing wisdom as the support of his throne, he allied himself with the king of Egypt by marriage, hired the king of Tyre, **Hiram Abiff**, as architect of the Temple at Jerusalem, answered the **Queen of Sheba**'s hard questions and became her lover, and through his trade policies became fabulously rich. Yet the size of his harem and the cost of his court drained the land with over-taxation; later he abandoned **Yahweh** for the worship of foreign gods.

Yet after he died his name came to personify wisdom. As a mythic rather than historical figure he is the prototypical magus. Though once an earthly king, he is also the Spirit of Universal Illumination, his name potent in itself. SOLOMON consists of three syllables, SOL-OM-ON: light, glory and truth respectively. His temple is tripartite and symbolic: the temple of universal creation, the temple of the human body, the temple of the **soul**. It is said to have been a house of **initiation**, containing a mass of **pagan** philosophic and phallic emblems. His quest for foreign gods was a quest for **Mystery** truths. So too the *Song of Songs*, that remarkable love poem, is addressed not merely to the Queen of Sheba, but to **Sophia**, the feminine spirit of later **Gnostic** wisdom, the counterpart or **shakti** of Solomon himself.

The Talmud presents him as a **Qabalist**, **alchemist** and **necromancer** who forced **demons** to reveal wisdom. A catalogue in the *Testament of Solomon* (*c.*AD 100–400) says an **angel** gave him a magic **ring** by which he made them tell their secret **names**. **Islamic myth** tells of the fate befalling those who foolishly release **djinns** from bottles in which he sealed them. The *Clavicula Salomonis* ('Key of Solomon') deals with conjuring spirits, and is said to offer insights into **Freemasonic** initiatory rites.

In his *Eighth Book of the Antiquities of the Jews*, the historian Flavius Josephus (AD 37–*c.*100) writes that the wisdom of Solomon exceeded that of the ancients, and that 'he was in no way inferior to the Egyptians, who are said to have been beyond all men in understanding' and that 'he left behind him the manner of using exorcisms, by which they drive away demons, so that they never return.'

SOLON (*c*.640–*c*.569 BC) (*See* **ATLANTIS, GREEK MYTH, PLATO**)
A Greek statesman who, commissioned in 594 BC to reform the constitution,
to the three existing electoral classes added a fourth, the labourers, giving
them a vote in the law-making assembly, also establishing the popular jury
courts. He is best remembered as the source of **Plato**'s tale of **Atlantis**.

SOMA (*See* **DIONYSUS, HAOMA, INDIAN MYTH**)
In the oldest Indian texts, this sweet, intoxicating beverage makes the gods
immortal, and thus is also called amrita (ambrosia). The equivalent of
Persian **haoma**, Greek nectar or Teutonic mead, it was loved by all the gods,
especially **Indra**, who would quaff thirty bowls before combat with **demons**
like **Vritra**. Derived from the juice of the now unknown soma plant (which
Indra found and brought from the mountains), it may have been a hallucinogenic wine distilled from the fruit of *Ficus religiosa*, the fig-tree under which
the Buddha sat, which contains the nerve hormone serotonin, as found in
psychedelic drugs. Originally drunk from a bowl that filled itself, later this
bowl became four cups, perhaps the phases of the **moon**-god Chandra. 'The
sun', said a poet, 'has the nature of **Agni**, the moon of soma.' The *Rig Veda*
(the ninth book calls it Father of All) refers to 'Brahmans drunk with soma'
as they offer this nectar to the gods. Made a god (like **Dionysus**), Soma
married the twenty-seven daughters of the **rishi Daksha**, and was said to be
ancestor of King Bharata of the lunar race.

SOPHIA (*See* **BLACK VIRGIN, GNOSTIC MYTH, LILITH, QUEEN
OF SHEBA, SOLOMON**)
In **Gnostic** lore the female epitome of wisdom, derived from older tradition
increasingly denied not only in **Judaism** but by the emergent patriarchy of
Pauline Christianity. Recalling that the word '**spirit**' (neuter in Greek,
masculine in Latin) is, in the original Hebrew form, feminine, the Gnostics
accepted women as well as men as priests; a process crushed in the late
second century and only now reborn in the struggle for the ordination of
women.
　　Sophia is also Mary the Magdalene ('reformed prostitute') as *Prunikos*,
'lewd': just as **Aphrodite**, Queen of Heaven, is *porné*, 'whore'. Wisdom,
crying her wares on the street, is open to whoever wants her. The Gnostics
describe Mary as the favourite disciple of **Christ**, who 'used to kiss her often
on the mouth' (Gospel of Philip). She may even have been his worldly wife.
Either way, lacking prudery, the Gnostics upheld the idea of one all-
embracing feminine wisdom, both **virgin** (originally meaning 'unmarried
woman', not one without sexual experience) and whore, calling it Sophia, the
Holy Spirit, as in Revelation xii:1 – 'a woman clothed with the sun, and the
moon under her feet, and upon her head a crown of twelve stars'.
　　The **Cathars** may have acknowledged her; the **head** Baphomet adored by
the **Knights Templar** may have been a symbol of her; the **Black Virgins**
found discreetly in Catholic churches throughout Europe represent her. Like
Lilith, a great survivor, she is 'that incomparable and to me unapproachable
woman,' as Russell Hoban writes in his novel *Pilgermann* (1983). 'Her name
is Sophia: Wisdom.'[1]

1. *Pilgermann*, Russell Hoban, Picador, London, 1983.

SORCERY (*See* **DIVINATION, MAGIC, NECROMANCY,
SHAMANISM, VOODOO, WITCHCRAFT**)
From Latin *sortiarus*, 'caster of lots' and Old French *sorcier*. Refers to the

practice of black magic, witchcraft, necromancy, divination, or to the casting of **curses**, **spells** or enchantments by the sorcerer, typically out of malice, for personal gain or to kill an enemy. Where a shaman seeks **spirit**-power to aid his people and is feared but respected, the sorcerer does harm and is feared, respected and hated, but often sought after.

The power of a Melanesian chief (*see* **Oceanic Myth**) to levy fines lay in a belief that he commanded ghosts who could inflict sickness or disaster were the fines unpaid. Fijian belief that sorcerers could steal the **soul** from the body was used to make criminals confess. West African wizards set snares for souls out of the bodies of their sleeping owners: catching one, they tied it up to shrivel it over a fire. Sickening, the owner had to pay to get his soul back. The Nande of Zaïre speak of the *avali*, women who eat the souls of others who then die of 'consumption'.

Sorcerers were said to cause harm by obtaining a person's cut **hair** or nail-parings, which were best burned or hidden. **Blood** or spittle also held power. In many cultures folk received two **names**, public and private, the latter kept secret lest (*see* **Isis**) a sorcerer work evil with it. Cattle were driven between **fire** to protect them against sorcery. Fire was also used to protect the hearth – **rowan** and **mistletoe** were said to keep evil at bay. African and Haitian (*see* **Voodoo**) wizards were said to revive 'dead' bodies and make these **zombies** work for them, maybe by using tetrodotoxin or other nerve-poisons causing catalepsy and apparent death. Sorcerers also sent spirit-animated **fetishes** to attack their victims, who died of fright.

SOTHIS (*See* **SIRIUS**)

SOUL (*See* **GREEK MYTH (2)**, *KA*, **SORCERY**, **SPIRIT**)
From Danish *sjoel*, or Swedish *sjal*: immaterial animating principle in human beings. Belief in it is found in most cultures and traditions. It is usually viewed as the spirit's vehicle. When the body dies it may linger a while before departing. Usually each person is said to have one soul, indwelling the body or associated with a particular organ (brain, **heart**, liver) or with the **blood**. Some cultures say people have two, three or as many as **seven** souls. The Caribs believed in one soul in the **head**, another in the heart, and others wherever an artery pulses. **Hawaii**'s Kahuna priests spoke of three souls: the low self, in the solar plexus (unconscious); the middle self (heart: consciousness), and the high self (head: 'superconscious'). At death the low self may leave the other two. Ancient Egyptians recognised several 'subtle bodies' (*see* *ka*), the soul proper being the *ba*, viewed as a **bird** (origin of the **Sirens**). The image of the soul as a bird is common.

Another belief is that the soul can temporarily leave the body without causing death, though risking capture or destruction by sorcery. If so, it may even be preferable to store the soul safely outside the body in a secret place. Folklore from India to Ireland tells of a **giant** or **wizard**, **invulnerable** and **immortal** because his soul is hidden. The hero seeks it out and destroys it, killing the ogre and winning the imprisoned princess (*see* **Koshchei**). Ravana, Indian demon-king, left his soul in a box on going to war: **Rama** could not kill him until it was found. Or the soul was said to live in a person's secret **name**: to learn or write down the name was to steal it. Some folk fear that to be photographed is to lose their soul.

A variation is to hide the soul in an animal. The **Fon** of Dahomey held that sorcerers united their soul with a specific beast (usually a leopard), the death of one meant the death of both. In the Cameroons it was said men have two souls, one in the body, the other in a beast. Nigerians posited four souls, one invariably in an animal. In Central America everyone had a familiar (**stag**, **dog**, **eagle**) and the death of this *nagual* killed the person. Australian **Aborigines** say **bats** hold women's souls, **owls** those of men. In Sumatra, Batak clans each had a **totem** animal they could not eat, the clan being descended from it and the soul being likely to transmigrate into it at death. **Pythagoreans** spoke of the soul transmigrating after death into animals or even beans. A related belief, as in the slaying of the divine **king** in ancient cultures, was that the dead king's soul entered his successor. So too the Dalai Lama of **Tibet** is seen as the **reincarnation** of all his predecessors.

From Australia and Malaysia to North America (**Eskimos** and Hurons), the soul has also been viewed as a mannikin living in the head or breast. Fat bodies have fat souls; thin bodies, thin souls. Not wholly impalpable, it can escape via mouth or nose if its owner is sick or asleep, or if **demons** or sorcerers try to extract it. An escaped soul must be recovered soon, or death results. A man's shadow or reflection may also be the seat of his soul. To stand on or attack either may lead to death and it is as dangerous to let another's shadow fall on you. The Greek myth of **Narcissus** may arise from the fear of seeing one's reflection in water, so too the custom of covering up mirrors after a death, or if a person is sick, in fear that the reflection may capture the soul. Portraits may also contain the soul of the person portrayed, as in Oscar Wilde's novel *The Portrait of Dorian Grey*.

SOUTH AMERICAN MYTH (*See* CONCORDANCE)

The beliefs of South American peoples (the Inca apart) before Europeans arrived (sixteenth century) remain obscure, religious ideas being vague and many tribes (especially of the Amazon) long remaining 'undiscovered'.

Of the same stock as the Asian migrants who crossed the Bering Strait into North and Central America, those continuing to the southern continent entered vast tracts of tropical jungle and, further south, the grasslands of the Pampas; the high chain of the Andes running down the west coast. Yet only the Inca developed a culture as sophisticated as those of the **Mayans**, Toltecs, Olmecs and even **Aztecs** of Central America. Even so, a general picture may be given, not least of a common **Flood**-tradition.

With the Inca civilisation in Peru to the south, Colombia, Ecuador and Venezuela to the northwest were occupied by organised societies with their own mythologies. The Chibchas of central Colombia worshipped Bochica, a **sun**-god and culture hero equivalent to **Quetzalcoatl** in Mexico. He was a bearded old man from abroad who instituted laws, agriculture and sun-worship. His wicked wife Chia, opposing him, made the River Funzha flood, so that only a few escaped. Bochica exiled her to the sky as the **moon** then re-made society before retiring to heaven after 2,000 years on earth as an ascetic. He also fought the evil storm-**demon** Fomagata long and hard before overcoming him. Annually **sacrificed** to him was a boy the Chibcha called the Guesa (vagabond), much honoured until, aged fifteen, he was bound to a sun-column and shot dead with arrows, his **heart** then being torn out.

The Caranquea of nearby Ecuador dedicated **totems** to Umina, god of **healing** and to the sun, to whom they sacrificed animals, women, children and captives. Priests **divined** the future from the entrails of animals. When a man died, his favourite wife was buried with him. A nearby tribe, the Canarians, claim descent from two brothers who escaped the Flood.

The Tupi of Brazil also speak of a god, Monan, who created mankind then destroyed the world with **fire** and flood. Able to change men into animals, he too brought laws and agriculture. Another Tupi hero, Maira-ata, foresaw the future with the help of **spirits**, and fathered the **twins** Ariconte and

Tamendonare, also said to have caused the Flood. The Tupi believed in many spirits and demons: Yurupari, haunting empty houses, burial sites and the Amazon jungle; Kurupira, a jungle imp who protected game but disliked men; the man-killing underwater Igpupiara; the Apoiaueue who brought rain when it was needed and who like **angels** told God what happens on earth.

The Caryan tribe of the Amazon also recalled the Flood. The Kiukuru of the Xingu River tell how in the beginning their creator, Kanassa, could not see what he was doing and so brought fire from heaven. The neighbouring Kamaiura agree that, in the beginning all was dark, but that Kuat the sun stole light from Urubutsin, the vulture king.

The Chaco of the Pampas tell how rain was produced by Kasogonaga, a female spirit of the air. To the west in Chile lived the Araucanians, who worshipped their **ancestors** and **fetishes**. Recognising no **creator**, they lacked temples, **idols** and formal religion. Of evil spirits demanding propitiatory sacrifices, the chief was Pillan, god of thunder, fire and the volcano. He controlled the Huecuvas, evil **shape-shifting** spirits, and also the Cherruve, human-headed **serpents** that caused ill-**omened** comets and shooting stars. The only good god was Auchimalgen the moon, wife of the sun, who protected men against the spirits whom she drove away. They too recalled the Flood (caused by volcanic eruption followed by violent earthquake), which a few escaped by crouching on a high mountain, Thegtheg, that floated on the waters.

SPEAR OF DESTINY (*See* HOLY LANCE)

SPELLS (*See* CHARMS, CURSES, *GEIS*, GLAMOUR, MAGIC, SORCERY, SPINDLE)

An incantation used by a **sorcerer** to control man or beast by paralysing the will by **curse**, or by imposing fatal prohibition to be undone only by **magic**, so 'spellbinding' or 'entrancing' the victim via hypnosis. Thus the death-spell cast by the uninvited thirteenth **fairy** on **Sleeping Beauty** is modified by another fairy to a state of sleep. In many cultures love-spells are used to make the desired one fall in love with the spellbinder: hunter-spells to trap beasts are also common. In Celtic lore, even kings feared the word-spells cast by poets and **bards**. The Gaelic term for 'spell' is *geis* or *geas*, from *guidh*, 'to entreat', meaning incantation made potent by the exercise of concentrated will-power. Such spells were usually chanted in verse, the bard directing the force by standing one-legged with one eye shut while pointing at the victim. Potent spells like '*fith-fáth*' ('fee-fa') imposed **invisibility** or (seemed to) **shape-shift** the victim into animal form (**Actaeon** into a **stag**; prince into frog) or transformed one object into another (**Cinderella**'s pumpkin into a carriage). Folklore offers many examples. Today the power to spellbind persists. **Hitler** and **Hollywood** both cast different kinds of spell over entire nations.

SPHINX (*See* EGYPTIAN MYTH, GREEK MYTH, PYRAMIDS, RIDDLES)

The epitome of enigma, in Greek myth a she-monster with woman's head and breasts, **lion**'s body, **serpent**'s tail and **eagle**'s wings. Sent by **Hera** to punish the people of Thebes, it settled on Mount Phicium on the road to the city, devouring all passers-by who could not answer a **riddle** taught it by the **Muses**.

More enigmatic is the original Sphinx, a huge stone statue with man's head and lion's body located 300 metres southwest of the Great **Pyramid** at Giza in Egypt. Some 200 feet long, 70 feet high and 38 feet wide across the shoulders, carved mostly from a single stone, a stele between its paws says it represents the **sun**-god Harmackis. Its age is as unknown as its original function. The tale is that it was buried in the desert until the god appeared in dream to the Pharaoh Thothmes IV (18th dynasty), declaring himself oppressed by the weight of sand about his body, whereupon Thothmes excavated and restored it. All efforts to find hidden chambers or passages in it have failed; an old claim that a tunnel leads from it to the Great Pyramid remains unproved. Yet as a symbol of the **Mysteries** it continues to fascinate. In combining human and animal elements it represents the union of physical with intellectual powers, also human mastery of bestial nature, also the four elements. The riddle of the Theban Sphinx has numerological meaning: 4+3+2 add up to 9, the **number** of man; 4 representing the ignorant man, 2 the intellectual man, and 3 the spiritual man. The Sphinx is the Mystery of Nature: whoever cannot solve her riddle must die stupidly.

SPIDER (*See* **FATES, HOPI, NAVAHO, NORNS, SPINDLE**)
Ambivalent, both creator and destroyer. It symbolises **mother**- or **moon**-goddesses as weavers or spinners of the web of destiny (**Fates** or **Norns**). As Cosmic or Great Spider it is the Creator, spinning the thread of life from its own body and weaving all men into the web of world-pattern. Amid its web it represents the world-centre, the sun surrounded by its rays or the year, weaving the web of time. In **Hindu** and **Buddhist** lore it is the weaver of **maya**, illusion; in some Indian schools the spider gods built and held together the embryonic universe with webs of invisible force. The North American **Hopi** tell how Spider Woman, Kotyangwuti, made the people of the First World by mixing saliva with earth; she also made the **twins** Poquanghoya and Palongawhoya who kept the world in order. The neighbouring **Navaho** tell how Spider Woman, Naste Estsan, helped the heroes Nayenezgani and Tobadzistsini to fulfil the task leading them to their father, the **sun**. Elsewhere in North America the web of Spider Man is said to connect heaven to earth. In West Africa **Anansi** (Mr Spider) is the great **trickster**, his exploits widely told. The Melanesian spider-**spirit** Marawa made man mortal yet often rescued the creator-spirit **Quat** from traps. In **Christian** lore a spider spun a web to hide the infant Jesus from his enemies. Spiders saved the lives of Mohammed and Frederick the Great, and inspired the Scots king Robert the Bruce to resist the English. In folk medicine, spider's web was used to bandage wounds and cure warts. The golden money spider was thought to enrich anyone on whose body it ran; if in the pocket, it ensured ready cash. In modern **comics** mythology Spiderman, who can shimmy like lightning up vertical walls, is among the many superheroes following **Superman**.

SPIDER WOMAN (*See* **HOPI, NAVAHO, SPIDER**)

SPINDLE (*See* **CORD, KNOT, SLEEPING BEAUTY, TABOO**)
Likewise a symbol of **mother**- and **moon**-goddesses as spinners of **fate** or destiny. These are usually triple (birth, life, death; past, present, future); two beneficent, the third cruel and destructive: thus the **fairy-tale** theme of the Good and Wicked **Witch**, as in **Sleeping Beauty** who, cursed by a Wicked Witch, pricks her finger on a spindle and falls into enchanted sleep. The theme expresses both our helplessness in the face of fate and the sense of a hidden design. In **Homer**, men's fortunes are spun or woven, then 'bound' on to them. The word 'destiny' is from Latin *destino*, to 'fix' or 'bind'.
  Sometimes the use of the spindle was **taboo**. The wives of Carpathian hunters were forbidden to spin during the hunt for fear that the game would

turn and wind, and the hunter be unable to hit it. In ancient Italy women walking on the roads could not spin or carry spindles openly, for fear the twirling would twist the corn-stalks. Among the **Ainu** of Japan a pregnant woman did not spin for two months prior to the birth, fearing the child's intestines might get entangled like thread.

SPIRAL (*See* DRAGON, LABYRINTH, LADDER, SERPENT)
In nature represented by snail shells, sea shells, the ear, animal horns, coiled **serpent**, coiled octopus, unfolding fronds and fir-cones, the motion through time of planets round the **sun** and the whirling of the macrocosmos (spiral galaxies), this ancient symbol suggests the winding path we follow through life. It implies eternal departure from one level, eternal return on another; ebb and flow; expansion and contraction; ascent and descent on Jacob's cosmic **ladder** of being; the Tree of Life and the Journey of the **Soul** which many of us, finding it difficult to climb the Holy **Mountain** of **Spirit** by a direct route, may well prefer to ascend by a roundabout spiral climb, as represented by the ziggurat form of the **pyramid**.

Yet the spiral may also be a negative vortex, not ascending to **heaven** but descending down to the **hell** of consciousness, contracting rather than expanding. The **seven** levels of **Dante**'s hell constitute such a negative spiral: to start upwards again, first you have to go all the way down.

Like **spider** and **spindle**, the spiral represents the **mother-goddess** as weaver of human **fates**. As **labyrinth**, it is the mazy road of life leading to the centre of being and to confrontation with the Minotaur, the hidden beast in us. The **treasure** guarded by **dragon** or **serpent** also lies at the heart of the spiral maze (the dragon itself being the spiral).

Such mazes are found in neolithic art from Australia to the cup-and-ring marks carved into European megaliths and burial mounds, as at New Grange in Ireland: follow the spiral serpent in; follow it out again. In Welsh myth, the 'Whirling Castle' of **Arianrhod** is a spiral maze of death-and-rebirth from which the poet **Taliesin** emerges three times.

Diviners derived auguries of the future from the spiralling entrails of **sacrificial** victims. The Kundalini serpent of **Tantric** yoga coils at the base of the spine and, when released, spirals up to the intellectual centres of the cortex, there to enlighten the seeker or drive him mad. The whirling **dance** of the **Dervish** (**Sufi** mystic) likewise invokes the spiral as a way to ecstatic spiritual knowledge.[1]

1. *The Mystic Spiral*, Jill Purce, Thames & Hudson, London, 1974.

SPIRIT (*See* HOLY GHOST, RELIGION, SOUL, SPIRITS)
From Latin *spirare*, 'to breathe'; life's **invisible**, intangible, **immortal** essence; never born so never dying; immaterial yet generating materiality; all-pervasive and universal creative force, the **soul** its vehicle in each individual being. Darwinian materialism and later scientific theory reject it as inessential or illusory, yet all **religions** insist that a spiritual reality underlies and pervades the transitory world of appearances.

In ancient **Mystery** ritual, myths of the descent to the **underworld** of deities (**Inanna, Ishtar, Persephone**) epitomise the descent of the spirit through the **seven** worlds until, naked in dark ignorance, it incarnates in the lowest world, **Hades**, imprisoned and forgetful of its origin. Locked in matter, it must recollect itself, as in the injunction at **Delphi**: 'Man, know thyself', or as in **Buddhist** doctrine that all material manifestations are **maya**, illusion, to be discarded so that the spirit's clear light again shines through matter. It is also widely claimed that, when we die to the world, we reunite with that eternal spirit which is our true essence, and that the world is a school in which the spirit is tested and trained.

SPIRITS (*See* DEMONS, DJINNS, ELEMENTALS, FAIRIES, SPIRIT)

Spirit is singular and all-pervasive, without individual personality or intention. Spirits are entities sharing the world with humanity but of a different order of being. The idea that the world is haunted, influenced or even ruled by such invisible but living beings who may or may not manifest in bodily form is less metaphysically elevated than belief in spirit, but just as common in primitive religion. Such entities are said to take many forms, some benevolent or neutral in regard to humanity, but usually malevolent or dangerous and to be feared, placated and guarded against by **amulet, charm** or other magical means. Some may be commanded by a **magus, shaman, sorcerer** or **witch** who, like **Solomon**, knows their secret **names** or by other means controls them, for good or ill. They may be **ancestors** (ghosts of the dead); **elementals** (natural forces personified) or potent supernatural beings (**demons, devas, djinns, fairies,** fallen **angels, ifrit, rakshasas,** etc.), either sent by God to punish the human race or working against God for the Evil One (**Ahriman, Devil,** etc.) to tempt and torment humanity. They may be able to revive dead bodies by entering the corpse, so communicating their messages to the living; possess living folk and make them act against their will, or lift up objects or persons and fly away with them. In principle **immortal,** they are intelligent and self-willed, and know the past and the future, which a powerful magician may force them to reveal. They come in every possible guise, inhabiting **animals, rivers, trees, stones, mountains, storms, fire** and any other phenomena that the **pagan** mind regards as imbued with the life-force.

Tales of such entities are found in every culture on earth. Belief in them persists (though in shadowy form) even in our seemingly materialistic culture, as in the annual celebration on 31 October of **Hallowe'en** (All Hallows Eve), when ancestral ghosts and all other sprites are set loose to do mischief or revisit the hearths of their living descendants.

SPRITES (*See* ELEMENTALS, SPIRITS)

STAG (*See* ACTAEON, CERNUNNOS, DEER, HORNED GODS, SHAPE-SHIFTING)

The **pagan** symbolism of the stag arises from specific qualities associated with its antlers, thus differentiating it from the symbolism of the **deer** in general. Fast, virile and aggressive during the rutting seasons, the wide-spreading antlers of these kings of the northern forests suggested the branches of trees. Antler-growth in spring (**sun** rising) and antler-loss in autumn (sun dying) endowed the stag with solar and fertility imagery.

So in **Celtic** lands the stag's antlers became emblematic of hunter and forest gods like **Cernunnos,** implying the same fierce masculine mastery as elsewhere indicated by the horns of **bull, ram** or **goat.** Antlers found in the **megalithic** chamber at New Grange, Ireland, suggest that the stag was the royal beast of the legendary **Tuatha dé Danaan,** just as the bull (**Minotaur**) represented the fecund might of Minos of Crete. The Danaan connection is also implied by the frequency in Irish and Welsh myth with which the stag appears as a supernatural messenger leading the hunter to the **otherworld,** as in the tales of **Pwyll** (who set his own hounds on a stag slain by the hounds of

Arawn, the otherworld king) and **Finn MacCool** (who hunted an enchanted stag, and whose son Oisin (fawn) was said to be half-human, half-deer). The Irish Morrigan became a stag as easily as a **crow**; in the *Mabinogion*, **Math** turns his nephews **Gwydion** and Gilfaethly into a stag and a hind; a supernatural stag helps **Culhwch** hunt the boar Twrch Trwyth. The *Mabinogion* also tells how, accompanied by his faithless wife **Blodeuwedd**, **Llew Llaw Gyffes** sees a stag baited to death, and almost immediately after is slain by her lover Gronw. So too in Greek myth, the hunter **Actaeon** spies on the goddess as she bathes naked; in revenge she turns him into a stag torn to pieces by his own hounds. Yet again: 'Long live the king (stag: human **soul**); the king must die.' Yet the image of a stag trampling a **serpent** underfoot is the victory of spirit over matter, good over evil; the soul of the slain stag-king lives on in his successor.

STAPLEDON, OLAF (1884–1950) (*See* **SCIENCE FICTION**)
Liverpool-born English writer and philosopher who in his later life produced a body of speculative literature characterised by its fecund imagination, grandeur of language, severity of logic and the cosmic range of its philosophical quest for a mythical system appropriate to modern needs. His first work of fiction, *Last and First Men* (1930) was acclaimed, though later nearly forgotten. Employing a time-scale of 2,000 million years, he describes the fate of seventeen human races subsequent to our own (the First Race). The tale is told by one of the Last (18th race) men, speaking through the 'docile but scarcely adequate brain' of a First Race man (Stapledon himself). He concludes that the First Race reached its apotheosis in **Socrates** (search for truth) and **Christ** (self-sacrifice to the Almighty). Later races, leaving earth for other planets, represent higher wisdom, though with frequent evolutionary degenerations en route to the climactic 18th men. The tone of the tale is serene yet severe.

Last Men in London (1932) led to *Odd John* (1935), the tale of a mutated **superman**, his superiority philosophic and intellectual, and restating the austere, remote wisdom of the 18th men. This was followed in 1937 by *Star Maker*, a masterpiece which some have compared with **Dante**'s *Divine Comedy* for the scale and precision of its vision. Ultimately the Star Maker is revealed to be as pitiless as **Shiva**, the dancing god who destroys to create.

STAR TREK (*See* **SCIENCE FICTION**)
First broadcast in the USA in 1966, this popular television series used old mythic themes in taking **Homer**'s *Odyssey* from the Aegean to Outer Space. Crew-members like the logical yet **pixie**-eared alien Vulcan Mr Spock (the sexually-ambiguous 'star' of the series) derive from old European folklore, evil aliens are **demonic sorcerers**, while the pseudo-scientific paraphernalia of instantaneous travel between worlds recasts the magic-carpet journey (*Arabian Nights*) in terms of a belief that science will make such marvels possible.

STAR WARS (*See* **HOLLYWOOD, SCIENCE FICTION**)

STONE (*See* **JEWELS, MEGALITHIC MYTHS, PHILOSOPHER'S STONE**)
Indestructible durability as in **pyramids**, megalithic circles and Gothic cathedrals. Stones carry a wide range of magical, mythical and healing associations. Precious stones possess their own symbolism. Meteoric stones like the Ka'aba in Mecca are widely viewed as sacred. In primitive belief

stones give birth to people, or people become stones, as by the **Medusa**'s glare or as in megalithic myth. Standing stones are *fir chreig* ('false men') in Gaelic lore. England's Rollright Stones are said to go down to a river to drink. In Lapland, stones moulded by water into odd shapes (*Seide*), set up as sacred, were viewed as a **prophetic** family. Animal-shaped stones owned by Melanesian **initiates** of the Ingiet, a secret society, were said to contain their **souls**: if their stone broke, they too died. The soul of Simeon, a Bulgarian prince, was held in a stone column at Constantinople. When the emperor Romanus Lecapenus removed its capital, he later learned that Simeon had instantly died of a stroke. In Greek myth, **Cronus** swallowed his new-born children, but **Rhea** saved **Zeus** her last-born by offering Cronus a stone wrapped in swaddling clothes, which he swallowed.

As column, pillar or megalith, stone represents the *axis mundi*, **omphalos** or phallic **lingam**: so too conical stones and cairns. Certain stones on Ural peaks were said by the Samoyeds to support the sky. Cubic stones are the foundation of sacred buildings, the rock on which the universe rests. The foundation stone of the Temple at Jerusalem was considered the centre of the earth; so too a stone at **Delphi** was the 'navel of the world'. At initiation a **Brahman** boy would tread right-footed on a stone as it was declared 'Tread on this stone: like a stone be firm.' The twelfth-century Danish historian Saxo tells how the ancient sages chose a king while standing on stones, so ensuring the durability of their decision. Likewise the custom of swearing oaths upon a stone, to indicate the reliability of the oath.

Round stones symbolise the **moon**, the feminine principle and fertility. If hollow, they symbolise the womb, as does the cromlech or dolmen (usually two uprights and a capstone). Cones or pillars or cubes may also symbolise the moon or **mother-goddess**. In Peru, people used stones of a certain shape to increase maize, potatoes or cattle. In Melanesia it was said that stones had powers according to their shape: a piece of coral resembling a bread-fruit would be laid under a bread-fruit tree, etc. Some stones were said to make **rain**: during droughts the *lapis manalis*, kept near a Temple of **Mars** outside Rome, was dragged into the city in hopes of a downpour.

Broken stones or pillars signify death or dismemberment, but the life-restoring mythic stone called *lapis exilis* ('paltry stone') is associated with the Philosopher's Stone, also with the **Holy Grail**.

STONEHENGE (*See* **MEGALITHIC MYTHS**)

STOORWORM (*See* **DRAGON, LOATHLY WORM, SERPENT**)

Derived from the Norse Midgard serpent and the Greek myth of **Perseus** and Andromeda, when this primeval British water monster crawled out of the sea, ocean, the waves swamped the land. Only by the sacrifice of maidens could it be propitiated. To avoid his daughter's death, a king offered her, half the realm and his **sword** (once **Odin**'s) to its killer. Heroic Assipattle thrust burning peats into its liver and amid its thrashing death agony its tail parted land to form the Skaggerak channel between Norway and Sweden; it vomited out its teeth to form the isles of Orkney, Shetland and Faroe; then curled into a ball, fell into the sea and formed Iceland, where hot springs exist because the Stoorworm's liver still burns.

STORK

A reptile-slaying water-bird of good omen and fertility, as in the fable that it brings babies. In Germany, children sing to the stork to bring them a little brother or sister. Bavarians say well-behaved baby boys come riding on its back, but naughty boys are carried in its bill. It is said if a Christmas mummer dressed as a stork nudges a woman, she will soon be pregnant, and that a wounded stork weeps human tears. Belief that storks can become people, or vice versa, existed from Arabia to Britain – Gervase of Tilbury (thirteenth century) speaks of people turning into storks. The belief arises perhaps from its size and upright posture. Long associated with springtime and thus new life, its old Germanic name, Adebar, means 'luck-bringer'. Its ancient reputation for filial piety is found from China to Egypt, where it is said that the young care for their parents in old age. Aristotle claims that the male stork kills his mate if she is unfaithful.

STORM-GODS (*See* **CONCORDANCE**)

STREIBER, WHITLEY (*See* **ABDUCTIONS, ROSWELL INCIDENT, UFOs**)

STUART, CHARLES EDWARD (*See* **BONNIE PRINCE CHARLIE**)

STURLUSSON, SNORRI (*See* ***EDDA*, NORSE MYTH**)

STYX (*See* **CHARON, RIVER MYTH, UNDERWORLD**)

SUFIS (*See* **DERVISHES, ISLAM, NASRUDDIN, OMAR, PERSIAN MYTH, RUMI**)

Believers in **reincarnation**, conscious evolution and human perfectability, the Sufi schools originated in Persia/Iran. Sufis claim to guard Islam's esoteric lore and to have preceded Mohammed, their eastern school deriving from **Zoroastrian** mysticism. The movement began as a revolt against rigid laws imposed by Islam on displacing Zoroastrianism in the mid-seventh century, later evolving into a pantheistic mysticism displaying **Buddhist** as well as Zoroastrian elements. While Buddhists deny deity and **soul**, Sufis admit both; while Buddhists seek via mental abstraction total cessation of thought and desire, Sufis seek via ecstatic devotion to God a state of all-enveloping love in which inferior desires are dissolved.

Long bridging gaps between disputing Moslem sects, Sufism's impact on Western thought remains largely unacknowledged. Idries Shah claims that Lully, Roger Bacon, **Paracelsus**, Aquinas and a number of popes were all Sufi-inspired, and that **Freemasonry, Rosicrucianism** and the Franciscan Order likewise bear the stamp of Sufi influence.[1]

The term 'Sufi' may derive from **Sophia**, wisdom, or may imply one wearing wool who pursues simplicity and poverty. Forming many orders including the dervishes, Sufism involves 'the grand idea of one universal creed which could be secretly held under any profession of outward faith.'[2] Sufism has inspired most of Persia's best poetry. Hiding their ideas behind the symbolism of 'The Beloved', poets like Rumi, Hafiz, Attar ('Parliament of Birds'; *see* **Simurgh**) and Saadi still command respect. Rumi's *Mathnawi* ranks next to the Koran. Of him Dr Johnson said, 'He makes plain to the Pilgrim the secrets of the Way of Unity, and unveils the Mysteries of the Path of Eternal Truth.' The popular Nasruddin tales began as Sufi teaching devices designed, **Zen**-like, to jolt the mind into lateral thought.

1. *The Sufis*, Idries Shah, Doubleday, New York, 1964.
2. *Reincarnation: The Phoenix Fire Mystery*, S.L. Cranston and Joseph Head, Julian Press, New York, 1977, p.169.

SUMERIAN MYTH (*See* CONCORDANCE)

Some 5,000 years ago, as societies developed by the Nile (Egypt) and Indus (northwest India), a non-Semitic people (perhaps central Asian) settled the Mesopotamian marshes between the Tigris and Euphrates. These Sumerians, the 'black-headed' people, developed organised agriculture and city-states: Uruk (Ur), Erech and Lagash, with Eridu to the south, Nippur to the north. The need for accounting techniques to collect and distribute grain surpluses to growing populations led them to develop pictographic script into the wedge-shaped cuneiform, stamped in clay tablets. Their early regional power was modified by Akkadian conquest under Sargon of Agade (2371–2316 BC). These Akkadians, Syrian Semites, built cities higher up the Euphrates (Borsippa, Babylon, Kish, Sippur and the unlocated Agade). Their influence on Sumeria is apparent in later **Babylonian** and **Assyrian** myth. Gods and myths were exchanged and assimilated by each city – but the Sumerian myth came first.

Reflecting a reliance on water, the Sumerian **creation myth** Enuma Elish (named for its first words, 'When on high') describes the world as a circle bounded by mountains that hold up the heavens. The world floats on Apsu, the abyss of sweet water, whose union with **Tiamat** (salt water, the chaotic primeval **dragon**) bears Mummu, the raging waves, then Lakhmu and Lakhamu, monsters who bear **Anu** (or Anshar: male, the celestial world) and Ki (or Kishar: female, the earth). These two bear the gods **Enlil** and **Enki/Ea**, also the Igigi (sky-deities) and **Anunnaki** ('Lords of the Dead'). Apsu and Tiamat, outraged, plot to kill their children. Enki seizes Apsu and Mummu, whereupon Tiamat bears monsters. Both she and they are slain (or tamed) by Enki's son **Marduk**, who becomes the great **sun**-god, humanity's creator.

Yet Enki also fathered Adapa (*see* **Adam**), the first man, mythical king of Eridu, said to have invented speech. Like **Gilgamesh**, he was angry at being denied **immortality**, yet had to accept disease and death as his lot.

Sumerian kings had authority from the gods, each city being owned by its god, his priests owning and working the land. Annually in each city holy marriage was celebrated between the king and a priestess representing the city-goddess. The king impersonated Dumuzi (*see* **Inanna**) while the priestess was Inanna. Only later, during Babylon's rise, did priestly power decline, the gods assuming new roles legitimising the earthly power of the kings, leading to the total authority of Assyrian despots like Ashurbanipal.

SUN (*See* CONCORDANCE, MOON)

Solar radiation makes earth-life possible. It is not surprising that the sun has been worshipped as a god since early times, either as Supreme Deity, or as the image of the godhead. **Flood**-myth recalls sunless epochs with horror – solar eclipses have long been regarded with fright and awe. Rites to make the sun shine (by prayer, propitiation or **sacrifice**) are found the world over. At an eclipse, the Ojibwas of North America shot fire-tipped arrows in the air to rekindle the dying light; the Senci of Peru did the same, but to expel the **dragon** devouring it. Norse myth says the **wolf Fenrir** (or his brood) will eat the sun, causing the Fimbulwinter, lasting three long years before **Ragnorak**. In ancient Egypt the Pharaoh, as epitome of **Ra** the sun-god, daily walked round the temple walls to ensure Ra's daily journey round the sky. **Brahmans** still claim that without their morning offering the sun cannot rise. The **Aztecs** annually sacrificed thousands of victims to their sun-god **Huitzilopochtli**, insisting on his continual need of flayed corpses and ripped-out hearts – perhaps reflecting their own dietary requirements.

Though sometimes a goddess (Japanese **Amaterasu**, Aboriginal Yhi), the sun is usually seen as a god, married to the **moon** and birthing the stars: *see* **Amon**-Ra, **Apollo, Baal, Slavonic** Dazhbog, **Inca** Inti, **Lug, Marduk, Phoebus, Shamash**. A common image was of the sun-god daily rising as a youth from his eastern palace to climb the sky in golden barge or **chariot** drawn by fiery **horses**. Reaching maturity at the zenith, he plunges into old age and nightly death in the west. Swallowed by the chaotic **dragon** of night (winter), he swims back to the east, or returns via the **underworld** to be reborn next morning (spring) as the newly young, all-conquering god.

So too solar imagery is that of the died-and-reborn **corn-god: Adonis, Attis, Tammuz,** etc., again including **Christ**, who brings the cosmic power down to earth, revives the world, suffers and is slain, and then rises from the dead. In Egyptian myth the rising sun is **Horus**, the noon sun is Ra, the setting (or dying) sun is **Osiris** (god of the dead), slain by **Set** in his guise as the dragon Apep, darkness or chaos, or winter. Ra, Horus, Osiris: Father, Son and **Holy Ghost**. The **dualist** battle is between Horus (light) and Set (darkness); **Ahura Mazda** and **Ahriman**; Lug and **Balor** or Christ and the **Devil**. It is a daily, monthly, annual, unending battle.

Solar symbols are various and, at first sight, sometimes contradictory. They include: a disc, revolving **wheel, swastika, spider** at the centre of its web, **eagle** (Amerindian **Thunderbird**), **hawk** (Horus), white or golden horse, **cock** crowing at break of dawn, **lion, ram,** the winged or plumed **serpent** (**Quetzalcoatl**), and the winged Chinese dragon. In **Qabalistic** lore, the central sephirah of the **Tree of Life** is Tiphareth, the sun, Christ-consciousness, the union of lower with upper worlds, a radiant child astride a lion, **soul** self-redeemed from its animal nature, transfigured and transformed. So too in occult belief the sun is but a local guarantor or expression of a wider cosmic soul: the star **Sirius** is said to be 'the Sun behind the Sun', regional governor in a cosmic administration of which our sun (son) is but a local district councillor.

SUN-GODS (*See* CONCORDANCE)

SUPERHEROES (*See* BATMAN, COMICS, SUPERMAN)

SUPERMAN (*See* COMICS, SCIENCE FICTION)
An American **comic** strip superhero created by writer Jerry Siegel and artist Joseph Shuster, later incorporated in contemporary Western pop mythology. The story-lines include time travel, journeys in space and attempts by supervillains to destroy him by exposing him to kryptonite, a mysterious substance. Sub-plots concern efforts to unmask his identity. Yet as Superman he remains aloof in his fight for 'truth, justice and the American way'.

SUPERNATURAL BEINGS (*See* CONCORDANCE)

SURYA (*See* INDIAN MYTH, SWASTIKA)
Aryan **sun**-god who like **Apollo, Dahzbog, Helios, Shamash** and others spends the day riding over the sky in his **chariot**, which is drawn by **seven** red mares, or by a single mare with seven heads. He is also called Savitri ('stimulator', 'enlightener'); Bhaga ('distributor of wealth'); Pushan ('benefactor'); Vivasvat ('father of humanity'). With golden hair, arms and hands, he is also 'the eye of **Varuna** and **Mitra**'. His wife is Ushas (Aurora), goddess of dawn. His **twin** sons are the Ashvins (sun-rays) who, in their own golden chariots, precede his daily rising. He was widely worshipped in the **Vedic** and **Puranic** periods, especially as Savitri. The

swastika symbol was a sign of his generosity.

SUSANOWO (*See* AMATERASU, JAPANESE MYTH)

SVAROG (*See* DAZHBOG, SLAVONIC MYTH)

SWAHILI (*See* AFRICAN MYTH, CREATION MYTH)

The **creation myth** of this **Islamic** central East African people of mixed Arab-Bantu descent tells how God first created light, then out of it the **souls** of all who will live in the future: first the souls of the **prophets**, then of saints and holy men, then of ordinary folk, as many as the stars in the sky. Also from this first light came the **angels**, who can never lie, being luminous. Then he created seven great things: Canopy, Throne, Pen, Book, Trumpet, Paradise and Hellfire. The Canopy covers God's Throne; the Pen daily inscribes the **fate** of all; the Book records the future, until the Last Day when the Trumpet sounds Final Judgement. Then the righteous go to Paradise, the Garden of Delight, but the wicked to the furnace of Gehennom.

Under his throne God created a huge **tree**, the Cedar of the End; on it millions of leaves, some fresh, others withering; each with a **name** on it. When a leaf falls, an angel reads the name and tells the Angel of Death, the Taker of Souls, who descends to earth to seek out the name's terrified owner, and to part body from soul.

Then he made the earth as **ocean**, the **sun** above it. He called up the continents; then islands. He made forests and grasslands. He made the sun sink in the west and removed the light, but hung stars in the sky under his throne. He made a heavenly **cock** to crow at dawn so that all earthly cocks, hearing it, would crow, waking folk up. He made four kinds of animal: those that swim, ruled by **Whale**; those that creep, ruled by **Python**; those that fly, ruled by **Eagle**; those on four legs, ruled by **Lion**. Also he made four intelligent classes of beings: angels, from light; **djinns**, from air; **shaitans**, from fire; and people, from earth. As for the flat earth with the ocean about it, this he placed on a four-horned **bull** which stands on a great **fish** that swims an ocean deeper than anything man ever saw.[1]

1. *African Mythology*, Jan Knappert, Aquarian Press, Wellingborough, 1990.

SWALLOW

The saying, 'One swallow does not make a summer', originates with the Greek philosopher Aristotle. Since early times the migratory return to northern lands of this darting, swooping small bird has been seen as the harbinger of springtime; and so it is associated with **resurrection**, new life, the **mother goddess**. Yet it was not seen as wholly beneficent. The Greeks disliked its chattering song; **diviners** found it ambiguous. The swallow fluttering round the head of **Alexander the Great** was seen as a portent of disaster, though returning swallows were said to predict the safe return of **Dionysus** (thus: growth of the vine). Weather was forecast from the flight of the swallow; still in Europe today low-flying swallows are said to mean bad weather approaching.

SWAN (*See* ANGUS MAC OG, BIRDS, SHAPE-SHIFTING, ZEUS)

Symbolising solitude, sincerity, purity and grace, the healing powers of the **sun** and **waters** united, this most graceful of large water-birds has since early times attracted a belief that people or gods may become swans. The typical tale is of a man who sees swans set down by the water, discard their feathers, and turn into lovely maidens. If he steals the feather-robe of one, she must be his wife until, finding it again, she takes wing and leaves him: a motif like that of the **seal**-woman or selkie. In Irish myth **Angus MacOg** falls for a swan-maiden and becomes a swan himself, their song so wondrous that all who hear it fall asleep. Less romantically, in Greek myth lecherous **Zeus** becomes a dazzling white swan to seduce Leda, wife of Tyndareus. That night she also lies with her husband, later giving birth to four children: Pollux and **Helen**, children of Zeus, and Castor and Clytemnestra, children of Tyndareus (*see* **Dioscuri**). So too the **rishis**, celestial poets of Indian myth, take swan-form when visiting mankind. The tale is also told of Prince Nala who, in love with Princess Damayanti (daughter of **Bhima**: *see Mahabharata*), seized one of a flock of golden-winged swans at play in his palace gardens. Begging release, the swan promises to argue Nala's love-suit to Damayanti, and so in time the two lovers are united.

The denial by Pliny (AD 23–79) that swans sing while dying shows this belief to be ancient. In *The Parliament of Fowles* Chaucer (1340–1400) refers to 'swan-song', while **Shakespeare**'s *Othello* resolves to 'play the swan, and die in music'. In the Finnish *Kalevala* a swan floats on the **underworld** river of Tuonela, singing the Song of the Dead, as interpreted by **Sibelius** in his tone-poem *The Swan of Tuonela*.

SWASTIKA (*See* **CROSS, SUN**)

Ancient worldwide symbol of an equal-armed cross with unidirectional rays extending from the tips of each arm. Though generally accepted as a symbol of the revolving **sun**, its precise meaning remains unknown. It may equally mean the stars revolving about the Pole, the four cardinal points, the four winds, the four seasons or the four quarters of the **moon**. It is also said to imply the union of the male and female principles, or to be a version of the **labyrinth**, of water in movement or of forked lightning. In any case its whirling motions implies fecundity and creative force. Though hijacked by the Nazis, it has nothing whatever to do with totalitarianism.

SWIFT, JONATHAN (1667–1745) (*See* **SCIENCE FICTION**)

Irish satirist, poet and cleric, famed as author of a fabulous adventure, part myth and part science fiction, first published in 1726 as *Travels into Several Nations of the World by Lemuel Gulliver, first a Surgeon, and then a Captain of Several Ships*, and since known simply as *Gulliver's Travels*. In each of its four books Gulliver is marooned in an alien culture, each satirising the absurdities Swift perceived in contemporary British culture.

SWINE (*See* **PIG**)

SWORD (*See* **EXCALIBUR**)

Symbolises power, protection, authority and the masculine principle. As a phallus (its sheath the receptive feminine) wielded by the solar **dragon**-slaying hero, it is a magical guarantor of the hero's prowess and strength, of his very masculinity; thus the frequent appearance in hero-myth of the supernatural sword gifted by the gods or **otherworld** powers, following a **test** by which the hero proves his right to wield it. **Arthur** alone can draw **Excalibur** from the **stone** into which his dying father **Uther** had plunged it; by this feat establishing himself as the true **king**. Likewise in **Norse myth** the hero Sigmund alone can pull the sword **Balmung** from the tree-post into which the god **Odin** had thrust it: with it he wins many battles until, in his final combat, Odin shatters it. Later it is reforged for his dragon-slaying son **Sigurd**. The tendency to name such swords as if they are alive is also notable: such as Excalibur, Balmung, Roland's Durendal. Metaphysically, the sword symbolises intellectual discrimination which cuts ignorance to the roots and slices through knotty problems, just as **Alexander the Great** sliced through the Gordian Knot.

SWORD-BRIDGE (*See* ARTHURIAN MYTH, BRIDGE, RAINBOW)

In **Arthurian myth** the **bridge** separating this world from the next, thus a version of the **rainbow**-bridge Bifrost of **Norse myth**, and of many similar bridges that in world myth epitomise the dangerous, narrow crossing. In the *Mabinogion* tale 'Culhwch and Olwen', King Arthur's ally Osla Big-Knife lays his knife over a river to help Arthur's army cross. In a later tale, Sir **Lancelot** has to cross a sword-bridge to rescue **Guinevere** from Melwas, the **otherworld** king who had abducted her. The theme was also used as one of the **tests** to be undergone by Grail Knights seeking to reach the castle of the **Holy Grail**.

SYLPHS (*See* ELEMENTALS)

SYMBOLISM

From Latin *symbolum*, 'token' or 'pledge', a symbol is an object or design that typifies or represents an abstract or spiritual state otherwise hard to express. Letters of the alphabet are symbols just as is a **totem** pole or the **cross**, **swastika** or Tree of Life. Symbols lead the mind beyond their own external, lower reality to the higher state they represent, so communicating truths either obscured by language limitations or too complex to be described. They function via the traditional understanding of what they represent; they trigger intuitive response.

SYMPLEGADES (*See* CLASHING ROCKS, GREEK MYTH)

T

TA'AROA (*See* CREATION MYTH, FLOOD MYTH, OCEANIC MYTH)

Supreme being in Tahitian myth of Polynesia. Breaking out of the darkness of the cosmic **egg**, he existed alone before creating a female being, his daughter, with whose aid he made the sea, sky and earth, fishing up the latter from the depths of the **ocean**. At last he took red earth and from it made man, who ate the earth until the breadfruit was created. Calling man by name, Ta'aroa put him to sleep, took a bone from his body, and from it made woman. Some claim that this myth is indigenous, others that it must be derived from the biblical account of **Eve**'s creation. Yet when in 1769 Captain Cook visited Tahiti, he noted how the temple called 'the god's house', said to have been built by Ta'aroa out of his own body, resembled 'the **Ark** of the Lord among Jews'. It is also said that Ta'aroa, angry with mankind, flooded the world, leaving only islands protruding. **Flood myth** at least is universal, owing nothing to the biblical account.

TABOO (*See GEIS*, OCEANIC MYTH, SPELLS)

Or tabu. A system of religious and social prohibition of a sort found in primitive cultures worldwide, as in the prohibitions called *geasa* placed upon ancient **Irish** kings and heroes, and more generally surviving as in superstitious belief in the bad luck caused by walking under **ladders** or breaking **mirrors**. In origin the word is Polynesian, referring to that which makes certain people or animals untouchable or unmentionable, so too certain acts or words; either because of their inherent sacred quality (so Jews cannot speak aloud **Yahweh**'s secret **name**), because of fear that to break the taboo is to incur divine or magical wrath; because the tabooed person or object is 'unclean' (**pigs, menstrual** woman, etc.); or to ensure protection from theft, trespass or other forms of harm, or to ensure safe birth (thus taboos against pregnant women crossing their legs, spinning or tying **knots**, etc.). Being supernatural in origin, a violated taboo need not be punished by man: the **Fates** will mete out the punishment. Tales all round the world warn against the breaking of taboo. There is the door that must not be entered (**Bluebeard**), the box not to be opened (**Pandora**), the fatal backwards look (**Lot's wife, Orpheus**), the requirement to get home by midnight (**Cinderella**), the fruit not to be eaten (**Adam** and **Eve**), the flesh not to be eaten (**Cuchulainn**), the horse from which the rider must not dismount (**Oisin**), and many, many more. All such tales refer to the common human perception that we live in a magical universe bound by laws which we break at our peril. Stray off the narrow path hedged on either side by a multitude of taboos, and we invite disaster.

TAGHAIRM (*See* CAT, DIVINATION, PROPHECY, SECOND SIGHT, SPIRITS)

A prophetic rite associated with Scots Gaels whereby, to learn the future, the seer or **shaman**, wrapped in the hide of a newly-slaughtered **bull**, lay all night near a waterfall, at the foot of a precipice or a similar wild place said to be haunted by **spirits** so that, spirit-possessed, he gained the knowledge required. This rite was also practised in Wales, as in the *Mabinogion* tale, 'The Dream of Rhonabwy', in which this warrior of Powys, while sleeping on the skin of a yellow heifer, dreams of King **Arthur**'s court. Another version is given in the tale of how two Highlanders, Allan and Lachlan, spitted then roasted black **cats** alive, causing such howling as to bring King Cat, the **Devil** himself, who, to save his subjects from more torture, granted the two men the long life and wealth they demanded.

TAHITI (*See* OCEANIC MYTH, TA'AROA)

TAIKOMOL (*See* FLOOD MYTH, NATIVE AMERICAN MYTH)

Creator-god and culture hero of the Yuki and associated tribes of Northern California. Alone in the universe, he made the world, then created human beings out of sticks. But the **flood** came, the earth disappeared. So he made a second world, one without daylight, **sun** or game to hunt, in which the people had to eat each other. Now naming himself 'He Who Walks Alone', Taikomol made a third world, with rivers and mountains, but this too was unstable, floating like a feather on the primeval waters. So at the North Pole he set a great **coyote**, elk and **deer**, making them lie down to render the earth more stable. Whenever they move, the earth quakes. Yet again he made human beings out of sticks, and gave them a **dance**. These people were immortal, but one sinned and died. Taikomol **resurrected** him, but all the other people were sickened by the corpse-stench, so Taikomol abandoned any idea of future resurrections. Despite this entry of death to the world, he bade them continue the **Ghost Dance** (not the same as that introduced in 1890 by the Paiute Wovoka), so that they might live well and long.

TÁIN BÓ CUALNGE (*See* BULL, CUCHULAINN, IRISH MYTH)

The best-known epic of the Ulster cycle of Old Irish literature, 'The Cattle Raid of Cooley' is also Western Europe's oldest epic, referring perhaps to events of the first century AD, written down from the oral tradition *c.*AD 650. The first extant manuscript is in the 'Book of the Dun Cow' (*c.*1100).

It tells how the war between Connaught and Ulster began with Queen Maeve of Connaught's fury at learning that her husband, King Ailill, had a White **Bull**, Finnbennach ('of the white horns'). Calved in her herds, it had gone over to Ailill's pastures, but he would not give it up. Her **Druid**, MacRoth, told her of its equal, the Donn Cualnge, the Brown Bull of Cooley, grazing on Ulster lands ruled by **Conchobar MacNessa**. Deciding to get it to spite Ailill, she sent MacRoth to Cooley, offering fifty heifers for a year's loan of it, plus other gifts, including herself. Agreement was reached, but MacRoth's drunken men boasted that Maeve could take the bull by force. Told that the arrangement was off, they left empty-handed. Maeve made Ailill declare war. Yet when Connaughtmen marched on Ulster with men of Munster and Leinster, she jealously rejected Leinster's finer warriors, who had encamped and lit fires while her Connaughtmen still sought a camp-site. Though fearing her rage, Ailill suggested that the Leinstermen disperse through the entire army.

They forded the River Shannon. That night a seer saw crows drinking the blood of Maeve's army. Yet next day they marched on. Ailill, and Fergus his champion, both hoping for peace, sent messengers to warn of the approaching army. But the Ulstermen lay under a *geis*, that for nine generations all their warriors would be as weak as women in childbirth. Only their champion, **Cuchulainn**, was not an Ulsterman. Alone he met and held off the Connaught army even as Maeve's men drove off the Brown Bull. Though badly wounded, Cuchulainn was healed by his father, the god **Lug**. Returning in a frenzy, he slew many. Maeve called on his foster-brother, Ferdiad, to fight him. For three days they fought a draw. Each night Cuchulainn sent Ferdiad healing herbs; Ferdiad sent him food. At last Cuchulainn slew his brother. Then in his grief he defeated the men of Connaught single-handed. The White and Brown Bulls fought to the death. At dawn the Brown Bull carried on his horns the gory remains of the White. Mortally wounded, the Brown Bull returned to Ulster, then dropped dead. Cuchulainn was persuaded to leave the men of Connaught alone. The Ulstermen returned home triumphant, but all were weary of the futile battle caused only by Maeve's jealousy of her husband's wealth.

TAIOWA (*See* CREATION MYTH, HOPI LORE)

TALIESIN (*See* ANEURIN, CERRIDWEN, GAMES, MERLIN, RIDDLES, WELSH MYTH)

As mysterious as **Merlin**, this Welsh **bard** is said in a former incarnation to have been the boy Gwion Bach who, accidentally tasting **Cerridwen**'s Brew of Inspiration, was pursued by this hag-goddess in **shape-shifting** flight until at last, as a hen catching up with him as a grain of corn, she ate him. But nine months later she bore a child. Like **Moses** abandoned to the waters, in his coracle the infant drifted into a **salmon**-weir, to be found by Prince Elphin, who named him Taliesin ('Radiant Brow'). When Elphin was imprisoned by a rival king, Maelgwyn, the youthful Taliesin released him by confounding Maelgwyn's sycophantic court-poets with **riddles** they could not answer, finally reducing them to mindless blabbering while bringing a **wind**-storm that led to Elphin's release. Among his riddles are a famous set of boasts as to his former incarnations; the epitome of poetic initiation and arrogance. 'Knowest thou what thou art in the hour of sleep?' he asks (in the thirteenth-century 'Book of Taliesin'). 'A mere body, a mere soul, or a secret retreat of light?' He goes on: 'I marvel that in their books they know not with certainty/ the properties of the soul, or what form are its members;/ Into what part, or when, it takes up its abode,/ Or by what wind or stream it is supplied.' Having made this statement, he goes on to tell of his many incarnations. He has been with God in the highest sphere, with Lucifer in the Pit of Hell, with **Noah** in the Ark, in India when Rome was built, and so on. He has been 'three times' in the whirling celestial castle of the goddess **Arianrhod**, he has been animal and man, male and female, black and white, and though originally he was little Gwion, at last he is Taliesin; the poet swallowed by the death-hag yet reborn so often that now he knows everything; the power of the true poet being to remember all things.

This mythic Taliesin has been identified with a sixth-century Welsh poet of the same name. In **Arthurian myth** he sails with Arthur to raid Annwn, the **otherworld**, to recover the spoils or **treasures** stolen from Britain.

TALISMAN (*See* AMULETS, CHARMS, SPELLS)

This is any wonder-working object or **charm** guaranteeing its owner power, as opposed to an **amulet**, which offers protection or prevents harm. The talisman is active and potent in itself, like the rabbit's foot, the magic **wand** or the amethyst worn to protect its owner from alcohol's effects. The holy relics of medieval Christendom, such as supposed pieces of the True **Cross**, or the bones of saints, were revered due to their talismanic properties, real or assumed. Possession of a talisman grants power to the owner: so by owning the magic lamp Aladdin (see *Arabian Nights*) is able to summon powerful **djinns** to serve him. Likewise, medieval alchemists sought the **Philosopher's Stone** as a means to **immortality** and power. Thus the talisman, like but unlike a **symbol**, is an object that brings to its owner specific benefits or worldly advantages. If it does not, it is useless.

TALOS (*See* ACHILLES HEEL, GREEK MYTH, JASON, ROBOTS)

TAMLIN (*See* FAIRIES, HALLOWE'EN)

In Scots lore this spellbound guardian of Carterhaugh, like **True Thomas** in bondage to the Queen of Faery, demanded of all maidens who went by 'their rings or green mantles, Or else their maidenhead'. Yet his true love Janet, unafraid of **fairy** bewitchment, went after him at Hallowe'en, braving all the enchanted denizens of fairyland to drag him off his milk-white **horse** as he rode by with the other sprites, and held him fast to the real world even as, still seized by spell, he **shape-shifted** into wild beasts. So she won him back to the human world, ignoring the death-**curse** put on her by the Faery Queen for taking away 'the bonniest knight/In a' my companie'.

The hero of this tale is not Tamlin but Janet, whose love restores a man lost in a dreamworld to the land of reality. She knows just what she wants, has no superstitious fear, and does what has to be done to get her potentially good man back from the illusions about to destroy him.

TAMMUZ (*See* ADONIS, BABYLONIAN MYTH, CORN-GODS, ISHTAR)

Derived from Dumuzi, consort of Sumerian **Inanna**, this Babylonian **corn-god** is essentially identical to the Phoenician **Adonis**. The youthful lover of the **mother-goddess Ishtar**, it is said her love was so terrible that annually it killed him, sending him down to the **underworld**, so that annually she had to follow him. During her absence from the world all reproduction and fertility ceased, until **Ereshkigal**, goddess of the underworld, let them both return to the upper world, so reviving nature.

TANE-MAHUTA (*See* HAWAII, MAORI MYTH, TANGAROA)

TANGAROA (*See* HAWAII, OCEANIC MYTH, QUAT)

A Polynesian sea-god, variously named with varying attributes according to the culture. Known in **Hawaii** as the evil-smelling squid-god Kanaloa, he was associated there with the **Christian Devil** and the land of the dead. The **Maori** of New Zealand say that he fled to the ocean when the storm-god Tawhiri-ma-tea raged in support of Rangi, their father, after Tane-mahuta the forest-god had forced Rangi off their mother the earth-goddess Papa and up into the sky. Another Maori myth has it that Tangaroa argued with his brother Vatea about who had fathered Papa's firstborn, so that Papa cut the child in half and gave each god his portion. Vatea cast his half into the sky, where it became the **sun**; Tangaroa kept his piece, but it began to decompose, so he too threw it into the sky, where it became the pale and pitted **moon**. Later Tane-mahuta supplied the human offspring of Tumatauenga, god of fierce human beings, with canoes, spears, fish-hooks and nets from his trees and plants, so that they might kill Tangaroa's offspring (fish). In revenge, Tangaroa took pleasure in sinking canoes, flooding the land and eating up the shoreline.

TANNHÄUSER (*See* **TEUTONIC MYTH, WAGNER**)
A thirteenth-century minnesinger (lyric poet) whose adventures in Germany
and on crusade to the Holy Land led to his identification with a knight in a
sixteenth-century ballad who, passing the Venusberg (localised as the
Hörselberg in Thuringia) is enticed within by the beautiful Frau Holde
(**Venus**). Giving himself up to revelry and love, at last he returns to the world
and goes on pilgrimage to Rome to seek absolution from Pope Urban IV, who
tells him he has as much chance of being forgiven as the papal staff has of
blossoming. By the time this happens three days later, Tannhäuser has
already returned to the Venusberg. This tale is the basis of **Wagner**'s opera
Tannhäuser.

TANTALUS (*See* **GREEK MYTH**)
In Greek myth this son of **Zeus** and king of Lydia abused the friendship of
the gods, either by betraying their secrets, by stealing nectar, by
demanding **immortality** or by serving the gods a dish of the flesh of his
own son Pelops. **Demeter** alone did not recognise what it was and ate part
of Pelops' shoulder. The gods restored Pelops to life and gave him a new
shoulder of ivory. Another version has it that he stole a **dog** from Zeus,
then lied to **Hermes** when asked if he had it. Whatever his sin, Tantalus
was doomed to a punishment famous throughout the ancient world: to
stand for ever in a lake of cool water that came up to his chin, but which
receded every time he bent to drink. About him swung boughs laden with
fruit, but each time he reached out, the wind carried the boughs away.
Writers after **Homer** added that a huge rock was suspended over his head,
threatening to crush him. The word 'tantalise' is derived from his name
and fate.

TANTRAS (*See* **DEVI, HINDUISM, INDIAN MYTH, SHIVA**)
From a Sanskrit term signifying a web, later meaning 'ritual' or 'rule', and
finally a treatise setting forth a religious ritual. Consisting of some
sixty-four books considered sacred by many **Hindus** on account of their
supposed authorship by Dattātreya, an incarnation of the *trimurti* (Hindu
trinity) of **Brahma**, **Vishnu** and **Shiva**, mostly they take the form of a
dialogue between Shiva and his wife **Devi**, his shakti or female counterpart. As **mother-goddess** and primal procreative power, she is seen as the
superior of the two. The topics covered include mysticism, white and
black **magic**, the arts of love (*maithuna*), **spells**, **charms**, **amulets** and
sacred gestures (*mudras*). The rites are performed by the Shaktas,
worshippers of Shakti. Those of the Right-Hand Path worship her in her
gentler aspects as Uma or **Parvati**; those of the Left-Hand Path pursue her
fierce, dark side as Durga or **Kali**. Complex breathing exercises and
techniques of meditation lead to self-control of mind, body and will. The
Left-Hand Path involves ritual sexual intercourse. Orgasm is withheld in
order to generate **kundalini**, an energy (symbolised as a sleeping **serpent**,
Shakti herself) said to lie dormant near the base of the spine. Kundalini is
thus raised through the seven *chakras* to the Shiva-power in the crown of
the head. The **alchemical** union of Shiva and Shakti is said to lead to
enlightenment and increased longevity. Yet it is also said that unskilled
interference with kundalini may cause madness or physical derangement,
while the sexual side of the worship has resulted in condemnation.
Originally composed *c.*AD 700, the oldest surviving Tantric texts date to
the tenth century, the original documents being destroyed by outraged
orthodox Hindus. Tantrism has always been practised in secret.

TAOISM (See CONCORDANCE)

From Tao, an old Chinese symbol of the essential interrelation between man, earth and heaven, often translated as 'The Way'. Representing a lateral, allusive philosophy, the essence of Taoism, one of the three main Chinese religions (see **Chinese Myth**) lies in the *Tao Te Ching* (*Book of the Way*), a collection of poems by the Chinese mystic **Lao Tsu**. All his life this older contemporary of **Confucius** (sixth century BC) taught that 'The Tao that can be told is not the eternal Tao.' Yet, claims legend, as he rode off into the western desert to die, sick of society, he was persuaded by a gatekeeper to write down his teaching for posterity. Thus:[1]

> The softest thing in the universe
> Overcomes the hardest thing in the universe.
> That without substance can enter where there is no room.
> Hence I know the value of non-action.
>
> Teaching without words and work without doing
> Are understood by very few.

The goal of Taoism (one branch esoteric and monastic, the other populist in its concentration on the magical powers attainable through harmony with the Tao), is the achievement of *wu-wei*, a state of positive inaction, creating harmony by integration with the universal flow of Tao.[2]

> The world is ruled by letting things take their course.
> It cannot be ruled by interfering.

1. *Tao Te Ching* (No. 43), Lao Tsu (trans. Gia-Fu Feng and Jane English), Wildwood House, Aldershot, 1973
2. *Ibid.*, (No. 48)

TARANIS (See CELTIC MYTH, TEUTATES)

TAROT (See DIVINATION, QABALAH)

A pack of 78 cards used for **divination**, divided into two sets: Major and Minor Arcana. The Major consists of 22 'trump' cards, each with a specific **symbolic** design (**Fool**, Magician, High Priestess, etc.). Twenty-one are numbered: the additional card, the Fool, is either unnumbered or is given as 0 or 22. The Minor contains 56 cards in four suits: Wands, Cups, Pentacles, Swords, each with four court cards: King, Queen, **Knight** and Page.

Tarot's origins are unknown. In 1781 Antoine Court de Gebelin, a French linguist, asserted that it derived from ancient Egyptian rites dedicated to the scribe-god **Thoth**. Others claim it originated in India, in Morocco as a graphic 'language', or even in **Atlantis**, or that the Gypsies brought it with them on arrival in Europe in 1417. The nineteenth-century French magus Eliphas Lévi associated the Major Arcana with **Qabalah**, assigning Hebrew letters and corresponding **number** significances to each of the 22 trumps.

There are about 160 different tarot decks available, the two most widely used being (1) the Grimaud 'Marseilles' pack (seventeenth century); (2) the Rider-Waite pack, designed by A.E. Waite and artist Pamela Coleman-Smith (early twentieth century). Others include the Tarot of the Witches, the Golden Dawn Tarot, the Aquarian Tarot, **Salvador Dali**'s Tarot, and Aleister Crowley's 'Thoth' pack. Though imagery differs among the many packs, all decks utilise a wide range of mythic symbology.

TARTARUS (*See* **AGHARTI, GREEK MYTH, HADES, UNDERWORLD**)

TARZAN (*See* **BURROUGHS, E.R.**)

TASK (*See* **HERO MYTH, QUEST, TEST**)
Though often indistinguishable from the folklore motifs of **quest** (the hero's search for something) and **test** (whereby the hero proves his worth or courage), in essence the task-motif involves the performance of a given act, often difficult or seemingly impossible, in order to save his life, win a bride, etc. Thus in the *Mabinogion* the Welsh hero **Culhwch**, under a *geis* that he should marry only Olwen, daughter of the **giant** Ysbaddaden, is presented by Ysbaddaden with many *anoethu* (impossible tasks) to accomplish before he can win her. Likewise the twelve labours of **Hercules**, undertaken in expiation for his murder of his family after the goddess **Hera** had driven him mad; the obtaining by **Perseus** of the various magic objects needed to slay the **Medusa** so that King Polydectes will leave his mother Danaë alone; the sowing by **Jason** of **dragon**'s teeth in order to gain the **Golden Fleece**, or the task imposed by **Hades** on **Sisyphus** in punishment for the latter's bad faith. Yet, as with the task imposed on Culhwch, the most common form of task is that imposed on the amorous suitor. So, in the Finnish *Kalevala*, Louhi, sorcerous ruler of Pohjola, offers Väinamöinen her daughter's hand in marriage, but only if he can forge the mysterious *sampo*. A variant from the Pacific coast of North America, *Sun Tests His Son-in-Law*, involves the unsuccessful attempts of the Sun to kill his son-in-law by assigning him dangerous tasks, like shooting game with blunt arrows. Other typical tasks in folklore include planting a vineyard or cutting down a forest overnight, answering **riddles** or making a princess laugh, recovering a **ring** from the sea, sorting mixed grain or separating lentils from the ashes in the hearth.

TEFNUT (*See* **EGYPTIAN MYTH**)

TELEMACHUS (*See* **GREEK MYTH (2), HOMER,** *ODYSSEY*)
A variation on the theme of the fatherless son (*see* **Perceval**). The name means 'decisive battle'. Son of **Odysseus** and Penelope, when at last after twenty years' absence from Ithaca, Odysseus is about to return home, the goddess **Athene** (disguised as the sage Mentor) urges Telemachus to stand up to the suitors besieging his mother and plundering Odysseus' wealth, then sends him to Sparta for news of his father. In his absence the suitors decide to murder him on his return. Odysseus returns, disguised as an old beggar; Telemachus also returns unexpectedly, much matured by his journey. Evading ambush, he is reunited with his father, who reveals himself to his son alone, telling the youth not to tell even Penelope. When Odysseus enters his own banqueting hall, Telemachus offers him hospitality but pretends not to know him. Obeying his father, he removes every spear from the walls of the hall and hides them. When Odysseus reveals himself, the suitors rush for the spears – which are no longer there. With Telemachus at his side, Odysseus slays them all but two, Medon the herald and Phemius the **bard**, who have not wronged him, and whose persons are sacrosanct.

TELLUS MATER (*See* **ROMAN MYTH, SILVANUS**)

TEMPLAR (*See* **KNIGHTS TEMPLAR**)

TENGRI (See CREATION MYTH)

Mongol sky-god and creator, author of all things, controller of destiny ('the sky decrees') and absolute ruler of the world. Belonging, like the Slavs, to the steppes and wide open spaces, the Mongols attributed great power to natural phenomena. Whoever saw a meteor (a 'crack in the sky'), could ask heaven a favour. The warlord Temujin (Genghis Khan: 1162–1227) considered himself favoured by heaven, declaring his many victories decreed by Tengri himself.

TEST (See HERO MYTH, POPOL VUH, QUEST, TASK)

A trial imposed on a would-be **hero** in order to prove himself, in many ways similar to the **task** and often undertaken for similar reasons: i.e., to satisfy a prospective but malevolent father-in-law who desires his death; to be accepted among a warrior-band like the Irish Fenians (see **Finn**), who had to pass tests of their learning, bravery and athleticism; to gain admission to a **mystery** cult (see **Popol Vuh**) by emerging alive from a **labyrinth** with many pitfalls or to undergo **shamanic initiation**, again involving a symbolic process of death-and-rebirth.

TETHYS (See GREEK MYTH, OCEAN)

TEUTATES (See CELTIC MYTH)

In his poem the *Pharsalia* the Roman poet Lucan (AD 39–65) mentioned three **Celtic** divinities encountered in Gaul by Caesar's armies: Esus, Taranis and Teutates; each propitiated by human **sacrifice**. Later commentaries tell how the cult of 'horrid Esus with his wild altars' involved men being stabbed (for **divinatory** purposes?), hung from trees and allowed to bleed to death. The name means 'Lord' or 'Good Master'. The cult of Taranis, the 'Thunderer', Lucan describes as 'more cruel than that of Scythian Diana'.[1] It appears to have involved the personification and invocation of **thunder** itself. The seven known surviving altars dedicated to this god range from Böckingen in Rhineland to Chester in Britain. As for Teutates, this was probably a title referring to the tribe of that name. Associated with **Mars** as a god of war, he may have been a tribal chief or protector. Those sacrificed to him were drowned. A panel on the Gundestrup Cauldron, found in Jutland and dated *c.*300 BC, shows a god (accompanied by cavalry and foot soldiers) thrusting a human victim into a tub of water.

1. *Celtic Myths and Legends*, T.W. Rolleston, Studio, London, p.86.

TEUTONIC MYTH (See CONCORDANCE)

Though broadly speaking the term 'Teutonic' covers the Scandinavians or Norse peoples as well as the Goths of the East and the Western Germans, ancestors of the modern Germans and English, here it is used to mean 'Germanic'. Yet just as Celtic myth is known not from mainland European but from Irish and Welsh texts, so too Germanic myth must be deduced from Norse texts (see **Edda**). Hardly anything is known of the earlier traditions of the Goths (Eastern Germans), mostly Christianised by the fourth century AD, following their contact with Byzantine civilisation. Christian evangelisation of the Western German or Anglo-Saxon world, begun in the seventh century, was completed by Charlemagne (AD 742–814). Roman authors such as Caesar and Tacitus in earlier contact with German tribes operated by hearsay and, in any case, romanised the gods. Donar (thunder-god) became **Jupiter**, **Woden** became **Mercury** and the sky-god Tiwaz (Norse **Tyr**) was identified with **Mars**. Of these, only Tiwaz (Anglo-Saxon Tiw, thus Tuesday) is more developed in the Germanic than in the Norse model. Donar is better known as the Norse **Thor**; so too Woden as **Odin**, though Woden (from Gothic *wut*, 'fury'), was associated with the **Wild Hunt** and the **Valkyries**. As for the Norse fertility deities, the **Vanir**, these remain hard to trace in Germany or England, though the earth-goddess best known as **Freya** or **Frigga** (Friday) seems to have been worshipped. There is less evidence of worship of her consort **Frey**. Even the degree to which there was Teuton–Celt cross-fertilisation remains vague.

TEZCATLIPOCA (*See* AZTEC MYTH)
Literally, 'Smoking Mirror', referring to the black obsidian mirror used by **Aztec diviners**. One of the original creator gods, he was both singular and quadrupal, each of his four faces associated with a cardinal direction and a colour sacred to him. Omnipotent, **invisible** and ubiquitous, he was once a **sun-god** but **Quetzalcoatl** cast him down, turning him into a **jaguar**, later into the constellation Ursa Major. He became **trickster**-god of the night, associated with **witches**, thieves and evildoers. Forever young, a youth was **sacrificed** to him each spring, having ruled a year in his name.

THANATOS (*See* GREEK MYTH, HYPNOS)

THEOSOPHY (*See* ATLANTIS, LEMURIA, NEOPLATONISM)
From Greek *theos* ('god') and **sophia** ('wisdom'), a movement founded in New York (1875) by Russian adventuress Helena Petrovna Blavatsky (1831–91) as the Theosophical Society. It promoted **reincarnation** and **karma**, rebirth of esoteric **Christianity** and a 'revival of the work of Ammonius Saccas', (*see* **Neoplatonism**) so as to 'reconcile all religious schools, sects and nations under a common system of ethics, based on eternal verities.' In *Isis Unveiled* (1877) Blavatsky outlined Theosophy's objectives as: (1) 'to form the nucleus of a Universal Brotherhood of Humanity, without distinction of race, creed, sex, caste or colour'; (2) 'to promote the study of Aryan and other Eastern literatures, religions and sciences', later expanded to 'the comparative study of ancient and modern religions, philosophies, and sciences'; and (3) 'to investigate unexplained laws of nature and the psychical powers of man.'

Pursued from America to India and back to Europe by accusations of fraud, and by now dying of Bright's disease, in *The Secret Doctrine* (1888) she maintained that the universe and humanity are older and more complex than science or **religion** realises. Yet fragments of a 'Parent doctrine . . . have survived geological and political cataclysms to tell the story.' Claiming that her account was dictated to her by discarnate teachers, she tells how, eighteen million years ago, 'Lords of Flame' impregnated terrene matter with the spark of life. Five 'Root Races' emerged, each perishing in a cataclysm. Each, save the first, arose in the last years of its predecessor. The first race were the Chhayas ('Shadows'): ethereal beings of fire-mist originating near the North Pole in an era before earth had condensed into solid form. Their 'continent', the 'Imperishable Sacred Land', is indestructible. The second 'Hyperborean' race inhabited northern Asia and was sufficiently physical to divide into two sexes. The third, 'Lemurian' race, anthropoid telepathic **giants**, occupied a continent sunk in the Indian Ocean a million years ago. Fourth, the Atlanteans were destroyed by **black magic** 800,000 years ago, but some survived until 12,000 years ago, when the last part of Atlantis sank. Modern humanity, the '**Aryan**', constitutes the fifth Root Race: we came into being about 850,000 years ago, before the first glacial period.

Claiming that pole-shift caused the Ice Ages, Blavatsky drew heavily on the book of **Enoch** and Egyptian records, commenting on a statement recorded by Herodotus (fifth century BC) that the sun has not always risen where it rises now (*see* **Velikovsky**). Insisting that the sixth Root Race will evolve from the present fifth to inhabit a renewed Lemuria, she prophesied that the seventh will leave Earth to inhabit the planet Mercury.

A century later, Theosophy retains a global following.[1]

1. *Isis Unveiled*, H.P. Blavatsky, Theosophical University Press, Pasadena, California, 1972; *The Secret Doctrine*, H.P. Blavatsky, Theosophical Publishing House, Wheaton, Illinois, 1988.

THERAVEDA (*See* BUDDHISM)

THESEUS (*See* GREEK MYTH, HERCULES, LABYRINTH, PROCRUSTES)

Like **Hercules** this mythic Athenian hero was said to have two fathers: **Poseidon** the sea-god, and the mortal Aegeus, King of Athens. Both slept with his mother Aethra on the same night. Also like Hercules he wore a **lion**-skin, slew monsters, and survived the **underworld**, only to die tragically – similarities invented by Athenian mythographers after the Battle of Marathon (490 BC). Crediting Theseus with inspiring this victory over the Persians, the Athenians, seeking a suitable founder-hero, compared him to Hercules. It was said he had enlarged the city, created a commonwealth, and (on conquering Crete) had minted coins stamped with the image of a **bull**. The myth is as follows:

Growing up with his mother, aged sixteen Theseus lifted a huge rock under which Aegeus had left his **sword** and sandals. En route to Athens he slew bandits and **giants** (*see* **Procrustes**). In Athens **Medea**, now married to Aegeus (*see* **Jason**) and fearing for Medus, her son by Aegeus, fled after failing to poison the hero. Crushing a revolt by Pallas, brother of Aegeus, and his fifty sons, Theseus now met Cretan ambassadors come to collect a tribute imposed by King Minos of Crete due to the murder by Aegeus of his son, Androgeus, friend of the Pallantids. Aegeus had feared he might support Pallantid revolt. Imposed every nine years, the tribute consisted of **seven** Athenian youths and seven maidens, to be thrown into the Cretan **labyrinth** built by **Daedalus** to house the bull-man, the Minotaur, monstrous offspring of Pasiphae, wife of Minos.

To slay this beast, (and defeat Crete), Theseus joined the victims. If victorious, he told Aegeus, his returning ship would fly a white sail. If not, the sail would be black. In Crete, he told Minos he was Poseidon's son. Minos hurled a **ring** into the sea. Theseus recovered the ring and also a crown, gifted by Thetis the **Nereid**. Ariadne, daughter of Minos, fell in love with him. Aided by her ball of thread, he slew the Minotaur, found his way out of the labyrinth, and in triumph left Crete with Ariadne and Phaedra her sister, but abandoned Ariadne on Naxos. She prayed for revenge. Nearing Athens, he forgot to change the black sail to white. Thinking him dead, Aegeus killed himself. Though now King of Athens, Theseus went on adventuring. With Hercules he attacked the **Amazons** and took Antiope, who bore him a son, Hippolytus. He rejected her to marry Phaedra, and slew her when she invaded the wedding. With King Peirithous of Thessaly he abducted **Helen**, but **Hades** trapped them when they invaded Tartarus to kidnap **Persephone**. Hercules rescued Theseus, but Peirithous was left behind to rot in the underworld.

Meanwhile Castor and Pollux (the **Dioscuri**) had come to Athens to reclaim Helen their sister, and Phaedra had fallen in love with Hippolytus. Rejected, she denounced him when Theseus returned to Athens. Deluded, Theseus called down Poseidon's wrath on his son, who was killed by a sea-monster. Realising his error, Theseus cursed Athens and left the city, to die on the Isle of Scyros where King Lycomedes, jealous of his fame, pushed him off a cliff.

The myth implies Athenian revolt against Cretan power, *c.*1400 BC. By slaying the Minotaur and marrying Ariadne (a **moon**-priestess), Theseus gained authority in Crete. By abandoning her, he ensured she would have no power in Athens. His other abductions of women (likewise his defeat of Medea and the Pallantids – 'Pallas' indicates the goddess **Athene**) also speak of a new masculine rejection of older goddess-worship and customs in the pre-**Homeric** period.

THETIS (*See* **ACHILLES, GREEK MYTH, NEREIDS, SHAPE-SHIFTING**)

THIRTEEN (*See* **NUMBER, ZODIAC**)

THOR (*See* **AESIR, NORSE MYTH, TEUTONIC MYTH, THUNDER**)

Or Teutonic Donar; thus Thursday (German Donnerstag). As late as the eleventh century this great Norse thunder-god, Christ's main opponent in northwest Europe, was worshipped by Dublin Vikings. Equivalent to **Jupiter**, **Indra** and **Zeus**, he was portrayed as hot-tempered, red-headed, bearded and rude, with a huge appetite. He represented the peasants while **Odin** represented the Aesir. Though older than Odin, the *Eddas* call him Odin's son by **Frigga**. Gaining the realm of Thrudvang in Asgard (land of the gods) he built Belskirnir, a palace with 540 halls to welcome his thralls after death. Though always fighting the **giants**, his first wife was the giantess Iarnsaxa. She bore two sons, Magni ('Strength') and Modi ('Courage'). His second wife was golden-haired Sif, a fertility-goddess. His sky-chariot was drawn by two **goats**, Tanngrisnr ('Toothgrinder') and Tanngniortr ('Tooth-gnasher'). He had three magic weapons: his **hammer** Mjollnir (thunderbolt; which like Indra's *vajra* returned to his hand after he hurled it), his **iron** glove, and his girdle of strength. Lacking Odin's or **Loki**'s wiles, he overcame his enemies by smashing them with his hammer. He liked Loki, who would obey no other god and whose wit restored Mjollnir to him after the giant Thrymr stole it (*see* **Jotunheim**). When not fighting giants, he enjoyed fishing for the serpent of Midgard. Its venom will kill him at **Ragnorak**, when all gods must die.

Thor's sign of the hammer was made much as **Christians** make the sign of the **Cross**. The first cup of drink at a banquet was dedicated to him, and babies were **named** with **water** and Thor's sign to signify that the father accepted the child as his own and would not kill it. His figure stood in many temples and where associated with other gods (as at Uppsala, Sweden) had the place of honour, being seated between Odin and **Frey**. His priests wore an arm-**ring** sacred to him, on which binding oaths were sworn, while into wooden images of him were driven iron nails, associated with the ritual kindling of fire. His favourite colour was red. In Scandinavia the **rowan** was sacred to him; in Germany, the **oak**, as befits the thunderer who hurls his lightning-hammer.

THOTH (See EGYPTIAN MYTH, HERMES, HERMES TRISMEGISTUS, MERCURY)

Or Tehuti; Egyptian scribe-god of wisdom and **magic**, record-keeper of the dead and inventor of writing. Represented as an ibis-headed man with the cresent **moon** above him and carrying a scribe's pen and ink-holder, or as a **dog**-headed ape, this chief deity of Khmun (Hermopolis) was, in the third millennium BC, viewed as the demiurge who hatched the world-**egg** and created the world by the sound of his voice alone. Later he was regarded as a son of **Ra** the **sun**-god, or as a brother of **Isis**, **Nepthys**, **Osiris** and **Set**, or as the vizier of the Osirian family. When Set murdered **Horus**, Thoth restored the young god to life and in Osirian legend became 'He who judges between the two companions', for also he ordered Set to return the stolen heritage of Horus. Tomb pictures show him reading the scales in which the **hearts** of the dead are weighed against the feather of truth and recording the result (*see* **Maat**); this because he was originally a moon-god measuring time, ebb and flow.

Thoth came to epitomise the wise and peaceful earthly ruler, inventor of all arts and sciences, the first magus and precursor of **Solomon**. The Greeks adopted him as Hermes; the Romans as Mercury. The **Neoplatonists** and **Gnostics** developed about him a body of lore which medieval **alchemists** and **Qabalists** ascribed to a magus said to have lived three generations after **Moses** – Hermes Trismegistus, 'possessor of three parts of the world's wisdom'. The **Tarot** is sometimes called 'The Book of Thoth'.

THREAD (See LABYRINTH, SPIDER, SPINDLE, THESEUS)

THREE (See DUALISM, NUMBER, SEVEN, TWELVE)

As with seven and twelve, three is a number with many connotations. It is beginning, middle and end; birth, life and death; father, mother and child; body, **soul** and **spirit**; past, present and future; new, full and old **moon**. It is the Christian Trinity, the **Hindu** trimurti (**Brahma**, **Shiva** and **Vishnu**); the **Taoist** Great Triad (heaven, man and earth). Three Wise Men bring three gifts to Christ who is tempted thrice, denied thrice by **Peter**, and who rises from death on the third day, is witnessed by three Marys, then appears three times to his Apostles. **Hermes Trismegistus** is Hermes the Thrice-Great, possessor of three parts of the world's wisdom. The Third Eye is said to be man's spiritual centre. There are three **Fates**, three **Norns**, three **Graces**, three **Gorgons**, **Sirens** and **Hesperides**. The Irish **Badb** or war-goddess is triple; Ireland is personified as three goddesses: Eriu, Fódla and Banbha. The lunar **hare** has three legs, the Chinese moon-toad likewise, the Hindu moon-chariot has three **wheels**. In folklore three wishes, chances or prophecies are typically offered by three **witches**, **fairies** or weird sisters, like those dooming **Cuchulainn**, who wore his hair in three braids and killed his enemies in groups of three. Goldilocks meets three bears, there are three little pigs, **Cinderella** and her two sisters are the archetypal triad (two bad, one good). 'The One gave rise to the Two, the two gave rise to the three; three gave rise to all numbers.'

THRESHOLD (See DOOR)

THUNDER/THUNDERBOLT (See HAMMER, OAK, VOLCANO)

The **bull**-roaring voice of the omnipotent angry sky-god, the copper kettles rattling in **Thor**'s sky-chariot, the harbinger of storm as likely to destroy as fructify via the downward flash and roar of the oak-blasting thunderbolt. Electrifying and vitalising, yet terrifying, the associations are naturally ambiguous. The thunderbolt is the hammer of **Zeus**, **Jupiter** or Thor, also the *vajra* of **Indra**, destroying all enemies. It is the celestial fire empowering the forges of smith-gods like **Hephaestus**, **Vulcan**, **Wayland** and **Goibniu**. It is the fecundating sky's penetration of receptive Mother Earth, bringing rain to nourish the crops and restore human hope. It is also the flash of **Shiva's** Third Eye, divine force slicing through illusion, destroying to create. It is the enlightening heavenly **fire Prometheus** stole and gave to humanity, with such dire consequences. In volcanic lands, thunder and the thunderbolt are also associated with the eruption of subterranean violence.

THUNDERBIRD (*See* EAGLE, NATIVE AMERICAN MYTH)

TIAMAT (*See* DRAGON, MARDUK, SERPENT, SUMERIAN MYTH)

In the Enuma Elish (creation myth) of Mesopotamia this personification of the raging, chaotic, salty sea (as opposed to Apsu, the abyss of 'sweet water' on which the earth floats) symbolises the primeval chaos to be overcome so that civilised society may develop. When the gods born of the mingling of Apsu and Tiamat began to contest their parents and conquered Apsu (i.e., when men first controlled the 'sweet water' to irrigate their lands), this **archetypal** she-**dragon** bore a legion of monsters, and would not be subdued. The young **sun-god Marduk** (epitome of his father **Enki**) netted her, shot an arrow into her open mouth, smashed her skull and cut her in two. Half her body became the heavens, the other half, the earth, on which Marduk built his palace. This may refer to the Mesopotamian spring floods. Tiamat's invading waters are dispersed by the sun and wind, leaving fertile ground behind. Whatever the rationalisation, the killing of Tiamat by Marduk is the prototype for all later dragon-slaying myths, from **Yahweh** slaying **Leviathan** to tales of **Sigurd**, **St George** and **St Michael**. In most versions, the monster is vulnerable in one spot only (Tiamat's open mouth); likewise usually the female dragon is untamed nature said to have been 'slain' (i.e., tamed) by masculine courage and knowledge.

TIBET (*See* AVALOKITESHVARA, BUDDHISM, REINCARNATION, SHAMBHALA)

This, the highest land in the world, has long been a source of mythic tales, of hidden civilisations like **Agharti** and **Shambhala**, and of the magic powers of its lamas (holy men). Of the same stock as Mongolians, Manchurians and northern Nepalese, Tibetans were once nature-worshippers, emphasising magical workings and belief in **demons**: this, the Bon cult, was modified by **Taoism** and **Confucianism**, but mainly by the austere Mahāyāna (Greater Vehicle) tradition of **Buddhism**. Acceptance of the **Buddha** as a true incarnation of the divine essence led by the mid-fifteenth century to the establishment in Lhasa (long a forbidden city) and other monastic centres (some 6,000 before the 1959 Chinese invasion) of a theocracy ruled by lamas regarded as the *tulkus* (**reincarnations**) of departed saints; at their head the Dalai Lama (Mongolian, 'broad ocean'), each such Dalai Lama being a new incarnation of **Avalokiteshvara**, the 'compassionate' **bodhisattva**. The Tibetan term for the Dalai Lama is Gyalpo Rimpoche ('Precious King').

In *Magic and Mystery in Tibet*, the French explorer Alexandra David-Neel (1867–1968), unique in that she herself became a lama, describes how *tulkus* may be reincarnations of not only saints or sages, but even of non-human entities. They can recall their former lives and, on dying, select their future parents. Many lamas are said to be *tulkus* of departed saints, but not every *tulku* is a lama. The present Dalai Lama may be but the *tulku* of another being living elsewhere. Traditionally two years pass after the death of a high lama before his *tulku* is sought. If he left no directions about his rebirth, an astrologer seeks signs to reveal the new *tulku*. When a child fitting the prescription is found, objects (books, rosaries, etc.) are set before it. Identification of those belonging to the late *tulku* is required. David-Neel describes seeing a boy who, brought as reincarnated *tulku* to an unknown house, told where a certain china cup, its location unknown even to the house-steward, would be found. The present Dalai Lama, the fourteenth, born in 1935, was recognised as the *tulku* of his predecessor in 1937. Enthroned in 1940, he went into exile in India in 1959, after the Chinese invasion. Today, the Chinese hook out the tongues of Tibetans about to be executed, fearing that before they die they will express long life for the Dalai Lama. It was predicted long ago that the fourteenth Dalai Lama would be the last.

Speaking of the pre-Chinese era, David-Neel describes other remarkable Tibetan powers: of **invisibility**, of the capacity to create mind-generated entities (*tulpas*), of holy men able to generate extra body-heat to survive Himalayan nights naked (*tumo*), of messages 'sent on the wind' (telepathy) and doctrines instructing the newly-dead how to avoid rebirth (see *Tibetan Book of the Dead*). Yet this 'original travelling sceptic', as one critic called her, also wrote: 'Tibetans do not believe in miracles, that is to say, in supernatural happenings. They consider the extraordinary facts which astonish us to be the work of natural energies which come into action in exceptional circumstances, or through the skill of someone who knows how to release them . . .'[1]

1. *Magic and Mystery in Tibet*, Alexandra David-Neel, Abacus, London, 1977.

TIBETAN BOOK OF THE DEAD (See BUDDHISM, REINCARNATION)

Or *Bardo Thödol* (*Liberation by Hearing on the After-Death Plane*). This eighth-century Mahāyāna **Buddhist** text consists of liturgies read over those dying or newly dead, describing the after-death hallucinations, the aim being to avoid unnecessary rebirth. The information comes from lamas said to recall their own former deaths. It is recognised that few avoid rebirth, due to their after-death involvement in **samsaric** delusion. Yet the chance of liberation exists. The text insists that the essence of consciousness is divine, and that identification with the divine is the purpose of life.

From a Western viewpoint the main problem is not only of accepting this metapsychology, or even the idea of rebirth, but the assertion that *all* metaphysical beings, deities and **demons** are unrecognised reflections of our own **soul**-activity. The purpose of the text is to explain this to the newly-dead person, so that the soul may recover the implicit divinity it forgot when previously born, and escape forever the illusions of **Maya**.[1]

1. *The Tibetan Book of the Dead* (ed. W.Y. Evans-Wentz), OUP, 1927.

TIGER (See ANIMALS, CAT, JAGUAR, LION)

Tyger, Tyger, burning bright
In the forests of the night,

What immortal hand or eye
Could frame thy fearful symmetry?[1]

Blake's famous poem 'The Tyger' expresses the ambivalent symbolism of this big striped **cat**: both solar and lunar, creator and destroyer, cruel greed and royal strength. In China, as a *yang* (male) symbol it, like the **lion** in the West, is King of the Beasts, depicting authority and courage; yet in conflict with the *yang* celestial **dragon** it is *yin*, female, a symbol of the earth. In Chinese **Buddhism**, as one of the Three Senseless Creatures, it symbolises anger (the **deer** is love-sickness, the **monkey** is greed). As a grave-guardian, it drives away **demons**, as a beast able to see in the dark, it is chthonic: to 'ride a tiger' means to face dangerous forces. In a Chinese version of 'Red Riding Hood', the tiger takes the place of the **wolf** to eat the old woman. Notorious throughout southeast Asia as a **shape-shifting** man-eater, it is said that, having eaten a man, the tiger can make his victim's physical ghost walk before him through the jungle to entice fresh prey. When the next victim has been devoured, the ghost of the first is freed. In Sumatra, people kill tigers only in self-defence or if one has killed a relative. The Bataks, bringing its carcase back to the village, pray its soul into an incense pot, burn incense and ask the spirits to tell the tiger why they had to kill it. They believe that human souls can migrate into tiger bodies. In Malaysia it is said that tigers live in a fabulous Tiger Village, the roofs of their houses thatched with human hair. A young boy 'given many stripes' by his teacher ran away and became the first tiger. Tiger claws and whiskers are potent **charms**. In India the tiger is the emblem of the warrior caste, the Kshatriyas. **Shiva** wears a tiger-skin; **Kali**-Durga the destroyer rides a tiger. Bengal hill-folk say that if a man kills a tiger without divine orders, he or a near relative will in turn be killed by a tiger. In Assam, it is said that women who eat tiger-meat become too assertive. Tigers are sensitive, easily insulted, and quick to anger, like Shere Khan in **Kipling**'s *The Jungle Book*.

1. 'The Tyger', from *Songs of Experience*, William Blake (1794).

TIME (*See* DIMENSIONS, FAIRIES, *KALPA*, *YUGA*)

In the seventeenth century Archbishop Ussher interpreted Holy Writ to claim that the world began in the year 4004 BC, and will endure 6,000 years until the final battle with **Antichrist**, this leading to a thousand-year Rule of the Saints and then . . . The End. The French seer Nostradamus (1503–66) used this **Christian** chronology, and the idea that time is a one-way river that flows from past to present, from Creation to Doomsday, to prophesy the year 1999 (6,000 years from 4004 BC) as the beginning of the End Times.

Yet in mythic tradition, as in Einstein's cosmology, time is much more complex, variable and cyclic. The **Mayans** of Yucatan, obsessed with measuring time, perceived a cyclic rhythm thought to repeat itself every 260 years, so that 'new' events were necessarily the echo of previous events obeying the same rhythm. Greek Stoics likewise held that the return of the planets to specific positions necessitated the re-enactment of cosmic events as reflected in human history. **Brahmanic** cosmology in India is also cyclic and eternal. When Brahma awakens from his cosmic sleep and breathes out, a new universe comes into being. 4,320,000,000 years later, he breathes in, returns to sleep, and that universe goes out of being.

In **Celtic** folklore, time is inconsistent, running at different rates in different realms. Those entering **fairy** mounds or the **otherworld** remain for what seems to be only a few hours, or a year and a day, then return to the daily world to find centuries gone. **Oisin**, made king in the Land of Youth, **Tir nan Og**, returns to Ireland to find 300 years gone. When inadvertently he dismounts from his **horse**, he dies of sudden old age. So too with **Bran MacFebal** and his crew when they return to Ireland from the Blessed Isles. Scotland's **True Thomas**, abducted to 'fair Elfland', was not seen again until 'seven years were gane and past'. **Sleeping Beauty**'s enchanted dream lasts a century before she receives the kiss that awakens her.

The mythic perception of time is endorsed by modern cosmology. The English astronomer Fred Hoyle calls the idea of time as an ever-rolling stream 'a grotesque and absurd illusion'. He says that everything that was and will be exists 'all the time', and that the consciousness creating a sense of past, present and future, is in fact an illusion.[1]

1. *Timewarps*, John Gribbin, Dent, London, 1979.

TIR NAN OG (*See* BRAN MACFEBAL, CELTIC MYTH, OISIN, OTHERWORLD, SIDHE)
Celtic **otherworld** paradise, Land of the Forever Young, variously sited over the Western **Ocean**, or in the **underworld** kingdom (*see* **Sidhe**) which the magical **Tuatha dé Danaan** established when defeated by the Children of Mil. Whatever the location, in Tir nan Og there is neither age, ugliness, pain nor decay; the banquet tables are always full, and there is no **time**.

TIRESIAS (*See* GREEK MYTH, PROPHECY, SERPENT, SHAPE-SHIFTING)
In Greek myth, a seer of Thebes who was out one day in the green wood (or on Mount Cyllene) when he saw two **serpents** copulating. Offended by the sight (or attacked by them), he struck at them with his staff, killing the female. For this crime he was turned into a woman and became a famous harlot. **Seven** years later he (she) saw the same sight at the same spot and again struck, now killing the male, and so regained his masculinity. Thus, when on **Olympus** the gods **Zeus** and **Hera** had an argument about who got more pleasure from love-making, men or women, they called on Tiresias to decide, he being the only one likely to know.

'If the parts of love-pleasure be counted as ten,' Tiresias answered, 'thrice three go to women, one only to men.'[1]

Hera was so exasperated that she blinded him, but Zeus gave him inner sight (prophetic powers) and a life extended to seven generations.

Later, Tiresias told **Oedipus** he had married his own mother, Jocasta, and informed **Odysseus** that he would not die of a comfortable old age.

The tale of mating serpents represents the generative force that plays through all pairs of opposites. By his initial blunder Tiresias learns the other side, then, learning that the two are in fact one, restores himself, being now 'immortal' insofar as he has seen through illusion to knowledge.

1. *The Greek Myths*, Robert Graves, Penguin, London, 1960, section 105.h.

TITANS (*See* GIANTS, GREEK MYTH, PROMETHEUS)
'Lords' or 'kings'. The first divine race in Greek myth, later honoured as the ancestors of humanity and as inventors of the arts and **magic**. Children of **Gaia** and **Ouranos**, originally they were deities ruling the **seven** days of the week, and were introduced by a Canaanite colony settled near Corinth early in the second millennium BC. With each Titan paired off with a Titaness, they numbered fourteen, later reduced to a mixed company of seven. They

included **Hyperion** and Theia (**sun**), Phoebe and **Atlas** (**moon**), Metis and Coeus (**Mercury**), Oceanus and Tethys (**Venus**), Dione and Crius (**Mars**), Themis and Eurymedon (**Jupiter**), **Rhea** and **Cronus** (**Saturn**). When the Hellenes conquered Greece, their **sky-god Zeus** threw down the Titans, including his 'father' Cronus, and established the Olympean pantheon. The Titans, except for Oceanus, revolted against the new order, launching furious attacks on Olympus, but in time were defeated and bound deep under the earth, for ever.

A generation later **Prometheus**, son of Eurymedon, took his revenge.

TLALOC (*See* **AZTEC MYTH**)

Originally Toltec, this god of mountains, **rain** and springs was adopted by the **Aztec** conquerors of Mexico. His image, painted black, wore a garland of white feathers, a green plume on top. He lived on a **mountain** with his wife (or sister, or both) Chalchiuhtlicue, goddess of springs and running water, who protected infants and marriages. The corn-goddesses also lived here with him, in Tlalocan, earthly paradise. Here he received the spirits of those killed by **thunderbolts**, drowning, leprosy and contagious disease. With four pitchers of water he fed the earth, each with different effect. The first made maize and fruit grow, the second produced the **spider**'s web and blighted cereals, the third turned everything to frost and the fourth destroyed all fruits. Needless to say, as an Aztec deity, he demanded human flesh. In fact his cult was more vicious than those of **Coatlicue, Huitzilopochtli** or **Tezcatlipoca**. Buying babies from their mothers, his priests killed, cooked and ate them. If the children wept before being slaughtered, this was cause for public joy. It meant fertilising rain was coming.

TOLKIEN, J(OHN) R(ONALD) R(EUEL) (1892–1973) (*See* **SCIENCE FICTION**)

South African born, this Oxford University professor of Anglo-Saxon (1925–45) and English literature (1945–59) wrote *Lord of the Rings* (1954–5), a very influential fantastic romance. Set in a mythical past ('Middle Earth', as in the Norse Midgard) and influenced by his philological interests, he began this trilogy as an undergraduate, to create a fantasy world in which his invented Elvish language could exist. As introduction, in 1937 he published *The Hobbit*, a tale for his children. Describing the war between good and evil kingdoms for possession of a magic **ring** able to determine the world's **fate**, *Lord of the Rings* is more detailed than any other modern invented fantasy world, not only in its subtle depiction of mythic beings (**elves, dwarves** and the hobbits, his own creation), but for its detailed background of invented languages and genealogies. A friend of fellow fantasy authors **C.S. Lewis** and Charles Williams, his tour-de-force became a major cult among the young during the 1960s.

TORTOISE (*See* **ANIMALS**)

Proverbial for persistence, endurance and sagacity, as in the fable of 'The Tortoise and the Hare', or the African tale of a tortoise which, caught by a **lion**, persuades the lion to put it in the river to soften its shell and make it good for eating and so escapes. Its slow movements and wrinkled skin make it look old and wise. The horny shield that covers its back and under which it can retreat if attacked make it seem invulnerable and always at home under its own roof, as in a **Swahili** song, 'I move house and yet I never move house; I am at home wherever I travel.' It is often depicted as supporting the world, its four feet the earth's four corners, as in Chinese symbolism. In Japanese lore it supports the cosmic **mountain**. In **Hindu** myth an **avatar** of **Vishnu**, its lower shell is the earth, its upper shell the heavens. It supports the **elephant** on whose back the world rests, it being female and lunar, the elephant male and solar. In Amerindian myth, the cosmic tree grows out of its back. As a water-creature it is associated with fertility, being an attribute of **Aphrodite** who rose from the sea.

TOTEM (*See* NATIVE AMERICAN MYTH, TABOO)

An Amerindian term, as in the Ojibwa *ototeman*, 'his sibling kin', the Cree *ototema*, 'his kin', and so on in other Algonquin dialects. It refers to the **animal** associated with a specific clan as **ancestor** or protector of that clan. But as with '**shaman**' and '**taboo**', the terms 'totem' and 'totemism' entered general usage after **J.G. Frazer** published studies (1887, 1899, 1905) defining a totem as 'a class of material objects which a savage regards with superstitious respect, believing that there exists between him and every member of the class an intimate and altogether special relation.' Thus totemism, wherever found, is the belief in a supernatural relationship between a group or individual and another being, usually an animal, bird, or fish, but sometimes a plant, river or tree. Without the protection of his totem a person cannot prosper. It accompanies him everywhere, like a shadow, punishing him if he breaks its taboos, commonly against eating it, also against intermarriage or blood-feud between those of the same totem.

The elaborate 'totem poles' carved with animal crests and set up as interior houseposts or in front of north Pacific coast houses are misnamed, being in origin grave-posts set beside the aboveground box graves of the region; the animals carved on them are heraldic or represent stories or events that happened to the householder.

TOWER OF BABEL (*See* BABEL)

TRANSFIGURATION (*See* BUDDHISM, CHRISTIANITY, HINDUISM)

Theological term for the visible manifestation of divinity, as by **Krishna** to **Arjuna** (Hindu), or the shining Buddha, or as in the Transfiguration of **Christ** who, taking the Apostles **Peter**, James and John with him up a mountain, was suddenly changed. His face shone like the sun, his clothes were dazzling white. They saw the prophets **Moses** and Elijah speak with him, then a shining cloud came over them and from it they heard the voice of God acknowledge Jesus as His son (Matthew xvii:1–5). The ecclesiastical feast commemorating this event is held on 6 August.

TRANSFORMATION (*See* SHAPE-SHIFTING)

TRANSMIGRATION OF SOULS (*See* METEMPSYCHOSIS, SOUL)

TRANSUBSTANTIATION (*See* CHRISTIANITY, RELIGION)

Theological term for the change said to occur in the consecrated elements in the Christian rite of Holy Communion; i.e., the transformation of the communion wafer and wine into the body and **blood** of Christ. The term was first used in the eleventh century, the dogma being recognised by the Church in 1215. The Council of Trent (1551) reasserted that the elements are transmuted into Christ's actual body and blood. Protestant denial of this claim and the assertion that transubstantiation is merely symbolic was one cause of the Thirty Years War (1618–48). In origin, the rite seems to have been borrowed from the Roman cult of **Mithras**.

TREASURE (*See* DRAGON, GOLD, HOLY GRAIL, JEWELS, QUEST)

In folklore and myth the hunt for treasure, usually buried underground or hidden in a cave, takes two forms. Either the treasure is earthly, in the form of gold and jewels, and the quest, if motivated by greed, usually ends in disaster; or it is spiritual, representing enlightenment or the gaining of knowledge or salvation, as in the quest for the Holy Grail. In either case **tests** are imposed, monsters must be overcome, supernatural aid is usually required and typically a dragon-guardian has to be slain; the dragon in such cases being the **loathly worm** zealously protecting what it cannot use. A good example of the treasure-tale is *King Solomon's Mines* (1885) by **H. Rider Haggard**, in which the heroes, aided by an ancient map, cross African deserts and mountain ranges to a **lost world**, at its heart a hollow **mountain** which they enter via **labyrinthine** caves past **ancestral** guardians to reach the treasure chamber itself. Trapped there by the **witch** Gagool, they escape via an underground **river** and return to civilisation with the fabulous treasure, though not before suffering enormous hardship.

TREE ALPHABET (*See* GRAVES, RIDDLES, TALIESIN, TREES)

As elucidated by Robert Graves (in *The White Goddess*) from a riddling poem called 'Câd Goddeu' ('The Battle of the Trees'), found in the thirteenth-century Welsh 'Hanes Taliesin' ('The Romance of Taliesin'), the oldest Irish alphabet, the Beth-Luis-Nion ('Birch-Rowan-Ash') is named after the first three of a set of trees whose initials form the sequence of its letters. Graves follows Edward Davies, a nineteenth-century Welsh scholar, in noting that in all Celtic languages trees mean letters, that **Druid** colleges were founded in woods or groves, and that the 'battle of the trees' was intellectual. He concludes that the Goidelic twenty-letter Ogham alphabet, attributed to the god **Ogma**, was in use long before the arrival via Italy of the original Greek alphabet said to have been imported from Phoenicia by the mythical **Cadmus**, though later the Gallic Druids added five imported letters to give a twenty-five letter alphabet. The 'Battle of the Trees' was thus a battle to establish one or another variant of an alphabet not yet in its final form. Yet it is necessary to say that Graves' argument is as complex (and speculative) as the riddling language in which the original 'Câd Goddeu' itself is cast.[1]

1. *The White Goddess*, Robert Graves, Faber & Faber, London, 1961 (1946).

TREE OF LIFE (*See* QABALAH, TREES)

TREES (*See* CONCORDANCE)

Rooted in **underworld** waters, its trunk the pillar of the daily world, its boughs reaching heaven, the tree represents the cosmos. Standing vertically, it symbolises the male principle and the *axis mundi*. Providing shelter and shade; fruit, nuts and syrup; dyes, bark, fibre and wood, it symbolises the nourishing earth-goddess. If evergreen, it symbolises **immortality**. If deciduous, annually shedding its leaves (dying) and in spring budding again, it is **resurrection**, reproduction, the died-and-reborn god.

Trees have long been revered as deities, or as the abode of deity or **spirits**, or as symbols of entry to deity's presence. Many early temples were forest groves, their doorways formed by the trees themselves, their altars a stone or rock before the tree. Later, trees were felled to build artificial temples, their trunks now pillars, the altar placed between them. Even when stone replaced wood the tree-motif persisted, as in Gothic cathedral pillars converging in stylised foliage at the vault, and in stained-glass windows admitting diffused sunlight, as if filtered through foliage.

The concept of gods dwelling in trees is universal. In Persia the cypress was sacred to **Ahura Mazda**. In India, the Buddha was said to have incarnated as a tree-spirit forty-three times. He was enlightened under the bo-tree (*ficus religiosa*). Egyptian gods were said to inhabit trees, especially the sycamore (*ficus sycomorus*). Rome was founded where the floating cradle of **Romulus** and Remus got tangled in the roots of another fig-tree, *ficus Ruminalis*. In Greece, laurel was sacred to **Apollo**; olive to **Athene**; cedar, myrtle, and **willow** to **Artemis**; while **Zeus** prophesied through the 'talking' **oaks** of Dodona (*see* **Oracle**).

In Arabia, the **djinn** were said to inhabit trees or thickets. In Greek and Roman lore, innumerable sylvan beings haunted the forests, from **Pan** and **Silvanus** to the dryads, **satyrs** and fauns, while the forests of India were haunted by the **shape-shifting Yakshas**.

Forest groves, in which Celtic **Druids** ('men of the oak') held their schools, were also places of human **sacrifice**. Most died-and-reborn gods are killed on a tree. The Norse god **Odin** hung self-impaled for nine days and nights from the world-tree **Yggdrasil** to gain knowledge of the **runes**. Christ was crucified on the 'Tree'. The **Tarot** Hanged Man is suspended upside down from a Tau cross of living wood. The coffin of **Osiris** was absorbed into the trunk of a tamarisk. Yet the corollary of death on a tree is birth from a tree. **Adonis** appeared when the tree into which his mother Myrrha had been transformed was struck by a **sword**. **Attis** was born out of an almond-tree; **Cybele** his mother imprisoned him in a pine-tree, from which every spring he was reborn. The pine cone remains a symbol of resurrection. In Norse myth, **Odin** with two other gods made Askr the first man from the **ash** tree, and Embla the first woman from the elm or vine.

As for the Tree of Life in the Garden of Paradise, a Sumerian seal shows the **earth-goddess** seated before this Tree, probably a date palm. It offers two fruits: enlightenment and **immortality**. Here the serpent-lord is a fertilising power. So too the **dragon** guarding the **apple**-tree of the **Hesperides** symbolises how hard it is to gain wisdom. In the biblical **garden** of **Eden** there are two trees. The fruit and sap of the Tree of Life, from a spring under which rise the Four Rivers, grant immortality, as does **haoma** from the Persian haoma tree, or **soma** from the Indian soma-plant (the bo-tree?). But the Tree of Knowledge, about which the serpent coils, is associated with the **Fall** of the primal **Adam** from his state of innocence and grace: knowledge may be used for good or evil. It is often depicted as the vine: *in vino veritas*.

This is also the tree the shaman climbs to seek spiritual knowledge, as with the bean-stalk that Jack climbs. In its most developed form this tree is the Sephirothic Tree of Life (*see* **Qabalah**).

Lastly, there is the Christmas tree, the cosmic tree of light, shining in the night, its lights and luminous balls symbolising **sun, moon** and stars; and its candles the **souls** of the dead, reborn upon its branches.

TRICKSTERS (*See* CONCORDANCE)

Sly humanised animal or prankster god, the trickster enlivens folklore the world over. Though amoral, greedy, lustful and selfish, good may come of his actions. Norse master-thief **Loki** causes the death of **Baldur**, yet by his witty disguise of **Thor** as blushing bride Thor recovers his stolen **hammer** (*see* **Jotunheim**). Polynesian Maui ropes the **sun** to slow it down so his mother has more time for her chores, and (like **Prometheus**) steals **fire**. The cunning of Reynard the **fox**, or Amerindian **coyote** or **raven**, or African **spider**-gods Tule or Anansi, is proverbial. Never lost for an answer or unable to get out of a tight spot (though often victims of their own deceit), tricksters love making folk quarrel.

The **Yoruba** (West Africa) tell how one day the god Edshu walks between two fields, a farmer working in each. He wears a hat, red one side, white the other, green before, black behind. Later one farmer asks the other 'Did you see that old man in the white hat?' The other insists 'It wasn't white, it was red!' Ending up fighting, they are taken to the headman for judgement. Revealing himself, Edshu shows the hat, saying 'They couldn't help but quarrel. I love causing trouble.' The moral is that the farmers fall out because neither sees the whole, only part. The colours of Edshu's hat are those of the four World Directions – i.e., he personifies the *axis mundi*. The moral is simple: Don't trust the evidence of your senses.[1]

Trickster tales are told as much to amuse as to edify, presenting life as belly laugh or Olympian absurdity. Typical motifs in Amerindian Coyote tales include: contests won by deception; scaring folk from food to eat it himself; shamming death to eat grave-offerings; tricking his victim over a cliff; pretending magic powers to win a bride; and many tales in which he falls victim of his own deceit. He is a buffoon, his tale a warning to all, like the man who lays a banana-skin then skids on it himself. Yet, though often killed, he always returns to life to continue working mischief.[2]

1. *The Hero with a Thousand Faces*, Joseph Campbell, Abacus, London, 1975, pp.41–2.
2. *Tales of the North American Indians* (ed. Stith Thompson), Indiana University Press, 1966 (1929).

TRIMURTI (*See* HINDUISM, THREE)

TRINITY (*See* CHRISTIANITY, HOLY GHOST, THREE)

TRIPLE GODDESS (*See* GRAVES, THREE)

TRISTAN (*See* ARTHURIAN MYTH)

Hero of the Arthurian romance, 'Tristan and Yseult' and nephew of King Mark of Cornwall, named Tristan ('Sorrow') after his mother, Elizabeth of Lyonesse (a legendary drowned land off the Cornish coast), dies bearing him. Reared by King Mark, he slays the Irish **giant** Morholt, whose corpse is sent back to Ireland with a splinter of Tristan's **sword** embedded in the skull. Sent to Ireland to find Mark a wife and wounded while **dragon**-slaying, he is healed by Yseult the Fair. Inheriting her **fairy** mother's powers, this princess is also Morholt's niece. Realising that a nick in Tristan's sword matches the splinter in Morholt's skull, she nearly kills him in his bath, but desists. On his recovery, he escorts her to Mark in Cornwall. En route by accident they drink the love-potion made by her mother for Mark and herself. They fall helplessly in love. Married to Mark, on the wedding-night she sends her maid in her place. At first deceived, Mark grows suspicious, imposing **tests** on them to prove their innocence. They elope into the woods, but Mark finds them asleep together with Tristan's sword between them. Thinking them innocent after all, he takes back Yseult. Tristan, exiled in Brittany, marries another

Yseult, Yseult of the White Hands, but in his grief cannot consummate the marriage, so that she grows jealous of Yseult the Fair.

Wounded by a poisoned spear through the loins (*see* **Fisher King**), he sends for Yseult the Fair to come and heal him, arranging that if the ship returns with her it will hoist white sails, if not, black (*see* **Theseus**). It returns white-sailed, but Yseult of the White Hands tells him that the sails are black. He abandons hope. When Yseult the Fair reaches him, he is dead. She too dies of grief. They are buried in Cornwall in two graves, from which two **trees** grow, branches intertwining.

The original Tristan may have been a Pictish king, Drust (*c*.AD 780). His legend (echoing that of **Lancelot** and **Guinevere**) passed from Scotland to Wales, Cornwall and Brittany, where by 1150 it had taken form. **Wagner**'s opera, *Tristan and Isolde*, is based on Gottfried von Strassburg's *Tristan*, perhaps the best of many medieval versions. The key is the love potion, symbolising a force that destroys innocent folk and everyone about them.

TRITON (*See* GREEK MYTH, MERMAIDS, NEREIDS, POSEIDON, PROTEUS)

Hesiod tells how this son of **Poseidon** and Amphitrite lived in a golden undersea palace. Human from waist up, fish from waist down, with his conch-shell trumpet he raised or calmed storms. During the war with the **giants** he aided **Olympian** victory by causing terror with its fearful sound. Later **Zeus** empowered him to withdraw the sea after the Deluge. He reared **Athene** as a companion for his daughter Pallas. Killing Pallas in play, Athene made the Palladium that kept **Troy** safe from enemies. In origin Libyan, Triton shared the gift of **prophecy** with Nereus and Proteus. Losing individual identity, he became a class of sea-beings, tritons and mermen, able to venture onto land. In essence, he personifies the sea's wild roar.

TROLLS (*See* DWARVES, ELEMENTALS, NORSE MYTH)

Originally elemental **giants**, later, especially in Sweden and Denmark, depicted as evil, ugly dwarves who inhabit **caves** and (like **fairies**) hollow hills. **Cannibals**, like **dragons** they guarded **treasure**, yet despite metal-working skills and great strength had little wit. They were said to hunt in dark forests and (like **vampires**) to die if the **sun** shone in their faces. In Scotland's Shetland and Orkney Isles the name survives as *trow*, a being hostile to man and as closely associated with the sea as with the hills.

TROY (*See* ATLANTIS, BRUTUS THE TROJAN, HELEN OF TROY, *ILIAD*, *ODYSSEY*)

TRUE THOMAS (*See* ABDUCTIONS, CURSES, FAIRIES, KIRK)

Alias Thomas of Ercildoune, or Thomas the Rhymer, quasi-historical thirteeth-century Scots seer who spent **seven** years in fairyland. A ballad tells how, as he 'lay on Huntlie bank', he sees a 'lady bright come riding down by the Eildon Tree'. She wears green, with fifty-nine silver bells woven into her horse's mane. He greets her as Queen of Heaven, but she claims only to be 'queen of fair Elfland', and warns him 'if ye dare to kiss my lips, Sure of your bodie I will be.' He 'kissed her rosy lips', and she tells him he must stay with her for seven years. So (*see* **Abductions**) away with her he goes, not unhappily, but heeding her advice not to speak in 'Elflyn land', or else he may never return to the world. He is said to be buried in a cemetery on a hill above Inverness called Tomnahurich, 'Hill of the Fairies'.

The tale typifies an old need to explain the knowledge of educated folk as magically gained. Similar stories were told of Roger Bacon (1214–94), Albertus Magnus (1206–80) and Michael Scott (1175?–1234). As late as the seventeenth century in Moray, northern Scotland, it was said that the alchemist and inventor Sir Robert Gordon of Gordonstoun had sold his soul to the **Devil** while being educated in Italy, that he was a warlock who hid in his library because he had no shadow, like a **vampire**, and that he had built the Round Square at Gordonstoun so that the Devil could not catch him in the corners.

TUATHA DÉ DANAAN (*See* DANU, FAIRIES, IRISH MYTH, SIDHE)

Irish: Children of the Goddess Danu. The *Lebor Gabala* (*Book of Invasions*) tells how this magical race wafted into Ireland on the air with their four great magical possessions (*see* **Irish Myth**), banished the Fir Bolg and defeated the demonic Fomorians, then themselves were defeated, though many centuries later, by the invading Milesians (Goidels), to retire into their **otherworld** kingdom (*see* **Sidhe, Tir nan Og**). There in their hollow hills they remain to this day as the fairy race, ageless and beautiful, still practising magic and controlling the supernatural. They included the gods **Angus MacOg**, the **Dagda, Diancecht, Goibniu, Lug, Nuadu** and **Ogma**.

TULE (*See* AFRICAN MYTH, SPIDER, TRICKSTERS)

In Zaïre and the Sudan it is said this spider-god descended from the sky, the seeds of all plants and **trees** in his bag. Sowing these, he rose up to the middle-sky and beat his **drum** while the plants sprang up. Yet there was no water, so he went looking for some, and reached a hut where an old woman had just scraped and cooked some yams. She denied having water, but he knew she could not have cooked without it. Turning into a spider, he crept up the doorpost and looked into her jar. It was full of water, which he sucked up with a reed. When she tried to kill him, he knocked over the jar, so its water spread over the earth. **Shape-shifting** back into human form, he promised to dig her fields if she made him a meal. As she did this he made a hoe, an axe and a bow and arrow, then shot a guinea fowl which he gave her. Pleased, she gave him the fruit of the Zamba-lindi tree, telling him to throw it down at the **crossroads** then look behind him. When he did this he saw a beautiful woman, whom he married.

TURTLE (*See* TORTOISE)

TWELVE (*See* NUMBER, SEVEN, THREE)

Or Duodecad, symbolising cosmic order, a complete cycle, both spiritual and temporal, being three (spirit) and four (matter) multiplied. Many **pagan** pantheons (like the **Olympian**) consist of twelve demigods and goddesses ruled by the Invincible One, Himself subject to the distant Sky-Father. There are twelve prophets, twelve patriarchs, twelve tribes and twelve apostles in Judaeo-Christian lore. There are twelve signs of the zodiac, twelve months of the year, twelve days of Christmas, twelve jurors, twelve knights of the Round Table, twelve paladins of **Charlemagne**; while **Mithra** like **Christ** had twelve disciples. Many of these groupings imply a hidden thirteenth behind the twelve: the judge, Christ, Mithra, Charlemagne, etc., while in literal terms there are not twelve but thirteen ($13 \times 128 = 364$) months (moons) in the year. Once (it seems) there were not twelve but thirteen signs in the zodiac, the thirteenth sign being Arachne the **spider**, between Taurus and Gemini, discarded when the Christian Church purged the old religions.[1]

1. *The Thirteenth Zodiac*, James Vogh, Granada/Mayflower, London, 1979.

TWILIGHT OF THE GODS (*See* AESIR, NORSE MYTH, RAGNORAK)

TWINS (*See* CONCORDANCE)

In myth, twins typically represent the two sides of human nature: thought and action, war and peace, ego and alter ego, light and dark, good and bad, or hairy and smooth. Abel's murder by **Cain** epitomises the enmity commonly found in tales of twins or brothers, so too the murder of **Osiris** by **Set**, or the rivalry between the royal twins Acrisius and Proetus in the Greek myth of **Perseus**. The latter tale refers to an epoch when some societies elected kings in pairs to rule for a year, the king **sacrificially** slain at midsummer by his tanist (brother), who then ruled until midwinter before himself being slain by the new king (*see* **cannibalism**). In the tale of the **Seven Against Thebes**, Polyneices and Eteocles, the twin sons born of the incestuous union of Jocasta their mother and **Oedipus**, their father and her son, agree to rule alternate years. Eteocles refuses to give up the throne and they end up killing each other. **Hercules** and **Theseus**, each fathered both by a god and a man, both have (actually or by implication) a twin brother. The **Dioscuri**, Castor and Pollux, one light and one dark, were fathered by **Zeus** in **swan**-form on the maiden Leda – unusually, they remained the best of friends.

The idea that one of two twins must be the child of a god or a devil, and only one is the father's child, is also common, as in Africa, where twins may bring ill-luck, have magical powers or influence the weather. The Tsimshian folk of British Columbia, Canada, also believed that twins control the weather, and that the wishes of twins always come true. The Kwakiutl of the same region say that twins are transformed **salmon**, hence twins cannot go near rivers lest they change back into salmon. In Mexico, the Tarascans say that twins are good at curing wounds or injuries, while elsewhere in Mexico it is said that twins can cure colic by kicking the sick animal seven times. Twins may also epitomise cosmic balance, as in the **Hopi** tale of how Poquanghoya and Palangawhoya, twin sons of **Spider** Woman, kept the world spinning on its axis, one at the North Pole and the other at the South Pole, until Sótuknang the Creator told them to leave their posts – which is how the Second World was destroyed.

TYPHON (*See* GREEK MYTH, SET)

In Greek myth a monster associated with storm and volcanic eruption; either the son of **Tartarus** and **Gaia**, taller than mountains with serpentine legs and thighs, a feathered and winged body and a hundred dragon heads, or a storm-wind who fathered other fearful monsters: the **chimera**, the **Sphinx**, the Nemean lion slain by **Hercules**, the vulture that ate **Prometheus**' liver.

Typhon was later identified with Egyptian **Set**, the killer of **Osiris**. It is said the Greek gods were so scared of Typhon they fled to Egypt where they took animal forms. This tale was invented to account for the Egyptian worship of gods with animal heads and to merge the two pantheons: thus **ram**-headed **Zeus-Ammon**, **cow**-headed **Hera-Isis** (or **Hathor**), ibis-headed **Hermes-Thoth**, **cat**-headed **Artemis**-Bast, and so on. **Athene** alone stood her ground, calling Zeus a coward. Zeus attacked Typhon with **thunderbolts** (just as **Yahweh** attacked **Leviathan** and **Indra** attacked **Vritra**). Typhon was wounded, but crushed Zeus in his coils, then cut the sinews of his hands and feet. Yet Hermes (or **Cadmus**) restored Zeus to full vigour, whereupon the god chased Typhon from Greece to Sicily, there burying him under Mount Etna, which belches fire to this day.

TYR (*See* **NORSE MYTH, TEUTONIC MYTH**)

Norse version of the Germanic sky-god Tiwaz. Snorri (*see* **Edda**) says men prayed to him for victory, and that he was as renowned for his wisdom as his courage. The name Tiwaz is cognate with Greek **Zeus** or Roman **Jupiter**, alias the Vedic Dyaus-Pita ('Sky-Father'). Human sacrifice was made to him, but also he was associated with the Thing, the popular assembly established to settle disputes and make law. Thus, either as Tyr or Tiwaz, this 'god' was early abstracted as the idea of justice, as neutral as the distant sky. In England he was called Tiw, a war-god associated with **horse**-riders who tamed the **wolf**, and was depicted as one-handed, having **sacrificed** his hand to the wolf to save his folk from destruction. The Norse version is that the wolf was **Fenrir**. It is said that Tyr will be slain by Garm the hell-hound in the final battle of the gods at **Ragnorak**.

U

UFOs (See **UNIDENTIFIED FLYING OBJECTS**)

ULGAN (See **ERLIK, SLAVONIC MYTH**)

ULSTER CYCLE (See **IRISH MYTH**)

ULYSSES (See **HOMER, JOYCE, *ODYSSEY***)

UNDEAD (See **VAMPIRISM**)

UNDERWORLD (See **CONCORDANCE**)
Anciently, the three worlds of gods, mortals, and the dead were commonly seen as being stacked atop each other. Gods inhabited the sky or **mountains**; mortals the earth; and the dead an underworld. Typically they were led there by a psychopomp (**Anubis, Mercury**) past gates guarded by monstrous **dogs** (**Cerberus**, or **Yama**'s hounds), or were ferried (by **Charon**) over a **river** of death (the **Styx**). On their arrival, facing the Lord of the Dead (Sumerian **Ereshkigal**, Egyptian **Osiris**, Greek **Hades**), their **souls** were judged.

Yet such judgement did not always imply punishment, nor even a permanent stay. Indeed, the Greek **Elysian Fields**, the Celtic **Tir nan Og**, or the Egyptian Fields of Aalu (nightly brightened by the sun-god **Ra** before his daily return to the Land of the Living) offered heroes eternal joy. Middle Eastern fertility gods (**Tammuz**) annually died and descended, to the underworld, only for their lovers (**Ishtar**) to follow them and beg the Lord of the Dead to free them so that the world might flower again.

The Greeks, early viewing the underworld as a realm of restless shades, elaborated this idea. **Persephone** denies her beloved **Adonis** return to earth, until **Zeus** orders her to release him for half of each year. Mortal **Tiresias** finds eternal life in Hades: heroes like **Hercules, Orpheus**, and **Theseus** raid the underworld but return to life, as do Celtic heroes (**Pwyll**; King **Arthur**). Most souls arriving in the Greek underworld went to the Elysian Fields. Only sinners were shut behind bronze-gated, triple-walled Tartarus. Here the **Titans** were jailed, also **Sisyphus, Tantalus** and Ixion, who, embracing a cloud that Zeus made to resemble **Hera**, was tied to a **wheel** spinning forever through the air.

The later **Christian** idea of **Hell** crewed by **demons** torturing sinners forever derives from the Judaic **Sheol**, but is also found in **Hindu, Islamic, Swahili, Jain, Native American**, and other myths. Yet even as **Dante** and Milton pictured hell as an inferno, other traditions saw the underworld as a lovely **fairy**-realm, or as the home of exotic beings (**Agharti**, Tir nan Og). And of the underworld **Mysteries** of **Eleusis**, Greek playwright Sophocles wrote 'Thrice blessed are those among men, who, after beholding these rites, go down to Hades. Only for them is there life, all the rest will suffer an evil lot.'[1]

1. *Occidental Mythology*, Joseph Campbell, Penguin, London, 1976, p.171.

UNDERWORLD DEITIES (*See* **CONCORDANCE**)

UNICORN (*See* **FABULOUS BEASTS, HORN**)
Portrayed as a white horse with a single horn projecting from its forehead, this lovely mythical beast has been euhemerised as narwhal or rhinoceros. In biblical myth it is said to be extinct because it was thrown out of the Ark and drowned. Roman naturalist Pliny the Elder (AD 23–79) refers to it (in an old English translation) as 'the most fell and furious beast . . . one black horne he hath in the midst of his forehead, bearing out two cubits in length: by report, this wild beast cannot possibly be caught alive.' Yet, though potent, it also represented purity and chastity: a **virgin**'s touch was said to tame it. Leonardo da Vinci (1452–1519) attributes this to its lust. It was said that if its horn was dipped in poisoned water, the water would be purified. This belief led many in Europe to buy 'unicorn's horn' for use as an ingredient in medicines. As late as 1789 in France it was used to detect poison in royal foods. It is also said that the gates to **Prester John**'s palace contained the horn of horned serpents to stop poison being smuggled in. In China, where ivory is still used to find poison, the unicorn (*k'i-lin*; with **dragon**, **phoenix** and **tortoise** one of the four animals of good omen) was said to live for a millennium. It had a **deer**'s body, an ox's tail and the hooves of a **horse**. It signified benevolence, good will, longevity, wise rule and illustrious children. A symbol of all virgin goddesses (**Artemis/Diana**), it represents perfection. Alchemically allied with the **lion**, it is quicksilver (**mercury**) where the lion is sulphur. Or it is lunar and the lion solar, their conflict symbolising the war of opposites. Yet, as a ninth-century Chinese author records, 'We know that a certain animal with a mane is a **horse** and that a certain animal with horns is a **bull**. We do not know what the unicorn looks like.'[1]

1. *The Book of Imaginary Beings*, Jorge Luis Borges, Penguin, London, 1974.

UNIDENTIFIED FLYING OBJECTS (UFOs) (*See* **ABDUCTIONS, FAIRIES, ROSWELL INCIDENT, VIMANAS**)
Folk-tales of anomalous objects seen in the sky are older than the modern reports of 'flying saucers', a term first used in 1878. Japanese records of 1180 mention a flying 'earthenware vessel'. Changing course in mid-air, it left a luminous trail. Medieval French chronicles tell of men seen on 'cloudships'. In 1491 seven men 'made of air' with 'shining shoes' visited Facius Cardan in Italy. A medieval Irish tale (also in the Norse *Speculum Regale*: thirteenth century) tells how[1]

> One day the monks of Clonmacnoise were holding a meeting on the floor of the church, and as they were at their deliberations there they saw a ship sailing over them in the air, going as if it were on the sea. When the crew of the ship saw the meeting and the inhabited place below them, they dropped anchor, and the anchor came right down onto the floor of the church, and the priests seized it. A man came down out of the ship after the anchor, and he was swimming as if he were in the water, till he reached the anchor; and they were dragging him down then. 'For God's sake let me go!' said he, 'for you are drowning me.' Then he left them, swimming in the air as before, taking his anchor with him.

Likewise in the USA in 1897 reports abounded of 'airships' from which, in one case, a man was seen descending a rope.

Hindu tales of flying craft (vimanas) and visions of prophets like Ezekiel and **Enoch** have been cited as 'proof' of alien intervention in human affairs. Typically such aliens are said to come from **Mars**, or from the assumed planets of nearby stars like **Sirius**, to breed with or genetically alter humanity. Psychologist Carl **Jung** speculated that UFOs are a symbolic manifestation of human unconscious content 'projected' into the sky, the disc or 'saucer' being a mandala, expressing collective anxiety about the bomb and modern science. Yet, uneasy about the notion of a 'materialised psychism', latterly he accepted that UFOs cannot be explained by psychic means alone.[2] **Hollow earth** theorists like Richard S. Shaver claim that UFOs are from inside the earth. Researchers like Jacques Vallée claim that the UFO enigma is associated with fairy lore and **trickster** entities.[3]

Of three modern groups of opinion, one insists on the objective 'outer space' reality of UFOs, with corollaries of threat and salvation. UFOs are the craft of god-like beings, their purpose humanly comprehensible, e.g., conquest, education, genetic experimentation, etc. The second insists on the 'psychic' aspect. UFO phenomena arise from forgotten **archetypes** buried deep in the collective **unconscious**. The third links UFOs with seismic-related sources and human perception of resulting phenomena, connecting electrical fields produced via pressure on rock crystals with phenomena visible not only as columns of light or as electrical events ('ball lightning'), but with direct stimulation of the percipient brain, leading to dreamlike states and complex visual imagery.[4]

Is this why UFO events are often perceived in the cultural terminology available – space visitors to a modern Westerner, the **Virgin Mary** to a Catholic, **demons** to a medieval **Qabalist**, or **Isis** to an ancient Egyptian?

1. *A Celtic Miscellany*, K.H. Jackson, Penguin, London, 1971, p.165.
2. *Flying Saucers: A Modern Myth of Things seen in the Sky*, C.G. Jung, Harcourt Brace, New York, 1959.
3. *Dimensions*, Jacques Vallée, Sphere, London, 1990.
4. *Earthlights*, Paul Devereux, Turnstone Press, Wellingborough, 1982.

UPANISHADS (See HINDUISM, INDIAN MYTH, PURANAS, VEDAS)

Speculative philosophical treaties in verse or prose marking the beginning of Hindu mysticism. Numbering about 150 works composed *c*.600–*c*.200 BC, they teach identification of **Brahman** with **Atman**; i.e., of the changeless power upholding the universe with the same changeless essence indwelling both the world-**spirit** and the individual human **soul**. Some, as the ascetics taught in the forests, are called Aranyakas ('forest treatises'). Composed during an era when the doctrine of **karma** had come to be viewed as self-evidently factual, and human life itself as obviously miserable, many are concerned with dream or dreamless sleep, states close to *moksha* ('release'); viewed in the *Chāndogya Upanishad* as a form of free being like that of the **wind**, able to roam at will, spaceless and timeless, like Brahman. So: 'The wind has no body. Clouds, thunder and lightning – these too have no body. So, just as these arise from space up there and plunge into the highest light, revealing theselves each in its own form, so too does this deep serenity arise out of this body and plunge into the highest light, revealing itself in its own form. Such a one is a super-man. . .'[1]

Other texts, attempting to describe the essentially indescribable by use of paradox, are reminiscent of **Lao Tsu** in the *Tao Te Ching*:[2]

> It moves. It moves not.
> It is far, yet It is near:
> It is within this whole universe,
> And yet It is without it.

1. *Hindu Scriptures* (trans. and ed. R.C. Zaehner), Dent Everyman, London, 1988, from *Chāndogya Upanishad*, VIII, xii, 2
2. *Ibid.*, from *Iśā Upanishad*, 5

URANUS (*See* ASTRONOMY AND MYTH, GREEK MYTH, OURANOS)

UROBOROS (*See* OUROBOUROS)

UTHER PENDRAGON (*See* ARTHURIAN MYTH, EXCALIBUR)

In his *History of the Kings of Britain* (1135), **Geoffrey of Monmouth** tells how the magician **Merlin** told the usurper Vortigern that the war between Britons and Saxons would go on until the **boar** of Cornwall (King **Arthur**) defeated the Saxons. Then Arthur's alleged father Uther Pendragon invaded England from Brittany with his brother, Aurelius Ambrosius, the rightful king, restored after they burned Vortigern alive in his castle. Poisoned, Aurelius was succeeded by Uther who, defeating the Saxons, held a feast in London. At it he fell in love with Ygraine, wife of Gorlois (Welsh for wolf) of Cornwall, one of Uther's supporters. Gorlois took Ygraine back to his castle at Tintagel, which Uther besieged. Merlin gave Uther a potion which made him look like Gorlois who, out attacking Uther's army, was slain while Uther made love to Ygraine and she conceived Arthur. **Shape-shifting** back into his own form, Uther married Ygraine who, apart from Arthur, bore him a daughter, Anna, who later married Lot of Lothian, bearing **Gawain** and **Mordred**. (Other accounts vary, giving Lot's wife as **Morgause**, daughter of Gorlois, and Lot's base as Orkney.) Uther gave Arthur into Merlin's hands, but was murdered. Buried in Stonehenge, he left the land in anarchy.

Uther may be from the Welsh *uthr*, 'cruel'. *Pendragon* means 'Chief' or 'Great **Dragon**'. Geoffrey is the first to present him as Arthur's father. There is no earlier evidence for this, but he may once have been identified with the Irish/British god **Bel** (Belinus).

UTNAPISHTIM (*See* FLOOD, GILGAMESH)

UTOPIA (*See* SCIENCE FICTION)

Term describing the Ideal State, coined by the English politician and lawyer Sir Thomas More (1478–1535), as the title of a humanist romance describing an imaginary isle of that name. Published in Latin in 1516, translated into English in 1551, in it More compared this ideal, rational, civilised society with the corruption of Europe. The word is a pun on *ou-topos*, 'nowhere'; and *eu-topos*, 'good place'. Later it came to be applied to all romances in which the author portrays an imaginary better world. Yet, in contradistinction to related tales of the **otherworld**, Promised Land or **heaven**, utopias are generally viewed not as a transcendental afterlife reward for the virtuous, but as a material state which may be achieved, elsewhere or elsewhen, by human effort and progress. The antonym 'dystopia' refers to works such as **Orwell's** *1984*, which portray cruel, fearful or tyrannical societies.

V

VÄINAMÖINEN (*See KALEVALA*)

VAJRA (*See INDRA, THUNDERBOLT*)

VALHALLA (*See AESIR, NORSE MYTH, ODIN, VALKYRIES*)
'Hall of the Slain', the great hall of the war-god **Odin** in Asgard, land of
the Norse gods, its rafters made of spears and its roof of shields; its 540
doors each wide enough for 800 men in line abreast. Here Odin receives
the Einheriar, warriors chosen from the slain and carried from the
battlefield by the **Valkyries**. They spend their days in combat, but each
night their wounds are healed; they enjoy a feast served by the Valkyries
and prepared by the cook, Andhrimnir, from a magic boar, Saehrimnir,
restored to life after each slaughter. Snorri in the *Edda* pictures Valhalla
as exclusively male, but there are references suggesting that women
suffering **sacrificial** death could also be admitted. When **Sigurd** the
Volsung is slain, Brynhild is by her own order burned with him on a huge
pyre, so that she might join him as his wife in the other world, though
they were kept apart in this.
   This is reminiscent of the Indian practice of suttee (*see* **Rishis**).

VALKYRIES (*See AESIR, NORSE MYTH, ODIN, VALHALLA,
WAGNER*)
Warrior-maidens, female spirits who serve **Odin**, riding over land and sea,
giving victory in battle according to Odin's command, and bearing away the
dead warriors to **Valhalla**, there serving these heroes at Odin's banquet-table.
They number (according to the source) three, or thrice nine (twenty-seven).
All are beautiful golden-haired maidens, their arms dazzling white, their
helms and armour shining. In Valhalla they wear white robes. They resemble
the **Norns**, or the **badb** of Irish myth; goddesses of **fate**, destiny and battle,
able both to protect and to condemn. Norse poets in the ninth and tenth
centuries depict them as the wives of mortal men. Human princesses may be
Valkyries.
   Several ideas here coincide: of priestesses overseeing the sacrificial
death (and **cannibalism**) of captives after battle ('valkyrie' means 'chooser
of the slain'); of armed women fighting with the men (as among the
Celts); of seeresses working spells to protect men in battle; or of female
tutelary or guardian spirits attached to and protecting particular families.
   The word **waelcyrge** (as above: 'chooser of the slain') occurs in Old
English word-lists (eighth century) as equivalent to Greek **Furies**. Votive
stones found on Hadrian's Wall on the Anglo-Scots border in 1883 are
dedicated to 'the God **Mars** Thincsus and to the two Alaisiagae, Bede and
Fimmilene'; the latter names meaning 'ruler of battle' and 'giver of free-
dom'.[1]
   Today the Valkyries remain well known through the music of Richard
Wagner, notably in his thunderous overture, 'The Ride of the Valkyries'.

1. *Gods and Myths of Northern Europe*, H.R. Ellis Davidson, Penguin, London, 1964, pp.61ff.

VAMPIRISM *(See* **ELEMENTALS, INCUBI)**
The ancient fear of 'undead' beings who by night rise from their graves to sustain an unnatural existence by drinking the **blood** of the living is the stuff not only of Translyvanian legend but of many modern horror tales and films. One strand of modern vampire-myth today lies in the old belief that to drink fresh **blood** is to absorb life-force. Another lies in the power of some people to drain the vitality of others and so wax stronger themselves – mental vampirism. A third aspect lies in the vampire's outlaw existence. A creature of night moving outside society's moral laws, it also denies all theological and biological laws. Being undead, it cannot die or be slain, only rendered inert by a stake through the heart. A vital fourth aspect, in this age of AIDS, is that it contaminates by blood-infection. The most famous fictional vampire of all, Dracula, specialised in turning the flower of Victorian English maidenhood into blood-sucking beasts of voracious sexual passion. Created in 1897 by the Irish novelist Bram Stoker (1847–1912), *Dracula* was based on a fifteenth-century Transylvanian count, Vlad the Impaler, the son of Dracul (Latin: *draco*, or '**dragon**') – thus 'Count Dracula'. Apparently his favourite pastime was to impale prisoners on pointed poles, feasting below them as they writhed to death. It is said that once he impaled 30,000 Turks in a day.

The combination of such horror, as with **Bluebeard** and an older body of vampire-myth (vampire perhaps from Turkish *ubyr*, 'ghost') based on ancient global fear of the hungry **spirits** of the dead, led in the eighteenth century to reports of a vampire epidemic in Wallachia, Moldavia and Transylvania (Austria, Hungary, Romania, and the Balkans). Here, the 'undead' were viewed as the restless ghosts of suicides, to be buried at **crossroads**, their graves spiked with crosses to prevent them from 'walking' (the **cross**, like a **knot**, 'binds' the fearful restless **spirit**). Here arose the modern myth of the bloodthirsty undead who walk at night, hate light, garlic, running water, **iron** and the cross, and who can be put to rest only by driving an iron stake through the **heart**.

Though dismissed as peasant superstition, the myth prospered; first in novels, then the cinema. The storytelling session that in 1816 led to **Mary Shelley**'s *Frankenstein* also led Byron's Dr Polidori to write a novel, *The Vampyre*. Thomas Prest's *Varney the Vampire* (1847) led to Sheridan le Fanu's *Carmilla* (the first female vampire), and to tales by de Maupassant, Tolstoy and so to Stoker's *Dracula*. Early cinema vampires in *Nosferatu* (1921) led to *The Lost Boys* (1987) and Coppola's 1992 remake of *Dracula*. The subject continues to fascinate. Today in the USA, social workers call child abuse the 'Dracula Syndrome', meaning the abused child abuses. Yet is vampirism only symbolic?

The Cypriot magus Daskalos described how in southern Greece an unmarried young girl fell in love with a fifty-year-old shepherd, Loizo, who died in a car crash. Five years later she said he came 'through the walls' to visit her by night. Examined, she was found to have been deflowered. A doctor said she had done this with her own fingers. On her neck Daskalos found two reddish spots. 'His kisses are strange,' she said. 'They are like sucking . . .' Daskalos sought out Loizo, to tell him he was dead, and to stop bothering the girl or else remain a vampire. Then Loizo left her alone. 'I never found out whether it was the dead shepherd who deflowered the girl or whether he made her break the hymen with her fingers,' Daskalos says. 'People get possessed by **elementals** which they themselves create as a result of their weaknesses. Only in rare cases do I encounter possession by beings who reside in the etheric world.'[1]

1. *The Magus of Strovolos*, Kyriacos C. Markides, Routledge & Kegan Paul, London, 1985, pp.162–4.

VANIR (*See* AESIR, FREY AND FREYA, NERTHUS, NORSE MYTH)

In Norse myth a class of fertility deities (name cognate with Latin **Venus**) later absorbed by the **Aesir**. Associated with Sweden, these benevolent deities provided sunlight and nourishing rain, and also protected trade and navigation. Chief among them were Njord, father of **Frey** and **Freya**, and the **earth mother Nerthus**, maybe or maybe not once the consort of Njord. Possibly once Njord and Nerthus were one and the same, Nerthus later being identified with both Njord and Frey. Njord was worshipped by seafaring and fishing communities along the west coast of Norway, also at inland cult centres associated with water. It is said the Aesir and Vanir waged war but finally made peace, the Vanir settling at Asgard as hostages, the wise **Mimir** and his robust yet silent (and obscure) companion Hoenir being exchanged in their place. This war has often been seen as a symbolic tale of conflict between followers of **Odin** and the Aesir and those of Frey and the Vanir, or of war between the gods of magic and those of fertility. In any case, the arrival of Frey, Freya and Njord at Asgard added a concern with soil fertility to the sovereignty and power that the Aesir already represented, implying that farming was overtaking war and the hunt.

VARAHA (*See* AVATAR, INDIAN MYTH, VISHNU)

This boar incarnation of the **Hindu** god **Vishnu** (his third **avatar**) was assumed to save the world from the **demon** Hiranyaksha ('Goldeneye'), who had carried the world to the bottom of the ocean. After a thousand-year battle Varaha killed the demon and restored the earth. It is also said that the world sank from overpopulation, but Varaha lifted it up on one tusk and restored it. Today it is said that earthquakes are caused when Varaha shifts the load from one tusk to the other.

VARUNA (*See* INDIAN MYTH, MITHRA, SURYA)

With **Agni**, **Indra** and Mitra one of the great gods of the early **Vedic** period in India. Originally king of the universe and bringer of rain, he dug the river-beds and the oceans, fixed the stars in the sky and set the **moon** in place, taught the birds to fly and the winds to blow. He may be loosely associated with the sky-god **Dyaus-Pita**, and both of them with the Greek **Ouranos**. As the moon he was associated with Mitra the sun-god (*see* **Mithra**). Absorbing Mitra and being displaced by Indra from his celestial functions, he became god of the rivers and of the western ocean, also the western quarter from which the **Aryans** originally entered India. A moral god who punished liars and evil-doers, he holds the noose used to fetter sinners. This noose, *Nagapasa*, was once a symbol of the river fishermen, who still worship him in many parts of India. He is depicted in sculptures as riding the Makara, a sea-monster, perhaps once a **dolphin**. Worshipped as rain-bringer from the west in the month of Kārttik (October–November) in eastern Bengal, in Gujarāt he is invoked as 'king of waters, who curbs the wicked, who made a road in the heavens to receive the rays of the sun'. He is also worshipped as a fertility deity at **Hindu** marriages.

VATEA (*See* OCEANIC MYTH, TANGAROA)

VAYU (*See* INDIAN MYTH, INDRA)

Vedic god of the winds, the breath of life sprung from the breath of the first or cosmic man, **Purusha**. As air, he is part of a triad with **Agni** (earth) and **Surya** (heaven). Riding a sky-chariot drawn by **deer**, he is also the charioteer of **Indra** the sky-god, guiding a golden chariot drawn by a thousand red **horses**. Among his sons are the monkey-god **Hanuman** and the Pandava hero **Bhima**. He rules the Himalayan northwest, from which cool winds blow down over the Indian plains. Forever travelling and of uncertain temper, it is said that, offended by **Indra**, he broke off the top of Mount **Meru** and threw it into the ocean, where it became Sri Lanka.

VEDĀNTA (*See* VEDAS)

VEDAS (*See BHAGAVAD GITA*, HINDUISM, INDIAN MYTH, UPANISHADS)

From the same source as the Icelandic *Edda*, the word 'Veda' means 'divine knowledge', and refers to a collection of prayers, hymns and ritualistic formulae composed in early **Sanskrit** during the late second millennium BC. There are four Vedas – the *Rig-Veda* (*Veda of Hymns*), the *Sāma-Veda* (*Veda of Chants*), the *Yajur-Veda* (*Veda of Sacrifice*) and the later (*c.*1000 BC) *Atharva-Veda*, or *Veda of Atharvan*, which consists mostly of magic charms.

Each Veda is subdivided into three parts: samhitā, collections of hymns and chants, brāhmana, expository texts and commentaries and *upanishads*, texts speculating on the nature of the universe.

Related and comparable to the mythology of Indo-European Greeks, these Vedic hymns (emanated from **Brahma** and revealed to the **rishis**) created the first stage of **Hindu** mythology, being addressed to the Vedic gods such as **Agni, Indra, Surya, Vayu, Varuna, Dyaus-Pita** and Prithivi, and to feared gods like **Yama, Vritra, Rudra** and the **Maruts**. Yet in no case does any one god, not even Indra, emerge as sole ruler, like **Zeus** or **Jupiter**, but all coalesce into the one supreme principle. 'They call it Indra, Mitra, Varuna, Fire, or again it is the celestial bird Garutmat. What is but one the wise call manifold. They call it Fire, Yama, Mātariśvan.'[1]

So, at the end of the Rig-Vedic period, the gods are replaced by new, functional deities like Prajāpati, 'Lord of Creatures', and **Purusha**, the Primal Man **sacrificed** so that creation may arise in all its multiplicity. Appearing in the tenth and last book of the *Rig-Veda*, they foreshadow the coming monotheistic pantheism characteristic of the *Upanishads* (*c.*600–*c.*200 BC) and all subsequent developments of Hinduism. The *Upanishads* are also known as the *Vedānta* or 'End of the Veda'.

The *Bhagavad Gita*, though later still (*c.*100 BC?), and well outside the Vedic canon, has long been held equal in philosophic authority.

1. *Hindu Scriptures* (trans. and ed. R.C. Zaehner), Dent Everyman, London, 1988, from *Rig-Veda*, I, clxiv, 46.

VELIKOVSKY, IMMANUEL (1895–1979)

Emigrating to the USA in 1939, this Russian-born psychoanalyst formulated a mythic-anthropological theory made notorious by the publication of *Worlds in Collision* (1950), in which he argued that ancient global myths present a distorted memory of an event so terrible as to cause racial amnesia. There was 'a great inundation,' says the **Mayan Popul Vuh**. 'People were drowned in a sticky substance raining from the sky.' This, claimed Velikovsky, was raw petroleum. Some rained down unignited, some caught fire. 'Then the heavens burst, and fragments rained down and killed everything and everybody,' say the Sashinaua of Brazil. The Persians watched in awe as one day lasted for three. The Chinese wrote of a time when the sun did not set for several days while the land burned. There were hurricanes, the planet tilted, the poles shifted. Populations died as the Israelites fled Egypt. Hydrocarbons drenching the earth in petroleum became edible as manna or ambrosia. Dark night shrouded the earth for many years. Later, Venus pulled Mars out of orbit; Mars drew near earth, causing new cataclysm. Earth's axis again shifted; the year lengthened from 360 to 365 days.

The publication of this thesis led to a campaign of vilification. Orthodox academia tried to suppress his ideas. His data were distorted, presentation of his views blocked, his book boycotted and derided, his supporters fired, his integrity impugned. Yet what had he done but challenge accepted myths?[1]

1. *Worlds in Collision*, Immanuel Velikovsky, Abacus, London, 1972.

VENUS (*See* APHRODITE, ROMAN MYTH)

From Latin *venustus* ('graceful', as Norse **Vanir**), like Feronia and Flora (*see* **Silvanus**) this ancient Italian goddess of growth and the beauty of ordered nature symbolised spring's fruitfulness. Worshipped especially in Rome, her status improved when in 46 BC Julius Caesar, who claimed to be her descendant via **Aeneas** the Trojan, dedicated a temple to Venus Genetrix in gratitude for his Civil War victories. By then for some two centuries she had already been identified with the Greek love-goddess **Aphrodite**, there being no native Roman goddess of love and human passion. More correctly she may be identified with Charis ('charity'), the Greek goddess of grace. In medieval times she epitomised earthly as opposed to spiritual love, as in the German myth of **Tannhäuser**, captive of pagan love in Venusberg.

VERNE, JULES (1828–1905) (*See* SCIENCE FICTION, POE, WELLS)

Born and brought up in the French port of Nantes, this lawyer's son came, with **H.G.Wells**, to be seen as one of the two founders of **science fiction**. Yet neither claimed to initiate a new genre: both worked within an existing popular tradition, while defining themes later central to the genre.

Moving to Paris, Verne wrote some twenty unpublished plays before discovering the work of **Edgar Allan Poe**. He began writing his own blend of adventure tales set in exotically remote locales and modernised by the insertion of quasi-scientific motifs. Imbued with an optimistic belief in progress typical of European culture of the era, his *Five Weeks in a Balloon* (1863, 1870) was the first of Verne's many *Voyages Extraordinaires* ('Extraordinary Journeys'). This was followed notably by *Journey to the Centre of the Earth* (1864, 1872), an exploration of the **Hollow Earth** theme that tells of the descent by three explorers through an extinct volcano to the interior of the earth, *From the Earth to the Moon* (1865, 1870, 1873), in which the adventurers are shot into space by a giant gun, *Twenty Thousand Leagues under the Seas* (1870, 1873), introducing Captain Nemo and his vast submarine, *Nautilus*, and, perhaps the best known, *Around the World in Eighty Days* (1873, 1874). These and other romances are set in a contemporary world and deal with it in pragmatic, realistic, conservative terms upholding the values of nineteenth-century middle-class Europe. Yet in late novels such as *Master of the World* (1904, 1914), doubts have crept into Verne's worldview; his megalomaniacal Robur, inventor of a flying machine, is portrayed as a dangerous madman, epitome of the 'mad scientist' who seeks uncontrolled development of scientific 'progress' at whatever cost to humanity or nature itself.

VESTA *(See* **AGNI, HESTIA, ROMAN MYTH, VIRGINITY)**
Roman goddess of the hearth and domestic fire. Originally associated with the agricultural divinities Janus Pater and Tellus Mater *(see* **Silvanus**) as protectress of sown fields, she derived both name and function (yet again) from a Greek original, **Hestia**. Both names derive from the Sanskrit root, *vas* ('shining'). Though **virgin**, she was a symbol of idealised maternity. Like Hestia worshipped in every house, her cult in Rome (said to have been initiated by **Romulus**) was conducted by the Vestal Virgins, priestesses who enjoyed vast prestige. Numbering six, chosen from patrician families by lot, they entered Vesta's college aged six to ten, and stayed there for thirty years. Those breaking their vow of absolute chastity were at first whipped to death; later they were whipped, then entombed alive. Their accomplice in love was also whipped to death. It is said that over eleven centuries only twenty Vestals broke their vow. After their thirty-year service they could marry, but few did. Any man condemned to death who met a Vestal immediately gained reprieve.

VILI AND VE *(See* **AESIR, ODIN, YMIR)**

VIMANAS *(See* **INDIAN MYTH,** *MAHABHARATA, RAMAYANA,* **UFOs)**
Recently certain old **Sanskrit** texts have stimulated interest for their seeming description of present-day destructive technology. Sections of the *Mahabharata* and the *Ramayana* have been quoted to support claims that accounts of aerial invasions, battles between vimanas ('celestial cars'), and the use of '**Brahma**'s deathful weapon flaming with celestial fire' literally describe aerial battles and annihilating weapons of a sort all too familiar. So, from the 'Droma Parva' section of the *Mahabharata*:[1]

The valiant Adwatthaman . . . invoked the Agneya weapon . . . The Sun seemed to turn round. The universe scorched with heats seemed to be in a fever. The elephants and other creatures of the land scorched by the energy of that weapon, ran in fright, breathing heavily and desirous of protection against that terrible force. The very water being heated, the creatures residing in [it] . . . seemed to burn . . . The steeds, O King, and the cars also burnt by the energy of that weapon, looked, O Sire, like the tops of trees burnt in a forest fire. Thousands of cars fell down on all sides. [From an 1888 translation.]

Further descriptions seem to describe the suffering of the survivors of the blast, the falling-out of their hair and teeth, the poisoning of the waters. Another account in the 'Droma Parva' describes the destruction of three 'cities' in the sky by a 'shaft inspired with the **Yuga** fire and composed of **Vishnu** and **Soma**.' The translator Chandra Roy notes in his commentary on another battle, involving a weapon called **Brahma**'s Rod: 'This . . . is infinitely more powerful even than **Indra**'s bolt. The latter can strike only once, but the former can smite whole countries and entire races from generation to generation.'
Have we but arrived where we were before? Was the destruction last time so great that we forgot *(see* **Velikovsky**), or blamed it on 'God'?

1. *Gods and Spacemen in the Ancient East*, W. Raymond Drake, Sphere, 1973, p.44.

VIRACOCHA (*See* INCA MYTH)

VIRGIL (70–19 BC) (*See* AENEAS, OVID, ROMAN MYTH)

Generally reckoned the greatest of ancient Roman poets, Publius Vergilius Maro was born near Mantua and educated at Milan and (after 53 BC) in Rome, where it is said the future emperor Augustus was his fellow-pupil. He lived in Rome thereafter and in 30 BC appeared his rustic *Georgics*. His remaining years were spent on composing *The Aeneid* which, though unfinished at his death, despite its air of effort and obvious imitation of **Homer**, quickly came to be celebrated as the Roman national epic. Notable for its dignity and perfect command of language and rhythm, for style it remains unsurpassed (*see* **Aeneas**).

VIRGIN MARY (*See* BLACK VIRGIN, CHRISTIANITY, VIRGINITY)

Christian dogma claims that the **angel** Gabriel 'was sent from God' (Luke i:26) to visit a virgin, Mary, living in Nazareth in Galilee and married to a carpenter, Joseph. Gabriel told her that she had 'found favour with God', who had chosen her to 'bring forth a son' called Jesus, of whose kingdom 'there shall be no end'. Amazed by this angelic visit (the Annunciation), Mary asked: 'How shall this be, seeing I know not a man?' Gabriel said: 'The Holy Ghost shall come upon thee, and the power of the Highest shall overshadow thee.' Whereupon Mary duly conceived Jesus **Christ**.

But the Church's promulgation of this inconsistent tale could not hide her relationship to earlier **moon**-goddesses and their died-and-reborn sons, brothers or consorts. **Inanna** and Dumuzi, **Ishtar** and **Tammuz**, **Isis** and **Osiris** all underlie this Christian myth. Notably, European reverence of Mary as Mother of God spread during the Crusades, Europeans making contact with these older myths. In medieval art the Virgin is often shown enthroned on the moon. The Church tried to stem the growth of her cult, but in time had to accept, for example, the worship in Catholic churches of the **Black Virgin**; essentially the old **pagan** fertility moon-goddess. She was also Mater Virgo, primal energy prior to its division into created multiplicity; equivalent to the sephirah Binah in **Qabalah**; and Stella Maris, star of the sea, immaculate womb, primeval ocean over which the Spirit moved. The Feast of Candlemas, dedicated to her, was once the Festival of Candles, dedicated to **Diana** and **Vesta**. It is celebrated on 2 February, once sacred to the Irish goddess **Brigit**. A similar feast of lamps was celebrated in Egypt, in honour of Isis. As comforter of those in despair many legends spread about her in European lore. She takes the place of a woman pledged by her husband to the **Devil**, who at the sight of her flees; her image stops a foolish nun leaving the convent; she eases the pain of poor **souls** in **purgatory** or retards the death of a sinner to save him from hell. Her cult as she who succours and cures continued to grow after the medieval era. Visions of the Virgin in the nineteenth century at La Salette and Lourdes in France, and at Knock in Ireland, in 1917 at Fatima in Portugal, and in the 1980s at Medugorje in Yugoslavia have reportedly led to mass healings and prophetic warnings. In 1950 the Bull *Munificentissimus Dei* proclaimed the dogma of the Virgin's bodily ascent into heaven.

VIRGINITY (*See* **BLACK VIRGIN, MOON, SOPHIA, VIRGIN MARY**)

Mythic references to 'virginity' or 'virgin birth' cause confusion due to the assumption that the term virgin means a female with unruptured hymen. Yet in earlier cultures it refers to an unmarried woman, even a prostitute, or to a married but barren woman. In patriarchal culture the unmarried (by implication virgin) woman belongs to her father, but in earlier times she was her own mistress until she married, with the right to do what she liked with her body. The painter Paul Gauguin in *Noa Noa* tells how any Tahitian woman slept with a stranger if she wished, giving herself not to him but to her instinct, so remaining one-in-herself: independent, virgin.

Thus in ancient Greece children born out of wedlock were *parthenioi*, or 'virgin-born'. The Latin term for the untouched virgin is *virgo intacta*.

So Greek **Artemis**, symbol of fierce virginity (*parthenos*), remained a 'virgin' despite arranging her impregnation by the sleeping Endymion and bearing fifty daughters. Priestesses of Roman **Vesta** ('Vestal Virgins'), their own chastity strictly guarded, called Vesta the mother-goddess and used phalluses as ritual objects. The Babylonian **Ishtar**, called Holy Virgin and Virgin Mother, was also the 'compassionate prostitute'. Women prostituting themselves in her temples were also 'virgins'. Greek **Aphrodite** was both 'virgin' and *porné*, 'whore' (*see* **Sophia**). Norse **Valkyries** entertaining slain heroes in **Valhalla** were 'virgin'; also Welsh **Arianrhod**, though she gave birth to **Dylan** and **Llew**. The Chinese Great Mother, Shing Moo, who conceived the Holy Child as immaculately as the **Virgin Mary**, was also the patroness of prostitutes.

Yet physical virginity traditionally implies spiritual merit. In medieval Europe it was said that only a virgin could tame a **unicorn**. The sacred (purifying) **fires** of Vesta in Rome, and **Brigit** in Ireland, could only be guarded by virgins. Sexual continence is widely believed to focus power. The religious of varied traditions are required to remain chaste in perpetuity, while temporary sexual abstinence is widely demanded of those about to perform religious rites or undergo **initiations**. Catholic dogma is that virginity is 'reverence for bodily integrity', a state said to produce a likeness to **Christ** and the **angels**. Yet it may be that neither Christ nor his mother were 'virgo intacta'. **Gnostic** insistence that Christ both married the Magdalene (meaning 'reformed prostitute') makes sense in the light of the above. As for his mother, see **Virgin Mary**.

VISHNU (*See* **ANANTA, BRAHMA, GARUDA, HINDUISM, KRISHNA, LAKSHMI, SHIVA**)

From **Sanskrit** *vish*, 'to pervade'. With **Brahma** the remote Creator and **Shiva** the stern Destroyer forming the **Hindu** trimurti (trinity), Vishnu the Preserver and Restorer is the best-loved and most complex of Indian deities. A Vedic **sun**-god associated pre-1000 BC with **Indra**, he is described of old as encompassing the cosmos in three steps (sunrise, noon, sunset; or birth, life and death; or past, present and future). By the **Puranic** era (*c*.800–600 BC), he is portrayed as sleeping in the cosmic **ocean**, on the coils of the **serpent Ananta**-Shesha, during the Night of Brahma. From his navel arises a **lotus**. On it sits the meditating Brahma. Does Brahma create Vishnu, or Vishnu, Brahma? And at what point does Vishnu become Shiva?

The Merciful Lord Vishnu incarnates his **avatars** on earth whenever evil threatens humanity. Of his ten best-known avatars, five have been human, five animal. He has manifested as **Krishna** and as **Rama**, and as Parasurama ('Rama with the axe') who destroyed the thousand-armed **demon** king of the

Himalayas, Kartavirya. As **Varaha** the Boar he uprooted the earth from the **ocean**, as Kurma the **tortoise** he supports the **elephant** who holds up the world; as Matsya the fish he towed **Manu** to safety amid the **flood**. He is a handsome youth with deep blue skin and four hands. One hand holds a conch shell (Panchajanya: representing his power over the waters), the second the chakra (**wheel** or **sun** disc), the third a club, the fourth a **lotus**. He carries the bow Sārnga and the **sword** Nandaka. When he comes down to earth he rides the giant man-**eagle Garuda**. He lives in his heaven Vaikuntha with his wife, Sri or **Lakshmi**. When he descends to earth to be reborn, Lakshmi descends with him. When he was incarnated as **Rama**, she was born as **Sita**. When he was born as Krishna the dancing musical god, she became not only Radha but Rukmini, both beloved of him.

Though like **Christ** he incarnates to combat evil, Vishnu is not an individual, but a condition. His forms are universal, but their source is singular. His worldly forms are **Maya**, illusion, a form of Vishnu himself, representing the material substance of the world. This too is illusion: the result of light playing on sound that plays on human desire. Images of Vishnu as 'kindly' are as false as images of **Kali** as 'cruel'. Thus to **Arjuna** he revealed seemingly a 'true' form; of writhing headless bodies and bodiless limbs, as awful as anything revealed by Shiva or Kali. In fact they are all one, their multiplex forms being but the human perception of things. Vishnu is the gentle side of Shiva: both are the perceptible aspect of Brahma, the unmanifest source of creation. Yet Vishnu remains more popular among Hindus today than the other two; he represents mercy, he drives disease and **demons** from the world; he maintains the world.

VOLCANOES (*See* HAWAII, MOUNTAINS, SINAI)

VOLSUNG (*See* NORSE MYTH, ODIN, SIGURD)

VOODOO (*See* FON, SORCERY, ZOMBIES)

One account claims that this Haitian spirit-religion is named after a twelfth-century **Gnostic** sect, the Waldensians or Vaudois. Accused of **cannibalism** and orgiastic devil-worship, their notoriety led **sorcery** to become known in France as *vauderie*, and witches as *vaudoises* – hence voodoo.[1] Another derivation is the word *vodun*, meaning 'god', 'spirit' or 'sacred object' in the language of the **Fon** of Dahomey in West Africa, many of whom were imported to Haiti as slaves by French plantation-owners. Yet as in Haiti voodoo is spelled 'vaudou', and as the cult relies both on Catholicism and European magical *grimoires*, it may be that both sources are correct. Pictures of Catholic saints are found in voodoo temples, identified with the individual voodoo gods and goddesses. St Patrick, driving the snakes from Ireland, is Damballah, the **serpent**-god, John the Baptist is Shango, a thunder-god.

Other loa (voodoo deities) include Ghede (alias Baron Samedi), the **sun**-god Legba, the **moon**-man Carrefour and the love-goddess, Erzulie.

Damballah (originally the Fon Da) manifests as a **rainbow**, twined round the world with his serpent-wife Ayida. He is one of three cosmic serpents in voodoo lore. Simbi is patron of springs and rivers, Petro is the 'snake up the tree', like the serpent in the Garden of **Eden**.

Notorious for use of sorcery to cause death or illness or to create **zombies**, this 'cult of the dead' is dominated by Ghede, lord of cemeteries and black magic, sinister in black top hat, long black tail coat and dark glasses. Wise, he waits at the **crossroads** for **souls** en route to *guinée*, the abode of the gods.

He is also the god of love, a counterpart of Erzulie, the loa of the elements and love. Though generous and free with her gifts, though powdered, perfumed and fabulously rich, she weeps for the brevity of life and love. The chief voodoo ceremony, on All Souls' Day, offers protection against evil creatures including the zombie, the *loup-garou* (a red-haired female **vampire** which makes incisions between the victim's toes) and the baka, **spirits** of black magicians who **shape-shift** into animal form and prowl by night, seeking victims.

The late Haitian dictator, François Duvalier ('Papa Doc') was reputed to use **black magic** against his enemies, and certainly had it used against him, his father's skeleton once being stolen from its grave by his enemies.

In 1947 the American film-maker Maya Deren, taking part in a voodoo dance, became possessed by Erzulie. While dancing she felt a numbness creeping up her legs, a 'white darkness' that flooded her body, threatening to explode her skull. Inwardly begging for mercy, she heard a shrill chorus crying 'Erzulie' in her mind, and she fainted. Later the *hungan* (priest) told her she had been 'mounted by Erzulie'.

The Catholic Church cannot persuade voodoo devotees that voodoo and Catholicism are at odds. 'The things of the Church are always affairs of magic,' one devotee told an anthropologist.[2]

1. *The Magical Arts*, Richard Cavendish, Arkana, London, 1984, p.296
2. 'Possessed by the gods', Francis King, in *The Unexplained*, Orbis, London, 1983, pp.2490–3.

VORTIGERN (*See* MERLIN, UTHER PENDRAGON, WELSH MYTH)

VRITRA (*See* INDIAN MYTH, INDRA, MARUTS)
In early **Vedic** lore the **Demon** of Drought who held the cloud-cattle (rain) captive in his mountain fortress until **Indra**, aided by the **Maruts**, came and slew him with the *vajra* or **thunderbolt**. This parallels the slaying of **Leviathan** by **Yahweh, Tiamat** by **Marduk** or **Typhon** by **Zeus**. Yet in the *Mahabharata* (fourth century BC), Vritra is described as the **atman** (spirit) of the universe, the slaying of whom by Indra was a crime.

VULCAN (*See* HEPHAESTUS, ROMAN MYTH)
Under the name 'Volcanus' this ancient Latin god predated even Jupiter; he was the original protector of Rome, **Juno** his consort. He was also allied with **Vesta**, considered as earth-goddess, and with Maia, mother of springs. Later as Vulcan he was god of the **thunderbolt** and **fire**, and thus of the hearth, also of the smithy. Taking on the attributes of **Hephaestus**, he was depicted as bearded and bonneted, with a slight facial deformity, the hammer, tongs and anvil of the smith close to hand.

W

WAGNER, RICHARD (1813–83) (*See* **MUSIC AND MYTH, NIBELUNGENLIED**)
German composer and littérateur who made wide use of Teutonic/Norse and Celtic mythic themes. In Paris (1839–42) he wrote his *Faust* overture and *The Flying Dutchman*. In Dresden he composed *Tannhäuser* (1845) and *Lohengrin* (1848), and began work on the book of *Der Ring des Nibelungen*, based on the old German epic, the *Nibelungenlied*. In Zurich, he composed parts of *Das Rheingold*, *Die Walküre* (*see* **Valkyries**), *Siegfried* (all part of the *Ring* cycle), and *Tristan und Isolde* (*see* **Tristan**). In 1882 *Parsifal* (*see* **Perceval**), his last and perhaps greatest work, was produced at Bayreuth.

Making wider use of mythical themes than any other composer, **Sibelius** included, Wagner was an innovator. Difficult and cantankerous, his notorious anti-Semitism and highly-coloured espousal of Teutonic myth later informed the worldview and Germanic nationalism of Adolf Hitler and the **Nazis**.

WAKAN TANKA (*See* **NATIVE AMERICAN MYTH, SIOUX**)

WAND (*See* **MAGIC**)
More than a prop used by stage magicians. Raised in the right hand of the Magician in the Rider-Waite **tarot**, this symbolic 'lightning rod' conducts cosmic energy down to earth; and as such has affinity with the rod or staff of **Moses** that turns into a **serpent**. Connection with the male imagery of phallus, tower, mace, sceptre, trident and crozier is likewise apparent.

An attribute of all **shamans**, magicians and **medicine** men, in medieval **fairy** lore the wand grants divine insight. The wand of **Hypnos** grants forgetfulness and sleep; the **angel** in the Book of Revelation strikes the Elect thrice between the eyes, causing them great suffering. The point touched is the 'third eye' (*see* **Shiva**), associated with the pineal gland.

WANDERING JEW (*See* **FLYING DUTCHMAN, JEWS AND ANTI-SEMITISM, SLEEPING EMPEROR**)
The legend of the Jew condemned to wander the earth until Judgement Day for insulting **Christ** on the way to Calvary is ascribed to Matthew of Paris, who said he heard the tale from an Armenian bishop in 1228, that the man's name was Ahasuerus, and that he had been a doorkeeper in Pilate's palace. By this name a 'Wandering Jew' declared himself in Hamburg in 1547, stating he had been a Jerusalem shoemaker who had refused to let Christ rest at his door. He had struck Jesus, who had said: 'I will stand here and rest, but thou shalt go on until the last day.' Another claimant, Isaac Laquedom, visited Moscow, Madrid and England. The myth flourished in the same era as that of the **Sleeping Emperor** (**Arthur, Charlemagne, Barbarossa**) who may return to lead the war against **Antichrist** in the Last Days. The **Flying Dutchman** is a later version of the same theme.

WAR-GODS (*See* **CONCORDANCE**)

WASHERWOMAN (*See* **BANSHEE**)

WASTELAND (*See* **ARTHURIAN MYTH, FISHER KING, HOLY GRAIL, PERCEVAL**)
A central theme in early **Celtic** and later **Arthurian** and **Grail** lore, based on the premise that 'land and king are one', and that a wounded, weak or spellbound king means a wounded, weak or spellbound land. The idea seems to originate in the ancient Irish law that no man with a physical defect or blemish could be king (*see* **Irish Myth, Nuadu**). An early version (*see* *Mabinogion*), tells how Gwawl, suitor of **Rhiannon**, loses her to King **Pwyll** of Dyfed via Pwyll's trickery, so that in the time of Pwyll's son, **Pryderi**, Gwawl's kin cast a spell on Dyfed, so that nothing will grow, no birds sing and folk starve. The later myth tells how the land of **Logres** becomes waste when the **Grail** or **Fisher King** is dealt the Dolorous Blow, a wound in the loins which saps his vitality and thus that of the land. To restore fertility, the Grail must be found and the right questions asked of it. In *Le Conte del Graal* (Chrétien de Troyes; *c*.1180) the knight **Perceval** sees the Grail but fails to ask the question, thus guaranteeing continued sterility. In the *Perlesvaus* (anon., *c*.1210), the land is waste, the Fisher King dead, his castle stolen by the King of Castle Mortal, lord of death. Perlesvaus storms the castle and regains the Grail which, once introduced to the rite of Mass, restores the fertility of the land.

Metaphysical symbolism aside (*see* **Holy Grail**), the theme simply states that weak government means a devasted 'body politic'. The wasteland is also internal, the empty dereliction of the wounded heart.

WATER (*See* **CONCORDANCE**)
In the present-day Western world it is hard to appreciate the awé, reverence and fear in which water in its various manifestations was once held. It takes prolonged drought, or torrential **rain** followed by severe flood, to remind us how we rely on it, and how either too little or too much of it can destroy us.

Yet water as manifested as **ocean** with neither beginning nor end has always stirred human imagination with images of a primal whole, a cosmic parent from which all life emerges and to which all returns. The Greeks imagined a vast **river**, Oceanus, girdling the entire universe. The Norse spoke of the serpent of Midgard, wrapped round the world, shaking its coils to cause tempest and flood. On this cosmic ocean during the long night of **Brahma** sleeps **Vishnu**, supported by the coils of the serpent **Ananta**-Shesha. In **Sumerian myth** it is both Apsu, the sweet waters on which the world floats, and **Tiamat**, the ferocious sea-**dragon** of primeval chaos that like **Balor, Leviathan** or **Typhon** must be tamed if human society is to flourish. Contrariwise, **Indra** slays **Vritra**, Demon of Drought, to free the cloud-cattle (i.e., so that rain may fall).

The magical Water of Life brings back the dead, cures all ills, and is frequently associated with the magical drinks of the gods: **soma, haoma**, nectar or ambrosia, or with wine, the fiery solar product of lunar water. **Christ** like **Dionysus** turns water into wine; passive fluid nature into potent spirit. The *axis mundi*, as the four great **rivers** that flow in the four cardinal directions, is nourishing and fertilising.

Rivers, lakes and **wells** are said to possess magical properties; they are regarded as deities or the home of deities, **elemental beings** or supernatural **shape-shifters** such as the Lady of the Lake, **Cerridwen**, or the deadly

kelpie, **mermaid**, **siren** or **rusalka**. They give birth, but also drown the unwary, or lead to the grave or **otherworld**. To cross the **Styx** is to die; to drink the Waters of Lethe is to forget; the Blessed Isles to which dead heroes go lie under the waves or over the Western Ocean.

As one of the four elements, water is the opposite of **fire** as earth is of air. Water and fire are the two conflicting opposites which ultimately interpenetrate: water is of the **earth mother**, fire is of the **Sky Father**. So the world is said from time to time to be destroyed first by fire and then by **flood**. So **Atlantis** sank; thus the tales of **Noah**, **Manu**, Utnapishtim, **Deucalion** and Pyrrha.

Throughout the world cults once worshipped or propitiated water divinities. Indeed, they are not yet entirely dead. Folk still throw pennies into wishing-wells. Nor was such cult-worship solely a product of superstition. The 'sixth sense' actively employed by water diviners or dowsers must once have been widespread. **Megalithic** stone circles are generally sited above a crossing of two underground streams: thus perhaps legends associated with circles like the Rollright Stones in Oxfordshire, that at night they go down to the river to drink (*see* **well**).

WATER CULTS (*See* **RIVER MYTH, WATER, WELL**)

WATER OF LIFE (*See* **WATER**)

WAYLAND SMITH (*See* **NORSE MYTH**)
Norse/Teutonic/Saxon smith-god, equivalent of the Irish **Goibniu** and Greek **Hephaestus**, and like the latter depicted as lame. He was said to have made many of the great magical weapons and gear of the gods, including the sword **Excalibur**, although the latter seems unlikely. His name is given in the Icelandic *Edda* as Volundr, who with his two brothers one day met three **swan**-maidens by a lake. For **seven** years they all lived together, but then the swans flew away. Sorrowing, the three brothers went in search of their lost loves. Wayland fell foul of a rival, King Nidud, who, claiming that the smith had stolen his **gold**, hamstrung him. In revenge Wayland lured Nidud's son and daughter to the remote isle on which he had set up his smithy. Killing the boy and raping the girl, he sent the boy's **head**, artfully bejewelled and silver-mounted, back to Nidud.

WEAVING (*See* **FATES, KNOT, NORNS, SPIDER, SPINDLE**)

WELL (*See* **CAVE, HEAD, WATER**)
Sweet-water wells have been sanctified since earliest times. Guaranteeing survival, their failure a disaster, they are also gateways into the body of the **mother-goddess** or the presence of wise but terrible **underworld** powers. **Serpents** were said to guard wells: Giraldus Cambrensis (*c.*1146–*c.*1230) mentions a well in Pembroke said to contain **treasure** guarded by a serpent. Pits or **caves** share similar symbolism, but the well offers the additional potency of water, and as such was widely associated, especially among the **Celts**, with the **oracular** wisdom said to emanate from the spirit-powers dwelling in its depths. Yet such wisdom could not be gained without offerings or **sacrifice**. Today a penny is thrown into the wishing-well as a casual jest, but once the sacrifice was often of human life or limb. The discovery in a well at Goadby in Leicestershire of two bodies buried head down emphasises numerous legends of decapitated heads placed in wells, either to placate the well-spirit or to act as a prophetic medium. In Norse

myth, to gain wisdom **Odin** drinks from the well of **Mimir** which lies under **Yggdrasil** the world-tree, but first must sacrifice an **eye**. The Irish hero **Finn** acquires wisdom from an **otherworld** well. Other Irish tales link wells or springs with the **hazel** tree and the **Salmon** of Knowledge.

Well-worship was so common that the Church had to accept it. In France, **pagan** wells lie under the cathedrals of Chartres, Nimes and Sangres; in Britain, under York Minster, Carlisle Cathedral and also at **Glastonbury**, where in the depths of the Chalice Well the **Holy Grail** is said to lie. The Church also took credit for the healing powers associated with wells. The water at Llandeilo Llwydarth in West Wales supposedly cured whooping cough, if drunk from a skull said to have been that of St Teilo. The tale of Ffynnawn Wenvrewy ('Winifred's Well'), also Welsh, tells how St Beuno cursed King Caradog who, enraged by fair Winifred's rejection in love, had cut off her head. On being cursed, Caradog 'melted into a dissolved lake'. Beuno rejoined her head to her body and she returned to life, while from the spot where her **blood** had fallen, the well sprang up.

Such beliefs persist. Today in Wales over 500 wells bear the names of early saints. In Scotland, wells hung about with rags may seem to be an eyesore, but remain intact due to a belief that anyone destroying the rags will take on the donor's illness. The Cloutie Well near Munlochy in Ross and Cromarty, northern Scotland, is overhung by some 50,000 rags, with more added every year.[1]

1. *Sacred Waters*, Janet and Colin Bord, Granada, London, 1985.

WELLS, H(ERBERT) G(EORGE) (1866–1946) (*See* SCIENCE FICTION, VERNE)

When young, this English author gained a scholarship to study in London under T.H. Huxley, an outspoken humanist and supporter of Darwinism. He then took up scientific journalism, writing articles such as 'The Man of the Year Million' (1893), describing humanity's evolved ancestors outliving the **sun**'s death while immersed in nutrient baths deep under the planetary surface. These led to short stories widely viewed as prototypical **science fiction** and to the novel *The Time Machine* (1895), the first 'modern' tale of **time** travel. Subsequent tales – *The Island of Doctor Moreau* (1896), *The Invisible Man* (1897) and *The War of the Worlds* (1898) not only firmly established Wells as a genuine seer in his capacity to embrace ideas which have since proved to be touchstones of modern mythic imagination (genetic engineering, fantasy fulfilment of the power of **invisibility**, invasion from outer space by a technologically-superior alien species), but revealed the conflict between his belief in Darwinian progress, and his desire to oppose the social inequity and hypocrisy of late Victorian society.

This conflict led to *When the Sleeper Wakes* (1899), in which the hero awakens from suspended animation into a totalitarian future to become the **messiah** of a social revolution. Though Wells followed this with *The First Men in the Moon* (1901), in which his heroes reach the **moon** via an anti-gravity device, increasingly he turned away from mythical fictions to futurological analysis and social crusade. Increasingly impatient with his fellow men, he continued to advertise an optimistic mythology of the future, as in the quasi-fictional *The Shape of Things to Come* (1933). Yet by the time World War II broke out, his former optimism had turned to despair. His final essay, *Mind at the End of its Tether* (1945), concluded that humanity is doomed because it cannot adapt to its new technological circumstances.

WELSH MYTH (*See* CONCORDANCE)

Progressively during the first millennium BC, the old Welsh stock was absorbed by incoming Goidelic Celts, their tongue the basis of Irish, Scots Gaelic and Manx. About 300 BC the Brythons arrived, their dialect the basis of Breton, Cornish and Welsh. In the first century AD the Romans conquered Wales. After they withdrew *c.*AD 410, the Welsh invited Cunedda Wledig from Lothian (*see* **Gododdin**) to settle in Wales and repel Irish pirates. From his stock arose the rulers of the four Welsh kingdoms (Dyfed, Gwynedd, Powys, Gwent). But *c.*420 the Celtic King Vortigern hired Saxon mercenaries to fight northern Picts. For this, his name became hated (*see* **Merlin**). The events on which **Arthurian myth** may be based, including the Battle of Badon Hill *c.*516, imply desperate war against incoming Saxons, defeats by whom near Bath in 577 and Chester *c.*613 forced the Welsh back into Wales.

Welsh myth covers an area from Brittany north to the Orkneys, notably as recorded in *The White Book of Rhydderch* (*c.*1300–25) and *The Red Book of Hergest* (*c.*1375–1425) (*see* **Mabinogion**). Other early material was ascribed to **bards** like Aneirin, **Taliesin** and Myrrdin. The oldest known elegy, the **Gododdin** (in the thirteenth-century *Book of Aneirin*) indicates ninth-century spelling, but the action is dated *c.*AD 600. Yet there is no proof that 'Aneirin' lived, nor that Myrrdin (Merlin) was a sixth-century bard. The mythic Merlin first appears in **Geoffrey of Monmouth's** *History of the Kings of Britain* (1135). As for Taliesin, a bard of that name wrote praise-verses to sixth-century kings like Brochwel Ysgythrog of Powys. Noted by Nennius in a seventh-century genealogy as 'renowned in poetry', the historic Taliesin is said to have died in a drunken brawl.

How far did **Christian** ethics affect the transmission of **pagan** material? The first Welsh collections, contemporary with Christianised Arthurian and **Holy Grail** myth, are five centuries later than the first Irish collections. Yet the *Mabinogion* often agrees with Irish tradition: in both lands the Celtic Church denied Rome until the eighth century. In Wales, pagan motifs survived. Churches were built on pagan **earth mounds** (Cascob and Darowen) or within **megalithic** stone circles (Ysbyty Confin). Legends tell how by night the 'Devil' would remove building-stones from an unpopular new site up to the old mound. Pelagian heresy, denying **original sin**, persisted. Tales of saints, from St Germanus (fifth century) to St David and St Beuno (*see* **well**) retain pagan magical elements, as many Welsh churches retain an association with 'holy' wells. Many old deities, though Christianised, also retained their functions. Cewydd, a rain-saint, is an old fertility god in disguise, while at Llansantffraed survives the name of Bridget, synonymous with Irish **Brigit**. There are over 200 Church dedications to the old **Mother Goddess**, disguised as the **Virgin Mary** and almost as many to 'Llanfihangel', or 'Church of the Chief Angel' (St **Michael**, the **dragon**-slaying angel).

To this day, the Red Dragon remains the Welsh national symbol.

WEREWOLF (*See* SHAMANISM, SHAPE-SHIFTING, VAMPIRISM, WOLF)

Literally, 'man-wolf', from Old English *wer*, man and *wulf*, wolf. As with the **vampire** myth, the idea that a man can **shape-shift** or be transformed into wolf-form at full **moon** remains potent: sexually predatory men are still called 'wolves'. In lands without wolves, the fiercest local beast fulfils the same function: the were**tiger** in India and East Asia, boar (Greece and Turkey), **hyena**, **lion**, leopard or **crocodile** (Africa), **bear** (North America), or **jaguar** (South America).

The origin of the idea is ancient. Greek historian Herodotus c.450 BC tells how Greeks and Scythians living by the Black Sea regarded the native Neurians as magicians able to take wolf-form at will, so as to indulge their obsessive **cannibal** appetite. Roman authors **Virgil** and Petronius record such tales, but not always about wolves – in *The Golden Ass* (c.AD 170) **Apuleius** describes the transformation of his unlucky hero into a donkey.

The transformation might be uncontrollable, or deliberately sought by wearing a wolf-skin. In medieval Germany, it was said a girdle made of the skin of a hanged man was effective. Use of a **charm** might be enough: no real change would occur, but observers would think they saw a wolf. In general European belief, the werewolf had to resume human form at daybreak by removing and hiding the skin. If anyone found and destroyed the skin, its owner died. A wounded werewolf returned instantly to human form; next day the wound would be seen on the corresponding part of his body.

Belief in lycanthropy (*lycos*, 'wolf'; *anthropos*, 'man') was so common in the fifteenth and sixteenth centuries that anyone suspected was destroyed. Between 1520 and 1630 in France over 30,000 cases were recorded. Cannibal appetite among half-starved peasants might explain part of the phenomenon, yet many so accused really thought themselves wolves. Traditionally, there are three types of werewolf – the hereditary, the voluntary and the benevolent. The first is passed down from generation to generation by a **curse**. The second arises from deliberate depravity. The third is one who, though so bound (as by heredity) feels nothing but human shame for his bestial affliction.

WHALE (*See* DOLPHIN, ESKIMO MYTH, RAVEN, TRICKSTERS, ZARATAN)

The largest animal ever on earth, symbolising the power of the cosmic sea, hence both regeneration and the grave. So Jonah, swallowed by the whale, 'dies'. Yet the whale's belly is also the womb, so he is 'reborn' (cast onto dry land) after the **three** days of the dark of the **moon**. In Greek myth **Hercules** destroys a sea-monster sent against Troy by **Poseidon** by diving down its open throat, cutting open its belly from inside and leaving it dead. The theme is of self-annihilation to gain a higher state of being. Yet when misidentified as **Leviathan**, the cosmic **serpent** slain by **Yahweh**, the whale becomes a disparaged monster. In **Christian** myth it represents the **Devil**, its jaws the gates of **hell**, its belly hell itself.

In Eskimo lore, Raven persuades a whale-cow to shut her eyes and open her mouth. Climbing into his raven-clothes, he picks up his **fire**-sticks, darts inside the whale and finds himself in a lamp-lit room. Here sits a beautiful girl, the whale's **soul**. She feeds him, but forbids him to touch a tube running along the ceiling. When she goes out, he licks a sweet drop of oil off it, then greedily breaks off a piece and eats it, so killing the whale-cow, for this is its heart-artery. Washed ashore, with Raven shut inside, the corpse is cut open by men. Leaving unnoticed, but realising he has left his fire-sticks, Raven takes human form and helps the men butcher the whale. When one finds his fire-sticks, he cries out that to find fire-sticks in a whale is bad luck and runs away, scaring the men into doing likewise. Later, of course, he returns to enjoy the feast on his own.

Elaborate **taboos** traditionally observed by whale-hunters typically involving fasting, ritual bathing, miming the whale's capture and avoiding women and liquor before the hunt. Eskimo hunters who had killed a white whale had to abstain from work for four days afterwards, this being the period the ghost of the whale was supposed to stay with its body.

WHEEL (*See* **BUDDHISM, CIRCLE, KARMA, RING**)
Associated with the symbology of the circle, ring, **cross** and **swastika**. A spinning circle suggests planets and stars in motion, the cosmos, a revolving plate to the Egyptians, an **egg** to the ancient Chinese. Or the wheel is the **sun** whirling in the sky, the hub the sun itself, its spokes the sun's rays. The wheel is the **chariot** of **Helios**, **Apollo** and other solar deities. The six-spoked wheel is an attribute of sky-gods like **Zeus** or **Jupiter**. In Greek myth, Ixion, who dared embrace an image of **Hera**, is bound forever to a flaming wheel endlessly crossing the skies. The third order of **angels** in Judaeo-**Christian** myth is that of Wheels or Thrones. The circular Chinese *yin-yang* symbol, divided into curved dark and light segments, is implicitly a wheel in motion. The **Gnostic** wheel is composed of four cone-shaped spokes each terminating in four circles. The **Vedic** god **Varuna** was represented by a wheel. The *Rig Veda* speaks of the god who directs 'the golden wheel of the sun', on which life relies and which nothing can stop. In Buddhist belief it is the Round of Existence, the Wheel of Law, Truth, **karma**, the endless revolution of human fate, time rolling on. In yoga, the **Sanskrit** word *chakra* denotes energy centres located along the vertical axis of the human body. Originally it meant sun, but came to mean wheel.

In a Buddhist myth of the Mystic Wheel, the chakravartin ('wheel-king', or 'universal monarch' who can ride his chariot over all the land without hindrance) purifies himself at his inauguration on the day of full **moon**. When the Wheel appears from the east he sprinkles water over it and invites it to 'Go forth and overcome'. It rolls eastward, he and his army follow, camping wherever it stops. By its power the kings of the east are beaten, then in turn those of the south, west and north. Thereafter fixed at the door to the chambers of the king in his palace, as his death approaches it falls off. When he dies it vanishes, and returns to his successor or a later king only if the law has been kept and the new monarch is righteous.

In northern Buddhism the concept of the Wheel of the Law (or of Life) manifests in painted meditational aids (mandalas), also as prayer-wheels or cylinders, to be turned by hand, water-power or the circulation of heat, but always in the direction of the sun (clockwise). A wheel turning anticlockwise (widdershins) implies evil. Witches **cursing** victims may dance naked, widdershins, while casting their spell. The wheel's solid outer rim suggests protection, as in the magic circle used by **necromancers** to protect them against the **demons** they summon, or as in the circle of wheeled wagons set up in **Wild West** myth against marauding attackers.

WILD HUNT (*See* **DOG, PWYLL**)
Ghostly hunters coursing the stormy night sky, restless **underworld** shades on skeletal horses accompanied by crimson-eyed white phantom hounds (*see* **Pwyll**) and led by the Lord of the Dead. In Wales this is Gwynn ap Nudd (Irish **Nuadu**), who leads the Cwn Annwn (hounds of hell) out over the night wastes to bear away the **souls** of the dying. In Devonshire, 'Wisht Hounds' career above midnight Dartmoor, in Yorkshire they are the Gabriel Hounds, and in Lancashire, ratchet hounds. Elsewhere in England, **Herne the Hunter** leads the pack, the wailing of which makes earthly dogs yelp in company.

WILD WEST (*See* **HOLLYWOOD, NATIVE AMERICAN MYTH**)
As morally stylised as **Greek** legend or **Arthurian** romance, the myth of the Wild West occupies a timeless frontier where the war between good and evil is decided as much by Colt 45 as by the **Bible**. The myth began even as the brief historical era birthing it ended. The deeds of some Western heroes

(Davy Crockett, Daniel Boone) are from the early nineteenth century, but the true Western belongs to the twenty-five years from the end of the American Civil War (1865) to the defeat of Native American resistance, *c.*1890 (*see* **Ghost Dance**).

Into this period is packed the imagery of Western myth – of a vast land which, in 1865, was 'wide open'. The **buffalo** still roamed the prairies. Native American tribes remained free. Yet by 1890 disease, despair and massacre had decimated both. The West had been taken over by immigrants already mythologising the 'frontier values' – self-reliance, courage and moral rectitude – said to have seen them through to the Pacific shore.

Demonisation of destroyed native societies typifies the myths of every conquering people. New about Wild West myth was the speed of its growth via Hollywood, a few years after the closure of the historical frontier. The popularity of the first Western movie, *The Great Train Robbery* (1903: a ten-minute tale of a train hold-up) led to many Westerns celebrating the creation of the new society which had created Hollywood itself. The true history of the West (historian John Unrue claims that of some 10,000 deaths on the trail between 1840 and 1860, only 362 were due to Indian attack) was less potent than the myth. The West was the Promised Land of the wagon-train on the Oregon Trail, the gunslinging outlaw, the lonesome cowboy, the whisky priest, the whore with a heart of gold, the devout frontier-wife who can shoot as well as knit – and of the eternal war between good and evil.

The heroes were historical figures already so mythologised that their actual lives had become irrelevant: Buffalo Bill, Wild Bill Hickok, Doc Holliday, Kit Carson. The Seventh Cavalry always turned up just in time to rescue the wagon-train from Indian attack. The villains were gunslingers (Billy the Kid), outlaws and thieves (the James Gang) or Red Indian war-bands (typically **Sioux**, Apache, Cheyenne or Comanche). Yet the villains were as attractive as the heroes. The whooping, painted, feathered redskin, implacable and cruel, was also a noble savage. Where not killing General Custer at the Little Big Horn in 1876, the red man was essential in proving the white hero's valour as was the saloon villain in provoking a shoot-out.

The classic Western myth is of the individual resisting evil, protected only by his courage, self-reliance, moral rectitude . . . and his six-shooter. But the Western evolved. During the 1920s, movie stars like William S. Hart were so moral they preferred their horses to their women (if any). In 1939 the director John Ford (1895–1973) made *Stagecoach*, making a star of the actor John Wayne (1907–79), whose taciturn character came to epitomise the hero who fights only if he must and only to retain his independence. Actors like Clark Gable, Gregory Peck, James Stewart, Gary Cooper and Joel McCrea starred in countless variations on this theme of personal honour. Cooper especially, in Fred Zinneman's *High Noon* (1950), remains memorable for his portrayal of an aging sheriff who refuses to leave town with Grace Kelly, his bride, just because four killers out for his blood will arrive on the noon train. His honour demands that he stay and face the deadly duel.

Yet times changed. In Ford's *The Searchers* (1956), Wayne is no hero but a man driven by racist hatred and crude desire for revenge to recover a girl abducted by redskins. The old morality was dead. The Western became elegaic or merely crude. In *The Wild Bunch* (1969), director Sam Peckinpah sends his out-of-date gunslingers to Mexico to die so violently that many Western fans were outraged by his apparent betrayal of the noble myth.

That the 'Western' has survived at all is due to actor/director Clint Eastwood. Star of the 1950s American tv Western series, *Rawhide*, in Spain in the 1960s he made three 'spaghetti westerns' (the *Dollar* trilogy) directed by Sergio Leone. Cast as the taciturn 'man with no name', a bounty-hunter who works for money not honour, and who shoots first, he tuned Western myth to a cynical modern era. Others copied this disenchantment with conventional Western morality (especially after the Vietnam war), but Eastwood's work as director-actor later sustained the genre virtually single-handed. His movies like *The Outlaw Josey Wales* (1976) and *Unforgiven* (1992) debunked the myth by 'realistically' portraying a West in which pure good or evil, black or white, never really existed. Also he introduced overtly mythic themes. In *High Plains Drifter* (1973) and *Pale Rider* (1985), he plays a gunslinger seeking vengeance not as a mere mortal but as Nemesis returned from the dead to exact punishment on his killers. This he does without rationalising or apologising for the supernatural emphasis (*Pale Rider* refers to the Book of Revelation). Thus he restored (or maintained) the Western as a mythic vehicle appropriate to and expressive of a fearful present.

For, as **science fiction** was never just about the future, the Western was never just about the past. Given new social demands, the rehabilitation of Native American culture was undertaken in *Dances with Wolves* (1990), directed by and starring Kevin Costner. It portrays a white man who joins the Sioux so completely that he rejects European culture as evil. Even the dialogue is in Sioux. So the Western morality play came full circle.

WILLIAM TELL (*See* ROBIN HOOD)

Swiss national hero in a legend of the fourteenth-century independence movement against the Habsburgs. It is said that Gessler, the governor of Uri, set up a cap in the marketplace and ordered all to bow to it. On 18 November 1307 the archer William Tell refused. Gessler commanded him to shoot an **apple** off his son's head with one shot. Tell placed a bolt in his crossbow and another in his belt, then shot the apple cleanly off. Gessler asked what the other bolt was for. Tell said it was for Gessler's own evil heart had the first shot missed. At this, Gessler had him bound and taken over the lake to jail, but Tell jumped ashore from the boat at a place later called Tell's Leap. Soon after, he slew Gessler. This act inflamed the Swiss desire for freedom and led to the formation of the Confederation.

For all its seemingly exact detail, the tale is as mythical as that of **Robin Hood**. The Greek archer Alcon, companion of **Hercules** as mentioned by **Virgil**, was noted for shooting rings off people's heads. In the Norse *Thidrek's Saga*, King Nidung orders the archer Egil to shoot an arrow off his son's head. The tale of the second arrow appears here, also in Saxo's twelfth-century Danish account of how in the year 950 Harold Bluetooth gave the braggart archer Tokko one chance to shoot the apple off his son's head. 'Tokko' means simpleton; Tell is derived from *toll*, meaning senseless or mad.

WILLOW (*See* ALDER, BEL, TREE ALPHABET, TREES, WITCHCRAFT)

'The Moon owns it,' writes Nicholas Culpeper (1616–54) in his *Complete Herbal*. Related to the **alder**, it was important in the worship of **Yahweh** at Jerusalem, where the Day of the Feast of Tabernacles, a fire and water ceremony, was called the Day of Willows. The Sumerian goddess Belili was a goddess of trees but above all of the willow; her son **Bel** (British Beli or Belinus) was perhaps a willow-god, supplanting the alder-god **Bran** before he became a god of light; thus the Goidelic *bile*, 'sacred tree'.

In the Beth-Luis-Nion **tree-alphabet** as adduced by **Graves**, the willow, *saille*, is the fifth letter, S, and the fifth month of the year. In Greek myth **Orpheus** holds a willow branch while in the **underworld**, and received the gift of mystic eloquence by touching willow-trees in a grove sacred to **Persephone**, goddess of the underworld. It is also sacred to **Hecate**, to **Circe** and **Hera** and to all **moon**-goddesses, as the tree that most loves water. Its connection with **witchcraft** throughout Northern Europe is so strong that the words 'witch', '*wicca*', 'wicked' and 'wicker' derive from the same ancient word for willow. The English 'witch's broom' was made of an **ash** stake, birch twigs and willow binding. It was said that witches were rendered harmless if detached from their broomstick and thrown into running water. **Druidic** human **sacrifices** were offered at full moon in wicker baskets, or burned alive in giant wicker cages: 'Wicker Men'. A traditional emblem of grief ('weeping willow'), it was once customary for rejected lovers to wear a willow sprig. In **Shakespeare**'s *Hamlet*, Ophelia hangs her wild flowers on a 'willow . . . aslant a brook', before she drowns herself. In *The Merchant of Venice*, the jilted queen of Carthage, Dido, stands 'with a willow in her hand, Upon the wild sea-banks . . .'

It was also a tree of enchantment, divination and prophecy, and sacred to poets, as in a gruesome old Irish poetic rite, the 'Dichetal do Chennaib' ('Recital from the Finger-ends'):[1]

> Willow wand, ear finger,
> By power of divination
> Force confessions from the mouth
> Of a mouldering corpse.

1. *The White Goddess*, Robert Graves, Faber & Faber, London, 1961, pp.173–4, 199.

WIND (*See* **RIDDLES, TALIESIN,** *UPANISHADS*, **VAYU**)

Symbolising the **spirit** moving over the dark, formless waters; the creative breath of life and the universe; a state of bodiless freedom and release from worldly cares as described in the Indian *Chāndogya Upanishad* ('The wind has no body'); or in the *Iśā Upanishad*, which refers to 'wind and immortal breath'. Transient and insubstantial, 'the wind' is the answer to a **riddle** by which Taliesin confounded the court-bards of King Maelgwyn, being the 'strong creature from before the **Flood**, without flesh, without bone, without vein, without blood . . . as wide as the surface of the earth, and it was not born, nor was it seen.' He gives the answer by producing a violent wind-storm. The sixteenth-century Scots Witches of Berwick were accused of trying to kill King James VI at sea by raising a storm against him. One technique was to dip a rag in water and beat it thrice on a stone, saying:[1]

> I knok this rag upone this stane
> To raise the wind in the divellis name,
> It shall not lye until I please again.

'Cunning men' from Scotland to Finland sold favourable winds to sailors in the form of knotted threads. Untying the first **knot** raised a breeze, the second, a moderate wind, and so on. Magic was also used to still or calm wind. In the reign of the emperor Constantine (fourth century AD), a certain Sopater was executed at Constantinople for magically binding the winds, the corn-ships from Egypt and Syria being becalmed and detained. There are tales of winds kept in bags. An Amerindian myth tells how **Coyote** snared

Wind but set him free when Wind promised in future to blow only four times, and not constantly. So too the universal belief in Four Winds, one for each quarter of the earth, usually depicted on old maps as cherubic heads with puffed-out cheeks emerging from clouds, or as old men blowing **horns**.

1. *The Golden Bough*, Sir James Frazer, Macmillan, London, 1963, p.81.

WINE (*See* DIONYSUS, SOMA, TRANSUBSTANTIATION)

WISHPOOSH (*See* COYOTE, NATIVE AMERICAN MYTH, TRICKSTERS)

The Nez Percé tribe (Pacific coast of the USA) tell how Coyote the trickster killed Wishpoosh, a beaver-monster that drowned any fisherman silly enough to approach the lake where he lived. Begged to help, Coyote made a long-handled spear, tied it to his wrist, then went fishing. Wishpoosh seized him and dragged him under the lake. They fought so hard that the mountains drew back in alarm. Wishpoosh tried to flee but, spearing him, Coyote went along with him, their fight now so fierce that rivers were widened, gorges created and holes torn through hills. Reaching the ocean Wishpoosh jumped in, eating **whales** to renew his strength. But Coyote turned himself into a fir-branch and floated out to Wishpoosh, who ate him. Inside the monster's stomach he returned to animal form and with a sharp knife stabbed Wishpoosh through the heart. From the corpse he created a new race of human beings: the Northwest tribes, including the Nez Percé. Yet he worked so fast he forgot to give them eyes and mouths. At last he realised his mistake, but his knife was dull, so that some of the mouths he made were crooked and others too big – which is why, say the Nez Percé, they have ugly mouths.

WITCHCRAFT (*See* AMULETS, BLACK MAGIC, CHARMS, SHAPE-SHIFTING, SORCERY)

Though once applied equally to male or female practitioners of sorcery or magic (black or white), since medieval times the stock image of the witch is of an evil crone who commands supernatural powers by virtue of a compact with the **Devil**. Such powers may include: **divination**, ability to fly and to **shape-shift** into animal form (**cat, deer, hare**, etc.), or to transform others into animals (Beauty and the Beast, **Circe**, etc.). Also **invisibility, invulnerability** and knowledge of drugs to produce love, fertility, death, or to prevent procreation may be among her powers. She can raise storms or make **wind** fall, cast **spells** and **curse** enemies or their cattle, englamour folk to see riches instead of rags, or make them fall into a magical sleep (**Sleeping Beauty**). On her broom or besom (variant of the magic **wand**) she flies by night to the sabbat, an orgy at which she worships Satan and plans evil, gaining power to do so by **sacrificing** new-born babes. She has a 'familiar', an animal (usually a cat) whose form she can take at will. She cannot weep, or at most only **three** tears, she fears running **water** and cold **iron**, and has a hidden nipple used to suckle her familiar, also a spot on her body that feels no pain. On seeing a broom she must stop to count the straws, or count seeds, grains or holes in a sieve, in which it is said she can sail out to sea (so sixteenth-century Scotland's Witches of Berwick were accused).

The word 'witch' is from Anglo-Saxon *wicca* (masc.) or *wicce* (fem.), being related to *wiccian*, to practise sorcery and Icelandic *vikja*, to exorcise. In origin witches, male or female, were neutral figures who might use their powers or knowledge of herbs for good or ill. Not until after the Crusades was witchcraft seen as anti-social or evil. But the Dominican Inquistion, founded to combat **Catharism**, and having broken both the Cathars and the **Knights Templar**, needed a new enemy to justify its continued existence.

In 1326 Pope John XXII agreed to Dominican demands for a war against witches. He made sorcery a new heresy, *Maleficium*, its essence being the making of pacts with the Devil. Yet persecution was slow to take root. In Paris in 1390 one Jehane de Brigue, accused by a dying man she had cured, under torture 'confessed' to owning a demonic familiar and was burned to death. The time was ripe. It was forty years since the Black Death had killed a third of Europe's population. European **Jews**, blamed for poisoning the **wells**, had been exterminated en masse. With Cathars, Templars and Jews already scapegoated for God's wrath, now it was Woman's turn. Had not **Eve** caused the **Fall**? Yet Dominican arguments against *Maleficium* only caught fire when Pope Innocent VIII issued a bull (1484) condemning 'Many persons of both sexes [who] have abandoned themselves to devils, **incubi and succubi**, and by their incantations, spells, conjurations and other accursed charms and crafts, enormities and horrid offences have slain unborn infants and the unborn offspring of cattle and blasted the produce of the earth.'[1]

In 1486 appeared *Malleus Maleficarum (The Hammer of the Witches)* by two German Dominicans, Kramer and Sprengler. Condoning torture to gain confession, denouncing carnal lust, it led to a hysteria amid which every ill was ascribed to witchcraft, yet also to fascination with the forbidden fruits it denounced. The climate of terror was maintained by Calvinist broadsides like Knox's *First Blast of the Trumpet against the Monstrous Regiment of Women* (c.1560) and Bodin's *Démonologie* (1580). In parts of Germany women were almost wiped out. At Bamburg between 1609 and 1633 over 900 women were tortured in the 'witches' chair'. Made of iron, it was covered with studs and heated over a fire. Confessions usually led to the stake.

The persecution was most marked in France, Germany, Switzerland and Scotland, where King James VI (later James I of England) was convinced that a storm nearly drowning him at sea was caused by the 'Witches of Berwick'. After torture, several were burned. Yet the fascination persisted. In 1662 Isobel Gowdie of Auldearn in Moray, northern Scotland, voluntarily confessed to intercourse with the Devil 'a meikle, blak, roch man' as 'cold within me as spring-well water'. Her fate is unclear, yet to those appalled by the customary cruelty a French writer explained 'the witches are so bent on [Satan's] devilish service that there is no torture or punishment that can frighten them; and they say that they go to a true martyrdom and to death, for love of him, as gaily as they go to a festival of pleasure and public rejoicing.'[2]

Britain's last witchcraft execution took place in the 1750s, but the last Witchcraft Act was repealed only in 1951, thirty years after Margaret Murray argued that witchcraft is a relic of a pre-Christian fertility religion.[3] Some historians claim there never were any witches, only a collective madness arising from sexual neurosis caused by the Church's moral imposition.[4] Yet there was an 'old religion', and its adherents, from **Gnostics** to **Cathars**, **Templars** and 'witches' were occasionally but effectively persecuted over a millennium until they were wiped out or silenced. It was a war against whatever contradicted Christian patriarchy. 'Scientific method' developed exactly as witchcraft (female religion) was most under attack – a bare millennium after worship of **Cybele**, **Isis** and other great **mother-goddesses** had been suppressed, with only the epicene **Virgin Mary** left behind.

Those practising withcraft are not now arrested. Their festivals are those of the old nature religion – **Beltane** (May Eve): the Summer Solstice; Lammas-tide (*Lugnasad*) on 1 August; Hallowe'en (Celtic Samhain: 31 October); the

Winter Solstice; and Candlemas (*Imbolc*; the old lambing festival) on 2 February. Their working unit is the coven of thirteen; their deity the mother-goddess; her consort the Horned God (**Cernunnos, Herne**, the **Green Man**).

1. *Bothwell and the Witches*, Godfrey Watson, Hale, London, 1975, p.16.
2. *Ibid.*, p.73
3. *The Witch-Cult in Western Europe*, Margaret Murray, OUP, 1921.
4. *Europe's Inner Demons*, Norman Cohn, Paladin, London, 1976.

WITCHDOCTOR (*See* AFRICAN MYTH, MEDICINE, SHAMAN, SORCERY)

In most Bantu languages the word *nganga* (**Swahili** *mganga*) translates as 'doctor', which in European terms may mean anything from **medicine** man or magician to herbalist, **shaman** or witchdoctor. Properly speaking, a witchdoctor is just that: a doctor who cures **witches**. Yet in African belief not all persons possessed by evil **spirits** are necessarily witches. Likewise few actual witches are thought curable, their desire to do evil being considered to be innate or inherited. So most 'witchdoctors' are, more precisely, 'witch-finders' or (in South Africa) 'witch-smellers', it being said that a witch smells of death and poison. The Zande *binza*, who knows which trees or plants give him power to 'see' witchcraft and drive it away from its intended victims, is a 'true' witchdoctor.[1]

1. *African Mythology*, Jan Knappert, Aquarian Press, Wellingborough, 1990.

WIZARD (*See* BLACK MAGIC, MAGIC, SORCERY)

General term for an enchanter, sorcerer, soothsayer, diviner or magician; a man who knows more than others and commands the power to perform incredible acts. Derived from the word 'wise', in most lands the wizard is not usually or necessarily represented as wicked (unless his wizardry be **sorcery**). He is simply a knowledgeable practitioner of magic. Even so, his character is ambiguous: it is sensible not to anger a wizard.

Yet in medieval and Renaissance Europe, denial by the **Christian** Church of any source of power or knowledge other than its own dogmatic authority led men like Ramon Lull (1235–1315), Albertus Magnus (1206–80), Roger Bacon (1214–94) and later **Cornelius Agrippa** (1486–1535) and **Paracelsus** (1493–1541) to be regarded solely as 'wizards', just because they enquired into the nature of phenomena. Latterly, during the mad time of the **witch**-hunts, any involvement with the occult was dangerous. Superstition ruled. Thus it was commonly thought that the power of wizards (and witches) lay in their **hair**. In France during the witch-trials it was customary to shave the heads and bodies of men and women charged with sorcery before handing them over to the torturer. This belief was also found in India and among the **Aztecs**, likewise among the Old Testament **Philistines**, as in the fate of **Samson**. Yet early Christian myth relies on wizardry. The defeat by the Apostle Peter of the **Gnostic** wizard Simon Magus is no less 'magical' than the conquest by **St Patrick** of the **Druids** of Ireland. In both cases, Peter and Patrick function as wizards, and the point asserted is that Christian magic is superior to any other magic. So in time any other form of 'magic' was simply demonised and punished. Despite this effective control-game, the **archetype** persisted.

So (in the Western tradition) **Merlin** remains the epitome of Celtic wizardry, along with **Math**, **Taliesin** and the magical Irish race, the **Tuatha dé Danaan**. The Finns were equally famed (and feared by neighbours) for their wizardry (see *Kalevala*). In modern lore the best-known wizard is Gandalf the Grey, portrayed by **J.R.R. Tolkien** in his epic fantasy, *The Lord of the Rings*. An awesome yet benign figure, he is contrasted with the wizards corrupted by the power of the **ring**. Another potent modern image of the wizard, complete with robe, magic **wand** and pointed hat decorated with astrological symbols, appears in 'The Sorcerer's Apprentice' sequence of **Disney**'s cartoon extravaganza, *Fantasia* (1940).

Odd, how after so many centuries of ecclesiastical indoctrination, the image of the wizard persists, even in the materialistic West.

WODEN/WOTAN (*See* ODIN, TEUTONIC MYTH)

WOLF (*See* COYOTE, DOG, FENRIR, HYENA, WEREWOLF)

Symbolises fierceness, cruelty, devouring evil and bloodthirstiness, as in the **Norse** myth of **Fenrir**, the giant wolf whose jaws gape so wide they stretch from earth to heaven. The Norse gods managed to bind him, yet at the cost of **Tyr** losing his hand to Fenrir's jaws. Yet eventually Fenrir (or one of his brood) will succeed in swallowing the sun, leading to three long years of unending night: the Fimbulwinter. In **Celtic** lore it is also said that a wolf swallows the sun every night. A she-wolf suckled **Romulus** and Remus, founders of Rome: appropriate, given Rome's military might. The wolf was also sacred to the war-gods **Mars** and **Ares**. The Norse god **Odin** rides a wolf, as do witches and warlocks, while some men become hungry **werewolves**, prowling the night in search of human flesh. In folklore both ancient and modern the wolf symbolises crafty rapaciousness. In many Native American myths, Wolf travels and shares adventures with **Coyote** the **trickster**. The Pawnee tribe held the Wolf Star sacred: this, probably **Sirius**, was closely connected with death. Elsewhere, Wolf is drowned, revived and ultimately becomes ruler of the Land of the Dead. As with the killing of other beasts, those slaying a wolf had to placate its spirit via rites of atonement.

In Europe, Little Red Riding-Hood narrowly survives her meeting with the wolf which first eats then disguises itself as her granny. The wolf was also widely regarded as a **corn**-spirit. From France to Russia folk would say, when the wind set the corn in motion, that 'The Wolf is in the corn', and would warn their children not to stray too far, or 'The Rye-Wolf will eat you!' The **Disney** cartoon, *The Three Little Pigs* (1933) made the Wolf a symbol of the Great Depression. 'Who's afraid of the Big Bad Wolf?', they all sang, but the only one to survive the wolf's attack was the one who built his house of brick, not of straw or wood.

WONDER-CHILD (*See* CONCORDANCE)

A common theme in religion or mythology is the birth of a child who proves even as an infant to possess extraordinary powers, thus revealing himself (the tale is invariably about a man-child) to be a god, or the **avatar** of a god, or to be destined for a heroic career as war-leader, monarch or saint. Sometimes his birth is resented by a god or goddess, or feared by a tyrant due to a **prophecy** that the child will destroy him. Thus, only four days old, the Greek god **Apollo** at Pytho (**Delphi**) slew the **serpent** which had molested his mother during her pregnancy. The hero **Hercules** went one better by bare-handedly strangling two serpents sent by **Hera** to destroy him (though by then he was at least eight months old). The Indian tyrant Kansa, fearing prophecy that Devaka's eighth child would kill him, locked her up, but when she bore **Krishna**, the gods put the guards to sleep and she escaped with the infant who, being an avatar of **Vishnu**, was equal to the occasion – for when they came to the River Yamuna he made the waters recoil. In Irish myth the Fomorian demon-king **Balor**, fearing a similar prophecy that his grandson will kill him, imprisons his daughter in an island **cave**. When she and her guardian-women are seduced and bear children, Balor tries to drown them all, but one, **Lug**, escapes, later to slay him. This is the same theme as that of **Moses** hidden in the bulrushes when Pharaoh orders the death of all new-born Hebrew boys, or of Herod, fearing the birth of the King of Jews, ordering the murder of all children under the age of two. Both **Moses** and **Christ** escape the fate aimed at them alone; aged twelve, Jesus impresses the Temple rabbis with his wisdom. Likewise in Welsh lore young **Taliesin**, abandoned by his mother **Cerridwen**, is found in a **salmon**-weir and as an infant confounds King Maelgwyn's court-**bards** with his **riddles** and his recollection of former incarnations. **Merlin**, too, born of union between a **virgin** and an **incubus**, is brought before villainous Vortigern, and likewise confounds the king's lying magicians with insight proving that he is more than a mere boy. Such tales are the very stuff of legend.

WONDJINA (*See* ABORIGINES)

WOODPECKER (*See* RAIN-MAKING)

Long considered a **rain-maker**, a **prophetic** bird and a guardian of **trees**. In Italy it is said, 'When the woodpecker pecks, expect rain or storm.' In France the tale goes that at the **Creation** the woodpecker was the only bird who refused to help God by hollowing out areas to be filled with water, so creating seas, lakes and ponds, perhaps because she feared to dirty her fine plumage. For this, she was condemned to peck wood and drink nothing but rain. Yet in older belief the woodpecker occupied an exalted position. Called 'the axe of **Ishtar**' in Babylonia, in Greece it was said that once the woodpecker occupied the throne of **Zeus** himself. Certainly the bird was consulted as an **oracle**, and was connected with fertility. In Greek lore one Celeus ('green woodpecker') tried to steal the honey nourishing the infant Zeus, and for this was turned into a green woodpecker. This and its association with ploughing may be explained by its habit of feeding on the ground, picking up ants, its beak functioning like a primitive plough.

WORD (*See* MUSIC AND MYTH, NAMES)

'In the beginning was the Word, and the Word was made flesh.' In various religious traditions the world's creation is associated with the idea of the *logos*, the Word made Flesh, as in the **Christian** mass: *Et Verbum caro factum est*, or as in the **Buddhist** mantra: *Aum mani padme hum* (the **jewel** of eternity in the **lotus** of birth and death). The tale is not only that of how at the Primal Instant a vast Word was spoken, bringing all worlds into material being, but of our endless recapitulation through language of **Mysteries** otherwise inexpressible. The Word is not just the spoken or written word, but the universal vibration underlying all created existence, the Song of the Spheres, the intelligence implicit in the very existence and formation of the world in which we live and love and suffer.

WORLD EGG (*See* EGG)

WORLD SERPENT (*See* DRAGON, SERPENT)

WORLD TREE (*See AXIS MUNDI*, **CROSS, TREES, YGGDRASIL**)

WORM (*See* **DRAGON, LOATHLY WORM, STOORWORM**)

WREN (*See* **BIRDS, DRUIDS**)
Symbolically ambiguous; in the West sometimes called the King of the Birds and taking the place of the **dove** as denoting **spirit**, but also malefic in its connection with **witchcraft**. Both connections arise from its ancient importance, particularly in the annual custom known as 'the hunting of the wren', this occurring at the time of the winter solstice, when from the Mediterranean to the north of Britain the bird was trapped, slain, hung on a pole, paraded about, then ritually eaten or buried in the churchyard; apparently due to its allegorical connection with the death of the **sun**. In parts of France, the youth who killed the wren was called the 'king'. In Ireland, Scotland and the Isle of Man, the wren was hunted on either Christmas Day or St Stephen's Day, and carried about to a song reverencing it as the King of Birds. Yet at no other time of year was the wren pursued. Indeed, in France it was said that to rob a wren's nest would lead to the robber's house being burned down or to his fingers being shrivelled. Sacred to the legendary Welsh poet **Taliesin**, its Welsh/British name, *dryw*, has been said to imply its connection with **Druid** mysticism. It was also associated with the robin to such a degree that robin and wren were commonly viewed as male and female of the same species. So, tradition claims:

> He who hunts the robin and the wren
> Shall never prosper, sea nor land.

and:

> The robin and the wren
> Are God Almighty's cock and hen.

What is the source of these beliefs? Living in **caves** and dark places, the wren symbolised powers contrary or complementary to the sun, as in the fable whereby through trickery it defeats the **eagle** in a contest to find which can fly highest. In France it was said that the wren snatched **fire** from the sun, but that while so doing it burst into flame, and passed the burning brand to the robin, whose feathers also caught fire. The Bretons claim that the wren stole fire not from **heaven** but **hell**, being scorched as she escaped through hell's keyhole. As for fiery Robin Redbreast, he too was a solar bird. The greedy black sparrow who murders him (in the old folk-song, 'Who Killed Cock Robin?') epitomises cold black winter.

But, like **Tammuz** or **Adonis**, both Robin and Wren are born again.

WYVERN (*See* **LAKE MONSTERS**)

X

XANADU (*See* **COLERIDGE**)

XIPETOTEC (*See* **AZTEC MYTH**)

'The flayed lord', this Aztec **corn**-god represented the newly-planted seed, **sacrificed** by being skinned just as the maize seed loses its skin when the shoot emerges from the earth. He was also the god of penitential torture as a route to spiritual liberation. He sent illnesses to mankind, and many human sacrifices were made to him. He was deeply involved in Mictlan, the Aztec **underworld** ruled by Mictlantecuhtli and his wife Mictlancihuatl. They governed the 'nine underground rivers' and the **souls** of the dead.

Other Aztec agricultural deities included Tzinteotl, presiding over procreation, Chicomecoatl, goddess of rural plenty, and **Xochiquetzal**.

XIUHTECUHTLI (*See* **AZTEC MYTH**)

The Aztec god of **fire**, perceived as a great pillar or **spindle** running from the top to the bottom of the cosmos, from the hearth of the **underworld** Mictlan to the hearth in the homes of human beings, and straight on up to the heavens. This deity also helped the **spirits** of the dead on their way down to Mictlan.

XOCHIPILI/XOCHIQUETZAL (*See* **AZTEC MYTH**)

God and goddess of the two sexes; of flowers, dancing and singing; red-faced Xochipili the personification of the spirit, and Xochiquetzal ('most precious flower'), goddess of the earth's bounties and giver of children.

XOLOTL (*See* **AZTEC MYTH**)

God of ball-play, protector of **twins**, this deformed deity with his burst **eye** and backward-turned feet was regarded as the bringer of misfortune, who as Lord of the Evening Star forced the sun down into night. Yet he was also viewed as **Quetzalcoatl**'s double.

Y

YAHWEH (*See* **EL, FREUD, JUDAISM, MOSES, NAMES**)
Or Jehovah, Jahweh, epitome of the 'jealous god' who acknowledges no
other, the **name** of this singular **Hebrew** deity derives from the Tetragrammaton, YHVH (yod he vau he), the four consonants comprising the secret
name of God, never spoken aloud save by the High Priest on the Day of
Atonement, in the Holy of Holies in the Temple at Jerusalem. The true
pronunciation is long lost. Yahweh/Jehovah are approximations, used to
define the Hebrew tribal deity, as distinct from God as the **Judaeo-Christian**
deity.

Yahweh's original nature remains open to conjecture, but the connection
of this **baal** (lord) of the Hebrews with the deities of neighbouring tribes is
clear from other names applied to him, including the Phoenician **El** and its
plural feminine form, **Elohim**; also Sabaoth, Shaddai and Adonai (*see*
Names). He gave the Law to **Moses** on Mount **Sinai**, named after **Sin**, the
Chaldean **moon**-god, and was probably connected with moon worship.
Freud's conjecture (*Moses and Monotheism*, 1939) that Yahweh was once an
Arabian volcano god is one of many theories; yet clearly he was once
connected with that very **serpent**-power which, in the myths of the Garden of
Eden and of **Leviathan**, he apparently **cursed** then overthrew. The tale of
Eden derives from an older Sumerian garden where the Serpent (cosmic
fertilising power) is consort of the **mother-goddess** (**Eve**). So the rod he gave
Moses becomes a serpent when cast down on the ground; in the desert, when
the Israelites complained, he 'sent fiery serpents among the people, and they
bit the people, so that many people died . . .' He commanded Moses to make
a bronze serpent and set it on a pole; this **idol** was long revered in Jerusalem,
until King Hezekiah (719–691 BC), broke it in pieces. So too the chief
protagonists of the Yahweh cult were the priestly tribe of Levi: i.e., of
Leviathan.[1]

Another aspect of Yahweh in relation to earlier deities is not only the curse
he puts on Woman, but his clear preference for the younger son (Abel versus
Cain, Isaac versus Ishmael, Jacob versus Esau, Joseph and Reuben) also (*see*
Cain) a preference for the nomadic shepherd over the farmer, as is appropriate for a god of patriarchal nomads.

Further aspects likewise drawn from older models but altered to suit
Hebrew needs include **creation** of the universe by the power of the **Word**,
going back to a much earlier Egyptian myth; the myth of the **flood**, from
an earlier Sumerian model (see **Gilgamesh**) and that of the Tower of
Babel, reversing the meaning of the ziggurat, which was built not to
threaten but to worship heaven, and to let the gods come down to earth to
be worshipped.

Also in the original Sumerian garden there is one Tree of Life, not two;
there is no **Fall**, no corruption of nature and no jealous God. In the biblical
version not only has sin overwhelmed the world, but the Cosmic Serpent has
split into two; one half the wrathful sky-god, the other the creeping, satanic
worm. Thus God became his own **Devil**.

1. *Occidental Mythology*, Joseph Campbell, Penguin, London, 1976, pp.29–31.

YAKSHA/YAKSHINI (*See* GANDHARVAS, INDIAN MYTH, RAKSHASA)

Though related to the revolting **Rakshasas**, these **shape-shifting** minor forest deities of Indian lore are also cousin to the nobler **Gandharvas**. Generally but not always benign, they are sometimes called the Punyajanas, the 'Good People', just as Scots and Irish countryfolk likewise cautiously referred to the **fairies** as the Daoine Sidhe. In general they represent the **elemental** forces, like the **fauns** and **satyrs** of Greek myth. The Yakshas, the males, may be of human size and even handsome, but sometimes appear as potbellied, hunchbacked black **dwarves**. They guard **treasure**, their king Kubera being the god of wealth, and protect the gates of his palace high in the Himalayas. They carry him through the sky with the speed of the **wind** wherever he wishes to go. When the hero **Bhima** came to the lake of Kubera in search of celestial **lotuses** for his Rakshasa queen, he killed many of the Yakshas, and put the rest to flight. The Yakshinis, female Yakshas, accost travellers losing their way in the forest. They resemble buxom, voluptuous women, but some, the Ashvamukhi, have the heads of **horses**.

YAMA (*See* HINDUISM, INDIAN MYTH, TWINS, YIMA)

The **Vedic** and later **Hindu** god of death; the 'restrainer'; the first man to be born on earth and thus the first to die. He and his sister Yami (or Yamuna, who became the south-flowing **River** Yamuna or Jumna) are identical to the Persian **Yima** and Yimeh. Children of the **sun**-god **Surya**, they are the primeval **twins** (*yama* means 'twin'), and became man and wife, for there were no other people on earth. When he died, Yama was first to find the road south to the Land of the Dead, a paradise where he became king over an ever-increasing number of **souls**. There with **Varuna** he sits under a tree, playing a flute and drinking **soma**. Once a form of Mitra (*see* **Mithra**) and called 'Noble Shepherd', his original role as friend of the dead gradually altered to that of the terrible judge. Seated on a **buffalo**, armed with a noose and a club, he sends out a pigeon or an **owl** to summon those about to die, and owns two ferocious four-eyed, big-snouted **dogs** past which those bound for the palace of death must hurry. Reaching it, the soul of the dead one meets Chitragupta, Recorder of the Dead who, like Egyptian **Thoth**, reads out the account of his deeds, the Agrasandhani. Then Yama, as 'King of Righteousness', Dharma-rajah, gives fair judgement, sending the soul either to Swarga, **heaven**, to one of the twenty-one **hells** (Naraka), or back to earth to be reborn. Victims sent to the hells must travel 200 leagues a day through scorching, treeless plains or against vicious winds, meeting **tigers**, venomous **serpents** and many other hardships before being plunged into inconceivable tortures in the lowest depths. As with the Greek **Styx** there is a river (Vaitarani) to separate the world of the living from that of the dead. The journey from the one to the other is said to take 4 hours 40 minutes: the body of the deceased cannot be cremated earlier than that.

YAMBE-AKKA

In Lapp (Northern Scandinavian) mythology this 'old woman of the dead' ruled the **underworld**, a gloomy realm entered via the mouth of a river plunging into the ice-bound Arctic Ocean. The Lapp underworld was thought to be much like the land of the living, save that the **souls** of the departed were able to walk on air. The dead were buried attired for a long journey, with a staff by them and birch-bark shoes on their feet. Their relatives cooked in the cemetery until the grave fell in, fearing that otherwise they might offend the ghost, who would return to haunt them.

YANG (See YIN)

YARILO (See CORN-GODS, KUPALA, MAY DAY, SLAVONIC MYTH)

Or Erilo, from *yary*, meaning 'ardent' or 'passionate'; also *yarovoi*, being corn sown in springtime. The cult of this Slavonic god of carnal love was so popular in White Russia that as late as the eighteenth century the Bishop of Voronezh (as disgusted as the Puritan Philip Stubbes was by the English **May Day** festivals) had great difficulty suppressing the festivals and 'satanic games' associated with it. Young and handsome, this god of fecundity was said to ride a white horse and wear a white cloak. Barefoot and crowned with wild flowers, in his left hand he carried ears of wheat. His festival was honoured at the time of the spring sowing, the village maidens electing the loveliest among them to play his part. Flower-bedecked, they danced in a long circle about her on her white horse to celebrate the festival in the new-sown fields. Later, in summer, they celebrated Yarilo's 'funeral', a straw image of the dead god being buried amid mass intoxication and **dance**.

Also see **Kupala**, a water-god whose rites were similarly orgiastic.

YEATS, W(ILLIAM) B(UTLER) (1865–1939) (See IRISH MYTH, JOYCE)

Irish poet whose fascination with **fairy** lore and the occult led him in 1888 to join the **Theosophical** Society and in 1889 to his first published poetry, *The Wanderings of Oisin*, a dialogue between **St Patrick** and the dying Fenian hero **Oisin**. In this and later work he rejected realism in his quest to tap what he called the *anima mundi* (World Soul), a universal treasure-house of imagery. 'The Irish bards . . .', he wrote, 'always were explicit rather than suggestive in dealing with the supernatural . . . They surround the vague with the definite.' Thus in his own art he utilised Irish mythic themes to create an extravagant yet utterly precise inner vision. So in *The Old Age of Queen Maeve* (1903), he tells how this mythic Queen of Connaught, cause of the war with Ulster (see *Táin*), is haunted by her memory. In *Baile and Aillinn* (1903), ideal lovers are transformed into **swans** and eternally linked by a **gold** chain (*see* **Angus Mac Og**). In *The Shadowy Waters* (1903), a man in love with eternity takes his ship so far out to sea that he sails out of the world (*see* **Bran MacFebal, Mael Dúin, St Brendan**).

Taking the secret **name** 'Diabolus est Deus Inversus' ('The Devil is God Reversed'), he joined the occult Order of the Golden Dawn but resigned in 1905. Yet esoteric symbolism persisted in his work. In 1917 he married Hyde Lees, a medium whose powers led him in 1925 to write *A Vision*, a thesis interpreting human character via the **moon**'s twenty-eight daily phases. Of such lunar knowledge, he warned: 'It is perhaps well that so few believe in it, for if many did many would go out of parliaments and libraries and run into the wilderness to so waste the body, and so hush the unquiet mind that, still living, they might pass the doors the dead pass daily; for who among the wise would trouble himself with making laws or in history or in weighing the earth if the things of eternity seemed ready to hand?'

Whether involved with the Irish Independence movement or with fairy lore and ancient myth, Yeats always remained true to his own vision.[1]

1. *The Poems*, W.B. Yeats (ed. Daniel Albright), Dent, London, 1990.

YETI (See BIGFOOT, FABULOUS BEASTS)

Or 'Abominable Snowman'. The best known of various hairy man-apes unknown to science yet said to survive in remote mountain forest regions. Evidence for the existence of the yeti (as with **lake monsters**) depends on sightings by mountaineers or folk living in the high Himalayas, its apparent habitat.

The Nepalese say there are three types of yeti: the small *yeh-teh*, the large *meh-teh* and the giant *dzu-teh*. Local reports are legion. The abbot of Thyangboche monastery under Mount Everest tells how yeti often visit the gardens.[1] In 1974 Lakhpa Domani, a Sherpa girl tending yaks at Pheriche in Nepal, was carried off by a huge apelike creature with black and red-brown hair, large eyes and prominent cheekbones. It dropped her as she fought it, but then killed two yaks before making off. In January 1987 in northern Kashmir a youth was attacked by a two-legged hairy creature some 4 feet tall. It ran off after he hit it with his fire-pot; two other villagers saw it jump a ditch.

In 1832 the Resident British Officer in Nepal described how his porters had fled a hairy beast they called *rakshas*, 'demon' (*see* **Rakshasa**). Later they told him how similar wild men had been feared for centuries.[2] In 1937 the mountaineer F.S. Smythe photographed yeti snow-prints at 16,500 feet, as did Eric Shipton on the Menlung glacier in 1951. These prints were so sharp as to be widely considered fraudulent, yet his partner, Michael Ward, insisted they were genuine. In 1970 on Annapurna, Don Whillans saw prints in the snow. Later in bright moonlight he looked out of his tent and through binoculars saw a black ape-like beast, then 'quite suddenly . . . as if it realised it was being watched, it shot across the whole slope of the mountain'.[3] In 1972 a US expedition found prints so clear that they took casts in plaster. In 1973, Lord Hunt, leader of the British 1953 Everest climb, who had previously heard 'high-pitched yelping cries' on the upper slopes, found prints: his 1978 photographs show footprints 14 inches long and 7 inches wide. He believes in 'an unidentified creature' still to be found.

No yeti bodies have been found. The 'yeti scalps' in some Himalayan monasteries are probably of goatskin, made to represent the yeti in ritual dances. Yet lack of yeti bodies does not prove lack of yeti. The reports of several species suggest anthropoids long adapted to a climate beyond easy reach of (and extermination by) *Homo sapiens*. If they do exist, it is probably better for them that they remain legendary.

1. *Arthur Clarke's Mysterious World*, Simon Welfare and John Fairley, Fontana, London, 1982, p.19.
2. *The Directory of Possibilities* (ed. Colin Wilson and John Grant), London, 1982.
3. *Ibid.*, p.199.

YEW (See IMMORTALITY, RESURRECTION, TREES)

Long-lived evergreen often found in churchyards; its symbolism ambivalent. Said to live over 3,000 years (unlikely), like other conifers it anciently represented **immortality**, and early became a symbol of life after death and of the **Resurrection**. Often incorporated in Eastertide church decorations and used on Palm Sunday, it was thought unlucky to bring it into a house, likewise to cut down or damage a growing yew, no doubt due to the idea that it gave protection against evil. Its berries were prized for their sticky sweetness, but its funereal associations (yew shoots were put into shrouds, and yew branches into the grave) also led it to be considered malign. This connotation was strengthened by the fact that bows and dagger-handles were made from its wood, and because its foliage is poisonous. The Latin *Taxus*, yew, may be connected with Greek *toxos*, bow, and *toxicon*, the poison with which arrows were smeared (thus the English word toxic). **Shakespeare** calls it the 'double fatal yew' (*Richard II*): Hamlet's uncle poisons the king by pouring its juice ('hebenon') into his ear. Thus regarded as a death-tree throughout Europe, and in Greece and Italy sacred to **Hecate**, in *Macbeth* Shakespeare refers to its use in **witchcraft** by noting how the **cauldron** of Hecate contains '*slips of yew/ Sliver'd in the moon's eclipse.*'

Representing the letter I (*Idho*) in the Celtic tree alphabet, it was one of the 'Five Magical Trees of Ireland', and in Roman Britain was connected with **Mercury** as psychopomp, leading the dead to Hecate's realm.[1]

1. *The White Goddess*, Robert Graves, Faber & Faber, London, 1961, pp.193–4.

YGGDRASIL (*See* ASH, *AXIS MUNDI*, CROSS, NORSE MYTH, TREES)

The cosmic ash-tree of **Norse myth**, *axis mundi* and column supporting the universe at the foot of which the gods sit in daily judgement, its trunk incorporates and branches overhang the three (or the nine) worlds. One of its three roots reaches down to Midgard and the Land of the **Giants**, at its foot the wisdom-**well** of **Mimir**; the second is in freezing Niflheim by the well of Hvergelmir, where the **dragon** Nidhoggr, the Dread Biter, gnaws perpetually at it; the third is in Asgard, realm of the gods, by the well of Urdr, guarded by the three **Norns**, spinners of human fate who judge not only men but the gods. Daily they water the tree and plaster it with nourishing clay. It may be that these three wells or springs (as named by Snorri in the *Eddas*), are in fact but one, with different names. In the topmost boughs of the tree sits Vithofnir, the golden **cockerel** who will crow at the dawning of **Ragnorak**. Other birds and animals living in its branches or round its roots include an **eagle** at war with the dragon, the squirrel Ratatosk, which runs up and down carrying messages between the dragon and the eagle, and four **stags** which also gnaw at its branches. The strife between the eagle and the dragon is said ultimately to destroy the tree, but it always springs up again. Dew comes from the tree and, when the deer feed on it, this becomes shining, inexhaustible mead which the slain warriors of **Valhalla** drink. Yggdrasil will survive Ragnorak, and succour a man and a woman within its trunk, feeding them on dew, so that they emerge to populate a new world.

The name 'Yggdrasil' means 'the ash-tree that is the horse of Yggr', Yggr being **Odin**, who gained the wisdom of the **runes** by impaling himself with his own spear and hanging from Yggdrasil for nine days and nights; a theme reminiscent of Christ's crucifixion, though done not to redeem mankind but to gain personal power. Likewise to gain wisdom by drinking from the well of Mimir, Odin willingly sacrificed an **eye**. Sacrificial trees existed throughout **pagan** northern Europe (*see* **Teutates**) until missionaries like St Boniface (*c*.674–754) cut them down. In time he too was cut down.

YGRAINE (*See* ARTHURIAN MYTH, UTHER PENDRAGON)

YHI (*See* ABORIGINES)

YIMA (*See* PERSIAN MYTH, YAMA)

In Persian lore the first man and first king of the world. He became ruler of the dead, and is thus the equivalent of the Vedic god **Yama**. Son of the sun-god Vivahvant, and husband of his sister Yimeh, he was the first to offer **haoma** to **Ahura Mazda**, who gave him a golden whip and a goad. When he lived on earth, the world was so beautiful and fruitful that men and their flocks increased until there was no more room for them. Three times Yima made the world stretch, each time making it a third larger (perhaps implying expansion of the territory he ruled), but he failed to keep up with the ever-growing population. So Ahura Mazda told him to follow the path of the sun to the south, and there to make an enclosure, the Var, and into it take the best of men, animals and plants, so that they might be protected against the bitter winters sent to destroy the evil on earth.

This land-based version of **Noah**'s Ark (winter instead of **flood**) may refer to the migration of Indo-European tribes from Russia into Iran. Yima was also a culture-hero who taught men to mould bricks and lay foundations; many ancient ruins are ascribed to him.

YIN AND YANG (*See* CHINESE MYTH, TAOISM)

Refers to the eternally interacting female (*yin*) and male (*yang*) principles of the universe in Chinese philosophy and religion; symbolising all pairs of complementary opposites forever shifting one into the other in a state of perpetual dynamic balance. Lamaist sects depict this principle as human figures engaged in sexual congress; the better-known **Taoist** image is of a circle bisected by a sine curve; the *yin* segment is dark; the *yang*, light. In each segment the opposite principle is depicted as a small circle, dark in the *yang*, light in the *yin*. This also symbolises the **cosmic egg**. The *yin* always comes first, representing primordial darkness before the *yang* light of creation. The *yin* is the primal cosmic **ocean**; passive, feminine, instinctual; the deep nourishing earth. The *yang* is the sky, the mountains, the dry light, air and fire, all solar animals and birds. Fabulous beasts like the **dragon** or **phoenix** symbolise the interaction of the two.

YMIR (*See* AESIR, CREATION MYTH, GIANTS, NORSE MYTH)

In Norse **creation myth** the first created being, a **giant** born of the ice melting from the streams of Niflheim (the cold, cloudy land north of the abyss) and sparks of **fire** from Muspelheim (a land of fire to the south). These mingled in the great void Ginnungagap and quickened into life, and so Ymir was born. There are several versions of what happened after this, as given by Snorri in the *Eddas*. One is that the Frost Giants came from his feet as he slept and, from his left armpit, the giant Buri was born. Or Buri was set free by the primordial **cow** Audhumla licking the salty sea ice. Buri's son Borr married Ymir's daughter, Bestia, who bore the first three Aesir (gods). These, **Odin**, Vili and Vé, killed Ymir, whose **blood** flooded the world, killing every Frost Giant except Bergelmir, who fathered a new race of giants forever hostile to the Aesir. Another version is that Audhumla licked the sons of Borr out of the sea-ice. A third version is that Audhumla emerged first from the ice, and that she nourished Ymir.

The essence of the myth is of the **sacrifice** of Ymir and the resulting formation of the world, as in the **Vedic** (Indian) myth of **Purusha**. It is possible that in origin both the Indian Purusha and the Norse Ymir were the same.

YOGA (*See* **BUDDHISM, HINDUISM**)
From a **Sanskrit** root *jog*, meaning 'yoke', 'union', 'conjunction' (as in the English conjugal), in India the technical term for one of the six Dársanas or philosophical schools, its foundation ascribed to Patanjali, author of the Yogasûtras (*c.*200 BC). The term describes the objective of the school: worldly withdrawal to attain union or at-one-ness (atonement) with the spiritual essence (**Brahma**), so relieving the **soul** of the five errors of mind (error, knowledge, imagination, memory and sleep). Yoga requires the practice of various asānas or bodily attitudes, these exercises leading to clarity of mind and also to siddhis; powers said to include telepathy, clairvoyance, clairaudience, suspended animation, **shape-shifting** and far memory. But these are secondary to gaining the goal of samādhi.

YONI (*See* **DEVI, HINDUISM, LINGA, TANTRAS**)
In India and Tibet, the vagina and vulva, usually including the womb, and symbolised as a round jar, the female creative energy as dedicated to the goddess **Devi** in her aspect as Shakti. It is worshipped on its own as a symbol of the **mother-goddess** and the earth's fertility or, more commonly, in combination with the male symbol (*see* **linga**). In the latter context it is the equivalent of the Chinese *yin* power, as the lingam is of *yang*. The oldest centres of yoni-worship were probably **river**-sources, springs and **wells**; wherever **water** gushes out or emerges from the earth.

YORUBA (*See* **AFRICAN MYTH, CREATION MYTH**)
In the beginning, say the Yoruba of Nigeria, below the **sun**-god Olorun was nothing but a world of **water** ruled by his brother Olokun. Olorun sent down his son Obatala to set the globe of the earth in the sea, where it broke into many pieces. The first creature to grow on one of the isles so formed was Agbon, the palm-tree. From it Obatala immediately made wine, which he drank, and so fell asleep. Olorun angrily sent down his daughter Oduduwa, the earth-goddess, along with Aje, goddess of wealth, who took the form of a hen which, immediately starting to scratch up the earth, made it habitable. Odudawa sowed the millet and other seeds Olorun had given her, so that the new earth fruited. Then, as Oludumare the Creator, Olorun came down to the world and, by the first palm-tree, which is the *axis mundi*, convened all the gods in the first great council. Each of these sixteen gods became the **ancestor** of a Yoruba clan, and each clan built a suburb of the holy city Ife-Ife round the centre that Olorun ruled. Yet they all quarrelled about their precedence, as people do, so that today the names of the Yoruba gods and goddesses vary as much as the above creation myth.

For, in another version, there were not 16 but 1,700 gods (Orisha), who demanded Oludumare's abdication. As a result, the universe came to a halt after just eight days. They begged his pardon, and he restored order.

Or, yet again, Olorun sent not Obatala to earth, but another god called Orishanla who, having created the firm earth, moulded the first sixteen human beings in various colours and shapes. Yet only Olorun could give them the breath of life. When Orishanla hid to see how Olorun did this, Olorun, who sees everything, cast him into a deep sleep, so that Orishanla never did learn the secret of life.

YSBADDADEN (*See* **CULHWCH, GIANTS, HAWTHORN**)

YSEULT (*See* **TRISTAN**)

YU (*See* **CHINESE MYTH, FLOOD**)

According to the Chinese *Shu Ching* (*Book of History*), this semi-legendary emperor and renowned hydraulic engineer was asked by Shun, a divine king, to contain the waters of the **flood**. For thirteen years, never once going home, he directed operations so that the flood-waters were not only drained from the land but organised irrigation began, so that the waters were tamed to fertilise the fields, leading to common agricultural advantage.

YUDHISTHIRA (*See* **DRAUPADI,** *MAHABHARATA*)

YUGA (*See* **BRAHMA, GOLDEN AGE, HINDUISM**)

Refers, in **Hindu** cosmogony, to each of the four ages of the world: *Krita Yuga* ('**Golden Age**'), *Treta Yuga* (Silver), *Dvapara Yuga* (Bronze) and *Kali Yuga* (Iron). Each endures 12,000 'divine years', a divine year being 360 solar years. The total of the four gives a single 'Day of **Brahma**'. At the end of each *Kali Yuga* the tired god closes his **eye** and falls asleep. All creation returns to the cosmic womb until, after a similar period of night, Brahma wakes up again, and a new universe comes into being. We are now, by common agreement, deep into the *Kali Yuga*, and may expect to sleep soon.

YULE (*See* **SATURN, TREES**)

From Gallic '*gule*', meaning **wheel**, alias the bottom point of the turning of the old year into the new, leading to twelve nights of chaos (the twelve Nights of Christmas) during which, following the winter solstice, the dead rule. Only after this period may the new year be created and born from the ashes of the old. Long before it was the festival of **Christ**'s birth it was the festival of **Adonis**, **Attis**, **Dionysus**, **Odin**, **Osiris**, and **Tammuz**, all slain either as part of the rite of seasonal fertility or as part of the quest for knowledge that leads the seeker through the belly of the **whale** to be reborn. The yule log is **oak**, the cosmic tree of **Druids** and other ancient priesthoods. The Christmas **tree** that stands in almost every house in the West once a year symbolises the light that will come out of the winter darkness. Out of despair, hope is born.

YURLUNGUR (*See* **ABORIGINES, PYTHON, SERPENT**)

The world-snake of Australian Aboriginal myth, the great Father **Python**, the **rainbow-serpent**. His voice is thunder, his existence guarantees the rain making desert survival possible, which when it falls brings the snakes out of the ground and green shoots from the soil. As in Chinese myth he is the celestial **dragon** of fertility, yet (as in the West) he is also the dreaded **Loathly Worm**. In primitive belief there is no real distinction between good and evil, fertility and death, for each guarantees the other.

Z

ZARATAN (See FABULOUS BEASTS, WHALE)

An old Moslem name for a genus of fabulous marine beast so vast yet still on the sea-surface that sailors think it an island and land on it, but then it sinks and drowns them. A mythic inflation of the whale, it is usually identified as such. On the first voyage of Sindbad, he and several shipmates land on a little island resembling a green meadow. They start to eat and drink, but the island trembles and begins to sink. The others escape, but Sindbad is left behind, clinging to a spar. In *Orlando Furioso*, the Italian poet Ariosto (1474–1533) retails the same account, of a whale mistaken for an island. A millennium earlier, while sailing to the Isles in the West, the Irish **St Brendan** and his monks land on the back of a whale. In a thirteenth-century account by the Persian al-Qaswini (in *Wonders of Creation*), the sailors land on an isle rich in greenery. They dig pits and light fires; the isle moves and turns out to be a vast turtle. The name 'zaratan' comes from the *Book of Animals* by the ninth-century Moslem zoologist, al-Jahiz, who reports the tale to debunk it, claiming that it 'outdoes even the boldest, most imaginative piece of fiction'. Maybe so, but it persists, being found in the Greek bestiary of Alexandria, where it stands for the whore of Proverbs; in a ninth-century Anglo-Saxon bestiary, where it is the **Devil**, and likewise in Milton's *Paradise Lost*, where it is Satan, 'stretched out huge in length'.

ZARATHUSTRA (See NIETZSCHE, PARSEES, ZOROASTER)

ZEN BUDDHISM (See BODHIDHARMA, BUDDHISM, JAPANESE MYTH)

Associated especially with Japan, which it reached following the spread in China during the sixth century AD of the Ch'an Tsung ('inner light') school of Buddhism as taught by **Bodhidharma**, the essence of Zen is the rejection of ritualised or habitual thought-patterns. The school possesses neither ritual, dogma nor written texts. Zen masters teach by example rather than words, so as not to betray what cannot accurately be written or spoken of. One teaching technique is a device called the *koan*, designed to baffle or corner the rationality of novices seeking enlightenment. It usually takes the form of a paradoxical or apparently meaningless question. Famously: 'What is the sound of one hand clapping?' The search for a rational answer (there is none) builds up mental tension until the aspirant reaches a point where all intellectual ideas and concepts dissolve. 'The mind has first to be attuned to the Unconscious,' wrote the modern Zen master Daisetz Teitaro Suzuki, explaining that Zen arts are meant not for utilitarian purposes or even aesthetic pleasure, but 'to train the mind; indeed, to bring it into contact with the ultimate reality . . . One has to transcend technique so that the art becomes an "artless art" growing out of the Unconscious.'[1]

1. *Zen in the Art of Archery*, Eugen Herrigel, Routledge & Kegan Paul, London, 1972, from the Foreword by D.T. Suzuki.

ZEND-AVESTA (*See* PARSEES, PERSIAN MYTH, ZOROASTRIANISM)

An erroneous name for the **Zoroastrian** sacred writings, the *Avesta*, derived from use of the phrase '*āpastāk va zand*' in reference to the original text. Zand, or zend, means 'commentary'. Zend-Avesta thus means a commentary or gloss on the *Avesta*, though there have been assertions that Zend was the ancient Persian language in which the Avesta was written. Yet the grammar and vocabulary of the Gathas (the earliest portions of the Avesta) closely match the **Sanskrit** of the *Rig-Veda*. Mingled with treatises on botany, astronomy, medicine, agriculture, philosophy, etc., the books, which supply our sole source of knowledge as to early Persian cults and myths, contain prayers, moral precepts and codes of conduct. It is said that the original work dates from the lifetime of **Zoroaster**, though its grammatical comparisons with the *Rig-Veda* suggest a revised dating of up to 700 years earlier both for the Avesta and for Zoroaster. It is said to have been destroyed, either during the invasion of **Alexander the Great** in 328 BC, or later, during the Arab conquests, and reconstructed either during the Sassanian period (AD 224–651), or by the **Parsees**, after their flight to India from the **Islamic** invasion during the mid-seventh century.

ZEUS (*See* GREEK MYTH)

Quintessential Indo-European sky-father, name derived from **Sanskrit** *dyaus* (*see* **Dyaus-Pita**), from *div*, 'to shine'. In Greek myth this omnipotent god, supreme over all other deities of **Olympus**, is said to be the youngest son of **Cronus** and **Rhea**, who saved him from being swallowed at birth by his father (the fate of his other brothers and sisters) by offering Cronos a **stone** wrapped in swaddling clothes. Cronus was duped: later Zeus made him vomit up his first five children, released the imprisoned offspring of **Ouranos** his castrated grandfather, defeated Cronus and the other **Titans**, then locked them up for ever in the bowels of the universe. Like **Indra**, **Thor** and **Jupiter** armed with the **thunderbolt**, with every attribute of divinity united in him but that of universal **creation**, this lord of the winds, cloud and rain, was worshipped on high places from Olympus to **Parnassus**; and as lord of **divination** was worshipped at the **oracles** of **Delphi** and Dodona. All-knowing, all-seeing, wise ruler over gods and mortals alike, he chastised the evil, protected the weak and ordained Fate. Yet, among his many functions, that of procreation was paramount.

As the god of Indo-Europeans (Achaeans) who *c.*1550 BC invaded Greece, he 'married' **Hera**, **mother-goddess** of the previous culture, thus associating her with his rule, but had many other liaisons. His first wife was Metis ('Wisdom') but, **Hesiod** says, **Gaia** and Ouranos warned him that her children would be stronger than he. Swallowing both mother and unborn child, he came to embody Wisdom (**Athene**, goddess of wisdom, was born from his brow). Next he married Themis, the law regulating social and moral order. Her children included the **Fates**. The Titaness Mnemosyne, his wife for nine nights, bore nine daughters, the **Muses**; the Oceanid Eurynome bore the Three **Graces**; **Demeter**, whom he raped in **bull**-form, bore **Persephone**. Only then, it is said, he came to Hera in the form of a **cuckoo**, on whom she took pity, for (as Pausanias tells it), the winter was cold, and the bird seemed frozen. But Hera gave in to him only when he promised to marry her. She became his wife, but the marriage was not successful: they fought constantly over his other amours; she never stopped persecuting his many other conquests and their offspring. He seduced numerous **nymphs**, including Mera, Antiope and Callisto; many other demi-goddesses and many mortal women, including Semele, mother of **Dionysus**, Danaë the mother of **Perseus** (to whom he manifested as a shower of **gold**), **Europa** (on whom in bull-form he fathered the Cretan **Minos**) and Leda, mother of the **twins** Castor and Pollux, whom he visited as a **swan**. Alcmene, whom he visited in the form of her husband, Amphitryon, bore **Hercules**. Indeed, Zeus was so busy with love-affairs it is a wonder he had time to consider the other affairs of gods and men, far less function as 'Ombrios', 'Rain-god'; 'Soter', 'Saviour', 'Gamelios', 'God of Marriage' and 'Teleios', 'Giver of Completeness'.

ZODIAC (*See* CIRCLE, TWELVE, WHEEL)

From Greek, meaning: 'circle of animals'. In apparent motion against the background stars, the **sun, moon** and planets ('wanderers') occupy a narrow band of constellations that form the zodiac. This circle of sky, called the ecliptic, is divided into **twelve** sectors, each of 30°, each forming one zodiacal sign. These signs, in astrological usage known as the 'star signs', were classified into various groups by Ptolemy in the first century AD. Thus six are masculine and six are feminine; four each are Cardinal, Fixed or Mutable; three each are Earth, Air, Fire or Water signs; and each is said to be governed by a particular Greek or Roman deity.

Aries (cardinal, fire) is said by Ptolemy to be ruled by **Athena**; Taurus (fixed, earth) by **Venus**; Gemini (mutable, air) by **Apollo**; Cancer (cardinal, water) by **Mercury**; Leo (fixed, fire) by **Jupiter**; Virgo (mutable, earth) by **Ceres**; Libra (cardinal, air) by **Vulcan**; Scorpio (fixed, water) by **Mars**; Sagittarius (mutable, fire) by **Diana**; Capricorn (cardinal, earth) by **Vesta**, Aquarius (fixed, air) by **Juno**; and Pisces (mutable, water) by **Neptune**.

Yet the signs are much older than the Ptolemaic attributions, dating back at least to 400 BC, and there are indications of an earlier thirteen-sign zodiac, equating to a thirteen-month year. The thirteenth sign has provisionally been identified as Arachne the **Spider** (see **Twelve**).

ZOMBIES (*See* AFRICAN MYTH, SORCERY, VOODOO, ZULU)

It is said of Haitian **voodoo** sorcerers that they can partially reanimate newly dead corpses, turning them into witless slaves called 'zombies'. The term derives from the African word *zumbi*, as found in the Congo, where it means '**fetish**' or 'enslaved spirit', referring to individuals physically alive who have lost their **souls**, or had them 'caught' by a magician, and who thus cannot distinguish between good and evil. Such loss is usually considered a result of sorcery. The **Zulu** of Natal say that such people 'walk zombe', and tell of two brothers, Sipo and Vamba. The latter became sick and suddenly old, and soon died. Sipo buried him, though his body was still soft: an indication of **sorcery**. Next morning the grave was open and the body gone. Sipo travelled in search of the sorcerer and came to a farm where an army of labourers worked without song or animation. Among them was Vamba, grey-faced and mute, his tongue slit. Sipo took his brother home, but Vamba soon died, and this time *rigor mortis* did set in.

In Dahomey (*see* **Fon**) the word refers to the **python**-god; in modern voodoo usage in Haiti the serpent-god Damballah is supposedly called upon to animate the corpse. Yet it may be that zombies are neither mythical nor the reanimated dead, but victims of coma brought on by the drug tetrodotoxin.

This, the 'fugu' poison of Japan, is found in blowfish tissue. A small dose causes external anaesthesia; a larger one is said to trigger 'out-of-the-body' experiences, while still greater quantities lead to the apparent death of the victim. Even the brain ceases detectable function. Deep in coma, the victim is buried, then later disinterred and 'reanimated' by the application of a partial antidote. Yet the reanimation is incomplete, the brain being permanently damaged; so creating the ideal witless slave who can never testify against the 'sorcerer' who uses him as cheap labour.

ZOROASTER/ZOROASTRIANISM (*See* CONCORDANCE)

The Persian/Iranian **prophet** Zoroaster (or Zarathustra) is said to have reconciled the **religion** of the **Magi** with that of the kings, so creating the system of belief that bears his name. He may have lived *c*.660–583 BC, during which era the *Avesta*, or Zoroastrian sacred writings, are said to have been set down. Yet comparison of these texts with the **Vedas** of India suggests a date for both prophet and texts as early as the fourteenth century BC.

Whatever his date of birth, the myth of Zoroaster's life is full of marvels. Born amid universal rejoicing, at his birth he did not wail, but laughed. Aged twenty, he left home to seek the holiest man in the land. Observing seven years of silence in a **mountain-cave**, he received **archangelic** revelations; thus he learned that **Ahura Mazda**, alias God the Creator, is One. Like **Buddha** or **Christ**, but before either, he began to wander and preach, travelling as far as Afghanistan. Receiving further revelations en route, he was **initiated** into the arts of domesticating animals, working metals, using healing herbs and the control of water for irrigation. Then Angra Mainya, alias the 'Destructive Spirit' (*see* **Ahriman**) came to tempt him, offering him an earthly kingdom, just as the **Devil** later tried to tempt Christ, but Zoroaster denied him. Later he converted kings and fought holy wars before he was assassinated, aged seventy-seven.

Zoroastrianism did not become Persia's official religion until the rise of the Sassanian dynasty in the third century AD, taking its surviving form only after the seventh century, when the **Parsees** (Persians) fled to India. The teaching involves the unity of creation in Ahura Mazda; a unity which, however, manifests in a dual form. Ahura Mazda is eternally opposed by Ahriman, or Angra Mainya, also called Druj, 'the Lie'. It is the task of all men to decide which side they are on: Good or Evil. Yet it is unclear how far Zoroaster preached this clear-cut **dualism** which in time became so much a part of Persian thought, and which has had such a deep influence on Judaeo-**Christian** concepts, of God and the Devil as two utterly opposed and separate forces.

ZULU (*See* ABAKULU-BANTU, AFRICAN MYTH)

The elaborate cosmology of the Zulu people of Natal in South Africa tells how their creator-god, Unkulunkulu, led the first men out of the reed-bed where they had emerged from an exploding reed stem. This 'old one' taught them all they knew, including all social and religious laws. Yet this High God is remote and incomprehensible: nothing is known of him save that he controls the lightning as uDumakade, 'he who thunders from far-off times'.

Such lightning is also seen as the excreta of a **thunderbird**. Harmless sheet lightning is said to be male; but dangerous forked lightning is seen as female. There is also a goddess said to make the **rain** and associated with the **rainbow**, which is believed to be the rafter of her sky-hut. She is a **virgin**, and once descended to earth to teach people how to make beer, and to plant seed and harvest it.

It is also said of Unkulunkulu that he sent the chameleon Unwaba to tell men they would never die, but Unwaba went so slow that the god changed his mind, and asked the lizard Intulo to carry another message, telling men they must die. Intulo not only overtook Unwaba but was back before Unwaba arrived, to find that Intulo's message had been accepted. Versions of this tale exist throughout Africa. The creator sends a dilatory **dog**, sheep or chameleon with one message, then changes his mind and sends a faster toad, lizard or **hare** with a contradictory announcement. No reason is given for the change of mind. Gods do not have to give reasons.

Unkulunkulu responded to this lost **immortality** by instituting marriage so that children might be born, and by providing men with doctors to treat illness, and with **fire** to prepare food.

The Zulu respect the **spirits** of their **ancestors**, said to live under the earth or in the sky, who send sickness if not regularly offered milk, beer and cattle. During illness, **diviners** are consulted to learn which ancestor is responsible. Male ancestors, thought to be reasonable, will repair ill-luck if propitiated, but capricious female ancestors may well let the misfortune continue even after due amends have been made.

Zulu *Isanusi* ('Wise Men') speak of an ancient brotherhood originating in Egypt at the time of Cheops, *c.*2600 BC. Its highest grade comprises the Abakulu-Bantu, perfected beings who, like the **Buddhist Bodhisattvas**, may choose whether or not to remain incarnate on this earth.

Concordance
of Themes

ABDUCTIONS
Abductions, Adonis, Enoch, Oisin, Persephone, Pied Piper, Tamlin, True Thomas, UFOs.

AFRICAN MYTH
Abakulu-Bantu, Adu Ogyinae, African Myth, Anansi, Ashanti, Bori, Buganda, Bunyoro, Bushmen, Crocodile, Dogon, Dragon, Drum, Fon, Ghoul, Hippopotamus, Hottentots, Huveane, Hydra, Hyena, Imana, Juju, Kalunga, Khadir, Kikuyu, Mangu, Medicine, Mokele, Mwuetsi, Ngai, Olorun, Python, Rain-Queens, Sorcery, Spider, Swahili, Voodoo, Yoruba, Zulu.

AMERINDIAN MYTH (*See* **NATIVE AMERICAN MYTH**)

ANGELS (*See* **SUPERNATURAL BEINGS**)

ANIMALS
Animals, Antelope, Bat, Bear, Bee, Buffalo, Bull, Cat, Cow, Coyote, Crocodile, Deer, Dog, Dolphin, Elephant, Fox, Goat, Hippopotamus, Horse, Hyena, Lamb, Lion, Monkey, Pig, Ram, Scorpion, Seals, Spider, Stag, Swine, Tiger, Tortoise, Turtle, Whale, Wolf.

ARTHURIAN MYTH (*See* **BRITISH, CELTIC, IRISH/SCOTTISH, WELSH MYTH**)
Arthurian Myth, Bedivere, Culhwch, Excalibur, Fisher King, Fool, Galahad, Games, Gawain, Geoffrey of Monmouth, Glastonbury, Green Knight, Guinevere, Holy Grail, Holy Lance, Joseph of Arimathea, Knight, Lancelot, Logres, *Mabinogion*, Malory, Merlin, Mordred, Morgan Le Fay, Morgause, Nimüe, Pelles, Perceval, Round Table, Sword-Bridge, Tristan, Uther, Wasteland, Ygraine, Yseult.

ARTIFICIAL BEINGS
Achilles Heel, Frankenstein, Golem, Robots, Science Fiction, Talos.

ASSYRIAN MYTH (*See* **BABYLONIAN, SUMERIAN MYTH**)
Assyrian Myth, Enlil, Ishtar, Marduk.

ASTRONOMY AND MYTH
Astronomy and Myth, Comets, Dogon, Greek Myth, Hyades, Inca Myth, Mayan Myth, Moon, Neptune, Orion, Pleiades, Roman Myth, Sirius, Sun, Zodiac.

AUTHORS
Aeschylus, Andersen, Apuleius, Aristophanes, Ballard, Barrie, Berossus, Blake, Borges, Bulfinch, Bulwer-Lytton, Burroughs E.R., Burroughs W.S., Campbell, Carroll, Clarke, Cocteau, Coleridge, Dante, Eliade, Frazer, Freud, Geoffrey of Monmouth, Graves, Haggard, Hesiod, Homer, Joyce, Jung, Kipling, Kirk, Lang, Lewis, Longfellow, Lovecraft, Macpherson, Malory, Mandeville, Omar, Orwell, Ovid, Rumi, Shakespeare, Shelley M.W., Shelley P.B., Stapledon, Streiber, Sturluson, Swift, Tolkien, Velikovsky, Verne, Virgil, Wells, Yeats.

AZTEC MYTH (*See* **NATIVE AMERICAN MYTH**)
Aztec Myth, Cannibalism, Coatlicue, Huitzilopochtli, Quetzalcoatl, Sacrifice, Tezcatlipoca, Tlaloc, Xipetotec, Xiuhtecuhtli, Xochipili/Xochiquetzal, Xolotl.

BABYLONIAN MYTH (*See* **ASSYRIAN, SUMERIAN MYTH**)
Anu, Babylonian Myth, Berossus, Enlil, Gilgamesh, Ishtar, Marduk, Shamash, Sin, Tiamat.

BIRDS
Cock, Crow, Cuckoo, Dove, Eagle, Goose, Hawk, Ibis, Owl, Peacock, Phoenix, Rain-Bird, Raven, Robin, Roc, Simurgh, Stork, Swallow, Swan, Thunderbird, Woodpecker, Wren.

BOOKS/TEXTS
Arabian Nights, Beowulf, Bhagavad Gita, Bible, Book of Invasions, *Edda, Gododdin, Iliad, Kalevala*, Koran, *Mabinogion, Mahabharata, Odyssey, Popol Vuh*, Puranas, *Ramayana*, Ras Shamrah, *Táin Bó Cualnge, Tibetan Book of the Dead, Upanishads*, Vedas.

BRITISH MYTH (*See* **ARTHURIAN, CELTIC, IRISH/SCOTTISH, WELSH MYTH**)
Abaros, Albion, Bel, Beltane, Beowulf, Blake, Brutus, Celtic Myth, Cernunnos, Fire-Festivals, Geoffrey of Monmouth, Giants, Glastonbury, Hallowe'en, Herne the Hunter, Irish Myth, Iseult, King Lear, May Day, Puck, Robin Hood, Scottish Myth, Shakespeare, Sheela-Na-Gig, Teutonic Myth, Vortigern, Welsh Myth, Wild Hunt.

BUDDHISM (*See* **INDIAN MYTH**)
Amida, Arhat, Avalokiteshvara, Bodhidharma, Bodhisattva, Buddha, Buddhism, Dharma, Hsi Wang Mu, Karma, Maitreya, Mara, Maya, Nirvana, Om, Samādhi, Samsara, Tibet, *Tibetan Book of the Dead*, Yoga.

CELTIC MYTH (*See* **BRITISH, IRISH/SCOTTISH, WELSH MYTH**)
Arthurian Myth, Bards, Celtic Myth, Druids, Epona, Esus, *Mabinogion*, Mabon, Maponus, Taranis, Teutates.

CHINESE MYTH
Bodhidharma, Chinese Myth, Chuang Tsu, Confucius, Dragon, Fox, Hsi Wang Mu, *Hsien*, Huang-Ti, Jade, Lao Tsu, Rain-Bird, *Yin* and *Yang*, Yu.

CHRISTIANITY (*See* **ARTHURIAN, JUDAEO-CHRISTIAN MYTH**)
Angels, Antichrist, Apocalypse, Armageddon, Bible, Christ, Christianity, Columba, Cross, Demons, Devil, Dove, Easter, Fall, Heaven, Hell, Holy Ghost, Holy Grail, Holy Lance, Joseph of Arimathea, Lamb, Loathly Worm, Magdalene, Manichaeism, Messiah, St Michael, New Jerusalem, Origen, Original Sin, St Patrick, St Paul, St Peter, Prester John, Purgatory, Rapture, Resurrection, Revelation, Satan, Second Coming, Shroud of Turin, Transfiguration, Transubstantiation, Trinity, Virgin Mary, Virginity.

CORN-GODS (*See* **FERTILITY**)

CREATION MYTH
Adam, Adu Ogyinae, Anu, Atum, Creation Myth, Cronus, Dogon, Ea/Enki, Erlik, Fon, Gaia, Huveane, Imana, Kici Manitou, Mwuetsi, Ngai, Swahili, Ta'aroa, Taiowa, Viracocha, Yahweh, Yoruba.

DEATH GODDESSES (*See* **GREAT GODDESS, MOON**)
Badb, Cailleach, Cerridwen, Coatlicue, Hecate, Kali, Karina, Lilith, Loathly Lady, Medusa, Morgan Le Fay, Morrigan, Owl, Triple Goddess.

DEMONS (*See* **SUPERNATURAL BEINGS**)
DOG/DOG-RELATED
Anubis, Cerberus, Coyote, Dog, Fenrir, Garm, Hecate, Sirius, Werewolf, Wolf.
DRAGON (*See* **SERPENT**)
Dragon, Fabulous Beasts, Fafnir, Grendel, Hydra, Leviathan, Loathly Worm, Tiamat.
DRAGON-SLAYERS
Beowulf, St George, Marduk, St Michael, Sigurd, Yahweh.
DYING GODS (*See* **FERTILITY**)
Adonis, Attis, Baal, Baldur, Christ, Corn-Gods, Dionysus, Dumuzi, Dying Gods, Galahad, Mithra, Odin, Orpheus, Osiris, Tammuz.
EARTH LORE/RELIGION
Dragon, Earth Mother, Earth Mounds, Glastonbury, Megalithic Myths, Sacred Geometry, Serpent, Stone.
EARTH MOTHER/GODDESS (*See* **GREAT GODDESS, MOON**)
EARTHLY PARADISE (*See* **OTHERWORLD**)
EGYPTIAN MYTH
Akhenaton, Amon, Anubis, Apis, Atlantis, Atum, Cleopatra, Egyptian Myth, Geb, Hathor, Horus, Ibis, Isis, *Ka*, Maat, Moses, Mysteries, Nepthys, Nuit, Nun, Osiris, Ptah, Pyramids, Ra, Set, Shu, Sothis, Sphinx, Tefnut, Thoth.
ELEMENTALS (*See* **SUPERNATURAL BEINGS**)
ESKIMO MYTH
Eskimo Myth, Fox, Native American Myth, Raven, Whale.
FABULOUS BEASTS
Basilisk, Behemoth, Bestiary, Bigfoot, Borges, Centaur, Chimera, Cyclopes, Dragon, Fabulous Beasts, Golem, Gorgon, Griffon, Harpies, Hydra, Kelpie, Kraken, Kujata, Lake Monsters, Lamia, Mandeville, Mermaids, Minotaur, Naga, Pegasus, Phoenix, Questing Beast, Rain-Bird, Roc, Sasquatch, Simurgh, Sirens, Sphinx, Unicorn, Yeti, Zaratan.
FAIRY LORE
Brownies, Changelings, Dimensions, Dwarves, Earth Mounds, Elves, Fairies, Gentry, Glamour, Illusion, Incubi, Iron, Kirk, Leprechaun, Oisin, Pixies, Sidhe, Tamlin, Tir nan Og, True Thomas, Tuatha dé Danaan.
FAIRY-TALES
Andersen, Bluebeard, Cinderella, Cocteau, Disney, Fairy-Tales, Grimm, Lang, Perrault, Sleeping Beauty.
FAMOUS MEN
Alexander, Ashoka, Barbarossa, Charlemagne, Cid, Hassan Ibn Sabbah, Kennedy, Mahdi.
FATHER-GODS
Baal, Dagda, Dyaus-Pita, El, Father-Gods, Indra, Jupiter, Kalunga, Thor, Yahweh, Zeus.
FEMMES FATALES
Cleopatra, Delilah, Draupadi, *Femmes Fatales*, Garbo, Helen of Troy, Jezebel, Monroe, Salome, Sirens.
FERTILITY ANIMALS AND THEMES
Abductions, Cannibalism, Castration, Circumcision, Cock, Corn-Gods, Hare, Rain-Making.
FERTILITY DEITIES/SPIRITS
Adonis, Attis, Baal, Baldur, Christ, Cybele, Diana, Dionysus, Dying Gods, Frey and Freya, Frigga, Hiram Abiff, Inanna, Ishtar, Lakshmi, Llew, Mithra, Ninkhursag, Orpheus, Osiris, Persephone, Priapus, Silvanus, Tam-

muz, Varuna, Xipetotec, Xochiquetzal.
FERTILITY FESTIVALS (*See* **SEASONAL FESTIVALS**)
FINNISH MYTH
Kalevala, Knot.
FIRE/FIRE DEITIES
Agni, Ahura Mazda, Bel/Belinus, Fire, Flood, Hephaestus, Hestia, Moloch, Pele, Prometheus, Sun, Vesta, Volcanoes, Vulcan, Water, Wren, Xiuhtecuhtli.
FIRE FESTIVALS
Beltane, Fire-Festivals, Hallowe'en.
FISH/FISH-MEN
Dolphin, Fintan, Fish, Fisher King, Flood, Manu, Oannes, Salmon, Whale.
FLIGHT, MAGICAL
Bellerophon, Daedalus, Flight, Golden Fleece, Pegasus, Roc, Santa Claus, Shamanism, Vimanas.
FLOOD MYTH
Ark, Atlantis, Deucalion, Enlil, Fire, Flood Myth, Gilgamesh, Manu, Maori Myth, Noah, Rainbow, South American Myth, Taikomol, Utnapishtim, Water, Yu.
FLORA (*See* **TREES**)
Apple, Fig, Gilgamesh, Golden Bough, Holly, *Hsien*, Lily, Lotus, Mandrake, Mistletoe, Narcissus, Rose, Silvanus.
FRUITS (*See* **FLORA**)
GAMES/MAGICAL CONTESTS/RIDDLES
Draupadi, Flying Dutchman, Games, Gawain, Gnostic Myth, Green Knight, Magical Contests, Riddles, Sphinx, Taliesin.
GHOSTS
Ancestor-Worship, Flying Dutchman, Ghost Dance, Ghost Wife, Holy Ghost, Necromancy, Phantom Hitch-Hikers, Spirits.
GIANTS
Aesir, Atlas, Balor, Cwlhwch, Earth Mounds, Enoch, Finn MacCool, Fire, Flood, Ghoul, Giants, Jotunheim, Megalithic Myths, Purusha, Titans, Ysbaddaden.
GRAIL MYTH (*See* **ARTHURIAN MYTH**)
GREAT GODDESS (*See* **DEATH GODDESS, MOON**)
Amaterasu, Astarte, Athene, Black Virgin, Cerridwen, Coatlicue, Cybele, Devi, Earth Mother, Eve, Gaia, Hera, Inanna, Ishtar, Isis, Kali, Lakshmi, Mati-Syra-Zemlya, Matrika, Mother Goddess, Nerthus, Parvati, Rhea, Saraswati, Sophia, Triple Goddess.
GREEK MYTH
Achilles, Actaeon, Aeneas, Aesop, Agamemnon, Amazons, Aphrodite, Apollo, Ares, Artemis, Athene, Atlas, Asclepius, Bellerophon, Cadmus, Calypso, Centaur, Cerberus, Charon, Circe, Clashing Rocks, Croesus, Cronus, Cyclopes, Daedalus, Danaë, Delphi, Demeter, Deucalion, Dionysus, Dioscuri, Eleusis, Empedocles, Eros, Europa, Eurydice, Fates, Furies, Gaia, Ganymede, Golden Fleece, Gorgon, Graces, Greek Myth, Hades, Harpies, Hecate, Helen, Helios, Hera, Hercules, Hermes, Hesiod, Hesperides, Hestia, Homer, Horae, Hyades, Hydra, Hyperion, Hypnos, Icarus, *Iliad*, Jason, Maenads, Medea, Medusa, Midas, Minos, Muses, Mysteries, Narcissus, Nereids, Nymphs, Ocean, Oceanus, *Odyssey*, Olympus, Orestes, Orion, Orpheus, Ouranos, Pan, Pandora, Paris, Parnassus, Pegasus, Persephone, Perseus, Phaethon, Phoebus, Plato, Pleiades, Polyphemus, Poseidon, Priam, Priapus, Procrustes, Prometheus, Proteus, Pythagoras, Python, Rhea, Satyrs, Scylla, Silenus, Sirens, Sisyphus, Sphinx, Styx,

Tantalus, Telemachus, Tethys, Theseus, Thetis, Tiresias, Titans, Triton, Troy, Typhon, Uranus, Zeus.

HEALING/HEALING DEITIES (*See* **IMMORTALITY**)
Asclepius, Christ, Diancecht, Gilgamesh, Healing, Thoth.

HERBS (*See* **FLORA**)

HERMETIC MYTH (*See* **MAGIC**)
Agrippa, Hermes Trismegistus, Paracelsus, Philosopher's Stone, Qabalah, Stone.

HERO MYTH
Beowulf, Bonnie Prince Charlie, Fairy-Tales, Gilgamesh, Hercules, Hero Myth, Hiawatha, Perseus, Popol Vuh, Quest, Robin Hood, Sigmund, Sigurd, Task, Test, Theseus, William Tell.

HINDUISM (*See* **INDIAN MYTH, RELIGION**)

HORNED GODS (*See* **RUSTIC DEITIES**)
Actaeon, Cernunnos, Green Man, Herne, Horned Gods, Pan, Robin Hood.

HORSE/HORSE-RELATED
Bellerophon, Centaur, Demeter, Epona, Horse, Pegasus, Poseidon, Rhiannon, Sleipnir.

HUNTER DEITIES
Artemis, Diana, Herne, Orion, Wild Hunt.

IMMORTALITY
Gilgamesh, Haggard, *Hsien*, Immortality, Jainism, Kali, Kali Yuga, Kalpa, Kamadeva, Khadir, Koshchei, Reincarnation.

INDIAN MYTH
Agni, Ahalya, Ananta, Arjuna, Aryan Controversy, Ashoka, Atman, Avatar, *Bhagavad Gita*, Bharata, Bhima, Bhishma, Brahma, Brahmanism, Buddha, Buddhism, Dakini, Daksha, Damayanti, Deva, Devi, Draupadi, Durga, Dyaus-Pita, Gandharvas, Ganesa, Garuda, Gommatesvara, Hanuman, Hinduism, Indian Myth, Indra, Jagannath, Jainism, Kali, Kali Yuga, *Kalpa*, Kartikeya, Kipling, Krishna, Lakshmi, Loka, *Mahabharata*, Manu, Mara, Maruts, Matrika, Maya, Meru, Mithra, Naga, Parvati, Prithivi, Puranas, Purusha, Rakshasas, Rama, Ramayana, Ravana, Rishis, Rudra, Sanskrit, Saraswati, Sati, Seven Wise Masters, Shiva, Sita, Surya, Tantras, Trimurti, Vajra, Varaha, Varuna, Vayu, Vedas, Vimanas, Vishnu, Vritra, Yama, Yoga, Yu, Yudhisthira, Yuga.

INSECTS (*See* **ANIMALS**)

INTOXICANTS
Amanita muscaria, Berserkers, Dionysus, Haoma, Soma.

IRISH/SCOTTISH MYTH
Angus MacOg, Badb, Balor, Banshee, Bodach, Bonnie Prince Charlie, Bran the Blessed, Bran MacFebal, St Brendan, Brigit, Cailleach, Celtic Myth, Changelings, St Columba, Conchobar, Cormac, Cuchulainn, Curses, Dagda, Danu, Deirdre, Diancecht, Diarmuid, Finn/Fingal, *Finnegans Wake*, Fintan, Fir Bolg, Fomorians, *Geis*, Glamour, Goibniu, Irish Myth, Joyce, Kirk, Lug, Macpherson, Mael Dúin, Maeve, Manannan Mac Lir, Milesians, Nuadu, Ogma, Oisin, Patrick, Salmon, Scottish Myth, Second Sight, Sidhe, Silver Bough, Taboo, Taghairm, Tain, Tamlin, Tir nan Og, Tristan, True Thomas, Tuatha dé Danaan, Ulster Cycle, Washerwoman, Welsh Myth, Yseult.

ISLAMIC/ARABIC MYTH
Angels, *Arabian Nights*, Azazel, Djinns, Ghoul, Hassan ibn Sabbah, Ifrit, Islam, Karina, Khadir, Kujata, Mahdi, Mohammed, Nasruddin, Ramadan, Rumi, Scheherazade, Seven Wise Masters, Shaitan, Solomon, Sufis.

JAINISM (*See* **INDIAN MYTH**)
Mahavira.
JAPANESE MYTH
Ainu, Amaterasu, Amida, Buddhism, Confucius, Demons, Izanagi, Izanami, Japanese Myth, Oni, Shinto, Susanowo, Zen.
JEWELS (*See* **METALS/MINERALS**)
JEWS
Jews and Anti-Semitism, Judaism, Nazi Myth, Protocols, Wandering Jew.
JUDAEO-CHRISTIAN MYTH (*See also* **CHRISTIANITY**)
Adam, Ark of the Covenant, Babel, Bible, Cain, Eden, Enoch, Eve, Fall, Hiram Abiff, Jews and Anti-Semitism, Jezebel, Judaism, Leviathan, Lot's Wife, Messiah, Methuselah, Moses, Names, Nimrod, Noah, Queen of Sheba, Resurrection, Salome, Samson, Scapegoats, Shemyaza, Sheol, Sin-Eating, Sinai, Solomon.
LOST WORLDS (*See* **OTHERWORLD, UNDERWORLD**)
Agharti, Atlantis, Cibola, El Dorado, Golden Age, Haggard, Hollow Earth, Hy-Brasil, Lemuria, Lost Worlds, Shambhala.
LOVE DEITIES
Aphrodite, Cupid, Eros, Freya, Frigga, Garbo, Ishtar, Kamadeva, Linga, Monroe, Venus, Yoni.
MAGIC/MAGICAL THEMES (*See* **HERMETIC MYTH**)
Amulets, Black Magic, Charms, Curses, Dimensions, Divination, Evil Eye, Fetish, Glamour, Illusion, Juju, Magic, Mangu, Medicine, Necromancy, Omens, Qabalah, Shamanism, Sorcery, Spells, Talisman, Voodoo, Willow, Wind, Witchcraft, Witchdoctor, Wizard, Zombies.
MAGICAL CONTESTS (*See* **GAMES**)
MAGICAL PROHIBITIONS
Blodeuwedd, Cuchulainn, *Geis*, Llew, Taboo.
MAGICAL SLEEP
Barbarossa, Charlemagne, Seven Sleepers, Sleeping Beauty, Sleeping Emperor.
MAGICAL WEAPONS
Excalibur, Hammer, Odin, Thunder, Vajra.
MAGICIANS/SORCERERS/WIZARDS
Agrippa, Circe, Faust, Hermes Trismegistus, Koshchei, Math, Medea, Merlin, Morgan Le Fay, Morgause, Nimüe, Odin, Paracelsus, Simon Magus, Solomon.
MAYAN MYTH
Ah Puch, Aztec Myth, Itzamna, Ixchel, Ixtab, Kukulcan, Mayan Myth, Popol Vuh.
MESSENGER/SCRIBAL DEITIES/WRITING (*See* **HERMETIC MYTH**)
Cadmus, Hermes, Mercury, Odin, Ogma, Runes, Thoth.
METALS/MINERALS
Dragon, Gold, Iron, Jade, Jewels, Pearl, Silver, Treasure.
MODERN MYTH (*See* **AUTHORS, MOTION PICTURES**)
Bermuda Triangle, Cinema, Comics, Hollywood, Men in Black, Neverland, New Age, Phantom Hitch-Hikers, Philadelphia Experiment, Robots, Rock-'n'Roll Myth, Roswell Incident, Santa Claus, Science Fiction, Star Trek, Star Wars, Superman, Supernatural Beings, Tarzan, UFOs, Wild West.
MOON (*See* **FERTILITY**)
Corn-Gods, Hare, Menstruation, Moon, Mother-Goddess, Soma, Sun, Virginity.

MOON DEITIES
Artemis, Astarte, Badb, Brigit, Demeter, Diana, Hecate, Inanna, Ishtar, Isis, Persephone, Sin, Soma, Virgin Mary.
MOTION PICTURES
Cinema, Dean, Disney, Garbo, Glamour, Hollywood, Monroe, Science Fiction, Wild West.
MOUNTAINS
Axis Mundi, Hawaii, Meru, Mountains, Olympus, Omphalos, Parnassus, Pele, Pyramids, Sinai.
MUSIC AND MYTH
Art and Myth, Beatles, Dance, Drum, Dylan, Muses, Music and Myth, Orpheus, Pied Piper, Presley, Pythagoras, Rock'n'Roll Myth, Sibelius, Wagner.
MYSTERIES, THE
Cave, Delphi, Demeter, Dionysus, Eleusis, Freemasonry, Inanna, Initiation, Isis, Labours, Labyrinth, Ladder, Moon, Mysteries, Orpheus, Pythagoras.
MYTHIC THEMES (*See* **SYMBOLISM**)
Abductions, Achilles Heel, Afterlife, Allegories, Ancestor-Worship, Archetypes, Art and Myth, Astronomy and Myth, Corn-Gods, Creation, Flood, Hero Myth, Initiation, Invisibility, Invulnerability, Kingship, Music and Myth, Mysteries, Purification, Quest, Riddles, Sacrifice, Task, Test, Tricksters, Underworld.
NATIVE AMERICAN MYTH
Awonawilona, Copper Woman, Coyote, Eskimo Myth, Ghost Dance, Ghost Wife, Glooscap, Gluscap, Hiawatha, Hopi, Igaluk, Kici Manitou, Medicine, Native American Myth, Navaho, Shamanism, Sioux, Spider, Taikomol, Taiowa, Thunderbird, Totem, Wakan Tanka, Wild West, Wishpoosh.
NAZI MYTH
Aryan Controversy, Cross, Hollow Earth, Jews and Anti-Semitism, Jung, Nazi Myth, Swastika, Wagner.
NORSE MYTH
Aesir, Ash, Baldur, Berserkers, *Edda*, Fafnir, Fenrir, Fimbulwinter, Frey and Freya, Frigga, Heimdall, Jotunheim, Loki, Midgard, Mimir, Mistletoe, Muspelheim, Nerthus, Niflheim, Njord, Norns, Norse Myth, Odin, Ragnarok, Runes, Saga, Sigmund, Sigurd, Teutonic Myth, Thor, Tyr, Valhalla, Valkyries, Vanir, Vili and Ve, Volsung, Wayland Smith.
NUMBER
Music and Myth, New Jerusalem, Number, Pythagoras, Qabalah, Riddles, Sacred Geometry, Seven, Thirteen, Three, Twelve.
OCEANIC MYTH
Aborigines, Ahoeitu, Aranda, Cargo Cult, Fiji, Hair, Head, Hawaii, Lizard Men, Maori Myth, Maui, Oceanic Myth, Pele, Quat, Rangi, Ta'aroa, Taboo, Tane-Mahuta, Tangaroa, Vatea, Wondjina, Yurlungur.
OTHERWORLD (*See* **LOST WORLDS, UNDERWORLD**)
Agharti, Dimensions, Earthly Paradise, Eden, Elysium, Er, Golden Age, Heaven, Hell, Hesperides, Hsi Wuang Mu, Hy-Brasil, Neverland, Ogygia, Shambhala, Tir nan Og, Utopia.
PERSIAN MYTH
Ahriman, Ahura Mazda, Dance, Dervishes, Deva, Dualism, Haoma, Magi, Manichaeism, Mithra, Persian Myth, Rumi, Simurgh, Sufis, Vedānta, Yima, *Zend-Avesta*, Zoroaster.
PHILOSOPHERS/PHILOSOPHIES (*See* **RELIGIONS**)
Empedocles, Gnostic Myth, Neoplatonism, Nietzsche, Origen, Plato, Plotinus, Pythagoras, Qabalah, Socrates, Solon, Sufis, Yoga, Zen.

PHOENICIAN MYTH (*See* **JUDAEO-CHRISTIAN MYTH**)
Adonis, Astarte, Baal, Bel, El, Hiram Abiff, Jezebel, Moloch, Phoenician Myth.
PLANTS (*See* **FLORA**)
PROPHECY/PROPHETS
Delphi, Divination, Enoch, Merlin, Omens, Oracle, Prophecy, Pyramids, Second Sight, Sibyl, Taghairm, Taliesin, Tarot, Tiresias.
PSYCHOLOGY/PSYCHOLOGISTS OF MYTH
Archetypes, Campbell, Collective Unconscious, Dreams, Eliade, Freud, Incest, Jung, Velikovsky, Virginity.
QUEENS OF HEAVEN
Hera, Inanna, Ishtar, Isis, Juno, Virgin Mary.
RAIN/RAIN DEITIES (*See* **FERTILITY**)
Ganymede, Indra, Rain-Bird, Rain-Making, Rain Queens, Rainbow, Varuna, Vritra, Woodpecker.
REINCARNATION (*See* **SURVIVAL**)
RELIGIONS/RELIGIOUS BELIEFS
Ancestor-Worship, Animism, Buddhism, Cathars, Christianity, Dualism, Gnostic Myth, Hinduism, Jainism, Judaism, Manichaeism, Original Sin, Paganism, Parsees, Religion, Resurrection, Shinto, Soul, Spirit, Taoism, Zen, Zoroaster.
REPTILES (*See* **ANIMALS**)
RIDDLES (*See* **GAMES, TRICKSTERS**)
RITES OF PASSAGE (*See* **MYSTERIES**)
Initiation, Labyrinth, Ladder, Menstruation, Shamanism.
RIVER DEITIES/MYTH (*See* **WATER DEITIES**)
ROMAN MYTH
Aeneas, Apuleius, Brutus, Ceres, Cupid, Cybele, Diana, Faunus, Fortuna, Genius, Golden Bough, Jove/Jupiter, Juno, Mars, Mercury, Minerva, Neptune, Ovid, Remus, Roman Myth, Romulus, Saturn, Sibyl, Tellus Mater, Venus, Vesta, Virgil, Vulcan, Wolf.
RUSTIC/SYLVAN DEITIES/THEMES (*See* **HORNED GODS**)
Elementals, Domovoi, Faunus, Flora, Green Man, Herne the Hunter, Paganism, Pan, Priapus, Silvanus.
SACRIFICE (*See* **DYING GODS, FERTILITY**)
Aztec Myth, Cannibalism, Castration, Corn-Gods, Moloch, Sacrifice, Sin-Eating.
SAINTS (*See* **CHRISTIANITY**)
SCIENCE FICTION
Ballard, Batman, Burroughs E.R., Burroughs W.S., Clarke, Comics, Frankenstein, Poe, Robots, Science Fiction, Superman, Verne, Wells.
SCOTTISH MYTH (*See* **IRISH/SCOTTISH MYTH**)
SEA DEITIES/MYTHS (*See* **WATER DEITIES/MYTHS**)
SEA MONSTERS (*See* **SERPENT/COSMIC SERPENT, WATER DEITIES**)
SEASONAL FESTIVALS
Attis, Beltane, Easter, Fire-Festivals, St George, Hallowe'en, May Day, Samhain, Saturn, Yule.
SECRET SOCIETIES
Freemasonry, Hiram Abiff, Knights Templar, Rosicrucians, Theosophy.
SERPENT/COSMIC SERPENT (*See* **DRAGON, FERTILITY**)
Adam, Adder, Ananta, Chinese Myth, Dragon, Eden, Kraken, Leviathan, Loathly Worm, Manu, Medusa, Naga, Ocean, Ourobouros, Python, Rain-

bow Snake, Serpent, Stoorworm, Tiamat, Typhon, Whale, World-Serpent, Yahweh, Yurlungur.

SHAPE-SHIFTING (*See* **TRICKSTERS**)
Acraeon, Buffalo, Cerridwen, Deer, Fox, Glamour, Hippopotamus, Lion, Manannan Mac Lir, Math, Pig, Poseidon, Proteus, Raven, Seals, Shape-Shifting, Tiresias, Werewolf, Zeus.

SKY/THUNDER GODS
Donar, Dyaus-Pita, Enlil, Hammer, Indra, Jupiter, Maruts, Odin, Ouranos, Perunu, Rangi, Sky, Tengri, Thunder, Thunderbird, Zeus.

SLAVONIC MYTH
Bogatyri, Byelun, Dazhbog, Domovoi, Erlik, Koschei, Kupala, Mati-Syra-Zemlya, Num, Perunu, Pyerun, Rusalka, Slavonic Myth, Svarog, Tengri, Yarilo.

SLEEPERS
Arthur, Barbarossa, Charlemagne, Sleeping Beauty, Sleeping Emperor.

SMITH GODS
Goibniu, Hephaestus, Iron, Vulcan, Wayland Smith.

SNAKE (*See* **SERPENT**)

SORCERY/SORCERERS (*See* **MAGIC/MAGICIANS**)

SOUTH AMERICAN MYTH
Chilean Fauna, Inca Myth, Jaguar, Manco Capac, Native American Myth, Pachacamac, Pachamama, South American Myth, Viracocha.

STORM-GODS (*See* **SKY/THUNDER GODS**)

SUMERIAN MYTH
Anu, Anunnaki, Assyrian Myth, Babylonian Myth, Berossus, Dumuzi, Ea/Enki, Enlil, Ereshkigal, Gilgamesh, Inanna, Nergal, Ninkhursag, Ninurta, Sumerian Myth, Tiamat.

SUN/SUN-GODS
Amaterasu, Apollo, Baal, Helios, Horus, Huitzilopochtli, Lug, Mabon, Maponus, Marduk, Phaethon, Ra, Shamash, Sun, Surya, Yhi.

SUPERNATURAL BEINGS
Angels, Azazel, Azrael, Badb, Banshee, Bori, Brownies, Cailleach, Dakini, Demons, Devas, Djinns, Domovoi, Dryads, Dwarves, Elementals, Elves, Fairies, Gandharvas, Ghouls, Gnomes, Ifrit, Incubi, Lemures, Leprechaun, Lorelei, Mermaids, Nereids, Nymphs, Oni, Pixies, Rakshasas, Rusalka, Satyrs, Spirits, Sprites, Supernatural Beings, Trolls, Yakshas.

SURVIVING DEATH
Afterlife, Er, Heaven, Hell, Metempsychosis, Otherworld, Purgatory, Pythagoras, Reincarnation, Resurrection, Underworld, Valhalla, Vampirism.

SYMBOLISM OF:
Altars, *Axis Mundi*, Blood, Boat, Bridge, Burial, Caduceus, Cannibalism, Castle, Castration, Cauldron, Cave, Chariot, Chastity, Circle, Circumcision, Colours, Comets, Cord, Cornucopia, Cross, Crossroads, Crown, Dance, Door, Dreams, Egg, Eye, Fool, Gold, Hair, Hammer, Head, Heart, Hermaphrodites, Icon, Idol, Iron, Jewels, Kingship, Knight, Knot, Ladder, Linga, Masks, Menstruation, Mirror, Names, Number, Ring, Sacrifice, Sin, Spindle, Spiral, Stone, Swastika, Sword, Time, Treasure, Wand, Weaving, Well, Wheel, Wind, Word, Yoni.

TABOO (*See* **MAGICAL PROHIBITIONS**)

TAOISM
Chinese Myth, Chuang Tsu, *Hsien*, Huang-Ti, Lao Tsu, Taoism.

TEUTONIC MYTH (*See* **NORSE MYTH**)
Donar, Easter, Lohengrin, Lorelei, *Nibelungenlied*, Siegfried, Tannhäuser, Teutonic Myth, Wagner, Woden.
THEOLOGY (*See* **RELIGIONS**)
TRANSFORMATIONS (*See* **SHAPE-SHIFTING**)
TREES
Alder, Apple, Ash, Birch, Bran, Golden Bough, Hawthorn, Hazel, Holly, Oak, Qabalah, Rowan, Shamanism, Silver Bough, Tree Alphabet, Tree of Life, Trees, Willow, World Tree, Yew, Yggdrasil.
TRICKSTERS
Anansi, Coyote, Loki, Maui, Mokele, Nasruddin, Raven, Riddles, Spider, Tricksters, Tule, Whale, Wishpoosh.
TWINS
Dioscuri, Frey and Freya, Perseus, Romulus and Remus, Seven Against Thebes, Twins, Yama.
UNDERWORLD (*See* **LOST WORLDS, OTHERWORLD**)
Annwn, Arawn, Gwyn ap Nudd, Hades, Hell, Hollow Earth, Kalunga, Pig, Sheol, Styx, Tartarus, Whale, Wild Hunt.
UNDERWORLD DEITIES
Adonis, Annwn, Anubis, Anunnaki, Cerberus, Charon, Ereshkigal, Hades, Hecate, Hel, Hypnos, Osiris, Persephone, Pwyll, Thoth, Yama, Yambe-Akka, Yima.
VIRGIN GODDESSES
Artemis, Athene, Inanna, Ishtar, Isis, Sophia, Virgin Mary, Virginity.
WAR-GODS
Ares, Huitzilopochtli, Ishtar, Kartikeya, Mars, Ninurta, Thor.
WATER DEITIES/BEINGS
Ganges, Kelpie, Kupala, Llŷr, Manannan Mac Lir, Mermaids, Neptune, Nereids, Oannes, Oceanus, Poseidon, Proteus, Rusalka, Selkie, Tangaroa, Tiamat, Triton.
WATER MYTH (*See* **FERTILITY, RAIN, SEA MONSTERS**)
Apsu, Ark, Berossus, Boat, Dolphin, Dylan, Flood Myth, Ocean, River Myth, Sea, Shape-Shifting, Styx, Wasteland, Water, Water of Life, Well, Whale.
WELSH MYTH
Annwn, Arianrhod, Blodeuwedd, Celtic Myth, Cerridwen, Culhwch, Dragon, Dylan, Elphin, *Gododdin*, Gwion Bach, Gwydion, Gwynn ap Nudd, Irish Myth, Llew, Lludd, Llŷr, *Mabinogion*, Manawyddan, Math, Melangell, Pryderi, Pwyll, Rhiannon, Scottish Myth, Taliesin, Tree Alphabet, Welsh Myth.
WITCHCRAFT (*See* **MAGIC/SORCERY**)
WONDER-CHILD
Apollo, Christ, Hercules, Merlin, Moses, Taliesin.
ZOROASTRIANISM
Ahriman, Ahura Mazda, Magi, Mithra, Parsees, Persian Myth, *Zend-Avesta*, Zoroaster, Zoroastrianism.

Select Bibliography

Bracketed dates refer to first edition of text cited, where known. Not every text referenced to encyclopedia entries is listed here; some listed here are not referenced in the encyclopedia nor is this listing in any way completely representative of the source materials.

Aeschylus, *The Oresteian Trilogy* (trans. Philip Vellacott), Penguin, London, 1956

Apuleius, Lucius, *The Golden Ass* (trans. Robert Graves), Penguin, London, 1985 (1950)

Arberry, Arthur J. (trans.), *The Koran*, OUP, 1964

Aristophanes, *The Wasps and Other Plays*, Penguin, London, 1970

Ashe, Geoffrey, *The Ancient Wisdom*, Macmillan, London, 1977

Baigent, Michael, Leigh, Richard and Lincoln, Henry, *The Holy Blood and the Holy Grail*, Corgi, London, 1983
  The Messianic Legacy, Corgi, London, 1987

Baigent, Michael and Leigh, Richard, *The Temple and the Lodge*, Corgi, London, 1990
  The Dead Sea Scrolls, Corgi, London, 1992

Batchelor, John, *The Ainu and their Folk-Lore*, Religious Tract Society, London, 1901

Begg, Ean, *Myth and Today's Consciousness*, Coventure, London, 1984
  The Cult of the Black Virgin, Arkana, London, 1985

Bellamy, H.S., *Moons, Myths and Man*, Faber & Faber, London, 1936

Berlitz, Charles, *The Bermuda Triangle*, Granada, London, 1975
  Atlantis, Fontana, London, 1985
  (with William Moore), *The Philadelphia Mystery*, Granada, London, 1980

Blake, William, *Poems and Prophecies*, Dent Everyman, London, 1972 (1927)

Blavatsky, H.P., *Isis Unveiled*, Theosophical University Press, Pasadena, California, 1972 (1877)

Bord, Janet and Colin, *Mysterious Britain*, Paladin, London, 1974
  Alien Animals, Granada, London, 1980
  Sacred Waters, Granada, London, 1985
  Modern Mysteries of the World, Grafton, London, 1989

Briggs, Katherine, *Nine Lives: Cats in Folklore*, Routledge & Kegan Paul, London, 1980

Brown, Joseph Epes, *The Sacred Pipe*, Penguin, London, 1981 (1953)

Brunton, Paul, *A Search in Secret Egypt*, Rider, London, 1969

Bryant, Page, *The Aquarian Guide to Native American Mythology*, Aquarian Press, London, 1991

Bucke, Richard M., *Cosmic Consciousness*, University Press, New York, 1961

Budge, Wallis (trans.), *The Egyptian Book of the Dead*, Routledge & Kegan Paul, London, 1969

Campbell, Joseph, *The Hero with a Thousand Faces*, Abacus, London, 1975 (1949)
  The Masks of God (4 vols), Penguin, London, 1976
Castaneda, Carlos, *The Teachings of Don Juan*, Penguin, London, 1970
  A Separate Reality, Penguin, London, 1973
Cavendish, Richard, *The Magical Arts*, Arkana, London, 1984 (1967)
  The Powers of Evil, Routledge & Kegan Paul, London, 1975
  King Arthur and the Grail, Paladin, London, 1980
Chadwick, Nora, *The Celts*, Pelican, London, 1970
Charpentier, Louis, *The Mysteries of Chartres Cathedral*, Avon, New York, 1975 (1966)
Chatwin, Bruce, *The Songlines*, Picador, London, 1988
Churchward, James, *The Lost Continent of Mu*, Paperback Library, New York, 1969
Clark, R.T. Rundle, *Myth and Symbol in Ancient Egypt*, Thames & Hudson, London, 1991 (1959)
Cohen, Daniel, *Myths of the Space Age*, Tower, New York, 1967
Cohn, Norman, *The Pursuit of the Millennium*, Paladin, London, 1970 (1957)
  Europe's Inner Demons, Paladin, London, 1976
Cooper, J.C., *An Illustrated Encyclopaedia of Traditional Symbols*, Thames & Hudson, London, 1978
Cottingley, Arthur, *A Dictionary of World Mythology*, OUP, 1986
Cranston, S.L., and Head, Joseph, *Reincarnation: The Phoenix Fire Mystery*, Julian Press, New York, 1977
Crossley-Holland, Kevin, *Northern Lights*, Faber & Faber, London, 1987
Crowley, Aleister, *The Book of Thoth*, Weiser, New York, 1984 (1944)
Currer-Briggs, Noel, *The Shroud and the Grail*, Weidenfeld & Nicolson, London, 1987

David-Neel, Alexandra, *Magic and Mystery in Tibet*, Abacus, London, 1977 (1931)
Davidson, H.R. Ellis, *Gods and Myths of Northern Europe*, Penguin, London, 1964
  (ed.), *The Seer in Celtic and Other Traditions*, John Donald, Edinburgh, 1989
Davis, Michael, *William Blake: A New Kind of Man*, University of California Press, Berkeley, 1977
Dee, John, *The Rosie Crucian Secrets*, Aquarian Press, Wellingborough, 1985
Devereux, Paul, *Earthlights*, Turnstone Press, Wellingborough, 1982
Donnelly, Ignatius, *Atlantis, the Antediluvian World*, Sidgwick & Jackson, London, 1970
Downing, Barry H., *The Bible and Flying Saucers*, Avon, New York, 1970
Drake, W. Raymond, *Gods and Spacemen in the Ancient East*, Sphere, London, 1973

Euripedes, *Works*, OUP, 1984
Evans-Wentz, W.Y., *The Tibetan Book of the Dead*, OUP, 1927
  The Fairy Faith in Celtic Countries, 1909

Feng, Gia-Fu, and English, Jane, *Tao Te Ching*, Wildwood House, Aldershot, 1973
Fortune, Dion, *The Mystical Qabalah*, Benn, London, 1966
Francis, David Pitt, *Nostradamus: Prophecies of Present Times?*, Aquarian Press, Wellingborough, 1985
Frazer, James, *The Golden Bough*, Macmillan, London, 1963 (1922)

Gardner, Gerald, *Witchcraft Today*, Rider, London, 1954

Ginzburg, Carlo, *Ecstasies*, Hutchinson, London, 1990

Goss, Michael, *The Evidence for Phantom Hitch-Hikers*, Aquarian Press, Wellingborough, 1984

Graves, Robert, *The Greek Myths* (2 vols), Penguin, London, 1960
  The White Goddess, Faber & Faber, London, 1961 (1946)

Graves, Tom, *Needles of Stone Revisited*, Gothic Image, Glastonbury, 1986

Green, Miranda J., *Dictionary of Celtic Myth and Legend*, Thames & Hudson, London, 1992

Green, Roger Lancelyn, *Myths of the Norsemen*, Puffin, London, 1989 (1960)

Gribbin, John, *Timewarps*, Dent, London, 1979

Guirdham, Arthur, *The Cathars and Reincarnation*, Turnstone Press, Wellingborough, 1982 (1970)
  The Great Heresy, Spearman, Sudbury, 1977

Gurdjieff, G.I., *Meetings with Remarkable Men*, Routledge & Kegan Paul, London, 1963

Hall, Manly P., *The Secret Teachings of All Ages*, Philosophical Research Society, Los Angeles, 1989 (1928)

Hancock, Graham, *The Sign and the Seal*, Heinemann, London, 1992

Harding, M. Esther, *Woman's Mysteries*, Rider, London, 1982 (1955)

Harvey, David, *The Power to Heal*, Aquarian Press, Wellingborough, 1983

Hendry, Allan, *The UFO Handbook*, Sphere, London, 1980

Herrigel, Eugen, *Zen in the Art of Archery*, Routledge & Kegan Paul, 1972 (1953)

Hesiod, *Theogony* (ed. F. Solansen), OUP, 1990

Hitching, Francis, *Earth Magic*, Picador, London, 1977

Hoeller, Stephan A., *The Gnostic Jung*, Quest, Wheaton, Illinois, 1982

Holiday, F.W., *The Great Orm of Loch Ness*, Faber & Faber, London, 1968
  The Dragon and the Disc, Sidgwick & Jackson, London, 1973

Holmyard, E.J., *Alchemy*, Penguin, London, 1968

Homer, *The Odyssey* (trans. Walter Shewring), OUP, 1980
  The Iliad (trans. Robert Fitzgerald), OUP

Howe, Ellic, *The Magicians of the Golden Dawn*, Routledge & Kegan Paul, London, 1972
  Astrology and the Third Reich, Aquarian Press

Huxley, Aldous, *The Doors of Perception/Heaven and Hell*, Granada, 1984 (1954/1956)

James, William, *The Varieties of Religious Experience*, Fontana, London, 1960

Jones, G. & T.J. (trans.), *The Mabinogion*, Dent, London, 1984 (1949)

Jung, C.G., *Dreams*, Ark Books, London, 1985
  Memories, Dreams and Reflections, Fontana, London, 1967
  (ed.) *Man and his Symbols*, Aldus Books, London, 1964

Jung, C.G., and Kerenyi, C., *Essays on a Science of Mythology*, Harper & Row, New York, 1963

Kipling, Rudyard, *Just So Stories*, Penguin, London, 1987 (1902)

Kirk, Rev. Robert, *The Secret Commonwealth of Elves, Fauns and Fairies*, Observer Press, Stirling, 1933 (1691)

Knappert, Jan, *The Aquarian Guide to African Mythology*, Aquarian Press, Wellingborough, 1990
  Indian Mythology, Aquarian Press, London, 1991

Knight, Gareth, *A Practical Guide to Qabalistic Symbolism* (2 vols), Helios, Cheltenham, 1965
  The Rose Cross and the Goddess, Aquarian Press, Wellingborough, 1985

Larousse Encyclopedia of Mythology, Hamlyn, London
Larsen, Stephen, *The Shaman's Doorway*, Harper Colophon, New York, 1977
Larson, Bob, *Larson's Book of Cults*, Tyndale, Illinois, 1989
Lemesurier, Peter, *The Great Pyramid Decoded*, Element Books, Shaftesbury, 1977
  The Armageddon Script, Element Books, Shaftesbury, 1981
LeShan, Lawrence, *The Science of the Paranormal*, Aquarian Books, Wellingborough, 1987
Lethbridge, T.C., *The Legend of the Sons of God*, Arkana, London, 1990 (1972)
Lewis, C.S., *Out of the Silent Planet*, Pan, London, 1952 (1938)
  Voyage to Venus (Perelandra), Pan, London, 1953 (1943)
  That Hideous Strength, Pan, London, 1955 (1945)
Lindsay, Hal, *The Late Great Planet Earth*, Zondervan, Michigan, 1970
Lorimer, David, *Survival?*, Routledge & Kegan Paul, London, 1984

Mackenzie, Alexander, *The Prophecies of the Brahan Seer*, Constable, London, 1977 (1877)
Mackenzie, Donald A., *Indian Myth and Legend*, Gresham, London, 1910
McNeill, Marian, *The Silver Bough* (4 vols), MacLellan, Glasgow, 1977
Mathers, S.L., *The Kabbalah Unveiled*, Routledge & Kegan Paul, London, 1951
Matthews, Caitlin and John, *The Western Way* (2 vols), Arkana, London, 1986
  British and Irish Mythology, Aquarian Press, London, 1988
Matthews, John, *The Grail*, Thames & Hudson, London, 1981
  (ed.), *An Arthurian Reader*, Aquarian Press, London, 1988
Michell, John, *The Flying Saucer Vision*, Sidgwick & Jackson, London, 1967
  City of Revelation, Abacus, London, 1973
  The Earth Spirit, Avon, New York, 1975
  The New View Over Atlantis, Thames & Hudson, London, 1983
  The Dimensions of Paradise, Thames & Hudson, London, 1989

Nicholls, Peter (ed.), *The Encyclopedia of Science Fiction*, Granada, London, 1981
Noone, Richard, *Ice: The Ultimate Disaster*, Genesis, Georgia, 1982

O'Brien, Christian, *The Megalithic Odyssey*, Turnstone, Wellingborough, 1983
  The Genius of the Few, Turnstone, Wellingborough, 1985
O'Flaherty, Wendy D. (ed.), *Hindu Myths*, Penguin, London, 1975
Ouspensky, P.D., *A New Model of the Universe*, Routledge & Kegan Paul, London, 1969
  In Search of the Miraculous, Routledge & Kegan Paul, London, 1969

Pagels, Elaine, *The Gnostic Gospels*, Pelican, London, 1982
Pálos, Stephan, *The Chinese Art of Healing*, Bantam, New York, 1972
Parrinder, E.G., *African Mythology*, Hamlyn, London, 1967
Pearsall, Ronald, *The Alchemists*, Weidenfeld & Nicolson, London, 1976

Pennick, Nigel, *Sacred Geometry*, Turnstone, Wellingborough, 1980
Perry, George, and Aldridge, Alan, *The Penguin Book of Comics*, Penguin, London, 1989 (1971)
Philpotts, Beatrice, *Mermaids*, Russell Ash/Windward, Leicester, 1980
Plato, *Timaeus and Critias* (trans. Desmond Lee), Penguin, London, 1971
Post, Laurens van der, *Jung and the Story of Our Time*, Penguin, London, 1978
Prophet, Elizabeth Clare, *Forbidden Mysteries of Enoch*, Summit University Press, USA, 1983
Purce, Jill, *The Mystic Spiral*, Thames & Hudson, London, 1974
Purucker, G. de, *An Occult Glossary*, Theosophical University Press, Pasadena, California, 1969 (1933)

Randles, Jenny and Fuller, Paul, *Crop Circles*, Hale, London, 1990
Reed, A.W., *Myths and Legends of Australia*, A.H. & A.W. Reed, Sydney, 1965
Regardie, Israel, *The Tree of Life*, Rider, London, 1937
  The Art of True Healing, Helios, Cheltenham, 1966
  The Philosopher's Stone, Llewellyn, USA, 1970
Robinson, James M. (ed.), *The Nag Hammadi Library*, Harper & Row, New York, 1981
Rolleston, T.W., *Celtic Myths and Legends*, Studio Press, London
Runciman, Steven, *The Medieval Manichee*, CUP, 1982 (1947)
Rush, Anne Kent, *Moon, Moon*, Random House, New York, 1976

Sandars, N.K. (ed.), *The Epic of Gilgamesh*, Penguin, London, 1972
Schuré, Edouard, *The Great Initiates*, Harper & Row, New York, 1980 (1889)
Shah, Idries, *The Secret Lore of Magic*, Muller, London, 1957
  The Sufis, Doubleday, New York, 1964
  The Hundred Tales of Wisdom, Octagon Press, London, 1978
  The Exploits of the Incomparable Mullah Nasruddin, Picador, London, 1970
Sophocles, *Electra and Other Plays* (trans. E.F. Watling), Penguin, London, 1969
Spence, Lewis, *Encyclopaedia of Occultism*, University Books, New York, 1960 (1920)
  The Magic Arts in Celtic Britain, Rider, London, 1970 (1946)
Steiner, Rudolf, *An Outline of Occult Science*, Rand McNally, New York, 1914
  Reincarnation and Immortality, Rudolf Steiner Publications, New York, 1970
Stevenson, Ian, *Twenty Cases Suggestive of Reincarnation*, American Society for Psychical Research, New York, 1966
Stewart, R.J., *The Prophetic Vision of Merlin*, Arkana, London, 1986
  Creation Myth, Element Books, Shaftesbury, 1989
  Robert Kirk: Walker between Worlds, Element Books, Shaftesbury, 1989
  Prophecy, Element Books, Shaftesbury, 1990
  Celtic Gods, Celtic Goddesses, Blandford, London, 1990
  Earth Light, Element Books, Shaftesbury, 1992
Stirling, William, *The Canon*, Garnstone Press, London, 1974 (1897)
Streiber, Whitley, *Communion*, Arrow/Hutchinson, London, 1988
  Transformation, Arrow/Hutchinson, London, 1989
  Majestic, Macdonald, London, 1990

Summers, Montague, *History of Witchcraft*, University Books, New York, 1956
   The Vampire in Europe, Aquarian Press, Wellingborough, 1980 (1929)
Sutherland, Elizabeth, *Ravens and Black Rain*, Corgi, London, 1987
Suzuki, D.T., *An Introduction to Zen Buddhism*, Rider, London, 1969

Tansley, David, *Omens of Awareness*, Spearman, Sudbury, 1977
Temple, Robert K.G., *The Sirius Mystery*, Futura, London, 1977
Thom, Alexander, *Megalithic Sites in Britain*, OUP, 1967
   Megalithic Lunar Observatories, OUP, 1971
Thomas, Keith, *Religion and the Decline of Magic*, Peregrine, London, 1978
Thompson, Stith, *Tales of the North American Indians*, Indiana University Press, 1966 (1929)
Thrum, Thomas G., *Hawaiian Folk Tales*, McClurg, Chicago, 1912
Tolstoy, Nikolai, *The Quest for Merlin*, Sceptre, London, 1988
Tompkins, Peter, *The Secrets of the Great Pyramid*, Allen Lane, London, 1973
   (with Bird, C.), *The Secret Life of Plants*, Harper & Row, New York, 1973
Trevelyan, Sir George, and Matchett, Edward, *Twelve Seats at the Round Table*, Spearman, Sudbury, 1976

Valiente, Doreen, *An ABC of Witchcraft Past and Present*, Hale, London, 1971, revised 1984
Vallée, Jacques, *Messengers of Deception*, And/Or Press, Berkeley, California, 1979
   Dimensions, Sphere, London, 1990
Vaughan, Alan, *Patterns of Prophecy*, Dell, New York, 1976
Velikovsky, Immanuel, *Worlds in Collision*, Abacus, London, 1972 (1950)
   Earth in Upheaval, Gollancz, London, 1956
   Mankind in Amnesia, Abacus, London, 1983
Virgil, *The Aeneid* (trans. W.F. Jackson Knight), Penguin, London, 1956
Vogh, James, *The Thirteenth Zodiac*, Granada/Mayflower, London, 1979

Waite, A.E., *The Pictorial Key to the Tarot*, Weiser, New York, 1977 (1910)
Waters, Frank, *Book of the Hopi*, Penguin, London, 1977 (1963)
Watson, Godfrey, *Bothwell and the Witches*, Hale, London, 1975
Watts, Alan, *The Way of Zen*, Penguin, London, 1957
Westwood, J., *Albion: A Guide to Legendary Britain*, Granada, London, 1985
White, John, *Pole Shift*, W.H. Allen, London, 1980
Wilhelm, Richard (trans.), *I Ching*, Routledge & Kegan Paul, London, 1951
   The Secret of the Golden Flower, Routledge & Kegan Paul, London, 1984 (1931)
Wilson, Colin, *The Occult*, Grafton/Collins, London, 1979 (1971)
   Mysteries, Grafton/Collins, London, 1979
   Starseekers, Hodder & Stoughton, London, 1980
   Beyond the Occult, Corgi, London, 1989
Wilson, Ian, *The Turin Shroud*, Penguin, London, 1979
Wilson, Peter Lamborn, *Angels*, Thames & Hudson, London, 1980
Wood, David, *Genisis*, Baton Press, Tunbridge Wells, 1985

Yates, Frances A., *Giordano Bruno and the Hermetic Tradition*, Routledge & Kegan Paul, London, 1964
   The Art of Memory, Routledge & Kegan Paul, London, 1966
   The Rosicrucian Enlightenment, Routledge & Kegan Paul, London, 1972

The Occult Philosophy, Routledge & Kegan Paul, London, 1979
Yeats, W.B., *The Poems* (ed. Daniel Albright), Dent, London, 1990

Zaehner, R.C. (trans. and ed.), *Hindu Scriptures*, Dent, London, 1988 (1938)
Zangger, Eberhard, *The Flood from Heaven*, Sidgwick & Jackson, London, 1992